Watkins

1000
83000

**The University of Chicago Spanish Dictionary**

Universidad de Chicago

# Diccionario
# Inglés-Español *y* Español-Inglés

## Edición Revisada

*Un Nuevo y Conciso Diccionario Que Contiene las Voces
y Locuciones Básicas de Ambos Idiomas*

Recopilación de
Carlos Castillo *y* Otto F. Bond

Con la ayuda de
Barbara M. García

Revisado por
D. Lincoln Canfield

The University of Chicago Press
Chicago & London

The University of Chicago

# Spanish Dictionary

**Revised Edition**

*A New Concise Spanish-English and English-Spanish
Dictionary of Words and Phrases Basic to the Written
and Spoken Languages of Today*

Compiled by
Carlos Castillo & Otto F. Bond

With the Assistance of
Barbara M. Garcia

Revised by
D. Lincoln Canfield

The University of Chicago Press
Chicago & London

THE UNIVERSITY OF CHICAGO PRESS, CHICAGO 60637
The University of Chicago Press, Ltd., London

© 1948, 1972 by The University of Chicago. All rights reserved
First Edition published 1948. Revised Edition 1972

Printed in the United States of America

International Standard Book Number: 0–226–09671–8 (clothbound)
Library of Congress Catalog Card Number: 78–177425

# Foreword

*The University of Chicago Spanish Dictionary* has been compiled for the general use of the American learner of Spanish and the Spanish-speaking learner of English, with special reference in either case to New World usages as found in the United States and in Spanish America.

With this purpose in mind, the editors and the author of the revisions of the new (1972) edition have selected the words to be defined, first according to the relative frequence of their occurrence, secondly in keeping with dialectal variations of the New World, both Anglo and Hispanic, and thirdly in accordance with the growth in the technological lexicon during the past two decades.

The Spanish-English section of this revised edition contains all the items listed in Juilland and Chang Rodríguez's *Frequency Dictionary of Spanish Words* (The Hague: Mouton & Co., 1964) which in turn follows Buchanan's *Graded Spanish Word Book* (Toronto: University of Toronto Press, 1929), L. Rodríguez Bou's *Recuento de Vocabulario Español* (Puerto Rico, 1952), and V. García Hoz's *Vocabulario Usual, Vocabulario Común y Vocabulario Fundamental* (Madrid, 1953). Furthermore, the original edition of the dictionary had listed all the items of Keniston's *Standard List of Spanish Words and Idioms* (Boston: D. C. Heath & Co., 1941), supplemented by many words occurring in textbooks and literary masterpieces of Spanish-speaking countries used in the United States and Canada in the instruction of Spanish at several levels. Hundreds of dialectal variants of Spanish America have been indicated in the Spanish-English section of the revised edition, and have been labeled according to the region or regions in which they are used. In the first edition these were all marked *Am.* New regionalisms have been added. In addition, many items related to developments in the fields of aviation, atomic energy, linguistics, and other areas of technological advancement have been added.

The words selected originally for definition in the English-Spanish section of the *Dictionary* were taken from the first nine thousand entries in Thorndike and Lorge's *Teacher's Word Book of 30,000 Words* (New York: Bureau of Publications, Teachers College, Columbia University, 1944), supplemented by residual words in the combined-words lists of Eaton, Buckingham-Dolch, and the *Interim Report on Vocabulary Selection* (London: P. S. King & Co., 1936). Additions to these in the revised edition include hundreds of terms related to technological developments of recent years as well as Spanish-American dialectal variants, with indications of regional usage wherever possible.

In order to coordinate the two parts and not leave undefined words used in definitions, it was necessary to introduce into each section a number of secondary entries which are a by-product of the primary definitions. This brought the total number of entries for the first edition to approximately 30,000 words and brings the total for the revised edition to about 32,000. Besides the approximately 500 new words in the Spanish-English section, more than 1500 items have been added to the English-Spanish section, and relatively few have been deleted.

No pretense is made to equalize the two parts in terms of the number of items for the simple reason that in the past three decades many more new terms of universal usage have been coined in English than in Spanish. Many of these have been taken bodily into Spanish.

The New World application of the *Dictionary* is further emphasized by its acceptance of American standards of speech in indicating the pronunciation of English entries and by the inclusion of American and Spanish-American equivalents and usages throughout. To enhance the usefulness and accuracy of the *Dictionary*, as has been stated, Spanish-American usages have been identified by words or abbreviations for specific countries or regions rather than by the general abbreviation *Am*. This latter abbreviation has been retained, however, to indicate general Spanish-American usage, usually with the implication of obsolescence in Spain. The abbreviation is also employed to identify words that are currently little used but which may occur in literary masterpieces of bygone days.

Certain auxiliary data have been provided at the beginning of each part, such as a list of abbreviations, an explanation of speech sounds; a summary of the use and value of suffixes; a list of numerals; a brief treatment of nouns, adjectives, and adverbs; and a table of irregular verb forms. In the Spanish-English section a superior number following a verb entry refers to a similarly numbered verb listed in the table preceding the section. Additional features of the Spanish-English part in the revised edition are a list of monetary units and values, a list of adjectives of nationality, and a rather extensive discussion of the Spanish of America and its regional dialects, with maps that indicate the occurrence of distinctive phonological and syntactic features.

One of the principal additions to the revised edition is the introduction of parenthetical identifying expressions to help the speaker of the first language distinguish among the several possible definitions that are traditionally given for a particular word. Hundreds of entries of this type have been added to both parts of the dictionary.

A dictionary should be an instrument for better understanding between peoples. It is the earnest wish of the editors of this one that it may serve that end.

# Part One Spanish-English

## List of Abbreviations

| | | | |
|---|---|---|---|
| *adj.* | adjective | *math.* | mathematics |
| *adv.* | adverb | *neut.* | neuter |
| *arith.* | arithmetic | *num.* | numeral |
| *conj.* | conjunction | *p.p.* | past participle |
| *contr.* | contraction | *pers.* | personal |
| *def.* | definite | *pers. pron.* | personal pronoun |
| *def. art.* | definite article | *pl.* | plural |
| *dem.* | demonstrative | *poss.* | possessive |
| *dem. adj.* | demonstrative adjective | *prep.* | preposition |
| *dem. pron.* | demonstrative pronoun | *pron.* | pronoun |
| *etc.* | et cetera | *refl.* | reflexive |
| *f.* | feminine noun | *refl. pron.* | reflexive pronoun |
| *fam.* | familiar | *rel.* | relative |
| *indef.* | indefinite | *rel. adv.* | relative adverb |
| *indef. art.* | indefinite article | *rel. pron.* | relative pronoun |
| *inf.* | infinitive | *sing.* | singular |
| *interj.* | interjection | *subj.* | subjunctive |
| *interr.* | interrogative | *v.* | verb |
| *irr.* | irregular | *v. irr.* | irregular verb |
| *m.* | masculine noun | | |

## Special Words and Abbreviations Used to Indicate Regional Occurrence

| | |
|---|---|
| *Am.*[1] | Spanish-American |
| *Andalusia* | |
| *Andes* | (Ecuador, Peru, Bolivia) |
| *Arg.* | Argentina |

[1] This abbreviation is employed to indicate general Spanish-American usage, usually with the implication of obsolescence in Spain. It is also used to identify words that are currently little used but which may occur in literary works of bygone days.

| | |
|---|---|
| *Bol.* | Bolivia |
| *Carib.* | (Cuba, Puerto Rico, Dominican Republic) |
| *C.A.* | Central America (Guatemala, El Salvador, Honduras, Nicaragua, Costa Rica) |
| *Ch.* | Chile |
| *Col.* | Colombia |
| *C.R.* | Costa Rica |
| *Cuba* | |
| *Ec.* | Ecuador |
| *Guat.* | Guatemala |
| *Hond.* | Honduras |
| *Mex.* | Mexico |
| *Nic.* | Nicaragua |
| *N.Sp.* | Northern Spain |
| *Pan.* | Panama |
| *Par.* | Paraguay |
| *Peru* | |
| *P.R.* | Puerto Rico |
| *Ríopl.* | Río de la Plata region (Eastern Argentina, Uruguay) |
| *S.A.* | South America |
| *Sal.* | El Salvador |
| *Spain* | |
| *Ur.* | Uruguay |
| *Ven.* | Venezuela |

## Spanish Pronunciation

The Spanish of Spain (except the southwest) has 24 phonemes, or minimum units of sound-meaning distinction. The Spanish of southwest Spain and most of Spanish America has 22 phonemes. These minimum units of sound are indicated in the following charts and descriptions by slashes, /b/, /e/, /č/, and stand for an abstract representation of a group or class of sounds, the individual members of which are variants or allophones. The latter are indicated by brackets: [b̦], [e], [ŷ]. Some of the phonemes of Spanish have two or three variants, depending on position within the phrase.

The two principal characteristics of Spanish pronunciation as contrasted with English are tenseness of articulation and continuity in transition from word to word within the breath group. Thus all the vowels have a clear nondiphthongal character and sound "clipped" to the English-speaking person. The consonants, especially /p/, /t/, /k/, /l/, /r/, /rr/, have much less vocalic interference than in English, and the first three have no aspiration. The glottal stop, so common in the Germanic languages, including English, is very rare in Spanish. The transition between vowels of contiguous words is smooth. **El hado, helado, el lado** sound very much alike. **Para hacerlo** is [paraasérlo] or in rapid speech [parasérlo]. So marked is the continuity that following sounds influence the preceding ones: **los dos niños** [lozdózniños]; **un peso** [umpéso] **en que** [éŋke].

The Consonantal Phonemes of the Spanish of Northern Spain

| | | | | | |
|---|---|---|---|---|---|
| /p/ | /b/ | /t/ | /d/ | /k/ | /g/ |
| | /f/ | /θ/ | /S/ | /y/ | /x/ |
| | | | /č/ | | |
| /m/ | | | /n/ | /ñ/ | |
| | | | /l/ | /ļ/ | |
| | | /r/ | /rr/ | | |

24

Phonetic Manifestations of the Phonemes of Spanish

| | Bilabial | | Labiodental | | Interdental | | Dental | | Alveolar | | Palatal | | Velar | | Glottal | |
|---|---|---|---|---|---|---|---|---|---|---|---|---|---|---|---|---|
| Voice | vs | vd | vs | vd | vs | vd | vs | vd | vs | vd | vs | vd | vs | vd | vs | vd |
| Occlusive | p | b | | | | | t | d | | | | | k | g | | |
| Fricative | φ | β | f | | θ | đ | | | | | | y | x | ǥ | h | |
| Sibilant | | | | | | | s | z | S | Z | (ŝ) | (ẑ) | | | | |
| Affricate | | | | | | | | | | | č | ŷ | | | | |
| Nasal | | | | | | | | | | n | | ñ | | ŋ | | |
| Lateral | | | | | | | | | | l | | ļ | | | | |
| Vibrant | | | | | | | | | | r rr | | | | | | |
| Semiconsonant | | w | | | | | | | | | | j | | | | |

The Vocalic Phonemes of Spanish

$$i \qquad\qquad u$$
$$e \qquad\quad o$$
$$a$$

The Consonantal Phonemes of Andalusian and Latin American Spanish

| /p/ | /b/ | /t/ | /d/ | /k/ | /g/ | |
|---|---|---|---|---|---|---|
| | /f/ | | /s/ | /y/ | /x/ | |
| | | | | /č/ | | |
| /m/ | | | /n/ | /ñ/ | | 22 or 23 |
| | | | /l/ | (/ḷ/) | [Bolivia, Paraguay, Peru] | |
| | | | /r/ | /rr/ | | |

## The Spanish Spelling System and the Sounds Represented

### I. The Vowels

1. **i** as a single vowel always represents [i], similar to the second vowel of *police*. Examples: **hilo, camino, piso.** As a part of a diphthong, it represents [j], much like English /y/ in *yes, year.* Examples: **bien** [bjen], **diablo** [djaƀlo], **ciudad, baile, reina, boina.** The first syllable of **baile** is much like *by* in English.

2. **e** represents [e], which has no exact equivalent in most English dialects. It is higher than the /e/ of *get* but without the diphthong of *they.* It is much more tense in articulation than either English sound. It varies slightly according to adjacent sounds. The vowel of **perro** is more open than that of **pero.** Generally it is more open in a closed syllable. Examples: **mesa, del, hablé, en, tres.**

3. **a** represents [a], which is similar to the first vowel of *mama*, stressed on the first syllable. Examples: **caso, cano, ¡ah!, América.** Even when not stressed, it has the same clear sound. English *America* has at least two neutral or *schwa* sounds [ə].

4. **o** represents [o], which is more like the Scotch-English sound of *auld* than the British or American *old.* It has no off-glide or diphthongal character such as is heard in the latter. It varies slightly according to adjacent sounds: the first syllable of **corro** is slightly more open than the first of **coro. Sol** is slightly more open than **no.** Examples: **boto, modo, señor, oso, amó.**

5. **u** represents [u], which always has the value of the sound indicated by English *oo* in *boot, fool*, never that of *book*, nor that of the *u* in *union.* Examples: **cura, agudo, uno.**
   a. Note that the spelling combinations **qui, que, gui, gue** represent [ki], [ke], [gi], [ge].
   b. **u** is used to represent the semiconsonant [w] in a diphthong: **cuida, cuento, cuadro, cuota** [kwíḍa], [kwénto], [kwáḍro], [kwóta].
   c. Likewise **u** is used to represent the semivocalic element of a diphthong: **bou, deuda, causa** [bow], [déwḍa], [káwsa].

### II. The Consonants

1. **p** represents [p], which never has the aspiration of English /p/ (*pill, papa*), but is like that of *spot.* Examples: **padre, capa, apuro, punto.**

2. **b** and **v** represent /b/, which has two variants, according to position in the phrase: [b], [ƀ]. These do not depend on spelling, which goes back centuries. Either letter represents [b] at the beginning of a breath group or when preceded by [m] (spelled either **m** or **n**), and is much like English /b/. Examples: **bomba, burro, en vez de, vine, invierno.** In spite of spelling, the last three examples are [embézɖe], [bíne], [imbjérno]. Either letter represents [ƀ] in all other situations. English has no equivalent. It is a /b/ with the lips slightly open. Examples: **haba, uva, Cuba, la vaca, habla, la barba.**

3. **m** represents [m], which is essentially the same as English /m/ (*much*). Examples: **madre, mano, cama.** [m] does not occur syllable final in Spanish. **Álbum** is pronounced [álƀun].

4. **f** represents [f], which is similar to the /f/ of English. In some areas and among certain strata of Hispanic society the articulation is bilabial rather than labiodental.

5. **t** represents [t], which never has the aspiration of English /t/ in prevocalic stressed position (*tea, two, ten*). It is more similar to the English /t/ of the cluster [st] (*stop, step*). Examples in Spanish: **tela, tino, tinta.** The point of articulation is dental.

6. **d** represents /d/, which has three variants according to position in the phrase: [d], [ɖ], [Ø]. At the beginning of the breath group or after /n/ and /l/, **d** represents [d], which is similar to the English /d/ of *dame, did, darn.* Examples: **donde, falda, conde.** In all other situations the letter represents [ɖ], or even [Ø]. There is a tendency in modern Spanish to move from the fricative [ɖ] (similar to the sound represented by the *th* in *mother, this, then*) to zero articulation [Ø]. Examples: **hado, cuerda, es de, dos dados, cuadro, padre, abad, usted, Madrid.** The last two words are usually pronounced without final consonant, and the consonant tends to be very weak in the ending /-ado/: **hablado, estado, mercado.**

7. **s** In Spain, except the southwest, this letter represents [S], an apico-alveolar sibilant, similar to the /s/ of southern Scotland and that of older speakers of the Midland dialect of the United States. Examples: **solo, casa, es.** Before a voiced consonant within the phrase it usually represents [Z]. Examples: **desde, mismo, es verde, los labios, las manos.**

In southwestern Spain and in all of Spanish America except a small area of Colombia, this letter represents [s], a dental sibilant of high resonance similar to the usual "feminine" sibilant of much of the United States. In some areas it is actually lisped. Before a voiced consonant within the phrase it usually represents [z], a voiced sibilant similar to the /z/ of English *razor, ooze,* Examples: **desde, mismo, es verde, los labios, las manos.** In the Caribbean and in coastal Spanish generally, there is a strong tendency to aspirate the /s/ syllable final, and the above voicing does not occur.

8. **z,** and **c** before **e** and **i** represent in Spain, except the southwest, [θ], an interdental fricative of tenser and more prolonged articulation than that represented by English *th* in *thin, cloth, ether.* Examples: **zagal, zorro, luz** [θagál], [θórro], [luθ]; or **luces, ciento, cerro** [lúθes], [θjento], [θerro].

In southwestern Spain and in Spanish America, these letters represent [s] (see paragraph 7). Examples: **zagal, zorro, luz, luces, ciento, cerro** [saǵál], [sórro], [lus], [lúses], [sjénto], [sérro]. Before a voiced consonant in the phrase, the **z** represents [z] (see paragraph 7). Examples: **en vez de, mayorazgo, la luz de.**

9. **l** always represents [l], a clear alveolar lateral that is rarely heard in English, except in Irish and Scotch dialects. It is never velar as in English *bell*, *full*. Examples: **lado, ala, el, al, sol.**

10. **n** represents /n/, which has variants according to the following consonants. It stands for [n] in all cases except before /b/, /p/, /m/, where it represents [m], and before /k/, /g/, /x/, where it represents [ŋ] (similar to the final consonant of *sing*). Examples of [n]: **no, nada, mano, aman;** of [m]: **en vez de, en Barcelona, un peso;** of [ŋ]: **anca, banco, en que, tengo, naranja.**

11. **ll** represents [ḷ] (a palatal lateral) in northern Spain and in Bolivia, Paraguay, and most of Peru, as well as in the Bogotá area of Colombia. This sound is similar to that heard in English *million*. In other parts of the Spanish-speaking world, *ll* represents [y]. Examples: **calle, llano, olla.**

12. **ñ** represents [ñ] among all speakers of Spanish. It is similar to the sound heard in English *canyon*, but is more one articulation than the English. Examples: **cañón, año, ñato.**

13. **ch** represents [č], which is similar to English /č/ (*church, cheek, reach*). Examples: **chato, chaleco, mucho.**

14. **y** represents [y], which varies regionally from [y] to [ž] (as in *azure*), and in most regions it represents [ŷ] (similar to *just* of English) in initial position in the phrase and after /l/ and /n/. Examples: **ayer, mayo** [ayér], [máyo]; **¡yo! un yugo, el yerno** [ŷo], [unŷúgo], [elŷérno]. In nearly all areas, Spanish /y/ has more palatal friction than English /y/.

15. a. **x** represents between vowels [ǵs] or simply [S] in Spain (see paragraph 7) and [ks] in Spanish America. Examples: **examen, próximo.**

    b. Before a consonant **x** represents [S] in Spain and [s] in Spanish America, except in affected speech, when one hears [ks]. Examples: **extranjero, experiencia.**

    c. In several Indian words of Mexico and Central America **x** represents [x] (see paragraph 20). **México** is one of these and is spelled **Méjico** in most of the Spanish-speaking world.

16. a. **c** represents [k] before **a, o, u, l,** or **r**. The [k] of Spanish does not have the aspiration of English /k/ in the unprotected prevocalic position (*can, quill, coal*) but is more like the sound in *scan*. Examples: **casa, cosa, cuna, quinto, queso, crudo, aclamar.** Note that **quinto** and **queso** are [kínto] and [késo]. The syllable final [k] in Spanish occurs only in "learned" terms and is dealt with in various ways by the people. In Spain generally it tends to voice to [g]: **técnico, acto, doctor** [tégnico], [ágto], [doǵtór], but today in Madrid and farther north, the latter becomes [doθtór]. In Central America, Cuba, Venezuela, and Colombia [kt] often becomes [pt] and vice versa; [ps] is [ks]: **Pepsi Cola** [péksi kóla].

b. **c** before **e** and **i** represents [θ] in Spain, except the southwest, and [s] in Spanish America (see paragraph 8).

17. **k** represents [k] in certain words of foreign origin, mainly Greek, German, and English: **kilo, kilómetro, kermesse, kiosko.**

18. **q** combined with **u** represents [k]. Examples: **queso, aquí, quien** [késo], [akí], [kjen]. **qu** occurs only before **e** and **i**.

19. a. **g** represents [g] before **a, o, u** when initial in the breath group or after /n/. Examples: **ganga, goma, guarda, tengo. gue, gui** represents [ge], [gi]; **güe, güi** represent [gwe], [gwi].
    Before **a, o, u** under other circumstances, **g** represents [ǥ], a voiced velar fricative. Examples: **la guerra** [laǥérra], **lago** [láǥo], **la goma** [laǥóma], **agrado** [aǥráḍo].

    b. **g** before **e, i,** represents [x], a palatal or velar fricative, which is also represented by **j**. Examples: **gente, giro** [xénte], [xíro]. In the Caribbean and Central America, as well as in southern Spain, the /x/ is simply [h].

20. **j** always represents /x/. The usual manifestation of this phoneme is [x], but in some areas (see paragraph 19) it is [h]. Examples: **jamás, jugo, jota** [xamás], [xúǥo], [xóta].

21. **h** represents a former aspiration that is no longer present except in some rural areas of southern Spain and Spanish America. Examples: **hoja** [óxa], **humo** [úmo], **harto** [árto].

22. **r** represents [r], an alveolar single flap, similar to the sound represented by *tt* in American English *kitty* in rapid speech. However, at the beginning of a word or after **n, l, s,** it represents [rr], a multiple vibrant (trill). Examples of [r]: **caro, farol, mero, tren, comer.** Examples of [rr] written **r: rosa, rana, Enrique, Israel, alrededor.**
    **rr** represents [rr] under all circumstances. Examples: **carro, correr, guerrero.**

# The Noun

## I. Gender[2]

### A. *Masculine Gender*

1. Names of male beings are naturally masculine: **el hombre** the man; **el muchacho** the boy; **el tío** the uncle; **el rey** the king; **el buey** the ox.

2. Nouns ending in **-o** are masculine: **el libro** the book; **el banco** the bank. *Exception*: **la mano** the hand.

3. Days of the week, months, rivers, oceans, and mountains are masculine: **el martes** Tuesday; **enero** January; **el Pacífico** the Pacific; **el Rin** the Rhine; **los Andes** the Andes.

4. Many nouns in **-l** or **-r,** and nouns of Greek origin ending in **-ma** are masculine: **el papel** the paper; **el azúcar** the sugar; **el favor**

[2] There is no general rule for the gender of nouns that are not treated in this section.

the favor; **el drama** the drama. *Common exceptions*: **la miel** the honey; **la sal** the salt; **la catedral** the cathedral; **la flor** the flower. Note that **mar** is both masculine and feminine.

B. *Feminine Gender*

1. Names of female persons or animals are naturally feminine: **la mujer** the woman; **la muchacha** the girl; **la tía** the aunt; **la vaca** the cow.

2. Nouns ending in **-a** are feminine: **la pluma** the pen; **la carta** the letter; **la casa** the house. *Common exceptions*: **el día** the day; **el mapa** the map; nouns of Greek origin ending in **-ma**: **el dogma** the dogma; **el programa** the program.

3. Letters of the alphabet are feminine: **la** *e*, **la** *s*, **la** *t*.

4. Nouns ending in **-ión, -tad, -dad, -tud, -umbre** are feminine: **la canción** the song; **la facultad** the faculty; **la ciudad** the city; **la virtud** the virtue; **la muchedumbre** the crowd. *Exceptions*: **el gorrión** the sparrow; **el sarampión** the measles.

C. *Formation of the Feminine*

1. Nouns ending in **-o** change **-o** to **-a**: **tío** uncle, **tía** aunt; **niño** boy, **niña** girl.

2. Nouns ending in **-ón, -or,** and **-án** add **-a**: **patrón** patron, **patrona** patroness; **pastor** shepherd, **pastora** shepherdess; **holgazán** lazy man, **holgazana** lazy woman.

3. Certain nouns have a special form for the feminine: **el poeta, la poetisa; el cantante, la cantatriz; el sacerdote, la sacerdotisa; el emperador, la emperatriz; el abad, la abadesa; el conde, la condesa; el duque, la duquesa.**

Note that (*a*) some nouns have different genders according to their meanings: **el corte** the cut or the cutting edge; **la corte** the court; **el guía** the guide; **la guía** the guidebook; **el capital** the capital (money); **la capital** the capital (city); (*b*) some nouns have invariable endings which are used for both the masculine and the feminine: **artista** (and all nouns ending in **-ista**), **amante, mártir, testigo, reo, demócrata, aristócrata, intérprete, consorte, comensal, homicida, suicida, indígena, cómplice, cliente.**

II. Plural of Nouns[3]

1. Nouns ending in an unaccented vowel add **-s** to form the plural: **el libro, los libros; la casa, las casas.**

2. Nouns ending in a consonant, in **-y**, or in an accented vowel add **-es**: **el papel, los papeles; la canción, las canciones: la ley, las leyes; el rubí, los rubíes.** The accepted plural, however, of **papá** is **papás**, and of **mamá** is **mamás**.

3. Nouns ending in unaccented **-es** and **-is** do not change in the plural: **el lunes** Monday, **los lunes** Mondays; **la tesis** the thesis, **las tesis** the theses.

Note that (*a*) nouns ending in **-z** change **z** to **c** before **-es**: **lápiz, lápices**; (*b*) nouns ending in **-ión** lose the written accent in the plural: **canción, canciones.**

[3] The plurals of certain masculine nouns may include the masculine and feminine genders: **los padres** the father(s) and mother(s), the parents; **los tíos** the uncle(s) and aunt(s); **los reyes** the king(s) and queen(s).

## The Adjective and the Adverb

### I. The Adjective

A. *Agreement.* The adjective in Spanish agrees in gender and number with the noun it modifies: **el lápiz rojo** the red pencil; **la casa blanca** the white house; **los libros interesantes** the interesting books; **las muchachas hermosas** the beautiful girls.

B. *Formation of the plural.* Adjectives follow the same rules as nouns for the formation of the plural: **pálido, pálidos** pale; **fácil, fáciles** easy; **cortés, corteses** courteous; **capaz, capaces** capable.

C. *Formation of the feminine.*

1. Adjectives ending in **-o** change **-o** to **-a: blanco, blanca.**

2. Adjectives ending in other vowels are invariable: **verde** green; **fuerte** strong; **indígena** indigenous, native; **pesimista** pessimistic; **baladí** trivial.

3. Adjectives ending in a consonant are invariable: **fácil** easy; **cortés** courteous. *Exceptions:* (*a*) adjectives ending in **-ón, -án, -or** (except comparatives) add **-a** to form the feminine: **holgazán, holgazana** lazy; **preguntón, preguntona** inquisitive; **hablador, habladora** talkative (Note that **mayor, mejor, menor, peor, superior, inferior, exterior, interior, anterior,** and **posterior** are invariable). **Superior** adds an **-a** when it is used as a noun meaning ("mother superior"). (*b*) adjectives of nationality ending in a consonant add **-a** to form the feminine: **francés, francesa** French; **español, española** Spanish; **alemán, alemana** German; **inglés, inglesa** English.

### II. The Adverb

Many adverbs are formed by adding **-mente** to the feminine form of the adjective: **claro, claramente; lento, lentamente; fácil, fácilmente.**

### III. Comparison of Adjectives and Adverbs

A. *Comparative of inequality.* The comparative of inequality is formed by placing **más** or **menos** before the positive form of the adjective or adverb: **más rico que** richer than; **menos rico que** less rich than; **más tarde** later; **menos tarde** less late. The superlative is formed by placing the definite article **el** before the comparative: **el más rico** the richest; **el menos rico** the least rich. Note the position of the article in the following examples: **la niña más linda** or **la más linda niña** the prettiest girl.

The following adjectives and adverbs have in addition irregular forms of comparison:

| Positive | Comparative | Superlative |
|---|---|---|
| bueno | mejor | el (la) mejor |
| malo | peor | el (la) peor |
| grande | mayor | el (la) mayor |
| pequeño | menor | el (la) menor |
| alto | superior | supremo |
| bajo | inferior | ínfimo |
| mucho | más | |
| poco | menos | |

B. *Comparative of equality*. With adjectives and adverbs the comparative of equality is formed with **tan . . . como: tan fácil como** as easy as; **tan bien como** as well as; with nouns the comparative of equality is formed with **tanto (tanta, tantos, tantas) . . . como: tanto dinero como** as much money as; **tantas personas como** as many people as.

C. *Absolute superlative of adjectives*. The absolute superlative of adjectives is formed by placing **muy** (very) before the adjective or by adding the suffix **-ísimo**:

| Positive | Absolute Superlative |
|---|---|
| feliz | muy feliz, felicísimo |
| fácil | muy fácil, facilísimo |
| importante | muy importante, importantísimo |
| limpio | muy limpio, limpísimo |
| feo | muy feo, feísimo |
| rico | muy rico, riquísimo |
| largo | muy largo, larguísimo |
| notable | muy notable, notabilísimo |

A few adjectives have, in addition, other forms derived from the Latin superlatives:

| bueno | muy bueno, bonísimo[4], óptimo |
|---|---|
| malo | muy malo, malísimo, pésimo |
| grande | muy grande, grandísimo, máximo |
| pequeño | muy pequeño, pequeñísimo, mínimo |

Some adjectives ending in **-ro** or **-re** revert to the corresponding Latin superlative:

| acre | muy acre, acrérrimo |
|---|---|
| célebre | muy célebre, celebérrimo |
| mísero | muy mísero, misérrimo |
| salubre | muy salubre, salubérrimo |

D. *Absolute superlative of adverbs*. The absolute superlative of adverbs not ending in **-mente** is formed in the same manner as that of adjectives:

| tarde | muy tarde, tardísimo |
|---|---|
| pronto | muy pronto, prontísimo |
| mucho | muchísimo |
| poco | poquísimo |
| cerca | muy cerca, cerquísima |
| lejos | muy lejos, lejísimos |

Superlative adverbs ending in **-mente** are formed by adding the suffix **-ísima** to the corresponding feminine adjective:

| claramente | muy claramente, clarísimamente |
|---|---|
| noblemente | muy noblemente, nobilísimamente |

## Common Spanish Suffixes

I. Diminutives

The most common diminutive endings in Spanish are:

| -ito, -ita | (-cito, -cita, -ecito, -ecita). Examples: **librito** (from **libro**), **casita** (from **casa**), **corazoncito** (from **corazón**), **mujercita** (from **mujer**), **cochecito** (from **coche**), **florecita** (from **flor**). |
|---|---|

[4] Also **buenísimo**.

| **-illo, -illa** | (**-cillo, -cilla, -ecillo, -ecilla**). Examples: **corderillo** (from **cordero**), **dolorcillo** (from **dolor**), **viejecillo** (from **viejo**), **piedrecilla** (from **piedra**). |
| **-ico, -ica** | (**-cico, -cica, -ecico, -ecica**). Examples: **niñico** (from **niño**), **hermanica** (from **hermana**), **corazoncico** (from **corazón**), **mujercica** (from **mujer**), **pobrecico** (from **pobre**). |
| **-uelo, -uela** | (**-zuelo, -zuela, -ezuelo, -ezuela**). Examples: **arroyuelo** (from **arroyo**), **mozuela** (from **moza**), **mujerzuela** (from **mujer**), **reyezuelo** (from **rey**), **piedrezuela** (from **piedra**). |
| **-ete, -eta** | Examples: **vejete** (from **viejo**), **vejeta** (from **vieja**). |
| **-uco, -uca** | Example: **casuca** (from **casa**). |
| **-ucho, -ucha** | Examples: **serrucho** (from **sierra**), **casucha** (from **casa**). |

## II. Augmentatives

The most common augmentative endings in Spanish are:

| **-acho, -acha** | Example: **ricacho** (from **rico**). |
| **-azo, -aza** | Examples: **gigantazo** (from **gigante**), **bribonazo** (from **bribón**), **manaza** (from **mano**), **bocaza** (from **boca**). |
| **-on, -ona** | Examples: **hombrón** (from **hombre**), **mujerona** (from **mujer**), **almohadón** (from **almohada**), **borrachón** (from **borracho**). |
| **-ote, -ota** | Examples: **grandote** (from **grande**), **muchachote** (from **muchacho**), **muchachota** (from **muchacha**). |

## III. Depreciatives

The most common depreciative endings in Spanish are:

| **-aco, -aca** | Example: **pajarraco** ugly bird. |
| **-ejo, -eja** | Example: **librejo** old, worthless book. |

Note that a depreciative or ironic connotation is often conveyed by many of the augmentatives and by the diminutive endings **-uelo, -ete, -uco, -ucho, -illo.**

## IV. Other Suffixes

| **-ada** | *a.* is sometimes equal to the English suffix *-ful:* **cucharada** spoonful; **palada** shovelful; |
| | *b.* often indicates a blow: **puñada** blow with the fist; **puñalada** stab or blow with a dagger; **topetada** butt, blow with the head; |
| | *c.* indicates a group or a crowd of: **peonada** a group or crowd of peons; **indiada** a group or crowd of Indians. |

| | |
|---|---|
| **-al, -ar** | denote a grove, field, plantation or orchard: **naranjal** orange grove; **cauchal** rubber plantation; **pinar** pine grove. |
| **-azo** | indicates a blow or explosion: **puñetazo** blow with the fist; **topetazo** butt, blow with the head; **escobazo** blow with a broom; **cañonazo** cannon shot. |
| **-dad, -tad** | are suffixes forming many abstract nouns and are usually equivalent to the English suffix *-ty*: **fraternidad** fraternity; **facultad** faculty; **cantidad** quantity; **calidad** quality. |
| **-dizo** | is an adjective-forming suffix which means sometimes *tending to*, or *in the habit of*: **resbaladizo** slippery; **olvidadizo** forgetful; **enojadizo** irritable, easily angered; **asustadizo** easily frightened, scary, timid; **movedizo** movable. |
| **-ería** | *a.* denotes a place where something is made or sold: **panadería** bakery; **librería** bookstore; **zapatería** shoestore; **pastelería** pastry shop;<br>*b.* indicates a profession, business or occupation: **carpintería** carpentry; **ingeniería** engineering;<br>*c.* means sometimes a collection: **pastelería** pastry, pastries;<br>*d.* is sometimes equivalent to English suffix *-ness*; it also suggests a single act or action: **tontería** foolishness; foolish act; **niñería** childishness; childish act. |
| **-ero** | *a.* indicates a person who makes, sells, or is in charge of: **panadero** baker; **librero** bookseller; **zapatero** shoemaker, **carcelero** jailer; **cajaro** cashier;<br>*b.* is an adjective-forming suffix; **parlero** talkative; **guerrero** warlike. |
| **-ez, -eza** | are used to make abstract nouns: **vejez** old age; **niñez** childhood; **viudez** widowhood; **grandeza** greatness. |
| **-ía** | *a.* is the ending of the names of many arts and sciences: **geología** geology; **geometría** geometry; **biología** biology;<br>*b.* see **-ería**. |
| **-iento** | indicates a *resemblance*, or a *tendency to*: **ceniciento** ashlike; **soñoliento** sleepy, drowsy. |
| **-ísimo** | is the ending of the absolute superlative: **hermosísimo** very beautiful. |
| **-izo** | is a suffix meaning *tending to* or *somewhat*: **rojizo** reddish. See **-dizo**. |
| **-mente** | is the adverbial ending attached to the feminine form of the adjective: **generosamente** generously; **claramente** clearly. |

| | |
|---|---|
| **-ón** | *a.* is an augmentative suffix; |
| | *b.* is also a suffix without an augmentative force, meaning *in the habit of,* or *full of:* **juguetón** playful; **preguntón** full of questions, inquisitive; **llorón** tearful; crybaby; |
| | *c.* indicates suddenness or violence of an action: **estirón** pull, tug, jerk; **apretón** squeeze. |
| **-or, -dor** | *a.* are equivalent to the English suffixes *-or, -er,* and indicate the agent or doer: **hablador** talker; **regulador** regulator; |
| | *b.* may also be used as adjectives: **hablador** talkative; **regulador** regulating. |
| **-oso** | is an adjective-forming suffix which usually means *having, full of,* or *characterized by:* **rocoso** rocky; **tormentoso** stormy; **fangoso** muddy; **herboso** grassy; **lluvioso** rainy; **maravilloso** marvelous; **famoso** famous. |
| **-udo** | is an adjective-forming suffix meaning *having* or *characterized by:* **zancudo** long-legged; **peludo** hairy; **panzudo** big-bellied; **caprichudo** stubborn. |
| **-ura** | is a suffix forming many abstract nouns: **negrura** blackness; **blancura** whiteness; **altura** height; **lisura** smoothness. |
| **-uzco** | indicates *resemblance* or *a tendency to;* it is akin to the English suffix *-ish:* **blancuzco** whitish; **negruzco** blackish. |

## Spanish Irregular and Orthographic Changing Verbs

The superior number, or numbers, after a verb entry indicate that it is conjugated like the model verb in this section which has the corresponding number. Only the tenses which have irregular forms or spelling changes are given. The irregular forms and spelling changes are shown in bold-face type.

1. pensar (if stressed, the stem vowel **e** becomes **ie**)
   *Pres. Indic.*   **pienso, piensas, piensa,** pensamos, pensáis, **piensan.**
   *Pres. Subj.*   **piense, pienses, piense,** pensemos, penséis, **piensen.**
   *Imper.*   **piensa** tú, **piense** Vd., pensemos nosotros, pensad vosotros, **piensen** Vds.

2. contar (if stressed, the stem vowel **o** becomes **ue**)
   *Pres. Indic.*   **cuento, cuentas, cuenta,** contamos, contáis, **cuentan.**
   *Pres. Subj.*   **cuente, cuentes, cuente,** centemos, contéis, **cuenten.**
   *Imper.*   **cuenta** tú, **cuente** Vd. contemos nosotros, contad vosotros, **cuenten** Vds.

3.*a.* sentir (if stressed, the stem vowel **e** becomes **ie;** if unstressed, the stem vowel **e** becomes **i** when the following syllable contains stressed **a, ie,** or **ió**)
   *Pres. Indic.*   **siento, sientes, siente,** sentimos, sentís, **sienten.**
   *Pres. Subj.*   **sienta, sientas, sienta, sintamos, sintáis, sientan.**

| | |
|---|---|
| *Pret. Indic.* | **sentí, sentiste, sintió,** sentimos, sentisteis, **sintieron.** |
| *Imp. Subj.* | **sintiera** or **sintiese, sintieras** or **sintieses, sintiera** or **sintiese, sintiéramos** or **sintiésemos, sintierais** or **sintieseis, sintieran** or **sintiesen.** |
| *Imper.* | **siente** tú, **sienta** Vd., **sintamos** nosotros, sentid vosotros, **sientan** Vds. |
| *Pres. Part.* | **sintiendo.** |

b. erguir (this verb has same vowel changes as *sentir*, but the initial **i** of the diphthong **ie** is changed to **y.** For regular spelling changes see No. 12,*a*)

| | |
|---|---|
| *Pres. Indic.* | **yergo, yergues, yergue,** erguimos, erguís, **yerguen.** |
| *Pres. Subj.* | **yerga, yergas, yerga, irgamos, irgáis, yergan.** |
| *Pret. Indic.* | erguí, erguiste, **irguió,** erguimos, erguisteis, **irguieron.** |
| *Imp. Subj.* | **irguiera** or **irguiese, irguieras** or **irguieses, irguiera** or **irguieses, irguiéramos** or **irguiésemos, irguierais** or **irguieseis, irguieran** or **irguiesen.** |
| *Imper.* | **yergue** tú, **yerga** Vd., **irgamos** nosotros, erguid vosotros, **yergan** Vds. |
| *Pres. Part.* | **irguiendo.** |

4. dormir (if stressed, the stem vowel **o** becomes **ue**; if unstressed, the stem vowel **o** becomes **u** when the following syllable contains stressed **a, ie,** or **ió**)

| | |
|---|---|
| *Pres. Indic.* | **duermo, duermes, duerme,** dormimos, dormís, **duermen.** |
| *Pres. Subj.* | **duerma, duermas, duerma, durmamos, durmáis, duerman.** |
| *Pret. Indic.* | dormí, dormiste, **durmió,** dormimos, dormisteis, **durmieron.** |
| *Imp. Subj.* | **durmiera** or **durmiese, durmieras** or **durmieses, durmiera** or **durmiese, durmiéramos** or **durmiésemos, durmierais** or **durmieseis, durmieran** or **durmiesen.** |
| *Imper.* | **duerme** tú, **duerma** Vd., **durmanos** nosotros, dormid vosotros, **duerman** Vds. |
| *Pres. Part.* | **durmiendo.** |

5. pedir (if stressed, the stem vowel **e** becomes **i**; if unstressed, the stem vowel **e** becomes **i** when the following syllable contains stressed **a, ie,** or **ió**)

| | |
|---|---|
| *Pres. Indic.* | **pido, pides, pide,** pedimos, pedís, **piden.** |
| *Pres. Subj.* | **pida, pidas, pida, pidamos, pidáis, pidan.** |
| *Pret. Indic.* | pedí, pediste, **pidió,** pedimos, pedisteis, **pidieron.** |
| *Imp. Subj.* | **pidiera** or **pidiese, pidieras** or **pidieses, pidiera** or **pidiese, pidiéramos** or **pidiésemos, pidierais** or **pidieseis, pidieran** or **pidiesen.** |
| *Imper.* | **pide** tú, **pida** Vd., **pidamos** nosotros, pedid vosotros, **pidan** Vds. |
| *Pres. Part.* | **pidiendo.** |

6. buscar (verbs ending in **car** change **c** to **qu** before **e**)

| | |
|---|---|
| *Pres. Subj.* | **busque, busques, busque, busquemos, busquéis, busquen.** |

*Pret. Indic.*    **busqué,** buscaste, buscó, buscamos, buscasteis, buscaron.

*Imper.*    busca tú, **busque** Vd., **busquemos** nosotros, buscad vosotros, **busquen** Vds.

7.   llegar (verbs ending in **gar** change the **g** to **gu** before **e**)

*Pres. Subj.*    **llegue, llegues, llegue, lleguemos, lleguéis, lleguen.**

*Pres. Indic.*    **llegué,** llegaste, llegó, llegamos, llegasteis, llegaron.

*Imper.*    llega tú, **llegue** Vd., lleguemos nosotros, llegad vosotros, **lleguen** Vds.

8.   averiguar (verbs ending in **guar** change the **gu** to **gü** before **e**)

*Pres. Subj.*    **averigüe, averigües, averigüe, averigüemos, averigüéis, averigüen.**

*Pret. Indic.*    **averigüé,** averiguaste, averiguó, averiguamos, averiguasteis, averiguaron.

*Imper.*    averigua tú, **averigüe** Vd., **averigüemos** nosotros, averiguad vosotros, **averigüen** Vds.

9.   abrazar (verbs ending in **zar** change **z** to **c** before **e**)

*Pres. Subj.*    **abrace, abraces, abrace, abracemos, abracéis, abracen.**

*Pret. Indic.*    **abracé,** abrazaste, abrazó, abrazamos, abrazasteis, abrazaron.

*Imper.*    abraza tú, **abrace** Vd., **abracemos** nosotros, abrazad vosotros, **abracen** Vds.

10.*a.* convencer (verbs ending in **cer** preceded by a consonant change **c** to **z** before **a** and **o**)

*Pres. Indic.*    **convenzo,** convences, convence, convencemos, convencéis, convencen.

*Pres. Subj.*    **convenza, convenzas, convenza, convenzamos, convenzáis, convenzan.**

*Imper.*    convence tú, **convenza** Vd., **convenzamos** nosotros, convenced vosotros, **convenzan** Vds.

*b.* esparcir (verbs ending in **cir** preceded by a consonant change **c** to **z** before **a** and **o**)

*Pres. Indic.*    **esparzo,** esparces, esparce, esparcimos, esparcís, esparcen.

*Pres. Subj.*    **esparza, esparzas, esparza, esparzamos, esparzáis, esparzan.**

*Imper.*    esparce tú, **esparza** Vd., **esparzamos** nosotros, esparcid vosotros, **esparzan** Vds.

*c.* mecer (some verbs ending in **cer** preceded by a vowel change **c** to **z** before **a** and **o**; see No. 13.*a*)

*Pres. Indic.*    **mezo,** meces, mece, mecemos, mecéis, mecen.

*Pres. Subj.*    **meza, mezas, meza, mezamos, mezáis, mezan.**

*Imper.*    mece tú, **meza** Vd., **mezamos** nosotros, meced vosotros, **mezan** Vds.

11.*a.* dirigir (verbs ending in **gir** change **g** to **j** before **a** and **o**)

*Pres. Indic.*    **dirijo,** diriges, dirige, dirigimos, dirigís, dirigen.

*Pres. Subj.*    **dirija, dirijas, dirija, dirijamos, dirijáis, dirijan.**

| | |
|---|---|
| *Imper.* | dirige tú, **dirija** Vd., **dirijamos** nosotros, dirigid vosotros, **dirijan** Vds. |

*b.* coger (verbs ending in **ger** change **g** to **j** before **o** and **a**)

| | |
|---|---|
| *Pres. Indic.* | **cojo,** coges, coge, cogemos, cogéis, cogen. |
| *Pres. Subj.* | **coja, cojas, coja, cojamos, cojáis, cojan.** |
| *Imper.* | coge tú, **coja** Vd., **cojamos** nosotros, coged vosotros, **cojan** Vds. |

12.*a.* distinguir (verbs ending in **guir** drop the **u** before **o** and **a**)

| | |
|---|---|
| *Pres. Indic.* | **distingo,** distingues, distingue, distinguimos, distinguís, distinguen. |
| *Pres. Subj.* | **distinga, distingas, distinga, distingamos, distingáis, distingan.** |
| *Imper.* | distingue tú, **distinga** Vd., **distingamos** nosotros, distinguid vosotros, **distingan** Vds. |

*b.* delinquir (verbs ending in **quir** change **qu** to **c** before **o** and **a**)

| | |
|---|---|
| *Pres. Indic.* | **delinco,** delinques, delinque, delinquimos, delinquís, delinquen. |
| *Pres. Subj.* | **delinca, delincas, delinca, delincamos, delincáis, delincan.** |

13.*a.* conocer (verbs ending in **cer** when preceded by a vowel insert **z** before **c** when **c** is followed by **o** or **a**; see No. 10.*c*)

| | |
|---|---|
| *Pres. Indic.* | **conozco,** conoces, conoce, conocemos, conocéis, conocen. |
| *Pres. Subj.* | **conozca, conozcas, conozca, conozcamos, conozcáis, conozcan.** |
| *Imper.* | conoce tú, **conozca** Vd., **conozcamos** nosotros, conoced vosotros, **conozcan** Vds. |

*b.* lucir (verbs ending in **cir** when preceded by a vowel insert **z** before **c** when **c** is followed by **o** or **a**; see No. 25)

| | |
|---|---|
| *Pres. Indic.* | **luzco,** luces, luce, lucimos, lucís, lucen. |
| *Pres. Subj.* | **luzca, luzcas, luzca, luzcamos, luzcáis, luzcan.** |
| *Imper.* | luce tú, **luzca** Vd., **luzcamos** nosotros, lucid vosotros, **luzcan** Vds. |

14. creer (unstressed **i** between vowels is regularly changed to **y**)

| | |
|---|---|
| *Pret. Indic.* | creí, creíste, **creyó,** creímos, creísteis, **creyeron.** |
| *Imp. Subj.* | **creyera** or **creyese, creyeras** or **creyeses, creyera** or **creyese, creyéramos** or **creyésemos, creyerais** or **creyeseis, creyeran** or **creyesen.** |
| *Pret. Part.* | **creyendo.** |

15. reír (like No. 5, except that when the **i** of the stem would be followed by **ie** or **ió** the two **i**'s are reduced to one)

| | |
|---|---|
| *Pres. Indic.* | **río, ríes, ríe,** reímos, reís, **ríen.** |
| *Pres. Subj.* | **ría, rías, ría, riamos, riáis, rían.** |
| *Pret. Indic.* | reí, reíste, **rió,** reímos, reísteis, **rieron.** |
| *Imp. Subj.* | **riera,** or **riese, rieras** or **rieses, riera,** or **riese, riéramos** or **riésemos, rierais** or **rieseis, rieran** or **riesen.** |
| *Imper.* | **ríe** tú, **ría** Vd., **ríamos** nosotros, reíd vosotros, **rían** Vds. |
| *Pres. Part.* | **riendo** |

16. podrir or pudrir

| | |
|---|---|
| *Pres. Indic.* | **pudro, pudres, pudre,** podrimos or pudrimos, podrís or pudrís, **pudren.** |
| *Pres. Subj.* | **pudra, pudras, pudra, pudramos, pudráis, pudran.** |
| *Imp. Indic.* | pudría or podría, etc. (Seldom *podría* because of confusion with *poder*) |
| *Pret. Indic.* | podrí or pudrí, podriste or pudriste, **pudrió,** podrimos or pudrimos, podristeis or pudristeis, **pudrieron.** |
| *Imp. Subj.* | **pudriera** or **pudriese, pudrieras** or **pudrieses, pudriera** or **pudriese, pudriéramos** or **pudriésemos, pudrierais** or **pudrieseis, pudrieran** or **pudriesen.** |
| *Fut. Indic.* | pudriré or podriré, etc. |
| *Cond.* | pudriría or podriría, etc. |
| *Pres. Part.* | **pudriendo.** |
| *Past Part.* | podrido or pudrido. |

17. enviar

| | |
|---|---|
| *Pres. Indic.* | envío, envías, envía, enviamos, enviáis, envían. |
| *Pres. Subj.* | envíe, envíes, enviemos, enviéis, envíen. |
| *Imper.* | envía tú, envíe Vd., enviemos nosotros, enviad vosotros, envíen Vds. |

18. continuar

| | |
|---|---|
| *Pres. Indic.* | continúo, continúas, continúa, continuamos, continuáis, continúan. |
| *Pres. Subj.* | continúe, continúes, continúe, continuemos, continuéis, continúen. |
| *Imper.* | continúa tú, continúe Vd., continuemos nosotros, continuad vosotros, continúen Vds. |

19. gruñir (**i** of the diphthong **ie** or **ió** is lost after **ñ**)

| | |
|---|---|
| *Pret. Indic.* | gruñí, gruñiste, **gruñó,** gruñimos, gruñisteis, **gruñeron.** |
| *Imp. Subj.* | **gruñera** or **gruñese, gruñeras** or **gruñeses, gruñera** or **gruñese, gruñéramos,** or **gruñésemos, gruñerais** or **gruñeseis, gruñeran** or **gruñesen.** |
| *Pres. Part.* | **gruñendo.** |

20. bullir (**i** of the diphthong **ie** or **ió** is lost after **ll**)

| | |
|---|---|
| *Pret. Indic.* | bullí, bulliste, **bulló,** bullimos, bullisteis, **bulleron.** |
| *Imp. Subj.* | **bullera** or **bullese, bulleras** or **bulleses, bullera** or **bullese, bulléramos** or **bullésemos, bullerais** or **bulleseis, bulleran** or **bullesen** |
| *Pres. Part.* | **bullendo.** |

21. andar

| | |
|---|---|
| *Pret. Indic.* | **anduve, anduviste, anduvo, anduvimos, anduvisteis, anduvieron.** |
| *Imp. Subj.* | **anduviera** or **anduviese, anduvieras** or **anduvieses, anduviera** or **anduviese, anduviéramos anduviésemos, anduvierais** or **anduvieseis, anduvieran** or **anduviesen.** |

22. asir

| | |
|---|---|
| *Pres. Indic.* | **asgo,** ases, ase, asimos, asís, asen. |
| *Pres. Subj.* | **asga, asgas, asga, asgamos, asgáis, asgan.** |
| *Imper.* | ase tú, **asga** Vd., **asgamos** nosotros, asid vosotros, **asgan** Vds. |

23. caber

| | |
|---|---|
| *Pres. Indic.* | **quepo,** cabes, cabe, cabemos, cabéis, caben. |
| *Pres. Subj.* | **quepa, quepas, quepa, quepamos, quepáis, quepan.** |
| *Pret. Indic.* | **cupe, cupiste, cupo, cupimos, cupisteis, cupieron.** |
| *Imp. Subj.* | **cupiera** or **cupiese, cupieras** or **cupieses, cupiera** or **cupiese, cupiéramos** or **cupiésemos, cupierais** or **cupieseis, cupieran** or **cupiesen.** |
| *Fut. Indic.* | **cabré, cabrás, cabrá, cabremos, cabréis, cabrán.** |
| *Cond.* | **cabría, cabrías, cabría, cabríamos, cabríais, cabrían.** |
| *Imper.* | cabe tú, **quepa** Vd., **quepamos** nosotros, cabed vosotros, **quepan** Vds. |

24. caer

| | |
|---|---|
| *Pres. Indic.* | **caigo,** caes, cae, caemos, caéis, caen. |
| *Pres. Subj.* | **caiga, caigas, caiga, caigamos, caigáis, caigan.** |
| *Pret. Indic.* | caí, caiste, **cayó,** caímos, caísteis, **cayeron.** |
| *Imp. Subj.* | **cayera** or **cayese, cayeras** or **cayases, cayera** or **cayese, cayéramos** or **cayésemos, cayerais** or **cayeseis, cayeran** or **cayesen.** |
| *Imper.* | cae tú, **caiga** Vd., **caigamos** nosotros, caed vosotros, **caigan** Vds. |
| *Pres. Part.* | **cayendo.** |

25. conducir (all verbs ending in **ducir** have the irregularities of conducir)

| | |
|---|---|
| *Pres. Indic.* | **conduzco,** conduces, conduce, conducimos, conducís, conducen. |
| *Pres. Subj.* | **conduzca, conduzcas, conduzca, conduzcamos, conduzcáis, conduzcan.** |
| *Pret. Indic.* | **conduje, condujiste, condujo, condujimos, condujisteis, condujeron.** |
| *Imp. Subj.* | **condujera** or **condujese, condujeras** or **condujeses, condujera** or **condujese, condujéramos** or **condujésemos, condujerais** or **condujeseis, condujeran** or **condujesen.** |
| *Imp.* | conduce tú, **conduzca** Vd., **conduzcamos** nosotros, conducid vosotros, **conduzcan** Vds. |

26. dar

| | |
|---|---|
| *Pres. Indic.* | **doy,** das, da, damos, dais, dan. |
| *Pres. Subj.* | dé, des, dé, demos, deis, den. |
| *Pret. Indic.* | **dí, diste, dió, dimos, disteis, dieron.** |
| *Imp. Subj.* | **diera** or **diese, dieras** or **dieses, deira** or **diese, diéramos** or **diésemos, dierais** or **dieseis, dieran** or **diesen.** |

27. decir

| | |
|---|---|
| *Pres. Indic.* | **digo, dices, dice,** decimos, decís, **dicen.** |
| *Pres. Subj.* | **diga, digas, diga, digamos, digáis, digan.** |
| *Pret. Indic.* | **dije, dijiste, dijo, dijimos, dijisteis, dijeron.** |
| *Imp. Subj.* | **dijera** or **dijese, dijeras** or **dijeses, dijera** or **dijese, dijéramos** or **dijésemos, dijerais** or **dijeseis, dijeran** or **dijesen.** |
| *Fut. Indic.* | **diré, dirás, dirá, diremos, deréis, dirán.** |
| *Cond.* | **diría, dirías, diría, diríamos, diríais, dirían.** |

| *Imper.* | **di** tú, **diga** Vd., **digamos** nosotros, decid vosotros, **digan** Vds. |
|---|---|
| *Pres. Part.* | **diciendo.** |
| *Past Part.* | **dicho.** |

NOTE. The compound verbs of *decir* have the same irregularities with the exception of the following:

- *a.* The future and conditional of the compound verbs *bendecir* and *maldecir* are regular: *bendeciré, maldeciré,* etc.; *bendeciría, maldeciría,* etc.
- *b.* The familiar imperative is regular: *bendice tu, maldice tu, contradice tu,* etc.
- *c.* The past participles of *bendecir* and *maldecir* are regular when used with *haber : bendecido, maldecido;* when used as an adjective with *estar,* the forms are: *bendito, maldito.*

28.   errar (like No. 1, except that the initial **ie** is spelled **ye**)

| *Pres. Indic.* | **yerro, yerras, yerra,** erramos, erráis, **yerran.** |
|---|---|
| *Pres. Subj.* | **yerre, yerres, yerre,** erremos, erréis, **yerren.** |
| *Imper.* | **yerra** tú, **yerre** Vd., erremos nosotros, errad vosotros, **yerren** Vds. |

29.   estar

| *Pres. Indic.* | **estoy, estás, está,** estamos, estáis, **están.** |
|---|---|
| *Pres. Subj.* | **esté, estés, esté,** estemos, estéis, **estén.** |
| *Pret. Indic.* | **estuve, estuviste, estuvo, estuvimos, estuvisteis, estuvieron.** |
| *Imp. Subj.* | **estuviera** or **estuviese, estuvieras** or **estuvieses, estuviera** or **estuviese, estuviéramos** or **estuviésemos, estuvierais** or **estuvieseis, estuvieran** or **estuviesen.** |
| *Imper.* | **está** tú, **esté** Vd., estemos nosotros, estad vosotros, **estén** Vds. |

30.   haber

| *Pres. Indic.* | **he, has, ha, hemos,** habéis, **han.** |
|---|---|
| *Pres. Subj.* | **haya, hayas, haya, hayamos, hayáis, hayan.** |
| *Pret. Indic.* | **hube, hubiste, hubo, hubimos, hubisteis, hubieron.** |
| *Imp. Subj.* | **hubiera** or **hubiese, hubieras** or **hubieses, hubiera** or **hubiese, hubiéramos** or **hubiésemos, hubierais** or **hubieseis, hubieran** or **hubiesen.** |
| *Fut. Indic.* | **habré, habrás, habrá, habremos, habréis, habrán.** |
| *Cond.* | **habría, habrías, habría, habríamos, habríais, habrían.** |

31.   hacer

| *Pres. Indic.* | **hago,** haces, hace, hacemos, hacéis, hacen. |
|---|---|
| *Pres. Subj.* | **haga, hagas, haga, hagamos, hagáis, hagan.** |
| *Pret. Indic.* | **hice, hiciste, hizo, hicimos, hicisteis, hicieron.** |
| *Imp. Subj.* | **hiciera** or **hiciese, hicieras** or **hicieses, hiciera** or **hiciese, hiciéramos,** or **hiciésemos, hicierais** or **hicieseis, hicieran** or **hiciesem.** |
| *Fut. Indic.* | **haré, harás, hará, haremos, haréis, harán.** |
| *Cond.* | **haría, harías, haría, haríamos, haríais, harían.** |
| *Imper.* | **haz** tú, **haga** Vd., **hagamos** nosotros, haced vosotros, **hagan** Vds. |
| *Past Part.* | **hecho.** |

32.*a.* huir

| | |
|---|---|
| *Pres. Indic.* | **huyo, huyes, huye,** huimos, huís, **huyen.** |
| *Pres. Subj.* | **huya, huyas, huya, huyamos, huyáis, huyan.** |
| *Pret. Indic.* | huí, huiste, **huyó,** huimos, huisteis, **huyeron.** |
| *Imp. Subj.* | **huyera** or **huyese, huyeras** or **huyeses, huyera** or **huyese, huyéramos** or **huyésemos, huyerais** or **huyeseis, huyeran** or **huyesen.** |
| *Imper.* | **huye** tú, **huya** Vd., **huyamos** nosotros, huid vosotros, **huyan** Vds. |
| *Pres. Part.* | **huyendo.** |

*b.* argüir

| | |
|---|---|
| *Pres. Indic.* | **arguyo, arguyes, arguye,** argüimos, argüís, **arguyen.** |
| *Pres. Subj.* | **arguya, arguyas, arguya, arguyamos, arguyáis, arguyan.** |
| *Pret. Indic.* | argüí, argüiste, **arguyó,** argüimos, argüisteis, **arguyeron.** |
| *Imp. Subj.* | **arguyera** or **arguyese, arguyeras** or **arguyeses, arguyera** or **arguyese, arguyéramos** or **arguyésemos, arguyerais** or **arguyeseis, arguyeran** or **arguyesen.** |
| *Imper.* | **arguye** tú, **arguya** Vd., **arguyamos** nosotros, agrüid vosotros, **arguyan** Vds. |
| *Pres. Part.* | **arguyendo.** |

33.   ir

| | |
|---|---|
| *Pres. Indic.* | **voy, vas, va, vamos, vais, van.** |
| *Pres. Subj.* | **vaya, vayas, vaya, vayamos, vayáis, vayan.** |
| *Imp. Indic.* | **iba, ibas, iba, íbamos, ibais, iban.** |
| *Pret. Indic.* | **fuí, fuiste, fué, fuimos, fuisteis, fueron.** |
| *Imp. Subj.* | **fuera** or **fuese, fueras** or **fueses, fuera** or **fuese, fuéramos** or **fuésemos, fuerais** or **fueseis, fueran** or **fuesen.** |
| *Imper.* | **ve** tú, **vaya** Vd., **vayamos (vamos)** nosotros, id vosotros, **vayan** Vds. |
| *Pres. Part.* | **yendo.** |

34.   jugar (cf. Nos. 2 and 7)

| | |
|---|---|
| *Pres. Indic.* | **juego, juegas, juega,** jugamos, jugáis, **juegan.** |
| *Pres. Subj.* | **juegue, juegues, juegue,** juguemos, juguéis, **jueguen.** |
| *Pret. Indic.* | **jugué,** jugaste, jugó, jugamos, jugasteis, jugaron. |
| *Imper.* | **juega** tú, **juegue** Vd., **jueguemos** nosotros, jugad vosotros, **jueguen** Vds. |

35.   adquirir

| | |
|---|---|
| *Pres. Indic.* | **adquiero, adquieres, adquiere,** adquirimos, adquirís, **adquieren.** |
| *Pres. Subj.* | **adquiera, adquieras, adquiera,** adquiramos, adquiráis, **adquieran.** |
| *Imper.* | **adquiere** tú, **adquiera** Vd., adquiramos nosotros, adquirid vosotros, **adquieran** Vds. |

36.   oír

| | |
|---|---|
| *Pres. Indic.* | **oigo, oyes, oye,** oímos, oís, **oyen.** |
| *Pres. Subj.* | **oiga, oigas, oiga, oigamos, oigáis, oigan.** |

*Pret. Indic.* oí, oíste, **oyó,** oímos, oísteis, **oyeron.**

*Imp. Subj.* **oyera** or **oyese, oyeras** or **oyeses, oyera** or **oyese, oyéramos** or **oyésemos, oyerais** or **oyeseis, oyeran** or **oyesen.**

*Imper.* **oye** tú, **oiga** Vd., **oigamos** nosotros, oíd vosotros, **oigan** Vds.

*Pres. Part.* **oyendo.**

37. oler (like No. 2, except that initial **ue** is spelled **hue**)

*Pres. Indic.* **huelo, hueles, huele,** olemos, oléis, **huelen.**

*Pres. Subj.* **huela, huelas, huela,** olamos, oláis, **huelan.**

*Imper.* **huele** tú, **huela** Vd., olamos nosotros, oled vosotros, **huelan** Vds.

38. placer

*Pres. Indic.* **plazco,** places, place, placemos, placéis, placen.

*Pres. Subj.* **plazca, plazcas, plazca, plazcamos, plazcáis, plazcan.** (There are also the antiquated forms **plegue** and **plega,** used now only in the third person in poetic language.)

*Pret. Indic.* In addition to the regular forms, there is the antiquated form **plugo,** used now only in poetic language.

*Imp. Subj.* In addition to the regular forms, there are the antiquated forms, **pluguiera** and **pluguiese,** used now only in poetic language.

39. poder

*Pres. Indic.* **puedo, puedes, puede,** podemos, podéis, **pueden.**

*Pres. Subj.* **pueda, puedas, pueda,** podamos, podáis, **puedan.**

*Pret. Indic.* **pude, pudiste, pudo, pudimos, pudisteis, pudieron.**

*Imp. Subj.* **pudiera** or **pudiese, pudieras** or **pudieses, pudiera** or **pudiese, pudiéramos** or **pudiésemos, pudierais** or **pudieseis, pudieran** or **pudiesen.**

*Fut. Indic.* **podré, podrás, podrá, podremos, podréis, podrán**

*Cond.* **podría, podrías, podría, podríamos, podríais, podrían.**

*Pres. Part.* **pudiendo.**

40. poner

*Pres. Indic.* **pongo,** pones, pone, ponemos, ponéis, ponen.

*Pres. Subj.* **ponga, pongas, ponga, pongamos, pongáis, pongan.**

*Pret. Indic.* **puse, pusiste, puso, pusimos, pusisteis, pusieron.**

*Imp. Subj.* **pusiera** or **pusiese, pusieras** or **pusieses, pusiera** or **pusiese, pusiéramos** or **pusiésemos, pusierais** or **pusieseis, pusieran** or **pusiesen.**

*Fut. Indic.* **pondré, pondrás, pondrá, pondremos, pondréis, pondrán.**

*Cond.* **pondría, pondrías, pondría, pondríamos, pondríais, pondrían.**

*Imper.* **pon** tú, **ponga** Vd., **pongamos** nosotros, poned vosotros, **pongan** Vds.

*Past Part.* **puesto.**

41. querer

*Pres. Indic.* **quiero, quieres, quiere,** queremos, queréis, **quieren.**

*Pres. Subj.* **quiera, quieras, quiera,** queramos, queráis, **quieran.**

| | |
|---|---|
| *Pret. Indic.* | **quise, quisiste, quiso, quisimos, quisisteis, quisieron.** |
| *Imp. Subj.* | **quisiera,** or **quisiese, quisieras** or **quisieses, quisiera** or **quisiese, quisiéramos** or **quisiémos, quisierais** or **quisieseis, quisieran** or **quisiesen.** |
| *Fut. Indic.* | **querré, querrás, querrá, querremos, querréis, querrán.** |
| *Cond.* | **querría, querrías, querría, querríamos, querríais, querrían.** |
| *Imper.* | **quiere** tú, **quiera** Vd., queramos nosotros, quered vosotros, **quieran** Vds. |

**42. saber**

| | |
|---|---|
| *Pres. Indic.* | **sé,** sabes, sabe, sabemos, sabéis, saben. |
| *Pres. Subj.* | **sepa, sepas, sepa, sepamos, sepáis, sepan.** |
| *Pret. Indic.* | **supe, supiste, supo, supimos, supisteis, supieron.** |
| *Imp. Subj.* | **supiera** or **supiese, supieras** or **supieses, supiera** or **supiese, supiéramos** or **supiésemos, supierais** or **supieseis, supieran** or **supiesen.** |
| *Fut. Indic.* | **sabré, sabrás, sabrá, sabremos, sabréis, sabrán.** |
| *Cond.* | **sabría, sabrías, sabría, sabríamos, sabríais, sabrían.** |
| *Imper.* | sabe tú, **sepa** Vd., **sepamos** nosotros, sabed vosotros, **sepan** Vds. |

**43. salir**

| | |
|---|---|
| *Pres. Indic.* | **salgo,** sales, sale, salimos, salís, salen. |
| *Pres. Subj.* | **salga, salgas, salga, salgamos, salgáis, salgan.** |
| *Fut. Indic.* | **saldré, saldrás, saldrá, saldremos, saldréis, saldrán.** |
| *Cond.* | **saldría, saldrías, saldría, saldríamos, saldríais, saldrían.** |
| *Imper.* | **sal** tú, **salga** Vd., **salgamos** nosotros, salid vosotros, **salgan** Vds. |

NOTE. The compound *sobresalir* is regular in the familiar imperative: sobresale tú.

**44. ser**

| | |
|---|---|
| *Pres. Indic.* | **soy, eres, es, somos, sois, son.** |
| *Pres. Subj.* | **sea, seas, sea, seamos, seáis, sean.** |
| *Imp. Indic.* | **era, eras, era, éramos, erais, eran.** |
| *Pret. Indic.* | **fuí, fuiste, fué, fuimos, fuisteis, fueron.** |
| *Imp. Subj.* | **fuera** or **fuese, fueras** or **fueses, fuera** or **fuese, fuéramos** or **fuésemos, fuerais** or **fueseis, fueran** or **fuesen.** |
| *Imper.* | **sé** tú, **sea** Vd., **seamos** nosotros, sed vosotros, **sean** Vds. |

**45. tener**

| | |
|---|---|
| *Pres. Indic.* | **tengo, tienes, tiene,** tenemos, tenéis, **tienen.** |
| *Pres. Subj.* | **tenga, tengas, tenga, tengamos, tengáis, tengan.** |
| *Pret. Indic.* | **tuve, tuviste, tuvo, tuvimos, tuvisteis, tuvieron.** |
| *Imp. Subj.* | **tuviera** or **tuviese, tuvieras** or **tuvieses, tuviera** or **tuviese, tuviéramos** or **tuviésemos, tuvierais** or **tuvieseis, tuvieran** or **tuviesen.** |

| *Fut. Indic.* | tendré, tendrás, tendrá, tendremos, tendréis, tendrán. |
| *Cond.* | tendría, tendrías, tendría, tendríamos, tendríais, tendrían. |
| *Imper.* | ten tú, tenga Vd., tengamos nosotros, tened vosotros, tengan Vds. |

46. traer

| *Pres. Indic.* | traigo, traes, trae, traemos, traéis, traen. |
| *Pres. Subj.* | traiga, traigas, traiga, traigamos, traigáis, traigan. |
| *Pret. Indic.* | traje, trajiste, trajo, trajimos, trajisteis, trajeron. |
| *Imp. Subj.* | trajera or trajese, trajeras or trajeses, trajera or trajese, trajéramos or trajésemos, trajerais or trajeseis, trajeran or trajesen. |
| *Imper.* | trae tú, traiga Vd., traigamos nosotros, traed vosotros, traigan Vds. |
| *Pres. Part.* | trayendo. |

47. valer

| *Pres. Indic.* | valgo, vales, vale, valemos, valéis, valen. |
| *Pres. Subj.* | valga, valgas, valga, valgamos, valgáis, valgan. |
| *Fut. Indic.* | valdré, valdrás, valdrá, valdremos, valdréis, valdrán. |
| *Cond.* | valdría, valdrías, valdría, valdríamos, valdríais, valdrían. |
| *Imper.* | val or vale tú, valga Vd., valgamos nosotros, valed vosotros, valgan Vds. |

48. venir

| *Pres. Indic.* | vengo, vienes, viene, venimos, venís, vienen. |
| *Pres. Subj.* | venga, vengas, venga, vengamos, vengáis, vengan. |
| *Pret. Indic.* | vine, viniste, vino, vinimos, vinisteis, vinieron. |
| *Imp. Subj.* | viniera or viniese, vinieras or vinieses, viniera or viniese, viniéramos or viniésemos, vinierais or vinieseis, vinieran or viniesen. |
| *Fut. Indic.* | vendré, vendrás, vendrá, vendremos, vendréis, vendrán. |
| *Cond.* | vendría, vendrías, vendría, vendríamos, vendríais, vendrían. |
| *Imper.* | ven tú, venga Vd., vengamos nosotros, venid vosotros, vengan Vds. |
| *Pres. Part.* | viniendo. |

49. ver

| *Pres. Indic.* | veo, ves, ve, vemos, veis, ven. |
| *Pres. Subj.* | vea, veas, vea, veamos, veáis, vean. |
| *Imp. Indic.* | veía, veías, veía, veíamos, veíais, veían. |
| *Imper.* | ve tú, vea Vd., veamos nosotros, ved vosotros, vean Vds. |
| *Past Part.* | visto. |

50. yacer

| *Pres. Indic.* | yazco, or yazgo, yaces, yace, yacemos, yacéis, yacen. |
| *Pres. Subj.* | yazca or yazga, yazcas or yazgas, yazca or yazga, yazcamos, or yazgamos, yazcáis or yazgáis, yazcan or yazgan. |

*Imper.*    yace tú, **yazca** or **yazga** Vd., **yazcamos** or **yazgamos** nosotros, yaced vosotros, **yazcan** or **yazgan** Vds.

51. Defective Verbs
   *a.* The following verbs are used only in the forms that have an **i** in the ending: abolir, agredir, aterirse, empedernir, transgredir.

   *b.* atañer
   This verb is used only in the third person. It is most frequently used in the present indicative: atañe, atañen.

   *c.* concernir
   This verb is used only in the third person of the following tenses:
   *Pres. Indic.*    **concierne, conciernen.**
   *Pres. Subj.*    **concierna, conciernan.**
   *Imp. Indic.*    concernía, concernían.
   *Imp. Subj.*    concerniera or concerniese, concernieran or concerniesen.
   *Pres. Part.*    concerniendo.

   *d.* soler
   This verb is used most frequently in the present and imperfect indicative. It is less frequently used in the present subjunctive.
   *Pres. Indic.*    **suelo, sueles, suele,** solemos, soléis, **suelen.**
   *Pres. Subj.*    **suela, suelas, suela,** solamos, soláis, **suelan.**
   *Imp. Indic.*    solía, solías, solía, solíamos, solíais, solían.
   The preterit is seldom used. Of the compound tenses, only the present perfect is commonly used: he solido, etc. The other tenses are very rare.

   *e.* roer
   This verb has three forms in the first person of the present indicative: **roo, royo, roigo,** all of which are infrequently used. In the present subjunctive the perferable form is **roa, roas, roa,** etc., although the forms **roya** and **roiga** are found.

52. *Irregular Past Participles*

| | |
|---|---|
| abrir—**abierto** | escribir—**escrito** |
| absorber—absorbido, **absorto** | freir—**frito,** freído |
| bendecir—bendecido, **bendito** | hacer—**hecho** |
| componer—**compuesto** | imprimir—**impreso** |
| cubrir—**cubierto** | inscribir—**inscrito, inscripto** |
| decir—**dicho** | maldecir—maldecido, **maldito** |
| deponer—**depuesto** | morir—**muerto** |
| descomponer—**descompuesto** | poner—**puesto** |
| describir—**descrito** | prescribir—**prescrito, prescripto** |
| descubrir—**descubierto** | proscribir—**proscrito, proscripto** |
| desenvolver—**desenvuelto** | proveer—proveído, **provisto** |
| deshacer—**deshecho** | resolver—**resuelto** |
| devolver—**devuelto** | revolver—**revuelto** |
| disolver—**disuelto** | romper—rompido, **roto** |
| encubrir—**encubierto** | satisfacer—**satisfecho** |
| entreabrir—**entreabierto** | subscribir—**subscrito** |
| entrever—**entrevisto** | ver—**visto** |
| envolver—**envuelto** | volver—**vuelto** |

## The Spanish Language in America
### Introduction

In a sense Latin is not dead. The speech of Roman soldiers, merchants, and colonists, the Latin of another day, was taken bodily to Iberia, to Gaul, to Dacia, and to many other regions. As it developed under some influence from the languages previously spoken in these areas, it became known eventually by several other names—Spanish, Portuguese, French, Italian, Romanian, etc.

The Latin of northern Spain came to be called Castilian since its speakers were from the province of Castilla (Latin *Castella*, "castles"), and although later it was often called Spanish (**español**), to this day the people of many regions of Spanish speech refer to their language as **castellano,** and the children of Argentina and Chile, for instance, study **composición castellana.**

Castilian, among other Latin dialects, became prominent in the Iberian peninsula because of the hegemony of north central Spain in the reconquest of the peninsula from the Moors during the Middle Ages and subsequently in the discovery and settlement of America. Thus its predominance over other manifestations of Latin is not due to its own nature but rather to non-linguistic factors: political and military power and organization, church-state relations, and finally literary ascendance.

The Spanish of Latin America, like most "colonial" speech, tends to be conservative in its structural changes compared with that of the mother country. In addition, it reflects regional traits of the southwestern part of Spain, notably Andalusia and adjacent areas, from where a large part of the sailors, conquistadores, and colonists came. In other words, the Spanish of America would seem to be Andalusian Castilian of the sixteenth and seventeenth centuries, as far as pronunciation and grammar are concerned. But in vocabulary hundreds of Indian words have entered the language, especially in Mexico, Guatemala, the Andes (Ecuador, Peru, and Bolivia), and in the Río de la Plata region. The Indian words of the Caribbean islands were taken to other parts of Latin America by the original Spanish settlers and often form a part of the general Spanish lexicon. It should be noted that these Indian languages belong to distinct, unrelated families, so that an **ahuacate** (avocado) in Mexico and Central America becomes a **palta** in the Andes. Although Spanish Americans generally have little difficulty understanding each other, the following variants represent rather extreme divergences:

|             | Little boy | bus       | blond  |
|-------------|------------|-----------|--------|
| *Mexico*    | **chamaco**| **camión**| **güero** |
| *Guatemala* | **patojo** | **camioneta** | **canche** |
| *El Salvador* | **cipote** | **camioneta** | **chele** |
| *Panamá*    | **chico**  | **chiva**  | **fulo** |
| *Colombia*  | **pelado** | **autobús**| **mono** |
| *Argentina* | **pibe**   | **colectivo** | **rubio** |
| *Chile*     | **cabro**  | **micro**  | **rubio** |
| *Cuba*      | **chico**  | **guagua** | **rubio** |

Although most of these words are actually Spanish (of Latin origin), several are from the Indian languages of the respective areas. The fact that there are differences of this sort is to be expected in a general culture that contains so many national boundaries.

Today Spanish (**castellano**) is the most extensive manifestation of the former spoken Latin. Those who think and express themselves in this language number about 200,000,000, and they live in some twenty countries, most of which have rapidly growing populations. It is estimated as of 1970 that by A.D. 2000 Spanish will be the language of nearly 500,000,000 people, most of whom will be **hispanoamericanos.** It is one of the principal languages of the world.

## The Pronunciation of Latin-American Spanish

The fundamental phonological traits of American Spanish are to be found in Castilla, but only changes that have taken place in the Andalusian dialect of Castilian have become established in America. Furthermore, these changes apparently took place between the fifteenth and the eighteenth centuries, during the settlement of Latin America. Evidence indicates that inaccessible areas of Spanish America (the mountainous regions of Mexico, Guatemala, Colombia, Ecuador, Peru, Bolivia, as well as Paraguay, inland Venezuela, and northern Argentina) received only the early changes of Andalusian Castilian, while the accessible coastal areas and port cities tend to reflect both early changes and those of the late colonial period. Thus it is that Cuban and Panamanian Spanish resemble that of present-day Sevilla more than does Mexican Spanish or that of Bogotá. In the meantime Madrid Spanish (called Castilian by many North Americans) developed one or two features that never reached America.

The outstanding common feature of American-Spanish pronunciation that goes back to the early colonial period is the so-called **seseo.** About the time of Columbus the people of southwestern Spain began to confuse the two sibilant sounds of **casa** [KáSa] ("house") and **caza** [kása] ("hunt") (the capital [S] representing a "thick" alveolar sound and the [s] representing a "normal" dental sound), with the result that only the dental sound survived. Since most settlers of America were from the south, this became the general Spanish-American tendency. **Coser** and **cocer** are alike in southern Spain and in Latin America. The sibilant is a delicate dental one. In northern and central Spain a distinction between these two sounds is still maintained, and the second or dental one has become interdental [θ], similar to the voiceless *th* of English. The former [S] is still apicoalveolar, and to the foreigner approaches the sound represented by English *sh*.

In the seventeenth and eighteenth centuries other changes occurred in the pronunciation of southern Spanish. As has been indicated, these became part of the Spanish of the accessible areas of America, but most did not reach the high mountains and plateaus. The first of these was the aspiration or even the loss of /s/ syllable final. **Estos** becomes [éhtoh] or even [éto], the result of what might be termed a "relaxed" articulation. About the same time the /l/ (written ll) tended to be "relaxed" to the extent that it coincided with the /y/ (written **y**), so that **valla** and **vaya** were levelled to [báya] in Andalusia and parts of America. Today Bolivia, Paraguay, and much of Peru and Ecuador still maintain a distinction. One of the latest levelings of Andalusia was the confusion of /l/ and /r/ syllable final. This is heard today in Puerto Rico, Panama, and Venezuela, and to a certain extent in Cuba, the Dominican Republic, and central Chile. **Puerta** sounds like [pwelta], **mar** like [mal] and the infinitives seem to end in /l/. A final Andalusian trait is the velar /n/ [ŋ] as a sign of open transition. **Enamora**

Map 1

 Vos used instead of tú in informal address.

In Chile the distinction is one of class: vos is used in the lower economic levels.

Map 2

Aspiration or loss of /s/ syllable final.

Map 3

Distinction between /ḷ/ and /y/.

Assibilation of /rr/ and /tr/.

is [enamóra], but **en amor** is [eɲamór]. English-speakers think of *ng* when they hear **son** and **pan** pronounced [soŋ] and [paŋ].

Perhaps the only outstanding feature of American Spanish that is not traceable to Andalusia is the assibilation of /rr/ [řř] and /r/ [ř] final and postconsonantal. This occurs in vast areas of America: Guatemala, Costa Rica, in the eastern cordillera of Colombia, highland Ecuador, Bolivia, Chile, western and northern Argentina, and Paraguay.

The maps show the distribution of the distinguishing features of Spanish-American pronunciation.

### Syntactic Features

The familiar form of address in Spanish, **tú,** is a direct descendant of the Latin *tu.* The Latin plural form *vos* also came down to Spanish, but by the late Middle Ages it had assumed the function of polite singular as well as familiar plural. To make the distinction, people began to say **vosotros** (you others) for the plural. In the sixteenth century there came into being a very polite form of address: **vuestra merced** (your mercy), used with the third person of the verb, as one might say, "Does his majesty wish to enter?" It has been shortened to **usted.** With this new polite form, **vos,** the former polite singular, lost prestige and became a familiar form. This was the state of affairs when the colonists came to America. As a result, vast sections of Latin America use **vos** instead of **tú** as the singular familiar form of address. All of Spanish America uses **ustedes** for the familiar plural as well as the polite plural. It will be noted in the map on page xxxiii that the **vos** areas are generally far from the old Viceroyalties of Mexico and Lima. Only in Chile is there a social distinction.

The verb used with **vos** is the modified plural of Old Spanish: **hablás, comés, vivís**; the imperative is **hablá, comé, viví.** The object pronoun and the possessive are from the singular, the object of the preposition, **vos: LLevate tu perro con vos.** Since the imperative of **ir** would be simply **i,** the verb **andar** is used instead: **¡andate!** Another interesting syntactic trait is the general tendency to differentiate gender of nouns of occupation and status of people and to create feminine forms where they may not have existed in so-called standard Spanish. **Presidenta, ministra, dependienta, liberala, abogada,** and **arquitecta** have been heard. Equally general are the tendencies to use adjectives as adverbs (**corre ligero, toca el piano lindo**) and to make certain adverbs "agree" with adjectives they modify (**media muerta; medias locas**) as well as to use the impersonal **haber** in the plural (**habían dos; ¿cuántos habrán?**).

### The Vocabulary of Spanish America

There are three main tendencies in the development of Hispanic-American lexical elements: (1) to use words that were popular at the time of the settlement of America, especially maritime terms or rural expressions, often out of popular etymology; (2) to adopt Indian words, especially those related to the domestic scene; and (3) to borrow directly from English and to develop cases of correlative analogy due to English influence.

Of the first category are such terms as **flota** for a bus line, **amarrar** for **atar; botar** for **echar; virar** for **volverse.** In the tropical zone of America (from Guatemala south through Peru), where there are no seasons of heat and cold, since these depend on altitude, the Spaniards began to call the wet periods **invierno** (winter) and the dry, **verano** (summer). The custom continues to this day in Guatemala, El Salvador, Honduras, Nicaragua, Costa Rica, Panama, Colombia, Venezuela, Ecuador, and Peru. One may ask, **¿qué tal el invierno?** ("How was the winter?") and receive the answer **¡copioso!** ("copious").

Indian words entered the Spanish of America by the hundreds. In the Caribbean the Spaniards learned **tabaco, canoa, huracán, maíz, ají;** in Mexico, from Náhuatl, **chocolate, tomate, coyote, chicle, cacao;** in the Andes, from Quechua, **pampa, quinina, cóndor, puma, poncho;** and in the Río de la Plata region, from Guaraní, **ananás, ñandú, ombú, yajá, tapioca.**

During the twentieth century the influence of English has been strong in Latin America, and the direct borrowings in some areas could be counted in the hundreds: **control, lonche, lonchería, sandwich, jaibol** ("highball"), **cóctel, ponche, bar, twist, chance, fútbol, béisbol, fildear** ("to field"), **jonrón** ("home run"), **noquear** ("to knock out"), **lobista,** and even such verbs as **taipear** ("to type") and **blofear** ("to bluff"). In the realm of correlative analogy or sense loans, English has tremendous influence, and **educación** ("upbringing") takes the place of **pedagogía, instrucción,** and **enseñanza; argumento** ("plot of a story") moves into the slot of **discusión; atender** ("to wait on") into that of **asistir; audiencia** into that of **concurrencia; acta** ("minutes") takes the place of **ley; complexión** ("physical constitution") takes the place of **tez.**

Regional Features: Mexico

Among speakers of Spanish, a Mexican is recognized by his intonation and by his tendency to lengthen the articulation of his /s/ and by his general preference for the consonant over the vowel. If intonation of Spanish is represented in a pattern of four levels, Mexicans, especially males in a "man-about-town" mood, tend to strike a terminal point between standard statement and emphatic statement, giving the utterance a "minor-key" effect. The tensely-grooved /s/ of Mexican Spanish leads to the virtual elimination of unstressed vowels, especially /e/, in rapid speech: **accidentes de coches** may tend to be [aksiḏénts ḏe kočs].

Typical adjectives of Mexico are **mero** and **puro.** The first of these is so popular that it means not only "mere" but "very," "real," "just," "same," and many other things, and is even used adverbially: **ya merito** ("It won't be long now").

As has been noted, Mexico is the center of Aztec vocabulary that has entered Spanish and eventually many languages of the world: **tomate, chocolate, cacao, coyote, chicle,** and hundreds of less common terms.

Guatemala

The Spanish of Guatemala is characterized by a strong assibilated /rr/ [řř] and by [ř] for /r/ except in intervocalic position. The **jota** tends to be [h] rather than [x], and velar /n/ marks open transition. Along with those of other Central-American areas, Guatemalan speakers tend to weaken intervocalic /y/ to the extent that **silla** sounds like [sía] and **bella** like [bea]. Through a process of ultracorrection, **vea** may become [béya]. Guatemalans generally pronounce their /s/ syllable final with clarity and tension.

A fairly universal feature of the Spanish of Guatemala is the **voseo,** or use of **vos** as the subject form of familiar address in the singular. The verb used with this is the plural familiar, but the pronoun objects and possessives are always singular. **Cuando te vayas, llévate tu perro contigo,** as one might say in Spain or in Mexico, would be **Cuando te vayás, llevate tu perro con vos** in Guatemala.

Little boys are **patojos** in Guatemala, and blonds are **canches.**

## El Salvador, Honduras, Nicaragua

Perhaps more than any other group of independent countries, these three form a linguistic unity in most respects. They represent in phonology a middle point between the highland conservatism (Mexico and the Andes, for instance) and the later trends of the lowlands (Cuba and Panamá, for example). The inhabitants of these countries call each other **guanacos, catrachos,** and **nicas** respectively, and are always talking of Central-American union.

The phonological phenomenon of recent discovery—although it is probably an "archaic" trait—is the occlusive pronunciation of /b/, /d/, /g/ after another consonant, a situation in which they would be fricative in "standard" Spanish.

It is in this region of Central America that one hears a lisped /s/ that approaches [θ] among many residents, and especially among the working classes. As in northern Mexico, the intervocalic /y/ (representing ortho-graphic **y** and **ll**) tends to be a semivowel or even disappears. The **jota** /x/ is [h] in all speakers, and there is a strong tendency to aspirate syllable final /s/.

The Salvador-Honduras-Nicaragua region is rich in forms of com-binative analogy, especially noun formation on the basis of other nouns. The suffixes **-ada** and **-ón** are of extensive application: **babosada, pende-jada, lambida, atolada, paisanada, perrada, barbón, narizón, pistón, quemazón;** and the longer diminutive form **-ecito** that might be used in Spain and in Mexico is simply **-ito: llavita, lucita, crucita, piedrita.** The place where things grow or are to be found is indicated by the suffix **-al: cañal, guacal, platanal, cafetal, piñal, pinal.**

Along with Guatemala and the other Central-American countries, except Panama, this region uses the **vos** form of familiar address, and in the way described for Guatemala: **Vení y decime, ¿ son vos y tu padre ladrones?**

Many indigenous words are used in everyday conversation, most of them from the Pipil, a sublanguage of the Náhuatl. A blond is a **chele,** a boy is a **cipote, pushco** is dirty, **peche** is slender, and there is the usual stock of Aztec terms that were imported after the conquest of Mexico.

## Costa Rica

Like Guatemala, Costa Rica is noted for its assibilated /rr/, along with assibilated /r/ syllable final. It also shares with Guatemala a fairly con-servative articulation of /s/ syllable final. As in all Central-American and Caribbean countries, the /n/ is velar when final, as a sign of open juncture: [eŋ amor] but [enamorár], and intervocalic /y/ weakens to the point of elimination through vocalization.

As a part of the syntactic structure of the dialect, **vos** and related forms operate where **tú** would prevail in Spain or Mexico today, and lexically, Costa Rica shows less Aztec influence than Guatemala, El Salvador, or Honduras.

Panama

The Spanish of Panama might be termed "trade route Spanish," in that it has the phonological character of parts of America that were in constant communication with Spain at the grass-roots level and yet were removed from the courtly influences of the viceregal centers (Mexico and Lima). It resembles strongly the Spanish of Cuba, Puerto Rico, and Venezuela and the northern coast of Colombia.

Along with other Caribbean residents, the Panamanians tend to aspirate their /s/ at the end of a syllable, or to eliminate it entirely.


Colombia

The development of the language in Colombia, which has three high mountain ranges and several important ports, might serve as an example of how American Spanish grew in disparate ways from Peninsular models. The relative inaccessibility of the high sierras and valleys makes it possible to find at least five distinct linguistic zones in the former Nueva Granada. The "dialects" therefore represent stages in the historical development of southern Peninsular Spanish, the most inaccessible regions generally representing the earliest and the most accessible in general representing the latest in Andalusian vogues, before independence.

Strange as it may seem, Colombian Spanish has two general traits in common with that of El Salvador, Honduras, and Nicaragua: the /x/ is [h] in all regions, and the /b/, /d/, /g/ are occlusive after any consonant. Thus **pardo, barba, algo, desde, las vacas,** all have occlusives where a Spaniard or a Mexican would use fricatives.

The Spanish of Bogotá has the conservative distinction of /ḷ/ and /y/ and, like that of Costa Rica and Guatemala, tends to assibilate the /rr/, the /tr/, and the /r/ final.

**Pastuso** Spanish (of Nariño) is in many ways Ecuadorean, and like the Spanish of highland Mexico, slights the vowel in favor of the consonant, tends to pronounce the /d/ of **-ado,** and uses an apicodental /s/, strong and well defined.

Antioquia's Spanish is unique in America in one way. The /s/ is apico-alveolar [S], like that of Spain, and although no distinction is made between **casa** and **caza,** the Colombian ambassador to Spain, an **antioqueño,** gave the impression of "talking like a Spaniard." The second distinguishing feature of this region's Spanish is the /y/ of such tenseness that it even becomes affricate intervocalically [maŷo, kabaŷo].

Colombia is unusually formal in most sections as far as direct address is concerned. Many speakers use **usted** almost exclusively—even to cats and dogs. Not only is this the case within the family, but some relatives speak to each other as **su merced.** The **voseo** prevails in Antioquia and in Santander and in the **Valle,** while Bogotá and the Coast always employ the **tuteo.**

Typical of Colombia are the idiomatic expressions ¡**siga!** and ¡**a la orden!** The first is said to invite one to enter, and the other to ask, "What can I do for you?" Black coffee, especially the demitasse, is a **tinto,** and to invite one to partake, one says: ¿**Le provoca un tinto?** This same sentence to a Spaniard might mean, "Does red wine make you fight?" Instead of sending regards with **saludos,** Colombians use **saludes** ("healths").

## Venezuela

The speech pattern of Venezuela is for the most part that of the Caribbean, and therefore late Andalusian. One "eats" his final /s/; /l/ and /r/ are confused at syllable end; /n/ is velar as a sign of finality; and as in El Salvador, Honduras, and Nicaragua, many people pronounce the /s/ as [θ].

As far as address is concerned, most of Venezuela is **tuteo** country, but sections near the Colombian frontier are **vos** areas.

## Ecuador

In a country where thousands speak Quechua (the language of the Incas) in preference to Spanish and where many are bilingual, the Spanish language of the upper inter-Andean region is very conservative in its phonological evolution. Ecuadoreans (except those of the coast) still distinguish /l/ and /y/ as [ž] and [y], still pronounce /s/ with deliberate tenseness and, like many Mexicans, slight the vowel in favor of the consonant. Because Quechua is so widely spoken, and because this language has a simple three-vowel system, the Spanish of the highlands tends to heighten /o/ to /u/ and /e/ to /i/. Unique in Latin America is the final /s/ as [z] before a vowel in the following word: [laz agwas].

## Peru

About 11,000,000 **peruanos,** or as their neighbors may say, **peruleros** or **cholos,** occupy the territory of the central Inca Empire of preconquest days. Their money is counted in **soles** and their babies are **guaguas.** Along with Ecuador and Bolivia, Peru belongs to heavily populated Andean Spanish America, and besides having many Quechua-speaking inhabitants, the region boasts a clear Spanish that gives evidence of sixteenth-century origin and viceregal nurture.

Except in Lima and along the northern coast, Peruvians still distinguish the /l/ and /y/, and the general impression of Peruvian Spanish is similar to that of Mexico, Bolivia, and Ecuador.

Nearly all of Peru uses the **tú** form of familiar address, and as one might expect, hundreds of Quechua words have entered the Spanish of everyday life. In fact, several **quechismos** have become universal terms: **pampa, cóndor, puma, puna, quinina, llama, alpaca, gaucho, china** ("sweetheart"), **poncho,** and many others.

## Chile

Linguistically, Chile can be divided into three sections, north, middle, and south. The north and the south resemble each other more than they do the middle. The heavily populated central valley partakes of many of the traits of late Andalusian, through the port of Valparaiso and the city of Santiago. Final /s/ is aspirated, /l/ and /r/ are confused in the syllable final situation, and /l/ and /y/ are not distinguished. Chiloé still distinguishes these latter two, and in the north there are vowel-heightening influences of Quechua. Two features that seem to characterize all Chilean Spanish are the /č/ of alveolar articulation rather than palatal and the /x/ with a palatal element of semiconsonantal nature before /e/. One seems to hear **la gente de Chile** as [la xjénte de tSíle].

Argentina, Uruguay, Paraguay

The Spanish of this vast territory is of two main types, according to the direction from which the settlers came. The western and northwestern sections were settled from Peru and Chile from about 1590. Although Buenos Aires and the humid Pampa were first settled about 1535, it was not until 1580 that a permanent settlement was established. The important factor producing the differences of today was the accessibility of Buenos Aires and surrounding country to constant influences from the ports of southern Spain in the colonial period. Thus the interior shows more conservative features: an /s/ of more tense articulation, a distinction between /l/ and /y/ in some areas, and the assibilated /rr/ of Costa Rica, Bogotá, and Guatemala.

The **porteño** of the Río de la Plata region is noted for his /y/ with strong [ž] articulation: **bayo, calle** [bážo], [káže].

Both Argentina and Uruguay are **voseo** territories, and the style has been recorded extensively in gaucho poetry. As a cattle region, the pampas have a lexicon that is rich in the terminology of the ranch and of horses. English and French are contributors to the vocabulary of the area, and one hears of **five o'clock tea a todas horas,** and the frequency of **chau** for "good-by" attests the influence of Italian, the original language of more than half of the inhabitants of Argentina. **Argentinos** are often called **che,** since they use this term to attract attention.

Paraguay, being more inaccessible, has two conservative features in its phonology: the distinction of /l/ and /y/, and the assibilation of /rr/. It is unique in that nearly all its inhabitants are bilingual. They speak the original Indian language, Guaraní, and Spanish. The occasion usually dictates which will be used, and speakers will often shift from one to the other in the same utterance.

Cuba, The Dominican Republic, and Puerto Rico

The Spanish of the Caribbean, like that of Panama, could be termed "trade route" Spanish, since it shows rather typically the American evolution of Andalusian trends of the seventeenth and eighteenth centuries, trends that do not seem to be present in the more inaccessible hinterland. Add to this the Afro-Cuban influences of slave days and the many American English loans of the twentieth century, and we have perhaps the least "conservative" Castilian.

Cubans tend to aspirate their syllable final /s/ or drop it altogether, and the tendency is as marked or more so in Puerto Rico and Santo Domingo. In all three, syllable final /l/ and /r/ are confused, most of all in Puerto Rico, where the /l/ is favored: **puerta, izquierdo** [pwélta], [ihkjéldo]. In contrast to Mexico, Ecuador, Peru, and Bolivia, where the vowel may be slighted, those of the Caribbean tend to slight the consonant in favor of the vowel. In Puerto Rico /rr/ is now velar in about half of the population. It resembles the **jota** of Spain: [x].

Cuba, Puerto Rico, and the Dominican Republic are **tuteo** countries.

This brief description of some of the features of the Castilian of America may help to show that distinctive features do not correspond to geographical or political entities to the extent that has been believed, and one might indicate as many as a hundred dialects—and yet it is all Spanish.

## Numerals—Números

| Cardinal Numbers | Números Cardinales | Ordinal Numbers | Números Ordinales[5] |
|---|---|---|---|
| 1........ one | uno, una | first | primero |
| 2........ two | dos | second | segundo |
| 3........ three | tres | third | tercero |
| 4........ four | cuatro | fourth | cuarto |
| 5........ five | cinco | fifth | quinto |
| 6........ six | seis | sixth | sexto |
| 7........ seven | siete | seventh | séptimo |
| 8........ eight | ocho | eighth | octavo |
| 9........ nine | nueve | ninth | noveno, nono |
| 10...... ten | diez | tenth | décimo |
| 11...... eleven | once | eleventh | undécimo |
| 12...... twelve | doce | twelfth | duodécimo |
| 13...... thirteen | trece | thirteenth | décimotercio |
| 14...... fourteen | catorce | fourteenth | décimocuarto |
| 15...... fifteen | quince | fifteenth | décimoquinto |
| 16...... sixteen | dieciseis, diez y seis | sixteenth | décimosexto |
| 17...... seventeen | diecisiete, diez y siete | seventeenth | décimoséptimo |
| 18...... eighteen | dieciocho, diez y ocho | eighteenth | décimoctavo |
| 19...... nineteen | diecinueve, diez y nueve | nineteenth | décimonono |
| 20...... twenty | veinte | twentieth | vigésimo |
| 21...... twenty-one | veintiuno, veinte y uno | twenty-first | vigésimo primero |
| 30...... thirty | treinta | thirtieth | trigésimo |
| 40...... forty | cuarenta | fortieth | cuadragésimo |
| 50...... fifty | cincuenta | fiftieth | quincuagésimo |
| 60...... sixty | sesenta | sixtieth | sexagésimo |
| 70...... seventy | setenta | seventieth | septuagésimo |
| 80...... eighty | ochenta | eightieth | octogésimo |
| 90...... ninety | noventa | ninetieth | nonagésimo |
| 100...... one hundred | ciento | (one) hundredth | centésimo |
| 101...... one hundred and one | ciento (y) uno | (one) hundred and first | centésimo primo |
| 200...... two hundred | doscientos | two-hundredth | ducentésimo |
| 300...... three hundred | trescientos | three-hundredth | tricentésimo |
| 400...... four hundred | cuatrocientos | four-hundredth | cuadringentésimo |
| 500...... five hundred | quinientos | five-hundredth | quingentésimo |
| 600...... six hundred | seiscientos | six-hundredth | sexagésimo |
| 700...... seven hundred | setecientos | seven-hundredth | septingentésimo |
| 800...... eight hundred | ochocientos | eight-hundredth | octingentésimo |
| 900...... nine hundred | novecientos | nine-hundredth | noningentésimo |
| 1000 .... one thousand | mil | (one) thousandth | milésimo |
| 100,000 .. one hundred thousand | cien mil | (one) hundred thousandth | cienmilésimo |
| 1,000,000 one million | un millón | (one) millionth | millonésimo |

## Nations, Cities, and Adjectives of Nationality

| | |
|---|---|
| Afganistán | afgano |
| Albania | albanés |
| Alto Volta | voltaico |
| Arabia Saudita | árabe saudita |

[5] The ordinals beyond the "tenth" are less used in Spanish than in English. They are often replaced by the cardinals: *Alfonso the Thirteenth* **Alfonso trece.**

| | |
|---|---|
| Argelia | argelino |
| Argentina | argentino |
| Asunción | asunceño |
| Basutolandia | basutolandés |
| Bechuanalandia | bechuanalandés |
| Bélgica | belga |
| Birmania | birmano |
| Bogotá | bogotano |
| Bolivia | boliviano |
| Brasil | brasileño |
| Bruselas | bruselense |
| Buenos Aires | bonaerense or porteño |
| Bulgaria | búlgaro |
| Burundi | burundi |
| Camboya | camboyano |
| Camerún | camerunés |
| Canadá | canadiense |
| Caracas | caraqueño |
| Ceilán | ceilanés |
| Colombia | colombiano |
| Congo (both) | congoleño |
| Costa de Marfil | marfileño |
| Costa Rica | costarricense |
| Cuba | cubano |
| Chad | chadiano |
| Checoslovaquia | checoslovaco |
| Chile | chileno |
| China | chino |
| Chipre | chipriota |
| Dahomey | dahomeyano |
| Dinamarca | dinamarqués or danés |
| Ecuador | ecuatoriano |
| El Salvador | salvadoreño |
| España | español |
| Estados Unidos de América | estadounidense |
| Etiopía | etíope |
| Filipinas | filipino |
| Finlandia | finlandés or finés |
| Francia | francés |
| Gabón | gabonés |
| Gambia | gambio |
| Ghana | ghanés |
| Ginebra | ginebrino |
| Grecia | griego |
| Guatemala | guatemalteco |
| Guayaquil | guayaquileño |
| Guinea | guineo |
| Haití | haitiano |
| Honduras | hondureño |
| Hungría | húngaro |

| | |
|---|---|
| Ifni | ifneño |
| India | indio |
| Indonesia | indonesio |
| Irak | iraqués |
| Irán | iranio |
| Irlanda | irlandés |
| Islandia | islandés |
| Israel | israelí |
| Italia | italiano |
| Jamaica | jamaicano |
| Japón | japonés |
| Jordania | jordanio |
| Jerusalém | jerosolimitano |
| Kenia | kenio |
| Kuwait | kuwaiteño |
| Laos | laosiano |
| La Paz | paceño |
| Líbano | libanés |
| Liberia | liberiano |
| Libia | libio |
| Lima | limeño |
| Lisboa | lisboeta or lisbonense |
| Londres | londinense |
| Luxemburgo | luxemburgués |
| Madagascar | malache |
| Madrid | madrileño |
| Malasia | malayo |
| Malavi | malavio |
| Malí | maliense |
| Managua | managüense |
| Marruecos | marroquí |
| Mauritania | mauritano |
| México (Mejico) | mejicano (mexicano) |
| Mongolia | mongol |
| Montevideo | montevideño or montevideano |
| Nepal | nepalés |
| Nicaragua | nicaragüense |
| Níger | nigerino |
| Nigeria | nigeriano |
| Noruega | noruego |
| Nueva York | neoyorquino |
| Nueva Zelandia | neozelandés |
| Paises Bajos | holandés |
| Pakistán | pakistano |
| Panamá | panameño |
| Paraguay | paraguayo |
| París | parisiense |
| Perú | peruano |
| Polonia | polaco |

| | |
|---|---|
| Portugal | portugués |
| Puerto Rico | puertorriqueño or portorriqueño |
| Reino Unido de Gran Bretaña e Irlanda del Norte | británico |
| República Arabe Unida | egipcio |
| República Centroafricana | centroafricano |
| República Dominicana | dominicano |
| República Socialista Soviética de Bielorrusia | bieloruso |
| República Socialista Soviética de Ucrania | ucranio |
| Río de Janeiro | carioca |
| Río Muni | ríomuniense |
| Rodesia | rodesio |
| Rumania | rumano |
| Rwanda | rwandés |
| San José | josefino |
| São Paulo | paulistano |
| Santa Cruz | cruceño |
| Santiago | santiagueño or santiaguino |
| Senegal | senegalés |
| Sierra Leona | leonense |
| Siria | sirio |
| Somalia | somalí |
| Suazilandia | suazilandés |
| Sudáfrica | sudafricano |
| Sudán | sudanés |
| Suecia | sueco |
| Tailandia | tailandés |
| Tanganyica | tanganyikano |
| Tanzania | tanzanio |
| Tegucigalpa | tegucigalpense |
| Tenerife | tinerfeño |
| Tetuán | tetuaní |
| Togo | togolés |
| Trinidad y Tobago | trinitario |
| Túnez | tunecí |
| Turquía | turco |
| Uganda | ugandés |
| Unión de Repúblicas Socialistas Soviéticas | ruso |
| Uruguay | uruguayo |
| Venecia | veneciano or véneto |
| Venezuela | venezolano |
| Viena | vienés |
| Yemen | yemenita |
| Yugoslavia | yugoslavo |
| Washington | washingtoniano |
| Zambia | zambio |
| Zanzíbar | zanzibareño |

## Monetary Units and Exchange Rates

| Country | Basic Unit | Standard Subdivision | Exchange Rate* | |
|---|---|---|---|---|
| Argentina | peso | 100 centavos | M$N | 0.003 |
| Bolivia | peso | 100 centavos | $b | 0.084 |
| Brazil | cruzeiro | 100 centavos | Cr$ | 0.260 |
| Chile | escudo | 100 centésimos | E° | 0.112 |
| Costa Rica | colon | 100 céntimos | ¢ | 0.128 |
| Cuba | peso | 100 centavos | $ | 1.000 |
| Dominican Republic | peso | 100 centavos | RD$ | 1.000 |
| Ecuador | sucre | 100 centavos | S/ | 0.045 |
| El Salvador | colon | 100 centavos | ¢ | 0.400 |
| Guatemala | quetzal | 100 centavos | Q | 1.000 |
| Haiti | gourde | 100 centimes | G | 0.200 |
| Honduras | lempira | 100 centavos | L | 0.500 |
| Mexico | peso | 100 centavos | Mex$ | 0.080 |
| Nicaragua | cordoba | 100 centavos | C$ | 0.142 |
| Panama | balboa | 100 centésimos | B | 0.800 |
| Paraguay | guarani | 100 céntimos | ₲ | 0.010 |
| Peru | sol | 100 centavos | S/ | 0.024 |
| Spain | peseta | 100 céntimos | Pts | 0.014 |
| Uruguay | peso | 100 centésimos | UR$ | 0.004 |
| Venezuela | bolívar | 100 céntimos | Bs | 0.220 |

* U.S. dollar = 1.000.

**A**

**a** *prep.* to; in, into; on; by.

**abacería** *f.* grocery; grocery store; **abacero** *m.* grocer.

**abad** *m.* abbot; **abadía** *f.* abbey.

**abadejo** *m. N.Sp.* codfish.

**abadesa** *f.* abbess.

**abajarse** *v.* to lower oneself, humiliate oneself.

**abajeño** *adj. Mex., C.A.* lowland; *n.* lowlander.

**abajo** *adv.* down, below; downstairs.

**abalanzar**[9] *v.* to balance; to hurl, impel; **-se** to hurl oneself; to rush (upon), swoop down (upon); *Am.* to rear, balk.

**abalear** *v.* to "shoot up."

**abanderado** *adj.* standard-bearing; *n.* standard-bearer.

**abandonamiento** = **abandono.**

**abandonar** *v.* to abandon, desert; to give up.

**abandono** *m.* abandon; desertion; neglect.

**abanicar**[6] *v.* to fan.

**abanico** *m.* fan.

**abaratar** *v.* to cheapen, lower the price of.

**abarcar**[6] *v.* to embrace, contain, include; *Carib., Ríopl.* to buy up, monopolize.

**abarrancarse**[6] *v.* to fall into an opening; to get into a difficult situation.

**abarrotería** *f. Mex., C.A., Andes* grocery, grocery store; **abarrotero** *m. Mex., C.A., Andes* grocer.

**abarrotes** *m. pl.* small packages (*in hold of a ship*); *Mex., C.A., Andes* groceries; **tienda de —** *Mex., C.A., Andes* grocery store.

**abastecer**[13] *v. irr.* to supply.

**abastecimiento** *m.* supply; provisions.

**abasto** *m.* supply; **no dar — a** to be unable to cope with.

**abatido** *adj.* dejected, depressed, crestfallen, humbled; fallen; lowered.

**abatimiento** *m.* discouragement, dejection, depression; descent, swoop, drop.

**abatir** *v.* to lower; to knock down; to depress; to humble; **-se** to become discouraged; to swoop down.

**abdicar**[6] *v.* to abdicate.

**abdomen** *m.* abdomen.

**abecedario** *m.* alphabet; primer.

**abedul** *m.* birch.

**abeja** *f.* bee; **abejera** *f.* beehive; **abejón** *m.* drone; bumblebee; **abejorro** *m.* bumblebee.

**aberración** *f.* aberration, mental or moral deviation.

**abertura** *f.* aperture, opening, hole, slit.

**abeto** *m.* fir (*tree and wood*).

**abierto** *p.p. of* **abrir** opened; *adj.* open; frank; *Am.* proud, self-satisfied; *Am.* generous.

**abigarrado** *adj.* motley; multicolored; variegated.

**abigeato** *m.* cattle stealing.

**abismado** *p.p.* absorbed, buried in thought; overwhelmed.

**abismal** *adj.* abysmal.

**abismar** *v.* to overwhelm; to depress; **-se** to be plunged (into); to bury oneself (*in thought, grief, etc.*).

**abismo** *m.* abyss, precipice, chasm.

**abjurar** *v.* to abjure; to renounce solemnly.

**ablandar** *v.* to soften.

**abnegación** *f.* abnegation, self-denial, self-sacrifice.

**abnegado** *adj.* self-sacrificing.

**abnegarse**[7] *v.* to deny oneself, sacrifice oneself.

**abobado** *adj.* stupid, silly.

**abocar**[6] *v.* to bite; to bring near; to flow into.

**abocinar** *v.* to flare; to fall on one's face.

**abochornar** *v.* to overheat; to embarrass; **-se** to get overheated; to blush; to be embarrassed.

**abofetear** *v.* to slap.

**abogacía** *f.* the legal profession; a law career.

**abogado** *m.* lawyer.

**abogar**[7] *v.* to advocate, plead in favor of; to intercede.

**abolengo** *m.* lineage, ancestry; inheritance, patrimony.

**abolición** *f.* abolition.

**abolir**[51] *v.* to abolish; to repeal.

**abolsarse** *v.* to bag (*said of trousers, skirts, etc.*).

**abollado** *p.p. & adj.* dented; bumped; bruised.

**abolladura** *f.* dent, bump.

**abollar** *v.* to dent; to bump; to crush, crumple; to bruise.

**abombar** *v.* to make bulge; **-se** *Ríopl.* to get drunk.

**abominable** *adj.* abominable, detestable.

**abominar** *v.* to abominate, abhor, detest.

**abonado** *m.* subscriber; *p.p. of* **abonar.**

**abonar** *v.* to credit with; to make a payment; to endorse, back (*a person*); to fertilize (*soil*); **-se** to subscribe.

**abonaré** *m.* promissory note; I.O.U.

**abono** *m.* (*monetario*) payment; installment; endorsement; guarantee; (*del suelo*) fertilizer; (*suscripción*) subscription.

**abordar** *v.* to board (*a ship*); to dock, put into port; to approach; to undertake, take up (*a matter, problem, etc.*).

**aborigen** *adj.* aboriginal, indigenous, native; **aborígenes** *m. pl.* aborigines, primitive inhabitants.

**aborrascarse**[6] *v.* to become stormy.

**aborrecer**[13] *v. irr.* to abhor, hate, detest.

**aborrecible** *adj.* abominable, hateful.

**aborrecimiento** *m.* abhorrence; hatred.

**abortar** *v.* to miscarry, have a miscarriage; to give birth prematurely; to fail.

**aborto** *m.* abortion, miscarriage; monster.

**abotagarse**[7] *v.* to bloat; to swell.

**abotonador** *m.* buttonhook.

**abotonar** *v.* to button, button up; to bud; **-se** to button up.

**abovedar** *v.* to vault, cover with a vault; to arch.

**abozalar** *v.* to muzzle.

**abra** *f.* cove; mountain gap or pass; dale; *Am.* breach (*in the jungle*); *Am.* leaf (*of a door*).

**abrasador** *adj.* burning, very hot.

**abrasar** *v.* to burn; to parch; **-se** to burn up, be consumed.

**abrazar**[9] *v.* to hug, embrace; to include.

**abrazo** *m.* hug, embrace.

**abrebotellas** *m.* bottle opener.

**abrelatas** *m.* can opener.

**abrevadero** *m.* drinking trough; watering place for cattle.

**abrevar** *v.* to water (*livestock*).

**abreviación** *f.* abbreviation.

**abreviar** *v.* to abbreviate, shorten, condense.

**abreviatura** *f.* abbreviation.

**abrigar**[7] *v.* to shelter, cover, protect; to wrap up; to harbor (*fear*), cherish (*hope*); **-se** to find shelter; to wrap oneself up.

**abrigo** *m.* shelter, cover, protection; wrap; overcoat.

**abril** *m.* April.

**abrillantar** *v.* to polish, shine; to glaze.

**abrir**[52] *v.* to open; to unlock.

**abrochar** *v.* to button; to clasp; to fasten.

**abrogación** *f.* repeal.

**abrogar**[7] *v.* to abrogate, repeal, annul.

**abrojo** *m.* thistle, thorn; **-s** reef.

**abrumador** *adj.* crushing, overwhelming; oppressive; fatiguing.

**abrumar** *v.* to crush, overwhelm; to trouble, annoy; **-se** to become foggy.

**abrupto** *adj.* abrupt, steep.

**absceso** *m.* abscess.

**absolución** *f.* absolution; acquittal.

**absoluto** *adj.* absolute; unconditional.

**absolver**[2,52] *v. irr.* to absolve, free from guilt; to pardon, acquit.

**absorbente** *adj.* & *m.* absorbent.

**absorber**[52] *v.* to absorb.

**absorción** *f.* absorption.

**absorto** *p.p. irr. of* **absorber** & *adj.* absorbed, engrossed; amazed.

**abstenerse**[45] *v. irr.* to abstain, refrain.

**abstinencia** *f.* abstinence; fasting.

**abstracción** *f.* abstraction, reverie.

**abstracto** *adj.* abstract.

**abstraer**[46] *v. irr.* to abstract; to withdraw, remove; **-se** to be lost in thought.

**abstraído** *adj.* lost in thought, absent-minded; aloof.

**absuelto** *p.p. of* **absolver** absolved, acquitted.

**absurdo** *adj.* absurd, ridiculous, senseless; *m.* absurdity.

**abuela** *f.* grandmother.

**abuelo** *m.* grandfather; **-s** grandparents; ancestors.

**abulia** *f.* abulia, loss of will power.

**abultado** *adj.* bulky, bulgy.

**abultar** *v.* to bulge; to be bulky; to enlarge.

**abundancia** *f.* abundance, plenty.

**abundante** *adj.* abundant, plentiful.

**abundar** *v.* to abound, be plentiful.

**aburrido** *p.p.* & *adj.* bored; boring, tiresome; weary.

**aburrimiento** *m.* weariness, dullness, boredom.

**aburrir** *v.* to bore, vex; **-se** to become bored or vexed.

**abusar** *v.* to abuse, mistreat; to misuse; **— de** to take unfair advantage of; to impose upon.

**abuso** *m.* abuse; misuse.

**acá** *adv.* here, over here; this way, hither.

**acabado** *m.* a finishing material: paint, varnish.

**acabamiento** *m.* finish, completion, end; death; *Am.* exhaustion, physical decline.

**acabar** *v.* to end, finish, complete; **— de** (+ *inf.*) to have just; **— por** (+ *inf.*) to end by; **— con** to put an end to, make short work of; to destroy; **-se** to be over, finished; to be consumed; *Am.* to wear oneself out; *Ríopl., Mex., C.A.* to age or decline in health.

**academia** *f.* academy; a special school; a scientific, literary, or artistic society.

**académico** *adj.* academic; *m.* academician, member of an academy.

**acaecer**[13] *v. irr.* to happen, occur.

**acaecimiento** *m.* event, happening.

**acalorado** *adj.* heated, excited, angry.

**acaloramiento** *m.* heat, ardor, excitement.

**acalorar** *v.* (*calentar*) to heat, warm; (*emocionar*) to excite.

**acallar** *v.* to silence; to calm, quiet.

**acampar** *v.* to encamp; to camp.

**acanalar** *v.* to groove; to flute (*as a column*); to form a channel in.

**acantilado** *adj.* sheer, steep (*cliff*); *m.* bluff, cliff.

**acantonar** *v.* to quarter (*troops*).

**acaparar** *v.* to corner (*the market*); to monopolize; to gather in (*for one's gain or profit*).

**acarear** *v.* to bring face to face; to confront.

**acariciar** *v.* to caress, pet; to cherish (*a hope or illusion*).

**acarreador** *m.* carter; carrier.

**acarrear** *v.* to cart, transport; to bring about (*harm, disaster*).

**acarreo** *m.* cartage, carriage, transport, haul.

**acaso** *adv.* perhaps; by chance; **por si — ** just in case; *m.* chance, accident.

**acatamiento** *m.* homage, reverence, respect.

**acatar** *v.* to revere, respect; to pay homage to; *Mex., C.A., Ven.* to realize; *Mex., C.A., Ven.* to notice, pay attention.

**acatarrar** *v.* to chill; *Mex., Ven.* to bother, annoy; **-se** to get chilled, catch cold; *Ríopl.* to get tipsy.

**acaudillar** *v.* to lead, command.

**acceso** *m.* access; entrance, admittance; attack; fit (*of madness, anger, etc.*).

**accesorio** *adj.* & *m.* accessory.

**accidentado** *adj.* seized with a fit; in a swoon; rough, uneven (*ground*).

**accidental** *adj.* accidental, casual.

**accidentarse** *v.* to have a seizure or fit; to swoon, faint.

**accidente** *m.* accident, mishap; chance; sudden fit, swoon.

**acción** *f.* (*física*) action; act; gesture; (*militar*) battle; (*de bolsa*) share of stock; — **de gracias** thanksgiving.

**accionar** *v.* to gesticulate, make gestures; *Am.* to act, be active.

**accionista** *m. & f.* shareholder, stockholder.

**acecinar** *v.* to dry-cure; to salt down.

**acechanza** *f.* snare; ambush.

**acechar** *v.* to lurk; to spy.

**acecho** *m.* ambush; spying; **al** (*or* **en**) — waiting in ambush, lying in wait.

**acedo** *adj.* rancid; acid; sour; harsh, disagreeable.

**aceitar** *v.* to oil, grease.

**aceite** *m.* oil; — **alcanforado** camphorated oil; — **de hígado de bacalao** cod-liver oil; — **de oliva** olive oil; — **de ricino** castor oil.

**aceitera** *f.* oil can; oil cruet (*bottle for the table*).

**aceitoso** *adj.* oily.

**aceituna** *f.* olive; **aceitunado** *adj.* olive green.

**aceituno** *m.* olive tree.

**aceleración** *f.* acceleration.

**acelerador** *m.* accelerator.

**acelerar** *v.* to accelerate, speed up; to quicken; to hurry, hasten.

**acémila** *f.* pack mule.

**acendrado** *adj.* pure, without blemish; purified.

**acendrar** *v.* to refine (*metals*); to purify, cleanse.

**acento** *m.* accent; emphasis.

**acentuar**[18] *v.* to accentuate, emphasize; to accent; **-se** to become worse (*as an illness*).

**acepción** *f.* acceptation, usual meaning.

**acepillar** *v.* to brush; to plane.

**aceptación** *f.* acceptance; approval.

**aceptar** *v.* to accept; to approve; to admit.

**acequia** *f.* irrigation canal or ditch; *Peru*, *Ch.* small stream; *Ven.*, *Mex.*, *Andes* sewer.

**acera** *f.* sidewalk.

**acerado** *adj.* steely, made of steel; steel-like; sharp.

**acerar** *v.* to steel.

**acerbo** *adj.* bitter; harsh, cruel.

**acerca de** *prep.* about, concerning.

**acercamiento** *m.* approach; approaching; rapprochement (*coming together*).

**acercar**[6] *v.* to bring near, draw up; **-se** to get near, approach.

**acero** *m.* steel.

**acérrimo** *adj.* very sour, very tart; very harsh; very strong, stanch, stalwart, steadfast.

**acertado** *adj.* accurate; right; sure.

**acertar**[1] *v. irr.* to hit (*the mark*); to hit upon; find by chance; to guess right; — **a** (+ *inf.*) to happen to.

**acertijo** *m.* riddle.

**aciago** *adj.* ill-fated, unlucky.

**acicalado** *p.p. & adj.* polished; dressed up; adorned; trim, neat.

**acicalar** *v.* to polish; to adorn; **-se** to dress up, doll up.

**acicate** *m.* spur; incentive.

**acidez** *f.* acidity, sourness.

**ácido** *m.* acid; *adj.* acid, sour.

**acierto** *m.* right guess; lucky hit; good aim; good judgment; **con** — effectively, successfully.

**aclamación** *f.* acclamation, applause.

**aclamar** *v.* to acclaim, cheer, hail, applaud.

**aclaración** *f.* explanation.

**aclarar** *v.* to clarify, explain; to clear up; to rinse; to dawn.

**aclimatar** *v.* to acclimatize, accustom to a climate or new environment.

**acobardar** *v.* to frighten, intimidate.

**acogedor** *adj.* friendly; hospitable.

**acoger**[11] *v.* to receive; to give shelter; **-se** to take refuge.

**acogida** *f.* reception, welcome; refuge.

**acogimiento** *m.* reception, welcome.

**acojinar** *v.* to cushion; to quilt.

**acolchar** *v.* to quilt.

**acólito** *m.* acolyte, altar boy.

**acometer** *v.* to attack; to undertake.

**acometida** *f.* **acometimiento** *m.* attack, assault.

**acomodadizo** *adj.* obliging; accommodating.

**acomodado** *adj.* well-off, wealthy; suitable, convenient; *p.p. of* **acomodar.**

**acomodador** *m.* usher (*in a theater*).

**acomodar** *v.* (*cosa*) to arrange, adjust; (*a una persona*) to lodge; to give employment to; **-se** to make oneself comfortable; to adapt oneself.

**acomodo** *m.* occupation, employment; arrangement.

**acompañador** *m.* companion; accompanist.

**acompañamiento** *m.* accompaniment; retinue, company.

**acompañante** *m.* companion; escort; attendant; accompanist.

**acompañar** *v.* to accompany; to escort; to be with; to enclose (*in a letter*).

**acompasado** *adj.* rhythmical; measured; slow, deliberate.

**acondicionado** *adj.* conditioned; comfortable; air-conditioned; *Am.* adequate, suitable.

**acondicionar** *v.* to condition; to prepare; to arrange; **-se** to become conditioned or prepared.

**acongojar** *v.* to grieve; **-se** to grieve; to be distressed.

**aconsejar** *v.* to advise, counsel.

**acontecer**[13] *v. irr.* to happen, occur.

**acontecimiento** *m.* event, happening.

**acopiar** *v.* to gather, accumulate, store up.

**acopio** *m.* storing; accumulation; stock, store, supply.

**acoplamiento** *m.* coupling; joint, connection.

**acoplar** v. to couple, connect; to fit or join together; to yoke; to pair, mate.

**acorazado** m. armored ship, battleship.

**acorazar**⁹ v. to armor.

**acordar** v. irr. (estar conforme) to arrange, to decide; (instrumento) to tune, put in harmony (stringed instrument); Peru, Ch., Ríopl., Mex., Cuba to grant; **-se** to remember.

**acorde** adj. in harmony; in tune; m. chord.

**acordelar** v. to measure with a cord; to rope off, put a cord around.

**acordeón** m. accordion.

**acordonar** v. to tie with a cord, string, or rope; to rope off, tie a rope around (a place); to mill (a coin).

**acornear** v. to gore, wound with a horn; to butt.

**acorralar** v. to corral; to surround.

**acortamiento** m. shortening.

**acortar** v. to shorten, diminish; **-se** to shrink; to be shy, bashful.

**acosar** v. to pursue, harass.

**acostado** adj. reclining, lying down, in bed; tilted.

**acostar**² v. irr. to put to bed; to lay down; **-se** to lie down, go to bed; to tilt.

**acostumbrado** adj. accustomed, used, usual, habitual.

**acostumbrar** v. to accustom, train; to be used to, be accustomed to; **-se** to get accustomed.

**acotación** f. marginal note; stage directions (for a play); boundary mark; mark on a map showing altitude.

**acotar** v. to mark off (with boundary marks); to make marginal notes or citations; to put the elevation marks on (maps).

**acre** adj. sour, tart, sharp; rude, harsh; m. acre.

**acrecentamiento** m. growth, increase.

**acrecentar**¹ v. irr. to increase; to advance, promote.

**acreditar** v. to credit; to bring fame or credit to; to accredit, authorize; **-se** to win credit or fame.

**acreedor** adj. worthy, deserving; m. creditor.

**acribillar** v. to riddle; to perforate; to pierce.

**acriollar** v. to make Spanish American; **-se** to become Spanish American like; to take on Spanish-American customs.

**acróbata** m. & f. acrobat.

**acta** f. minutes (of a meeting); document; **levantar —** to write the minutes.

**actitud** f. attitude; posture, pose.

**activar** v. to activate, make active; to speed up, hasten.

**actividad** f. activity; energy.

**activista** m. & f. activist.

**activo** adj. active, lively; m. assets.

**acto** m. act; action, deed; ceremony; **— continuo** (or **seguido**) immediately after; **en el —** immediately.

**actor** m. actor; **actriz** f. actress.

**actuación** f. action; intervention, par-

ticipation, performance; **-es** legal proceedings.

**actual** adj. present (time); of the present month; **-mente** adv. at present, nowadays.

**actualidad** f. present time; **-es** latest news, fashions, or events; **de —** current, up-to-date.

**actuar**¹⁸ v. to act, perform a function or act; to set in motion, cause to act.

**acuarela** f. water color.

**acuario** m. aquarium.

**acuartelar** v. to quarter (troops).

**acuático** adj. aquatic; **deportes -s** water sports.

**acuchillar** v. to knife; to stab; to slash.

**acudir** v. to go or come (to aid, or in response to a call); to attend, be present; to resort or turn to for help.

**acueducto** m. aqueduct, water channel or pipe.

**acuerdo** m. agreement; decision, resolution; opinion; remembrance; **estar de —** to be in agreement; **ponerse de —** to come to an agreement; **tomar un —** to take a decision.

**acullá** adv. yonder, over there.

**acumulación** f. accumulation.

**acumulador** m. storage battery.

**acumular** v. to accumulate, gather, pile up.

**acuñación** f. coinage, minting; wedging.

**acuñar** v. to mint, coin; to wedge.

**acuoso** adj. watery.

**acurrucarse**⁶ v. to cuddle, nestle; to huddle.

**acusación** f. accusation, charge.

**acusado** p.p. & adj. accused; m. defendant.

**acusar** v. to accuse, denounce; to acknowledge (receipt).

**acuse** m. acknowledgment (of receipt).

**acústica** f. acoustics (science of sound).

**achacar**⁶ v. to impute, attribute.

**achacoso** adj. sickly.

**achaparrado** adj. shrub, of shrub size; squat, squatty.

**achaque** m. slight chronic illness; excuse; pretext; infirmity.

**achicar**⁶ v. to shorten; to make small; to bail (water); to humiliate; Col. to kill; Ríopl. to tie, fasten; **-se** to get smaller; to shrink.

**adagio** m. adage, proverb, wise saying; adagio (musical Spanish America).

**adaptar** v. to adapt, fit, adjust.

**adecuado** adj. adequate, fit, suitable.

**adecuar** v. to fit, adapt.

**adefesio** m. absurdity, nonsense; ridiculous sight, dress, or person.

**adelantado** p.p. & adj. anticipated; advanced; ahead; forward, bold; **por —** in advance; m. governor of a province (in colonial Spanish America).

**adelantamiento** m. advancement, progress, betterment.

**adelantar** v. to advance; to move forward; to progress; to better; **-se** to get ahead.

**adelante** adv. forward, ahead; **en —** from now on.

**adelanto** *m.* advance; advancement, progress; betterment.

**adelgazar**[9] *v.* to thin out, taper; **-se** to get thin, slender.

**ademán** *m.* gesture, gesticulation; attitude.

**además** *adv.* moreover, besides; **— de** *prep.* in addition to, besides.

**adentro** *adv.* within, inside; **tierra —** inland; **mar —** out to sea; **hablar para sus -s** to talk to oneself.

**aderezamiento** *m.* dressing; adornment, decoration.

**aderezar** *v.* (*embellecer*) to fix up, adorn, beautify, garnish; (*condimentar*) to season, prepare; (*almidonar*) to starch, stiffen.

**aderezo** *m.* (*adorno*) adornment, garnish, trappings, finery, set of jewels; (*alimento*) seasoning; (*almidón*) starch, stiffener, filler (*used in cloth*).

**adestrado** *adj.* trained, skilled.

**adestrar**[1] *v. irr.* to train; to guide.

**adeudado** *adj.* indebted; in debt; *p.p.* of **adeudar.**

**adeudar** *v.* to owe; to debit, charge; **-se** to run into debt.

**adeudo** *m.* debt, indebtedness; duty (*on imports*); debit, charge.

**adherencia** *f.* adherence; attachment.

**adherir**[3] *v. irr.* to adhere, stick.

**adhesión** *f.* adhesion; attachment.

**adicto** *adj.* addicted; devoted; *m.* addict; follower.

**adiestrado** = **adestrado.**

**adiestramiento** *m.* training; drill.

**adiestrar** = **adestrar.**

**adinerado** *adj.* wealthy.

**¡adiós!** *interj.* good-bye!; farewell!; hello!; *Am.* you don't say!

**aditamento** *m.* addition; annex.

**adivinación** *f.* divination, prediction; guess.

**adivinanza** *f.* conundrum, riddle.

**adivinar** *v.* to guess.

**adivino** *m.* fortuneteller; soothsayer.

**adjetivo** *m. & adj.* adjective.

**adjudicar**[6] *v.* to adjudge, award, assign; **-se** to appropriate.

**adjuntar** *v.* to put with; to bring together; to enclose (*in a letter*).

**adjunto** *adj.* adjoining; attached, enclosed.

**adminículo** *m.* accessory; gadget.

**administración** *f.* administration, management; headquarters; *Ven., Mex., Cuba* extreme unction, last sacrament.

**administrador** *m.* administrator, manager.

**administrar** *v.* to administer; to manage; **-se** *Ven., Mex., Cuba* to receive the extreme unction or last sacrament.

**administrativo** *adj.* administrative.

**admirable** *adj.* admirable, wonderful.

**admiración** *f.* admiration, wonder; **punto de —** exclamation point.

**admirador** *m.* admirer.

**admirar** *v.* to admire; **-se** to be astonished or amazed; to wonder.

**admisible** *adj.* admissible, allowable.

**admisión** *f.* admission; acceptance; acknowledgment.

**admitir** *v.* to admit; to let in; to accept; to allow, permit.

**adobar** *v.* to fix, cook, prepare (*food*); to tan (*hides*); to pickle (*meats, fish*).

**adobe** *m.* adobe, sun-dried mud brick.

**adobo** *m.* mending; sauce for seasoning or pickling; mixture for dressing skins or cloth; rouge.

**adoctrinamiento** *m.* indoctrination, teaching, instruction.

**adoctrinar** *v.* to indoctrinate, teach, instruct.

**adolecer**[13] *v. irr.* to suffer (*from an illness, defect, etc.*).

**adolescencia** *f.* adolescence.

**adolescente** *adj.* adolescent.

**adonde** *rel. adv.* where; **¿adónde?** *interr. adv.* where to?; where?

**adoptar** *v.* to adopt; to accept (*an opinion*).

**adoptivo** *adj.* adoptive, related by adoption; adopted.

**adoración** *f.* adoration, worship.

**adorar** *v.* to adore, worship.

**adormecer**[13] *v. irr.* to make sleepy or drowsy; to lull; **-se** to get sleepy; to get numb; to fall asleep.

**adormilado** *adj.* drowsy.

**adornar** *v.* to adorn, decorate, ornament.

**adorno** *m.* adornment, ornament, decoration.

**adquirir**[35] *v. irr.* to acquire, gain, win, obtain.

**adquisición** *f.* acquisition; attainment.

**adrede** *adv.* on purpose, intentionally.

**aduana** *f.* customhouse.

**aduanero** *m.* customhouse officer; *adj.* customhouse.

**aduar** *m.* gypsy camp; *Ríopl.* Indian camp or ranch.

**aducir**[25] *v. irr.* to cite, allege, offer as proof.

**adueñarse** *v.* to take possession.

**adulación** *f.* flattery.

**adulador** *m.* flatterer.

**adular** *v.* to flatter.

**adulterar** *v.* to adulterate, corrupt, make impure.

**adulterio** *m.* adultery.

**adúltero** *m.* adulterer.

**adulto** *m. & adj.* adult.

**adusto** *adj.* stern, severe, austere.

**advenedizo** *m.* newcomer, stranger; upstart; *Mex., Carib., Andes* novice, beginner; *adj.* newly arrived; upstart; *Mex., Carib., Andes* inexperienced.

**advenimiento** *m.* advent, arrival, coming.

**adverbio** *m.* adverb.

**adversario** *m.* adversary, opponent; foe.

**adversidad** *f.* adversity; calamity.

**adverso** *adj.* adverse; contrary; unfavorable.

**advertencia** *f.* notice; warning; advice.

**advertir**[3] *v. irr.* to notice; to warn; to advise.

**adyacente** *adj.* adjacent.
**aéreo** *adj.* aerial; airy; **correo — air** mail.
**aerodinámico** *adj.* aerodynamic; *f.* aerodynamics.
**aeródromo** *m.* airport.
**aerofluyente** *adj.* streamlined.
**aeronave** *f.* airship.
**aeropista** *f.* landing strip; runway.
**aeroplano** *m.* airplane.
**aeropuerto** *m.* airport.
**afabilidad** *f.* friendliness, pleasantness, courtesy; **afable** *adj.* affable, pleasant, courteous.
**afamado** *adj.* famous.
**afán** *m.* eagerness, anxiety, ardor.
**afanar** *v.* to urge, press; **-se** to hurry; to worry; to work eagerly; to toil.
**afanoso** *adj.* laborious; hardworking.
**afasia** *f.* aphasia.
**afear** *v.* to make ugly; to disfigure; to blame, censure, condemn.
**afección** *f.* affection, fondness; disease.
**afectado** *p.p.* & *adj.* affected; *Am.* hurt, harmed; *Am.* **estar — del corazón** to have heart trouble.
**afectar** *v.* (*promover*) to affect, move; (*fingir*) to pretend to have or feel; *Am.* to hurt, to harm, to injure.
**afecto** *m.* affection; *adj.* fond; **— a** fond of; given to; prone to.
**afectuoso** *adj.* affectionate, tender.
**afeitada** *f. Am.* shave, shaving.
**afeitar** *v.* to shave; **-se** to shave oneself; to put on make-up.
**afeite** *m.* make-up, cosmetics.
**afeminado** *adj.* effeminate.
**aferrado** *adj.* stubborn, obstinate; *p.p.* of **aferrar.**
**aferramiento** *m.* grasping, seizing; attachment; stubbornness; tenacity.
**aferrar** *v.* to seize, grasp, grapple; **-se** to take or seize hold of; to cling; **-se a una opinión** to cling to an opinion.
**afianzar**[9] *v.* to fasten, secure; to steady; to give bail or bond.
**afición** *f.* taste, inclination; fondness, affection.
**aficionado** *adj.* fond; *m.* amateur, fan.
**aficionar** *v.* to inspire a liking or fondness; **-se a** to become fond of.
**afiche** *m. Ríopl.*, poster.
**afilador** *m.* grinder, sharpener.
**afilar** *v.* to sharpen; to grind; *Am.* to make love to, woo; *Am.* to flatter; *Am.* **— con** to flirt with.
**afín** *adj.* kindred, related; **ideas afines** related ideas.
**afinador** *m.* piano tuner.
**afinar** *v.* to refine, polish; to tune.
**afinidad** *f.* affinity; similarity; relationship.
**afirmación** *f.* affirmation, assertion.
**afirmar** *v.* to affirm, assert; to make firm; *Am.* **— un golpe** to deal a blow.
**afirmativa** *f.* affirmative.
**afirmativo** *adj.* affirmative.
**aflicción** *f.* affliction, trouble, pain, grief.
**afligir**[11] *v.* to afflict, trouble, grieve;

*Ríopl., Ven.* to mistreat, harm, beat, strike; **-se** to worry, grieve.
**aflojar** *v.* to slacken; to loosen, unfasten; to let go; *Mex., Ríopl., Carib.* to let go of money, spend easily; *Mex., Ríopl., Carib.* **— un golpe** to give a blow.
**afluente** *m.* tributary; *adj.* abundant.
**afluir**[32] *v. irr.* to flow (into).
**afortunado** *adj.* fortunate; lucky.
**afrenta** *f.* affront, offense, insult.
**afrentar** *v.* to insult, offend, dishonor.
**afrentoso** *adj.* outrageous, shameful, disgraceful.
**africano** *adj.* & *m.* African.
**afrontar** *v.* to face; to confront.
**afuera** *adv.* out, outside; **-s** *f. pl.* outskirts.
**agachar** *v.* to lower; to bend down; **-se** to stoop, bend down, duck; to crouch; *Am.* to give in, yield; *Col.* **-se con algo** to make away with or steal something.
**agalla** *f.* gill; tonsil; *Col., Ven.* greed; **tener -s** to have guts, have courage; *Ríopl., Ch., Carib.* to be unscrupulous and bold in business deals; *Ríopl., Ch., Carib.* to be greedy or stingy; *C.A.* to be smart, astute, cunning.
**agarrar** *v.* to seize, grasp, grab; **-se** to cling, hold on.
**agarro** *m.* clench, clutch, grasp, grip, grab; **agarrón** *m.* tight clench, sudden grasp, grab; *Mex., Col., Ven., C.A.* pull, tug.
**agasajar** *v.* to entertain; to flatter.
**agasajo** *m.* entertainment, kind reception; friendliness; flattery.
**agazapar** *v.* to nab, seize (*a person*); **-se** to crouch; to squat.
**agencia** *f.* agency; *Ch.* pawnshop.
**agenciar** *v.* to negotiate; to procure by negotiation; to promote.
**agente** *m.* agent; *Am.* officer, official.
**ágil** *adj.* agile, nimble, limber.
**agilidad** *f.* agility, nimbleness.
**agitación** *f.* agitation; excitement.
**agitador** *m.* agitator; *adj.* agitating; stirring.
**agitar** *v.* to agitate, excite; to stir; to wave; to shake.
**aglomeración** *f.* conglomeration, heap, pile, mass.
**aglomerar** *v.* to mass together; to cluster; **-se** to crowd together, pile up.
**agobiar** *v.* to oppress, weigh down; to overwhelm.
**agolparse** *v.* to crowd together, jam.
**agonía** *f.* agony.
**agonizante** *adj.* dying; *m.* dying person.
**agonizar**[9] *v.* to be dying.
**agorero** *adj.* ominous, of bad omen; prophetic; *m.* augur, prophet, fortune-teller.
**agostar** *v.* to parch, dry up; to pasture; to plow (*in August*).
**agosto** *m.* August; harvest; **hacer su —** to make hay while the sun shines.
**agotado** *adj.* & *p.p.* exhausted; out-of-print.
**agotamiento** *m.* exhaustion; draining.

**AD**

**agotar** *v.* to exhaust, use up; to drain off; **-se** (*acabarse*) to be exhausted, used up; (*terminarse la edición*) to go out of print.

**agraciado** *adj.* graceful; *m.* winner (*of a favor, prize, etc.*).

**agraciar** *v.* to grace; to adorn.

**agradable** *adj.* agreeable, pleasant.

**agradar** *v.* to please, be agreeable (to).

**agradecer**[13] *v. irr.* to thank for; to be grateful for.

**agradecido** *adj.* thankful, grateful.

**agradecimiento** *m.* gratitude, thankfulness.

**agrado** *m.* agreeableness; liking, pleasure; **de su —** to his liking.

**agrandar** *v.* to enlarge; to aggrandize, make greater.

**agravar** *v.* to aggravate, make worse; to make heavier; to oppress; **-se** to get worse.

**agraviar** *v.* to offend, insult, affront.

**agravio** *m.* offense, insult, affront.

**agredir**[51] *v.* to assail, assault, attack.

**agregado** *m.* attaché, person attached to a staff; aggregate, collection.

**agregar**[7] *v.* to add; to join; to attach.

**agresivo** *adj.* aggressive, offensive.

**agresor** *m.* agressor; assailant.

**agreste** *adj.* rustic; wild (*fruit, flower, etc.*).

**agriar**[17] *v.* to sour, make sour; **-se** to sour, turn sour, become sour.

**agrícola** *adj.* agricultural.

**agricultor** *m.* agriculturist, farmer.

**agricultura** *f.* agriculture.

**agridulce** *adj.* bittersweet, tart.

**agrietarse** *v.* to crack; to chap (*said of the skin*).

**agrimensura** *f.* survey, surveying (*of land*).

**agrio** *adj.* sour; disagreeable.

**agropecuario** *adj.* farming (*crops and cattle*).

**agrupación** *f.* group; bunch; grouping; gathering.

**agrupar** *v.* to group, bunch up.

**agrura** *f.* sourness.

**agua** *f.* water; rain; **— abajo** downstream; **— arriba** upstream; **aguas inmundas** *f.* sewage.

**aguacate** *m. Am.* avocado, alligator pear; *Am.* avocado tree; *Am.* phlegmatic person.

**aguacero** *m.* shower.

**aguada** *f.* watering place; supply of drinking water; flood in a mine; wall wash; water color.

**aguadero** *m.* watering place.

**aguado** *adj.* watery; watered; *Am.* soft, unstarched; *Am.* weak, limp; *Andes* insipid, uninteresting, dull; **sopa aguada** thin soup; *p.p. of* **aguar**.

**aguaitar** *v. Col., Ven., Andes, Ch.* to spy; to watch; to wait for.

**aguantar** *v.* to endure, bear; to resist; **-se** to be silent, restrain oneself.

**aguante** *m.* endurance, fortitude, resistance.

**aguar**[9] *v.* to water, dilute with water; to spoil (*pleasure*); *Ríopl., Ven., C.A.*

to water (*livestock*); **-se** to become diluted; to get watery; to fill up with water; **se aguó la fiesta** the party was spoiled.

**aguardar** *v.* to wait; to wait for.

**aguardentoso** *adj.* alcoholic; hoarse, raucous.

**aguardiente** *m.* brandy, hard liquor; **— de caña** rum.

**aguarrás** *m.* turpentine, oil of turpentine.

**aguazal** *m.* marsh, swamp.

**agudeza** *f.* sharpness; keenness; wit; witty remark or saying.

**agudo** *adj.* sharp; sharp-pointed; keen, witty; acute; shrill.

**agüero** *m.* augury, prediction; sign, omen; *Ríopl., Mex., Carib.* fortune-teller.

**aguijar** *v.* (*picar*) to prick, goad, spur; (*animar*) to encourage, excite.

**aguijón** *m.* prick; sting; spur, goad.

**aguijonear** *v.* to goad; to prick.

**águila** *f.* eagle; **es un —** he is a shark.

**aguileño** *adj.* aquiline; eaglelike.

**aguinaldo** *m.* Christmas or New Year's gift; bonus.

**aguja** *f.* needle; crochet hook; watch hand; church spire; railroad switch.

**agujerear** *v.* to pierce, perforate; to riddle.

**agujero** *m.* hole; needle peddler; needle box; pincushion.

**aguzar**[9] *v.* to sharpen; to goad, stimulate; **— las orejas** to prick up one's ears.

**ahí** *adv.* there; **por —** over there.

**ahijado** *m.* godchild.

**ahinco** *m.* effort, eagerness, zeal.

**ahogar**[7] *v.* to drown; to choke, strangle; to smother; to quench, extinguish.

**ahogo** *m.* suffocation; breathlessness; anguish, grief.

**ahondar** *v.* to deepen; to dig; to penetrate, go deep into.

**ahora** *adv.* now; **— mismo** right now; **por —** for the present; **— que** *Am.* as soon as; **ahorita** instantly, this very minute; **ahoritica, ahoritita** *Am.* this very second, in a jiffy.

**ahorcar**[6] *v.* to hang, kill by hanging.

**ahorrar** *v.* to save; to spare; to avoid.

**ahorro** *m.* saving, economy; **caja de -s** savings bank.

**ahuecar**[6] *v.* to make hollow; to hollow out; **— la voz** to speak in a hollow voice; *Am.* ¡**ahueca**! get out of here!; **-se** to become puffed up, get conceited.

**ahuehuete** *m. Am.* a Mexican cypress.

**ahumado** *adj.* smoked; smoky.

**ahumar** *v.* to smoke; to fume.

**ahuyentar** *v.* to drive away; to scare away; **-se** to go away, flee; *Ven., Carib., Mex.* to stop frequenting a place.

**aindiado** *adj.* Indian-like.

**airar** *v.* to annoy, irritate; **-se** to get angry.

**aire** *m.* air; wind; tune; appearance; conceit; **-cito** *m.* breeze; a little tune; a certain air or appearance.

**airear** *v.* to air, ventilate.

**airoso** *adj.* windy; airy; graceful, elegant; lively, spirited.

**aislador** *m.* insulator; isolator; *adj.* insulating; isolating.

**aislamiento** *m.* isolation; insulation.

**aislar** *v.* to isolate, place apart; to insulate.

**ajar** *v.* to crumple, wither.

**ajedrez** *m.* chess.

**ajeno** *adj.* (*de otro*) another's; (*inconciente*) unaware; (*extranjero*) alien; — **a mi voluntad** beyond my control; — **de cuidados** free from cares.

**ajetrearse** *v.* to hustle and bustle; to get tired out.

**ajetreo** *m.* bustle, hustle; hubbub; fuss; fatigue.

**ají** *m. S.A., Carib.* chili pepper, chili sauce.

**ajo** *m.* garlic; garlic clove; garlic sauce; swear word.

**ajuar** *m.* furniture set; trousseau, bride's outfit; bride's portion or dowry.

**ajustado** *adj.* tight, fitting tight; agreed upon (*as a price*); — **a la ley** in accordance with the law; *p.p. of* **ajustar.**

**ajustamiento** *m.* adjustment.

**ajustar** *v.* to adjust; to fit tight; to regulate; to tighten; to settle (*accounts*); to hire (*a person*); *Col.* to stint, scrimp, save; *C.A.* — **una bofetada** to give a good slap; *C.A., Mex.* **hoy ajusta quince años** he is just fifteen years old today; -**se** to come to an agreement.

**ajuste** *m.* adjustment, fit; agreement; settlement (*of accounts*).

**ajusticiar** *v.* to execute, put to death.

**al** = **a** + **el** to the.

**ala** *f.* wing; hat brim.

**alabanza** *f.* praise.

**alabar** *v.* to praise.

**alacena** *f.* cupboard; closet; *Am.* booth, stall, market stand.

**alacrán** *m.* scorpion.

**alado** *adj.* winged.

**alambicado** *p.p.* & *adj.* distilled; over-refined, over-subtle (*applied to style*).

**alambique** *m.* still.

**alambrada** *f.* wire entanglement.

**alambrado** *m.* wire fence; wire screening; wiring.

**alambre** *m.* wire.

**alameda** *f.* poplar grove; park.

**álamo** *m.* poplar.

**alancear** *v.* to lance, spear.

**alano** *m.* mastiff.

**alarde** *m.* boast, bluff, brag.

**alardear** *v.* to boast, brag.

**alargar**[7] *v.* to lengthen; to prolong; to stretch out, extend.

**alarido** *m.* shout, scream, howl.

**alarma** *f.* alarm.

**alarmar** *v.* to alarm.

**alazán** *adj.* chestnut-colored; sorrel.

**alba** *f.* dawn; alb (*white robe worn by priest*).

**albacea** *m.* executor.

**albañal** *m.* sewer.

**albañil** *m.* mason, brickmason; **albañilería** *f.* masonry.

**albaricoque** *m.* apricot; **albaricoquero** *m.* apricot tree.

**albayalde** *m.* white lead.

**albazo** *m. Mex.* early morning serenade; *Mex.* bad surprise, surprise attack at dawn.

**albear** *v.* to show white (*in the distance*); *Am.* to rise at dawn.

**albedrío** *m.* free will.

**albéitar** *m.* veterinary.

**alberca** *f.* water reservoir, tank; pool.

**albergar**[7] *v.* to house, shelter, lodge; -**se** to take shelter; to lodge.

**albo** *adj.* white; *Am.* white-footed (*horse*).

**albóndiga** *f.* meat ball; fish ball.

**albor** *f.* dawn; whiteness.

**alborada** *f.* dawn; reveille (*morning bugle call*).

**alborear** *v.* to dawn.

**alborotador** *m.* agitator, troublemaker.

**alborotar** *v.* to disturb, upset; *Am.* to excite, arouse enthusiasm; -**se** to get upset; to mutiny; to riot; *Am.* to get excited; *Am.* to rear, balk (*said of a horse*).

**alboroto** *m.* uproar, disturbance; riot; *Am.* excitement, enthusiasm; *Col., C.A.* popcorn, candied popcorn ball.

**alborozado** *adj.* elated, excited.

**alborozar**[9] *v.* to gladden; -**se** to rejoice.

**alborozo** *m.* joy, delight.

**albricias** *f. pl.* good news; reward (*for good news*).

**alcachofa** *f.* artichoke; *Ch.* sock, blow.

**alcahuete** *m.* procurer, pander; go-between; **alcahueta** *f.* bawd, procuress, go-between.

**alcaide** *m.* warden (*of a fortress, prison, etc.*).

**alcalde** *m.* mayor; justice of the peace; — **mayor** mayor.

**alcance** *m.* (*extensión*) reach, scope; (*capacidad*) talent, capacity; (*noticias*) last minute news, newspaper extra; **cortos -s** meagre intellect; **dar — a** to catch up with.

**alcancía** *f.* money box (*with slit for coin*); savings bank.

**alcanfor** *m.* camphor.

**alcantarillado** *m.* sewage system.

**alcanzado** *adj.* needy; broke, short of funds.

**alcanzar**[9] *v.* to reach; to overtake; to obtain; to befall; to be enough; *Am.* to hand, pass, put within reach.

**alcayata** *f.* wall hook; meat hook.

**alcázar** *m.* castle, fortress.

**alcoba** *f.* alcove, bedroom.

**alcohol** *m.* alcohol; **alcohólico** *adj.* alcoholic.

**alcor** *m.* hill.

**alcornoque** *m.* cork tree; cork wood; blockhead, dunce.

**alcuza** *f.* oil can; cruet, oil bottle.

**aldaba** *f.* knocker (*of a door*); crossbar, bolt, latch; handle (*of a door, chest,* *etc.*);[1] **tener buenas -s** to have "pull", influential connections.

**aldabón** *m.* large iron knocker; large handle; **aldabonazo** *m.* knock, knocking.

**aldea** *f.* village; **aldehuela** *f.* little village, hamlet.

**aldeano** *adj.* rustic, countrified; *m.* villager; peasant.

**aleación** *f.* alloy; alloying.

**alear** *v.* to alloy, mix (*metals*); to flutter; to flap (*wings, arms, etc.*).

**aleccionar** *v.* to coach; to teach, instruct; to train; to drill.

**aledaños** *m. pl.* borders, frontiers.

**alegar**[7] *v.* to allege, assert; *Am.* to argue, dispute.

**alegato** *m.* allegation; assertion.

**alegrar** *v.* to cheer up, gladden; to brighten; **-se** to be glad, rejoice; to get tipsy.

**alegre** *adj.* merry, gay, joyful, cheerful, bright; tipsy.

**alegría** *f.* joy, mirth, gaiety, merriment.

**alejamiento** *m.* withdrawal; retirement, aloofness.

**alejar** *v.* to remove, move away from; **-se** to move away; to withdraw, be aloof.

**alelado** *adj.* stupefied, open-mouthed; silly.

**alemán** *adj. & m.* German.

**alentar**[1] *v. irr.* to breathe; to encourage, cheer, cheer up; **-se** to take heart; *Am.* to recover (*from illness*).

**alergia** *f.* allergy.

**alero** *m.* eaves; projecting edge.

**alerón** *m.* aileron; flap.

**alerto** *adj.* alert, watchful; ¡**alerta**! attention! look out!; **estar alerta** to be on the alert.

**aleta** *f.* small wing; flap; fin (*of a fish*).

**aletargado** *adj.* drowsy, sluggish.

**aletargarse**[7] *v.* to fall into a state of lethargy; to become drowsy.

**aletazo** *m.* flap, blow with a wing.

**aletear** *v.* to flap, flutter.

**aleteo** *m.* flapping, flutter (*of wings*).

**aleve** *adj.* treacherous.

**alevosía** *f.* treachery.

**alevoso** *adj.* treacherous.

**alfabeto** *m.* alphabet.

**alfalfa** *f.* alfalfa; **alfalfar** *m.* alfalfa field.

**alfarería** *f.* pottery; **alfarero** *m.* potter.

**alfeñicar**[6] *v.* to frost with sugar (*a cake, cookie, etc.*); **-se** to get frail, delicate; to act affectedly.

**alfeñique** *m.* sugar paste; delicate person.

**alférez** *m.* ensign; second lieutenant.

**alfil** *m.* bishop (*in chess*).

**alfiler** *m.* pin; brooch; **-es** pin money; **ponerse de veinticinco -es** to doll up, dress up.

**alfombra** *f.* carpet; **alfombrilla** *f.* (*para el suelo*) carpet, rug; (*enfermedad*) measles; *Mex.* plant of the vervain family; *Carib.* black smallpox; *Carib.* skin eruption.

**alforja** *f.* saddlebag; knapsack; food

provisions for a trip; *Am.* **pasarse a la otra —** to take undue liberties.

**alforza** *f.* tuck, fold, pleat; scar.

**algarabía** *f.* jargon; chatter; uproar.

**algarrobo** *m.* locust tree; carob tree.

**algazara** *f.* clamor; shouting; uproar.

**álgebra** *f.* algebra.

**algo** *pron.* something; *adv.* somewhat.

**algodón** *m.* cotton; **algodonal** *m.* cotton plantation.

**alguacil** *m.* policeman, constable.

**alguien** *pron.* somebody, someone.

**algún(o)** *adj.* some; any; *pron.* someone.

**alhaja** *f.* jewel.

**alharaca** *f.* rumpus, clamor, racket.

**aliado** *adj.* allied; *m.* ally.

**alianza** *f.* alliance, union; *Andes* wedding ring; *Am.* mixture of liquors.

**aliar**[17] *v.* to ally; to unite; **-se** to form an alliance; to unite.

**alicaído** *adj.* crestfallen, downcast, discouraged; drooping.

**alicates** *m. pl.* pliers, small pincers.

**aliciente** *m.* inducement, incentive, attraction.

**alienista** *m.* alienist (*doctor who treats mental diseases*).

**aliento** *m.* (*de los pulmones*) breath; (*ánimo*) encouragement.

**aligerar** *v.* to lighten; to hasten.

**alimentación** *f.* nourishment, food, nutrition; feeding.

**alimentar** *v.* to feed, nourish.

**alimenticio** *adj.* nutritious, nourishing.

**alimento** *m.* food.

**alinear** *v.* to line up, put into line; to range; **-se** to fall in line, form into a line.

**aliño** *m.* ornament, decoration; neatness; condiment, dressing, seasoning.

**alisar** *v.* to smooth; to polish; to plane.

**alistamiento** *m.* enlistment; enrollment.

**alistar** *v.* to enlist; to enroll; to make ready; **-se** to enlist; to get ready; *Am.* to dress up.

**aliviar** *v.* to lighten; to alleviate, relieve, remedy, soothe; **-se** to get better, recover.

**alivio** *m.* relief, remedy; aid, help; improvement.

**aljibe** *m.* cistern, reservoir, tank; water tanker; *Ríopl.* well, artesian well, spring.

**alma** *f.* soul, spirit; inhabitant.

**almacén** *m.* warehouse; department store; store.

**almacenaje** *m.* storage.

**almacenar** *v.* to store, store up; to put in storage.

**almacenista** *m. & f.* department store owner; warehouse owner or manager; wholesale merchant.

**almanaque** *m.* almanac, calendar.

**almeja** *f.* clam.

**almendra** *f.* almond; **almendrado** *m.* almond paste; **almendro** *m.* almond tree.

**almíbar** *m.* syrup.

**almidón** *m.* starch; *Col., Ven.* paste (*for gluing*).

**almidonar** *v.* to starch.
**alminar** *m.* turret.
**almirante** *m.* admiral.
**almirez** *m.* metal mortar.
**almohada** *f.* pillow; **almohadón** *m.* large cushion or pillow.
**almohaza** *f.* currycomb (*for grooming horses*).
**almoneda** *f.* auction.
**almorzar**²,⁹ *v. irr.* to lunch, eat lunch.
**almuerzo** *m.* lunch.
**alojamiento** *m.* lodging.
**alojar** *v.* to lodge; to house; to quarter (*troops*); **-se** to lodge, room.
**alondra** *f.* lark.
**alpaca** *f.* alpaca (*sheeplike animal of South America*); alpaca wool; alpaca cloth.
**alpargata** *f.* sandal (*usually of canvas and with hemp sole*).
**alquería** *f.* farmhouse.
**alquilar** *v.* to rent; to hire; **-se** to hire out.
**alquiler** *m.* rent, rental; **de —** for rent, for hire.
**alquitrán** *m.* tar.
**alrededor** *adv.* about, around; **— de** *prep.* around; **-es** *m. pl.* environs, outskirts.
**altanería** *f.* haughtiness.
**altanero** *adj.* haughty, proud.
**altar** *m.* altar; **— mayor** high altar.
**altavoz** *m.* loud-speaker.
**alteración** *f.* alteration, change; disturbance.
**alterar** *v.* to alter, change; to disturb.
**altercar**⁶ *v.* to argue, dispute; to quarrel.
**alternar** *v.* to alternate; to take turns; **— con** to rub elbows with, be friendly with.
**alternativa** *f.* alternative, choice, option.
**alternativo** *adj.* alternating, alternative.
**alterno** *adj.* alternate.
**alteza** *f.* highness (*title*); lofty height.
**altibajo** *m.* downward thrust (*in fencing*); **-s** ups and downs; uneven ground.
**altiplanicie** *f.* upland; high plateau.
**altiplano** *m. Am.* high plateau.
**altisonante** *adj.* high-sounding.
**altitud** *f.* altitude.
**altivez** *f.* haughtiness, arrogance.
**altivo** *adj.* haughty, proud, arrogant.
**alto** *adj.* (*tamaño*) high; *m.* height; upper story (*of a building*); *Am.* heap, pile; **-s** *Am.* upper floors; *v.* **hacer —** to halt, stop; **pasar por —** to omit, overlook; **¡ — !** halt!
**altoparlante** *m.* loud-speaker.
**altura** *f.* height, altitude.
**alud** *m.* avalanche.
**aludir** *v.* to allude, refer indirectly.
**alumbrado** *m.* lighting; *adj.* lit, lighted; tipsy.
**alumbramiento** *m.* childbirth; lighting.
**alumbrar** *v.* to light, give light; to enlighten; to give birth; **-se** to get tipsy.
**aluminio** *m.* aluminum.

**alumnado** *m.* student body.
**alumno** *m.* student.
**alusión** *f.* allusion.
**alza** *f.* rise; lift (*for shoes*).
**alzada** *f.* height (*of a horse*).
**alzamiento** *m.* raising, lifting; uprising, insurrection.
**alzar**⁹ *v.* to lift, raise; to cut (*cards*); **-se** to rebel, rise up in arms; *Col.*, *Ven.*, *C.A.*, *Mex.*, *Andes* to puff up with pride; **-se con algo** to run off with something, steal something.
**allá** *adv.* there, over there; **más —** farther.
**allanar** *v.* to level, even off; to invade, break into (*a house*); to raid; **— una dificultad** to smooth out a difficulty.
**allegado** *adj.* near; related; allied; *m.* relative; partisan, follower.
**allegar**⁷ *v.* to accumulate, heap up, gather.
**allende** *adv.* on the other side; beyond; **— el mar** across the sea, overseas.
**allí** *adv.* there; **por —** through that place, around there.
**ama** *f.* mistress, owner; **— de leche** wet nurse; **— de llaves** housekeeper.
**amabilidad** *f.* kindness, courtesy.
**amable** *adj.* kind, amiable.
**amador** *m.* lover.
**amaestrar** *v.* to teach, coach, train.
**amagar**⁷ *v.* to threaten; to feint, make a threatening motion; to strike at.
**amago** *m.* threat; indication.
**amalgamar** *v.* to amalgamate, combine, mix, blend.
**amamantar** *v.* to nurse, suckle.
**amanecer**¹³ *v. irr.* to dawn; **— malo** to wake up ill; *m.* dawn, sunrise.
**amanecida** *f.* dawn, sunrise.
**amansar** *v.* to tame; to subdue; to pacify.
**amante** *m.* lover; **— de** fond of.
**amañarse** *v. Ec.*, *Col.*, *Ven.* to be accustomed; to acclimate oneself.
**amapola** *f.* poppy.
**amar** *v.* to love.
**amargar**⁷ *v.* to embitter, make bitter.
**amargo** *adj.* bitter; *m.* bitters; *Am.* mate (*Paraguayan tea*) without sugar.
**amargor** *m.* bitterness.
**amargura** *f.* bitterness; grief.
**amarillear** *v.* to show or have a yellowish tinge; to turn yellow.
**amarillento** *adj.* yellowish.
**amarillo** *adj.* yellow.
**amarra** *f.* cable; rope; strap.
**amarrar** *v.* to tie, fasten, rope; to moor (*a ship*); *Am.* **amarrárselas** to get "tight," drunk.
**amasar** *v.* to knead, mix; to mash; *Am.* to amass, accumulate (*a fortune*).
**amatista** *f.* amethyst.
**ambages** *m. pl.* circumlocutions; **hablar sin —** to go straight to the point, speak plainly, not to beat about the bush.
**ámbar** *m.* amber; **ambarino** *adj.* amber; like amber.
**ambición** *f.* ambition; aspiration.

**ambicionar** *v.* to seek, aspire after; to covet.

**ambicioso** *adj.* ambitious, eager; greedy, grasping.

**ambiente** *m.* atmosphere, environment.

**ambigüedad** *f.* ambiguity.

**ambiguo** *adj.* ambiguous; uncertain, doubtful.

**ámbito** *m.* precinct, enclosure.

**ambos** *adj.* & *pron.* both.

**ambulancia** *f.* ambulance; field hospital.

**ambulante** *adj.* walking; itinerant; moving; wandering.

**amedrentar** *v.* to scare, frighten.

**amenaza** *f.* menace, threat.

**amenazador, amenazante** *adj.* threatening.

**amenazar**[9] *v.* to menace, threaten.

**amenguar**[8] *v.* to lessen, diminish; to defame, dishonor.

**amenidad** *f.* pleasantness.

**amenizar**[9] *v.* to make pleasant, cheer, brighten.

**ameno** *adj.* pleasant, agreeable.

**americana** *f.* suit coat.

**americano** *adj.* & *m.* American.

**ametrallador** *m.* gunner; **ametralladora** *f.* machine gun.

**amigable** *adj.* friendly; affable, pleasant.

**amígdala** *f.* tonsil; **amigdalitis** *f.* tonsilitis.

**amigo** *m.* friend; **— de** fond of.

**aminorar** *v.* to lessen.

**amistad** *f.* friendship; friendliness.

**amistoso** *adj.* friendly.

**amo** *m.* master, owner, boss.

**amodorrado** *adj.* drowsy.

**amodorrar** *v.* to make drowsy; **-se** to become drowsy.

**amolador** *m.* grinder, sharpener; *adj.* grinding, sharpening.

**amolar** *v. irr.* to grind, hone, sharpen; to annoy; *Col., Mex., C.A.* to ruin, harm; **-se** *Mex., C.A., Col.* to go to rack and ruin.

**amoldar** *v.* to mold; to shape; to adjust; to adapt.

**amonestación** *f.* admonition, advice, warning; **-es** marriage bans (*or* banns).

**amonestar** *v.* to admonish, advise, warn.

**amoníaco** *m.* ammonia.

**amontonamiento** *m.* accumulation, pile, heap.

**amontonar** *v.* to heap up, pile up, crowd up.

**amor** *m.* love; **— propio** self-esteem.

**amoratado** *adj.* livid, bluish, purplish.

**amordazar**[9] *v.* to gag; to muzzle.

**amorío** *m.* love affair; love-making.

**amoroso** *adj.* loving, tender, affectionate.

**amortajar** *v.* to shroud.

**amortiguador** *m.* shock absorber; silencer, muffler.

**amortiguar**[8] *v.* to muffle; to deafen (*a sound*); to deaden (*a blow or sound*); to soften, tone down (*a color or sound*).

**amortizar**[9] *v.* to pay on account; to liquidate, pay (*a debt*); to provide a sinking fund.

**amoscarse**[6] *v.* to get peeved, annoyed; *Am.* to blush, be inhibited or embarrassed.

**amostazar**[9] *v.* to anger, irritate; **-se** to get angry or irritated.

**amotinar** *v.* to incite to rebellion; **-se** to mutiny; to riot.

**amparar** *v.* to protect; to defend; *Am.* to grant mining rights; **-se** to seek protection or refuge; to protect oneself.

**amparo** *m.* protection; habeas corpus (*protection against imprisonment*); *Am.* mining rights.

**ampliación** *f.* enlargement, widening.

**ampliar**[17] *v.* to enlarge, widen.

**amplificador** *m.* amplifier.

**amplificar**[6] *v.* to amplify, expand, extend, enlarge; to magnify.

**amplio** *adj.* ample; wide, large, roomy.

**amplitud** *f.* breadth, extent, width.

**ampolla** *f.* (*condición*) blister, water bubble; (*vasija*) narrow-necked bottle or vase, cruet.

**ampollar** *v.* to blister; **-se** to blister.

**ampuloso** *adj.* inflated, wordy, bombastic, pompous.

**amputar** *v.* to amputate, cut off.

**amueblar** *v.* to furnish (*with furniture*).

**ánade** *m.* & *f.* duck; **anadeja** *f.* duckling.

**anadear** *v.* to waddle.

**anales** *m. pl.* annals, historical records.

**analfabeto** *adj.* & *m.* illiterate; **analfabetismo** *m.* illiteracy.

**análisis** *m.* analysis.

**analizar**[9] *v.* to analyze, examine.

**analogía** *f.* analogy, similarity.

**análogo** *adj.* analogous, similar, comparable.

**ananá, ananás** *f.* pineapple. *See* **piña.**

**anaquel** *m.* shelf; bookshelf; **anaquelería** *f.* shelves, bookshelves, library stacks.

**anaranjado** *adj.* orange-colored; *m.* orange color.

**anarquía** *f.* anarchy.

**anatomía** *f.* anatomy.

**anca** *f.* haunch, hind quarter, rump; *Andes* popcorn.

**ancianidad** *f.* old age.

**anciano** *adj.* old, aged; *m.* old man.

**ancla** *f.* anchor.

**anclar** *v.* to anchor.

**ancho** *adj.* wide, broad; loose; roomy; *Col., Ven.* self-satisfied, conceited; **a sus anchas** at one's ease; comfortable; leisurely; *m.* width.

**anchoa, anchova** *f.* anchovy.

**anchura** *f.* width, breadth; comfort, ease.

**anchuroso** *adj.* vast, extensive; spacious.

**andada** *f. Mex., Ven.* walk, stroll; **-s** track, footprints; **volver a las -s** to fall back into one's old ways or habits.

**andadura** *f.* gait, pace.

**andaluz** *adj.* Andalusian, of or pertaining to Andalusia, Spain; *m.* Andalusian, native of Andalusia.

**andamiada** *f.*, **andamiaje** *m.* scaffolding; framework.

**andamio** *m.* scaffold, scaffolding.

**andanada** *f.* (*localidad*) grandstand; (*descarga*) broadside; **soltar una —** to discharge a broadside; to reprimand.

**andante** *adj.* walking; errant, wandering; moderately slow (*music*); **caballero —** knight-errant.

**andanzas** *f. pl.* rambles, wanderings.

**andar**[21] *v. irr.* to walk; to go, go about; to run (*as a watch or machinery*); **— con cuidado** to be careful; **anda en quince años** he is about fifteen; **a todo —** at full (walking) speed; **a más —** walking briskly; **¡anda!** move on!; **¿qué andas haciendo?** what are you doing?; *Am.* **— andando** to be walking around; *Am.* **¡ándale!** hurry!

**andariego** *adj.* fond of walking; roving; *m.* walker.

**andas** *f. pl.* portable platform; litter.

**andén** *m.* railway station platform; *C.A., Col.. Ven.,* sidewalk.

**andino** *adj.* Andean, of or from the Andes.

**andrajo** *m.* rag.

**andrajoso** *adj.* ragged, in rags.

**anécdota** *f.* anecdote, story.

**anegar**[7] *v.* to drown; to flood.

**anejo** *adj.* annexed, attached.

**anestésico** *m. & adj.* anesthetic.

**anexar** *v.* to annex.

**anexo** *m.* annex; *adj.* annexed, joined.

**anfiteatro** *m.* amphitheater.

**anfitrión** *m.* generous host.

**ángel** *m.* angel.

**angélico** *adj.* angelic.

**angina** *f.* angina, inflammation of the throat; *Mex., Ven.* tonsil; **— del pecho** angina pectoris.

**anglosajón** *adj. & m.* Anglo-Saxon.

**angostar** *v.* to narrow; **-se** to narrow, become narrow; to contract.

**angosto** *adj.* narrow.

**angostura** *f.* narrowness; narrows (*narrow part of a river, valley, strait, etc.*).

**anguila** *f.* eel.

**angular** *adj.* angular; **piedra —** cornerstone.

**ángulo** *m.* angle, corner.

**anguloso** *adj.* angular, sharp-cornered.

**angustia** *f.* anguish, sorrow, grief, worry.

**angustiar** *v.* to distress, grieve, worry.

**angustioso** *adj.* anguished, worried, grievous; distressing.

**anhelante** *adj.* anxious, desirous, longing; panting.

**anhelar** *v.* to long for; to breathe hard; to pant.

**anhelo** *m.* longing.

**anheloso** *adj.* anxious; eager.

**anidar** *v.* to nest; to nestle; to dwell; to shelter.

**anillo** *m.* ring.

**ánima** *f.* soul, spirit.

**animación** *f.* animation, liveliness, life.

**animal** *m.* animal; *adj.* animal; stupid; beastly; **animalejo** *m.* little animal; **animalucho** *m.* insignificant animal; hideous little beast.

**animar** *v.* to animate, give life to; to inspire, encourage.

**ánimo** *f.* spirit, mind; courage, valor; intention.

**animosidad** *f.* animosity, ill will; courage, energy.

**animoso** *adj.* spirited; courageous.

**aniñado** *adj.* boyish; childish; **aniñada** girlish.

**aniquilar** *v.* to annihilate, wipe out, destroy completely.

**aniversario** *m.* anniversary.

**anoche** *adv.* last night.

**anochecer**[13] *v. irr.* to grow dark; to be or arrive at nightfall; *m.* nightfall.

**anochecida** *f.* nightfall.

**anonadar** *v.* to annihilate; to humiliate.

**anónimo** *adj.* anonymous; nameless; *m.* anonymous letter or note.

**anormal** *adj.* abnormal.

**anotación** *f.* annotation; note.

**anotar** *v.* to annotate, provide with notes; to write down.

**anquilosado** *adj.* stiff-jointed; gnarled.

**anquilosarse** *v.* to become stiff in the joints; to become mentally stagnant.

**ansia** *f.* anxiety, anguish; longing, eagerness; **-s** anguish; *Col., Ven., P.R.* nausea.

**ansiar**[17] *v.* to long for, desire eagerly.

**ansiedad** *f.* anxiety; worry.

**ansioso** *adj.* anxious, troubled; eager.

**antagonismo** *m.* antagonism.

**antagonista** *m. & f.* antagonist, adversary, opponent.

**antaño** *adv.* yesteryear, formerly; **días de —** days of old.

**ante** *prep.* before, in the presence of; **— todo** above all; *m.* elk; buckskin.

**anteanoche** *adv.* night before last.

**anteayer** *adv.* day before yesterday.

**antebrazo** *m.* forearm.

**antecámara** *f.* antechamber, waiting room.

**antecedente** *m.* antecedent; *adj.* antecedent, preceding.

**antecesor** *m.* ancestor; predecessor.

**antedicho** *adj.* aforesaid.

**antelación** *f.* precedence, priority (*in time*).

**antemano: de —** beforehand.

**antena** *f.* antenna (*of a radio or wireless*); lateen yard (*of a ship*); **-s** antennae, feelers; **— emisora** *f.* broadcasting antenna; **— receptora** *f.* receiving antenna; **— parabólica** *f.* parabolic (*TV*) antenna.

**antenoche = anteanoche.**

**anteojera** *f.* blinder.

**anteojo** *m.* spyglass; small telescope; eyeglass; **-s** spectacles; **-s de larga vista** field glasses.

**antepasado** *adj.* passed; **año —** year before last; *m.* ancestor.

**antepecho** *m.* sill, railing.
**anteponer**[40] *v. irr.* to place before; to prefer.
**antepuesto** *p.p. of* **anteponer.**
**anterior** *adj.* front, toward the front; earlier, previous; **el día —** the day before.
**antes** *adv.* before, formerly; **— de** *prep.* before; **— (de) que** *conj.* before.
**antesala** *f.* anteroom, waiting room.
**antiaéreo** *adj.* antiaircraft.
**anticipación** *f.* anticipation, advance consideration; **con —** in advance.
**anticipado** *adj.* early, ahead of time; advanced (*payment*); **por —** in advance; *p.p. of* **anticipar** anticipated.
**anticipar** *v.* to anticipate; to advance, pay in advance; **-se** to get ahead (of).
**anticipo** *m.* advance, advance payment.
**anticlericalismo** *m.* anticlericalism (*opposition or antagonism to the clergy*).
**anticuado** *adj.* antiquated, out-of-date.
**antídoto** *m.* antidote.
**antigualla** *f.* antique; anything old.
**antigüedad** *f.* antiquity, ancient times; **-es** antique objects, antiques.
**antiguo** *adj.* ancient, old; antique.
**antílope** *m.* antelope.
**antiparras** *f. pl.* goggles; spectacles.
**antipatía** *f.* antipathy, dislike; mutual antagonism.
**antipático** *adj.* disagreeable; unlikeable, unpleasant.
**antipoliomielítico** *adj.* antipolio.
**antiséptico** *adj.* & *m.* antiseptic.
**antojadizo** *adj.* fanciful, whimsical.
**antojarse** *v.* : **antojársele a uno** to take a notion or fancy to; to strike one's fancy; to want, desire.
**antojo** *m.* whim, notion, fancy.
**antorcha** *f.* torch.
**antracita** *f.* anthracite, hard coal.
**anual** *adj.* annual, yearly.
**anuario** *m.* annual, yearbook.
**anublar** *v.* to cloud; to dim, obscure; **-se** to become cloudy.
**anudar** *v.* to knot; **anudársele a uno la garganta** to choke up with emotion.
**anulación** *f.* voiding, cancellation.
**anular** *v.* to annul, void, cancel, abolish.
**anunciador** *m.* announcer; advertiser; *adj.* announcing; advertising.
**anunciante** *m.* & *f.* announcer, advertiser.
**anunciar** *v.* to announce; to advertise.
**anuncio** *m.* announcement; advertisement.
**anzuelo** *m.* fishhook; lure, attraction.
**añadidura** *f.* addition.
**añadir** *v.* to add.
**añejado** *adj.* aged (*wine, cheese, etc.*).
**añejo** *adj.* old; of old vintage; stale.
**añicos** *m. pl.* bits, shatters, fragments; **hacer(se) —** to shatter, break into a thousand pieces.
**añil** *m.* indigo (*plant*); indigo blue.
**año** *m.* year; **— bisiesto** leap year; **¿cuántos -s tiene Vd?** how old are you?
**añoranza** *f.* nostalgia, longing.

**añorar** *v.* to long for, yearn for, be homesick for; to make reminiscences.
**añoso** *adj.* old, aged.
**aojar** *v.* to bewitch; to cast the evil eye.
**apabullar** *v.* to crush, crumple.
**apacentar**[1] *v. irr.* to graze, pasture; to feed (*the spirit, desires, passions, etc.*); **-se** to graze, pasture.
**apacibilidad** *f.* gentleness, mildness, pleasantness; **apacible** *adj.* pleasant, quiet, gentle.
**apaciguamiento** *m.* appeasement.
**apaciguar**[8] *v.* to pacify, calm, appease; **-se** to calm down.
**apachurrar** *v. Mex., C.A., Carib., Andes* to crush. *See* **despachurrar.**
**apadrinar** *v.* to sponsor; to act as a godfather; to act as a second in a duel.
**apagar**[7] *v.* to put out, extinguish; to deafen (*a sound*).
**apagón** *m.* blackout.
**apalabrar** *v.* to speak for, engage, reserve; **-se con** to make a verbal agreement with.
**apalear** *v.* to beat up, thrash; to thresh.
**aparador** *m.* sideboard; cupboard; showcase; show window; workshop.
**aparato** *m.* apparatus; pomp.
**aparatoso** *adj.* pompous, ostentatious.
**aparcero** *m.* co-owner of land; *Am.* pal, comrade.
**aparear** *v.* to mate; to match; to pair; **-se** to mate; to match; to pair.
**aparecer**[13] *v. irr.* to appear, show up.
**aparecido** *m.* ghost, specter, phantom.
**aparejar** *v.* to prepare; to harness; to rig; to equip.
**aparejo** *m.* harness; packsaddle; rigging (*of a boat*); preparation; fishing tackle; **-s** equipment, tools.
**aparentar** *v.* to appear, seem; to pretend, feign, affect.
**aparente** *adj.* apparent.
**aparición** *f.* apparition, ghost; appearance.
**apariencia** *f.* appearance.
**apartado** *m.* compartment; **— postal** post office letter box; *p.p. of* **apartar.**
**apartamento** *m.* apartment.
**apartamiento** *m.* separation; retirement; aloofness; retreat, refuge; *Am.* apartment, flat.
**apartar** *v.* to set apart, separate; to remove; *Am.* **— las reses** to sort out cattle; **-se** to withdraw; to step aside; to go away.
**aparte** *adv.* apart; aside; *m.* aside (*in a play*); new paragraph; *Am.* sorting out of cattle.
**apasionado** *adj.* passionate; very fond (of); impassioned, emotional.
**apasionar** *v.* to arouse passion; to fill with passion; **-se** to become impassioned; to fall ardently in love.
**apatía** *f.* apathy, indolence, indifference.
**apático** *adj.* apathetic, indifferent, indolent.
**apear** *v.* (*de caballo*) dismount; (*bajar*) to lower, take down; to shackle (*a horse*); to fell (*a tree*); *Ríopl.* to fire, dismiss from a position; **— el**

**tratamiento** to omit the title (*in addressing a person*); **-se** to get off, alight; *Am.* **-se por la cola** (*or por las orejas*) to go off at a tangent, make an irrelevant remark.

**apechugar**[7] *v.* to push with the chest; to push ahead; **— con** to accept reluctantly; to go through with (*something*) courageously; *P.R.* to snatch, take possession of.

**apedrear** *v.* to stone, hit with stones.

**apegado** *adj.* devoted, attached; *p.p.* of **apegarse.**

**apegarse**[7] *v.* to become attached (to); to become fond (of).

**apego** *m.* attachment, fondness.

**apelación** *f.* appeal.

**apelar** *v.* to appeal.

**apelotonar** *v.* to form or roll into a ball; to pile up, bunch together.

**apellidar** *v.* to call, name; **-se** to be named; to have the surname of.

**apellido** *m.* surname.

**apenar** *v.* to grieve, afflict; **-se** to be grieved; *Col., Ven., C.A., Carib.* to feel embarrassed, feel ashamed.

**apenas** *adv.* hardly, scarcely; *conj.* as soon as.

**apéndice** *m.* appendix.

**apercibir** *v.* to prepare beforehand; to supply; to warn, advise; to perceive; **-se a la pelea** to get ready to fight; *Am.* **-se de** to notice.

**apergaminado** *adj.* parchment-like; dried up.

**aperitivo** *m.* aperitif, appetizer; cocktail.

**aperlado** *adj.* pearly, pearl-colored.

**apero** *m.* farm equipment; **-s** tools, implements; *Ríopl., Ch., Mex., Ven., Andes* saddle and trappings.

**apertura** *f.* opening (*act of opening or beginning*).

**apestar** *v.* to infect; to corrupt; to sicken; to stink; **-se** to turn putrid, become corrupted; *Am.* to catch cold.

**apestoso** *adj.* putrid, foul-smelling.

**apetecer**[13] *v. irr.* to desire, crave.

**apetecible** *adj.* desirable; appetizing.

**apetencia** *f.* hunger, appetite; desire.

**apetito** *m.* appetite; hunger.

**apetitoso** *adj.* appetizing; gluttonous.

**apiadarse** *v.* to pity; **— de** to pity, take pity on.

**ápice** *m.* apex, top, summit.

**apilar** *v.* to pile up, stack, heap.

**apiñado** *p.p.* of **apiñar** & *adj.* crowded, jammed; cone-shaped, shaped like a pine cone.

**apiñamiento** *m.* crowd, jam (*of people or animals*); crowding together.

**apiñar** *v.* to cram together; to crowd; **-se** to pile up, crowd together.

**apio** *m.* celery.

**apisonar** *v.* to pack down, flatten by pounding.

**aplacar**[6] *v.* to appease, pacify, soothe.

**aplanamiento** *m.* flattening, leveling; dejection, depression.

**aplanar** *v.* to level; to flatten; to astonish; *Am.* **— las calles** to tramp the streets; **-se** to be flattened out; to be

leveled to the ground; to lose one's strength; *Col.* to give in, yield.

**aplastar** *v.* to squash, crush, flatten; *Am.* to tire out, break (*a horse*); **-se** *Am.* to plump oneself down; *Col., Andes* to overstay a call (*remaining seated*).

**aplaudir** *v.* to applaud, clap; to approve, praise.

**aplauso** *m.* applause; praise, approval.

**aplazamiento** *m.* postponement; adjournment.

**aplazar**[9] *v.* to postpone; to adjourn.

**aplicable** *adj.* applicable, suitable, fitting.

**aplicación** *f.* application; effort, diligence; **-es** appliqué (*trimming laid on a dress*).

**aplicado** *adj.* industrious, diligent.

**aplicar**[6] *v.* to apply; to put on, lay on; **-se** to apply oneself, work hard.

**aplomado** *adj.* gray, lead-colored; *p.p.* of **aplomar.**

**aplomar** *v.* to plumb (*a wall*); to make vertical; to make heavier; **-se** *Am.* to become ashamed or embarrassed; *Am.* to be slow.

**aplomo** *m.* assurance, confidence, self-possession, serenity; **estar —** to be plumb, vertical.

**apocado** *adj.* cowardly; timid; *p.p.* of **apocar.**

**apocamiento** *m.* timidity; bashfulness; belittling.

**apocar**[6] *v.* to lessen; to belittle, give little importance to; **-se** to humble oneself.

**apodar** *v.* to nickname.

**apoderado** *m.* attorney; proxy, substitute.

**apoderar** *v.* to empower, give power of attorney; **-se de** to take possession of, seize.

**apodo** *m.* nickname.

**apogeo** *m.* apogee (*point at which a planet, satellite, or rocket is at the greatest distance from the earth*); highest point, height (*of glory, fame, etc.*).

**apolillado** *adj.* moth-eaten; worm-eaten.

**apología** *f.* apology.

**apoplejía** *f.* apoplexy, stroke.

**aporrear** *v.* to beat; to maul; *Am.* to beat (*in a game*), defeat.

**aportación** *f.* contribution.

**aportar** *v.* to bring; to contribute; to arrive in port; to reach an unexpected place (*after having gone astray*); **-se** *Am.* to appear, approach.

**aporte** *m.* contribution.

**aposento** *m.* room; lodging.

**apostar**[2] *v. irr.* to bet; to post, station.

**apóstol** *m.* apostle; religious leader.

**apostólico** *adj.* apostolic (*pertaining to the apostles, or to the Pope and his authority*).

**apostura** *f.* elegant bearing, graceful carriage.

**apoyar** *v.* to lean, rest; to back, support; to aid, favor; to confirm; **-se** to lean (on).

**apoyo** *m.* support; favor, protection.

**apreciable** *adj.* estimable, esteemed; valuable; appraisable; noticeable.

**apreciación** *f.* appreciation; valuation; estimation.

**apreciar** *v.* to appreciate, value, esteem; to price, fix the price of; to appraise.

**aprecio** *m.* esteem, high regard; appraisal, valuation, estimate; *Mex.*, *Ven.*, *Cuba* **hacer —** to notice, pay attention.

**aprehender** *v.* to apprehend, seize, arrest.

**aprehensión, aprensión** *f.* apprehension; fear, dread; seizure, arrest; *Am.* prejudice.

**aprehensor, aprensor** *m.* captor.

**apremiante** *adj.* pressing, urgent.

**apremiar** *v.* to press, urge onward, hurry.

**apremio** *m.* pressure; urgency.

**aprender** *v.* to learn.

**aprendiz** *m.* apprentice.

**aprendizaje** *m.* apprenticeship; learning (*act of learning*).

**apresar** *v.* to seize, grab; to capture; to imprison.

**aprestar** *v.* to prepare, make ready; **-se** to get ready.

**apresto** *m.* preparation; readiness.

**apresurado** *adj.* hasty.

**apresurar** *v.* to hurry, hasten; **-se** to hurry, hasten.

**apretado** *adj.* tight; compact; stingy, miserly; difficult, dangerous; *p.p. of* **apretar.**

**apretar**[1] *v. irr.* to press, squeeze, tighten; to urge on; *Am.* to increase in strength or intensity (*as rain, wind, etc.*); *Am.* to redouble one's effort; **— a correr** to start to run; **-se** *Col.* to gorge, overeat.

**apretón** *m.* sudden pressure; squeeze; dash, short run; **— de manos** handshake.

**apretura** *f.* jam, crush; tight squeeze; narrow place; difficulty, predicament; dire poverty.

**aprieto** *m.* tight spot, difficulty.

**aprisa** *adv.* quickly, fast, speedily.

**aprisco** *m.* sheepfold.

**aprisionar** *v.* to imprison; to tie, fasten.

**aprobación** *f.* approbation, approval; consent; pass, passing grade.

**aprobar**[2] *v. irr.* to approve; to pass (*in an examination*).

**aprontar** *v.* to make ready; to expedite; to hand over without delay; *Am.* to pay in advance.

**apropiación** *f.* appropriation; confiscation.

**apropiado** *adj.* appropriate, proper, fitting, suitable; *p.p. of* **apropiar.**

**apropiar** *v.* to fit; to adapt; **-se** to take possession (of); to confiscate.

**aprovechable** *adj.* available; usable, fit to use.

**aprovechado** *adj.* diligent, industrious; *p.p. of* **aprovechar.**

**aprovechamiento** *m.* use, utilization; exploitation; profit, benefit; progress.

**aprovechar** *v.* to profit, be profitable; to progress, get ahead; to utilize; **-se de** to take advantage of; **¡que aproveche!** may you enjoy it!

**aproximado** *adj.* approximate; near; nearly correct.

**aproximar** *v.* to place or bring near; to approximate; **-se** to get near, approach.

**aproximativo** *adj.* approximate.

**aptitud** *f.* aptitude, capacity, ability.

**apto** *adj.* apt; competent.

**apuesta** *f.* bet, wager.

**apuesto** *adj.* smart, stylish; good-looking.

**apuntación** *f.* note; memorandum; musical notation, set of musical symbols or signs.

**apuntalar** *v.* to prop; to shore up.

**apuntar** *v.* (*señalar*) to point; (*arma*) to aim; (*escribir*) to write down; (*a un actor*) to prompt; (*remendar*) to mend, to stitch; to sharpen; (*brotar*) to begin to show; **— el día** to begin to dawn; **-se** to sprout.

**apunte** *m.* note, memorandum.

**apuñalar** *v.* to stab.

**apuración** *f.* worry; trouble.

**apurado** *adj.* worried; needy; difficult; dangerous; in a hurry.

**apurar** *v.* (*acabar*) to exhaust, to drain to the last drop; (*preocupar*) to worry, annoy; (*acelerar*) to hurry, press; **-se** to be or get worried; to hurry up.

**apuro** *m.* need; worry; predicament; *Am.* rush, hurry.

**aquejar** *v.* to grieve, afflict.

**aquel, aquella** *dem. adj.* that (*at a distance*); **aquellos, aquellas** those; **aquél, aquélla** *m., f. dem. pron.* that one; the former; **aquello** that, that thing; **aquéllos, aquéllas** *m., f. pl.* those; the former.

**aquí** *adv.* here; **por —** this way; through here; around here.

**aquietar** *v.* to quiet, calm; to hush; **-se** to calm down, become calm.

**aquilón** *m.* north wind.

**ara** *f.* altar.

**árabe** *adj. & m.* Arab; Arabic.

**arado** *m.* plow; *Am.* plowed land, piece of cultivated land.

**aragonés** *adj.* Aragonese, of or from Aragón, Spain; *m.* Aragonese.

**arancel** *m.* tariff; **— de aduanas** customs, duties; **arancelario** *adj.* pertaining to tariff.

**araña** *f.* spider; chandelier.

**arañar** *v.* to scratch; to claw.

**araño** *m.* scratch; **arañazo** *m.* big scratch.

**arar** *v.* to plow.

**arbitración** *f.* arbitration.

**arbitrador** *m.* arbitrator; referee, umpire.

**arbitraje** *m.* arbitration.

**arbitrar** *v.* to arbitrate; to umpire.

**arbitrario** *adj.* arbitrary.

**arbitrio** *m.* free will; scheme, means; compromise, arbitration; sentence (*of a judge*); judgment.

**árbitro** *m.* arbitrator, sole judge, umpire.

**árbol** *m.* tree; mast; **arbolado** *adj.* wooded; *m.* grove of trees.

**arboleda** *f.* grove.

**arbusto** *m.* shrub.

**arca** *f.* ark; chest, coffer; **arcón** *m.* large coffer or chest; bin.

**arcada** *f.* arcade; archway.

**arcaico** *adj.* archaic.

**arcano** *adj.* hidden, secret; *m.* secret, mystery.

**arce** *m.* maple, maple tree.

**arcilla** *f.* clay.

**arco** *m.* arc; arch; bow; violin bow; — **iris** rainbow.

**archipiélago** *m.* archipelago (*group of many islands*).

**archisabido** *adj.* very well-known.

**archivo** *m.* archives; file; public records; *Am.* office, business office; **archivero** *m.* keeper of archives; city clerk.

**arder** *v.* to burn; to be consumed (*with fever or passion*); *Col., Carib.* to smart, sting.

**ardid** *m.* trick, scheme.

**ardiente** *adj.* ardent, burning, fervent; passionate; fiery.

**ardilla** *f.* squirrel.

**ardite** *m.* ancient coin of small value; bit, trifle; **no valer un —** not to be worth a penny.

**ardor** *m.* ardor; heat; fervor, eagerness.

**ardoroso** *adj.* ardent, fiery.

**arduo** *adj.* arduous, hard, difficult.

**área** *f.* area.

**arena** *f.* sand; arena; **-s** kidney stones; **arenal** *m.* sand pit.

**arenga** *f.* address, speech.

**arenisco** *adj.* sandy; gritty; **piedra arenisca** sandstone.

**arenoso** *adj.* sandy; gritty.

**arenque** *m.* herring.

**arepa** *f. Col., Ven., Carib.* a fried (*griddle*) cake made of corn meal that corresponds to the Mexican tortilla.

**arete** *m.* earring.

**argamasa** *f.* mortar.

**argentar** *v.* to plate (*with silver*); to polish.

**argentino** *adj.* silvery; Argentine; *m.* Argentine; Argentine gold coin worth 5 pesos.

**argolla** *f.* large iron ring; *Am.* plain finger ring, engagement ring; *Am.* **tener —** to be lucky.

**argucia** *f.* cunning, astuteness; scheme; subtlety.

**argüir**[32] *v. irr.* to argue; to deduce, infer.

**argumentación** *f.* argumentation, argument, reasoning.

**argumento** *m.* reasoning; substance, subject matter, resumé (*of a play or story*)

**aridez** *f.* barrenness; dryness; drought.

**árido** *adj.* arid, dry, barren; **-s** *m. pl.* grains and dry vegetables; **medida para -s** dry measure.

**ariete** *m.* ram, battering ram; — **hidráulico** hydraulic ram.

**arisco** *adj.* gruff, harsh, unsociable; *Am.* shy, distrustful.

**arista** *f.* sharp edge; ridge; beard (*of wheat or corn*).

**aristocracia** *f.* aristocracy.

**aristócrata** *m. & f.* aristocrat.

**aristocrático** *adj.* aristocratic.

**aritmética** *f.* arithmetic.

**arma** *f.* arm, weapon; branch (*of the army*); **-s** armed forces; — **arrojadiza** missile weapon; — **blanca** sword or knife; **de -s tomar** ready for any emergency; ready to fight.

**armada** *f.* armada, fleet.

**armador** *m.* shipbuilder; assembler.

**armadura** *f.* armor; armature (*of a generator or dynamo*); framework; mounting.

**armamento** *m.* armament; equipment.

**armar** *v.* to arm; to set up, assemble, rig up; — **una pendencia** to start a quarrel; *Col.* — **un trique** to lay a snare, set a trap; *Am.* **-se** to balk, to be stubborn; *Ven., Mex.* **-se con alguna cosa** to refuse to return something.

**armario** *m.* wardrobe, clothes closet; cabinet.

**armatoste** *m.* unwieldy object or machine; clumsy thing; heavy, clumsy fellow.

**armazón** *f.* framework, skeleton; *m.* skeleton (*of an animal*); *Am.* shelf, set of shelves.

**armella** *f.* staple; screw eye.

**armiño** *m.* ermine.

**armisticio** *m.* armistice.

**armonía** *f.* harmony.

**armónico** *adj.* harmonic; harmonious.

**armonioso** *adj.* harmonious, musical.

**armonizar**[9] *v.* to harmonize.

**arnés** *m.* harness; coat of mail; **-es** harness and trappings; equipment, outfit.

**aro** *m.* hoop; rim (*of a wheel*); *Am.* finger ring; *Ch., Ríopl.* earring.

**aroma** *f.* aroma, scent, perfume.

**aromático** *adj.* aromatic, fragrant, spicy; **sales aromáticas** smelling salts.

**arpa** *f.* harp.

**arpía** *f.* shrew.

**arpón** *m.* harpoon, spear.

**arqueado** *adj.* arched.

**arquear** *v.* to arch.

**arquitecto** *m.* architect.

**arquitectónico** *adj.* architectural.

**arquitectura** *f.* architecture.

**arrabal** *m.* outlying district; **-es** outskirts, suburbs.

**arracada** *f.* earring.

**arraigar**[7] *v.* to root, take root; **-se** to become rooted, attached.

**arrancado** *adj. Mex., Carib., C.A., Andes* without money, broke.

**arrancar**[6] *v.* to uproot; to pull out; to start, start out; *Ch., Mex.* to flee, run away.

**arranque** *m.* start; pull; uprooting; automobile starter; **— de ira** fit or outburst of anger; **punto de —** starting point.

**arrasar** *v.* to level; to tear down, raze; to fill to the brim; **-se** to clear up (*said of the sky*); **-se de lágrimas** to fill up with tears.

**arrastrado** *adj.* poor, destitute; mean, vile; wretched; rascally; **llevar una vida arrastrada** to lead a dog's life.

**arrastrar** *v.* to drag, haul; *Ven.* to harrow (*land*); **-se** to drag along, crawl.

**arrayán** *m.* myrtle.

**¡arre!** *interj.* gee! get up there!

**arrear** *v.* to drive (*mules, cattle*); *Guat.* to rustle, steal cattle; *Am.* **-le a uno una bofetada** to give a person a slap.

**arrebatamiento** *m.* snatch; ecstasy; rage.

**arrebatar** *v.* to snatch away; **-se de cólera** to have a fit of anger.

**arrebatiña** *f.* grab, snatch; scramble; **arrebatón** *m.* quick or violent grab.

**arrebato** *m.* rage; rapture, ecstasy; fit.

**arrebol** *m.* red color of the sky; rouge; **-es** red clouds.

**arreciar** *v.* to increase in intensity, get stronger.

**arrecife** *m.* reef.

**arredrar** *v.* to frighten, intimidate; **-se** to be or get scared.

**arreglar** *v.* to arrange, put in order; to regulate; to fix; to adjust, settle; *Am.* to pay (*a debt*); *Am.* to correct, punish; **-se** to doll up, fix oneself up; to settle differences, come to an agreement.

**arreglo** *m.* arrangement; adjustment; settlement; conformity, agreement; **con — a** according to.

**arrellanarse** *v.* to sprawl, lounge; to be self-satisfied.

**arremangado** *adj.* & *p.p.* turned up; **nariz arremangada** turned up nose.

**arremangar**[7] *v.* to tuck up, turn up, roll up (*the sleeves, trousers, etc.*); **-se** to roll up one's sleeves; **-se los pantalones** to roll up one's trousers.

**arremeter** *v.* to attack, assail, assault.

**arremetida** *f.* thrust, push, attack.

**arremolinarse** *v.* to whirl, swirl; to eddy; to mill around.

**arrendamiento** *m.* renting; lease; rental, rent.

**arrendar**[1] *v. irr.* to rent, lease, let; to hire; to tie (*a horse*); to bridle; *Am.* to head for.

**arrendatario** *m.* renter, tenant.

**arreo** *m.* raiment; ornament; *Am.* driving of horses or mules; *Ríopl., Ch., Mex., Ven.* drove of horses or mules; **-s** trappings; equipment; finery; *adv.* uninterruptedly, without interruption.

**arrepentido** *adj.* repentant; *p.p. of* **arrepentirse.**

**arrepentimiento** *m.* repentance, regret.

**arrepentirse**[3] *v. irr.* to repent, regret.

**arrestado** *adj.* daring, rash; *p.p. of* **arrestar.**

**arrestar** *v.* to arrest; *Am.* to return, strike back (*a ball*); *Peru* to reprimand; **-se** to dare, venture.

**arresto** *m.* arrest, imprisonment; detention; daring, rashness; rash act.

**arriar**[17] *v.* to haul down, lower (*the flag*); to lower (*the sails*); to slacken (*a rope*).

**arriba** *adv.* above; upstairs; **de — abajo** from top to bottom; up and down; **río —** upstream; **¡ — !** hurrah!

**arribada** *f.* arrival; *Am.* back talk, impudent answer.

**arribar** *v.* to arrive; to put into port; *Am.* to prosper, better one's lot.

**arribo** *m.* arrival.

**arriendo** = **arrendamiento.**

**arriero** *m.* muleteer.

**arriesgado** *adj.* risky, daring.

**arriesgar**[7] *v.* to risk; **-se** to dare, run a risk.

**arrimar** *v.* to bring or place near; to lay aside; to strike (*a blow*); **-se** to lean (on); to get near; to seek shelter.

**arrinconar** *v.* to corner; to put in a corner; to lay aside; to slight, neglect; **-se** to retire; to live a secluded life.

**arriscado** *adj.* bold; daring; brisk; spirited (*horse*); craggy, rugged.

**arriscar**[6] *v.* to risk, venture; *Mex.* to roll up, curl up, tuck up, fold back; *Col.* to have vim and vigor; *Am.* **— a** to reach, amount to; **-se** to get angry; *Peru., C.A.* to dress up, doll up.

**arroba** *f.* weight of 25 pounds.

**arrobamiento** *m.* trance, rapture.

**arrobarse** *v.* to be entranced; to be in a trance; to be enraptured.

**arrodillarse** *v.* to kneel.

**arrogancia** *f.* arrogance, pride.

**arrogante** *adj.* arrogant, haughty, proud.

**arrogarse**[7] *v.* to appropriate, usurp, assume (*power or rights*).

**arrojadizo** *adj.* missile; **arma arrojadiza** missile weapon.

**arrojado** *adj.* daring, rash, fearless; *p.p. of* **arrojar.**

**arrojar** *v.* to throw, hurl, cast; to expel; *Am.* to throw up, vomit; **— un saldo de** to show a balance of; **-se a** to hurl oneself upon or at; to dare to.

**arrojo** *m.* boldness, daring.

**arrollador** *adj.* sweeping, overwhelming, violent; winding (*that serves to wind or roll up*).

**arrollar** *v.* to roll up; to sweep away; to trample upon; to destroy.

**arropar** *v.* to wrap, cover; *Col.* to snap up, accept on the spot (*a deal*); **-se** to wrap up, cover up.

**arrostrar** *v.* to face, defy; **-se** to dare, dare to fight face to face.

**arroyada** *f.* gully, valley of a stream; bed (*formed by a stream*); river flood.

**arroyo** *m.* brook, small stream, rivulet; gutter; **arroyuelo** *m.* rivulet.

**arroz** *m.* rice; **arrozal** *m.* rice field.

**arruga** *f.* wrinkle.

**arrugar**[7] *v.* to wrinkle; *Carib.* to bother, annoy; **-se** to get wrinkled; *Mex., Col.* to crouch with fear, be afraid.

**arruinar** *v.* to ruin, destroy; **-se** to become ruined; *Am.* to go "broke", lose all one's fortune.

**arrullar** *v.* to lull; to coo.

**arrullo** *m.* lullaby; cooing.

**arrumbar** *v.* to lay aside (*as useless*), put away in a corner, discard; to dismiss, remove (*from office or a position of trust*); to take bearings; **— a su adversario** to corner one's opponent, overpower him.

**arsenal** *m.* arsenal; navy yard.

**arsénico** *m.* arsenic.

**arte** *m.* & *f.* art; skill, ability; cunning; craft; **por — de** by way or means of; **bellas -s** fine arts.

**artefacto** *m.* piece of workmanship, manufactured object; handiwork; contrivance.

**arteria** *f.* artery.

**artero** *adj.* crafty, astute.

**artesa** *f.* trough.

**artesano** *m.* artisan, craftsman; **artesanía** *f.* arts and crafts; workmanship, craftsmanship.

**artesonado** *m.* ceiling decorated with carved panels.

**ártico** *adj.* arctic.

**articulación** *f.* articulation; pronunciation; joint.

**articular** *v.* to articulate; to join, unite.

**artículo** *m.* article; **— de fondo** editorial.

**artífice** *m.* artisan, craftsman.

**artificial** *adj.* artificial.

**artificio** *m.* artifice, clever device; craft, skill; cunning, deceit.

**artificioso** *adj.* cunning, astute, deceitful; skillful.

**artillería** *f.* artillery, gunnery; **— de plaza** (*or* **de sitio**) heavy artillery; **— de montaña** light mountain artillery.

**artillero** *m.* artilleryman, gunner.

**artimaña** *f.* trick.

**artista** *m.* & *f.* artist.

**artístico** *adj.* artistic.

**arveja** *f. C.A., Col., Ven.* pea. *Also referred to as* **alverja.**

**arzobispo** *m.* archbishop.

**arzón** *m.* saddletree.

**as** *m.* ace.

**asa** *f.* handle.

**asado** *m.* roast; *p.p.* & *adj.* roasted.

**asador** *m.* spit (*for roasting*).

**asaltador** *m.* assailant; highway robber.

**asaltar** *v.* to assault, attack; **-le a uno una idea** to be struck by an idea; *Ríopl., Carib.* **— la casa de un amigo** to give a surprise party.

**asalto** *m.* assault, attack; *Am.* surprise party.

**asamblea** *f.* assembly, legislature; meeting.

**asar** *v.* to roast; **-se** to roast; to feel hot.

**asaz** *adv.* enough, very.

**ascendencia** *f.* ancestry; origin.

**ascendente** *adj.* ascendant, ascending, upward, rising.

**ascender**[1] *v. irr.* to ascend, climb; to promote; to amount (to).

**ascendiente** *m.* ancestor; influence.

**ascensión** *f.* ascension; ascent.

**ascenso** *m.* ascent, rise; promotion.

**ascensor** *m.* elevator.

**asco** *m.* disgust, loathing; nausea; **me da —** it makes me sick; it disgusts me; *Mex., Ven.* **poner a uno del —** to call a person all kinds of bad names; to soil.

**ascua** *f.* ember.

**aseado** *adj.* clean, neat; *p.p.* of **asear.**

**asear** *v.* to adorn; to make neat and clean; **-se** to clean oneself up.

**asechanza** = **acechanza.**

**asediar** *v.* to besiege, attack.

**asedio** *m.* siege.

**asegurar** *v.* to assure; to secure; to affirm; to insure; **-se** to make sure; to hold on; to get insured.

**asemejar** *v.* to liken, compare; **-se a** to resemble.

**asentaderas** *f. pl.* buttocks.

**asentador** *m.* razor strop.

**asentar** *v.* (*poner*) to set; to put down in writing; (*afirmar*) to assert; to iron out; to establish; (*afilar*) to hone, strop; **-se** to settle.

**asentimiento** *m.* assent, acquiescence, agreement.

**asentir**[3] *v. irr.* to assent, agree.

**aseo** *m.* neatness, cleanliness.

**asequible** *adj.* obtainable, available.

**aserción** *f.* assertion, affirmation.

**aserradero** *m.* sawmill.

**aserrar**[1] *v. irr.* to saw.

**aserrín** *m.* sawdust.

**aserto** *m.* assertion.

**asesinar** *v.* to assassinate, murder.

**asesinato** *m.* assassination, murder.

**asesino** *m.* assassin, murderer; *adj.* murderous.

**asestar** *v.* to point, aim, direct; **— un golpe** to deal a blow; **— un tiro** to fire a shot.

**aseveración** *f.* assertion, affirmation, contention.

**aseverar** *v.* to assert, affirm.

**asfalto** *m.* asphalt.

**asfixia** *f.* suffocation.

**asfixiar** *v.* to suffocate, smother.

**así** *adv.* so, thus, like this; therefore; **— —** so-so; **— que** so that; **— que** (*or* **como**) *conj.* as soon as; *Ríopl., Ch., Ven., Mex., Andes* **— no más** so-so; just so.

**asiático** *adj.* & *m.* Asiatic.

**asidero** *m.* handle; hold.

**asiduo** *adj.* assiduous, diligent, persevering.

**asiento** *m.* seat; site, location; bottom; entry (*in bookkeeping*); **-s** dregs, sediment.

**asignación** *f.* assignment; allowance.

**asignar** *v.* to assign; to allot; to attribute; to appoint.

**asilado** *m.* inmate (*of an asylum*).

**asilar** *v.* to house, shelter; to put in an asylum.

**asilo** *m.* asylum, refuge, shelter.

**asimilar** *v.* to assimilate, digest, absorb; to liken, compare.

**asimismo** *adv.* likewise, also.

**asir**[22] *v. irr.* to seize, take hold of.

**asistencia** *f.* presence; attendance; assistance, help; *Mex.* sitting room; **-s** allowance; *Col.*, *Ven.*, *Mex.* **casa de —** boarding house.

**asistente** *m.* assistant; helper; military orderly; *Col.*, *Ven.*, *P.R.* servant; **los -s** those present.

**asistir** *v.* to attend, be present; to help; *Am.* to board, serve meals.

**asno** *m.* ass, donkey.

**asociación** *f.* association.

**asociado** *m.* associate.

**asociar** *v.* to associate; **-se** to join; to associate.

**asolamiento** *m.* devastation, ravage, havoc, destruction.

**asolar**[2] *v. irr.* to raze; to lay waste; to parch; **-se** to dry up, become parched; to settle (*as liquids*).

**asoleado** *adj.* sunny; *p.p. of* **asolear.**

**asolear** *v.* to sun; **-se** to bask in the sun; to get sunburnt.

**asomar** *v.* to show, appear; **— la cabeza** to stick one's head out; **-se** to look out (*of a window*); to peep out (*or* into); *Peru* to draw near, approach.

**asombrar** *v.* (*hacer sombra*) to cast a shadow, darken; (*asustar*) to astonish, amaze, frighten; **-se** to be astonished, amazed.

**asombro** *m.* astonishment, amazement; fright.

**asombroso** *adj.* astonishing, amazing.

**asomo** *m.* sign, indication; conjecture, suspicion; **ni por —** by no means.

**aspa** *f.* wing of a windmill; blade (*of a propeller*); reel (*for winding yarn*).

**aspecto** *m.* aspect, look, appearance.

**aspereza** *f.* roughness, ruggedness; harshness; severity.

**áspero** *adj.* rough, uneven, harsh; gruff.

**aspiración** *f.* aspiration, ambition, longing; inhalation, breathing in.

**aspiradora** *f.* vacuum cleaner.

**aspirante** *m. & f.* applicant; candidate.

**aspirar** *v.* (*anhelar*) to aspire, long for, seek; (*inspirar*) to breathe in, to inhale; to aspirate (*a sound*).

**asquear** *v.* to disgust, nauseate, sicken.

**asqueroso** *adj.* loathsome, disgusting, sickening, filthy.

**asta** *f.* horn; antler; mast, pole, staff, flagstaff; lance; **a media —** at half mast.

**asterisco** *m.* asterisk, star (*used in printing*).

**astilla** *f.* chip; splinter; splint.

**astillar** *v.* to chip; to splinter; **-se** to splinter, break into splinters.

**astillero** *m.* dry dock; shipyard; lumber yard; rack (*for lances or spears*).

**astro** *m.* star; planet.

**astronauta** *m. & f.* astronaut.

**astronomía** *f.* astronomy; **astrónomo**

*m.* astronomer.

**astucia** *f.* shrewdness, cunning; trick.

**asturiano** *adj.* Asturian, of or from Asturias, Spain; *m.* Asturian.

**astuto** *adj.* astute, shrewd, wily, crafty.

**asueto** *m.* recess, vacation; **día de —** holiday.

**asumir** *v.* to assume.

**asunto** *m.* topic, subject matter; business; affair.

**asustadizo** *adj.* shy, scary, easily frightened, jumpy.

**asustar** *v.* to frighten, scare.

**atacante** *m.* attacker; *adj.* attacking.

**atacar**[6] *v.* to attack; to tighten, fasten; to ram; to plug, wad (*a gun*).

**atadura** *f.* tie, knot; fastening.

**atajar** *v.* to intercept; to interrupt, cut off; to take a short cut; to cross out.

**atajo** *m.* short cut; interception; *Am.* drove. *See* **hatajo.**

**atalaya** *f.* lookout, watchtower; *m.* lookout, watchman, guard.

**atañer**[19,51] *v.* to concern.

**ataque** *m.* attack; fit.

**atar** *v.* to tie, fasten; **-se** to get tied up; to be puzzled or perplexed.

**atareado** *adj.* busy, over-worked.

**atarear** *v.* to overwork, load with work; **-se** to toil, work hard; to be very busy.

**atascadero** *m.* muddy place; obstruction.

**atascar**[6] *v.* to stop up; to jam, obstruct; **-se** to get stuck; to stick; to jam, get obstructed; to stall.

**ataúd** *m.* coffin.

**ataviar**[17] *v.* to attire, deck, adorn; **-se** to dress up, doll up.

**atavío** *m.* attire, costume; ornaments, finery.

**atemorizar**[9] *v.* to frighten, scare.

**atención** *f.* attention, care, thought; courtesy; **-es** business, affairs; **en — a** having in mind, considering.

**atender**[1] *v. irr.* to heed, pay attention; to attend to, take care of; to take into account or consideration.

**atendido** *adj. Am.* attentive, courteous.

**atenerse**[45] *v. irr.* to rely (on); to accept, abide (by).

**atenido** *adj. Mex.*, *Carib.*, *C.A.*, *Andes* habitually dependent on another; *p.p. of* **atenerse.**

**atentado** *m.* offense, violation; crime, violence.

**atentar**[1] *v. irr.* to attempt, try; **— contra la vida de alguien** to attempt the life of someone.

**atento** *adj.* attentive; courteous, polite.

**atenuar**[18] *v.* to attenuate, lessen; to tone down; to dim; to make thin or slender.

**ateo** *m.* atheist; *adj.* atheistic.

**aterciopelado** *adj.* velvety.

**aterido** *adj.* stiff, numb from cold.

**aterirse**[3,51] *v. irr.* to become numb with cold.

**aterrador** *adj.* terrifying, appalling.

**aterrar** *v.* to terrify, frighten.

**aterrizaje** *m.* landing (*of a plane*); **pista de —** landing strip.

**aterrizar**[9] *v.* to land (*said of a plane*).

**aterronar** *v.* to make lumpy, form into lumps; **-se** to lump, form into lumps, become lumpy.

**aterrorizar**[9] *v.* to terrify, frighten, appal.

**atesorar** *v.* to treasure; to hoard, lay up, accumulate.

**atestado** *adj.* crowded, jammed, stuffed; witnessed; *p.p.* of **atestar.**

**atestar** *v.* (*legal*) to attest, testify, witness; (*llenar*) to fill up, cram, stuff, crowd; **-se de** to stuff oneself with, to get stuffed with.

**atestiguar**[8] *v.* to testify, witness; to attest.

**atiborrar** *v.* to stuff; **-se** to stuff oneself.

**atiesar** *v.* to stiffen.

**atildado** *adj.* spruce, trim; painstaking in dress or style.

**atinar** *v.* to hit the mark; to guess right.

**atisbar** *v.* to spy, look cautiously; to watch, pry; to catch a glimpse of; to peek.

**atisbo** *m.* glimpse; insight; peek; spying.

**atizar**[9] *v.* to poke, stir (*the fire*); to kindle, rouse; to trim (*a wick*); **— un bofetón** to give a wallop.

**atlántico** *adj.* Atlantic; **el Atlántico** the Atlantic.

**atlas** *m.* atlas.

**atleta** *m.* & *f.* athlete.

**atlético** *adj.* athletic.

**atletismo** *m.* athletics.

**atmósfera** *f.* atmosphere, air.

**atmosférico** *adj.* atmospheric.

**atole** *m.* *Am.* Mexican drink made of corn meal.

**atolondrado** *p.p.* & *adj.* confused, muddled; stunned; heedless, harebrained, thoughtless.

**atolondramiento** *m.* thoughtlessness, recklessness; confusion, perplexity.

**atolondrar** *v.* to confuse, muddle, perplex; to stun; **-se** to get muddled, confused; to get stunned.

**átomo** *m.* atom; small particle, tiny bit.

**atónito** *adj.* astonished, amazed.

**atontado** *adj.* stupefied, stupid, stunned.

**atontar** *v.* to stupefy, stun; to confuse.

**atorar** *v.* to jam; to stop up, clog; *Am.* to hold up, stop; **-se** to get stuck (*in the mud*); to get clogged; to get jammed; to choke (*with food*).

**atormentar** *v.* to torment; to worry, afflict; to tease, bother, vex.

**atornasolado** = **tornasolado.**

**atornillar** *v.* to screw; *Am.* to bother, torment.

**atorrante** *m.* & *f.* *Col., Ch., Ríopl., Bol.* vagabond, tramp.

**atrabancar**[6] *v.* to rush awkwardly; to run over; **-se** *Ríopl.* to get involved in difficulties; *Ríopl.* to rush into things.

**atrabiliario** *adj.* melancholy; bad-tempered.

**atracar** *v.* (*llenar*) to cram, stuff; (*amarrar*) to moor, to approach land; (*atacar*) to hold up, assault; *Am.* to seize; *Col.* to pursue, harass; *Am.* to treat severely; *Mex., C.A.* to thrash, beat; **— al muelle** to dock, moor to the wharf; **-se** to stuff oneself, overeat; *Ch.* to have a fist fight; *Ríopl.* to falter, stutter; **-se a** to come alongside of (*a ship*).

**atracción** *f.* attraction.

**atraco** *m.* holdup, assault; *Am.* **darse un — de comida** to stuff oneself, gorge.

**atracón** *m.* stuffing, gorging; *C.A.* violent quarrel; **darse un — de comida** to stuff oneself, gorge.

**atractivo** *adj.* attractive; *m.* attractiveness, charm.

**atraer**[46] *v. irr.* to attract.

**atragantarse** *v.* to gobble up; to choke (*with food*).

**atrancar**[6] *v.* to bolt, fasten with a bolt; *Am.* **-le a una cosa** to face something, stand up against something; **-se** to get crammed, obstructed; *Am.* to be stubborn, stick to one's opinion; *Col.* to stuff oneself, choke (*with food*).

**atrapar** *v.* to trap, ensnare; to seize, grab; to overtake.

**atrás** *adv.* back; behind; backward; *Am.* **echarse —** (*or* **para —**) to back out, go back on one's word.

**atrasado** *adj.* late; behind time; backward; behind (*in one's work, payments, etc.*); slow (*said of a clock*); *p.p.* of **atrasar.**

**atrasar** *v.* to delay; to be slow or behind time; **-se** to get behind, lose time; *Am.* to suffer a setback (*in one's health or fortune*).

**atraso** *m.* backwardness; delay; setback; **-s** arrears.

**atravesar**[1] *v. irr.* to cross; to walk across; to go through; to pierce; *Am.* to buy wholesale.

**atreverse** *v.* to dare, risk; to be insolent, saucy.

**atrevido** *adj.* bold, daring; insolent.

**atrevimiento** *m.* boldness, daring; insolence.

**atribuir**[32] *v. irr.* to attribute, ascribe, impute.

**atribular** *v.* to grieve, distress; **-se** to grieve; to be distressed.

**atributo** *m.* attribute, quality.

**atril** *m.* lectern, reading desk; book stand; music stand.

**atrincherar** *v.* to entrench, fortify with trenches; **-se** to entrench oneself.

**atrio** *m.* court, patio in front of a church; entrance hall.

**atrocidad** *f.* atrocity.

**atronador** *adj.* thunderous, deafening.

**atronar**[2] *v. irr.* to deafen; to stun.

**atropellar** *v.* to run over, run down; to knock down; to trample upon; to insult; **— por** to knock down, overcome with violence; **-se** to rush.

**atropello** *m.* violent act; insult; outrage; trampling.

**atroz** *adj.* atrocious, awful; inhuman.

**atún** *m.* tunny fish, tuna fish.

**aturdido** *adj.* & *p.p.* stupid, awkward; stunned, bewildered.

**aturdimiento** *m.* daze, bewilderment, confusion.

**aturdir** *v.* to stun; to deafen; to bewilder.

**audacia** *f.* daring, boldness.

**audaz** *adj.* daring, bold.

**audiencia** *f.* audience, hearing; court of justice.

**auditor** *m.* judge advocate.

**auditorio** *m.* audience.

**auge** *f.* boom (*in the market*); boost (*in prices*); topmost height (*of fortune, fame, dignity, etc.*); **estar** (*or* **ir**) **en —** to be on the increase.

**augurar** *v.* to foretell, predict.

**augusto** *adj.* venerable; majestic.

**aula** *f.* schoolroom, classroom; lecture hall.

**aullar** *v.* to howl; to shriek; to bawl.

**aullido** *m.* howl.

**aumentar** *v.* to augment, increase.

**aumento** *m.* increase, advance, rise.

**aun** (**aún**) *adv.* even, still, yet.

**aunque** *conj.* though, although.

**aura** *f.* breeze; favor, applause; *Am.* bird of prey, buzzard, vulture.

**áureo** *adj.* golden.

**aureola** *f.* aureole, halo.

**aureomicina** *f.* Aureomycin (*trademark for chlortetracycline*).

**aurora** *f.* dawn; beginning; **— boreal** aurora borealis, northern lights.

**auscultar** *v.* to sound, examine by listening to (*the chest, lungs, heart, etc.*).

**ausencia** *f.* absence.

**ausentarse** *v.* to absent oneself; to be absent; to leave.

**ausente** *adj.* absent.

**auspicios** *m. pl.* auspices, patronage; omens.

**austeridad** *f.* austerity, severity, sternness, harshness.

**austero** *adj.* austere, stern, strict; harsh.

**austral** *adj.* southern.

**austríaco** *adj.* & *m.* Austrian.

**austro** *m.* south wind.

**auténtico** *adj.* authentic, true, genuine.

**auto** *m.* auto, automobile; one-act play; writ, order; **— sacramental** one-act religious play; **-s** proceedings.

**autobús** *m.* bus, autobus.

**autóctono** *adj.* indigenous, native.

**automático** *adj.* automatic.

**automotriz** *adj.* automotive, self-moving.

**automóvil** *m.* automobile, auto.

**automovilista** *m.* & *f.* motorist.

**autonomía** *f.* autonomy.

**autopista** *f.* expressway, superhighway, freeway, throughway, turnpike.

**autor** *m.* author.

**autoridad** *f.* authority.

**autoritario** *adj.* authoritative; authoritarian, domineering; bossy.

**autorización** *f.* authorization, sanction.

**autorizar**[9] *v.* to authorize, give power (to).

**auxiliar** *v.* to aid, help; *adj.* auxiliary, helping, assisting; *m.* assistant.

**auxilio** *m.* aid, help.

**avaluación** *f.* valuation, appraisal, assessment.

**avaluar**[18] *v.* to value, appraise.

**avalúo** *m.* valuation, appraisal.

**avance** *m.* advance, progress, headway; advanced payment; attack.

**avanzada** *f.* advance guard; outpost; advanced unit, spearhead.

**avanzar**[9] *v.* to advance.

**avaricia** *f.* avarice, greed.

**avariento** *adj.* avaricious, miserly; *m.* miser.

**avaro** *adj.* miserly, greedy; *m.* miser.

**avasallar** *v.* to subject, dominate, subdue.

**ave** *f.* bird; fowl; **— de corral** domestic fowl; **— de rapiña** bird of prey.

**avecindarse** *v.* to settle, locate, establish oneself, take up residence (*in a community*).

**avellana** *f.* hazelnut; **avellano** *m.* hazel; hazelnut tree; **avellanado** *adj.* hazel, light brown.

**avena** *f.* oats.

**avenencia** *f.* harmony, agreement; conformity.

**avenida** *f.* avenue; flood.

**avenir**[48] *v. irr.* to adjust; to reconcile; **-se a** to adapt oneself to; **-se con alguien** to get along with someone.

**aventador** *m.* fan (*for fanning a fire*); ventilator; winnower (*machine for separating wheat from chaff*).

**aventajar** *v.* to excel; to be ahead (of); **-se a** to get ahead of.

**aventar**[1] *v. irr.* to fan; to winnow, blow chaff from grain; to throw out, expel; *Am.* to pitch, throw; *Am.* to dry sugar (*in the open*); *Am.* to rouse (*game*); **-se** to be full of wind; to flee, run away; *Am.* to attack, hurl oneself (*on someone*).

**aventura** *f.* adventure; risk, danger; chance.

**aventurado** *adj.* adventurous, risky; bold, daring.

**aventurar** *v.* to venture, risk; **-se a** to risk, run the risk of; to dare.

**aventurero** *adj.* adventurous; *m.* adventurer.

**avergonzar**[2,9] *v. irr.* to shame; **-se** to feel ashamed.

**avería** *f.* damage; aviary, birdhouse; *Am.* misfortune; *Mex.*, *Cuba* mischief.

**averiar**[17] *v.* to damage, spoil, hurt; **-se** to become damaged; to spoil.

**averiguar**[8] *v.* to find out; to investigate.

**aversión** *f.* aversion, dislike; reluctance.

**avestruz** *m.* ostrich.

**avezado** *p.p.* & *adj.* accustomed; trained, practiced.

**aviación** *f.* aviation.

**aviador** *m.* aviator, flyer; purveyor, provider; *Am.* moneylender (*to miners or laborers*), promoter.

**aviar**[17] *v.* to equip; to supply; to prepare, make ready; *Am.* to lend money or equipment; **estar aviado** to be surrounded by difficulties; to be in a fix.

**ávido** *adj.* eager; greedy.
**avinagrado** *adj.* sour; acid; cross.
**avinagrar** *v.* to sour, make sour or acid; **-se** to sour, become sour.
**avío** *m.* provision, supply; preparation; *Cuba, Mex.* loan of money or equipment; **-s** equipment; **-s de pescar** fishing tackle.
**avión** *m.* airplane; martin (*a bird similar to a swallow*).
**avisar** *v.* to inform, give notice, advise; to announce; to warn.
**aviso** *m.* notice, advice, announcement; warning.
**avispa** *f.* wasp; **avispero** *m.* wasp's nest; **avispón** *m.* hornet.
**avispado** *adj.* lively, keen, clever, wide-awake; *Am.* frightened, scared.
**avispar** *v.* to spur, incite; **-se** to be on the alert; to be uneasy; *Am.* to become frightened, scared.
**avistar** *v.* to glimpse, catch sight of; **-se** to see each other, meet.
**avivar** *v.* to enliven, give life to; to revive; to brighten; to quicken.
**avizor** *adj.* alert, watchful.
**avizorar** *v.* to spy, watch closely.
**aya** *f.* child's nurse, governess; **ayo** *m.* tutor, guardian.
**ayer** *adv.* yesterday.
**ayuda** *f.* aid, help.
**ayudante** *m.* assistant.
**ayudar** *v.* to aid, help.
**ayunar** *v.* to fast.
**ayunas: en —** fasting; **en — de** totally ignorant of.
**ayuno** *m.* fast; **— de** wholly ignorant of.
**ayuntamiento** *m.* municipal government; town hall.
**azabache** *m.* jet; **-s** jet ornaments.
**azada** *f.* spade; hoe; **azadón** *m.* hoe.
**azafrán** *m.* saffron.
**azahar** *m.* orange or lemon blossom.
**azar** *m.* hazard; chance; accident; disaster.
**azogue** *m.* quicksilver.
**azolvar** *v.* to clog, obstruct; **-se** to clog, get clogged.
**azorar** *v.* to disturb, startle; to bewilder; **-se** to be startled, astonished; to be bewildered, perplexed; to be uneasy.
**azotaina** *f.* flogging, lashing, beating.
**azotar** *v.* to whip, lash, beat; *Am.* to thresh (*rice*); **— las calles** to "beat the pavement", walk the streets.
**azote** *m.* whip; lash with a whip; scourge; affliction, calamity.
**azotea** *f.* flat roof.
**azteca** *adj., m. & f.* Aztec.
**azúcar** *m.* sugar.
**azucarar** *v.* to sugar; to sweeten; **-se** to become sweet; *Am.* to crystallize, turn to sugar.
**azucarera** *f.* sugar bowl; sugar mill.
**azucarero** *adj.* sugar (*used as adj.*); *m.* sugar manufacturer, producer or dealer; sugar bowl.
**azucena** *f.* white lily.
**azufre** *m.* sulphur.

**azul** *adj.* blue; **— celeste** sky-blue; **— marino** navy blue; **— turquí** indigo; *Am.* **tiempos -es** hard times.
**azulado** *adj.* bluish.
**azular** *v.* to dye or color blue.
**azulejo** *m.* glazed tile; *Am.* bluebird; *adj.* bluish.
**azuzar**[9] *v.* to urge, egg on; to incite.

## B

**baba** *f.* drivel, slaver, saliva; slime, slimy secretion; *Am.* small alligator.
**babear** *v.* to drivel; to slobber.
**babero** *m.* baby's bib.
**babor** *m.* port, port side (*of a ship*).
**babosear** *v.* to slaver, drivel; to keep one's mouth open; to act like a fool.
**baboso** *adj.* driveling, slobbering; slimy; foolishly sentimental; *Am.* silly, idiotic, foolish; **babosa** *f.* slug (*creature like a snail, but without a shell*).
**babucha** *f.* slipper; *Riopl.* **a —** pickaback, on the back or shoulders.
**bacalao, bacallao** *m. Andalusia, Am.* codfish.
**bacilo** *m.* bacillus.
**bacín** *m.* pot, chamber pot; **bacinica** *f.* chamber pot.
**bacteria** *f.* bacterium; **-s** bacteria.
**bacteriología** *f.* bacteriology.
**bacteriológico** *adj.* bacteriological, pertaining to bacteriology.
**báculo** *m.* staff, cane; aid, support.
**bache** *m.* rut, hole in the road.
**bachiller** *m.* bachelor (*one who holds degree*); talkative person; **bachillerato** *m.* bachelor's degree; studies for the bachelor's degree.
**badajo** *m.* clapper of a bell; foolish talker.
**badana** *f.* sheepskin.
**bagaje** *m.* baggage; army pack mule.
**bagatela** *f.* trifle.
**bagazo** *m.* waste pulp (*of sugarcane, olives, grapes, etc.*).
**bagual** *adj. Riopl.* wild, untamed, unruly; *Riopl.* rude, discourteous; *Riopl.* lanky, awkward; *m. Riopl.* wild horse.
**bahía** *f.* bay, harbor.
**bailador** *m.* dancer; *adj.* dancing.
**bailar** *v.* to dance; to spin around.
**bailarín** *m.* dancer; **bailarina** *f.* dancer.
**baile** *m.* dance; ball; ballet.
**bailotear** *v.* to jig, jiggle; to dance poorly; to dance around.
**baja** *f.* fall (*of prices*); war casualty; **dar de —** to discharge, muster out.
**bajada** *f.* descent; slope, dip (*on a road*); **de —** on the way down; **subidas y -s** ups and downs.
**bajar** *v.* to go down; to drop (*as price or value*); to lower; to take or carry down; to humble; **-se** to get down or off; to alight; *Am.* to stop at a hotel.
**bajel** *m.* boat, ship.
**bajeza** *f.* vile act or remark; meanness; baseness; degradation.
**bajío** *m.* shoal, sand bank; *Am.* lowland.
**bajo** *adj.* low; short; soft, bass (*tone or voice*); shallow (*water*); subdued

(*color*); humble; base; **piso —** first
floor, ground floor; *prep.* under, underneath; *m.* bass.

**bala** *f.* bullet, shot, ball; bale (*of cotton*).

**balada** *f.* ballad.

**baladí** *adj.* trivial; flimsy.

**balance** *m.* balance; equilibrium; balance sheet; rocking, rolling.

**balancear** *v.* to balance; to rock, roll;
to swing, sway; to waver.

**balanceo** *m.* rocking, rolling; swinging;
balancing; wavering; wobbling.

**balanza** *f.* balance, scale.

**balar** *v.* to bleat.

**balaustrada** *f.* balustrade, banister,
railing.

**balaustre** *m.* banister.

**balazo** *m.* shot; bullet wound; *adj. Ch.*
clever, cunning.

**balbucear** *v.* to stammer, stutter; to
babble.

**balbuceo** *m.* babble.

**balcón** *m.* balcony.

**baldado** *m.* cripple; *adj. & p.p.* crippled.

**baldar** *v.* to cripple; to trump (*a card*).

**balde** *m.* pail; bucket; **de —** free of
charge; **en —** in vain.

**baldío** *adj.* barren; fallow, uncultivated;
*m.* fallow land; wasteland.

**baldón** *m.* infamy, insult.

**baldosa** *f.* floor tile; paving stone.

**balido** *m.* bleat, bleating.

**balneario** *m.* bathing resort; *adj.* pertaining to bathing resorts or medicinal
springs.

**balompié** *m.* football.

**balota** *f.* ballot.

**balotar** *v.* to ballot, vote.

**balsa** *f.* (*de agua*) pond, pool; (*embarcación*) raft; *Am.* marsh; *Am.* a
species of ceiba (*a tropical tree*).

**bálsamo** *m.* balsam, balm.

**baluarte** *m.* bulwark.

**ballena** *f.* whale; whalebone.

**bambolear** *v.* to sway, swing, rock; **-se**
to stagger; to sway.

**bambú** *m.* bamboo.

**banana** *f.* banana; **banano** *m.* banana
tree.

**banasta** *f.* large basket.

**banca** *f.* bench; card game; banking;
banking house.

**bancario** *adj.* bank, pertaining to a
bank.

**bancarrota** *f.* bankruptcy; failure, collapse.

**banco** *m.* bank; bench, stool; school (*of
fish*); *Mex.* pile of grain; *Am.* small
hill on a plain.

**banda** *f.* (*musical*) band; (*cinta*) ribbon,
sash; (*grupo*) gang, group, party;
flock; (*lindero*) side, edge, border.

**bandada** *f.* flock of birds; *Am.* gang.

**bandeja** *f.* tray; *Mex., Ven., Col.* bowl.

**bandera** *f.* banner, flag; *Ríopl., Cuba,
Mex.* **parar uno —** to take the lead,
be a gangleader.

**banderilla** *f.* dart with a small flag or
streamers (*used in bullfights*); **clavar a
uno una —** tog oad or taunt someone; **tercio de —** the **banderilla**

phase of the bullfight; *Am.* **pegar una
—** to touch for a loan.

**banderillero** *m.* bullfighter who sticks
the **banderillas** into the bull.

**banderín** *m.* small flag; signal flag;
pennant; recruiting office.

**banderola** *f.* streamer, small banner or
flag; pennant.

**bandidaje** *m.* banditry, highway robbery; bandits.

**bandido** *m.* bandit, gangster.

**bando** *m.* (*decreto*) decree, proclamation; (*partido*) party, faction.

**bandolero** *m.* bandit.

**bandurria** *f.* bandore (*stringed instrument*); *Am.* a species of wading bird.

**banquero** *m.* banker.

**banqueta** *f.* bench (*without a back*);
stool; footstool; *Mex.* sidewalk.

**banquete** *m.* banquet.

**banquetear** *v.* to banquet, feast.

**banquillo** *m.* bench, stool.

**bañada** *f.* shower, spray; dip, bath.

**bañar** *v.* to bathe, wash; to dip; **-se** to
take a bath.

**bañera** *f.* bathtub.

**bañista** *m. & f.* bather.

**baño** *m.* (*aseo*) bath; bathtub; (*acabado*)
cover, coating; **— de María** double
boiler; *Am.* **— ruso** steam bath.

**baqueta** *f.* rod; whip; **-s** drumsticks;
**tratar a la —** to treat scornfully,
despotically.

**baquiano, baqueano** *m. Ríopl., Ven.,
Andes* native guide (*through the wilderness, pampas, etc.*); *adj. Ríopl., Andes*
having an instinctive sense of direction.

**bar** *m.* bar, taproom, tavern.

**baraja** *f.* pack of cards.

**barajar** *v.* to shuffle; to mix, jumble together; to scuffle, wrangle; *Am.* to
hinder, obstruct.

**baranda** *f.* railing; **barandal** *m.*
banister, railing.

**barandilla** *f.* balustrade, rail, railing.

**barata** *f.* barter, exchange; *Am.* bargain sale; *Peru, Ch.* cockroach.

**baratear** *v.* to sell cheap; to cheapen; to
cut the price of.

**baratija** *f.* trinket, trifle.

**barato** *adj.* cheap; *m.* bargain sale;
money given by the winning gambler.

**baratura** *f.* cheapness.

**baraúnda** *f.* clamor, uproar, clatter.

**barba** *f.* chin; beard; **-s** whiskers.

**barbacoa** *f. Am.* barbecue; barbecued
meat.

**barbado** *adj.* bearded.

**barbaridad** *f.* cruelty, brutality; rudeness; **una — de** a lot of; **¡que —!**
what nonsense!; what an atrocity!

**barbarie** *f.* barbarousness; savagery;
lack of culture, ignorance; cruelty,
brutality.

**bárbaro** *adj.* barbarous, cruel, savage;
crude, coarse; *m.* barbarian.

**barbechar** *v.* to plow; to fallow.

**barbecho** *m.* first plowing; plowed land;
fallow, fallow land.

**barbería** *f.* barbershop.

**barbero** *m.* barber; *Am.* flatterer.

**barbilla** *f.* point of the chin.

**barbón, barbudo** *adj.* bearded.

**barca** *f.* boat, launch, barge.

**barco** *m.* boat, ship.

**bardo** *m.* bard, minstrel, poet.

**barítono** *m.* baritone.

**barniz** *m.* varnish; glaze; printer's ink.

**barnizar**[9] *v.* to varnish; to glaze.

**barómetro** *m.* barometer.

**barquero** *m.* boatman; bargeman.

**barquillo** *m.* rolled wafer; ice-cream cone.

**barquinazo** *m.* tumble, bad fall, hard bump, somersault; *Am.* lurch (*of a vehicle or boat*).

**barra** *f.* bar; rod; railing; sand bar; claque, audience; **— de jabón** bar of soap.

**barrabasada** *f.* mischief, mean prank; rash, hasty act.

**barraca** *f.* hut, cabin; *Andes* large shed, warehouse.

**barranca** *f.*, **barranco** *m.* ravine, gorge; *Am.* cliff.

**barreminas** *m.* mine-sweeper.

**barrena** *f.* auger, drill; gimlet (*small tool for boring holes*); spinning dive (*of a plane*).

**barrenar** *v.* to drill, bore; to scuttle (*a ship*); to blast (*a rock*).

**barrendero** *m.* sweeper.

**barrer** *v.* to sweep; to sweep away; *Am.* to defeat; *Am.* **al —** altogether, as a whole.

**barrera** *f.* barrier; obstacle.

**barreta** *f.* small iron bar; *Mex., Cuba, Col.* pick, pickaxe.

**barrica** *f.* cask, keg.

**barrida** *f. Am.* sweep, sweeping.

**barrido** *m.* sweep, sweeping; sweepings; *p.p. of* **barrer.**

**barriga** *f.* belly; bulge.

**barrigón, barrigudo** *adj.* big-bellied.

**barril** *m.* barrel, keg.

**barrio** *m.* district, neighborhood, quarter; **-s bajos** slums.

**barro** *m.* (*tierra*) mud, clay; (*granillo*) pimple; *Am.* **hacer** (*or* **cometer**) **un —** to commit a blunder.

**barroso** *adj.* muddy; pimply; reddish.

**barrote** *m.* short, thick bar; brace; rung (*of a ladder or chair*).

**barruntar** *v.* to foresee; to have a presentiment; to conjecture.

**barrunto** *m.* foreboding, presentiment; guess; hint, indication, sign.

**bártulos** *m. pl.* household goods; implements, tools.

**barullo** *m.* hubbub, racket, disorder.

**basa** *f.* base, pedestal; basis, foundation.

**basar** *v.* to base; to put on a base.

**basca** *f.* nausea, sickness to one's stomach; **tener -s** to be nauseated, sick to one's stomach.

**báscula** *f.* scale (*for weighing*), platform scale.

**base** *f.* base, basis, foundation.

**básico** *adj.* basic.

**basquear** *v.* to heave, try to vomit; to be nauseated, sick to one's stomach.

**basquetbol** *m.* basketball.

**bastante** *adj.* enough, sufficient; *adv.* enough.

**bastar** *v.* to be enough; to suffice.

**bastardilla** *f.* italic type, italics.

**bastardo** *adj.* bastard.

**bastidor** *m.* wing (*of a stage*); frame; embroidery frame; window sash; easel (*support for a picture, blackboard, etc.*); **entre -es** behind the scenes, off stage.

**bastilla** *f.* hem.

**bastimento** *m.* supply, provisions; vessel, ship.

**basto** *adj.* coarse; *m.* club (*in cards*); *Am.* saddle pad.

**bastón** *m.* cane, walking stick.

**basura** *f.* rubbish, scraps; garbage; refuse.

**basurero** *m.* garbage or rubbish dump; manure pile; garbage man, rubbish man; street cleaner.

**bata** *f.* lounging robe; housecoat, wrapper, dressing gown; smock; **batín** *m.* smock.

**batahola** *f.* hubbub, racket, uproar.

**batalla** *f.* battle; struggle.

**batallar** *v.* to battle, fight, struggle.

**batallón** *m.* battalion.

**batata** *f.* sweet potato.

**bate** *m. Am.* baseball bat.

**batea** *f.* tray; trough; bowl; barge; *Am.* washtub.

**bateador** *m. Am.* batter (*in baseball*).

**batear** *v. Am.* to bat.

**batería** *f.* battery (*military, naval, or electric*); **— de cocina** set of kitchen utensils; **— de jazz** a jazz combo; *Mex.* **dar —** to raise a rumpus; to plod, work hard.

**batidor** *m.* beater; scout.

**batintín** *m.* gong.

**batir** *v.* (*combatir*) to beat, whip, defeat; (*reconocer*) reconnoiter, explore; (*mover*) to flap; *Ch.* to rinse (*clothes*); *Ríopl.* to denounce; **-se** to fight; **— palmas** to clap, applaud.

**batisfera** *f.* bathysphere.

**baturrillo** *m.* medley, mixture; hodgepodge.

**batuta** *f.* orchestra conductor's baton or wand; **llevar la —** to lead; to be the leader.

**baúl** *m.* trunk, chest; **— mundo** large trunk.

**bautismo** *m.* baptism, christening; **nombre de —** Christian name.

**bautista** *m. & f.* Baptist; baptizer.

**bautizar**[9] *v.* to baptize, christen.

**bautizo** *m.* christening, baptism.

**baya** *f.* berry.

**bayeta** *f.* flannel; flannelette; **bayetón** *m.* thick wool cloth; *Col.* long poncho lined with flannel.

**bayo** *adj.* bay, reddish-brown.

**baza** *f.* trick (*cards played in one round*); **meter —** to meddle; to butt into a conversation; **no dejar meter —** not to let a person put a word in edgewise.

**bazar** *m.* bazaar; department store.

**bazo** *m.* spleen.
**bazofia** *f.* scraps, refuse, garbage; dregs.
**beatitud** *f.* bliss, blessedness.
**beato** *adj.* blessed; beatified; devout; overpious; hypocritical.
**bebé** *m.* baby.
**bebedero** *m.* drinking trough; watering place; spout.
**bebedor** *m.* drinker; drunkard.
**beber** *v.* to drink; to drink in, absorb.
**bebida** *f.* drink, beverage; **dado a la — given to drink.
**beca** *f.* scholarship, fellowship; sash worn over the academic gown.
**becario** *m.* scholar, fellow, holder of a scholarship.
**becerro** *m.* young bull (*less than a year old*); calf; calfskin.
**becuadro** *m.* natural sign (*in music*).
**bedel** *m.* beadle.
**befa** *f.* scoff, jeer.
**befar** *v.* to scoff, jeer at, mock.
**bejuco** *m.* cane; **silla de —** cane chair.
**beldad** *f.* beauty.
**belga** *adj., m. & f.* Belgian.
**bélico** *adj.* warlike.
**beligerante** *adj., m. & f.* belligerent.
**bellaco** *adj.* sly, deceitful; *m.* villain; rascal.
**bellaquear** *v.* to cheat; to play tricks; *Am.* to rear, stand up on the hind legs; *Am.* to balk; *Am.* to be touchy, oversensitive.
**bellaquería** *f.* cunning, trickery; sly act or remark.
**belleza** *f.* beauty.
**bello** *adj.* beautiful.
**bellota** *f.* acorn.
**bemol** *adj.* flat (*in music*); **tener -es** to have difficulties.
**bendecir**[27,52] *v. irr.* to bless.
**bendición** *f.* benediction, blessing; *Mex., C.A., Col., Ven.* **echarle la — a una cosa** to give something up for lost.
**bendito** *adj.* blessed; saintly; **es un —** he is a saint, he is a simple soul; *p.p. of* **bendecir.**
**benefactor** *m.* benefactor; patron.
**beneficencia** *f.* beneficence, kindness, charity.
**beneficiar** *v.* to benefit, do good; to cultivate (*land*); to exploit (*a mine*); to treat (*metals*); *Col., Ven.* to slaughter (*cattle*) for marketing.
**beneficio** *m.* (*provecho*) benefit, profit; exploitation of a mine; (*cultivo*) cultivation of land; *Am.* fertilizer; *Am.* slaughtering (*of cattle*).
**benéfico** *adj.* beneficent, good, kind.
**benemérito** *m.* worthy, notable; *adj.* worthy.
**benevolencia** *f.* benevolence, kindness.
**benévolo** *adj.* benevolent, good, kindly.
**benigno** *adj.* benign, gentle, mild, kind.
**beodo** *adj.* drunk; *m.* drunkard.
**berenjena** *f.* eggplant; *Mex., C.A.* kind of squash; **berenjenal** *m.* eggplant patch; **meterse uno en un —** to get into a mess.

**bergantín** *m.* brigantine, brig (*square-rigged ship with two masts*).
**bermejo** *adj.* crimson, bright red.
**bermellón** *adj.* vermilion (*bright red*).
**berrear** *v.* to bellow; to scream; to sing off key.
**berrido** *m.* bellow, bellowing; scream.
**berrinche** *m.* fit of anger; tantrum.
**berza** *f.* cabbage.
**besar** *v.* to kiss.
**beso** *m.* kiss.
**bestia** *f.* beast.
**bestialidad** *f.* bestiality, brutality.
**besugo** *m.* sea bream (*a fish*).
**besuquear** *v.* to kiss repeatedly.
**betabel** *f. Mex.* beet.
**betún** *m.* bitumen (*combustible mineral*); black pitch; shoeblacking.
**Biblia** *f.* Bible.
**bíblico** *adj.* Biblical.
**biblioteca** *f.* library; set of volumes; bookcase.
**bibliotecario** *m.* librarian.
**bicicleta** *f.* bicycle; **biciclista, bicicletista** *m. & f.* bicyclist, bicycle rider.
**bicho** *m.* insect, bug; any small animal; an insignificant person.
**biela** *f.* connecting rod (*of an engine*).
**bien** *adv.* well; **— que** although; **ahora — now then; **más —** rather; **si — although; *m.* good, benefit; **-es** property; **-es inmuebles** real estate; **-es raíces** real estate.
**bienaventurado** *adj.* blessed, happy.
**bienaventuranza** *f.* blessedness; beatitude; bliss.
**bienestar** *m.* well-being, comfort, welfare.
**bienhechor** *m.* benefactor.
**bienvenida** *f.* welcome.
**bienvenido** *adj.* welcome.
**biftec, bistec, bisté** *m.* beefsteak.
**bifurcación** *f.* fork, forking, branching out; railway junction; branch railroad.
**bifurcarse**[6] *v.* to fork, branch off, divide into two branches.
**bigamía** *f.* bigamy.
**bigote** *m.* mustache.
**bikini** *m.* bikini bathing suit.
**bilis** *f.* bile.
**billar** *m.* billiards; billiard room.
**billete** *m.* ticket; note; bill, banknote.
**billón** *m.* billion.
**bimestre** *m.* two-month period; bimonthly salary, rent, etc.; *adj.* bimonthly; **bimestral** *adj.* bimonthly.
**biografía** *f.* biography.
**biología** *f.* biology.
**biombo** *m.* folding screen.
**birlar** *v.* to snatch away; to steal; to kill or knock down with one blow.
**bisabuelo** *m.* great-grandfather; **bisabuela** *f.* great-grandmother.
**bisagra** *f.* hinge.
**bisiesto** *adj.* leap (*year*).
**bisojo** *adj.* squint-eyed.
**bisonte** *m.* bison; the American buffalo.
**bisturí** *m.* bistoury, surgical knife.
**bitoque** *m.* barrel plug, stopper; *Am.* faucet; *Col., Cuba, Mex.* injection point (*of a syringe*).

**BA**

**bizarría** f. gallantry, bravery; generosity.

**bizarro** adj. gallant, brave; generous.

**bizco** adj. cross-eyed.

**bizcocho** m. hardtack, hard biscuit; cake; cookie; — **borracho** cake dipped in wine.

**biznieto** m. great-grandson; **biznieta** f. great-granddaughter.

**blanco** adj. (color) white; m. white man; (nada escrito) blank, blank sheet; (objeto de tiro) target, goal.

**blancura** f. whiteness.

**blancuzco, blanquecino, blanquizco** adj. whitish.

**blandir** v. to brandish, flourish, swing.

**blando** adj. bland, smooth; soft; **blanducho** adj. flabby; soft.

**blandura** f. softness; mildness, gentleness.

**blanquear** v. to whiten, bleach; to whitewash; to show white; to begin to turn white.

**blanqueo** m. whitening, bleach, bleaching.

**blanquillo** adj. whitish; white (flour); m. Mex., C.A. egg; Peru, Ch., Andes white peach.

**blasfemar** v. to blaspheme, curse, swear.

**blasfemia** f. blasphemy.

**blasón** m. coat of arms; honor, glory.

**blasonar** v. to boast.

**blindaje** m. armor, armor plating.

**blindar** v. to armor.

**bloc** m. Am. tablet, pad of paper.

**blocaje** m. action of blocking.

**blondo** adj. blond.

**bloque** m. block (of stone, wood, etc.); Am. tablet, pad of paper; Cuba, Mex., Ríopl. political bloc.

**bloquear** v. to blockade.

**bloqueo** m. blockade.

**blusa** f. blouse.

**boato** m. pomp, ostentation.

**bobada** f. foolishness, folly.

**bobalicón** adj. foolish, silly; m. simpleton, blockhead, dunce.

**bobear** v. to act like a fool; to fool around; to gawk, stare foolishly.

**bobería** f. foolishness, folly; nonsense; foolish remark.

**bobina** f. bobbin, reel; electric coil; — **distribuidora** feeding reel; — **receptora** rewind reel (on a tape recorder).

**bobo** adj. simple, foolish, stupid; m. booby, fool, dunce.

**boca** f. mouth; opening; — **abajo** face downward; — **arriba** face upward; **a — de jarro** at close range; **bocaza** f. large mouth.

**bocacalle** f. street intersection.

**bocado** m. mouthful, morsel, bite; bit (of a bridle); **bocadillo, bocadito** m. snack; sandwich; tidbit; Am. piece of candy.

**bocanada** f. mouthful; puff (of smoke).

**boceto** m. sketch; outline; skit.

**bocina** f. horn; trumpet; automobile horn; speaking tube; megaphone.

**bochorno** m. sultry weather; suffocating heat; blush, flush; embarrassment.

**bochornoso** adj. sultry; embarrassing.

**boda** f. marriage, wedding; — **de negros** a noisy party; **-s de Camacho** lavish feast, banquet.

**bodega** f. cellar; wine cellar; storeroom; warehouse; Cuba, Ven., Col. grocery store; **bodeguero** m. keeper of a wine cellar; liquor dealer; Cuba, Ven., Col. grocer.

**bodoque** m. wad; lump; dunce; Am. bump, swelling.

**bofe** m. lung; P.R. snap, easy job; **echar uno los -s** to throw oneself into a job; to work hard; Am. **ser un —** to be a bore; to be repulsive.

**bofetada** f. slap; **bofetón** m. big slap, blow, hard sock, wallop.

**boga** f. vogue, fashion; rowing; m. rower.

**bogar**[7] v. to row.

**bohemio** adj. & m. Bohemian.

**bohío** m. Carib., Ven. cabin, shack, hut.

**boina** f. cap.

**bola** f. (esfera) ball, bowling; (mentira) fib, lie; (betún) shoe polish; Am. disturbance, riot, false rumor; **no dar pie con —** not to do things right; not to hit the mark; to make mistakes; Am. **darle a la —** to hit the mark.

**boleada** f. Ríopl. lassoing with **boleadoras**; Ríopl. hunting expedition (with **boleadoras**); Mex. shoeshine; Col. affront, insult.

**boleadoras** f. pl. Am. lasso with balls at the ends.

**bolear** v. to play billiards; to bowl; to lie, fib; Am. to lasso with **boleadoras**; Am. to entangle; Am. to polish (shoes); Am. to dismiss; Am. to blackball, vote against; Am. to flunk; **-se** Am. to rear, balk (said of a horse); Am. to blush, be ashamed.

**boleta** f. certificate; pass; pay order; Mex., C.A. ballot; Ch. first draft of a deed.

**boletín** m. bulletin.

**boleto** m. Am. ticket; **boletería** f. Am. ticket office.

**boliche** m. bowl (wooden ball for bowling); bowling alley; Ríopl. cheap tavern; Ch. gambling joint; Ríopl. cheap store or shop, notions store, variety store.

**bolita** f. small ball; Am. ballot (small ball used in voting); Col., Ven. marble; Am. armadillo.

**bolo** m. one of the ninepins (used in bowling); dunce, stupid fellow; **-s** bowls, bowling; **jugar a los -s** to bowl.

**bolsa** f. bag, purse; stock exchange; Ríopl. pocket.

**bolsillo** m. pocket; pocketbook.

**bolsista** m. stockbroker, market operator.

**bollo** m. bun, muffin; bump, lump; puff (in a dress); tuft (on upholstery); Andes loaf of bread; Am. a kind of tamale; **-s** Am. difficulties, troubles.

**bomba** *f*. pump; lamp globe; bomb; — **atómica** atomic bomb; — **de hidrógeno** hydrogen bomb; *Carib*. false news; *Am*. stanza improvised by a dancer; *Ríopl*. firecracker, skyrocket; *Mex*., *Col*. satirical remark; *Am*. large drum; — **para incendios** fire engine; *Am*. **estar con una** — to be drunk; **bombita** *f*. soap bubble; *Col*. shame, embarrassment.

**bombachas** *f*. *pl*. *Am*. loose-fitting breeches.

**bombacho** *adj*. loose-fitting (*trousers or breeches*).

**bombardear** *v*. to bomb.

**bombardeo** *m*. bombardment, bombing; **avión de** — bomber, bombing plane.

**bombardero** *m*. bombardier; bomber.

**bombear** *v*. (*echar bombas*) to bomb; (*alabar*) to praise, extol; *Am*. to pump; *Col*. to fire, dismiss; *Am*. to puff hard on a cigar or cigarette.

**bombero** *m*. fireman; pumper.

**bombilla** *f*. electric-light bulb; *Am*. kerosene lamp tube; *Am*. small tube for drinking **mate**.

**bombo** *m*. large drum; bass drum; player on a bass drum; *Mex*., *Col*., *Ch*. pomp, ostentation; *Ríopl*. buttocks, rump; **dar** — to praise, extol (*in the press or newspapers*); *Col*., *Ríopl*. **darse** — to put on airs; *Am*. **irse uno al** — to fail; *adj*. stunned; *Am*. lukewarm; *Am*. slightly rotten; *Am*. stupid, silly, simple; *Cuba* **fruta bomba** papaya (*tropical fruit*).

**bombón** *m*. bonbon, candy; — **de altea** marshmallow.

**bonachón** *adj*. good-natured; naïve, simple.

**bonanza** *f*. fair weather; prosperity; rich vein of ore.

**bondad** *f*. goodness.

**bondadoso** *adj*. good, kind.

**boniato** *m*. *Am*. sweet potato.

**bonito** *adj*. pretty; *m*. striped tunny (*a fish*).

**bono** *m*. certificate; bond.

**boñiga** *f*. dung, manure.

**boqueada** *f*. gape, gasp.

**boquear** *v*. to open one's mouth; to gape, gasp; to be dying.

**boquete** *m*. breach, gap, hole, opening.

**boquiabierto** *adj*. openmouthed.

**boquilla** *f*. (*abertura*) little mouth; small opening; (*de cigarro*) holder; (*de instrumento*) mouthpiece.

**borbollón, borbotón** *m*. spurt; spurting; big bubble; bubbling up; **a -es in** spurts.

**borbotar** *v*. to bubble up; to spurt, gush forth; to boil over.

**bordado** *m*. embroidery.

**bordadura** *f*. embroidery.

**bordar** *v*. to embroider.

**borde** *m*. border, edge.

**bordear** *v*. to skirt, go along the edge of; *Am*. to trim with a border; *Am*. to make a **bordo** (*small, temporary dam*); **-se** *Ch*., *Mex*., *Ven*. to approach, get near.

**bordo** *m*. board, side of a ship; tack (*of a ship*); *Mex*., *Ven*. ridge (*of a furrow*); *Mex*. small dam; **a** — on board.

**borla** *f*. (*indumentaria*) tassel; doctor's cap; (*titulo*) doctor's degree; (*cosmético*) powder puff; tuft; **tomar uno la** — to get a doctor's degree.

**borlarse** *v*. *Am*. to get a doctor's degree.

**borrachera** *f*. drunkenness; drunken spree.

**borrachín** *m*. toper.

**borracho** *adj*. drunk; *m*. drunkard; **borrachón** *m*. drunkard, heavy drinker.

**borrador** *m*. rough draft; *Am*. rubber eraser.

**borrar** *v*. to blot out; to erase.

**borrasca** *f*. storm, tempest.

**borrascoso** *adj*. stormy.

**borrego** *m*. lamb; fool, simpleton; *Mex*., *C.A*. false news.

**borrico** *m*. donkey, ass; fool; sawhorse.

**borrón** *m*. blotch (*of ink*), blot.

**borronear** *v*. to blot, blotch; to scribble; to blur; to make a rough sketch.

**boruca** *f*. racket, noise.

**boscaje** *m*. grove, thicket, woods; landscape (*picture of natural scenery*).

**bosque** *m*. forest, woods; **bosquecillo** *m*. small forest, grove.

**bosquejar** *v*. to sketch; to outline.

**bosquejo** *m*. sketch, plan, outline, rough draft.

**bostezar**[9] *v*. to yawn.

**bostezo** *m*. yawn.

**bota** *f*. (*calzado*) boot; (*bolsa*) leather wine bag; *adj*. *Am*. stupid, clumsy; *Mex*. drunk.

**botar** *v*. (*echar*) to launch; to fling; to throw away; (*rebotar*) to bounce; *Ven*. to waste, squander; *Am*. to fire, dismiss; **-se** *Am*. to lie down.

**botarate** *m*. fool; braggart; *Mex*., *Carib*. spendthrift.

**bote** *m*. (*jarro*) small jar; (*embarcación*) boat; (*rebote*) bounce; (*golpe*) blow; jump; *Ríopl*. liquor bottle; *Mex*., *C.A*. jail; **estar de** — **en** — to be crowded, completely filled up.

**botella** *f*. bottle.

**botica** *f*. drugstore.

**boticario** *m*. druggist.

**botija** *f*. earthen jug; fat person; *Am*. buried treasure; *Am*. belly; *Col*. **poner a uno como** — **verde** to dress down, scold, insult a person.

**botín** *m*. booty, plunder; high shoe; *Am*. sock.

**botiquín** *m*. medicine cabinet; medicine kit; *Am*. liquor store, wine shop.

**botón** *m*. bud; button; knob; handle; **-es** bellboy.

**bóveda** *f*. arched roof; vault, underground cellar; burial place.

**boxeador** *m*. boxer.

**boxear** *v*. to box, fight with the fists.

**boxeo** *m*. boxing.

**boya** *f*. buoy; float net; *Am*. crease, dent; *Am*. rich mineral vein; *Am*. **estar en la buena** — to be in good humor.

**bozal** *m.* (*de animal*) nuzzle; (*cascabel*) bells on a harness; (*novicio*) novice; (*negro*) Negro native of Africa; *Am.* headstall (*of a halter*); *Spain* person (*especially a Negro*) who speaks broken Spanish; *Am.* coarse, crude individual; *adj.* green, inexperienced; wild, untamed; stupid.

**bozo** *m.* down (*on the upper lip*); mustache; outside part of the mouth; headstall (*of a halter*).

**bracear** *v.* to swing one's arms; to struggle; to crawl, swim with a crawl.

**bracero** *m.* laborer; **de — ** arm in arm; **servir de — a una señora** to serve as an escort, give a lady one's arm.

**bracete: de — ** arm in arm.

**bramante** *m.* hemp cord, hemp string; Brabant linen; *adj.* roaring, bellowing.

**bramar** *v.* to bellow, roar, howl; to rage.

**bramido** *m.* roar; howl; bellow.

**brasa** *f.* red-hot coal.

**brasero** *m.* brazier (*pan for burning coal*), grate; hearth; *Ríopl.* brick cooking stove.

**bravata** *f.* bravado, boastfulness, defiance.

**bravear** *v.* to bluster; to bully.

**bravío** *adj.* savage, wild; rustic.

**bravo** *adj.* (*agresivo*) wild, ferocious, harsh; ill-tempered; (*valiente*) brave; *Carib.*, *C.A.*, *Andes* angry; *Am.* hot, highly seasoned.

**bravura** *f.* fierceness; courage; bravado, show of boldness.

**braza** *f.* fathom; stroke.

**brazada** *f.* armful; movement of the arms (*swimming stroke*); **a una — ** at arm's length.

**brazalete** *m.* bracelet.

**brazo** *m.* arm; branch; **-s** day laborers; *Ríopl.*, *Cuba* **de — ** arm in arm; **luchar a — partido** to wrestle; to fight hand to hand.

**brea** *f.* pitch; tar; canvas.

**brecha** *f.* breach, gap.

**bregar**[7] *v.* to struggle; to fight.

**breña** *f.* rough, craggy ground covered with brambles; bramble; **breñal** *m.* brambles; bush country.

**breve** *adj.* brief, short; **en — ** shortly.

**brevedad** *f.* brevity, shortness.

**bribón** *adj.* idle, indolent; *m.* rascal, rogue; **bribonazo** *m.* scoundrel, cheat.

**brida** *f.* bridle; rein.

**brigada** *f.* brigade.

**brillante** *adj.* brilliant, bright; *m.* diamond.

**brillantez** *f.* brilliance, dazzle.

**brillar** *v.* to shine.

**brillo** *m.* luster, sparkle, shine.

**brincar**[6] *v.* to hop, skip, jump, bounce.

**brinco** *m.* hop, skip, bounce, leap.

**brindar** *v.* to toast, drink to the health of; to offer.

**brindis** *m.* toast (*to a person's health*).

**brío** *m.* vigor, liveliness; valor, courage.

**brioso** *adj.* lively; brave.

**brisa** *f.* breeze.

**británico** *adj.* British.

**brizna** *f.* particle, chip, fragment; blade of grass.

**brocal** *m.* curb, curbstone (*of a well*).

**brocha** *f.* painter's brush; loaded dice; **cuadro de — gorda** badly done painting; **pintor de — gorda** house painter; **brochada** *f.* stroke of the brush, brush stroke; **brochazo** *m.* blow with a brush; brush stroke.

**broche** *m.* brooch; clasp, clip, fastener; hook and eye.

**broma** *f.* jest, joke; fun, merriment; *Am.* disappointment, irritation; **de — ** in jest; **fuera de — ** all joking aside.

**bromear** *v.* to joke, jest.

**bronca** *f.* quarrel, dispute, wrangle; **armar una — ** to cause a disturbance, raise a rumpus.

**bronce** *m.* bronze.

**bronceado** *adj.* bronzed; bronze-colored; *m.* bronze finish.

**bronco** *adj.* hoarse; raspy, harsh; coarse, rough; uncouth; wild, untamed (*horse*).

**bronquio** *m.* bronchus, bronchial tube.

**broquel** *m.* buckler, shield (*worn on the arm*).

**brotar** *v.* to shoot forth; to bud; to break out (*on the skin*); to gush, flow; to spring forth.

**broza** *f.* brushwood, underbrush; rubbish, refuse, trash; coarse, hard brush.

**bruces: de — ** face downward.

**bruja** *f.* witch; hag; owl; *adj. Mex.* broke, poor; **brujo** *m.* sorcerer, magician, wizard.

**brújula** *f.* (*compás*) compass; magnetic needle; (*mira*) peephole; gunsight.

**bruma** *f.* mist, fog; **brumoso** *adj.* foggy, misty, hazy.

**bruñir**[19] *v. irr.* to burnish, polish; to put on make-up.

**brusco** *adj.* blunt, rude, abrupt.

**brutal** *adj.* brutal, beastly, savage.

**brutalidad** *f.* brutality.

**bruto** *adj.* (*tonto*) stupid, brutal; (*burdo*) coarse, rough; **peso — ** gross weight; **diamante en — ** diamond in the rough, unpolished diamond; *m.* brute, beast.

**bucal** *adj.* oral, pertaining to the mouth.

**bucear** *v.* to dive; to dive into, plunge into; to explore thoroughly a subject.

**bucle** *m.* curl, ringlet.

**buche** *m.* crop (*of a bird*); mouthful (*of water*); wrinkle, bag (*in clothes*); *Ríopl.*, *Mex.*, *Ven.* goiter.

**budín** *m.* pudding.

**buen(o)** *adj.* good; kind; useful; well, in good health; **de buenas a primeras** all of a sudden, unexpectedly, on the spur of the moment; **por la(s) buena(s) o por la(s) mala(s)** willingly or unwillingly, by hook or crook.

**buey** *m.* ox.

**búfalo** *m.* buffalo.

**bufanda** *f.* muffler, scarf.

**bufar** v. to snort; to puff with anger; **-se** *Mex.* to swell, bulge (*as a wall*).
**bufete** m. desk, writing table; lawyer's office.
**bufido** m. snort.
**bufón** m. buffoon, jester, clown; *adj.* comical, funny; **bufonada** f. wisecrack; jest.
**bufonear** v. to clown; to jest.
**buhardilla** f. garret, attic; skylight.
**buho** m. owl.
**buhonero** m. peddler.
**buitre** m. vulture.
**buje** m. bushing; axle box.
**bujía** f. candle; candle power; candlestick; spark plug.
**bula** f. bull (*papal document*); papal seal.
**buldozer** m. bulldozer.
**bulevar** m. boulevard.
**bulto** m. (*cuerpo*) body, bundle, shadow, lump, swelling; (*tamaño*) bulk, volume; **a —** haphazardly, by guess; **escurrir el —** to dodge; **imagen de —** statue, sculpture; **una verdad de —** an evident truth.
**bulla** f. shouting, uproar; noisy crowd.
**bullicio** m. noise, uproar.
**bullicioso** *adj.* boisterous, noisy; gay, lively; turbulent, stormy.
**bullir**[20] v. *irr.* to boil; to buzz about; to bustle; to stir, move; *Am.* to deride.
**buñuelo** m. fritter; botch, poor piece of work.
**buque** m. ship, boat.
**burbuja** f. bubble.
**burdo** *adj.* coarse.
**burgués** *adj.* bourgeois, middle-class.
**burla** f. jest, mockery; **de —** in jest.
**burlador** m. practical joker; jester; scoffer; seducer.
**burlar** v. to mock, ridicule, deceive; **-se de** to scoff at; to make fun of.
**burlón** m. jester, teaser.
**burro** m. ass, donkey; *Mex., Cuba, Ríopl.* stepladder; *adj.* stupid; **burrito** m. small donkey; *Am.* saddle rack.
**busca** f. search; hunting party; *Am.* **-s** profit on the side; graft.
**buscar**[6] v. to seek, search, look for; *Andes* to provoke.
**búsqueda** f. search.
**busto** m. bust (*upper part of body*).
**butaca** f. armchair; orchestra seat; **butacón** m. large armchair.
**buzo** m. diver.
**buzón** m. mailbox; letter drop.

## C

**cabal** *adj.* complete, entire; exact; **estar uno en sus -es** to be in one's right mind.
**cabalgar**[7] v. to ride, mount (*a horse*); to ride horseback.
**caballa** f. horse mackerel.
**caballada** f. herd of horses; *Am.* nonsense, stupidity, blunder.
**caballejo** m. nag; poor horse.
**caballeresco** *adj.* gentlemanly; knightly; chivalrous, gallant.
**caballería** f. cavalry; horsemanship; mount, horse; knighthood; chivalry.

**caballeriza** f. stable; horses of a stable.
**caballerizo** m. groom, stableman.
**caballero** m. gentleman; knight, horseman; *adj.* gentlemanly.
**caballerosidad** f. chivalry, gentlemanly conduct.
**caballeroso** *adj.* chivalrous, gentlemanly.
**caballete** m. (*de casa*) ridge of a roof; (*madero*) sawhorse; (*de la cara*) bridge of the nose.
**caballo** m. horse; knight (*in chess*); *Am.* stupid or brutal person; **a —** on horseback; **caballuco** m. nag.
**cabaña** f. hut, cabin; *Am.* cattle ranch.
**cabecear** v. to nod; to shake the head; to pitch (*as a boat*); *Am.* to begin to rise or fall (*said of a river*).
**cabeceo** m. nodding; pitching (*of a boat*).
**cabecera** f. head (*of bed or table*); seat, chief city (*of a district*).
**cabecilla** f. small head; m. ringleader.
**cabellera** f. head of hair, long hair; wig; tail of a comet.
**cabello** m. hair; **traer algo por los -s** to bring in a far-fetched fact or quotation; **-s de ángel** cotton candy.
**cabelludo** *adj.* hairy; **cuero —** scalp.
**caber**[23] v. *irr.* to fit into, go into; to have enough room for; to befall; **no cabe duda** there is no doubt; **no cabe más** there is no room for more; **no — uno en sí** to be puffed up with pride; **no cabe en lo posible** it is absolutely impossible.
**cabestro** m. halter; leading ox; *Carib., Mex.* rope, cord; *Am.* advance payment; **cabestrillo** m. sling (*for an arm*).
**cabeza** f. (*parte superior*) head; upper part; (*director*) chief, leader; capital (*of a district*); *Carib.* source (*of a river*); **— de playa** beachhead; **— de puente** bridgehead; **— sonora** recording head.
**cabezada** f. butt (*with the head*); bump on the head; nod; shake of the head; pitching (*of a ship*); headgear (*of a harness*).
**cabezazo** m. butt (*with the head*); bump on the head.
**cabezudo** *adj.* big-headed; hard-headed, pig-headed, stubborn, headstrong.
**cabezón** *adj.* big-headed; pig-headed, stubborn; *Ch.* strong (*liquor*); m. large head; cavesson (*iron noseband used in breaking a horse*); *Col.* rapids or whirlpool in a river.
**cabida** f. space, room, capacity; **tener — con alguien** to have influence with someone.
**cabildo** m. cathedral chapter; municipal council; council room; town hall.
**cabina** f. cabin (*of an airplane*).
**cabizbajo** *adj.* crestfallen, downcast; pensive.
**cable** m. cable.
**cablegrafiar**[17] v. to cable.
**cablegrama** m. cablegram.

**cabo** *m.* (*cosa*) end, tip, handle; piece of rope; (*geográfico*) cape, headland; (*persona*) foreman, corporal; **al —** finally; **al fin y al —** anyway, in the long run; **de — a rabo** from beginning to end; **estar al — de** to be well informed about; **llevar a —** to carry out, finish.

**cabra** *f.* goat; *Col.* fraud, trick; *Am.* loaded dice; *Am.* light two-wheeled carriage; **cabrillas** *f. pl.* whitecaps (*small waves with white crests*); Pleiades (*constellation*); game of skipping stones on the water.

**cabrío** *adj.* goatish; **macho —** he-goat; *m.* herd of goats.

**cabriola** *f.* caper, leap, hop, skip; somersault; **hacer -s** to cut capers; to prance.

**cabriolar** *v.* to prance; to caper; to romp, frolic, frisk.

**cabrito** *m.* kid; **cabritilla** *f.* kid, kidskin.

**cabrón** *m.* he-goat; cuckold (*man whose wife is unfaithful*).

**cacahuate** *m. Mex., C.A.* peanut; *Spain* **cacahuete, cacahuey.**

**cacao** *m.* cocoa.

**cacarear** *v.* to cackle; to boast; *Am.* to run away from a fight.

**cacareo** *m.* cackle.

**cacería** *f.* hunt, hunting.

**cacerola** *f.* saucepan.

**cacha** *f.* handle (*of a knife or pistol*); *Am.* the horns of a bull; *C.A.* **hacer la —** to complete a task, to get.

**cacharro** *m.* earthen pot or vase; broken piece of a pot; crude utensil; *Am.* cheap trinket.

**cachaza** *f.* slowness; calm; rum.

**cachazudo** *adj.* slow, easy going.

**cachetada** *f. Am.* slap on the face.

**cachete** *m.* cheek; slap on the cheek.

**cachimbo** *m. Am.* pipe (*for smoking*); *Cuba* small sugar mill; also **cachimba.**

**cachivache** *m.* piece of junk; worthless fellow; *Mex., Carib., Ven.* trinket.

**cachorro** *m.* cub; small pistol; *Am.* rude, ill-bred person.

**cachucha** *f.* cap; rowboat; popular Andalusian dance, song and music; *Am.* slap.

**cacique** *m.* chief; political boss; *Mex.* tyrant; *Ch., Ven.* one who leads an easy life.

**caciquismo** *m.* political bossism (*rule by political bosses*).

**cacto** *m.* cactus.

**cacumen** *m.* acumen, keen insight.

**cada** *adj.* each, every; **— uno** each one; **— y cuando que** whenever; *Am.* **a — nada** every second.

**cadalso** *m.* gallows; scaffold, platform.

**cadáver** *m.* corpse; **cadavérico** *adj.* deadly, ghastly, pale, like a corpse.

**cadena** *f.* chain.

**cadencia** *f.* cadence.

**cadencioso** *adj.* rhythmical.

**cadera** *f.* hip.

**cadete** *m.* cadet.

**caducar**[6] *v.* to dote, be in one's dotage; to lapse, expire; to become extinct, fall into disuse.

**caduco** *adj.* decrepit, very old, feeble; perishable.

**caer**[24] *v. irr.* to fall; to fall down; to fall off; **-se** to fall down, tumble; **— a** to face, overlook; **— bien** to fit, be becoming; **— en cama** to fall ill; **— en la cuenta** to catch on, get the point; **— en gracia** to please; **al — de la noche** at nightfall; **dejar —** to drop.

**café** *m.* coffee; café; *Am.* annoyance, bad time.

**cafeína** *f.* caffein.

**cafetal** *m.* coffee plantation.

**cafetera** *f.* coffeepot; woman café owner, coffee vendor or merchant; coffee-bean picker.

**cafetería** *f.* café, bar, lunchroom.

**cafetero** *adj.* pertaining to coffee; *m.* coffee grower; coffee merchant; owner of a café or coffee-house; *Am.* coffee drinker.

**cafeto** *m.* coffee bush.

**caída** *f.* fall, drop; descent; **a la — del sol** (*or* **de la tarde**) at sunset.

**caimán** *m.* cayman, alligator.

**caja** *f.* case, box; **— de ahorros** savings bank; **— de cambios** transmission (*automobile*); **— de píldora** pillbox; **— fuerte** safe; **echar a uno con -s destempladas** to give someone the gate.

**cajero** *m.* cashier; box maker.

**cajetilla** *f.* small box; package of cigarettes.

**cajón** *m.* large box, chest; drawer; vendor's booth or stand; *Ch., Mex.* narrow canyon; **— de muerto** coffin; *Mex.* **— de ropa** dry-goods and clothing store.

**cal** *f.* lime (*mineral*).

**calabaza** *f.* pumpkin, squash; gourd; an ignorant person; **dar -s** to jilt, turn down (*a suitor*); to flunk, fail.

**calabozo** *m.* dungeon; prison cell.

**calado** *m.* drawn work; openwork (*in wood, metal, linen, etc.*), fretwork; draft (*of a ship*).

**calamar** *m.* squid, cuttlefish.

**calambre** *m.* cramp.

**calamidad** *f.* calamity, misfortune.

**calandria** *f.* lark, skylark.

**calar** *v.* (*penetrar*) to pierce, penetrate; to soak through; to make openwork (*in cloth, metal*); (*probar*) to probe, search into; **-se el sombrero** to put on one's hat; to pull down one's hat.

**calavera** *f.* skull; *m.* madcap, rounder, reckless fellow; *Mex.* taillight.

**calcar**[6] *v.* to trace; to copy, imitate.

**calceta** *f.* hose, stocking; **hacer —** to knit; **calcetería** *f.* hosiery shop; hosiery (*business of making hose*).

**calcetín** *m.* sock.

**calcinar** *v.* to burn, char, heat.

**calcio** *m.* calcium.

**calco** *m.* tracing, traced copy; exact copy; imitation.

**calculadora** *f.* calculator (*machine for performing mathematical operations*); **— electrónica** computer.

**calcular** *v.* to calculate, figure, estimate.

**cálculo** *m.* calculation, estimate; calculus; gravel (*in the gall bladder, kidney, etc.*).

**caldear** *v.* to heat; to weld; **-se** *Am.* to become overheated, excited; *Am.* to get "lit up", get drunk.

**caldera** *f.* boiler; caldron, kettle; **calderilla** *f.* copper coin.

**caldo** *m.* broth; gravy.

**calefacción** *f.* heat, heating.

**calendario** *m.* calendar; almanac.

**caléndula** *f.* marigold.

**calentador** *m.* heater.

**calentar**[1] *v. irr.* to warm, heat; to spank; *Am.* to annoy, bother; **-se** to warm oneself; to become heated, excited; to be in heat; *Am.* to become angry.

**calentura** *f.* fever; *Col.* fit of temper; **— de pollo** feigned illness; **calenturón** *m.* high fever.

**calenturiento** *adj.* feverish; *Ch.* tubercular.

**caletre** *m.* judgment, acumen, keen insight.

**calibrar** *v.* to gauge, measure; to measure the caliber of.

**calibre** *m.* caliber; bore, gauge (*of a gun*); diameter (*of a pipe, tube, wire*).

**calicanto** *m.* stone masonry.

**calicó** *m.* calico, cotton cloth.

**calidad** *f.* quality.

**cálido** *adj.* warm, hot.

**caliente** *adj.* warm, hot; heated; fiery; *Am.* angry; *Col.* bold, brave; *m. Am.* brandy in hot water; **calientito** *adj.* nice and warm.

**calificación** *f.* qualification; grade, mark (*in a course or examination*); judgment.

**calificar**[6] *v.* to qualify; to rate, consider, judge; to grade; *Am.* to compute (*election returns*); **-se** *Ch.* to qualify or register (*as a voter*).

**caligrafía** *f.* penmanship.

**calina** *f.* haze, mist.

**cáliz** *m.* chalice, communion cup; cup, goblet; calyx (*of a flower*).

**calma** *f.* calm, quiet.

**calmante** *adj.* soothing; *m.* sedative.

**calmar** *v.* to calm, quiet, soothe.

**calmo** *adj.* calm, quiet.

**calmoso** *adj.* calm; soothing; phlegmatic, slow.

**calor** *m.* heat, warmth; ardor.

**calorífero** *m.* heater, radiator; furnace.

**calosfrío, calofrío** *m.* chill.

**calumnia** *f.* slander.

**calumniar** *v.* to slander.

**caluroso** *adj.* (*literal*) hot, warm; (*figurado*) heated, excited; cordial, enthusiastic.

**calva** *f.* bald head; bald spot; barren spot.

**calvario** *m.* Calvary, place of the Cross; suffering, tribulation.

**calvo** *adj.* bald; barren.

**calza** *f.* wedge; shoehorn; *Col., Ven.* gold inlay, tooth filling; **-s** breeches.

**calzada** *f.* paved road; highway; *Mex., Carib.* wide avenue.

**calzado** *m.* footwear.

**calzador** *m.* shoehorn.

**calzar**[9] *v.* to put on (*shoes, gloves, spurs*); to put a wedge under a wheel; *Am.* to fill (*a tooth*).

**calzón** *m.* (*or* **calzones**) breeches, short trousers; *Mex., Ven.* drawers; *Mex.* white cotton trousers; **calzoncillos** *m. pl.* drawers, men's shorts; **calzoneras** *f. pl. Mex.* trousers open down the sides.

**callado** *adj.* silent, quiet.

**callar** *v.* to be silent; to hush; **-se** to be or keep silent.

**calle** *f.* street.

**calleja** *f.* small street, alley, lane; **callejuela** *f.* small, narrow street; lane.

**callejear** *v.* to walk the streets, ramble.

**callejero** *m.* street-rambler, street-stroller; street-loiterer; *adj.* fond of walking the streets; rambling.

**callejón** *m.* alley; lane; narrow pass; **— sin salida** blind alley.

**callo** *m.* callus, corn; **-s** tripe (*food*).

**calloso** *adj.* callous, hard.

**cama** *f.* bed, couch, cot; litter; **caer en — to** fall ill; **guardar — to** be confined to bed; *Am.* **tenderle uno la — a otro** to help one in his love affairs; to set a trap for someone; **camastro** *m.* poor, uncomfortable bed.

**camada** *f.* litter; brood.

**cámara** *f.* chamber, hall, parlor; house (*of a legislative body*); cabin, stateroom; chamber (*of a gun*); **— de aire** inner tube; **— fotográfica** camera.

**camarada** *m.* comrade; **camaradería** *f.* comradeship, companionship.

**camarera** *f.* waitress; chambermaid; stewardess.

**camarero** *m.* waiter; chamberlain; steward; valet.

**camarilla** *f.* political lobby; small group of politicians; "kitchen cabinet", group of unofficial advisers; small room.

**camarón** *m.* shrimp.

**camarote** *m.* cabin, stateroom.

**cambalache** *m.* swap, barter, exchange.

**cambalachear** *v.* to swap, barter, exchange.

**cambiador** *m.* barterer; money changer; *Am.* switchman.

**cambiante** *adj.* changing; exchanging; **-s** *m. pl.* iridescent colors.

**cambiar** *v.* to change; to exchange; to shift; **— de marcha** to shift gears.

**cambiavía** *m. Carib., Mex., Andes* railway switchman. *See* **guardagujas** *and* **cambiador.**

**cambio** *m.* change; exchange; railway switch; **libre —** free trade; **en —** on the other hand; in exchange.

**cambista** *m.* exchange broker, banker; *Am.* railway switchman.

**camello** *m.* camel.

**camilla** f. stretcher; cot; **camillero** m. stretcher bearer.

**caminante** m. & f. walker, traveler.

**caminar** v. to travel; to walk; Am. to progress, prosper.

**caminata** f. long walk; hike; jaunt.

**camino** m. road; course; Ríopl. table runner; Am. hall runner; **— de hierro** railroad; **— real** highway; **de — on** the way.

**camión** m. truck; wagon; Mex. bus; **camionero** m. truck driver; **camioneta** f. small truck; C.A. bus.

**camisa** f. shirt; **— de fuerza** straitjacket; **meterse en — de once varas** to attempt more than one can manage, bite off more than one can chew; **camiseta** f. undershirt.

**camisón** m. long shirt; Am. nightgown; Am. gown, dress.

**camote** m. Am. a kind of sweet potato.

**campamento** m. encampment; camp.

**campana** f. bell; Ríopl., Andes spy, lookout (for thieves); **campanada** f. stroke of a bell; Am. **por — de vacante** once in a blue moon, very seldom.

**campanario** m. bell tower.

**campanilla** f. small bell; bubble; uvula; tassel; bell-flower.

**campanillazo** m. loud ring of a bell.

**campanilleo** m. ringing; tinkling.

**campaña** f. level, open country; campaign; period of active service.

**campear** v. to pasture; to grow green (said of the fields); to excel; to be prominent, stand out; to be in the field; Ríopl. to search the plains for lost cattle; Col., Ven. to act the bully.

**campechano** adj. frank, open.

**campéon** m. champion; defender

**campeonato** m. championship.

**campesino** adj. rural, rustic; m. peasant, countryman; farmer.

**campestre** adj. rural, rustic.

**campiña** f. large field; open country.

**campo** m. country; field; camp; **a — raso** in the open; **a — traviesa** (or **travieso**) cross-country.

**camposanto** m. churchyard, cemetery.

**camuesa** f. pippin (a variety of apple).

**camuflaje** m. camouflage.

**can** m. dog; trigger (of a gun).

**cana** f. white hair, grey hair; Carib. a kind of palm; **echar una — al aire** to go out for a good time; to go out on a fling.

**canadiense** adj., m. & f. Canadian.

**canal** m. canal, channel; f. eaves trough.

**canalla** f. rabble, mob; m. mean fellow.

**canana** f. cartridge belt; **-s** Col., Ven. handcuffs.

**canapé** m. couch, lounge, sofa; settee.

**canario** m. canary; native of the Canary Islands; interj. great Scott!

**canasta** f. basket; crate.

**cancelación** f. cancellation.

**cancelar** v. to cancel.

**canciller** m. chancellor.

**canción** f. song; a kind of lyric poem; **volver a la misma —** to repeat, harp on the same thing.

**cancha** f. court (for tennis, etc.); sports ground or field; cockpit, enclosure for cockfights; Peru roasted corn or beans; Am. **¡abran —!** gangway!; make room!

**candado** m. padlock; Col. goatee.

**candela** f. candle; fire, forest fire; light.

**candelero** m. candlestick.

**candente** adj. incandescent, white-hot, red-hot.

**candidato** m. candidate.

**candidatura** f. candidacy.

**candidez** f. candor, simplicity.

**cándido** adj. candid, simple, innocent; white.

**candil** m. lamp; Ríopl., Mex. chandelier; **candileja** f. small oil lamp; oil receptacle (of a lamp); **-s** footlights (of a stage).

**candor** m. candor, simplicity, innocence; frankness, sincerity.

**canela** f. cinnamon; an exquisite thing.

**cangrejo** m. crab.

**canguro** m. kangaroo.

**caníbal** m. cannibal.

**canica** f. marble (small glass or marble ball).

**canilla** f. long bone (of the arm or leg); cock (of a barrel), faucet; spool (for a sewing machine); C.A. slender leg; Ch., Col., Ríopl. calf (of the leg); Mex., Ven. **tener —** to have physical strength; **canillita** m. Ríopl., Ch., C.A., Andes newspaper boy.

**canino** adj. canine; **tener un hambre canina** to be ravenous; to be hungry as a dog.

**canje** m. interchange, exchange.

**canjear** v. to exchange, interchange.

**cano** adj. grey-headed, grey-haired.

**canoa** f. canoe.

**canon** m. canon; precept, rule, principle.

**canónigo** m. canon (churchman).

**canonizar**[9] v. to canonize, saint.

**canoso** adj. grey, grey-haired.

**cansado** adj. tired; tiresome, boring.

**cansancio** m. fatigue, weariness.

**cansar** v. to tire, fatigue; **-se** to get tired.

**cantar** v. to sing; to squeal, confess; Am. **— alto** to ask a high price; **— claro** (or **-las claras**) to speak with brutal frankness; m. song, epic poem.

**cántaro** m. pitcher, jug.

**cantatriz** f. singer.

**cantera** f. quarry; Ríopl., Mex., Carib. stone block.

**cántico** m. canticle, religious song.

**cantidad** f. quantity.

**cantilena** f. song, ballad; monotonous repetition.

**cantimplora** f. canteen; metal vessel for cooling water; Col. flask for carrying gunpowder.

**cantina** f. mess hall; wine cellar; wine shop; canteen; Carib., Mex., Ríopl. barroom, tavern; Col. saddlebag.

**cantinela** = **cantilena**.

**cantinero** m. bartender; tavern keeper.

**canto** *m.* song; singing; canto (*division of a long poem*); stone; edge; *Col.* lap; *Am.* piece.

**cantón** *m.* canton, region; corner; *Am.* cotton cloth.

**cantor** *m.* singer; song bird.

**canturrear, canturriar** *v.* to hum, sing softly.

**canturreo** *m.* hum, humming.

**caña** *f.* cane, reed; tall, thin glass; stem; *Ríopl., Col., Ven.* sugar-cane brandy; *Am.* a kind of dance; *Am.* bluff, boast.

**cañada** *f.* narrow canyon, dale, dell, gully, ravine; *Am.* brook.

**cáñamo** *m.* hemp; hemp cloth; *Am.* hemp cord, rope; **cañamazo** *m.* canvas.

**cañaveral** *m.* cane field; reed patch; sugar-cane plantation.

**cañería** *f.* conduit, pipe line; tubing, piping; gas or water main.

**caño** *m.* pipe, tube; spout; sewer; narrow channel; *Ven.* branch of a river, stream.

**cañón** *m.* (*arma*) cannon, gun; barrel (*of a gun*); (*topográfico*) ravine, gorge, canyon; (*tubo*) pipe, tube; (*figurado*) beard stubble; pinfeather; quill (*of a feather*); chimney shaft; **cañonazo** *m.* cannon shot.

**cañonear** *v.* to cannonade, bombard.

**cañoneo** *m.* cannonade; bombardment.

**cañonero** *m.* gunboat; gunner; **lancha cañonera** gunboat.

**caoba** *f.* mahogany.

**caos** *m.* chaos, confusion.

**capa** *f.* (*ropa*) cape, cloak; (*cubierta*) covering, coating; layer; scum; **so — de** under the guise of, under pretense of.

**capacidad** *f.* capacity; ability.

**capacitar** *v.* to enable, prepare, fit, qualify; *Col.* to empower, authorize.

**capataz** *m.* boss, foreman, overseer.

**capaz** *adj.* capable, able, competent; spacious, roomy.

**capellán** *m.* chaplain, priest, clergyman.

**caperuza** *f.* pointed hood.

**capilla** *f.* chapel; hood.

**capirote** *m.* hood; **tonto de —** dunce, plain fool.

**capital** *m.* capital, funds; *f.* capital, capital city; *adj.* capital; **capitalismo** *m.* capitalism; **capitalista** *m.* & *f.* capitalist; *adj.* capitalistic.

**capitalizar**[9] *v.* to capitalize.

**capitán** *m.* captain.

**capitanear** *v.* to command, lead.

**capitolio** *m.* capitol.

**capitular** *v.* to surrender; to come to an agreement.

**capítulo** *m.* chapter.

**caporal** *m.* boss, leader; *Am.* foreman in a cattle ranch.

**capote** *m.* cloak (*with sleeves*); bullfighter's cloak; *Ch.* thrashing, beating; **decir para su —** to say to oneself; *Am.* **de —** in an underhanded way; *Ven., Carib.* **dar —** to get ahead; to deceive.

**capricho** *m.* caprice, whim, notion.

**caprichoso** *adj.* capricious, whimsical; changeable, fickle.

**caprichudo** *adj.* whimsical; stubborn, willful.

**cápsula** *f.* capsule; percussion cap, cartridge shell; metal cap (*on bottles*).

**captar** *v.* to win, attract; to capitivate; *Am.* to get, tune in on (*a radio station*).

**captura** *f.* capture.

**capturar** *v.* to capture, arrest.

**capucha** *f.* hood.

**capullo** *m.* cocoon; bud; acorn cup.

**cara** *f.* face; expression, countenance; front; **de —** opposite; **echar** (*or* **dar**) **en —** to reproach, blame; **sacar la — por alguien** to take someone's part, defend him.

**carabina** *f.* carbine, rifle.

**caracol** *m.* snail; winding stairs; *Am.* embroidered blouse; *Am.* curl.

**caracolear** *v.* to caper, prance around (*said of horses*); *Col.; Ven.* to muddle, entangle; *Am.* to sidestep an obligation.

**caracoleo** *m.* prancing around; winding, turn.

**carácter** *m.* character; temper.

**característico** *adj.* characteristic; **característica** *f.* characteristic, trait.

**caracterizar**[9] *v.* to characterize.

**¡caramba!** *interj.* great guns! great Scott!

**carámbano** *m.* icicle.

**caramelo** *m.* caramel.

**caramillo** *m.* reed pipe, small flute; **armar un —** to raise a rumpus, create a disturbance.

**carancho** *m.* *Ríopl.* hawk, buzzard.

**carátula** *f.* mask; *Col., Ven., Ríopl., Carib., Andes* title page of a book; *C.A., Mex., Andes* dial, face of a watch.

**caravana** *f.* caravan.

**carbólico** *adj.* carbolic.

**carbón** *m.* carbon; coal; **— de leña** charcoal; **carbono** *m.* carbon.

**carbonera** *f.* coal bin; coal cellar; woman coal or charcoal vendor; *Am.* coal mine; **carbonero** *m.* coal dealer; charcoal vendor; *adj.* coal, relating to coal or charcoal.

**carburador** *m.* carburetor.

**carcajada** *f.* loud laughter, peal of laughter.

**cárcel** *f.* jail, prison.

**carcelero** *m.* jailer; *adj.* relating to a jail.

**carcomido** *adj.* worm-eaten; decayed.

**cardar** *v.* to card, comb (*wool*).

**cardenal** *m.* cardinal; cardinal bird; bruise.

**cárdeno** *adj.* dark-purple.

**cardo** *m.* thistle; a kind of cactus.

**carear** *v.* to confront, bring face to face; to compare; **-se** to meet face to face.

**carecer**[13] *v. irr.* to lack, be in need of.

**carencia** *f.* lack, want.

**carente** *adj.* lacking.

**carero** *adj.* overcharging; profiteering; *m.* profiteer.

**carestía** *f.* dearth, scarcity; high price.

**careta** *f.* mask.

**carga** *f.* load, burden; freight; cargo; charge of gunpowder; **volver a la —** to insist again and again.

**cargado** *p.p.* & *adj.* loaded; strong (*as tea or coffee*); cloudy, sultry; **— de espaldas** round-shouldered, stoop-shouldered.

**cargador** *m.* loader; stevedore; *Am.* carrier, errand boy, mover.

**cargamento** *m.* cargo.

**cargar**⁶ *v.* (*poner carga*) to load; to charge; (*atacar*) to charge; (*molestar*) to bother, annoy; *Am.* to carry, lug; *Am.* to punish; **— con** to carry away; to assume (*responsibility*); **— con el muerto** to get the blame (*unjustly*).

**cargo** *m.* charge, position, duty, burden; loading; accusation; **hacerse — de** to take charge of; to realize.

**carguero** *adj.* load-carrying; freight-carrying; *m.* *Am.* beast of burden; *Am.* skilled loader of pack animals; *Am.* patient, long-suffering person.

**caribe** *adj.* Caribbean; *m.* Carib, Caribbean Indian; cannibal; savage.

**caricatura** *f.* caricature; cartoon.

**caricia** *f.* caress.

**caridad** *f.* charity; alms.

**caries** *f.* decay (*of a bone*); tooth cavity.

**cariño** *m.* affection, love; *Am.* gift.

**cariñoso** *adj.* affectionate, loving.

**caritativo** *adj.* charitable.

**carmesí** *adj.* & *m.* crimson.

**carmín** *m.* crimson.

**carnal** *adj.* carnal, sensual.

**carnaval** *m.* carnival.

**carne** *f.* meat; flesh; **— de gallina** "goose flesh", "goose pimples"; **echar -s** to put on weight, get fat; *Am.* **— de res** beef.

**carneada** *f.* *Ríopl.* butchering, slaughtering.

**carnear** *v.* *Ríopl.* to butcher; *Ríopl.* to kill.

**carnero** *m.* (*animal*) ram, male sheep; (*carne*) mutton; *Am.* a weak-willed person; *Am.* waste basket; *Am.* **— de la tierra** llama (*or any fleece-bearing animal*); *Am.* **cantar uno el —** to die.

**carnicería** *f.* (*tienda*) meat market; (*matanza*) butchery, slaughter; *C.A.*, *Ec.* slaughterhouse.

**carnicero** *m.* butcher; *adj.* carnivorous, flesh-eating; cruel.

**carnívoro** *adj.* carnivorous.

**carnosidad** *f.* fleshiness, fatness; abnormal growth (*on animal or plant tissues*).

**carnoso** *adj.* fleshy; meaty; pulpy.

**caro** *adj.* expensive; dear; *adv.* at a high price.

**carona** *f.* saddle pad.

**carozo** *m.* cob, corncob.

**carpa** *f.* carp (*fresh-water fish*); *Am.* canvas tent, circus tent; **— dorada** goldfish.

**carpeta** *f.* (*cubierta*) table cover; desk pad; (*cartera*) portfolio, letter case or file; *Andes* office desk; *Am.* bookkeeping department; **carpetazo: dar —** to table (*a motion*); to set aside, pigeonhole or dismiss.

**carpintería** *f.* carpentry; carpenter's workshop.

**carpintero** *m.* carpenter; **pájaro —** woodpecker.

**carraspear** *v.* to cough up; to clear one's throat; to be hoarse.

**carraspera** *f.* hoarseness.

**carrera** *f.* career; race, run; course; stocking run.

**carreta** *f.* long, narrow wagon; cart; *Col.*, *Ven.* wheelbarrow.

**carretaje** *m.* cartage (*transporting by cart, truck, etc.*); price paid for cartage.

**carrete** *m.* spool; reel; **— distribuidor** feeding reel; **— receptor** take-up reel (*tape recorder*).

**carretel** *m.* reel, spool, bobbin; fishing reel; log reel (*of a boat*).

**carretera** *f.* highway.

**carretero** *m.* carter, teamster; cart maker; **camino —** highway.

**carretilla** *f.* wheelbarrow; small cart; baggage truck; *Ríopl.* wagon; *Am.* jaw; *Col.* string, series (*of lies, blunders, etc.*); *Am.* firecracker; **repetir de —** to rattle off, repeat mechanically.

**carretón** *m.* truck; wagon, cart.

**carril** *m.* rail; rut; furrow.

**carrillo** *m.* (*de la cara*) cheek; (*mecánico*) pulley; cart.

**carrizo** *m.* reed; reed grass.

**carro** *m.* cart; cartload; *Am.* car, auto, streetcar, coach; *Am.* **pararle a uno el —** to restrain someone; *Am.* **pasarle a uno el —** to suffer an injury or misfortune; **carroza** *f.* large and luxurious carriage; chariot; *Am.* hearse.

**carrocería** *f.* chassis; frame for a parade float.

**carroña** *f.* dead and decaying flesh; putrid, decaying carcass.

**carruaje** *m.* carriage, vehicle.

**carta** *f.* (*misiva*) letter; (*naipe*) card; (*documento*) charter; map; **— blanca** full authority, freedom to act; **— de naturaleza** naturalization papers; **— de venta** bill of sale; *Ch.* **retirar —** to repent, back down; *Am.* **ser la última — de la baraja** to be the worst or most insignificant person or thing.

**cartearse** *v.* to correspond, write to each other.

**cartel** *m.* poster, handbill; cartel, written agreement; **cartela** *f.* tag, slip of paper, small card, piece of cardboard; **cartelera** *f.* billboard; **cartelón** *m.* large poster.

**cartera** *f.* (*objeto*) wallet; briefcase; desk pad; (*puesto*) portfolio, cabinet post; **carterista** *m.* & *f.* pickpocket.

**cartero** *m.* mailman, letter carrier, postman.

**cartilla** *f.* primer; note, short letter; **leerle a uno la —** to scold, lecture someone concerning his duties.

**cartografiar**[17] *v.* to chart; to make charts.

**cartón** *m.* cardboard; pasteboard; **cartulina** *f.* fine cardboard.

**cartuchera** *f.* cartridge belt.

**cartucho** *m.* cartridge; roll of coins; paper cone or bag.

**casa** *f.* (*doméstica*) house, home; household; (*negocio*) business firm; square (*of a chessboard*); *Am.* bet, wager; **— de empeños** pawnshop; **— de huéspedes** boardinghouse; **echar la — por la ventana** to spend recklessly, squander everything; **poner —** to set up housekeeping.

**casabe, cazabe** *m. Am.* cassava; *Am.* cassava bread.

**casaca** *f.* long military coat; **volver —** to be a turncoat, change sides or parties.

**casamiento** *m.* wedding; marriage.

**casar** *v.* to marry; to match; *Am.* to graft (*trees*); **-se** to get married.

**cascabel** *m.* jingle bell, tinkle bell; snake's rattle; *Am.* rattlesnake; **cascabela** *f. C.R.* rattlesnake.

**cascada** *f.* cascade, waterfall.

**cascajo** *m.* coarse gravel; crushed stone; pebble; fragment; rubbish.

**cascanueces** *m.* nutcracker.

**cascar**[6] *v.* to crack, break; **-se** to crack or break open.

**cáscara** *f.* shell, husk, hull, rind; bark of a tree; *Ríopl.* **dar a uno — de novillo** to give someone a whipping; **cascarudo** *adj.* having a thick husk; having a thick rind.

**cascarrabias** *m. & f.* crab, grouch, illtempered person; *adj.* grouchy, cranky, irritable.

**casco** *m.* helmet; hoof; skull; broken piece of earthenware; cask; empty bottle; hull of a ship; *Mex., Ríopl.* compound, main buildings of a farm; **caliente de -s** hot-headed; **ligero de -s** light-headed, frivolous; **romperse los -s** to rack one's brain.

**caserío** *m.* hamlet, small settlement.

**casero** *adj.* domestic; homemade; *m.* landlord; janitor, caretaker; *Ch.* customer; *Col., Peru, Ven.* delivery boy; **casera** *f.* landlady; housekeeper.

**caseta** *f.* small house, cottage; booth, stall.

**casi** *adv.* almost.

**casilla** *f.* (*puesto*) stall, booth; (*apartado*) post office box; pigeonhole; **sacarle a uno de sus -s** to change someone's way of life or habits; to irritate, annoy, try someone's patience; **salirse de sus -s** to lose one's temper; to do something out of the way.

**casino** *m.* club, society; clubhouse; recreation hall.

**caso** *m.* case; point; matter; event; **— que** (*or* **en — de que**) in case that; **dado —** supposing; **hacer — de** to pay attention to; **hacer — omiso de**

to omit; **no viene al —** that is not to the point.

**casorio** *m.* wedding, marriage.

**caspa** *f.* dandruff.

**casta** *f.* race, breed; caste, distinct class; quality, kind.

**castaña** *f.* chestnut; jug; knot or roll of hair; *Am.* small barrel; *Mex.* trunk, large suitcase.

**castañetear** *v.* to rattle the castanets; to chatter (*said of the teeth*); to crackle (*said of the knees or joints*); **— con los dedos** to snap one's fingers.

**castañeteo** *m.* rattle or sound of castanets; chatter, chattering (*of the teeth*).

**castaño** *m.* chestnut (*tree and wood*); *adj.* chestnut-colored.

**castañuela** *f.* castanet.

**castellano** *adj. & m.* Castilian.

**castidad** *f.* chastity.

**castigar**[7] *v.* to chastise, punish.

**castigo** *m.* punishment; correction.

**castillo** *m.* castle.

**castizo** *adj.* pure, correct (*language*); pure-blooded.

**casto** *adj.* chaste, pure.

**castor** *m.* beaver; beaver cloth.

**casual** *adj.* casual, accidental.

**casualidad** *f.* chance, accident.

**casuca** *f.* little house; hut, shanty.

**casucha** *f.* hut, hovel, shack.

**catadura** *f.* aspect, appearance.

**catalán** *adj.* Catalan, Catalonian, of or from Catalonia, Spain; *m.* Catalan.

**catalejo** *m.* telescope.

**catalogar**[7] *v.* to catalogue.

**catálogo** *m.* catalogue.

**catar** *v.* to look at, examine; to taste, sample.

**catarata** *f.* cataract; waterfall.

**catarro** *m.* catarrh, cold.

**catástrofe** *f.* catastrophe, mishap.

**catear** *v.* to explore, look around; *Ch., C.A., Mex.* to search or raid (*a home*); *Am.* to explore for ore; *Col., Ríopl.* to test, try.

**catecismo** *m.* catechism.

**cátedra** *f.* class; subject; chair, professorship.

**catedral** *f.* cathedral.

**catedrático** *m.* professor.

**categoría** *f.* category, rank; kind, class.

**categórico** *adj.* categorical, positive.

**catequizar**[9] *v.* to catechize, give religious instruction (to); to induce, persuade.

**católico** *adj.* Catholic; universal; *m.* Catholic; **catolicismo** *m.* Catholicism.

**catre** *m.* cot, small bed; *Am.* raft, float; *C.A.,* camp stool, folding stool; **— de tijera** folding cot.

**catrín** *m. Am.* dandy; *adj. Mex., C.A.* over-elegant, dressy.

**cauce** *m.* river bed.

**caución** *f.* precaution; security, guarantee; bail.

**cauchero** *m. Am.* rubber gatherer; *Am.* rubber producer; *adj. Am.* rubber, pertaining to rubber.

**caucho** *m.* rubber; — **sintético** synthetic rubber; *Am.* rubber tree; *Col.* rubber raincoat or cloak; **cauchal** *m.* rubber grove or plantation.

**caudal** *m.* (*monetario*) wealth; (*torrente*) river current; volume of water.

**caudaloso** *adj.* wealthy; abundant.

**caudillaje** *m.* military leadership; *Am.* political bossism; *Am.* tyranny.

**caudillo** *m.* leader, chief; *Am.* political boss.

**causa** *f.* cause; case, lawsuit; *Am.* light lunch, snack.

**causar** *v.* to cause.

**cautela** *f.* caution; cunning, craftiness; trick, deception.

**cauteloso** *adj.* cautious; crafty.

**cautivar** *v.* to capture; to charm, fascinate.

**cautiverio** *m.* captivity.

**cautivo** *m.* captive, war prisoner.

**cauto** *adj.* cautious.

**cavar** *v.* to dig, spade; to excavate.

**caverna** *f.* cavern, cave.

**cavernoso** *adj.* cavernous, like a cavern; hollow; **voz cavernosa** deep, hollow voice.

**cavidad** *f.* cavity.

**cayado** *m.* shepherd's crook, staff.

**cayo** *m.* key, island reef.

**caza** *f.* hunt, hunting; wild game; *m.* attack plane; **dar —** to pursue, track down.

**cazador** *adj.* hunting; *m.* hunter.

**cazar**[9] *v.* to chase, hunt; to track down.

**cazatorpedero** *m.* destroyer, torpedo-boat.

**cazo** *m.* dipper; pot, pan.

**cazuela** *f.* stewing pan; earthenware cooking pan; topmost theatre gallery; *Ven.* stewed hen; *P.R.* candied sweet potatoes with spices.

**cebada** *f.* barley; *Am.* brewing of **mate**; **cebadal** *m.* barley field.

**cebar** *v.* to feed, fatten (*animals*); to encourage, nourish (*a passion*); to prime (*a gun, pump, etc.*); to bait (*a fishhook*); *Ríopl.* to brew and serve **mate** or tea; **-se** to vent one's fury.

**cebo** *m.* feed (*for animals*); bait; incentive.

**cebolla** *f.* onion.

**cecear** *v.* to lisp.

**ceceo** *m.* lisp, lisping.

**cecina** *f.* dried beef, jerked beef.

**cedazo** *m.* sieve.

**ceder** *v.* to cede, transfer; to yield, surrender, submit; to diminish, abate.

**cedro** *m.* cedar.

**cédula** *f.* slip of paper; certificate; — **de vecindad** (*or* — **personal**) official identification card.

**céfiro** *m.* zephyr, soft breeze; *Am.* fine muslin.

**cegar**[1,7] *v. irr.* to blind; to become blind; to confuse; to fill up, stop up (*a hole*).

**ceguedad, ceguera** *f.* blindness.

**ceiba** *f.* *Am.* ceiba, silk-cotton tree.

**ceja** *f.* eyebrow; brow of a hill.

**cejar** *v.* to go backward; to back; to back down, give in, yield; to slacken.

**cejijunto** *adj.* frowning; with knitted eyebrows.

**celada** *f.* ambush, snare, trap.

**celaje** *m.* colored clouds; skylight; presage, portent; *P.R.* shadow, ghost; *Am.* **como un —** like lightning.

**celar** *v.* to guard, watch; to watch over jealously; to conceal.

**celda** *f.* cell.

**celebración** *f.* celebration.

**celebrar** *v.* to celebrate; to praise, honor; to be glad.

**célebre** *adj.* famous; funny, witty; *Col.* graceful, pretty (*woman*).

**celebridad** *f.* fame, renown; celebrity, famous person; celebration.

**celeridad** *f.* swiftness, speed.

**celeste** *adj.* celestial, heavenly.

**celestial** *adj.* celestial, heavenly, divine.

**célibe** *adj.* unmarried; *m. & f.* unmarried person.

**celo** *m.* (*humano*) zeal, ardor; envy; (*animal*) heat (*sexual excitement in animals*); **-s** jealousy, suspicion; **tener -s** to be jealous.

**celosía** *f.* window lattice; Venetian blind.

**celoso** *adj.* jealous; zealous, eager; suspicious.

**célula** *f.* cell.

**celuloide** *m.* celluloid.

**cellisca** *f.* sleet; rain and snow.

**cementar** *v.* to cement.

**cementerio** *m.* cemetery.

**cemento** *m.* cement; — **armado** reinforced concrete.

**cena** *f.* supper.

**cenagal** *m.* quagmire, muddy ground, swamp.

**cenagoso** *adj.* muddy, miry.

**cenar** *v.* to eat supper.

**cencerrada** *f.* racket, noise (*with cowbells, tin cans, etc.*); tin pan serenade.

**cencerrear** *v.* to make a racket (*with cowbells, tin cans, etc.*).

**cencerro** *m.* cowbell.

**cendal** *m.* gauze; thin veil.

**cenicero** *m.* ash tray; ash pit; ash pan.

**cenicienta** *f.* a Cinderella.

**ceniciento** *adj.* ashen, ash-colored.

**cenit** *m.* zenith.

**ceniza** *f.* ashes, cinders.

**cenizo** *adj.* ash-colored.

**censo** *m.* census.

**censor** *m.* censor.

**censura** *f.* censure, criticism, disapproval; censorship.

**censurador** *m.* censor, critic; critical person; *adj.* critical.

**censurar** *v.* to censure, criticize, reprove; to censor.

**centavo** *m.* cent.

**centella** *f.* lightning, flash; spark.

**centelleante** *adj.* sparkling, flashing.

**centellear** *v.* to twinkle; to sparkle, glitter; to flash.

**centelleo** *m.* glitter, sparkle.

**centenar** *m.* one hundred; field of rye.

**centenario** *m.* centennial, one hundredth anniversary; *adj.* centennial; old, ancient.

**centeno** *m.* rye.
**centésimo** *adj.* & *m.* hundredth.
**centímetro** *m.* centimeter (*one hundredth part of a meter*).
**céntimo** *m.* one hundredth part of a **peseta**.
**centinela** *m.* sentry, sentinel.
**central** *adj.* central; *f.* main office; headquarters; *Am.* main sugar mill or refinery.
**centrar** *v.* to center.
**céntrico** *adj.* central.
**centro** *m.* center, middle.
**ceñidor** *m.* girdle, belt, sash.
**ceñir**⁵,¹⁹ *v. irr.* (*rodear*) to gird, girdle; to tighten; to encircle; (*abreviar*) to diminish; to limit; **-se a** to limit oneself to.
**ceño** *m.* frown; scowl; **fruncir el —** to frown; to scowl.
**cepa** *f.* stump, stub (*of a tree or plant*); vinestock; origin, stock (*of a family*); *Am.* mass of plants growing from a common root; *Am.* excavation (*for a building*), hole, pit (*for planting trees*); **de buena —** of good stock.
**cepillo** *m.* brush; alms box; carpenter's plane; *Am.* flatterer; **— de dientes** toothbrush.
**cepo** *m.* branch, stock.
**cera** *f.* wax.
**cerámica** *f.* ceramics, pottery.
**cerca** *adv.* near, near by; **— de** *prep.* near, nearly; *f.* fence, low wall.
**cercado** *m.* enclosure; fenced-in garden; fence; *Am.* Peruvian political division; *p.p. of* **cercar**.
**cercanía** *f.* proximity; **-s** surroundings, vicinity.
**cercano** *adj.* near; neighboring.
**cercar**⁶ *v.* to fence, enclose; to surround; to besiege.
**cercenar** *v.* to clip off; to curtail, diminish, reduce.
**cerciorar** *v.* to assure, affirm; **-se** to ascertain, find out.
**cerco** *m.* fence, enclosure; siege; circle; *Ch.* small farm or orchard.
**cerda** *f.* bristle; *Am.* **ir en -s** to go halves or share in a deal.
**cerdo** *m.* hog, pig; pork.
**cerdoso** *adj.* bristly.
**cereal** *m.* cereal, grain.
**cerebro** *m.* brain.
**ceremonia** *f.* ceremony.
**ceremonial** *adj.* & *m.* ceremonial.
**ceremonioso** *adj.* ceremonious.
**cereza** *f.* cherry; **cerezo** *m.* cherry tree; cherry wood.
**cerilla** *f.* wax taper; wax match; ear-wax.
**cerillo** *m. Mex., C.A., Ven., Andes* match.
**cerner**¹ *v. irr.* to sift; to drizzle; *Am.* to strain through a sieve; **-se** to hover (*as a bird or plane*).
**cero** *m.* zero; nothing.
**cerquita** *adv.* quite near, nice and near.
**cerrado** *adj.* closed; cloudy; thick (*beard*); reserved (*person*); dull; *Am.* stubborn.

**cerradura** *f.* locking, closing; lock; **— de golpe** spring lock.
**cerrajería** *f.* locksmith's shop; locksmith's trade.
**cerrajero** *m.* locksmith.
**cerrar**¹ *v. irr.* to close, shut, lock; **-se** to close; **-se el cielo** to become overcast or cloudy.
**cerrazón** *f.* cloudiness, darkness.
**cerro** *m.* hill.
**cerrojo** *m.* latch, bolt.
**certamen** *m.* contest, literary contest; debate; competition.
**certero** *adj.* accurate, exact; well-aimed; **tirador —** good shot.
**certeza** *f.* certainty.
**certidumbre** *f.* certainty.
**certificado** *adj.* certified, registered; *m.* certificate.
**certificar**⁶ *v.* to certify; to register (*a letter*).
**cervato** *m.* fawn, young deer.
**cerveza** *f.* beer; **cervecería** *f.* beer tavern; brewery.
**cesante** *adj.* unemployed.
**cesar** *v.* to cease, stop; to quit.
**cesta** *f.* basket; a kind of racket for playing jai alai (*Basque ball game*).
**cesto** *m.* large basket, hamper.
**cetrino** *adj.* greenish-yellow, lemon-colored; citronlike; melancholy, gloomy.
**cetro** *m.* scepter, staff.
**cibernética** *f.* cybernetics, computer science.
**cicatero** *adj.* miserly, stingy.
**cicatriz** *f.* scar.
**cicatrizar**⁹ *v.* to heal, close (*a wound*).
**ciclo** *m.* cycle; period of time; school term.
**ciclón** *m.* cyclone.
**ciclotrón** *m.* cyclotron.
**ciego** *adj.* blind; **a ciegas** blindly; *m.* blindman.
**cielo** *m.* sky; heaven; **— de la boca** palate; **poner en el —** to praise, extol; **poner el grito en el —** to "hit the ceiling"; **cielito** *m. Am.* gaucho group dance and tune.
**ciempiés, cientopiés** *m.* centipede.
**ciénaga** *f.* swamp, bog, quagmire, marsh.
**ciencia** *f.* science; learning; skill; **a** (*or* **de**) **— cierta** with certainty.
**cieno** *m.* mud, mire.
**científico** *adj.* scientific; *m.* scientist.
**cierre** *m.* clasp, fastener; zipper; closing, fastening, locking; method of closing.
**cierto** *adj.* certain, true, sure; **por —** certainly; *Col., C.A.* **ciertas hierbas** so-and-so (*person not named*).
**ciervo** *m.* deer; **cierva** *f.* doe, hind, female deer.
**cierzo** *m.* north wind.
**cifra** *f.* cipher, number; figure; abridgment, summary; code; monogram; emblem.
**cifrar** *v.* to write in code; to summarize; **— la esperanza en** to place one's hope in.
**cigarra** *f.* cicada, locust.

**cigarrera** *f.* cigar or cigarette case; woman cigar maker or vendor.

**cigarrillo** *m.* cigarette.

**cigarro** *m.* cigar; cigarette.

**cigüeña** *f.* stork; crank, handle (*for turning*).

**cigüeñal** *m.* crankshaft.

**cilíndrico** *adj.* cylindrical.

**cilindro** *m.* cylinder; *Mex.* hand organ.

**cima** *f.* peak, summit, top; **dar —** to complete, carry out.

**cimarrón** *adj. Ríopl., Mex., Carib., Ven., Andes* wild, untamed; *Am.* **mate —** black, bitter **mate.**

**cimarronear** *v. Ríopl.* to drink **mate** without sugar.

**cimbrar, cimbrear** *v.* to brandish, flourish, swing; to shake; to bend; *Am.* to swing around, change suddenly one's direction; **— a uno de un golpe** to knock a person down with a blow; **-se** to swing, sway; to vibrate, shake.

**cimiento** *m.* foundation, base; source, root; **abrir los -s** to break ground for a building.

**cinc** *m.* zinc.

**cincel** *m.* chisel.

**cincelar** *v.* to chisel; to engrave.

**cincha** *f.* cinch, girth; *Am.* blows with the flat of a sword; *Col., Ríopl.* **a revienta -s** unwillingly; hurriedly; at breakneck speed.

**cinchar** *v.* to cinch, tighten the saddle girth; *Am.* to hit with the flat of a sword.

**cine, cínema** *m.* cinema, motion picture, movie; **cinematógrafo** *m.* motion picture.

**cinematografía** *f.* cinematography, the science of motion picture photography.

**cíngulo** *m.* girdle, cord, belt.

**cínico** *adj.* cynical, sarcastic, sneering; *m.* cynic.

**cinta** *f.* ribbon, band; tape; strip; movie film; coarse fishing net; *Am.* tin can.

**cintarada** *f.* beating, flogging; **cintarazo** *m.* blow with the flat of a sword.

**cintilar** *v.* to sparkle, twinkle; to glimmer.

**cinto** *m.* belt; girdle.

**cintura** *f.* waist; **meter en —** to subdue, subject.

**cinturón** *m.* belt; **— de seguridad** safety belt.

**ciprés** *m.* cypress.

**circo** *m.* circus.

**circuito** *m.* circuit.

**circulación** *f.* circulation; traffic.

**circular** *v.* to circulate; to circle; *adj.* circular; *f.* circular letter, notice.

**círculo** *m.* circle; group; club; clubhouse.

**circundante** *adj.* surrounding.

**circundar** *v.* to surround.

**circunferencia** *f.* circumference.

**circunlocución** *f.* circumlocution, roundabout expression.

**circunspección** *f.* circumspection, decorum, prudence, restraint.

**circunspecto** *adj.* circumspect, prudent.

**circunstancia** *f.* circumstance.

**circunstante** *adj.* surrounding; present; **-s** *m. pl.* bystanders, onlookers, audience.

**circunvecino** *adj.* neighboring, surrounding.

**cirio** *m.* wax candle; saguaro cactus.

**ciruela** *f.* plum; prune; **— pasa** prune, dried prune; **ciruelo** *m.* plum tree.

**cirugía** *f.* surgery.

**cirujano** *m.* surgeon.

**cisne** *m.* swan; *Ríopl.* powder puff.

**cisterna** *f.* cistern.

**cita** *f.* date, appointment; citation, summons; quotation.

**citación** *f.* citation, quotation; summons.

**citar** *v.* (*convocar*) to make a date or appointment with; (*referir*) to cite, quote; (*incitar*) incite, provoke; to summon.

**ciudad** *f.* city.

**ciudadano** *m.* citizen; resident of a city; *adj.* of or pertaining to a city; **ciudadanía** *f.* citizenship.

**ciudadela** *f.* citadel.

**cívico** *adj.* civic.

**civil** *adj.* civil; polite, courteous.

**civilidad** *f.* civility, courtesy.

**civilización** *f.* civilization.

**civilizador** *adj.* civilizing; *m.* civilizer.

**civilizar**[9] *v.* to civilize.

**cizaña** *f.* weed; vice; discord; **sembrar —** to sow discord.

**clamar** *v.* to clamor, shout; to whine.

**clamor** *m.* clamor, shout; whine; knell.

**clamoreo** *m.* clamoring; shouting.

**clamorear** *v.* to clamor, shout; to toll, knell.

**clandestino** *adj.* clandestine, underhanded, secret.

**clara** *f.* white of egg; bald spot; thin spot (*in a fabric*); **a las -s** clearly, openly, frankly.

**claraboya** *f.* skylight.

**clarear** *v.* (*poner claro*), to clarify, make clear; (*haber más luz*) to grow light, begin to dawn; to clear up; *Am.* to pierce through and through; **-se** to become transparent; to reveal oneself.

**claridad** *f.* clarity, clearness; blunt remark, slam; fame.

**claridoso** *adj. Mex., Ven., C.A.* blunt, outspoken, plainspoken.

**clarificar**[6] *v.* to clarify, make clear.

**clarín** *m.* bugle; bugler; organ stop; *Am.* song bird.

**clarinete** *m.* clarinet; clarinet player.

**clarito** *adj. & adv.* quite clear, nice and clear.

**clarividencia** *f.* clairvoyance; keen insight.

**claro** *adj.* clear; light (*color*); illustrious; *adv.* clearly; *m.* skylight; space, gap; clearing (*in a forest*); **pasar la noche de — en —** not to sleep a wink; *Mex., Carib.* **en —** without eating or sleeping; *Am.* **poner en —** to copy (*a rough draft*).

**clase** *f.* class; classroom; kind, sort.
**clásico** *adj.* classic, classical.
**clasificación** *f.* classification.
**clasificar**[6] *v.* to classify.
**claustro** *m.* cloister; meeting of a university faculty; **— de profesores** university faculty.
**cláusula** *f.* clause.
**clausura** *f.* closing; seclusion, monastic life.
**clavado** *m. Mex.* a dive.
**clavar** *v.* to nail; to fix; to deceive, cheat; **-se** to be deceived; *Mex.* to fall into a trap; *Mex.* to dive.
**clave** *f.* key, code; keystone; clef.
**clavel** *m.* carnation, pink.
**clavetear** *v.* to nail; to stud with nails.
**clavícula** *f.* collarbone.
**clavija** *f.* peg; electric plug; peg (*of a stringed instrument*).
**clavijero** *m.* hat or clothes rack.
**clavo** *m.* nail; clove (*spice*); sharp pain or grief; sick headache; *Mex.* rich mineral vein; *Am.* bother, worry; *Col.* surprise, disappointment; *Ríopl.* drug on the market (*unsaleable article*); **dar en el —** to hit the nail on the head; *Am.* **meter a uno en un —** to put a person in a predicament; *Am.* **ser un —** to be punctual, exact.
**clemencia** *f.* mercy; **clemente** *adj.* merciful.
**clerical** *adj.* clerical, of a clergyman or the clergy.
**clérigo** *m.* clergyman.
**clero** *m.* clergy.
**cliché** *m.* photographic plate; also **clisé.**
**cliente** *m. & f.* client; customer; **clientela** *f.* cleintele, clients; customers.
**clima** *m.* climate.
**clímax** *m.* climax.
**clínica** *f.* clinic.
**clíper** *m.* clipper.
**cloaca** *f.* sewer.
**cloquear** *v.* to cluck.
**cloqueo** *m.* cluck, clucking.
**cloro** *m.* chlorine.
**club** *m.* club, society.
**clueca** *f.* brooding hen.
**coacción** *f.* compulsion, force; enforcement.
**coagular** *v.* to coagulate, thicken, clot; to curd, curdle; **-se** to coagulate, clot; to curd, curdle.
**coágulo** *m.* coagulation, clot.
**coartar** *v.* to restrain, limit.
**coba** *f.* flattery; fib; **dar —** to flatter; to tease.
**cobarde** *adj.* cowardly; timid; weak; *m.* coward.
**cobardía** *f.* cowardice.
**cobertizo** *m.* shed; shanty.
**cobertor** *m.* bedcover, quilt.
**cobertura** *f.* cover, covering.
**cobija** *f.* cover; shelter; roof; *Am.* blanket; *Am.* shawl, serape, poncho; **-s** *Am.* bedclothes.
**cobijar** *v.* to cover; to shelter.
**cobrador** *m.* collector; ticket collector.
**cobranza** *f.* collection (*of a sum of money*); cashing.

**cobrar** *v.* to collect (*bills, debts*); to charge; to cash (*a draft, check, etc.*); to recover, regain; to gain, acquire; *Am.* to demand payment; **— cariño a** to take a liking to.
**cobre** *m.* copper; copper kitchen utensils; *Am.* copper coin; **-s** brass musical instruments; **batir el —** to hustle, work with energy; *Am.* **mostrar el —** to show one's worse side.
**cobrizo** *adj.* coppery, copper-colored.
**cobro** *m.* collection (*of bills*); **poner en —** to put in a safe place; **ponerse en —** to take refuge, get to a safe place.
**coca** *f. Am.* coca (*South American shrub and its leaves*); *Am.* cocaine; *Am.* coca tea; *Am.* eggshell; *Am.* fruit skin or rind; *Am.* **de —** free of charge; in vain.
**cocaína** *f.* cocaine.
**cocear** *v.* to kick.
**cocer**[2,10] *v. irr.* to cook; to boil; to bake.
**cocido** *m.* Spanish stew; *p.p. of* **cocer.**
**cociente** *m.* quotient.
**cocimiento** *m.* cooking; baking; liquid concoction (*generally made of medicinal herbs*).
**cocina** *f.* kitchen; cuisine, cooking; **— económica** stove, range.
**cocinar** *v.* to cook.
**cocinero** *m.* cook.
**coco** *m.* coconut; coconut palm; bogeyman, goblin; *Am.* derby hat; *Mex., Carib., Ríopl.* head; *Am.* blow on the head; **hacer -s a** to make eyes at, flirt with; *Col., Ven., Andes* **pelar a —** to crop the hair; **cocotal** *m.* grove of coconut palms; coconut plantation; **cocotero** *m.* coconut palm.
**cocodrilo** *m.* crocodile.
**coche** *m.* coach; car; taxi.
**cochero** *m.* coachman; cabman; taxi driver.
**cochinada** *f.* filth, filthiness; filthy act or remark; dirty trick; herd of swine.
**cochinilla** *f.* cochineal (*insect*).
**cochino** *m.* hog, pig; dirty person; *Ch.* stingy person; *Am.* **— de monte** wild boar; *adj.* filthy, dirty; *Ch.* miserly, stingy.
**codazo** *m.* nudge; poke (*with the elbow*).
**codear** *v.* to elbow; to nudge; **-se con alguien** to rub elbows with someone.
**codicia** *f.* greed; greediness.
**codiciar** *v.* to covet.
**codicioso** *adj.* covetous, greedy.
**código** *m.* code of laws.
**codo** *m.* elbow; bend; **alzar** (*or* **empinar**) **el —** to drink too much; **hablar por los -s** to talk too much; **meterse** (*or* **estar metido**) **hasta los -s** to be up to the elbows, be very busy.
**codorniz** *f.* partridge.
**coetáneo** *adj.* contemporary.
**cofrade** *m. & f.* fellow member (*of a brotherhood, club, society, etc.*).
**cofradía** *f.* brotherhood; sisterhood; guild; trade union.
**cofre** *m.* coffer, jewel box; chest, trunk.

Cl

**coger**[11] v. to seize; to catch; to grasp; to gather; *Am.* **-se una cosa** to steal something.

**cogote** m. nape, back of the neck.

**cohechar** v. to bribe.

**coheredero** m. joint heir.

**coherente** adj. coherent; connected.

**cohete** m. skyrocket; rocket; *Ríopl.* **al — in vain, uselessly.

**cohetería** f. rocketry; rocket weaponry; shop for making fireworks.

**cohibición** f. repression, inhibition, restraint.

**cohibido** p.p. & adj. inhibited; embarrassed, uneasy.

**cohibir** v. to restrain, repress; to inhibit.

**coincidencia** f. coincidence.

**coincidir** v. to coincide.

**cojear** v. to limp; **cojeamos del mismo pie** we both have the same weakness.

**cojera** f. limp, lameness.

**cojín** m. cushion; pad; **cojincillo** m. pad.

**cojinete** m. small pillow or cushion, pad; bearing, ball bearing.

**cojo** adj. lame, crippled; one-legged.

**col** f. cabbage; **— de Bruselas** Brussels sprouts.

**cola** f. (*rabo*) tail; train of a dress; (*hilera de gente*) line of people; **piano de —** grand piano; **piano de media —** baby grand; **hacer —** to stand in line; *Am.* **comer —** to be the last one in a contest.

**colaboración** f. collaboration, mutual help.

**colaborar** v. to collaborate, work together.

**coladera** f. colander, strainer, sieve; *Mex.*, *Ven.* drain.

**colar**[2] v. irr. to strain, filter; to bleach with lye; **-se** to slip in or out, sneak in.

**colcha** f. quilt; bedspread; **-s** *Ríopl.* saddle and trappings; *Ríopl.* gaucho clothing.

**colchón** m. mattress.

**colear** v. to wag the tail; to grab a bull by the tail and throw him over; *Am.* to flunk (*a student*); *Am.* to trail, tag behind (*a person*); *Col.* to bother, nag, harass; *Am.* to smoke one cigarette after another.

**colección** f. collection; set; gathering.

**coleccionar** v. to collect, make a collection.

**coleccionista** m. & f. collector (*of stamps, curios, etc.*).

**colecta** f. collection of voluntary gifts; assessment; collect (*a short prayer of the mass*).

**colectivo** adj. collective; m. *Am.* small bus.

**colector** m. collector; water pipe, drain.

**colega** m. & f. colleague, fellow worker.

**colegiatura** f. college fellowship or scholarship; *C.A.* tuition in a college.

**colegio** m. boarding school; school, academy; college, body of professional men.

**colegir**[5,11] v. to gather; to conclude, infer.

**cólera** f. anger, rage; m. cholera (*disease*).

**colérico** adj. irritable; angry.

**coleto** m. leather jacket; one's inner self; *Am.* impudence, shamelessness; **decir para su —** to say to oneself; **echarse al —** to drink down; to devour.

**colgadero** m. hanger; hook, peg; hat or clothes rack.

**colgadura** f. drape, hanging; drapery; tapestry.

**colgante** adj. hanging; dangling; **puente —** suspension bridge.

**colgar**[2,7] v. irr. (*suspender*) to hang, suspend; to dangle; to drape (*walls*); (*achacar*) to impute, attribute; *Cuba* to flunk, fail (*a student*); *Col.* **-se** to fall behind.

**colibrí** m. hummingbird.

**coliflor** f. cauliflower.

**coligarse**[7] v. to league together, band together.

**colilla** f. small tail; butt (*of a cigarette*), stub (*of a cigar*).

**colina** f. hill.

**colindante** adj. contiguous, neighboring, adjacent.

**colindar** v. to border (on); to be adjoining.

**colisión** f. collision, clash.

**colmar** v. to fill to the brim; **— de** to fill with; to shower with (*gifts, favors, etc.*); **-le a uno el plato** to exhaust one's patience.

**colmena** f. beehive; *Mex.* bee.

**colmillo** m. eyetooth, canine tooth; tusk; fang.

**colmo** m. overfullness; limit; **— de la locura** height of folly; **¡eso es el —!** that's the limit! adj. overfull, filled to the brim.

**colocación** f. placing, arrangement; position, job.

**colocar**[6] v. to place; to put in place, arrange; to give employment to.

**colocho** m. *C.A.* curly hair; wood shavings.

**colombiano** adj. Colombian, of or pertaining to Colombia, South America.

**colon** m. colon (*of the large intestine*).

**colonia** f. colony; silk ribbon; *Mex.*, *Carib.* city district; *Am.* sugar plantation.

**coloniaje** m. *Am.* colonial period.

**colonial** adj. colonial.

**colonización** f. colonization.

**colonizador** m. colonizer, colonist; adj. colonizing.

**colonizar**[9] v. to colonize.

**colono** m. colonist, settler; tenant farmer; *Carib.* owner of a sugar plantation; *Am.* bootlicker, flatterer.

**coloquio** m. conversation, talk; literary dialogue; *Col.* street comedy, farce.

**color** m. color; coloring; paint; rouge; **so — de** under the pretext of.

**coloración** f. coloring.

**colorado** *adj.* red, reddish; colored; **ponerse —** to blush.

**colorante** *adj.* & *m.* coloring.

**colorar** *v.* to color; to stain; to dye.

**colorear** *v.* to color; to redden; to give color to.

**colorete** *m.* rouge.

**colorido** *m.* coloring; color; *adj.* colored; colorful.

**colosal** *adj.* colossal, huge.

**columbrar** *v.* to see faintly; to glimpse.

**columna** *f.* column.

**columpiar** *v.* to swing; **-se** to swing; to sway.

**columpio** *m.* swing.

**collado** *m.* hillock, knoll.

**collar** *m.* necklace; dog collar; *Am.* collar (*of a draft horse*); **collera** *f.* collar (*for draft animals*).

**coma** *f.* comma; *m.* coma, stupor, prolonged unconsciousness.

**comadre** *f.* (*amiga*) woman friend; (*chismosa*) gossip; (*partera*) midwife; (*alcahueta*) go-between; *name used to express kinship between mother and godmother*; **comadrona** *f.* midwife.

**comadreja** *f.* weasel.

**comandancia** *f.* command; position and headquarters of a commander.

**comandante** *m.* major; commander.

**comandar** *v.* to command (*troops*).

**comandita** *f.* silent partnership; **sociedad en —** limited company.

**comando** *m.* military command.

**comarca** *f.* district, region.

**comba** *f.* bulge, warp.

**combar** *v.* to warp, bend, twist; **-se** to warp; to sag; to bulge.

**combate** *m.* combat, battle, fight.

**combatiente** *m.* combatant, fighter.

**combatir** *v.* to combat; to fight.

**combinación** *f.* combination.

**combinar** *v.* to combine, unite.

**comburente** *m.* the chemical agent that causes combustion, e.g., oxygen; *adj.* causing combustion.

**combustible** *adj.* combustible; *m.* fuel.

**combustión** *f.* combustion.

**comedero** *m.* trough (*for feeding animals*); *adj.* edible, eatable.

**comedia** *f.* comedy; farce.

**comediante** *m.* actor, comedian.

**comedido** *adj.* courteous, polite; obliging; *p.p.* of **comedirse**.

**comedirse**[5] *v. irr.* to be civil, polite, obliging; *Ec.* to meddle; *Am.* **— a hacer algo** to volunteer to do something.

**comedor** *m.* dining room; great eater.

**comején** *m.* termite.

**comelón** *m. Am.* big eater. *See* **comilón**.

**comendador** *m.* commander (*of certain military orders*).

**comensal** *m.* & *f.* table companion; dinner guest.

**comentador** *m.* commentator.

**comentar** *v.* to comment.

**comentario** *m.* commentary, explanation.

**comentarista** *m.* & *f.* commentator.

**comenzar**[1,9] *v. irr.* to begin.

**comer** *v.* to eat; to dine; to take (*in chess or checkers*); **dar de —** to feed; **ganar de —** to earn a living; **-se** to eat; to eat up; to skip (*a letter, syllable, word, etc.*); *Ríopl., Col.* **-se uno a otro** to deceive each other.

**comercial** *adj.* commercial.

**comerciante** *m.* merchant; storekeeper.

**comerciar** *v.* to trade; to have dealings (with).

**comercio** *m.* commerce, trade.

**comestible** *adj.* edible, eatable; **-s** *m. pl.* food, groceries.

**cometa** *m.* comet; *C.A.* person seldom seen; *f.* kite.

**cometer** *v.* to commit; to entrust; to use (*a figure of speech*).

**cometido** *m.* commission, assignment, charge; task, duty.

**comezón** *f.* itch.

**comicios** *m. pl.* primaries, elections.

**cómico** *adj.* comic, of comedy; comical, funny, amusing; *m.* comedian, actor.

**comida** *f.* meal; dinner; good; **comidilla** *f.* small meal; gossip; **la comidilla de la vecindad** the talk of the town.

**comienzo** *m.* beginning; origin.

**comilitona** *f.* spread, big feast.

**comilón** *m.* big eater.

**comillas** *f. pl.* quotation marks.

**comisario** *m.* commissary, deputy, delegate; manager; *Am.* police inspector.

**comisión** *f.* commission; committee.

**comisionado** *adj.* commissioned, charged, delegated; *m.* commissioner; *Am.* constable.

**comisionar** *v.* to commission.

**comistrajo** *m.* mess, strange food concoction, mixture.

**comité** *m.* committee, commission.

**comitiva** *f.* retinue, group of attendants or followers.

**como** *adv.* & *conj.* as, like, such as; if, provided that, since, when; *Mex., Ven.* about, approximately; **¿cómo?** *interr. adv.* how?; what (did you say)?; *Am.* **¡cómo no!** yes, of course!

**cómoda** *f.* bureau, chest of drawers.

**comodidad** *f.* comfort; convenience.

**cómodo** *adj.* comfortable; convenient; *m. Am.* bedpan.

**compacto** *adj.* compact.

**conpadecer**[13] *v. irr.* to pity, sympathize with; **-se con** to be in harmony with; **-se de** to take pity on.

**compadrazgo** *m.* compaternity (*spiritual affinity between the godfather and the parents of a child*); friendship; relationship; clique, group of friends.

**compadre** *m.* (*amigo*) pal, crony, comrade; (*padrino*) cosponsor; *name used to express kinship between father and godfather.*

**compañero** *m.* companion; partner; mate; **compañerismo** *m.* companionship.

**compañía** *f.* company; *Am.* **— del ahorcado** silent companion, poor company.

**comparación** *f.* comparison.
**comparar** *v.* to compare.
**comparativo** *adj.* comparative.
**comparecer**[13] *v. irr.* to appear (*before a judge or tribunal*).
**compartimiento** *m.* compartment.
**compartir** *v.* to share; to divide into shares.
**compás** *m.* compass; measure; beat; **llevar el —** to beat time.
**compasión** *f.* compassion, pity.
**compasivo** *adj.* compassionate, sympathetic.
**compatible** *adj.* compatible, in harmony.
**compatriota** *m. & f.* compatriot, fellow countryman.
**compeler** *v.* to compel, force.
**compendiar** *v.* to abstract, summarize, condense.
**compendio** *m.* summary, condensation.
**compensación** *f.* compensation; recompense.
**compensar** *v.* to balance; to make equal; to compensate, recompense.
**competencia** *f.* competition, rivalry; competence, ability.
**competente** *adj.* competent; capable; adequate.
**competidor** *m.* competitor; rival; *adj.* competing.
**competir**[5] *v. irr.* to compete, vie.
**compilar** *v.* to compile.
**compinche** *m.* chum, pal, comrade.
**complacencia** *f.* complacency, satisfaction, contentment.
**complacer**[38] *v. irr.* to please, humor; to comply; **-se** to take pleasure or satisfaction (in).
**complaciente** *adj.* obliging, agreeable, willing to please.
**complejidad** *f.* complexity.
**complejo** *adj. & m.* complex.
**complemento** *m.* complement; object (*of a verb*).
**completamiento** *m.* completion.
**completar** *v.* to complete; to finish.
**completo** *adj.* complete, full, perfect.
**complicar**[6] *v.* to complicate.
**cómplice** *m. & f.* accomplice, companion in crime.
**complot** *m.* plot, conspiracy; intrigue.
**componenda** *f.* adjustment; compromise.
**componente** *adj.* component, constituent; *m.* component, essential part.
**componer**[40] *v. irr.* to fix, repair; to fix up; to adorn, trim; to compose; to set up (*type*); to settle (*a dispute*); *Col.* to set (*bones*).
**comportamiento** *m.* conduct, behavior.
**composición** *f.* composition; settlement.
**compositor** *m.* composer.
**compostura** *f.* (*arreglo*) repair; settlement, adjustment; (*aseo*) neatness, composition; (*dignidad*) composure, dignity.
**compota** *f.* fruit preserves; **— de manzana** applesauce.

**compra** *f.* purchase; buying; **ir de -s** to go shopping.
**comprador** *m.* buyer, purchaser.
**comprar** *v.* to buy, purchase.
**comprender** *v.* to understand, grasp, comprehend; to comprise, embrace.
**comprensible** *adj.* comprehensible, understandable.
**comprensión** *f.* understanding; comprehension; keenness.
**comprensivo** *adj.* comprehensive; understanding.
**compresión** *f.* compression.
**compresor** *m.* compressor.
**comprimir** *v.* to compress; to repress.
**comprobación** *f.* confirmation, check, proof, test.
**comprobante** *adj.* proving, verifying; *m.* proof; evidence; certificate; voucher; warrant.
**comprobar**[2] *v. irr.* to verify; to check; to prove.
**comprometer** *v.* (*exponer*) to compromise; to endanger; to bind; to force; (*concordar*) to come to an agreement; **-se** to promise, bind oneself; to become engaged; to compromise oneself.
**compromiso** *m.* (*convenio*) compromise; (*obligación*) engagement; appointment; (*dificultad*) predicament, trouble.
**compuerta** *f.* sluice (*gate to control the flow of water*), floodgate.
**compuesto** *p.p. of* **componer** & *adj.* repaired; fixed, adorned; composed; composite; compound; *m.* composite; compound.
**compungirse**[11] *v.* to feel regret or remorse.
**computadora electrónica** *f.* electronic computer.
**computar** *v.* to compute, calculate.
**cómputo** *m.* computation, calculation.
**comulgar**[7] *v.* to commune, take communion.
**común** *adj.* common; **por lo —** generally; *m.* toilet; **el — de las gentes** the majority of the people; the average person.
**comunero** *adj.* common, popular; *Am.* pertaining to a community; *m.* commoner (*one of the common people*); *Col., Ven., Andes* member of an Indian community.
**comunicación** *f.* communication.
**comunicar**[6] *v.* to communicate; to notify; **-se** to communicate; to correspond; to be in touch (with); to connect.
**comunicativo** *adj.* communicative, talkative.
**comunidad** *f.* community; commonwealth; the common people; commonness; guild.
**comunión** *f.* communion; political party.
**comunismo** *m.* communism; **comunista** *m. & f.* communist; *adj.* communistic, communist.

**con** *prep.* with; **— ser** in spite of being; **— tal que** provided that; **— todo** however.

**concavidad** *f.* hollow, cavity; hollowness.

**cóncavo** *adj.* concave, hollow.

**concebible** *adj.* conceivable.

**concebir**[5] *v. irr.* to conceive; to imagine; to understand, grasp.

**conceder** *v.* to concede, grant; to admit.

**concejal** *m.* councilman, alderman.

**concentración** *f.* concentration.

**concentrar** *v.* to concentrate.

**concepción** *f.* conception.

**concepto** *m.* concept, idea, thought.

**concernir**[51] *v. irr.* to concern.

**concertar**[1] *v. irr.* (*arreglar*) to arrange, plan, settle; to conclude (*a treaty or business deal*); (*concordar*) to harmonize; to agree.

**concesión** *f.* concession, grant; granting; acknowledgment.

**conciencia** *f.* conscience.

**concienzudo** *adj.* conscientious.

**concierto** *m.* concert; harmony; agreement; **de —** by common agreement.

**conciliar** *v.* to conciliate, win over; to reconcile, bring into harmony; **— el sueño** to get to sleep.

**concilio** *m.* council.

**concision** *f.* conciseness, brevity.

**conciso** *adj.* concise, brief.

**conciudadano** *m.* fellow citizen, fellow countryman.

**concluir**[32] *v. irr.* to conclude, finish; to infer.

**conclusión** *f.* conclusion.

**concordancia** *f.* concord, agreement, harmony.

**concordar**[2] *v. irr.* to agree; to be in harmony; to put in harmony.

**concordia** *f.* concord, harmony, agreement.

**concretar** *v.* to summarize, condense; to limit; **-se a** to limit oneself to.

**concreto** *adj.* concrete, real, specific; **en —** concretely; to sum up; *m. Am.* concrete.

**concupiscente** *adj.* sensual.

**concurrencia** *f.* gathering, audience; concurrence, simultaneous meeting or happening; competition.

**concurrido** *adj.* well-patronized, well-attended, much frequented.

**concurrir** *v.* to concur, meet together; to happen at the same time or place; to attend; to agree.

**concurso** *m.* gathering; contest; competitive examination; assistance.

**concha** *f.* shell; shellfish; prompter's box; *Mex.* **tener —** to be indifferent, unruffled, tough.

**conchabar** *v.* to unite, join; *Mex., S.A.* to hire (*labor*); **-se** to join, gang together; to conspire; *Ríopl.* to hire oneself out, get a job.

**conchabo** *m. Am.* hiring of a laborer or servant; *Ríopl.* job, menial job.

**conde** *m.* count; **condesa** *f.* countess.

**condecoración** *f.* decoration; badge, medal.

**condecorar** *v.* to decorate (*with a badge or medal*).

**condena** *f.* term in prison, sentence, penalty.

**condenación** *f.* condemnation; conviction (*of a prisoner or criminal*); damnation.

**condenar** *v.* to condemn; to sentence; *Am.* to annoy, irritate; **-se** to be damned, go to hell.

**condensar** *v.* to condense.

**condescendencia** *f.* condescension, patronizing attitude.

**condescender**[1] *v. irr.* to condescend; to comply, yield.

**condición** *f.* condition.

**condimentar** *v.* to season.

**condimento** *m.* condiment, seasoning.

**condiscípulo** *m.* schoolmate, classmate.

**condolerse**[2] *v. irr.* to condole (with), sympathize (with), be sorry (for).

**cóndor** *m. Am.* condor, vulture; *Am.* gold coin of Ecuador, Chile and Colombia.

**conducir**[25] *v. irr.* to conduct, lead; to drive (*an auto*); **-se** to behave, act.

**conducta** *f.* conduct; behavior; convoy, escort; management.

**conducto** *m.* conduit, pipe, channel; **por — de** through.

**conductor** *adj.* conducting; *m.* leader; chauffeur; guide; conductor (*electrical*); *Am.* conductor, ticket collector (*on trains, buses, streetcars*); *Am.* teamster, driver.

**conectar** *v.* to connect.

**conejera** *f.* burrow; rabbit warren (*piece of land for breeding rabbits*); den, joint, dive (*of ill repute*).

**conejo** *m.* rabbit; *Am.* guinea pig; **conejillo de Indias** guinea pig.

**conexión** *f.* connection.

**conexo** *adj.* connected; coherent.

**confección** *f.* making; confection; manufactured article; workmanship; concoction, compound.

**confeccionar** *v.* to make; to manufacture; to mix, put up (*a prescription*).

**confederación** *f.* confederation, alliance, league.

**confederar** *v.* to confederate; **-se** to confederate, form into a confederacy.

**conferencia** *f.* lecture; conference, meeting.

**conferenciante** *m. & f.* lecturer.

**conferencista** *m. & f.* lecturer.

**conferir**[3] *v. irr.* to confer; to give, bestow.

**confesar**[1] *v. irr.* to confess.

**confesión** *f.* confession.

**confesionario** *m.* confessional, confessional box.

**confesor** *m.* confessor.

**confiado** *adj.* confident, trusting, credulous; presumptuous, self-confident.

**confianza** *f.* confidence, trust; familiarity; informality; **reunión de —** informal gathering or party.

**confianzudo** *adj.* over-friendly, over-familiar; *Am.* meddlesome.

**confiar**[17] *v.* to confide, entrust; to trust, hope firmly.

**confidencia** *f.* confidence, trust; secret, confidential remark; **confidencial** *adj.* confidential.

**confidente** *m.* confidant; spy, secret agent; settee or sofa for two people, love seat; *adj.* faithful, trustworthy.

**confín** *m.* limit, border, boundary; *adj.* bordering, limiting.

**confinar** *v.* to border (upon); to confine, exile to a specific place.

**confirmación** *f.* confirmation.

**confirmar** *v.* to confirm.

**confiscar**[6] *v.* to confiscate.

**confitar** *v.* to candy (*with sugar syrup*); to make into candy or preserves; to sweeten.

**confite** *m.* candy, bonbon; **confitería** *f.* confectionery; candy shop; **confitura** *f.* confection.

**conflicto** *m.* conflict.

**confluencia** *f.* junction (*of two rivers*).

**conformar** *v.* to adapt, adjust; **-se** to conform, comply; to agree; to be resigned (to); to be satisfied.

**conforme** *adj.* in agreement; resigned, satisfied; alike, similar; **— a** in accordance with.

**conformidad** *f.* conformity; agreement, harmony; compliance; **— con la voluntad de Dios** resignation to the will of God; **en — con** in compliance with; **estar de — con** to be in accordance or agreement with.

**confortar** *v.* to comfort, console.

**confraternidad** *f.* brotherhood.

**confrontar** *v.* to confront; to face; to compare, check.

**confundir** *v.* to confound, confuse, mix up; to bewilder; to shame.

**confusión** *f.* confusion.

**confuso** *adj.* confused, bewildered; blurred; vague.

**congelado** *p.p.* & *adj.* frozen; icy.

**congelar** *v.* to congeal, freeze.

**congenial** *adj.* congenial.

**congeniar** *v.* to be congenial (with); to harmonize, be in harmony (with).

**congoja** *f.* anguish, grief, anxiety.

**congratular** *v.* to congratulate.

**congregación** *f.* congregation, assembly; religious fraternity.

**congregar**[7] *v.* to congregate, call together; to assemble; **-se** to congregate, assemble.

**congresista** *m.* congressman; *f.* congresswoman.

**congreso** *m.* congress, assembly; **— de los Diputados** House of Representatives.

**conjetura** *f.* conjecture, guess, surmise.

**conjeturar** *v.* to conjecture, guess, surmise.

**conjugación** *f.* conjugation; coupling, joining together.

**conjugar**[7] *v.* to conjugate.

**conjunción** *f.* conjunction; union, combination.

**conjunto** *m.* total, whole, entirety; **en —** as a whole; *adj.* joined; related, allied.

**conjuración** *f.* conspiracy, plot.

**conjurado** *m.* conspirator.

**conjurar** *v.* to conspire, plot; to join a conspiracy; to entreat; to conjure; to ward off.

**conmemorar** *v.* to commemorate.

**conmemorativo** *adj.* memorial, serving to commemorate.

**conmigo** with me.

**conminación** *f.* threat.

**conminatorio** *adj.* threatening.

**conmoción** *f.* commotion.

**conmovedor** *adj.* moving, touching; stirring.

**conmover**[2] *v. irr.* to move, touch, affect (*with emotion*); to stir (*emotions*).

**conmutador** *m.* electric switch; **cuadro —** switchboard.

**connatural** *adj.* inborn.

**cono** *m.* cone; pine cone.

**conocedor** *adj.* knowing, aware, expert; *m.* connoisseur, judge, expert; **ser — de** to be judge of.

**conocer**[13] *v. irr.* (*tener idea de*) to know, be acquainted with; to recognize; (*llegar a conocer*) to meet; **se conoce que** it is clear or evident that.

**conocido** *p.p.* & *adj.* known; well-known; *m.* acquaintance.

**conocimiento** *m.* (*inteligencia*) knowledge, understanding; acquaintance; (*documento*) bill of lading; **-s** knowledge, learning; **poner en —** to inform.

**conque** *conj.* so then, well then, and so.

**conquista** *f.* conquest.

**conquistador** *m.* conqueror; *adj.* conquering, victorious.

**conquistar** *v.* to conquer, defeat; to win.

**consabido** *adj.* aforementioned, aforesaid.

**consagración** *f.* consecration.

**consagrar** *v.* to consecrate.

**consciencia** *f.* consciousness.

**consciente** *adj.* conscious.

**consecución** *f.* attainment.

**consecuencia** *f.* consequence; result; **a — de** as a result of; **por** (*or* **en**) **—** therefore; consequently.

**consecuente** *adj.* consequent, logical; consistent; *m.* consequence, result.

**consecutivo** *adj.* consecutive, successive.

**conseguir**[5,12] *v. irr.* to get, obtain; to reach, attain.

**conseja** *f.* old wives' tale, fable.

**consejero** *m.* adviser, counselor.

**consejo** *m.* counsel, advice; council; council hall.

**consentimiento** *m.* consent.

**consentir**[3] *v. irr.* to consent, permit; to pamper, spoil.

**conserje** *m.* janitor, caretaker.

**conserva** *f.* preserve; pickled fruit or vegetables; *Ch.* filling (*for tarts or candy*).

**conservación** *f.* conservation.

**conservador** *m.* conservative; preserver; guardian; *adj.* conservative.

**conservar** *v.* to conserve, keep; to preserve.

**considerable** *adj.* considerable.

**consideración** *f.* consideration.

**considerado** *adj.* considerate, thoughtful; respected; prudent.

**considerar** *v.* to consider; to treat with consideration.

**consigna** *f.* watchword, password; *Am.* checkroom.

**consignar** *v.* to consign; to deliver; to deposit; to assign; to check (*baggage*).

**consigo** with oneself; with himself (herself, themselves).

**consiguiente** *adj.* consequent; *m.* consequence; **por —** consequently.

**consistente** *adj.* firm, substantial.

**consistir** *v.* to consist; to be based on; **¿en qué consiste?** why?; what is the explanation for it?

**consocio** *m.* associate, partner.

**consolación** *f.* consolation.

**consolar**[2] *v. irr.* to console, cheer.

**consolidar** *v.* to consolidate, make solid; to unite, combine.

**consonante** *m.* perfect rhyme; *f.* consonant; *adj.* in harmony.

**consorte** *m. & f.* consort; mate; companion.

**conspicuo** *adj.* conspicuous.

**conspiración** *f.* conspiracy, plot.

**conspirador** *m.* conspirator, plotter.

**conspirar** *v.* to conspire, plot.

**constancia** *f.* (*firmeza*) constancy; perseverance; (*certeza*) evidence, certainty; *Am.* documentary proof, record.

**constante** *adj.* constant; continual; firm, faithful.

**constar** *v.* to be evident, clear; to consist (of), be composed (of); to be on record.

**constatación** *f. Am.* proof, check, evidence.

**constelación** *f.* constellation.

**constipado** *adj.* suffering from a cold; *m.* cold in the head.

**constipar** *v.* to stop up (*the nasal passages*); to cause a cold; **-se** to catch cold.

**constitución** *f.* constitution.

**constitucional** *adj.* constitutional.

**constituir**[32] *v. irr.* to constitute, form; to set up, establish; **-se en** to set oneself up as.

**constitutivo** = **constituyente**.

**constituyente** *adj.* constituent.

**constreñir**[5,19] *v. irr.* to constrain; to compel, oblige.

**construcción** *f.* construction; structure; building.

**construir**[32] *v. irr.* to construct, build.

**consuelo** *m.* consolation, comfort; relief; cheer.

**consuetudinario** *adj.* habitual, customary; **derecho —** common law.

**cónsul** *m.* consul.

**consulado** *m.* consulate.

**consulta** *f.* consultation; opinion.

**consultar** *v.* to consult.

**consultorio** *m.* office for consultation; doctor's office or clinic.

**consumado** *p.p. of* **consumar;** *adj.* consummate, perfect, complete; accomplished.

**consumar** *v.* to consummate, complete.

**consumidor** *m.* consumer; *adj.* consuming.

**consumir** *v.* to consume; to waste; **-se** to be consumed; to burn out; to be exhausted; to waste away.

**consumo** *m.* consumption (*of food, provisions, etc.*).

**consunción** *f.* consumption (*illness*).

**contabilidad** *f.* accounting; bookkeeping.

**contacto** *m.* contact.

**contado : al —** in cash; **de —** immediately; **por de —** of course; **contados** *adj.* few, scarce, rare.

**contador** *m.* accountant; purser; cashier; counter; meter (*for water, gas, or electricity*); **— geiger** Geiger counter; Geiger-Müller counter.

**contaduría** *f.* accountant's or auditor's office; box office; cashier's office; accounting.

**contagiar** *v.* to infect; to corrupt; to contaminate.

**contagio** *m.* contagion; infection.

**contagioso** *adj.* contagious; infectious.

**contaminar** *v.* to contaminate, defile; to corrupt.

**contar**[2] *v. irr.* to count; to tell, relate; **— con** to count on, rely on; **a — desde** starting from, beginning with.

**contemplación** *f.* contemplation; gazing; meditation.

**contemplar** *v.* to contemplate, gaze at; to examine; to meditate.

**contemporáneo** *adj.* contemporary.

**contender**[1] *v. irr.* to contend, fight; to compete.

**contener**[45] *v. irr.* to contain; to restrain, check; **-se** to refrain; to restrain oneself.

**contenido** *m.* contents; *adj.* restrained, moderate.

**contentamiento** *m.* contentment, joy.

**contentar** *v.* to give pleasure, make happy; **-se** to be satisfied, pleased; *Am.* to make up, renew friendship.

**contento** *adj.* content, contented, satisfied, glad; *m.* gladness, contentment.

**contera** *f.* metal tip (*of a cane, umbrella, etc.*); tip, end; refrain of a song; **por —** as a finishing touch.

**contertulio** *m.* fellow-member.

**contestación** *f.* answer, reply; argument.

**contestar** *v.* to answer, reply.

**contextura** *f.* texture, composition; structure (*of animal or vegetable tissues*).

**contienda** *f.* fight; dispute; contest.

**contigo** with you (with thee).

**contiguo** *adj.* contiguous, next, neighboring.

**continental** *adj.* continental.

**continente** *m.* continent; countenance; *adj.* continent, moderate, sober.

**contingencia** *f.* contingency, possibility; risk.

**contingente** *adj.* contingent, accidental; *m.* quota; military contingent.

**continuación** *f.* continuation; continuance; **a —** below, as follows.

**continuar**[18] *v.* to continue; to last.

**continuidad** *f.* continuity.

**continuo** *adj.* continuous, connected; continual; steady, constant.

**contonearse** *v.* to strut, swagger; to waddle.

**contoneo** *m.* strut; waddle.

**contorno** *m.* (*circuito*) environs, surrounding country (*usually used in plural*); (*línea*) contour, outline.

**contra** *prep.* against; **el pro y el —** the pro and con; *f.* opposition; *Am.* antidote, remedy; **-s** *Am.* play-off, final game (*to determine the winner*); **llevar a uno la —** to contradict a person, take the opposite view.

**contraalmirante** *m.* rear admiral.

**contrabajo** *m.* bass fiddle, string bass.

**contrabandear** *v.* to smuggle.

**contrabandista** *m.* smuggler.

**contrabando** *m.* contraband; smuggled goods; smuggling.

**contracción** *f.* contraction; *Ch., Peru* diligence, application, devotion.

**contradecir**[27] *v. irr.* to contradict.

**contradicción** *f.* contradiction.

**contradictorio** *adj.* contradictory, contrary, opposing.

**contradicho** *p.p.* of **contradecir**.

**contraer**[46] *v. irr.* to contract; **— matrimonio** to get married; **-se** to shrink; to contract.

**contrafuerte** *m.* buttress; spur (*of a mountain*); **-s** secondary chain of mountains.

**contrahacer**[31] *v. irr.* to counterfeit; to forge; to copy, imitate; to mimic.

**contrahecho** *p.p.* of **contrahacer** & *adj.* counterfeit; forged; deformed.

**contralor** *m.* *Am.* controller or comptroller (*of accounts or expenditures*). See **controlador**.

**contraorden** *f.* countermand; cancellation of an order.

**contrapelo : a —** against the grain.

**contrapesar** *v.* to counterbalance, balance; to offset.

**contrapeso** *m.* counterpoise, counterweight, counterbalance; *Am.* fear, uneasiness.

**contrariar**[17] *v.* to oppose; to contradict; to irritate, vex.

**contrariedad** *f.* opposition; contradiction; bother, irritation; disappointment.

**contrario** *adj.* contrary; opposite; *m.* opponent.

**contrarrestar** *v.* to counteract; to resist, oppose; to strike back (*a ball*).

**contraseña** *f.* password, watchword; mark; check (*for baggage*); **— de salida** theatre check (*to re-enter during the performance*).

**contrastar** *v.* (*contrapesar*) to contrast; to test (*scales, weights, measures, etc.*); to assay (*metals*); (*resistir*) to resist, oppose.

**contraste** *m.* contrast; assay, test; assayer, tester; assayer's office.

**contrata** *f.* contract, bargain, agreement.

**contratar** *v.* to contract for; to trade; to engage, hire (*men*); **-se** to come to, or make, an agreement.

**contratiempo** *m.* accident, mishap.

**contratista** *m.* & *f.* contractor.

**contrato** *m.* contract.

**contraventana** *f.* shutter.

**contribución** *f.* contribution; tax.

**contribuir**[32] *v. irr.* to contribute.

**contribuyente** *m.* contributor; taxpayer; *adj.* contributing.

**control** *m.* *Am.* control.

**controlador** *m.* *Am.* controller.

**controlar** *v.* *Am.* to control.

**controversia** *f.* controversy.

**contumacia** *f.* stubbornness, obstinacy; contempt of court, failure to appear in court; rebelliousness.

**contumaz** *adj.* stubborn; rebellious.

**contusión** *f.* bruise.

**convalecer**[13] *v. irr.* to convalesce, recover from an illness.

**convecino** *adj.* near, neighboring; *m.* neighbor.

**convencedor** *adj.* convincing.

**convencer**[10] *v.* to convince.

**convencimiento** *m.* conviction, belief; convincing.

**convención** *f.* convention, assembly; pact, agreement; *Ríopl., Col., Ven., Mex., Carib.* political convention; **convencional** *adj.* conventional.

**convenido** *adj.* agreed; O.K., all right; *p.p.* of **convenir**.

**conveniencia** *f.* convenience; comfort; utility, profit.

**conveniente** *adj.* convenient, useful, profitable; fit, proper, suitable; opportune.

**convenio** *m.* pact, agreement.

**convenir**[48] *v. irr.* to agree; to convene, assemble; to be suitable, proper, advisable; to suit, fit; **-se** to agree.

**conventillo** *m.* *Ríopl., Ch.* tenement house.

**convento** *m.* convent.

**convergente** *adj.* convergent, coming together.

**converger**,[11] **convergir**[11] *v.* to converge.

**conversación** *f.* conversation.

**conversar** *v.* to converse.

**conversión** *f.* conversion.

**convertir**[3] *v. irr.* to convert.

**convicción** *f.* conviction.

**convicto** *p.p. irr.* of **convencer;** convicted, guilty.

**convidado** *m.* guest; *Am.* **— y con ollita** guest who abuses hospitality.

**convidar** *v.* to invite; **-se** to volunteer one's services; to invite oneself.

**convincente** *adj.* convincing.

**convite** *m.* invitation; banquet.

**convocación** *f.* convocation.
**convocar**[6] *v.* to convoke, call together.
**convoyar** *v.* to convoy, escort.
**convulsión** *f.* convulsion.
**convulsivo** *adj.* convulsive; **tos convulsiva** whooping cough.
**conyugal** *adj.* conjugal, pertaining to marriage or a married couple; **vida —** married life.
**cónyuge** *m.* husband; *f.* wife.
**cooperación** *f.* cooperation.
**cooperador** *adj.* cooperating, cooperative; *m.* cooperator, co-worker.
**cooperar** *v.* to cooperate.
**cooperativo** *adj.* cooperative; **cooperativa** *f.* cooperative, cooperative society.
**coordinación** *f.* coordination.
**coordinar** *v.* to coordinate.
**copa** *f.* (*vaso*) goblet; (*de árbol*) treetop; (*de sombrero*) crown; (*palo de la baraja*) card in the suit of copas (*Spanish deck of cards*); *Am.* **empinar la —** to drink, get drunk.
**copartícipe** *adj.* participant; *m.* & *f.* joint partner.
**copete** *m.* tuft; crest; top, summit; ornamental top on furniture; **de —** of high rank, important; proud; **estar uno hasta el —** to be stuffed; to be fed up; **tener mucho —** to be arrogant, haughty.
**copia** *f.* copy; imitation; abundance.
**copiar** *v.* to copy.
**copioso** *adj.* copious, abundant.
**copita** *f.* little glass; little drink.
**copla** *f.* couplet; stanza (*of variable length and meter*); popular song.
**copo** *m.* (*de nieve*) snowflake; (*mechón*) wad, tuft (*of wool or cotton*).
**coqueta** *f.* coquette, flirt.
**coquetear** *v.* to flirt.
**coquetería** *f.* coquetry, flirting.
**coraje** *m.* courage, valor; anger.
**coral** *m.* coral; *Am.* red poisonous snake; **-es** coral beads; *adj.* choral, pertaining to a choir; **coralino** *adj.* coral, like coral.
**coraza** *f.* cuirass, armor; armor plate or plating; shell (*of a turtle*).
**corazón** *m.* heart; core, center.
**corazonada** *f.* presentiment, foreboding; hunch.
**corbata** *f.* necktie; cravat; *Am.* colorful kerchief, scarf.
**corcel** *m.* charger, steed.
**corcova** *f.* hump, hunch; **corcovado** *adj.* hunchbacked; *m.* hunchback.
**corcovear** *v.* to prance about, leap; *Am.* to kick, protest against.
**corchete** *m.* hook and eye.
**corcho** *m.* cork; beehive; *adj. Am.* corklike, spongy.
**cordel** *m.* cord, rope.
**cordero** *m.* lamb; lambskin.
**cordial** *adj.* cordial, friendly; **dedo —** middle finger.
**cordialidad** *f.* cordiality, friendliness, warmth.
**cordillera** *f.* mountain range.
**cordobés** *adj.* Cordovan, of or pertaining to Cordova; *m.* native of Cordova.
**cordón** *m.* cord; braid; cordon, line of soldiers; *Ríopl.* **— de la acera** curb, curbstone of the sidewalk; **cordonería** *f.* lace or cord maker's shop; collection of cords and laces; cordmaker's work; braiding.
**cordoncillo** *m.* small cord, drawstring, lace, lacing; braid; mill (*ridged edge of a coin*); ridge, rib (*of certain fabrics*).
**cordura** *f.* good judgment, wisdom; sanity.
**cornada** *f.* goring; butt with the horns; **dar -s** to gore, horn, butt with the horns.
**corneta** *f.* cornet; bugle; horn; *m.* bugler.
**cornisa** *f.* cornice.
**coro** *m.* choir; chorus.
**corona** *f.* crown; wreath.
**coronar** *v.* to crown; to top.
**coronel** *m.* colonel.
**coronilla** *f.* small crown; crown of the head; **estar uno hasta la —** to be fed up, be satiated.
**corpanchón** *m.* large body; carcass.
**corpiño** *m.* bodice.
**corporación** *f.* corporation.
**corporal** *adj.* corporal, of the body; *m.* corporal (*small piece of linen used at Mass*).
**corpóreo** *adj.* corporeal, bodily; tangible, material.
**corpulento** *adj.* corpulent, fat, stout.
**corral** *m.* yard; corral, cattle yard; **corralón** *m.* large corral; *Am.* lumber warehouse.
**correa** *f.* leather strap; resistance; *Ch.* **-s** leather blanket carrier; *Am.* **tener muchas -s** to be phlegmatic, calm.
**corrección** *f.* correction; correctness.
**correcto** *adj.* correct, proper.
**corredizo** *adj.* sliding, slipping; **nudo —** slip knot.
**corredor** *m.* (*que corre*) runner, racer; (*pasillo*) corridor; gallery around a patio; (*revendedor*) broker; *Carib., Andes* covered porch; *Am.* beater of wild game; *adj.* running; speedy.
**corregidor** *m.* corrector; Spanish magistrate.
**corregir**[5,11] *v. irr.* to correct; to reprove; to punish; **-se** to mend one's ways.
**correligionario** *adj.* of the same religion; of the same political party or sympathies; *m.* coreligionist.
**correntada** *f. Ch., Ríopl., C.A., Carib.* strong river current.
**correo** *m.* mail; mail service; postman; post office; **— aéreo** air mail.
**correón** *m.* large strap.
**correoso** *adj.* flexible; leathery, tough; **correosidad** *f.* toughness; flexibility.
**correr** *v.* (*caminar*) to run; to blow (*said of the wind*); (*encarrera*) to race; to chase; (*pasar*) to pass, elapse (*time*); to draw (*a curtain*); *Am.* to dismiss, throw out; **-se** to slip through; to slide; to be embarrassed.

**correría** f. foray, raid for plunder; excursion, short trip; **-s** wanderings, travels; raids.

**correspondencia** f. correspondence; letters, mail; agreement; interchange.

**corresponder** v. to reciprocate, return (*love, favors*); to belong; to concern; to correspond (*one thing with another*).

**correspondiente** adj. corresponding, agreeing; respective; m. correspondent.

**corresponsal** m. correspondent; agent; newspaper reporter.

**corretear** v. to run around; to roam, rove; *Am.* to pursue, chase.

**corrida** f. race; *Ch.* row, file; *P.R.* night spree; *Am.* beating up of game; **— del tiempo** swiftness of time; **— de toros** bullfight; **de —** without stopping.

**corrido** adj. embarrassed, ashamed; worldly-wise; flowing, fluent; **de —** without stopping; m. *Mex., Col., Ven., Ríopl., Andes* popular ballad.

**corriente** adj. (*que corre*) running; flowing, fluent; (*común*) usual, common, ordinary; *Am.* frank, open; ¡ **—** ! all right! O.K.!; **el ocho del —** the eighth of the current month; **estar al —** to be up-to-date; to be well-informed (*about current news*); **poner a uno al —** to keep someone posted or well informed; f. current; flow; course; *Am.* **hay que llevarle la —** one must humor him.

**corrillo** m. circle or group of gossipers.

**corro** m. group of talkers or spectators.

**corroer**[51] v. irr. to corrode.

**corromper** v. to corrupt; to seduce; to bribe; **-se** to rot; to become corrupted.

**corrompido** adj. corrupt, rotten, spoiled; degenerate; p.p. of **corromper.**

**corrupción** f. corruption.

**corrupto** adj. corrupt, rotten.

**corsé** m. corset.

**cortada** f. *Col., Ven., Carib.* cut, slash.

**cortador** m. cutter.

**cortadura** m. cut; gash; slash.

**cortante** adj. cutting; sharp.

**cortaplumas** m. penknife.

**cortar** v. to cut; to cut off; to cut out; to cut down; to interrupt; *Ven.* to harvest, pick (*fruit*); to gossip, speak ill of someone; **-se** to be embarrassed, ashamed; to sour, curdle (*said of milk*); *Am.* to become separated, cut off; *Mex., Cuba* to leave in a hurry; *Am.* to die.

**corte** m. cut; cutting; cutting edge; fit, style; *Carib., Mex., Ríopl.* cut (*in cards*); *Am.* harvest; *Am.* weeding; *Am.* gracefulness in dancing; f. royal court; retinue; *P.R., Ven.* court of justice; **-s** Spanish parliament; **hacer la —** to court, woo; *Am.* **darse uno — to** put on airs.

**cortedad** f. smallness; timidity; bashfulness, shyness.

**cortejar** v. to court, woo.

**cortejo** m. cortege, procession; retinue; courtship; suitor.

**cortés** adj. courteous, polite.

**cortesana** f. courtesan, prostitute.

**cortesano** m. courtier; adj. courtlike; courteous.

**cortesía** f. courtesy, politeness.

**corteza** f. bark; crust; peel.

**cortijo** m. farmhouse.

**cortina** f. curtain.

**corto** adj. short; scanty; bashful.

**corveta** f. buck, leap, bound (*of a horse*); **hacer -s** to prance.

**corvo** adj. *see* **curvo.**

**cosa** f. thing; **— de** approximately, about; **no es —** it is not worth anything; **otra —** something else; **como si tal —** serene, as if nothing had happened; *Am.* **ni por una de estas nueve -s** absolutely not, not for anything in the world.

**cosecha** f. crop; harvest.

**cosechar** v. to reap; to harvest.

**coser** v. to sew; to stitch.

**cosmético** m. & adj. cosmetic.

**cosquillas** f. pl. ticklishness; tickling; **hacer —** to tickle; to excite (*one's desire or curiosity*); **tener —** to be ticklish.

**cosquillear** v. to tickle; to excite (*one's curiosity or desire*).

**cosquilleo** m. tickle, tickling sensation.

**cosquilloso** adj. ticklish; touchy.

**costa** f. coast; cost, expense, price; **a toda —** at all costs, by all means.

**costado** m. side; flank.

**costal** m. sack; **estar hecho un — de huesos** to be nothing but skin and bones; to be very thin.

**costanero** adj. coastal, relating to a coast; sloping.

**costar**[2] v. irr. to cost; **— trabajo** to be difficult.

**costarricense** adj., m. & f. Costa Rican.

**coste, costo** m. cost; expense.

**costear** v. (*pagar*) to defray or pay costs; to pay, be profitable; (*pasar junto a*) to navigate along the coast; to go along the edge of; **no costea** it does not pay.

**costero** adj. coastal; **navegación costera** coastal navigation.

**costilla** f. rib; chop, cutlet.

**costoso** adj. costly, expensive.

**costra** f. crust; scab.

**costroso** adj. crusty, scabby.

**costumbre** f. custom, habit.

**costura** f. sewing; stitching; seam.

**costurera** f. seamstress.

**costurero** m. sewing table or cabinet; sewing box; sewing room.

**costurón** m. coarse stitching; large seam; patch, mend; big scar.

**cotejar** v. to confront, compare.

**cotejo** m. comparison.

**cotense** m. *Ch., Mex.* burlap.

**cotidiano** adj. daily.

**cotizable** adj. quotable (*price*).

**cotización** f. quotation of prices; current price.

**cotizar**[9] v. to quote (*prices*); *Ch.* to

**contribute** one's share or quota; *Am.* to prorate, distribute proportionally.

**coto** *m.* enclosure; landmark; limitation; limit, boundary; **poner — a** to set a limit to; to put an end to.

**cotorra** *f.* small parrot; magpie; talkative person, chatterbox.

**cotorrear** *v.* to chatter; to gossip.

**covacha** *f.* small cave; grotto; *Mex., Cuba, Andes* hut, shanty; *Col.* cubbyhole, small dark room.

**coyote** *m. Am.* coyote, prairie wolf; *Mex.* shyster, tricky, lawyer; *C.A.* agent, broker (*often illegal*).

**coyuntura** *f.* joint; articulation; occasion; precise moment.

**coz** *f.* kick; recoil of a gun; butt of a firearm; **dar** (*or* **tirar**) **coces** to kick.

**cráneo** *m.* cranium, skull.

**craso** *adj.* fat; thick, coarse, gross; **ignorancia crasa** gross ignorance.

**cráter** *m.* crater of a volcano.

**creación** *f.* creation.

**creador** *m.* creator; *adj.* creating, creative.

**crear** *v.* to create.

**crecer**[13] *v. irr.* to grow; to increase; **-se** to swell (*as a river*); to become or feel important.

**crecida** *f.* river flood.

**crecido** *adj.* grown, increased; large; swollen.

**creciente** *adj.* growing, increasing; crescent (*moon*); *f.* river flood; *m.* crescent.

**crecimiento** *m.* growth, increase.

**credenciales** *f. pl.* credentials.

**crédito** *m.* credit; credence, belief; fame, reputation; letter of credit; **dar a —** tó loan on credit.

**credo** *m.* creed; **en un —** in a jiffy, in a minute.

**crédulo** *adj.* credulous, too ready to believe.

**creencia** *f.* belief, faith.

**creer**[14] *v.* to believe; to think, suppose; **¡ya lo creo!** I should say so!; yes, of course!

**creíble** *adj.* credible, believable.

**crema** *f.* cream; custard; cold cream.

**crepitar** *v.* to crackle, snap; to creak; to rattle.

**crepuscular** *adj.* twilight.

**crepúsculo** *m.* twilight.

**crespo** *adj.* curly; artificial (*style*); angry; crisp.

**crespón** *m.* crepe.

**cresta** *f.* crest; top, summit; tuft, comb (*of a bird*).

**cretona** *f.* cretonne.

**creyente** *m. & f.* believer; *adj.* believing.

**creyón** *m. Am.* crayon.

**cría** *f.* brood; suckling; breeding.

**criadero** *m.* tree nursery; breeding place; hotbed; rich mine.

**criado** *m.* servant; *adj.* bred; **mal —** ill-bred; **criada** *f.* maid, servant.

**criador** *m.* breeder, raiser, rearer; creator; *adj.* creating, creative; breeding; nourishing.

**crianza** *f.* breeding; nursing; manners.

**criar**[17] *v.* to breed; to bring up, rear, educate; to nurse.

**criatura** *f.* creature; baby, child.

**criba** *f.* sieve.

**cribar** *v.* to sift.

**crimen** *m.* crime.

**criminal** *adj., m. & f.* criminal.

**crin** *f.* mane.

**crinudo** *adj. Am.* with a long or thick mane.

**criollo** *m. Am.* Creole; native of America (*especially Spanish America*); *adj. Am.* national, domestic (*not foreign to Spanish America*).

**crisantema** *f.*, **crisantemo** *m.* chrysanthemum.

**crisis** *f.* crisis.

**crisol** *m.* crucible, melting pot; hearth of a blast furnace.

**crispar** *v.* to contract (*muscles*); to clench (*fists*); to put (*nerves*) on edge.

**cristal** *m.* crystal; glass; mirror; lens.

**cristalería** *f.* glassware shop or factory; glassware.

**cristalino** *adj.* crystalline, transparent, clear; *m.* lens of the eye.

**cristalizar**[9] *v.* to crystallize.

**cristiandad** *f.* Christianity; Christendom.

**cristianismo** *m.* Christianity.

**cristiano** *m.* Christian; person; **hablar en —** to speak clearly; *adj.* Christian.

**criterio** *m.* criterion, rule, standard; judgment.

**crítica** *f.* criticism; censure; gossip.

**criticador** *adj.* critical; *m.* critic, faultfinder.

**criticar**[6] *v.* to criticize; to censure; to find fault with.

**crítico** *adj.* critical; *m.* critic, judge; *Am.* faultfinder, slanderer; **criticón** *m.* critic, knocker, faultfinder; *adj.* critical, over-critical, faultfinding.

**croar** *v.* to croak.

**cromo** *m.* chromium.

**cromosoma** *m.* chromosome.

**crónica** *f.* chronicle, history; **cronista** *m. & f.* chronicler.

**crónico** *adj.* chronic.

**cronómetro** *m.* chronometer, timepiece.

**croquis** *m.* rough sketch.

**cruce** *m.* crossing; crossroads; crossbreeding.

**crucero** *m.* (*cruciforme*) crossing; crossbearer; crossroads; transept (*of a church*); crossbeam; cross (*a constellation*); (*buque*) cruiser.

**cruceta** *f.* crosspiece; crosstree; universal joint (*automobile*).

**crucificar**[6] *v.* to crucify.

**crucifijo** *m.* crucifix.

**crucigrama** *m.* crossword puzzle.

**crudo** *adj.* raw; uncooked; unripe; harsh; **agua cruda** hard water; **petróleo —** crude oil; *Mex.* **estar —** to have a hang-over; **cruda** *f. Mex.* hang-over.

**cruel** *adj.* cruel.

**crueldad** *f.* cruelty.

**crujido** *m.* creak, crack, creaking; rustle.

**crujir** *v.* to creak, crackle; to grate (*one's teeth*); to rustle; to crunch.

**cruz** *f.* cross.

**cruzada** *f.* crusade; holy war; campaign.

**cruzado** *m.* crusader; *adj.* crossed; cross, crosswise, transverse.

**cruzamiento** *m.* crossing; crossroads.

**cruzar**[9] *v.* to cross; *Am.* to fight, dispute; **-se con** to meet.

**cuaco** *m. Mex.* horse; *Am.* cassava flour.

**cuaderno** *m.* notebook; memorandum book; booklet; *Mex., Ven.* pamphlet.

**cuadra** *f.* hall, large room; stable; hospital or prison ward; *Am.* city block; *Am.* reception room.

**cuadrado** *adj.* square; *m.* square; square ruler; die, metal block or plate.

**cuadrante** *m.* dial, face of a clock or watch; sundial; quadrant (*fourth part of circle; instrument used in astronomy*).

**cuadrar** *v.* (*cuadriforme*) to square; to form into a square; (*agradar*) to please; to conform; to harmonize; to set well; *Am.* to be becoming (*said of clothes*); *Am.* to be ready; *Am.* to contribute a large sum; *Am.* to come out well, succeed; **-se** to stand at attention.

**cuadricular** *v.* to square off, divide into squares.

**cuadrilla** *f.* group, troupe, gang; armed band; quadrille, square dance.

**cuadro** *m.* square; picture; scene; frame; flower bed; *Am.* blackboard; *Ch.* slaughterhouse.

**cuajada** *f.* curd.

**cuajado** *p.p.* & *adj.* coagulated, curdled; filled, covered; **— de** full or covered with (*flowers, dew, etc.*).

**cuajar** *v.* to coagulate, thicken, curd, curdle; to turn out well; to jell; to please; *Am.* to chatter, prattle; **-se** to coagulate, curd; to become crowded, be filled; **la cosa no cuajó** the thing did not work, did not jell.

**cuajarón** *m.* clot.

**cual** *rel. pron.* which; **cada —** each one; **— más, — menos** some people more, others less; **el —, la —, los -es, las -es** which; who; **lo —** which; *adv.* as, like; **¿cuál?** *interr. pron.* which one? what?

**cualidad** *f.* quality; trait.

**cualquier(a)** *indef. adj.* & *pron.* any, anyone; whichever; **un hombre cualquiera** any man whatever.

**cuando** *rel. adv.* & *conj.* when; **aun —** even though; **¿cuándo?** *interr. adv.* when?

**cuantía** *f.* quantity; rank, importance.

**cuantioso** *adj.* plentiful, abundant; numerous.

**cuanto** *rel. adj.* & *pron.* as much as, as many as; all that; **— antes** as soon as possible, immediately; **en —** *conj.* as soon as; **en — a** as for, with regard to; **unos -s** a few; **¿cuánto?** *interr. adj.* & *pron.* how much?; **¿cuántos?** how many?

**cuaquerismo** *m.* the Quaker sect, or doctrine.

**cuáquero** *m.* Quaker.

**cuarentena** *f.* quarantine; forty units of anything; period of forty days, months, or years.

**cuarentón** *m.* man in his forties; **cuarentona** *f.* woman in her forties.

**cuaresma** *f.* Lent.

**cuarta** *f.* fourth, fourth part; span of a hand; *Am.* horse whip; *P.R.* **echar — to beat, flog.**

**cuartear** *v.* to quarter, divide into quarters; *P.R.* to whip; **-se** to crack, split (*said of walls or ceilings*); *Mex.* to back down, go back on one's word.

**cuartel** *m.* quarter, one fourth; quarters, barracks; district; quarter, mercy; **no dar —** to give no quarter.

**cuartelada** *f.* military coup d'état, uprising, insurrection.

**cuartelazo** *m. Am.* military coup d'état, insurrection.

**cuarterón** *m.* quarter, fourth part; fourth of a pound; panel (*of a door or window*); *adj.* & *m.* quarter-breed (*one fourth Indian and three fourths Spanish*); quadroon (*person of quarter negro blood*).

**cuarteto** *m.* quartet; quatrain (*stanza of four lines*).

**cuartilla** *f.* (*hoja*) sheet of paper; (*medida*) about 4 quarts; about 1½ pecks; fourth of an **arroba** (about 6 pounds); *Am.* three cents' worth; *Am.* **no valer uno —** not to be worth a penny.

**cuartillo** *m.* fourth of a peck; about a pint; fourth of a **real.**

**cuarto** *m.* room; quarter, one fourth; **tener -s** to have money; *adj.* fourth.

**cuarzo** *m.* quartz.

**cuate** *adj.*, *m.* & *f. Mex.* twin; pal, buddy.

**cuatrero** *m.* horse thief, cattle thief; *Am.* Indian who speaks "broken" Spanish.

**cuba** *f.* cask, barrel; tub, vat; bigbellied person; drunkard.

**cubano** *adj.* & *m.* Cuban.

**cubeta** *f.* small barrel or keg; bucket, pail.

**cúbico** *adj.* cubic.

**cubierta** *f.* cover; covering; envelope; deck (*of a ship*); *Am.* sheath.

**cubierto** *p.p.* of **cubrir;** *m.* cover; place setting for one person at a table.

**cubo** *m.* cube; bucket, pail; hub of a wheel; mill pond; *Am.* finger bowl.

**cubremesa** *f.* table cover.

**cubrir**[52] *v.* to cover; to hide; to coat; to settle, pay (*a bill*); **-se** to cover oneself; to put on one's hat.

**cucaracha** *f.* cockroach.

**cuclillas : en —** in a squatting position; **sentarse en —** to squat.

**cuclillo** *m.* cuckoo.

**cuco** *adj.* dainty, cute; sly, shrewd; *m.* cuckoo; a kind of caterpillar; card game; *Ríopl.* peach, peach tree; *Am.* **hacer — a** to make fun of; to fool.

**cucurucho** *m.* paper cone; *Am.* peak, summit; *Peru, C.A., Mex.* cowl, cloak with a hood (*worn by penitents in Holy Week processions*).

**cuchara** *f.* spoon; scoop; *Am.* mason's trowel; **media —** mediocre person; *Am.* mason's helper; *Am.* **hacer —** to pout; *Am.* **meter uno su —** to butt into a conversation; to meddle; **cucharada** *f.* spoonful; scoop; **cucharón** *m.* large spoon; ladle; dipper; scoop.

**cuchichear** *v.* to whisper.

**cuchicheo** *m.* whispering, whisper.

**cuchilla** *f.* large knife, cleaver; blade (*of any cutting instrument*); *Peru* penknife; *Ríopl., Mex., P.R.* mountain ridge; *Am.* gore (*in a garment*); *Am.* narrow tract of land.

**cuchillada** *f.* thrust with a knife, stab, slash; cut, gash.

**cuchillo** *m.* knife; gore (*in a garment*); **— de monte** hunting knife; **cuchillería** *f.* cutlery; cutlery shop.

**cueca** *f. Am.* a Chilean dance.

**cuello** *m.* neck; collar.

**cuenca** *f.* river basin; narrow valley; wooden bowl; socket of the eye.

**cuenco** *m.* earthen bowl.

**cuenta** *f.* (*cálculo*) count, calculation; bill; account; (*bolita*) bead (*of a rosary or necklace*); **a fin de -s** in the final analysis; **caer en la —** to see, get the point; **darse —** to realize; *Col.* **de toda —** anyway; **eso corre de mi —** that is my responsibility; I'll take charge of that; **eso no me tiene —** that does not pay me; it is of no profit to me; **en resumidas -s** in short; *P.R.* **hacerle — una cosa a uno** to be useful or profitable for one; **tomar en —** to take into account; **tomar una cosa por su —** to take charge of something, take the responsibility for it; **vamos a -s** let's understand or settle this.

**cuentagotas** *m.* dropper (*for counting drops*).

**cuento** *m.* story, tale; **— de nunca acabar** never-ending tale; **déjese de -s** come to the point; **no viene a —** it is not opportune or to the point.

**cuerda** *f.* cord, string, rope; chord; watch spring; **dar — a** to wind (*a watch*).

**cuerdo** *adj.* sane; wise.

**cuereada** *f. Mex., C.A., Col., Ven.* flogging, whipping; *Am.* skinning of an animal.

**cuerear** *v. Am.* to flog, whip; *Am.* to harm, dishonor; *Am.* to beat (*in a game*); *Am.* to skin (*an animal*).

**cuerno** *m.* horn; antenna, feeler; **poner -s a** to be unfaithful to, deceive (*a husband*); *Am.* **mandar al —** to send to the devil.

**cuero** *m.* hide, skin; leather; wineskin; *Col., Ven.* whip; **en -s** naked.

**cuerpeada** *f. Ríopl.* dodge; evasion.

**cuerpo** *m.* body; bulk; corps; **en —** without hat or coat; **luchar — a —**

to fight in single combat; *Am.* **sacar el —** to dodge; to escape, avoid doing something.

**cuervo** *m.* crow; raven; *Ven.* buzzard; *Am.* dishonest priest; *Ríopl., Ch.* **hacer uno la del —** to leave abruptly and not return.

**cuesta** *f.* hill, slope; **a -s** on one's shoulders or back; in one's care; **— abajo** downhill; **— arriba** uphill.

**cuestión** *f.* question; controversy, dispute; problem, matter.

**cuestionario** *m.* questionnaire, list of questions.

**cueva** *f.* cave, cavern; cellar.

**cuico** *m. Mex.* cop, policeman; *Am.* gossiper, tattletale, "squealer"; *Ch., Bol., Peru* half-breed; *Ríopl.* short, chubby person.

**cuidado** *m.* care, attention; worry, misgiving; **al — de** in care of; **tener —** to be careful; **¡ —!** look out!; be careful! **¡cuidadito!** be very careful!

**cuidadoso** *adj.* careful; attentive; anxious.

**cuidar** *v.* to take care of, look after, keep; to make or do carefully.

**cuita** *f.* grief, care, anxiety; misfortune; *C.A.* bird dung.

**cuitado** *adj.* unfortunate; timid, shy.

**culata** *f.* haunch, buttock; rear; butt (*of a firearm*).

**culatazo** *f.* blow with the butt of a rifle; recoil, kick of a firearm.

**culebra** *f.* snake; coil; *Mex.* money belt.

**culebrear** *v.* to zigzag; to twist, wriggle.

**culminación** *f.* culmination, climax.

**culminar** *v.* to culminate; to come to a climax.

**culpa** *f.* fault; guilt; blame; **echar la — a** to blame; **tener la —** to be to blame.

**culpabilidad** *f.* guilt; **culpable** *adj.* guilty.

**culpar** *v.* to blame; to declare guilty.

**cultivación** *f.* cultivation.

**cultivador** *m.* cultivator; **máquina cultivadora** cultivator.

**cultivar** *v.* to cultivate.

**cultivo** *m.* cultivation, culture.

**culto** *adj.* cultured; *m.* cult, worship; religious sect; **rendir — a** to pay homage to; to worship.

**cultura** *f.* culture; cultivation.

**cumbre** *f.* summit; top.

**cumpleaños** *m.* birthday.

**cumplido** *adj.* (*completo*) complete, full; perfect; (*cortés*) courteous; *p.p.* fulfilled; due, fallen due; **tiene tres años -s** he is just over three years old; *m.* courtesy, attention; compliment.

**cumplimentar** *v.* to compliment; to congratulate; to pay a courtesy visit.

**cumplimiento** *m.* fulfilment; courtesy; completion; compliment; **de —** formal, ceremonious.

**cumplir** *v.* to fulfill; to comply; to carry out; to fall due; **— años** to have a birthday; to be (*so many*) years old.

**cúmulo** *m.* pile, heap; accumulation; cumulus (*mass of clouds*).

**cuna** f. cradle; origin; Am. coffin for the poor; Am. dive, den (for gambling and dancing).

**cundir** v. to spread (as news, disease, liquids); to propagate, extend, multiply.

**cuña** f. wedge; splinter; Ch., Ríopl. influential person.

**cuñado** m. brother-in-law; **cuñada** f. sister-in-law.

**cuota** f. quota; dues, fee; — de entrada admission fee.

**cuotidiano** adj. everyday, daily.

**cupé** m. coupé.

**cupón** m. coupon.

**cúpula** f. dome.

**cura** f. cure; m. curate, priest.

**curación** f. cure.

**curandero** m. healer (not a doctor); quack; medicine man (among Indians).

**curar** v. to cure, heal; to treat; to cure (meats, tobacco); to tan (skins); Am. to load (dice), fix (cards); — de to take care of; -se to cure oneself; to get well; Ríopl. to get drunk.

**curiosear** v. to snoop, peek, peer, pry; to observe with curiosity.

**curiosidad** f. curiosity; neatness, daintiness.

**curioso** adj. curious; neat, dainty; **libros raros y -s** rare books.

**curro** adj. showy, gaudy, flashy; m. dandy.

**currutaco** m. fop, dandy; adj. affected (in one's dress).

**cursi** adj. common, in bad taste; cheap, ridiculous; **cursilería** f. bad taste, cheapness, false elegance; group of cheap, ridiculous people.

**curso** m. course, direction; scholastic year; course of study.

**curtidor** m. tanner.

**curtiduría** f. tannery.

**curtir** v. to tan; to harden, accustom to hardships; Col., Ven. to dirty, soil; -se to get tanned or sunburned; to become accustomed to hardships.

**curva** f. curve.

**curvo** adj. curved; bent, crooked; arched.

**cúspide** f. summit, peak, top; spire, steeple.

**custodia** f. custody; guard, guardian; monstrance (vessel in which the consecrated Host is exposed).

**custodiar** v. to guard, watch; to keep in custody.

**custodio** m. guardian, keeper.

**cutícula** f. cuticle.

**cutis** m. skin; complexion.

**cuyo** rel. poss. adj. whose, of whom, of which.

## CH

**chabacano** adj. crude, unpolished; inartistic; cheap, in bad taste; m. Mex. a variety of apricot.

**chacota** f. fun; jest; **echar a —** to take as a joke; **hacer — de** to make fun of.

**chacotear** v. to frolic, joke, make merry; to be boisterous; to show off.

**chacra** f. Ec., Peru, Ch. small farm; Col., Ec. cultivated field.

**chagra** f. Col., Ec. farm, piece of farm land; m. & f. Ec. peasant; adj. uncivilized, unrefined.

**chal** m. shawl.

**chalán** m. horse trader; Am. broncobuster, horse breaker.

**chaleco** m. waistcoat, vest.

**chalupa** f. sloop, sailboat; launch; Mex., Col., Ven., Ríopl. canoe; P.R. raft; Mex. Mexican tortilla with sauce.

**chamaco** m. Mex., C.A. boy; **chamaquito** m. Mex., C.A. little boy.

**chamarra** f. coarse wool jacket or sweater; Mex. sheepskin jacket, leather jacket; Am. heavy wool blanket.

**chamarreta** f. short loose jacket; Am. square poncho.

**chambergo** m. gaucho sombrero.

**chambón** adj. clumsy, awkward, unskillful; m. bungler, clumsy performer, awkward workman; clumsy player.

**champaña** f. champagne.

**champú** m. shampoo.

**champurrado** m. Mex. a mixed drink of chocolate and **atole;** Col. a mixed alcoholic beverage.

**champurrar,** Am. **champurrear** v. to mix (drinks).

**chamuscada, chamuscadura** f. Am. singe, scorch.

**chamuscar**[6] v. to scorch; to singe; to sear; Am. to sell at a low cost; -se to get scorched, singed, or seared; Am. to get peeved, offended.

**chamusquina** f. singe, scorch.

**chancear** v. to fool, joke, jest.

**chancero** m. jester, joker; adj. jolly.

**chancla** f. slipper; old shoe; **chancleta** f. slipper; m. Am. good-for-nothing.

**chanclo** m. galosh, overshoe; clog; rubber overshoe; -s rubbers.

**chancho** m. S.A. pig, pork.

**changador** m. Ríopl. carrier, porter; Am. handy man, person who does odd jobs.

**chango** m. Mex. monkey; **ponerse —** to be alert, wary.

**chantaje** m. blackmail, blackmailing.

**chanza** f. joke, jest.

**chapa** f. metal plate; veneer (thin leaf of wood); rosy spot on the cheeks; Mex., C.A., Andes lock; Am. Indian spy; -s game of tossing coins; **hombre de —** serious, reliable man.

**chapado** adj. veneered (covered with a thin layer of wood or other material); — a la antigua old-fashioned.

**chapalear = chapotear.**

**chaparro** m. scrub oak; short, chubby person; Am. a kind of tropical shrub with rough leaves; Am. short whip; adj. Mex., C.A. short, squatty.

**chaparrón** m. downpour, heavy shower.

**chapitel** *m.* spire, steeple; capital (*of a column*).

**chapotear** *v.* to splash, paddle in the water.

**chapoteo** *m.* splash.

**chapucear** *v.* to fumble; to botch, bungle, do or make clumsily; *Am.* to deceive, trick.

**chapulín** *m. Mex., C.A.* grasshopper.

**chapurrar** *v.* to speak (*a language*) brokenly; to mix (*drinks*).

**chapuz** *m.* dive, duck, ducking.

**chapuza** *f.* botch, clumsy piece of work; *Am.* foul trick, fraud.

**chapuzar**⁹ *v.* to duck; to dive.

**chaqueta** *f.* jacket; **chaquetón** *m.* long jacket, coat.

**charamusca** *f. Mex.* twisted candy stick or cane; *Col., Ven.* brushwood, firewood; *C.A.* hubbub, uproar.

**charamusquero** *m. Am.* candy-stick maker or vendor.

**charca** *f.* pond.

**charco** *m.* puddle, pool; **pasar el —** to cross the pond, cross the ocean.

**charla** *f.* chat, chatter, prattle.

**charladuría** *f.* chatter, gossip.

**charlar** *v.* to chat, chatter, prate.

**charlatán** *m.* chatterer, prater; gossiper; charlatan, quack.

**charol** *m.* varnish; patent leather; *Col.* tray; **charola** *f. Mex.* tray.

**charolar** *v.* to varnish, polish.

**charqui** *m.* jerky, jerked beef.

**charro** *m. Spain* a villager of Salamanca province; *Mex.* Mexican horseman of special costume and cultural status.

**charrúa** *m. & f. Am.* Charruan Indian (*Indian of Uruguay*).

**chascarrillo** *m.* joke, funny story.

**chasco** *m.* joke, prank; surprise; disillusionment, disappointment; **llevarse —** to be disappointed, surprised or fooled; *adj. Am.* thick, curly (*hair*); *Am.* ruffled (*plumage*).

**chasquear** *v.* to play a trick on; to disappoint; to crack (*a whip*); to smack (*the lips*); to click (*the tongue*); to crack, snap; *Col., Ven.* to chatter (*said of the teeth*); *Am.* to munch (*food*); **-se** to be disappointed or disillusioned; to be tricked or fooled.

**chasqui** *m. Andes, Ríopl.* courier, messenger.

**chasquido** *m.* crack of a whip; crackle; smack (*of the lips*); click (*of the tongue*).

**chata** *f.* bedpan; scow, barge, flat-bottomed boat; *Am.* platform wagon, platform car, flatcar; **chatita** *f. Mex.* "honey", "cutie", "funny face".

**chato** *adj.* snub-nosed, flat-nosed; flat; flattened; squatty; *Mex.* **quedarse uno —** to be left flat or in the lurch; to be disappointed.

**chaval** *m.* lad; young man.

**chayote** *m. Am.* vegetable pear (*a tropical fruit growing on a vine*); *Am.* dunce, silly fool.

**che** *interj. Ríopl.* word used to attract attention among intimates; say! listen! hey!; nickname for citizens of Argentina.

**cheque** *m.* check, bank check.

**chica** *f.* little girl; girl; maid, servant.

**chicle** *m. Am.* chicle; *Am.* chewing gum.

**chico** *adj.* small, little; *m.* child, boy; *Col.* each game of billiards; *Am.* = **chicozapote** (*tropical fruit and tree from which chicle is extracted*).

**chicote** *m.* cigar; piece of rope; *Am.* whip; *Col., Ven.* cigar butt.

**chicotear** *v. Ríopl., Col., Peru* to lash, whip, flog; *Am.* to fight, quarrel; *Am.* to kill.

**chicoteo** *m. Ríopl.* whipping; *Am.* shooting, killing; *Am.* crackling, rattling (*as of machine guns*); *Am.* quarreling.

**chicha** *f. Peru, Col., Ch., Ríopl., C.A.* chicha (*a popular alcoholic beverage*); *Peru* thick-soled shoe; **no ser ni — ni limonada** to be worth nothing, be neither fish nor fowl.

**chícharo** *m.* pea; *Col.* bad cigar; *Am.* apprentice.

**chicharra** *f.* cicada, locust; talkative person; *Mex.* person with a shrill voice; *Am.* rickety, squeaky car; *Ch.* harsh-sounding musical instrument or bell; *C.A., Mex., Cuba* piece of fried pork skin.

**chicharrón** *m.* crackling, crisp piece of fried pork skin; burned piece of meat; sunburnt person; *Am.* dried-up, wrinkled person; *Am.* bootlicker, flatterer.

**chiche** *m. Mex., C.A.* breast, teat; wet nurse.

**chichón** *m.* bump, lump; *Am.* joker, jester; **chichona** *adj. Mex., C.A.* large-breasted.

**chiflado** *adj.* "cracked", "touched", crazy; *p.p. of* **chiflar.**

**chifladura** *f.* craziness, mania; mockery, jest.

**chiflar** *v.* to whistle; to hiss; *Am.* to sing (*said of birds*); **-se** to lose one's head; to become unbalanced, crazy.

**chiflido** *m.* whistle; hiss; *Am.* **en un —** in a jiffy, in a second.

**chile** *m.* chili, red pepper.

**chileno** *adj. & m.* Chilean.

**chillante** *adj.* flashy, bright, showy, loud; shrieking.

**chillar** *v.* to shriek, scream; to hiss; *Am.* to shout, protest, moan; *Am.* to "squeal", turn informer; *Ríopl., Ven., C.A., P.R.* **no —** not to say a word; *Mex.***-se** to be piqued, offended.

**chillido** *m.* shriek, scream.

**chillón** *adj.* shrieking, screaming; shrill; loud, gaudy; *Col., Andes* whining, discontented; *Ríopl.* touchy.

**chimenea** *f.* chimney; fireplace, hearth.

**china** *f.* (*de la China*) Chinese woman; China silk or cotton; porcelain; (*piedra*) pebble; marble; *Andes, Ch.,*

*Ríopl., Col.* girl, young woman (*usually half-breed or Indian*); *Am.* servant girl; *P.R.* sweet orange; *Col.* spinning top; **chinita** *f. Am.* little Indian girl; darling.

**chinche** *f.* bedbug; thumbtack; tiresome person, bore; *Col., Ven., Ríopl.* touchy or irritable person; *Am.* plump, squatty person.

**chinchorro** *m. Ven., Col.* hammock.

**chino** *adj.* Chinese; *Mex.* curly; *m. Ríopl.* Chinese; Chinaman; *Am.* pig; *Am.* half-breed (*Negro and Indian, white and Indian*); *Am.* Indian; *Col.* house servant; *Am.* coarse, rough, ugly person; *Col.* straight, coarse hair.

**chiquero** *m.* pigsty, pigpen; pen for bulls; goat shelter.

**chiquilín** *m. Am.* tot, little boy; **chiquilina** *f. Am.* little girl.

**chiquito** *adj.* tiny, very small; *m.* tiny tot, tiny child; **chiquitico** *adj.* tiny.

**chiripa** *f.* stroke of good luck.

**chiripá** *m. Ríopl.* loose riding trousers (*square of cloth draped from the waist and between the legs*).

**chirola** *f. Mex., Ven., Ríopl.* "jug", jail; *Am.* coin of low value.

**chirona** *f.* "jug"; jail.

**chirriado** *adj. Col.* attractive; lively.

**chirriar**[17] *v.* to squeak, creak; to sizzle; to chirp; to sing out of tune; *Col.* to go on a spree.

**chirrido** *m.* creak, squeak; chirp; squeaking, creaking; chirping.

**chisguete** *m.* squirt.

**chisme** *m.* gossip, piece of gossip; trifle, trinket, knickknack, gadget.

**chismear** *v.* to gossip; to tattle.

**chismería** *f.* gossiping, talebearing.

**chismero** *adj.* gossiping; *m.* gossip.

**chismoso** *adj.* gossiping; *m.* gossip, talebearer, tattletale.

**chispa** *f.* spark; small diamond; wit; *Col.* false rumor, lie; *Am.* two-wheeled cart; *Mex.* brazen, shameless woman; *Am.* **da —** it clicks, works, functions; *Am.* **ponerse —** to get drunk.

**chispeante** *adj.* sparkling.

**chispear** *v.* to spark; to sparkle; to twinkle; to drizzle.

**chisporrotear** *v.* to sputter, throw off sparks.

**chiste** *m.* joke, jest; **dar en el —** to guess right, hit the nail on the head.

**chistera** *f.* top hat; fish basket.

**chistoso** *adj.* funny, amusing, humorous.

**¡chito! ¡chitón!** *interj.* hush!

**chiva** *f.* female goat; *Am.* goatee; *Pan., Col.* flivver, small bus; **chivo** *m.* he-goat; *Am.* fit of anger; *Am.* insulting remark; *Am.* **estar hecho un —** to be very angry; *adj. Am.* angry; **chivato** *m. Cuba* informer, squealer.

**chocante** *adj.* striking, surprising; shocking; disgusting; *Col., Andes* tiresome, annoying, impertinent.

**chocar**[6] *v.* to bump, collide, clash; to fight; to shock, surprise, disgust; **me**

**choca ese hombre** I loathe that man.

**chocarrear** *v.* to tell coarse jokes; to clown.

**chocarrería** *f.* coarse joke; **chocarrero** *adj.* coarse, vulgar; clownish.

**choclo** *m.* overshoe; clog; *Mex.* low shoe or slipper; *Andes, Col., Ch., Ríopl.* ear of corn; *Am.* corn stew; *Am.* spike, ear of wheat.

**chocolate** *m.* chocolate.

**chochear** *v.* to be in one's dotage, act senile.

**chochera, chochez** *f.* senility, dotage; **chocheras, chocheces** senile actions or habits.

**chocho** *adj.* doting; *m.* childish old man.

**chófer** *m.* chauffeur.

**cholo** *m. Andes, Ríopl., Ch.* half-breed; *Am.* half-civilized Indian; *adj. Am.* coarse, rude; *C.R.* dark-skinned; *Ch.* black (*dog*).

**chopo** *m.* black poplar; *adj. Am.* stupid.

**choque** *m.* collision, bump; shock; clash, conflict; dispute.

**chorizo** *m.* sausage; *Am.* string of things; *Am.* fool.

**chorrazo** *m.* spurt, large stream or jet.

**chorrear** *v.* to drip; to spout.

**chorro** *m.* spurt, jet; stream, flow; *Am.* strand of a whip; *Am.* river rapids.

**choteador** *m. Am.* joker, jester.

**chotear** *v. Cuba* to make fun of, jeer, jest, mock, kid; *Mex., C.A.* to idle, fool around; *Am.* to pamper.

**choteo** *m. Cuba* joking, jeering, kidding.

**choza** *f.* hut, cabin.

**chubasco** *m.* squall, sudden shower; **aguantar el —** to weather the storm.

**chuchería** *f.* trifle, trinket; knickknack; tidbit.

**chueco** *adj. Am.* crooked, bent; *Col.* crook-legged, bow-legged, knock-kneed; *Am.* worn-out, dejected; *Mex.* disgusted, annoyed; *Am.* **comerciar en —** to trade in stolen goods.

**chuleta** *f.* cutlet, chop; blow, slap.

**chulo** *m.* dandy; effeminate man; clownish fellow; bullfighter's assistant; *Col.* buzzard; *Am.* coarse, thick brush; *adj. C.A., Col., Mex.* good-looking, pretty.

**chumpipe** *m. C.A.* turkey; also **chompipe.**

**chupada** *f.* sucking; suction; suck, sip; *Mex., C.A., Ven., Andes* puff from a cigarette; *Ríopl.* big swallow of liquor.

**chupador** *m.* sucker; teething ring; *Am.* toper, heavy drinker; *Am.* smoker.

**chupaflor, chuparrosa** *m. Am.* hummingbird.

**chupar** *v.* to suck; to sip; to absorb, take in; *Am.* to smoke; *C.A., Ríopl., Andes* to drink, get drunk; **-se** to shrivel up.

**churrasco** *m. Ríopl., Andes* roasted meat; *Ríopl., Andes* barbecued meat; *Ríopl., Andes* large piece of meat for barbecuing.

**CH**

**churrasquear** *v. Ríopl., Andes* to barbecue, roast over coals; *Ríopl., Andes* to prepare (*meat*) for barbecuing; *Ríopl., Andes* to eat barbecued meat.

**churrasquito** *m.* small piece of roast.

**churrigueresco** *adj.* baroque, ornate (*architecture*).

**chuscada** *f.* jest, joke.

**chusco** *adj.* funny, witty; ridiculous; *Peru* **perro** — mongrel dog.

**chusma** *f.* rabble, mob.

**D**

**dable** *adj.* feasible, possible.

**daca** = **da acá.**

**dádiva** *f.* gift.

**dadivoso** *adj.* liberal, generous.

**dado** *m.* die; **-s** dice.

**dador** *m.* giver.

**daga** *f.* dagger.

**dama** *f.* lady; **jugar a las -s** to play checkers.

**damisela** *f.* damsel, girl.

**danza** *f.* dance.

**danzante** *m. & f.* dancer.

**danzar**⁹ *v.* to dance.

**danzarina** *f.* dancer.

**dañar** *v.* to harm, hurt, damage; **-se** to spoil, rot; to get hurt; to get damaged.

**dañino** *adj.* harmful; destructive.

**daño** *m.* damage, harm, loss.

**dañoso** *adj.* harmful.

**dar**²⁶ *v. irr.* (*hacer don*) to give, confer; (*golpear*) to strike, hit; (*emitir*) give off, emit; — **a luz** to give birth to; to publish; — **con** to encounter, find; — **de comer** to feed; — **de sí** to give, stretch; — **en** to hit upon; to persist in; — **largas a un asunto** to prolong or postpone a matter; *C.A., Ven., Col.* — **cuero** (**guasca, puños**) to beat, thrash, lash; **lo misma da** it makes no difference; **-se** to give up; **dárselas de** to boast of.

**dardo** *m.* dart, arrow.

**dares y tomares** *m. pl.* give-and-take, dispute; dealings.

**dársena** *f.* dock, wharf.

**datar** *v.* to date; — **de** to date from.

**dátil** *m.* date (*fruit of the date palm*).

**dato** *m.* datum, fact; **-s** data.

**de** *prep.* of, from; about, concerning; in (*after a superlative*); if (*before inf.*); — **no llegar** if he does not arrive; **el** — **la gorra azul** the one with the blue cap; **el mejor** — **América** the best in America; **más** — **lo que dice** more than he says.

**debajo** *adv.* under, underneath; — **de** *prep.* under.

**debate** *m.* debate; dispute, quarrel.

**debatir** *v.* to debate, argue, discuss; to fight; **-se** to struggle.

**debe** *m.* debit.

**debelar** *v.* to subdue, defeat.

**deber** *v.* to owe; to have to (must, should, ought); **debe de ser** it must be, probably is; **¡me la debes!** I have an account to settle with you!

**deber** *m.* duty, obligation; debt; debit; debit side (*in bookkeeping*).

**debido** *adj.* due, owing; just, appropriate.

**débil** *adj.* weak, feeble.

**debilidad** *f.* debility, weakness.

**debilitación** *f.*, **debilitamiento** *m.* weakening; weakness.

**debilitar** *v.* to weaken.

**débito** *m.* debt; debit.

**debutar** *v.* to make a debut, make a first public appearance.

**década** *f.* decade, ten years; series of ten.

**decadencia** *f.* decadence, decline, falling off.

**decaer**²⁴ *v. irr.* to decay, decline, wither, fade; to fall to leeward.

**decaimiento** *m.* decline, decay; dejection; weakness.

**decano** *m.* dean; senior member of a group.

**decantado** *p.p. & adj.* much talked about; overrated.

**decapitar** *v.* to behead.

**decencia** *f.* decency; **decente** *adj.* decent; respectable; fair.

**decenio** *m.* decade.

**decepción** *f.* disillusion, disappointment.

**decepcionante** *adj.* disappointing.

**decepcionar** *v.* to disillusion, disappoint.

**decibel** *m.* decibel (*unit for the measurement of the intensity of sound*).

**decidir** *v.* to decide, resolve; **-se a** to make up one's mind to; to decide to.

**décima** *f.* tenth; tithe; stanza of ten octosyllabic lines.

**décimo** *adj.* tenth.

**decir**²⁷ *v. irr.* to say; to tell; to speak; **es** — that is; **querer** — to mean, signify.

**decisión** *f.* decision.

**decisivo** *adj.* decisive, final.

**declamar** *v.* to declaim, recite.

**declaración** *f.* declaration; statement; deposition, testimony.

**declarar** *v.* to declare, state, affirm; to testify; **-se** to propose, declare one's love; to give one's views or opinion.

**declinar** *v.* to decline; to go down; to lose vigor, decay; to bend down.

**declive** *m.* declivity, slope.

**decoración** *f.* decoration, ornament; stage setting.

**decorar** *v.* to decorate, adorn.

**decorativo** *adj.* decorative, ornamental.

**decoro** *m.* decorum, propriety, dignity; honor.

**decoroso** *adj.* decorous, becoming, proper, decent.

**decrépito** *adj.* decrepit, old, feeble.

**decretar** *v.* to decree.

**decreto** *m.* decree; decision, order.

**dechado** *m.* model, pattern, example.

**dedal** *m.* thimble.

**dedicar**⁶ *v.* to dedicate; to devote; **-se** to apply oneself.

**dedicatoria** *f.* dedication, inscription.

**dedo** *m.* (*de la mano*) finger; (*del pie*)

toe; **— del corazón** middle finger;
**— meñique** little finger; **— pulgar**
thumb; **no mamarse el —** not to
be easily fooled; **dedillo** *m.* small
finger; **saber al dedillo** to know
perfectly, know by heart.

**deducción** *f.* deduction; inference.

**deducir**[25] *v. irr.* to deduce, conclude;
to deduct.

**defecto** *m.* defect, fault.

**defectuoso** *adj.* defective, faulty.

**defender**[1] *v. irr.* to defend.

**defensa** *f.* defense; *Am.* automobile
bumper.

**defensivo** *adj.* defensive; *m.* defense,
safeguard; **defensiva** *f.* defensive.

**defensor** *m.* defender.

**deficiencia** *f.* deficiency; **deficiente**
*adj.* deficient.

**déficit** *m.* deficit, shortage.

**definición** *f.* definition.

**definido** *adj.* definite; *p.p. of* **definir.**

**definir** *v.* to define, explain; to determine.

**definitivo** *adj.* definitive, conclusive,
final; **en definitiva** in short, in conclusion; definitely.

**deformación** *f.* deformation, deformity.

**deformar** *v.* to deform; **-se** to become
deformed; to lose its shape or form.

**deforme** *adj.* deformed; ugly.

**deformidad** *f.* deformity.

**defraudar** *v.* to defraud, cheat, rob of.

**defunción** *f.* death, decease.

**degenerado** *adj. & m.* degenerate.

**degenerar** *v.* to degenerate.

**deglución** *f.* swallowing.

**deglutir** *v.* to swallow.

**degollar**[2] *v. irr.* to behead; to slash the
throat; to cut (*a dress*) low in the neck.

**degradar** *v.* to degrade; to debase.

**degüello** *m.* beheading; throat-slashing.

**dehesa** *f.* pasture, grazing ground.

**deidad** *f.* deity.

**dejadez** *f.* lassitude, languor, listlessness; self-neglect, slovenliness.

**dejado** *adj.* indolent, listless; slovenly.

**dejar** *v.* (*abandonar*) to leave; to quit;
to abandon; to omit; (*permitir*) to
permit, let; (*soltar*) to let go; **— de**
stop, cease; **— caer** to drop; *Am.*
**no -se** not to be an easy mark, not to
let others pick on one.

**dejo** *m.* (*sabor*) aftertaste; slight taste;
(*acento*) slight accent, peculiar inflection.

**del = de + el** of the.

**delantal** *m.* apron.

**delante** *adv.* before, in front; **— de**
*prep.* in front of.

**delantera** *f.* lead, forepart, front.

**delantero** *adj.* front, foremost, first.

**delatar** *v.* to denounce, accuse, inform
against.

**delator** *m.* accuser, informer.

**delegación** *f.* delegation.

**delegado** *m.* delegate.

**delegar**[7] *v.* to delegate.

**deleitable** *adj.* delightful, enjoyable.

**deleitar** *v.* to delight, please.

**deleite** *m.* delight, joy, pleasure.

**deleitoso** *adj.* delightful.

**deletrear** *v.* to spell.

**deleznable** *adj.* perishable; brittle.

**delfín** *m.* dolphin; dauphin.

**delgadez** *f.* thinness; slimness; fineness.

**delgado** *adj.* thin, slender, slim.

**deliberado** *adj.* deliberate; *p.p. of*
**deliberar.**

**deliberar** *v.* to deliberate, consider,
ponder.

**delicadeza** *f.* fineness; delicacy; softness, exquisiteness.

**delicado** *adj.* delicate; weak, frail; exquisite, dainty; tender.

**delicia** *f.* delight.

**delicioso** *adj.* delicious, delightful.

**delincuente** *adj., m. & f.* delinquent.

**delineación** *f.*, **delineamiento** *m.* delineation, design, outline, drawing;
portrayal.

**delinear** *v.* to delineate, sketch, outline.

**delirante** *adj.* delirious, raving.

**delirar** *v.* to be delirious; to rave, talk
wildly or foolishly.

**delirio** *m.* delirium, temporary madness; wild excitement; foolishness.

**delito** *m.* crime; misdemeanor.

**demacrado** *adj.* scrawny, emaciated,
thin.

**demanda** *f.* demand; petition; question; claim; complaint; lawsuit.

**demandado** *m.* defendant; *p.p. of* **demandar.**

**demandante** *m. & f.* plaintiff.

**demandar** *v.* to demand; to petition;
to sue, file a suit; to indict.

**demás** *indef. adj. & pron.*: **los —** the
rest; the others; **las — personas** the
other people; **lo —** the rest; **por —**
useless; uselessly; **por lo —** as to the
rest; moreover.

**demasía** *f.* excess; boldness, insolence;
offense, outrage; **en —** excessively.

**demasiado** *adv.* too much, excessively;
too; *adj.* too much, excessive.

**demente** *adj.* demented, insane, crazy.

**democracia** *f.* democracy; **demócrata**
*m. & f.* democrat; **democrático** *adj.*
democratic.

**demoler**[2] *v. irr.* to demolish, tear down.

**demonio** *m.* demon, devil; evil spirit.

**demontre** *m.* devil; ¡**—**! the deuce!

**demora** *f.* delay.

**demorar** *v.* to delay; to retard; **-se** to
linger; to be delayed.

**demostración** *f.* demonstration; proof,
explanation.

**demostrar**[2] *v. irr.* to demonstrate,
show, prove, explain.

**demostrativo** *adj.* demonstrative.

**demovilizar**[9] *v.* to demobilize.

**demudar** *v.* to change, alter; to disguise; **-se** to change color or one's
facial expression; to turn pale.

**dengoso, denguero** *adj.* affected;
finicky.

**dengue** *m.* primness; coyness, affectation; dengue, breakbone fever; *Am.*

marigold; *Col.* zigzag; *Am.* swagger;
**hacer -s** to act coy, make grimaces.
**denigrar** *v.* to blacken, defame, revile,
insult.
**denodado** *adj.* dauntless, daring.
**denominación** *f.* denomination; name,
title, designation.
**denominar** *v.* to name, call, entitle.
**denostar**[2] *v. irr.* to insult, outrage,
revile.
**denotar** *v.* to denote, indicate, mean.
**densidad** *f.* density.
**denso** *adj.* dense, compact; thick.
**dentado** *adj.* toothed, notched.
**dentadura** *f.* set of teeth.
**dentar**[1] *v. irr.* to tooth, furnish (*a saw*)
with teeth; to indent; to cut teeth,
grow teeth (*referring to a child*).
**dentellada** *f.* bite; tooth mark; **a -s**
with big bites.
**dentición** *f.* teething.
**dentífrico** *m.* dentrifice, tooth cleanser;
**pasta dentífrica** toothpaste; **polvos
dentífricos** toothpowder.
**dentista** *m.* dentist.
**dentro** *adv.* inside, within; **— de** *prep.*
inside of; **por —** on the inside.
**denuedo** *m.* spirit, courage, daring.
**denuesto** *m.* affront, insult.
**denuncia** *f.* denunciation, condemnation, accusation; miner's claim.
**denunciar** *v.* to denounce, accuse; to
proclaim, advise, give notice; to claim
(*a mine*).
**deparar** *v.* to furnish, offer, supply.
**departamento** *m.* department; compartment; apartment.
**departir** *v.* to talk, converse.
**dependencia** *f.* dependence; dependency; branch office.
**depender** *v.* to depend, rely (on).
**dependiente** *m.* clerk; dependent, subordinate; *adj.* dependent.
**deplorar** *v.* to deplore, lament, regret.
**deponer**[40] *v. irr.* to set aside; to depose,
remove (*an official*); to testify, declare;
to have a bowel movement; *Am.* to
vomit.
**deportar** *v.* to deport, banish.
**deporte** *m.* sport; pastime, recreation.
**deportista** *m.* sportsman; *f.* sports-
woman.
**deportivo** *adj.* sport, sports (*used
as an adj.*); **copa deportiva** loving
cup.
**deposición** *f.* declaration, assertion;
testimony; dismissal, removal (*from
office or power*); bowel movement.
**depositar** *v.* to deposit; to deliver, intrust.
**depositario** *m.* receiver, trustee.
**depósito** *m.* deposit; storage; warehouse; **— de agua** reservoir.
**depravado** *adj.* depraved, corrupt, degenerate.
**depravar** *v.* to corrupt, pervert, contaminate.
**depreciar** *v.* to depreciate, lessen the
value of.
**depresión** *f.* depression; dip, sag.
**deprimente** *adj.* depressing.

**deprimir** *v.* to depress; to press down;
to humiliate, belittle.
**depuesto** *p.p.* of **deponer.**
**depurar** *v.* to purify.
**derecha** *f.* right hand; right side; right
wing (*in politics*); **a la —** to the right;
**derechazo** *m.* a blow with the right
hand, a right (*boxing*).
**derecho** *adj.* right; straight; *m.* law;
duty, tax; fee.
**derechura** *f.* straightness.
**deriva** *f.* drift (*of a boat or plane*); **irse**
(*or* **andar**) **a la —** to drift, be drifting.
**derivar** *v.* to derive; to come (from).
**derogar**[7] *v.* to revoke, repeal, abolish.
**derramamiento** *m.* spill, spilling,
shedding; overflow; scattering; **— de
sangre** bloodshed.
**derramar** *v.* to spill; to spread, scatter;
to shed.
**derrame** *m.* spill, spilling, shedding;
overflow; discharge (*of secretion, blood,
etc.*); slope.
**derredor** *m.* circuit; contour; **al —**
around; **en —** around.
**derrengado** *p.p. & adj.* lame, crippled;
dislocated (*said of hip or spine*).
**derrengar**[1,7] *v. irr.* to dislocate or
sprain (*hip or spine*); to cripple; to
bend.
**derretimiento** *m.* thaw, thawing, melting.
**derretir**[5] *v. irr.* to melt, dissolve; **-se** to
be consumed; to melt.
**derribar** *v.* to demolish, knock down,
fell; to overthrow; **-se** to lie down,
throw oneself down.
**derrocamiento** *m.* overthrow.
**derrocar**[6] *v.* to fling down; to fell; to
overthrow.
**derrochador** *m.* squanderer, spendthrift; *adj.* wasteful, extravagant.
**derrochar** *v.* to waste; to squander.
**derroche** *m.* waste; dissipation, lavish
spending.
**derrota** *f.* rout, defeat; ship's route or
course.
**derrotar** *v.* to defeat; to squander; to
destroy, ruin; to lose or shift its
course (*said of a ship*).
**derrotero** *m.* course, direction; ship's
course; book of marine charts.
**derrumbadero** *m.* precipice.
**derrumbamiento** *m.* landslide; collapse.
**derrumbar** *v.* to fling down; *Am.* to
knock down; *Am.* to go down in a
hurry; **-se** to crumble away; to topple
over; *Col., Ven.* to dwindle (*as a
business*).
**derrumbe** *m.* landslide; collapse.
**desabotonar** *v.* to unbutton.
**desabrido** *adj.* tasteless, insipid; harsh;
sour.
**desabrigar**[7] *v.* to uncover; **-se** to uncover oneself.
**desabrimiento** *m.* tastelessness; harshness; sourness.
**desabrochar** *v.* to unfasten, unbutton,
unclasp; **-se** to unbutton oneself, unfasten one's clothes.

**DE**

**desacato** *m.* irreverence, disrespect; profanation.

**desacierto** *m.* mistake, error.

**desacostumbrado** *adj.* unaccustomed; unusual; *p.p. of* **desacostumbrar.**

**desacostumbrar** *v.* to disaccustom, rid of a habit; **-se** to become unaccustomed; to lose a custom.

**desacreditar** *v.* to discredit; to disgrace.

**desacuerdo** *m.* disagreement; discord; blunder; forgetfulness.

**desafiar**[17] *v.* to challenge; to compete; to defy.

**desafinado** *adj.* out of tune.

**desafinar** *v.* to be discordant; to be out of tune; **-se** to get out of tune.

**desafío** *m.* challenge, defiance; duel; contest.

**desafortunado** *adj.* unfortunate, unlucky.

**desafuero** *m.* violation; outrage, abuse.

**desagradable** *adj.* disagreeable, unpleasant.

**desagradar** *v.* to displease.

**desagradecido** *adj.* ungrateful.

**desagrado** *m.* displeasure; discontent.

**desagraviar** *v.* to make amends; to compensate for a damage or injury; to right a wrong; to apologize; to vindicate.

**desagravio** *m.* reparation; compensation for a wrong or injury; vindication; apology.

**desaguadero** *m.* drain, drain pipe, water outlet.

**desaguar**[8] *v.* to drain, draw off; to flow (into); *Ch.* to wash (*something*) two or more times; *Am.* to extract the juice from; *Col., Ven., Mex.* to urinate; **-se** to drain.

**desagüe** *m.* drainage; drain.

**desaguisado** *m.* outrage, violence, wrong.

**desahogado** *p.p. & adj.* (*aliviado*) relieved; (*espacioso*) roomy, spacious; **estar —** to be in easy or comfortable circumstances; to be well-off.

**desahogar**[7] *v.* to relieve from pain or trouble; **-se** to find relief or release; to unbosom oneself, disclose one's feelings.

**desahogo** *m.* relief from pain or trouble; release; ease, comfort, relaxation; freedom, unrestraint.

**desairar** *v.* to slight, snub, disdain; to rebuff; to disappoint; to neglect.

**desaire** *m.* rebuff, snub, slight, disdain.

**desalentar**[1] *v. irr.* to put out of breath; to discourage; **-se** to get discouraged.

**desaliento** *m.* discouragement, dejection.

**desaliñado** *adj.* disheveled, slovenly, unkempt, untidy; disorderly.

**desaliño** *m.* slovenliness, untidiness; neglect, carelessness; disorder.

**desalmado** *adj.* soulless, cruel, inhuman.

**desalojar** *v.* to dislodge; to evict, expel from a lodging; to vacate.

**desamarrar** *v.* to untie, unfasten; to unmoor (*a ship*).

**desamparar** *v.* to abandon, forsake.

**desamparo** *m.* desertion, abandonment.

**desamueblado** *adj.* unfurnished.

**desangrar** *v.* to bleed, draw blood from; to drain; **-se** to bleed, lose blood.

**desanimado** *adj.* discouraged; lifeless; dull (*said of a party, meeting, etc.*).

**desanimar** *v.* to dishearten, discourage.

**desaparecer**[13] *v. irr.* to disappear; to hide; **-se** to disappear, vanish.

**desaparición** *f.* disappearance.

**desapasionado** *adj.* dispassionate; free from passion; calm; impartial.

**desapego** *m.* aloofness, indifference, detachment.

**desapercibido** *adj.* unprepared; unprovided; unnoticed.

**desaprobación** *f.* disapproval.

**desaprobar**[2] *v. irr.* to disapprove.

**desarmar** *v.* to disarm; to dismount, take apart.

**desarme** *m.* disarmament.

**desarraigar**[7] *v.* to root out, uproot.

**desarreglado** *p.p. & adj.* disordered; disorderly; slovenly.

**desarreglar** *v.* to disarrange, disorder, disturb, upset.

**desarreglo** *m.* disorder, confusion.

**desarrollar** *v.* to unroll, unfold; to develop, explain; **-se** to develop; to unfold.

**desarrollo** *m.* development.

**desaseado** *adj.* unkempt, untidy.

**desaseo** *m.* slovenliness, untidiness.

**desasir**[22] *v. irr.* to loosen, unfasten; **-se** to get loose (from); to let go (of).

**desasosiego** *m.* unrest, uneasiness, restlessness.

**desastrado** *adj.* unfortunate, unhappy; ragged, dirty, untidy.

**desastre** *m.* disaster.

**desastroso** *adj.* disastrous, unfortunate.

**desatar** *v.* to untie, loosen; to dissolve; to unravel, clear up; **-se** to let loose, let go; to break loose; **-se en improperios** to let out a string of insults.

**desatención** *f.* inattention, lack of attention; discourtesy.

**desatender**[1] *v. irr.* to disregard, pay no attention (to); to slight, neglect.

**desatento** *adj.* inattentive; discourteous.

**desatinado** *adj.* senseless; reckless.

**desatinar** *v.* to act foolishly; to talk nonsense; to blunder; to rave; to lose one's bearings.

**desatino** *m.* blunder, error; folly, nonsense.

**desatracar**[6] *v.* to push off (*from shore or from another ship*); to cast off, unmoor.

**desavenencia** *f.* disagreement, discord; dispute, misunderstanding.

**desayunarse** *v.* to eat breakfast; **— con la noticia** to hear a piece of news for the first time.

**desayuno** *m.* breakfast.

**desazón** *f.* uneasiness, anxiety; insipidity, flatness, tastelessness; displeasure.

**desbandarse** *v.* to disband, scatter, disperse; to desert the army or a party.

**desbaratar** *v.* to destroy, ruin; to upset, disturb; to disperse, put to flight; to talk nonsense; **-se** to be upset, be in disorder; to fall to pieces.

**desbocado** *adj.* runaway (*horse*), dashing headlong; foul-mouthed, abusive; broken-mouthed (*jar, pitcher, etc.*).

**desbordamiento** *m.* overflow, flood.

**desbordante** *adj.* overflowing; *Am.* frantic.

**desbordar** *v.* to overflow, flood; **-se** to spill over; to get overexcited.

**descabalar** *v.* to break (*a given amount, making it thereby incomplete*).

**descabello** *m.* the act of killing the bull by piercing the brain with the sword.

**descabezado** *p.p.* beheaded; *adj.* headless; harebrained, thoughtless.

**descabezar**[9] *v.* to behead; to chop off the head or tip of; — **el sueño** to take a nap; **-se** to break one's head; to rack one's brain.

**descaecido** *adj.* feeble, weak; — **de ánimo** depressed, dejected, despondent.

**descaecimiento** *m.* languor, weakness; depression, dejection.

**descalabradura** *f.* blow or wound on the head; scar on the head.

**descalabrar** *v.* to wound on the head; to hurt, injure; to damage; **-se** to suffer a head wound or skull fracture.

**descalabro** *m.* loss, misfortune.

**descalzar**[9] *v.* to take off (*someone's*) shoes or (and) stockings; **-se** to take off one's shoes or (and) stockings; to lose a shoe (*said of horses*).

**descalzo** *adj.* barefoot; shoeless.

**descaminar** *v.* to mislead, lead astray; **-se** to go astray.

**descamisado** *adj.* shirtless; in rags; *m.* ragamuffin, ragged fellow.

**descansar** *v.* to rest.

**descanso** *m.* rest; staircase landing.

**descarado** *adj.* shameless, impudent, brazen.

**descarga** *f.* discharge; unloading.

**descargar**[7] *v.* to discharge; to unload.

**descargo** *m.* discharge (*of a duty or obligation*); unloading; relief.

**descargue** *m.* unloading; discharge.

**descarnado** *adj.* fleshless, scrawny.

**descarnar** *v.* to pull the flesh from the bone; to corrode, eat away; **-se** to become thin, emaciated.

**descaro** *m.* effrontery, shamelessness, impudence, audacity.

**descarriar**[17] *v.* to mislead, lead astray; to separate (*cattle*) from the herd; **-se** to stray; to go astray.

**descarrilar** *v.* to derail (*cause a train to run off the track*); to wreck (*a train*); **-se** to get or run off the track; to go astray.

**descartar** *v.* to discard; to put aside.

**descascarado** *p.p.* & *adj.* peeled off; chipped off.

**descascarar** *v.* to shell, hull, husk; to peel; to chip off (*plaster*); *Am.* to defame, discredit; *Col.* to flay; **-se** to chip off, peel off.

**descendencia** *f.* descent, lineage; descendants, offspring.

**descendente** *adj.* descending, downward.

**descender**[1] *v. irr.* to descend, go down; to get down; to come (from), originate.

**descendiente** *m.* & *f.* descendant; *adj.* descending.

**descendimiento** *m.* descent.

**descenso** *m.* descent; fall.

**descifrar** *v.* to decipher, puzzle out, figure out.

**descolgar**[2,7] *v. irr.* to unhang, take down; to let down; **-se** to climb down (*a rope, tree, etc.*); to drop in, appear unexpectedly.

**descolorar** *v.* to discolor; to fade; **-se** to fade, lose its color; to discolor.

**descolorido** *adj.* pale.

**descollar**[2] *v. irr.* to excel; to stand out, tower (above).

**descomedido** *adj.* rude, discourteous, impolite; unobliging.

**descompletar** *v.* to make incomplete, break (*a unit, sum, set, etc.*).

**descomponer**[40] *v. irr.* (*estorbar*) to upset, disturb; (*echar a perder*) to put out of order; to decompose; **-se** to decompose, rot; to become upset, ill; to get out of order; *Col., Ven., C.A., Carib., Mex.* **se me descompuso el brazo** I dislocated my arm, my arm got out of joint.

**descomposición** *f.* decomposition; decay, corruption; disorder, confusion.

**descompuesto** *p.p. of* **descomponer**; *adj.* out of order; insolent; brazen; immodest.

**descomunal** *adj.* colossal, enormous, monstrous.

**desconcertante** *adj.* disconcerting, disturbing, confusing, baffling, embarrassing.

**desconcertar**[1] *v. irr.* to disconcert, bewilder, confuse; to disturb; **-se** to be confused, perplexed.

**desconcierto** *m.* disorder; confusion; disagreement; feeling of discomfort.

**desconchadura** *f.* chip (*chipped off place*); chipping off, peeling off (*of plaster, varnish, etc.*).

**desconchar** *v.* to scrape off (*plaster or stucco*); **-se** to peel off, chip off (*as plaster*).

**desconectar** *v.* to disconnect.

**desconfiado** *adj.* distrustful, suspicious.

**desconfianza** *f.* mistrust, distrust.

**desconfiar**[17] *v.* to distrust; to lose confidence.

**desconocer**[13] *v. irr.* to fail to recognize or remember; to disown; to disregard, slight; not to know.

**desconocido** *adj.* unknown; unrecognizable; *m.* stranger.

**desconocimiento** *m.* disregard; igno-rance.

**desconsolado** *p.p.* & *adj.* disconsolate, forlorn; disheartened, grieved.

**desconsolador** *adj.* disheartening, sad-dening.

**desconsolar**[2] *v. irr.* to sadden, grieve; to discourage; **-se** to become disheart-ened, grieved.

**desconsuelo** *m.* dejection, sadness, dis-tress.

**descontar**[2] *v. irr.* to discount, deduct; to allow for.

**descontentadizo** *adj.* discontented, fretful, hard to please.

**descontentar** *v.* to displease.

**descontento** *adj.* discontent, dis-pleased; *m.* discontent, displeasure.

**descorazonado** *adj.* disheartened, dis-couraged, depressed.

**descorchar** *v.* to uncork; to remove the bark from (*a cork tree*); to force or break open.

**descortés** *adj.* discourteous, rude, im-polite.

**descortesía** *f.* discourtesy, rudeness, impoliteness.

**descortezar**[9] *v.* to bark, strip the bark from (*trees*); to remove the crust or shell from; to peel; to civilize, remove the rough manners from.

**descoser** *v.* to rip, unsew, unstitch; **-se** to rip, come unstitched; to talk too much or indiscreetly.

**descosido** *m.* rip; *adj.* too talkative, in-discreet; disorderly; *p.p. of* **descoser.**

**descostrar** *v.* to flake; to scale off; to remove the crust from; **-se** to flake, scale off.

**descoyuntado** *p.p.* & *adj.* dislocated, out of joint.

**descoyuntar** *v.* to dislocate, put out of joint; **-se** to get out of joint.

**descrédito** *m.* discredit.

**descreído** *adj.* incredulous, unbeliev-ing; *m.* unbeliever.

**descreimiento** *m.* unbelief, lack of faith.

**describir**[52] *v.* to describe.

**descripción** *f.* description.

**descriptivo** *adj.* descriptive.

**descrito** *p.p. irr. of* **describir.**

**descuartizar**[9] *v.* to quarter (*an animal*); to tear or cut into parts.

**descubierto** *p.p. of* **descubrir** & *adj.* (*sin cubierta*) uncovered; hatless, bareheaded; (*hallado*) discovered; *m.* deficit, shortage; **al —** openly, in the open; **en —** uncovered, unpaid.

**descubridor** *m.* discoverer.

**descubrimiento** *m.* discovery; find; invention.

**descubrir**[52] *v.* to discover; to uncover; **-se** to uncover; to take off one's hat.

**descuento** *m.* discount; deduction.

**descuidado** *adj.* careless, negligent; untidy, slovenly; unaware; thought-less.

**descuidar** *v.* to neglect; to overlook; to be careless or negligent; **-se** to be careless or negligent.

**descuido** *m.* carelessness; neglect; oversight; disregard; inattention; slip, error.

**desde** *prep.* from; since; **— luego** of course; **— que** *conj.* since, ever since.

**desdecir**[27] *v. irr.* to be out of harmony (with); to detract (from); **-se** to re-tract; to contradict oneself.

**desdén** *m.* disdain, scorn.

**desdentado** *adj.* toothless.

**desdeñar** *v.* to disdain, scorn.

**desdeñoso** *adj.* disdainful, scornful.

**desdicha** *f.* misfortune; misery; pov-erty.

**desdichado** *adj.* unfortunate; unhappy, wretched; miserable; *m.* wretch.

**desdoblamiento** *m.* unfolding.

**desdoblar** *v.* to unfold; to spread out.

**desdorar** *v.* to remove the gilt from; to tarnish; to dishonor.

**desdoro** *m.* tarnish, blemish; dishonor.

**deseable** *adj.* desirable.

**desear** *v.* to desire, want.

**desecación** *f.*, **desecamiento** *m.* dry-ing; drainage.

**desecar**[6] *v.* to dry; to dry up; to drain (*land*).

**desechar** *v.* to discard; to reject; to re-fuse, decline; *Col.* to cut across, take a short cut.

**desecho** *m.* remainder, residue; waste material; piece of junk; discard; **-s** refuse, scraps, junk; **hierro de —** scrap iron; **papel de —** wastepaper, scraps of paper.

**desembalar** *v.* to unpack.

**desembarazar**[9] *v.* to rid, free, clear; *Ch.* to give birth; **-se** to get rid of.

**desembarazo** *m.* freedom, ease, natu-ralness; *Ch.* childbirth.

**desembarcadero** *m.* dock, wharf, pier.

**desembarcar**[6] *v.* to disembark, land; to unload; to go ashore.

**desembarco, desembarque** *m.* land-ing; unloading.

**desembocadura** *f.* mouth (*of a river, canal, etc.*); outlet.

**desembocar**[6] *v.* to flow (into); to lead (to).

**desembolsar** *v.* to disburse, pay out.

**desembolso** *m.* disbursement, outlay, expenditure.

**desembragar**[7] *v.* to throw out the clutch; to disconnect.

**desemejante** *adj.* unlike.

**desempacar**[6] *v.* to unpack.

**desempeñar** *v.* to recover, redeem, take out of pawn; **— un cargo** to perform the duties of a position; **— un papel** to play a part; **-se** to get out of debt.

**desempeño** *m.* fulfillment, carrying out, discharge; performance (*of a duty*); acting (*of a role*); redeeming (*of a thing pawned*).

**desempleado** *adj.* unemployed.

**desempleo** *m.* unemployment.

**desempolvar** *v.* to dust, remove the dust from.

**desencadenar** *v.* to unchain, free from chains; to loosen, set free; **-se**

to free oneself; to break loose.

**desencajado** *p.p. & adj.* disjointed; disfigured; sunken (*eyes*); emaciated.

**desencantar** *v.* to disillusion, disappoint.

**desencanto** *m.* disillusion, disappointment.

**desenfado** *m.* ease, freedom; calmness.

**desenfrenado** *p.p. & adj.* unbridled; wanton, reckless; loose, immoral.

**desenganchar** *v.* to unhitch; to unhook; to unfasten.

**desengañador** *adj.* disappointing, disillusioning.

**desengañar** *v.* to undeceive, disillusion, disappoint.

**desengaño** *m.* disillusion, disappointment, blighted hope.

**desengranar** *v.* to throw out of gear.

**desenmarañar** *v.* to untangle; to unravel.

**desenmascarar** *v.* to unmask.

**desenredar** *v.* to disentangle, unravel.

**desenrollar** *v.* to unroll.

**desensartar** *v.* to unstring; to unthread; to unfasten from a ring.

**desensillar** *v.* to unsaddle.

**desentenderse**[1] *v. irr.* to neglect, ignore, pay no attention to; to pretend not to see, hear or understand.

**desentendido** *adj.* unmindful, heedless; *p.p. of* **desentenderse; hacerse el —** to pretend not to notice.

**desenterrar**[1] *v. irr.* to unearth, dig up.

**desentonado** *adj.* inharmonious, out of tune.

**desentonar** *v.* to be out of tune; to be out of harmony; to sing off key, play out of tune.

**desenvoltura** *f.* freedom, ease, abandon; boldness, impudence.

**desenvolver**[2,52] *v. irr.* to unroll, unfold; to unwrap; to develop.

**desenvolvimiento** *m.* development, unfolding.

**desenvuelto** *adj.* free, easy; forward, bold; shameless, brazen; *p.p. of* **desenvolver.**

**deseo** *m.* desire, wish.

**deseoso** *adj.* desirous, eager.

**desequilibrado** *adj.* unbalanced; *p.p. of* **desequilibrar.**

**desequilibrar** *v.* to unbalance; to derange.

**desequilibrio** *m.* lack of balance; derangement, mental disorder.

**deserción** *f.* desertion.

**desertar** *v.* to desert; to abandon; **-se de** to desert.

**desertor** *m.* deserter; quitter.

**desesperación** *f.* despair; desperation; fury.

**desesperado** *adj.* desperate; despairing; hopeless; *p.p. of* **desesperar.**

**desesperanzado** *p.p. & adj.* discouraged; hopeless; desperate, in despair.

**desesperanzar**[9] *v.* to discourage, deprive of hope; **-se** to be discouraged; to despair, lose one's hope.

**desesperar** *v.* to despair, lose hope; to make (*someone*) despair; **-se** to despair, be desperate; to be furious.

**desfachatez** *f.* shamelessness, effrontery, impudence.

**desfalcar**[6] *v.* to embezzle; to remove a part of.

**desfalco** *m.* embezzlement; diminution, decrease.

**desfallecer**[13] *v. irr.* to grow weak; to faint.

**desfallecimiento** *m.* faintness; weakness; languor; swoon, faint.

**desfavorable** *adj.* unfavorable.

**desfigurar** *v.* to disfigure; to deface; to distort.

**desfiladero** *m.* narrow passage, narrow gorge; road on the edge of a precipice.

**desfilar** *v.* to march, parade, pass by.

**desfile** *m.* parade.

**desgana** *f.* lack of appetite; reluctance.

**desgarrado** *p.p.* torn; *adj.* shameless; impudent.

**desgarradura** *f.* tear.

**desgarrar** *v.* to tear, rend; to expectorate, cough up; **-se** to tear; to separate oneself (from).

**desgastar** *v.* to waste, consume, wear away; **-se** to waste away, lose one's strength or vigor; to wear off.

**desgaste** *m.* waste; wear and tear.

**desgracia** *f.* misfortune, mishap; disgrace.

**desgraciado** *adj.* unfortunate, wretched.

**desgranar** *v.* to thrash, thresh (*grain*); to remove the grain from; to shell (*peas, beans, etc.*).

**desgreñado** *adj.* disheveled.

**deshabitado** *adj.* uninhabited, deserted; empty, vacant.

**deshacer**[31] *v. irr.* to undo; to dissolve; to destroy; to untie; **-se** to dissolve; to melt; to waste away; **-se de** to get rid of.

**desharrapado, desarrapado** *adj.* ragged, shabby, tattered.

**deshecha** *f.* simulation, pretense; **hacer la —** to feign, pretend.

**deshecho** *p.p. of* **deshacer** & *adj.* undone; ruined, destroyed, in pieces; violent (*said of rainstorms*); worn-out, fatigued; *Am.* disorderly, untidy.

**deshelar**[1] *v. irr.* to melt; to thaw; **-se** to melt; to thaw.

**desherbar**[1] *v. irr.* to weed.

**deshielo** *m.* thaw.

**deshierbe** *m.* weeding.

**deshilachar** *v.* to ravel, fray.

**deshilar** *v.* to unravel; **-se** to unravel; to fray.

**deshojar** *v.* to strip off the leaves, petals, or pages; **-se** to lose its leaves (*said of a plant or book*); to lose petals.

**deshollejar** *v.* to husk, hull; to peel, pare, skin; to shell (*beans*).

**deshonesto** *adj.* immodest; unchaste, lewd.

**deshonra** *f.* dishonor; disgrace.

**deshonrar** v. to dishonor, disgrace; to insult, offend; to seduce.

**deshonroso** adj. dishonorable; shameful.

**deshora** f. inopportune time; **a —** (or **a -s**) unexpectedly; **comer a —** to piece, eat between meals.

**deshuesar** v. to stone, remove the pits or stones from (fruits); to bone, remove the bones from (an animal).

**desidia** f. indolence, laziness.

**desidioso** adj. indolent, negligent, lazy; listless.

**desierto** adj. deserted, uninhabited; alone, lonely; m. desert, wilderness.

**designación** f. designation; appointment.

**designar** v. to designate, appoint, select; to design, plan, intend.

**designio** m. design, plan, purpose.

**desigual** adj. unequal; uneven; variable, changeable.

**desigualdad** f. inequality; unevenness; roughness (of the ground).

**desilusión** f. disillusion, disappointment.

**desilusionar** v. to disillusion, disappoint; **-se** to become disillusioned; to lose one's illusions.

**desinencia** f. termination, ending (of a word).

**desinfectante** adj. disinfecting; m. disinfectant.

**desinfectar** v. to disinfect.

**desinflado** adj. deflated, not inflated, flat.

**desinterés** m. disinterestedness, unselfishness, impartiality.

**desinteresado** adj. disinterested, unselfish, fair, impartial.

**desistir** v. to desist, stop, cease.

**deslavado** p.p. & adj. half-washed; weakened; faded; pale; saucy.

**deslavar** v. to wash away; to fade; to wash superficially.

**desleal** adj. disloyal, faithless.

**desleír**[15] v. irr. to dissolve; to dilute, make thin or weak; **-se** to become diluted.

**deslindar** v. to mark off, mark the boundaries of.

**desliz** m. slip, slide; error.

**deslizador** m. glider.

**deslizamiento** m. slip, slipping; glide; sliding, skidding.

**deslizar**[9] v. to slip, slide; **-se** to slip; to skid: to glide; to slip out.

**deslucido** p.p. & adj. tarnished; dull; discredited; dingy, shabby; awkward, ungraceful; inelegant.

**deslucir**[13] v. irr. to tarnish, dull the luster of; to discredit.

**deslumbrador** adj. dazzling, glaring.

**deslumbramiento** m. dazzle, glare; daze, confusion.

**deslumbrar** v. to dazzle.

**deslustrado** adj. & p.p. tarnished; dim, dull; opaque.

**deslustrar** v. to tarnish; to soil, stain (one's honor or reputation).

**deslustre** m. tarnish; disgrace.

**desmadejado** p.p. & adj. enervated, exhausted; depressed.

**desmadejar** v. to enervate, weaken.

**desmán** m. misconduct, abuse, insult; calamity, disaster.

**desmantelar** v. to dismantle, strip of furniture, equipment, etc.

**desmañado** adj. unskillful, awkward, clumsy.

**desmayar** v. to dismay; to lose strength, courage; **-se** to faint.

**desmayo** m. faint, swoon; dismay, discouragement.

**desmazalado** adj. dejected, depressed.

**desmejorar** v. to impair; to make worse; **-se** to grow worse; to waste away, lose one's health.

**desmentir**[3] v. irr. to contradict; to give the lie; **-se** to contradict oneself; to retract, take back one's word.

**desmenuzar**[9] v. to crumble, break into bits; to mince; to shred; **-se** to crumble, fall to pieces.

**desmerecer**[13] v. irr. to become unworthy of; to deteriorate, lose merit or value; to be inferior to.

**desmigajar** v. to crumb (bread); to crumble; **-se** to crumble.

**desmochar** v. to cut off, chop off (the top or tip).

**desmolado** adj. toothless, without molars.

**desmontar** v. to dismount; to cut down (a forest); to clear or level off (ground); to dismantle, take apart; to tear down; **-se** to dismount, alight, get off.

**desmoronar** v. to crumble; **-se** to crumble down, fall gradually to pieces.

**desnatar** v. to skim, take the cream from (milk).

**desnaturalizado** adj. unnatural, cruel; **alcohol —** denatured alcohol (made unfit for drinking); **madre desnaturalizada** unnatural mother (one without motherly instincts).

**desnudar** v. to undress, uncover; **-se** to undress.

**desnudez** f. nudity, nakedness.

**desnudo** adj. nude, naked, bare.

**desobedecer**[13] v. irr. to disobey.

**desobediencia** f. disobedience; **desobediente** adj. disobedient.

**desocupación** f. unemployment; idleness; vacationing.

**desocupado** adj. unoccupied; unemployed, idle; empty, vacant.

**desocupar** v. to empty, vacate; **-se de un negocio** to get rid of, or not pay attention to, a business.

**desoír**[36] v. irr. to turn a deaf ear to, not to heed; to refuse (a petition).

**desolación** f. desolation; ruin; loneliness; anguish, affliction, grief.

**desolado** adj. desolate; p.p. of **desolar**.

**desolar**[2] v. irr. to lay waste, ruin; **-se** to be in anguish; to grieve.

**desollar**[2] v. irr. to skin, flay; to fleece, extort money from.

**desorbitado**[3] adj. out of its orbit; out of

place or proportion; decentered; *Ch.,
Andes* popeyed, with bulging eyes;
*Am.* crazy, eccentric.

**desorden** *m.* disorder, confusion.

**desordenado** *adj.* disorderly; lawless;
unsettled; *p.p. of* **desordenar.**

**desordenar** *v.* to disturb, confuse, upset.

**desorientar** *v.* to throw off one's bearings; to lead astray; to misdirect, mislead; to confuse; **-se** to lose one's
bearings; to go astray, get lost.

**despabilado** *adj.* wakeful; wide-awake;
bright, lively.

**despabilar** *v.* to snuff, trim the wick of
(*a candle*); to enliven, awaken (*the
mind*), sharpen (*the wits*); **-se** to wake
up, rouse oneself, shake off drowsiness.

**despacio** *adv.* slowly.

**despacioso** *adj.* slow.

**despachar** *v.* to dispatch; to send; to
facilitate; to ship.

**despacho** *m.* (*oficina*) office, bureau;
salesroom; (*comunicación*) dispatch;
(*envío*) sending; shipment; (*sin demora*) promptness; *Ch.* country store,
farm store.

**despachurrar** *v.* to crush, squash.

**desparejo** *adj.* unequal, uneven.

**desparpajar** *v.* to upset, disarrange; to
rant, talk too much; *Mex.* to disperse,
scatter.

**desparpajo** *m.* ease, freedom of man-
.ner; freshness, pertness; *Col.* dispersion, scattering; *Am.* disorder,
jumble.

**desparramar** *v.* to scatter, spread; to
spill; to squander; **-se** to "spread"
oneself, spend lavishly; to scatter; to
spill.

**desparramo** *m. Ch., C.A.* scattering,
spreading, spilling; *Ríopl., Carib.*
disorder, commotion.

**despatarrarse** *v.* to sprawl; to fall
sprawling to the ground.

**despecho** *m.* spite; grudge; despair;
weaning; **a — de** in spite of.

**despedazar**[9] *v.* to break, cut, tear into
pieces.

**despedida** *f.* farewell; departure; dismissal.

**despedir**[5] *v. irr.* (*cesar*) to discharge,
dismiss; (*emitir*) emit, throw off, give
off; to see (*a person*) off (*at a station,
airport, etc.*); **-se** to take leave, say
good-bye.

**despegar**[7] *v.* to detach; to unfasten; to
take off (*said of a plane*); *Am.* to unhitch; **no — los labios** not to say
a word, not to open one's mouth; **-se**
to grow apart; to come loose or
become detached.

**despego** = **desapego.**

**despegue** *m.* takeoff (*of an airplane*).

**despejado** *adj.* clear, cloudless; smart,
bright; *p.p. of* **despejar.**

**despejar** *v.* to clear; to remove obstacles
from; **-se** to clear up (*as the sky*); to
clear one's mind.

**despellejar** *v.* to skin, flay.

**despensa** *f.* pantry; storeroom (*for
food*); food provisions.

**despensero** *m.* butler; steward.

**despeñadero** *m.* steep cliff, precipice.

**despeñar** *v.* to fling down a precipice;
**-se** to fall down a precipice; to throw
oneself down a cliff.

**despepitar** *v.* to seed, remove the seeds
from; **-se** to talk or shout vehemently;
to rave, talk wildly; **-se por una cosa**
to long for something; to be crazy
about something.

**desperdiciado** *adj.* wasteful; *p.p. of*
**desperdiciar.**

**desperdiciar** *v.* to squander; to waste.

**desperdicio** *m.* waste; extravagance;
**-s** leftovers, garbage; residue.

**desperdigar**[7] *v.* to disperse; to scatter;
to strew.

**desperezarse**[9] *v.* to stretch oneself.

**desperfecto** *m.* damage; flaw, defect.

**despertador** *m.* alarm clock.

**despertar**[1] *v. irr.* to awaken; to wake
up; **-se** to wake up.

**despiadado** *adj.* pitiless, heartless,
cruel.

**despierto** *adj.* awake; wide-awake.

**despilfarrado** *adj.* wasteful, extravagant; ragged; *p.p. of* **despilfarrar.**

**despilfarrar** *v.* to squander; to waste.

**despilfarro** *m.* extravagance, squander-
ing; waste.

**despistar** *v.* to throw off the track.

**desplante** *m.* arrogance; impudent remark or act.

**desplazar**[9] *v.* to displace.

**desplegar**[1,7] *v. irr.* to unfold; to unfurl; to show, manifest.

**desplomar** *v.* to cause (*a wall*) to lean;
**-se** to slump; to topple over, tumble
down, collapse.

**desplome** *m.* collapse; toppling over;
landslide.

**desplumar** *v.* to pick, pluck (*a fowl*);
to fleece, skin, rob, strip; **-se** to molt,
shed the feathers.

**despoblado** *adj.* uninhabited, desolate;
**— de árboles** treeless; *m.* open country; uninhabited place; wilderness.

**despojar** *v.* to despoil, rob; to strip (of),
deprive (of); **-se** to undress; to deprive oneself.

**despojo** *m.* plundering, robbery; spoil,
booty; leftover, scrap; **-s** remains.

**desportilladura** *f.* chip; nick.

**desportillar** *v.* to chip; to nick.

**desposar** *v.* to marry; **-se** to become
formally engaged; to get married.

**déspota** *m. & f.* despot, tyrant.

**despótico** *adj.* despotic, tyrannical.

**despotismo** *m.* despotism, tyranny.

**despreciable** *adj.* contemptible; worthless; insignificant, negligible.

**despreciar** *v.* to despise, scorn.

**desprecio** *m.* scorn, contempt.

**desprender** *v.* to unfasten, loosen; to
detach; **-se** to get loose, come un-
fastened; to climb down; to get rid
(of); to be inferred, be deduced.

**desprendimiento** *m.* detachment; generosity; unfastening; landslide.

**DE**

**despreocupado** *p.p.* & *adj.* unbiased; liberal, broadminded; unconventional, carefree; *Am.* careless, slovenly; *Am.* indifferent to criticism.

**desprestigiar** *v.* to discredit, harm the reputation of; **-se** to lose one's prestige.

**desprestigio** *m.* discredit, loss of prestige.

**desprevenido** *adj.* unprepared; unaware.

**despropósito** *m.* absurdity, nonsense.

**desprovisto** *adj.* destitute; lacking; devoid.

**después** *adv.* after, afterward; then, later; — **de** *prep.* after; — **(de) que** *conj.* after.

**despuntado** *adj.* blunt, dull; *p.p.* of **despuntar.**

**despuntar** *v.* (*quitar la punta* ) to blunt; to cut off (*a point*); nip; (*brotar*) to bud or sprout; (*sobresalir*) to excel; to be clever, witty; — **el alba** to begin to dawn.

**desquitar** *v.* to retrieve, restore (*a loss*); **-se** to get even, take revenge; to win back one's money; to make up (for).

**desquite** *m.* retaliation, revenge; getting even; recovery of a loss; return game or match.

**desrazonable** *adj.* unreasonable.

**destacado** *adj.* outstanding; *p.p.* of **destacar.**

**destacamento** *m.* military detachment.

**destacar**[6] *v.* to detach (*troops*); to make stand out; to stand out; **hacer** — to emphasize; to make stand out; **-se** to stand out.

**destapar** *v.* to uncover; to uncork; *Am.* to start running; **-se** to uncover, get uncovered; to get uncorked; *Am.* to burst out talking.

**destartalado** *adj.* in disorder; in rack and ruin; dismantled, stripped of furniture.

**destechado** *adj.* roofless.

**destellar** *v.* to flash; to sparkle, twinkle; to gleam.

**destello** *m.* flash, sparkle, gleam.

**destemplado** *adj.* out of tune, out of harmony; immoderate; **sentirse** — not to feel well; to feel feverish.

**desteñir**[5,19] *v. irr.* to discolor; to fade; to bleach; **-se** to become discolored; to fade.

**desternillarse** *v.* — **de risa** to split one's sides with laughter.

**desterrado** *m.* exile; outcast; *p.p.* & *adj.* exiled, banished.

**desterrar**[1] *v. irr.* to exile, banish; to remove earth (from).

**destetar** *v.* to wean.

**destierro** *m.* exile.

**destilación** *f.* distillation.

**destiladera** *f.* still; *Am.* filter.

**destilar** *v.* to distill; to drip, trickle; to filter.

**destilería** *f.* distillery.

**destinación** *f.* destination.

**destinar** *v.* to destine; to employ.

**destinatario** *m.* addressee.

**destino** *m.* destiny, fate; destination; employment, job.

**destituido** *adj.* destitute; *p.p.* of **destituir.**

**destituir**[32] *v. irr.* to deprive.

**destornillador** *m.* screwdriver.

**destornillar** *v.* to unscrew.

**destrabar** *v.* to unlock, unfasten; to untie; to separate; to unfetter.

**destreza** *f.* dexterity, skill, ability.

**destronar** *v.* to dethrone, depose, overthrow.

**destrozar**[9] *v.* to shatter, cut to pieces; to destroy; to squander.

**destrozo** *m.* destruction; ruin.

**destrucción** *f.* destruction.

**destructivo** *adj.* destructive.

**destructor** *adj.* destructive; *m.* destroyer.

**destruir**[32] *v. irr.* to destroy; to ruin.

**desunir** *v.* to divide, separate.

**desusado** *adj.* unusual, unaccustomed; obsolete, out of use.

**desuso** *m.* disuse; obsoleteness.

**desvaído** *adj.* lanky, tall and awkward; gaunt; dull, faded.

**desvainar** *v.* to shell (*peas, beans, etc.*).

**desvalido** *adj.* abandoned; destitute; helpless.

**desvalijar** *v.* to ransack the contents of a valise; to rob.

**desván** *m.* garret, attic.

**desvanecer**[13] *v. irr.* to fade, dissolve; to make vain; to make dizzy; **-se** to evaporate; to vanish; to fade out, disappear; to get dizzy.

**desvanecido** *adj.* (*desmayado*) dizzy, faint; (*orgulloso*) proud, haughty; *p.p.* of **desvanecer.**

**desvanecimiento** *m.* dizziness, faintness; vanity.

**desvariar**[17] *v.* to rave, be delirious; to rant, talk excitedly; to talk nonsense.

**desvarío** *m.* raving; delirium; madness; inconstancy.

**desvelado** *adj.* sleepless, awake; watchful; *p.p.* of **desvelar.**

**desvelar** *v.* to keep (*another*) awake; **-se** to keep awake; to have insomnia, lose sleep; to be worried, anxious.

**desvelo** *m.* lack of sleep; restlessness; vigilance, watchfulness; worry, anxiety.

**desvencijado** *adj.* tottering, rickety, shaky, falling apart.

**desventaja** *f.* disadvantage.

**desventura** *f.* misfortune, unhappiness.

**desventurado** *adj.* unfortunate, unhappy, miserable, wretched.

**desvergonzado** *adj.* shameless, brazen.

**desvergüenza** *f.* shamelessness; disgrace; shame; insolence; impudent word.

**desvestir**[5] *v. irr.* to undress; **-se** to undress.

**desviación** *f.* deviation, turning aside, shift; detour.

**desviar**[17] *v.* to deviate, turn aside; to swerve; **-se** to shift direction; to branch off, turn off the main road; to swerve.

**desvío** *m.* deviation, turning aside; indifference, coldness; side track, railroad siding; detour.

**desvirtuar**[18] *v.* to impair, diminish the value or quality of.

**desvivirse** *v.* — **por** to long for; to be excessively fond of, be crazy about, make a fuss over; to do one's best for; **ella se desvive por complacerme** she does her utmost to please me.

**desyerbar** = **desherbar.**

**detallar** *v.* to detail, report in detail; to retail.

**detalle** *m.* detail; retail; **¡ahí está el — !** that's the point.

**detallista** *m.* & *f.* retailer; detailer, person fond of detail.

**detective, detectivo** *m.* detective.

**detención** *f.* detention, arrest; stop, halt; delay.

**detener**[45] *v. irr.* to detain, stop; to arrest; **-se** to halt; to delay oneself, stay.

**detenimiento** *m.* detention; delay; care, deliberation.

**deteriorar** *v.* to deteriorate, damage; **-se** to deteriorate, become impaired or damaged; to wear out.

**deterioro** *m.* deterioration, impairment.

**determinación** *f.* determination; firmness.

**determinar** *v.* to determine; to decide; **-se** to resolve, decide.

**detestable** *adj.* detestable; hateful.

**detestar** *v.* to detest.

**detonación** *f.* detonation, report (*of a gun*), loud explosion; pop.

**detonar** *v.* to detonate, explode with a loud noise; to pop.

**detrás** *adv.* behind; — **de** *prep.* behind; **por —** from the rear, by the rear, from behind.

**deuda** *f.* debt; indebtedness.

**deudo** *m.* relative, kinsman.

**deudor** *m.* debtor; *adj.* indebted, obligated.

**devanar** *v.* to spool, wind on a spool; **-se los sesos** to rack one's brain.

**devaneo** *m.* frenzy; dissipation; wandering; idle pursuit; giddiness.

**devastar** *v.* to devastate, lay waste, destroy.

**devenir**[48] *v. irr.* to befall; to become, be transformed into.

**devoción** *f.* devotion; piety; attachment.

**devocionario** *m.* prayer book.

**devolución** *f.* return, giving back; replacement.

**devolver**[2,52] *v. irr.* to return, give back, pay back.

**devorador** *adj.* devouring; absorbing; ravenous; *m.* devourer.

**devorar** *v.* to devour, gobble up.

**devoto** *adj.* devout, religious, pious; very fond (of).

**devuelto** *p.p. of* **devolver.**

**día** *m.* day; **al otro —** on the next day; **hoy —** nowadays; **un — sí y otro no** every other day.

**diablo** *m.* devil, demon.

**diablura** *f.* deviltry, mischief, devilish prank.

**diabólico** *adj.* diabolic, devilish, fiendish.

**diácono** *m.* deacon.

**diadema** *f.* diadem, crown.

**diáfano** *adj.* transparent, clear; sheer.

**diagnosticar**[6] *v.* to diagnose.

**diagrama** *m.* diagram; graph.

**dialecto** *m.* dialect.

**dialogar**[7] *v.* to dialogue.

**diálogo** *m.* dialogue.

**diamante** *m.* diamond.

**diámetro** *m.* diameter.

**diantre** *m.* devil.

**diapasón** *m.* pitch (*of a sound*); tuning fork.

**diapositiva** *f. Spain* slide, lantern slide.

**diario** *adj.* daily; *m.* newspaper; daily expense; journal, diary.

**diarrea** *f.* diarrhea.

**dibujante** *m.* & *f.* draftsman; designer.

**dibujar** *v.* (*diseñar*) to draw, make a drawing of; (*describir*) depict, portray; describe; **-se** to appear, show.

**dibujo** *m.* drawing; delineation, portrayal, picture; — **natural** drawing of the human figure, drawing from life.

**dicción** *f.* diction; word; choice of words, style.

**diciembre** *m.* December.

**dictado** *m.* dictation; title; dictate; **escribir al —** to take dictation.

**dictador** *m.* dictator.

**dictadura** *f.* dictatorship.

**dictamen** *m.* opinion, judgment.

**dictaminar** *v.* to give an opinion or judgment.

**dictar** *v.* to dictate.

**dicha** *f.* happiness; good luck.

**dicharachero** *adj.* fond of making wisecracks; witty.

**dicharacho** *m.* wisecrack, smart remark; malicious remark.

**dicho** *p.p. of* **decir** said; — **y hecho** no sooner said than done; *m.* saying, popular proverb.

**dichoso** *adj.* happy, lucky.

**diente** *m.* tooth; tusk; — **de león** dandelion; **de -s afuera** insincerely; *Am.* **pelar el —** to smile affectedly.

**diéresis** *f.* diaeresis (*as in* **vergüenza**).

**diesel** *m.* diesel; diesel motor.

**diestra** *f.* right hand.

**diestro** *adj.* skillful; right; *m.* matador; skillful swordsman; halter.

**dieta** *f.* diet; assembly; salary, fee.

**diezmo** *m.* tithe.

**difamación** *f.* libel, slander.

**difamador** *m.* slanderer.

**difamar** *v.* to defame, libel, malign, slander.

**difamatorio** *adj.* scandalous, slandering.

**diferencia** *f.* difference.

**diferenciar** *v.* to differentiate, distinguish; to differ, disagree; **-se** to distinguish oneself; to become different.

**diferente** *adj.* different.

**diferir**[3] *v. irr.* to defer, put off, delay; to differ, disagree; to be different.

**difícil** *adj.* difficult.

**dificultad** *f.* difficulty.

**dificultar** *v.* to make difficult; **— el paso** to impede or obstruct the passage; **-se** to become difficult.

**dificultoso** *adj.* difficult, hard.

**difteria** *f.* diphtheria.

**difundir** *v.* to diffuse, spread out, scatter; to broadcast by radio.

**difunto** *adj.* deceased, dead; *m.* corpse.

**difusión** *f.* diffusion, spreading, scattering; wordiness; broadcasting.

**difuso** *adj.* diffuse; diffused, widespread.

**digerible** *adj.* digestible.

**digerir**[3] *v. irr.* to digest.

**dignarse** *v.* to deign, condescend.

**dignatario** *m.* dignitary (*person in a high office*).

**dignidad** *f.* dignity.

**digno** *adj.* worthy; dignified.

**digresión** *f.* digression.

**dije** *m.* trinket, small piece of jewelry; locket; woman of fine qualities, a "jewel"; *Am.* locket or charm.

**dilación** *f.* delay.

**dilatado** *adj.* vast, spacious; extensive; *p.p. of* **dilatar.**

**dilatar** *v.* to dilate, widen, enlarge; to expand; to lengthen, extend; to spread out; to defer, put off, retard; **-se** to expand; to be diffuse, wordy; *Am.* to delay oneself, take long.

**diligencia** *f.* diligence, care, industry; speed; stagecoach; business, errand.

**diligente** *adj.* diligent; quick, speedy.

**diluir**[32] *v. irr.* to dilute.

**diluvio** *m.* flood.

**dimensión** *f.* dimension.

**dimes:** **— y diretes** quibbling, arguing; **andar en — y diretes** to quibble, argue.

**diminución** *f.* diminution, decrease.

**diminutivo** *adj.* diminutive, tiny; diminishing; *m.* diminutive.

**diminuto** *adj.* tiny, little.

**dimisión** *f.* resignation (*from an office*).

**dimitir** *v.* to resign, give up (*a position, office, etc.*).

**dinámica** *f.* dynamics; **dinámico** *adj.* dynamic.

**dinamismo** *m.* vigor, forcefulness; dynamic force or energy.

**dinamita** *f.* dynamite.

**dínamo** *m.* dynamo.

**dinastía** *f.* dynasty.

**dineral** *m.* a lot of money.

**dinero** *m.* money; currency; *Peru* Peruvian silver coin equivalent to about ten cents; **— contante y sonante** ready cash, hard cash.

**dios** *m.* god; **Dios** God; **a la buena de —** without malice; without plan, haphazard, at random.

**diosa** *f.* goddess.

**diplomacia** *f.* diplomacy; tact.

**diplomático** *adj.* diplomatic; tactful; *m.* diplomat.

**diputación** *f.* deputation; committee.

**diputado** *m.* deputy; representative.

**diputar** *v.* to depute, delegate, commission.

**dique** *m.* dike; barrier; **— de carena** dry dock.

**dirección** *f.* direction, course; advice, guidance; management; board of directors; office of the board of directors; address.

**directivo** *adj.* directive, directing, guiding; **mesa directiva** board of directors.

**directo** *adj.* direct, straight.

**director** *m.* director, manager; *adj.* directing.

**directorio** *adj.* directory, directive, directing; *m.* directory, book of instructions; directorate, board of directors.

**dirigente** *adj.* directing, leading; *m.* leader, director.

**dirigir**[11] *v.* to direct, manage, govern; to guide; to address (*letters, packages*); to dedicate; **-se a** to address (*a person*); to go to or toward.

**discernimiento** *m.* discernment, keen judgment, insight, discrimination.

**discernir**[3] *v. irr.* to discern; to distinguish; to discriminate.

**disciplina** *f.* discipline, training; rule of conduct; order; any art or science; scourge, whip.

**disciplinar** *v.* to discipline, train; to drill; **-se** to discipline oneself; to scourge oneself.

**discípulo** *m.* pupil; disciple.

**disco** *m.* disk; discus; phonograph record.

**díscolo** *adj.* unruly, disobedient; unfriendly.

**discordancia** *f.* discord, disagreement.

**discordia** *f.* discord.

**discreción** *f.* discretion; keenness; wit; **darse (*or* rendirse) a —** to surrender unconditionally; **discrecional** *adj.* optional.

**discrepancia** *f.* discrepancy.

**discreto** *adj.* discreet, prudent; clever.

**disculpa** *f.* excuse; apology.

**disculpable** *adj.* excusable.

**disculpar** *v.* to excuse, free from blame; **-se** to excuse oneself, apologize.

**discurrir** *v.* (*charlar*) to discuss; (*recorrer*) to ramble about; (*imaginar*) to invent, think out.

**discursear** *v.* to make speeches.

**discurso** *m.* discourse; speech; reasoning; lapse of time.

**discusión** *f.* discussion.

**discutible** *adj.* debatable, questionable.

**discutir** *v.* to discuss.

**disecar**[6] *v.* to dissect; to stuff and mount (*the skins of animals*).

**diseminación** *f.* dissemination, spread, scattering.

**diseminar** *v.* to disseminate, scatter, spread.

**disensión** *f.* dissension, dissent, disagreement.

**disentería** *f.* dysentery.

**disentir**[3] *v. irr.* to dissent, differ, disagree.

**diseñador** *m.* designer.

**diseñar** *v.* to design; to sketch, outline.

**diseño** *m.* design; sketch, outline.

**disertar** *v.* to discourse, discuss.

**disforme** *adj.* deformed; ugly, hideous; out of proportion.

**disfraz** *m.* disguise, mask; masquerade costume.

**disfrazar**[9] *v.* to disguise, conceal; **-se** to disguise oneself; to masquerade.

**disfrutar** *v.* to enjoy; to reap benefit or advantage; to make use of.

**disfrute** *m.* enjoyment, benefit, use.

**disgustar** *v.* to disgust, displease; **-se** to get angry; to get bored.

**disgusto** *m.* displeasure; unpleasantness; annoyance; quarrel; grief; disgust.

**disidente** *m.* & *f.* dissident; protester.

**disimulado** *adj.* underhanded, sly, cunning; *p.p. of* **disimular.**

**disimular** *v.* to feign, hide, mask; to overlook, excuse.

**disimulo** *m.* dissimulation, feigning, pretense; slyness; reserve.

**disipación** *f.* dissipation; waste, extravagance.

**disipar** *v.* to dissipate, scatter; to squander; **-se** to vanish.

**dislocar**[6] *v.* to dislocate, put out of joint; **-se** to become dislocated, get out of joint.

**disminución = diminución.**

**disminuir**[32] *v. irr.* to diminish, decrease, lessen.

**disociación** *f.* dissociation, separation.

**disociar** *v.* to dissociate, separate.

**disolución** *f.* dissolution, breaking up; dissoluteness, lewdness.

**disoluto** *adj.* dissolute, loose, immoral, dissipated.

**disolver**[2,52] *v. irr.* to dissolve; to melt.

**disonancia** *f.* discord.

**disparada** *f.* *C.A.*, *Mex.*, *Carib.*, *Ríopl.* rush, run.

**disparar** *v.* to shoot, fire, discharge; to throw; **-se** to run away, dart out.

**disparatado** *adj.* absurd, foolish, senseless.

**disparatar** *v.* to talk nonsense; to blunder; to act foolishly.

**disparate** *m.* nonsense, blunder.

**disparidad** *f.* inequality.

**disparo** *m.* shooting, discharge, explosion; shot; sudden dash, run.

**dispensa** *f.* dispensation; exemption.

**dispensar** *v.* to excuse, absolve, pardon; to grant, give.

**dispensario** *m.* dispensary; pharmaceutical laboratory; pharmacopoeia (*book containing list and description of drugs*).

**dispersar** *v.* to disperse, scatter.

**dispersión** *f.* dispersion, dispersal.

**displicencia** *f.* displeasure, discontent, dislike.

**displicente** *adj.* unpleasant, disagreeable, cross.

**disponer**[40] *v. irr.* (*arreglar*) to dispose;

to arrange, put in order; to prepare; (*mandar*) to order, command; **-se** to get ready; to make one's will and testament.

**disponible** *adj.* spare, available; on hand.

**disposición** *f.* disposition; arrangement; order, command; aptitude; disposal.

**dispuesto** *p.p. of* **disponer** & *adj.* disposed; ready; fit; smart, clever.

**disputa** *f.* dispute.

**disputar** *v.* to dispute.

**distancia** *f.* distance.

**distante** *adj.* distant.

**distar** *v.* to be distant, far (from).

**distender**[1] *v. irr.* to distend, stretch; to inflate; **-se** to distend, expand.

**distinción** *f.* distinction.

**distinguido** *adj.* & *p.p.* distinguished.

**distinguir**[12] *v.* to distinguish; **-se** to distinguish oneself, excel; to differ, be different.

**distintivo** *adj.* distinctive, distinguishing; *m.* distinguishing characteristic; mark, sign; badge.

**distinto** *adj.* distinct, plain, clear; different.

**distracción** *f.* distraction; diversion, amusement; lack of attention.

**distraer**[46] *v. irr.* to distract; to divert, amuse; to lead astray; to divert (*funds*); **-se** to have a good time; to be absentminded; to be inattentive.

**distraído** *adj.* distracted; inattentive; absentminded; *Am.* slovenly, untidy.

**distribución** *f.* distribution, apportionment.

**distribuidor** *m.* distributor; *adj.* distributing.

**distribuir**[32] *v. irr.* to distribute; to sort, classify.

**distrito** *m.* district; region.

**disturbio** *m.* disturbance.

**disuelto** *p.p. of* **disolver.**

**divagación** *f.* rambling, digression.

**divagar**[7] *v.* to ramble; to digress.

**diván** *m.* divan, sofa.

**divergencia** *f.* divergence; difference (*of opinion*).

**divergir**[11] *v.* to diverge; to differ.

**diversidad** *f.* diversity; variety.

**diversión** *f.* amusement.

**diverso** *adj.* diverse; different; **-s** several, various.

**divertido** *adj.* amusing, funny.

**divertir**[3] *v. irr.* to amuse, entertain; to divert, turn aside; **-se** to have a good time, amuse oneself.

**dividendo** *m.* dividend.

**dividir** *v.* to divide, split.

**divinidad** *f.* divinity, deity; ¡**qué —**! what a beauty!

**divino** *adj.* divine.

**divisa** *f.* device, emblem.

**divisar** *v.* to sight; to make out, distinguish.

**división** *f.* division.

**divorciar** *v.* to divorce; to separate.

**divorcio** *m.* divorce.

**divulgar**[7] *v.* to divulge, spread, make public, give out.

**diz** = **dice; dizque** they say that...

**dobladillar** *v.* to hem.

**dobladillo** *m.* hem; — **de ojo** hemstitch.

**doblar** *v.* to bend, fold; to double; to toll, knell; *Ríopl.* to knock down; — **la esquina** to turn the corner; **-se** to stoop; to bend down; to give in.

**doble** *adj.* double, twofold; double-faced, hypocritical; *Am.* broke, poor; *m.* fold; toll, tolling of bells, knell.

**doblegar**[7] *v.* to bend; to fold; **-se** to bend over; to stoop; to submit, yield.

**doblez** *m.* fold, crease; duplicity, hypocrisy.

**docena** *f.* dozen.

**docente** *adj.* teaching; educational; **cuerpo** — faculty (*of a school*).

**dócil** *adj.* docile, obedient, manageable, meek; flexible; **docilidad** *f.* obedience, meekness, gentleness; flexibility.

**docto** *adj.* learned; expert.

**doctor** *m.* doctor.

**doctorar** *v.* to grant a doctor's degree to; **-se** to get a doctor's degree.

**doctrina** *f.* doctrine.

**documentar** *v.* to document.

**documento** *m.* document.

**dogal** *m.* halter; noose.

**dogma** *m.* dogma; **dogmático** *adj.* dogmatic, pertaining to dogma; positive.

**dolencia** *f.* ailment; ache, aching.

**doler**[2] *v. irr.* to ache, hurt, cause pain; to cause grief; **-se de** to feel pity for, feel sorry for; to repent from.

**doliente** *adj.* sorrowful; suffering; aching; *m.* sick person, patient; mourner.

**dolor** *m.* pain, ache; sorrow, grief.

**dolorido** *adj.* aching, sore; afflicted; repentant; doleful.

**doloroso** *adj.* painful; sorrowful.

**doma** *f.* breaking of horses.

**domador** *m.* horsebreaker, bronco-buster.

**domar** *v.* to tame, subdue.

**domeñar** *v.* to tame; to subdue; to dominate.

**domesticar**[6] *v.* to domesticate, tame.

**doméstico** *adj.* domestic; *m.* house servant.

**domiciliar** *v.* to house, lodge; *Ríopl.* to address (*a letter*); **-se** to take up residence; to settle down; to dwell, reside.

**domicilio** *m.* home, dwelling.

**dominación** *f.* domination, rule, authority.

**dominador** *adj.* dominant, dominating; domineering, bossy; *m.* ruler, boss.

**dominante** *adj.* dominant; domineering; tyrannical; prevailing, predominant.

**dominar** *v.* to dominate, rule, lead; to stand out, tower above; to master.

**dómine** *m.* teacher; pedagogue; pedant.

**domingo** *m.* Sunday; — **de ramos** Palm Sunday.

**dominio** *m.* domain; dominion; authority; mastery (*of a science, art, language, etc.*).

**dominó** *m.* domino.

**don** *m.* gift; ability, knack; Don (*title used only before Christian names of men*).

**donación** *f.* donation; grant.

**donador** *m.* donor, giver.

**donaire** *m.* grace, elegance; wit; humor; witty remark.

**donairoso** *adj.* elegant, graceful; witty.

**donar** *v.* to donate.

**doncella** *f.* virgin, maiden; maidservant; *Col.* felon (*sore or inflammation near a finger or toenail*).

**donde** *rel. adv.* where, in which; **a** — (**adonde**) where, to which; *C.A.*, *Ríopl.* to the house of; **de** — from where, from which; **en** — where, in which; **por** — where, through which; wherefore; — **no** otherwise; if not; **¿dónde?** *interr. adv.* where?; **¿por** — ? which way?

**dondequiera** *adv.* wherever; anywhere.

**donjuanismo** *m.* Don Juanism, conduct reminiscent of Don Juan Tenorio.

**donoso** *adj.* witty, gay; graceful.

**doña** *f.* Doña (*title used only before Christian names of women*).

**dorado** *p.p.* & *adj.* gilded, gilt; golden; *m.* gilding; *Am.* a kind of hummingbird; **doradillo** *adj. Am.* honey-colored, golden (*applied to horses*).

**dorar** *v.* to gild.

**dormir**[4] *v. irr.* to sleep; **-se** to go to sleep, fall asleep; to become numb.

**dormitar** *v.* to doze.

**dormitorio** *m.* dormitory; bedroom.

**dorso** *m.* back, reverse.

**dosel** *m.* canopy.

**dosis** *f.* dose.

**dotación** *f.* endowment, endowing; donation, foundation; dowry; complement (*personnel of a warship*); office force.

**dotar** *v.* to endow; to provide with a dowry.

**dote** *m.* & *f.* dowry; *f.* natural gift, talent, or quality.

**draga** *f.* dredge, dredging machine.

**dragado** *m.* dredging.

**dragaminas** *m.* mine sweeper.

**dragar**[7] *v.* to dredge.

**dragón** *m.* dragon.

**drama** *m.* drama.

**dramático** *adj.* dramatic; *m.* dramatic actor; playwright, dramatist.

**dramatizar**[9] *v.* to dramatize.

**dramaturgo** *m.* playwright, dramatist.

**drenaje** *m. Am.* drainage.

**drenar** *v. Am.* to drain.

**dril** *m.* drill (*strong cotton or linen cloth*).

**droga** *f.* (*medicina*) drug, medicine; (*mentira*) lie, fib; trick; (*molestia*) bother, nuisance; *Peru, Carib.* bad debt; *Ríopl.* drug on the market, unsalable article.

**droguería** *f.* drugstore; drug business.

**droguero** *m.* druggist; *Am.* cheat, debt evader.

**droguista** *m.* & *f.* druggist; cheat, crook.

**ducha** *f.* shower bath; douche.

**ducho** *adj.* expert, skillful.

**duda** *f.* doubt.

**dudable** *adj.* doubtful.

**dudar** *v.* to doubt; to hesitate.

**dudoso** *adj.* doubtful; uncertain.

**duela** *f.* stave (*of a barrel*); *Mex., Andes* long, narrow floor board.

**duelo** *m.* (*luto*) grief, sorrow; mourning; mourners; (*pleito*) duel; **estar de —** to be in mourning; to mourn.

**duende** *m.* goblin.

**dueña** *f.* owner, landlady; duenna, chaperon or governess.

**dueño** *m.* owner; master.

**dueto, duo** *m.* duet.

**dulce** *adj.* sweet; pleasant, agreeable; fresh (*water*); soft (*metal*); *m.* sweet-meat; candy; preserves; *Am.* sugar, honey; **dulcería** *f.* candy shop.

**dulcificar**⁶ *v.* to sweeten; to soften.

**dulzón** *adj.* over-sweet, sickeningly sweet.

**dulzura** *f.* sweetness; meekness.

**duna** *f.* dune, sand dune.

**duplicado** *adj.* & *m.* duplicate; **por —** in duplicate; *p.p. of* **duplicar.**

**duplicar**⁶ *v.* to duplicate, double; to repeat.

**duplicidad** *f.* duplicity, deceit, deceitfulness, treachery.

**duque** *m.* duke.

**duquesa** *f.* duchess.

**durabilidad** *f.* durability, durable quality, wear.

**durable** *adj.* durable.

**duración** *f.* duration.

**duradero** *adj.* durable, lasting.

**durante** *prep.* during, for.

**durar** *v.* to last, endure; to wear well.

**durazno** *m.* peach; peach tree; **duraznero** *m.* peach tree.

**dureza** *f.* hardness; harshness.

**durmiente** *adj.* sleeping; *m.* sleeper; crossbeam; *Col., Ven., Mex., Ch.* railroad tie.

**duro** *adj.* (*sólido*) hard; firm, solid; untiring; (*cruel*) cruel; harsh; rigid; (*tacaño*) stubborn; stingy; **a duras penas** with difficulty; *Am.* **— y parejo** eagerly, tenaciously; *Am.* **hacer —** to resist stubbornly; *m.* **duro** (*Spanish dollar*).

### E

**e** *conj.* and (*before words beginning with* **i** *or* **hi**).

**ébano** *m.* ebony.

**ebrio** *adj.* drunk.

**ebullición** *f.* boiling, bubbling up.

**eclesiástico** *adj.* ecclesiastic, belonging to the church; *m.* clergyman.

**eclipsar** *v.* to eclipse; to outshine, surpass.

**écloga** *f.* eclogue, pastoral poem, idyll.

**eco** *m.* echo.

**economía** *f.* economy; **— política** economics, political economy.

**económico** *adj.* economic; economical, saving; **economista** *m.* economist.

**economizar**⁹ *v.* to economize, save.

**ecuación** *f.* equation.

**ecuador** *m.* equator.

**echar** *v.* (*tirar*) to throw, cast; to expel; to throw out; (*emitir*) to give off; to sprout; **— a correr** to run away; **-(se) a perder** to spoil; **— a pique** to sink; **-(se) a reír** to burst out laughing; **— carnes** to get fat; **— de menos** to miss; **— de ver** to notice; to make out; **— mano** to seize; **— papas** to fib; **— raíces** to take root; **— suertes** to draw lots; **-se** to lie down; *Am.* **echársela** to boast.

**edad** *f.* age.

**edén** *m.* Eden; paradise.

**edición** *f.* edition; publication.

**edificación** *f.* edification (*moral or spiritual uplift*); construction.

**edificar**⁶ *v.* to construct, build; to edify, uplift.

**edificio** *m.* edifice, building.

**editar** *v.* to publish.

**editor** *m.* publisher; *adj.* publishing.

**editorial** *adj.* publishing, editorial; *m.* editorial; *f.* publishing house.

**edredón** *m.* down quilt, comforter, quilted blanket.

**educación** *f.* education, training; breeding, manners.

**educador** *m.* educator; *adj.* educating.

**educando** *m.* pupil; inmate (*of an orphanage, boarding school, etc.*).

**educar**⁶ *v.* to educate, teach, train, raise, bring up.

**educativo** *adj.* educational.

**efectivo** *adj.* effective; real; in operation, active; *m.* cash.

**efecto** *m.* (*resultado*) effect, result; (*fin*) end, purpose; **-s** goods, personal property; **en —** in fact, actually; **llevar a —** to carry out; **surtir —** to come out as expected; to give good results.

**efectuar**¹⁸ *v.* to effect, bring about.

**eficacia** *f.* efficacy; efficiency; effectiveness.

**eficaz** *adj.* effective; active; efficient.

**eficiencia** *f.* efficiency; **eficiente** *adj.* efficient.

**efímero** *adj.* ephemeral, short-lived, brief.

**efluvio** *m.* emanation, exhalation, vapors.

**efusión** *f.* effusion, unrestrained expression of feeling, gushy manner; **— de sangre** bloodshed.

**efusivo** *adj.* effusive, too demonstrative, over-emotional.

**egipcio** *adj.* & *m.* Egyptian.

**egocéntrico** *adj.* egocentric, self-centered.

**egoísmo** *m.* selfishness.

**egoísta** *adj.* selfish; *m.* & *f.* selfish person.

**egolatría** *f.* self-worship.

**eje** *m.* axis; axle.

DI

**ejecución** *f.* execution; carrying out.

**ejecutar** *v.* to execute; to carry out; to perform, do.

**ejecutivo** *adj.* executive; active; *m.* executive.

**ejecutor** *m.* executor; **— de la justicia** executioner.

**ejemplar** *adj.* exemplary, model; *m.* copy; specimen.

**ejemplo** *m.* example; model, pattern.

**ejercer**[10] *v.* to practice (*a profession*); to exert.

**ejercicio** *m.* exercise; practice; military drill; exercise (*of authority*); **hacer —** to take exercise.

**ejercitar** *v.* to practice, exercise; to drill, train; **-se** to train oneself; to practice.

**ejército** *m.* army.

**ejido** *m.* public land, common.

**ejote** *m. Mex., Guat.* string bean.

**el** *def. art. m.* the; **— de** the one with, that one with; **— que** *rel. pron.* he who, the one that; **él** *pers. pron.* he; him, it (*after a prep.*).

**elaboración** *f.* manufacture, making; development.

**elaborar** *v.* to elaborate.

**elasticidad** *f.* elasticity.

**elástico** *adj.*, elastic; flexible; *m.* elastic; elastic tape; wire spring; **-s** *Am.* suspenders.

**elección** *f.* election; choice.

**electo** *adj.* elect, chosen; *m.* elect, person chosen.

**elector** *m.* elector, voter; *adj.* electoral, electing.

**electoral** *adj.* electoral.

**electricidad** *f.* electricity.

**electricista** *m.* electrician; electrical engineer.

**eléctrico** *adj.* electric, electrical.

**electrizar**[9] *v.* to electrify; to thrill, excite; *Am.* to anger, irritate.

**electrocardiógrafo** *m.* electrocardiograph.

**electroimán** *m.* electromagnet.

**electrónico** *adj.* electronic; **electrónica** *f.* electronics.

**elefante** *m.* elephant.

**elegancia** *f.* elegance, grace, distinguished manner.

**elegante** *adj.* elegant, graceful, polished; stylish.

**elegir**[5,11] *v. irr.* to elect, choose.

**elemental** *adj.* elementary; elemental, fundamental.

**elemento** *m.* element; **-s** elements, fundamentals; personnel; **— químicos** chemical elements, simple substances; *Am.* **ser** (*or* **estar**) **hecho un —** to be an idiot, a fool.

**elevación** *f.* elevation; height; rise; rapture.

**elevador** *m. Am.* elevator, hoist.

**elevar** *v.* to elevate, raise, lift; **-se** to go up; to soar.

**eliminación** *f.* elimination, removal.

**eliminar** *v.* to eliminate.

**elocuencia** *f.* eloquence.

**elocuente** *adj.* eloquent.

**elogiar** *v.* to praise.

**elogio** *m.* praise.

**elote** *m. Mex., C.A.* ear of corn, corn on the cob.

**elucidación** *f.* elucidation, explanation.

**elucidar** *v.* to elucidate, illustrate, explain.

**eludir** *v.* to elude, avoid, dodge.

**ella** *pers. pron.* she; her, it (*after a prep.*).

**ello** *pron.* it; **— es que** the fact is that.

**emanación** *f.* emanation, flow; fumes, vapor, odor; manifestation.

**emanar** *v.* to emanate, spring, issue.

**emancipación** *f.* emancipation.

**emancipar** *v.* to emancipate, set free; **-se** to become free.

**embajada** *f.* embassy; errand, mission.

**embajador** *m.* ambassador.

**embalador** *f.* packer.

**embalaje** *m.* packing.

**embalar** *v.* to pack; to bale, crate.

**embaldosar** *v.* to pave with flagstones or tiles.

**embalsamar** *v.* to embalm; to scent, perfume.

**embarazar**[9] *v.* (*impedir*) to hinder, to obstruct; (*preñar*) to make pregnant; **-se** to become pregnant; to become embarrassed.

**embarazo** *m.* (*obstáculo*) impediment, obstacle; (*preñez*) pregnancy; (*timidez*) bashfulness, awkwardness.

**embarazoso** *adj.* embarrassing; cumbersome, unwieldly.

**embarcación** *f.* ship, boat; embarkation.

**embarcadero** *m.* wharf, pier.

**embarcador** *m.* shipper.

**embarcar**[6] *v.* to embark; to ship; *Am.* to ship by train or any vehicle; **-se** to embark, sail; to engage (in); *Am.* to board, get on a train.

**embarco** *m.* embarkation.

**embargar**[7] *v.* to impede; to restrain; to attach, confiscate; to lay an embargo on; **estar embargado de emoción** to be overcome with emotion.

**embargo** *m.* embargo, restriction on commerce; attachment, confiscation; **sin —** nevertheless.

**embarque** *m.* shipment.

**embarrado** *p.p.* & *adj.* smeared; plastered; muddy.

**embarrar** *v.* to smear, daub.

**embaucador** *m.* cheat, impostor.

**embaucar**[6] *v.* to fool, trick, swindle, deceive.

**embebecido** *p.p.* & *adj.* absorbed; amazed.

**embebecimiento** *m.* absorption; rapture.

**embeber** *v.* to imbibe, absorb; to soak; to shrink; **-se** to be fascinated; to be absorbed.

**embelesar** *v.* to enrapture, delight, charm.

**embeleso** *m.* delight, ecstasy.

**embellecer**[13] *v. irr.* to embellish, beautify, adorn.

**embestida** *f.* sudden attack, onset, assault.

**embestir**[5] *v. irr.* to attack, assail.

**embetunar** *v.* to cover with pitch; to black.

**emblanquecer**[13] *v. irr.* to whiten; to bleach; to become white; **-se** to whiten, become white.

**emblema** *m.* emblem.

**embobar** *v.* to fool; to amuse; to fascinate; to amaze; **-se** to be amazed; to be fascinated.

**embobinado** *m.* reel assembly (*of a tape recorder or computer*).

**embocadura** *f.* mouth (*of a river*); entrance (*through a narrow passage*); mouthpiece (*of a wind instrument*); bit (*of a bridle*); taste, flavor (said of *wines*).

**embolado** *m.* bull whose horns have been tipped with balls; impotent, ineffectual person; *p.p.* of **embolar.**

**embolar** *v.* (*al toro*) to tip a bull's horns with balls; (*dar lustre*) to polish, to black; **-se** *C.A.* to get drunk.

**émbolo** *m.* piston; plunger (*of a pump*); embolus (*clot in a blood vessel*).

**embolsar** *v.* to put into a pocket or purse; **-se** to pocket, put into one's pocket.

**emborrachar** *v.* to intoxicate; **-se** to get drunk.

**emborronar** *v.* to blot; to scribble.

**emboscada** *f.* ambush.

**emboscar**[6] *v.* to ambush; **-se** to lie in ambush; to go into a forest.

**embotado** *adj.* dull, blunt; *p.p.* of **embotar.**

**embotamiento** *m.* dullness, bluntness; dulling, blunting.

**embotar** *v.* to dull, blunt; to enervate, weaken.

**embotellador** *m.* bottling machine; **embotelladora** bottling works.

**embotellar** *v.* to bottle; to bottle up; *Am.* to jail.

**embozado** *adj.* cloaked; muffled, covered up to the face.

**embozar**[7] *v.* to muffle; to cloak, conceal, disguise; to muzzle; **-se** to muffle oneself, wrap oneself.

**embragar**[7] *v.* to engage or throw in the clutch.

**embrague** *m.* clutch (*of a machine*); coupling.

**embriagar**[7] *v.* to intoxicate; **-se** to get drunk, intoxicated.

**embriaguez** *f.* intoxication; drunkenness.

**embrollar** *v.* to involve, ensnare, entangle; to confuse.

**embrollo** *m.* confusion, tangle; trickery, lie, deception.

**embromar** *v.* to chaff, make fun of, "kid"; *Am.* to bother, molest; *Am.* to delay unnecessarily; *Col., Ven.* to ruin, harm; **-se** *Am.* to be bothered, disgusted; *Mex.* to get delayed.

**embrujar** *v.* to bewitch, enchant.

**embrujo** *m.* charm, enchantment; glamour.

**embrutecer**[13] *v. irr.* to stupefy, render brutish; to dull the mind, make insensible.

**embudo** *m.* funnel; trick.

**embuste** *m.* lie, fraud; trinket.

**embustero** *m. liar; adj.* deceitful, tricky.

**embutido** *m.* sausage; inlaid work; *Am.* insertion of embroidery or lace; *p.p.* of **embutir.**

**embutir** *v.* to insert, inlay; to stuff.

**emerger**[11] *v.* to emerge, come out.

**emigración** *f.* emigration.

**emigrante** *m. & f.* emigrant.

**emigrar** *v.* to emigrate; to migrate.

**eminencia** *f.* eminence; height.

**eminente** *adj.* eminent, high, lofty.

**emisión** *f.* issue (*of bonds, money, etc.*); radio broadcast.

**emisor** *adj.* emitting; broadcasting; *m.* radio transmitter; **emisora** *f.* broadcasting station.

**emitir** *v.* to emit, give off; to utter; to send forth; to issue; to broadcast.

**emoción** *f.* emotion.

**emocional** *adj.* emotional.

**emocionante** *adj.* moving, touching, thrilling.

**emocionar** *v.* to cause emotion, touch, move; **-se** to be touched, moved, stirred.

**emotivo** *adj.* emotional.

**empacador** *m.* packer.

**empacar**[6] *v.* to pack up, wrap up, bale, crate; *Ríopl.* to goad, irritate (*an animal*); **-se** to be stubborn; to get angry; *Ríopl.* to balk; *Ríopl.* to put on airs.

**empachado** *p.p. & adj.* (*relleno*) clogged; stuffed; upset from indigestion; (*tímido*) embarrassed; bashful.

**empachar** *v.* to stuff, cram; to cause indigestion; **-se** to get upset; to get clogged; to be stuffed; to suffer indigestion; to get embarrassed.

**empacho** *m.* indigestion; bashfulness; **no tener — en** to have no objection to; to feel free to.

**empalagar**[7] *v.* to cloy; to pall on, become distasteful; to disgust.

**empalagoso** *adj.* cloying; sickeningly sweet; boring, wearisome.

**empalizada** *f.* stockade, palisade.

**empalmar** *v.* to splice; to join; **— con** to join (*as railroads or highways*).

**empalme** *m.* junction; joint, connection; splice.

**empanada** *f.* pie, meat pie; swindle, fraud.

**empanizar**[9] *v. Carib., C.A., Mex.* to bread.

**empañado** *adj. & p.p.* tarnished; dim, blurred.

**empañar** *v.* to blur, dim, tarnish.

**empapada** *f. Am.* drenching, soaking.

**empapar** *v.* to soak, drench, saturate.

**empapelador** *m.* paper hanger.

**empapelar** *v.* to paper; to wrap in paper.

**empaque** *m.* (*bulto*) packing; (*parecer*) looks, appearance, air; airs, importance; *Am., Peru* impudence.

**empaquetar** *v.* to pack; to pack in; to make a package; **-se** to dress up, doll up.

**emparedado** *adj.* shut up, confined between walls; *m.* sandwich; prisoner confined in a narrow cell.

**emparejar** *v.* to even up, level off; to match; to pair off; to overtake, catch up with.

**emparentado** *adj. & p.p.* related by marriage.

**emparentar** *v.* to become related by marriage.

**emparrado** *m.* vine arbor.

**empastar** *v.* to paste; to fill (*a tooth*); to bind (*books*); **-se** *Ch.* to get lost in the pasture; *Mex.* to become overgrown with grass.

**empaste** *m.* tooth filling; binding (*of a book*).

**empatar** *v.* (*igualar*) to tie (*in a game*), have an equal score; to have an equal number of votes; (*impedir*) to hinder, obstruct; *Col., Ven., Carib.* to tie, join.

**empate** *m.* tie, draw, equal score, equal number of votes; hindrance, obstruction; *Am.* joint, junction.

**empecinado** *adj. Am.* stubborn.

**empedernido** *adj.* hardened, hardhearted.

**empedernir**[51] *v.* to harden, toughen; **-se** to become hardened.

**empedrado** *m.* cobblestone pavement; *p.p. & adj.* paved with stones.

**empedrar**[1] *v. irr.* to pave with stones.

**empeine** *m.* instep; groin (*hollow between lower part of abdomen and thigh*).

**empellón** *m.* push, shove; **a -es** by pushing.

**empeñar** *v.* (*dar en prenda*) to pawn; (*obligar*) to oblige, compel; **-se** to persist, insist; to apply oneself; to go into debt; **-se por** to plead for, intercede for; **se empeñaron en una lucha** they engaged in a fight.

**empeño** *m.* (*fianza*) pledge, pawn; (*deseo*) persistence, insistence; eagerness, perseverance; *Am.* pawnshop; **tener — en** to be eager to.

**empeorar** *v.* to impair; to make worse; to grow worse; **-se** to grow worse.

**empequeñecer**[13] *v. irr.* to diminish, make smaller; to belittle.

**emperador** *m.* emperor; **emperatriz** *f.* empress.

**emperifollar** *v.* to decorate, adorn; **-se** to dress up, deck out, doll up.

**empero** *conj.* however, nevertheless.

**empezar**[1,9] *v. irr.* to begin.

**empiezo** *m. Carib., Mex., C.A.* beginning.

**empinado** *adj.* steep; lofty.

**empinar** *v.* to raise, lift; to incline, bend; **— el codo** to drink; **-se** to stand on tiptoes; to rear (*said of horses*); to rise high; *Am.* to overeat.

**empiojado** *adj.* lousy, full of lice.

**emplasto** *m.* plaster, poultice.

**empleado** *m.* employee; *p.p. of* **emplear.**

**emplear** *v.* to employ; to invest, spend; **-se en** to be employed in.

**empleo** *m.* employment, position, job; employ; occupation; aim; investment.

**emplumar** *v.* to feather; to adorn with feathers; to tar and feather; *C.A.* to deceive; *Ec.* to send away to a house of correction or prison; *Am.* **— con algo** to run away with something, steal it; *Ch., Col., Ven.* **-las** (*or* **emplumárselas**) to take to one's heels, flee, escape.

**empobrecer**[13] *v. irr.* to impoverish; **-se** to become poor.

**empobrecimiento** *m.* impoverishment.

**empolvado** *adj.* dusty, covered with dust or powder.

**empolvar** *v.* to sprinkle powder; to cover with dust; **-se** to get dusty; to powder one's face.

**empollar** *v.* to hatch, brood.

**emponzoñar** *v.* to poison.

**emprendedor** *adj.* enterprising.

**emprender** *v.* to undertake.

**empreñar** *v.* to impregnate, make pregnant.

**empresa** *f.* enterprise, undertaking; symbol; company, management.

**empresario** *m.* manager; impresario; promoter.

**empréstito** *m.* loan.

**empujar** *v.* to push, shove.

**empuje** *m.* push; shove; impulse; energy.

**empujón** *m.* shove, push.

**empuñar** *v.* to grasp, grab, clutch, seize.

**émulo** *m.* rival, competitor.

**en** *prep.* in, on, upon.

**enaguas** *f. pl.* underskirt, petticoat; short skirt.

**enajenamiento** *m.* trance; abstraction; absence of mind; transfer (*of property*); **— mental** mental disorder; **— de los sentidos** loss of consciousness.

**enajenar** *v.* (*distraer*) to enrapture, charm; to deprive (*of one's sense*); (*trasladar*) to transfer property; to dispossess; **— el afecto de** to alienate the affection of; **-se** to be enraptured, be in a trance.

**enaltecer**[13] *v.* to extol, exalt.

**enamorado** *adj.* in love; *m.* lover.

**enamorar** *v.* to make love, woo, court; to enamor; **-se** to fall in love.

**enano** *m.* dwarf; *adj.* dwarfish, tiny, little.

**enarbolar** *v.* to hoist, lift, raise on high; to brandish (*a sword, cane, etc.*); **-se** to rear, balk.

**enarcado** *p.p.* arched.

**enarcar**[6] *v.* to arch; to hoop (*barrels, kegs, etc.*); **— las cejas** to arch one's eyebrows.

**enardecer**[13] *v. irr.* to excite, kindle, fire with passion; **-se** to become excited; to become passionate; to get angry.

**enardecimiento** *m.* ardor, passion, unbridled enthusiasm; inflaming.

**encabezado** *m.* headline; heading.

**encabezamiento** *m.* heading; headline; list or roll of taxpayers; registration of taxpayers.

**encabezar**[9] *v.* to give a heading or title to; to head; to lead; to make up (*a list or tax roll*); to strengthen (*wine*).

**encabritarse** *v.* to rear, rise up on the hind legs.

**encadenar** *v.* to chain; to link together.

**encajar** *v.* to thrust in, fit into, insert; **-se** to squeeze into; to intrude, meddle.

**encaje** *m.* lace; adjustment; fitting together; socket, groove, hole; inlaid work.

**encajonar** *v.* to box (*put or pack in a box*).

**encallar** *v.* to strand, run aground; to get stuck.

**encamado** *p.p.* confined in bed.

**encaminar** *v.* to direct, guide; **-se** to betake oneself, go (toward); to start out on a road.

**encanecer**[13] *v. irr.* to get grey, get grey-haired.

**encanijado** *adj.* emaciated, thin, sickly.

**encanijarse** *v.* to get thin, emaciated.

**encantado** *p.p.* & *adj.* delighted, charmed; enchanted.

**encantador** *adj.* charming; *m.* charmer, enchanter.

**encantamiento** *m.* enchantment.

**encantar** *v.* to charm, enchant.

**encanto** *m.* charm, enchantment, delight.

**encapillar** *v. P.R.* to confine in the death cell.

**encapotado** *p.p.* & *adj.* cloaked; overcast, cloudy; in a bad humor.

**encapotarse** *v.* to become overcast, cloudy; to cover up, put on a cloak or raincoat; to frown.

**encapricharse** *v.* to persist in one's whims; to get stubborn.

**encaramar** *v.* to raise; to elevate; to extol; **-se** to climb; to climb upon, get upon, perch upon; *Ch.* to be ashamed; *Carib.* to go to one's head (*said of liquor*).

**encarar** *v.* to face; to aim; **-se con** to face; to confront.

**encarcelación** *f.* imprisonment.

**encarcelamiento** = **encarcelación**.

**encarcelar** *v.* to imprison, jail.

**encarecer**[13] *v. irr.* (*alzar precio*) to go up in value; to make dear, raise the price of; (*ponderar*) to exaggerate; to extol; to recommend highly, to enhance.

**encarecidamente** *adv.* earnestly.

**encargar**[7] *v.* (*dar cargo*) to put in charge; to entrust; to commission; (*aconsejar*) to recommend, advise; (*pedir*) to order; to beg; **-se de** to take charge of.

**encargo** *m.* recommendation, advice; charge; order; commission; errand.

**encariñado** *adj.* & *p.p.* attached, fond, enamored.

**encariñamiento** *m.* affection, fondness, attachment.

**encariñar** *v.* to awaken love or affection; **-se** to become fond (of), attached (to).

**encarnado** *adj.* flesh-colored; red; *p.p*

*of* **encarnar.**

**encarnar** *v.* to incarnate, embody; to bait (*a fishhook*).

**encarnizado** *adj.* bloody; hard-fought, fierce.

**encarnizar**[9] *v.* to infuriate, enrage; **-se** to get furous, enraged; to fight with fury.

**encasillar** *v.* to pigeonhole, put in a pigeonhole or compartment; to put in a stall; to classify, sort out.

**encender**[1] *v. irr.* to light, kindle; to set on fire; **-se** to take fire, be on fire; to get red.

**encendido** *adj.* red; *p.p. of* **encender;** *m.* ignition (*of a motor*).

**encerado** *m.* blackboard; oilcloth; wax coating; *p.p.* & *adj.* waxed; wax-colored; **papel —** wax paper.

**encerar** *v.* to wax; to thicken (*lime*).

**encerramiento** *m.* enclosure, confinement; locking up; retreat; prison.

**encerrar**[1] *v. irr.* to enclose; to lock up; to contain; **-se** to lock oneself up, go into seclusion.

**encía** *f.* gum (*of the teeth*).

**enciclopedia** *f.* encyclopedia.

**encierro** *m.* confinement; retreat; prison.

**encima** *adv.* above, overhead, over, on top; besides, in addition; **— de** on top of; **por — de** over; *Am.* **de —** besides, in addition; *Col., C.A., Ríopl., Carib.* **echárselo todo —** to spend everything on clothes.

**encina** *f.* live oak.

**encinta** *adj.* pregnant.

**encintado** *m.* curb (*of a sidewalk*).

**enclaustrar** *v.* to cloister.

**enclavar** *v.* to nail, fix, fasten.

**enclenque** *adj.* sickly, wan; weak, feeble.

**encoger**[11] *v.* to shrink, shrivel, shorten, contract; **-se** to shrink; to shrivel; **-se de hombros** to shrug one's shoulders.

**encogido** *p.p.* & *adj.* shrunk, shrivelled; timid, shy.

**encogimiento** *m.* shrinking; timidity; **— de hombros** shrug.

**encolerizar**[9] *v.* to anger; **-se** to get angry.

**encomendar**[1] *v. irr.* (*encargar*) to charge, advise; to entrust; (*recomendar*) to recommend, commend; **-se** to put oneself in the hands (of); to send regards; to pray (to).

**encomiar** *v.* to extol, praise.

**encomienda** *f.* charge, commission; recommendation; royal land grant (*including Indian inhabitants*); *Am.* warehouse (*for agricultural products*); *Am.* parcel-post package.

**encomio** *m.* encomium, high praise.

**enconado** *p.p.* & *adj.* inflamed; infected; sore; angry.

**enconar** *v.* to inflame; to infect; to irritate; **-se** to become inflamed, infected; to get irritated.

**encono** *m.* rancor, animosity, ill will; *Cuba, Mex.* inflammation, swelling.

EM

**encontrado** *adj.* opposite; opposing; contrary; *p.p. of* **encontrar.**

**encontrar**² *v. irr.* to encounter, meet; to find; **-se** to meet; to coincide; to be; to be found, be situated; to collide; to conflict; **-se con** to come across, meet up with.

**encontrón, encontronazo** *m.* bump, collision; **darse un —** to collide (with) bump (into); to bump into each other.

**encordelar** *v.* to string; to tie with strings.

**encorvar** *v.* to curve, bend; **-se** to bend down; to stoop.

**encrespar** *v.* (*rizar*) to curl; to ruffle; (*agitar*) to irritate; **-se** to curl; to get ruffled; to become involved or entangled (*a matter or affair*); to become rough (*said of the sea*).

**encrucijada** *f.* crossroads, street intersection; ambush.

**encuadernación** *f.* binding (*of books*).

**encuadernar** *v.* to bind (*books*).

**encuadrar** *v.* to enclose in a frame; to encompass; to fit (into); *Am.* to suit; *Ven.* to summarize briefly, give a synthesis of.

**encubierto** *p.p. of* **encubrir.**

**encubrir**⁵² *v.* to cover, hide.

**encuentro** *m.* (*hallazgo*) encounter, meeting; find, finding; (*conflicto*) conflict, clash; collision; **salir al — de** to go out to meet; to make a stand against, oppose; *Am.* **llevarse de —** to run over, knock down; to drag along.

**encuerado** *adj. Am.* naked.

**encuerar** *v. Am.* to strip of clothes; *Am.* to skin, fleece, strip of money; **-se** *Am.* to strip, get undressed.

**encuesta** *f.* search, inquiry, investigation; survey.

**encumbrado** *p.p. & adj.* elevated; exalted; high, lofty.

**encumbramiento** *m.* elevation; exaltation; height; eminence.

**encumbrar** *v.* to elevate; to exalt, extol; **-se** to climb to the top; to rise up; to hold oneself high; to soar.

**encurtido** *m.* pickle; *p.p. of* **encurtir.**

**encurtir** *v.* to pickle.

**enchilada** *f. Mex., C.A.* rolled **tortilla** served with chili.

**enchuecar**⁶ *v.* to bend, twist; **-se** *Col., Ven., Mex., Ríopl.* to get bent or twisted.

**enchufar** *v.* to plug in; to telescope; to fit (*a tube or pipe*) into another.

**enchufe** *m.* socket; plug; electric outlet; *Spain* influence; position obtained through influence.

**ende : por —** hence, therefore.

**endeble** *adj.* weak, feeble; flimsy.

**endemoniado** *adj.* possessed by the devil; devilish, fiendish; mischievous.

**endentar**¹ *v. irr.* to indent, form notches in; to furnish (*a saw, wheel, etc.*) with teeth; to mesh.

**enderezar**⁹ *v.* to straighten; to set upright; to right, correct; to direct; to

address; **-se** to go straight (to); to straighten up.

**endeudado** *p.p. & adj.* indebted; in debt.

**endeudarse** *v.* to get into debt, become indebted.

**endiablado** *adj.* devilish; possessed by the devil; ugly; mean, wicked; *Col., Ven., Mex., Ríopl.* dangerous, risky.

**endomingado** *p.p. & adj.* dressed up in one's Sunday, or best, clothes.

**endosante** *m.* endorser.

**endosar** *v.* to endorse (*a check, draft, etc.*).

**endose, endoso** *m.* endorsement.

**endulzar**⁹ *v.* to sweeten; to soften.

**endurecer**¹³ *v. irr.* to harden; **-se** to get hardened; to get cruel.

**enemigo** *m.* enemy; devil; *adj.* hostile; unfriendly; **ser — de una cosa** to dislike a thing.

**enemistad** *f.* enmity, hatred.

**enemistar** *v.* to cause enmity between; **-se con** to become an enemy of.

**energía** *f.* energy; **— nuclear** nuclear energy.

**enérgico** *adj.* energetic.

**enero** *m.* January.

**enervar** *v.* to enervate, weaken.

**enfadar** *v.* to anger; **-se** to get angry.

**enfado** *m.* anger, disgust.

**enfadoso** *adj.* annoying.

**enfardar** *v.* to bale, pack.

**énfasis** *m.* emphasis; **enfático** *adj.* emphatic.

**enfermar** *v.* to become ill; to make ill; to weaken; **-se** to become ill.

**enfermedad** *f.* sickness, illness.

**enfermería** *f.* infirmary.

**enfermero** *m.* male nurse; **enfermera** *f.* nurse (*for the sick*).

**enfermizo** *adj.* sickly; unhealthy.

**enfermo** *adj.* sick, ill; feeble; *m.* patient.

**enflaquecer**¹³ *v. irr.* to become thin; to make thin; to weaken.

**enfocar**⁶ *v.* to focus.

**enfrenar** *v.* to bridle; to brake, put the brake on; to check, curb.

**enfrentar** *v.* to put face to face; **-se con** to confront, face, meet face to face.

**enfrente** *adv.* in front, opposite; **— de** in front of, opposite.

**enfriamiento** *m.* cooling; chill; refrigeration.

**enfriar**¹⁷ *v.* to cool, chill; *Carib.* to kill; **-se** to cool, cool off; to get chilled.

**enfurecer**¹³ *v. irr.* to infuriate, enrage; **-se** to rage; to get furious; to get rough, stormy (*said of the sea*).

**enfurruñarse** *v.* to get angry; to grumble.

**engalanar** *v.* to adorn, decorate; **-se** to dress up, primp.

**enganchamiento = enganche.**

**enganchar** *v.* to hitch; to hook; to ensnare; to draft; to attract into the army; *Col., Ven., Mex., Ríopl.* to hire (*labor with false promises*); **-se** to engage, interlock; to get hooked; to enlist in the army.

**enganche** *m.* hooking; coupling; draft

(*into the army*); *Col.*, *Ven.*, *Mex.*, *Ríopl.* enrolling of laborers (*for a rubber plantation or other risky business under false promises*); *Mex.* down payment.

**engañador** *adj.* deceitful, deceiving; *m.* deceiver.

**engañar** *v.* to deceive; to while away (*time*); to ward off (*hunger or sleep*); **-se** to deceive oneself; to be mistaken.

**engaño** *m.* deceit, trick, fraud; mistake, misunderstanding; *Ch.*, *C.A.* bribe.

**engañoso** *adj.* deceitful; tricky; misleading.

**engastar** *v.* to mount, set (*jewels*).

**engaste** *m.* setting (*for a gem or stone*).

**engatusar** *v.* to coax, entice; to fool.

**engendrar** *v.* to engender, beget, produce; to cause.

**engolfarse** *v.* to get deep (into); to go deeply (into); to become absorbed, lost in thought.

**engomar** *v.* to gum; to glue.

**engordar** *v.* to fatten; to get fat; to get rich.

**engorroso** *adj.* cumbersome; bothersome.

**engranaje** *m.* gear, gears, gearing.

**engranar** *v.* to gear, throw in gear; to mesh gears.

**engrandecer**[13] *v. irr.* to aggrandize, make greater; to magnify; to exalt.

**engrane** *m.* engagement (*of gears*); gear.

**engrasar** *v.* to lubricate, grease; to stain with grease; to fertilize, manure; to dress (*cloth*).

**engreído** *adj.* & *p.p.* conceited, vain; *Col.* attached, fond.

**engreír**[15] *v. irr.* to make vain, conceited; **-se** to puff up, get conceited; *Col.* to become fond (of), become attached (to).

**engrosar**[2] *v. irr.* to enlarge; to thicken; to fatten; to get fat.

**engrudo** *m.* paste (*for gluing*).

**engullir**[20] *v.* to gobble, devour; to gorge.

**enhebrar** *v.* to thread (*a needle*); to string (*beads*).

**enhiesto** *adj.* straight, upright, erect.

**enhorabuena** *f.* congratulation; *adv.* safely; well and good; all right; with much pleasure.

**enigma** *m.* enigma, riddle, puzzle.

**enjabonar** *v.* to soap; to soft-soap, flatter.

**enjaezar**[9] *v.* to harness.

**enjalbegar**[7] *v.* to whitewash; **-se** to paint (*one's face*).

**enjambre** *m.* swarm of bees; crowd.

**enjaular** *v.* to cage; to confine; to jail.

**enjuagar**[7] *v.* to rinse, rinse out.

**enjuague** *m.* mouth wash; rinse; rinsing; scheme, plot.

**enjugar**[7] *v.* to dry; to wipe; **-se** to dry oneself.

**enjuiciar** *v.* to indict; to prosecute, bring suit against; to try (*a case*); to judge.

**enjundia** *f.* substance, essence; fat; force, strength.

**enjuto** *adj.* dried; thin, skinny; **-s** *m. pl.* dry kindling.

**enlace** *m.* link; tie, bond; marriage.

**enladrillado** *m.* brick pavement or floor.

**enladrillar** *v.* to pave with bricks.

**enlatar** *v.* to can; *Col.* to roof with tin.

**enlazar**[9] *v.* to join, bind, tie; to rope; *Ven.*, *Mex.* to lasso; **-se** to join; to marry; to become related through marriage.

**enlodar** *v.* to cover with mud; to smear, sully, soil, dirty; **-se** to get in the mud; to get muddy.

**enloquecer**[13] *v. irr.* to make crazy; to drive mad; to lose one's mind; **-se** to go crazy.

**enlosado** *m.* flagstone pavement; *p.p. of* **enlosar**.

**enlosar** *v.* to pave with flagstones.

**enmantecado** *m. Am.* ice cream. *See* **mantecado**.

**enmantecar**[6] *v.* to butter; to grease (*with lard or butter*).

**enmarañar** *v.* to entangle; to snarl; to confuse, mix up.

**enmascarar** *v.* to mask; **-se** to put on a mask; to masquerade.

**enmendar**[1] *v. irr.* to amend, correct; to indemnify, compensate; **-se** to reform, mend one's ways.

**enmienda** *f.* correction; amendment; reform; indemnity, compensation.

**enmohecer**[13] *v.* to rust; to mold; **-se** to rust, become rusty; to mold.

**enmudecer**[13] *v. irr.* to silence; to remain silent; to lose one's voice; to become dumb.

**ennegrecer**[13] *v. irr.* to blacken; to darken; **-se** to become dark; to get cloudy.

**ennoblecer**[13] *v. irr.* to ennoble, dignify.

**enojadizo** *adj.* irritable, ill-tempered.

**enojado** *adj.* angry.

**enojar** *v.* to make angry, vex, annoy; **-se** to get angry.

**enojo** *m.* anger; annoyance.

**enojoso** *adj.* annoying, bothersome.

**enorgullecer**[13] *v. irr.* to fill with pride; **-se** to swell up with pride; to be proud.

**enorme** *adj.* enormous.

**enramada** *f.* arbor, bower; shady grove.

**enrarecer**[13] *v. irr.* to rarefy, thin, make less dense (*as air*); **-se** to become rarefied; to become scarce.

**enrarecimiento** *m.* rarity, thinness (*of the air*); rarefaction (*act of making thin, rare or less dense*).

**enredadera** *f.* climbing vine.

**enredar** *v.* (*enmarañar*) to entangle, snare; to snarl; to mix up; to wind (*on a spool*); (*enemistar*) to raise a rumpus; **-se** to get tangled up, mixed up; to get trapped; **-se con** to have an affair with.

**enredista** *m. Am.* liar; *Am.* talebearer.

**enredo** *m.* tangle; confusion; lie; plot.

**enredoso** *adj.* tangled up; *Am.* tattler.

**enrejado** *m.* trellis; grating.

**enrevesado** *adj.* turned around; intricate, complicated; unruly.

**enriquecer**[13] *v. irr.* to enrich; to become rich; **-se** to become rich.

**enrojecer**[13] *v. irr.* to redden; **-se** to get red, blush.

**enrollar** *v.* to roll, roll up; to coil.

**enronquecer**[13] *v. irr.* to make hoarse; to become hoarse; **-se** to become hoarse.

**enroscar**[6] *v.* to coil; to twist, twine; **-se** to coil; to curl up.

**ensacar**[6] *v.* to sack, bag, put in a bag or sack.

**ensalada** *f.* salad; hodgepodge, mixture.

**ensalzar**[9] *v.* to exalt, praise.

**ensanchar** *v.* to widen, enlarge; **-se** to expand; to puff up.

**ensanche** *m.* widening, expansion, extension.

**ensangrentado** *adj.* gory, bloody; *p.p. of* **ensangrentar.**

**ensangrentar** *v.* to stain with blood; **-se** to be covered with blood; to get red with anger.

**ensartar** *v.* to string; to thread; to link; to rattle off (*tales, stories, etc.*); *Ch.* to tie to a ring; *Am.* to swindle, trick; **-se** *Andes* to fall into a trap.

**ensayar** *v.* to try; to attempt; to test; to rehearse; **-se** to practice, train oneself.

**ensayo** *m.* trial, attempt; rehearsal; test; experiment; essay.

**ensenada** *f.* small bay, cove.

**enseñanza** *f.* teaching; education, training.

**enseñar** *v.* to show; to teach; to train; to point out.

**enseres** *m. pl.* household goods; utensils; implements; equipment.

**ensillar** *v.* to saddle; *Ch.* to abuse, mistreat, domineer; *Ríopl.* — **el picazo** to get angry.

**ensimismarse** *v.* to become absorbed in thought; *Col., Ven., Ch.* to become conceited or vain.

**ensoberbecer**[13] *v. irr.* to make proud or haughty; **-se** to puff up with pride; to become haughty; to get rough, choppy (*said of the sea*).

**ensordecer**[13] *v. irr.* to deafen; to become deaf.

**ensortijar** *v.* to curl; to ring the nose of (*an animal*); **-se** to curl.

**ensuciar** *v.* to dirty, soil; to stain; **-se** to get dirty; to soil oneself.

**ensueño** *m.* illusion, dream.

**entablar** *v.* to board up; to plank; to splint; — **una conversación** to start a conversation; — **un pleito** to bring a lawsuit.

**entablillar** *v.* to splint; *Mex.* to cut (*chocolate*) into tablets or squares.

**entallar** *v.* to fit closely (*a dress*); to carve.

**entapizar**[9] *v.* to cover with tapestry; to drape with tapestries; to upholster.

**entarimar** *v.* to floor (*with boards*).

**ente** *m.* entity, being; queer fellow.

**enteco** *adj.* sickly, skinny.

**entender**[1] *v. irr.* to understand; — **de** to know, be an expert in; — **en** to take care of; to deal with; **-se con** to have dealings or relations with; to have an understanding with.

**entendido** *p.p.* understood; *adj.* wise, prudent; well-informed; able, skilful; **no darse por** — to pretend not to hear or understand; not to take the hint.

**entendimiento** *m.* understanding; intellect; mind.

**enterado** *p.p.* & *adj.* informed; aware.

**enterar** *v.* to inform, acquaint; **-se** to know, learn, find out; to understand, get the idea.

**entereza** *f.* entirety; integrity; fortitude; serenity; firmness; perfection.

**enternecedor** *adj.* touching, moving, pitiful.

**enternecer**[13] *v. irr.* to soften, touch, stir, move; **-se** to become tender; to be touched, stirred.

**entero** *adj.* (*completo*) entire, whole; (*justo*) just, right; firm; *m.* integer, whole number; *Col.* payment, reimbursement; *Ch.* balance of an account; **caballo** — stallion.

**enterramiento** *m.* burial.

**enterrar**[1] *v. irr.* to bury; *Am.* to sink, stick into.

**entibiar** *v.* to make lukewarm; **-se** to become lukewarm.

**entidad** *f.* entity; unit, group, organization; **de** — of value or importance.

**entierro** *m.* burial; funeral; grave; *Am.* hidden treasure.

**entintar** *v.* to ink; to stain with ink; to dye.

**entoldar** *v.* to cover with an awning; **-se** to puff up with pride; to become overcast, cloudy.

**entonación** *f.* intonation.

**entonar** *v.* to sing in tune; to start a song (*for others to follow*); to be in tune; to harmonize; **-se** to put on airs.

**entonces** *adv.* then, at that time; **pues** — well then.

**entornado** *adj.* half-open; half-closed, ajar.

**entornar** *v.* to half-open.

**entorpecer**[13] *v. irr.* to stupefy; to benumb, make numb; to delay, obstruct; to thwart, frustrate.

**entorpecimiento** *m.* numbness; dullness; delay, obstruction.

**entrada** *f.* (*apertura*) entrance; entry; gate; opening; (*acción o privilegio*) entering, admission; entrée (*dish or dinner course*); *Am.* attack, assault, goring; *Mex.* beating; **-s** cash receipts.

**entrambos** *adj.* & *pron.* both.

**entrampar** *v.* to trap, ensnare; to trick; to burden with debts; **-se** to get trapped or entangled; to run into debt.

**entrante** *adj.* entering; incoming; **el año** — next year.

**entraña** *f.* entrail; innermost recess; heart; disposition, temper; **-s** entrails, "innards", insides; **hijo de mis -s**

child of my heart; **no tener -s** to be cruel.

**entrar** *v.* to enter, go in, come in; to attack; **me entró miedo** I became afraid; **-se** to slip in, get in, sneak in; to enter.

**entre** *prep.* between; among; **dijo — sí** he said to himself; **— tanto** meanwhile; *Am.* **— más habla menos dice** the more he talks the less he says.

**entreabierto** *p.p. of* **entreabrir;** *adj.* ajar, half-open, partly open.

**entreabrir**[52] *v.* to half-open.

**entreacto** *m.* intermission; intermezzo (*entertainment between the acts*); small cigar.

**entrecano** *adj.* greyish.

**entrecejo** *m.* space between the eyebrows; **fruncir el —** to wrinkle one's brow.

**entrecortado** *adj.* hesitating, faltering (*speech*); breathless, choking; *p.p.* interrupted.

**entrecortar** *v.* to cut halfway through or in between; to interrupt at intervals.

**entrecruzar**[9] *v.* to intercross, cross; to interlace; **-se** to cross.

**entredicho** *m.* prohibition, injunction.

**entrega** *f.* (*acto de ceder*) delivery; surrender; (*parte suelta*) installment (*of a book*); **novela por -s** serial novel.

**entregar**[7] *v.* to deliver, hand over; **-se** to surrender, submit, give up; to devote oneself (to); to abandon oneself (to).

**entrelazar**[9] *v.* to interlace; to weave together.

**entremés** *m.* relish, side dish (*of olives, pickles, etc.*); one-act farce (*formerly presented between the acts of a play.*)

**entremeter** *v.* to insert; to place between; **-se** to meddle; to intrude.

**entremetido** *adj.* meddlesome; *m.* meddler; intruder.

**entremetimiento** *m.* intrusion, meddling.

**entremezclar** *v.* to intermix, intermingle.

**entrenador** *m. Am.* trainer.

**entrenamiento** *m. Am.* training, drill.

**entrenar** *v. Am.* to train, drill; **-se** *Am.* to train.

**entresacar**[6] *v.* to pick out, select.

**entresuelo** *m.* mezzanine; second floor.

**entretanto** *adv.* meanwhile.

**entretejer** *v.* to weave together; to intertwine.

**entretener**[45] *v. irr.* to delay, detain; to amuse, entertain; **-se** to amuse oneself; to delay oneself; **— el tiempo** to while away the time.

**entretenido** *adj.* entertaining, amusing; *p.p. of* **entretener.**

**entretenimiento** *m.* entertainment; pastime; delay.

**entrever**[49] *v.* to glimpse, catch a glimpse of; to half-see, see vaguely.

**entreverar** *v.* to intermingle, intermix.

**entrevista** *f.* interview; date, appointment.

**entrevistar** *v.* to interview; **-se con** to have an interview with.

**entrevisto** *p.p. of* **entrever.**

**entristecer**[13] *v. irr.* to sadden, make sad; **-se** to become sad.

**entrometer** = **entremeter.**

**entrometido** = **entremetido.**

**entumecer**[13] *v. irr.* to make numb; **-se** to get numb; to surge; to swell.

**entumido** *adj.* numb, stiff; *Am.* timid, shy, awkward.

**entumirse** *v.* to get numb.

**enturbiar** *v.* to make muddy; to muddle; to disturb; to obscure; **-se** to get muddy; to get muddled.

**entusiasmar** *v.* to excite, fill with enthusiasm; **-se** to get enthusiastic, excited.

**entusiasmo** *m.* enthusiasm.

**entusiasta** *m. & f.* enthusiast; **entusiástico** *adj.* enthusiastic.

**enumeración** *f.* enumeration, counting.

**enumerar** *v.* to enumerate.

**enunciar** *v.* to express, state, declare.

**envainar** *v.* to sheathe.

**envalentonar** *v.* to make bold or haughty; **-se** to get bold; to brag, swagger.

**envanecer**[13] *v. irr.* to make vain; **-se** to become vain.

**envasar** *v.* to pack, put up in any container; to bottle; to can.

**envase** *m.* packing; container, jar, bottle, can (*for packing*).

**envejecer**[13] *v. irr.* to make old; to grow old, get old; **-se** to grow old, get old.

**envenenamiento** *m.* poisoning.

**envenenar** *v.* to poison; to infect.

**envergadura** *f.* span (*of an airplane*); spread (*of a bird's wings*); breadth (*of sails*).

**envés** *m.* back or wrong side.

**enviado** *m.* envoy.

**enviar**[17] *v.* to send; **— a uno a paseo** to give someone his walking papers.

**enviciar** *v.* to vitiate, corrupt; **-se** to become addicted (to), overly fond (of)

**envidar** *v.* to bid (*in cards*); to bet.

**envidia** *f.* envy.

**envidiable** *adj.* enviable, desirable.

**envidiar** *v.* to envy.

**envidioso** *adj.* envious.

**envilecer**[13] *v. irr.* to revile, malign, degrade; **-se** to degrade or lower oneself.

**envilecimiento** *m.* degradation, humiliation, shame.

**envío** *m.* remittance, sending; shipment.

**envite** *m.* bid; stake (*in cards*); offer; push.

**envoltorio** *m.* bundle, package.

**envoltura** *f.* wrapping, cover; wrapper.

**envolver**[2,52] *v. irr.* to involve, entangle; to wrap; to wind (*a thread, rope, etc.*); to surround; **-se** to become involved, entangled; to cover up, wrap up.

**envuelto** *p.p. of* **envolver.**

**enyesar** *v.* to plaster; to chalk.

**enzolvar** *v. Am.* to clog, obstruct; *Am.* **-se** to clog, get clogged. *See* **azolvar.**

**¡epa!** *interj. Ríopl., Ven., Col., Mex.* hey! listen! stop! look out!

**épico** *adj.* epic.

**epidemia** *f.* epidemic.

**episodio** *m.* episode.

**epístola** *f.* epistle; letter.

**epitafio** *m.* epitaph.

**época** *f.* epoch.

**epopeya** *f.* epic poem.

**equidad** *f.* equity, justice, fairness.

**equidistante** *adj.* equidistant, equally distant, halfway, midway.

**equilibrar** *v.* to balance, poise.

**equilibrio** *m.* equilibrium, balance; poise.

**equipaje** *m.* baggage, luggage; equipment, outfit; crew.

**equipar** *v.* to equip, fit out; to man, equip and provision (*a ship*).

**equipo** *m.* (*materiales*) equipment, equipping; outfit; (*grupo*) work crew; sport team; **— de novia** trousseau.

**equitación** *f.* horsemanship; horseback riding.

**equitativo** *adj.* fair, just.

**equivalente** *adj.* equivalent.

**equivaler**[47] *v. irr.* to be equivalent.

**equivocación** *f.* error, mistake.

**equivocado** *p.p.* & *adj.* mistaken.

**equivocar**[6] *v.* to mistake; **-se** to be mistaken; to make a mistake.

**equívoco** *adj.* equivocal, ambiguous, vague; *Am.* mistaken; *m.* pun, play on words; *Am.* mistake, error.

**era** *f.* era, age; threshing floor.

**erario** *m.* public treasury.

**erguido** *adj.* erect; *p.p. of* **erguir.**

**erguir**[3] *v. irr.* to erect, set upright; to lift (*the head*); **-se** to sit up or stand erect; to become proud and haughty.

**erial** *m.* uncultivated land; *adj.* unplowed, untilled.

**erigir**[11] *v.* to erect, build; to found.

**erizado** *adj.* bristly, prickly; **— de** bristling with.

**erizar**[9] *v.* to set on end, make bristle; **-se** to bristle; to stand on end (*hair*).

**erizo** *m.* hedgehog, porcupine; thistle; **— de mar** sea urchin; **ser un —** to be irritable, harsh.

**ermitaño** *m.* hermit.

**erosion** *f.* erosion.

**errabundo** *adj.* wandering.

**errado** *adj.* mistaken, wrong, in error; *p.p. of* **errar.**

**errante** *adj.* errant, roving, wandering.

**errar**[28] *v. irr.* to err, make mistakes; to miss (*target, road*); to rove, wander.

**errata** *f.* misprint, printer's error.

**erróneo** *adj.* erroneous, mistaken, wrong, incorrect.

**error** *m.* error, fault, mistake.

**eructar** *v.* to belch.

**eructo** *m.* belch.

**erudición** *f.* erudition, learning.

**erudito** *adj.* erudite, scholarly, learned; *m.* scholar.

**erupción** *f.* eruption; outburst; rash.

**esbelto** *adj.* slender.

**esbozar**[9] *v.* to sketch, outline.

**esbozo** *m.* sketch, outline.

**escabechar** *v.* to pickle.

**escabeche** *m.* pickled fish; pickle (*solution for pickling*).

**escabel** *m.* stool; footstool.

**escabrosidad** *f.* roughness, unevenness; harshness; improper word or phrase.

**escabroso** *adj.* rough; rugged; scabrous, rather indecent.

**escabullirse**[20] *v. irr.* to slip away; to slip through; to scoot, scamper, scurry.

**escala** *f.* ladder; scale; port of call; stopover; **hacer — en** to stop over at; **escalafón** *m.* army register.

**escalar** *v.* to scale; to climb.

**escaldar** *v.* to scald; to make red-hot; **-se** to get scalded.

**escalera** *f.* stairs, staircase; ladder; **— mecánica** escalator.

**escalfar** *v.* to poach (*eggs*).

**escalinata** *f.* flight of stairs (*usually on the outside*).

**escalofriarse**[17] *v.* to become chilled.

**escalofrío** *m.* chill; **-s** chills and fever.

**escalón** *m.* step (*of a ladder or staircase*); stepping stone; *Am.* **-es** tribe of **quichua** Indians.

**escalonar** *v.* to echelon (*arrange in step-like formation*); to terrace; **-se** to rise in terraces.

**escama** *f.* scale, fish scale; flake.

**escamoso** *adj.* scaly.

**escamotear** *v.* to whisk out of sight; to steal or snatch away with cunning; to conceal by a trick or sleight of hand.

**escandalizar**[9] *v.* to scandalize, shock; **-se** to be shocked.

**escándalo** *m.* scandal; bad example.

**escandaloso** *adj.* scandalous, shocking; *Mex., C.A., Col., Andes* showy, loud (*color*).

**escapada** *f.* escape, flight.

**escapar** *v.* to escape, flee, avoid; **-se** to run away, escape.

**escaparate** *m.* show window; glass case, glass cabinet or cupboard.

**escapatoria** *f.* escape, loophole, excuse.

**escape** *m.* escape; vent, outlet; exhaust; **a —** rapidly, at full speed.

**escarabajo** *m.* black beetle.

**escaramuza** *f.* skirmish; quarrel.

**escarbar** *v.* to scrape, scratch; to dig out; to pry into, investigate.

**escarcear** *v. Ch., Ríopl.* to prance.

**escarcha** *f.* frost; frosting.

**escarchar** *v.* to frost; to freeze.

**escardar** *v.* to weed; to weed out.

**escarlata** *f.* scarlet; scarlet fever; scarlet cloth; **escarlatina** *f.* scarlet fever.

**escarmentar**[1] *v. irr.* to punish (*as an example or warning*); to profit by one's misfortunes, punishment, etc.; **— en cabeza ajena** to profit by another's mistake or misfortune.

**escarmiento** *m.* lesson, example, warning; punishment.

**escarnecer**[13] *v. irr.* to jeer, insult, mock.

**escarnio** *m.* scoff, jeer.

**escarpa** *f.* steep slope, bluff, cliff; scarp (*of a fortification*).

**escarpado** *adj.* steep; rugged.

**escarpia** *f.* hook (*for hanging something*).

**escasear** *v.* to be scarce; to grow less, become scarce; to stint.

**escasez** *f.* scarcity, lack, scantiness.

**escaso** *adj.* scarce, limited; scant; scanty; stingy.

**escatimar** *v.* to stint, skimp; to curtail.

**escena** *f.* scene; scenery; theatre, stage.

**escenario** *m.* stage.

**escenificación** *f.* dramatization, stage adaptation.

**escepticismo** *m.* scepticism; doubt, unbelief.

**escéptico** *m.* & *adj.* sceptic.

**esclarecer**[13] *v. irr.* to lighten, illuminate; to elucidate, make clear, explain.

**esclarecimiento** *m.* clarification, illumination, illustration; worth, nobility.

**esclavitud** *f.* slavery.

**esclavizar**[9] *v.* to enslave.

**esclavo** *m.* slave.

**esclusa** *f.* lock (*of a canal*); sluice, floodgate.

**escoba** *f.* broom.

**escobazo** *m.* blow with a broom.

**escobilla** *f.* whisk broom; small broom.

**escocer**[2,10] *v. irr.* to sting, smart.

**escocés** *adj.* Scotch; *m.* Scotch; Scotchman.

**escoger**[11] *v.* to choose, select, pick out.

**escolar** *adj.* scholastic, academic; *m.* scholar, student.

**escolástico** *adj.* & *m.* scholastic.

**escolta** *f.* escort; convoy.

**escoltar** *v.* to escort; to convoy.

**escollo** *m.* reef; danger; obstacle.

**escombro** *m.* debris, rubbish; mackerel.

**esconder** *v.* to hide, conceal; **-se** to hide, go into hiding.

**escondidas: a —** on the sly, under cover; *Am.* **jugar a las —** to play hide-and-seek.

**escondite** *m.* hiding place; *Spain* **jugar al —** to play hide-and-seek.

**escondrijo** *m.* hiding place.

**escopeta** *f.* shotgun.

**escopetazo** *m.* gunshot; gunshot wound; sudden bad news; *Am.* offensive or ironic remark.

**escoplo** *m.* chisel.

**escoria** *f.* slag; scum; **escorial** *m.* dump, dumping place; pile of slag.

**escorpión** *m.* scorpion.

**escote** *m.* low neck; **convite a —** Dutch treat (*where everyone pays his share*).

**escotilla** *f.* hatchway; **escotillón** *m.* hatch, hatchway; trap door.

**escozor** *m.* smarting sensation, sting.

**escribano** *m.* court clerk; lawyer's clerk; notary.

**escribiente** *m.* clerk, office clerk.

**escribir**[52] *v.* to write.

**escrito** *p.p. of* **escribir** written; *m.* writing, manuscript.

**escritor** *m.* writer.

**escritorio** *m.* desk; office.

**escritura** *f.* writing, handwriting; deed, document; **Sagrada Escritura** Holy Scripture.

**escrúpulo** *m.* scruple, doubt.

**escrupuloso** *adj.* scrupulous; particular, exact.

**escrutador** *adj.* scrutinizing, examining; peering; penetrating; *m.* scrutinizer, examiner; inspector of election returns.

**escrutar** *v.* to scrutinize.

**escrutinio** *m.* scrutiny, careful inspection.

**escuadra** *f.* squadron; fleet; square (*instrument for drawing or testing right angles*).

**escuadrón** *m.* squadron.

**escualidez** *f.* squalor.

**escuálido** *adj.* squalid, filthy; thin, emaciated.

**escuchar** *v.* to listen; to heed.

**escudar** *v.* to shield.

**escudero** *m.* squire.

**escudo** *m.* shield; escutcheon, coat of arms; gold crown (*ancient coin*); *Am.* Chilean gold coin.

**escudriñar** *v.* to scrutinize, search, pry into.

**escuela** *f.* school.

**escuelante** *m.* & *f. Col.* schoolboy; schoolgirl.

**escueto** *adj.* plain, unadorned, bare.

**esculcar**[6] *v. Am.* to search; *Carib.*, *Col.*, *Ven.* to frisk (*a person's pockets*).

**esculpir** *v.* to sculpture; to engrave.

**escultor** *m.* sculptor.

**escultura** *f.* sculpture.

**escupidera** *f.* cuspidor.

**escupir** *v.* to spit.

**escurrir** *v.* to drip; to drain; to trickle; **-se** to ooze out, trickle; to slip out, sneak out.

**ese, esa** *dem. adj.* that; **esos, esas** those; **ése, ésa** *m.*, *f. dem. pron.* that one; **ésos, ésas** *m.*, *f. pl.* those.

**esencia** *f.* essence.

**esencial** *adj.* essential.

**esfera** *f.* sphere; clock dial.

**esférico** *adj.* spherical.

**esforzado** *adj.* strong; valiant; courageous.

**esforzar**[2,9] *v. irr.* to give or inspire strength; to encourage; **-se** to make an effort; to strive, try hard.

**esfuerzo** *m.* effort; spirit, courage, vigor; stress.

**esfumar** *v.* to shade, tone down; **-se** to vanish, disappear.

**esgrima** *f.* fencing.

**esgrimir** *v.* to fence; to brandish; to wield (*the sword or pen*).

**eslabón** *m.* link of a chain; steel knife sharpener; black scorpion.

**eslabonar** *v.* to link; to join; to connect.

**esmaltar** *v.* to enamel; to beautify, adorn.

**esmalte** *m.* enamel; enamel work; smalt (*a blue pigment*).

**esmerado** *adj.* painstaking, careful, conscientious; *p.p. of* **esmerar.**

**esmeralda** *f.* emerald; *Am.* an eel-like fish; *Col.* hummingbird; *Mex.* variety of pineapple.

**esmerar** *v.* to polish, clean; **-se** to strive, take special pains, use great care.

**esmero** *m.* care, precision.

**esmoquin** *m.* tuxedo, dinner coat.

**eso** *dem. pron.* that, that thing, that fact; **— es** that is it; **a — de** at about (*referring to time*); *Am.* **¡eso!** that's right!

**espaciar**[17] *v.* to space; to spread; to expand; **-se** to enlarge (*upon a subject*); to relax, amuse oneself.

**espacio** *m.* space; interval; slowness, delay; *adv. Mex.* slowly.

**espacioso** *adj.* spacious; slow.

**espada** *f.* sword; skilled swordsman; matador (*bull-fighter who kills the bull*); **-s** swords (*Spanish card suit*).

**espalda** *f.* back, shoulders; **-s** back, back part; **a -s** behind one's back; **de -s** on one's back; **dar la — a** to turn one's back on; **espaldilla** *f.* shoulder blade.

**espaldar** *m.* back (*of a chair*); trellis (*for plants*); backplate of a cuirass (*armor*).

**espantadizo** *adj.* scary, shy, timid.

**espantajo** *m.* scarecrow.

**espantapájaros** *m.* scarecrow.

**espantar** *v.* to frighten, scare; to scare away; *Col.* to haunt; **-se** to be scared; to be astonished; *Mex.* **espantárselas** to be wide-awake, catch on quickly.

**espanto** *m.* fright, terror; astonishment; *Col., Ven., Mex.* ghost.

**espantoso** *adj.* frightful, terrifying; wonderful.

**español** *adj.* Spanish; *m.* Spaniard; Spanish language.

**esparadrapo** *m.* court plaster, adhesive tape. *See* **tela adhesiva.**

**esparcir**[10] *v.* to scatter, spread; **-se** to relax, amuse oneself.

**espárrago** *m.* asparagus.

**esparto** *m.* esparto grass (*used for making ropes, mats, etc.*).

**espasmo** *m.* spasm; horror.

**espátula** *f.* spatula.

**especia** *f.* spice.

**especial** *adj.* special; **en —** in particular, specially.

**especialidad** *f.* specialty.

**especialista** *m. & f.* specialist.

**especializar**[9] *v.* to specialize; **-se en** to specialize in.

**especie** *f.* species; kind, sort; pretext; idea.

**especificar**[6] *v.* to specify; to name.

**específico** *adj.* specific; *m.* specific (*medicine*).

**espécimen** *m.* specimen, sample.

**espectacular** *adj.* spectacular.

**espectáculo** *m.* spectacle.

**espectador** *m.* spectator.

**espectro** *m.* spectre, ghost; spectrum.

**especulación** *f.* speculation.

**especulador** *m.* speculator.

**especular** *v.* to speculate.

**especulativo** *adj.* speculative.

**espejismo** *m.* mirage; illusion.

**espejo** *m.* mirror; model; **— de cuerpo entero** full-length mirror.

**espeluznante** *adj.* hair-raising, terrifying.

**espeluznarse** *v.* to be terrified; to bristle with fear.

**espera** *f.* wait; stay (*granted by judge*); delay; extension of time (*for payment*); **sala de —** waiting room; **estar en — de** to be waiting for; to be expecting.

**esperanza** *f.* hope; expectation.

**esperanzado** *adj.* hopeful.

**esperanzar**[9] to give hope to.

**esperar** *v.* (*tener esperanza*) to hope; to expect; to trust; (*permanecer*) to wait, wait for; **— en alguien** to place hope or confidence in someone.

**esperezarse** = **desperezarse.**

**esperpento** *m.* ugly thing; nonsense.

**espesar** *v.* to thicken; to make dense; **-se** to thicken; to become thick or dense.

**espeso** *adj.* thick, dense; compact; slovenly; *Ríopl.* bothersome, boring.

**espesor** *m.* thickness.

**espesura** *f.* density, thickness; thicket; thickest part (*of a forest*).

**espetar** *v.* to spring (*a joke, story, etc.*) on (*a person*), surprise with (*a joke, speech, story, etc.*); to pop (*a question*); to run a spit through (*meat, fish, etc. for roasting*); to pierce; **-se** to be stiff, pompous.

**espía** *m. & f.* spy.

**espiar**[17] *v.* to spy; *Col., Mex.* **-se** to bruise the hoofs, get lame (*said of horses*).

**espiga** *f.* ear of wheat; peg; spike.

**espigar**[7] *v.* to glean; to grow spikes (*said of corn or grain*); **-se** to grow tall and slender.

**espina** *f.* thorn; sharp splinter; fish bone; spine; fear, suspicion; **darle a uno mala —** to arouse one's suspicion.

**espinaca** *f.* spinach.

**espinazo** *m.* spine, backbone.

**espinilla** *f.* shin (*front part of leg*); blackhead (*on the skin*).

**espino** *m.* hawthorn; thorny shrub; thorny branch.

**espinoso** *adj.* thorny; difficult, dangerous.

**espionaje** *m.* espionage, spying.

**espiral** *adj. & f.* spiral.

**espirar** *v.* to exhale; to emit, give off; to die. *See* **expirar.**

**espíritu** *m.* spirit; soul; courage; vigor; essence; ghost.

**espiritual** *adj.* spiritual.

**espita** *f.* spigot, faucet, tap; toper, drunkard.

**esplendidez** *f.* splendor.

**espléndido** *adj.* splendid.

**esplendor** *m.* splendor.

**esplendoroso** *adj.* resplendent, shining.

**espliego** *m.* lavender (*plant*).

**espolear** *v.* to spur; to incite.

**espoleta** *f.* bomb fuse.

**espolón** *m.* spur (*on a cock's leg*); ram (*of a boat*); spur; buttress.

**espolvorear** *v.* to powder, sprinkle with powder.

**esponja** *f.* sponge; sponger, parasite; *Col., Peru, Ch., Ríopl.* souse, habitual drunkard.

**esponjado** *adj.* fluffy; spongy; puffed up; *p.p. of* **esponjar.**

**esponjar** *v.* to fluff; to make spongy or porous; **-se** to fluff up; to become spongy or porous; to swell, puff up; to puff up with pride.

**esponjoso** *adj.* spongy.

**esponsales** *m. pl.* betrothal.

**espontaneidad** *f.* spontaneity, ease, naturalness.

**espontáneo** *adj.* spontaneous.

**esposa** *f.* wife; **-s** handcuffs.

**esposo** *m.* husband.

**espuela** *f.* spur.

**espulgar**[7] *v.* to delouse, remove lice or fleas from; to scrutinize.

**espuma** *f.* foam, froth; scum; **— de jabón** suds.

**espumar** *v.* to skim; to froth, foam.

**espumarajo** *m.* froth, foam (*from the mouth*); **echar -s** to froth at the mouth; to be very angry.

**espumoso** *adj.* foamy.

**esputo** *m.* sputum, spit, saliva.

**esquela** *f.* note, letter; announcement.

**esqueleto** *m.* skeleton; carcass; framework; *Mex., C.A., Col., Ven.* blank (*to fill out*); *Am.* outline.

**esquema** *f.* scheme, outline.

**esquí** *m.* ski, skiing; **— náutico, — acuático** water ski.

**esquiar**[17] *v.* to ski.

**esquila** *f.* small bell; cow bell; sheepshearing.

**esquilar** *v.* to shear; to clip; to crop.

**esquina** *f.* corner, angle; **esquinazo** *m.* corner; *Am.* serenade; **dar esquinazo** to avoid meeting someone; to "ditch" someone.

**esquivar** *v.* to avoid, dodge; to shun; **-se** to withdraw, shy away.

**esquivez** *f.* shyness; aloofness; disdain.

**esquivo** *adv.* reserved, unsociable; shy; disdainful, aloof.

**estabilidad** *f.* stability.

**estable** *adj.* stable, firm, steady.

**establecer**[13] *v. irr.* to establish; to found; to decree, ordain.

**establecimiento** *m.* establishment; foundation; statute, law.

**establo** *m.* stable; **establero** *m.* groom.

**estaca** *f.* stake, club; stick; picket.

**estacada** *f.* stockade; picket fence; *Am.* predicament.

**estacar**[6] *v.* to stake; to tie to a stake; to stake off, mark with stakes; *Am.* to fasten down with stakes; **-se** to remain stiff or rigid.

**estación** *f.* station; season; railway station.

**estacionar** *v.* to station; to place; to park (*a car*); **-se** to remain stationary; to park.

**estacionario** *adj.* stationary; motionless.

**estada** *f.* sojourn, stay.

**estadía** *f.* detention, stay; stay in port (*beyond time allowed for loading and unloading*); *C.A., Carib.* sojourn, stay (*in any sense*).

**estadio** *m.* stadium.

**estadista** *m.* statesman.

**estadística** *f.* statistics.

**estado** *m.* state, condition; station, rank; estate; **— mayor** army staff; **hombre de —** statesman; *Am.* **en — interesante** pregnant.

**estadounidense** *adj.* from the United States, American.

**estafa** *f.* swindle, fraud, trick.

**estafador** *m.* swindler, crook.

**estafar** *v.* to swindle, defraud, cheat.

**estallar** *v.* to explode, burst; to creak, crackle.

**estallido** *m.* explosion, outburst; crash; creaking; crack (*of a gun*), report (*of a gun or cannon*).

**estambre** *m.* woolen yarn; stamen (*of a flower*).

**estampa** *f.* image; print; stamp; cut, picture; footprint; figure, appearance.

**estampado** *m.* print, printed fabric; printing.

**estampar** *v.* to stamp, print.

**estampida** *f.* crack, sharp sound; *Col., Ven., C.A.* stampede (*sudden scattering of a herd of cattle or horses*).

**estampido** *m.* crack, sharp sound; report of a gun.

**estampilla** *f.* stamp, seal; *Mex., C.A., Andes* postage stamp.

**estancar**[6] *v.* to stem; to stanch; to stop the flow of; to corner (*a market*); **-se** to stagnate, become stagnant.

**estancia** *f.* (*permanencia*) stay; (*lugar*) hall, room; mansion; *Ríopl.* farm, cattle ranch; *Carib.* main building of a farm or ranch.

**estanciero** *m. Ríopl.* rancher, ranchowner, cattle raiser; *adj.* pertaining to an **estancia.**

**estanco** *m.* monopoly; government store (*for sale of monopolized goods such as tobacco, stamps and matches*); tank, reservoir; *Ec., C.A.* liquor store.

**estándar** *m. Am.* standard, norm.

**estandardizar, estandarizar**[9] *v. Am.* to standardize.

**estandarte** *m.* standard, flag, banner.

**estanque** *m.* pond, pool, reservoir.

**estanquillo** *m.* tobacco store; *Am.* small store; *C.A., Mex.* small liquor store, tavern.

**estante** *m.* shelf; bookshelf; *Am.* prop, support; **estantería** *f.* shelves; bookcases.

**estaño** *m.* tin.

**estaquilla** *f.* peg; spike.

**estar**[29] *v. irr.* to be; **-le bien a uno** to be becoming to one; **— de prisa** to be in a hurry; **¿a cuántos estamos?** what day of the month is it today?; **-se** to keep, remain.

**estático** *adj.* static; **estática** *f.* statics; radio static.

**estatua** *f.* statue.

**estatura** *f.* stature, height.

**estatuto** *m.* statute.

**este, esta** *dem. adj.* this; **estos, estas** these; **éste, ésta** *m.,f. dem. pron.* this one, this thing; the latter; **esto** this, this thing; **éstos, éstas** *m., f. pl.* these; the latter.

**este** *m.* east; east wind.

**estela** *f.* wake of a ship.

**estenógrafo** *m.* stenographer.

**estentóreo** *adj.* loud, thundering (*voice*).

**estepa** *f.* steppe, treeless plain.

**estera** *f.* matting; mat.

**estercolar** *v.* to manure, fertilize with manure.

**estercolero** *m.* manure pile, manure dump; manure collector.

**estereoscopio** *m.* stereoscope.

**estereotipo** *m.* stereotype.

**estéril** *adj.* sterile, barren.

**esterilidad** *f.* sterility, barrenness.

**esterilizar**[9] *v.* to sterilize.

**esterlina** *adj.* sterling; **libra —** pound sterling.

**estero** *m.* estuary.

**estertor** *m.* death-rattle; snort.

**estético** *adj.* aesthetic; **estética** *f.* aesthetics.

**estetoscopio** *m.* stethoscope.

**estibador** *m.* stevedore, longshoreman.

**estibar** *v.* to stow (*in a boat*); to pack down, compress.

**estiércol** *m.* manure; fertilizer.

**estigma** *m.* stigma; brand, mark of disgrace; birthmark.

**estilar** *v.* to use, be accustomed to using; **-se** to be in style (*said of clothes*).

**estilete** *m.* stiletto, narrow-bladed dagger; stylet (*instrument for probing wounds*); long, narrow sword.

**estilo** *m.* style; fashion.

**estima** *f.* esteem.

**estimación** *f.* esteem, regard; valuation.

**estimar** *v.* to esteem, regard highly; to estimate, appraise; to judge, think.

**estimulante** *adj.* stimulant, stimulating; *m.* stimulant.

**estimular** *v.* to stimulate, excite, goad.

**estímulo** *m.* stimulation, incitement; stimulus.

**estío** *m.* summer.

**estipulación** *f.* stipulation, specification, provision, proviso.

**estipular** *v.* to stipulate, specify.

**estirado** *p.p. & adj.* stretched; extended, drawn out; stuck-up, conceited.

**estirar** *v.* to stretch, extend; **— la pata** to die; **-se** to stretch out; *Am.* to die.

**estirón** *m.* hard pull, tug; stretch; **dar un —** to grow suddenly (*said of a child*).

**estirpe** *f.* lineage, family, race.

**estival** *adj.* summer, relating to the summer.

**estocada** *f.* thrust, stab; stab wound.

**estofa** *f.* stuff, cloth; class, quality; **gente de baja —** low class people, rabble.

**estofado** *m.* stew, stewed meat; *p.p.* of **estofar.**

**estofar** *v.* to quilt; to stew.

**estoico** *adj. & m.* stoic.

**estola** *f.* stole; **— de visón** mink wrap.

**estómago** *m.* stomach.

**estopa** *f.* burlap; oakum (*loose fiber of old ropes*).

**estoque** *m.* long, narrow sword.

**estorbar** *v.* to hinder; to obstruct.

**estorbo** *m.* hindrance; nuisance, bother.

**estornudar** *v.* to sneeze.

**estornudo** *m.* sneeze.

**estrado** *m.* dais (*platform for a throne, seats of honor, etc.*); main part of a parlor or drawing room.

**estragado** *p.p. & adj.* corrupted; spoiled; ruined; tired, worn out.

**estragar**[7] *v.* to corrupt, contaminate; to spoil; to ruin.

**estrago** *m.* havoc, ruin; massacre.

**estrangulador** *m.* strangler, choke (*of an automobile*); *adj.* strangling.

**estrangular** *v.* to strangle; to choke, throttle.

**estratagema** *f.* stratagem, scheme.

**estrategia** *f.* strategy.

**estratégico** *adj.* strategic; *m.* strategist, person trained or skilled in strategy.

**estrato** *m.* stratum, layer (*of mineral*).

**estratorreactor** *m.* supersonic jet plane.

**estratosfera** *f.* stratosphere.

**estrechar** *v.* to tighten; to narrow down; to embrace, hug; **— la mano** to squeeze, grasp another's hand; to shake hands.

**estrechez, estrechura** *f.* narrowness; tightness; austerity; dire straits; poverty; closeness.

**estrecho** *adj.* narrow; tight; *m.* strait, narrow passage.

**estrella** *f.* star; **— de mar** starfish.

**estrellado** *adj.* starry; spangled with stars; **huevos -s** fried eggs.

**estrellar** *v.* to shatter; to dash to pieces; to star, spangle with stars; **-se** to shatter, break into pieces; to fail.

**estremecer**[13] *v. irr.* to shake; **-se** to shiver, shudder; to vibrate.

**estremecimiento** *m.* shiver, shudder; vibration; shaking.

**estrenar** *v.* to wear for the first time; to perform (*a play*) for the first time; to inaugurate; to begin.

**estreno** *m.* début, first appearance or performance.

**estreñimiento** *m.* constipation.

**estreñir**[5,19] *v. irr.* to constipate; **-se** to become constipated.

**estrépito** *m.* racket, noise, crash.

**estrepitoso** *adj.* noisy; boisterous.

**estriado** *p.p. & adj.* fluted, grooved; streaked.

**estriar**[17] *v.* to groove; to flute (*as a column*).

**estribación** f. spur (*of a mountain or mountain range*).

**estribar** v. to rest (upon); **eso estriba en que ...** the basis or reason for it is that ...

**estribillo** m. refrain.

**estribo** m. (*de caballo o vehículo*) stirrup; footboard, running board; (*apoyo*) support; brace; spur (*of a mountain*); **perder los -s** to lose one's balance; to lose control of oneself.

**estribor** m. starboard.

**estricto** adj. strict.

**estrofa** f. strophe, stanza.

**estropajo** m. fibrous mass (*for scrubbing*); **tratar a uno como un —** to treat someone scornfully.

**estropear** v. to spoil, ruin, damage; to cripple.

**estructura** f. structure.

**estructural** adj. structural.

**estruendo** m. clatter; clamor, din, racket.

**estruendoso** adj. thunderous, uproarious, deafening.

**estrujamiento** m. crushing, squeezing.

**estrujar** v. to squeeze, press, crush.

**estrujón** m. squeeze, crush; smashing.

**estuario** m. estuary.

**estuco** m. stucco.

**estuche** m. jewel box; instrument case, kit; small casket; sheath.

**estudiantado** m. the student body (*of a school or college*).

**estudiante** m. & f. student.

**estudiar** v. to study.

**estudio** m. study; studio.

**estudioso** adj. studious; m. learner.

**estufa** f. heater; stove; hothouse; steam room; steam cabinet.

**estupefacto** adj. stunned; speechless.

**estupendo** adj. stupendous, marvelous.

**estupidez** f. stupidity.

**estúpido** adj. stupid.

**etapa** f. stage, lap (*of a journey or race*); army food rations; epoch, period.

**éter** m. ether.

**etéreo** adj. ethereal; heavenly.

**eternidad** f. eternity.

**eternizar**[9] v. to prolong excessively; to perpetuate, make eternal.

**eterno** adj. eternal, everlasting.

**ética** f. ethics; **ético** adj. ethical, moral.

**etiqueta** f. etiquette; formality; tag; **de —** formal (*dress, function, etc.*).

**eucalipto** m. eucalyptus.

**europeo** adj. & m. European.

**evacuación** f. evacuation; bowel movement.

**evacuar**[18] v. to evacuate, empty; to vacate.

**evadir** v. to evade, elude; **-se** to slip away, escape.

**evaluar**[18] v. to evaluate, appraise.

**evangelio** m. gospel.

**evaporar** v. to evaporate; **-se** to evaporate; to vanish, disappear.

**evasión** f. evasion, dodge, escape.

**evasiva** f. evasion, dodge, escape.

**evasivo** adj. evasive.

**evasor** m. evader, dodger.

**evento** m. event.

**evidencia** f. evidence.

**evidenciar** v. to prove, show, make evident.

**evidente** adj. evident.

**evitable** adj. avoidable.

**evitar** v. to avoid, shun.

**evocar**[6] v. to evoke, call forth.

**evolución** f. evolution.

**evolucionar** v. to evolve; to perform maneuvers; to go through changes.

**exacerbar** v. to exasperate, irritate; to aggravate, make worse.

**exactitud** f. exactness, precision; punctuality.

**exacto** adj. exact, precise; punctual.

**exagerar** v. to exaggerate.

**exaltación** f. exaltation; excitement.

**exaltado** adj. elated; excited; hotheaded.

**exaltar** v. to exalt, elevate, glorify; to praise; **-se** to get excited; to become upset emotionally.

**examen** m. examination; inspection.

**examinar** v. to examine; to inspect.

**exangüe** adj. lacking blood; anemic; exhausted.

**exánime** adj. lifeless, motionless; weak, faint.

**exasperar** v. to exasperate, irritate, annoy.

**excavar** v. to excavate, dig, dig out.

**excedente** m. surplus; adj. exceeding, extra.

**exceder** v. to exceed, surpass; to overdo; **-se** to go beyond the proper limit; to misbehave.

**excelencia** f. excellence, superiority; excellency (*title*).

**excelente** adj. excellent.

**excelso** adj. lofty, elevated; sublime; **El Excelso** the Most High.

**excéntrico** adj. eccentric; queer, odd.

**excepción** f. exception.

**excepcional** adj. exceptional, unusual.

**excepto** adv. except, with the exception of.

**exceptuar**[18] v. to except.

**excesivo** adj. excessive.

**exceso** m. excess; crime; **— de equipaje** excess baggage; **en —** in excess, excessively.

**excitación** f. excitement.

**excitante** adj. exciting; stimulating.

**excitar** v. to excite, stir; **-se** to get excited.

**exclamación** f. exclamation.

**exclamar** v. to exclaim.

**excluir**[32] v. irr. to exclude.

**exclusivo** adj. exclusive.

**excomunicar**[6] v. to excommunicate.

**excomunión** f. excommunication.

**excrecencia, excrescencia** f. excrescence (*abnormal growth or tumor*).

**excremento** m. excrement.

**excursión** f. excursion, tour, outing.

**excusa** f. excuse.

**excusado** p.p. & adj. excused; exempt; superfluous; unnecessary; reserved. private; m. toilet.

**excusar** v. (*disculpar*) to excuse; to exempt; (*evitar*) to avoid, shun; **-se** to excuse oneself, apologize; to decline.

**exención** f. exemption.

**exentar** v. to exempt. *See* **eximir**.

**exento** adj. exempt, freed; free, unobstructed.

**exequias** f. pl. obsequies, funeral rites.

**exhalar** v. to exhale; to emit, give off; to breathe forth; **-se** to evaporate; to run away.

**exhibición** f. exhibition; exposition; *Mex.* payment of an installment.

**exhibir** v. to exhibit; *Mex.* to pay for in installments (*stocks, policies, etc.*); **-se** to exhibit oneself, show off.

**exhortar** v. to exhort, admonish.

**exigencia** f. demand; urgent want; emergency.

**exigente** adj. demanding, exacting; urgent.

**exigir**[11] v. to require; to demand; to exact.

**exiguo** adj. scanty, meager.

**eximio** adj. very distinguished.

**eximir** v. to exempt, except, excuse; **-se de** to avoid, shun.

**existencia** f. existence; **-s** stock on hand, goods; **en —** in stock, on hand.

**existente** adj. existent, existing; in stock.

**existir** v. to exist.

**éxito** m. outcome, result; success; **tener buen (mal) —** to be successful (unsuccessful).

**éxodo** m. exodus, emigration.

**exonerar** v. to exonerate, free from blame; to relieve of a burden or position; to dismiss.

**exorbitante** adj. exorbitant, excessive, extravagant.

**exótico** adj. exotic, foreign, strange; quaint.

**expansión** f. expansion; relaxation; recreation.

**expansivo** adj. expansive; demonstrative, effusive.

**expatriar** v. to expatriate, exile; **-se** to expatriate oneself, renounce one's citizenship; to emigrate.

**expectación** f. expectation.

**expectativa** f. expectation; hope, prospect; **estar en — de algo** to be expecting, or on the lookout for, something.

**expectorar** v. to expectorate, cough up.

**expedición** f. expedition; dispatch, promptness; papal dispatch or bull.

**expedicionario** adj. expeditionary; m. member of an expedition; explorer.

**expediente** m. certificate; papers pertaining to a business matter; expedient, means; dispatch, promptness.

**expedir**[5] v. irr. to dispatch; to issue officially; to remit, send.

**expeler** v. to expel, eject.

**experiencia** f. experience; experiment.

**experimentado** adj. & p.p. experienced.

**experimental** adj. experimental.

**experimentar** v. to experiment, try, test; to experience, feel.

**experimento** m. experiment, trial.

**experto** adj. expert, skillful; m. expert.

**expiación** f. expiation, atonement.

**expiar**[17] v. to atone for; to make amends for; to purify.

**expirar** v. to die; to expire, come to an end.

**explayar** v. to extend; **-se** to become extended; to relax in the open air; to enlarge upon a subject; **-se con un amigo** to unbosom oneself, speak with utmost frankness with a friend.

**explicable** adj. explainable.

**explicación** f. explanation.

**explicar**[6] v. to explain; **— una cátedra** to teach a course; **-se** to explain oneself; to account for one's conduct.

**explicativo** adj. explanatory, explaining.

**explícito** adj. explicit, express, clear, definite.

**exploración** f. exploration.

**explorador** m. explorer, scout; adj. exploring.

**explorar** v. to explore.

**explosión** f. explosion.

**explosivo** adj. & m. explosive.

**explotación** f. exploitation; operation of a mine; development of a business; plant.

**explotar** v. to exploit, operate, develop; to utilize, profit by; to make unfair use of; *Am.* to explode.

**exponer**[40] v. irr. (*dejar ver*) to expose, reveal; to show, exhibit; to display; (*sin protección*) to leave unprotected, to expose (*film*); (*explicar*) to expound; to explain; **-se a** to expose oneself to; to run the risk of.

**exportación** f. exportation; export.

**exportar** v. to export.

**exposición** f. exposition; exhibition; explanation; exposure.

**exprés** m. *Am.* express; *Am.* express company.

**expresar** v. to express; **-se** to express oneself, speak.

**expresión** f. expression; utterance; **-es** regards.

**expresivo** adj. expressive; affectionate.

**expreso** adj. expressed; express, clear, exact; fast; m. express train.

**exprimir** v. to squeeze, extract (*juice*); to wring out; to express, utter.

**expuesto** p.p. of **exponer** & adj. exposed; expressed; displayed; risky, dangerous; **lo —** what has been said.

**expulsar** v. to expel, eject.

**expulsión** f. expulsion, expelling.

**exquisitez** f. exquisiteness.

**exquisito** adj. exquisite.

**extasiado** adj. rapt, in ecstasy; p.p. of **extasiar**.

**extasiar**[17] v. to delight; **-se** to be in ecstasy; to be entranced.

**éxtasis** m. ecstasy.

**extender**[1] v. irr. to extend; to spread; to unfold; to draw up (*a document*); **-se** to extend, spread; to expatiate, be too wordy.

**extensión** *f*. extension; extent; expanse; expansion.

**extensivo** *adj*. extensive.

**extenso** *p.p. irr. of* **extender** extended; *adj*. extensive, vast, spacious; **por —** extensively, in detail.

**extenuado** *adj*. wasted, weak, emaciated.

**exterior** *adj*. exterior, outer; *m*. exterior; outside; outward appearance.

**exterminar** *v*. to exterminate.

**exterminio** *m*. extermination, destruction.

**externo** *adj*. external, outward.

**extinguir**[12] *v*. to extinguish, put out; to destroy.

**extinto** *adj*. extinct.

**extintor** *m*. extinguisher; **— de espuma** fire extinguisher.

**extirpar** *v*. to eradicate, pull out by the roots, root out, remove completely; to destroy completely.

**extorsión** *f*. extortion.

**extorsionar** *v*. *Am*. to extort, extract money, blackmail.

**extorsionista** *m*. *Am*. extortioner, profiteer, racketeer.

**extracto** *m*. extract; abstract, summary.

**extraer**[46] *v. irr*. to extract.

**extranjero** *adj*. foreign; *m*. foreigner.

**extrañamiento** *m*. wonder, surprise, amazement.

**extrañar** *v*. to wonder at; to banish; *Am*. to miss (*a person or thing*); **-se** to marvel, be astonished.

**extrañeza** *f*. strangeness; surprise, astonishment; oddity, odd thing.

**extraño** *adj*. strange; rare; odd; *m*. stranger.

**extraordinario** *adj*. extraordinary.

**extravagancia** *f*. extravagance; folly.

**extravagante** *adj*. extravagant, fantastic; queer, odd.

**extraviar**[17] *v*. to lead astray; to strand; to misplace; **-se** to lose one's way; to get stranded; to get lost; to miss the road.

**extravío** *m*. deviation, straying; error; misconduct; damage.

**extremado** *adj*. extreme; extremely good or extremely bad; *p.p. of* **extremar.**

**extremar** *v*. to carry to an extreme; **-se** to take great pains, exert great effort.

**extremidad** *f*. extremity; extreme degree; remotest part; **-es** extremities, hands and feet.

**extremo** *adj*. extreme, last; farthest; excessive; utmost; *m*. extreme, highest degree or point; end, extremity; extreme care; **con (en** *or* **por) —** very much, extremely.

**exuberante** *adj*. exuberant; luxuriant.

## F

**fa** *m*. fourth note of the musical scale (*solfa syllables*).

**fábrica** *f*. manufacture; factory, mill; structure.

**fabricación** *f*. manufacture.

**fabricante** *m*. manufacturer, maker.

**fabricar**[6] *v*. to manufacture, make; to construct, build; to fabricate, make up, invent.

**fabril** *adj*. manufacturing.

**fábula** *f*. fable, tale; falsehood.

**fabuloso** *adj*. fabulous; false, imaginary.

**facción** *f*. faction, band, party; battle; **-es** features; **estar de —** to be on duty.

**faceto** *adj*. *Am*. cute, funny; *Am*. affected.

**fácil** *adj*. easy; docile, yielding, manageable; likely; probable.

**facilidad** *f*. facility, ease; opportunity.

**facilitar** *v*. to facilitate, make easy; to furnish, give; **— todos los datos** to furnish all the data.

**facón** *m*. *Ríopl., Bol.* dagger, large knife; **faconazo** *m*. *Ríopl., Bol.* stab.

**factible** *adj*. feasible.

**factor** *m*. factor; element, joint cause; commercial agent; baggage man.

**factoría** *f*. trading post; *Am*. factory.

**factura** *f*. (*cuenta*) invoice, itemized bill; (*hechura*) make; workmanship, form; *Am*. roll, biscuit, muffin; **—simulada** temporary invoice, memorandum.

**facturar** *v*. to invoice, bill; to check (*baggage*).

**facultad** *f*. faculty; ability, aptitude; power, right; permission; branch of learning; school or college of a university.

**facultativo** *m*. doctor, physician.

**facundia** *f*. eloquence, fluency, facility in speaking, gift of expression.

**facha** *f*. appearance, figure, aspect, looks.

**fachada** *f*. façade, front (*of a building*); title page.

**fachenda** *f*. ostentation, vanity.

**fachendoso** *adj*. vain, boastful, ostentatious.

**faena** *f*. task, job, duty; *Carib., Mex., C.A.* extra job; *Ch.* work crew, labor gang.

**faja** *f*. sash; girdle; band; *Am*. belt, waist band.

**fajar** *v*. to girdle; to bind, wrap, or bandage with a strip of cloth; *Am*. to beat, strike, thrash; *Am*. **— un latigazo a uno** to whip, thrash someone; **-se** to put on a sash or belt; to tighten one's sash or belt; *Am*. **-se con** to have a fight with, come to blows with.

**fajo** *m*. bundle; sheaf.

**falaz** *adj*. illusive, illusory; deceitful, deceiving.

**falda** *f*. skirt; lap; hat brim; foothill, slope; **faldón** *m*. coattail; shirttail.

**faldear** *v*. to skirt (*a hill*).

**falsario** *m*. crook, forger; liar.

**falsear** *v*. to falsify, misrepresent; to counterfeit; to forge; to pick (*a lock*); to flag, grow weak; to hit a wrong note.

**falsedad** *f*. falsehood, lie; deceit.

**falsificación** *f*. falsification, forgery; counterfeit.

**falsificar**[6] *v.* to falsify, make false; to counterfeit; to forge.

**falso** *adj.* false; untrue, unreal; deceitful; counterfeit; sham; *C.A.* cowardly; *m.* inside facing of a dress; lining; *Mex.* false testimony, slander; **en —** upon a false foundation; without proper security; *Am.* **coger a uno en —** to catch one lying.

**falta** *f.* (*defecto*) lack, want; fault, mistake; defect; absence; (*infracción*) misdemeanor, offense; **a — de** for want of; **hacer —** to be necessary; to be missing; **me hace —** I need it; **sin —** without fail.

**faltar** *v.* to be lacking, wanting; to be absent or missing; to fail, be of no use or help; to fail to fulfill (*a promise or duty*); to die; *Mex., C.A.* to insult; **— poco para las cinco** to be almost five o'clock; **¡no faltaba más!** that's the last straw!; why, the very idea!

**falto** *adj.* lacking; deficient, short; *Am.* foolish, simple.

**faltriquera** *f.* pocket.

**falla** *f.* fault, defect; failure; fault (*fracture in the earth's crust*); *Ríopl.* baby's bonnet.

**fallar** *v.* (*juzgar*) to render a verdict; (*fracasar*) to fail, be deficient; to default; to miss; to fail to hit; to give way, break; to trump.

**fallecer**[13] *v. irr.* to die.

**fallecimiento** *m.* decease, death.

**fallido** *adj.* frustrated; bankrupt.

**fallo** *m.* verdict, judgment; decision; *adj.* lacking (*a card, or suit, in card games*); *Ch.* silly, foolish.

**fama** *f.* fame, reputation; rumor, report; *Ch.* bull's-eye, center of a target.

**famélico** *adj.* ravenous, hungry, starved.

**familia** *f.* family.

**familiar** *adj.* domestic, homelike; familiar, well-known; friendly, informal; colloquial (*phrase or expression*); *m.* intimate friend; member of a household; domestic servant; familiar spirit, demon; *Am.* relative.

**familiaridad** *f.* familiarity, informality.

**familiarizar**[9] *v.* to familiarize, acquaint; **-se** to acquaint oneself, become familiar (with).

**famoso** *adj.* famous; excellent.

**fanal** *m.* beacon, lighthouse; lantern; headlight; bell jar, glass cover.

**fanático** *adj. & m.* fanatic.

**fanatismo** *m.* fanaticism.

**fanega** *f.* Spanish bushel; **— de tierra** land measure (*variable according to region*).

**fanfarrón** *m.* braggart, boaster; bluffer.

**fanfarronada** *f.* boast, brag, swagger, bluff.

**fanfarronear** *v.* to bluff, brag; to swagger.

**fango** *m.* mud, mire.

**fangoso** *adj.* muddy, miry.

**fantasear** *v.* to fancy; to imagine.

**fantasía** *f.* fantasy, imagination, fancy, whim; **-s** string of pearls; *Ven.* **tocar por —** to play by ear.

**fantasma** *m.* phantom, image; vision, ghost; *f.* scarecrow.

**fantasmagórico** *adj.* fantastic, unreal, illusory.

**fantástico** *adj.* fantastic.

**fardel** *m.* knapsack, bag; bundle.

**fardo** *m.* bundle; bale; *Ríopl., Andes* **pasar el —** to "pass the buck", shift the responsibility to someone else.

**faringe** *f.* pharynx.

**faríngeo** *adj.* pharyngeal.

**farmacéutico** *m.* pharmacist, druggist; *adj.* pharmaceutical (*pertaining to a pharmacy or pharmacists*).

**farmacia** *f.* pharmacy; drugstore.

**faro** *m.* lighthouse; beacon; *Am.* headlight.

**farol** *m.* (*linterna*) lantern; street lamp; (*fachendoso*) conceit, self-importance; *Ríopl.* balcony; *Am.* presumptuous man; *Am.* bluff; **darse —** to show off; to put on airs.

**farola** *f.* street light; lamppost.

**farolero** *adj.* vain, ostentatious; *m.* lamp maker or vendor; lamplighter (*person*).

**farra** *f.* *Ríopl., Ch., Col., Ven., Andes* spree, revelry, wild party, noisy merrymaking; *Ríopl., Ch., Col., Ven., Andes* **ir de —** to go on a spree.

**farsa** *f.* farce; company of actors; sham, fraud.

**farsante** *m.* charlatan, bluffer; quack; comedian; wag.

**fascinación** *f.* fascination; glamour.

**fascinador** *adj.* fascinating, glamorous; charming.

**fascinar** *v.* to fascinate, bewitch, charm; to allure.

**fase** *f.* phase, aspect.

**fastidiar** *v.* to annoy, bother; to bore; *Col., P.R.* to hurt, harm, ruin.

**fastidio** *m.* boredom; disgust; nuisance, annoyance.

**fastidioso** *adj.* annoying, bothersome; boring, tiresome.

**fatal** *adj.* fatal; mortal, deadly; unfortunate.

**fatalidad** *f.* fatality, destiny; calamity, misfortune.

**fatiga** *f.* fatigue, weariness; toil; **-s** hardships.

**fatigar**[7] *v.* to fatigue, weary; to bother.

**fatigoso** *adj.* fatiguing, tiring.

**fatuo** *adj.* foolish, stupid; vain; **fuego —** will-o'-the-wisp.

**favor** *m.* favor; kindness; help, aid; protection; *Am.* ribbon bow; **a — de** in favor of; **hágame el —** please.

**favorable** *adj.* favorable.

**favorecer**[13] *v. irr.* to favor, help, protect.

**favoritismo** *m.* favoritism.

**favorito** *adj. & m.* favorite.

**faz** *f.* face.

**fe** *f.* faith; **— de bautismo** baptismal certificate.

**fealdad** *f.* ugliness, homeliness; foulness, foul or immoral action.

**febrero** *m.* February.

**febril** *adj.* feverish.
**fécula** *f.* starch.
**fecundar** *v.* to fertilize.
**fecundo** *adj.* fruitful, fertile, productive.
**fecha** *f.* date.
**fechar** *v.* to date.
**fechoría** *f.* misdeed, misdemeanor.
**federación** *f.* federation, union.
**federal** *adj.* federal.
**felicidad** *f.* happiness; **¡-es!** congratulations!
**felicitación** *f.* congratulation.
**felicitar** *v.* to congratulate.
**feligrés** *m.* parishioner.
**feliz** *adj.* happy; lucky.
**felpudo** *adj.* plushy, like plush; *m.* small plushlike mat; door mat.
**femenil** *adj.* womanly, feminine.
**femenino** *adj.* feminine.
**fementido** *adj.* false; treacherous.
**fenecer**[13] *v. irr.* to die; to finish, end.
**fénico** *adj.* carbolic; **acido —** carbolic acid.
**fénix** *m.* phoenix (*mythical bird*).
**fenómeno** *m.* phenomenon.
**feo** *adj.* ugly, homely; *Am.* bad (*referring to taste or odor*); **feote** *adj.* hideous, very ugly.
**féretro** *m.* bier; coffin.
**feria** *f.* fair; market; *Mex.* change (*money*); *Am.* tip; **-s** *Am.* present given to servants or the poor during holidays.
**feriante** *m. & f.* trader at fairs; trader; peddler.
**fermentar** *v.* to ferment.
**fermento** *m.* ferment; yeast, leaven.
**ferocidad** *f.* ferocity, fierceness.
**feroz** *adj.* ferocious, wild, fierce.
**férreo** *adj.* ferrous (*pertaining to or derived from iron*); ironlike; harsh; **vía férrea** railroad.
**ferretería** *f.* hardware shop; hardware.
**ferrocarril** *m.* railroad.
**ferroviario** *adj.* railway, railroad (*used as adj.*); *m.* railroad man; railroad employee.
**fértil** *adj.* fertile, productive; **fertilidad** *f.* fertility.
**fertilizar**[9] *v.* to fertilize.
**ferviente** *adj.* fervent, ardent.
**fervor** *m.* fervor, zeal, devotion.
**fervoroso** *adj.* fervent, ardent; pious, devout; zealous.
**festejar** *v.* to feast, entertain; to celebrate; to woo; *Mex.* to thrash, beat.
**festejo** *m.* entertainment, festival, celebration; courtship; *Am.* revelry.
**festín** *m.* feast; banquet.
**festividad** *f.* festival; holiday; holy day; festivity, gaiety, rejoicing.
**festivo** *adj.* festive, gay; **día —** holiday.
**fétido** *adj.* foul, foul-smelling.
**fiado** *p.p.* of **fiar; al —** on credit.
**fiador** *m.* guarantor, backer, bondsman; *Ec., Ch.* chin strap, hat guard.
**fiambre** *m.* cold meat; cold or late news; *Ríopl., Mex., Col., Ven.* cold meat salad; *Am.* flop, failure (*referring to a party*).

**fianza** *f.* bond, security, surety, guarantee; bail.
**fiar**[17] to trust; to guarantee, back; *Am.* to borrow on credit; **-se de** to place confidence in.
**fibra** *f.* fiber; **fibroso** *adj.* fibrous.
**ficción** *f.* fiction.
**ficticio** *adj.* fictitious.
**ficha** *f.* (*pieza*) chip; token; domino; (*tarjeta*) file card; *Am.* check (*used in barbershops and stores*); *Am.* rascal, scamp; **fichero** *m.* file, card index, filing cabinet.
**fidedigno** *adj.* trustworthy, reliable.
**fidelidad** *f.* fidelity, faithfulness.
**fideo** *m.* vermicelli, thin noodle; thin person.
**fiebre** *f.* fever; excitement, agitation; *Ch.* astute person.
**fiel** *adj.* faithful; true, accurate; *m.* public inspector; pointer of a balance or scale; pin of the scissors; **los -es** the worshipers, the congregation.
**fieltro** *m.* felt; felt hat; felt rug.
**fiera** *f.* wild beast; *Am.* go-getter, hustler; **ser una — para el trabajo** to be a demon for work.
**fiereza** *f.* ferocity, fierceness; cruelty; ugliness.
**fiero** *adj.* fierce, ferocious, wild; cruel; ugly, horrible; huge; *m.* threat; **echar** (*or* **hacer**) **-s** to threaten; to boast.
**fierro** *m. Am.* iron; *Am.* iron bar; *Am.* cattle brand; **-s** *Am.* tools, implements. *See* **hierro.**
**fiesta** *f.* festivity, celebration, entertainment; holiday; **estar de —** to be in a holiday mood; **hacer -s a uno** to fawn on a person.
**fiestero** *adj.* fond of parties, fond of entertaining; gay, festive; playful; *m.* merrymaker.
**figón** *m.* cheap eating house, "joint."
**figura** *f.* figure; shape, form; countenance; face card.
**figurado** *adj.* figurative.
**figurar** *v.* to figure; to form; to represent, symbolize; **-se** to imagine; **se me figura** I think, guess, or imagine.
**figurín** *m.* fashion plate; dandy.
**fijar** *v.* to fix, fasten; to establish; **-se** to settle; **-se en** to notice, pay attention to.
**fijeza** *f.* firmness, solidity, steadiness.
**fijo** *adj.* fixed; firm; secure.
**fila** *f.* row, tier; rank.
**filamento** *m.* filament.
**filete** *m.* (*moldura*) edge, rim; (*carne*) fillet, tenderloin; (*freno*) snaffle bit (*for horses*); hem; screw thread.
**filial** *adj.* filial.
**filmar** *v.* to film, screen (*a play or novel*).
**filo** *m.* cutting edge; *Andes* hunger; **por —** exactly; *Am.* **de —** resolutely.
**filón** *m.* seam, layer (*of metallic ore*).
**filoso** *adj. Am.* sharp, sharp-edged.
**filosofía** *f.* philosophy.
**filosófico** *adj.* philosophic, philosophical.
**filósofo** *m.* philosopher.

**FA**

**filtrar** *v.* to filter; **-se** to leak through, leak out; to filter.

**filtro** *m.* filter.

**filudo** *adj. Am.* sharp, sharp-edged.

**fin** *m.* end, ending; purpose; **al —** at last; **al — y al cabo** at last; anyway; in the end; **a — de que** so that; **a -es del mes** toward the end of the month; **en —** in conclusion; well; in short.

**finado** *m.* the deceased.

**final** *adj.* final.

**finalizar**[9] *v.* to finish; to end.

**financiamiento** *m. Am.* financing.

**financiar** *v. Am.* to finance.

**financiero** *adj.* financial; *m.* financier.

**financista** *m. Am.* financier.

**finanza** *f. Am.* finance; **-s** *Am.* public treasury, government funds.

**finca** *f.* real estate; property; country house; *Am.* ranch, farm.

**fincar** *v.* to buy real estate; *Am.* to rest (on), be based (on); *Am.* to build a farmhouse or country house.

**fineza** *f.* fineness; nicety; courtesy; favor, kindness; present.

**fingimiento** *m.* pretense, sham.

**fingir**[11] *v.* to feign, pretend, fake; to imagine.

**finiquito** *m.* settlement (*of an account*); quittance, final receipt; **dar —** to finish up.

**fino** *adj.* fine; nice; delicate; sharp; subtle; refined.

**finura** *f.* fineness; nicety; subtlety; courtesy, good manners.

**fiordo** *m.* fjord.

**firma** *f.* signature; firm, firm name.

**firmamento** *m.* firmament, sky.

**firmante** *m. & f.* signer.

**firmar** *v.* to sign.

**firme** *adj.* firm; solid, hard; **de —** without stopping, hard, steadily.

**firmeza** *f.* firmness.

**fiscal** *m.* public prosecutor, district attorney; *adj.* fiscal.

**fisgar**[7] *v.* to pry; to snoop; to spy on.

**fisgón** *m.* snoop, snooper; *adj.* snooping; curious.

**fisgonear** *v.* to pry about; to snoop.

**física** *f.* physics.

**físico** *adj.* physical; *Am.* vain, prudish; affected; *Am.* real; *m.* physicist.

**fisiología** *f.* physiology.

**fisiológico** *adj.* physiological.

**fisionomía** *f.* face, features.

**flaco** *adj.* lean, skinny; frail, weak; **su lado —** his weak side, his weakness.

**flacura** *f.* thinness.

**flama** *f.* flame.

**flamante** *adj.* bright, shiny; brand-new.

**flameante** *adj.* flaming, flashing.

**flamear** *v.* to flame; to flap, flutter (*in the wind*).

**flamenco** *adj.* Flemish; *C.A., P.R.* skinny; *m.* Flemish, Flemish language; flamingo; Andalusian dance.

**flan** *m.* custard.

**flanco** *m.* flank, side.

**flanquear** *v.* to flank.

**flaps** *m. pl.* flaps (*of an airplane*).

**flaquear** *v.* to weaken, flag.

**flaqueza** *f.* thinness, leanness; weakness, frailty.

**flauta** *f.* flute; **flautista** *m. & f.* flute player.

**fleco** *m.* fringe; bangs, fringe of hair.

**flecha** *f.* arrow, dart.

**flechar** *v.* to dart, shoot (*an arrow*); to strike, wound or kill with an arrow; to cast an amorous or ardent glance; *Ven.* to prick, sting; *Am.* to burn (*said of the sun*).

**fletamento** *m.* charter, charter party (*of a ship*).

**fletar** *v.* to charter (*a ship*); to freight; *Ch.* to hire (*pack animals*); *Peru* to let loose (*strong words*); *Am.* to scatter (*false rumors*); **-se** *Col., Mex., Carib., Ch.* to run away, slip away; *Am.* to slip in uninvited; *Am.* **salir fletado** to leave on the run.

**flete** *m.* freight, freightage; cargo; load; *Am.* fine horse, race horse; *Am.* bother, nuisance; *Col., Ven.* **salir sin -s** to leave in a hurry.

**flexibilidad** *f.* flexibility; **flexible** *adj.* flexible.

**flexión** *f.* bending, bend; sag.

**flojear** *v.* to slacken; to weaken; to idle, to be lazy.

**flojedad** *f.* laxity, looseness; slackness; laziness; slack.

**flojera** = **flojedad.**

**flojo** *adj.* (*mal atado*) lax; loose, slack; (*sin fuerza*) lazy; weak.

**flor** *f.* flower, blossom; compliment; **— de la edad** prime; **— de lis** iris (*flower*); **— y nata** the best, the cream, the chosen few; **a — de** flush with; **echar -es** to throw a bouquet; to compliment, flatter.

**floreado** *p.p. & adj.* flowered; made of the finest wheat.

**florear** *v.* to decorate with flowers; to brandish, flourish; to make a flourish on the guitar; to flatter, compliment; to bolt, sift out (*the finest flour*); *Am.* to flower, bloom; *Am.* to choose the best; **-se** *C.A.* to shine, excel; *Am.* to burst open like a flower.

**florecer**[13] *v. irr.* to flower, bloom; to flourish, thrive.

**floreciente** *adj.* flourishing, thriving; prosperous.

**florecimiento** *m.* flourishing, flowering, bloom.

**floreo** *m.* flourish; idle talk; flattery, compliment.

**florería** *f.* florist's shop.

**florero** *m.* florist; flower vase; flatterer; *adj.* flattering.

**floresta** *f.* wooded place, grove; arbor.

**florete** *m.* fencing foil.

**florido** *adj.* flowery.

**flota** *f.* fleet; *Col.*, **echar -s** to brag, boast.

**flotador** *m.* floater; float; pontoon (*of a hydroplane*); *adj.* floating.

**flotante** *adj.* floating; *m. Col., Ven.* bluffer, braggart.

**flotar** *v.* to float.
**flote: a —** afloat.
**fluctuación** *f.* fluctuation; wavering, hesitation.
**fluctuar**[18] *v.* to fluctuate; to waver; to hesitate.
**fluente** *adj.* fluent, flowing.
**fluidez** *f.* fluidity, easy flow, fluency.
**flúido** *adj.* fluid, flowing, fluent; *m.* fluid.
**fluir**[32] *v. irr.* to flow.
**flujo** *m.* flux; flow; flood tide.
**fluorescente** *adj.* fluorescent.
**flux** *f.* flush (*in cards*); *P.R., Col., Ven.* suit of clothes; **hacer —** to use up one's funds, lose everything; *Am.* **tener uno —** to be lucky.
**foca** *f.* seal, sea lion.
**foco** *m.* focus, center; *Am.* electric-light bulb.
**fofo** *adj.* spongy, porous; light (*in weight*); soft.
**fogata** *f.* fire, blaze, bonfire.
**fogón** *m.* hearth, fireplace; grill (*for cooking*); vent of a gun; *C.A., Mex.* fire, bonfire; **fogonazo** *m.* flash (*of gunpowder*).
**fogoso** *adj.* fiery, ardent; lively, spirited.
**follaje** *m.* foliage.
**folletín** *m.* small pamphlet; serial story.
**folleto** *m.* pamphlet.
**fomentar** *v.* to foment, encourage, promote, foster.
**fomento** *m.* promotion, encouragement; development; aid.
**fonda** *f.* inn; restaurant.
**fondear** *v.* to cast anchor; to sound, make soundings; to search (*a ship*); to sound out; **-se** *Cuba* to save up for the future.
**fondero** *m. Am.* innkeeper.
**fondillos** *m. pl.* seat of trousers.
**fondista** *m. & f.* innkeeper.
**fondo** *m.* (*hondura*) bottom; depth; background; back, rear end; (*esencia*) mature, heart, inner self; fund; *Cuba, Ven.* underskirt; **-s** funds; **a —** thoroughly; **echar a —** to sink.
**fonducho** *m.* cheap eating place.
**fonema** *m.* phoneme.
**fonética** *f.* phonetics, study of pronunciation.
**fonógrafo** *m.* phonograph.
**fonología** *f.* phonology.
**forajido** *m.* outlaw, fugitive; highwayman, bandit.
**foráneo** *adj.* foreign; *m.* outsider, stranger.
**forastero** *m.* stranger; foreigner; outsider; *adj.* foreign.
**forcejear, forcejar** *v.* to struggle; to strive; to oppose, resist.
**forja** *f.* forge; forging; blacksmith's shop.
**forjador** *m.* forger (*of metals*); smith, blacksmith; inventor (*of lies, stories, tricks, etc.*).
**forjar** *v.* to forge; to form, shape; to invent, feign, fake.
**forma** *f.* form, shape, figure; manner; format (*size and shape of a book*);

host (*unleavened bread for communion*).
**formación** *f.* formation.
**formal** *adj.* formal; serious, trustworthy, punctual; reliable.
**formalidad** *f.* formality; seriousness, reliability; gravity, dignity; punctuality; red tape.
**formalismo** *m.* formality, red tape (*excess of formalities*); **formalista** *adj.* fond of excessive formalities, fond of red tape.
**formalizar**[9] *v.* to give proper form to; to legalize; to make official; **-se** to settle down, become serious.
**formar** *v.* to form; to shape, mold; **-se** to get into line; to be molded, educated; to take form.
**formidable** *adj.* formidable; fearful.
**formón** *m.* wide chisel.
**fórmula** *f.* formula.
**formular** *v.* to formulate, word.
**fornido** *adj.* stout, strong, sturdy.
**foro** *m.* stage; back, rear (*of a stage*); forum, court; bar (*profession of law*).
**forraje** *m.* forage, green grass, fodder, feed.
**forrajear** *v.* to forage, gather forage.
**forrar** *v.* to line; to cover, put a sheath, case, or covering on; **-se** *Ríopl., C.A.* to eat well; *Am.* to supply oneself with provisions; *Ríopl., Mex., Cuba* to save money.
**forro** *m.* lining; sheathing; casing; covering; book cover.
**fortalecer**[13] *v. irr.* to fortify; to strengthen.
**fortaleza** *f.* fortress; fortitude; strength, vigor; *Ch.* stench, stink.
**fortificación** *f.* fortification; fort.
**fortificar**[6] *v.* to fortify.
**fortuito** *adj.* fortuitous, accidental, unexpected.
**fortuna** *f.* fortune; fate, chance; wealth; **por —** fortunately.
**forzar**[9] *v. irr.* to force; to compel; to take (*a fort*); to rape; **— la entrada en** to break into.
**forzozo** *adj.* compulsory; necessary.
**fosa** *f.* grave; cavity.
**fosco** *adj.* dark; cross, irritable, frowning.
**fosfato** *m.* phosphate.
**fosforecer**[13], **fosforescer** *v.* to glow.
**fósforo** *m.* phosphorus; match.
**fósil** *adj. & m.* fossil.
**foso** *m.* hole, pit; stage pit; ditch.
**fotograbado** *m.* photoengraving.
**fotografía** *f.* photograph; photography.
**fotografiar**[17] *v.* to photograph.
**fotógrafo** *m.* photographer.
**fracasado** *adj.* failed; *m.* failure.
**fracasar** *v.* to fail; to come to ruin; to crumble to pieces.
**fracaso** *m.* failure, ruin; calamity; crash.
**fracción** *f.* fraction.
**fractura** *f.* fracture; break, crack.
**fracturar** *v.* to fracture, break.
**fragancia** *f.* fragrance, scent, perfume.
**fragante** *adj.* fragrant; **en —** in the act.

FI

**fragata** *f.* frigate.
**frágil** *adj.* fragile, breakable; frail, weak.
**fragmento** *m.* fragment.
**fragor** *m.* clang, din; crash.
**fragoroso** *adj.* deafening, thunderous.
**fragoso** *adj.* rugged, craggy, rough, uneven; noisy.
**fragua** *f.* forge; blacksmith's shop.
**fraguar** *v.* to forge; to scheme, hatch (*a plot*).
**fraile** *m.* friar; priest; **frailuco** *m.* little old friar.
**frambuesa** *f.* raspberry; **frambueso** *m.* raspberry bush.
**francés** *adj.* French; *m.* Frenchman; French language.
**franco** *adj.* (*sincero*) frank, open, candid, sincere; (*exento*) free; *m.* franc; **francote** *adj.* very frank, blunt, outspoken.
**franela** *f.* flannel.
**franja** *f.* fringe, border; stripe; braid.
**franquear** *v.* to exempt; to free; to frank (*a letter*); to dispatch, send; to make grants; **— el paso** to permit the passage (of); **-se** to unbosom oneself, disclose one's innermost thoughts and feelings.
**franqueo** *m.* postage; franking (*of a letter*); freeing (*of slaves or prisoners*).
**franqueza** *f.* frankness; freedom.
**franquicia** *f.* franchise, grant, privilege; freedom or exemption (*from fees*).
**frasco** *m.* flask, vial, small bottle.
**frase** *f.* phrase; sentence.
**fraternal** *adj.* fraternal, brotherly.
**fraternidad** *f.* fraternity; brotherhood.
**fraude** *m.* fraud.
**fraudulento** *adj.* fraudulent, tricky, deceitful, dishonest.
**fray** *m.* (*contr. of* **fraile**, *used before Christian name*) friar.
**frazada** *f.* blanket.
**frecuencia** *f.* frequency; **con —** frequently.
**frecuentar** *v.* to frequent.
**frecuente** *adj.* frequent.
**fregadero** *m.* sink.
**fregado** *m.* scrub, scrubbing; *p.p. of* **fregar**; *adj. Ch., Andes* bothersome, annoying; *Col.* stubborn; *Mex., C.A.* brazen.
**fregar**[7] *v. irr.* to scour; to scrub; to rub; to wash (*dishes*); *Am.* to molest, annoy.
**fregona** *f.* scrub woman; dishwasher, kitchen maid.
**freír**[15] *v. irr.* to fry; to tease, bother.
**frenesí** *m.* frenzy, madness.
**frenético** *adj.* frantic; furious; in a frenzy.
**freno** *m.* bridle; brake; control; bit (*for horses*).
**frente** *f.* forehead; countenance; *m.* front; **en — de** in front of; **— a** in front of, facing; **hacer —** to face.
**fresa** *f.* strawberry.
**fresca** *f.* fresh air; fresh remark.
**fresco** *adj.* (*bastante frío*) fresh; cool, (*sereno*) calm, serene; (*descarado*) forward, bold; *m.* coolness; cool air;

fresco (*painting*); *C.A., Col.* refreshment; **al —** in the open air; **pintura al —** painting in fresco.
**frescor** *m.* freshness, coolness.
**frescura** *f.* (*temperatura baja*) freshness; coolness; (*serenidad*) calm; freedom; ease; (*insolencia*) boldness, impudence; impudent remark.
**fresno** *m.* ash, ash tree.
**fresquecillo** *adj.* nice and cool; *m.* cool air, fresh breeze; **fresquecito, fresquito** *adj.* nice and cool.
**frialdad** *f.* coldness; coolness, indifference.
**fricción** *f.* friction, rub, rubbing.
**friccionar** *v.* to rub; to massage.
**friega** *f.* rub, rubbing; *Am.* bother, nuisance, irritation; *Am.* flogging, beating.
**frigorífico** *adj.* freezing; *m. Spain* refrigerator, icebox; *Ríopl.* meat-packing house.
**frijol** *m.* bean; kidney bean, navy bean.
**frío** *adj.* cold; frigid; cool, indifferent; *m.* cold; **-s** *Mex.* chills and fever; *Col., C.A., Ven.* malaria.
**friolento** *adj.* cold-blooded, sensitive to cold; chilly.
**friolera** *f.* trifle.
**fritada** *f.* dish of fried food.
**frito** *p.p. irr. of* **freír** fried; *m.* fry, dish of fried food.
**fritura** *f.* fry, dish of fried food; fritter.
**frivolidad** *f.* frivolity; **frívolo** *adj.* frivolous.
**fronda** *f.* leaf; fern leaf; foliage.
**frondoso** *adj.* leafy.
**frontera** *f.* frontier, border; **fronterizo** *adj.* frontier (*used as an adj.*); opposite, facing.
**frontero** *adj.* facing, opposite.
**frontis** *m.* façade, front (*of a building*).
**frontispicio** *m.* front, façade (*front of a building*); title page.
**frontón** *m.* main wall of a handball court; handball court; jai alai court; game of *pelota*.
**frotación** *f.* friction, rubbing.
**frotar** *v.* to rub; to scour.
**frote** *m.* rubbing; friction.
**fructificar**[6] *v.* to fruit, bear or produce fruit; to yield profit.
**fructuoso** *adj.* fruitful.
**frugal** *adj.* frugal, economical, saving, thrifty; **frugalidad** *f.* frugality, thrift.
**fruncir**[10] *v.* to wrinkle; to gather in pleats; to contract, shrivel; **— las cejas** to frown; to knit the eyebrows; **— los labios** to purse or curl the lips.
**fruslería** *f.* trifle, trinket.
**frustración** *f.* frustration; failure.
**frustrar** *v.* to frustrate, thwart, foil; **-se** to fail, be thwarted.
**fruta** *f.* fruit (*not a vegetable*); **frutería** *f.* fruit store.
**frutero** *m.* fruit vendor; fruit dish; *adj.* fruit (*used as adj.*); **buque —** fruit boat; **plato —** fruit dish.
**fruto** *m.* fruit (*any organic product of the earth*); result; benefit, profit.
**¡fuche!** *interj. Mex.* phew! ugh! pew!

phooey!

**fuego** *m.* (*incendio*) fire; (*pasión*) passion; (*erupción*) skin eruption; *Am.* cold sore; **-s artificiales** fireworks; **hacer —** to fire, shoot; **estar hecho un —** to be very angry; **romper —** to begin to fire, start shooting.

**fuelle** *m.* (*instrumento*) bellows; (*arruga*) pucker, wrinkle, fold; (*hablador*) tattletale, windbag, gossiper.

**fuente** *f.* fountain; source, origin; spring; platter, serving dish.

**fuera** *adv.* outside, out; **— de** *prep.* outside of; in addition to.

**fuereño** *m. Mex., Ven., Andes* outsider, stranger.

**fuero** *m.* law, statute; power, jurisdiction; code of laws; exemption, privilege.

**fuerte** *adj.* (*robusto*) strong; loud; secure, fortified; (*grave*) grave, serious; (*áspero*) excessive; *Ch.* stinking; *m.* fort; forte, strong point; forte (*music*); *Mex.* alcohol, liquor; *adv.* strongly; excessively; loud; hard.

**fuerza** *f.* force; power, strength; violence, compulsion; **a — de** by dint of; **a la —** (**por —, por la —, de por —,** *Am.* **de —**) by force, forcibly; necessarily; **ser —** to be necessary.

**fuete** *m. Col., Cuba, Ríopl., Mex., Ven., Andes* whip; **fuetazo** *m. Am.* lash.

**fuga** *f.* flight, escape; leak, leakage; fugue (*musical composition*).

**fugarse**[7] *v.* to flee, escape.

**fugaz** *adj.* fleeing; fleeting, brief, passing.

**fugitivo** *adj.* fugitive; fleeting, passing; perishable; *m.* fugitive.

**fulano** *m.* so-and-so (*referring to person*).

**fulgor** *m.* radiance, brilliance.

**fulgurar** *v.* to gleam, flash, shine.

**fulminar** *v.* to thunder, thunder forth; to utter (*threats*).

**fulo** *m. Pan.* blond.

**fullero** *m.* cardsharp; crooked gambler; cheat.

**fumada** *f.* puff, whiff (*of smoke*).

**fumadero** *m.* smoking room.

**fumador** *m.* smoker, habitual smoker.

**fumar** *v.* to smoke (*tobacco*); *Am.* **-se a uno** to swindle or cheat someone.

**fumigar**[7] *v.* to fumigate.

**función** *f.* (*actividad*) function; functioning; (*empleo*) office; occupation; (*espectáculo*) show, performance; religious festival.

**funcionamiento** *m.* functioning, action, working, operation.

**funcionar** *v.* to function; to work, run (*said of machines*).

**funcionario** *m.* public employee, officer or official.

**funda** *f.* cover, case; *Col.* skirt; **— de almohada** pillowcase.

**fundación** *f.* foundation.

**fundador** *m.* founder.

**fundamental** *adj.* fundamental.

**fundamento** *m.* foundation, groundwork; basis; *Col.* skirt.

**fundar** *v.* to found, establish; to erect; to base, ground.

**fundir** *v.* to smelt, fuse, melt; to cast, mold; *Am.* to ruin; **-se** to fuse, melt together; to unite; *Ríopl., Mex.* to be ruined.

**fundo** *m.* farm, country estate; property, land.

**fúnebre** *adj.* funeral; funereal, gloomy, dismal.

**funeral** *adj.* & *m.* funeral.

**funeraria** *f.* undertaking establishment, funeral parlor.

**funesto** *adj.* ill-fated, unlucky; sad, unfortunate.

**fungosidad** *f.* fungus, fungous growth.

**furgón** *m.* freight car, boxcar; **furgonada** *f.* carload.

**furia** *f.* fury, rage; speed.

**furibundo** *adj.* furious.

**furioso** *adj.* furious.

**furor** *m.* fury, rage, anger; frenzy.

**furtivo** *adj.* furtive, sly, secret.

**fuselaje** *m.* fuselage (*of an airplane*).

**fusible** *adj.* fusible; *m.* electric fuse.

**fusil** *m.* gun, rifle.

**fusilar** *v.* to shoot, execute.

**fusión** *f.* fusion; melting; **— nuclear** nuclear fusion.

**fustigar**[7] *v.* to lash, whip; to censure severely, scold sharply.

**fútil** *adj.* futile, useless; trivial; **futilidad** *f.* futility, uselessness.

**futuro** *adj.* future; *m.* fiancé, future husband; future.

## G

**gabacho** *adj.* from or of the Pyrenees; Frenchlike; *Am.* **me salió —** it turned out wrong; *m.* Frenchman (*used depreciatively*).

**gabán** *m.* overcoat.

**gabeta = gaveta.**

**gabinete** *m.* cabinet (*of a government*); study; library room; dressing room; sitting room; private room; dentist's office; laboratory; *Am.* glassed-in **mirador.**

**gaceta** *f.* gazette, official newspaper; professional periodical; *Am.* any newspaper.

**gacetilla** *f.* short newspaper article; column of short news items; gossip column; *m.* & *f.* newsmonger, tattletale; **gacetillero** *m.* newspaper reporter; newsmonger.

**gacha** *f.* watery mass or mush; *Col.* china or earthenware bowl; **-s** porridge, mush; caresses; **-s de avena** oatmeal.

**gacho** *adj.* drooping; bent downward; turned down; stooping; slouching; with horns curved downward; **sombrero —** slouch hat; **a gachas** on all fours; **con las orejas gachas** with drooping ears; crestfallen, discouraged.

**gafas** *f. pl.* spectacles; grappling hooks.

**gaita** *f.* flageolet, a kind of flute; *Am.* good-for-nothing, lazy bum; **— gallega** bagpipe; **sacar la —** to stick out one's neck; **gaitero** *m.* piper, bagpipe player.

**gaje** *m.* fee; **-s** wages, salary; fees.

**gala** *f.* elegance; full dress or uniform; ostentation; *Am.* award, prize, tip; **-s** finery, regalia, best clothes; **-s de novia** trousseau; **hacer — de** to boast of.

**galán** *m.* gallant, lover; leading man (*in a play*).

**galante** *adj.* gallant, attentive to ladies; polite.

**galanteador** *m.* gallant, lady's man; flatterer.

**galantear** *v.* to court, woo; to make love.

**galanteo** *m.* wooing, courtship.

**galantería** *f.* gallantry, compliment, attention to ladies; courtesy; gracefulness; generosity.

**galardón** *m.* recompense, reward.

**galeote** *m.* galley slave.

**galera** *f.* galley; large wagon; women's jail; printer's galley; *Mex.* jail; *Ch.*, *Ríopl.* tall hat.

**galerada** *f.* galley, galley proof; wagon load, van load.

**galería** *f.* gallery; corridor.

**galgo** *m.* greyhound; *adj. Col.* gluttonous, always hungry.

**galicismo** *m.* gallicism.

**galillo** *m.* uvula.

**galón** *m.* galloon, braid, trimming; gallon.

**galoneado** *adj.* gallooned, trimmed with braid.

**galopada** *f.* gallop; **pegar una —** to break into a gallop.

**galopar** *v.* to gallop.

**galope** *m.* gallop; **a** (**al** *or* **de**) **—** at a gallop; speedily.

**galopear** = **galopar.**

**galpón** *m. Ríopl., Andes* large open shed.

**gallardete** *m.* streamer.

**gallardía** *f.* elegance; gracefulness; bravery.

**gallardo** *adj.* elegant, graceful; brave.

**gallego** *adj.* Galician, from or of Galicia, Spain; *m.* Galician; *Carib.*, *Ríopl.* Spaniard (*used as a nickname*).

**galleta** *f.* cracker; hardtack, hard biscuit; hard cookie; blow, slap; small pot; *Ríopl.* bread of coarse meal or bran; *Ch.* reproof; *Am.* **colgarle la — a uno** to fire, dismiss someone; *Am.* **tener —** to have strength, muscle.

**gallina** *f.* hen; *m. & f.* chickenhearted person.

**gallinero** *m.* chicken coop, house, or yard; flock of chickens; basket for carrying chickens; poultryman; noisy gathering; top gallery of a theater.

**gallo** *m.* cock, rooster; aggressive, bossy person; cork float; false note (*in singing*); frog (*in one's throat*); *Am.* secondhand clothing; *Am.* fire wagon; *Mex., Ríopl.* serenade.

**gamo** *m.* buck, male deer.

**gamuza** *f.* chamois, chamois skin (*soft leather made from the skin of sheep,*

*goats, deer, etc*).

**gana** *f.* desire, appetite; **de buena** (**mala**) **—** willingly (unwillingly); **tener —** (*or* **-s**) to feel like, want to; **no me da la —** I don't want to.

**ganadero** *m.* cattleman; cattle dealer; *adj.* cattle, pertaining to cattle.

**ganado** *m.* cattle; herd; livestock; **— mayor** cattle; horses; mules; **— menor** sheep; **— de cerda** swine.

**ganador** *m.* winner; *adj.* winning.

**ganancia** *f.* profit, gain; *Am.* something to boot, something extra.

**ganancioso** *adj.* winning; profitable; *m.* winner.

**ganar** *v.* to win; to profit, gain; to earn; to get ahead of.

**gancho** *m.* hook; hooked staff; *Mex.*, *Cuba, Ríopl., Col., C.A.* hairpin; *Am.* bait, lure, trick; **aguja de —** crochet hook; **echar a uno el —** to hook someone; **tener —** to be attractive, alluring.

**gandul** *m.* bum, loafer.

**ganga** *f.* bargain; snap, easy job; kind of prairie hen.

**gangoso** *adj.* twangy, nasal (*voice*).

**gangrena** *f.* gangrene.

**gangrenar** *v.* to gangrene, cause gangrene; **-se** to gangrene.

**ganoso** *adj.* desirous; *Am.* lively, spirited (*horse*).

**ganso** *m.* goose, gander; lazy, slovenly person; dunce.

**ganzúa** *f.* hook; picklock (*tool for picking locks*); *m. & f.* burglar.

**garabato** *m.* hook; scrawl, scribble; **hacer -s** to scribble, write poorly.

**garaje** *m.* garage.

**garantía** *f.* to guaranty; security; bail, bond.

**garantizar**[9] *v.* to guarantee, vouch for.

**garañón** *m.* jackass, male ass; male camel (*for breeding*); *Ríopl., Mex.*, *C.A.* stallion.

**garapiñar** *v.* to candy (*almonds, fruits, etc.*).

**garbanzo** *m.* chickpea.

**garbo** *m.* elegance, graceful air, good carriage.

**garboso** *adj.* graceful; elegant; sprightly.

**garduña** *f.* marten.

**garfio** *m.* hook.

**garganta** *f.* throat, neck; gorge, ravine; **gargantilla** *f.* necklace.

**gárgara** *f.* gargling; **-s** *Am.* gargle, gargling solution; **hacer -s** to gargle.

**gargarear** *v. Am.* to gargle.

**gargarismo** *m.* gargling; gargle, gargling solution.

**gargarizar**[9] *v.* to gargle.

**garita** *f.* sentry box; watchman's booth; *Col.* vendor's booth.

**garito** *m.* gambling house, gambling joint; gambler's winnings.

**garra** *f.* claw, paw; hook; *Am.* strength; *Col.* leather or cloth remnant; *Am.* skinny person or animal; *Am.* margin of profit in a business deal; **echar la —** to arrest; to grab; *Mex., C.A.*,

*Ven., Andes* **hacer -s** to tear to pieces.
**garrafa** *f.* decanter; **garrafón** *m.* large decanter; demijohn.
**garrapata** *f.* tick (*an insect*).
**garrapatear** *v.* to scribble, scrawl, write poorly.
**garrocha** *f.* pole; iron-pointed staff; *Am.* goad (*for goading oxen*).
**garrote** *m.* club, cudgel, heavy stick; *Mex., Ur.* brake; **dar —** to strangle; *Am.* to brake, set the brakes; **garrotazo** *m.* blow with a club; huge stick.
**garrotero** *m. Mex., Ven.* brakeman; *Am.* beater (*one who beats with a club*); *adj. Am.* stingy.
**garrucha** *f.* pulley.
**garúa** *f. C.A., Ríopl., Ven., Andes* drizzle.
**garza** *f.* heron.
**garzo** *adj.* blue, bluish; blue-eyed.
**gas** *m.* gas, vapor; *Col., Ríopl., Ven.* gasoline.
**gasa** *f.* gauze.
**gaseosa** *f.* soda water; soda pop.
**gaseoso** *adj.* gaseous.
**gasolina** *f.* gasoline.
**gastador** *adj.* lavish, extravagant, wasteful; *m.* spendthrift, lavish spender.
**gastar** *v.* to spend; to wear; to use; to waste; **-se** to wear out; to get old.
**gasto** *m.* expense, expenditure; wear.
**gatas : a —** on all fours; **andar a —** to creep, crawl; **salir a —** to crawl out of a difficulty.
**gateado** *adj.* catlike; veined, streaked; *m. Am.* light-colored horse with black streaks.
**gatear** *v.* to creep, crawl; to walk on all fours; to claw, scratch; to steal.
**gatillo** *m.* kitten; trigger; forceps (*for extracting teeth*); petty thief.
**gato** *m.* cat; moneybag; jack (*for lifting weights*); sneak thief; sly fellow; *Am.* trigger; *Am.* outdoor market; *Am.* hot-water bottle; *Am.* a gaucho song and tap dance (*by extension,* the dancer); *Am.* blunder.
**gatuperio** *m.* fraud, intrigue.
**gauchada** *f. Ríopl.* gaucho deed or exploit.
**gauchaje** *m. Ríopl.* band of Gauchos, Gaucho folk.
**gauchesco** *adj. Am.* relating to Gauchos.
**gaucho** *m. Am.* Gaucho, Argentine and Uruguayan cowboy; *Ríopl., Ven.* good horseman; *adj. Am.* relating to Gauchos, Gaucho-like; *Am.* sly, crafty.
**gaveta** *f.* drawer.
**gavilla** *f.* sheaf; gang, band (*of rogues, thieves, etc.*).
**gaviota** *f.* sea gull.
**gaza** *f.* loop; *Carib.* noose of a lasso.
**gazmoñería** *f.* prudery, affected modesty; **gazmoño** *adj.* prudish, affected, coy.
**gaznate** *m.* windpipe; a kind of fritter; *Andes* a sweetmeat made of pineapple or coconut.
**gelatina** *f.* gelatin; jelly.
**gema** *f.* gem, jewel; bud.

**gemelo** *m.* twin; **-s** twins; binoculars, opera glasses, field glasses; cuff links.
**gemido** *m.* moan; wail, cry.
**gemir**[b] *v. irr.* to moan; to wail, cry.
**gendarme** *m. Mex., Ven., Ríopl., C.A.* policeman.
**generación** *f.* generation.
**generador** *m.* generator; **— molecular** atom smasher.
**general** *adj. & m.* general; **por lo —** generally.
**generalidad** *f.* generality; majority.
**generalizar**[9] *v.* to generalize; **-se** to spread, become general.
**género** *m.* (*clase*) kind, sort, class; gender; (*tela*) goods, material, cloth; **— humano** human race.
**generosidad** *f.* generosity.
**generoso** *adj.* generous; best (*wine*).
**genial** *adj.* genial, jovial, pleasant.
**genio** *m.* genius; temperament, disposition; spirit.
**gente** *f.* (*personas*) people; crowd; (*pueblo*) race, nation; clan; *Am.* **— bien** upper-class or important person; *Am.* **ser —** to be a somebody; to be cultured; to be socially important.
**gentil** *adj.* graceful; genteel; courteous; gentile; *m.* pagan; gentile.
**gentileza** *f.* grace, courtesy; nobility; favor.
**gentío** *m.* crowd, throng.
**gentuza** *f.* rabble.
**genuino** *adj.* genuine.
**geofísica** *f.* geophysics.
**geografía** *f.* geography; **geográfico** *adj.* geographical.
**geología** *f.* geology; **geológico** *adj.* geological.
**geometría** *f.* geometry; **geométrico** *adj.* geometric.
**geranio** *m.* geranium.
**gerencia** *f.* management, administration.
**gerente** *m.* manager.
**germen** *m.* germ; origin, source.
**germinar** *v.* to germinate.
**gerundio** *m.* gerund; present participle.
**gesticular** *v.* to gesticulate.
**gestión** *f.* action, step, maneuver; intervention; **-es** negotiations.
**gestionar** *v.* to manage; to take steps; to negotiate or carry out (*a deal, transaction, etc.*).
**gesto** *m.* face, expression; grimace; gesture; **estar de buen** (*or* **mal**) **—** to be in a good (*or* bad) humor; **hacer -s a** to make faces at.
**giba** *f.* hump, hunch.
**gigante** *adj.* gigantic; *m.* giant.
**gigantesco** *adj.* gigantic.
**gimnasia** *f.* gymnastics; **gimnasio** *m.* gymnasium; German institute (*for secondary instruction*).
**gimotear** *v.* to whimper, whine.
**gimoteo** *m.* whimper, whining.
**ginebra** *f.* gin (*liquor*).
**gira** *f.* excursion, tour; outing, picnic.
**girador** *m.* drawer (*of a check or draft*).
**girar** *v.* to revolve, rotate, whirl; to

**GA**

send, issue, or draw (*checks*, *drafts*, etc.); to manage (*a business*).

**girasol** *m.* sunflower.

**giratorio** *adj.* rotary, revolving.

**giro** *m.* (*movimiento circular*) rotation; bend, turn; (*dirección*) direction, trend; (*estructura*) turn of phrase; (*monetario*) draft; — **postal** money order; *adj.* yellowish (*rooster*); *Am.* black and white (*rooster*); *Am.* cocky.

**gitano** *adj.* gypsy; gypsylike; sly, clever; *m.* gypsy.

**gitomate** *Am.* = **jitomate**.

**glacial** *adj.* glacial, icy, very cold.

**glaciar** *m.* glacier.

**glándula** *f.* gland.

**glasear** *v.* to glaze (*paper*, *fruits*, etc.), make glossy.

**globo** *m.* globe, sphere; world; balloon.

**gloria** *f.* glory; gloria (*song of praise to God*).

**gloriarse**[17] *v.* to glory (in), delight (in), be proud (of); to boast (of).

**glorieta** *f.* arbor, bower; secluded nook in a park (*with benches*).

**glorificar**[6] *v.* to glorify; -**se** to glory (in), take great pride (in).

**glorioso** *adj.* glorious.

**glosar** *v.* to gloss, comment upon, explain (*a text*).

**glosario** *m.* glossary.

**glotal** *adj.* glottal.

**glotis** *f.* glottis.

**glotón** *adj.* gluttonous; *m.* glutton.

**glotonería** *f.* gluttony.

**gobernador** *adj.* governing; *m.* governor, ruler.

**gobernante** *adj.* governing, ruling; *m.* governor, ruler.

**gobernar**[1] *v. irr.* to govern, rule; to lead, direct; to steer (*a boat*).

**gobierno** *m.* government; management; control; helm, rudder.

**goce** *m.* enjoyment; joy.

**goleta** *f.* schooner, sailing vessel.

**golfo** *m.* gulf; open sea; faro (*gambling game*); vagabond, bum, ragamuffin.

**golondrina** *f.* swallow; swallow fish.

**golosina** *f.* sweet, dainty, tidbit; trifle; appetite, desire.

**goloso** *adj.* sweet-toothed, fond of sweets; gluttonous.

**golpazo** *m.* bang, whack, heavy blow, hard knock.

**golpe** *m.* blow, hit, stroke; knock; beat; *Col.* facing (*of a garment*); *Am.* sledge hammer; — **de fortuna** stroke of good luck; — **de gente** crowd, throng; — **de gracia** death blow; finishing stroke; **de** — suddenly; **de un** — all at once; **pestillo de** — spring latch; *Am.* **al** — instantly, at once; *Am.* **al** — **de vista** at one glance.

**golpear** *v.* to strike, hit; to knock; to beat; *Am.* to knock at a door.

**golpetear** *v.* to tap, knock or pound continuously; to flap; to rattle.

**golpeteo** *m.* tapping, pounding, knocking; flapping; rattling.

**gollería** *f.* dainty, delicacy; super-

fluous thing.

**goma** *f.* gum; rubber; elastic; eraser; tire; — **de repuesto** spare tire; *Am.* **estar de** — to have a hang-over (*after excessive drinking*).

**gomero** *adj.* rubber, pertaining to rubber; *m. Ríopl.* gum or rubber tree; *Am.* rubber producer; *Am.* rubber-plantation worker; *Ven.* glue container or bottle.

**gomífero** *adj.* rubber-bearing, rubber-producing.

**gomoso** *adj.* gummy, sticky; *m.* dandy.

**gordiflón** *adj.* fat; chubby.

**gordo** *adj.* fat; plump; *m.* suet, fat; **gorda** *f. Mex.* thick tortilla or corn-meal cake; **se armó la gorda** all hell broke loose; there was a big rumpus.

**gordura** *f.* fatness; stoutness; fat.

**gorgojo** *m.* weevil; puny person; *Am.* wood borer, wood louse; **gorgojoso** *adj.* infested with weevils.

**gorila** *m.* gorilla.

**gorjeador** *m.* warbler; *adj.* warbling; **pájaro** — warbler.

**gorjear** *v.* to warble; to chirp.

**gorjeo** *m.* warble; warbling.

**gorra** *f.* cap; bonnet; **de** — at another's expense; **vivir de** — to sponge, live at another's expense.

**gorrión** *m.* sparrow.

**gorro** *m.* cap; bonnet.

**gorrón** *m.* sponge, parasite; bum; rake (*dissolute fellow*).

**gota** *f.* (*líquido*) drop; (*enfermedad*) gout; **sudar la** — **gorda** to sweat profusely, toil, work hard.

**gotear** *v.* to drip; to leak; to dribble, trickle; to sprinkle, begin to rain; -**se** to leak.

**goteo** *m.* trickle, drip.

**gotera** *f.* leak, hole (*in the roof*); eaves, trough; -**s** *Mex.* surroundings, out-skirts.

**gotero** *m. Carib.*, *Mex.* dropper (*for counting drops*).

**gótico** *adj.* Gothic; *m.* Goth; Gothic language.

**gozar**[9] *v.* to enjoy; to possess, have; -**se** to rejoice.

**gozne** *m.* hinge.

**gozo** *m.* pleasure, joy.

**gozoso** *adj.* joyful, glad, merry.

**gozque, gozquejo, gozquecillo** *m.* a small dog.

**grabación** *f.* recording (*tape*).

**grabado** *adj.* engraved; recorded; *m.* engraving; woodcut, print; — **al agua fuerte** etching.

**grabadora** *f.* tape recorder.

**grabar** *v.* to engrave; to carve; to fix, impress; to record on tape; — **al agua fuerte** to etch.

**gracejada** *f. C.A.* clownish act or expression.

**gracejo** *m.* grace; cuteness; humor, wit.

**gracia** *f.* (*humorismo*) witty remark; joke; humor; (*garbo*) grace; gracious act; (*favor*) favor; pardon; **caer en** — to please; **hacer** — to amuse, make (*someone*) laugh; **¡-s!** thanks!;

**dar -s** to thank.

**gracioso** *adj.* (*chistoso*) amusing; funny; witty; (*con garbo*) graceful, attractive; *m.* comedian, clown.

**grada** *f.* step of a staircase; harrow; **-s** steps; seats of an amphitheater; bleachers.

**gradación** *f.* gradation.

**gradería** *f.* series of steps; rows of seats (*in an amphitheater or stadium*); — **cubierta** grandstand; **-s** bleachers.

**grado** *m.* (*medida*) degree; step; (*título*) degree; **de** (**buen**) — willingly, with pleasure; **de mal** — unwillingly; **de — en —** by degrees, gradually.

**graduación** *f.* graduation; military rank.

**gradual** *adj.* gradual; *m.* response sung at mass.

**graduar**[18] *v.* to graduate, give a diploma, rank or degree to; to gauge; to classify, grade; **-se** to graduate, take a degree.

**gráfico** *adj.* graphic; vivid, lifelike; **gráfica** *f.* graph, diagram, chart.

**grafito** *m.* graphite.

**grajo** *m.* jay.

**grama** *f.* grama grass.

**gramática** *f.* grammar; **gramatical** *adj.* grammatical; **gramático** *adj.* grammatical; *m.* grammarian.

**gramo** *m.* gram.

**gran** *contr. of* **grande.**

**grana** *f.* cochineal, kermes (*insects used for producing a red dye*); scarlet color; scarlet cloth; any small seed.

**granada** *f.* pomegranate; grenade, shell, small bomb; — **de mano** hand grenade.

**granado** *m.* pomegranate tree; *adj.* notable; illustrious; select.

**grande** *adj.* large, big; great, grand; *Mex., C.A., Ven., Andes* **mamá** (**papá**) — grandmother (grandfather); *m.* grandee (*Spanish or Portuguese nobleman*); **en —** on a large scale.

**grandeza** *f.* greatness; grandeur, splendor; bigness; size; grandeeship; body of grandees.

**grandiosidad** *f.* grandeur, grandness; greatness; **grandioso** *adj.* grandiose, great, grand, magnificent.

**granero** *m.* granary; grain bin; country or region rich in grain.

**granito** *m.* granite; small grain; small pimple.

**granizada** *f.* hailstorm; shower, volley.

**granizar**[9] *v.* to hail.

**granizo** *m.* hail; hailstorm; web or film in the eye; *adj. Mex.* spotted (*horse*).

**granja** *f.* grange, farm; country house.

**granjear** *v.* to earn, gain; to acquire, obtain; *Ch., C.A.* to steal; **-se** to win for oneself (*favor, goodwill, esteem, etc.*).

**granjería** *f.* farming; business profit.

**granjero** *m.* farmer.

**grano** *m.* (*cereal*) grain; seed; grain (*unit of measure*); **ir al —** to come to the point.

**granuja** *m.* ragamuffin, urchin; scamp.

**granular** *v.* to granulate; **-se** to become granulated; to break out with pimples.

**grapa** *f.* clamp; staple; (*carbunclo*) pimple.

**grasa** *f.* grease; fat; tallow; *Mex., Ríopl., Ven.* shoe polish; *Am.* **dar —** to polish (*shoes*).

**grasiento** *adj.* greasy, oily.

**grasoso** *adj.* greasy, oily.

**gratificación** *f.* gratuity, bonus, tip; recompense, reward.

**gratis** *adv.* gratis, for nothing, free of charge.

**gratitud** *f.* gratitude.

**grato** *adj.* pleasing, pleasant; gratuitous; **su grata** your favor, your letter.

**gratuito** *adj.* gratuitous, free, free of charge.

**grava** *f.* gravel.

**gravamen** *m.* burden; mortgage.

**grave** *adj.* grave; serious; weighty, heavy; grievous; deep, low (*in pitch*).

**gravedad** *f.* (*fuerza*) gravity; (*seriedad*) seriousness, gravity; (*tono*) depth (*of a sound*).

**gravoso** *adj.* burdensome; **serle a uno —** to be burdensome; to weigh on one's conscience.

**graznar** *v.* to caw, croak, squawk, cackle, quack.

**graznido** *m.* caw, croak, squawk, cackle, quack.

**greca** *f.* fret; ornamental design.

**greda** *f.* clay, chalk; chalk cleaner.

**gremio** *m.* guild, society, brotherhood; trade union; fold (*referring to the Church*).

**greña** *f.* shock of hair, tangled mop of hair (*usually* **greñas**); **greñudo** *adj.* shaggy, with long, unkempt hair.

**grey** *f.* flock; congregation (*of a church*).

**griego** *adj.* Greek, Grecian; *m.* Greek.

**grieta** *f.* crevice; crack; fissure.

**grifo** *m.* faucet; *Am.* cheap tavern (*where* **chicha** *is sold*); *Peru* gas station; *Am.* colored person; *Col.* drug addict; *Am.* drunkard; *adj.* curly, kinky, woolly (*hair*); *Col.* vain, conceited; **letra grifa** script; **ponerse —** to bristle, stand on end (*said of hair*).

**grillo** *m.* cricket; sprout, shoot; **-s** fetters; obstacle, hindrance.

**grima** *f.* uneasiness; displeasure, disgust; *Ríopl., Carib.* sadness, compassion, pity; *Am.* bit, small particle; **dar —** to disgust; to make uneasy; *Am.* to make sad, inspire pity.

**gringo** *adj. Ch., Ríopl.* (*Italian*) foreign (*not Spanish*); *m. Ch., Ríopl.* (*Italian*) foreigner (*not Spanish*); *Mex., C.A., Andes, Col., Ven.* Yankee or English-speaking person.

**gripe** *f.* grippe, flu, influenza.

**gris** *adj.* grey; **grisáceo** *adj.* greyish.

**grita** *f.* shouting, hooting; clamor, uproar.

**gritar** *v.* to shout, cry.

**gritería** *f.* shouting, clamor, uproar.

**grito** *m.* shout, cry; **poner el — en el**

**cielo** to complain loudly, "hit the ceiling".

**grosella** *f.* currant; **— blanca** gooseberry; **grosellero** *m.* currant bush.

**grosería** *f.* rudeness; coarseness; crudeness; insult.

**grosero** *adj.* rough, coarse; rude, impolite.

**grosor** *m.* thickness.

**grotesco** *adj.* grotesque, fantastic; absurd.

**grúa** *f.* crane, derrick.

**gruesa** *f.* gross, twelve dozen.

**grueso** *adj.* (*voluminoso*) fat, stout; thick; bulky, big, heavy; (*burdo*) dense; coarse; *m.* thickness; bulk; density; main part; **en —** in gross, in bulk, by wholesale.

**grulla** *f.* crane (*bird*).

**gruñido** *m.* growl, grumble; grunt.

**gruñir**[19] *v. irr.* to grunt; to growl; to snarl; to grumble.

**gruñón** *adj.* growling; grunting; grumbly; *m.* growler; grumbler.

**grupa** *f.* rump; **volver -s** to turn around (*usually on horseback*).

**grupo** *m.* group; set.

**gruta** *f.* grotto, cavern.

**guacal** *m. Col., Mex., C.A.* crate (*for transporting fruit, vegetables, etc.*). Also **huacal.**

**guacamayo** *m. Am.* macaw (*large parrot*); *Am.* flashily dressed person.

**guacamole** *m. Mex., C.A., Cuba* avocado salad; also **guacamol.**

**guacho** *m.* birdling, chick; young animal; *Andes, Ríopl.* orphan; *Andes, Ríopl.* foundling, abandoned child; *adj. Am.* odd, not paired; *Andes, Ríopl.* forlorn, alone, abandoned.

**guadal** *m. Am.* small dune, sand hill; *Ven.* quagmire, bog, swamp; *Am.* growth of bamboo grass.

**guadaña** *f.* scythe.

**guagua** *f. Carib., Ven.* bus; trifle, insignificant thing; *m. & f. Andes, Ch., Ríopl.* baby; **de —** for nothing, gratis, free.

**guaje** *m. Am.* a species of gourd; *Am.* vessel or bowl made of a gourd; *Am.* simpleton, fool; *Am.* trifle, trinket, piece of junk; *adj. Am.* foolish; *Am.* **hacerse uno —** to play the fool; *Am.* **hacer a uno —** to fool, deceive someone.

**guajiro** *m.* Indian of the Guajira peninsula (*in Venezuela and Colombia*); *Cuba* rustic, peasant.

**guajolote** *m. Mex.* turkey; *Am.* fool.

**guanaco** *m. Andes, Ch., Ríopl.* guanaco (*a kind of llama*); *Am.* tall, lanky, gawky person; *Am.* fool, simpleton; nickname for Salvadoreans.

**guanajo** *m. Am.* turkey; *Am.* fool, dunce.

**guano** *m. Carib.* palm tree; *Carib.* palm leaves (*used for thatching*); *Am.* guano, bird dung, fertilizer.

**guantada** *f.* wallop, blow, slap.

**guante** *m.* glove; *Andes* whip, scourge; **echar el — a uno** to seize or grab a

person; **guantelete** *m.* gauntlet.

**guapo** *adj.* handsome, good-looking; ostentatious, showy; daring, brave; *Ch., Andes* harsh, severe; *Carib., Mex.* angry; *m.* brawler, quarreler, bully.

**guarache** *m. Mex.* Mexican leather sandal; *Mex.* tire patch. *Also* **huarache.**

**guaraní** *adj.* pertaining to the Guarani Indians of Paraguay; *m. & f.* Guarani Indian.

**guarapo** *m. Col., C.A., Andes* juice of the sugar cane; *Col., C.A., Andes* sugar-cane liquor; *Col., C.A., Andes* low-grade brandy.

**guarda** *m. & f.* guard; keeper; *Ríopl.* ticket collector on a streetcar; *f.* custody, care, keeping; observance of a law; **-s** outside ribs of a fan; flyleaves.

**guardabarros, guardafango** *m.* fender.

**guardabosques** *m.* forest ranger, forester, forest keeper.

**guardabrisa** *f.* windshield.

**guardafrenos** *m.* brakeman.

**guardagujas** *m.* switchman.

**guardapapeles** *m.* file, filing cabinet or box.

**guardapelo** *m.* locket.

**guardar** *v.* to guard, watch over; to keep; to store; to observe (*laws, customs*); **-se de** to guard against, keep from, avoid.

**guardarropa** *m.* wardrobe; cloakroom; keeper of a cloakroom.

**guardía** *f.* guard, body of guards; defense, protection; *m.* guard, guardsman.

**guardiamarina** *f.* midshipman.

**guardián** *m.* guardian, keeper; guardian, superior of a Franciscan monastery.

**guarecer**[13] *v. irr.* to protect, shelter; **-se** to take shelter.

**guarida** *f.* den, cave, lair.

**guarismo** *m.* number.

**guarnecer**[13] *v. irr.* to garnish, decorate; to adorn; to trim; to harness; to garrison; to set (*jewels*).

**guarnición** *f.* adornment; trimming; setting of a jewel; guard of a sword; garrison; **-es** trappings, harness.

**guaro** *m. C.A.* rum.

**guasca** *f. Andes, Ch., Ríopl.* leather thong; *Andes, Ch., Ríopl.* rope, cord; *Andes, Ch.* whip; *Andes, Ch., Ríopl.* **dar —** to whip, beat, thrash.

**guaso** *m. Am.* stag, male deer; *Ch., Andes, Ríopl.* peasant; *Cuba* halfbreed; *Am.* lasso; *adj. Am.* rustic, peasantlike.

**guasón** *adj.* funny, comical; *m.* joker, jester.

**guata** *f. Am.* padding; *Ven.* fib; *Col.* a species of potato; *Ch., Andes* paunch, belly; *Am.* **echar —** to get fat.

**guatemalteco** *m. & adj.* Guatemalan.

**guayaba** *f.* guava (*pear-shaped tropical fruit*); **guayabo** *m.* guava tree; *Am.* lie, fraud, trick.

**gubernativo** *adj.* governmental, administrative.

**guedeja** *f.* forelock; lock of hair; lion's mane.

**güero** *adj. Mex.* blond; *m. Ven.* cassava liquor. *See* **huero.**

**guerra** *f.* war; — **a muerte** war to the finish; **dar** — to bother, trouble

**guerrear** *v.* to war; *Am.* to do mischief or to bother (*said of children*).

**guerrero** *adj.* warlike, martial; *m.* warrior, soldier.

**guerrilla** *f.* small war; skirmish; body of soldiers; band of fighters.

**guerrillero** *m.* guerrilla fighter.

**guía** *m. & f.* guide, leader; *f.* guidebook, directory; signpost; shoot, sprout; *Ríopl.* garland of flowers.

**guiar**[17] *v.* to guide; to drive (*a car*).

**guija** *f.* pebble; **guijarro** *m.* pebble.

**guijo** *m.* gravel.

**guinda** *f.* a kind of cherry.

**guindilla** *f. Spain* small hot pepper.

**guiñada** *f.* wink.

**guiñapo** *m.* tag, tatter, rag; ragamuffin, ragged person.

**guiñar** *v.* to wink.

**guiño** *m.* wink.

**guión** *m.* hyphen; repeat sign (*in music*); cross (*carried before a prelate in a procession*); guide, leader (*among birds and animals*); leader in a dance.

**guirnalda** *f.* garland, wreath.

**guisa** *f.* way, manner; **a** — **de** like, in the manner of.

**guisado** *m.* stew.

**guisante** *m.* pea; — **de olor** sweet pea.

**guisar** *v.* to cook; to prepare, arrange.

**guiso** *m.* dish, dish of food.

**guisquil** *m. C.A.* chayote (*a pear-shaped fruit*).

**guitarra** *f.* guitar.

**gula** *f.* gluttony.

**gusano** *m.* worm; caterpillar; — **de la conciencia** remorse; — **de luz** glowworm; *Col., Mex.* **matar el** — to satisfy a need or desire (*particularly hunger or thirst*).

**gustar** *v.* (*agradar*) to please, be pleasing; (*saborear*) to taste; to experience; **-le a uno una cosa** to like something; — **de** to have a liking for, be fond of.

**gusto** *m.* (*agrado*) pleasure; whim, fancy; (*sabor*) taste; flavor; **dar** — to please; **estar a** — to be comfortable, contented; **tener** — **en** to be glad to; **tomar el** — **a una cosa** to become fond of something.

**gustoso** *adj.* (*con agrado*) glad; pleasant; willing; merry; (*sabroso*) tasty; *adv.* willingly.

## H

**haba** *f.* large bean; Lima bean.

**haber**[30] *v. irr.* to have (*auxiliary verb*); **habérselas con** to have it out with; **ha de llegar mañana** he is to arrive tomorrow; **ha de ser verdad** it must be true; **hay** (**había, hubo,** *etc.*) there is, there are (there was, there were, *etc.*); **hay que** ( + *inf.*)

it is necessary; **no hay de qué** you are welcome; **¿qué hay?** what's the matter?

**haber** *m.* credit, credit side (*in bookkeeping*); **-es** property, goods, cash, assets.

**habichuela** *f.* bean; — **verde** string bean.

**hábil** *adj.* skilful, capable, able.

**habilidad** *f.* ability, skill.

**habilitar** *v.* to enable; to equip; to qualify.

**habitación** *f.* apartment; room; lodging.

**habitante** *m.* inhabitant; resident.

**habitar** *v.* to inhabit; to live, reside.

**hábito** *m.* habit; custom.

**habitual** *adj.* habitual, customary.

**habituar**[18] *v.* to accustom; **-se** to get used, accustomed.

**habla** *f.* speech; language, dialect; **al** — within speaking distance; in communication (with).

**hablador** *m.* talker; gossip; *adj.* talkative.

**habladuría** *f.* gossip, rumor; empty talk; impertinent remark.

**hablar** *v.* to speak; to talk; — **alto** (*or* **en voz alta**) to speak loudly; — **bajo** (**quedo** *or* **en voz baja**) to speak softly; — **por los codos** to chatter constantly.

**hablilla** *f.* gossip, rumor, malicious tale.

**hacedero** *adj.* feasible.

**hacedor** *m.* maker; **el Supremo Hacedor** the Maker.

**hacendado** *m.* landholder; *Ríopl., Ch., Ven.* owner of a farm, plantation, or ranch.

**hacendoso** *adj.* industrious, diligent.

**hacer**[31] *v. irr.* (*crear*) to do; to make; (*formar*) to form; to accustom; (*causar*) to cause, order (*followed by inf.*); — **caso** to mind, pay attention; — **frío** (**calor**) to be cold (warm); — **la maleta** to pack one's suitcase; — **un papel** to play a part; *Am.* — **aprecio** to pay attention; *Ríopl., Mex.* — **caras** (*or* **caritas**) to flirt; **no le hace** it makes no difference; **-se** to become, grow, get to be; **-se a** to get used to; **-se de rogar** to want to be coaxed.

**hacia** *prep.* toward; about; — **adelante** forward; — **atrás** backward.

**hacienda** *f.* estate; property; finance; large farm; *Ríopl.* cattle, livestock.

**hacina** *f.* shock (*of grain*), stack, pile.

**hacinar** *v.* to shock (*grain*); to stack, pile up; to accumulate.

**hacha** *f.* ax; hatchet; torch.

**hachero** *m.* axman, woodcutter.

**hada** *f.* fairy.

**hado** *m.* fate, fortune, destiny.

**halagar**[7] *v.* to coax; to flatter; to allure, attract.

**halago** *m.* flattery; caress; allurement.

**halagüeño** *adj.* alluring, attractive; flattering; promising.

**halar = jalar.**

GR

**halcón** *m*. falcon.
**hálito** *m*. breath; vapor.
**hallar** *v*. to find; to discover, find out; **-se** to be; to fare, get along.
**hallazgo** *m*. find; discovery; reward (*for finding something*).
**hamaca** *f*. hammock.
**hambre** *f*. hunger; famine; appetite; **tener —** to be hungry; **hambruna** *f*. *Am*. great hunger, starvation.
**hambrear** *v*. to starve; to be hungry.
**hambriento** *adj*. hungry; greedy; *C.A.*, *Mex.*, *Andes* stingy.
**hampa** *f*. underworld.
**hangar** *m*. hangar.
**haragán** *adj*. lazy, indolent; *m*. loafer, idler.
**haraganear** *v*. to lounge, loaf, be lazy.
**haraganería** *f*. laziness.
**harapiento** *adj*. tattered, ragged.
**harapo** *m*. rag, tatter; **andar hecho un —** to be in tatters.
**haraposo** *adj*. tattered, ragged.
**harina** *f*. flour; **eso es — de otro costal** that is something entirely different; **harinoso** *adj*. floury; flour-like.
**harmonía** *f*. harmony.
**hartar** *v*. to fill up, gorge; to sate, satiate; **-se** to have one's fill; to overeat, eat too much.
**harto** *adj*. full; sated, satiated; fed up; too much; *adv*. too much; *Mex.*, *C.A.*, *Col.*, *Ven.*, *Ríopl.*, *Andes* much, very much.
**hasta** *prep*. till, until; up to; **— luego** good-bye, see you later; *conj*. even; **— que** until.
**hastiar**[17] *v*. to surfeit; to cloy; to disgust.
**hastío** *m*. surfeit, excess; boredom; loathing, disgust.
**hato** *m*. herd; flock; sheepfold; shepherd's hut; gang, crowd; pile; *Col.*, *Ven*. cattle ranch.
**haya** *f*. beech; **hayuco** *m*. beechnut.
**haz** *f*. face; surface; *m*. fagot, bundle, bunch.
**hazaña** *f*. deed, exploit, feat.
**he** (*used with* **aquí** *or* **allí**) behold, here is, here you have; **heme aquí** here I am; **helo aquí** here it is.
**hebilla** *f*. buckle.
**hebra** *f*. thread; fiber; fine string; *Am*. **de una —** all at once, at one stroke; *Am*. **ni —** absolutely nothing; **hebroso** *adj*. fibrous, stringy.
**hecatombe** *m*. massacre, great slaughter; hecatomb (*sacrifice of 100 oxen*).
**hechicera** *f*. witch, enchantress; hag.
**hechicería** *f*. witchcraft; magic; charm; enchantment.
**hechicero** *adj*. bewitching, charming; *m*. magician; charmer; sorcerer.
**hechizar**[9] *v*. to bewitch; to charm.
**hechizo** *m*. charm; enchantment.
**hecho** *m*. fact; act, deed; **de —** in fact; *p.p. of* **hacer** done, made.
**hechura** *f*. make; shape, cut; workmanship.
**heder**[1] *v. irr*. to stink; to reek.

**hediondez** *f*. stink, stench.
**hediondo** *adj*. foul-smelling, stinking; filthy; *m*. *Ríopl*. skunk.
**hedor** *m*. stink, stench.
**helada** *f*. frost.
**helado** *adj*. frozen; freezing; frosty; icy; *m*. ice cream; ice, sherbet; **heladería** *f*. *Am*. ice-cream parlor.
**heladora** *f*. freezer.
**helar**[1] *v. irr*. to freeze.
**helecho** *m*. fern.
**hélice** *f*. screw propeller; helix, spiral.
**helicóptero** *m*. helicopter.
**helio** *m*. helium.
**helipuerto** *m*. heliport.
**hembra** *f*. female; staple; nut (*of a screw*); **macho y —** hook and eye.
**hemisferio** *m*. hemisphere.
**henchir**[5] *v. irr*. to swell, stuff, fill.
**hendedura, hendidura** *f*. crack, crevice, fissure.
**hender**[1] *v. irr*. to split, crack, cleave.
**henequén** *m*. *Mex.*, *Ven.*, *C.A.*, *Col*. sisal, sisal hemp.
**heno** *m*. hay; **henil** *m*. hayloft.
**heraldo** *m*. herald.
**herbazal** *m*. field of grass.
**herboso** *adj*. grassy; weedy.
**heredad** *f*. parcel of land; rural property; estate.
**heredar** *v*. to inherit; to bequeath, leave in a will.
**heredero** *m*. heir; successor; **heredera** *f*. heiress.
**hereditario** *adj*. hereditary.
**hereje** *m*. heretic; **cara de —** hideous face.
**herejía** *f*. heresy; offensive remark.
**herencia** *f*. inheritance; heritage; heredity.
**herida** *f*. wound; injury.
**herido** *adj*. wounded; *m*. wounded man; *Am*. small drainage channel.
**herir**[3] *v. irr*. to wound; to hurt; to strike; to offend.
**hermana** *f*. sister.
**hermanastro** *m*. stepbrother, half brother; **hermanastra** *f*. stepsister, half sister.
**hermandad** *f*. brotherhood, fraternity.
**hermano** *m*. brother.
**hermético** *adj*. hermetic; airtight; tight-lipped; close-mouthed; **hermetismo** *m*. complete silence.
**hermosear** *v*. to beautify, adorn.
**hermoso** *adj*. beautiful, handsome.
**hermosura** *f*. beauty.
**héroe** *m*. hero; **heroína** *f*. heroine.
**heroico** *adj*. heroic.
**heroísmo** *adj*. heroism.
**herradura** *f*. horseshoe.
**herraje** *m*. ironwork; iron trimmings; horseshoes and nails; *Am*. silver saddle trimmings; *Am*. horseshoe.
**herramienta** *f*. set of tools; iron tool.
**herrar**[1] *v. irr*. to shoe (*a horse*); to brand; to trim with iron.
**herrería** *f*. blacksmith's shop or trade; forge; ironworks.
**herrero** *m*. blacksmith.
**herrete** *m*. metal tip (*for a shoelace, for*

*instance*); *Am.* branding iron.

**hervidero** *m.* bubbling sound (*of boiling water*); bubbling spring; swarm, crowd; **un — de gente** a swarm of people.

**hervir**[3] *v. irr.* to boil; **— de gente** to swarm with people.

**hervor** *m.* boiling; boiling point; **soltar el —** to come to a boil.

**hez** *f.* scum; **la — del pueblo** the scum of society; **heces** dregs, sediment.

**hidalgo** *m.* hidalgo (*Spanish nobleman*); *adj.* noble, courteous.

**hidalguía** *f.* nobility; generosity; courtesy.

**hidráulico** *adj.* hydraulic; **fuerza hidráulica** water power; **ingeniero —** hydraulic engineer.

**hidroavión** *m.* hydroplane, seaplane.

**hidrógeno** *m.* hydrogen.

**hidroplano** *m.* hydroplane.

**hiedra** *f.* ivy.

**hiel** *f.* gall, bile; bitterness.

**hielo** *m.* ice; frost.

**hierba** *f.* grass; herb; weed; *Ríopl., Andes* mate (*Paraguayan tea*); *Mex., Ven., Cuba* marihuana (*a narcotic*); *C.A.* **ciertas -s** so-and-so (*person not named*).

**hierbabuena** *f.* mint. *Also* **yerbabuena.**

**hierro** *m.* iron; brand; iron tool, instrument, or weapon; **-s** irons, chains, handcuffs.

**hígado** *m.* (*órgano*) liver; (*valentía*) courage; valor; **malos -s** ill will.

**higiene** *f.* hygiene; **higiénico** *adj.* hygienic, sanitary.

**higo** *m.* fig; **higuera** *f.* fig tree; **higuerilla** *f. Am.* castor-oil plant.

**hija** *f.* daughter; native daughter.

**hijo** *m.* son; native son; offspring; fruit, result.

**hilachas** *f. pl.* lint; **mostrar uno la hilacha** to show one's worst side or nature; **hilachos** *m. pl. Am.* rags, tatters.

**hilado** *m.* yarn; *p.p. of* **hilar.**

**hilandera** *f.* spinner.

**hilandería** *f.* spinning mill; art of spinning; spinning.

**hilandero** *m.* spinner; spinning room.

**hilar** *v.* to spin, make into thread; **— muy delgado** to be very subtle.

**hilas** *f. pl.* lint, fine ravelings (*for dressing wounds*).

**hilaza** *f.* coarse thread; yarn.

**hilera** *f.* file, row, line; **— de perlas** strand or string of pearls.

**hilo** *m.* (*hebra*) thread; fine yarn; string; (*alambre*) filament; thin wire; (*tela*) linen; **a —** without interruption; **al — along the thread; *Am.* very well, all right; **de, —** straight, without stopping; *Am.* **de un —** constantly, without stopping; **tener el alma en un —** to be frightened to death; to be in great anxiety or suspense.

**hilván** *m.* basting stitch; basting; *Am.* hem.

**hilvanar** *v.* to baste; to put together,

connect; to do hastily; *Am.* to hem.

**himno** *m.* hymn.

**hincapié : hacer —** to emphasize, stress; to insist (upon).

**hincar**[6] *v.* to drive, thrust (into); **-se** (*or* **-se de rodillas**) to kneel down.

**hinchado** *adj. & p.p.* swollen; inflated; presumptuous.

**hinchar** *v.* to swell; **-se** to swell; swell up, puff up.

**hinchazón** *f.* swelling; inflation; conceit; bombast, inflated style.

**hinojos : de —** on one's knees.

**hipérbole** *f.* hyperbole.

**hiperbólico** *adj.* hyperbolic.

**hipo** *m.* hiccough; sob; longing; grudge, ill will.

**hipocresía** *f.* hypocrisy.

**hipócrita** *adj.* hypocritical, insincere; *m. & f.* hypocrite.

**hipódromo** *m.* race track.

**hipoteca** *f.* mortgage.

**hipotecar**[6] *v.* to mortgage.

**hipótesis** *f.* hypothesis, theory.

**hirviente** *adj.* boiling.

**hispanista** *m. & f.* Hispanist; one who is interested in Hispanic studies.

**hispano** *adj.* Hispanic, Spanish; *m.* Spaniard.

**hispanoamericano** *adj.* Spanish-American.

**histérico** *adj.* hysterical.

**historia** *f.* history; story; tale, fable; **dejarse de -s** to stop fooling and come to the point; **historieta** *f.* story, anecdote.

**historiador** *m.* historian.

**historial** *m.* record, data (*concerning a person or firm*); *adj.* historic.

**histórico** *adj.* historic, historical.

**hocico** *m.* snout; **caer de -s** to fall on one's face; **meter el — en todo** to meddle, stick one's nose in everything.

**hogaño** *adv.* nowadays.

**hogar** *m.* hearth, fireplace; home.

**hogareño** *adj.* home-loving, domestic; homelike.

**hoguera** *f.* bonfire.

**hoja** *f.* leaf; petal; sheet of paper or metal; blade; **— de lata** tin plate.

**hojalata** *f.* tin plate.

**hojaldre** *m. & f.* puff pastry.

**hojarasca** *f.* fallen leaves; dry foliage; superfluous ornament; trash; useless words.

**hojear** *v.* to leaf, turn the pages of; to browse.

**hojuela** *f.* leaflet, small leaf; thin leaf (*of metal*); flake; thin pancake; **— de estaño** tin foil.

**¡hola!** *interj.* hello!; ho!; ah!

**holandés** *adj.* Dutch; *m.* Dutchman; Dutch language.

**holgado** *adj.* (*libre*) free, at leisure; comfortable; (*ancho*) wide, loose; roomy, spacious; *p.p. of* **holgar.**

**holgar** *v. irr.* to rest; to loaf; **-se** to be glad; to relax, have a good time; **huelga decir** needless to say.

**holgazán** *m.* idler, loafer; *adj.* lazy,

idle.

**holgazanear** v. to loiter, lounge, idle, bum around.

**holgazanería** f. idleness, laziness.

**holgorio** m. spree.

**holgura** f. (*descanso*) ease; rest, comfort; (*lugar*) roominess, plenty of room.

**holocausto** m. holocaust, burnt offering, sacrifice.

**hollar** v. to tread, trample upon.

**hollejo** m. skin, peel; husk.

**hollín** m. soot.

**hombrada** f. manly act; show of bravery.

**hombre** m. man; **hombría** f. manliness, manly strength; **— de bien** honesty.

**hombro** m. shoulder; **arrimar** (*or* **meter**) **el —** to help.

**hombruno** adj. mannish, masculine.

**homenaje** m. homage, honor.

**homicida** m. murderer; f. murderess; adj. homicidal, murderous.

**homicidio** m. homicide, murder.

**homogéneo** adj. homogeneous, of the same kind or nature.

**honda** f. sling, slingshot.

**hondo** adj. deep; low; m. bottom, depth.

**hondonada** f. hollow, dip, gully, ravine.

**hondura** f. depth; **meterse en -s** to go beyond one's depth; to get into trouble.

**honestidad** f. chastity, modesty, decency; decorum, propriety.

**honesto** adj. chaste, modest, decent; just; honest.

**hongo** m. mushroom; fungus; derby hat.

**honor** m. honor; glory; dignity.

**honorario** m. fee (*for professional services*); adj. honorary.

**honorífico** adj. honorary; **mención honorífica** honorable mention.

**honra** f. honor; reputation; **-s** obsequies, funeral rites.

**honradez** f. honesty, honor, integrity.

**honrado** adj. honest, honorable; honored.

**honrar** v. to honor; **-se** to be honored; to consider it an honor.

**honroso** adj. honorable; honoring.

**hora** f. hour; time; **-s** canonical hours, office (*required daily prayers for priests and nuns*); **es — de** it is time to; **no ver la — de** (+ *inf.*) to be anxious to; **¿qué — es?** what time is it?

**horadar** v. to pierce, bore, perforate.

**horario** m. schedule, timetable; hour hand.

**horca** f. (*cadalso*) gallows; (*horcón*) pitchfork; *P.R.* birthday present; **— de ajos** string of garlic.

**horcajadas: a —** astride (*with one leg on each side*); **ponerse a —** to straddle.

**horcón** m. forked pole, forked prop; *Mex., Cuba, Ven.* post, roof support; *Am.* roof.

**horda** f. horde.

**horizontal** adj. horizontal.

**horizonte** m. horizon.

**horma** f. form, mold; block (*for shaping a hat*); shoe last; shoe tree.

**hormiga** f. ant.

**hormigón** m. concrete.

**hormiguear** v. to swarm; to be crawling with ants; **me hormiguea el cuerpo** I itch all over.

**hormigueo** m. itching, creeping sensation; tingle, tingling sensation.

**hormiguero** m. ant hill; ant nest; swarm; **oso —** anteater.

**hornada** f. batch of bread, baking.

**hornear** v. to bake (*in an oven*).

**hornilla** f. burner; grate (*of a stove*).

**hornillo** m. kitchen stove; hot plate.

**horno** m. furnace; oven; kiln (*for baking bricks*).

**horquilla** f. hairpin; forked pole; small pitchfork.

**horrendo** adj. horrible, hideous.

**horrible** adj. horrible.

**horripilante** adj. horrifying.

**horror** m. horror; atrocity; **dar —** to cause fright; to horrify; **tenerle — a uno** to feel a strong dislike for one.

**horrorizar**[9] v. to horrify, shock, terrify.

**horroroso** adj. horrid; frightful, hideous.

**hortaliza** f. vegetables; vegetable garden.

**hortelano** m. gardener.

**hosco = fosco.**

**hospedaje** m. board and lodging; lodging.

**hospedar** v. to lodge, give lodging; **-se** to take lodging; to room; to stop (*at a hotel*).

**hospedero** m. innkeeper.

**hospicio** m. asylum; orphanage, orphan asylum; poorhouse; **hospiciano** m. inmate of a poorhouse or asylum.

**hospital** m. hospital; **— de primera sangre** first-aid station.

**hospitalidad** f. hospitality.

**hostia** f. host (*consecrated wafer*).

**hostigar**[7] v. to harass, vex; to beat, lash; *C.A., Col.* to cloy.

**hostil** adj. hostile; **hostilidad** f. hostility.

**hotel** m. hotel; villa; **hotelero** m. hotel-keeper; adj. pertaining to hotels.

**hoy** adv. today; **— día** nowadays; **de — en adelante** from now on; **— por —** at present; **de — más** henceforth.

**hoya** f. pit, hole; grave; valley; *Am.* river basin.

**hoyo** m. hole; pit; grave; *Ríopl., Carib.* dimple.

**hoyuelo** m. dimple; tiny hole.

**hoz** f. sickle; narrow ravine.

**hozar**[9] v. to root, turn up the earth with the snout (*as hogs*).

**huacal = guacal.**

**huarache = guarache.**

**huaso = guaso.**

**hueco** adj. (*vacío*) hollow, empty; (*vano*) vain, affected; puffed up; high-sounding; m. gap, space, hole.

**huelga** f. labor strike; rest; leisure;

**declararse en** — to strike.
**huelguista** *m.* striker.
**huella** *f.* trace; footprint.
**huérfano** *adj.* & *m.* orphan.
**huero** *adj.* empty; rotten, spoiled (*egg*). See **güero.**
**huerta** *f.* orchard and vegetable garden; irrigated land.
**huerto** *m.* small orchard and vegetable garden; garden patch.
**hueso** *m.* bone; stone, pit; big seed; **la sin** — the tongue; **soltar la sin** — to talk too much; **no dejarle un** — **sano** to pick him to pieces.
**huésped** *m.* (*convidado*) guest; (*anfitrión*) host; **ser** — **en su casa** to be seldom at home.
**hueste** *f.* host, army, multitude.
**huesudo** *adj.* bony.
**huevo** *m.* egg; — **duro** hard-boiled egg; — **estrellado** fried egg; — **pasado por agua** soft-boiled egg; **-s revueltos** scrambled eggs; *Mex., C.A., Col., Ven.* **-s tibios** soft-boiled eggs; *Col., Ven.* **-s pericos** scrambled eggs; *Ven., Andes* **costar un** — to be very expensive.
**huída** *f.* flight; escape.
**huir**[32] *v. irr.* to flee, escape; to avoid, shun.
**huizache** *m. Mex., C.A.* huisache (*a species of acacia*).
**hule** *m.* rubber; oilcloth; *Col., Ven.* rubber tree.
**hulla** *f.* soft coal.
**humanidad** *f.* humanity, mankind; **-es** humanities, letters.
**humanitario** *adj.* humanitarian, humane, kind, charitable.
**humano** *adj.* human; humane; *m.* man, human being.
**humareda** *f.* cloud of smoke.
**humeante** *adj.* smoking, smoky; steaming.
**humear** *v.* to smoke, give off smoke; to steam; *Am.* to fumigate.
**humedad** *f.* humidity, moisture, dampness.
**humedecer**[13] *v. irr.* to moisten, wet, dampen.
**húmedo** *adj.* humid, moist, wet, damp.
**humildad** *f.* humility; humbleness; meekness.
**humilde** *adj.* humble, lowly, meek.
**humillación** *f.* humiliation; submission.
**humillar** *v.* to humiliate, humble, lower, crush; **-se** to humiliate oneself; to bow humbly.
**humillos** *m. pl.* airs, conceit, vanity.
**humo** *m.* smoke, fume, vapor; **-s** conceit, vanity.
**humor** *m.* humor; mood, disposition.
**humorada** *f.* pleasantry, witty remark; caprice, notion.
**humorismo** *m.* humor, humorous style.
**humorístico** *adj.* humorous.
**humoso** *adj.* smoky.
**hundimiento** *m.* sinking, collapse, cave-in.

**hundir** *v.* (*sumir*) to sink, submerge; (*batir*) to crush, oppress; to destroy; **-se** to sink; to collapse, cave in.
**huracán** *m.* hurricane.
**huraño** *adj.* diffident, shy, bashful; unsociable.
**¡hurra!** *interj.* hurrah!
**hurtadillas : a** — on the sly, secretly, stealthily.
**hurtar** *v.* to steal, rob; **-se** to withdraw, slip away; to hide; — **el cuerpo** to dodge; to flee.
**hurto** *m.* robbery, theft; stolen article; **a** — stealthily, on the sly.
**husmear** *v.* to scent, smell, follow the track of; to nose, pry (into).
**husmeo** *m.* sniff, sniffing, smelling; prying.
**huso** *m.* spindle.

# I

**ibérico, ibero** *adj.* Iberian; **iberoamericano** *adj.* Ibero-American (*Spanish or Portuguese American*).
**ida** *f.* departure; sally; **billete de** — **y vuelta** round-trip ticket; **-s y venidas** goings and comings.
**idea** *f.* idea; notion.
**ideal** *m.* & *adj.* ideal.
**idealismo** *m.* idealism.
**idealista** *adj.* idealistic; *m.* & *f.* idealist; dreamer.
**idear** *v.* to form an idea of; to devise, think out, plan.
**ídem** idem (*abbreviation*: id.), ditto, the same.
**idéntico** *adj.* identical.
**identidad** *f.* identity.
**identificar**[6] *v.* to identify.
**idilio** *m.* idyl.
**idioma** *m.* language, tongue.
**idiota** *m.* & *f.* idiot; *adj.* idiotic, foolish.
**idiotismo** *m.* idiom; idiocy.
**idolatrar** *v.* to idolize, worship.
**ídolo** *m.* idol.
**idóneo** *adj.* fit, suitable; qualified.
**iglesia** *f.* church.
**ignición** *f.* ignition.
**ignominia** *f.* infamy, shame, disgrace.
**ignominioso** *adj.* ignominious; infamous, shameful, disgraceful.
**ignorancia** *f.* ignorance.
**ignorante** *adj.* ignorant.
**ignorar** *v.* to be ignorant of, not to know.
**ignoto** *adj.* unknown, undiscovered.
**igual** *adj.* (*semejante*) equal; (*liso*) even, smooth; uniform; (*siempre*) constant; **serle** — **a uno** to be all the same to one, make no difference to one; *m.* equal; **al** — equally.
**igualar** *v.* to equal; to equalize; to match; to level, smooth; to adjust; to be equal.
**igualdad** *f.* equality.
**igualitario** *adj.* equalitarian (*promoting the doctrine of equality*).
**iguana** *f.* iguana.
**ijada** *f.* loin; flank (*of an animal*); pain in the side; **ijar** *m.* flank (*of an animal*).

HO

**ilegal** *adj.* illegal, unlawful.
**ilegítimo** *adj.* illegitimate; illegal.
**ileso** *adj.* unharmed, uninjured, unhurt, safe and sound.
**ilícito** *adj.* illicit, unlawful.
**ilimitado** *adj.* unlimited.
**iluminación** *f.* illumination.
**iluminar** *v.* to illuminate; to light; to enlighten.
**ilusión** *f.* illusion.
**ilusivo** *adj.* illusive.
**iluso** *adj.* deluded; *m.* visionary, dreamer.
**ilusorio** *adj.* illusive; deceptive; worthless.
**ilustración** *f.* illustration; elucidation, explanation.
**ilustrador** *m.* illustrator.
**ilustrar** *v.* to illustrate.
**ilustre** *adj.* illustrious, distinguished.
**imagen** *f.* image.
**imaginable** *adj.* imaginable, conceivable.
**imaginación** *f.* imagination.
**imaginar** *v.* to imagine.
**imaginario** *adj.* imaginary.
**imaginativo** *adj.* imaginative; **imaginativa** *f.* imagination.
**imán** *m.* magnet; attraction.
**imbécil** *adj.* imbecile, stupid.
**imborrable** *adj.* indelible, not erasable; unforgettable.
**imbuir**[32] *v. irr.* to imbue; to instill, infuse, inspire (with).
**imitación** *f.* imitation.
**imitador** *m.* imitator; follower; *adj.* imitative, imitating.
**imitar** *v.* to imitate.
**impaciencia** *f.* impatience.
**impaciente** *adj.* impatient.
**impar** *adj.* odd; **número —** odd number.
**imparcial** *adj.* impartial; **imparcialidad** *f.* impartiality, fairness, justice.
**impasible** *adj.* impassive, insensitive, insensible, unfeeling, unmoved.
**impávido** *adj.* fearless; calm; *Am.* impudent, brazen.
**impedimento** *m.* impediment, hindrance, obstacle.
**impedir**[5] *v. irr.* to impede, prevent, hinder.
**impeler** *v.* to impel, push; to incite, spur.
**impenetrable** *adj.* impenetrable; impervious; incomprehensible.
**impensado** *adj.* unforeseen, unexpected; offhand, done without thinking; **impensadamente** *adv.* offhand, without thinking; unexpectedly.
**imperar** *v.* to rule, command, dominate.
**imperativo** *adj.* imperative; urgent, compelling; *m.* imperative mood.
**imperceptible** *adj.* imperceptible.
**imperdible** *m.* safety pin; *adj.* safe, that cannot be lost.
**imperecedero** *adj.* imperishable, enduring, everlasting.
**imperfecto** *adj.* imperfect; *m.* imperfect tense.

**imperial** *adj.* imperial; *f.* coach top; top seats on a coach or bus.
**impericia** *f.* inexperience.
**imperio** *m.* empire; command, rule; sway, influence.
**imperioso** *adj.* imperious, arrogant, domineering; urgent.
**impermeable** *adj.* waterproof, impervious, rainproof; *m.* raincoat.
**impersonal** *adj.* impersonal.
**impertinencia** *f.* impertinence; impudence; insolent remark or act; **decir -s** to talk nonsense; to make insolent remarks.
**impertinente** *adj.* impertinent, impudent; meddlesome; irrelevant, not to the point; **-s** *m. pl.* lorgnette (*eyeglasses mounted on a handle*).
**ímpetu** *m.* impetus; violent force; impulse; *C.A., Ríopl.* vehement desire; **— de ira** fit of anger.
**impetuoso** *adj.* impetuous, violent.
**impío** *adj.* impious, irreligious; profane.
**implacable** *adj.* implacable, relentless.
**implantación** *f.* implantation, establishment, introduction (*of a system*).
**implantar** *v.* to implant, establish, introduce.
**implicar**[6] *v.* to imply; to implicate, involve.
**implorar** *v.* to implore, entreat, beg.
**imponente** *adj.* imposing.
**imponer**[40] *v. irr.* to impose; to invest (*money*); **— miedo** to inspire fear; **— respeto** to inspire or command respect; **-se** to inspire fear or respect; to dominate; *Am.* **-se a** to get accustomed or used to.
**importancia** *f.* importance.
**importante** *adj.* important.
**importar** *v.* to be important; to matter; to amount to; to be necessary; to concern; to import.
**importe** *m.* amount, price, value.
**importunar** *v.* to importune, nag, tease, pester.
**importuno** *adj.* annoying, persistent.
**imposibilidad** *f.* impossibility.
**imposibilitado** *p.p.* & *adj.* disabled, unfit; helpless.
**imposibilitar** *v.* to make impossible; to disable.
**imposible** *adj.* impossible; intolerable, unbearable; *Col., Ven.* disabled (*because of illness*); *Am.* slovenly, untidy.
**imposición** *f.* imposition; burden; tax.
**impostor** *m.* impostor, cheat; **impostura** *f.* imposture, fraud, deceit.
**impotencia** *f.* impotence.
**impotente** *adj.* impotent, powerless.
**impreciso** *adj.* vague, indefinite; inaccurate.
**impregnar** *v.* to impregnate, saturate.
**imprenta** *f.* press; printing shop; printing.
**imprescindible** *adj.* essential, indispensable.
**impresión** *f.* impression; printing; mark; footprint.

**impresionante** *adj.* impressive.
**impresionar** *v.* to impress; to move, affect, stir; **-se** to be stirred, moved.
**impreso** *p.p. irr. of* **imprimir** printed; impressed, imprinted; *m.* printed matter.
**impresor** *m.* printer.
**imprevisión** *f.* carelessness, lack of foresight.
**imprevisto** *adj.* unforeseen, unexpected.
**imprimir** *v.* to print; to imprint, impress.
**improbable** *adj.* improbable, unlikely.
**improperio** *m.* affront, insult.
**impropio** *adj.* improper; unsuitable.
**improvisar** *v.* to improvise.
**improviso** *adj.* unforeseen; **de —** suddenly; *Col., Ven., Mex.* **en un —** in a moment, in the twinkling of an eye.
**imprudencia** *f.* imprudence, indiscretion, rash act.
**imprudente** *adj.* imprudent; unwise; indiscreet.
**impuesto** *p.p. of* **imponer** imposed; informed; *Am.* **estar — a** to be used or accustomed to; *m.* tax, duty.
**impulsar** *v.* to impel, push, move; to force.
**impulso** *m.* impulse; push.
**impureza** *f.* impurity.
**impuro** *adj.* impure.
**imputar** *v.* to impute, attribute.
**inacabable** *adj.* unending, endless.
**inacabado** *adj.* unfinished.
**inaccesible** *adj.* inaccessible, unobtainable.
**inacción** *f.* inaction, inactivity, idleness.
**inaceptable** *adj.* unacceptable, unsatisfactory.
**inactividad** *f.* inactivity.
**inactivo** *adj.* inactive.
**inadecuado** *adj.* inadequate.
**inadvertencia** *f.* oversight; inattention, heedlessness.
**inadvertido** *adj.* careless, heedless; unnoticed.
**inafectado** *adj.* unaffected.
**inagotable** *adj.* inexhaustible.
**inaguantable** *adj.* insufferable, unbearable.
**inalámbrico** *adj.* wireless.
**inalterable** *adj.* unalterable, unchangeable.
**inalterado** *adj.* unchanged.
**inamovible** = **inmovible.**
**inanición** *f.* starvation.
**inanimado** *adj.* inanimate, lifeless.
**inapetencia** *f.* lack of appetite.
**inaplicable** *adj.* inapplicable, unsuitable; **— al caso** irrelevant.
**inapreciable** *adj.* invaluable; inappreciable, too small to be perceived, very slight.
**inasequible** *adj.* inaccessible, not obtainable; hard to attain or obtain.
**inaudito** *adj.* unheard-of; unprecedented.
**inauguración** *f.* inauguration.
**inaugurar** *v.* to inaugurate, begin, open.

**incaico, incásico** *adj.* Incan (*of or pertaining to the Incas*).
**incalculable** *adj.* incalculable; innumerable, untold.
**incandescente** *adj.* incandescent.
**incansable** *adj.* untiring, tireless.
**incapacidad** *f.* incompetence, inability, unfitness.
**incapacitar** *v.* to cripple, disable, handicap, unfit, make unfit.
**incapaz** *adj.* incapable, unable.
**incauto** *adj.* unwary, heedless, reckless.
**incendiar** *v.* to set fire to; **-se** to catch fire.
**incendio** *m.* conflagration, fire.
**incentivo** *m.* incentive, inducement.
**incertidumbre** *f.* uncertainty, doubt.
**incesante** *adj.* incessant.
**incidental** *adj.* incidental.
**incidente** *adj.* incidental; *m.* incident.
**incienso** *m.* incense.
**incierto** *adj.* uncertain, doubtful; unstable; unknown; untrue.
**incisión** *f.* incision, cut, slit, gash.
**incitamiento** *m.* incitement, inducement, incentive.
**incitar** *v.* to incite, rouse, stir up.
**incivil** *adj.* uncivil, rude, impolite.
**inclemencia** *f.* inclemency, severity, harshness; **inclemente** *adj.* unmerciful, merciless.
**inclinación** *f.* inclination, affection; tendency, bent; bow; incline, slope.
**inclinar** *v.* (*bajar*) to incline; (*persuadir*) to persuade; **-se** to bow; to stoop; to incline, slope, slant; to lean, bend.
**incluir**[32] *v. irr.* to include; to inclose.
**inclusive** *adv.* inclusive, including; even; **inclusivo** *adj.* inclusive; comprehensive.
**incluso** *adj.* inclosed; included; including; even.
**incógnito** *adj.* unknown; **de —** incognito (*with one's name or rank unknown*); **incógnita** *f.* unknown quantity (*in mathematics*).
**incoherente** *adj.* incoherent, disconnected, rambling.
**incoloro** *adj.* colorless.
**incombustible** *adj.* incombustible; fireproof.
**incomodar** *v.* to inconvenience, disturb, trouble, annoy.
**incomodidad** *f.* inconvenience, discomfort; bother, annoyance.
**incómodo** *adj.* inconvenient, bothersome: uncomfortable.
**incomparable** *adj.* incomparable.
**incompasivo** *adj.* merciless, pitiless.
**incompatible** *adj.* incompatible; unsuitable, uncongenial.
**incompetencia** *f.* incompetence, inability, unfitness; **incompetente** *adj.* incompetent, unfit.
**incompleto** *adj.* incomplete.
**incomprensible** *adj.* incomprehensible.
**incondicional** *adj.* unconditional.
**inconexo** *adj.* unconnected; incoherent, disconnected.
**inconfundible** *adj.* unmistakable.
**incongruente** *adj.* unsuitable, not ap-

IL

propriate; not harmonious.

**inconquistable** *adj.* unconquerable.

**inconsciencia** *f.* unconsciousness; unawareness.

**inconsciente** *adj.* unconscious; unaware.

**inconsecuente** *adj.* inconsistent; illogical.

**inconsiderado** *adj.* inconsiderate, thoughtless.

**inconstancia** *f.* inconstancy, changeableness, fickleness.

**inconstante** *adj.* inconstant, fickle, changeable, variable.

**incontable** *adj.* countless, innumerable.

**inconveniencia** *f.* inconvenience; trouble.

**inconveniente** *adj.* inconvenient; improper; *m.* obstacle; objection.

**incorporar** *v.* to incorporate, unite; to embody; to include; **-se** to sit up; **-se a** to join.

**incorrecto** *adj.* incorrect.

**incredulidad** *f.* incredulity, unbelief.

**incrédulo** *adj.* incredulous, unbelieving; *m.* unbeliever.

**incréible** *adj.* incredible, unbelievable.

**incremento** *m.* increment, increase.

**incrustar** *v.* to inlay; to encrust (*cover with a crust or hard coating*); **-se en** to penetrate, impress itself deeply into.

**incubadora** *f.* incubator.

**inculcar**[6] *v.* to inculcate, instill, impress.

**inculto** *adj.* uncultured; uncultivated; unrefined.

**incumbencia** *f.* concern, duty, obligation; **no es de mi —** it does not concern me, it is not within my province.

**incurable** *adj.* incurable.

**incurrir** *v.* to incur, fall (into); **— en un error** to fall into or commit an error; **— en el odio de** to incur the hatred of.

**incursión** *f.* raid, invasion.

**indagación** *f.* investigation, inquiry.

**indagador** *m.* investigator; inquirer; *adj.* investigating; inquiring.

**indagar**[7] *v.* to find out, investigate; to inquire.

**indebido** *adj.* undue, improper; illegal; **indebidamente** *adv.* unduly; illegally.

**indecencia** *f.* indecency, obscenity, indecent act or remark.

**indecente** *adj.* indecent, improper.

**indecible** *adj.* inexpressible, untold.

**indeciso** *adj.* undecided; doubtful, uncertain.

**indefectible** *adj.* unfailing; **-mente** unfailingly.

**indefenso** *adj.* defenseless, unprotected.

**indefinible** *adj.* indefinable.

**indefinido** *adj.* indefinite.

**indeleble** *adj.* indelible.

**indemnizatión** *f.* indemnity, compensation.

**indemnizar**[9] *v.* to indemnify, compensate.

**independencia** *f.* independence.

**independiente** *adj.* independent.

**indescriptible** *adj.* indescribable.

**indeseable** *adj.* undesirable, unwelcome.

**indiada** *f. Ríopl., C.A., Col.* community, group, or crowd of Indians; *Col., Ven., Carib., Andes* an Indianlike remark or act; *Am.* an uncontrollable fit of anger.

**indianista** *m. & f.* student of Indian culture; *adj.* pertaining to Indian culture.

**indiano** *adj.* of or pertaining to the West or East Indies; *m.* Spaniard who goes back to settle in his country after having lived for some time in Spanish America.

**indicación** *f.* indication.

**indicar**[6] *v.* to indicate, show, point out.

**indicativo** *adj.* indicative; *m.* indicative, indicative mood.

**índice** *m.* index; catalogue; sign; pointer; forefinger.

**indicio** *m.* indication, sign.

**indiferencia** *f.* indifference.

**indiferente** *adj.* indifferent.

**indígena** *adj.* indigenous, native; *m. & f.* native inhabitant; *Am.* Indian.

**indignación** *f.* indignation.

**indignado** *p.p. & adj.* indignant, irritated, angry.

**indignar** *v.* to irritate, anger; **-se** to become indignant, angry.

**indignidad** *f.* indignity, affront, insult; unworthy or disgraceful act.

**indigno** *adj.* unworthy; low, contemptible.

**indio** *adj. & m.* Indian; Hindu.

**indirecta** *f.* hint, indirect remark, innuendo, insinuation.

**indirecto** *adj.* indirect.

**indisciplinado** *adj.* undisciplined, untrained.

**indiscreto** *adj.* indiscreet, imprudent, unwise, rash.

**indiscutible** *adj.* indisputable, unquestionable.

**indispensable** *adj.* indispensable.

**indisponer**[40] *v. irr.* to indispose; to make ill; **— a uno con otro** to prejudice someone against another; **-se** to become ill; **-se con** to fall out with, quarrel with.

**indisposición** *f.* indisposition, upset, slight illness; reluctance, unwillingness.

**indispuesto** *p.p. of* **indisponer** *& adj.* indisposed, unwilling; ill.

**indisputable** *adj.* unquestionable.

**indistinto** *adj.* indistinct, dim, vague, not clear.

**individual** *adj.* individual.

**individualidad** *f.* individuality.

**individuo** *adj.* individual; indivisible; *m.* individual; person; member.

**indócil** *adj.* unruly, disobedient, headstrong.

**indocto** *adj.* uneducated, ignorant.

**índole** *f.* disposition, temper; kind, class.

**indolencia** *f*. indolence, laziness; in-sensitiveness, indifference.

**indolente** *adj*. indolent, lazy; insensi-tive, indifferent.

**indomable** *adj*. indomitable, uncon-querable; unmanageable; untamable.

**indómito** *adj*. untamed; uncontrollable, unruly.

**inducir**[25] *v*. *irr*. to induce; to persuade.

**indudable** *adj*. unquestionable, cer-tain.

**indulgencia** *f*. indulgence, tolerance, forgiveness; remission of sins.

**indulgente** *adj*. indulgent, lenient.

**indultar** *v*. to pardon, set free; to ex-empt.

**indulto** *m*. pardon, forgiveness; ex-emption; privilege.

**indumentaria** *f*. costume, dress; man-ner of dressing.

**industria** *f*. industry; cleverness, skill; **de** — intentionally, on purpose.

**industrial** *adj*. industrial; *m*. indus-trialist; manufacturer.

**industrioso** *adj*. industrious.

**inédito** *adj*. unpublished.

**inefable** *adj*. ineffable, inexpressible.

**ineficaz** *adj*. ineffective; inefficient.

**inepto** *adj*. incompetent; unsuitable.

**inequívoco** *adj*. unmistakable.

**inercia** *f*. inertia, lifelessness; inactivity.

**inerme** *adj*. unarmed, defenseless.

**inerte** *adj*. inert; inactive, sluggish, slow.

**inesperado** *adj*. unexpected.

**inestable** *adj*. unstable; unsettled; un-steady.

**inestimable** *adj*. inestimable, invalu-able.

**inevitable** *adj*. inevitable, unavoidable.

**inexacto** *adj*. inexact, inaccurate.

**inexperiencia** *f*. inexperience.

**inexperto** *adj*. unskilful, unskilled, in-experienced.

**inexplicable** *adj*. inexplicable.

**inextinguible** *adj*. inextinguishable, unquenchable.

**infalible** *adj*. infallible.

**infame** *adj*. infamous; *m*. scoundrel.

**infamia** *f*. infamy, dishonor; wicked-ness.

**infancia** *f*. infancy.

**infante** *m*. infant; infante (*royal prince of Spain, except the heir to the throne*); infantryman.

**infantería** *f*. infantry.

**infantil** *adj*. infantile, childlike, child-ish.

**infatigable** *adj*. tireless, untiring.

**infausto** *adj*. unfortunate; unhappy.

**infección** *f*. infection; **infeccioso** *adj*. infectious.

**infectar** *v*. to infect; to corrupt; **-se** to become infected.

**infeliz** *adj*. unhappy, unfortunate; *m*. poor wretch.

**inferior** *adj*. inferior; lower; *m*. inferior.

**inferioridad** *f*. inferiority.

**inferir**[3] *v*. *irr*. (*concluir*) to infer; to imply; (*causar*) to inflict.

**infernal** *adj*. infernal.

**infestar** *v*. to infest, invade, overrun, plague; to corrupt, infect.

**inficionar** *v*. to infect; to contaminate.

**infiel** *adj*. unfaithful, faithless; infidel; inaccurate.

**infiernillo** *m*. chafing dish.

**infierno** *m*. hell; **en el quinto** — very far away.

**infiltrar** *v*. to filter through; **-se** to leak (into), filter (through), infiltrate.

**infinidad** *f*. infinity; **una** — **de** a large number of.

**infinito** *adj*. infinite; *adv*. infinitely; *m*. infinity.

**inflamación** *f*. inflammation.

**inflamado** *p.p*. & *adj*. inflamed; sore.

**inflamar** *v*. to inflame, excite; to kindle, set on fire; **-se** to become inflamed.

**inflar** *v*. to inflate; to exaggerate; **-se** to become inflated; to swell up with pride.

**inflexible** *adj*. inflexible, stiff, rigid; unbending.

**inflexión** *f*. inflection.

**infligir**[11] *v*. to inflict.

**influencia** *f*. influence.

**influenza** *f*. influenza, grippe, flu.

**influir**[32] *v*. *irr*. to influence.

**influjo** *m*. influence; influx, inward flow.

**influyente** *adj*. influential.

**información** *f*. information.

**informal** *adj*. informal; unconvention-al; unreliable, not dependable, not punctual.

**informar** *v*. to inform; to give form to; to give a report; to present a case; **-se** to find out.

**informe** *m*. report, account; informa-tion; brief; *adj*. formless, shapeless.

**infortunio** *m*. misfortune, mishap; misery.

**infracción** *f*. infraction, breach, viola-tion (*of a law*, *treaty*, *etc.*).

**infractor** *m*. transgressor, lawbreaker, violator (*of a law*).

**infrascrito** *m*. undersigned, subscriber, signer (*of a letter*, *document*, *etc.*); **el** — **secretario** the secretary whose signature appears below.

**infringir**[11] *v*. to infringe, break, violate.

**infructuoso** *adj*. fruitless.

**ínfulas** *f*. *pl*. airs, false importance; **darse** — to put on airs.

**infundado** *adj*. groundless, without foundation.

**infundir** *v*. to infuse, inspire; to instill.

**infusión** *f*. infusion (*liquid extract ob-tained by steeping*); infusion, inspi-ration; **poner en** — to steep (*as tea leaves*).

**ingeniería** *f*. engineering.

**ingeniero** *m*. engineer.

**ingenio** *m*. genius; talent; ingenuity; mentality, mental power, mind; wit; — **de azúcar** sugar refinery; sugar plantation.

**ingeniosidad** *f*. ingenuity, cleverness.

**ingenioso** *adj*. ingenious, clever.

**ingenuidad** *f*. candor, frankness; un-affected simplicity.

IN

**ingenuo** *adj.* frank, sincere; simple, unaffected; naive.

**ingerir** = **injerir**.

**ingestión** *f.* ingestion.

**ingle** *f.* groin.

**inglés** *adj.* English; **a la inglesa** in the English fashion; *Am.* **ir a la inglesa** to go Dutch treat; *m.* Englishman; the English language.

**ingobernable** *adj.* ungovernable, unruly, uncontrollable.

**ingratitud** *f.* ingratitude.

**ingrato** *adj.* ungrateful, thankless; harsh; cruel; disdainful.

**ingrediente** *m.* ingredient.

**ingresar** *v.* to enter; **— en** to join (*a society, club, etc.*).

**ingreso** *m.* entrance; entry; **-s** receipts, profits; revenue.

**inhábil** *adj.* unskilled; unskilful; unfit.

**inhabilidad** *f.* inability; unfitness.

**inhabilitar** *v.* to disqualify; to unfit, disable.

**inherente** *adj.* inherent.

**inhospitalario** *adj.* inhospitable.

**inhumano** *adj.* inhuman, cruel.

**iniciador** *m.* initiator; pioneer; *adj.* initiating.

**inicial** *adj.* & *f.* initial.

**iniciar** *v.* to initiate; to begin.

**iniciativa** *f.* initiative.

**inicuo** *adj.* wicked.

**iniquidad** *f.* iniquity, wickedness; sin.

**injerir**³ *v. irr.* to inject, insert; **-se** to interfere, meddle.

**injertar** *v.* to graft.

**injerto** *m.* graft.

**injuria** *f.* affront, insult; harm, damage.

**injuriar** *v.* to insult, offend; to harm, damage.

**injurioso** *adj.* insulting, offensive; harmful.

**injusticia** *f.* injustice.

**injustificado** *adj.* unjustified; unjustifiable.

**injusto** *adj.* unjust, unfair.

**inmaculado** *adj.* immaculate, clean; pure.

**inmediación** *f.* vicinity; nearness; **-es** environs, outskirts.

**inmediato** *adj.* near, close; *Am.* **de —** immediately; suddenly; **inmediatamente** *adv.* immediately, at once.

**inmensidad** *f.* immensity, vastness; vast number.

**inmenso** *adj.* immense, vast, huge; boundless.

**inmersión** *f.* immersion, dip.

**inmigración** *f.* immigration.

**inmigrante** *adj.*, *m.* & *f.* immigrant.

**inmigrar** *v.* to immigrate.

**inmiente** *adj.* imminent.

**inmiscuir**³² *v. irr.* to mix; **-se** to meddle, interfere.

**inmoble** *adj.* motionless; unshaken.

**inmoral** *adj.* immoral; **inmoralidad** *f.* immorality.

**inmortal** *adj.* immortal; **inmortalidad** *f.* immortality.

**inmovible** *adj.* immovable, fixed; steadfast.

**inmóvil** *adj.* motionless, still; immovable.

**inmundicia** *f.* filth, dirt; nastiness.

**inmundo** *adj.* filthy, dirty; impure; nasty.

**inmune** *adj.* immune; exempt.

**inmunidad** *f.* immunity.

**inmutable** *adj.* unchangeable, invariable.

**inmutar** *v.* to alter, change; **-se** to show emotion (*either by turning pale or blushing*).

**innato** *adj.* innate, natural, inborn.

**innecesario** *adj.* unnecessary.

**innegable** *adj.* undeniable, not to be denied.

**innocuo** *adj.* innocuous, harmless; **innocuidad** *f.* harmlessness.

**innovación** *f.* innovation; novelty.

**innumerable** *adj.* innumerable.

**inobservancia** *f.* nonobservance, violation (*of a law*), lack of observance (*of a law, rule, or custom*).

**inocencia** *f.* innocence.

**inocente** *adj.* innocent; *m.* innocent person; **inocentón** *adj.* quite foolish or simple; easily fooled; *m.* dupe, unsuspecting victim.

**inocular** *v.* to inoculate.

**inodoro** *adj.* odorless; *m. C.A., Ven., Col.* toilet, water closet.

**inofensivo** *adj.* inoffensive; harmless.

**inolvidable** *adj.* unforgettable.

**inopinado** *adj.* unexpected.

**inoportuno** *adj.* inopportune, untimely, unsuitable.

**inquietar** *v.* to worry, disturb, make uneasy; **-se** to become disturbed, uneasy.

**inquieto** *adj.* restless; uneasy, anxious.

**inquietud** *f.* restlessness; anxiety, uneasiness; fear.

**inquilino** *m.* tenant, renter; lodger.

**inquina** *f.* aversion, grudge, dislike.

**inquirir**³⁵ *v. irr.* to inquire, investigate; to find out.

**inquisición** *f.* inquisition; inquiry, investigation.

**insaciable** *adj.* insatiable, never satisfied, greedy.

**insalubre** *adj.* unhealthy, unhealthful, unwholesome.

**insano** *adj.* insane, crazy; unhealthy.

**inscribir**⁵² *v.* to inscribe; to register, enroll; to record; **-se** to register.

**inscripción** *f.* inscription; registration.

**inscripto, inscrito** *p.p. of* **inscribir**.

**insecto** *m.* insect.

**inseguro** *adj.* insecure; unsafe; doubtful, uncertain.

**insensato** *adj.* senseless; foolish.

**insensibilidad** *f.* insensibility, unconsciousness; lack of feeling.

**insensible** *adj.* insensible; unfeeling; imperceptible.

**inseparable** *adj.* inseparable.

**inserción** *f.* insertion; insert.

**insertar** *v.* to insert.

**inserto** *adj.* inserted.

**inservible** *adj.* useless.

**insidioso** *adj.* insidious; sly, crafty.

**insigne** *adj.* famous.

**insignia** *f.* badge, medal, decoration; flag, pennant; **-s** insignia.

**insignificante** *adj.* insignificant.

**insinuación** *f.* insinuation; intimation, hint.

**insinuar**[18] *v.* to insinuate, hint; **-se** to insinuate oneself (*into another's friendship*); to creep (into) gradually.

**insipidez** *f.* flatness, tastelessness, dullness; **insípido** *adj.* insipid; tasteless.

**insistencia** *f.* insistence, persistence, obstinacy; **insistente** *adj.* insistent, persistent.

**insistir** *v.* to insist; to persist.

**insociable** *adj.* unsociable.

**insolación** *f.* sunstroke.

**insolencia** *f.* insolence.

**insolentarse** *v.* to sauce, become insolent, act with insolence.

**insolente** *adj.* insolent.

**insólito** *adj.* unusual; uncommon.

**insolvente** *adj.* insolvent, bankrupt.

**insomne** *adj.* sleepless.

**insondable** *adj.* fathomless, deep; impenetrable.

**insoportable** *adj.* unbearable.

**insospechado** *adj.* unsuspected.

**inspección** *f.* inspection.

**inspeccionar** *v.* to inspect.

**inspector** *m.* inspector; overseer.

**inspiración** *f.* inspiration; inhalation, breathing in.

**inspirar** *v.* to inspire; to inhale.

**instalación** *f.* installation.

**instalar** *v.* to install.

**instancia** *f.* instance, urgent request; petition; **a -s de** at the request of.

**instantánea** *f.* snapshot.

**instantáneo** *adj.* instantaneous; sudden.

**instante** *m.* instant, moment; **al —** at once, immediately; **por -s** continually; from one moment to another; *adj.* instant, urgent.

**instar** *v.* to urge, press; to be urgent.

**instigar**[7] *v.* to instigate, urge on, incite.

**instintivo** *adj.* instinctive.

**instinto** *m.* instinct.

**institución** *f.* institution; establishment, foundation; **-es** institutes, collection of precepts and principles.

**instituir**[32] *v. irr.* to institute; **— por heredero** to appoint as heir.

**instituto** *m.* institute; established principle, law, or custom; **— de segunda enseñanza** high school.

**institutriz** *f.* governess.

**instrucción** *f.* instruction; education.

**instructivo** *adj.* instructive.

**instruir**[32] *v. irr.* to instruct, teach; to inform.

**instrumento** *m.* instrument.

**insuficiencia** *f.* insufficiency, deficiency; incompetence; dearth, scarcity, lack.

**insuficiente** *adj.* insufficient.

**insufrible** *adj.* insufferable, unbearable.

**ínsula** *f.* island.

**insultante** *adj.* insulting, abusive.

**insultar** *v.* to insult; **-se** to be seized with a fit.

**insulto** *m.* insult; sudden fit or attack.

**insuperable** *adj.* insuperable; insurmountable.

**insurgente** *adj.*, *m. & f.* insurgent.

**insurrección** *f.* insurrection, uprising, revolt.

**insurrecto** *m.* insurgent, rebel; *adj.* rebellious.

**intacto** *adj.* intact.

**intachable** *adj.* faultless, irreproachable.

**integral** *adj.* integral; *f.* integral (*math*).

**integrante** *adj.* integral; integrating.

**integridad** *f.* integrity; wholeness; honesty; purity.

**íntegro** *adj.* whole, complete; honest, upright.

**intelecto** *m.* intellect.

**intelectual** *adj.* intellectual.

**inteligencia** *f.* intelligence.

**inteligente** *adj.* intelligent.

**intemperancia** *f.* intemperance, excess.

**intemperie** *f.* open air; bad weather; **a la —** unsheltered, outdoors, in the open air; exposed to the weather.

**intención** *f.* intention; **intencional** *adj.* intentional.

**intendente** *m.* manager, superintendent, supervisor; *Ríopl.* governor of a province; *Am.* police commissioner.

**intensidad** *f.* intensity; stress.

**intenso** *adj.* intense; intensive; ardent, vehement.

**intentar** *v.* to attempt, try; to intend.

**intento** *m.* intent, purpose, intention; **de —** on purpose.

**intercalar** *v.* to insert, place between.

**intercambio** *m.* interchange; exchange.

**interceder** *v.* to intercede.

**interceptar** *v.* to intercept.

**intercesión** *f.* intercession, mediation.

**interdicción** *f.* interdiction; prevention.

**interés** *m.* interest.

**interesante** *adj.* interesting.

**interesar** *v.* to interest; to give an interest or share; **-se** to be or become interested.

**interferencia** *f.* interference.

**ínterin** *m.* interim, meantime; **en al —** in the meantime.

**interino** *adj.* acting, temporary.

**interior** *adj.* interior; inner; internal; *m.* interior, inside.

**interjección** *f.* interjection, exclamation.

**interlocutor** *m.* participant in a dialogue.

**intermedio** *adj.* intermediate; intervening; *m.* intermission; interval; **por — de** by means of, through the intervention of.

**interminable** *adj.* interminable, unending, endless.

**intermisión** *f.* intermission, interruption, pause, interval.

**intermitente** *adj.* intermittent, occurring at intervals; **calentura** (*or* **fiebre**) **—** intermittent fever.

**internacional** *adj.* international.
**internado** *m.* a boarding student.
**internar** *v.* to intern, confine; **-se** to penetrate, go into the interior.
**interno** *adj.* internal; interior; *m.* boarding-school student.
**interoceánico** *adj.* interoceanic; transcontinental.
**interpelar** *v.* to interrogate, question, demand explanations; to ask the aid of.
**interponer**[40] *v. irr.* to interpose, put between, insert; to place as a mediator; **-se** to intervene, mediate.
**interpretación** *f.* interpretation.
**interpretar** *v.* to interpret.
**intérprete** *m.* & *f.* interpreter.
**interpuesto** *p.p. of* **interponer.**
**interrogación** *f.* interrogation, question; **signo de —** question mark.
**interrogador** *m.* questioner; *adj.* questioning.
**interrogar**[7] *v.* to interrogate, question.
**interrogativo** *adj.* interrogative.
**interrogatorio** *m.* interrogation, questioning.
**interrumpir** *v.* to interrupt.
**interrupción** *f.* interruption.
**interruptor** *m.* interrupter; electric switch.
**intersección** *f.* intersection.
**intervalo** *m.* interval.
**intervención** *f.* intervention; mediation; participation; auditing of accounts.
**intervenir**[48] *v. irr.* to intervene; to mediate; to audit (*accounts*).
**interventor** *m.* inspector; controller, comptroller; auditor.
**intestino** *m.* intestine; *adj.* intestine, internal.
**intimación** *f.* intimation; hint, insinuation, suggestion.
**intimar** *v.* to announce, notify; to intimate, hint; to become intimate, become friendly.
**intimidad** *f.* intimacy.
**intimidar** *v.* to intimidate.
**íntimo** *adj.* intimate.
**intitular** *v.* to entitle; to give a title to (*a person or a thing*); **-se** to be entitled, be called; to call oneself (*by a certain name*).
**intolerable** *adj.* intolerable.
**intolerancia** *f.* intolerance; **intolerante** *adj.* intolerant, narrow-minded.
**intoxicante** *m.* poison.
**intoxicar**[6] *v.* to poison.
**intranquilo** *adj.* disturbed, uneasy.
**intranquilidad** *f.* uneasiness, restlessness.
**intransigencia** *f.* uncompromising act or attitude; intolerance.
**intransigente** *adj.* uncompromising, unwilling to compromise or yield; intolerant.
**intratable** *adj.* unsociable; rude; unruly.
**intravenoso** *adj.* intravenous (*within a vein or the veins; into a vein*).
**intrepidez** *f.* fearlessness, courage.

**intrépido** *adj.* intrepid, fearless.
**intriga** *f.* intrigue; scheme; plot.
**intrigante** *m.* & *f.* intriguer, plotter; *adj.* intriguing.
**intrigar**[7] *v.* to intrigue.
**intrincado** *adj.* intricate, complicated, entangled.
**introducción** *f.* introduction.
**introducir**[25] *v. irr.* to introduce; **-se** to introduce oneself; to get in; to penetrate.
**intromisión** *f.* meddling; insertion.
**intruso** *adj.* intrusive, intruding; *m.* intruder.
**intuición** *f.* intuition.
**intuir**[32] *v. irr.* to sense, feel by intuition.
**inundación** *f.* inundation, flood.
**inundar** *v.* to inundate, flood.
**inusitado** *adj.* unusual, rare.
**inútil** *adj.* useless.
**inutilidad** *f.* uselessness.
**inutilizar**[9] *v.* to make useless, put out of commission; to disable; to ruin, spoil.
**invadir** *v.* to invade.
**invalidar** *v.* to render invalid; to void, annul.
**inválido** *adj.* invalid; void, null; sickly, weak; *m.* invalid.
**invariable** *adj.* invariable.
**invasión** *f.* invasion.
**invasor** *m.* invader; *adj.* invading; **ejército —** invading army.
**invencible** *adj.* invincible, unconquerable.
**invención** *f.* invention.
**invendible** *adj.* unsaleable.
**inventar** *v.* to invent.
**inventariar**[17] *v.* to inventory, take an inventory of.
**inventario** *m.* inventory.
**inventiva** *f.* inventiveness, power of inventing, ingenuity.
**inventivo** *adj.* inventive.
**invento** *m.* invention.
**inventor** *m.* inventor; storyteller, fibber.
**invernáculo** *m.* greenhouse, hothouse.
**invernadero** *m.* winter quarters; winter resort; winter pasture; greenhouse, hothouse.
**invernal** *adj.* wintry, winter.
**invernar**[1] *v. irr.* to winter, spend the winter.
**inverosímil, inverisímil** *adj.* unlikely, improbable.
**inversión** *f.* inversion; investment.
**inverso** *adj.* inverse, inverted; reverse; **a** (*or* **por**) **la inversa** on the contrary.
**invertir**[3] *v. irr.* to invert; to reverse; to invest; to employ, spend (*time*).
**investigación** *f.* investigation.
**investigador** *m.* investigator; *adj.* investigating.
**investigar**[7] *v.* to investigate.
**invicto** *adj.* unconquered; always victorious.
**invierno** *m.* winter; *C.A., Col., Ven., Ec., Peru* the rainy season.
**invisible** *adj.* invisible.
**invitación** *f.* invitation.
**invitar** *v.* to invite.

**invocar**[6] *v.* to invoke.
**involuntario** *adj.* involuntary.
**inyección** *f.* injection.
**inyectado** *p.p.* injected; *adj.* blood-shot, inflamed.
**inyectar** *v.* to inject.
**ir**[33] *v. irr.* to go; to walk; **— corriendo** to be running; **— entendiendo** to understand gradually; to begin to understand; **— a caballo** to ride horseback; **— a pie** to walk; **— en automóvil** to drive, ride in an automobile; **no irle ni venirle a uno** to make no difference to one; **¿cómo le va?** how are you?; **no me va nada en eso** that doesn't concern me;**¡vamos!** let's go! come on!; **¡vaya!** well now!; **¡vaya un hombre!** what a man!; **-se** to go, go away; to escape; **-se abajo** to fall down, topple over; to collapse; **-se a pique** to founder, sink.
**ira** *f.* ire, anger.
**iracundo** *adj.* irritable; angry.
**iris** *m.* iris (*of the eye*); **arco —** rainbow.
**irisado** *adj.* iridescent, rainbow-hued.
**ironía** *f.* irony.
**irónico** *adj.* ironic, ironical.
**irracional** *adj.* irrational, unreasonable.
**irradiar** *v.* to radiate.
**irreal** *adj.* unreal.
**irreflexión** *f.* thoughtlessness.
**irreflexivo** *adj.* thoughtless.
**irrefrenable** *adj.* uncontrollable.
**irregular** *adj.* irregular.
**irreligioso** *adj.* irreligious.
**irremediable** *adj.* irremediable; hopeless, incurable.
**irreprochable** *adj.* irreproachable, flawless.
**irresistible** *adj.* irresistible.
**irresoluto** *adj.* irresolute, undecided, hesitating.
**irrespetuoso** *adj.* disrespectful.
**irreverencia** *f.* irreverence.
**irreverente** *adj.* irreverent.
**irrigación** *f.* irrigation.
**irrigar**[7] *v.* to irrigate.
**irrisión** *f.* mockery, ridicule, derision.
**irritación** *f.* irritation.
**irritante** *adj.* irritating.
**irritar** *v.* to irritate.
**irrumpir** *v.* to enter violently; to invade.
**irrupción** *f.* sudden attack, raid, invasion.
**isla** *f.* island.
**isleño** *m.* islander.
**islote** *m.* islet, small rocky island.
**istmo** *m.* isthmus.
**italiano** *adj.* & *m.* Italian.
**itinerario** *m.* itinerary; timetable, schedule; railroad guide.
**izar**[9] *v.* to hoist; to heave.
**izquierda** *f.* left hand; left side; left wing (*in politics*); **a la —** to the left; **izquierdista** *m.* & *f.* leftist, radical.
**izquierdo** *adj.* left; left-handed.

# J

**jabalí** *m.* wild boar.
**jabalina** *f.* javelin; wild sow.
**jabón** *m.* soap; *Ríopl.* fright, fear; **dar**
— to soft-soap, flatter; **dar un —** to give a good scolding; to beat, thrash.
**jabonadura** *f.* washing, soaping; **-s** suds, lather; **dar a uno una —** to reprimand or scold someone.
**jabonar** *v.* (*lavar*) to lather, soap; (*reprender*) to scold; reprimand.
**jabonera** *f.* soap dish; woman soap vendor or maker.
**jaca** *f.* pony; small horse; **jaco** *m.* small nag; poor horse.
**jacal** *m. Mex.* shack, adobe hut; **jacalucho** *m. Am.* poor, ugly shack.
**jacinto** *m.* hyacinth.
**jactancia** *f.* boast, brag; boasting.
**jactancioso** *adj.* braggart, boastful.
**jactarse** *v.* to brag, boast.
**jaculatoria** *f.* short, fervent prayer.
**jadeante** *adj.* breathless, panting, out of breath.
**jadear** *v.* to pant.
**jadeo** *m.* pant, panting.
**jaez** *m.* harness; kind, sort; **jaeces** trappings.
**jalar** *v.* to pull; to haul; to jerk; *C.A.* to court, make love; *Ven., Andes* to flunk (*a student*); *Mex.* **¡jala!** (*or* **¡jálale!**) get going! get a move on there!; **-se** *Am.* to get drunk; *Mex.* to go away, move away.
**jalea** *f.* jelly.
**jalear** *v.* to shout (*to hunting dogs*); to rouse, beat up (*game*); to shout and clap (*to encourage dancers*).
**jaleo** *m.* shouting and clapping (*to encourage dancers*); an Andalusian dance; revelry, merrymaking; jesting; gracefulness.
**jaletina** *f.* gelatin.
**jalón** *m.* marker (*for boundaries*); *Am.* pull, jerk, tug; *Mex., C.A.* swallow of liquor; *Bol., C.A.* stretch, distance.
**jalonear** *v. C.A., Mex.* to pull, jerk.
**jamás** *adv.* never.
**jamón** *m.* ham; *P.R.* fix, difficulty.
**japonés** *adj.* & *m.* Japanese.
**jaque** *m.* check (*in chess*); braggart, bully; **— mate** checkmate (*in chess*); **tener a uno en —** to hold someone under a threat.
**jaqueca** *f.* headache; sick headache.
**jara** *f.* rockrose (*shrub*); *Ven., Col.* reed; **jaral** *m.* bramble of rockroses; *Am.* reeds, clump of reeds.
**jarabe** *m.* syrup; sweet beverage; *Mex., C.A.* a kind of tap dance; *Mex.* song and musical accompaniment of the **jarabe.**
**jarana** *f.* merrymaking, revelry; trick; fib; jest; *Col., Ec., Carib.* a dance; *Mex.* small guitar; **ir de —** to go on a spree.
**jarcia** *f.* rigging (*ropes, chains, etc. for the masts, yards and sails of a ship*); fishing tackle; pile, heap; jumble of things.
**jardín** *m.* flower garden.
**jardinero** *m.* gardener.
**jarra** *f.* jar, vase, pitcher; **de** (*or* **en**) **-s** akimbo (*with hands on the hips*).
**jarro** *m.* jar, jug, pitcher.

IN

**jarrón** *m.* large vase or jar.
**jaspe** *m.* jasper; veined marble; **jaspeado** *adj.* veined, streaked, mottled.
**jaula** *f.* cage; cagelike cell or prison; *Am.* roofless cattle car or freight car.
**jauría** *f.* pack of hounds.
**jazmín** *m.* jasmine.
**jefatura** *f.* position of chief; headquarters of a chief.
**jefe** *m.* chief, leader, head.
**jengibre** *m.* ginger.
**jerez** *m.* sherry wine.
**jerga** *f.* (*tela*) thick coarse cloth; straw mattress; (*dialecto*) jargon; slang; *Am.* saddle pad; *Col.* poncho made of coarse cloth.
**jergón** *m.* (*material*) straw mattress; ill-fitting suit or dress; (*persona*) big clumsy fellow; *Ríopl.*, *Mex.*, *Ven.* cheap coarse rug.
**jerigonza** *f.* jargon; slang.
**jeringa** *f.* syringe; **jeringazo** *m.* injection; squirt.
**jeringar**[7] *v.* to inject; to squirt; to bother, molest, vex, annoy.
**jesuita** *m.* Jesuit.
**jeta** *f.* snout; thick lips.
**jiba** = **giba**.
**jíbaro** *adj.* *P.R.* rustic, rural, rude, uncultured; *m.* *P.R.* bumpkin, peasant.
**jícara** *f.* chocolate cup; *Am.* small bowl made out of a gourd; *Am.* any small bowl; *Am.* bald head.
**jilguero** *m.* linnet.
**jinete** *m.* horseman, rider.
**jineteada** *f.* *Ríopl.*, *C.A.* roughriding, horse-breaking.
**jinetear** *v.* to ride horseback; to perform on horseback; *Am.* to break in (*a horse*); *Am.* to ride a bronco or bull.
**jira** *f.* excursion, tour; outing, picnic; strip of cloth.
**jirafa** *f.* giraffe; boom mike (*broadcasting*).
**jitomate** *m.* *Mex.* tomato. *Also* **gitomate**.
**jofaina** *f.* basin, washbowl.
**jolgorio** = **holgorio**.
**jornada** *f.* day's journey; military expedition; working day; act (*of a Spanish play*).
**jornal** *m.* day's wages; bookkeeping journal; **a —** by the day.
**jornalero** *m.* day laborer.
**joroba** *f.* hump; nuisance, annoyance.
**jorobado** *adj.* hunchbacked; annoyed, bothered, in a bad fix; *m.* hunchback.
**jorobar** *v.* to bother, pester, annoy.
**jorongo** *m.* *Mex.* Mexican poncho.
**jota** *f.* name of the letter *j*; iota (*anything insignificant*); Aragonese and Valencian dance and music; *Am.* (= **ojota**) leather sandal; **no saber una —** not to know anything.
**joven** *adj.* young; *m.* & *f.* youth; young man; young woman.
**jovial** *adj.* jovial, jolly, merry; **jovialidad** *f.* gaiety, merriment, fun.
**joya** *f.* jewel; piece of jewelry; **-s** jewels; trousseau.
**joyería** *f.* jeweler's shop.

**joyero** *m.* jeweler; jewel box.
**juanete** *m.* bunion.
**jubilación** *f.* retirement (*from a position or office*); pension.
**jubilar** *v.* to pension; to retire; **-se** to be pensioned or retired; to rejoice; *Col.* to decline, fall into decline; *Ven.*, *Guat.* to play hooky or truant.
**jubileo** *m.* jubilee; time of rejoicing; concession by the Pope of plenary (*complete*) indulgence.
**júbilo** *m.* joy, glee.
**jubiloso** *adj.* jubilant, joyful.
**jubón** *m.* jacket; bodice.
**judía** *f.* bean; string bean; Jewess; **-s tiernas** (*or* **verdes**) string beans.
**judicial** *adj.* judicial; **-mente** *adv.* judicially.
**judío** *adj.* Jewish; *m.* Jew.
**judo** *m.* judo.
**juego** *m.* game; play; sport; gambling; pack of cards; set; **— de palabras** pun, play on words; **— de te** tea set; **hacer —** to match; **poner en —** to coordinate; to set in motion.
**juerga** *f.* spree, revelry, wild festivity; **irse de —** to go out on a spree; **juerguista** *m.* & *f.* merrymaker.
**jueves** *m.* Thursday.
**juez** *m.* judge; juror, member of a jury; **— arbitrador** (*or* **árbitro**) arbitrator, umpire.
**jugada** *f.* play, move; stroke; trick.
**jugador** *m.* player; gambler; **— de manos** juggler.
**jugar**[34] *v. irr.* to play; to gamble; to toy; **— a la pelota** to play ball; *Am.* **— a dos cartas** to be double-faced.
**jugarreta** *f.* bad play, wrong play; mean trick; tricky deal; *Am.* noisy game.
**jugo** *m.* juice; sap.
**jugosidad** *f.* juiciness; **jugoso** *adj.* juicy.
**juguete** *m.* plaything, toy; jest, joke; **— cómico** skit; **por** (*or* **de**) **—** jokingly.
**juguetear** *v.* to play around, romp, frolic; to toy; to tamper (with), fool (with).
**juguetón** *adj.* playful.
**juicio** *m.* judgment; sense, wisdom; opinion; trial; **perder el —** to lose one's mind, go crazy.
**juicioso** *adj.* judicious, wise; sensible.
**julio** *m.* July.
**jumento** *m.* ass, donkey.
**junco** *m.* rush, reed; junk (*Chinese sailboat*).
**jungla** *f.* *Am.* jungle.
**junio** *m.* June.
**junquillo** *m.* reed; jonquil (*yellow flower similar to the daffodil*), species of narcissus.
**junta** *f.* (*reunión*) meeting, conference; (*funcionarios*) board, council.
**juntar** *v.* to join, unite; to connect; to assemble; to collect; **-se** to assemble, gather; to be closely united; to associate (with).
**junto** *adj.* joined, united; **-s** together; *adv.* near; **— a** near to, close to; **en —**

all together, in all; **por —** all together, in a lump; wholesale.

**juntura** *f.* juncture; junction; joint, seam.

**jurado** *m.* jury; juror, juryman; *adj. & p.p.* sworn.

**juramentar** *v.* to swear in; **-se** to take an oath, be sworn in.

**juramento** *m.* oath; vow; curse.

**jurar** *v.* to swear, vow; to take oath; to curse.

**jurisconsulto** *m.* jurist, expert in law; lawyer.

**jurisdicción** *f.* jurisdiction.

**jurisprudencia** *f.* jurisprudence, law.

**juro: de — adv.** certainly, of course.

**justa** *f.* joust, tournament, combat (*between horsemen with lances*); contest.

**justicia** *f.* justice; court of justice; judge; police.

**justiciero** *adj.* strictly just, austere (*in matters of justice*).

**justificación** *f.* justification.

**justificante** *adj.* justifying; *m.* voucher; written excuse; proof.

**justificar**⁶ *v.* to justify; to vindicate, clear of blame.

**justo** *adj.* just; pious; exact, correct; tight; *adv.* duly; exactly; tightly; *m.* just man; **los -s** the just.

**juvenil** *adj.* juvenile, young, youthful.

**juventud** *f.* youth; young people.

**juzgado** *m.* court, tribunal.

**juzgar**⁷ *v.* to judge.

### K

**kermesse** *f.* country fair; bazaar for charity.

**kerosena** *f.* kerosene, coal oil.

**kilo** *m.* kilo, kilogram.

**kilogramo** *m.* kilogram.

**kilometraje** *m.* number of kilometers.

**kilómetro** *m.* kilometer.

### L

**la** *def. art. f.* the; **— de** the one with, that one with; *obj. pron.* her; it; **— que** *rel. pron.* she who, the one that; which.

**la** *m.* sixth note on the musical scale.

**laberinto** *m.* labyrinth, maze; labyrinth, internal ear.

**labia** *f.* fluency, talkativeness, gift of gab; **tener mucha —** to be a good talker.

**labial** *adj.* labial.

**labio** *m.* lip.

**labiodental** *adj.* labiodental.

**labor** *f.* (*trabajo*) labor, work; (*cosido*) embroidery; needlework; (*agrícola*) tillage; **— de punto** knitting; **laborable** *adj.* workable; tillable; **día laborable** work day; **laboral** *adj.* pertaining to labor.

**laboratorio** *m.* laboratory.

**laboriosidad** *f.* laboriousness, industry.

**laborioso** *adj.* laborious; industrious.

**labrado** *p.p. & adj.* (*agrícola*) tilled, cultivated; (*hecho*) wrought; manufactured; carved; *m.* carving; **— en madera** woodwork, carving; **-s** cultivated lands.

**labrador** *m.* farmer; peasant.

**labranza** *f.* farming, tillage, plowing; cultivated land, farm.

**labrar** *v.* (*la tierra*) to till, cultivate, farm; to plow; (*crear*) to carve; to embroider; to work (*metals*); to build (*a monument*).

**labriego** *m.* peasant.

**laca** *f.* lacquer; shellac.

**lacayo** *m.* lackey, footman, flunky.

**lacio** *adj.* withered; languid; limp; straight (*hair*).

**lacra** *f.* trace of an illness; blemish, defect; *Am.* sore, ulcer, scab, scar.

**lacre** *m.* red sealing wax; *adj. Am.* red.

**lactar** *v.* to nurse, suckle; to feed with milk.

**lácteo** *adj.* milky; **fiebre láctea** milk fever; **régimen —** milk diet; **Vía Láctea** Milky Way.

**ladear** *v.* to tilt, tip; to go along the slope or side of; to turn aside (*from a way or course*); **-se** to tilt; to sway; to incline or lean (towards); to move to one side; *Am.* to fall in love.

**ladeo** *m.* inclination, tilt.

**ladera** *f.* slope.

**ladino** *adj.* crafty, sly, shrewd; conversant with two or three languages; *m.* Sephardic Jew (*Spanish-speaking*); Romansch (*a Romance language of Switzerland*); *Guat.* Spanish-speaking person (*as opposed to one who speaks an Indian language*); *Am.* mestizo, half-breed; *Mex., Ven.* talker, talkative person.

**lado** *m.* side; **al —** near, at hand, at one's side; **de —** tilted, obliquely; sideways; **a —** side by side; **¡a un —!** gangway! **hacerse a un —** to move over, step aside, move to one side; *Mex., Ven.* **echársela de —** to boast.

**ladrar** *v.* to bark.

**ladrido** *m.* bark, barking.

**ladrillo** *m.* brick.

**ladrón** *m.* thief, robber; **ladronzuelo** *m.* petty thief.

**lagartija** *f.* small lizard.

**lagarto** *m.* lizard; rascal, sly fellow.

**lago** *m.* lake.

**lágrima** *f.* tear; **llorar a — viva** to weep abundantly.

**lagrimear** *v.* to weep, shed tears.

**laguna** *f.* lagoon; gap, blank space.

**laico** *adj.* lay; *m.* layman.

**laja** *f.* slab; flat stone.

**lamedero** *m.* salt lick (*for cattle*).

**lamentable** *adj.* lamentable, pitiful.

**lamentación** *f.* lamentation.

**lamentar** *v.* to lament, deplore; **-se** to moan, complain, wail.

**lamento** *m.* lament, moan, cry.

**lamer** *v.* to lick; to lap.

**lamida** *f. Mex., C.A.* lick; also **lambida**.

**lámina** *f.* metal plate; sheet of metal; engraving; book illustration.

**lámpara** *f.* lamp.

**lampiño** *adj.* hairless; beardless.

**lana** *f.* wool; *Am.* tramp, vagabond.

**lanar** *adj.* wool-bearing; of wool.
**lance** *m.* occurrence, event; cast, throw, move, turn; accident; quarrel; predicament.
**lancear** *v.* to lance, spear.
**lancha** *f.* launch; boat; slab; **lanchón** *m.* barge.
**langosta** *f.* lobster; locust.
**languidecer**[13] *v. irr.* to languish.
**languidez** *f.* languor, faintness, weakness.
**lánguido** *adj.* languid.
**lanilla** *f.* nap (*of cloth*).
**lanudo** *adj.* woolly; *Ven.* coarse, crude, ill-bred; *Am.* dull, slow, weak-willed; *Ch., C.A., Col.* wealthy.
**lanza** *f.* lance, spear; *Col.* swindler, cheat; *m.* **lanzabombas** bomb launcher; *m.* **lanzacohetes** rocket launcher; *m.* **lanzallamas** flame thrower.
**lanzada** *f.* thrust (*with a spear*).
**lanzadera** *f.* shuttle.
**lanzamiento** *m.* launching (*boat or rocket*).
**lanzar**[9] *v.* to fling, throw; to eject; to launch; **-se** to rush, fling oneself; to dart out.
**lanzazo** *m.* thrust with a lance.
**lapicero** *m.* pencil (*a mechanical pencil, one with an adjustable lead*).
**lápida** *f.* slab, tombstone; stone tablet.
**lapidar** *v.* to stone; *Col., Ch.* to cut precious stones.
**lápiz** *f.* pencil; crayon; **— para los labios** lipstick.
**lapso** *m.* lapse.
**lardo** *m.* lard.
**largar**[7] *v.* to loosen; to let go; to set free; to unfold (*a flag or sails*); *Am.* to hurl, throw; *Col.* to strike (*a blow*); *Ríopl.* to give, hand over; **-se** to go away, slip away; to leave.
**largo** *adj.* long; generous; *m.* length; largo (*music*); **a la larga** in the long run; slowly; **a lo —** along; lengthwise; **¡— de aquí!** get out of here!
**largor** *m.* length.
**largucho** *adj.* lanky.
**largueza** *f.* generosity, liberality; length.
**larguísimo** *adj.* very long.
**largura** *f.* length.
**laringe** *f.* larynx.
**laríngeo** *adj.* laryngeal.
**larva** *f.* larva.
**las** *def. art. f. pl.* the; *obj. pron.* them; **— que** *rel. pron.* those which; which.
**lascivia** *f.* lewdness.
**lascivo** *adj.* lascivious, lewd.
**lástima** *f.* pity; compassion, grief.
**lastimadura** *f.* sore, hurt.
**lastimar** *v.* to hurt; to offend; **-se** to get hurt; **-se de** to feel pity for.
**lastimero** *adj.* pitiful; mournful.
**lastimoso** *adj.* pitiful.
**lastre** *m.* ballast, weight.
**lata** *f.* (*metal*) tin plate; tin can, can; (*madero*) small log; thin board; (*pesadez*) annoyance; embarrassment; boring speech; *Am.* gaucho saber;

*Am.* prop.
**latente** *adj.* latent.
**lateral** *adj.* lateral, side; [l] (*phonetically*).
**latido** *m.* palpitation, throb, beat; bark, howl.
**latifundio** *m.* large landed estate.
**latigazo** *m.* lash, stroke with a whip; crack of a whip; harsh reprimand; unexpected blow or offense.
**látigo** *m.* whip; *Am.* whipping, beating; *Ch.* end or goal of a horse race.
**latín** *m.* Latin language.
**latino** *adj.* Latin; *m.* Latinist, Latin scholar; Latin.
**latir** *v.* to throb, beat, palpitate; to bark.
**latitud** *f.* latitude; extent, breadth.
**latón** *m.* brass.
**latrocinio** *m.* larceny, theft, robbery.
**laúd** *m.* lute; catboat (*long, narrow boat with a lateen sail*).
**laudable** *adj.* laudable, praiseworthy.
**laurel** *m.* laurel; laurel wreath.
**lauro** *m.* laurel; glory, fame.
**lava** *f.* lava; washing of minerals.
**lavable** *adj.* washable.
**lavabo** *m.* lavatory, washroom; washstand; washbowl.
**lavadero** *m.* washing place.
**lavado** *m.* wash, washing; laundry, laundry work.
**lavador** *m.* washer; cleaner; *adj.* washing; cleaning; **lavadora** *f.* washer, washing machine.
**lavadura** *f.* washing; slops, dirty water.
**lavamanos** *m.* lavatory, washbowl, washstand.
**lavandera** *f.* laundress, washerwoman.
**lavandería** *f.* laundry.
**lavar** *v.* to wash; to launder; to whitewash.
**lavativa** *f.* enema; syringe; bother, nuisance.
**lavatorio** *m.* washing (*act of washing*); wash (*liquid or solution for washing*); lavatory (*ceremonial act of washing*); washbowl, washstand; *Am.* washroom.
**lavazas** *f. pl.* slops, dirty water.
**lazada** *f.* bow, bowknot; *Am.* throwing of the lasso, lassoing.
**lazar**[9] *v.* to rope, lasso; to noose.
**lazarillo** *m.* blindman's guide.
**lazo** *m.* (*nudo*) bow, knot; slipknot; lasso, lariat; (*vínculo*) tie, bond; (*trampa*) snare, trap; trick.
**le** *obj. pron.* him; you (*formal*); to him; to her; to you (*formal*).
**leal** *adj.* loyal.
**lealtad** *f.* loyalty.
**lebrel** *m.* greyhound.
**lebrillo** *m.* earthenware basin or tub.
**lección** *f.* lesson; reading; **dar la —** to recite the lesson; **dar —** to teach; **tomarle a uno la —** to have someone recite his lesson.
**lector** *m.* reader; lecturer.
**lectura** *f.* reading; **libro de —** reader.
**lechada** *f.* whitewash; *Am.* milking.
**leche** *f.* milk; *Col., Ven., C.A., Andes, Ríopl.* luck (*in games*).

**lechería** f. dairy, creamery; **lechero** adj. milk; milch, giving milk (applied to animals); Am. lucky (in games of chance); m. milkman; **lechera** f. milkmaid; milk can; milk pitcher.

**lecho** m. bed; river bed.

**lechón** m. suckling pig; pig.

**lechoso** adj. milky; m. papaya tree; **lechosa** f. papaya (tropical fruit).

**lechuga** f. lettuce.

**lechuza** f. screech owl, barn owl.

**leer**[14] v. to read.

**legación** f. legation.

**legado** m. (donación) legacy; legato; (representante) representative, ambassador.

**legal** adj. legal, lawful; truthful; reliable; Col., Ven., Andes excellent, best; Am. just, honest.

**legalizar**[9] v. to legalize.

**legar**[7] v. to will, bequeath; to send as a delegate.

**legendario** adj. legendary.

**legión** f. legion.

**legislación** f. legislation.

**legislador** m. legislator; adj. legislating, legislative.

**legislar** v. to legislate.

**legislativo** adj. legislative.

**legislatura** f. legislature, legislative assembly.

**legítimo** adj. legitimate; real, genuine.

**lego** adj. lay; ignorant; m. layman.

**legua** f. league (about 3 miles).

**leguleyo** m. shyster.

**legumbre** f. vegetable.

**leída** f. Am. reading. See **lectura**.

**leísta** m. & f. one who uses the pronoun le for masculine direct object (le conozco).

**lejanía** f. distance; distant place.

**lejano** adj. distant; remote.

**lejía** f. lye; harsh reprimand.

**lejos** adv. far, far away; **a lo** — in the distance; Am. **a un** — in the distance; **de** (or **desde**) — from afar; m. view, perspective; background.

**lelo** adj. silly, stupid, foolish.

**lema** m. motto; theme; slogan.

**lencería** f. dry goods; dry-goods store; linen room or closet.

**lengua** f. tongue; language; interpreter; — **de tierra** point, neck of land.

**lenguado** m. flounder, sole (a fish).

**lenguaje** m. language (manner of expression).

**lenguaraz** adj. talkative, loose-tongued.

**lengüeta** f. small tongue; **lengüetada** f. lick.

**lente** m. & f. lens; **-s** m. pl. eyeglasses.

**lenteja** f. lentil; lentil seed; **lentejuela** f. spangle.

**lentitud** f. slowness.

**lento** adj. slow; dull.

**leña** f. firewood; kindling; beating.

**leñera** f. woodshed; woodbox.

**leñador** m. woodcutter, woodman.

**leño** m. log; timber; piece of firewood.

**león** m. lion; **leona** f. lioness; **leonera** f. lion's den or cage; dive, gambling

joint; disorderly room.

**leontina** f. Mex., Carib., Col. watch chain.

**leopardo** m. leopard.

**leopoldina** f. Mex., Ven. watch chain.

**lerdo** adj. dull, heavy, stupid, slow.

**les** obj. pron. to them; to you (formal).

**lesión** f. wound, injury.

**lesionar** v. to injure; to wound; to hurt; to damage.

**lesna** = **lezna**.

**letargo** m. lethargy, stupor, drowsiness.

**letra** f. letter (of the alphabet); printing type; hand, handwriting; letter (exact wording or meaning); words of a song; — **abierta** letter of credit; — **de cambio** draft, bill of exchange; — **mayúscula** capital letter; — **minúscula** small letter; **al pie de la** — literally; **-s** letters, learning.

**letrado** adj. learned; m. lawyer.

**letrero** m. notice, poster, sign; legend (under an illustration).

**leva** f. levy, draft; weighing anchor, setting sail; **echar** — to draft, conscript; Col. **echar -s** to boast.

**levadura** f. leaven, yeast.

**levantamiento** m. (revuelta) uprising, revolt, insurrection; (altura) elevation; lifting, raising; adjournment (of a meeting); — **de un plano** surveying.

**levantar** v. to raise, lift; to set up; to erect; to rouse, stir up; to recruit; Ch. to break land, plow; — **el campo** to break camp; — **la mesa** to clear the table; — **la sesión** to adjourn the meeting; — **un plano** to survey, map out; — **falso testimonio** to bear false witness; **-se** to stand up, get up, rise; to rebel.

**levante** m. east; east wind.

**levantisco** adj. turbulent; rebellious.

**levar** v. to weigh (anchor); — **el ancla** to weigh anchor; **-se** to weigh anchor, set sail.

**leve** adj. light; slight, unimportant.

**levita** f. frock coat; m. Levite, member of the tribe of Levi.

**léxico** m. lexicon, dictionary; vocabulary; glossary.

**ley** f. law; rule; loyalty; standard quality; **de buena** — of good quality; **plata de** — sterling silver; **-es** jurisprudence, law; system of laws.

**leyenda** f. legend; reading; inscription.

**lezna** f. awl.

**liar**[17] v. to tie, bind; to roll up; to deceive; **-se** to bind oneself; to get tangled up.

**libelo** m. libel.

**libélula** f. dragon fly.

**liberación** f. liberation; deliverance.

**liberal** adj. liberal; generous; **liberalidad** f. liberality; generosity.

**libertad** f. liberty.

**libertador** m. liberator, deliverer.

**libertar** v. to liberate, free, set free; **-se** to get free; to escape.

**libertinaje** m. license, licentiousness, lack of moral restraint.

**libertino** m. libertine (person without

**LA**

moral restraint).

**libra** f. pound; Libra (sign of the Zodiac).

**librador** m. drawer (of a bill, draft, etc.); deliverer, liberator; measuring scoop.

**libranza** f. bill of exchange, draft.

**librar** v. to free, set free; to issue; to draw (a draft); **— guerra** to wage war; **-se** to save oneself; to escape; **-se de** to get rid of, escape from.

**libre** adj. free; unmarried; loose; vacant.

**librea** f. livery (uniform).

**librería** f. bookstore.

**librero** m. bookseller; Am. bookcase, bookshelves.

**libreta** f. notebook, memorandum book.

**libro** m. book; **— de caja** cashbook; **— mayor** ledger.

**licencia** f. license; permission; furlough, leave; looseness; license to practice.

**licenciado** m. licenciate (person having a degree approximately equivalent to a master's degree); Ríopl., Mex., C.A. lawyer.

**licenciar** v. to license; to give a license or permit; to dismiss, discharge (from the army); to confer the degree of **licenciado**; **-se** to get the degree of **licenciado**.

**licenciatura** f. degree of **licenciado**.

**licencioso** adj. licentious, lewd.

**liceo** m. lyceum; high school; Col. primary school or high school.

**lícito** adj. lawful; permissible, allowable.

**licor** m. liquid; liquor.

**lid** f. fight; contest.

**líder** m. Am. leader.

**lidiar** v. to fight; to combat; to contend.

**liebre** f. hare; coward.

**lienzo** m. cotton or linen cloth; canvas; painting.

**liga** f. (alianza) league; alliance; (cinta) garter; alloy; birdlime.

**ligadura** f. binding; tie, bond.

**ligar**[7] v. to bind, tie, unite; to alloy (combine metals); **-se** to unite, combine, form an alliance.

**ligereza** f. lightness; swiftness; flippancy; frivolity.

**ligero** adj. (leve) light; (rápido) swift; nimble; flippant; adv. Am. quickly; **a la ligera** quickly, superficially.

**lija** f. sandpaper.

**lijar** v. to sandpaper.

**lila** f. lilac; pinkish-purple.

**lima** f. file; lime (fruit); finishing, polishing.

**limar** v. to file; to file down; to smooth, polish.

**limeño** adj. of or from Lima, Peru.

**limitación** f. limitation; district.

**limitar** v. to limit; to restrict; to bound.

**límite** m. limit; boundary.

**limo** m. slime.

**limón** m. lemon; lemon tree; **limonada** f. lemonade; **limonero** m. lemon tree; lemon dealer or vendor.

**limosna** f. alms, charity.

**limosnero** m. beggar.

**limpiabotas** m. bootblack; Ch. bootlicker, flatterer.

**limpiadientes** m. toothpick.

**limpiar** v. to clean; to wipe; to cleanse, purify; Am. to beat up, whip, lash.

**límpido** adj. limpid, clear.

**limpieza** f. cleanliness, neatness; purity; honesty.

**limpio** adj. clean; neat; pure; **poner en —** to make a clean copy; Am. **— y soplado** absolutely broke, wiped out.

**linaje** m. lineage, family, race.

**linaza** f. linseed.

**lince** m. lynx; sharp-sighted person.

**linchar** v. to lynch.

**lindar** v. to border, adjoin.

**linde** m. & f. limit, border, boundary; landmark.

**lindero** adj. bordering upon; m. Carib., C.A. landmark; boundary.

**lindeza** f. prettiness; exquisiteness; neatness; witty act or remark.

**lindo** adj. pretty; **de lo —** wonderfully; very much; to the utmost.

**línea** f. line; limit.

**lineal** adj. lineal, linear.

**lino** m. linen; flax; **linón** m. lawn, thin linen or cotton.

**linotipia** f. linotype.

**linterna** f. lantern.

**lío** m. (bulto) bundle; (enredo) fib; mess, confusion; **armar un —** to raise a rumpus; to cause confusion; **hacerse un —** to be confused, get tangled up; **meterse en un —** to get oneself into a mess.

**liquidación** f. liquidation; settlement (of an account).

**liquidar** v. to liquidate; to settle (an account).

**líquido** m. liquid.

**lira** f. lyre, small harp; a type of metrical composition; lira (Italian coin).

**lírico** adj. lyric, lyrical; Am. fantastic; m. Ríopl. visionary, dreamer.

**lirio** m. lily.

**lirismo** m. lyricism (lyric quality); Am. idle dream, fantasy.

**lisiado** adj. lame, hurt, injured.

**liso** adj. smooth, even; flat; evident, clear; Am. crafty, sly; Col., Ven., C.A., Andes fresh, impudent.

**lisonja** f. flattery.

**lisonjear** v. to flatter; to fawn on; to please.

**lisonjero** adj. flattering, pleasing; m. flatterer.

**lista** f. list; strip; stripe; **pasar —** to call the roll.

**listado** adj. striped.

**listar** v. to register, enter in a list; Ríopl., Mex., Ven. to stripe, streak.

**listo** adj. ready, prompt; clever; Ríopl., Ch. mischievous.

**listón** m. ribbon, tape; strip.

**lisura** f. smoothness; sincerity, frankness; Am. freshness, impudence; Andes insulting or filthy remark.

**litera** f. berth (on a boat or train);

litter (*for carrying a person*).
**literario** *adj.* literary.
**literato** *adj.* literary, learned; *m.* literary man, writer.
**literatura** *f.* literature.
**litigio** *m.* litigation, lawsuit.
**litoral** *adj.* seaboard, coastal; *m.* coast, shore.
**litro** *m.* liter (*about 1.05 quarts*).
**liviandad** *f.* lightness; frivolity; lewdness.
**liviano** *adj.* (*leve*) light; slight, unimportant; (*lascivo*) frivolous, fickle; lewd; unchaste.
**lívido** *adj.* livid, having a dull-bluish color; pale.
**lo** *obj. pron.* him; you (*formal*); it; so; *dem. pron.* **— de** that of, that affair of, that matter of; **— bueno** the good, what is good; **sé — bueno que Vd. es** I know how good you are; **— que** that which, what.
**loable** *adj.* laudable, worthy of praise.
**loar** *v.* to praise.
**lobanillo** *m.* growth, tumor.
**lobo** *m.* wolf.
**lóbrego** *adj.* dark, gloomy.
**lobreguez** *f.* darkness, gloominess.
**lóbulo** *m.* lobe.
**local** *adj.* local; *m.* place, quarters; site; premises.
**localidad** *f.* location; locality, town; place; seat (*in a theater*).
**localización** *f.* localization, localizing.
**localizar**⁹ *v.* to localize.
**loco** *adj.* insane, mad, crazy; **— de remate** stark mad; *m.* lunatic, insane person.
**locomotor** *adj.* locomotive.
**locomotora** *f.* locomotive; **— diesel** diesel locomotive.
**locuaz** *adj.* loquacious, talkative.
**locución** *f.* phrase; diction.
**locura** *f.* madness, insanity.
**locutor** *m.* radio announcer.
**lodazal** *m.* muddy place; mire.
**lodo** *m.* mud; **lodoso** *adj.* muddy, miry.
**logaritmo** *m.* logarithm.
**logia** *f.* lodge (*secret society*).
**lógica** *f.* logic; reasoning.
**lógico** *adj.* logical.
**lograr** *v.* to gain, obtain, accomplish; **— (+ inf.)** to succeed in; **-se** to succeed; to turn out well.
**logrero** *m.* usurer; profiteer.
**logro** *m.* profit, gain; usury; attainment; realization.
**loísta** *m. & f.* one who uses the pronoun *lo* for the masculine direct object (*lo conozco*).
**loma** *f.* small hill; **lomerío** *m. Am.* group of hills.
**lombriz** *f.* earthworm.
**lomo** *m.* back (*of an animal, book, knife, etc.*); loin; ridge between two furrows; *Mex., Ven.* **hacer —** to bear with patience, resign oneself.
**lona** *f.* canvas.
**lonche** *m. Col., Ven., Mex.* lunch; **lonchería** *f. Col., Ven., Mex.* lunchroom.

**longaniza** *f.* pork sausage.
**longevidad** *f.* longevity, long life; span of life, length of life.
**longitud** *f.* longitude; length.
**longitudinal** *adj.* longitudinal, lengthwise; **-mente** *adv.* longitudinally, lengthwise.
**lonja** *f.* (*mercado*) exchange; market; (*carne*) slice of meat; (*correa*) leather strap; *Ríopl.* raw hide.
**lontananza** *f.* background; **en —** in the distance, in the background.
**loro** *m.* parrot.
**los** *def. art. m. pl.* the; *obj. pron.* them; **— que** *rel. pron.* those which; which.
**losa** *f.* flagstone; slab; gravestone.
**lote** *m.* lot, share, part; *Am.* remnant lot; *Col.* swallow of liquor; *Am.* blockhead, dunce.
**lotear** *v. Am.* to subdivide into lots; *Am.* to divide into portions.
**lotería** *f.* lottery; raffle.
**loza** *f.* fine earthenware; crockery; **— fina** chinaware.
**lozanía** *f.* luxuriance (*rich foliage or growth*); vigor.
**lozano** *adj.* luxuriant; exuberant, vigorous, lusty.
**lubricar**⁶ *v.* to lubricate, or grease.
**lucero** *m.* morning star; any bright star; star on the forehead of certain animals; splendor, brightness.
**lúcido** *adj.* lucid, clear; shining, bright.
**luciente** *adj.* shining, bright.
**luciérnaga** *f.* firefly; glowworm.
**lucimiento** *m.* splendor; brilliance; success.
**lucir**¹³ *v. irr.* (*brillar*) to shine; to illuminate; to brighten; (*superar*) to excel; (*alardear*) to show off; **-se** to shine, be brilliant; to show off; to be successful.
**lucrativo** *adj.* lucrative, profitable.
**lucro** *m.* profit, gain.
**luctuoso** *adj.* sad, mournful, dismal.
**lucha** *f.* fight, struggle; dispute; wrestling match.
**luchador** *m.* fighter; wrestler.
**luchar** *v.* to fight; to wrestle; to struggle; to dispute.
**luego** *adv.* soon, presently; afterwards, then, next; **desde —** immediately, at once; naturally; **— de** after; **— que** as soon as; **hasta —** good-bye, so long; **— —** right away.
**luengo** *adj.* long; **-s años** many years.
**lugar** *m.* (*sitio*) place; site; town; space; (*empleo*) position, employment; (*ocasión*) time, occasion, opportunity; **dar — a** to give cause or occasion for; **hacer** (*or* **dar**) **—** to make room; **en — de** instead of.
**lúgubre** *adj.* mournful, gloomy.
**lujo** *m.* luxury, extravagance.
**lujoso** *adj.* luxurious; elegant; showy.
**lujuria** *f.* lust, lewdness, sensuality.
**lujurioso** *adj.* lustful, lewd, sensual.
**lumbre** *f.* fire; brightness.
**luminoso** *adj.* luminous, bright, shining.
**luna** *f.* moon; mirror, glass for mirrors.

**lunar** *adj.* lunar; *m.* mole; blemish; spot.
**lunático** *adj.* & *m.* lunatic.
**lunes** *m.* Monday; *Ch.* **hacer San Lunes** to lay off on Monday.
**lunfardo** *m.* social dialect of the Buenos Aires underworld.
**lustre** *m.* luster, shine; glory.
**lustroso** *adj.* lustrous, glossy, shining.
**luto** *m.* mourning; sorrow, grief.
**luz** *f.* light; clarity; hint, guidance; **dar a —** to give birth; to publish; **entre dos luces** at twilight.

## LL

**llaga** *f.* wound; ulcer, sore.
**llama** *f.* flame; llama (*a South American beast of burden*).
**llamada** *f.* call; beckon, sign; knock; reference mark (*as an asterisk*).
**llamador** *m.* knocker (*of a door*); caller.
**llamamiento** *m.* call, calling; calling together; appeal.
**llamar** *v.* to call; to summon; to name; to invoke; **— a la puerta** to knock at the door; **-se** to be called, named; *Am.* to break one's word or promise.
**llamarada** *f.* flash; sudden flame or blaze; sudden flush, blush.
**llamativo** *adj.* showy, loud, gaudy, flashy; thirst-exciting.
**llameante** *adj.* flaming.
**llana** *f.* mason's trowel.
**llanero** *m. Ven., Col.* plainsman.
**llaneza** *f.* simplicity; frankness; sincerity; plainness.
**llano** *adj.* plain, simple; even, smooth, level; frank; *m.* plain, flat ground.
**llanta** *f. Spain* rim of a wheel; *Am.* tire; tire casing; *Peru* large sunshade (*used in Peruvian markets*).
**llanto** *m.* crying, weeping; tears.
**llanura** *f.* extensive plain; prairie; evenness, flatness.
**llapa** *f. Andes, Ríopl.* a small gift from the vendor to the purchaser; also **yapa, ñapa.**
**llave** *f.* key; faucet; clef; **— de tuercas** wrench; **— inglesa** monkey wrench; **— maestra** master key.
**llavera** *f. Am.* housekeeper.
**llavero** *m.* key ring; key maker; keeper of the keys.
**llavín** *m.* small key.
**llegada** *f.* arrival.
**llegar**[7] *v.* to arrive; to reach; to amount; **— a ser** to get or come to be; **— a las manos** to come to blows; **-se** to approach, get near.
**llenar** *v.* to fill; to stuff; **-se** to fill up; to overeat; **-se de** to get filled with; to get covered with, spattered with.
**lleno** *adj.* full; *m.* fullness, completeness; **de —** totally, completely; **un — completo** a full house (*said of a theater*).
**llenura** *f.* fullness; abundance.
**llevadero** *adj.* bearable, tolerable.
**llevar** *v.* (*transportar*) to carry; to bear; to transport; to wear (*conducir*) to take; to lead; (*cobrar*) to charge; to

ask a certain price; to keep (*accounts*); **— ventaja** to be ahead, have the advantage; **— un año a** to be one year older than; **— un mes aquí** to have been here one month; **— un castigo** to suffer punishment; **-se** to carry away; **-se bien con** to get along with.
**llorar** *v.* to cry, weep.
**lloriquear** *v.* to whimper, whine, weep.
**lloriqueo** *m.* whimper, whining.
**lloro** *m.* weeping.
**llorón** *adj.* weeping; **sauce —** weeping willow; *m.* weeper, crybaby, whiner.
**llorona** *f.* weeping woman; **-s** *Am.* large spurs.
**lloroso** *adj.* tearful; weeping.
**llovedizo** *adj.* rain (*used as adj.*); **agua llovediza** rain water.
**llover**[2] *v. irr.* to rain, shower.
**llovizna** *f.* drizzle.
**lloviznar** *v.* to drizzle, sprinkle.
**lluvia** *f.* rain; shower.
**lluvioso** *adj.* rainy.

## M

**macana** *f. Am.* club, cudgel, stick; *Am.* lie, absurdity, nonsense.
**macanudo** *adj. Ríopl.* tremendous! great!
**macarrón** *m.* macaroon; **-es** macaroni.
**maceta** *f.* (*tiesto*) flowerpot; (*martillo*) small mallet; stonecutter's hammer; handle of tools; *Am.* head; *adj. Am.* slow.
**macilento** *adj.* thin, emaciated; pale.
**macizo** *adj.* solid, firm; massive; *m.* massiveness; firmness; thicket; clump.
**machacar**[6] *v.* to pound, crush; to insist, harp on.
**machacón** *adj.* persistent; tenacious.
**machete** *m.* machete, large heavy knife; **machetazo** *m.* large machete; blow with a machete.
**machismo** *m.* the quality of being a male; proven daring.
**macho** *m.* male; he-mule; hook (*of a hook and eye*); abutment; pillar; stupid fellow; sledgehammer; *C.R.* a blond; North American; *Am.* **pararle a uno el —** to halt or repress a person; *adj.* masculine, male; strong.
**machucar**[6] *v.* to pound, beat, bruise; *Am.* to crush; *Am.* to break (*a horse*).
**machucón** *m.* smash; bruise.
**madeja** *f.* skein; mass of hair; limp, listless person.
**madera** *f.* wood; timber; lumber; **maderero** *m.* lumberman, lumber dealer.
**maderaje** *m.* timber, lumber; timber work; woodwork.
**maderamen** *m.* timber; timber work; woodwork.
**madero** *m.* beam; plank; timber; piece of lumber; blockhead, dunce.
**madrastra** *f.* stepmother.
**madre** *f.* mother; womb; root, origin; river bed; **salirse de —** to overflow (*said of rivers*).
**madrepeña** *f. Am.* moss.

**madreperla** *f.* mother-of-pearl.
**madreselva** *f.* honeysuckle.
**madriguera** *f.* burrow; den, lair.
**madrileño** *adj.* Madrilenian, from or pertaining to Madrid; *m.* Madrilenian.
**madrina** *f.* (*patrocinadora*) godmother; bridesmaid; sponsor; (*correa*) strap for yoking two horses; (*ganado*) leading mare; prop; *Am.* small herd of tame cattle (*used for leading wild cattle*).
**madrugada** *f.* dawn; early morning; **de —** at daybreak.
**madrugador** *m.* early riser.
**madrugar**[7] *v.* to rise early; to be ahead of others; to "get the jump" on someone.
**madurar** *v.* to mature; to ripen.
**madurez** *f.* maturity; ripeness.
**maduro** *adj.* ripe; mature; prudent, wise; *Am.* bruised, sore.
**maestría** *f.* mastery; great skill.
**maestro** *m.* master, teacher; chief craftsman; *adj.* master; masterly, skillful; **llave maestra** master key; **obra maestra** masterpiece.
**magia** *f.* magic; charm.
**mágico** *adj.* magic; *m.* magician.
**magín** *m.* imagination, fancy.
**magisterio** *m.* teaching profession.
**magistrado** *m.* magistrate, judge.
**magistral** *adj.* masterly; masterful; authoritative.
**magnánimo** *adj.* magnanimous, noble, generous.
**magnético** *adj.* magnetic; attractive.
**magnetofónico** *adj.* recording (*tape or wire*).
**magnetófono** *m.* tape recorder.
**magnificencia** *f.* magnificence, splendor.
**magnífico** *adj.* magnificent, splendid.
**magnitud** *f.* magnitude, greatness.
**mago** *m.* magician, wizard; **los tres Reyes Magos** the Three Wise Men.
**magra** *f.* slice of ham.
**magro** *adj.* lean.
**maguey** *m.* maguey, century plant.
**magullar** *v.* to bruise; to maul; to mangle; *Ríopl.*, *Ch.*, *Col.*, *Andes*, *P.R.* to crumple.
**mahometano** *adj.* & *m.* Mohammedan.
**maíz** *m.* corn; **maizal** *m.* cornfield.
**majada** *f.* sheepfold; dung, manure; *Ríopl.*, *Ch.* flock of sheep or goats.
**majadería** *f.* foolishness, nonsense.
**majadero** *adj.* foolish; bothersome.
**majar** *v.* to pound; to crush; to bruise; to crumple; to mash; to annoy, bother.
**majestad** *f.* majesty; dignity.
**majestuoso** *adj.* majestic, stately.
**majo** *adj.* gaudy, showy; gaily attired; pretty; *m.* dandy; **maja** *f.* belle.
**mal** *m.* evil; illness; harm; wrong. *See* **malo.**
**malabarista** *m.* & *f.* juggler; *Ch.* sly thief.
**malacate** *m.* hoist, hoisting machine; winch; *Am.* spindle (*for cotton*); *Am.* **parecer uno un —** to be constantly

on the go, be in constant motion.
**malagueña** *adj.* song and dance of Málaga.
**malandanza** *f.* misfortune.
**malaventura** *f.* misfortune, disaster.
**malazo** *adj.* perverse, evil, wicked; vicious.
**malbaratar** *v.* to undersell, sell at a loss; to squander.
**malcontento** *adj.* discontented; *m.* malcontent, troublemaker.
**malcriado** *adj.* ill-bred, rude.
**maldad** *f.* badness, evil, wickedness.
**maldecir**[27,52] *v. irr.* to curse; to damn.
**maldición** *f.* curse.
**maldispuesto** *adj.* unwilling, not inclined.
**maldito** *p.p.* of **maldecir** & *adj.* cursed; wicked; damned; *Am.* tricky; *Am.* bold, boastful.
**maleante** *m.* crook, rogue, rascal, villain.
**malecón** *m.* mole; dike.
**maledicencia** *f.* slander.
**maleficio** *m.* spell, charm, witchery.
**maléfico** *adj.* evil, harmful.
**malestar** *m.* indisposition; slight illness; discomfort.
**maleta** *f.* travelling bag; suitcase; *Col.*, *Ven.*, *C.A.* bundle of clothes; *Col.* hump (*on the back*); *Am.* saddlebag; *C.A.* rogue, rascal; *Am.* lazy fellow.
**maletín** *m.* small valise, satchel.
**malevo** *adj. Bol.*, *Ríopl.* bad, wicked.
**malévolo** *adj.* bad, evil, wicked.
**maleza** *f.* underbrush; thicket; weeds.
**malgastar** *v.* to squander, waste.
**malhechor** *m.* malefactor, evildoer, criminal.
**malhora** *f. Ríopl.*, *C.A.*, *Ven.* trouble, misfortune.
**malhumorado** *adj.* ill-humored.
**malicia** *f.* malice; wickedness; shrewdness; suspicion; *Ch.* bit of brandy or cognac added to another drink.
**maliciar** *v.* to suspect.
**malicioso** *adj.* malicious; wicked; shrewd; suspicious.
**maligno** *adj.* malign, malignant; pernicious, harmful.
**malmandado** *adj.* disobedient; stubborn.
**mal(o)** *adj.* bad, evil; wicked; ill; difficult; *Am.* **a la mala** treacherously; *Ríopl.* **de malas** by force; **estar de malas** to be out of luck; **por la mala** unwillingly, by force; **venir de malas** to come with evil intentions; **mal** *adv.* badly; poorly; wrongly.
**malograr** *v.* to waste, lose; **-se** to turn out badly; to fail.
**malón** *m.* mean trick; *Ríopl.* surprise Indian raid; *Ven.* tin-pan serenade, boisterous surprise party.
**malpagar**[7] *v.* to underpay, pay poorly.
**malparto** *m.* miscarriage, abortion.
**malquerencia** *f.* aversion, dislike, ill will.
**malsano** *adj.* unhealthy; sickly.
**malta** *f.* malt.

LU

**maltratar** *v.* to treat badly; to misuse, abuse.

**maltrato** *m.* mistreatment, abuse.

**maltrecho** *adj.* battered, bruised, injured.

**malvado** *adj.* wicked; malicious.

**malversación** *f.* graft, corruption, misuse of public funds.

**malversar** *v.* to misuse (*funds in one's trust*); to embezzle.

**malla** *f.* mesh; coat of mail; *Ch.* species of potato; **hacer —** to knit.

**mamá** *f.* mamma.

**mamada** *f.* suck, sucking.

**mamar** *v.* to suckle; to suck; to gorge; **-se** *Ríopl., C.A.* to get drunk; *Col.* to go back on one's promise; *Am.* to fold up, crack up; **-se a uno** to get the best of someone, deceive someone; *Col., C.A.* to kill someone.

**mamífero** *m.* mammal; *adj.* mammalian, of mammals.

**mamón** *adj.* suckling; *m.* suckling (*very young animal or child*); shoot, sucker (*of a tree*); *Ríopl.* cherimoya (*tree and fruit*); *Am.* papaya (*tree and fruit*); *Mex.* a kind of cake; *C.A.* public employee.

**mampara** *f.* screen.

**mampostería** *f.* masonry, stone masonry.

**manada** *f.* herd; drove; pack; flock.

**manantial** *m.* spring; source, origin.

**manar** *v.* to spring, flow (from); to abound.

**manaza** *f.* large hand.

**manazo** *m. Ríopl.* slap. *See* **manotazo.**

**mancarrón** *m.* one-armed or one-handed man; cripple; old nag; *Ríopl., Andes* crude, clumsy fellow; *Am.* disabled workman; *Am.* dike, small dam.

**mancebo** *m.* youth, young man; bachelor.

**mancera** *f.* handle of a plough.

**mancilla** *f.* stain, spot; dishonor.

**manco** *adj.* one-armed; one-handed; maimed; lame (*referring to an arm or the front leg of an animal*); faulty, defective; *m. Ch.* nag.

**mancuerna** *f.* pair of animals tied together; *Mex., C.A. f. pl.* cuff links.

**mancha** *f.* spot, stain, blemish; *Am.* cloud, swarm; *Ven., Cuba, Col.* roving herd of cattle.

**manchar** *v.* to stain, soil, spot; to tarnish.

**manchego** *adj.* of or belonging to La Mancha (*region of Spain*); *m.* inhabitant of La Mancha.

**manchón** *m.* large stain; large patch.

**mandadero** *m.* messenger, errand boy.

**mandado** *m.* (*orden*) command, order; (*recado*) errand; *p.p. of* **mandar; bien —** well-behaved; **mal —** ill-behaved.

**mandamiento** *m.* command, order; writ; commandment.

**mandar** *v.* (*pedir*) to command, order; rule; (*enviar*) to send; to bequeath, will; *Col., Ven.* to throw, hurl; **—**

**hacer** to have made, order; *Col., Ven., Mex., Carib., Andes —* **una bofetada** to give a slap; *Col., Ven., Mex., Carib., Andes —* **una pedrada** to throw a stone; **-se** *Am.* to be impudent; **-se mudar** *Ríopl., Carib.* to go away.

**mandatario** *m.* attorney, representative; *Am.* magistrate, chief.

**mandato** *m.* mandate; order, command; term of office.

**mandíbula** *f.* jaw, jawbone.

**mando** *m.* command, authority, power.

**mandón** *adj.* bossy, domineering; *m.* bossy person; *Am.* boss or foreman of a mine; *Am.* race starter.

**maneador** *m. Ríopl., Ven., Col.* hobble, leather lasso (*for the legs of an animal*); *Am.* whip; *Ven., Andes* halter.

**manear** *v.* to hobble, lasso, tie the legs of (*an animal*); **-se** *Col., Ven.* to get tangled up.

**manecilla** *f.* small hand; hand of a watch or clock.

**manejable** *adj.* manageable.

**manejar** *v.* to manage, handle; to drive (*a car*); **-se** to move about, get around (*after an illness or accident*); *Carib., Ven.* to behave oneself.

**manejo** *m.* handling; management; trick, intrigue.

**manera** *f.* manner, way, mode; side opening in a skirt; front opening in breeches; **-s** customs; manners, behavior; **a — de** (*or* **a la — de**) like, in the style of; **de — que** so that; **sobre —** exceedingly; extremely.

**manga** *f.* sleeve; bag; hose (*for watering*); body of troops; *Am.* multitude, herd, swarm; *Am.* cattle chute (*narrow passageway*); *Am.* corral; **— de agua** waterspout, whirlwind over the ocean; *Am.* **— de hule** raincape; **por angas o por -s** by hook or crook, in one way or another.

**mangana** *f.* lariat, lasso.

**manganeso** *m.* manganese.

**mango** *m.* handle; *Am.* mango (*tropical tree and its fruit*).

**manguera** *f.* hose (*for water*); waterspout; *Ríopl.* large corral (*for livestock*).

**manguito** *m.* muff; knitted half-sleeve (*worn on the forearm*); oversleeve.

**maní** *m. Carib., C.A., Ch., Andes, Ven., Col.* peanut; **manicero** *m. Carib., C.A., Ch., Andes, Ven., Col.* peanut vendor.

**manía** *f.* mania, frenzy; craze, whim.

**maniatar** *v.* to tie the hands; to handcuff; to hobble (*an animal*).

**maniático** *m.* crank, queer fellow; *adj.* cranky, queer, odd.

**manicomio** *m.* insane asylum.

**manicura** *f.* manicure; manicurist.

**manicurar** *v.* to manicure.

**manido** *adj.* rotting; *Ríopl., Carib., Col., Andes* trite, commonplace.

**manifestación** *f.* manifestation; demonstration.

**manifestar**[1] *v. irr.* to manifest; to show.

**manifiesto** *adj.* manifest, clear, plain; *m.* manifesto, public declaration; customhouse manifest.

**manigua** *f. Col., Ríopl., Cuba, P.R.* Cuban jungle or thicket; *Carib.* **coger** — to get feverish; *Ríopl., Carib.* **irse a la** — to rise up in rebellion.

**manija** *f.* handle; crank; fetter.

**manilla** *f.* small hand; bracelet; **-s de hierro** handcuffs.

**maniobra** *f.* maneuver; operation.

**maniobrar** *v.* to maneuver.

**manipulación** *f.* manipulation.

**manipular** *v.* to manipulate, handle.

**maniquí** *m.* manikin, model, dummy, figure of a person; puppet.

**manivela** *f.* crank.

**manjar** *m.* dish, food; choice bit of food.

**mano** *f.* (*del cuerpo*) hand; forefoot; (*reloj*) clock hand; (*acabado*) coat of paint or varnish; quire (*25 sheets*) of paper; *Am.* adventure, mishap; *Am.* handful; — **de obra** workmanship; labor; **a** — at hand; by hand; *Am.* **estamos a** — we are even, we are quits; *Am.* **doblar las -s** to give up; **ser** — to be first (*in a game*); to lead (*in a game*); **venir a las -s** to come to blows.

**manojo** *m.* handful; bunch.

**manopla** *f.* gauntlet; heavy glove; huge hand.

**manosear** *v.* to handle, touch, feel with the hand; *Am.* to fondle, pet, caress.

**manotada** *f.* slap, blow; sweep of the hand; *Col.* handful, fistful; **manotazo** *m.* slap.

**manotear** *v.* to gesticulate; to strike with the hands; *Ríopl.* to embezzle, steal; *Am.* to snatch away (*what is given*).

**mansalva: a** — without danger or risk; treacherously; **matar a** — to kill without warning or without giving a person a chance to defend himself.

**mansedumbre** *f.* meekness; gentleness.

**mansión** *f.* sojourn, stay; abode, dwelling.

**manso** *adj.* meek; mild, gentle; tame; *Ríopl., Ch.* cultivated (*plant*), civilized (*Indian*); *m.* leading sheep, goat, or ox.

**manta** *f.* blanket; large shawl; tossing in a blanket; *Mex., C.A., Ven., Ríopl.* coarse cotton cloth; *Am.* poncho; *Am.* — **mojada** dull person, dunce; **darle a uno una** — to toss someone in a blanket.

**mantear** *v.* to toss (*someone*) in a blanket.

**manteca** *f.* fat; lard; butter; *Am.* — **de cacao** cocoa butter; *Am.* — **de coco** coconut oil; **mantequera** *f.* churn; butter dish; woman who makes or sells butter.

**mantecado** *m.* ice cream.

**mantel** *m.* tablecloth; altar cloth; *C.A., Mex.* **estar de -es largos** to dine in style.

**mantener**[45] *v. irr.* to maintain; to support; to sustain; to defend; **-se** to continue, remain; to support oneself; **-se firme** to remain firm; **-se quieto** to stay or keep quiet.

**mantenimiento** *m.* maintenance, support; sustenance; livelihood.

**mantequilla** *f.* butter; **mantequillería** *f. Am.* creamery, dairy (*for making butter*).

**mantilla** *f.* mantilla (*Spanish veil or scarf for the head*); saddlecloth.

**manto** *m.* mantle, cloak; cape; large mantilla; mantel, mantelpiece.

**mantón** *m.* large shawl; — **de Manila** embroidered silk shawl.

**manuable** *adj.* handy, easy to handle.

**manual** *adj.* manual; handy; *m.* manual, handbook.

**manubrio** *m.* crank; handle.

**manufacturar** *v.* to manufacture.

**manufacturero** *adj.* manufacturing; *m.* manufacturer.

**manuscrito** *adj.* written by hand; *m.* manuscript.

**manutención** *f.* maintenance; support; conservation.

**manzana** *f.* apple; block of houses; *Ríopl., Ch., Col., Ven., C.A.* Adam's apple; **manzano** *m.* apple tree.

**maña** *f.* skill, knack; cunning; **malas -s** bad tricks or habits.

**mañana** *f.* morning; *Ríopl.* **media** — mid-morning snack; *adv.* tomorrow, in the near future; **pasado** — day after tomorrow; **muy de** — very early in the morning; *m.* morrow; **mañanitas** *f. pl. Mex., C.A.* popular song sung early in the morning to celebrate a birthday, saint's day, etc.

**mañanero** *m.* early riser; *adj.* early rising; **mañanista** *m. & f. Am.* procrastinator, one who puts things off until tomorrow.

**mañero** *adj.* astute, artful, clever; *Am.* tricky; *Ch.* shy (*animal*); *Ríopl.* indolent, lazy (*child*).

**mañoso** *adj.* skillful; clever; sly; tricky; deceitful; *Am.* slow, lazy; *Am.* greedy, gluttonous (*child*).

**mapa** *m.* map, chart.

**mapache** *m. Ch.* raccoon.

**mapurite, mapurito** *m. Col., Ven.* skunk. *See* **zorrino, zorrillo.**

**máquina** *f.* machine; engine; — **de coser** sewing machine; — **de escribir** typewriter.

**maquinación** *f.* machination, scheming, plotting; plot, scheme.

**maquinador** *m.* schemer, plotter.

**maquinal** *adj.* mechanical, automatic; **-mente** *adv.* mechanically, automatically, in a mechanical manner.

**maquinar** *v.* to plot, scheme.

**maquinaria** *f.* machinery; mechanism; mechanics.

**maquinista** *m.* engineer, locomotive engineer; machinist; mechanic.

**mar** *m. & f.* sea; — **alta** rough sea; — **llena** high tide (*see* **pleamar**); — **de fondo** swell; **a -es** abundantly; **baja**

— low tide; **en alta** — on the high seas; **la** — **de cosas** a lot of things.

**maraca** f. *Carib., Col., Ven.* maraca (*rhythm instrument made of a dried gourd filled with seeds or pebbles*).

**maraña** f. tangle; snarl; thicket; maze; plot, intrigue.

**maravedí** m. maravedi (*an old Spanish coin*).

**maravilla** f. wonder, marvel; marigold; **a las mil -s** wonderfully, perfectly.

**maravillar** v. to astonish, dazzle; **-se** to wonder, marvel.

**maravilloso** adj. marvellous, wonderful.

**marbete** m. label, stamp; baggage tag or check.

**marca** f. mark, stamp; sign; brand, make; gauge, rule; march, frontier province; — **de fábrica** trademark; **de** — of excellent quality.

**marcar**[6] v. to mark, stamp, brand; to note, observe.

**marcial** adj. martial, warlike; frank, abrupt.

**marco** m. frame; mark (*German coin*); mark (*unit of weight, equal to 8 ounces*).

**marcha** f. march; course, progress; speed; gait; running, functioning; movement of a watch.

**marchamo** m. customhouse mark; *Am.* tax on each slaughtered animal.

**marchante** m. (*vendedor*) merchant, dealer; (*cliente*) customer, regular client.

**marchar** v. to march, mark step; to walk; to parade; to run (*said of machinery*); **-se** to go away.

**marchitar** v. to wither; **-se** to wither; to fade; to shrivel up.

**marchito** adj. withered; faded; shriveled up.

**marea** f. tide; *Ríopl., Ch.* sea fog.

**mareado** adj. seasick; dizzy.

**marear** v. (*navegar*) to navigate, sail; (*fastidiar*) to annoy, upset (*a person*); to make dizzy; **-se** to get seasick, nauseated; dizzy.

**mareo** m. seasickness; nausea; vexation, annoyance.

**marfil** m. ivory; *Ven.* fine-toothed comb.

**margarita** f. marguerite, daisy; pearl.

**margen** m. & f. margin, border; river bank; **dar** — **a** to give an occasion to.

**maricón** adj. sissy, effeminate; m. sissy.

**marido** m. husband.

**marimba** f. marimba.

**marina** f. (*costa*) seacoast, shore; (*fuerza naval*) fleet; navy; (*arte u oficio*) seascape; seamanship; — **de guerra** navy; — **mercante** merchant marine.

**marinero** m. mariner, seaman, sailor.

**marino** adj. marine; m. mariner, seaman, sailor.

**mariposa** f. butterfly; moth; *Am.* blindman's buff (*a game*).

**mariscal** m. marshal; blacksmith; — **de campo** field marshal.

**marisco** m. shellfish.

**marítimo** adj. maritime, marine.

**marmita** f. kettle, boiler, teakettle.

**mármol** m. marble.

**marmóreo** adj. marble, of marble, like marble.

**maroma** f. rope; *Am.* somersault; *Am.* acrobatic performance; *Col.* sudden change of political views; **andar en la** — to walk the tightrope; **maromero** m. *Carib.* acrobat.

**marqués** m. marquis.

**marquesa** f. marquise; *Ch.* couch.

**marrano** m. pig, hog; filthy person.

**marrazo** m. *Am.* bayonet, dagger.

**marrón** adj. maroon.

**marroquí** adj. from Morocco; pl. **marroquíes.**

**marrullero** adj. sly, wily.

**martes** m. Tuesday; — **de carnestolendas** Shrove Tuesday (*Tuesday before Lent*).

**martillar** v. to hammer, pound.

**martillo** m. hammer.

**martinete** m. pile driver; drop hammer; hammer of a piano.

**mártir** m. & f. martyr.

**martirio** m. martyrdom; torture, torment.

**martirizar**[9] v. to martyr; to torture, torment.

**marzo** m. March.

**mas** conj. but.

**más** adj. more; most; adv. more; most; plus; — **bien** rather; — **de** more than, over; — **que** more than; **no ... — que** only; **a** — **de** in addition to; **a lo** — at the most; **está de** — it is superfluous, unnecessary; *Am.* **no** — only; *Am.* **no quiero** — **nada** (*instead of* **no quiero nada** —) I don't want anything more.

**masa** f. (*volumen*) mass; volume; (*pueblo*) crowd, the masses; (*pasta*) dough, paste; mortar; — **coral** glee club, choral society; **agarrarle a uno con las manos en la** — to catch someone in the act; **masilla** f. putty.

**masaje** m. massage.

**mascada** f. chewing; *Am.* mouthful; *Ríopl.* chew or quid of tobacco; *Am.* reprimand, scolding; *Mex.* silk handkerchief, scarf.

**mascar**[6] v. to chew.

**máscara** f. mask; **-s** masquerade; m. & f. masquerader; **mascarada** f. masquerade.

**masculino** adj. masculine.

**mascullar** v. to mumble; to munch.

**masón** m. mason, freemason; **masonería** f. masonry, freemasonry.

**masticar**[6] v. to chew.

**mástil** m. mast; post.

**mastín** m. mastiff.

**mastuerzo** m. (*flor*) nasturtium; (*tonto*) simpleton, fool.

**mata** f. shrub, plant, bush; grove; clump of trees; *Ven., Col.* thicket; jungle; — **de pelo** head of hair.

**matadero** m. slaughterhouse; hard

work.

**matador** *m.* killer, murderer; bull-fighter who kills the bull.

**matanza** *f.* massacre, butchery; slaughter of livestock; *Mex.* slaughterhouse.

**matar** *v.* to kill; to murder; **-se** to commit suicide; to overwork; **-se con alguien** to fight with somebody.

**matasanos** *m.* quack, quack doctor.

**mate** *m.* checkmate (*winning move in chess*); *Ríopl., Ch.* Paraguayan tea (*used also in Argentina and Uruguay*); *Andes, Col.* teapot (*for* **mate**), any small pot; *Am.* bald head; *adj.* unpolished, dull (*surface*).

**matear** *v.* to plant seeds or shoots; to hunt among the bushes; *Ríopl., Ch.* to drink **mate;** *Am.* to checkmate (*make the winning move in chess*).

**matemáticas** *f. pl.* mathematics.

**matemático** *adj.* mathematical; *m.* mathematician.

**materia** *f.* matter; material; subject; pus; **— prima** (*or* **primera —** ) raw material.

**material** *adj.* material; rude, coarse; *m.* ingredient; material; equipment; *Ven.* **de —** made of adobe.

**maternal** *adj.* maternal.

**maternidad** *f.* maternity, motherhood.

**materno** *adj.* maternal.

**matinal** *adj.* morning, of the morning.

**matiné** *m. Am.* matinée.

**matiz** *m.* tint, shade, color, hue; shading.

**matizar**[9] *v.* to blend (*colors*); to tint; to shade, tone down.

**matón** *m.* bully.

**matorral** *m.* thicket.

**matoso** *adj.* bushy; weedy, full of weeds.

**matrero** *adj.* astute, shrewd; cunning, sly; *m. Col.* trickster, swindler; *Ríopl.* bandit, outlaw, cattle thief.

**matrícula** *f.* register, list; matriculation, registration; certificate of registration.

**matricular** *v.* to matriculate, enroll, register.

**matrimonio** *m.* matrimony, marriage; married couple.

**matriz** *f.* matrix, mold, form; womb; screw nut; *adj.* main, principal, first; **casa —** main office (*of a company*).

**matungo** *m. Ríopl.* nag, old worn-out horse.

**matutino** *adj.* morning, of the morning.

**maullar** *v.* to mew.

**maullido, maúllo** *m.* mew.

**máxima** *f.* maxim, rule; proverb.

**máxime** *adj.* principally, especially.

**máximo** *adj. & m.* maximum.

**maya** *f.* daisy; May queen; *m. & f.* Maya, Mayan Indian; *m.* Mayan language.

**mayo** *m.* May; Maypole; *Am.* Mayo Indian (*from Sonora, Mexico*); *Am.* language of the Mayo Indian.

**mayonesa** *f.* mayonnaise; dish served with mayonnaise.

**mayor** *adj.* greater; larger; older; great-est; largest; oldest; main; major; high (*altar, mass*); *m.* major; chief; **-es** elders; ancestors; **— de edad** of age; **por —** (*or* **al por —**) wholesale; *f.* major premise (*of a syllogism*).

**mayoral** *m.* head shepherd; stagecoach driver; foreman; overseer, boss.

**mayorazgo** *m.* primogeniture (*right of inheritance by the first-born*); first-born son and heir; family estate left to the eldest son.

**mayordomo** *m.* majordomo, steward, butler; manager of an estate.

**mayorear** *v. Am.* to wholesale, sell at wholesale.

**mayoreo** *m. Am.* wholesale.

**mayoría** *f.* majority.

**mayorista** *m. Am.* wholesale dealer.

**maza** *f.* mace (*weapon, staff*); **— química** chemical mace.

**mazmorra** *f.* dungeon.

**mazo** *m.* mallet; sledgehammer; bunch, handful.

**mazorca** *f.* ear of corn; *Ríopl.* tyrannical government; *Am.* cruel torture (*imposed by tyrants*).

**me** *obj. pron.* me; to me; for me; myself.

**mecánico** *adj.* mechanical; *m.* mechanic, machinist, repairman; driver, chauffeur.

**mecanismo** *m.* mechanism.

**mecanografía** *f.* stenography, typewriting.

**mecanógrafo** *m.* stenographer, typist.

**mecate** *m. Mex., C.A., Col., Ven.* rope, cord.

**mecedor** *m.* swing; *adj.* swinging, rocking.

**mecedora** *f.* rocking chair.

**mecer**[10] *v.* to swing, rock, sway; to shake.

**mecha** *f.* wick; lock of hair; fuse; strip of salt pork or bacon (*for larding meat*); *Ven.* tip of a whip; *Am.* scare, fright; *Andes, Col.* fib; *Andes, Col.* jest, joke; *Col.* trifle, worthless thing.

**mechar** *v.* to lard (*meat or fowl*).

**mechero** *m.* (*canutillo*) lamp burner; gas jet; candlestick socket; (*encendedor*) pocket lighter; large wick; *Col.* disheveled hair; *Am.* joker, jester.

**mechón** *m.* large wick; large lock of hair.

**medalla** *f.* medal.

**médano** *m.* dune, sand hill, sand bank; *Ríopl., Carib.* sandy marshland.

**media** *f.* stocking; *Col., Ríopl., Ven.* **— corta** (*or* **— —** ) sock.

**mediación** *f.* mediation.

**mediador** *m.* mediator.

**mediados: a — de** about the middle of.

**medianero** *m.* mediator; go-between; *adj.* mediating; intermediate; **pared medianera** partition wall.

**medianía** *f.* mediocrity; average; middle ground; moderate circumstances; moderation; *Col.* partition wall.

**mediano** *adj.* medium; moderate; middle-sized; average; mediocre.

**medianoche** f. midnight.

**mediante** adj. intervening; **Dios —** God willing; prep. by means of, through, with the help of.

**mediar** v. to mediate, intervene; to intercede; to arrive at, or be in, the middle.

**medible** adj. measurable.

**medicamento** m. medicament, medicine.

**medicastro** m. quack, quack doctor.

**medicina** f. medicine.

**medicinar** v. to doctor, treat, prescribe medicine for; **-se** to take medicine.

**medición** f. measurement; measuring.

**médico** m. doctor, physician; adj. medical.

**medida** f. measure; measurement; gauge, rule; **— para áridos** dry measure; **a — del deseo** according to one's desire; **a — que** as, in proportion as; at the same time as.

**medio** adj. half; middle; intermediate; medium, average; **media noche** midnight; **hacer una cosa a medias** to do something halfway; **ir a medias** to go halves; adv. half, not completely; m. middle; means, way; medium; environment; **-s** means, resources; **meterse de por —** to intervene, meddle in a dispute.

**mediocre** adj. mediocre; **mediocridad** f. mediocrity.

**mediodía** m. midday, noon; south.

**medioeval, medieval** adj. medieval.

**medir**⁵ v. irr. to measure; to scan (verses); Col., Ven., Mex. **— las calles** to walk the streets, be out of a job; **-se** to measure one's words or actions; Mex., C.A., Ven., Col., Ríopl. **-se con otro** to try one's strength or ability against another; to fight with another.

**meditación** f. meditation.

**meditar** v. to meditate; to muse.

**medrar** v. to flourish, thrive; to prosper.

**medroso** adj. timid, faint-hearted; fearful, dreadful.

**médula** f. marrow; pith; **— oblongada** medulla oblongata (the posterior part of the brain tapering off into the spinal cord).

**megáfono** m. megaphone.

**mejicano** adj. Mexican; m. Mexican; the Aztec language; inhabitant of Mexico City. Also **mexicano.**

**mejilla** f. cheek.

**mejor** adj. better; **el —** the best; adv. better; **a lo —** suddenly, unexpectedly; **tanto —** so much the better.

**mejora** f. betterment; improvement.

**mejoramiento** m. improvement.

**mejorar** v. to better, improve; to get better, recover; **-se** to get better, recover.

**mejoría** f. betterment, improvement; superiority.

**melado** adj. honey-colored; m. sugarcane syrup; honey cake.

**melancolía** f. melancholy, gloom.

**melancólico** adj. melancholy, gloomy.

**melaza** f. molasses.

**melena** f. mane.

**melindre** m. (acto) affectation; affected act or gesture; recollect; (comestible) fritter, marzipan (sweetmeat made of almond paste).

**melindroso** adj. affected; too particular, finicky, fussy.

**melocotón** m. peach; **melocotonero** m. peach tree.

**melodía** f. melody; **melodioso** adj. melodious.

**melón** m. melon; cantaloupe; muskmelon; melon vine.

**melosidad** f. sweetness; softness, gentleness.

**meloso** adj. honeyed; soft, sweet; m. Am. honey-voiced person; Am. overaffectionate person.

**mella** f. nick; dent; **hacer —** to make a dent or impression; to cause pain, worry, or suffering.

**mellar** v. to notch; to nick; to dent; to impair, damage.

**mellizo** adj. & m. twin.

**membrete** m. heading; letterhead; memorandum.

**membrillo** m. quince (tree and its fruit).

**membrudo** adj. sinewy, robust, strong, muscular.

**memorable** adj. memorable, notable.

**memorándum** m. memorandum, note; memorandum book, notebook.

**memoria** f. memory; remembrance; reminiscence; memoir, note, account; memorandum; **de —** by heart; **hacer — to** remember, recollect; **— de gallo** poor memory; **-s** regards; memoirs.

**memorial** m. memorandum book; memorial, brief, petition.

**mención** f. mention.

**mencionar** v. to mention.

**mendigar**⁷ v. to beg; to ask alms.

**mendigo** m. beggar.

**mendrugo** m. crumb of bread.

**menear** v. to move, shake, stir; to wiggle; to wag; **-se** to hustle about; to wag; to wiggle.

**meneo** m. shaking; swaying; wagging; wiggle; wiggling.

**menester** m. need; job, occupation; **-es** bodily needs; implements, tools; tasks, chores; **ser —** to be necessary.

**menesteroso** adj. needy, in want.

**mengua** f. diminution, decrease; waning; poverty, want; discredit.

**menguante** adj. waning, diminishing, declining.

**menguar**⁸ v. to diminish, decrease; to wane.

**menjurje** m. stuff, mixture.

**menor** adj. smaller, lesser, younger; smallest, least, youngest; minor; m. & f. **— de edad** minor; m. minor (music); Minorite, Franciscan; f. minor premise (of a syllogism); **por — (al por —)** at retail; in small quantities.

**menoría = minoría.**

**menos** *adv.* less; least; except; *adj.* &
*pron.* less, least; *m.* minus; **— de** (*or*
**— que**) less than; **a lo —** (**al —**, *or*
**por lo —**) at least; **a — que** unless;
**echar de —** to miss, feel or notice
the absence of; **no puede — de hacerlo** he cannot help doing it; **venir
a —** to decline; to become weak or
poor.

**menoscabar** *v.* to diminish, lessen; to
impair, damage; **— la honra de** to
undermine the reputation of.

**menoscabo** *m.* impairment; damage;
diminution, lessening.

**menospreciar** *v.* to despise, scorn; to
underestimate.

**menosprecio** *m.* scorn, contempt; un-
derestimation.

**mensaje** *m.* message.

**mensajero** *m.* messenger.

**menstruo** *m.* menstruation.

**mensual** *adj.* monthly.

**mensualidad** *f.* monthly allowance;
monthly payment.

**mensurable** *adj.* measurable.

**menta** *f.* mint; peppermint; *Ríopl.*
rumor, hearsay; *Ríopl., Andes* **por -s**
by hearsay; *Ríopl.* **persona de —**
famous person.

**mentado** *adj.* famous; *p.p.* mentioned.

**mental** *adj.* mental.

**mentalidad** *f.* mentality.

**mentar**[1] *v. irr.* to mention; to call,
name.

**mente** *f.* mind; intellect.

**mentecato** *adj.* foolish, simple; *m.*
fool.

**mentir**[3] *v. irr.* to lie, tell lies.

**mentira** *f.* lie, falsehood, fib; white
spot on the fingernails.

**mentiroso** *adj.* lying, deceptive, false;
*m.* liar, fibber; **mentirosillo** *m.* little
fibber.

**mentís: dar un —** to give the lie (to).

**mentón** *m.* chin.

**menú** *m.* menu.

**menudear** *v.* to occur frequently; to
repeat over and over; to fall inces-
santly (*as rain, stones, projectiles, etc.*);
to tell in detail; *Am.* to retail, sell at
retail; *Am.* to meet together often.

**menudeo** *m.* retail; **vender al —** to
retail, sell at retail.

**menudo** *adj.* minute, small; insignificant; exact, detailed; **dinero —**
change; **a —** often; **por —** in detail;
retail; *m.* entrails, "innards"; change,
small coins.

**meñique** *adj.* tiny, wee; **dedo —** little
finger.

**meollo** *m.* marrow; pith; kernel; substance; brain; brains.

**meple** *m. Ríopl.* maple.

**merca** *f.* purchase.

**mercachifle** *m.* peddler, vendor;
cheap merchant; cheap fellow.

**mercader** *m.* trader, merchant.

**mercadería** *f.* merchandise; trade.

**mercado** *m.* market; mart.

**mercancía** *f.* merchandise; goods.

**mercantil** *adj.* mercantile, commercial.

**mercar**[6] *v.* to purchase, buy.

**merced** *f.* favor; present, gift; mercy;
**Vuestra Merced** Your Honor; **a —
de** at the mercy of; at the expense of.

**mercería** *f.* notions (*pins, buttons, etc.*);
notions store; *Ríopl., P.R.* drygoods
store.

**mercurio** *m.* mercury; quicksilver.

**merecedor** *adj.* worthy, deserving.

**merecer**[13] *v. irr.* to deserve.

**merecido** *adj.* & *p.p.* deserved; *m.* deserved punishment.

**merecimiento** *m.* merit.

**merendar**[1] *v. irr.* to have an afternoon
snack or refreshment; *Carib., Ven.*
**-se uno a alguien** to fleece or skin
someone (*in a game or business deal*);
to kill someone.

**merendero** *m.* lunchroom.

**meridiano** *adj.* & *m.* meridian.

**meridional** *adj.* southern; *m.* southerner.

**merienda** *f.* light afternoon meal;
afternoon refreshments.

**mérito** *m.* merit; **de —** notable.

**merito** *dim. of* **mero**.

**meritorio** *adj.* meritorious, worthy, deserving; *m.* employee without salary
(*learning trade or profession*).

**merluza** *f.* hake (*species of codfish*);
drunken state.

**merma** *f.* reduction, decrease.

**mermar** *v.* to dwindle; to decrease,
reduce.

**mermelada** *f.* marmalade.

**mero** *adj.* mere, pure; *Mex., C.A.*
exact, real; **la mera verdad** the real
truth; *adv. Mex., C.A.* very, very
same, exactly; *Mex., C.A.* soon;
*Col.* only; *Mex., C.A.* **una mera de
las tres** only one of the three; *Mex.,
C.A.* **ya —** (*or* **merito**) very soon;
*Mex., C.A.* **allí —** (*or* **merito**) right
there; *m.* species of perch; *Ch.*
species of thrush.

**merodear** *v.* to rove in search of
plunder.

**mes** *m.* month.

**mesa** *f.* table; executive board; staircase landing; mesa, plateau; **levantar
la —** to clear the table; **poner la —**
to set the table; *Col., Carib., C.A.,
Mex.* **quitar la —** to clear the table.

**mesada** *f.* monthly salary or allowance.

**mesarse** *v.* to tear (*one's hair or beard*).

**mesero** *m. Mex., C.A., Ven., Col.*
waiter.

**meseta** *f.* plateau; staircase landing.

**mesón** *m.* inn (*usually a large one-story
shelter for men and pack animals*).

**mesonero** *m.* innkeeper.

**mestizo** *adj.* half-breed; hybrid; **perro
—** mongrel dog; *m.* mestizo, half-
breed.

**mesura** *f.* moderation; composure; dignity; politeness.

**mesurado** *adj.* moderate, temperate;
dignified.

**meta** *f.* goal; objective.

**metáfora** *f.* metaphor.

ME

**metal** *m.* metal.
**metálico** *adj.* metallic, metal; *m.* specie, coined money; cash in coin.
**metalurgia** *f.* metallurgy.
**metate** *m. Mex.* flat stone (*used for grinding corn, etc.*).
**metátesis** *f.* metathesis.
**meteorito** *m.* meteorite.
**meteoro** *m.* meteor.
**meteorología** *f.* meteorology; **meteorológico** *adj.* meteorological; **oficina meteorológica** weather bureau.
**meter** *v.* to put (in); to get (in); to insert; to smuggle; to make (*noise, trouble, etc.*); to cause (*fear*); *Carib.* to strike (*a blow*); *Ríopl., Carib.* **-le** to hurry up; **-se** to meddle, interfere; to plunge (into); **-se monja** (*Am.* **-se de monja**) to become a nun; also **-se a monja**; **-se con** to pick a quarrel with.
**metódico** *adj.* methodical.
**método** *m.* method.
**métrico** *adj.* metric.
**metro** *m.* meter; subway.
**metrópoli** *f.* metropolis.
**metropolitano** *adj.* metropolitan; *m.* archbishop.
**mexicano = mejicano** (*pronounced identically*).
**mezcal** *m. Mex.* mescal (*a species of* **maguey** *and an alcoholic beverage made from it*).
**mezcla** *f.* mixture; mortar; mixed cloth; **mezclilla** *f.* mixed cloth (*generally black and white*); tweed.
**mezclar** *v.* to mix, blend; **-se** to mix, mingle; to meddle.
**mezcolanza** *f.* jumble, mess, mixture.
**mezquindad** *f.* meanness; stinginess; dire poverty.
**mezquino** *adj.* poor, needy; mean, stingy; meager; small, tiny; *m. Col., Mex.* wart (*usually on a finger*).
**mi** *adj.* my.
**mí** *pers. pron.* (*used after prep.*) me, myself.
**miaja = migaja.**
**miau** *m.* mew.
**mico** *m.* long-tailed monkey; *C.A.* jack (*for lifting heavy objects*).
**microbio** *m.* microbe.
**micrófono** *m.* microphone.
**microscopio** *m.* microscope; **— electrónico** electron microscope; **microscópico** *adj.* microscopic.
**miedo** *m.* fear; dread; **tener —** to be afraid.
**miedoso** *adj.* afraid, fearful, timid.
**miel** *m.* honey; molasses.
**miembro** *m.* member; limb.
**mientes** *f. pl.* thought, mind; **parar — en** to consider, reflect on; **traer a las — to recall; venírsele a uno a las —** to occur to one, come to one's mind.
**mientras** *conj.* while; **— que** while; **— tanto** in the meantime, meanwhile; **— más . . . — menos . . .** the more . . . the less . . .
**miércoles** *m.* Wednesday.
**mies** *f.* ripe grain; harvest; **-es** fields of grain.

**miga** *f.* crumb; soft part of bread; substance; **-s** crumbs; fried crumbs of bread; **hacer buenas -s** (*or* **malas -s**) **con** to get along well (*or* badly) with.
**migaja** *f.* crumb; bit, fragment, small particle.
**migración** *f.* migration.
**milagro** *m.* miracle; wonder.
**milagroso** *adj.* miraculous.
**milicia** *f.* militia; military science; military profession.
**militar** *adj.* military; *m.* soldier, military man; *v.* to serve in the army; to militate, fight (against).
**milpa** *f. Mex., C.A.* cornfield.
**milla** *f.* mile.
**millar** *m.* thousand; **-es** thousands, a great number.
**millón** *m.* million; **millonario** *adj.* & *m.* millionaire; **millonésimo** *adj.* & *m.* millionth.
**mimar** *v.* to pamper, spoil, humor; to pet.
**mimbre** *m.* wicker; **mimbrera** *f.* willow.
**mímico** *adj.* mimic.
**mimo** *m.* pampering; caress; coaxing.
**mimoso** *adj.* tender, sensitive; delicate; finicky, fussy.
**mina** *f.* mine; source; fortune.
**minar** *v.* to mine; to undermine; to sow with explosive mines.
**mineral** *m.* mineral; mine; ore; wealth, fortune; *adj.* mineral.
**minería** *f.* mining; miners.
**minero** *m.* miner; wealth, fortune; source; *adj.* mining; **compañía minera** mining company.
**miniatura** *f.* miniature.
**mínimo** *adj.* least, smallest; *m.* minimum.
**minino** *m.* kitten, kitty, pussy.
**ministerio** *m.* ministry; administration, ministering; portfolio (*office of a cabinet member*); minister's office.
**ministrar** *v.* to minister; to give (*money, aid, etc.*).
**ministro** *m.* minister; cabinet member; office of justice.
**minoría** *f.* minority.
**minoridad** *f.* minority (*in age*).
**minucioso** *adj.* minute, detailed; scrupulous.
**minúsculo** *adj.* small; **letra minúscula** small letter.
**minuta** *f.* minutes; memorandum; first draft (*of a contract, deed, etc.*); memorandum list; lawyer's bill; *Am.* **a la —** breaded and fried (*said of meat or fish*).
**minuto** *m.* minute; **minutero** *m.* minute hand.
**mío** *poss. adj.* my, of mine; *poss. pron.* mine; *Ríopl., Ch.* **detrás —** behind me.
**miope** *adj.* shortsighted, nearsighted; *m. & f.* nearsighted person.
**mira** *f.* (*de puntería*) gun sight; guiding point; (*intención*) intention, design; outlook; **estar a la — de** to be on

the lookout for; to be on the alert for; **poner la — en** to fix one's eyes on; to aim at.

**mirada** *f.* glance, gaze, look.

**mirador** *m.* mirador, enclosed balcony (*commanding an extensive view*); watchtower; lookout site; onlooker, spectator; *Ríopl.* penthouse (*small house built on a roof for recreation*).

**miramiento** *m.* consideration, respect, regard; reverence; circumspection, prudence.

**mirar** *v.* to look; to glance; to behold; to see; **— por alguien** to take care of someone; **¡mira (tú)!** look!

**miríada** *f.* myriad, multitude, great number.

**mirlo** *m.* blackbird.

**mirón** *m.* bystander, onlooker, spectator; *adj.* curious.

**mirto** *m.* myrtle.

**misa** *f.* mass; **— del gallo** midnight mass.

**misceláneo** *adj.* miscellaneous.

**miserable** *adj.* miserable, unhappy; forlorn; miserly, stingy; mean.

**miseria** *f.* misery; poverty; stinginess; bit, trifle.

**misericordia** *f.* mercy, compassion, pity.

**misericordioso** *adj.* merciful, compassionate.

**mísero** *adj.* miserable, unhappy; forlorn; stingy.

**misión** *f.* mission.

**misionero** *m.* missionary.

**mismo** *adj.* same; self, very; **ahora —** right away.

**misterio** *m.* mystery; secret.

**misterioso** *adj.* mysterious.

**místico** *adj.* mystical, mystic; *m.* mystic.

**mitad** *f.* half; middle.

**mitigar**[7] *v.* to mitigate, soften, soothe.

**mitin** *m.* meeting.

**mito** *m.* myth; **mitología** *f.* mythology.

**mitra** *f.* bishop's miter.

**mixto** *adj.* mixed; half-breed; *m.* composite; match; explosive compound.

**mobiliario** *m.* furniture.

**moblaje** = **mueblaje**.

**mocedad** *f.* youth; youthfulness; youthful prank.

**mocetón** *m.* tall, robust lad.

**moción** *f.* motion.

**mocoso** *adj.* sniffling; *m.* brat, scamp; sniffling boy.

**mochar** *v. Am.* to cut off, chop off, cut, trim (*see* **desmochar**); *Am.* to snitch, pilfer; *Col.* to depose, dismiss, put out of a job.

**mochila** *f.* knapsack; soldier's kit.

**mocho** *adj.* cut off; cropped, shorn; *Am.* maimed, mutilated; *Mex.* reactionary, conservative; *m.* butt of a firearm; *Col., Ven.* nag; *Carib.* cigar butt.

**moda** *f.* mode, custom, style, fashion; **de —** fashionable.

**modelar** *v.* to model.

**modelo** *m.* model, copy, pattern; *m.* & *f.* life model.

**moderación** *f.* moderation.

**moderado** *adj.* moderate; conservative.

**moderar** *v.* to moderate, temper; to regulate; to restrain.

**moderno** *adj.* modern.

**modestia** *f.* modesty.

**modesto** *adj.* modest.

**módico** *adj.* moderate, reasonable (*price*).

**modificación** *f.* modification.

**modificar**[6] *v.* to modify.

**modismo** *m.* idiom.

**modista** *f.* dressmaker; milliner.

**modo** *m.* mode, manner, way; mood (*grammar*); **a** (*or* **al**) **— de** like, in the manner of; **de — que** so that; and so; **de todos -s** at any rate, anyway.

**modorra** *f.* drowsiness; gid (*a disease of sheep*).

**modular** *v.* to modulate, tone down.

**mofa** *f.* scoff, jeer, taunt; mockery.

**mofar** *v.* to mock, scoff, jeer; **-se de** to make fun of, scoff at.

**moflete** *m.* fat cheek; **mofletudo** *adj.* fat-cheeked.

**mohín** *m.* grimace; wry face.

**mohino** *adj.* moody, discontented, sad, melancholy; black (*referring to a horse, cow, or bull*).

**moho** *m.* rust; mold.

**mohoso** *adj.* musty, moldy; rusty.

**mojada** *f.* drench, drenching, wetting.

**mojado** *adj.* wet, damp, moist; *p.p. of* **mojar**.

**mojadura** *f.* wetting, dampening, drenching.

**mojar** *v.* to dampen, wet, moisten; *Ríopl., Ch.* to accompany (*a song*); *Am.* to bribe; *Ríopl., Carib., Mex.* to celebrate by drinking; *Am.* **mojársele a uno los papeles** to get things mixed up.

**mojicón** *m.* punch, blow; muffin, bun.

**mojigatería** *f.* prudery; false humility; affected piety.

**mojigato** *adj.* prudish; affectedly pious, overzealous (*in matters of religion*); hypocritical; *m.* prude; hypocrite.

**mojón** *m.* landmark; milestone; heap, pile.

**molde** *m.* mold, cast; form; pattern, model; **venir de —** to come pat, be to the point; **letras de —** printed letters; print.

**moldear** *v.* to mold; to cast; to decorate with moldings.

**moldura** *f.* molding.

**mole** *f.* mass, bulk; *adj.* soft, mild; *m. Mex.* **— de guajolote** a Mexican dish of turkey served with a chili gravy.

**molécula** *f.* molecule.

**moler**[2] *v. irr.* to mill; to grind; to tire, fatigue; to wear out, destroy; to bother; **— a palos** to give a thorough beating.

**molestar** *v.* to molest, disturb; to bother, annoy.

**molestia** *f.* bother, annoyance; discomfort.

**molesto** *adj.* bothersome, annoying; uncomfortable.

**molicie** *f.* softness; fondness for luxury.

**molienda** *f.* grind, grinding, milling; portion to be, or that has been, ground; grinding season (*for sugar cane or olives*); fatigue, weariness; bother.

**molinero** *m.* miller.

**molinete** *m.* small mill; ventilating fan; pin wheel; twirl, whirl, flourish.

**molinillo** *m.* small mill or grinder; chocolate beater; restless person.

**molino** *m.* mill; restless person; **— de viento** windmill.

**mollera** *f.* crown of the head; judgment, good sense; **ser duro de —** to be stubborn; **no tener sal en la —** to be dull, stupid.

**momentáneo** *adj.* momentary; sudden, quick.

**momento** *m.* moment; importance; momentum; **al —** immediately, without delay; **a cada —** continually; frequently.

**mona** *f.* female monkey; mimic; drunkenness; **dormir la —** to sleep it off; **pillar una —** to get drunk.

**monada** *f.* (*típico de mono*) monkeyshine; monkey face; (*cosa graciosa*) cute little thing; cute gesture; nonsense; flattery.

**monarca** *m.* monarch.

**monarquía** *f.* monarchy.

**monasterio** *m.* monastery.

**mondadientes** *m.* toothpick.

**mondar** *v.* to pare; to peel; to prune; to clean out; *Am.* to beat, thrash; *Am.* to beat, defeat; **-se los dientes** to pick one's teeth.

**moneda** *f.* coin; money; **— corriente** currency; **— menuda** (*or* **suelta**) change, small coins; **casa de —** mint.

**monería** *f.* monkeyshine, antic; trifle, trinket; cute little thing.

**monetario** *adj.* monetary, pertaining to money; financial.

**monigote** *m.* puppet, ridiculous figure; dunce.

**monitorear** *v.* to monitor (*a radio or TV program*).

**monja** *f.* nun.

**monje** *m.* monk.

**mono** *m.* monkey; silly fool; mimic; coveralls; *Ch.* pile of fruit or vegetables (*in a market*); **-s** *Ch.* worthless household utensils and furniture; *Am.* **meterle a uno los -s en el cuerpo** to frighten, terrify someone; *adj.* pretty, neat, cute; *Am.* sorrel, reddishbrown; *Col.* blond.

**monologar**[7] *v.* to soliloquize, talk to oneself; to recite monologues; to monopolize the conversation.

**monólogo** *m.* monologue.

**monopolio** *m.* monopoly.

**monopolizar**[9] *v.* to monopolize; to corner (*a market*).

**monosílabo** *adj.* monosyllabic, of one syllable; *m.* monosyllable.

**monotonía** *f.* monotony; **monótono** *adj.* monotonous,

**monserga** *f.* gabble.

**monstruo** *m.* monster.

**monstruosidad** *f.* monstrosity; monster, freak.

**monstruoso** *adj.* monstrous.

**monta** *f.* amount, sum; value, importance; **de poca —** of little value or importance.

**montaje** *m.* assembly, assembling (*of machinery*); mount, support for a cannon.

**montante** *m.* broadsword; transom; upright; post; *Carib., Ven.* sum, amount, cost; *f.* high tide.

**montaña** *f.* mountain; **— rusa** roller coaster.

**montañés** *adj.* mountain (*used as adj.*) of, from or pertaining to the mountains; *m.* mountaineer; native of the province of Santander, Spain.

**montañoso** *adj.* mountainous.

**montar** *v.* to mount; to ride horseback; to amount (to); to set (*jewels*); to cock (*a gun*); to assemble, set up (*machinery*); *Carib., C.A.* to organize, establish.

**montaraz** *adj.* wild, primitive, uncivilized; *m.* forester.

**monte** *m.* mount, mountain; forest; thicket; monte (*a card game*); *C.A., Mex.* grass, pasture; *Am.* country, outskirts; **montecillo** *m.* mound, small hill; **montepío** *m.* pawnshop.

**montera** *f.* cap; *Andes* Bolivian coneshaped hat (*worn by Indians*).

**montés** *adj.* wild, mountain (*used as adj.*); **cabra —** mountain goat; **gato —** wildcat.

**montículo** *m.* mound.

**montón** *m.* pile, heap; mass, great number; **a -es** in abundance, in heaps, by heaps.

**montonera** *f.* *Col., Ven., Ríopl.* band of mounted rebels or guerrilla fighters; *Col.* pile of wheat, hay, straw, etc.; *Am.* pile, heap (*of anything*).

**montuoso** *adj.* hilly; mountainous.

**montura** *f.* mount, horse; saddle and trappings.

**monumento** *m.* monument; **monumental** *adj.* monumental.

**moño** *m.* knot or roll of hair; bow of ribbon; crest, tuft of feathers; *Mex.* forelock (*lock of hair on the fore part of the head*); *Am.* crest, peak (*of anything*); *Col.* whim; *Am.* a Colombian popular dance; **-s** frippery, gaudy ornaments; *Col.* **estar con el — torcido** to be in an ugly humor.

**mora** *f.* blackberry; mulberry; brambleberry; *Ch.* blood pudding, sausage.

**morada** *f.* dwelling, residence; stay.

**morado** *adj.* purple.

**morador** *m.* dweller, resident.

**moral** *adj.* moral; *f.* ethics, moral philosophy; morale; *m.* mulberry tree; blackberry bush.

**moraleja** *f.* moral, lesson, maxim.

**moralidad** *f.* morality.

**moralista** *m.* & *f.* moralist.

**morar** *v.* to live, dwell, reside.

**morbidez** *f.* softness; mellowness.

**mórbido** *adj.* morbid; soft.

**morboso** *adj.* morbid, unhealthy, diseased.

**morcilla** *f.* blood pudding, blood sausage; gag (*an amusing remark by a comedian*).

**mordacidad** *f.* sharpness (*of tongue*).

**mordaz** *adj.* biting, cutting, sarcastic.

**mordaza** *f.* gag (*for the mouth*).

**mordedor** *adj.* biting; snappy; *m.* biter; slanderer.

**mordedura** *f.* bite; sting.

**mordelón** *adj. Col., Ven.* biting, snappy; *m. Am.* biter; *Mex.* public official who accepts a bribe.

**morder**[2] *v. irr.* to bite; to nip; to gnaw; to corrode; to backbite, slander; *Ven.* to swindle; *Mex., C.A.* to "shake down", exact a bribe.

**mordida** *f. Am.* bite; *Mex., C.A., Carib., Ven.* graft, money obtained by graft.

**mordiscar**[6], **mordisquear** *v.* to nibble; to gnaw.

**mordisco** *m.* bite; nibble.

**moreno** *adj.* brown; dark, brunette; *m. Ríopl., Carib., Mex., Ven., Andes* colored person.

**moretón** *m.* bruise, black-and-blue mark.

**morfema** *m.* morpheme.

**morfina** *f.* morphine; **morfinómano** *m.* morphine addict, drug fiend.

**moribundo** *adj.* dying.

**morir**[4,52] *v. irr.* to die; **-se** to die; to die out, be extinguished.

**morisco** *adj.* Moorish; Moresque, in the Moorish style; *m.* Morisco (*Christianized Moor*); language of the Moriscos.

**moro** *adj.* Moorish; *Mex., Ven., Ríopl., Cuba* dappled, spotted (*horse*); *Col., Ch., Andes* unbaptized; *m.* Moor; *Am.* frosted cookie.

**morocho** *adj. Am* robust, strong; *Ríopl.* of dark complexion; *Ch.* rough, tough; *Andes* of low social condition.

**morral** *m.* nose bag; knapsack; hunter's bag.

**morriña** *f.* melancholy, blues, sadness.

**morsa** *f.* walrus.

**mortaja** *f.* shroud; *Am.* cigarette paper.

**mortal** *adj.* mortal; fatal; deadly; *m.* mortal; **mortalidad** *f.* mortality; death rate.

**mortandad** *f.* mortality, death rate; massacre, slaughter.

**mortecino** *adj.* deathly pale; dying; **hacer la mortecina** to pretend to be dead.

**morterete** *m.* small mortar, small cannon.

**mortero** *m.* mortar (*for grinding*).

**mortífero** *adj.* deadly, fatal.

**mortificar**[6] *v.* to mortify; to torment; to vex, annoy; **-se** to do penance; to be grieved; *Mex., C.A., Ven.* to be embarrassed.

**mortuorio** *adj.* funeral; funereal, mournful; *m.* funeral, burial.

**mosaico** *adj.* & *m.* mosaic.

**mosca** *f.* fly; bore; bother; *Am.* sponger, parasite; *Mex., C.A., Ven.* bull's-eye, center of a target; **moscón** *m.* large fly; *Am.* **ir de moscón** to go along as a chaperone.

**mosquear** *v.* to brush off or drive away flies; to whip, beat; *Ríopl.* to rage, be furious; **-se** to show pique or resentment; *Ch.* to go away.

**mosquito** *m.* mosquito; gnat; *Am.* Mosquito Indian of Nicaragua; **mosquitero** *m.* mosquito net.

**mostacho** *m.* mustache.

**mostaza** *f.* mustard; mustard seed; bird shot.

**mostrador** *m.* demonstrator; store counter; clock dial.

**mostrar**[2] *v. irr.* to show; to demonstrate; to exhibit.

**mostrenco** *adj.* (*sin dueño*) ownerless; homeless; stray (*animal*); (*torpe*) slow, dull; fat, heavy; *m.* dunce; *C.A.* worthless animal.

**mota** *f.* mote, speck; knot in cloth; slight defect; mound, knoll; *Col., Ven., Carib.* powder puff; *Am.* tuft.

**mote** *m.* motto; slogan; nickname; *Andes, Ch., Col.* stewed corn; *Andes* grammatical error (*made by illiterate people and children*); *Am.* **— pelado** hominy.

**motear** *v.* to speck, speckle; to spot; *Am.* to mispronounce, enunciate badly.

**motejar** *v.* to jeer at; to call bad names; to insult; to censure; **— de** to brand as.

**motín** *m.* mutiny; riot.

**motivar** *v.* to cause; to give a cause for.

**motivo** *m.* motive, reason; motif, theme; *m.* **con — de** because of; on the occasion of; *adj.* motive.

**motocicleta** *f.* motorcycle; **motociclista** *m.* & *f.* motorcyclist, motorcycle rider.

**motor** *m.* motor; **— de reacción** jet engine; *adj.* motor, causing motion.

**motorista** *m.* & *f.* motorist; motorman, motorwoman.

**motriz** *adj.* motive, impelling, driving; **fuerza —** power, driving force.

**movedizo** *adj.* movable; shaky; shifting; **arena movediza** quicksand.

**mover**[2] *v. irr.* (*físicamente*) to move; (*persuadir*) to persuade; to stir, excite; to touch, affect; **-se** to move.

**movible** *adj.* movable; mobile; fickle.

**móvil** *m.* motive, inducement, incentive; *adj.* mobile, movable; unstable.

**movilización** *f.* mobilization.

**movilizar**[9] *v.* to mobilize.

**movimiento** *m.* movement; motion; commotion, disturbance.

**moza** *f.* maid; girl; last hand of a game; *Ch.* last song or dance of a fiesta.

**mozalbete** *m.* youth, lad.

**mozárabe** *adj.* Mozarabic (*Christian in*

*Moslem Spain*).

**mozo** *adj.* young; unmarried; *m.* youth; manservant; waiter; porter; errand boy; **buen —** handsome man.

**mozuela** *f.* lass, young girl.

**mozuelo** *m.* lad, young boy.

**mucama** *f. Andes, Ríopl.* servant girl; **mucamo** *m. Andes, Ríopl.* servant.

**mucoso** *adj.* mucous; slimy; **membrana mucosa** mucous membrane.

**muchacha** *f.* child; girl; servant, maid.

**muchacho** *m.* child; boy, lad.

**muchedumbre** *f.* multitude; crowd.

**mucho** *adj.* much, a lot of; long (*referring to time*); **-s** many; *adv.* much; a great deal; **ni con —** not by far, not by a long shot; **ni — menos** not by any means, nor anything like it; **por — que** no matter how much; **no es — que** it is no wonder that.

**muda** *f.* change; change of clothes; molt (*act or time of shedding feathers*); *Ríopl.* relay of draft animals.

**mudable** *adj.* changeable; fickle.

**mudanza** *f.* change; removal; inconstancy.

**mudar** *v.* to change; to remove; to molt; **— de casa** to move; **— de traje** to change one's suit or costume; **-se** to change one's clothes; to change one's habits; to move, change one's abode.

**mudez** *f.* muteness, dumbness.

**mudo** *adj.* mute, dumb; silent; *m.* dumb person.

**mueblaje** *m.* furniture.

**mueble** *m.* piece of furniture; **-s** furniture, household goods; *adj.* movable; **bienes -s** chattels, movable possessions.

**mueca** *f.* grimace; wry face.

**muela** *f.* (*diente*) molar tooth; (*piedra*) millstone; grindstone; **— cordal** (*or* **— del juicio**) wisdom tooth.

**muelle** *adj.* soft; voluptuous; *m.* spring; wharf; loading platform; **— real** main spring of a watch.

**muerte** *f.* death.

**muerto** *p.p. of* **morir** *& adj.* dead; withered; faded; **naturaleza muerta** still life; *m.* corpse.

**muesca** *f.* notch; groove.

**muestra** *f.* sample; pattern, model; shop sign; sign, indication; presence, bearing; face, dial (*of a clock or watch*); **muestrario** *m.* book or collection of samples.

**mugido** *m.* moo; mooing, lowing of cattle.

**mugir**[11] *v.* to moo, low.

**mugre** *f.* dirt, grime.

**mugriento** *adj.* grimy, dirty.

**mujer** *f.* woman; wife.

**mujeril** *adj.* womanly, feminine; womanish, like a woman.

**mula** *f.* mule; *Am.* cushion for carrying loads; *Am.* worthless merchandise; *Ríopl.* cruel, treacherous person; *Am.* **echar a uno la —** to give someone the dickens, scold someone.

**muladar** *m.* rubbish pile or dump;

dunghill, pile of manure.

**mulato** *adj. & m.* mulatto.

**muleta** *f.* crutch; red cloth draped over a rod (*used by bullfighters*).

**muletilla** *f.* cane with a crutchlike handle; red cloth draped over a rod (*used by bullfighters*); cliché (*hackneyed or trite phrase*); refrain; repetitious word or phrase; braid frog (*fastener for a coat*).

**mulo** *m.* mule.

**multa** *f.* fine.

**multicolor** *adj.* many-colored, motley.

**múltiple** *adj.* multiple.

**multiplicación** *f.* multiplication.

**multiplicar**[6] *v.* to multiply.

**multiplicidad** *f.* multiplicity, manifold variety.

**múltiplo** *m.* multiple number.

**multitud** *f.* multitude; crowd.

**mullido** *adj.* soft; fluffy; *m.* stuffing for mattresses or pillows; soft cushion or mattress.

**mullir**[20] *v.* to fluff; to soften.

**mundanal** *adj.* worldly.

**mundano** *adj.* mundane, worldly.

**mundial** *adj.* universal; **la guerra —** the World War.

**mundo** *m.* world; trunk; **todo el —** everybody.

**munición** *f.* ammunition; buckshot; **-es de guerra** war supplies.

**municipal** *adj.* municipal; **municipalidad** *f.* municipality; town hall; city government.

**municipio** *m.* municipality.

**muñeca** *f.* doll; wrist; manikin (*figure for displaying clothes*); **muñeco** *m.* boy doll; dummy, puppet.

**muñón** *m.* stump (*of an arm or leg*).

**muralla** *f.* surrounding wall; rampart.

**murciano** *adj.* of or from Murcia, Spain; *m.* native of Murcia.

**murciélago** *m.* bat.

**murga** *f.* brass band.

**murmullo** *m.* murmur, rumor; whisper; muttering.

**murmuración** *f.* slander, gossip; grumbling.

**murmurar** *v.* to murmur; to slander, gossip; to whisper; to grumble.

**muro** *m.* wall.

**murria** *f.* sulkiness, sullenness, melancholy, blues; **tener —** to be sulky; to have the blues.

**musa** *f.* Muse; muse, poetic inspiration; poetry; **-s** fine arts.

**muscular** *adj.* muscular.

**musculatura** *f.* muscles; muscular system.

**músculo** *m.* muscle.

**musculoso** *adj.* muscular; sinewy.

**muselina** *f.* muslin.

**museo** *m.* museum.

**musgo** *m.* moss.

**musgoso** *adj.* mossy.

**música** *f.* music.

**musical** *adj.* musical.

**músico** *adj.* musical; *m.* musician.

**musitar** *v.* to mutter, mumble; to whisper.

**muslo** *m.* thigh.
**mustio** *adj.* sad; withered; humble.
**mutilar** *v.* to mutilate; to butcher; to mar.
**mutismo** *m.* muteness, silence.
**mutuo** *adj.* mutual; reciprocal.
**muy** *adv.* very; greatly; most.

# N

**nabo** *m.* turnip.
**nácar** *m.* mother-of-pearl; pearl color.
**nacarado** *adj.* pearly.
**nacer**[13] *v. irr.* (*salir del vientre*) to be born; (*brotar*) to spring, originate; to bud; to sprout, grow (*said of plants*); **— de pie** (*or* **— de pies**) to be born lucky.
**naciente** *adj.* rising (*sun*); *m.* orient, east.
**nacimiento** *m.* birth; origin; beginning; descent; source; crèche (*representation of the Nativity*).
**nación** *f.* nation.
**nacional** *adj.* national; *m.* national, citizen.
**nacionalidad** *f.* nationality.
**nada** *f.* nothingness; *indef. pron.* nothing, not . . . anything; *adv.* not at all; **de —** you are welcome, don't mention it (*as a reply to* «**gracias**»); *Am.* **a cada —** constantly; **una nadita** a trifle, just a little.
**nadada** *f.* swim.
**nadador** *m.* swimmer; *Ven.* fish-net float.
**nadar** *v.* to swim; to float.
**nadería** *f.* a mere nothing, trifle, worthless thing.
**nadie** *indef. pron.* nobody, no one, not . . . anyone.
**nafta** *f.* naphtha.
**naguas** = **enaguas.**
**náhuatl** *adj.* the language of the Aztec Indians.
**naipe** *m.* playing card.
**nalgas** *f. pl.* buttocks; rump; **nalgada** *f.* spank; **-s** spanking.
**nana** *f.* grandma; lullaby; *Mex.*, *Ríopl.*, *Ven.* child's nurse; *Spain* nice old lady.
**naranja** *f.* orange; **— tangerina** tangerine; **naranjada** *f.* orangeade; orange juice; orange marmalade; **naranjal** *m.* orange grove; **naranjo** *m.* orange tree.
**narciso** *m.* narcissus; daffodil; fop, dandy.
**narcótico** *adj. & m.* narcotic.
**narcotizar**[9] *v.* to dope, drug with narcotics.
**nariz** *f.* nose; nostril; **narices** nostrils.
**narración** *f.* narration, account, story.
**narrar** *v.* to narrate, tell, relate.
**narrativo** *adj.* narrative; **narrativa** *f.* narrative.
**nata** *f.* cream; best part; scum; **-s** whipped cream with sugar; custard; **natoso** *adj.* creamy.
**natación** *f.* swimming.
**natal** *adj.* natal; native; **natalicio** *m.* birthday; **natalidad** *f.* birth rate.

**natillas** *f. pl.* custard.
**nativo** *adj.* native.
**natural** *adj.* natural; native; simple, unaffected; *m. & f.* native; *m.* nature, disposition; **al —** without affectation; **del —** from nature, from life.
**naturaleza** *f.* nature; disposition; nationality; naturalization; **— muerta** still life.
**naturalidad** *f.* naturalness; simplicity; birthright.
**naturalista** *adj.* naturalistic; *m. & f.* naturalist.
**naturalización** *f.* naturalization.
**naturalizar**[9] *v.* to naturalize; to acclimatize, accustom to a new climate; **-se** to become naturalized.
**naufragar**[7] *v.* to be shipwrecked; to fail.
**naufragio** *m.* shipwreck; failure, ruin.
**náufrago** *m.* shipwrecked person.
**náusea** *f.* nausea; **dar -s** to nauseate, sicken; to disgust; **tener -s** to be nauseated, be sick to one's stomach.
**nauseabundo** *adj.* nauseating, sickening.
**nauseado** *adj.* nauseated, sick to one's stomach.
**náutica** *f.* navigation (*science of navigation*).
**navaja** *f.* jackknife, pocketknife; penknife; razor.
**navajazo** *m.* stab with a jackknife or razor; stab wound.
**naval** *adj.* naval.
**navarro** *adj.* Navarrese, of or pertaining to Navarre, Spain; *m.* Navarrese.
**nave** *f.* ship, boat; nave; **— cósmica** spaceship; **— cósmica pilotada** manned space vehicle.
**navegable** *adj.* navigable.
**navegación** *f.* navigation; sea voyage; **— aérea** aviation.
**navegador navegante** *m.* navigator; *adj.* navigating.
**navegar**[7] *v.* to navigate; to sail.
**navidad** *f.* Nativity; Christmas; **-es** Christmas season.
**navío** *m.* vessel, ship; **— de guerra** warship.
**neblina** *f.* fog, mist.
**necedad** *f.* foolishness, nonsense.
**necesario** *adj.* necessary.
**neceser** *m.* toilet case; sewing kit.
**necesidad** *f.* necessity, need, want.
**necesitado** *adj.* needy; in need, destitute, poor; *p.p. of* **necesitar;** *m.* needy person.
**necesitar** *v.* to need; to necessitate.
**necio** *adj.* stupid, ignorant; foolish; stubborn; *Col.* touchy.
**nefando** *adj.* abominable; wicked.
**negación** *f.* negation, denial; negative (*negative particle*).
**negar**[1,7] *v. irr.* to deny; to refuse; to prohibit; to disown; **-se** to refuse, decline.
**negativa** *f.* negative; denial, refusal.
**negativo** *adj.* negative.
**negligencia** *f.* negligence, neglect, carelessness.
**negligente**[7] *adj.* negligent, neglectful,

MO

careless.

**negociación** *f.* negotiation; business; business house; management; transaction, deal.

**negociante** *m.* merchant, trader, dealer; businessman; *adj.* negotiating.

**negociar** *v.* to negotiate; to trade; to transact.

**negocio** *m.* business; business deal; negotiation, transaction; *Ríopl., Carib., C.A., Ven., Andes* store; **hombre de -s** businessman.

**negrear** *v.* to become black; to appear black, look black (*in the distance*).

**negro** *adj.* black; dark; sad, gloomy; unfortunate; *m.* black color; negro; *Ríopl., C.A., Ven., Col.* dear, darling; **negra** *f.* negress; *Ríopl., C.A., Ven., Col.* dear, darling.

**negrura** *f.* blackness.

**negruzco** *adj.* blackish.

**nena** *f.* baby girl; **nene** *m.* baby boy.

**nepotismo** *m.* nepotism.

**nervio** *m.* nerve.

**nervioso, nervoso** *adj.* nervous; sinewy, strong.

**nerviosidad, nervosidad** *f.* nervousness; flexibility; vigor.

**nervudo** *adj.* sinewy, tough, powerful.

**neto** *adj.* clear, pure; net (*profit, price, etc.*); **netamente** *adv.* clearly, distinctly.

**neumático** *m.* tire; *adj.* pneumatic.

**neutralidad** *f.* neutrality.

**neutralizar**[9] *v.* to neutralize, counteract.

**neutro** *adj.* neutral; neuter; sexless.

**nevada** *f.* snowfall.

**nevado** *adj.* snowy, white as snow; covered with snow.

**nevar**[1] *v. irr.* to snow.

**nevasca** *f.* snowstorm.

**nevera** *f.* icebox; refrigerator; ice storehouse; ice or ice-cream vendor (*woman*).

**ni** *conj. & adv.* nor; not even; neither; **— siquiera** not even.

**nicho** *m.* niche; recess, hollow in a wall.

**nidada** *f.* nestful of eggs; brood of chicks; hatch, brood.

**nido** *m.* nest; abode; *Am.* **patearle el — a alguien** to "upset the applecart", upset someone's plans.

**niebla** *f.* fog, mist; confusion.

**nieto** *m.* grandson, grandchild; **nieta** *f.* granddaughter.

**nieve** *f.* snow; *Mex., Ríopl., Ven.* sherbet, ice cream; **tiempo de -s** snowy season.

**nimio** *adj.* miserly, stingy; *Am.* very small, insignificant.

**ninfa** *f.* nymph.

**ningun(o)** *indef. adj. & pron.* no one, none, not . . . any; nobody.

**niña** *f.* girl; baby girl; *Andes, Ríopl., Mex., Carib.* lady, mistress (*title of respect and endearment given to adults*); **— del ojo** pupil of the eye.

**niñada** *f.* childishness, childish act or remark.

**niñera** *f.* child's nurse.

**niñería** *f.* childish act; child's play; trifle; foolishness.

**niñez** *f.* infancy; childhood.

**niño** *m.* child, boy; infant; *Am.* master (*title of respect given to a young man by his servants*); *adj.* childlike, childish; very young, immature.

**níquel** *m.* nickel.

**niquelado** *adj.* nickel-plated; *m.* nickel plating; nickel plate.

**nitidez** *f.* clarity, clearness.

**nítido** *adj.* clear.

**nitrato** *m.* nitrate; saltpeter.

**nitro** *m.* niter, saltpeter.

**nitrógeno** *m.* nitrogen.

**nivel** *m.* level.

**nivelar** *v.* to level; to grade; to equalize.

**no** *adv.* no; not; nay; **— bien** as soon as; **un — sé qué** something indefinable; **por sí o por —** just in case, anyway.

**noble** *adj.* noble; *m.* nobleman.

**nobleza** *f.* nobility; nobleness.

**noción** *f.* notion, idea.

**nocivo** *adj.* noxious, harmful, injurious.

**nocturno** *adj.* nocturnal, night, nightly; *m.* nocturne (*musical or lyrical composition*).

**noche** *f.* night; darkness; **a la —** tonight; **de —** by (at) night; **por (en) la —** at night, in the evening; **dejar a uno a buenas -s** to leave a person in the lurch.

**Nochebuena** *f.* Christmas Eve.

**nocherniego** *m.* night owl (*person*).

**nodriza** *f.* child's nurse; wet nurse.

**nogal** *m.* walnut (*tree and wood*).

**nomás** *Am.* = **no más** just; only.

**nombradía** *f.* renown, fame.

**nombramiento** *m.* nomination; appointment; naming.

**nombrar** *v.* to nominate; to name; to appoint.

**nombre** *m.* name; fame; noun; watchword; **— de pila** (*or* **— de bautismo**) Christian name.

**nomeolvides** *f.* forget-me-not.

**nómina** *f.* list (*of names*); pay roll.

**nominación** *f.* nomination; appointment.

**nominal** *adj.* nominal; **valor —** small, insignificant value.

**nominar** *v.* to nominate.

**non** *adj.* odd, uneven; *m.* odd number, uneven number; **estar** (*or* **quedar**) **de —** to be left alone, be left without a partner or companion.

**nonada** *f.* trifle, mere nothing.

**nopal** *m.* nopal, prickly pear tree (*species of cactus*).

**nordeste** *adj. & m.* northeast.

**noria** *f.* draw well; chain pump.

**norma** *f.* norm, standard, model.

**normal** *adj.* normal; standard; *f.* perpendicular line.

**normalizar**[9] *v.* to normalize, make normal; to standardize.

**noroeste** *adj. & m.* northwest.

**nortada** *f.* strong north wind.

**nortazo** *m. Mex., Ven.* sudden gust of wind, strong north wind.

**norte** *m.* north; north wind; guide;

North Star; direction.

**norteamericano** *adj.* North American; American (*from or of the United States*).

**norteño** *adj.* northern; *m.* northerner.

**noruego** *adj.* & *m.* Norwegian.

**nostalgia** *f.* nostalgia, longing, homesickness.

**nostálgico** *adj.* homesick; lonesome; longing.

**nota** *f.* note; mark; fame.

**notable** *adj.* notable; noticeable.

**notar** *v.* to note, observe; to mark; to write down.

**notario** *m.* notary.

**noticia** *f.* notice, information; news; **recibir -s** to receive word, hear (from).

**noticiario** *m.* news sheet, news column, news bulletin; **noticiero** *m.* = **noticiario**; *adj.* news (*used as adj.*); newsy, full of news.

**noticioso** *adj.* newsy, full of news; well-informed.

**notificación** *f.* notification, notifying; notice; summons.

**notificar**[6] *v.* to notify.

**notorio** *adj.* well-known; obvious, evident.

**novato** *m.* novice, beginner.

**novedad** *f.* novelty; latest news, event, or fashion; change; newness; **hacerle a uno —** to seem strange or new to one; to excite one's curiosity or interest; **sin —** as usual; well.

**novel** *adj.* new, inexperienced.

**novela** *f.* novel; fiction.

**novelesco** *adj.* novelistic, fictional; fantastic.

**novelista** *m.* & *f.* novelist.

**novia** *f.* fiancée; sweetheart; bride.

**noviazgo** *m.* betrothal, engagement; courtship.

**novicio** *m.* novice; beginner; apprentice; *adj.* inexperienced.

**noviembre** *m.* November.

**novilla** *f.* heifer, young cow.

**novillada** *f.* herd of young bulls; bullfight (*using young bulls*).

**novillero** *m.* a novice bullfighter; a fighter of 3-year-old bulls.

**novillo** *m.* young bull; steer; **-s** bullfight (*using young bulls*); **hacer -s** to play hooky, cut classes; to play truant.

**novio** *m.* fiancé; sweetheart; bridegroom.

**nubarrón** *m.* large storm cloud.

**nube** *f.* cloud; film on the eyeball; **poner por las -s** to praise to the skies.

**nublado** *m.* storm cloud; imminent danger; *adj.* cloudy.

**nublar** *v.* to cloud; to darken, obscure; **-se** to grow cloudy.

**nubloso** *adj.* cloudy; gloomy.

**nuca** *f.* nape.

**nuclear** *adj.* nuclear.

**núcleo** *m.* nucleus; kernel.

**nudillo** *m.* small knot; knuckle; loop, knitted stitch.

**nudo** *m.* (*vínculo*) knot; joint; union,

bond, tie; (*crisis*) crisis, turning point (*of a play*); knot, nautical mile; **— ciego** hard knot.

**nudoso** *adj.* knotty, gnarled, knotted.

**nuera** *f.* daughter-in-law.

**nueva** *f.* news.

**nuevecito** *adj.* nice and new, brand-new.

**nuevo** *adj.* new; newly arrived; **de —** again; **¿qué hay de —?** what's new? what's the news?

**nuez** *f.* walnut; nut; **— (*or* — de Adán)** Adam's apple; **— moscada (*or* — de especia**) nutmeg.

**nulidad** *f.* nullity (*state or quality of being null*); incompetence; nonentity, a nobody.

**nulo** *adj.* null, void; useless.

**numeral** *adj.* & *m.* numeral.

**numerar** *v.* to number; to calculate; to enumerate.

**numérico** *adj.* numerical.

**numero** *m.* number; numeral.

**numeroso** *adj.* numerous.

**nunca** *adv.* never; **no ... — not ...** ever; **mas que —** more than ever.

**nuncio** *m.* herald, messenger; nuncio, Papal envoy.

**nupcial** *adj.* nuptial, relating to marriage or weddings.

**nupcias** *f. pl.* nuptials, wedding.

**nutria** *f.* otter.

**nutrición** *f.* nutrition; nourishment.

**nutrido** *adj.* full, abundant; substantial; *p.p. of* **nutrir.**

**nutrimento, nutrimiento** *m.* nutrition; nourishment, food.

**nutrir** *v.* to nourish, feed.

**nutritivo** *adj.* nutritious, nourishing.

**nylon** *m.* nylon.

## Ñ

**ñandu** *m.* nandu; American ostrich.

**ñapa** *f. Andes, Ríopl., Cuba, Ven., Col.* additional amount, something extra; *Am.* **de —** to boot, in addition, besides.

**ñato** *adj. C.A., Col., Ven., Andes* flat-nosed, pug-nosed, snub-nosed; *Am.* ugly, deformed; *Am.* insignificant.

**ñoñería** *f.* silly remark or action; *Am.* dotage.

**ñoño** *adj.* feeble-minded; silly; *Am.* old, decrepit, feeble; *Col., Ec.* old-fashioned, out of style.

## O

**o** *conj.* or, either.

**oasis** *m.* oasis.

**obedecer**[13] *v. irr.* to obey; **— a cierta causa** to arise from, be due to, a certain cause; **esto obedece a que ...** this is due to the fact that ...

**obediencia** *f.* obedience.

**obediente** *adj.* obedient.

**obertura** *f.* musical overture.

**obispo** *m.* bishop; *Cuba, Andes* **a cada muerte de (*or* por la muerte de un) —** once in a blue moon.

**objeción** *f.* objection.

**objetar** *v.* to object.

NE

**objetivo** *adj.* objective; *m.* objective (*lens of any optical instrument*); objective.

**objeto** *m.* object, purpose, aim; thing.

**oblea** *f.* wafer.

**oblicuo** *adj.* oblique, slanting, bias.

**obligación** *f.* obligation; duty; bond, security; engagement.

**obligar**[7] *v.* to oblige; to obligate, bind, compel, put under obligation; **-se** to bind oneself, obligate oneself.

**obligatorio** *adj.* obligatory; compulsory; binding.

**oboe** *m.* oboe.

**óbolo** *m.* mite, small contribution.

**obra** *f.* (*resultado de acción*) work; act; labor, toil; (*creación artística*) book; building (*under construction*); masterpiece of art; repair; **— de** approximately; **por — de** through, by virtue or power of; **hacer mala —** to interfere, hinder; **poner por —** to undertake, begin; to put into practice.

**obrar** *v.* to work; to act; to operate; to function; to perform; to make; to do; **obra en nuestro poder** we are in receipt of; **la carta que obra en su poder** the letter that is in his possession.

**obrero** *m.* workman, laborer.

**obscenidad** *f.* obscenity.

**obsceno** *adj.* obscene.

**obscurecer**[13] *v. irr.* to obscure, darken; to tarnish; to grow dark; **-se** to get dark or cloudy.

**obscuridad** *f.* obscurity; darkness; dimness.

**obscuro** *adj.* obscure; dark; dim; **a obscuras** (= **a oscuras**) in the dark; *m.* shade (*in painting*).

**obsequiar** *v.* to regale, entertain; to court; *Am.* to give, make a present of.

**obsequio** *m.* attention, courtesy; gift; **en — de** for the sake of, in honor of.

**obsequioso** *adj.* attentive, courteous, obliging; obsequious, servile.

**observación** *f.* observation; remark.

**observador** *m.* observer; *adj.* observing.

**observancia** *f.* observance (*of a law, rule, custom, etc.*).

**observante** *adj.* observant (*of a law, custom, or rule*).

**observar** *v.* to observe; to watch; to remark.

**observatorio** *m.* observatory.

**obsesión** *f.* obsession.

**obsesionar** *v.* to obsess.

**obstáculo** *m.* obstacle.

**obstante: no —** notwithstanding; nevertheless.

**obstar** *v.* to hinder, impede, obstruct.

**obstinación** *f.* obstinacy, stubbornness.

**obstinado** *adj.* obstinate, stubborn.

**obstinarse** *v.* to persist (in); to be obstinate, stubborn (about).

**obstrucción** *f.* obstruction.

**obstruir**[32] *v. irr.* to obstruct, block.

**obtener**[45] *v. irr.* to obtain, get; to attain.

**obtenible** *adj.* obtainable, available.

**obturador** *m.* choke (*of an automobile*); throttle; plug, stopper; shutter (*of a camera*).

**obviar** *v.* to obviate, clear away, remove.

**obvio** *adj.* obvious.

**ocasión** *f.* occasion, opportunity; cause; danger, risk; **de —** reduced, bargain; **avisos de —** want "ads" (*advertisements*); *Am.* **esta —** this time.

**ocasional** *adj.* occasional.

**ocasionar** *v.* to occasion, cause.

**ocaso** *m.* sunset; setting (*of any star or planet*); west; decadence, decline, end.

**occidental** *adj.* occidental, western.

**occidente** *m.* occident, west.

**océano** *m.* ocean.

**ocelote** *m.* ocelot.

**ocio** *m.* leisure, idleness; recreation, pastime.

**ociosidad** *f.* idleness, leisure.

**ocioso** *adj.* idle; useless.

**octubre** *m.* October.

**ocular** *adj.* ocular; **testigo —** eye witness; *m.* eyepiece, lens (*for the eye in a microscope or telescope*).

**oculista** *m. & f.* oculist; *Am.* flatterer.

**ocultar** *v.* to hide, conceal.

**oculto** *adj.* hidden, concealed; *m. Am.* species of mole (*small animal*).

**ocupación** *f.* occupation; employment.

**ocupante** *m. & f.* occupant.

**ocupar** *v.* to occupy; to employ; **-se en** (*Am.* **-se de**) to be engaged in; to pay attention to, be interested in.

**ocurrencia** *f.* occurrence, event; witticism, joke; bright or funny idea.

**ocurrente** *adj.* witty, funny, humorous; occurring.

**ocurrir** *v.* to occur.

**ocurso** *m. Ríopl.* petition, application.

**oda** *f.* ode.

**odiar** *v.* to hate.

**odio** *m.* hatred.

**odioso** *adj.* odious, hateful.

**odre** *m.* wine bag; drunk.

**oeste** *m.* west; west wind.

**ofender** *v.* to offend; to displease; **-se** to get offended; to become angry, take offense.

**ofensa** *f.* offense.

**ofensivo** *adj.* offensive; obnoxious; attacking; **ofensiva** *f.* offensive.

**ofensor** *m.* offender; *adj.* offending.

**oferta** *f.* offer; promise.

**oficial** *m.* official, officer; skilled workman; *adj.* official.

**oficiar** *v.* to officiate, serve, minister, perform the duties of a priest or minister; to communicate officially; **— de** to serve as, act as.

**oficina** *f.* office; shop; **oficinesco** *adj.* clerical, pertaining to an office.

**oficio** *m.* office, position; trade; function; official communication; religious office (*prayers*).

**oficioso** *adj.* officious, meddlesome.

**ofrecer**[13] *v. irr.* to offer; to promise; **-se** to offer, occur, present itself; to offer oneself, volunteer; **¿qué se le ofrece a Vd.?** what do you wish?

**ofrecimiento** *m.* offer; offering.

**ofrenda** *f.* offering, gift.

**ofuscamiento** *m.* clouded vision, blindness; cloudiness of the mind, bewilderment, mental confusion.

**ofuscar**⁶ *v.* to darken, cast a shadow on; to blind; to cloud; to bewilder, confuse.

**ogro** *m.* ogre.

**oído** *m.* hearing; ear; **al —** confidentially; **de** (*or* **al**) **—** by ear; **de -s** (*or* **de oídas**) by hearsay or rumor.

**oidor** *m.* hearer, listener; judge.

**oír**³⁶ *v. irr.* to hear; to listen; to understand; **— misa** to attend mass; **— decir que** to hear that; **— hablar de** to hear about.

**ojal** *m.* buttonhole; hole.

**¡ojalá!** *interj.* God grant!; I hope so!; **— que** would that. I hope that.

**ojazo** *m.* large eye.

**ojeada** *f.* glimpse, quick glance.

**ojear** *v.* to eye, stare; to bewitch; to beat up, rouse (*wild game*).

**ojera** *f.* dark circle under the eye; eyecup.

**ojeriza** *f.* grudge, spite.

**ojeroso** *adj.* with dark circles under the eyes.

**ojiva** *f.* pointed arch; **ojival** *adj.* pointed (*arch*); **ventana ojival** window with a pointed arch.

**ojo** *m.* (*órgano*) eye; (*agujero*) keyhole; hole; **¡—!** careful! look out!; **a —** by sight, by guess; **a -s vistas** visibly, clearly; **— de agua** spring (*of water*); **— de buey** porthole; **mal** (*or* **mal de**) **—** evil eye; *Am.* **hacer —** to cast the evil eye; *Am.* **pelar el —** to be alert, keep one's eye peeled; *Mex., Ven.* **poner a uno los -s verdes** to deceive someone; **tener entre -s a** to have ill will toward, have a grudge against.

**ojota** *f. Andes, Ch., Ríopl.* leather sandal.

**ola** *f.* wave.

**oleada** *f.* big wave; swell; surge; abundant yield of oil.

**oleaje, olaje** *m.* swell, surge, succession of waves.

**oleo** *m.* oil, holy oil; **pintura al —** oil painting.

**oleoso** *adj.* oily.

**oler**³⁷ *v. irr.* to smell; to scent; **— a** to smack of; to smell like; *Am.* **olérselas** to suspect it, "smell a rat".

**olfatear** *v.* to scent, sniff, smell.

**olfateo** *m.* sniff, sniffing.

**olfato** *m.* sense of smell.

**oligarquía** *f.* oligarchy.

**oliva** *f.* olive; olive tree; **olivar** *m.* olive grove; **olivo** *m.* olive tree.

**olmo** *m.* elm.

**olor** *m.* (*en el olfato*) smell, odor, fragrance; (*fama*) smack, trace, suspicion; *Am.* spice; **olorcillo** *m.* faint odor.

**oloroso** *adj.* fragrant.

**olote** *m. Mex., C.A.* cob, corncob.

**olvidadizo** *adj.* forgetful.

**olvidar** *v.* to forget; to neglect; **-se de** to forget; **olvidársele a uno algo** to forget something.

**olvido** *m.* forgetfulness; oblivion; neglect; **echar al —** to cast into oblivion; to forget on purpose.

**olla** *f.* pot, kettle; olla (*vegetable and meat stew*); **— podrida** Spanish stew of mixed vegetables and meat.

**ombligo** *m.* navel; middle, center.

**ombú** *m.* umbra tree.

**omisión** *f.* omission; oversight, neglect.

**omiso** *adj.* careless, neglectful; *N. Arg.* guilty; **hacer caso —** to omit.

**omitir** *v.* to omit; to overlook.

**ómnibus** *m.* omnibus, bus.

**omnipotente** *adj.* omnipotent, almighty.

**onda** *f.* wave; ripple; sound wave; scallop.

**ondear** *v.* to wave; to waver; to ripple; to sway, swing.

**ondulación** *f.* undulation, waving motion; wave; **— permanente** permanent wave.

**ondulado** *p.p.* & *adj.* wavy; scalloped (*edge*); **— permanente** permanent wave.

**ondulante** *adj.* wavy, waving.

**ondular** *v.* to undulate, wave.

**onza** *f.* ounce; ounce, wildcat; *Ríopl., Bol.* small tiger.

**opacidad** *f.* opacity; sadness.

**opaco** *adj.* opaque, dim, dull.

**ópalo** *m.* opal.

**ópera** *f.* opera.

**operación** *f.* operation; business transaction.

**operador** *m.* operator, surgeon.

**operar** *v.* to operate; to take effect, work; to speculate (*in business*); to manipulate, handle.

**operario** *m.* operator, workman, worker.

**opereta** *f.* operetta.

**opinar** *v.* to express an opinion; to think; to judge; to argue.

**opinión** *f.* opinion; reputation.

**opio** *m.* opium.

**oponer**⁴⁰ *v. irr.* to oppose; **-se** to disapprove; **-se a** to oppose, be against.

**oporto** *m.* port wine.

**oportunidad** *f.* opportunity.

**oportuno** *adj.* opportune; convenient, timely.

**oposición** *f.* opposition; competition; **-es** competitive examinations.

**opositor** *m.* opponent; competitor.

**opresión** *f.* oppression.

**opresivo** *adj.* oppressive.

**opresor** *m.* oppressor.

**oprimir** *v.* to oppress; to crush; to press down.

**oprobio** *m.* infamy; insult; shame; dishonor.

**optar** *v.* to choose, select; **— por** to decide upon; to choose.

**óptica** *f.* optics.

**óptico** *adj.* optical, optic; *m.* optician.

**optimismo** *m.* optimism; **optimista** *m.* & *f.* optimist; *adj.* optimistic.

**óptimo** *adj.* very good, very best.

**opuesto** *p.p.* of **oponer** opposed; *adj.* opposite; contrary.

**opulencia** *f.* opulence, abundance,

**OB**

wealth.

**opulento** *adj.* opulant, wealthy.

**oquedad** *f.* cavity, hollow; chasm.

**ora** *conj.* now, then; whether; either.

**oración** *f.* oration; prayer; sentence.

**oráculo** *m.* oracle.

**orador** *m.* orator, speaker.

**oral** *adj.* oral.

**orar** *v.* to pray.

**oratoria** *f.* oratory, eloquence.

**oratorio** *m.* oratory, private chapel; oratorio (*a religious musical composition*); *adj.* oratorical, pertaining to oratory.

**orbe** *m.* orb, sphere, globe; the earth; world, universe.

**órbita** *f.* orbit; eye socket.

**orden** *m.* (*colocación*) order; succession, series; class, group; relation; proportion; *f.* (*mando*) order, command; (*sociedad*) honorary or religious order; *m.* & *f.* sacrament of ordination; **a sus órdenes** at your service.

**ordenado** *p.p.* & *adj.* ordered; ordained; orderly; neat.

**ordenanza** *f.* ordinance, decree, law; command, order; *m.* orderly (*military*).

**ordenar** *v.* to arrange, put in order; to order, command; to ordain; **-se** to become ordained.

**ordeña** *f.* milking.

**ordeñar** *v.* to milk.

**ordinariez** *f.* commonness, lack of manners.

**ordinario** *adj.* ordinary; usual; common, coarse; *m.* ordinary (*a bishop or judge*); ordinary mail; daily household expense; **de —** usually, ordinarily.

**orear** *v.* to air; **-se** to be exposed to the air; to dry in the air.

**oreja** *f.* ear; hearing; loop; small flap; *Am.* handle (*shaped like an ear*); **orejano** *adj.* unbranded (*cattle*); *Ven., Col.* cautious; *m. Cuba* aloof, unsociable person; **orejera** *f.* ear muff, ear flap; **orejón** *m.* pull by the ear; *Col.* rancher or inhabitant of the **sabana**; *adj. Col.* long-eared, longhorned; *Col.* unbranded (*cattle*); *Col.* coarse, crude, uncouth.

**orfandad** *f.* orphanage (*state of being an orphan*).

**orfanato** *m.* orphanage, orphan asylum.

**orfanatorio** *Am.* = **orfanato**.

**orfebre** *m.* goldsmith; silversmith.

**orfeón** *m.* glee club, choir.

**orgánico** *adj.* organic.

**organillo** *m.* hand organ, hurdy-gurdy.

**organismo** *m.* organism.

**organización** *f.* organization.

**organizador** *m.* organizer.

**organizar⁹** *v.* to organize; to arrange.

**órgano** *m.* organ; **organillo** *m.* hand organ.

**orgía** *f.* orgy, wild revel.

**orgullo** *m.* pride; haughtiness, arrogance.

**orgulloso** *adj.* proud; haughty, arrogant.

**oriental** *adj.* oriental, eastern.

**orientar** *v.* to orientate, orient; **-se** to orient oneself, find one's bearings.

**oriente** *m.* orient, east; east wind; source, origin.

**orificación** *f.* gold filling.

**orificio** *m.* orifice, small hole, aperture, outlet.

**origen** *m.* origin; source.

**original** *adj.* original; strange, quaint; *m.* original; manuscript, copy; queer person; **originalidad** *f.* originality.

**originar** *v.* to originate, cause to be; **-se** originate, arise.

**orilla** *f.* shore, bank; beach; edge, border; **-s** *Am.* outskirts, environs.

**orillar** *v.* to border, trim the edge of; to skirt, go along the edge of; to reach the edge or shore.

**orín** *m.* rust; **orines** *m. pl.* urine.

**orina** *f.* urine.

**orinar** *v.* to urinate.

**oriol** *m.* oriole.

**oriundo** *adj.* native; **ser — de** to hail from, come from.

**orla** *f.* border; trimming, fringe.

**orlar** *v.* to border, edge, trim with a border or fringe.

**ornado** *adj.* ornate; *p.p.* adorned, ornamented.

**ornamentar** *v.* to ornament, adorn.

**ornamento** *m.* ornament; decoration; **-s** sacred vestments.

**ornar** *v.* to adorn.

**oro** *m.* gold; gold ornament; **-s** "gold coins" (*Spanish card suit*).

**orondo** *adj.* self-satisfied, puffed up, vain; *Am.* serene, calm.

**oropel** *m.* tinsel.

**orquesta** *f.* orchestra.

**orquídea** *f.* orchid.

**ortiga** *f.* nettle.

**ortografía** *f.* orthography, spelling.

**ortográfico** *adj.* orthographic (*pertaining to orthography or spelling*).

**oruga** *f.* caterpillar.

**orzuelo** *m.* sty (*on the eyelid*).

**osadía** *f.* boldness, daring.

**osado** *adj.* bold, daring.

**osar** *v.* to dare, venture.

**oscilación** *f.* oscillation, sway; fluctuation, wavering.

**oscilar** *v.* to oscillate, swing, sway; to waver.

**oscurecer** = **obscurecer**.

**oscuridad** = **obscuridad**.

**oscuro** = **obscuro**.

**oso** *m.* bear; **— blanco** polar bear; **— hormiguero** anteater; **— marino** seal.

**ostentación** *f.* ostentation, show, display.

**ostentar** *v.* to display, show; to show off; to boast.

**ostentoso** *adj.* ostentatious, showy.

**ostión** *m.* large oyster.

**ostra** *f.* oyster.

**otate** *m. Mex., C.A.* species of bamboo; *Mex., C.A.* bamboo stick or cane.

**otero** *m.* hillock, small hill, knoll.

**otoñal** *adj.* autumnal, of autumn.

**otoño** *m.* autumn, fall.

**otorgar**[7] *v.* to grant; to promise; to consent to.

**otro** *adj.* another; **otra vez** again; *Am.* **como dijo el —** as someone said.

**otrora** *adv.* formerly, in other times.

**ovación** *f.* ovation, enthusiastic applause.

**oval, ovalado** *adj.* oval; **óvalo** *m.* oval.

**oveja** *f.* sheep.

**ovejero** *m.* shepherd; sheep dog.

**ovejuno** *adj.* sheep, pertaining or relating to sheep.

**overo** *adj.* peach-colored (*applied to horses and cattle*); *Ríopl.* mottled, spotted; *Ríopl.* multicolored; *Ríopl.* **ponerle a uno —** to insult someone.

**overol, overoles** *m.* *Ch., Col.* overalls.

**ovillar** *v.* to ball, wind or form into a ball; **-se** to curl up into a ball.

**ovillo** *m.* ball of yarn or thread; tangle; **hacerse uno un —** to curl up into a ball; to become entangled, confused.

**oxidado** *p.p.* rusted; *adj.* rusty.

**oxidar** *v.* to oxidize; to rust; **-se** to become oxidized; to rust.

**oxígeno** *m.* oxygen.

**oyente** *m. & f.* listener, auditor, hearer; *adj.* listening.

### P

**pabellón** *m.* pavilion; canopy; banner, flag; shelter, covering; external ear.

**pabilo** *m.* wick; snuff (*of a candle*).

**pacer**[13] *v. irr.* to pasture; to graze.

**paciencia** *f.* patience.

**paciente** *adj.* patient; *m. & f.* patient.

**pacienzudo** *adj.* patient, long-suffering.

**pacificar**[6] *v.* to pacify; to appease.

**pacífico** *adj.* pacific, peaceful, calm.

**pacto** *m.* pact, agreement.

**padecer**[13] *v. irr.* to suffer.

**padecimiento** *m.* suffering.

**padrastro** *m.* stepfather; hangnail.

**padre** *m.* father; **-s** parents; ancestors; *adj. Am.* very great, stupendous.

**padrenuestro** *m.* paternoster, the Lord's Prayer.

**padrino** *m.* godfather; sponsor, patron; second in a duel; best man (*at a wedding*).

**paella** *f.* a popular rice dish with chicken, vegetables, etc.

**paga** *f.* payment; pay, salary.

**pagadero** *adj.* payable.

**pagado** *p.p. & adj.* paid; self-satisfied, conceited; **— de sí mismo** pleased with oneself.

**pagador** *m.* payer; paymaster; paying teller (*in a bank*).

**paganismo** *m.* paganism, heathenism.

**pagano** *adj.* pagan; *m.* pagan; payer; dupe, sucker.

**pagar**[7] *v.* to pay; to pay for; to requite, return (*love*); **-se de** to be proud of; to boast of; to be pleased with; *Ríopl.* **-se de palabras** to let oneself be tricked; *Am.* **— a nueve** to pay in excess.

**pagaré** *m.* promissory note; I.O.U.

**página** *f.* page.

**paginar** *v.* to page.

**pago** *m.* (*premio*) payment; prize, reward; (*distrito*) country district; *Ríopl.* one's native farm land or district; *adj.* paid; *Am.* **estar -s** to be quits.

**paila** *f.* large pan; *C.A.* saucer.

**país** *m.* nation, country; region.

**paisaje** *m.* landscape.

**paisanaje** *m.* peasantry, country people; civilians; *Andes* gang of farm laborers.

**paisano** *m.* countryman; peasant; fellow countryman; civilian.

**paja** *f.* straw; chaff; rubbish; *Andes* grass for pasture; **echar -s** to draw lots; **por quítame allá esas -s** for an insignificant reason or pretext; **en un quítame allá esas -s** in a jiffy, in a second; **a humo de -s** thoughtlessly; lightly; **no lo hizo a humo de -s** he did not do it without a special reason or intention.

**pajar** *m.* straw loft, barn.

**pájaro** *m.* bird; shrewd, cautious person; *Ch.* absent-minded person; *Ch., Ríopl.* person of suspicious conduct; **— carpintero** woodpecker; **— mosca** humming bird.

**paje** *m.* page, valet, attendant.

**pajizo** *adj.* made of straw; covered with straw; straw colored.

**pajonal** *m.* plain or field of tall coarse grass.

**pala** *f.* shovel; trowel; scoop; paddle; blade of an oar; racket; upper (*of a shoe*); cunning, craftiness; **meter la —** to deceive with cunning; *Am.* **hacer la —** to deceive with cunning; to stall, pretend to work; to flatter; **palada** *f.* scoop, shovelful; stroke of an oar.

**palabra** *f.* word; promise; **de —** by word of mouth; **cuatro -s** a few words; **empeñar la —** to promise, pledge; **tener la —** to have the floor; *Am.* **¡—!** I mean it, it is true!

**palabrero** *adj.* wordy, talkative.

**palabrita** *f.* a little word, a few words; a word of advice.

**palacio** *m.* palace; **palaciego** *m.* courtier; *adj.* relating to a palace or court; court (*used as an adj.*).

**paladar** *m.* palate; taste, relish.

**paladear** *v.* to relish, taste with relish.

**paladín** *m.* knight; champion, defender.

**palanca** *f.* lever; crowbar; bar used for carrying a load.

**palangana** *f.* washbowl, basin; *S.A.* platter; *Ch.* large wooden bowl; *m. Andes* bluffer, charlatan.

**palatal** *adj.* palatal.

**palco** *m.* theater box; **— escénico** stage.

**palenque** *m.* palisade, fence; enclosure; *Ríopl.* hitching post or plank.

**paleta** *f.* small flat shovel; mason's trowel; shoulder blade; blade (*of a rudder, of a ventilating fan*); paddle (*of a paddle wheel*); painter's palette; *Am.* candy, sweetmeat or ice cream attached to a stick; *Am.* a wooden

**OP**

paddle to stir with, or for beating clothes; **en dos -s** in a jiffy, in a second; **paletilla** *f.* shoulder blade.

**palidecer** [13] *v. irr.* to turn pale.

**palidez** *f.* pallor, paleness.

**pálido** *adj.* pallid, pale.

**palillo** *m.* small stick; toothpick; **tocar todos los -s** (*Ch.* **menear uno los -s**) to try every possible means.

**paliza** *f.* beating (*with a stick*), thrashing.

**palizada** *f.* palisade; stockade.

**palma** *f.* palm tree; palm leaf; palm of the hand; **batir -s** to clap, applaud; **llevarse la —** to triumph, win, carry off the honors; to be the best.

**palmada** *f.* slap; clap.

**palmario** *adj.* clear, evident.

**palmatoria** *f.* small candlestick with handle.

**palmear** *v.* to clap, applaud; *Am.* to pat, clap on the back; *Ríopl.* to flatter.

**palmera** *f.* palm tree.

**palmo** *m.* span (*about 9 inches*); **— a —** slowly, foot by foot.

**palmotear** *v.* to clap, applaud.

**palo** *m.* stick; pole; log; mast; wood; blow with a stick; suit (*in a deck of cards*); *Am.* tree; *Ríopl.* reprimand, reproof; *P.R., Ven.* large swallow of liquor; **— del Brasil** Brazil wood; *Ven.* **— a pique** rail fence, barbed wire fence; *Mex., C.A.* **a medio —** half-done; half-drunk; *Am.* **a — entero** drunk.

**paloma** *f.* dove, pigeon; pleasant, mild person; **-s** whitecaps.

**palomar** *m.* dovecot (*shelter for doves or pigeons*).

**palomilla** *f.* little dove; moth; small butterfly; **-s** small whitecaps.

**palomita** *f.* little dove; **-s** *Am.* popcorn.

**palpable** *adj.* palpable (*that can be felt or touched*); clear, obvious, evident.

**palpar** *v.* to feel; to touch; to grope.

**palpitación** *f.* palpitation; beat, throb.

**palpitante** *adj.* palpitating, throbbing, trembling; exciting; **la cuestión —** the burning question.

**palpitar** *v.* to palpitate; to throb, beat.

**palta** *f. Col., Ven., Andes, Ríopl., Ch.* avocado, alligator pear; **palto** *m. Col., Ven., Andes, Ríopl., Ch.* avocado tree. See **aguacate**.

**palúdico** *adj.* marshy; **fiebre palúdica** malarial, or marsh fever; malaria; **paludismo** *m.* malaria.

**pampa** *f. Am.* pampa (*vast treeless plain of South America*); *Am.* prairie; *Ch.* drill field (*military*); *m. & f.* pampa Indian of Argentina; *m. Am.* language of the pampa Indian; *adj. Am.* pertaining to the pampa Indian; *Ríopl.* **caballo —** horse with head and body of different colors; *Ríopl.* **trato —** dubious or dishonest deal; *Am.* **estar a la —** to be in the open; *Ríopl.* **tener todo a la —** to be ragged or to be indecently exposed; *Ch.* **quedar en —** to be left without

clothes; to be left in the lurch.

**pampeano** *adj. Ríopl.* of, or pertaining to, the pampa.

**pampero** *adj. Ríopl.* of, or pertaining to, the pampas; *m. Ríopl.* inhabitant of the pampas; *Ríopl.* violent wind of the pampa.

**pan** *m.* bread; loaf of bread; wheat; **-es** fields of grain; breadstuffs; *Am.* **echar -es** to brag, boast.

**pana** *f.* corduroy.

**panadería** *f.* bakery.

**panadero** *m.* baker; *Ch.* flatterer.

**panal** *m.* honeycomb; sweetmeat (*made of sugar, egg white, and lemon*).

**panamericano** *adj.* Pan-American.

**pandearse** *v.* to bulge, warp; to sag.

**pandeo** *m.* sag; bulge.

**pandilla** *f.* gang, band.

**panela** *f. Col., C.A.* unrefined sugar.

**panfleto** *m. Am.* pamphlet.

**pánico** *m.* panic; *adj.* panic, panicky.

**panne** *f.* accident, car trouble.

**panocha** *f.* ear of corn; *Mex.* Mexican raw sugar; *Col., C.R.* a kind of tamale.

**panqué** *m. Col., C.A., Mex.* small cake, cup cake; *Am.* pancake.

**pantalón** *m.* trousers; pants; **un par de -es** a pair of trousers.

**pantalla** *f.* light shade; screen; fireplace screen; motion-picture screen; *C.R.* fan, palm leaf fan; *P.R.* earring.

**pantano** *m.* swamp; dam; difficulty.

**pantanoso** *adj.* swampy, marshy; muddy.

**panteón** *m.* cemetery.

**pantera** *f.* panther.

**pantorrilla** *f.* calf (*of the leg*).

**pantufla** *f.* bedroom slipper.

**panza** *f.* paunch, belly.

**panzón, panzudo** *adj.* big-bellied.

**pañal** *m.* diaper; **estar en -es** to be in one's infancy; to have little or no knowledge of a thing.

**paño** *m.* cloth (*any cloth, especially woolen*); blotch or spot on the skin; film on the eyeball; *Mex., Cuba* parcel of tillable land; *Mex.* kerchief, shawl; **— de manos** towel; **— de mesa** tablecloth; **al —** off-stage; **-s** clothes, garments; **-s menores** underwear; **pañero** *m.* clothier.

**pañolón** *m.* scarf, large kerchief; shawl.

**pañuelo** *m.* handkerchief.

**papa** *m.* Pope; *f.* potato; fib, lie; *Am.* snap, easy job; **-s** pap (*soft food for babies*); soup; *Ríopl., Ch.* **cosa —** something good to eat; excellent thing; **echar -s** to fib, lie; *Am.* **importarle a uno una —** not to matter to one a bit; *Am.* **no saber ni —** not to a know a thing; to be completely ignorant.

**papá** *m.* papa; *Mex., C.A., Andes* **— grande** grandfather.

**papagayo** *m.* parrot; talker, chatterer.

**papal** *adj.* papal.

**papalote, papelote** *m. Carib., Mex.* kite.

**papamoscas** *m.* flycatcher (*a bird*); simpleton, half-wit, dunce.

**papanatas** *m.* simpleton, fool, dunce.
**paparrucha** *f.* fib, lie; **paparruchero** *m.* fibber.
**papaya** *f.* papaya.
**papel** *m.* (*hoja*) paper; sheet of paper; document; (*parte dramática*) role; — **de estraza** brown wrapping paper — **de lija** sandpaper; — **de seda** tissue paper; — **moneda** paper money; — **secante** blotting paper; **hacer el — de** to play the role of; **hacer buen** (*or* **mal**) — to cut a good (*or* bad) figure.
**papelera** *f.* folder, file, case or device for keeping papers; *Am.* wastepaper basket; **papelero** *m.* paper manufacturer; *adj.* pertaining to paper; vain, ostentatious.
**papelería** *f.* stationery store; stationery; lot of papers.
**papeleta** *f.* card, file card, slip of paper.
**papelucho** *m.* worthless piece of paper.
**papera** *f.* goiter; **-s** mumps.
**paquete** *m.* package; bundle; dandy; packet boat (*mail boat*); *adj. Am.* dolled up, dressed up; *Riopl., Col.* important, pompous; *Riopl., Col.* insincere.
**par** *adj.* even; *m.* pair, couple; peer; **a la** — at par; jointly; at the same time; **al — de** on a par with; **bajo** — below par; **sin** — peerless, without an equal, having no equal; **sobre** — above par; **de** — **en** — wide-open.
**para** *prep.* for; to; toward; in order to; ¿— **qué?** what for; — **que** so that; — **siempre** forever; — **mis adentros** to myself; **sin qué ni** — **qué** without rhyme or reason; *m. Riopl.* Paraguayan tobacco; *Riopl.* Paraguayan (*used as nickname*).
**parabién** *m.* congratulations; **dar el** — to congratulate.
**parabrisa** *m.* windshield.
**paracaídas** *m.* parachute; **paracaidista** *m. & f.* parachutist.
**parachoques** *m.* bumper.
**parada** *f.* stop; stopping place; bet, stake; military review; *P.R.* parade; *Riopl.* boastfulness; *Riopl.* **tener mucha** — to dress very well.
**paradero** *m.* stopping place; whereabouts; end.
**parado** *p.p. & adj.* stopped; unoccupied, unemployed; fixed, motionless; *Ch., P.R.* standing, erect, straight up; *Ch., P.R.* stiff, proud; *Riopl.* cold, unenthusiastic; *P.R., Ch., Andes* **caer uno** — to land on one's feet; to be lucky; *Am.* **estar bien** — to be well-fixed, well-established; to be lucky; *m. Am.* air, appearance.
**paradoja** *f.* paradox.
**parafina** *f.* paraffin.
**paraguas** *m.* umbrella; **paragüero** *m.* umbrella stand; umbrella maker or seller.
**paraguayo** *adj. & m.* Paraguayan.
**paraíso** *m.* paradise, heaven; upper gallery (*in a theater*).
**paraje** *m.* place; spot; situation.

**paralelo** *adj.* parallel; similar; *m.* parallel; similarity; **paralela** *f.* parallel line; **paralelismo** *m.* parallelism.
**parálisis** *f.* paralysis.
**paralizar**[9] *v.* to paralyze; to stop.
**páramo** *m.* high, bleak plain; cold region; *Andes* blizzard or a cold drizzle.
**parangón** *m.* comparison.
**parangonar** *v.* to compare.
**paraninfo** *m.* assembly hall, lecture hall, auditorium.
**parapeto** *m.* parapet.
**parar** *v.* to stop; to end, end up, come to an end; to parry (*in fencing*); to set up (*type*); *Am.* to stand, place in upright position; — **atención** to notice; — **mientes en** to observe, notice; *Riopl.* — **las orejas** to prick up one's ears; to pay close attention; **-se** to stop; *Am.* to stand up, get up.
**pararrayos** *m.* lightning rod.
**parásito** *m.* parasite; *adj.* parasitic.
**parasol** *m.* parasol.
**parcela** *f.* parcel of land; particle, small piece.
**parcial** *adj.* partial; *m.* follower, partisan; **parcialidad** *f.* partiality; faction, party.
**parche** *m.* mending patch; sticking plaster; medicated plaster; drum.
**pardal** *m.* sparrow; linnet; sly fellow.
**pardear** *v.* to grow dusky; to appear brownish-grey.
**pardo** *adj.* dark-grey; brown; dark; cloudy; *m.* leopard; *Carib., Riopl.* mulatto; **pardusco** *adj.* greyish; brownish.
**parear** *v.* to pair, couple, match, mate.
**parecer**[13] *v. irr.* to seem; to appear, show up; **-se** to resemble each other, look alike; *m.* opinion; appearance, looks; **al** — apparently, seemingly.
**parecido** *adj.* alike, similar; **bien** — good-looking; *p.p. of* **parecer**; *m.* similarity, likeness, resemblance.
**pared** *f.* wall; — **maestra** main wall; — **medianera** partition wall.
**pareja** *f.* pair; couple; match; partner; *Am.* team of two horses; *Riopl.* horse race.
**parejero** *m. Riopl.* race horse; *Riopl.* over-familar person, backslapper, hail-fellow-well-met.
**parejo** *adj.* even; smooth; equal; *adv. Riopl.* hard.
**parentela** *f.* relatives, kin.
**parentesco** *m.* kinship, relationship.
**paréntesis** *m.* parenthesis; digression; **entre** — by the way.
**paria** *m. & f.* outcast.
**paridad** *f.* par, equality.
**pariente** *m. & f.* relative, relation.
**parir** *v.* to give birth; to bear (*children*).
**parlamentar** *v.* to converse; to parley, discuss terms with an enemy.
**parlamentario** *adj.* parliamentary; *m.* member of parliament; envoy to a parley.
**parlamento** *m.* speech (*of a character in a play*); parley; parliament, legislative assembly.

PA

**parlanchín** *adj.* talkative; *m.* talker, chatterer.
**parlero** *adj.* talkative; gossipy; chattering, chirping.
**parlotear** *v.* to prate, prattle, chatter, chat.
**parloteo** *m.* chatter, prattle, idle talk.
**paro** *m.* work stoppage; lockout; *Am.* throw (*in the game of dice*); *Am.* — **y pinta** game of dice.
**parodia** *f.* parody, take-off, humorous imitation.
**parodiar** *v.* to parody, take off, imitate.
**parótidas** *f. pl.* mumps.
**parpadear** *v.* to wink; to blink; to flutter the eyelids; to twinkle.
**parpadeo** *m.* winking; blinking; fluttering of the eyelids; twinkling.
**párpado** *m.* eyelid.
**parque** *m.* park; *Am.* ammunition.
**parra** *f.* grapevine; earthenware jug.
**parrafada** *f.* chat.
**párrafo** *m.* paragraph; **echar un — con** to have a chat with.
**parranda** *f.* revel, orgy, spree; *Col.* gang, band; **andar** (*or* **ir**) **de** — to go on a spree.
**parrandear** *v.* to revel, make merry, go on a spree.
**parrilla** *f.* grill, gridiron, broiler; grate.
**párroco** *m.* parish priest.
**parroquia** *f.* parish; parish church; clientele, customers.
**parroquiano** *m.* client, customer; parishioner; *adj.* parochial, of a parish.
**parsimonia** *f.* thrift, economy; moderation; prudence.
**parsimonioso** *adj.* thrifty; stingy; cautious; slow.
**parte** *f.* part; share; place; party (*legal term*); **-s** qualities; **parte** *m.* notice, announcement; *Am.* unnecessary excuses or explanations; **de algún tiempo a esta** — for some time past; **de — de** on behalf of; in favor of; **de — a** — through, from one side to the other; **dar** — to inform; **echar a mala** — to take amiss; **en** — partly; **por todas -s** everywhere; *m.* telegram; message.
**partera** *f.* midwife.
**partición** *f.* partition, division.
**participación** *f.* participation, share; notice.
**participante** *m. & f.* participant; *adj.* participating, sharing.
**participar** *v.* to participate, share; to inform, notify.
**partícipe** *m. & f.* participant; *adj.* participating.
**participio** *m.* participle.
**partícula** *f.* particle.
**particular** *adj.* particular, special; peculiar; private, personal; odd, strange; **en** — specially; **lecciones -es** private lessons; *m.* private citizen; individual; point, detail; matter.
**partida** *f.* (*salida*) departure, leave; (*entidad*) item, entry; record; band, group; squad; shipment; game; set (*in tennis*); *Am.* part in the hair; —

**de bautismo** (**de matrimonio** *or* **de defunción**) birth (marriage, *or* death) certificate; — **de campo** picnic; — **de caza** hunting party; — **doble** double-entry bookkeeping; *Mex.*, *Ríopl.* **confesar la** — to tell the truth, speak plainly; **jugar una mala** — to play a mean trick.
**partidario** *m.* partisan, follower, supporter.
**partido** *m.* party, faction, group; contest, game; profit; district; *Bol.* **a** (*or* **al**) — in equal shares; *Am.* **dar** — to give a handicap or advantage (*in certain games*); **darse a** — to yield, give up; **sacar** — **de** to derive advantage from, make the best of; **tomar un** — to decide, make a decision.
**partir** *v.* (*dividir*) to split, divide; to crack, break; (*salir*) to depart, leave; **a** — **de hoy** starting today; from this day on; *Am.* **a** (*or* **al**) — in equal parts; *Am.* — **a uno por el eje** to ruin someone.
**partitura** *f.* musical score.
**parto** *m.* childbirth, delivery; product, offspring; **estar de** — to be in labor.
**parvada** *f.* pile of unthreshed grain; brood; *Andes* flock (*of birds or children*).
**parvedad** *f.* smallness; trifle; snack, bit of food.
**párvulo** *m.* child; *adj.* small; innocent.
**pasa** *f.* raisin; woolly hair of negros.
**pasada** *f.* passing, passage; *Am.* stay *Am.* embarrassment, shame; **una mala** — a mean trick; **de** — on the way; incidentally, by the way; **dar una** — **por** to pass by, walk by.
**pasadizo** *m.* aisle; narrow hall; narrow passageway.
**pasado** *m.* past; *p.p.* past, gone; *adj.* overripe, spoiled *Mex.* dried (*fruits*). *Col.* thin, bony (*animal*); — **mañana** day after tomorrow; **el año** — last year; **en días -s** in days gone by.
**pasaje** *m.* passage; fare, ticket; total number of passengers; *Carib.*, *Mex. Col.* private alley; *Col.*, *Ven.* anecdote.
**pasajero** *adj.* passing, temporary, fleeting, transitory; *m.* passenger; guest (*of a hotel*).
**pasamano** *m.* railing, hand rail; gangplank; gangway (*of a ship*).
**pasaporte** *m.* passport.
**pasar** *v.* to pass; to cross; to surpass, exceed; to pierce; to go forward; to go over (in, by, to); to enter; to carry over, take across; to happen; to get along; to swallow; to overlook; to tolerate; to suffer; — **las de Caín** to have a hard time; — **por alto** to omit, overlook; — **por las armas** to execute; **-se** to transfer, change over; to get overripe, spoiled; to exceed, go beyond; **se me pasó decirte** I forgot to tell you; *Ch.* **pasársela a uno** to deceive someone, break someone's confidence; **un buen** —

enough to live on.

**pasarela** *f.* gangplank.

**pasatiempo** *m.* pastime; *Am.* cookie.

**pascua** *f.* Easter; Jewish Passover; — **florida** (*or* **de resurrección**) Easter Sunday; — **de Navidad** Christmas.

**pase** *m.* pass, permit; thrust (*in fencing*); pass (*with the cape in bullfighting*).

**pasear** *v.* to walk; to take a walk; to ride; **-se** to take a walk; to parade; **-se en automóvil** to take an automobile ride; **-se a caballo** to go horseback riding.

**paseo** *m.* walk, ride; parade; public park; boulevard; — **en automóvil** automobile ride; **dar un** — to take a walk.

**pasillo** *m.* aisle; hallway, corridor; short step; short skit; *Col., Ec.* a type of dance music; *Mex.* runner, hall carpet.

**pasión** *f.* passion; suffering.

**pasivo** *adj.* passive; inactive; *m.* liabilities, debts; debit, debit side (*in bookkeeping*).

**pasmar** *v.* to astound, stun; **-se** to be amazed, stunned; to marvel; to get a sudden chill; to get frostbitten; *P.R.* to become dried up, shriveled up; *P.R., Mex.* to get bruised by the saddle or pack (*said of horses and mules*).

**pasmo** *m.* amazement, astonishment; wonder, awe.

**pasmoso** *adj.* astonishing, astounding; marvellous.

**paso** *m.* pass; step; pace; gait; passage; passing; skit; incident; *P.R., Ch., Andes* ford; *Mex.* ferry, ferryboat wharf; *adv.* slowly; **de** — by the way, in passing; **al** — **que** while; **salir del** — to get out of a difficulty; *Am.* **marcar el** — to mark step, obey humbly; *adj.* dried (*figs, grapes, prunes, etc.*); **paso a nivel** grade crossing.

**pasta** *f.* paste; dough; noodles; book cover, binding; *Am.* cookie, cracker; **de buena** — of good temper or disposition.

**pastal** *m. Am.* range, grazing land, large pasture.

**pastar** *v.* to pasture, graze.

**pastear** *v. Mex., Ríopl.* to graze, pasture.

**pastel** *m.* pie; pastry roll; filled pastry; trick, fraud; secret pact, plot; pastel crayon; **pintura al** — pastel painting.

**pastelería** *f.* pastry shop, bakery; pastry.

**pastelero** *m.* pastry cook; *Cuba* turncoat (*person who changes easily from one political party to another*); *Ríopl.* political intriguer.

**pasterizar**[9], **pasteurizar**[9] *v.* to pasteurize.

**pastilla** *f.* tablet (*of medicine, candy, etc.*); bar (*of chocolate*); cake (*of soap*).

**pastizal** *m.* pasture, grassland.

**pasto** *m.* pasture; grassland; grazing; nourishment; *Am.* grass; **a todo** —

without restraint.

**pastor** *m.* shepherd; pastor.

**pastoral** *adj.* pastoral; *f.* pastoral play; idyll; pastoral letter; **pastorela** *f.* pastoral, pastoral play; **pastoril** *adj.* pastoral.

**pastoso** *adj.* pasty, soft; mellow (*said of the voice*); *Am.* grassy.

**pastura** *f.* pasture; fodder, feed.

**pata** *f.* foot, leg (*of an animal, table, chair, etc.*); female duck; — **de gallo** crow's-foot (*wrinkle at the corner of the eye*); *Ch., Andes* — **de perro** wanderer; *Ríopl.* **hacer** — **ancha** to stand firm, face a danger; **meter la** — to put one's foot in it, make an embarrassing blunder; **-s arriba** upside down, head over heels.

**patacón** *m. Ríopl.* silver coin worth about one peso.

**patada** *f.* kick; stamp (*with the foot*); footprint; "kick", intoxicating effect; **a -s** with kicks; in great abundance; *Andes* **en dos -s** in a jiffy, in a second.

**patalear** *v.* to kick around; to stamp.

**pataleo** *m.* kicking; stamping.

**pataleta** *f.* convulsion; fainting fit.

**patán** *m.* boor, ill-mannered person; rustic; *adj.* rude, boorish, ill-mannered.

**patata** *f.* potato.

**patear** *v.* to kick; to stamp the foot; to tramp about; to trample on; to humiliate; *Am.* to kick, spring back (*as a gun*); *Ch.* to have a kick or intoxicating effect.

**patentar** *v.* to patent.

**patente** *adj.* patent, evident, clear; *f.* patent; grant; privilege; *Carib.* **de** — excellent, of best quality.

**patentizar**[9] *v.* to evidence, reveal, show.

**paternal** *adj.* paternal; fatherly.

**paternidad** *f.* paternity, fatherhood; authorship.

**paterno** *adj.* paternal, fatherly.

**patético** *adj.* pathetic.

**patibulario** *adj.* harrowing, frightful, hair-raising; criminal.

**patíbulo** *m.* scaffold, gallows.

**patilla** *f.* small foot or paw; *Col., Ven.* watermelon; *Ríopl.* stone or brick bench (*near a wall*); *Ríopl.* railing of a balcony; *Ch.* slip from a plant; **-s** side whiskers; **Patillas** the Devil.

**patín** *m.* skate; a small patio; goosander (*a kind of duck*); — **de ruedas** roller skate; **patinadero** *m.* skating rink.

**patinar** *v.* to skate; to skid.

**patio** *m.* patio, open court, courtyard; *Am.* railway switchyard; *Am.* **pasarse uno al** — to take undue liberties.

**patituerto** *adj.* crook-legged; knock-kneed; bow-legged.

**patizambo** *adj.* knock-kneed.

**pato** *m.* duck; **pagar el** — to be the goat; to get the blame; *Ríopl.* **andar** — to be flat broke, penniless; *Am.* **hacerse** — to play the fool; *Mex., Ríopl.* **pasarse de** — **a ganso** to take undue liberties; *Am.* **ser el — de la boda** to be the life of the party; **patito** *m.* duckling.

**patochada** *f.* stupidity, blunder, nonsense.

**patojo** *adj.* crooked-legged; bowlegged; *m. & f. Guat.* child; young person.

**patraña** *f.* fabulous tale; lie, falsehood.

**patria** *f.* fatherland, native country.

**patriarca** *m.* patriarch; **patriarcal** *adj.* patriarchal.

**patrimonio** *m.* patrimony; inheritance.

**patrio** *adj.* native, of one's native country; paternal, belonging to the father.

**patriota** *m. & f.* patriot.

**patriótico** *adj.* patriotic.

**patriotismo** *m.* patriotism.

**patrocinar** *v.* to patronize, favor, sponsor.

**patrocinio** *m.* patronage, protection.

**patrón** *m.* (*protector*) patron; patron saint; sponsor; (*amo*) master, boss; proprietor, landlord; host; skipper; (*dechado*) pattern, standard, model; **patrona** *f.* landlady; patroness; hostess.

**patronato** *m.* board of trustees; foundation (*for educational, cultural, or charitable purposes*).

**patrono** *m.* patron, protector; trustee; patron saint.

**patrulla** *f.* patrol; squad, gang.

**patrullar** *v.* to patrol.

**pausa** *f.* pause, stop, rest.

**pausar** *v.* to pause.

**pauta** *f.* norm, rule, standard; guide lines (*for writing*).

**pava** *f.* turkey hen; *Ríopl.* kettle, teapot, teakettle; *Andes, Ch.* jest, coarse joke; **pelar la —** to talk by night at the window (*said of lovers*).

**pavesa** *f.* cinder; small firebrand; burnt wick or snuff of a candle; **-s** cinders.

**pavimentar** *v.* to pave.

**pavimento** *m.* pavement.

**pavo** *m.* turkey; *Ch.* sponger, parasite; **— real** peacock; **comer —** to be a wallflower at a dance; *adj.* silly, foolish; vain.

**pavón** *m.* peacock.

**pavonearse** *v.* to strut, swagger.

**pavoneo** *m.* strut, swagger.

**pavor** *m.* awe, dread, terror.

**pavoroso** *adj.* frightful, dreadful.

**payador** *m. Ríopl.* one who sings an improvised song accompanied on the guitar.

**payasada** *f.* clownish act or remark.

**payasear** *v.* to clown, play the fool.

**payaso** *m.* clown.

**paz** *f.* peace.

**pazguato** *adj.* simple, dumb, stupid; *m.* simpleton.

**peaje** *m.* toll (*for crossing a bridge or ferry*).

**peal = pial.**

**pealar = pialar.**

**peatón** *m.* pedestrian.

**peca** *f.* freckle.

**pecado** *m.* sin.

**pecador** *m.* sinner; *adj.* sinful.

**pecaminoso** *adj.* sinful.

**pecar**[6] *v.* to sin; **— de bueno** to be too good; **— de oscuro** to be exceedingly unclear, too complicated.

**pecera** *f.* fish bowl.

**pecoso** *adj.* freckly, freckled.

**peculado** *m.* embezzlement.

**peculiar** *adj.* peculiar; **peculiaridad** *f.* peculiarity.

**pechada** *f. Ríopl.* bump, push, shove with the chest; *Am.* bumping contest between two riders; *Ríopl., Ch.* overthrowing an animal (*by bumping it with the chest of a horse*).

**pechar** *v. Ríopl., Ch., Bol.* to bump, push, shove with the chest; *Ríopl., Ch., Bol.* to drive ones' horse against; *Ch., Ríopl.* to borrow, strike (*someone*) for a loan.

**pechera** *f.* shirtfront; chest protector; bib (*of an apron*).

**pecho** *m.* chest; breast; bosom; heart; courage; **dar el —** to nurse; **tomar a -s** to take to heart; *P.R., Col.* **a todo —** shouting; *Am.* **en -s de camisa** in shirt sleeves.

**pechuga** *f.* breast, breast meat of a fowl; bosom; *C.A., Col., Ch., Andes* courage, nerve, audacity, impudence.

**pedagogía** *f.* pedagogy, science of education.

**pedagógica** *adj.* pedagogic, relating to education or teaching.

**pedagogo** *m.* pedagogue, teacher, educator.

**pedal** *m.* pedal.

**pedalear** *v.* to pedal.

**pedante** *adj.* pedantic, affected, vain, superficial; *m.* pedant; **pedantesco** *adj.* pedantic.

**pedazo** *m.* piece, portion, bit; **hacer -s** to tear or break into pieces; **caerse a -s** to fall into pieces.

**pedernal** *m.* flint.

**pedestal** *m.* pedestal, base.

**pedestre** *adj.* pedestrian, walking, going on foot; commonplace, vulgar, low.

**pedido** *m.* commercial order; request, petition; *p.p.* of **pedir.**

**pedigüeño** *adj.* begging, demanding.

**pedir**[5] *v. irr.* to ask, beg, petition; to ask for; to demand; to require; to order (*merchandise*); **a — de boca** exactly as desired.

**pedo** *m.* wind, flatulence; *Mex.* **andar —** to be drunk.

**pedrada** *f.* hit or blow with a stone; throw with a stone; mark or bruise made by a stone (*thrown*); **a -s** by stoning; with stones; **dar una —** to hit with a stone; **echar a alguien a -s** to someone someone out; **matar a -s** to stone to death.

**pedregal** *m.* rocky ground, ground strewn with rocks.

**pedregoso** *adj.* rocky, stony, pebbly.

**pedrería** *f.* precious stones; precious stone ornament; jewelry.

**pedrusco** *m.* boulder.

**pedúnculo** *m.* stem (*of a leaf, flower or fruit*), stalk.

**pegajoso** *adj.* sticky; contagious.

**pegar**[7] *v.* (*golpear*) to hit, strike, slap, beat; (*adherir*) to stick, paste, glue; to sew on (*a button*); to infect; to be becoming; to be fitting, opportune, to the point; *Am.* to tie, fasten; *Am.* to yoke; — **fuego** to set on fire; — **un chasco** to play a trick; to surprise, disappoint; — **un susto** to give a scare; — **un salto (una carrera)** to take a jump (a run); **-se** to stick, cling; **pegársela a uno** to fool somebody.

**pegote** *m.* sticky thing; sticking plaster; clumsy patch; sponger; thick, sticky concoction; clumsy addition or insertion (*in a literary or artistic work*).

**peinado** *m.* coiffure, hairdo; hairdressing; *p.p.* combed; groomed; *adj.* effeminate; **bien** — spruce, trim.

**peinador** *m.* hairdresser; short wrapper or dressing gown; **peinadora** *f.* woman hairdresser.

**peinar** *v.* to comb; *Ríopl.* to flatter.

**peine** *m.* comb.

**peineta** *f.* large ornamental comb.

**peladilla** *f.* small pebble.

**pelado** *p.p.* & *adj.* peeled; plucked; skinned; hairless; featherless; barren, treeless, bare; penniless, broke; *m. Mex.* ragged fellow (*generally a peon*); *Mex.* ill-bred person; *Col.* child.

**pelafustán** *m.* tramp, vagabond.

**pelagatos** *m.* ragged fellow, tramp.

**pelaje** *m.* animal's coat, fur; external appearance.

**pelar** *v.* to cut the hair of; to pluck the feathers or hair from; to peel, shell, skin, husk; to fleece, rob; *Am.* to beat, thrash; *Am.* to slander; *C.R.* — **los dientes** to show one's teeth; to smile affectedly; *C.A., Mex., Carib., Col., Andes* — **los ojos** to keep one's eyes peeled; to open one's eyes wide; **-se** to peel off; to lose one's hair; *Col., Ven.* to be confused; *Col., Ven.* to be careless, unaware; *Col., Ven.* to slip away; *Col., Ven.* to die; **pelárselas por algo** to be dying for something, want something very much.

**peldaño** *m.* step (*of a staircase*).

**pelea** *f.* fight, quarrel.

**pelear** *v.* to fight; to quarrel.

**peletería** *f.* fur store; fur trade; furs; *Am.* leather goods, leather shop; *Cuba* shoe store.

**película** *f.* thin skin; membrane; film; motion-picture film.

**peligrar** *v.* to be in danger.

**peligro** *m.* danger.

**peligroso** *adj.* dangerous.

**pelillo** *m.* short, fine hair; **-s** trouble, nuisance; **echar -s a la mar** to "bury the hatchet", become reconciled; **no pararse en -s** not to stop at small details, not to bother about trifles; **no tener -s en la lengua** to speak frankly.

**pelirrojo** *adj.* redheaded, red-haired.

**pelo** *m.* (*cabello*) hair; (*haz*) nap (*of cloth*); (*fibra*) grain (*in wood*); **al** — perfectly; agreed; apropos, to the point; along the grain; **eso me viene al** — that suits me perfectly; **con todos sus -s y señales** with every possible detail; *Am.* **por** (*or* **en**) **un** — on the point of, almost, by a hair's breadth; **montar en** — to ride bareback; **tomar el** — **a** to kid, make fun of; *Ríopl., Carib., Mex., Andes* **no aflojar un** — not to yield an inch.

**pelota** *f.* ball; ball game; *Am.* boat made of cowhide; **en** — (*or* **en -s**) naked; *Am.* **darle a la** — to hit upon by chance; **pelotilla** *f.* pellet, little ball.

**pelotari** *m.* pelota (*jai-alai*) player.

**pelotera** *f.* brawl, row, riot; *C.A., Ven.* crowd.

**pelotón** *m.* large ball; crowd, gang; heap, pile; platoon of soldiers; firing squad.

**peluca** *f.* wig.

**peludo** *adj.* hairy; shaggy; *m.* plush carpet with shaggy pile; *Am.* a species of armadillo; *Ríopl.* **agarrar un** — to get drunk.

**peluquería** *f.* barbershop, hairdresser's shop.

**peluquero** *m.* hairdresser, barber.

**pelusa** *f.* down; fuzz; nap (*of cloth*).

**pellejo** *m.* hide; skin; peel; **salvar el** — to save one's skin, escape punishment; *Am.* **jugarse el** — to gamble one's life.

**pellizcar**[6] *v.* to pinch, nip.

**pellizco** *m.* pinching, nipping; pinch, nip.

**pena** *f.* penalty; grief, worry; hardship; toil; *Mex., Carib., C.A., Col., Ven.* embarrassment; **a duras -s** with great difficulty; hardly; **me da** — it grieves me; *C.A., Ven., Col., Carib.* it embarrasses me; **valer la** — to be worthwhile; **tener** (*or* **estar con**) **mucha** — to be terribly sorry; *Am.* to be greatly embarrassed.

**penacho** *m.* tuft, crest; plume.

**penal** *adj.* penal; **código** — penal code.

**penalidad** *f.* hardship; trouble; penalty.

**penar** *v.* to suffer; to worry, fret; to impose a penalty; — **por** to long for; to suffer because of.

**penca** *f.* leaf of a cactus plant; *Am.* sweetheart; *Ven.* **coger una** — to get drunk.

**penco** *m.* nag, horse; *Am.* boor.

**pendencia** *f.* quarrel; scuffle, fight.

**pendenciero** *adj.* quarrelsome.

**pender** *v.* to hang; to dangle; to depend.

**pendiente** *f.* slope; *m.* earring; pendant; *Am.* watch chain; *adj.* hanging, dangling; pending.

**pendón** *m.* banner.

**péndulo** *m.* pendulum.

**penetración** *f.* penetration; acuteness; keen judgment.

**penetrante** *adj.* penetrating; acute; keen.

**penetrar** *v.* to penetrate; to pierce; to fathom, comprehend.

**penicilina** *f.* penicillin.

**península** *f.* peninsula.

**peninsular** *adj.* peninsular.

**penitencia** *f.* penance.

**penitenciaría** *f.* penitentiary.

**penitente** *adj.* repentant, penitent; *m. & f.* penitent.

**penoso** *adj.* painful; hard, difficult; embarrassing; fatiguing; *Mex., Carib., C.A., Ven., Col.* timid, shy.

**pensador** *m.* thinker; *adj.* thinking.

**pensamiento** *m.* thought; mind; pansy.

**pensar**[1] *v. irr.* to think; to think over; to intend.

**pensativo** *adj.* pensive.

**pensión** *f.* pension; board; scholarship for study; boardinghouse; *Col.* apprehension, anxiety; **— completa** room and board.

**pensionado** *m.* pensioner (*person receiving a pension*); *adj. & p.p.* pensioned.

**pensionar** *v.* to pension.

**pensionista** *m. & f.* boarder; pensioner (*person receiving a pension*).

**pentagrama** *m.* musical staff.

**penúltimo** *adj.* next to the last.

**penumbra** *f.* partial shadow, dimness.

**penumbroso** *adj.* dim.

**peña** *f.* rock, large stone.

**peñasco** *m.* large rock; crag.

**peñascoso** *adj.* rocky.

**peón** *m.* unskilled laborer; foot soldier; spinning top; pawn (*in chess*); *Ch., Ríopl., C.A., Carib., Mex.* farm hand; *Am.* apprentice; *Mex.* **— de albañil** mason's helper.

**peonada** *f.* gang of laborers or peons.

**peor** *adj. & adv.* worse; worst; **— que** worse than; **— que** — that is even worse; **tanto** — so much the worse.

**pepa** *f. Andes, Col., Ven., Ch., Mex., Ríopl.* seed (*of an apple, melon, etc.*); *Am.* marble (*to play with*); **Pepa** nickname for **Josefa.**

**pepenar** *v. Mex.* to pick up; *Am.* to seize, grab.

**pepino** *m.* cucumber.

**pepita** *f.* seed (*of an apple, melon, etc.*); pip (*a disease of birds*); nugget (*lump of gold or other minerals*); *Am.* fruit stone, pit; **Pepita = Josefita** *dim. of* **Josefa.**

**pequeñez** *f.* smallness; childhood; trifle; meanness.

**pequeño** *adj.* small, little; young; low, humble; *m.* child.

**pera** *f.* pear; goatee; sinecure, easy job; *Am.* Peruvian alligator pear (*see* **aguacate**); *Am.* **hacerle a uno la —** to play a trick on someone; **peral** *m.* pear tree; pear orchard.

**percal** *m.* percale (*fine cotton cloth*).

**percance** *m.* misfortune, accident; occurrence.

**percepción** *f.* perception; idea.

**perceptible** *adj.* perceptible, noticeable.

**percibir** *v.* to perceive; to collect, receive.

**percudido** *adj.* dirty, grimy.

**percudir** *v.* to soil, make dirty or grimy; **-se** to get grimy.

**percha** *f.* clothes or hat rack; pole; perch, roost; perch (*a fish*); **perchero** *m.* clothes or hat rack.

**perder**[1] *v. irr.* to lose; to squander; to ruin, harm; to miss (*a train*); **— de vista** to lose sight of; **-se** to lose one's way; to get lost; to go astray; to get spoiled; to become ruined.

**perdición** *f.* perdition, damnation, hell, ruin.

**pérdida** *f.* loss; damage.

**perdidamente** *adv.* excessively.

**perdido** *p.p. & adj.* lost; strayed; mislaid; ruined; **estar — por alguien** to be crazy about, or very fond of, someone; *m.* rake, dissolute fellow; bum, vagabond.

**perdigón** *m.* young partridge; bird shot, buckshot; losing gambler.

**perdiz** *f.* partridge.

**perdón** *m.* pardon; forgiveness; remission.

**perdonar** *v.* to pardon; to forgive.

**perdulario** *m.* rake, dissolute person; reckless fellow; good-for-nothing; tramp.

**perdurable** *adj.* lasting, everlasting.

**perdurar** *v.* to last, endure.

**perecedero** *adj.* perishable.

**perecer**[13] *v. irr.* to perish; to die; **-se** to long (for), pine (for).

**peregrinación** *f.* pilgrimage; long journey.

**peregrino** *m.* pilgrim; *adj.* foreign, strange; rare; beautiful, perfect; travelling, wandering; **ave peregrina** migratory bird, bird of passage.

**perejil** *m.* parsley; **-es** frippery, showy clothes or ornaments.

**perenne** *adj.* perennial, enduring, perpetual.

**pereza** *f.* laziness; idleness.

**perezoso** *adj.* lazy; *m. Am.* sloth (*an animal*); *Am.* safety pin; *Am.* bed cushion.

**perfección** *f.* perfection; **a la —** to perfection, perfectly.

**perfeccionamiento** *m.* perfecting, perfection; completion.

**perfeccionar** *v.* to perfect, finish, complete.

**perfecto** *adj.* perfect.

**perfidia** *f.* perfidy, treachery.

**pérfido** *adj.* perfidious, treacherous, faithless.

**perfil** *m.* profile; outline; *Am.* pen or pen point.

**perfilar** *v.* to silhouette; to outline; **-se** to show one's profile; to be silhouetted.

**perforación** *f.* perforation, hole; puncture; perforating, boring, drilling.

**perforar** *v.* to perforate, pierce; to drill, bore.

**perfumar** *v.* to perfume, scent.

**perfume** *m.* perfume; fragrance.

**perfumería** *f.* perfumery; perfume shop.

**pergamino** *m.* parchment.

**pericia** *f.* expertness, skill.

**perico** *m.* parakeet, small parrot; *Col.* **huevos -s** scrambled eggs.

**perifollos** *m. pl.* frippery, finery, showy ornaments.

**perifrasear** *v.* to paraphrase.

**perigeo** *m.* perigee.

**perilla** *f.* small pear; pear-shaped ornament; knob; pommel of a saddle; goatee; **de —** apropos, to the point.

**perímetro** *m.* perimeter.

**periódico** *m.* newspaper; periodical; *adj.* periodic, periodical.

**periodismo** *m.* journalism; **periodista** *m. & f.* journalist; newspaper editor or publisher; **periodístico** *adj.* journalistic.

**período** *m.* period; cycle; sentence.

**peripecia** *f.* vicissitude, change in fortune; unforeseen incident.

**peripuesto** *adj.* dressed up, dolled up, decked out.

**perito** *adj.* learned; experienced; skillful; skilled; *m.* expert.

**perjudicar**[6] *v.* to damage, impair, harm.

**perjudicial** *adj.* harmful, injurious.

**perjuicio** *m.* damage, ruin, mischief; harm.

**perjurar** *v.* to perjure oneself; to commit perjury; to curse, swear.

**perjurio** *m.* perjury.

**perla** *f.* pearl; **de -s** perfectly, just right, to the point.

**perlino** *adj.* pearly, pearl-colored.

**permanecer**[13] *v. irr.* to remain, stay.

**permanencia** *f.* permanence, duration; stability; stay, sojourn.

**permanente** *adj.* permanent.

**permiso** *m.* permission; permit.

**permitir** *v.* to permit, let; to grant.

**permuta** *f.* exchange, barter.

**permutar** *v.* to exchange; to barter; to change around.

**pernetas : en —** barelegged, with bare legs.

**pernicioso** *adj.* pernicious, harmful.

**perno** *m.* bolt; spike; **-s** *Am.* tricks, frauds.

**pero** *conj.* but, except, yet; *m.* objection, exception; defect; a variety of apple tree; a variety of apple; **perón** *m. Am.* a variety of apple.

**perogrullada** *f.* platitude, trite or commonplace remark.

**peroración** *f.* peroration, speech, harangue.

**perorar** *v.* to make an impassioned speech; to declaim, harangue; to plea, make a plea.

**perorata** *f.* harangue, speech.

**perpendicular** *adj., m. & f.* perpendicular.

**perpetuar**[18] *v.* to perpetuate.

**perpetuo** *adj.* perpetual; **perpetua** *f.* everlasting.

**perplejidad** *f.* perplexity.

**perplejo** *adj.* perplexed, bewildered.

**perra** *f.* bitch, female dog; drunkenness; **— chica** five-centime copper coin; **— grande** (*or* **gorda**) ten-centime copper coin.

**perrada** *f.* pack of dogs; **hacer una —** to play a mean trick.

**perrera** *f.* kennel; toil, hard work, hard job; tantrum; *Carib., Mex., Ven.* brawl, dispute.

**perrilla** *f. Am.* sty (*on the eyelid*). *See* **orzuelo.**

**perro** *m.* dog; **— de busca** hunting dog; **— dogo** bulldog; **— de lanas** poodle; *adj.* dogged, tenacious; *Mex., C.A.* hard, selfish, mean, stingy; *Ven.*, vagabond.

**perruno** *adj.* canine, doglike.

**persecución** *f.* persecution; pursuit.

**perseguidor** *m.* pursuer; persecutor.

**perseguimiento** *m.* pursuit; persecution.

**perseguir**[5,12] *v. irr.* to pursue; to persecute; to harass, annoy.

**perseverancia** *f.* perseverance.

**perseverar** *v.* to persevere.

**persiana** *f.* Venetian blind; window shade.

**persistencia** *f.* persistence; **persistente** *adj.* persistent.

**persistir** *v.* to persist.

**persona** *f.* person; personage.

**personaje** *m.* personage; character (*in a book or play*).

**personal** *adj.* personal; *m.* personnel.

**personalidad** *f.* personality; individuality; person, personage.

**perspectiva** *f.* perspective; view; appearance; outlook; prospect.

**perspicacia** *f.* keenness of mind, penetration, keen insight.

**perspicaz** *adj.* keen, shrewd.

**persuadir** *v.* to persuade.

**persuasión** *f.* persuasion.

**persuasivo** *adj.* persuasive.

**pertenecer**[13] *v. irr.* to belong; to pertain; to concern.

**perteneciente** *adj.* pertaining, belonging, concerning.

**pértiga** *f.* pole, bar, rod; **salto con —** pole vault.

**pertinente** *adj.* pertinent, to the point, apt, fitting.

**pertrechos** *m. pl.* military supplies; tools, implements.

**perturbación** *f.* uneasiness, agitation, disturbance.

**perturbar** *v.* to perturb, disturb.

**peruano** *adj. & m.* Peruvian.

**perulero** *adj. m. & f.* Peruvian (*slang expression*).

**perversidad** *f.* perversity, wickedness.

**perverso** *adj.* perverse, wicked; *m.* pervert.

**pervertir**[3] *v. irr.* to pervert; to; corrupt to distort; **-se** to become perverted; to go wrong.

**pesa** *f.* weight (*for scales*); **— de reloj** clock weight; **-s y medidas** weights and measures.

**pesadez** *f.* heaviness; dullness, drowsiness; slowness; bother; stubbornness.

**pesadilla** *f.* nightmare.

**pesado** *adj.* heavy; sound (*sleep*); tiresome, boring; annoying; slow; dull.

**pesadumbre** *f.* grief, sorrow; weight, heavinesss.

**pésame** *m.* condolence, expression of sympathy.

**pesantez** *f.* gravity; heaviness.

**pesar** *v.* (*penar*) to cause grief, sorrow, or regret; (*tener gravedad*) to weigh; to consider, to have weight, value, or importance; *m.* grief, sorrow; **a — de** in spite of.

**pesaroso** *adj.* grieved, sad; repentant.

**pesca** *f.* fishing; catch, fish caught.

**pescadería** *f.* fish market; **pescadero** *m.* fishmonger, dealer in fish.

**pescado** *m.* fish (*especially after being caught*); salted codfish.

**pescador** *m.* fisherman.

**pescar**[6] *v.* to fish; to catch; to catch unaware, catch in the act.

**pescozón** *m.* blow on the back of the head or neck.

**pescuezo** *m.* neck.

**pesebre** *m.* manger.

**peseta** *f.* peseta (*monetary unit of Spain*).

**pesimismo** *m.* pessimism; **pesimista** *m.* & *f.* pessimist; *adj.* pessimistic.

**pésimo** *adj.* very bad.

**peso** *m.* weight; weighing; burden; importance; *Am.* peso (*monetary unit of several Spanish American countries*).

**pesquera** *f.* fishery (*place for catching fish*); **pesquería** *f.* fishery; fishing.

**pesquero** *adj.* fishing; **buque —** fishing boat; **industria pesquera** fishing industry.

**pesquisa** *f.* investigation, inquiry; *m. Am.* police investigator.

**pestaña** *f.* eyelash; edging, fringe; **quemarse las -s** to burn the midnight oil, study hard at night.

**pestañear** *v.* to blink; to wink; to flicker.

**peste** *f.* pest, pestilence, plague; epidemic; stench, stink, foul odor; overabundance, excess; *Am.* smallpox; *Col.* head cold; **echar -s** to utter insults.

**pestillo** *m.* bolt; latch; lock.

**petaca** *f.* tobacco pouch; cigar case; leather covered hamper (*used as a pack*); *Mex., Ven.* leather covered trunk, suitcase; *adj. Andes* heavy, clumsy.

**pétalo** *m.* petal.

**petate** *m.* bundle; impostor; *Mex., C.A., Ven., Col.* mat (*of straw or palm leaves*); *Am.* dunce; *Andes* coward; **liar el —** to pack up and go; *Mex.* to die; *Col., Ven.* **dejar a uno en un —** to ruin a person, leave him penniless.

**petición** *f.* petition, request.

**petirrojo** *m.* robin, robin redbreast.

**petiso** *adj. Ríopl., Ch., Andes* small, short, dwarfish; *m. Am.* small horse, pony.

**pétreo** *adj.* stone, stony.

**petróleo** *m.* petroleum.

**petrolero** *m.* oil man; dealer in petroleum; **compañía petrolera** oil company.

**petulancia** *f.* flippancy; insolence; **petulante** *adj.* pert, impertinent, flippant.

**pez** *m.* fish; *f.* pitch, tar.

**pezón** *m.* nipple; stem, stalk (*of a fruit, leaf or flower*); small point of land.

**pezuña** *f.* hoof.

**piadoso** *adj.* pious; kind, merciful.

**pial** *m. Mex.* lasso, lariat (*thrown in order to trip an animal*); *Ríopl.* snare, trap.

**pialar** *v.* to lasso by tripping with a **pial.**

**piano** *m.* piano; **— de cola** grand piano; **— vertical** upright piano.

**piar**[17] *v.* to peep, chirp; to cry, whine.

**pica** *f.* pike, spear; picador's goad or lance; stonecutter's hammer; *Ven.* tapping of rubber trees; *Col.* trail; *Col., Ch.* pique, resentment; *Am.* cockfight.

**picada** *f.* prick; bite (*as of an insect or fish*); puncture; sharp pain; dive (*of a plane*); *Cuba, Ríopl.* path, trail (*cut through a forest*); *Am.* narrow ford; *Col., Ven., Mex.* peck.

**picadillo** *m.* meat and vegetable hash; minced meat, mincemeat.

**picador** *m.* picador (*mounted bullfighter armed with a goad*); horse-breaker; chopping block; *Ven.* tree tapper.

**picadura** *f.* biting; pricking; bite; prick; sting; puncture; cut tobacco.

**picante** *adj.* (*acerbo*) pricking, biting, stinging; (*con chile o ají*) spicy; highly seasoned; *m.* strong seasoning; *Am.* highly seasoned sauce (*usually containing chili pepper*).

**picapleitos** *m.* quarrelsome person (*one who likes to pick a fight*); shyster.

**picaporte** *m.* latch; latchkey; door knocker.

**picar**[6] *v.* to prick; to pierce; to bite (*said of fish or insects*); to sting; to peck; to nibble; to mince, chop up; to goad; to stick, poke; to hew, chisel; to pique, vex; to itch, smart, burn; *Am.* to chop (*wood*); *Am.* to open a trail; *Am.* to tap (*a tree*); *Am.* to slaughter (*cattle*); **— muy alto** to aim very high; **— en** to border on, be somewhat of; *Mex., Ven.* **¡picale!** hurry! **-se** to be piqued, angry; to be motheaten; to begin to sour; to begin to rot; *C.A., Ven.* to get tipsy; **-se de** to boast of.

**picardía** *f.* roguishness; offensive act or remark; roguish trick; mischief.

**picaresco** *adj.* picaresque, roguish.

**pícaro** *m.* rogue, rascal; *adj.* roguish; mischievous; crafty, sly; low, vile; **picarón** *m.* big rascal.

**picazón** *f.* itch, itching.

**pico** *m.* beak, bill; sharp point; peak; pickaxe, pick, spout; mouth; additional amount, a little over; *C.A., Carib., Ríopl., Ven.* a small balance; *Mex.* a goodly sum; **tener el — de**

**oro** to be very eloquent; **tener mucho — to** be very talkative.

**picotada** *f.*, **picotazo** *m.* peck.

**picotear** *v.* to peck; to chatter; *Am.* to mince, cut into small pieces.

**pichel** *m.* pitcher; mug.

**pichón** *m.* pigeon; *C.A.* any male bird (*except a rooster*); *Am.* dupe, easy mark; *Am.* novice, inexperienced person, apprentice; *adj. Am.* timid, shy.

**pie** *m.* foot; leg; stand; stem; base; *Am.* down payment; *Mex.* strophe, stanza; *Am.* **— de amigo** wedge; prop; **— de banco** silly remark; **a — juntillas** steadfastly, firmly; **al — de la letra** to the letter, literally, exactly; **de —** (*or* **en —**) standing; **a cuatro -s** on all fours; **dar —** to give an opportunity or occasion; *Am.* **estar a — en** to be ignorant of; **ir a —** to walk.

**piececito, piecito** *m.* little foot.

**piedad** *f.* piety; pity; mercy; **monte de — pawnshop.**

**piedra** *f.* stone; gravel; hailstone; *Ven.* piece of a domino set; **— angular** (*or* **fundamental**) cornerstone; **— caliza** limestone; **— pómez** pumice, pumice stone; **a — y lodo** shut tight; **ser — de escándalo** to be an object of scandal.

**piel** *f.* skin; hide; leather; fur.

**piélago** *m.* high sea; sea; great abundance, great plenty.

**pienso** *m.* feed; thought; **ni por —** not even in thought.

**pierna** *f.* leg; **dormir a — suelta** to sleep like a log, sleep soundly; *Am.* **ser una buena —** to be a good fellow, be always in a good mood.

**pieza** *f.* (*pedazo*) piece; part; (*cuarto*) room; (*comedia*) play; **de una —** solid, in one piece; *Am.* **ser de una —** to be an honest, upright man.

**pigmento** *m.* pigment.

**pijama** *m.* pajamas.

**pila** *f.* (*pieza cóncava*) basin; baptismal font; trough; (*cúmulo*) pile; heap; electric battery; **— atómica** atomic pile; *Am.* fountain; *Andes* hairless dog; *Am.* bald head; **nombre de —** Christian name; *Andes* **andar —** to go naked; *Mex.* **tener las -s** (*or* **tener por -s**) to have a lot, have heaps.

**pilar** *m.* pillar, column; basin of a fountain.

**pilcha** *f. Ríopl.* any article of clothing; *Am.* mistress; **-s** *Ríopl.* belongings.

**píldora** *f.* pill.

**pilmama** *f. Mex.* child's nurse, wet nurse.

**pilón** *m.* basin (*of a fountain*); watering trough; sugar loaf; large wooden or metal mortar (*for grinding grain*); counterpoise; *Mex.* an additional amount, premium (*given to a buyer*); *Mex.* **de —** to boot, in addition, besides; **piloncillo** *m. Am.* unrefined sugar loaf.

**pilotar, pilotear** *v.* to pilot.

**pilote** *m.* pile (*for building*).

**piloto** *m.* pilot; *Mex.* generous entertainer or host.

**pillaje** *m.* pillage, plunder.

**pillar** *v.* to pillage, plunder; to pilfer; to seize, snatch, grasp; to catch; *Am.* to surprise, catch in the act.

**pillo** *adj.* roguish; sly, crafty; *m.* rogue, rascal; *Am.* a species of heron; *Am.* long-legged person; **pilluelo** *m.* little rascal, scamp.

**pimentero** *m.* pepper plant; pepperbox, pepper shaker.

**pimentón** *m.* large pepper; cayenne, red pepper; paprika.

**pimienta** *f.* black pepper.

**pimiento** *m.* green pepper; red pepper.

**pimpollo** *m.* rosebud; bud; shoot, sprout; attractive youth.

**pináculo** *m.* pinnacle, top, summit.

**pinar** *m.* pine grove.

**pincel** *m.* artist's brush; **pincelada** *f.* stroke of the brush.

**pinchar** *v.* to prick; to puncture.

**pinchazo** *m.* prick; puncture; stab.

**pingajo** *m.* tag, tatter, rag.

**pingo** *m. Ríopl., Andes* saddle horse; *Mex.* devil.

**pingüe** *adj.* abundant, copious; fat, greasy.

**pino** *m.* pine; *Am.* filling for a meat pie; **hacer -s** (*or* **hacer pinitos**) to begin to walk (*said of a baby*); to begin to do things (*said of a novice*).

**pinta** *f.* spot, mark; outward sign, aspect; pint; *Mex.* **hacer —** to play hooky, cut class.

**pintar** *v.* to paint; to describe, depict; to feign; to begin to turn red, begin to ripen (*said of fruit*); to fancy, imagine; *Mex.* to play hooky, play truant; *Am.* to fawn, flatter; **no — nada** to be worth nothing, count for nothing; **las cosas no pintaban bien** things did not look well; *Mex.* **— venados** to play hooky; **-se** to put on make-up; *Am.* to excel (in); to praise oneself; *Ven.* to go away.

**pintarrajear** *v.* to daub; to smear with paint or rouge.

**pinto** *adj. Am.* spotted, speckled.

**pintor** *m.* painter, artist; **— de brocha gorda** house painter; poor artist; *adj. Am.* boastful, conceited.

**pintoresco** *adj.* picturesque.

**pintura** *f.* painting; picture; paint, color; description.

**pinzas** *f. pl.* pincers; tweezers; claws (*of lobsters, crabs, etc.*); *Ríopl., Mex., Carib.* pliers, tongs.

**piña** *f.* pineapple; pine cone; piña cloth; cluster; *Cuba* pool (*a billiard game*).

**piñata** *f.* pot; hanging pot or other container (*filled with candies, fruit, etc.*).

**piñón** *m.* pine nut; nut pine; pinion.

**pío** *adj.* pious, devout; kind; merciful; dappled, spotted (*horse*); **obras pías** pious works, charitable deeds.

**piojo** *m.* louse.

**piojoso** *adj.* lousy; mean, stingy.

**pipa** *f.* tobacco pipe; keg, barrel; reed

PE

pipe (*musical instrument*); fruit seed (*of a lemon, orange, melon*); *Col.* green coconut; *Am.* potato; *Ven.* **estar —** to be drunk; *m. Am.* species of green frog.

**pipiar**[17] *v.* to peep, chirp.

**pipiolo** *m.* novice, beginner; *Am.* child, youngster.

**pique** *m.* pique, resentment; chigger (*insect*); flea; *Am.* small chili pepper; *Am.* trail; **a — de** in danger of, on the point of; **echar a —** to sink (*a ship*); to destroy; **irse a —** to capsize; to sink.

**piquete** *m.* prick; bite, sting (*of insects*); small hole; picket, stake; picket (*military*); *Am.* small band of musicians; *Am.* small corral; *Am.* cutting edge of scissors.

**piragua** *f. Ríopl., Carib., Ven., Col., Andes* Indian canoe.

**pirámide** *f.* pyramid.

**pirata** *m.* pirate.

**piratear** *v.* to pirate.

**piropo** *m.* flattery, compliment; a variety of garnet (*a semiprecious stone*); **echar un —** to "throw a bouquet"; to compliment.

**pirueta** *f.* whirl; somersault; caper; **hacer -s** to cut capers; to turn somersaults; to do stunts.

**pisada** *f.* footstep; footprint; **dar una —** to step on, stamp on; **seguir las -s de** to follow in the fooststeps of; to imitate.

**pisapapeles** *m.* paperweight.

**pisar** *v.* to step on, tread upon; to trample under foot; to pound; to cover (*said of a male bird*).

**piscina** *f.* swimming pool, swimming tank; fish pond.

**pise** *m. Ven.* rut; *Am.* tread (*of a wheel*). See **rodadura.**

**piso** *m.* floor; story; pavement; apartment, flat; tread; *Ríopl., Mex., Carib., Ven.* fee for pasturage rights; *Am.* table scarf; *Am.* stool, footstool; *Am.* small rug.

**pisón** *m.* heavy mallet (*for pounding, flattening, crushing*).

**pisotear** *v.* to tramp, tramp on, trample; to tread.

**pisotón** *m.* hard step, stamp (*of the foot*); **dar un —** to step hard, stamp (upon).

**pista** *f.* track, trace, trail; clew; race track; **— de aterrizaje** landing field.

**pistola** *f.* pistol; **pistolera** *f.* holster.

**pistón** *m.* piston; *Col.* cornet.

**pita** *f. Am.* agave or century plant; *Am.* fiber, or thread made from the fiber, of the agave or maguey.

**pitar** *v.* to toot; to whistle; *Ríopl., Andes* to smoke; *Ven.* to hiss; *Carib., Mex.* to slip away, escape; *Am.* **-se una cosa** to steal something; *Ch., Col., Ven., C.A.* (*pitado*) **salir pitando** to leave on the run.

**pitazo** *m.* toot, whistle, blast.

**pitillo** *m.* cigarette; **pitillera** *f.* cigarette case.

**pito** *m.* whistle; cigarette; *Am.* tick (*an insect*); **no vale un —** it is not worth a straw; *Am.* **no saber ni — de una cosa** not to know anything about a subject.

**pizarra** *f.* slate; blackboard; **pizarrín** *m.* slate pencil; **pizarrón** *m.* blackboard.

**pizca** *f.* pinch, small bit; *Mex.* harvest.

**placa** *f.* badge, insignia; plaque, tablet; metal plate; photographic plate; license plate; *Ven.* scab or skin blemish.

**placentero** *adj.* pleasant, agreeable.

**placer**[38] *v. irr.* to please, content; *m.* pleasure; sand bank, shoal; placer (*place where gold is obtained by washing*); *Am.* pearl fishing.

**placero** *m.*, **placera** *f.* market vendor.

**plácido** *adj.* placid, calm.

**plaga** *f.* plague; calamity.

**plagar**[7] *v.* to plague, infest; **-se de** to become plagued or infested with.

**plagiar** *v.* to plagiarize, steal and use as one's own (*the writings, ideas, etc. of another*); to kidnap, abduct.

**plan** *m.* plan; design; project; drawing; mine floor; *Am.* clearing; *Am.* building grounds of a ranch.

**plana** *f.* page; plain, flat country; mason's trowel; tally sheet; **enmendar la — a uno** to correct a person's mistakes.

**plancha** *f.* flatiron; metal plate; gangplank; blunder; *Cuba* railway flatcar; *Ven., Col.* dental plate; **— de blindaje** armor plate; **hacer una —** to make a ridiculous blunder; **tirarse una —** to place oneself in a ridiculous situation.

**planchado** *m.* ironing; clothes ironed or to be ironed; *adj. Am.* smart, clever; *Am.* brave; *Ven.* dolled up, dressed up; *Am.* broke, penniless.

**planchar** *v.* to iron; to smooth out; *Mex.* to leave (*someone*) waiting; *Am.* to strike with the flat of a blade; *Am.* to flatter; *Mex., Ven.* **— el asiento** to be a wallflower at a dance.

**planeador** *m.* glider airplane.

**planear** *v.* to plan; to glide (*said of an airplane or bird*).

**planeo** *m.* planning; glide, gliding (*of an airplane*).

**planeta** *m.* planet.

**plano** *adj.* plane, flat, level; *m.* plane; plan; map; **de —** flatly, clearly, openly; **dar de —** to hit with the flat of anything.

**planta** *f.* (*ser orgánico*) plant; plantation; (*proyecto*) plan; ground plan, ground floor; (*del pie*) sole of the foot; **— baja** ground floor; **buena —** good looks; **echar -s** to brag.

**plantación** *f.* plantation; planting.

**plantar** *v.* to plant; to strike (*a blow*); **-se** to stand firm; to balk; *Am.* to doll up, dress up; **dejar a uno plantado** to "stand someone up", keep someone waiting indefinitely.

**plantear** *v.* to plan; to establish; to carry out; to state, present (*a prob-*

*lem*); to try.

**plantel** *m.* establishment; firm; plant; nursery.

**plantío** *m.* planting; plantation; recently planted garden; tree nursery.

**plasma** *m.* plasma.

**plástico** *adj.* plastic.

**plata** *f.* silver; silver money; **hablar en — to** speak in plain language; *Carib., C.A., Ven., Col.* money.

**plataforma** *f.* platform; **— de lanzamiento** launching pad.

**platanal, platanar** *m.* grove of banana trees; banana plantation.

**plátano** *m.* banana; banana tree; plane tree.

**platea** *f.* main floor of a theatre; a lower box seat.

**plateado** *adj.* silver-plated; silvery.

**platear** *v.* to silver, plate, cover with silver.

**platel** *m.* platter; tray.

**platero** *m.* silversmith; jeweler.

**plática** *f.* conversation, talk, chat; informal lecture.

**platicador** *m.* talker; *adj.* talkative.

**platicar**[6] *v.* to converse, talk, chat.

**platillo** *m.* saucer; pan (*of a pair of scales*); cymbal; stew.

**platino** *m.* platinum.

**plato** *m.* plate; dish; dinner course; **— de tocadiscos** turntable.

**platón** *m.* large plate; platter.

**platudo** *adj. Am.* wealthy, rich.

**playa** *f.* beach, shore; *Ven.* wide, open space in front of a ranch house; *Ríopl., Andes* **— de estacionamiento** parking lot.

**plaza** *f.* (*pública*) plaza, public square; public market; (*empleo*) job; employment; *Ríopl., Ch., Cuba, Ven.* park, promenade; **— de armas** parade ground; public square; fortress; **— fuerte** fortress; **— de gallos** cockpit (*for cockfights*); **— de toros** bull ring; **sacar a —** to bring out into the open, make public; **sentar —** to enlist; **plazoleta, plazuela** *f.* small square, court.

**plazo** *m.* term, time; **a —** on credit; in installments.

**pleamar** *m.* flood tide, high tide.

**plebe** *f.* rabble; masses.

**plebeyo** *adj.* plebeian.

**plebiscito** *m.* plebiscite, direct vote.

**plegadizo** *adj.* folding; pliable, easily bent.

**plegar**[1,7] *v.* to fold; to pleat; to crease; **-se** to bend, yield, submit.

**plegaria** *f.* supplication, prayer; prayer hour.

**pleito** *m.* litigation, lawsuit; dispute; debate; duel; **— de acreedores** bankruptcy proceedings; **pleitista** *m. & f.* quarrelsome person.

**plenipotenciario** *m.* plenipotentiary (*diplomatic agent having full power or authority*); *adj.* plenipotentiary, having full power.

**plenitud** *f.* plenitude, fullness, completeness; abundance.

**pleno** *adj.* full, complete; **sesión plena** joint session; **en — día** in broad daylight, openly; **en — rostro** (*or* **en plena cara**) right on the face; *m.* joint session (*of a legislative body*).

**pliego** *m.* sheet of paper; sealed letter or document.

**pliegue** *m.* fold, crease, pleat.

**plomada** *f.* plumb, lead weight, plumb bob.

**plomazo** *m. Col., Ven., Mex.* shot, bullet.

**plomería** *f.* plumbing; plumber's shop; lead roof.

**plomero** *m.* plumber.

**plomizo** *adj.* leaden, lead-colored.

**plomo** *m.* lead; plumb, lead weight; bullet; boring person; **a —** vertical; vertically; *adj. Carib., Mex.* lead-colored.

**pluma** *f.* (*de ave*) feather; plume; (*instrumento*) pen; quill; **— estilográfica** (*or* **— fuente**) fountain pen; **plumada** *f.* dash, stroke of the pen, flourish; **plumaje** *m.* plumage; plume, **plumero** *m.* feather duster; box for feathers; feather ornament (*on hats, helmets, etc.*); **plumón** *m.* down; feather mattress; **plumoso** *adj.* downy, feathery.

**plural** *adj.* plural.

**pluvial** *adj.* rain (*used as adj.*); **capa —** cope (*long cape used by priests during certain religious ceremonies*).

**pluviómetro** *m.* rain gauge.

**población** *f.* (*acto*) populating; settlement; (*numero*) population; (*lugar*) town, city.

**poblado** *m.* inhabited place; village; *p.p.* populated; covered with growth.

**poblador** *m.* settler (*of a colony*).

**poblar**[2] *v. irr.* to populate, people; to to colonize, settle; to stock (*a farm*); to breed; **-se** to become covered (*with leaves or buds*).

**pobre** *adj.* poor; *m.* poor man; beggar; **pobrete** *m.* poor devil, poor wretch; **pobretón** *m.* poor old fellow, poor wretch.

**pobreza** *f.* poverty; need; lack, scarcity; barrenness.

**pocilga** *f.* pigsty, pigpen.

**pocillo** *m.* cup.

**poco** *adj.* little, scanty; small; short (*time*); **-s** few, some; *m.* a little, a bit; *adv.* little; **a —** presently, after a short time; **a — rato** (*or* **al — rato**) after a short while; **— a —** slowly, little by little; **a los -s meses** after a few months; **por — me caigo** I almost fell; **tener en — a** to hold in low esteem.

**podadera** *f.* pruning hook or knife.

**podar** *v.* to prune, trim, cut off.

**podenco** *m.* hound.

**poder**[39] *v. irr.* to be able; can; may; **él puede mucho** (*or* **poco**) he has much (*or* little) power; **puede que** it is possible that, it may be that, perhaps; **hasta más no —** to the utmost, to the limit; **no — más** not to be able to do more; to be exhausted; **no puede menos de hacerlo** he cannot help doing it; **no — con la carga** not to be equal to the burden, not to be able to lift the load; *Col., Ven.* **-le a uno algo** to be worried or affected by something, *m.* power, authority.

**poderío** *m.* power, dominion; might; wealth.

**poderoso** *adj.* powerful; wealthy.

**podre** *f.* pus; decayed matter; **podredumbre** *f.* corruption, decay; pus; rotten matter.

**podrido** *adj.* rotten; *p.p. of* **podrir.**

**podrir**[16] = **pudrir**[16].

**poema** *m.* poem.

**poesía** *f.* poetry; poem.

**poeta** *m.* poet; **poetastro** *m.* bad poet.

**poético** *asj.* poetic; **poética** *f.* poetics.

**poetisa** *f.* poetess.

**polaco** *adj.* Polish; *m.* Polish, Polish language; Pole.

**polaina** *f.* legging.

**polar** *adj.* polar.

**polea** *f.* pulley.

**polen** *m.* pollen.

**policía** *f.* police; *m.* policeman.

**policial** *m. Col., Ven.* policeman.

**polilla** *f.* moth; larva of the moth.

**política** *f.* politics; policy; *Am.* **— de campanario** politics of a clique.

**politicastro** *m.* bad or incapable politician.

**político** *adj.* political; politic; polite; **madre política** mother-in-law; *m.* politician.

**póliza** *f.* policy, written contract; draft; customhouse certificate; **— de seguros** insurance policy.

**polizonte** *m.* policeman.

**polo** *m.* pole (*of a magnet or of an axis*); polo (*a game*); **— acuático** water polo.

**poltrón** *adj.* lazy, idle; **silla poltrona** easy chair.

**polvareda** *f.* cloud of dust; **armar** (*or* **levantar**) **una —** to kick up the dust; to raise a rumpus.

**polvera** *f.* powder box; compact; powder puff.

**polvo** *m.* dust; powder; pinch of snuff or powder; **— férrico** iron oxide filings (*coating for recording tape*); **-s** toilet powder; **-s para dientes** tooth powder; **limpio de — y paja** entirely free; net; *Am.* cleaned out, without a penny; *Am.* innocent, ignorant, unaware; *Mex., Col., Ven.* **tomar el —** to escape, "beat it".

**pólvora** *f.* gunpowder; fireworks.

**polvorear** *v.* to powder, sprinkle with powder.

**polvoriento** *adj.* dusty.

**polvorín** *m.* powder magazine; priming powder; powder flask; *Am.* tick (*parasitic insect*); *Ríopl.* spitfire, quicktempered person.

**polla** *f.* pullet (*young hen*); young lass; pool (*in cards*).

**pollada** *f.* hatch, brood; flock of chicks.

**pollera** *f.* woman who raises and sells

chickens; chicken coop; a bell-shaped basket for chickens; petticoat; *Ríopl., Ch., Col., Andes* skirt.

**pollino** *m.* young donkey, ass.

**pollo** *m.* young chicken; nestling, young bird; *Spain* young man; **polluelo** *m.* chick.

**pompa** *f.* pomp; pageant, procession; bubble; pump.

**pomposo** *adj.* pompous.

**pómulo** *m.* cheek bone.

**ponche** *m.* punch (*a beverage*); **ponchera** *f.* punch bowl.

**poncho** *m. Andes, Ch., Ríopl.* poncho; cape.

**ponderación** *f.* pondering, careful consideration, weighing; exaggeration.

**ponderar** *v.* (*pensar*) to ponder, consider, weigh; (*exagerar*) to exaggerate; to extol.

**ponderativo** *adj.* exaggerating.

**ponderoso** *adj.* ponderous, heavy.

**poner**[40] *v. irr.* to put; to place; to set; to lay; to suppose; **— como nuevo a alguien** to cover someone with insults; **— en claro** to clarify; **— en limpio** to recopy, make a clean copy; **— todo de su parte** to do one's best; **pongamos que . . .** let us suppose that . . .; **-se** to place oneself; to become; **-se a** to begin to; **-se al corriente** to become informed; **-se de pie** to stand up; *Carib., Mex., Ch., Andes* **-se bien con alguien** to ingratiate oneself with someone, get on his good side; *Am.* **ponérsela** to get drunk.

**poniente** *m.* west; west wind; **el sol —** the setting sun.

**pontón** *m.* pontoon; scow, flat-bottomed boat; log bridge; pontoon bridge.

**ponzoña** *f.* venom, poison.

**ponzoñoso** *adj.* venomous, poisonous.

**popa** *f.* poop, stern; **viento en —** speedily; going well.

**popote** *m. Mex.* straw for brooms; *Mex.* drinking straw or tube.

**populacho** *m.* populace, rabble.

**popular** *adj.* popular.

**popularidad** *f.* popularity.

**populoso** *adj.* populous, densely populated.

**poquito** *adj.* very little; *Cuba, Ven., Col.* timid, shy; *m.* a small bit; **a -s** in small quantities.

**por** *prep.* by; for; for the sake of, on account of, on behalf of; because of; through; along; on exchange for; in the place of; during; about, around; to, with the idea of; **— ciento** percent; **— consiguiente** consequently; **— entre** among, between; **— escrito** in writing; **— poco se muere** he almost died; **está — hacer** it is yet to be done; **él está — hacerlo** he is in favor of doing it; **recibir — esposa** to receive as a wife; **tener —** to consider, think of as; **¿ — que?** *interr. adv.* why? for what reason?

**porcelana** *f.* porcelain, china; enamel.

**porcentaje** *m.* percentage.

**porción** *f.* portion; part, share; **una — de gente** a lot of people.

**porche** *m.* porch.

**pordiosear** *v.* to beg.

**pordiosero** *m.* beggar.

**porfía** *f.* stubbornness, obstinacy; persistence, insistence; **a —** in competition; with great insistence.

**porfiado** *adj.* stubborn, obstinate, persistent.

**porfiar**[17] *v.* to persist; to insist; to dispute obstinately; to argue.

**pormenor** *m.* detail.

**pormenorizar**[9] *v.* to detail, tell in detail; to itemize.

**poro** *m.* pore.

**poroso** *adj.* porous.

**poroto** *m. Ch., Ríopl., Andes* bean; *Ch., Ríopl., Andes* runt.

**porque** *conj.* because; so that.

**porqué** *m.* cause, reason, motive.

**porquería** *f.* filth; filthy act or word; nasty piece of food; trifle, worthless object.

**porra** *f.* club, stick; *Am.* **mandar a uno a la —** to send someone to the devil; **porrazo** *m.* blow; knock; bump; **porrón** *m.* wine vessel with long snout.

**porta** *f.* porthole; cover for a porthole; goal (*in football*).

**portaaviones** *m.* airplane carrier.

**portada** *f.* façade, front (*of a building*); title page.

**portador** *m.* carrier; bearer; tray.

**portal** *m.* portal; entrance, vestibule; portico, porch; *Am.* Christmas crèche; **-es** arcades, galleries; **portalón** *m.* large portal; gangway (*of a ship*).

**portamonedas** *m.* pocketbook, coin purse.

**portapapeles** *m.* briefcase.

**portaplumas** *m.* penholder.

**portar** *v. Am.* to carry; **-se** to behave.

**portátil** *adj.* portable.

**portaviones** *m.* aircraft carrier; also **portaaviones**.

**portavoz** *m.* megaphone; mouthpiece; spokesman.

**portazgo** *m.* toll.

**portazo** *m.* bang or slam of a door; **dar un —** to bang or slam the door.

**porte** *m.* portage, cost of carriage; freight; postage; manner, bearing; size, capacity; *Am.* birthday present; *C.A.* size.

**portear** *v.* to carry on one's back; *Am.* to get out in a hurry.

**portento** *m.* portent; wonder, marvel.

**portentoso** *adj.* marvelous, extraordinary, amazing, terrifying.

**porteño** *adj.* from a port; *Ríopl.* from Buenos Aires.

**portería** *f.* porter's quarters; main door of a building.

**portero** *m.* doorkeeper, doorman; janitor.

**pórtico** *m.* portico, porch.

**portilla** *f.* porthole; small gate or passageway.

**portón** *m.* gate.

**portugués** *adj.* Portuguese; *m.* Portu-guese; Portuguese language.

**porvenir** *m.* future.

**pos : en — de** after; in pursuit of.

**posada** *f.* lodging; inn; boardinghouse; dwelling, home; *Mex.* **las -s** a Christmas festivity lasting nine days; **posadero** *m.* innkeeper.

**posaderas** *f. pl.* posterior, buttocks, rump.

**posar** *v.* to lodge; to rest; to sit down; to pose (*as a model*); to perch (*said of birds*); **-se** to settle (*said of sediment*); to perch (*said of birds*).

**posdata** *f.* postscript.

**poseedor** *m.* possessor, owner.

**poseer**[14] *v.* to possess, own; to master, know well; **-se** to have control of oneself.

**posesión** *f.* possession.

**posesivo** *adj. & m.* possessive.

**posesor** *m.* possessor, owner.

**posibilidad** *f.* possibility.

**posible** *adj.* possible; **hacer lo —** to do one's best; **-s** *m. pl.* goods, property, means.

**posición** *f.* position; posture; status, rank, standing; placing.

**positivo** *adj.* positive; effective; true; practical.

**posponer**[40] *v. irr.* to postpone, put off; to put after; to subordinate.

**pospuesto** *p.p.* of **posponer.**

**posta** *f.* (*bala*) small bullet; (*apuesta*) bet, wager; (*relevo*) relay (*of post horses*); post station; **-s** buckshot; **por la —** posthaste; fast, speedily; *m.* postboy, courier, messenger.

**postal** *adj.* postal; **tarjeta —** postcard.

**postdata** = **posdata.**

**poste** *m.* post, pillar.

**postergar**[7] *v.* to delay; to postpone; to disregard someone's right.

**posteridad** *f.* posterity.

**posterior** *adj.* posterior, back, rear; later.

**postigo** *m.* wicket, small door or gate; shutter; peep window.

**postizo** *adj.* false, artificial; *m.* switch, false hair.

**postración** *f.* prostration, collapse, exhaustion; dejection, lowness of spirits.

**postrar** *v.* to prostrate; to humiliate; to throw down; to weaken, exhaust; **-se** to kneel to the ground; to be weakened, exhausted; to collapse.

**postre** *m.* dessert; **a la —** at last.

**postrer(o)** *adj.* last; hindmost, nearest the rear.

**postulante** *m. & f.* petitioner; applicant; candidate.

**póstumo** *adj.* posthumous, after one's death.

**postura** *f.* posture, position; bid; wager; pact, agreement; egg-laying.

**potable** *adj.* drinkable; **agua —** drinking water.

**potaje** *m.* pottage, thick soup; porridge; mixed drink.

**pote** *m.* pot; jar; jug; *Carib., Ven., Mex., Ríopl.* flask; *Am.* buzzard.

**potencia** *f.* potency; power; faculty,

ability; powerful nation.

**potente** *adj.* potent, powerful, strong.

**potestad** *f.* power; dominion, authority.

**potranca** *f.* filly, young mare.

**potrero** *m.* herdsman of colts; fenced-in pasture land; *Carib., Mex., C.A., Ven., Col., Ch.* cattle ranch, stock farm.

**potro** *m.* colt; rack, torture; *Col., Ven., Mex., Ch., Riopl.* wild horse.

**poyo** *m.* stone or brick bench (*usually built against a wall*).

**pozo** *m.* well; hole, pit; mine shaft; hold of a ship; *Am.* pool, puddle; *Riopl., Ch., Ven., Col., Mex.* spring, fountain.

**práctica** *f.* practice; exercise; custom, habit; method.

**practicante** *m. & f.* doctor's assistant; hospital intern.

**practicar**[6] *v.* to practice; to put into practice.

**práctico** *adj.* practical; experienced, skilful; *m.* **— de puerto** harbor pilot.

**pradera** *f.* prairie; meadow.

**prado** *m.* meadow, field; lawn.

**preámbulo** *m.* preamble, introduction, prologue.

**precario** *adj.* precarious.

**precaución** *f.* precaution.

**precaver** *v.* to guard (against), keep (from); to warn, caution; **-se** to guard oneself (against); to take precautions.

**precavido** *adj.* cautious, on guard.

**precedencia** *f.* precedence; priority.

**precedente** *adj.* preceding; *m.* precedent.

**preceder** *v.* to precede; to have precedence.

**precepto** *m.* precept; rule; order.

**preceptor** *m.* teacher, tutor.

**preciado** *adj.* prized, esteemed; precious, valuable.

**preciar** *v.* to appraise; to value; **-se de** to boast of, be proud of.

**precio** *m.* price; value, worth; esteem.

**precioso** *adj.* precious, valuable; fine, exquisite; beautiful.

**precipicio** *m.* precipice; ruin.

**precipitación** *f.* precipitation; rush, haste, hurry.

**precipitado** *adj.* precipitate, hasty, rash; *m.* precipitate (*chemical term*).

**precipitar** *v.* to precipitate; to hasten, rush; to hurl, throw headlong; **-se** to throw oneself headlong; to rush (into).

**precipitoso** *adj.* precipitous, steep; rash.

**precisar** *v.* to determine precisely; to force, compel, make necessary; *Riopl., Col., Ven., Mex., Andes;* to be necessary or urgent; *Am.* to need.

**precisión** *f.* precision, exactness; accuracy; compulsion, force, necessity; *Am.* haste.

**preciso** *adj.* necessary; precise, exact; clear; *m. Am.* small travelling bag.

**precoz** *adj.* precocious.

**precursor** *m.* precursor, forerunner.

**predecir**[27] *v. irr.* to predict, prophesy, forecast, foretell.

**predestinar** *v.* to predestine.

**predicación** *f.* preaching.

**predicado** *adj. & m.* predicate; *p.p. of* **predicar.**

**predicador** *m.* preacher.

**predicar**[6] *v.* to preach.

**predicción** *f.* prediction.

**predilección** *f.* predilection, preference, liking.

**predilecto** *adj.* favorite, preferred.

**predisponer**[40] *v. irr.* to predispose, bias, prejudice.

**predispuesto** *p.p. of* **predisponer** & *adj.* predisposed, prejudiced, biased.

**predominante** *adj.* predominant; prevailing, ruling.

**predominar** *v.* to predominate, prevail.

**predominio** *m.* predominance; sway, influence.

**prefacio** *m.* preface.

**prefecto** *m.* prefect (*military or civil chief; sometimes a mayor, sometimes governor of a province, as in Peru*).

**preferencia** *f.* preference; **de —** with preference; preferably.

**preferente** *adj.* preferable; preferred; preferential; **acciones -s** preferred shares.

**preferible** *adj.* preferable.

**preferir**[3] *v. irr.* to prefer.

**prefijar** *v.* to prefix; to set beforehand (*as a date*).

**prefijo** *m.* prefix.

**pregonar** *v.* to proclaim, cry out; to make known.

**pregunta** *f.* question; **hacer una —** to ask a question.

**preguntar** *v.* to ask, inquire.

**preguntón** *adj.* inquisitive.

**prejuicio** *m.* prejudice.

**prelado** *m.* prelate.

**preliminar** *adj. & m.* preliminary.

**preludiar** *v.* to be the prelude or beginning of; to initiate, introduce; to try out (*a musical instrument*).

**preludio** *m.* prelude; introduction.

**prematuro** *adj.* premature, untimely.

**premeditado** *adj.* premeditated, deliberate.

**premiar** *v.* to reward.

**premio** *m.* prize; reward; recompense; premium; **a —** with interest, at interest.

**premisa** *f.* premise (*either of the first two propositions of a syllogism*).

**premura** *f.* pressure, urgency, haste.

**prenda** *f.* (*fianza*) pawn, pledge, security; token; (*partes del vestido*) article of clothing; anything vauable; loved person; jewel; **-s** good qualities, gifts, talents; **— de vestir** garment; **juego de -s** game of forfeits; **en — de** as a proof of, as a pledge of.

**prendar** *v.* to pawn, pledge; to charm, please; **-se de** to get attached to; to fall in love with.

**prendedor** *m.* clasp; stickpin; tie pin; brooch; *Am.* lighter.

**prender** *v.* (*asir*) to seize, catch, grab; to bite (*said of an insect*); to fasten,

clasp; to arrest, imprison; (*empezar*)
to take root; to begin to burn; catch
fire; *Ríopl.*, *Carib.*, *C.A.*, *Mex.* to
light (*a lamp*); *Am.* to start, begin,
undertake; — **el fuego** to start the
fire; *Col.* **-las** to take to one's heels;
**-se** to dress up.

**prendero** *m.* pawnbroker; second-hand
dealer.

**prensa** *f.* press; printing press.

**prensar** *v.* to press.

**preñado** *adj.* pregnant; full.

**preñez** *f.* pregnancy.

**preocupación** *f.* preoccupation; worry;
bias, prejudice.

**preocupar** *v.* to preoccupy; to worry;
to prejudice; **-se** to be preoccupied;
to worry; to be prejudiced.

**preparación** *f.* preparation.

**preparar** *v.* to prepare; **-se** to get ready;
to be prepared.

**preparativo** *adj.* preparatory; *m.* preparation.

**preparatorio** *adj.* preparatory.

**preposición** *f.* preposition.

**prerrogativa** *f.* prerogative, right, privilege.

**presa** *f.* prey; dam; fang, tusk; claw;
**hacer** — to seize.

**presagiar** *v.* to foretell.

**presagio** *m.* presage, omen, sign.

**presbítero** *m.* priest.

**prescindir** *v.* to disregard, set aside,
leave aside; to omit; to dispense
(with).

**prescribir**[52] *v.* to prescribe.

**prescrito** *p.p.* of **prescribir**.

**presencia** *f.* presence; figure, bearing;
— **de ánimo** presence of mind,
serenity.

**presenciar** *v.* to see, witness; to be
present at.

**presentación** *f.* presentation; personal
introduction; *Ven.* petition.

**presentar** *v.* to present; to introduce;
**-se** to appear, present oneself; to introduce oneself; to offer one's services; *Am.* to have recourse to justice,
file suit.

**presente** *adj.* present; *m.* present, gift;
**al** — now, at the present time; **por
el** (**la**, *or* **lo**) — for the present;
**mejorando lo** — present company
excepted; **tener** — to bear in mind.

**presentimiento** *m.* presentiment, foreboding.

**presentir**[3] *v. irr.* to have a presentiment, foreboding or hunch.

**preservación** *f.* preservation.

**preservar** *v.* to preserve, guard, protect, keep.

**presidencia** *f.* presidency; office of
president; presidential term; chairmanship.

**presidencial** *adj.* presidential.

**presidente** *m.* president; chairman;
presiding judge.

**presidiario** *m.* prisoner, convict.

**presidio** *m.* garrison; fortress; penitentiary, prison; **diez años de** — ten
years at hard labor (*in a prison*).

**presidir** *v.* to preside; to direct.

**presilla** *f.* loop, fastener; clip.

**presión** *f.* pressure.

**preso** *m.* prisoner; *p.p. irr.* of **prender**
imprisoned.

**prestado** *adj.* & *p.p.* loaned, lent; **dar**
— to lend; **pedir** — to borrow.

**prestamista** *m.* & *f.* moneylender.

**préstamo** *m.* loan.

**prestar** *v.* to loan, lend; *Col.*, *Ven.*,
*C.A.*, *Andes* to borrow; — **ayuda** to
give help; — **atención** to pay attention; *Andes* **presta acá** give it here,
give it to me; **-se** to lend oneself or
itself.

**presteza** *f.* promptness, speed.

**prestidigitación** *f.* juggling, sleight of
hand.

**prestidigitador** *m.* juggler.

**prestigio** *m.* prestige; influence, authority; good reputation.

**presto** *adj.* quick; nimble; prompt;
ready; *adv.* soon, at once; **de** —
quickly, promptly.

**presumido** *adj.* conceited, presumptuous; *p.p.* of **presumir**.

**presumir** *v.* to presume; to boast; to
show off; *Am.* to court, woo; — **de
valiente** to boast of one's valor.

**presunción** *f.* presumption, assumption; conceit, arrogance.

**presunto** *adj.* presumed; supposed;
prospective; **heredero** — heir apparent.

**presuntuoso** *adj.* presumptuous, conceited.

**presuponer**[40] *v. irr.* to presuppose,
take for granted, imply; to estimate.

**presupuesto** *p.p.* of **presuponer** pre-
supposed; estimated; *m.* budget, estimate.

**presuroso** *adj.* quick, prompt; hasty.

**pretencioso** *adj.* presumptuous; conceited.

**pretender** *v.* to pretend; to solicit, seek;
to claim; to try; to court.

**pretendiente** *m.* pretender, claimant;
suitor; office seeker.

**pretensión** *f.* pretension; claim; presumption; pretense.

**pretérito** *adj.* preterite, past; *m.* preterite, the past tense.

**pretexto** *m.* pretext, pretense, excuse.

**pretil** *m.* stone or brick railing; *Am.*
ledge; *Mex.*, *Ven.* stone or brick
bench (*built against a wall*).

**pretina** *f.* belt, girdle; waistband.

**prevalecer**[13] *v. irr.* to prevail.

**prevaleciente** *adj.* prevalent, current.

**prevención** *f.* prevention; foresight,
preparedness; bias, prejudice; provision, supply; admonition, warning;
police station; guardhouse.

**prevenido** *adj.* & *p.p.* prepared, ready;
forewarned; cautious; supplied.

**prevenir**[48] *v. irr.* to prevent, avoid; to
prepare beforehand; to foresee; to
warn; to predispose; **-se** to get prepared, get ready.

**prever**[49] *v. irr.* to foresee.

**previo** *adj.* previous; *m. Am.* prelimi-

**PO**

nary examination.
**previsión** *f.* foresight.
**previsto** *p.p. of* **prever**.
**prieto** *adj.* dark, black; tight; compact; *Riopl.*, *Ven.*, *Col.*, *Mex.*, *C.A.*, *Andes* dark-complexioned, swarthy.
**prima** *f.* female cousin; premium; prime (*first of the canonical hours*).
**primacía** *f.* priority, precedence; superiority.
**primario** *adj.* primary, principal.
**primavera** *f.* spring; primrose; print, flowered silk cloth.
**primaveral** *adj.* spring, pertaining to spring.
**primer(o)** *adj.* first; former; leading, principal; **primera enseñanza** primary education; **primera materia** raw material; **de buenas a primeras** all of a sudden, unexpectedly; **a primera luz** at dawn; *adv.* first; rather.
**primicia** *f.* first fruit; first profit; **-s** first fruits.
**primitivo** *adj.* primitive; primary; original.
**primo** *m.* cousin; simpleton, sucker, dupe; **— hermano** (*or* **— carnal**) first cousin; *Carib.* **coger a uno de — to** deceive someone easily; *adj.* first; **número —** prime number.
**primogénito** *adj.* & *m.* first-born; **primogenitura** *f.* birthright; rights of the first-born.
**primor** *m.* beauty; excellence; exquisiteness; skill, ability.
**primoroso** *adj.* excellent, fine, exquisite; skillful.
**prímula** *f.* primrose.
**princesa** *f.* princess.
**principal** *adj.* principal; renowned, famous; **piso —** main floor (*usually, the second floor*); *m.* principal, capital sum; chief, head.
**príncipe** *m.* prince; *adj.* princeps, first (*edition*).
**principiante** *m.* beginner.
**principiar** *v.* to begin.
**principio** *m.* principle; beginning; origin, source; entrée (*main dinner course*); **a -s de** towards the beginning of.
**pringue** *m.* & *f.* grease drippings (*from bacon, ham, etc.*).
**prioridad** *f.* priority; precedence.
**prisa** *f.* speed, haste; **de** (*or* **a**) **— quick-** ly, speedily; **a todo —** with the greatest speed; **eso corre —** that is urgent; **dar — a** to hurry; **darse —** to hurry; **tener** (*or* **estar de**) **—** to be in a hurry.
**prisión** *f.* prison; imprisonment; seizure; shackle; **-es** shackles, fetters, chains.
**prisionero** *m.* prisoner.
**prisma** *f.* prism.
**pristino** *adj.* first, early, former, primitive.
**privación** *f.* privation; want, lack; loss.
**privado** *adj.* private; personal; unconscious; *p.p.* deprived; *m.* favorite.
**privar** *v.* (*destituir*) to deprive; to

prohibit; (*tener aceptación*) to enjoy the favor of someone; to be in vogue; **-le a uno del sentido** to stun, daze; **ya no privan esas costumbres** those customs are no longer in vogue or in existence; **-se** to lose consciousness; **-se de** to deprive oneself of.
**privativo** *adj.* exclusive; particular, distinctive.
**privilegiado** *adj.* privileged.
**privilegiar** *v.* to favor; to give a privilege to.
**privilegio** *m.* privilege; exemption; patent; copyright; **— de invención** patent on an invention.
**pro** *m.* & *f.* profit, advantage; **en — de** on behalf of; **en — y en contra** pro and con, for and against; **hombre de — man** of worth.
**proa** *f.* prow.
**probabilidad** *f.* probability.
**probable** *adj.* probable.
**probar²** *v. irr.* (*examinar*) to test; to taste; to prove; to try; to try on; (*gustar*) to suit, agree with; **no me prueba el clima** the climate does not agree with me.
**probeta** *f.* test tube; pressure gauge.
**probidad** *f.* integrity, uprightness, honesty.
**problema** *m.* problem.
**procedente** *adj.* proceeding (from), originating; according to law.
**proceder** *v.* to proceed; to originate; to behave; to take action (against); *m.* behavior, conduct.
**procedimiento** *m.* procedure; method; process; conduct.
**prócer** *m.* distinguished person; hero; great statesman.
**procesado** *p.p.* & *adj.* relating to, or included in, a lawsuit; accused, prosecuted; *m.* defendant.
**procesar** *v.* to prosecute; to accuse; to indict; to sue.
**procesión** *f.* procession; parade.
**proceso** *m.* process; lawsuit, legal proceedings; lapse of time; **— verbal** minutes, record.
**proclama** *f.* proclamation, ban; marriage banns.
**proclamación** *f.* proclamation.
**proclamar** *v.* to proclaim.
**procurador** *m.* attorney.
**procurar** *v.* (*pretender*) to try, endeavor; (*obtener*) to procure, obtain, get.
**prodigar⁷** *v.* to lavish; to bestow upon; to squander, waste.
**prodigio** *m.* prodigy, wonder, marvel; miracle.
**prodigioso** *adj.* prodigious, marvelous; fine, exquisite.
**pródigo** *adj.* prodigal, wasteful; lavish; generous; *m.* spendthrift.
**producción** *f.* production; produce.
**producir²⁵** *v. irr.* to produce; to bring about; to yield; **-se** to express oneself, explain oneself; *Col.*, *Ven.* to occur, happen.
**productivo** *adj.* productive; fruitful; profitable.

**producto** *m.* product; yield; result.
**productor** *m.* producer; *adj.* producing, productive.
**proeza** *f.* prowess; *Col.* boast, exaggeration.
**profanación** *f.* profanation.
**profanar** *v.* to profane; to defile.
**profano** *adj.* profane, not sacred; irreverent; lay, uninformed (*about a branch of learning*).
**profecía** *f.* prophecy; prediction.
**proferir**³ *v. irr.* to utter, express, speak.
**profesar** *v.* to profess; to avow, confess.
**profesión** *f.* profession; avowal, declaration.
**profesional** *adj.*, *m.* & *f.* professional.
**profesionista** *m.* & *f. Am.* professional.
**profesor** *m.* professor, teacher; **profesorado** *m.* faculty; body of teachers; teaching profession; professorship.
**profeta** *m.* prophet.
**profético** *adj.* prophetic.
**profetizar**⁹ *v.* to prophesy.
**proficiente** *adj.* proficient, skilled.
**profilaxis** *f.* prophylaxis (*disease prevention*).
**prófugo** *adj.* & *m.* fugitive.
**profundidad** *f.* profundity, depth.
**profundizar**⁹ *v.* to deepen; to go deep into.
**profundo** *adj.* profound; deep; low.
**profuso** *adj.* profuse; lavish.
**programa** *m.* program; plan.
**progresar** *v.* to progress.
**progresista** *m.*, *f.* & *adj.* progressive.
**progresivo** *adj.* progressive.
**progreso** *m.* progress.
**prohibición** *f.* prohibition; ban.
**prohibir** *v.* to prohibit, forbid.
**prójimo** *m.* neighbor, fellow being; *Ríopl., Carib., C.A.* **ese —** that fellow.
**prole** *f.* progeny, offspring.
**proletariado** *m.* proletariat, working class.
**proletario** *adj.* proletarian, belonging to the working class; plebeian; *m.* proletarian.
**prolijo** *adj.* prolix, too long, drawn out, too detailed; boring, tedious.
**prologar**⁷ *v.* to preface, write a preface for.
**prólogo** *m.* prologue.
**prolongación** *f.* prolongation, extension; lengthening.
**prolongar**⁷ *v.* to prolong, lengthen, extend.
**promediar** *v.* to average; to divide or distribute into two equal parts; to mediate; **antes de — el mes** before the middle of the month.
**promedio** *m.* middle; average.
**promesa** *f.* promise.
**prometedor** *adj.* promising, hopeful.
**prometer** *v.* to promise; to show promise; *Ríopl., C.A.* to affirm, assure; **-se** to become engaged, betrothed.
**prometido** *adj.* & *p.p.* betrothed; *m.* fiancé, betrothed; promise.
**prominente** *adj.* prominent.
**promisorio** *adj.* promissory.
**promoción** *f.* promotion, advance-

ment.
**promontorio** *m.* promontory, headland, cape; anything bulky; bulge.
**promotor** *m.* promoter.
**promovedor** *m.* promoter.
**promover**² *v. irr.* to promote; to advance.
**promulgación** *f.* promulgation, publication, proclamation (*of a law*).
**promulgar**⁷ *v.* to promulgate, proclaim, announce publicly.
**pronombre** *m.* pronoun.
**pronosticar**⁶ *v.* to prophesy, predict.
**pronóstico** *m.* forecast; prediction; omen.
**prontitud** *f.* promptness; quickness.
**pronto** *adj.* quick, speedy; ready; prompt; *adv.* soon; quickly; **de —** suddenly; **al —** at first; **por de** (*or* **por lo**) **—** for the present; *m.* sudden impulse.
**pronunciación** *f.* pronunciation.
**pronunciar** *v.* to pronounce; to utter; **-se** to rise up in rebellion.
**propagación** *f.* propagation, spread, spreading.
**propaganda** *f.* propaganda.
**propagar**⁷ *v.* to propagate, reproduce; to spread.
**propalar** *v.* to spread (*news*).
**propasarse** *v.* to overstep one's bounds; to exceed one's authority, go too far.
**propensión** *f.* tendency, inclination; bent, natural tendency or ability.
**propenso** *adj.* prone, susceptible, inclined.
**propicio** *adj.* propitious, favorable.
**propiedad** *f.* property; ownership; attribute, quality; propriety, appropriateness.
**propietario** *m.* proprietor, owner.
**propina** *f.* tip (*voluntary gift of money for service*).
**propinar** *v.* to give (*something to drink*); to give (*a beating, kick, slap*); *Am.* to tip, give a tip to; **— una paliza** to give a beating.
**propio** *adj.* proper; suitable; own; same; **amor —** vanity, pride, self-esteem; *m.* messenger.
**proponer**⁴⁰ *v. irr.* to propose; to resolve; to present; **-se** to resolve, make a resolution.
**proporción** *f.* proportion; dimension; ratio; opportunity, chance.
**proporcionar** *v.* to proportion; to adapt, adjust; to furnish, supply; give.
**proposición** *f.* proposition; proposal; assertion.
**propósito** *m.* purpose, aim, design; **a —** apropos, suitable, fitting; by the way; **de —** on purpose; **fuera de —** irrelevant, beside the point.
**propuesto** *f.* proposal, offer; proposition.
**propuesto** *p.p.* of **proponer.**
**propulsar** *v.* to propel.
**propulsión** *f.* propulsion; **— a chorro** (*por reacción*) jet propulsion; **— a cohete** rocket propulsion.
**propulsor** *m.* propeller; *adj.* propelling.

**prorratear** *v.* to prorate, distribute or assess proportionally; to average.

**prorrateo** *m.* apportionment, proportional distribution.

**prórroga** *f.* renewal, extension of time.

**prorrogar**[7] *v.* to put off, postpone; to adjourn; to extend (*time limit*).

**prorrumpir** *v.* to break forth; **— en llanto** to burst into tears; **—en una carcajada** to let out a big laugh.

**prosa** *f.* prose.

**prosaico** *adj.* prosaic; dull; tedious.

**proscribir**[52] *v.* to proscribe, banish; to outlaw.

**proscripción** *f.* banishment.

**proscripto, proscrito** *p.p. of* **proscribir;** *m.* exile, outlaw.

**proseguir**[5, 12] *v. irr.* to continue; to follow.

**prosperar** *v.* to prosper.

**prosperidad** *f.* prosperity; success.

**próspero** *adj.* prosperous; successful.

**próstata** *f.* prostate.

**prostituir**[32] *v.* to prostitute, corrupt.

**prostituta** *f.* prostitute.

**protagonista** *m. & f.* protagonist (*main character or actor*).

**protección** *f.* protection; support.

**proteccionista** *adj.* protective; **tarifa — protective tariff;** *m. & f.* protectionist (*follower of the economic principles of protection*).

**protector** *m.* protector, guardian; *adj.* protecting, protective.

**protectorado** *m.* protectorate.

**proteger**[11] *v.* to protect; to shelter; to defend.

**proteína** *f.* protein.

**proteínico** *adj.* related to the proteins.

**protesta** *f.* protest; protestation.

**protestación** *f.* protestation, solemn declaration; protest.

**protestante** *m.* Protestant; one who protests.

**protestar** *v.* (*confesar*) to assert, assure; to avow publicly; (*negar*) to protest; **— una letra** to protest a draft.

**protón** *m.* proton.

**protoplasma** *m.* protoplasm.

**protuberancia** *f.* protuberance, bulge.

**protuberante** *adj.* protuberant, prominent, bulging.

**provecho** *m.* profit; benefit; utility; advantage; **hombre de —** worthy, useful man.

**provechoso** *adj.* profitable; useful; beneficial; advantageous.

**proveedor** *m.* provisioner, provider; supply man.

**proveer**[14, 52] *v. irr.* to provide; to supply; to confer, bestow; to decide; **-se de** to supply oneself with.

**provenir**[48] *v. irr.* to originate, arise, come (from).

**proverbio** *m.* proverb.

**providencia** *f.* providence; foresight; Providence, God; legal decision, sentence; provision, measure; **tomar una — to** take a step or measure.

**providencial** *adj.* providential.

**provincia** *f.* province.

**provincial** *adj.* provincial.

**provinciano** *adj. & m.* provincial.

**provisión** *f.* provision; supply, stock.

**provisorio** *adj.* provisional, temporary.

**provisto** *p.p. of* **proveer.**

**provocación** *f.* provocation; dare, defiance.

**provocador** *adj.* provoking; **—** provoker.

**provocar**[6] *v.* to provoke; to excite, rouse; to stimulate.

**proximidad** *f.* proximity, nearness.

**próximo** *adj.* next; neighboring; near; **del — pasado** of last month.

**proyección** *f.* projection; jut.

**proyectar** *v.* to project; to plan; to throw; to cast; **-se** to be cast (*as a shadow*).

**proyectil** *m.* projectile.

**proyectista** *m. & f.* designer; schemer, planner.

**proyecto** *m.* project; plan; **— de ley** bill (*in a legislature*).

**prudencia** *f.* prudence, practical wisdom, discretion.

**prudente** *adj.* prudent, wise, discreet.

**prueba** *f.* proof; trial; test; fitting; sample; evidence; *Andes, Ríopl., Col., C.A.* acrobatic performance, stunt, trick, sleight of hand; **a — de incendio** fireproof.

**prurito** *m.* itch; keen desire.

**púa** *f.* prick; barb; prong; thorn; quill (*of a porcupine, etc.*); sharp, cunning person; *Ríopl.* cock's spur; **alambre de -s** barbed wire.

**publicación** *f.* publication.

**publicar**[6] *v.* to publish; to reveal; to announce.

**publicidad** *f.* publicity.

**público** *adj. & m.* public.

**puchero** *m.* pot, kettle; meat and vegetable stew; pout; **hacer -s** to pout.

**pucho** *m.* cigar or cigarette butt; *C.A.* something of little value.

**pudiente** *adj.* powerful; rich, wealthy; *m.* man of means.

**pudín** *m.* pudding.

**pudor** *m.* modesty; shyness.

**pudrir**[16] *v.* to rot; to vex, annoy; **-se** to rot.

**pueblero** *m.* *Ríopl.* townsman (*as opposed to countryman*).

**pueblo** *m.* town, village; people, race, nation; populace; common people.

**puente** *m.* bridge; *Carib., Mex., Ríopl.* dental bridge; *Am.* knife and fork rest; **— colgante** suspension bridge; **— levadizo** drawbridge.

**puerca** *f.* sow.

**puerco** *m.* pig, hog; **—espin** porcupine; **— jabalí** wild boar; *adj.* filthy, dirty; coarse, ill-bred.

**pueril** *adj.* puerile, childish.

**puerta** *f.* door; gate; entrance; **— accesoria (excusada,** *or* **falsa)** side door; **— de golpe** spring door; trap door; **— franca** open door; free entrance or entry; **— trasera** back door;

**a — cerrada** secretly, behind closed doors; *Am.* **en —** in view, in sight, very near.

**puerto** *m.* port; harbor; refuge; mountain pass; **— franco** free port.

**pues** *conj.* since, because, for, inasmuch as; then; *adv.* then; well; **— bien** well then, well; **— que** since.

**puesta** *f.* set, setting (*of a star or planet*); stake at cards; **— de sol** sunset.

**puestero** *m. Carib., Mex., Ríopl.* vendor, seller (*at a stand or stall*); *Ríopl.* man in charge of livestock on Argentine ranches.

**puesto** *p.p.* of **poner** placed, put, set; **mal** (*or* **bien**) **—** badly (*or* well) dressed; *m.* place; vendor's booth or stand; post, position, office; military post; *Andes, Ríopl.* station for watching and taking care of cattle on a ranch; **— de socorros** first-aid station; **— que** *conj.* since.

**pugilato** *m.* boxing.

**pugilista** *m.* boxer, prize fighter.

**pugna** *f.* struggle; conflict; **estar en — con** to be in conflict with; to be opposed to.

**pugnar** *v.* to fight; to struggle; to strive; to persist.

**pujanza** *f.* push, force, power.

**pujar** *v.* to make a strenuous effort; to grope for words; to falter; to outbid (*offer a higher bid than*); *C.A.* to grunt; *Am.* to reject; *Ven.* to dismiss; *Am.* **— para adentro** to forbear, keep silent; *Am.* **andar pujado** to go around crestfallen; to be in disgrace.

**pujido** *m. Am.* grunt (*due to strenuous effort*).

**pulcritud** *f.* neatness, trimness; excellence, perfection.

**pulcro** *adj.* neat, trim; beautiful.

**pulga** *f.* flea; *Ríopl.* small and insignificant person; **tener malas -s** to be ill-tempered; *Col., Andes* **ser de pocas -s** to be touchy, oversensitive; **pulgón** *m.* blight, plant louse.

**pulgada** *f.* inch.

**pulgar** *m.* thumb.

**pulido** *adj.* polished, refined; polite; neat; exquisite.

**pulimentar** *v.* to polish.

**pulimento** *m.* polish; gloss.

**pulir** *v.* to polish.

**pulmón** *m.* lung.

**pulmonar** *adj.* pulmonary, pertaining to the lungs.

**pulmonía** *f.* pneumonia.

**pulpa** *f.* pulp.

**pulpería** *f. Ríopl., C.A., Ch., Ven., Andes* country general store; *Am.* tavern.

**pulpero** *m. Ríopl., C.A., Ch., Ven., Andes* owner of a country store or tavern.

**púlpito** *m.* pulpit.

**pulpo** *m.* octopus.

**pulque** *m. Mex.* pulque (*fermented juice of the maguey*).

**pulsación** *f.* pulsation, beat, throb; pulse, beating.

**pulsar** *v.* to pulsate, throb, beat; to feel the pulse of; to sound out; examine; to play (*the harp*); *Mex., C.A.* to judge or try the weight of (*by lifting*).

**pulsera** *f.* bracelet; wrist bandage; **reloj de —** wrist watch.

**pulso** *m.* pulse; steadiness; tact; *Ríopl., Carib., Col.* bracelet, wrist watch; **un hombre de —** a prudent, steady man; *Cuba, Mex.* **beber a —** to drink straight down, gulp down; **levantar a —** to lift with the strength of the wrist or hand; **sacar a — un negocio** to carry out a deal by sheer perseverance.

**pulular** *v.* to swarm; to multiply rapidly; to sprout, bud.

**pulverizar**[9] *v.* to pulverize.

**pulla** *f.* taunt; mean dig, quip, cutting remark; filthy word or remark.

**puma** *f.* puma, mountain lion.

**puna** *f. Andes* cold, arid tableland of the Andes; *Ríopl.* desert; *Andes* sickness caused by high altitude.

**pundonor** *m.* point of honor.

**punta** *f.* point, tip; bull's horn; cigar or cigarette butt; *Ven.*, gang, band, herd, a lot (*of things, people, etc.*); *Am.* small leaf of fine tobacco; *Am.* jeer, cutting remark; **-s** point lace; scallops; **de —** on end; **de -s** (*or* **de puntillas**) on tiptoe; *Am.* **a — de** by dint of, by means of; **estar de — con** to be on bad terms with; **sacar — a un lápiz** to sharpen a pencil; **tener sus -s de poeta** to be something of a poet.

**puntada** *f.* stitch; hint; *Andes* prick, pricking, sting, sharp pain; **no he dado — en este asunto** I have left this matter completely untouched.

**puntal** *m.* prop; support, basis; bull's horn; *Col.* snack (*between meals*).

**puntapié** *m.* kick (*with the toe of the shoe*).

**puntazo** *m. Col., Ven., Mex., Cuba* stab, jab.

**puntear** *v.* to pluck (*the strings of a guitar*); to play (*a guitar*); to make dots; to engrave, draw or paint by means of dots; to stitch; to tack (*said of a boat*).

**puntería** *f.* aim.

**puntero** *m.* pointer; chisel; blacksmith's punch; *C.A., Col., Ch.* clock or watch hand; *Am.* leader of a parade; *Cuba, Mex., Ven., Col.* leading ox (*or other animal*); *Am.* guide.

**puntiagudo** *adj.* sharp, sharp-pointed.

**puntilla** *f.* small point; tip; small dagger; tracing point; point lace; *Ven.* penknife; *Am.* toe rubber; *Am.* ridge (*of a hill*); **de -s** on tiptoe; **puntillazo** *m.* stab (*with a dagger*).

**punto** *m.* (*parada*) period; stop; point; dot; (*puntada*) stitch; mesh; (*sitio*) place; moment; (*mira*) gun sight; **— de admiración** exclamation mark; **— de interrogación** question mark; **— y coma** semicolon; **dos -s** colon; **al —** at once, immediately; **a — de** on the point of; **de —** knitted, porous knit, stockinet or jersey weave; **en** — exactly, on the dot; **a — fijo** with certainty; **subir de** — to increase or get worse.

**puntuación** *f.* punctuation.

**puntual** *adj.* punctual, prompt; exact.

**puntualidad** *f.* punctuality, promptness; certainty.

**puntuar**[18] *v.* to punctuate.

**punzada** *f.* puncture; prick; sharp pain.

**punzante** *adj.* sharp; pricking; piercing, penetrating.

**punzar**[9] *v.* to puncture; to sting; to prick; to punch, perforate.

**punzón** *m.* punch, puncher; pick; awl.

**puñada** *f.* punch, box, blow with the fist.

**puñado** *m.* fistful, handful; **a -s** abundantly; by handfuls.

**puñal** *m.* dagger.

**puñalada** *f.* stab; sharp pain; **coser a -s** to stab to death.

**puñetazo** *m.* punch, blow with the fist.

**puño** *m.* fist; fistful, handful; cuff; hilt, handle; *Ven.*, *Col.* blow with the fist; **a — cerrado** firmly; **ser como un** — to be stingy; **tener -s** to be strong, courageous.

**pupila** *f.* pupil (*of the eye*).

**pupilo** *m.* ward; boarding-school pupil; boarder.

**pupitre** *m.* desk, school desk.

**puré** *m.* purée, thick soup.

**pureza** *f.* purity; chastity.

**purga** *f.* purge, laxative, physic.

**purgante** *adj.* purgative, laxative; *m.* purgative, physic, laxative.

**purgar**[7] *v.* to purge; to purify; to atone for; **-se** to purge oneself; to take a laxative.

**purgatorio** *m.* purgatory.

**purificar**[6] *v.* to purify.

**puro** *adj.* (*limpio*) pure; clean; chaste; (*sólo*) mere, only, sheer; **a pura fuerza** by sheer force; **a puros gritos** by just shouting; *m.* cigar.

**púrpura** *f.* purple; purple cloth.

**purpúreo** *adj.* purple.

**pus** *m.* pus.

**puta** *f.* whore, prostitute.

**putativo** *adj.* reputed, supposed; **padre** — foster father.

**putrefacción** *f.* putrefaction, decay, rotting.

**putrefacto** *adj.* putrid, rotten, decayed.

# Q

**que** *rel. pron.* that; which; who; whom; **el** — who; which; the one who; the one which; *conj.* that; for, because; **más** (**menos**) — more (less) than; **el mismo** — the same as; — (= *subj.*) let, may you, I hope that; **por mucho** no matter how much; **quieras** — **no** whether you wish or not.

**qué** *interr. adj. & pron.* what?; what a!; *interr. adv.* how; ¡ — **bonito!** how beautiful!; **¿a** —? what for?; **¿para** —? what for?; **¿por** —? why?; **¿—**

**tal?** how?; hello!; ¡— **más da!** what's the difference!; **¡a mí** —! so what! and what's that to me!

**quebracho** *m.* quebracho, breakax wood.

**quebrada** *f.* ravine; gorge; failure, bankruptcy; *Ríopl.*, *Col.*, *Ven.*, *C.A.*, *Mex.* brook.

**quebradizo** *adj.* breakable; brittle; fragile; delicate.

**quebrado** *adj.* broken; weakened; ruptured; bankrupt; rough or rugged (*ground*); *m.* common fraction; *Ven.* navigable waters between reefs.

**quebrantar** *v.* to break; to break open; to pound, crush; to violate (*a law*); to weaken; to vex; *Mex.*, *Col.* to tame, break in (*a colt*); — **el agua** to take the chill off the water.

**quebranto** *m.* breaking; grief, affliction; discouragement; damage, loss.

**quebrar**[1] *v. irr.* to break; to crush; to interrupt; to wither (*said of the complexion*); to become bankrupt; **-se** to break; to get broken; to be ruptured; **-se uno la cabeza** to rack one's brain.

**quebrazón** *m. Ven.*, *Col.* breakage, breaking.

**quechua** *adj. Am.* Quichuan; *m. & f.* Quichua, Quichuan Indian; *m.* Quichuan language.

**quedar** *v.* to stay; to remain; to be left over; to be left (*in a state or condition*); — **en** to agree to; *Am.* — **de** to agree to; — **bien** to acquit oneself well; to come out well; *Am.* to suit, become (*said of a dress, hat, etc.*); *Am.* — **bien con alguien** to please someone; **-se** to remain; **-se con una cosa** to keep something; to take something (*buy it*); *Am.* **-se como si tal cosa** to act as if nothing had happened.

**quedo** *adj.* quiet, still; gentle; *adv.* softly; in a low voice; **quedito** *adj.* nice and quiet; *adv.* very softly.

**quehacer** *m.* work, occupation; task, duty, chore.

**queja** *f.* complaint; groan, moan; grudge.

**quejarse** *v.* to complain; to grumble; to moan; to lament.

**quejido** *m.* moan; groan.

**quejoso** *adj.* complaining, whining.

**quejumbre** *f.* whine, moan; murmur, complaint; **-s** *m. Cuba*, *Ven.* grumbler, whiner; **quejumbroso** *adj.* whining, complaining.

**quemada** *f.* burned forest; *Am.* burn.

**quemado** *m.* burned portion of a forest; *Col.* burned field; *Am.* hot alcoholic drink; *adj.* dark, tan; *Am.* peeved, piqued; *Col.*, *Ven.*, *Cuba*, *Mex.* ruined; *p.p.* of **quemar.**

**quemadura** *f.* burn; scald; smut (*plant disease*).

**quemar** *v.* to burn; to scald; to scorch; to sell at a loss; to annoy; *Am.* to deceive, swindle; **-se** to burn; to be hot.

**quemazón** *f.* (*calor*) burn, burning;

great heat; fire, conflagration; (*desazón*) pique, anger; bargain sale; *Am.* mirage on the pampas.

**querella** *f.* quarrel; complaint; controversy.

**querellarse** *v.* to complain.

**querencia** *f.* affection; longing; favorite spot; haunt; stable.

**querer**[41] *v. irr.* to want, wish, desire; to will; to be willing; to love; **— decir** to mean; **sin —** unwillingly; **no quiso hacerlo** he refused to do it; **quiere llover** it is trying to rain, it is about to rain; **como quiera** in any way; **como quiera que** since; no matter how; **cuando quiera** whenever; **donde quiera** wherever; anywhere; **-se** to love each other; *Ríopl., Ven., Col.* to be on the point of, be about to; **se quiere caer esa pared** that wall is about to fall.

**querido** *p.p.* wanted, desired; *adj.* beloved, dear; *m.* lover; **querida** *f.* darling; mistress.

**quesería** *f.* dairy, creamery, cheese factory; **quesera** *f.* dairy, cheese factory; cheese dish; dairymaid, woman cheese vendor or cheesemaker; **quesero** *adj.* pertaining to cheese; *m.* cheesemaker.

**queso** *m.* cheese; *Ven.* **— de higos** fig paste.

**quicio** *m.* hinge of a door; **sacar a uno de —** to exasperate someone.

**quichua** = **quechua.**

**quiebra** *f.* (*rotura*) break; crack; fissure; fracture; (*pérdida*) loss, damage; bankruptcy.

**quien** *rel. pron.* who, whom; he who, she who; **quién** *interr. pron.* who? whom?

**quienquiera** *pron.* whoever, whosoever, whomsoever.

**quieto** *adj.* quiet, still; calm.

**quietud** *f.* quiet, stillness, calmness.

**quijada** *f.* jaw; jawbone.

**quilate** *m.* carat (*twenty-fourth part in weight and value of gold*); unit of weight for precious stones and pearls; **-s** qualities; degree of perfection or purity.

**quilla** *f.* keel.

**quimera** *f.* absurd idea, wild fancy.

**química** *f.* chemistry.

**químico** *adj.* chemical; *m.* chemist.

**quina, quinina** *f.* quinine.

**quincalla** *f.* hardware.

**quincallería** *f.* hardware; hardware store; hardware trade.

**quincena** *f.* fortnight; semimonthly pay.

**quinta** *f.* (*casa*) villa, country house; (*militar*) draft, military conscription; (*cartas*) sequence of five cards.

**quintaesencia** *f.* quintessence, pure essence, purest form.

**quiosco** *m.* kiosk, small pavilion.

**quirúrgico** *adj.* surgical.

**quisquilloso** *adj.* touchy, oversensitive.

**quisto: bien —** well-liked, well received, welcome; **mal —** disliked;

unwelcome.

**quitamanchas** *m.* cleaner, stain remover.

**quitar** *v.* to remove; to take away (off, *or* from); to rob of; to deprive of; to subtract; to parry (*in fencing*); **-se** to take off (*clothing*); to remove oneself, withdraw; **-se de una cosa** to give up something, get rid of something; **-se a alguien de encima** to get rid of someone; **¡quita allá!** don't tell me that!; **¡quítese de aquí!** get out of here!

**quitasol** *m.* large sunshade, parasol.

**quite** *m.* parry (*in fencing*); dodge, dodging; *Ven., Col., Mex.* **andar a los -s** to be on the defensive; to take offense easily; to be afraid of one's own shadow; **eso no tiene —** that can't be helped.

**quizá, quizás** *adv.* perhaps, maybe.

## R

**rabadilla** *f.* end of the spinal column; tail of a fowl; rump.

**rábano** *m.* radish; **tomar el — por las hojas** to take one thing for another; to misinterpret something.

**rabia** *f.* rabies; rage; **tener — a alguien** to hate someone; *Ríopl., Carib., Mex.* **volarse de —** to get furious, angry.

**rabiar** *v.* to have rabies; to rage; to rave; to suffer a severe pain; **— por** to be dying to or for, be very eager to; **quema que rabia** it burns terribly.

**rabieta** *f.* tantrum, fit of temper.

**rabino** *m.* rabbi.

**rabioso** *adj.* rabid (*having rabies*), mad; furious, angry, violent.

**rabo** *m.* tail; **de cabo a —** from beginning to end; **mirar con el — del ojo** to look out of the corner of one's eye.

**racimo** *m.* bunch; cluster.

**raciocinio** *m.* reasoning.

**ración** *f.* ration; allowance; supply.

**racional** *adj.* rational; reasonable.

**racionamiento** *m.* rationing.

**racionar** *v.* to ration.

**radar** *m.* radar.

**radaroscopio** *m.* radarscope.

**radiación** *f.* radiation; **— cósmica** cosmic radiation.

**radiactividad** *f.* radioactivity.

**radiactivo** *adj.* radioactive.

**radiador** *m.* radiator.

**radiante** *adj.* radiant; shining; beaming.

**radiar** *v.* to radiate; to radio; to broadcast.

**radical** *adj.* (*básico*) fundamental, basic; radical; (*extremista*) extreme; *m.* radical; root of a word.

**radicar**[6] *v.* to take root; to be, be found (*in a certain place*); **-se** to take root; to locate, settle.

**radio** *m.* radius; radium; *m. & f.* radio.

**radiodifundir** *v.* to broadcast by radio. *See* **difundir.**

**radiodifusión** *f.* broadcasting. *See* **difusión.**

**radiodifusora, radioemisora** *f.*

broadcasting station.
**radioescucha** *m. & f.* radio listener.
**radiofónico** *adj.* radio (*used as adj.*);
 **estación radiofónica** radio station.
**radiografía** *f.* radiography, X-ray
 photography; X-ray picture.
**radiografiar**[17] *v.* to take X-ray pictures.
**radiolocutor** *m.* radio announcer. *See*
 **locutor.**
**radiotelefonía** *f.* radiotelephony, radio,
 wireless.
**radiotelegrafía** *f.* radiotelegraphy,
 radio, wireless telegraphy.
**radioyente** = **radioescucha.**
**raer**[24] *v. irr.* to scrape off; to rub off; to
 scratch off; to fray; to erase.
**ráfaga** *f.* gust of wind; flash of light.
**raído** *p.p. & adj.* scraped off; rubbed
 off; frayed; worn, threadbare.
**raigón** *m.* large root; root of a tooth.
**raíz** *f.* root; origin; foundation; —
 **cuadrada** square root; **a — de** close
 to, right after; **de —** by the roots,
 completely; **echar raíces** to take
 root, become firmly fixed.
**raja** *f.* slice; splinter; crack; split,
 crevice; **hacer -s** to slice; to tear into
 strips; to cut into splinters; **hacerse
 uno -s** to wear oneself out (*by dancing,
 jumping or any violent exercise*).
**rajadura** *f.* crack, crevice.
**rajar** *v.* to split; to crack; to cleave; to
 slice; to chatter; to brag; *Col., Cuba,
 Mex., Andes* to defame, insult; *Col.*
 to flunk, fail (*a student*); **-se** to split
 open; to crack; *Mex.* to get afraid,
 back down.
**rajatablas** *m. Col.* reprimand, scolding; **a —** in great haste.
**ralea** *f.* breed, race, stock; species, kind.
**ralear** *v.* to thin out, make less dense;
 to become less dense.
**ralo** *adj.* sparse, thin, thinly scattered.
**rallador** *m.* grater.
**rallar** *v.* to grate; to grate on, annoy;
 *Am.* to goad, spur.
**rama** *f.* branch, limb; **en —** crude,
 raw; **andarse por las -s** to beat
 about the bush, not to stick to the
 point.
**ramada** *f.* branches, foliage; arbor;
 *Am.* shed, tent.
**ramaje** *m.* foliage; branches.
**ramal** *m.* strand (*of a rope, etc.*);
 branch; branch railway line; halter.
**ramera** *f.* harlot, prostitute.
**ramificarse**[6] *v.* to branch off, divide
 into branches.
**ramillete** *m.* bouquet; flower cluster.
**ramo** *m.* bunch (*of flowers*), bouquet;
 line, branch (*of art, science, industry,
 etc.*); branch, bough; **domingo de -s**
 Palm Sunday.
**ramonear** *v.* to cut off twigs or tips of
 branches; to nibble grass, twigs, or
 leaves; *Am.* to eat scraps or leftovers.
**rampa** *f.* ramp; apron (*airport*); **— de
 cohetes, — de lanzamiento** launching ramp.
**ramplón** *adj.* coarse; crude, uncouth;

slovenly.
**ramplonería** *f.* coarse act or remark;
 crudeness, coarseness; slovenliness.
**rana** *f.* frog.
**rancio** *adj.* rancid, stale; old (*wine*);
 **linaje —** old, noble lineage.
**ranchero** *m. Mex.* rancher, farmer;
 **ranchería** *f.* group of huts; *Col.* inn
 (*for* **arrieros**).
**rancho** *m.* camp; hamlet; mess (*meal
 for a group and the group itself*);
 *Carib., Ven., Col., Andes, Ríopl.* hut;
 *Carib., Ven., Col., Andes, Ríopl.*
 country house; *Mex.* ranch, small
 farm (*usually for cattle raising*).
**rango** *m.* rank, position.
**ranura** *f.* groove; slot.
**rapar** *v.* to shave off; to crop (*hair*); to
 strip bare, rob of everything.
**rapaz** *adj.* rapacious, grasping, greedy;
 *m.* lad; **rapaza** *f.* lass, young girl.
**rapé** *m.* snuff (*pulverized tobacco*).
**rapidez** *f.* rapidity, speed.
**rápido** *adj.* rapid, swift; *m.* rapids.
**rapiña** *f.* plunder; **ave de —** bird of
 prey.
**rapiñar** *v.* to plunder; to steal.
**raposa** *f.* fox.
**raptar** *v.* to kidnap, abduct.
**rapto** *m.* (*delito*) abduction, kidnapping; (*sentimiento*) ecstasy, rapture;
 outburst.
**raqueta** *f.* racket (*used in games*);
 tennis.
**raquítico** *adj.* rickety, feeble, weak,
 skinny, sickly.
**rareza** *f.* rarity; oddity; strangeness;
 freak; curiosity; queer act or remark;
 peculiarity; **por —** seldom.
**raro** *adj.* rare; thin, not dense; scarce;
 strange, odd; ridiculous; **rara vez** (*or*
 **raras veces**) rarely, seldom.
**ras : a — de** flush with, even with; **al
 — con** flush with; **estar — con —**
 to be flush, perfectly even.
**rascacielos** *m.* skyscraper.
**rascar**[6] *v.* to scratch; to scrape; *Andes*
 to dig up potatoes; *Am.* **— uno para
 adentro** to seek one's own advantage,
 look out for oneself.
**rasete** *m.* sateen.
**rasgado** *adj.* torn; open; *Col.* generous;
 *Am.* outspoken; **ojos -s** large, wide-
 open eyes.
**rasgadura** *f.* tear, rip, rent.
**rasgar**[7] *v.* to tear; to rip.
**rasgo** *m.* (*propiedad*) trait, characteristic; (*rúbrica*) stroke of the pen,
 flourish; (*hazaña*) feat; *Am.* irrigation ditch; **— de terreno** a
 parcel of land; **-s** features; traits.
**rasgón** *m.* large tear, rent, rip.
**rasguñar** *v.* to scratch; to claw.
**rasguño** *m.* scratch.
**raso** *adj.* (*llano*) plain; flat, smooth;
 (*despejado*) clear, cloudless; *Ríopl.,
 Mex.* even, level (*when measuring
 wheat, corn, etc.*); *Am.* scarce, scanty;
 **soldado —** private; **al —** in the open
 air; *m.* satin.
**raspadura** *f.* scrape; scraping; erasure;

shaving (*of wood or metal*).

**raspar** *v.* to scrape, scrape off; to steal; *Andes* to scold, upbraid; *Col.* to leave.

**rastra** *f.* drag; sled; large rake; harrow; **a -s** dragging; unwillingly.

**rastreador** *m.* trailer, tracker, tracer.

**rastrear** *v.* to trail, track, trace; to rake, harrow; to drag (*a dragnet*); to skim, scrape the ground.

**rastrero** *adj.* low, vile.

**rastrillar** *v.* to rake; to comb (*flax or hemp*); *Ven.* to scrape; *Am.* to shoot; *Am.* to barter, exchange; *Am.* to pilfer, steal (*in stores*).

**rastrillo** *m.* rake; *Am.* barter, exchange; *Am.* business deal.

**rastro** *m.* track, trail, scent; trace, sign; rake, harrow; slaughterhouse.

**rastrojo** *m.* stubble.

**rasura** *f.* shave, shaving.

**rasurar** *v.* to shave.

**rata** *f.* rat; *m.* pickpocket.

**ratear** *v.* to pilfer; to pick pockets; to creep, crawl.

**ratería** *f.* petty larceny; meanness.

**ratero** *m.* pickpocket; *adj.* contemptible, mean.

**ratificar**⁶ *v.* to ratify.

**rato** *m.* short time, little while; **buen —** pleasant time; long time; **-s perdidos** leisure hours; **a -s** at intervals, from time to time; **pasar el —** to while away the time, kill time; *Am.* **¡hasta cada — !** so long!; see you later!

**ratón** *m.* mouse; *Am.* **tener un —** to have a hangover; **ratonera** *f.* mousetrap.

**raudal** *m.* torrent, downpour, flood; *Ríopl., Ch., Col., Ven., Andes* rapids.

**raudo** *adj.* rapid, swift.

**raya** *f.* line; dash; stripe; boundary line; part in the hair; *Mex.* pay, wage; *Mex.* **día de —** payday; **tener a —** to keep within bounds; to hold in check; **pasar de la —** to overstep one's bounds, take undue liberties; *m.* sting ray (*a species of fish*).

**rayador** *m. Mex.* paymaster; *Am.* umpire in a game.

**rayar** *v.* to line, make lines on; to streak; to scratch, mark; to cross out; *Mex.* to pay or collect wages; *Am.* to stop a horse all of a sudden; *Am.* to spur a horse to run at top speed; **— el alba** to dawn; **— en** to border on; *Am.* **-se uno** to help oneself; to get rich.

**rayo** *m.* ray, beam; lightning, thunderbolt; spoke; **-s X** X-rays; **-s infrarrojos** infrared rays.

**raza** *f.* race; clan; breed; fissure, crevice; **caballo de —** thoroughbred horse.

**razón** *f.* (*facultad*) reason; (*justicia*) right, justice; (*cuenta*) ratio; account, information, word, message; **— social** firm, firm name; **a — de** at the rate of; **¡con — !** no wonder!; **dar —** to inform; **dar la — a una persona** to admit that a person is right; **perder la —** to lose one's mind; **poner en —**

to pacify; **tener —** to be right.

**razonable** *adj.* reasonable.

**razonamiento** *m.* reasoning.

**razonar** *v.* to reason; to discourse, talk; to argue.

**reabierto** *p.p.* of **reabrir**.

**reabrir**⁵² *v.* to reopen.

**reacción** *f.* reaction; **— nuclear** nuclear reaction; **— en cadena** chain reaction.

**reaccionar** *v.* to react.

**reaccionario** *adj.* & *m.* reactionary.

**reacio** *adj.* stubborn, obstinate.

**reactor** *m.* reactor; **— atómico** atomic reactor; **— nuclear** nuclear reactor.

**reajustar** *v.* to readjust.

**reajuste** *m.* readjustment.

**real** *adj.* real; royal; *m.* army camp; fairground; real (*Spanish coin worth one fourth of a peseta*); **-es** *Andes* money (*in general*); **levantar el —** (*or* **los -es**) to break camp.

**realce** *m.* (*adorno*) embossment, raised work, relief; (*lustre*) prestige; lustre, splendor; **dar —** to enhance; to emphasize.

**realeza** *f.* royalty (*royal dignity*).

**realidad** *f.* reality; truth; fact; **en —** really, truly, in fact.

**realismo** *m.* realism; royalism.

**realista** *adj.* realistic; royalist; *m.* realist; royalist.

**realización** *f.* realization, fulfillment; conversion into money, sale.

**realizar**⁹ *v.* to realize, fulfill, make real; to convert into money; to sell out.

**realzar**⁹ *v.* to emboss; to raise; to enhance; to make stand out; to emphasize.

**reanimar** *v.* to revive; to comfort; to cheer; to encourage.

**reanudación** *f.* renewal.

**reanudar** *v.* to renew, resume, begin again.

**reaparecer**¹³ *v. irr.* to reappear.

**reasumir** *v.* to resume.

**reata** *f.* lariat, rope, lasso.

**reavivar** *v.* to revive.

**rebaja** *f.* deduction; reduction; discount.

**rebajar** *v.* to diminish; to lower, reduce; to tone down (*a painting*); to humiliate; **-se** to lower or humble oneself.

**rebanada** *f.* slice.

**rebanar** *v.* to slice.

**rebaño** *m.* flock; herd.

**rebatir** *v.* to beat over and over; to repel, resist; to refute; to rebut (*come back with an argument*); to argue; to parry (*in fencing*).

**rebato** *m.* alarm, call to arms; surprise attack.

**rebelarse** *v.* to rebel.

**rebelde** *adj.* rebellious; *m.* rebel; defaulter (*one who fails to appear in court*).

**rebeldía** *f.* rebelliousness; defiance; default, failure to appear in court; **en —** in revolt.

**RA**

**rebelión** f. rebellion, revolt.

**rebencazo** m. Ríopl., Ch., Andes crack of a whip; Am. lash, stroke with a whip.

**rebenque** m. rawhide whip.

**reborde** m. edge, border.

**rebosante** adj. brimming, overflowing.

**rebosar** v. to overflow, brim over; to abound.

**rebotar** v. to rebound, bounce back or again; to make rebound; to repel, reject; to annoy, vex; **-se** to become vexed, upset; Col., Mex. to become cloudy or muddy (said of water); Am. **rebotársele a uno la bilis** to get angry, become upset.

**rebote** m. rebound, bounce; **de —** on the rebound; indirectly.

**rebozar**[9] v. to muffle up; **-se** to muffle oneself up; to wrap oneself up.

**rebozo** m. shawl; **sin —** frankly, openly.

**rebullir**[20] v. irr. to stir, move; to boil up.

**rebusca** f. research; search; searching; gleaning; residue.

**rebuscar**[6] v. to search thoroughly; to pry into; to glean.

**rebuznar** v. to bray.

**rebuzno** m. bray.

**recabar** v. to obtain, gain by entreaty.

**recado** m. message; errand; gift; daily food supply, daily marketing; precaution; equipment; Ríopl., Andes saddle and trappings; **— de escribir** writing materials; **-s a** regards to.

**recaer**[24] v. irr. to fall (upon); to fall again; to relapse; to have a relapse.

**recaída** f. relapse; falling again.

**recalar** v. to saturate, soak through; to reach port; to come within sight of land; to land, end up, stop at; Am. **— con alguien** to "land" on somebody, take it out on somebody.

**recalcar**[6] v. to emphasize; to harp on; to press down.

**recalcitrante** adj. obstinate, disobedient, stubborn.

**recalentar**[1] v. irr. to reheat, warm over; to overheat, heat too much.

**recamar** v. to embroider (usually with gold or silver).

**recámara** f. dressing room; Mex., C.A., Col. bedroom; Ríopl., Col. chamber for an explosive charge.

**recapitular** v. to recapitulate, sum up, tell briefly.

**recargo** m. overload; extra load; extra charge; increase (of fever); new charge, new accusation.

**recatado** adj. cautious, prudent; modest; p.p. concealed.

**recatar** v. to cover, conceal; **-se** to show timidity; to be cautious; to hide (from), shun.

**recato** m. caution, prudence; reserve, restraint, secrecy; modesty.

**recaudación** f. collection, collecting; office of tax collector.

**recaudador** m. tax collector.

**recaudar** v. to collect (money, taxes,

rents, etc.).

**recaudo** m. collection, collecting; precaution; bond, security; Mex. spices, seasonings; Am. daily supply of vegetables; **estar a buen —** to be safe; **poner a buen —** to place in safety.

**recelar** v. to suspect, fear; **-se de** to be suspicious or afraid of.

**recelo** m. suspicion, fear.

**receloso** adj. suspicious, distrustful, fearful.

**recepción** f. reception; admission.

**receptáculo** m. receptacle.

**receptivo** adj. receptive, capable of receiving, quick to receive.

**receptor** m. receiver; adj. receiving.

**receta** f. recipe; prescription.

**recetar** v. to prescribe (a medicine).

**recibidor** m. receiver; reception room.

**recibimiento** m. reception; welcome; reception room; parlor.

**recibir** v. to receive; to admit, accept; to go out to meet; **— noticias de** to hear from; **-se de** to receive a title or degree of.

**recibo** m. (monetario) receipt; (acción) reception; (sala) reception room; parlor; **sala de —** reception room; **estar de —** to be at home for receiving callers; **ser de —** to be acceptable, be fit for use.

**reciedumbre** f. strength, force, vigor.

**recién** adv. recently, lately, newly (used before a past participle); Ríopl., Ch., Andes just now; Ríopl., Ch., Andes a short time ago; Ríopl., Ch., Andes **— entonces** just then.

**reciente** adj. recent, new.

**recinto** m. enclosure; precinct.

**recio** adj. strong, robust; harsh; hard, severe; fast; adv. strongly; harshly; rapidly; hard; loud.

**recipiente** m. receptable, container; recipient, receiver (he who receives).

**recíproco** adj. reciprocal, mutual.

**recitación** f. recitation, recital.

**recital** m. musical recital.

**recitar** v. to recite.

**reclamación** f. protest, complaint; claim, demand.

**reclamador** m. claimant; complainer.

**reclamante** m. & f. claimant; complainer; adj. complaining; claiming.

**reclamar** v. (protestar) to complain, protest (against); (exigir) to claim, demand; to lure, call back (a bird).

**reclamo** m. (protesta) protest; claim; advertisement; (llamada) call; bird call; decoy bird; lure.

**reclinar** v. to recline, lean; **-se** to recline, lean back.

**recluir**[32] v. irr. to seclude, shut up; **-se** to isolate oneself.

**recluso** m. recluse, hermit; adj. shut in, shut up.

**recluta** f. recruiting; Am. roundup of cattle; m. recruit.

**reclutamiento** m. recruiting; levy, draft.

**reclutar** v. to recruit, enlist; Am. to round up (cattle).

**recobrar** *v.* to recover, regain; **-se** to recover; to recuperate.

**recobro** *m.* recovery.

**recodo** *m.* bend, turn; elbow (*of a road*).

**recoger**[11] *v.* (*juntar*) to gather; to collect; to pick up; (*ceñir*) to take in, tighten; (*abrigar*) to shelter; **-se** to retire, go home; to withdraw; to seclude oneself; to take shelter.

**recogimiento** *m.* seclusion; concentration of thought, composure; retreat; collecting, gathering.

**recolección** *f.* collecting, gathering; harvest, crop; summary.

**recolectar** *v.* to harvest; to gather.

**recomendable** *adj.* praiseworthy, laudable; advisable.

**recomendación** *f.* recommendation; request.

**recomendar**[1] *v. irr.* to recommend; to commend, praise; to enjoin, urge; to advise.

**recompensa** *f.* recompense; compensation.

**recompensar** *v.* to recompense, reward; to compensate.

**reconcentrar** *v.* to concentrate, bring together; to hide in the depth of one's heart; **-se** to concentrate, become absorbed in thought, collect one's thoughts.

**reconciliación** *f.* reconciliation.

**reconciliar** *v.* to reconcile; **-se** to become reconciled.

**recóndito** *adj.* hidden, concealed; profound.

**reconocer**[13] *v. irr.* to recognize; to admit, acknowledge; to examine carefully; to reconnoiter, scout, explore.

**reconocimiento** *m.* recognition; acknowledgment; gratitude; examination; scouting, exploring.

**reconstruir**[32] *v. irr.* to reconstruct, rebuild.

**recontar**[2] *v. irr.* to recount; to tell, relate.

**recopilar** *v.* to compile; to digest, make a digest of.

**recordación** *f.* recollection; remembrance.

**recordar**[2] *v. irr.* to remember; to recall; to remind; *Am.* to rouse, awaken; **-se** to remember; to wake up.

**recordativo** *m.* reminder; *adj.* reminding.

**recordatorio** *m.* reminder.

**recorrer** *v.* to go over; to travel over; to read over; to look over; to overhaul.

**recorrido** *m.* trip, run; mileage, distance traveled.

**recortar** *v.* to trim, clip; to shorten; to cut out (*figures*); to pare off; **-se** to project itself (*as a shadow*); to outline itself.

**recorte** *m.* clipping; cutting; outline; *Mex.* gossip, slander.

**recostar** *v.* to recline, lean; **-se** to recline, lean back.

**recoveco** *m.* turn, bend; nook; sly or underhanded manner.

**recreación** *f.* recreation.

**recrear** *v.* to entertain, amuse; to gratify, please; **-se** to amuse oneself; to take delight (in).

**recreo** *m.* recreation, entertainment; place of amusement.

**recrudecer**[13] *v.* to recur, break out again, flare up, become worse (*said of an illness or evil*).

**rectángulo** *m.* rectangle; *adj.* rectangular, right-angled.

**rectificar**[6] *v.* to rectify, correct, amend; to refine (*liquors*).

**rectitud** *f.* rectitude, uprightness, righteousness; straightness; accuracy.

**recto** *adj.* straight; right; just, honest; **ángulo —** right angle; *m.* rectum; *adv. C.A.* straight ahead.

**rector** *m.* college or university president; principal; rector, curate, priest.

**recua** *f.* drove of pack animals; drove, crowd.

**recuento** *m.* recount.

**recuerdo** *m.* remembrance; recollection; souvenir, keepsake; memory; **-s** regards; *adj. Riopl., Col., Ven.* awake.

**reculada** *f.* recoil.

**recular** *v.* to recoil, spring back; to fall back, go back, retreat; to yield, back down.

**recuperación** *f.* recovery.

**recuperar** *v.* to recuperate, recover, regain; **-se** to recuperate, recover one's health.

**recurrir** *v.* to resort (to); to have recourse (to).

**recurso** *m.* recourse, resort; petition, appeal; **-s** means, resources; **sin —** without remedy; without appeal.

**recusar** *v.* to reject, decline.

**rechazar**[9] *v.* to reject; to repel, drive back; to rebuff.

**rechifla** *f.* hooting; hissing; ridicule.

**rechiflar** *v.* to hoot; to hiss; to ridicule.

**rechinamiento** *m.* creak; squeak; squeaking; gnashing.

**rechinar** *v.* to squeak; to creak; *Am.* to be furious, angry; *Am.* to grumble, growl; **— los dientes** to gnash one's teeth.

**rechino** = **rechinamiento.**

**rechoncho** *adj.* plump; chubby; squat.

**rechuparse** *v.* to smack one's lips.

**red** *f.* net; netting; network; snare; **redecilla** *f.* small net; mesh; hair net.

**redacción** *f.* (*acto*) wording; editing; (*lugar*) newspaper offices; editorial department; (*cuerpo*) editorial staff.

**redactar** *v.* to word, compose; to edit.

**redactor** *m.* editor.

**redargüir**[32] *v. irr.* to retort, answer back; to contradict, call in question; to reargue.

**rededor** *m.* surroundings; **al** (*or* **en**) **—** around, about.

**redención** *f.* redemption.

**redentor** *m.* redeemer, savior; **el Redentor** the Savior.

**RE**

**redil** *m.* sheepfold.
**redimir** *v.* to redeem; to ransom; to set free.
**rédito** *m.* interest, revenue, yield.
**redituar**[18] *v.* to produce, yield (*interest*).
**redoblar** *v.* to double; to clinch (*a nail*); to reiterate, repeat; to roll (*a drum*).
**redoble** *m.* roll (*of a drum*).
**redoma** *f.* flask, vial.
**redomón** *m. Ríopl.* half-tame horse or bull; *adj. Ríopl.* half-civilized, rustic.
**redonda** *f.* surrounding district, neighborhood; whole note (*music*); **a la —** all around, round-about.
**redondear** *v.* to round, make round; to round off; to round out.
**redondel** *m.* arena, bull ring; circle.
**redondo** *adj.* round; whole, entire; clear, evident; *Andes* stupid; *Mex.* honest; **en —** all around.
**redopelo : a —** against the grain.
**redor** *m.* round mat; **en —** around.
**reducción** *f.* reduction; cut, discount; decrease.
**reducido** *p.p.* & *adj.* reduced; compact, small.
**reducir**[25] *v. irr.* to reduce; to diminish; to convert (into); to reset (*a bone*); **-se** to adapt oneself, adjust oneself; to be constrained, forced.
**reedificar**[6] *v.* to rebuild, reconstruct.
**reelección** *f.* re-election.
**reelegir**[11] *v.* to re-elect.
**reembolsar** *v.* to reimburse, refund, repay, pay back.
**reembolso** *m.* reimbursement, refund.
**reemitir** *v.* to emit again; to issue again; to rebroadcast; to relay (*a broadcast*).
**reemplazable** *adj.* replaceable.
**reemplazar**[9] *v.* to replace; to substitute.
**reemplazo** *m.* replacement; substitute, substitution.
**refacción** *f.* (*alimento*) light lunch, refreshment; (*compostura*) repair, reparation; *Mex., Col.* spare part; *Carib.* help, aid, loan.
**refajo** *m.* underskirt; short skirt.
**referencia** *f.* reference; narration, account.
**referente** *adj.* referring.
**referir**[3] *v. irr.* to refer; to narrate; to relate; **-se** to refer (to), relate (to).
**refinamiento** *m.* refinement.
**refinar** *v.* to refine; to purify.
**refinería** *f.* refinery.
**reflector** *m.* reflector; floodlight.
**reflejar** *v.* to reflect; to think over; **-se** to be reflected.
**reflejo** *m.* reflection, image; reflex; *adj.* reflected; reflex.
**reflexión** *f.* reflection; meditation, consideration.
**reflexionar** *v.* to reflect, meditate, think over.
**reflexivo** *adj.* reflexive; reflective, thoughtful.
**reflujo** *m.* ebb; ebb tide.
**reforma** *f.* reform; reformation; improvement.

**reformador** *m.* reformer.
**reformar** *v.* to reform; to correct, amend; to improve; **-se** to reform.
**reformista** *m.* & *f.* reformer.
**reforzar**[2,9] *v. irr.* to reinforce; to strengthen.
**refracción** *f.* refraction.
**refractario** *adj.* refractory; impervious; rebellious, unruly; stubborn.
**refrán** *m.* popular proverb or saying.
**refrenar** *v.* to restrain, keep in check; to curb; to rein.
**refrendar** *v.* to legalize by signing; to countersign (*confirm by another signature*); **— un pasaporte** to visé a passport.
**refrescante** *adj.* refreshing.
**refrescar**[6] *v.* to refresh, renew; to cool; to get cool (*said of the weather*); **-se** to cool off; to take the fresh air; to take a cooling drink or refreshment; *Cuba, C.A.* to take an afternoon refreshment.
**refresco** *m.* refreshment.
**refresquería** *f. Mex., C.A., Ven.* refreshment shop, outdoor refreshment stand.
**refriega** *f.* strife, fray, scuffle.
**refrigeración** *f.* refrigeration; light meal or refreshment.
**refrigerador** *m. Am.* refrigerator, freezer; *adj.* refrigerating, freezing; refreshing.
**refrigerio** *m.* refreshment; relief, comfort; coolness.
**refuerzo** *m.* reinforcement.
**refugiado** *m.* refugee; *p.p. of* **refugiar.**
**refugiar** *v.* to shelter; **-se** to take shelter or refuge.
**refugio** *m.* refuge, shelter.
**refulgente** *adj.* refulgent, radiant, shining.
**refundir** *v.* to remelt, refound, recast (*metals*); to recast, rewrite, reconstruct.
**refunfuñar** *v.* to grumble, mumble, growl, mutter.
**refunfuño** *m.* grumble, growl; **refunfuñón** *adj.* grouchy; grumbly, grumbling.
**refutar** *v.* to refute.
**regadera** *f.* sprinkler; *Mex.* shower, bath.
**regadío** *adj.* irrigable, that can be irrigated; irrigated; *m.* irrigated land; **tierras de —** irrigable lands.
**regalar** *v.* (*dar*) to give, present as a gift; to regale; (*recrear*) to entertain; to delight, please; **-se** to treat oneself well, live a life of ease.
**regalo** *m.* present, gift; pleasure, delight; dainty, delicacy; luxury, comfort.
**regañadientes : a —** much against one's wishes; unwillingly.
**regañar** *v.* to growl; to grumble; to quarrel; to scold.
**regaño** *m.* scolding, reprimand.
**regañón** *adj.* grumbling; scolding; quarrelsome; *m.* growler, grumbler, scolder.

**regar**[1,7] *v. irr.* to irrigate; to water; to sprinkle, scatter; *Col.* to spill, throw off (*said of a horse*); **-se** *Am.* to scatter, disperse (*said of a group, herd, etc.*).

**regatear** *v.* to haggle, bargain; to dispute; to sell at retail; to race (*in a regatta or boat race*).

**regazo** *m.* lap.

**regentar** *v.* to direct, conduct, manage; **— una cátedra** to teach a course (*at a university*).

**regente** *m.* regent; manager; *adj.* ruling.

**regidor** *m.* councilman, alderman; *adj.* governing, ruling.

**régimen** *m.* regime; government, rule, management; **— lácteo** milk diet.

**regimiento** *m.* regiment; (*administrativo*) administration; municipal council; position of alderman.

**regio** *adj.* regal, royal; splendid, magnificent.

**región** *f.* region.

**regir**[5,11] *v. irr.* to rule, govern; to direct, manage; to be in force (*said of a law*); to move (*said of the bowels*).

**registrador** *m.* registrar, recorder; city clerk, official in charge of records; inspector (*in a customhouse*); searcher; *adj.* registering; **caja registradora** cash register.

**registrar** *v.* to examine, inspect, scrutinize; to register, record; **-se** to register, enroll.

**registro** *m.* search, inspection; registration; census; registration office; register; record; registration certificate; watch regulator; bookmark; organ stop; *Ven.* wholesale textile store.

**regla** *f.* (*precepto*) rule; ruler; order; precept, principle; (*medida*) measure, moderation; menstruation; **en —** in order, in due form; **por — general** as a general rule; usually.

**reglamento** *m.* regulations, rules; rule, bylaw.

**regocijado** *adj.* joyful, merry, gay; *p.p. of* **regocijar.**

**regocijar** *v.* to gladden, delight; **-se** to be glad; to rejoice.

**regocijo** *m.* joy; rejoicing.

**regordete** *adj.* plump.

**regresar** *v.* to return.

**regreso** *m.* return; **estar de —** to be back.

**reguero** *m.* stream, rivulet; trickle; irrigation ditch.

**regulación** *f.* regulation; adjustment.

**regulador** *m.* regulator; controller, governor (*of a machine*); *adj.* regulating.

**regular** *v.* to regulate; to adjust; *adj.* regular; ordinary; moderate; fair, medium; **por lo —** as a rule, usually; *adv.* fairly well.

**regularidad** *f.* regularity.

**regularizar**[9] *v.* to regulate, make regular.

**rehacer**[31] *v. irr.* to remake; to make over; to repair; **-se** to recover one's strength; to rally.

**rehén** *m.* hostage; **en rehenes** as a hostage.

**rehuir**[32] *v. irr.* to shun, avoid; to shrink (from).

**rehusar** *v.* to refuse; **-se a** to refuse to.

**reina** *f.* queen.

**reinado** *m.* reign.

**reinante** *adj.* reigning; prevailing.

**reinar** *v.* to reign; to rule; to prevail.

**reincidir** *v.* to relapse, slide back (into).

**reino** *m.* kingdom.

**reintegro** *m.* reimbursement, refund.

**reír**[15] *v. irr.* to laugh; **-se de** to laugh at; *Ríopl., Andes, Col., Ven., Carib.* **— de dientes para afuera** to laugh outwardly, laugh hypocritically.

**reiterar** *v.* to reiterate, repeat.

**reja** *f.* grate, grating; plowshare (*blade of the plow*); plowing; *Carib., C.A.* jail.

**rejilla** *f.* small grating, lattice; small latticed window; fireplace grate; cane upholstery; *Ch.* wire dish-cover.

**rejonear** *v.* to fight a bull from horseback (*Portuguese style*).

**rejuvenecer**[13] *v. irr.* to rejuvenate, make young; **-se** to become rejuvenated.

**relación** *f.* relation; story, account; long speech in a play; *Ríopl.* verse recited alternately by a couple in a folk dance; **-es** personal relations, connections; acquaintances.

**relacionar** *v.* to relate, connect; **-se** to be related, connected; to become acquainted, establish friendly connections.

**relajación** *f.*, **relajamiento** *m.* relaxation; laxity; slackening; hernia.

**relajar** *v.* to relax; to slacken; to release from a vow or oath; **-se** to get a hernia or rupture; to become weakened; to become lax (*said of laws, customs, etc.*).

**relajo** *m. Carib., Mex.* disorderly conduct; lewdness; scandal.

**relamerse** *v.* to lick one's lips; to gloat; to boast; to slick oneself up.

**relámpago** *m.* lightning; flash.

**relampaguear** *v.* to lighten; to flash; to sparkle.

**relampagueo** *m.* flashing; sheet lightning.

**relatar** *v.* to relate, narrate.

**relativo** *adj.* relative; **— a** relative to, regarding.

**relato** *m.* narration, account, story.

**relé** *m.* relay; **— de televisión** television relay system.

**relegar**[7] *v.* to relegate, banish; to postpone; to set aside, put away.

**relente** *m.* night dampness; *Am.* fresh night breeze.

**relevar** *v.* to relieve; to release; to absolve; to replace, substitute; to emboss; to make stand out in relief.

**relevo** *m.* relief (*from a post or military duty; person who relieves another from the performance of a duty*).

**relicario** *m.* reliquary (*small box or*

*casket for keeping relics*); *Col., Ven., Cuba, Mex., Andes* locket.

**relieve** *m.* relief, embossment, raised work; **-s** scraps, leftovers; **de —** in relief; prominent, outstanding; **poner de —** to make stand out; to emphasize.

**religión** *f.* religion.

**religiosidad** *f.* religiousness, piety; faithfulness.

**religioso** *adj.* religious; faithful; punctual; *m.* friar, monk.

**relinchar** *v.* to neigh.

**relincho** *m.* neigh.

**reliquia** *f.* relic; vestige; **-s** relics, remains.

**reloj** *m.* clock; watch; **— de pulsera** wristwatch; **— de sol** (*or* **— solar**) sundial; **— despertador** alarm clock.

**reluciente** *adj.* shining; sparkling.

**relucir**[13] *v. irr.* to glitter, sparkle; to shine.

**relumbrante** *adj.* brilliant, flashing, resplendent.

**relumbrar** *v.* to glare; to glitter.

**relumbre** *m.* glare, glitter.

**rellenar** *v.* to refill; to fill up; to pad; to stuff.

**relleno** *adj.* stuffed; *m.* meat stuffing; filling.

**remachar** *v.* to clinch; to hammer down; to flatten; to rivet; to fix firmly; **-se** *Am.* to be tight-lipped, stubbornly silent.

**remache** *m.* clinching; fastening, securing; riveting; rivet.

**remanente** *m.* remainder, balance; remnant; residue.

**remar** *v.* to row; to struggle.

**rematado** *adj. & p.p.* (*acabado*) finished; (*vendido en subasta*) sold at auction; **loco —** completely crazy.

**rematar** *v.* (*acabar*) to finish; to end; to give the final or finishing stroke; (*vender*) to auction; (*afianzar*) to fasten (*a stitch*); *Am.* to stop (*a horse*) suddenly; *Am.* to buy or sell at auction; **-se** to be finished, be completely destroyed or ruined.

**remate** *m.* (*fin*) finish, end; (*postura*) highest bid at an auction; sale at auction; (*punta*) pinnacle, spire; *Am.* selvage, edge of a fabric; **de —** absolutely, without remedy; **loco de —** completely crazy, stark mad.

**remedar** *v.* to imitate; to mimic.

**remediar** *v.* to remedy; to help; to avoid.

**remedio** *m.* remedy; help; amendment; recourse, resort; **sin —** without help, unavoidable; **no tiene —** it can't be helped.

**remedo** *m.* imitation; mockery.

**remembranza** *f.* remembrance, memory.

**rememorar** *v.* to remember, call to mind.

**remendar**[1] *v. irr.* to mend, patch; to darn; to repair.

**remendón** *m.* cobbler, shoe repairman; mender, patcher.

**remero** *m.* rower.

**remesa** *f.* shipment; remittance, payment.

**remesar** *v.* to remit; to ship.

**remiendo** *m.* mend; mending; patch; darn; repair; **a -s** piecemeal, piece by piece.

**remilgado** *adj.* prudish, prim, affected.

**remilgo** *m.* prudery, primness, affectation.

**reminiscencia** *f.* reminiscence.

**remisión** *f.* (*disculpa*) remission; forgiveness; (*remesa*) remittance, remitting; (*diminución*) abatement, slackening; *Mex., Ven.* anything shipped or sent.

**remitente** *m. & f.* sender; shipper.

**remitir** *v.* (*enviar*) to remit; to send; (*diferir*) to defer; to pardon; to refer; to abate; **-se** to defer, yield (*to another's judgment*).

**remo** *m.* oar; hard and long work; leg of a horse; **al —** at the oar; at hard labor.

**remojar** *v.* to soak; to steep; *Am.* to tip, bribe.

**remojo** *m.* soaking; steeping; *Am.* tip, bribe.

**remolacha** *f.* beet.

**remolcador** *m.* towboat, tug, tugboat; **lancha remolcadora** tugboat.

**remolcar**[6] *v.* to tow, tug; to take (*a person*) in tow.

**remolino** *m.* swirl, whirl; whirlwind; whirlpool; commotion; *Ríopl.* pin wheel; *Am.* ventilating wheel (*fan*); **— de gente** throng, crowd.

**remolón** *adj.* indolent, lazy.

**remolque** *m.* tow; towrope; **llevar a — to** tow; to take in tow.

**remontar** *v.* (*alzar*) to elevate, raise; (*reparar*) to repair, patch up; to resole; to revamp; *Am.* to go up; *Ríopl., Carib., C.A., Ven., Col.* to go upstream; **-se** to rise; to soar, fly upward; to date (from), go back (to); *Ríopl.* to take to the woods or hills.

**rémora** *f.* impediment, obstacle, hindrance.

**remordimiento** *m.* remorse.

**remoto** *adj.* remote, distant; improbable.

**remover**[2] *v. irr.* to remove; to dismiss; to stir.

**rempujar** *v.* to jostle, push.

**rempujón** *m.* jostle, push.

**remuda** *f.* change; substitution; replacement; change of clothes; spare tire; relay of horses; *Am.* spare horse, spare pack animal.

**remudar** *v.* to change; to replace.

**remuneración** *f.* remuneration, compensation, pay, reward.

**remunerar** *v.* to remunerate, compensate, pay, reward (*for services*).

**renacer**[13] *v. irr.* to be reborn; to spring up, grow up again.

**renacimiento** *m.* renascence, renaissance; revival; rebirth.

**renco** *adj.* lame.

**rencor** *m.* rancor, resentment, hatred, grudge.

**rencoroso** *adj.* resentful, spiteful.

**rendición** *f.* surrender; submission; yield, profit.

**rendido** *p.p.* & *adj.* tired out, fatigued; devoted; obsequious, servile.

**rendija** *f.* crack, crevice.

**rendimiento** *m.* yield, output, profit; surrender, submission; fatigue.

**rendir**[5] *v. irr.* to subdue; to surrender, hand over; to yield, produce; to fatigue; to render, do (*homage*); *Cuba*, *Ven.* **— la jornada** to end or suspend the day's work; **-se** to surrender, give up; to become fatigued, worn out.

**renegado** *m.* renegade, traitor; *adj.* renegade, disloyal; wicked.

**renegar**[1, 7] *v. irr.* to deny insistently; to detest; to blaspheme, curse; **— de** to deny, renounce (*one's faith*); *Am.* to hate, protest against.

**renglón** *m.* line (*written or printed*); item; *Ríopl.*, *Col.*, *Ven.*, *Mex.*, *Carib.*, *Andes* line of business, specialty.

**renombrado** *adj.* renowned, famous.

**renombre** *m.* renown, fame.

**renovación** *f.* renovation, restoration; renewal.

**renovar**[2] *v. irr.* to renovate; to renew; to replace.

**renquear** *v.* to limp.

**renta** *f.* rent, rental; income; revenue.

**renuencia** *f.* reluctance, unwillingness.

**renuente** *adj.* reluctant, unwilling.

**renuevo** *m.* (*vástago*) sprout, shoot; (*acto*) renovation, restoration.

**renunciar** *v.* to renounce; to resign; to refuse; to renege (*fail to follow suit in cards*).

**reñidor** *adj.* quarrelsome.

**reñir**[5, 19] *v. irr.* to quarrel; to fight; to scold.

**reo** *adj.* guilty; *m.* culprit, criminal; defendant.

**reojo : mirar de —** to look out of the corner of one's eye; to look scornfully.

**repantigarse**[7] *v.* to lounge, stretch out (*in a chair*).

**reparación** *f.* reparation; repair; indemnity.

**reparar** *v.* (*renovar*) to repair; to regain; to recover; (*corregir*) to make amends for, atone for; to remedy; to ward off (*a blow*); *Am.* to rear, buck (*said of horses*); **— en** to observe, notice.

**reparo** *m.* (*arreglo*) repair; restoration; (*observación*) notice; observation; (*duda*) doubt, objection; (*abrigo*) shelter; parry (*fencing*); *Mex.* sudden bound or leap of a horse.

**repartimiento** *m.* distribution, division; assessment.

**repartir** *v.* to distribute; to allot.

**reparto** *m.* distribution; mail delivery; cast of characters.

**repasar** *v.* to review, look over, go over again; to mend (*clothes*); to pass by

again.

**repaso** *m.* review; revision.

**repelente** *adj.* repellent, repulsive, repugnant.

**repeler** *v.* to repel; to reject.

**repente** *m.* sudden movement; *Am.* attack, fit; **de —** suddenly.

**repentino** *adj.* sudden.

**repercutir** *v.* to resound, echo back; to rebound; to reflect back (*as light*).

**repetición** *f.* repetition.

**repetido** *p.p.* repeated; **repetidas veces** repeatedly, often.

**repetir**[5] *v. irr.* to repeat; to belch.

**repicar**[6] *v.* (*tañer*) to chime, ring; (*hacer menudo*) to mince, chop fine; *Carib.*, *Ven.* to drum, tap (*with the fingers or heels*); **-se** to boast; to be conceited.

**repique** *m.* (*tañido*) chime, ringing, peal; (*acción de picar*) mincing, chopping.

**repiquetear** *v.* to chime, ring; to jingle; *Am.* to tap (*with fingers or heels*).

**repiqueteo** *m.* chiming, ringing; jingling, tinkling; *Ríopl.*, *Carib.*, *Ven.* clicking sound of heels.

**repisa** *f.* shelf, ledge; sill; wall bracket; **— de ventana** window sill.

**replegar**[1, 7] *v. irr.* to fold, pleat; **-se** to retreat, fall back.

**réplica** *f.* reply, answer, retort; replica, copy; *Am. m.* examiner.

**replicar**[6] *v.* to reply, answer back; to retort.

**repliegue** *m.* fold, crease; retreat (*of troops*).

**repollo** *m.* cabbage.

**reponer**[40] *v. irr.* (*devolver*) to replace, put back; to restore; (*contestar*) to reply, retort; **-se** to recover one's health or fortune; to collect oneself, become calm.

**reportaje** *m.* newspaper report; reporting.

**reportar** *v.* to check, control, restrain; to attain, obtain; to bring; to carry; *Am.* to report; **-se** to control oneself.

**reporte** *m.* report, news.

**repórter, reportero** *m.* reporter.

**reposado** *p.p.* & *adj.* reposed; quiet, calm; restful.

**reposar** *v.* to repose; to rest; to lie buried; **-se** to settle (*said of sediment*).

**reposición** *f.* replacement; recovery (*of one's health*).

**reposo** *m.* repose, rest; calm.

**repostada** *f.* sharp answer, back talk.

**reprender** *v.* to reprimand, scold.

**reprensible** *adj.* reprehensible, deserving reproof.

**reprensión** *f.* reproof, rebuke.

**represa** *f.* dam; damming, stopping; *Col.*, *Ven.* reservoir.

**represalia** *f.* reprisal.

**represar** *v.* to bank, dam; to recapture (*a ship*) from the enemy; to repress, check.

**representación** *f.* representation; play, performance; authority, dignity; petition, plea.

**RE**

**representante** *adj.* representing; *m.* & *f.* representative; actor.

**representar** *v.* (*declarar*) to represent; to declare, state; to express, show; (*actuar*) to act, play, perform; **-se** to imagine, picture to oneself.

**representativo** *adj.* representative.

**represión** *f.* repression, control, restraint.

**reprimenda** *f.* reprimand, rebuke.

**reprimir** *v.* to repress, check, curb; **-se** to repress oneself; to refrain.

**reprobar**[2] *v. irr.* to reprove, blame; to condemn; to flunk, fail.

**reprochar** *v.* to reproach.

**reproche** *m.* reproach.

**reproducción** *f.* reproduction.

**reproducir**[25] *v. irr.* to reproduce.

**reptil** *m.* reptile.

**república** *f.* republic.

**republicano** *adj.* & *m.* republican.

**repudiar** *v.* to repudiate; to disown.

**repuesto** *m.* stock, supply, provisions; sideboard; **de —** spare, extra; *p.p.* of **reponer** & *adj.* recovered (*from an illness, loss, fright, etc.*); replaced; restored.

**repugnancia** *f.* repugnance, disgust; aversion; dislike, reluctance.

**repugnante** *adj.* repugnant, disgusting, loathsome.

**repugnar** *v.* to be repugnant; to disgust; to oppose, contradict.

**repulido** *adj.* polished up, slick; shiny; spruce.

**repulsa** *f.* repulse; rebuff; rebuke.

**repulsar** *v.* to repulse, repel, reject.

**repulsivo** *adj.* repulsive, repugnant.

**reputación** *f.* reputation.

**reputar** *v.* to repute.

**requebrar**[1] *v. irr.* to compliment; to flatter; to flirt with; to court, woo; to break again.

**requemado** *p.p.* & *adj.* burned; parched; tanned, sunburned.

**requemar** *v.* to parch, dry up; to burn; to overcook; **-se** to become overheated; to burn inwardly; to get tanned, sunburned.

**requerimiento** *m.* requisition; requirement; summons; **-s** amorous advances, insinuations.

**requerir**[3] *v. irr.* (*exigir*) to require; to need; to summon; (*indagar*) to examine, investigate; (*avisar*) to notify; **— de amores** to court, woo.

**requesón** *m.* cottage cheese.

**requiebro** *m.* flattery; compliment.

**requisito** *m.* requirement, requisite; **— previo** prerequisite.

**res** *f.* head of cattle; any large animal.

**resabio** *m.* disagreeable aftertaste; bad habit.

**resaca** *f.* undertow; surge, surf; redraft (*of a bill of exchange*); *Am.* beating, thrashing; *Mex., Ríopl.* mud and slime (*left by a flood*).

**resaltar** *v.* to stand out; to project, jut out; to rebound, bounce or spring back; to be evident, obvious.

**resarcir**[10] *v.* to indemnify, compensate,

repay; to make amends for; **-se de** to make up for.

**resbaladero** *m.* slide, slippery place.

**resbaladizo** *adj.* slippery.

**resbalar** *v.* to slide; **-se** to slip; to slide; to skid; **resbalársele a uno una cosa** to let a thing slide off one's back, be impervious to a thing.

**resbalón** *m.* sudden or violent slip; slide; error; **darse un —** to slip.

**resbaloso** *adj.* slippery.

**rescatar** *v.* to ransom; to redeem; to barter, exchange, trade; *Am.* to resell.

**rescate** *m.* ransom; redemption; barter, exchange.

**rescoldo** *m.* embers, hot cinders, hot ashes; doubt, scruple.

**resecar**[6] *v.* to dry up; to parch.

**reseco** *adj.* very dry; dried up, parched; thin, skinny.

**resentimiento** *m.* resentment; impairment, damage (*to one's health*).

**resentirse**[3] *v. irr.* (*tener pesar*) to show resentment, hurt, or grief; to resent; (*empeorar*) to weaken; to become worse.

**reseña** *f.* military review; book review; brief account; sign, signal.

**reseñar** *v.* to review (*a book*); to review (*troops*); to outline briefly, give a short account of.

**resero** *m. Ríopl.* cowboy, herdsman; *Am.* dealer in livestock.

**reserva** *f.* reserve; reservation; exception; caution; **a — de** reserving the right to, intending to; **sin —** without reserve, frankly.

**reservación** *f.* reservation.

**reservar** *v.* to reserve; to put aside; to postpone; to exempt; to keep secret; **-se** to conserve one's strength, spare oneself (*for another time*).

**resfriado** *m.* cold (*illness*); *p.p.* of **resfriar**; *adj. Ríopl.* indiscreet.

**resfriar**[17] *v.* to cool; to chill; **-se** to catch cold; to cool.

**resfrío** *m.* chill; cold.

**resguardar** *v.* to guard, defend; to shield; **-se de** to guard oneself against; to seek shelter from.

**resguardo** *m.* defense; security; guarantee; guard.

**residencia** *f.* residence; office or post of a resident foreign minister; *Am.* luxurious dwelling.

**residente** *adj.* resident, residing; *m.* & *f.* resident, dweller; resident foreign minister; *Col., C.A., Ríopl.* alien resident.

**residir** *v.* to reside; to live, dwell; to be inherent, belong (to).

**residuo** *m.* residue; remainder.

**resignación** *f.* resignation.

**resignar** *v.* to resign; to hand over; **-se** to resign oneself.

**resina** *f.* resin.

**resistencia** *f.* resistance.

**resistente** *adj.* resistant; resisting.

**resistir** *v.* to resist; to tolerate, endure; **-se** to resist, struggle.

**resolución** *f.* (*ánimo*) resolution; courage, determination; (*resultado*) solution; **en —** in brief.

**resolver**[2,52] *v. irr.* to resolve, decide; to solve; to dissolve; **-se** to resolve, decide; to be reduced (to), dissolve (into).

**resollar**[2] *v. irr.* to breathe hard; to pant.

**resonar**[2] *v. irr.* to resound.

**resoplar** *v.* to puff, breathe hard; to snort.

**resoplido** *m.* puff, pant; snort.

**resorte** *m.* spring; elasticity; means (*to attain an object*); *Col.* elastic, rubber band; *Ven.* **no es de mi —** it doesn't concern me.

**respaldar** *v.* to endorse; to guarantee; *Am.* to back, support; **-se** to lean back; *Ch.* to protect one's rear.

**respaldo** *m.* back (*of a chair or sheet of paper*); protecting wall; endorsement; *Am.* protection, security, guarantee.

**respectivo** *adj.* respective.

**respecto** *m.* respect, relation, reference; point, matter; (**con**) **— a** (*or* **— de**) with respect to, with regard to.

**respetable** *adj.* respectable.

**respetar** *v.* to respect.

**respeto** *m.* respect; reverence, regard; consideration.

**respetuoso** *adj.* respectful; respectable.

**respingar**[7] *v.* to buck; to balk (*said of a horse*); to grumble; to curl up (*said of the edge of a garment*).

**respingo** *m.* buck, balking; muttering, grumbling.

**respiración** *f.* respiration, breathing.

**respirar** *v.* to breathe.

**respiro** *m.* breathing; breath; respite, pause, moment of rest; extension of time (*for payment*).

**resplandecer**[13] *v. irr.* to shine; to glitter.

**resplandeciente** *adj.* resplendent, shining.

**resplandor** *m.* splendor, brilliance, brightness; *Am.* sun's glare.

**responder** *v.* to respond; to answer; to correspond, harmonize; to answer (for), be responsible (for).

**respondón** *adj.* saucy, pert, insolent (*in answering*).

**responsabilidad** *f.* responsibility.

**responsable** *adj.* responsible.

**respuesta** *f.* response; answer, reply.

**resquebradura, resquebrajadura** *f.* fissure, crevice, crack.

**resquebrajar** = **resquebrar.**

**resquebrar**[1] *v. irr.* to crack; to split.

**resquicio** *m.* crack, slit, crevice; opening; *Col., Ven., Mex.* vestige, sign, trace.

**resta** *f.* subtraction (*as an arithmetical operation*); remainder.

**restablecer**[13] *v. irr.* to re-establish; to restore; **-se** to recover.

**restante** *adj.* remaining; *m.* residue, remainder.

**restañar** *v.* to staunch (*a wound*); to check the flow of.

**restar** *v.* to deduct; to subtract; to remain, be left over; to strike back (*a ball*).

**restauración** *f.* restoration.

**restaurante** *m.* restaurant.

**restaurar** *v.* to restore; to recover; to re-establish; to repair.

**restitución** *f.* restitution, restoration, return.

**restituir**[32] *v. irr.* to return, give back; to restore.

**resto** *m.* rest, remainder; stakes at cards; return (*of a tennis ball*); player who returns the ball; **-s** remains.

**restorán** *m. Am.* restaurant.

**restregar**[1,7] *v. irr.* to rub hard; to scrub.

**restricción** *f.* restriction; restraint; curb; limitation.

**restringir**[11] *v.* to restrict; to restrain; to limit.

**resucitar** *v.* to resuscitate, bring to life; to come to life; to revive.

**resuelto** *p.p. of* **resolver** resolved, determined; *adj.* resolute, bold; quick.

**resuello** *m.* breath; breathing, panting.

**resulta** *f.* result; effect, consequence; **de -s** as a result, in consequence.

**resultado** *m.* result, effect, consequence.

**resultante** *adj.* resulting; *f.* resultant (*force*).

**resultar** *v.* to result; to spring, arise as a consequence; to turn out to be; **resulta que** it turns out that.

**resumen** *m.* résumé, summary; **en —** summing up, in brief.

**resumidero** *m. Am.* = **sumidero.**

**resumir** *v.* to summarize, sum up; **-se** to be reduced or condensed.

**resurgir**[11] *v.* to arise again; to reappear.

**retablo** *m.* altarpiece; religious picture hung as a votive offering; series of pictures that tell a story.

**retaguardia** *f.* rear guard.

**retal** *m.* remnant.

**retar** *v.* to challenge, defy; to reprimand, scold; *Ch., Andes* to insult.

**retardar** *v.* to retard, delay.

**retazo** *m.* remnant; piece; fragment.

**retener**[45] *v. irr.* to retain; to keep; to withhold; to detain.

**retintín** *m.* jingle, tinkle; sarcastic tone or ring.

**retirada** *f.* retreat; withdrawal.

**retirado** *p.p.* & *adj.* retired; distant, remote; isolated; pensioned.

**retirar** *v.* to withdraw; to take away; **-se** to retire, withdraw; to retreat.

**retiro** *m.* retreat; retirement; withdrawal; place of refuge; pension of a retired officer.

**reto** *m.* challenge; defiance; *Ríopl.* scolding; *Andes* insult.

**retobado** *adj. Col., Ríopl.* saucy; *Andes* stubborn, unruly; *Andes* peevish; *Am.* sly, astute.

**retobar** *v. Col., Andes* to cover with leather; *Am.* to wrap with leather, oilcloth, or burlap; *Am.* to tan (*leather*); **-se** *Ríopl.* to rebel, talk back, act saucy; *Andes, Col.* to become disagreeable and aloof.

**retocar**[6] *v.* to retouch, touch up; to

**RE**

finish, perfect.

**retoñar** v. to sprout; to bud; to sprout again; to reappear.

**retoño** m. sprout, shoot; bud.

**retoque** m. retouching; finishing touch.

**retorcer**[2,10] v. irr. to twist; to retort; to distort; **-se** to wriggle; to squirm.

**retorcimiento** m. twisting; squirming.

**retórica** f. rhetoric.

**retornar** v. to return; to give back.

**retorno** m. return; repayment; barter.

**retozar**[9] v. to gambol, frisk about, frolic, romp; to stir within (said of passions).

**retozo** m. frolic; **retozón** adj. frisky, playful.

**retractarse** v. to retract, take back one's word.

**retraer**[46] v. irr. to withdraw, draw back, take back; **-se de** to withdraw from; to keep aloof or away from; to shun.

**retraimiento** m. retirement; reserve, aloofness, shyness.

**retranca** f. Cuba brake; **retranquero** m. Am. brakeman.

**retrancar**[6] v. Cuba to brake, put the brake on; Cuba **se ha retrancado el asunto** the affair has come to a standstill.

**retrasado** p.p. & adj. behind, behind time; backward; postponed, delayed.

**retrasar** v. to delay, retard; to set back; to go backward; **-se** to fall behind; to be late, behind time.

**retraso** m. delay.

**retratar** v. to portray; to photograph; to copy, imitate; **-se** to be portrayed; to be photographed; to be reflected.

**retrato** m. portrait; photograph; copy, imitation; reflection.

**retrete** m. toilet, water closet; place of retreat.

**retroceder** v. to turn back; to fall back, draw back; to recede.

**retroceso** m. retrogression, backward step; retreat; setback, relapse.

**retruécano** m. pun.

**retumbar** v. to resound; to rumble.

**retumbo** m. loud echo or sound; rumble (of thunder, cannon, etc.).

**reuma** m. & f., **reumatismo** m. rheumatism.

**reunión** f. reunion; meeting.

**reunir** v. to reunite; to unite; to group; to gather; to assemble; to collect; **-se** to meet, assemble; to reunite.

**revancha** f. revenge; return game or match.

**revelación** f. revelation.

**revelador** adj. revealing; m. developer (in photography).

**revelar** v. to reveal; to develop (a film).

**revendedor** m. retailer; reseller; ticket scalper.

**reventa** f. resale.

**reventar**[1] v. irr. (estallar) to burst; to burst forth; to explode; to smash; (fatigar) to fatigue, exhaust; to bother; **-se** to burst; to blow out, explode.

**reventón** m. burst, bursting; blowout; steep hill; hard work, toil; adj. burst-

ing.

**reverdecer**[13] v. irr. to grow fresh and green again; to gain new strength and vigor.

**reverencia** f. reverence; bow.

**reverenciar** v. to revere, venerate.

**reverendo** adj. reverend; Cuba, Ríopl., Mex., Andes large, big (ironically).

**reverente** adj. reverent.

**reverso** m. reverse; back side.

**revertir**[3] v. irr. to revert.

**revés** m. reverse; back, wrong side; back stroke or slap; backhanded thrust (in fencing); misfortune; **al —** backwards; wrong side out; in the opposite way; from left to right.

**revestir**[5] v. irr. to dress, clothe; to coat, cover with a coating; **-se** to dress, put on an outer garment or vestment; to be invested (with power, authority, etc.); **-se de paciencia** to arm oneself with patience.

**revisar** v. to revise; to review; to examine, inspect.

**revisión** m. revision; review (of a case), new trial.

**revisor** m. corrector; inspector, overseer.

**revista** f. (inspección) review; inspection; (publicación) magazine, journal; (proceso) second trial or hearing; **pasar —** to pass in review; to examine carefully; to review (troops).

**revistar** v. to review, inspect (troops).

**revivir** v. to revive.

**revocación** f. repeal, cancellation.

**revocar**[6] v. to revoke, repeal.

**revolcar**[6] v. (derribar) to knock down; to turn over and over; to floor, defeat; (suspender) to fail, flunk; **-se** to wallow; to roll over and over; to flounder.

**revolotear** v. to fly about, flutter around; to hover; to circle around.

**revoltijo, revoltillo** m. jumble, mixture, mess; tangle, muddle; **revoltillo de huevos** scrambled eggs.

**revoltoso** adj. turbulent, unruly, rebellious; mischievous; intricate; m. agitator, troublemaker; rebel.

**revolución** f. revolution.

**revolucionario** adj. revolutionary; m. revolutionist, revolutionary.

**revolver**[2] v. irr. to revolve; to turn over; to stir up; to mix up; to turn around swiftly (a horse); **-se** to move back and forth; to roll over and over; to change (said of the weather).

**revólver** m. revolver, pistol.

**revuelo** m. whirl; stir, commotion; flying around.

**revuelta** f. revolt, revolution; second turn; turn, bend; quarrel, fight; Am. sudden turning of a horse.

**revuelto** p.p. of **revolver** & adj. confused; mixed up; intricate, complicated; choppy (sea); changeable (weather); **huevos -s** scrambled eggs.

**rey** m. king.

**reyerta** f. quarrel, dispute.

**rezagado** adj. back, behind; m. straggler, slowpoke, latecomer.

**rezagar**[7] *v.* to leave behind; to separate (*the weak cattle*) from the herd; *Am.* to reserve, set aside; **-se** to lag behind.

**rezar**[9] *v.* to pray; to say or recite (*a prayer*); to mutter, grumble; **así lo reza el libro** so the book says; **eso no reza conmigo** that has nothing to do with me.

**rezo** *m.* prayer.

**rezongar**[7] *v.* to grumble, growl, mutter.

**rezongón** *adj.* growling, grumbling; *m.* grumbler, growler; scolder.

**rezumar** *v.* to ooze; to leak; **se rezuma** it oozes, it seeps through.

**ría** *f.* mouth of a river, estuary.

**riachuelo** *m.* rivulet, brook.

**ribazo** *m.* bank, ridge.

**ribera** *f.* shore, bank, beach.

**ribereño** *adj.* of, pertaining to, or living on, a river bank.

**ribete** *m.* trimming, border, edge, binding; addition; **tiene sus -s de poeta** he is something of a poet.

**ribetear** *v.* to bind, put a binding on; to border, trim the edge or border of.

**ricacho** *adj.* quite rich (*often said sarcastically*); **ricachón** *adj.* extremely rich, disgustingly rich.

**rico** *adj.* rich, wealthy; delicious; exquisite; **ricote = ricacho.**

**ridiculizar**[9] *v.* to ridicule, deride.

**ridículo** *adj.* ridiculous; queer, strange; *m.* ridicule; ridiculous situation; **hacer el —** to be ridiculous; to act the fool.

**riego** *m.* irrigation; watering.

**riel** *m.* rail; **-es** track, railroad track.

**rienda** *f.* rein, bridle; moderation, restraint; **a — suelta** with free rein, without restraint; violently, swiftly; **soltar la —** to let loose, act without restraint; **tirar las -s** to draw rein, tighten the reins; to restrain.

**riente** *adj.* laughing, smiling.

**riesgo** *m.* risk.

**rifa** *f.* raffle; scuffle, quarrel.

**rifar** *v.* to raffle; to scuffle, quarrel.

**rifle** *m.* rifle.

**rigidez** *f.* rigidity, stiffness; severity, strictness.

**rígido** *adj.* rigid, stiff; severe, strict.

**rigor** *m.* rigor; severity; harshness; rigidity, stiffness; **en —** in reality; strictly; **ser de —** to be absolutely indispensable, be required by custom.

**rigoroso, riguroso** *adj.* rigorous; harsh; severe; strict.

**rima** *f.* rhyme; **-s** poems.

**rimar** *v.* to rhyme.

**rimbombante** *adj.* high-sounding; resounding.

**rimero** *m.* pile, heap.

**rincón** *m.* corner; nook; *Am.* narrow valley.

**rinconada** *f.* corner; nook.

**rinconera** *f.* corner cupboard, corner table, corner bracket.

**ringlera** *f.* tier, row, line.

**rinoceronte** *m.* rhinoceros.

**riña** *f.* quarrel, dispute, fight.

**riñón** *m.* kidney; center, interior.

**río** *m.* river.

**ripio** *m.* rubble, stone or brick fragments; padding (*in a verse, speech, etc.*), useless word.

**riqueza** *f.* riches; wealth.

**risa** *f.* laugh; laughter; **reventar de —** to burst with laughter; **tomar a —** to take lightly; to laugh off.

**risada** *f.* gale of laughter, loud laugh.

**risco** *m.* rocky cliff, crag; honey fritter.

**risible** *adj.* laughable, ridiculous.

**risotada** *f.* guffaw, big laugh.

**ristra** *f.* string (*of onions, garlic, etc.*); series, row.

**risueño** *adj.* smiling; pleasant; delightful.

**rítmico** *adj.* rhythmical.

**ritmo** *m.* rhythm.

**rito** *m.* rite, ceremony.

**rival** *m.* & *f.* rival, competitor; enemy.

**rivalidad** *f.* rivalry, competition; enmity.

**rivalizar**[9] *v.* to rival, compete.

**rizado** *p.p.* curled; *adj.* wavy, curly; *m.* curling; curls.

**rizar**[9] *v.* to curl; to ripple; to ruffle, gather into ruffles; **-se** to curl one's hair; to curl.

**rizo** *m.* curl; *adj.* curly; **rizoso** *adj.* curly.

**roano** *adj.* roan (*red, bay, or chestnut-colored, mixed with white; applied to a horse*).

**robar** *v.* to rob, steal; to abduct, kidnap.

**roble** *m.* oak tree; oak wood; **robledal, robledo** *m.* oak grove.

**robo** *m.* robbery, theft; loot, plunder.

**robusto** *adj.* robust, vigorous.

**roca** *f.* rock, boulder; rocky cliff, crag.

**rocalloso** *adj.* rocky.

**roce** *m.* graze; friction; contact; **no tener — con** to have no contact with (*a person*).

**rociada** *f.* sprinkling; spray; dew; sprinkle, shower; volley of harsh words.

**rociar**[17] *v.* to sprinkle; to spray; to fall (*said of dew*).

**rocín** *m.* nag, hack; draft horse; coarse, ill-bred man; *Ríopl., Mex., Andes* riding horse.

**rocío** *m.* dew; sprinkle; shower; spray; *adj. Am.* reddish, roan (*horse*).

**rocoso** *adj.* rocky.

**rodada** *f.* rut, wheel track; *Ríopl.* tumble, fall.

**rodado** *adj.* dapple (*horse*); *p.p.* of **rodar.**

**rodadura** *f.* rolling; rut; **— del neumático** tire tread.

**rodaja** *f.* disk; small wheel; round slice.

**rodaje** *m.* works (*of a watch*); **— de película** the filming of a movie.

**rodar**[2] *v. irr.* to roll; to revolve; to roam, wander about; to fall down (*rolling*); *Am.* **— a patadas** to kick down.

**rodear** *v.* to go around; to go by a roundabout way; to surround, encircle; *Ríopl., Cuba, Ven.* to round up (*cattle*).

**RE**

**rodela** *f.* round shield; *Mex.* padded ring for carrying loads on the head; *Am.* round slice; *Am.* kettle lid; *Am.* hoop; *Am.* game of rolling a hoop.

**rodeo** *m.* detour, roundabout way; circumlocution, roundabout expression; dodge, evasion; corral, stockyard; rodeo, roundup.

**rodilla** *f.* knee; **de -s** on one's knees; **hincarse de -s** to kneel down.

**rodillo** *m.* roller; rolling pin; road roller.

**roer**[51] *v. irr.* to gnaw; to corrode, eat away; to torment, harass.

**rogar**[2,7] *v. irr.* to pray, beg, beseech; **hacerse de —** to let oneself be coaxed.

**rojez** *f.* redness.

**rojizo** *adj.* reddish.

**rojo** *adj.* red; red, radical.

**rojura** *f.* redness.

**rollizo** *adj.* plump; *m.* log.

**rollo** *m.* roll; bundle; rolling pin; log.

**romadizo** *m.* nasal catarrh, head cold.

**romance** *adj.* Romance, Romanic (*language*); *m.* Romance language; Spanish language; romance, chivalric novel; ballad; eight-syllable meter with even verses rhyming in assonance; **en buen —** in plain language.

**románico** *adj.* Romanesque (*architecture*); Romance (*language*).

**romano** *adj.* & *m.* Roman.

**romanticismo** *m.* romanticism.

**romántico** *adj.* romantic; sentimental; *m.* romantic; sentimentalist.

**romería** *f.* pilgrimage.

**romero** *m.* pilgrim; rosemary (*shrub*).

**romo** *adj.* blunt; snub-nosed.

**rompe: de — y rasga** resolute, bold; **al — ** *Am.* suddenly.

**rompecabezas** *m.* puzzle, riddle.

**rompeolas** *m.* breakwater, mole.

**romper**[52] *v.* to break; to shatter; to tear; to wear through; *Ven.* to leave suddenly or on the run; **— el alba** to dawn; **— a** to start to; **-se** to break.

**rompiente** *m.* shoal, sand bank, reef; **-s** breakers, surf.

**rompimiento** *m.* rupture, break; crack; breach; quarrel.

**ron** *m.* rum.

**roncar**[6] *v.* to snore; to roar; to brag.

**ronco** *adj.* hoarse; harsh-sounding.

**roncha** *f.* hive; welt.

**ronda** *f.* patrol; night serenaders; round (*of a game, of drinks, etc.*); *Ríopl., C.A., Andes* ring-around-a-rosy (*a children's game*); **hacer la — a** to court; *Am.* to surround, trap (*an animal*).

**rondar** *v.* to go around, hover around; to patrol; to make the rounds; to serenade.

**ronquera** *f.* hoarseness.

**ronquido** *m.* snore; snort.

**ronronear** *v.* to purr.

**ronroneo** *m.* purr.

**ronzal** *m.* halter.

**roña** *f.* scab, mange; filth; infection; stinginess; trickery; *Ríopl., Col., Ven.,*

*Cuba* ill will, grudge; *Am.* **hacer —** to fake an illness.

**roñoso** *adj.* scabby, mangy; dirty; stingy; *Carib., Mex.* spiteful; *Am.* fainthearted, cowardly.

**ropa** *f.* clothing, clothes; **— blanca** linen; **— vieja** old clothes; stew made from leftover meat; **a quema —** at close range (*when shooting*); suddenly, without warning.

**ropaje** *m.* clothes, clothing, apparel; robe.

**ropero** *m.* clothier; wardrobe, clothespress; wardrobe keeper; *Am.* clothes rack.

**roqueño** *adj.* rocky; hard, like rock.

**rosa** *f.* rose; red spot on the skin; rose color; *Ch., Mex.* rosebush; **— de los vientos** (*or* **— náutica**) mariner's compass.

**rosado** *adj.* rosy, rose-colored; frosted (*drink*); *Am.* roan, reddish-brown (*horse*).

**rosal** *m.* rosebush.

**rosario** *m.* rosary; **— de desdichas** chain of misfortunes.

**rosbif** *m.* roast beef.

**rosca** *f.* screw and nut; screw thread; spiral, twist; ring-shaped roll; *Mex., Ven., Col.* ring-shaped cushion (*for carrying loads on the head*); *Am.* circle of card players.

**roseta** *f.* rosette; small rose; **-s** popcorn; **rosetón** *m.* large rosette; rose window.

**rosillo** *adj.* light red; roan (*horse*).

**rostro** *m.* face; **hacer —** to face.

**rota** *f.* rout, defeat; ship's course; Rota (*ecclesiastical court*); rattan palm tree.

**rotación** *f.* rotation.

**rotario** *m.* member of the Rotary Club.

**rotativo** *adj.* rotary; *f.* printing press.

**rotatorio** *adj.* rotary.

**roto** *p.p. irr. of* **romper** & *adj.* broken; shattered; torn; worn out, ragged; *m. Ch.* person of the poorer class.

**rotular** *v.* to label; to letter.

**rótulo** *m.* title, inscription; label.

**rotundo** *adj.* round; sonorous; **una negativa rotunda** a flat denial.

**rotura** *f.* breach, opening; break; tear, rip; rupture; fracture.

**roturar** *v.* to break ground; to plow (*new ground*).

**rozadura** *f.* friction; chafe; chafing.

**rozamiento** *m.* friction; rubbing.

**rozar**[9] *v.* to graze; to scrape; to chafe; to clear of underbrush; **-se con alguien** to have connections, contact, or dealings with someone.

**rozón** *m.* graze, sudden or violent scrape; short, broad scythe.

**ruana** *f. Col., Ven.* a woolen poncho.

**ruano = roano.**

**rubí** *m.* ruby.

**rubicundo** *adj.* reddish; ruddy, healthy red; reddish-blond.

**rubio** *adj.* blond, blonde.

**rubor** *m.* blush; bashfulness, shyness.

**ruborizarse**[9] *v.* to blush; to feel ashamed.

**rúbrica** *f.* scroll, flourish (*added to a signature*); title, heading; **de —** according to ritual, rule, or custom.

**rucio** *adj.* grey (*horse or donkey*); **— rodado** dapple-grey.

**rudeza** *f.* rudeness; coarseness; roughness.

**rudo** *adj.* rude; coarse; rough; stupid.

**rueca** *f.* distaff (*used for spinning*).

**rueda** *f.* (*maquina*) wheel; circle; spread of a peacock's tail; round object; (*grupo*) circle; group; **en —** in turn; in a circle; **hacer la — a** to court; to flatter.

**ruedo** *m.* circuit, tour; border, rim; circumference.

**ruego** *m.* prayer, supplication, request.

**rufián** *m.* ruffian; bully.

**rugido** *m.* roar; rumbling.

**rugir**[11] *v.* to roar; to bellow.

**rugoso** *adj.* wrinkled; furrowed.

**ruibarbo** *m.* rhubarb.

**ruidazo** *m.* big noise.

**ruido** *m.* noise; din; dispute; talk, rumor; **hacer** (*or* **meter**) **—** to make a noise; to create a sensation; to cause a disturbance.

**ruidoso** *adj.* noisy; loud; sensational.

**ruin** *adj.* (*vicioso*) vile, base, mean; vicious (*animal*); (*mezquino*) small; petty; puny; stingy.

**ruina** *f.* ruin; destruction; downfall.

**ruindad** *f.* baseness; meanness; stinginess; mean or vile act.

**ruinoso** *adj.* ruinous; in a state of ruin or decay.

**ruiseñor** *m.* nightingale.

**rumba** *f.* Ven., Col., Carib., Mex., Ríopl. rumba (*dance and music*); Carib., Ven., Andes spree; Carib., Ven., Andes **irse de —** to go on a spree.

**rumbear** *v.* Ríopl., Andes to head (towards), take a certain direction; Am. to cut a path through a forest; Am. to go on a spree.

**rumbo** *m.* (*ruta*) direction, course; route; (*pompa*) pomp; ostentation; Am. cut on the head; Am. revel, noisy spree; **hacer — a** to head or sail towards; Am. **ir al —** to be going in the right drection, be on the right track.

**rumboso** *adj.* pompous, ostentatious; generous.

**rumiar** *v.* to ruminate; to chew the cud; to ponder, meditate.

**rumor** *m.* rumor, report; murmur; rumble.

**runfla** *f.* series (*of things of the same kind*); sequence (*in cards*).

**runrún** *m.* rumor; murmur.

**ruptura** *f.* rupture; break; fracture.

**rural** *adj.* rural.

**ruso** *adj.* Russian; *m.* Russian; Russian language.

**rústico** *adj.* rustic, rural; crude, coarse; *m.* peasant; **en** (*or* **a la**) **rústica** unbound, paper-bound.

**ruta** *f.* route, course, way.

**rutina** *f.* routine.

**S**

**sábado** *m.* Saturday.

**sábana** *f.* bed sheet; altar cloth.

**sabana** *f. Col.* savanna, treeless plain; Col. **ponerse en la —** to become suddenly rich.

**sabandija** *f.* small reptile; small lizard.

**sabañón** *m.* chilblain.

**sabedor** *adj.* knowing; aware, informed.

**saber**[42] *v. irr.* to know; to know how to, be able to; to learn, find out; Ríopl., Ven., Col. to be in the habit of; **— a** to taste of, taste like; **sabe bien** it tastes good; **a —** namely; that is; Am. **¡a — si venga!** who knows whether he will come!; **un no sé qué** an indefinable something; **¿sabe Vd. a la plaza?** do you know the way to the square?; *m.* knowledge, learning.

**sabiduría** *f.* wisdom; knowledge.

**sabiendas : a —** consciously, knowingly.

**sabio** *adj.* wise; judicious; learned; *m.* savant, scholar; sage, wise man.

**sable** *m.* saber; **sablazo** *m.* blow with a saber; saber wound; **dar un sablazo** to strike for a loan.

**sabor** *m.* savor, taste, flavor.

**saborear** *v.* to savor, flavor, season; to relish, taste with pleasure; to enjoy; **-se** to eat or drink with relish; to smack one's lips.

**sabotaje** *m.* sabotage.

**sabotear** *v.* to sabotage.

**sabroso** *adj.* savory, tasty; delicious; delightful.

**sabueso** *m.* hound.

**sacabocados** *m.* punch (*tool*).

**sacacorchos** *m.* corkscrew.

**sacamuelas** *m. & f.* tooth puller; quack dentist.

**sacar**[6] *v.* to draw, draw out, pull out, get out, or take out; to get, obtain; to infer; to make (*a copy*); to take (*a snapshot or picture*); to stick out (*one's tongue*); to serve (*a ball*); **— a bailar** to ask to dance, lead on to the dance floor; **— a luz** to publish; **— el cuerpo** to dodge; **— en claro** (*or* **en limpio**) to deduce, conclude; Am. **— el sombrero** to take off one's hat; Am. **¡sáquese de allí!** get out of there!

**sacarina** *f.* saccharine.

**sacerdocio** *m.* priesthood.

**sacerdote** *m.* priest.

**saciar** *v.* to satiate, satisfy; **-se** to be satiated, satisfied completely.

**saco** *m.* sack, bag; sackful, bagful; loose-fitting coat; sack, plundering; Am. suit coat; **— de noche** overnight bag, satchel.

**sacramento** *m.* sacrament.

**sacrificar**[6] *v.* to sacrifice.

**sacrificio** *m.* sacrifice.

**sacrilegio** *m.* sacrilege.

**sacrílego** *adj.* sacrilegious.

**sacristán** *m.* sacristan, sexton; Am. busybody, meddler.

**sacro** *adj.* sacred.

RO

**sacrosanto** *adj.* sacrosanct, holy and sacred.

**sacudida** *f.* shake, jolt, jerk.

**sacudimiento** *m.* shaking; shake, jerk; shock, jolt.

**sacudir** *v.* to shake; to jerk; to beat; to beat the dust from; to shake off; **-se** to shake oneself; to brush oneself off; **-se de alguien** to shake someone off, get rid of someone.

**sádico** *adj.* sadistic, cruel.

**saeta** *f.* arrow, dart.

**sagacidad** *f.* sagacity.

**sagaz** *adj.* sagacious, shrewd.

**sagrado** *adj.* sacred; consecrated; *m.* asylum, refuge.

**sahumar** *v.* to perfume with incense; to fumigate.

**sahumerio** *m.* vapor, fume; incense; burning of incense; fumigation.

**sainete** *m.* one-act comedy or farce; delicacy, tasty tidbit; flavor, relish; sauce.

**sajón** *adj.* & *m.* Saxon.

**sal** *f.* salt; wit, humor; grace; *Mex., Cuba, C.A., Col., Andes* misfortune, bad luck.

**sala** *f.* parlor; hall, large room; **— de justicia** courtroom.

**salado** *adj.* salty; salted; witty; charming; *Am.* costly; *Mex., Cuba, C.A., Col., Andes* **estar —** to be unlucky; *m. Am.* salt pit, salt mine.

**salar** *v.* to salt; to cure or preserve with salt; *Mex., Cuba, C.A., Col., Andes* to bring bad luck (to); *Am.* to dishonor; *Am.* to ruin, spoil; *Am.* to bribe; *Am.* to feed salt to cattle; *m. Am.* salt pit.

**salario** *m.* salary, wages.

**salchicha** *f.* sausage; **salchichón** *m.* large sausage.

**saldar** *v.* to balance, settle (*an account*).

**saldo** *m.* balance, settlement (*of an account*); bargain sale.

**saledizo** = **salidizo**.

**salero** *m.* (*vaso*) saltcellar, saltshaker; place for storing salts; salt lick; (*gracia*) wit, grace, charm; *Am.* salt dealer.

**salida** *f.* departure; exit; sally; outlet; way out; loophole; outskirts; outcome; jut, projection; outlay, expenditure; witty remark; **— de pie de banco** silly remark, nonsense; **— del sol** sunrise; *Cuba* **— de teatro** evening wrap.

**salidizo** *m.* jut, ledge, projection; *adj.* salient, jutting, projecting.

**saliente** *adj.* salient, standing out; projecting; *m.* salient, salient angle; jut, projection.

**salina** *f.* salt mine or pit; salt works.

**salir**[43] *v. irr.* (*partir*) to go out; to leave, depart; to get out (*of*); to come out; to sprout; to come (*from*); (*resultar*) to turn out to be; **— bien** to turn out well; to come out well; **— a su padre** to turn out to be or look like his father; *Am.* **— a mano** to come out even; **-se** to get out, slip out; to leak

out; **-se con la suya** to get one's own way.

**salitral** *m.* saltpeter bed or mine.

**salitre** *m.* saltpeter; **salitrera** *f.* saltpeter mine or bed; **salitroso** *adj.* nitrous, abounding in saltpeter.

**saliva** *f.* saliva.

**salmo** *m.* psalm.

**salmodiar** *v.* to chant; to talk in a monotone or singsong.

**salmón** *m.* salmon.

**salmuera** *f.* brine.

**salobre** *adj.* briny, salty.

**salón** *m.* salon, hall, large room; salted meat or fish.

**salpicadura** *f.* spatter, splash.

**salpicar**[6] *v.* to sprinkle, spray, spatter.

**salpicón** *m.* hash; hodgepodge; *Ec.* fruit drink.

**salpimentar**[1] *v. irr.* to salt and pepper.

**salpimienta** *f.* salt and pepper.

**salpullido** *m.* rash, skin eruption.

**salsa** *f.* sauce; gravy; *Am.* sound whipping or beating; **salsera** *f.* sauce dish

**saltamontes** *m.* grasshopper.

**saltar** *v.* (*brincar*) to jump; to jump over; to leap; to bounce; to skip; (*estallar*) to burst, break into pieces; to come off; **— a la vista** to be obvious, evident; **— a tierra** to disembark, land; *Mex.* **— las trancas** to lose one's patience; to lose one's head.

**salteador** *m.* bandit, highway robber.

**saltear** *v.* to assault, attack; to hold up, rob; to take by surprise; to jump or skip around.

**salto** *m.* jump; leap; precipice; gap; **— de agua** waterfall; **a -s** by jumps; **en un** (*or* **de un**) **—** in a jiffy; quickly; **dar un —** to jump, leap.

**saltón** *adj.* jumping, skipping, hopping; jumpy; protruding; *Col.* half-cooked; **ojos -es** popeyes, bulging eyes; *m.* grasshopper.

**salubre** *adj.* healthy, healthful.

**salubridad** *f.* healthfulness, health; sanitation.

**salud** *f.* health; welfare; salvation; **¡—!** greetings!; your health!

**saludable** *adj.* wholesome, healthful beneficial.

**saludador** *m.* greeter; healer, quack.

**saludar** *v.* to salute, greet; to fire a salute.

**saludo** *m.* salute, nod, greeting.

**salutación** *f.* salutation; greeting.

**salva** *f.* salvo, salute with guns; greeting, welcome.

**salvación** *f.* salvation.

**salvado** *m.* bran.

**salvador** *m.* savior, rescuer; Savior; *adj.* saving.

**salvaguardar** *v.* to safeguard, defend, protect.

**salvaguardia** *m.* safeguard, protection; guard; *f.* safe-conduct paper, passport; password.

**salvajada** *f.* savage act or remark.

**salvaje** *adj.* savage, wild; *m.* savage.

**salvajez** *f.* wildness, savagery.

**salvajismo** *m.* savagery; *Am.* savage act or remark. *See* **salvajada.**

**salvamento** *m.* salvation, rescue; place of safety; salvage (*rescue of property*); **bote de —** lifeboat.

**salvar** *v.* (*librar*) to save; to except; to exclude; (*vencer*) to clear, jump over; **-se** to be saved; to save oneself, escape.

**salvavidas** *m.* life preserver; **lancha —** lifeboat.

**¡salve!** *interj.* hail!; **Salve** *f.* Salve Regina, prayer to the Virgin Mary.

**salvia** *f.* sage (*a plant*).

**salvo** *adj.* saved; safe; *prep.* save, except but; **a —** safe, without injury; **en —** in safety; out of danger.

**salvoconducto** *m.* safe-conduct, pass.

**san** *adj.* (*contr. of* **santo**) saint.

**sánalotodo** *m.* cure-all.

**sanar** *v.* to heal, cure; to recover, get well.

**sanatorio** *m.* sanitarium.

**sanción** *f.* sanction.

**sancionar** *v.* to sanction; to authorize, ratify.

**sandalia** *f.* sandal.

**sandez** *f.* stupidity; folly; foolish remark.

**sandía** *f.* watermelon.

**sandio** *adj.* silly, foolish.

**saneamiento** *m.* sanitation; drainage of land.

**sanear** *v.* to make sanitary (*land, property, etc.*); to drain, dry up (*land*).

**sangrar** *v.* to bleed; to drain; to tap (*a tree*); to pilfer; to exploit (*someone*); to indent (*a line*).

**sangre** *f.* blood; **— fría** calmness, coolness of mind; **a — fría** in cold blood.

**sangría** *f.* a refreshing Spanish drink made of red wine, fruit juice, and sugar.

**sangriento** *adj.* bleeding; bloody; bloodstained; bloodthirsty, cruel.

**sanguijuela** *f.* leech.

**sanguinario** *adj.* bloody, cruel; bloodthirsty, murderous.

**sanidad** *f.* health; soundness; healthfulness; sanitation; **— publica** health department.

**sanitario** *adj.* sanitary.

**sano** *adj.* (*de salud*) sound, healthy; healthful; sane, sensible; (*integro*) whole; unbroken; undamaged; **— y salvo** safe and sound.

**sanseacabó** that's all; that's the end.

**santiamén : en un —** in a jiffy.

**santidad** *f.* sanctity, holiness, saintliness; **su Santidad** his Holiness.

**santificar**[6] *v.* to sanctify; to consecrate.

**santiguar**[8] *v.* to bless; to make the sign of the cross; to beat, hit, punish; **-se** to cross oneself; to show astonishment (*by crossing oneself*).

**santísimo** *adj.* most holy; *m.* the Holy Sacrament.

**santo** *adj.* saintly, holy; sacred; **esperar todo el — día** to wait the whole blessed day; **— y bueno** well and good; *Ríopl., Col., Ven., Mex., Carib.,*

*Andes* **¡santa palabra!** that's my final and last word! *m.* saint; saint's day; *Mex., Ven.* **tener el — de espaldas** to have a streak of bad luck; **santurrón** *m.* religious hypocrite, affectedly pious person.

**santuario** *m.* sanctuary; *Col.* buried treasure; *Am.* Indian idol.

**saña** *f.* fury, rage.

**sañudo** *adj.* furious, enraged.

**sapo** *m.* toad; *Col.* despicable little man; *Col.* chubby person; *Am.* sly person; **echar -s y culebras** to swear, curse.

**saque** *m.* serve, service (*in tennis*); server.

**saquear** *v.* to sack, plunder, pillage, loot.

**saqueo** *m.* sacking, pillaging, plunder; loot, booty.

**saquillo** *m.* small bag, handbag, satchel.

**sarampión** *m.* measles.

**sarao** *m.* soirée, evening party.

**sarape** *m. Mex.* serape, blanket.

**sarcasmo** *m.* sarcasm.

**sarcástico** *adj.* sarcastic.

**sardina** *f.* sardine.

**sargento** *m.* sergeant.

**sarmentoso** *adj.* vinelike; full of vine shoots; gnarled, knotty.

**sarmiento** *m.* shoot or branch of a vine.

**sarna** *f.* itch; mange.

**sarnoso** *adj.* itchy, scabby, mangy.

**sarpullido = salpullido.**

**sarro** *m.* tartar (*on teeth*); crust, sediment (*in utensils*).

**sarta** *f.* string (*of beads*); series.

**sartén** *f.* frying pan.

**sastre** *m.* tailor.

**satánico** *adj.* satanic, devilish.

**satélite** *m.* satellite; suburban development; **— artificial** artificial satellite.

**satén** *m.* sateen.

**sátira** *f.* satire.

**satírico** *adj.* satirical.

**satirizar**[9] *v.* to satirize.

**satisfacción** *f.* satisfaction; apology; excuse; **tomar —** to vindicate oneself; to take revenge; **dar una —** to offer an apology; to apologize.

**satisfacer**[31] *v. irr.* to satisfy; to pay (*a debt*); **— una letra** to honor a draft; **-se** to be satisfied; to take satisfaction.

**satisfactorio** *adj.* satisfactory.

**satisfecho** *p.p. of* **satisfacer** satisfied, gratified; *adj.* content, contented.

**saturar** *v.* to saturate; to satiate.

**sauce** *m.* willow.

**savia** *f.* sap.

**saxófono** *m.* saxophone; also **saxofón.**

**sazón** *f.* (*época*) season, opportune time; (*sabor*) taste, flavor; ripeness; **a la —** then, at that time; **en —** in season; ripe; opportunely; *adj. Ríopl., Mex., Cuba* ripe.

**sazonado** *adj. & p.p.* seasoned; mellow, ripe; expressive (*said of a phrase*).

**sazonar** *v.* to season; to flavor; **-se** to become seasoned; to ripen, mature.

**se** *obj. pron.* (*before* **le, la, lo, las,** *and* **los**) to him, to her; to you (*formal*); to them; *refl. pron.* himself, herself,

**SA**

yourself (*formal*), yourselves (*formal*) themselves; *reciprocal pron.* each other, one another.

**sebo** *m.* tallow, fat.

**secador** *m. Am.* dryer (*clothes, hair*).

**secante** *adj.* drying, blotting; **papel —** blotter; *f.* secant (*math.*).

**secar**[6] *v.* to dry; to wipe dry; **-se** to dry or wipe oneself; to dry up; to wither; to get thin.

**sección** *f.* section; division; cutting.

**seccionar** *v.* to section.

**seco** *adj.* (*sin humedad*) dry; dried; withered; (*áspero*) harsh; abrupt; plain, unadorned; **en —** on dry land, out of the water; **parar en —** to stop short, stop suddenly; **a secas** plain; alone, without anything else; *Mex., Carib., Ríopl., Andes* simply, straight to the point; **comer pan a secas** to eat just bread; *Mex., Ven.* **bailar a secas** to dance without musical accompaniment.

**secreción** *f.* secretion.

**secretar** *v.* to secrete.

**secretaría** *f.* secretary's office; position of secretary.

**secretario** *m.* secretary; confidant; **secretaria** *f.* woman secretary; secretary's wife.

**secretear** *v.* to whisper; **-se** to whisper to each other.

**secreto** *adj.* secret, hidden; secretive; *m.* secret; secrecy; secret place; **— a voces** open secret; **en —** secretly; **hablar en —** to whisper.

**secta** *f.* sect.

**secuaz** *m.* partisan, follower.

**secuela** *f.* sequel, outcome, consequence.

**secuencia** *f.* sequence.

**secuestrador** *m.* kidnapper; confiscator.

**secuestrar** *v.* to seize; to kidnap; to confiscate.

**secuestro** *m.* kidnapping; seizure.

**secular** *adj.* secular; lay, worldly; centennial; *m.* secular, secular priest.

**secundar** *v.* to second, favor, back up.

**secundario** *adj.* secondary.

**sed** *f.* thirst; craving, desire; **tener —** to be thirsty.

**seda** *f.* silk; **como una —** soft as silk; sweet-tempered; smoothly, easily.

**sedal** *m.* fishing line.

**sedán** *m.* sedan.

**sedativo** *adj.* & *m.* sedative.

**sede** *f.* seat, see; **Santa Sede** Holy See.

**sedentario** *adj.* sedentary.

**sedeño** *adj.* silky, silken.

**sedería** *f.* silk goods; silk shop.

**sedero** *m.* silk dealer or weaver; *adj.* silk, pertaining to silk; **industria sedera** silk industry.

**sedición** *f.* sedition.

**sedicioso** *adj.* seditious, turbulent.

**sediento** *adj.* thirsty; dry, parched; anxious, desirous.

**sedimento** *m.* sediment; dregs, grounds.

**sedoso** *adj.* silken, silky.

**seducción** *f.* seduction.

**seducir**[25] *v. irr.* to seduce; to entice; to charm.

**seductivo** *adj.* seductive, alluring; inviting, enticing.

**seductor** *adj.* tempting, fascinating; *m.* seducer; tempter; charming person.

**segador** *m.* harvester, reaper; **segadora** *f.* harvester, mowing machine; woman reaper.

**segar**[1,7] *v. irr.* to mow, reap; to cut off.

**seglar** *adj.* secular, lay; *m.* layman.

**segmento** *m.* segment.

**seguida** *f.* succession; series, continuation; **de —** without interruption, continuously; **en —** at once, immediately.

**seguido** *p.p.* followed; continued; *adj.* continuous; straight, direct; *adv.* without interruption; *Am.* often; *Col., Ven.* **de —** at once, immediately.

**seguidor** *m.* follower.

**seguimiento** *m.* pursuit.

**seguir**[5,12] *v. irr.* to follow; to continue; to pursue; **-se** to follow as a consequence.

**según** *prep.* according to; *conj.* as; according to; **— y conforme** (*or* **— y como**) exactly as, just as; that depends.

**segundar** *v.* to repeat a second time; to second.

**segundero** *m.* second hand (*of a watch or clock*).

**segundo** *adj.* & *m.* second.

**seguridad** *f.* security; safety; certainty; **alfiler de —** safety pin.

**seguro** *adj.* secure; sure, certain; safe; *Ríopl., Mex., Carib., Andes* honest, trustworthy; *m.* assurance; insurance; safety device; **a buen — (al —,** *or* **de —)** truly, certainly; **en —** in safety; **sobre —** without risk; without taking a chance; *Am.* **irse uno del —** to lose one's temper; *Ch., Mex., Cuba, Andes* **a la segura** without risk.

**selección** *f.* selection choice.

**seleccionar** *v.* to select, choose.

**selecto** *adj.* select, choice.

**selva** *f.* forest; jungle.

**sellar** *v.* (*imprimir*) to stamp; to seal; (*cerrar*) to close tightly, seal; (*concluir*) to conclude.

**sello** *m.* seal; stamp; *Am.* official stamped paper.

**semáforo** *m.* traffic light.

**semana** *f.* week; week's wages; **días de —** week days; **entre —** during the week.

**semanal** *adj.* weekly; **-mente** *adv.* weekly, every week.

**semanario** *m.* weekly publication; *adj.* weekly.

**semblante** *m.* countenance; facial expression; appearance.

**semblanza** *f.* portrait, literary sketch.

**sembrado** *m.* sown ground; cultivated field.

**sembrar**[1] *v. irr.* to sow; to scatter.

**semejante** *adj.* similar, like; such a; *m.* fellow man; **nuestros -s** our fellow men.

**semejanza** *f.* resemblance, similarity; simile; **a — de** in the manner of.

**semejar** *v.* to resemble; **-se** to resemble.

**semental** *adj.* sowing (*crops*); breeding (*animals*); used as stud.

**semiconsonante** *f.* semiconsonant.

**semilla** *f.* seed.

**semillero** *m.* seed bed; plant nursery; **— de vicios** hotbed of vice.

**seminario** *m.* seminary; plant nursery, seed plot.

**semivocal** *f.* semivowel.

**sempiterno** *adj.* everlasting; evergreen.

**senado** *m.* senate.

**senador** *m.* senator.

**sencillez** *f.* simplicity; plainness.

**sencillo** *adj.* simple; easy; plain; unadorned; unaffected; *m.* loose change, small coins.

**senda** *f.* path; way, course.

**sendero** *m.* path.

**sendos** *adj. pl.* one for each of two or more persons or things.

**senectud** *f.* senility, old age.

**senil** *adj.* senile.

**seno** *m.* (*pecho*) breast, bosom; (*hueco*) cavity, hollow; womb; lap; cove, bay; innermost recess; sinus (*cavity in a bone*); sine (*math.*); *C.A.* armpit.

**sensación** *f.* sensation.

**sensacional** *adj.* sensational.

**sensatez** *f.* prudence, common sense.

**sensato** *adj.* sensible, wise, prudent.

**sensibilidad** *f.* sensibility; sensitiveness.

**sensible** *adj.* sensitive; perceptible; regrettable.

**sensitivo** *adj.* sensitive.

**sensual** *adj.* sensual; sensuous.

**sensualidad** *f.* sensuality; lewdness.

**sentada** *f.* sitting; **de una —** at one sitting.

**sentado** *adj.* seated, sitting; **dar por —** to take for granted.

**sentar**¹ *v. irr.* to seat; to set; to establish; to become, suit, fit; to agree with one (*as food or climate*); **-se** to sit down; to settle down; *Col.* **-se en la palabra** to do all the talking, monopolize the conversation.

**sentencia** *f.* sentence; verdict; judgment, maxim, proverb; statement.

**sentenciar** *v.* to sentence; to pass judgment on; to decide.

**sentido** *p.p.* felt; experienced; *adj.* heartfelt, filled with feeling; sensitive; touchy; **darse por —** to take offense; to have one's feelings hurt; **estar — con alguien** to be offended or peeved at someone; *m.* sense; meaning; judgment; **aguzar el —** to prick up one's ears; **perder el —** to faint.

**sentimental** *adj.* sentimental.

**sentimentalismo** *m.* sentimentalism, sentimentality.

**sentimiento** *m.* sentiment; sensation, feeling; grief, regret.

**sentir**³ *v. irr.* to feel; to sense; to hear; to regret; **-se** to feel (*well, strong, sad, etc.*); to feel oneself, consider oneself;

to feel resentment; to feel a pain; **sin —** without being realized or felt; inadvertently; unnoticed; *m.* feeling; judgment, opinion.

**señá** *familiar contraction of* **señora**.

**seña** *f.* sign, mark; signal; password; **-s** address (*name and place of residence*); **por más -s** as an additional proof.

**señal** *f.* (*marca*) sign, mark; signal; trace, vestige; scar; (*indicio*) reminder; indication; token, pledge; *Ríopl.*, *Andes* earmark, brand (*on the ear of livestock*); **en — de** in proof of, in token of.

**señalar** *v.* to mark; to point out; to indicate; to determine, fix; to appoint; to signal; to assign; *Am.* to earmark, brand (*cattle*); **-se** to distinguish oneself.

**señor** *m.* mister; sir; owner; master, lord; gentleman; **el Señor** the Lord.

**señora** *f.* lady; madam; mistress; Mrs.

**señorear** *v.* to lord it over, domineer; to dominate; to master, control.

**señoría** *f.* lordship.

**señoril** *adj.* lordly.

**señorío** *m.* dominion, rule; domain of a lord; lordship; dignity; mastery, control; body of noblemen.

**señorita** *f.* miss; young lady.

**señorito** *m.* master, young gentleman.

**señuelo** *m.* decoy; lure, bait; *Ven.* leading or guiding oxen.

**separación** *f.* separation.

**separado** *p.p.* & *adj.* separate; separated; **por —** separately.

**separar** *v.* to separate; to set aside; to remove (from); to dismiss (from); **-se** to separate; to retire, resign; to withdraw, leave.

**separata** *f.* reprint (*of an article*).

**septentrional** *adj.* northern.

**septiembre** *m.* September.

**sepulcral** *adj.* sepulchral (*pertaining to sepulchers or tombs*); **lápida —** tombstone.

**sepulcro** *m.* sepulcher, tomb, grave.

**sepultar** *v.* to bury; to hide.

**sepultura** *f.* burial; grave; **dar —** to bury.

**sequedad** *f.* dryness; gruffness.

**sequía** *f.* drought.

**séquito** *m.* retinue, following.

**ser**⁴⁴ *v. irr.* to be; to exist; to happen, occur; **— de** (*or* **para**) **ver** to be worth seeing; *m.* being; essence, nature; existence; *Am.* **estar en un —** to be always in the same condition.

**serenar** *v.* to pacify; to calm down; *Col.* to drizzle, rain gently; **-se** to become serene, calm down; to clear up (*said of the weather*).

**serenata** *f.* serenade.

**serenidad** *f.* serenity, calm.

**sereno** *adj.* serene, calm; clear, cloudless; *m.* night humidity, dew; night watchman; **al —** in the night air.

**serie** *f.* series.

**seriedad** *f.* seriousness; gravity; earnestness; dignity.

**serio** *adj.* serious; grave; earnest; dig-

**SE**

nified; formal; **en —** seriously.
**sermón** *m.* sermon; reproof.
**sermonear** *v.* to preach; to admonish, reprimand.
**serpentear** *v.* to wind, twist, turn, zigzag.
**serpiente** *f.* serpent, snake.
**serrado** *adj.* toothed, notched (*like a saw*); jagged.
**serrana** *f.* mountain girl; **serranilla** *f.* lyric poem with a rustic theme.
**serranía** *f.* mountainous region; chain of mountains.
**serrano** *m.* mountaineer; *adj.* of, pertaining to, or from the mountains.
**serrar = aserrar.**
**serrín** *m.* sawdust.
**serrucho** *m.* handsaw.
**servible** *adj.* serviceable, useful.
**servicial** *adj.* helpful, obliging.
**servicio** *m.* service; table service; tea or coffee set; chamber pot; *Am.* toilet, water closet.
**servidor** *m.* servant; waiter; **— de Vd.** at your service; **su seguro —** yours truly.
**servidumbre** *f.* domestic help, servants; servitude, slavery; service.
**servil** *adj.* servile; **servilón** *adj.* very servile; *m.* bootlicker, great flatterer.
**servilismo** *m.* servility, servile behavior or attitude, servile submission.
**servilleta** *f.* napkin.
**servir**[5] *v. irr.* to serve; to be of use; **— de** to serve as, act as; to be used as; **— para** to be good for; to be used for; **-se** to serve or help oneself; to be pleased to; **-se de** to make use of; **sírvase Vd. hacerlo** please do it.
**sesgado** *adj.* slanting, oblique, bias.
**sesgar**[7] *v.* to slant; to cut on the bias; to follow an oblique line.
**sesgo** *m.* bias; slant; diagonal cut; turn; **al —** on the bias; diagonally, obliquely.
**sesión** *f.* session; meeting, conference.
**seso** *m.* brain; wisdom, intelligence; **devanarse los -s** to rack one's brain.
**sestear** *v.* to snooze, take a nap.
**sesudo** *adj.* sensible, wise, prudent; *Mex., C.A.* stubborn.
**seta** *f.* mushroom.
**seto** *m.* fence; hedge.
**seudónimo** *m.* pseudonym, pen name.
**severidad** *f.* severity; strictness; seriousness.
**severo** *adj.* severe; strict; stern.
**sevillano** *adj.* of, from, or pertaining to Seville, Spain.
**sexo** *m.* sex.
**sexual** *adj.* sexual.
**si** *conj.* if; whether; **¡— ya te lo dije!** but I already told you!; **— bien** although; **por — acaso** just in case.
**sí** *adv.* yes; **— que** certainly, really; **un — es no es** a trifle, somewhat; *m.* assent, consent; *refl. pron.* (*used after a prep.*) himself, herself, yourself (*formal*), themselves; **de por —** separately, by itself; **estar sobre —** to be on the alert.

**sicología** *f.* psychology.
**sicológico** *adj.* psychological.
**sicólogo** *m.* psychologist.
**sidra** *f.* cider.
**siega** *f.* reaping, mowing; harvesting; harvest, harvest season.
**siembra** *f.* sowing; seedtime, sowing time; sown field.
**siempre** *adv.* always; *Mex., C.A., Col., Andes* in any case, anyway; **para** (*or* **por) —** forever, for always; **por — jamás** forever and ever; **— que** whenever; provided that; *Am.* **— sí me voy** I've decided to go anyway.
**siempreviva** *f.* evergreen; everlasting.
**sien** *f.* temple (*of the forehead*).
**sierpe** *f.* serpent, snake.
**sierra** *f.* saw; rocky mountain range.
**siervo** *m.* serf; slave; servant.
**siesta** *f.* siesta, afternoon nap; early afternoon; **dormir la —** to take an afternoon nap.
**sifón** *m.* siphon; siphon bottle; trap (*in plumbing fixtures*).
**sigilo** *m.* secret; secrecy.
**siglo** *m.* century; period, epoch; the world, worldly matters.
**significación** *f.* meaning; significance.
**significado** *m.* significance, meaning.
**significar**[6] *v.* to signify; to mean; to make known, show; to matter, have importance.
**significativo** *adj.* significant.
**signo** *m.* sign; mark; symbol.
**siguiente** *adj.* following.
**sílaba** *f.* syllable.
**silabario** *m.* speller, spelling book.
**silbar** *v.* to whistle; to hiss.
**silbato** *m.* whistle.
**silbido** *m.* whistle; hiss.
**silenciador** *m.* silencer; muffler (*of an automobile*).
**silencio** *m.* silence; pause; *adj. Am.* silent, quiet, motionless.
**silencioso** *adj.* silent, quiet.
**silueta** *f.* silhouette.
**silvestre** *adj.* wild, uncultivated.
**silvicultor** *m.* forester; **silvicultura** *f.* forestry.
**silla** *f.* chair; saddle; **— de montar** saddle; *Ven.* **— de balanza** rocking chair. *See* **mecedora.**
**sillón** *m.* large chair; easy chair; *Am.* **— de hamaca** rocking chair.
**sima** *f.* chasm, abyss.
**simbólico** *adj.* symbolic.
**simbolismo** *m.* symbolism.
**símbolo** *m.* symbol; **— de la fe** (*or de los Apóstoles*) the Apostle's creed.
**simetría** *f.* symmetry.
**simétrico** *adj.* symmetrical.
**simiente** *f.* seed.
**símil** *m.* simile; similarity; *adj.* similar.
**simpatía** *f.* sympathy; accord, harmony; liking.
**simpático** *adj.* sympathetic, congenial; pleasant, agreeable, nice.
**simpatizar**[9] *v.* to be attractive to; to get on well with; to be congenial; **no me simpatiza** I don't like him.
**simple** *adj.* simple; mere; plain; pure,

unmixed; naïve, innocent; silly, fool-ish; *m.* simpleton.

**simpleza** *f.* simplicity; simpleness, stupidity, foolishness.

**simplicidad** *f.* simplicity; candor.

**simplificar**[6] *v.* to simplify.

**simplista** *adj.* simplistic; *m. & f.* a person who is inclined to over-simplify.

**simplón** *m.* simpleton.

**simulacro** *m.* mimic battle, sham or mock battle; image, vision.

**simular** *v.* to simulate, feign.

**simultáneo** *adj.* simultaneous.

**sin** *prep.* without; besides, not count-ing; **— que** *conj.* without; **— embar-go** nevertheless, still, yet; **— qué ni para qué** without rhyme or reason.

**sinapismo** *m.* mustard plaster; irritat-ing person, nuisance, pest, bore.

**sincerar** *v.* to square, justify, excuse; **-se** to square oneself (with), justify oneself (with).

**sinceridad** *f.* sincerity.

**sincero** *adj.* sincere.

**síncopa** *f.* syncopation; syncope.

**sindicar**[6] *v.* to syndicate; **-se** to syndi-cate, form a syndicate.

**sindicato** *m.* syndicate.

**síndico** *m.* receiver (*person appointed to take charge of property under litigation or to liquidate a bankrupt business*); trustee.

**sinecura** *f.* sinecure (*easy and well paid position*).

**sinfonía** *f.* symphony.

**singular** *adj.* singular; unique; striking; odd, strange.

**singularizar**[9] *v.* to single out, choose; to distinguish; **-se** to distinguish one-self; to be singled out.

**siniestro** *adj.* sinister; left (*side*); *m.* unforeseen loss, damage; **siniestra** *f.* left hand; left-hand side.

**sinnúmero** *m.* great number, endless number.

**sino** *conj.* but; *prep.* except; **no hace — lo que le mandan** he only does what he is told; **— que** *conj.* but; *m.* fate, destiny.

**sinónimo** *m.* synonym; *adj.* synon-ymous.

**sinrazón** *f.* injustice, wrong.

**sinsabor** *m.* displeasure; trouble, grief, distress.

**sintaxis** *f.* syntax.

**síntesis** *f.* synthesis; summary.

**sintético** *adj.* synthetic.

**sintetizar**[9] *v.* to synthesize.

**síntoma** *m.* symptom; indication, sign.

**sintonizar**[9] *v.* to tune in (on).

**sinuoso** *adj.* sinuous, winding; wavy.

**sinvergüenza** *m. & f.* shameless per-son; scoundrel.

**siquiatra** *m. & f.* psychiatrist, alienist.

**siquiatría** *f.* psychiatry.

**siquiera** *adv.* at least; even; **ni —** not even; *conj.* even though.

**sirena** *f.* siren; whistle, foghorn.

**sirviente** *m.* servant; waiter; **sirvienta** *f.* housemaid; waitress.

**sisa** *f.* petty theft; dart (*made in a gar-ment*).

**sisal** *m. Am.* sisal or sisal hemp (*fiber used in ropemaking*).

**sisar** *v.* to take in (*a garment*); to pilfer; to cheat out of, defraud.

**sisear** *v.* to hiss.

**siseo** *m.* hiss, hissing.

**sistema** *m.* system.

**sistemático** *adj.* systematic.

**sitial** *m.* chair of a presiding officer; place of honor.

**sitiar** *v.* to besiege; to surround.

**sitio** *m.* site, location; place, spot, space; siege; *Am.* cattle ranch; *Mex.* taxicab station; **poner — a** to lay siege to.

**sito** *adj.* situated, located.

**situación** *f.* situation; position; loca-tion; state, condition; *Mex., Carib., Ven., Col.* **hombre de la —** man of the hour, man of influence.

**situado** *p.p.* situated; placed.

**situar**[18] *v.* to locate; to place; **-se** to station oneself, place oneself; to be located, placed, situated.

**so :** **— capa de** under the guise of; **— pena de** under penalty of; **— pretex-to de** under the pretext of.

**sobaco** *m.* armpit.

**sobar** *v.* (*ablandar*) to rub; to knead; to massage; to touch, handle; to fondle, pet; (*fastidiar*) to bother; to beat, slap; *Col., Ven., Mex.* to set bones; *Col.* to flay, skin; *Am.* to win (*in a fight*); *Am.* to tire out (*a horse*).

**soberanía** *f.* sovereignty.

**soberano** *adj. & m.* sovereign.

**soberbia** *f.* pride, arrogance; ostenta-tion, pomp.

**soberbio** *adj.* proud, haughty, arrogant; pompous; superb, magnificent; spir-ited (*horse*).

**sobornar** *v.* to bribe.

**soborno** *m.* bribery; bribe; *Andes* over-load (*on a pack animal*), extra load.

**sobra** *f.* surplus, excess; **-s** leftovers, leavings; **de —** more than enough; superfluous, unnecessary.

**sobrado** *m.* attic; loft; *Am.* pantry shelf; **-s** *Col., Ven.* leftovers, leavings; *adj.* leftover; excessive; superfluous; for-ward, brazen; **sobradas veces** many times, repeatedly.

**sobrante** *adj.* leftover, surplus, excess, spare; *m.* surplus, excess, remainder.

**sobrar** *v.* to exceed; to remain, be left over; to be more than enough.

**sobre** *prep.* (*encima de*) over; above; on, upon; (*acerca de*) about; approxi-mately; besides; **— manera** ex-cessively; **estar — sí** to be cautious, on the alert; **— que** besides, in addition to the fact that; *m.* en-velope; address (*on an envelope*).

**sobrecama** *f.* bedspread.

**sobrecarga** *f.* overload; overburden.

**sobrecargar**[7] *v.* to overload; to over-burden.

**sobrecargo** *m.* purser (*on a ship*); *f.* airline hostess.

**sobrecoger**[11] *v.* to surprise, catch un-

aware; to startle; **-se** to be startled;
**-se de miedo** to be seized with fear.
**sobreexcitación** *f.* overexcitement;
thrill.
**sobreexcitar** *v.* to overexcite.
**sobrehumano** *adj.* superhuman.
**sobrellevar** *v.* to endure, bear; to tolerate; to lighten (*another's burden*).
**sobremesa** *f.* table runner; after dinner
conversation at the table; **de —** during the after dinner conversation.
**sobrenadar** *v.* to float.
**sobrenatural** *adj.* supernatural.
**sobrenombre** *m.* surname; nickname.
**sobrentender**[1] *v. irr.* to assume, understand; **-se** to be assumed, be obvious,
be understood.
**sobrepasar** *v.* to exceed; to excel; **-se**
to overstep, go too far.
**sobreponer**[40] *v. irr.* to lay on top; **-se**
to dominate oneself; **-se a** to overcome; to dominate.
**sobrepuesto** *p.p. of* **sobreponer**; *m.*
appliqué (*trimming laid on a dress*);
*C.A.* mend, patch.
**sobrepujar** *v.* to exceed, excel, surpass;
to outweigh.
**sobresaliente** *adj.* outstanding; projecting; excellent; *m. & f.* substitute
(*a person*); understudy (*substitute actor*).
**sobresalir**[43] *v. irr.* to stand out; to project, jut out; to excel.
**sobresaltar** *v.* to startle, frighten; to
assail; to stand out clearly; **-se** to be
startled, frightened.
**sobresalto** *m.* start, scare, fright, shock;
**de —** suddenly.
**sobrescrito** *m.* address (*on an envelope*).
**sobrestante** *m.* overseer; boss, foreman.
**sobresueldo** *m.* overtime pay, extra pay
or wages.
**sobretodo** *m.* overcoat.
**sobrevenir**[48] *v. irr.* to happen, occur,
come unexpectedly; to follow, hap-
pen after.
**sobreviviente** *m. & f.* survivor; *adj.*
surviving.
**sobrevivir** *v.* to survive.
**sobriedad** *f.* sobriety, soberness, temperance, moderation.
**sobrina** *f.* niece.
**sobrino** *m.* nephew.
**sobrio** *adj.* sober, temperate, moderate.
**socarrón** *adj.* cunning, sly, crafty.
**socarronería** *f.* craftiness, slyness, cunning.
**socavar** *v.* to dig under; to undermine.
**socavón** *m.* tunnel; cave, cavern; underground passageway.
**social** *adj.* social; sociable, friendly.
**socialista** *adj.* socialist, socialistic; *m.
& f.* socialist.
**sociedad** *f.* society; partnership; company, firm, corporation; **— anónima**
(*or* **— por acciones**) stock company.
**socio** *m.* associate, partner; member.
**sociología** *f.* sociology.
**socorrer** *v.* to help, aid, assist.
**socorro** *m.* help, aid, assistance, relief;
*Am.* partial advance payment on a

workman's wages.
**sodio** *m.* sodium.
**soez** *adj.* low, vile, vulgar; coarse, ill-
mannered.
**sofá** *m.* sofa, davenport.
**sofocante** *adj.* suffocating, stifling.
**sofocar**[6] *v.* to suffocate, choke; to
smother; to bother; to embarrass.
**sofoco** *m.* suffocation, choking; upset,
annoyance; embarrassment.
**sofrenar** *v.* to check; to control; to
reprimand.
**soga** *f.* rope; *Ven., Col., Andes, Ch.*
leather lasso or rope.
**sojuzgamiento** *m.* subjugation, subjection.
**sojuzgar**[7] *v.* to subjugate, subdue, subject.
**sol** *m.* sun; sunshine; sol (*fifth note of
the scale*); *Am.* sol (*monetary unit of
Peru*); **de — a —** from sunrise to
sunset; **hace —** it is sunny; **tomar
el —** to bask in the sun; to enjoy the
sunshine.
**solana** *f.* sunny place; sunroom; sun
porch; intense sunlight; **solanera** *f.*
sunburn; sunny place.
**solapa** *f.* lapel.
**solapado** *adj.* sly, crafty, cunning, deceitful, underhanded.
**solar** *m.* lot, plot of ground; ancestral
mansion, manor; *Carib., Mex.* tenement house; *Mex., Ven.* back yard;
*Col.* town lot, field (*for growing alfalfa,
corn, etc.*); *adj.* solar, of the sun.
**solar**[2] *v. irr.* to sole (*shoes*); to pave,
floor.
**solariego** *adj.* manorial, pertaining to a
manor; **casa solariega** ancestral
manor or mansion.
**solaz** *m.* solace, comfort; relaxation,
recreation.
**solazar**[9] *v.* to console, cheer, comfort;
**-se** to seek relaxation or pleasure; to
enjoy oneself.
**soldado** *m.* soldier; **— raso** private; **—
de línea** regular soldier.
**soldadura** *f.* soldering; welding; solder.
**soldar**[2] *v. irr.* to solder; to weld.
**soleado** *adj.* sunny; *p.p.* sunned.
**solear = asolear.**
**soledad** *f.* solitude; loneliness; homesickness; lonely retreat.
**solemne** *adj.* solemn; imposing; **—
disparate** downright foolishness,
huge blunder.
**solemnidad** *f.* solemnity; solemn ceremony.
**soler**[2,51] *v. irr.* to have the custom of, be
in the habit of.
**solferino** *adj.* reddish-purple.
**solicitante** *m. & f.* solicitor; applicant.
**solicitar** *v.* to solicit; to apply for; to
beg, ask for; to court, woo.
**solícito** *adj.* solicitous, careful; anxious,
concerned, diligent.
**solicitud** *f.* solicitude; care, concern,
anxiety.
**solidaridad** *f.* solidarity; union; bond,
community of interests.
**solidez** *f.* solidity; compactness.

**solidificar**[6] *v.* to solidify.
**sólido** *adj.* solid; firm; strong; *m.* solid.
**soliloquio** *m.* soliloquy, monologue.
**solista** *m.* & *f.* soloist.
**solitaria** *f.* tapeworm.
**solitario** *adj.* solitary; lonely; *m.* recluse, hermit; solitaire (*card game*); solitaire (*gem set by itself*).
**solo** *adj.* sole, only; single; alone; lonely; **a solas** alone; *m.* solo; **sólo** *adv.* only.
**solomillo, solomo** *m.* sirloin; loin; loin of pork.
**soltar**[2] *v. irr.* to loosen, untie, unfasten; to let loose; to set free; to let go; to let out; to utter; **-se** to set oneself free; to come loose; to lose restraint; to loosen up; **-se a** to begin to, start to.
**soltero** *adj.* single, unmarried; *m.* bachelor; **soltera** *f.* spinster; **solterón** *m.* old bachelor; **solterona** *f.* old maid.
**soltura** *f.* looseness; freedom; facility, ease; agility, nimbleness; release (*of a prisoner*).
**solución** *f.* solution; loosening, untying.
**solventar** *v.* to pay (*a bill*), settle (*an account*); to solve (*a problem or difficulty*).
**sollozar**[9] *v.* to sob.
**sollozo** *m.* sob.
**sombra** *f.* (*oscuridad*) shadow; shade; darkness; (*abrigo*) shelter, protection; (*imagen*) image, reflection (*in the water*); *Am.* guide lines (*under writing paper*); *Ven.* awning, sunshade; **hacer —** to shade; to cast a shadow (on).
**sombreado** *adj.* shady; shaded.
**sombrear** *v.* to shade; **-se** *Mex., Ven., Col.* to seek the shade, stand in the shade.
**sombrerería** *f.* hat shop.
**sombrero** *m.* hat; **— de copa** top hat, high hat; **— hongo** derby; **— de jipijapa** Panama hat; *C.A., Col., Ven.* **— de pelo** top hat.
**sombrilla** *f.* parasol, sunshade.
**sombrío** *adj.* somber, gloomy; shady.
**somero** *adj.* superficial, shallow; summary, concise.
**someter** *v.* to submit; to subject; **-se** to submit.
**sometimiento** *m.* submission; subjection.
**somnolencia** *f.* drowsiness, sleepiness; **con —** sleepily.
**son** *m.* sound; tune; rumor; **en — de guerra** in a warlike manner; **sin ton ni —** without rhyme or reason.
**sonaja** *f.* jingles, tambourine (*to accompany certain dances*); rattle; **sonajero** *m.* child's rattle.
**sonante** *adj.* sounding; ringing; sonorous; **en dinero — y contante** in hard cash.
**sonar**[2] *v. irr.* to sound; to ring; to sound familiar; **— a** to sound like; seem like; **-se** to blow one's nose; **se**

**suena que** it is rumored that.
**sonda** *f.* plumb, string with lead weight (*for sounding the depth of water*); sounding; surgeon's probe.
**sondar** = **sondear.**
**sondear** *v.* to sound, fathom; to sound out; to probe; to examine into.
**sondeo** *m.* sounding, fathoming.
**soneto** *m.* sonnet.
**sonido** *m.* sound.
**sonoro** *adj.* sonorous; **consonante sonora** voiced consonant.
**sonreír**[15] *v. irr.* to smile; **-se** to smile.
**sonriente** *adj.* smiling, beaming, radiant.
**sonrisa** *f.* smile.
**sonrojarse** *v.* to blush.
**sonrojo** *m.* blush.
**sonrosado** *adj.* rosy.
**sonsacar**[6] *v.* to lure away; to draw (*someone*) out; to extract (*a secret*); to take on the sly.
**sonsonete** *m.* singsong; rhythmical tapping sound.
**soñador** *m.* dreamer.
**soñar**[2] *v. irr.* to dream; **— con** (*or* **— en**) to dream of; **— despierto** to daydream.
**soñoliento** *adj.* sleepy, drowsy.
**sopa** *f.* soup; sop; **estar hecho una —** to be sopping wet; *Am.* **es un -s** he is a fool.
**sopapo** *m.* chuck, tap, pat (*under the chin*); slap.
**sopetón** *m.* box, slap; **de —** all of a sudden, unexpectedly.
**soplar** *v.* (*despedir aire*) to blow; to blow away; to blow up, inflate; (*robar*) to swipe, steal; (*informar*) to prompt; to "squeal" on, inform against; *Col., Ven., Mex., Cuba, Andes* **— una bofetada** to strike a blow; **-se** to swell up, puff up; to eat up, gobble up; to gulp down; **se sopló el pastel** he gobbled up the pie; *Am.* **-se a uno** to deceive someone, get the best of someone.
**soplete** *m.* blow torch; blowpipe.
**soplo** *m.* (*de aire*) blowing; puff, gust of wind; breath; (*aviso*) whispered warning or advice; "squealing", informing; **en un —** in a jiffy, in a second.
**soplón** *m.* informer, "squealer" (*one who tells on someone*), tattletale.
**soportal** *m.* arcade.
**soportar** *v.* to support, hold up, bear; to stand, endure, tolerate.
**soporte** *m.* support.
**sorber** *v.* to sip; to suck; to swallow; to absorb; to snuff up one's nose.
**sorbete** *m.* sherbet; fruit ice; *C.A., Mex., Ven.* cone, ice-cream cone; *Am.* silk top hat.
**sorbo** *m.* sip, swallow, gulp; sniff.
**sordera, sordez** *f.* deafness.
**sórdido** *adj.* sordid.
**sordina** *f.* mute (*of a musical instrument*).
**sordo** *adj.* deaf; silent, noiseless; dull; muffled; **consonante sorda** voiceless

**SO**

consonant; *m.* deaf person; **hacerse el —** to pretend not to hear; to turn a deaf ear.

**sordomudo** *adj.* deaf and dumb; *m.* deaf-mute.

**sorna** *f.* slyness, cunning; sneer.

**soroche** *m. Andes* shortness of breath, sickness caused by high altitude; *Am.* blush, flush.

**sorprendente** *adj.* surprising.

**sorprender** *v.* to surprise; **-se** to be surprised.

**sorpresa** *f.* surprise.

**sortear** *v.* to draw lots; to raffle; to dodge; to shun; to fight (*bulls*) skillfully.

**sorteo** *m.* drawing or casting of lots; raffle.

**sortija** *f.* ring; finger ring; ringlet, curl.

**sosa** *f.* soda.

**sosegado** *adj.* calm, quiet, peaceful.

**sosegar**[1],[7] *v.* to calm, quiet; to be quiet; **-se** to quiet down.

**sosiego** *m.* calm, peace, quiet.

**soslayo : al —** obliquely; slanting; on the bias; **de —** oblique, slanting; at a slant; sideways; **mirada de —** side glance; **pegar de —** to glance, hit at a slant.

**soso** *adj.* flat, tasteless, insipid; dull, silly; awkward.

**sospecha** *f.* suspicion; mistrust.

**sospechar** *v.* to suspect; to mistrust.

**sospechoso** *adj.* suspicious; *m.* suspect.

**sostén** *m.* support; prop; supporter; brassière.

**sostener**[45] *v. irr.* to sustain; to hold; to support, maintain; to defend, uphold; to endure.

**sostenido** *p.p.* & *adj.* sustained; supported, held up; *m.* sharp (*in music*).

**sota** *f.* jack (*at cards*); *m. Am.* foreman, boss, overseer.

**sotana** *f.* cassock (*black outer robe of a priest*).

**sótano** *m.* cellar, basement.

**soto** *m.* grove; thicket.

**sotreta** *m. Andes, Ríopl.* nag, old horse.

**soviet** *m.* soviet; **soviético** *adj.* soviet, of, or pertaining to, soviets.

**suave** *adj.* soft; smooth; mild; bland; gentle.

**suavidad** *f.* softness; smoothness; mildness; gentleness.

**suavizar**[9] *v.* to smooth; to soften.

**subalterno** *adj.* & *m.* subordinate.

**subasta** *f.* public auction.

**subastar** *v.* to sell at auction.

**súbdito** *m.* subject.

**subida** *f.* rise; ascent; carrying up; **de — on** the way up; **muchas -s y bajadas** many ups and downs; much going up and down.

**subir** *v.* to ascend, go up, climb; to raise, lift; to carry up; to mount; **— al tren** to board the train, get on the train.

**súbito** *adj.* sudden; **de —** suddenly.

**sublevación** *f.* revolt, uprising, insurrection.

**sublevar** *v.* to excite to rebellion; **-se** to revolt.

**sublime** *adj.* sublime.

**submarino** *m.* & *adj.* submarine; *m.* **— atómico** atomic submarine.

**subordinado** *adj.* & *m.* subordinate.

**subordinar** *v.* to subordinate; to subdue.

**subrayar** *v.* to underline; to emphasize.

**subsanar** *v.* to mend, remedy, repair (*a damage, error, defect, etc.*); to make up for (*an error, fault, etc.*); to excuse (*a fault or error*).

**subscribir = suscribir.**

**subscripción = suscripción.**

**subscriptor = suscritor.**

**subsecretario** *m.* undersecretary.

**subsecuente** *adj.* subsequent.

**subsiguiente** *adj.* subsequent.

**subsistencia** *f.* living, livelihood; sustenance; permanence.

**subsistir** *v.* to subsist; to exist; to last.

**substancia = sustancia.**

**substancial = sustancial.**

**substancioso = sustancioso.**

**substituíble = sustituíble.**

**substantivo = sustantivo.**

**substitución = sustitución.**

**substituir = sustituir.**

**substituto = sustituto.**

**substracción = sustracción.**

**substraer = sustraer.**

**subsuelo** *m.* subsoil.

**subteniente** *m.* second lieutenant.

**subterráneo** *adj.* subterranean, underground; *m.* underground; cave, tunnel, vault.

**suburbano** *adj.* suburban; *m.* suburban resident.

**suburbio** *m.* suburb.

**subvención** *f.* subsidy.

**subvencionar** *v.* to subsidize.

**subyugar** *v.* to subdue.

**succión** *f.* suction.

**suceder** *v.* to happen, occur; to succeed, follow.

**sucesión** *f.* succession; heirs, offspring.

**sucesivo** *adj.* successive; **en lo — hereafter,** in the future.

**suceso** *m.* event; outcome, result.

**sucesor** *m.* successor.

**suciedad** *f.* dirt, filth; filthiness; filthy act or remark.

**sucinto** *adj.* compact, concise, brief.

**sucio** *adj.* dirty; foul, filthy.

**suculento** *adj.* juicy.

**sucumbir** *v.* to succumb; to yield.

**sucursal** *f.* branch, branch office (*of a post office, bank, etc.*); *adj.* branch (*used as an adj.*).

**suche** *adj. Ven.* sour, unripe; *m. Andes* pimple; *Ch.* office boy, insignificant employee; *Andes* suche (*a tree*).

**sud** *m.* south; south wind; **sudeste** *m.* & *adj.* southeast; **sudoeste** *m.* & *adj.* southwest.

**sudamericano** *adj.* & *m.* South American.

**sudar** *v.* to sweat, perspire; to ooze; to toil.

**sudor** *m.* sweat, perspiration; toil.

**sudoroso** *adj.* sweaty, sweating, perspiring.

**sueco** *adj.* Swedish; *m.* Swede; Swedish language; **hacerse el —** to pretend not to see or understand.

**suegra** *f.* mother-in-law.

**suegro** *m.* father-in-law.

**suela** *f.* sole of a shoe; shoe leather.

**sueldo** *m.* salary.

**suelo** *m.* soil, ground; floor; pavement; bottom.

**suelto** *adj.* (*no atado*) loose; free, easy; (*ágil*) agile, nimble; blank (*verse*); *m.* small change; short newspaper article, news item.

**sueño** *m.* sleep; dream; sleepiness, drowsiness; **en -s** in one's sleep; **conciliar el —** to get to sleep; **tener —** to be sleepy.

**suero** *m.* serum.

**suerte** *f.* (*fortuna*) fate; fortune; chance; luck; (*clase*) sort, kind; way, manner; (*truco*) trick; **de — que** so that, in such a way that; and so; **echar -s** to cast lots; **tener —** to be lucky; **tocarle a uno la —** to fall to one's lot; to be lucky.

**suéter** *m. Am.* sweater.

**suficiente** *adj.* sufficient; competent, able.

**sufijo** *m.* suffix; *adj.* suffixed.

**sufragar**[7] *v.* to defray, pay; to help, aid; *Am.* **— por** to vote for.

**sufragio** *m.* suffrage; vote; help, aid.

**sufrido** *adj.* suffering, long-suffering, patient; **mal —** impatient.

**sufridor** *m.* sufferer; *adj.* suffering.

**sufrimiento** *m.* suffering; patience, endurance.

**sufrir** *v.* to suffer; to endure; to allow, permit; to sustain; to undergo; **— un examen** to take an examination.

**sugerencia** *f. Am.* suggestion, hint.

**sugerir**[3] *v. irr.* to suggest; to hint.

**sugestión** *f.* suggestion; hint.

**sugestivo** *adj.* suggestive.

**suicida** *m. & f.* suicide (*person who commits suicide*).

**suicidarse** *v.* to commit suicide.

**suicidio** *m.* suicide (*act of suicide*).

**suizo** *adj. & m.* Swiss.

**sujeción** *f.* subjection; control; submission.

**sujetapapeles** *m.* paper clip.

**sujetar** *v.* to subject; to control; to subdue; to fasten; to grasp, hold; **-se** to subject oneself; to submit; to adhere (to).

**sujeto** *adj.* subject; liable; fastened; under control; *m.* subject matter; subject; fellow, individual.

**sulfamida** *f.* common name for the sulfa drugs.

**sulfato** *m.* sulphate.

**sulfurarse** *v.* to get angry.

**sulfúrico** *adj.* sulphuric.

**sulfuro** *m.* sulphide.

**sultán** *m.* sultan.

**suma** *f.* sum; addition; substance; summary; **en —** in short.

**sumador** *adj.* adding; **máquina sumadora** adding machine.

**sumar** *v.* to add; to add up (to), amount (to); to sum up; **-se a** to join.

**sumario** *m.* summary; indictment; *adj.* summary, brief, concise; swift (*punishment*).

**sumergible** *adj.* submergible; *m.* submarine.

**sumergir**[11] *v.* to submerge, plunge, sink; to immerse; **-se** to submerge; to sink.

**sumidero** *m.* sink; sewer, drain.

**suministrar** *v.* to give, supply with, provide with.

**sumir** *v.* to sink; to submerge; to immerse; *Ríopl., Mex., Carib.* to dent; **-se** to sink; *Andes* to shrink, shrivel; *Andes* to cower, crouch in fear; *Am.* **-se el sombrero hasta las cejas** to pull one's hat over one's eyes.

**sumisión** *f.* submission; obedience.

**sumiso** *adj.* submissive; obedient; meek.

**sumo** *adj.* supreme, highest, high; greatest; **— pontífice** Sovereign Pontiff (*the Pope*); **a lo —** at the most.

**suntuoso** *adj.* sumptuous, magnificent, luxurious.

**superabundancia** *f.* superabundance, great abundance, overflow.

**superar** *v.* to surpass; to exceed; to overcome.

**superávit** *m.* surplus.

**superficial** *adj.* superficial; shallow; frivolous; **superficialidad** *f.* superficiality, shallowness, frivolity.

**superficie** *f.* surface; area.

**superfluo** *adj.* superfluous.

**superintendente** *m.* superintendent; supervisor; overseer.

**superior** *adj.* superior; higher; better; upper; *m.* superior; father superior; **superiora** *f.* superior, mother superior.

**superioridad** *f.* superiority; excellence.

**superlativo** *adj. & m.* superlative.

**supersónico** *adj.* supersonic.

**superstición** *f.* superstition.

**supersticioso** *adj.* superstitious.

**supervivencia** *f.* survival.

**superviviente = sobreviviente.**

**suplantar** *v.* to supplant; to forge (*a document or check*).

**suplementar** *v.* supplement.

**suplementario** *adj.* supplementary, extra.

**suplemento** *m.* supplement; supply, supplying.

**suplente** *adj., m. & f.* substitute.

**súplica** *f.* entreaty; request; petition; prayer.

**suplicante** *adj.* suppliant, beseeching; *m. & f.* suppliant; petitioner.

**suplicar**[6] *v.* to beg, entreat, implore; to pray humbly; to appeal, petition.

**suplicio** *m.* torture; torment; anguish; execution; instrument of torture; scaffold, gallows.

**suplir** *v.* to supply; to make up for; to substitute, take the place of (*temporarily*).

**SO**

**suponer**[40] *v. irr.* to suppose; to assume; to be important.

**suposición** *f.* supposition; assumption.

**supremacía** *f.* supremacy.

**supremo** *adj.* supreme; final, last.

**supresión** *f.* suppression; omission; elimination.

**suprimir** *v.* to suppress; to abolish; to omit.

**supuesto** *p.p. of* **suponer** supposed, assumed; **— que** supposing that; since; **por —** of course, naturally; *m.* supposition; assumption.

**supuración** *f.* formation or discharge of pus.

**supurar** *v.* to fester, form or discharge pus.

**sur** *m.* south; south wind; **sureste** *m.* southeast; **suroeste** *m.* southwest.

**suramericano = sudamericano.**

**surcar**[6] *v.* to furrow; to plow; to plow through; to cut through.

**surco** *m.* furrow; rut; groove; wrinkle.

**sureño** *adj.* southern, from the south; *m.* a southerner.

**surgir**[11] *v.* to surge, rise; to spurt, spout; to appear.

**surtido** *m.* stock, supply, assortment; *adj.* assorted.

**surtidor** *m.* supplier; spout, jet.

**surtir** *v.* to provide, supply, stock (with); to spout, spurt; **— efecto** to produce the desired result; **— un pedido** to fill an order.

**susceptible** *adj.* susceptible; sensitive; touchy.

**suscitar** *v.* to raise, stir up, provoke.

**suscribir**[52] *v.* to subscribe; to endorse; to agree (to); **-se** to subscribe.

**suscripción** *f.* subscription.

**suscrito** *p.p. of* **suscribir.**

**suscritor** *m.* subscriber.

**susodicho** *adj.* aforesaid, above-mentioned.

**suspender** *v.* (*colgar*) to suspend; to hang; (*detener*) to stop; to defer; (*no aprobar*) to fail, flunk; to dismiss temporarily; to astonish.

**suspensión** *f.* suspension; postponement, delay; uncertainty; cessation; a system of supporting devices (*automobile*).

**suspenso** *adj.* suspended; hanging; pending; perplexed, astonished; **en —** in suspense; *m.* failure (*in an examination*).

**suspicaz** *adj.* suspicious.

**suspirar** *v.* to sigh; to sigh (for), long (for).

**suspiro** *m.* sight; brief pause (*in music*).

**sustancia** *f.* substance; essence; *Andes* broth.

**sustancial** *adj.* substantial; nourishing.

**sustancioso** *adj.* substantial; nourishing.

**sustantivo** *m.* noun; *adj.* substantive; real; independent.

**sustentar** *v.* to sustain; to support; to feed, nourish; to maintain; uphold.

**sustento** *m.* sustenance; food; support.

**sustitución** *f.* substitution.

**sustituíble** *adj.* replaceable.

**sustituir**[32] *v. irr.* to substitute.

**sustituto** *m.* substitute.

**susto** *m.* scare, fright.

**sustracción** *f.* subtraction.

**sustraer**[46] *v. irr.* to subtract; to remove, withdraw; **-se a** to evade, avoid, slip away from.

**susurrar** *v.* to whisper; to murmur; to rustle; **-se** to be whispered or rumored about.

**susurro** *m.* whisper; murmur; rustle.

**sutil** *adj.* subtle; keen; clever; crafty; thin, fine, delicate.

**sutileza, sutilidad** *f.* subtlety; keenness, cleverness; cunning; thinness, fineness.

**suyo** *adj.* his, of his; her, of hers; your, of yours (*formal*); their, of theirs; *pron.* his, hers, yours (*formal*), theirs; **de —** naturally, by nature; **salirse con la suya** to get one's own way; **hacer de las suyas** to be up to one's tricks; **los -s** his (hers, theirs); his (her, their) own people.

# T

**tabaco** *m.* tobacco; *Carib., Ven., Col.* cigar; snuff; *Col.* blow with the fist; **tabaquería** *f.* tobacco store, cigar store.

**tábano** *m.* horsefly, gadfly.

**taberna** *f.* tavern, bar, liquor store.

**tabernáculo** *m.* tabernacle.

**tabique** *m.* partition, partition wall.

**tabla** *f.* board, plank; plate of metal; slab; table, list; strip of ground; *Col.* chocolate tablet; **-s** draw, tie (*in games*); stage boards, the stage; **a raja —** cost what it may; *Am.* in great haste; **hacer — rasa de algo** to disregard, omit, or ignore something; *Am.* to clear away all obstacles in the way of something.

**tablado** *m.* platform, stage; scaffold; floor boards.

**tablero** *m.* board; panel; timber, piece of lumber; chessboard, checkerboard; store counter; large work table; gambling table; *Col., Ven., Mex.* blackboard; **poner al —** to risk, endanger; **— de mando** control panel.

**tableta** *f.* tablet; small thin board; memorandum pad.

**tabletear** *v.* to rattle; to make a continuous rattling or tapping sound.

**tableteo** *m.* rattling sound; tapping.

**tablilla** *f.* tablet; slat, small thin board; splint; small bulletin board; **-s** wooden clappers.

**tablón** *m.* plank; large, thick board.

**taburete** *m.* stool; footstool.

**tacañería** *f.* stinginess, tightness, miserliness.

**tacaño** *adj.* stingy, tight, miserly; sly.

**tácito** *adj.* tacit, implied; silent.

**taciturno** *adj.* taciturn, silent, sullen; sad.

**taco** *m.* wad; roll; plug, stopper; billiard cue; bite, snack; swear word; *Mex., C.A.* Mexican folded tortilla sandwich; *Am.* leather legging; *Ch.*, *Andes* short, fat person; *Mex.* heel of a shoe; *Am.* pile, heap; **echar -s** to curse, swear; *Mex.* **darse uno —** to strut, put on airs.

**tacón** *m.* heel of a shoe.

**taconear** *v.* to click the heels, walk hard on one's heels.

**taconeo** *m.* click, clicking (*of the heels*).

**táctica** *f.* tactics.

**tacto** *m.* tact; touch, sense of touch.

**tacha** *f.* flaw, defect, blemish.

**tachar** *v.* (*borrar*) to cross out; to scratch out; to blot out; (*culpar*) to blame; to find fault with; to censure.

**tachón** *m.* stud; trimming, braid; blot.

**tachonar** *v.* to stud, ornament with studs; to adorn with trimming.

**tachuela** *f.* tack, small nail; *Am.* metal dipper; *Am.* runt, "shorty".

**tafetán** *m.* taffeta; **— inglés** court plaster.

**tahur** *m.* gambler; cardsharp.

**taimado** *adj.* sly, crafty; *Am.* sullen, gloomy, gruff.

**taita** = **tatita**. See **tata**.

**tajada** *f.* slice; cut.

**tajalápiz** *m.* pencil sharpener.

**tajante** *adj.* cutting, sharp.

**tajar** *v.* to slice; to cut; to sharpen (*a pencil*).

**tajo** *m.* cut; gash; cutting edge; sheer cliff; chopping block.

**tal** *adj.* such; such a; **— cual** such as; so-so, fair; **— vez** perhaps; **el — Pedro** that fellow Peter; **un — García** a certain García; **— para cual** two of a kind; **un — por cual** a nobody; *adv.* just as, in such a way; **estaba — como le dejé** he was just as I left him; **con — (de) que** provided that; **¿qué — ?** how are you?; hello!

**talabarte** *m.* sword belt.

**taladrar** *v.* to bore, drill; to pierce; to penetrate.

**taladro** *m.* auger, drill; bore, drill hole; *Am.* mine tunnel.

**tálamo** *m.* bridal bed or chamber.

**talante** *m.* disposition; mood; appearance, manner.

**talco** *m.* talc (*a soft mineral*); **— en polvo** talcum powder.

**talega** *f.* money bag, sack.

**talento** *m.* talent; ability, natural gift.

**talentoso** *adj.* talented, gifted.

**talismán** *m.* talisman, charm.

**talón** *m.* heel; stub, check, coupon.

**talonario** *m.* stub book; **libro —** stub book.

**talonear** *v.* to tap with one's heel; to walk briskly.

**taloneo** *m.* tapping with the heel; loud footsteps.

**talla** *f.* (*altura*) stature, height; (*labrado*) carving; (*lance entero*) round of a card game; (*rescate*) ransom; *Am.* chat; *Am.* thrashing, beating.

**tallar** *v.* to carve; to cut (*stone*); to appraise; to deal (*cards*); *Am.* to court, make love; *Andes, Col.* to

bother, disturb.

**tallarín** *m.* noodle.

**talle** *m.* figure, form; waist; fit (*of a dress*); looks, appearance; *Ven.* bodice.

**taller** *m.* workshop; laboratory; studio; factory.

**tallo** *m.* stalk; stem; shoot, sprout.

**tamal** *m.* *Mex.*, *C.A.* tamale; *Am.* vile trick, intrigue; *Am.* clumsy bundle.

**tamaño** *m.* size; *adj.* such a; of the size of; **— disparate** such a (big) mistake; **— como un elefante** big as an elephant; **tamañito** *adj.* very small; **tamañito así** about this little; **se quedó tamañito** he was (left) astonished, amazed.

**tambalearse** *v.* to totter, stagger, sway, reel.

**también** *adv.* also, too; likewise.

**tambor** *m.* drum; drum-like object; drummer; pair of embroidery hoops; *Mex.* bedspring, spring mattress; **— de freno** brake drum; **tambora** *f.* bass drum; **tamboril** *m.* small drum; **tamborilero** *m.* drummer.

**tamborilear** *v.* to drum; to extol.

**tamiz** *m.* fine sieve.

**tamizar** *v.* to sift; to blend.

**tampoco** *conj.* either (*after a negative*); **no lo hizo —** he did not do it either; **ni yo —** nor I either.

**tan** *adv.* (*contr. of* **tanto**) so, as; such a.

**tanda** *f.* turn; round, bout; task; gang, group; shift, relay; *Col.*, *Ven.*, *Mex.*, *Carib.* section of a theatrical performance.

**tangente** *adj. & f.* tangent; **salirse por la —** to go off at a tangent; to avoid the issue.

**tangible** *adj.* tangible.

**tango** *m.* tango.

**tanque** *m.* tank; reservoir; *Col.*, *Ven.* pond; *Mex.* swimming pool.

**tantán** *m.* clang; knock! knock!; sound of a bell, drum, etc.

**tantear** *v.* to probe, test; to sound out, feel out; to estimate, calculate approximately; *Cuba, Ven., Ríopl.* to grope, feel one's way; *Am.* to lie in wait; *Mex.* to fool, make a fool of; *Ven., Mex., C.A.* **¡tantee Vd.!** just imagine!

**tanteo** *m.* trial, test; calculation, estimate; score; **al —** by guess; hit or miss.

**tanto** *adj., pron. & adv.* so much, as much; so; **-s** so many, as many; *m.* certain amount; counter, chip (*to keep score*); **cuarenta y -s** forty odd; **el — por ciento** percentage, rate; **un — (or algún —)** somewhat; **— como** as well as; as much as; **— ... como** both ... and; **— en la ciudad como en el campo** both in the city and in the country; **entre (or mientras) —** meanwhile; **por lo —** therefore.

**tañer** *v.* to play (*an instrument*); to ring.

**tañido** *m.* sound, tune; ring; twang (*of a guitar*).

**tapa** *f.* cover; lid; book cover; heel

lift.

**tapacubos** *m.* hubcap.

**tapadera** *f.* cover, lid; one who shields another.

**tapar** *v.* to cover; to plug, stop up; to veil; to hide; *Am.* to fill (*a tooth*); *Am.* to crush, crumple; *Am.* to cover with insults; **-se** to cover up; to wrap oneself up.

**taparrabo** *m.* loincloth; trunks.

**tapera** *f. Am.* ruins; *Ríopl., Andes* abandoned room or house.

**tapete** *m.* rug; table scarf.

**tapia** *f.* adobe wall; wall fence.

**tapiar** *v.* to wall up; to block up (*a door or window*).

**tapicería** *f.* tapestry; upholstery; tapestry shop; tapestry making.

**tapiz** *m.* tapestry.

**tapón** *m.* plug, stopper, cork; bottle cap.

**taquigrafía** *f.* shorthand.

**taquígrafo** *m.* stenographer.

**taquilla** *f.* ticket office; box office; file (*for letters, papers, etc.*); *Am.* tavern, liquor store.

**tararear** *v.* to hum.

**tarareo** *m.* hum, humming.

**tarascada** *f.* snap, bite; snappy or harsh answer.

**tardanza** *f.* delay; slowness.

**tardar** *v.* to delay; to be late; to be long (in); to take long (in); **-se** to delay oneself; to be delayed; **a más —** at the very latest.

**tarde** *f.* afternoon; *adv.* late; **de — en —** from time to time, now and then.

**tardío** *adj.* late; slow.

**tardo** *adj.* slow, lazy; tardy, late; stupid, dull; **tardón** *adj.* very slow; *m.* slowpoke, slow person.

**tarea** *f.* task, job; anxiety, care.

**tarifa** *f.* tariff; list of duties, taxes, or prices; fare.

**tarima** *f.* wooden platform; low bench.

**tarjeta** *f.* card; **— postal** postcard.

**tarro** *m.* earthen jar; *Mex.* horn (*of an animal*); *Ch., Cuba, Andes* can; *Andes* top hat.

**tarta** *f.* tart.

**tartamudear** *v.* to stutter, stammer.

**tartamudeo** *m.* stammer, stammering.

**tartamudo** *m.* stutterer, stammerer; *adj.* stuttering, stammering.

**tartera** *f.* griddle; baking pan.

**tarugo** *m.* wooden block; wooden peg; blockhead, dunce; *adj. Andes* mischievous, devilish.

**tasa** *f.* measure; standard; rate; appraisal; valuation.

**tasación** *f.* assessment, valuation, appraisal.

**tasajo** *m.* piece of jerked beef.

**tasar** *m.* to measure; to appraise; to rate.

**tata** *f.* daddy, dad; *Mex., Andes* chief (*said by Indians to a superior*); **tatita** *m.* daddy; *Mex., Andes* dear chief or daddy (*said by Indians*).

**tataranieto** *m.* great-great-grandson.

**tauromaquia** *f.* bullfighting.

**taxear** *v.* to taxi (*said of a plane*).

**taxi, taxímetro** *m.* taxi, taxicab.

**taxista** *m. & f.* taxi driver.

**taza** *f.* cup; bowl; basin of a fountain.

**tazón** *m.* large cup; bowl; basin of a fountain.

**té** *m.* tea; *f.* T-square, T-shaped ruler.

**te** *obj. pron.* you (*fam. sing.*); to you; for you; yourself.

**teatral** *adj.* theatrical.

**teatro** *m.* theater; stage; scene, setting; **hacer —** to put on airs, show off.

**tecla** *f.* key (*of a piano, typewriter, etc.*); **dar uno en la —** to hit the nail on the head, find the right way to do something.

**teclado** *m.* keyboard.

**teclear** *v.* to finger the keys; to play the piano; to type.

**tecleo** *m.* fingering; movement of the keys (*typewriter, piano*).

**técnica** *f.* technique.

**técnico** *adj.* technical; *m.* technical expert, technician.

**tecolote** *m. Am.* owl.

**techado** *m.* roof; shed; *p.p. of* **techar.**

**techar** *v.* to roof.

**techo** *m.* roof; ceiling.

**techumbre** *f.* roof; ceiling.

**tedio** *m.* tediousness; boredom; bother.

**tedioso** *adj.* tedious, boring, tiresome.

**teja** *f.* tile; linden tree; *Am.* rear part of a saddle; **de -s abajo** here below, in this world.

**tejado** *m.* roof; shed.

**tejamanil** *m.* shingle; small thin board.

**tejar** *m.* tile factory; *v.* to cover with tiles.

**tejedor** *m.* weaver.

**tejer** *v.* to weave; to interlace; to braid; to knit.

**tejido** *m.* textile, fabric; texture; weave; weaving; tissue.

**tejo** *m.* disk; quoit; weight.

**tejón** *m.* badger; bar of gold.

**tela** *f.* cloth; membrane; web; film (*on the surface of liquids*); **— adhesiva** adhesive tape; **— de cebolla** onion skin; flimsy fabric; *Am.* **— emplástica** court plaster; **— metálica** wire screen; **poner en — de juicio** to call in question.

**telar** *m.* loom.

**telaraña** *f.* cobweb, spider's web.

**teleférico** *m.* telpher; car suspended on aerial cables.

**telefonear** *v.* to telephone.

**telefónico** *adj.* telephonic, telephone (*used as adj.*); **receptor —** telephone receiver.

**teléfono** *m.* telephone; **telefonista** *m. & f.* telephone operator.

**telegrafía** *f.* telegraphy.

**telegrafiar**[17] *v.* to telegraph.

**telegráfico** *adj.* telegraphic.

**telégrafo** *m.* telegraph; **— sin hilos** (*or* **— inalámbrico**) wireless telegraph; **telegrafista** *m. & f.* telegraph operator.

**telegrama** *m.* telegram.

**telescopio** *m.* telescope.

**telesquí** *m.* ski lift.
**teletipo** *m.* teletype.
**televisión** *f.* television.
**telón** *m.* theater curtain; — **de boca** drop curtain; — **de foro** drop scene.
**tema** *m.* theme; subject; *f.* fixed idea, mania.
**temblar**[1] *v. irr.* to tremble; to shake; to quiver.
**temblón** *adj.* tremulous, trembling, shaking, quivering.
**temblor** *m.* tremor, trembling; shiver; quake; — **de tierra** earthquake.
**tembloroso** *adj.* trembling, shaking.
**temer** *v.* to fear; to dread; to suspect.
**temerario** *adj.* rash, reckless.
**temeridad** *f.* temerity, recklessness; folly.
**temeroso** *adj.* fearful; suspicious; timid.
**temible** *adj.* terrible, dreadful.
**temor** *m.* fear; dread, suspicion.
**tempano** *m.* thick slice or chunk (*of anything*); kettledrum; drumhead (*parchment stretched over the end of a drum*); — **de hielo** block of ice; iceberg.
**temperamento** *m.* temperament; climate.
**temperatura** *f.* temperature.
**tempestad** *f.* tempest, storm.
**tempestuoso** *adj.* tempestuous, stormy.
**templado** *p.p.* & *adj.* (*moderado*) tempered; tuned; moderate; temperate; lukewarm; (*valiente*) brave; *Andes* in love; *Am.* half-drunk; *Am.* hard, severe; **estar mal** — to be in a bad humor.
**templanza** *f.* temperance; moderation; mildness.
**templar** *v.* to temper; to moderate; to calm; to soften; to tune; **-se** to be tempered, moderate; to control oneself; *Andes* to fall in love; *Col.* to take to one's heels; *Am.* to stuff oneself.
**temple** *m.* temper; temperament; valor, courage; harmony (*of musical instruments*); *Am.* sweetheart; **de mal** — in a bad humor.
**templo** *m.* temple; church.
**temporada** *f.* period of time, season; — **de ópera** opera season.
**temporal** *adj.* temporal; secular, worldly; temporary; *m.* weather; storm; spell of rainy weather.
**tempranero** *adj.* habitually early or ahead of time; **ser** — to be an early riser.
**temprano** *adj.* early; premature; *adv.* early.
**tenacidad** *f.* tenacity; tenaciousness; perseverance.
**tenacillas** *f. pl.* small tongs; pincers, tweezers; sugar tongs; curling iron.
**tenaz** *adj.* tenacious; firm; strong, resistant; stubborn.
**tenazas** *f. pl.* pincers; pliers; tongs; forceps (*for pulling teeth*); **tenazuelas** *f. pl.* tweezers, small pincers.
**tendedero** *m.* place to hang or spread clothes; clothesline.

**tendencia** *f.* tendency, inclination.
**tender**[1] *v. irr.* (*extender*) to spread out; to hang to dry; to stretch out; to lay out; (*propender*) to tend, have a tendency, move (*toward*); *Mex.*, *C.A.*, *Ríopl.*, *Andes* to make (*a bed*); **-se** to stretch oneself out; to lay all one's cards on the table; to run at full gallop.
**ténder** *m.* tender (*of a train*).
**tendero** *m.* storekeeper; tentmaker.
**tendón** *m.* tendon, sinew.
**tenducho** *m.* wretched little shop.
**tenebroso** *adj.* dark, shadowy; gloomy.
**tenedor** *m.* table fork; holder, possessor, keeper; — **de libros** bookkeeper.
**teneduría** *f.* office and position of bookkeeper; — **de libros** bookkeeping.
**tener**[45] *v. irr.* to have; to possess; to hold; — **en mucho** to esteem highly; — **por** to consider, judge; — **que** (+ *inf.*) to have to; — **gana** (or — **ganas**) **de** to desire, feel like; — **miedo** (**sueño, frío, hambre,** *etc.*) to be afraid (sleepy, cold, hungry, *etc.*); — **. . . años** to be . . . years old; **-se** to stand firm; to hold on.
**tenería** *f.* tannery.
**teniente** *m.* first lieutenant; substitute, deputy.
**tenis** *m.* tennis.
**tenor** *m.* tenor; text, literal meaning; kind, sort, nature.
**tensión** *f.* tension; strain.
**tenso** *adj.* tense; tight, taut.
**tentación** *f.* temptation.
**tentáculo** *m.* tentacle, feeler.
**tentador** *adj.* tempting; *m.* tempter; the devil.
**tentalear** *v.* to grope, feel around; to finger, touch; to fumble (*for something*).
**tentar**[1] *v. irr.* to tempt; to touch, feel with the fingers; to grope; to attempt, try; to test; to probe, examine with a probe.
**tentativa** *f.* attempt, trial.
**tentativo** *adj.* tentative.
**tenue** *adj.* delicate, thin; flimsy; worthless.
**teñir**[5,19] *v. irr.* to dye; to tinge; to darken (*the color of a painting*).
**teologal, teológico** *adj.* theological.
**teología** *f.* theology.
**teoría** *f.* theory.
**teórico** *adj.* theoretical.
**tequila** *m. Mex.* tequila (*liquor made from the maguey plant*).
**tercero** *adj.* third; *m.* third person; mediator; go-between; tertiary (*member of the third order of St. Francis*).
**terciar** *v.* (*atravesar*) to sling across one's shoulders; (*dividir*) to divide into three parts; (*intervenir*) to intervene, mediate; to meddle, join (*in*); (*equilibrar*) to balance the load on a pack animal; *Mex.*, *Col.* to load or carry on the back; *Am.* to adulterate, add water to; *Am.* to mix.
**tercio** *adj.* third; *m.* one third; half of a mule load; military regiment or

**TA**

division; *Col., Carib., Mex.* bale, bundle; **hacer uno mal —** to hinder, interfere; **— de varas** the banderilla part of the bullfight.

**terciopelo** *m.* velvet.

**terco** *adj.* obstinate, stubborn; hard; *Am.* harsh, severe.

**tergiversar** *v.* to distort, twist.

**terminación** *f.* termination, end; ending.

**terminal** *adj.* terminal, final.

**terminante** *adj.* closing, ending; decisive, final.

**terminar** *v.* to terminate, end; to finish; **-se** to end.

**término** *m.* end; completion; goal, object; boundary, limit; terminal; term; word, phrase; **en otros -s** in other words; **por — medio** on an average; as a rule; **primer —** foreground.

**termo** *m.* thermos bottle.

**termómetro** *m.* thermometer.

**termonuclear** *adj.* thermonuclear.

**Termos** *f.* Thermos bottle (*trademark*).

**termóstato** *m.* thermostat.

**ternera** *f.* calf; veal.

**terneza** *f.* tenderness; softness; affection; affectionate word; caress.

**terno** *m.* group or combination of three; suit of clothes; *Carib., Mex.* set of jewels (*earrings, necklace, and brooch*); *Am.* cup and saucer; **echar** (*or* **soltar**) **un —** to utter a bad word; to curse, swear.

**ternura** *f.* tenderness.

**terquedad** *f.* obstinacy, stubbornness.

**terrado** *m.* terrace; flat roof.

**terramicina** *f.* Terramycin.

**terraplén** *m.* railroad embankment.

**terrateniente** *m. & f.* landholder.

**terraza** *f.* terrace, veranda; flat roof.

**terremoto** *m.* earthquake.

**terrenal** *adj.* earthly, worldly.

**terreno** *m.* land; ground; field; *adj.* earthly, worldly.

**terrestre** *adj.* terrestrial; earthly.

**terrible** *adj.* terrible.

**terrífico** *adj.* terrific.

**territorio** *m.* territory.

**terrón** *m.* clod; lump (*of sugar*).

**terror** *m.* terror.

**terso** *adj.* polished, smooth.

**tertulia** *f.* evening party; social gathering; club; conversation; *Ríopl., Cuba, Ven.* theater gallery.

**tertuliano, tertulio** *m.* member of a **tertulia.**

**tesis** *f.* thesis.

**tesón** *m.* grit, endurance, pluck, persistence.

**tesonero** *adj. Mex., Cuba, Andes* tenacious, stubborn, persevering, persistent.

**tesorería** *f.* treasury; **tesorero** *m.* treasurer.

**tesoro** *m.* treasure; treasury.

**testa** *f.* head; crown of the head; front.

**testamento** *m.* testament; will.

**testarudez** *f.* stubbornness, obstinacy.

**testarudo** *adj.* stubborn.

**testigo** *m. & f.* witness; *m.* testimony,

proof, evidence; **— de cargo** witness for the prosecution; **— de vista** eyewitness.

**testimoniar** *v.* to give testimony of; to serve as a witness.

**testimonio** *m.* testimony; proof, evidence; **levantar falso —** to bear false witness.

**testuz** *m.* nape; crown of the head (*of certain animals*).

**teta** *f.* teat, nipple; breast; udder.

**tetera** *f.* teapot; teakettle; *Mex., Cuba, Col.* **tetero** nursing bottle.

**tétrico** *adj.* sad, melancholy, gloomy.

**textil** *adj.* textile.

**texto** *m.* text; quotation; textbook.

**tez** *f.* complexion, skin.

**ti** *pers. pron.* (*used after prep.*) you; yourself (*fam. sing.*).

**tía** *f.* aunt; older woman; *Ven.* **— rica** pawnshop; **no hay tu —** there is no use or hope; there is no way out of it; **quedarse una para —** to remain an old maid.

**tibio** *adj.* tepid, lukewarm; indifferent; *Am.* annoyed, angry.

**tiburón** *m.* shark.

**tico** *adj. & m. Am.* Costa Rican (*humorous nickname*).

**tiempo** *m.* time; weather; tense; **a —** in time, on time; **a su —** in due time, at the proper time; **a un —** at one and the same time; **andando el —** in time, as time goes on.

**tienda** *f.* store; tent; **— de campaña** camping tent, army tent.

**tienta** *f.* probe (*surgical instrument*); **a -s** gropingly, feeling one's way; **andar a -s** to grope, feel one's way.

**tiento** *m.* touch; tact; blind man's stick; steady hand; blow; tentacle, feeler (*of an insect*); *Andes, Ríopl.* saddle strap, leather strap, thong; *Am.* snack; *Am.* swallow of liquor; **dar un —** to make a trial or attempt; **hacer algo con mucho —** to do something with great care or caution; **perder el —** to lose one's skill; *Andes* **tener a uno a los -s** to keep someone within sight; *Ven.* **tener la vida en un —** to be in great danger.

**tierno** *adj.* tender; soft; young; recent, new; sensitive; affectionate; *Am.* green, unripe.

**tierra** *f.* earth; land; ground; soil; native land; **— adentro** inland; **— firme** mainland; solid ground; **dar en — con alguien** to overthrow someone; **echar por —** to knock down; to demolish; **tomar —** to land.

**tieso** *adj.* stiff, rigid; stuck-up; firm; stubborn.

**tiesto** *m.* flowerpot; broken piece of earthenware; *Am.* pot.

**tiesura** *f.* stiffness.

**tifo** *m.* typhus; **tifoidea** *f.* typhoid fever.

**tifón** *m.* typhoon; waterspout.

**tifus** *m.* typhus.

**tigre** *m.* tiger.

**tijera** *f.* (*usually* **tijeras**) scissors; sawhorse; **silla de —** folding chair; **tener buena —** (*or* **tener buenas -s**) to have a sharp tongue; to be a gossip.

**tijeretada** *f.*, **tijeretazo** *m.* snip, cut, clip (*with the scissors*).

**tijeretear** *v.* to snip, cut, clip (*with scissors*); to criticize others, gossip.

**tildar** *v.* to accent (*a word*); to put a tilde over the **n;** to stigmatize.

**tilde** *f.* tilde (*mark over an* **n**); blemish; jot, bit, speck; *Col.* accent mark.

**timbrar** *v.* to stamp, mark with a seal.

**timbre** *m.* revenue stamp; seal; crest (*on a coat of arms*); call bell; timbre (*quality of tone, tone color*); merit, fame; glorious deed; *Am.* postage stamp.

**timidez** *f.* timidity; shyness.

**tímido** *adj.* timid; shy.

**timón** *m.* helm; rudder; beam of a plow.

**timonear** *v.* to steer (*a ship*).

**timorato** *adj.* timorous, timid.

**tímpano** *m.* eardrum; kettledrum.

**tina** *f.* large earthen jar; vat, tank, tub; bathtub.

**tinaco** *m.* tank, vat, tub.

**tinaja** *f.* large earthen jar.

**tinieblas** *f. pl.* darkness; obscurity; ignorance, confusion; Tenebrae (*Holy Week religious service*).

**tino** *m.* acumen, keen insight, good judgment; tact; accurate aim; good sense of touch; tank, vat.

**tinta** *f.* ink; dye; tint, hue; **-s** paints; **— simpática** invisible ink; **saber de buena —** to know on good authority.

**tinte** *m.* tint, hue; tinge; color; dye; dyeing.

**tinterillo** *m.* shyster. *See* **picapleitos.**

**tintero** *m.* inkwell, inkstand; ink roller (*printing*); *Am.* writing materials, desk set.

**tintinear** *v.* to tinkle.

**tintineo** *m.* tinkle, tinkling.

**tinto** *adj.* tinged; red (*wine*); *Am.* dark-red; *p.p. irr. of* **teñir.**

**tintorería** *f.* cleaner's and dyer's shop.

**tintorero** *m.* dyer.

**tintura** *f.* tincture; tint, color; dye.

**tinturar** *v.* to tincture; to tinge; to dye.

**tiñoso** *adj.* scabby, mangy; stingy.

**tío** *m.* uncle; old man; good old man; fellow, guy; *Ríopl., Mex., Ven., Andes* **el cuento del —** deceitful story (*told to extract money*).

**tiovivo** *m.* merry-go-round.

**típico** *adj.* typical; *Am.* corrected (*edition*).

**tiple** *m. & f.* high soprano singer; *m.* treble; soprano voice; treble guitar.

**tipo** *m.* type; class; model, standard; fellow, guy; *Am.* rate of interest; *Am.* **— de cambio** rate of exchange; **buen —** good-looking fellow.

**tipografía** *f.* typography, printing; press, printing shop.

**tira** *f.* strip; stripe; *Mex.* **estar hecho -s** to be in rags; *Ven.* **sacar a uno las -s** to tan one's hide, beat one to pieces.

**tirabuzón** *m.* corkscrew.

**tirada** *f.* throw; issue, edition, printing;

*Am.* tirade, long speech; *Am.* sly trick; *Am.* dash (*on horseback*); **de una —** all at once, at one fell swoop.

**tirador** *m.* shooter; thrower; slingshot; bell cord; handle; printer; *Am.* leather belt with pockets; **— de goma** slingshot.

**tiranía** *f.* tyranny.

**tiránico** *adj.* tyrannical.

**tirano** *adj.* tyrannical; *m.* tyrant.

**tirante** *adj.* pulling; stretched, taut; strained; *m.* trace (*of a harness*); brace; **-s** suspenders; supporters (*for stockings*).

**tirantez** *f.* tension, tightness; strain; pull.

**tirar** *v.* (*lanzar*) to throw; to throw away; to shoot, fire; (*imprimir*) to draw; to print; (*atraer*) to pull; to attract; *Am.* to cart; **— a** to tend toward; to resemble; to aim at; **— de** to pull, tug; **— bien a la espada** to handle a sword well; **ir tirando** to get along; **a todo** (*or* **a más**) **—** at the most; *Am.* **al —** haphazardly; **-se** to throw oneself; to lie down; *Mex., C.A., Col., Ven., Ríopl., Andes* **tirársela de** to boast of.

**tiritar** *v.* to shiver.

**tiro** *m.* (*disparo*) throw; shot; (*pieza*) piece of artillery; (*alcance*) range of a gun; shooting range; (*carga*) charge of a gun; team (*of horses*); chimney draft; mine shaft; *Am.* issue, printing; *Am.* cartage, transport; **-s** *Am.* suspenders; **— al blanco** target practice; *Ch., Andes* **al —** at once; *Ven.* **de a —** (*or* **de al**) all at once; completely; **caballo de —** draft horse; **ni a -s** absolutely not (*not even if you shoot me*).

**tirón** *m.* jerk, sudden pull; **de un —** all at once, with one big pull.

**tironear** *v. C.A., Mex., Ríopl.* to pull, jerk; *Col.* to attract.

**tirotear** *v.* to shoot around; to shoot at random; **-se** to exchange shots.

**tiroteo** *m.* shooting; exchange of shots; skirmish.

**tirria** *f.* aversion, grudge; **tenerle — a una persona** to have a strong dislike for someone; to hold a grudge against someone.

**tísico** *adj.* tubercular, consumptive.

**tisis** *f.* tuberculosis, consumption.

**títere** *m.* puppet; ridiculous little fellow; **-s** puppet show.

**titilación** *f.* flicker; twinkle; **titileo** *m.* flickering; twinkling; glimmer.

**titilar** *v.* to flicker; to twinkle.

**titubear** *v.* to hesitate; to totter, stagger; to grope; to stutter, stammer.

**titubeo** *m.* hesitation, wavering.

**titular** *v.* to entitle; to name; **-se** to be called or named; to call oneself; to receive a title; *adj.* titular, in name only.

**título** *m.* (*letrero*) title; heading; sign; inscription; (*derecho*) claim, legal right; (*grado*) degree, diploma; credential; titled person; merit; bond, certificate; **a — de** under the pre-

**TE**

text of; in the capacity of.

**tiza** *f.* chalk.

**tiznado** *adj.* sooty, covered with soot; smutty; dirty; *Ven.* drunk; *p.p.* of **tiznar.**

**tiznar** *v.* to smudge, smut; to smear with soot.

**tizne** *m.* soot; smut; **tiznón** *m.* smudge.

**tizón** *m.* firebrand (*piece of burning wood*); rust, blight (*on plants*); stain (*on one's honor*).

**toalla** *f.* towel.

**tobillo** *m.* ankle.

**tocadiscos** *m.* record player; phonograph.

**tocado** *m.* headdress; hairdo, coiffure; *adj.* "touched", half-crazy; *p.p.* of **tocar.**

**tocador** *m.* dressing table; boudoir, dressing room; dressing case; player (*of a musical instrument*).

**tocar**[6] *v.* to touch; to play (*an instrument*); to toll, ring; to knock, rap; — **en** to stop over in; **-le a uno** to fall to one's lot; to be one's share; to be one's turn; to concern one; **-se** to fix one's hair; to become "touched", go slightly crazy.

**tocayo** *m.* namesake.

**tocino** *m.* bacon; salt pork; lard.

**tocón** *m.* stub, stump (*of a tree, arm or leg*).

**todavía** *adv.* still; yet; even.

**todo** *adj.* all, whole; every, each; — **hombre** every man; **-s los días** every day; **a — correr** at full or top speed; *m.* whole; all; everything; **-s** everybody; **ante —** first of all; **así y — in spite of that; con —** in spite of that; **del —** wholly.

**todopoderoso** *adj.* almighty.

**toga** *f.* gown, robe (*worn by a judge, professor, etc.*); Roman toga.

**toldería** *f. Ríopl.* Indian camp, Indian village.

**toldo** *m.* awning; pomp, vanity; *Ríopl.* Indian hut.

**tolerancia** *f.* tolerance, toleration; **tolerante** *adj.* tolerant.

**tolerar** *v.* to tolerate; to allow; to overlook, let pass.

**tolete** *m. Col., Mex., Cuba* stick, club, cudgel; *Am.* raft.

**toma** *f.* taking; seizure, capture; dose; tap (*of a water main*); *Am.* irrigation ditch; **— de corriente** plug, electric outlet.

**tomar** *v.* (*asir*) to take; to grasp, catch; to capture; (*beber*) to drink; **— a pechos** to take to heart, take seriously; **-lo a mal** to take it amiss; **— el pelo a** to make fun of, make a fool of; **— por la derecha** to turn to the right; **-se con** to quarrel with.

**tomate** *m.* tomato.

**tomillo** *m.* thyme.

**tomo** *m.* tome, volume; *Am.* heavy person; *Am.* dull, silent person; *Am.* **buen —** a heavy drinker; **de — y lomo** bulky; important.

**ton: sin — ni son** without rhyme or reason.

**tonada** *f.* tune, song; *Andes* singsong; *Andes, Mex., Carib., Ríopl.* local accent; **tonadilla** *f.* little tune; short popular song.

**tonel** *m.* keg, cask, barrel.

**tonelada** *f.* ton.

**tonelaje** *m.* tonnage.

**tónico** *adj.* & *m.* tonic.

**tono** *m.* tone; tune; key, pitch; accent; manner; vigor, strength; **de buen —** of good taste, stylish; **subirse de —** to put on airs.

**tontera** = **tontería.**

**tontería** *f.* foolishness; stupidity.

**tonto** *adj.* foolish; stupid; **a tontas y a locas** recklessly, without thought; *m.* fool; dunce; *Col., Ch.* a game of cards.

**topar** *v.* to collide with, run into, bump into; to encounter; to find; to run across; to butt; *Am.* to gamble; *Col.* to fight with the fists; *Carib., Mex., Ríopl., Andes, Col.* to meet, greet.

**tope** *m.* butt, bump, collision; encounter; bumper; **hasta el —** up to the top; **estar hasta los -s** to be filled up.

**topetada** *f.*, **topetazo** *m.* butt; bump, blow on the head; **topetón** *m.* hard bump, collision; butt.

**topetear** *v.* to butt; to bump.

**tópico** *m.* topic, subject.

**topo** *m.* mole (*small animal*); dunce; awkward person.

**toque** *m.* touch; ringing; beat (*of a drum*); tap, sound (*of a trumpet, clarinet, etc.*); assay; **piedra de —** touchstone; **¡allí está el — !** there is the difficulty!; there is the real test!

**toquilla** *f.* triangular handkerchief; ribbon; hatband.

**torbellino** *m.* whirlwind; rush, bustle, confusion.

**torcedura** *f.* twist; sprain, strain.

**torcer**[2,10] *v. irr.* to twist; to turn; to bend; to sprain; to distort; **-se** to become twisted, bent, or sprained; to get crooked; to go astray; to turn sour (*said of wine*); *Am.* to get offended, angry.

**torcido** *p.p.* & *adj.* twisted, turned, bent; crooked; angry, resentful; *Am.* unfortunate, unlucky; **estar — con** to be on unfriendly terms with; *m.* twisted roll of candied fruit; coarse silk twist; *Mex., Carib.* gesture or look of disdain; *Andes* lasso made of twisted leather.

**tordillo** *adj.* greyish, dapple-grey.

**tordo** *adj.* dapple-grey; *m.* thrush; dapple-grey horse.

**torear** *v.* to perform in a bullfight; to incite, provoke (*a bull*); to tease.

**torero** *m.* bullfighter; *adj.* relating to bullfighting.

**tormenta** *f.* storm, tempest; misfortune.

**tormento** *m.* torment; torture; rack (*instrument of torture*); anguish; pain.

**tornar** *v.* to return; to turn; to change, alter; **— a hacerlo** to do it again.

**tornasolado** *adj.* iridescent, rainbow-colored; changeable (*silk*).

**tornear** *v.* to turn in a lathe; to do lathe work; to fight in a tournament.

**torneo** *m.* tournament.

**tornillo** *m.* screw; clamp, vise; **faltarle a uno un —** to have little sense, "have a screw loose".

**torno** *m.* turn; lathe; turnstile; revolving server; winch or windlass (*machine for lifting or pulling, turned by a crank*); **— de hilar** spinning wheel; **en —** around.

**toro** *m.* bull; *Mex., Col.* difficult question; **-s** bullfight; *Am.* **estar en las astas del —** to be in a predicament.

**toronja** *f.* grapefruit.

**torpe** *adj.* stupid, dull; clumsy; slow; lewd.

**torpedear** *v.* to torpedo.

**torpedo** *m.* torpedo; **torpedero** *m.* torpedo boat.

**torpeza** *f.* stupidity, dullness; clumsiness; slowness; moral turpitude, lewdness.

**torre** *f.* tower; turret; castle (*in chess*).

**torrente** *m.* torrent; flood; **— de voz** powerful voice.

**torreón** *m.* large tower (*of a fortress, castle, etc.*).

**tórrido** *adj.* torrid.

**torsión** *f.* twist; sprain.

**torta** *f.* torte, round cake; round loaf.

**tortilla** *f.* omelet; *Mex., C.A.* tortilla (*flat, thin cornmeal cake*).

**tórtola** *f.* turtledove.

**tortuga** *f.* tortoise; turtle.

**tortuoso** *adj.* tortuous, twisting, winding; sly.

**tortura** *f.* torture; grief, affliction.

**torturar** *v.* to torture.

**torvo** *adj.* grim, stern, severe.

**tos** *f.* cough; **— ferina** whooping cough.

**tosco** *adj.* coarse, harsh, rough.

**toser** *v.* to cough; *Am.* to brag, boast.

**tosquedad** *f.* coarseness, crudeness, roughness; rudeness.

**tostada** *f.* toast, toasted bread; *Am.* boring visit or conversation; *Ven.* toasted **tortilla; dar** (*or* **pegar**) **una — a uno** to play a mean trick on someone; *Am.* to make someone very angry.

**tostado** *p.p.* & *adj.* toasted; roasted; tanned; *Am.* worn out, tired out; *m.* toasting; *Am.* roasted corn.

**tostador** *m.* toaster.

**tostar**[2] *v. irr.* to toast; to tan; to overheat; to roast (*coffee*).

**tostón** *m.* toast dipped in oil; small roasted pig; *Mex., C.A.* coin worth half a Mexican peso.

**total** *adj.* & *m.* total.

**totalidad** *f.* entirety, whole.

**totalitario** *adj.* totalitarian.

**tóxico** *adj.* toxic.

**toxina** *f.* toxin (*poison produced within animals and plants*).

**toza** *f.* wooden block; stump; log; piece of bark.

**traba** *f.* bond, tie; binding or locking device; fastener, fetter, shackle; hindrance, obstacle.

**trabado** *adj. Col., Ríopl., Mex.* tonguetied; *p.p. of* **trabar.**

**trabajador** *adj.* industrious; *m.* worker, laborer.

**trabajar** *v.* to work; to labor; to strive.

**trabajo** *m.* work; labor; difficulty, obstacle; trouble; hardship.

**trabajoso** *adj.* laborious, difficult; troublesome; *Am.* unobliging; *Am.* demanding.

**trabalenguas** *m.* tongue twister.

**trabar** *v.* to join, fasten; to clasp; to shackle; to brace; to impede; **— amistad con alguien** to become friends with someone; **— batalla** to join in battle; **— conversación** to be engaged in conversation; to engage in conversation; **-se** *Ríopl., Mex., Ven.* to stammer; **-se de palabras** to get into an argument.

**tracción** *f.* traction.

**tractor** *m.* tractor.

**tradición** *f.* tradition.

**tradicional** *adj.* traditional.

**traducción** *f.* translation.

**traducir**[25] *v. irr.* to translate; to interpret.

**traductor** *m.* translator.

**traer**[46] *v. irr.* to bring; to carry; to lead, conduct; to have; to bring about; to wear; **— a uno inquieto** to keep one disturbed; **— a uno a mal —** to mistreat someone; to bother someone; **-se bien** to dress well; to carry oneself well.

**trafagar**[7] *v.* to traffic, trade; to roam about; to bustle, hustle; to toil.

**tráfago** *m.* trade, commerce; bustle, hustle; toil.

**traficante** *m.* trader; dealer; tradesman.

**traficar**[6] *v.* to traffic, trade; *Ven.* to pass or move back and forth (*as traffic*). *See* **transitar.**

**tráfico** *m.* traffic; trade, commerce.

**tragaluz** *f.* skylight.

**tragar**[7] *v.* to swallow; to gulp; to engulf, swallow up.

**tragedia** *f.* tragedy.

**trágico** *adj.* tragic.

**trago** *m.* swallow, gulp; misfortune; *Am.* brandy, hard liquor; **a -s** slowly, by degrees; **echar un —** to take a drink; **tragón** *m.* glutton; *adj.* gluttonous.

**traición** *f.* treason; treachery; **a —** treacherously; deceitfully.

**traicionar** *v.* to betray.

**traicionero** *adj.* treacherous; deceitful; *m.* traitor.

**traído** *adj.* used, old, worn out; **muy — y llevado** very worn out; *p.p. of* **traer.**

**traidor** *adj.* treacherous; *m.* traitor; betrayer.

**traje** *m.* dress; suit; gown; **— de etiqueta** (**— de ceremonia**, *or Am.* **— de parada**) formal gown; formal suit; dress uniform; **— de luces**

bullfighter's costume; *Col.*, *C.A.*, *Mex.*, *Ríopl.* — **sastre** woman's tailor-made suit.

**trajeado** *p.p.* & *adj.* dressed, clothed.

**trajín** *m.* traffic, going and coming; hustle, bustle, commotion.

**trajinar** *v.* to carry, cart back and forth; to go back and forth; to bustle, hustle.

**trama** *f.* plot; scheme; conspiracy; woof (*horizontal threads of a fabric*).

**tramar** *v.* to weave; to plot; to scheme.

**tramitar** *v.* to transact; to take legal steps; to negotiate.

**trámite** *m.* transaction, procedure, step, formality.

**tramo** *m.* stretch, lap, span; short distance; regular interval; flight of stairs.

**trampa** *f.* trap; snare; hatch, trap door; hinged section of a counter; spring door; fraud; trick.

**trampear** *v.* to trick, cheat, swindle.

**trampista** *m.* & *f.* cheat, crook, swindler.

**trampolín** *m.* springboard.

**tramposo** *adj.* deceitful, tricky; *m.* swindler, cheat.

**tranca** *f.* crossbar, bolt; pole, prop; club, stick; *Ven.*, *Ríopl.* rustic gate; *Ríopl.* fence with gates; *Mex.*, *Ven.* **saltar las -s** to jump over the fence; to lose one's patience, rebel, get angry; *Ch.*, *Ríopl.*, *Andes*, *Mex.* **tener una —** to be drunk.

**trance** *m.* critical moment; dangerous situation; **el último —** the last moment of life; **a todo —** at any cost, cost what it may.

**tranco** *m.* stride, long step; threshold; **a -s** hurriedly; **en dos -s** in a jiffy; *Ríopl.* **al —** striding, with long steps.

**tranquear** *v.* to stride along.

**tranquera** *f.* stockade, wooden fence; *Ríopl.*, *Cuba*, *Ven.* large gate (*made with* **trancas**).

**tranquilidad** *f.* tranquillity, peacefulness.

**tranquilizar**[9] *v.* to quiet, calm down; to pacify; **-se** to become tranquil, calm down.

**tranquilo** *adj.* tranquil, peaceful.

**transacción** *f.* transaction, negotiation; compromise.

**transar** *v. Am.* to compromise, yield, give in.

**transatlántico** *adj.* transatlantic; *m.* transatlantic steamer.

**transbordar = trasbordar.**

**transbordo = trasbordo.**

**transcendencia** *f.* consequence, importance; penetration.

**transcendental** *adj.* consequential, important, far-reaching.

**transcurrir** *v.* to pass, elapse.

**transcurso** *m.* passing, lapse (*of time*).

**transeúnte** *m.* passer-by; pedestrian; transient; *adj.* transient.

**transferencia** *f.* transference, transfer.

**transferir**[3] *v. irr.* to transfer.

**transformación** *f.* transformation.

**transformador** *m.* transformer.

**transformar** *v.* to transform.

**transgredir**[51] *v.* to transgress.

**transgresión** *f.* transgression.

**transgresor** *m.* transgressor, offender.

**transición** *f.* transition.

**transigente** *adj.* compromising, yielding, pliable.

**transigir**[11] *v.* to compromise, yield, make concessions; to settle by compromise.

**transistor** *m.* transistor.

**transitable** *adj.* passable (*road*).

**transitar** *v.* to pass or move back and forth (*as traffic*).

**tránsito** *m.* transit; traffic; passing; passage; transition; **de —** on the way, in transit, passing through.

**transitorio** *adj.* transitory.

**transmisión** *f.* transmission; **— automática** automatic transmission.

**transmisor** *m.* transmitter; *adj.* transmitting.

**transmitir** *v.* to transmit.

**transparencia** *f.* transparency.

**transparente** *adj.* transparent; lucid, clear; *m.* window shade; stained-glass window.

**transponer**[40] *v. irr.* to transpose; to transfer; to transplant; to go beyond, go over to the other side; **-se** to hide from view, go behind; to set, go below the horizon.

**transportación** *f.* transportation, transport.

**transportar** *v.* to transport; to transpose (*music*); **-se** to be transported, carried away by strong feeling; to be in ecstasy.

**transporte** *m.* transport; transportation; transport vessel; ecstasy; **— de locura** fit of madness.

**transpuesto** *p.p.* of **transponer.**

**transversal** *adj.* transversal, transverse; **sección —** cross section.

**transverso** *adj.* transverse, cross.

**tranvía** *m.* streetcar; streetcar track.

**trapacear** *v.* to swindle, cheat; to racketeer.

**trapacería** *f.* racket, fraud, swindle.

**trapacero** *m.* racketeer; cheat, swindler; *adj.* cheating, deceiving.

**trapacista** *m.* & *f.* racketeer; swindler, cheat.

**trapeador** *m. Am.* mopper; *Andes*, *Ven.*, *Col.*, *C.A.*, *Mex.*, *Cuba* mop.

**trapear** *v. Am.* to mop; *Am.* to beat up, give (*someone*) a licking.

**trapiche** *m.* sugar mill; press (*for extracting juices*); *Andes* grinding machine (*for pulverizing minerals*).

**trapisonda** *f.* escapade, prank; brawl; noisy spree.

**trapo** *m.* rag; *C.A.*, *Ven.*, *Ur.* cloth; **-s** clothes; **a todo —** at full sail; speedily; **poner a uno como un —** to make one feel like a rag; **sacarle a uno los -s al sol** to exhibit somebody's dirty linen; **soltar el —** to burst out laughing or crying.

**traposo** *adj. Am.* ragged, tattered, in

rags.

**tráquea** *f.* trachea, windpipe.

**traquetear** *v.* to rattle; to shake; to jolt; to crack, crackle.

**traqueteo** *m.* rattling; shaking; jolting; cracking, crackling; *Ríopl.. Col., Ven., C.A., Mex., Carib., Andes* uproar, din; *Am.* noisy, disorderly traffic.

**tras** *prep.* after; in search of; behind, in back of; **— de** behind, after; besides, in addition to; *interj.* ¡ **—** ! bang!

**trasbordar** *v.* to transfer.

**trasbordo** *m.* transfer.

**trascendencia** = **transcendencia**.

**trascendental** = **transcendental**.

**trasegar**[1,7] *v. irr.* to upset, overturn; to change from one place to another; to pour from one container to another.

**trasero** *adj.* rear, hind, back; *m.* rump.

**trasladar** *v.* to move, remove; to transfer; to postpone; to translate; to transcribe, copy.

**traslado** *m.* transfer; transcript, written copy.

**traslucirse**[13] *v. irr.* to be translucent; to be transparent, clear, evident.

**trasnochar** *v.* to sit up all night; to stay awake all night; to spend the night out.

**traspalar** *v.* to shovel.

**traspapelar** *v.* to mislay, misplace (*a paper, letter, document, etc.*); **-se** to become mislaid among other papers.

**traspasar** *v.* to pass over, cross over; to go beyond; to pass through; to pierce; to transfer (*property*); to trespass.

**traspaso** *m.* transfer; transgression, trespass.

**traspié** *m.* stumble, slip; **dar un —** to stumble or trip.

**trasplantar** *v.* to transplant.

**trasponer**[40] = **transponer**.

**trasquila, trasquiladura** *f.* shearing, clip, clipping; bad haircut.

**trasquilar** *v.* to shear; to clip; to crop; to cut badly (*hair*).

**trastazo** *m.* thump, blow.

**traste** *m.* fret, stop (*of a guitar*); *Am.* utensil, implement; **dar al — con** to destroy, ruin.

**trasto** *m.* household utensil; piece of junk; rubbish, trash; **-s** utensils; implements; **-s de pescar** fishing tackle.

**trastornar** *v.* to overturn; to upset; to disturb.

**trastorno** *m.* upset; disorder; disturbance.

**trastrocar**[2,6] *v. irr.* to invert, change; to upset.

**trasudar** *v.* to perspire, sweat slightly.

**trasudor** *m.* slight perspiration or sweat.

**tratable** *adj.* friendly, sociable; manageable.

**tratado** *m.* treaty; treatise.

**tratamiento** *m.* treatment; title of courtesy; form of address.

**tratante** *m. & f.* dealer, tradesman, trader.

**tratar** *v.* to treat; to handle; to dis-

cuss; to have social relations with; **— con** to have dealings with; **— de** to try to; to treat of, deal with; **-le a uno de** to address someone as; to treat someone as; **— en** to deal in; **-se bien** to treat oneself well; to behave well; **-se de** to be a question of; **no se trata de eso** that isn't the question, that isn't the point.

**trato** *m.* (*acuerdo*) treatment; deal, pact; trade; (*manera*) manner, behavior; social relations; dealings; *Am.* **— pampa** unfair deal; ¡**— hecho!** it's a deal!; **tener buen —** to be affable, sociable.

**través** *m.* crossbeam; reverse, misfortune; **a** (*or* **al**) **— de** through, across; **de —** across; **dar al — con** to ruin, destroy; to squander; **mirar de —** to squint in a sinister manner.

**travesaño** *m.* crosspiece, crossbar; bolster, long bedpillow; *Ven., Andes* railway tie.

**travesear** *v.* to romp, frisk, frolic; to fool around; to misbehave.

**travesía** *f.* crossing; sea voyage; wind blowing towards a coast; *Am.* wasteland, desert land; *Am.* partition wall or fence.

**travesura** *f.* mischief; prank; lively wit.

**traviesa** *f.* railway tie; rafter, crossbeam; *Col.* midyear crop.

**travieso** *adv.* mischievous; lively; restless; **a campo —** (*or* **a campo traviesa**) cross-country.

**trayecto** *m.* run, stretch, lap, distance (*traveled over*).

**trayectoria** *f.* path (*of a bullet, missile, etc.*).

**traza** *f.* (*plan*) plan; design; plot; invention; (*apariencia*) appearance; semblance; aspect; indication, sign; **darse -s** to use one's wits or ingenuity; **tener -s de** to have the appearance or signs of; **tiene** (*or* **lleva**) **-s de no acabar nunca** it looks as if he would never end.

**trazado** *m.* draft, plan, sketch, outline; drawing; *p.p. & adj.* traced, sketched, outlined.

**trazar**[9] *v.* to trace, sketch; to draw, mark out; to plan.

**trébol** *m.* clover.

**trecho** *m.* space, distance; lap (*in a race*); **a -s** by or at intervals; **de — en —** at certain points or intervals; from time to time.

**tregua** *f.* truce; rest, respite.

**tremedal** *m.* quagmire, bog.

**tremendo** *adj.* tremendous, huge; terrible.

**trementina** *f.* turpentine.

**tremolar** *v.* to flutter, wave (*as a flag*).

**trémolo** *m.* tremolo (*of the voice*), quaver.

**trémulo** *adj.* tremulous, trembling, quivering; flickering.

**tren** *m.* train; *Am.* traffic; **— correo** mail train; **— de aterrizaje** landing gear; *Ven., Carib.* **— de lavado**

**TR**

laundry; *Cuba, Ven.* — **de mudadas** moving company; — **de recreo** excursion train; — **mixto** freight and passenger train.

**trenza** *f.* tress; braid; *Mex., Cuba, Ven.* string (*of garlic, onions, etc.*); **trencilla** *f.* braid.

**trenzar**⁹ *v.* to braid; **-se** to braid one's hair; *Ríopl., Andes, Col.* to fight hand to hand.

**trepar** *v.* to climb; to clamber; **-se** to climb; to clamber; to perch.

**trepidación** *f.* jar, vibration; trembling, shaking.

**trepidar** *v.* to shape, vibrate, tremble, jar.

**treta** *f.* trick, wile; **malas -s** bad tricks, bad habits.

**triángulo** *m.* triangle.

**tribu** *f.* tribe.

**tribulación** *f.* tribulation, trouble.

**tribuna** *f.* rostrum (*speaker's platform*).

**tribunal** *m.* tribunal; court of justice; body of judges.

**tributar** *v.* to pay tribute, pay homage.

**tributario** *adj. & m.* tributary.

**tributo** *m.* tribute; contribution, tax.

**trifulca** *f.* fight, quarrel, wrangle, row.

**trigo** *m.* wheat.

**trigueño** *adj.* swarthy; brunet; dark.

**trillado** *p.p.* beaten; *adj.* trite, hackneyed, commonplace; **camino —** beaten path.

**trilladora** *f.* threshing machine.

**trillar** *v.* to thresh; to beat, mistreat; *Cuba* to cut a path.

**trimestre** *m.* quarter, period of three months; quarterly payment, income, or salary; **trimestral** *adj.* quarterly.

**trinar** *v.* to trill (*in singing*); to warble; to quaver (*said of the voice*); to get furious.

**trinchante** *m.* carving fork; carving knife; carver.

**trinchar** *v.* to carve (*meat*).

**trinche** *m. Col., Ven., C.A., Mex.* fork; *Am.* carving table; *Am.* **plato —** carving platter.

**trinchera** *f.* trench; ditch; *C.A., Ven., Andes* stockade, fence; *Am.* curved knife.

**trinchero** *m.* carving table; **plato —** carving platter.

**trineo** *m.* sleigh; sled.

**trino** *m.* trill (*in singing*).

**tripa** *f.* intestine, bowel; paunch, belly; **-s** entrails, insides.

**triple** *adj. & m.* triple.

**triplicar**⁶ *v.* to triplicate, triple, treble.

**tripulación** *f.* crew, ship's company.

**tripular** *v.* to man (*a ship*).

**trique** *m.* crack, snap; *Mex.* utensil, trinket; *Col.* clever trick in a game; *Am.* drink made from barley; **-s** *Mex.* poor household utensils, goods, etc.

**triscar**⁶ *v.* to romp, frisk, frolic; to stamp or shuffle the feet; *Am.* to tease, make fun of.

**triste** *adj.* sad; sorrowful; *Mex.* bashful, backward; *m. Ríopl.* melancholy love song.

**tristeza** *f.* sadness; sorrow; *Am.* tick fever.

**tristón** *adj.* wistful, quite sad, melancholy.

**triunfal** *adj.* triumphal.

**triunfante** *adj.* triumphant.

**triunfar** *v.* to triumph; to trump (*at cards*).

**triunfo** *m.* triumph; trump card; trophy.

**trivial** *adj.* trivial, commonplace, trite.

**triza** *f.* shred, fragment, small piece; cord, rope (*for sails*); **hacer -s** to tear into shreds; to tear to pieces.

**trocar**²,⁶ *v. irr.* to change; to barter, exchange; to do one thing instead of another; **-se** to change; to be transformed; to exchange.

**trocha** *f.* path, trail; *Ríopl.* gauge (*of a railway*); *Col.* trot; *Am.* slice or serving of meat.

**trofeo** *m.* trophy; booty, spoils.

**troj, troje** *m.* barn, granary.

**trole** *m.* trolley.

**tromba** *f.* waterspout.

**trombón** *m.* trombone.

**trompa** *f.* trumpet; trunk of an elephant; large spinning top; *Am.* snout; *Col.* cowcatcher (*of a locomotive*).

**trompada** *f.* blow with the first; bump.

**trompeta** *f.* trumpet; *m.* trumpeter; useless individual; *Andes* drunk, drunkard; *Andes* bold, shameless fellow.

**trompetear** *v.* to trumpet, blow the trumpet.

**trompo** *m.* spinning top; stupid fellow, dunce.

**tronada** *f.* thunderstorm.

**tronar**² *v. irr.* to thunder; to explode, burst; *Mex., C.A.* to execute by shooting; — **los dedos** to snap one's fingers; **por lo que pueda —** just in case.

**tronco** *m.* tree trunk; log; stem; trunk (*of the human body*); team (*of horses*).

**tronchar** *v.* to bend or break (*a stalk or trunk*); to chop off; to break off; **-se** to break off or get bent (*said of a stalk or trunk*); *Col.* to get twisted or bent.

**tronera** *f.* opening; porthole (*through which to shoot*); small, narrow window; pocket of a billiard table; *m.* madcap, reckless fellow.

**tronido** *m.* thunder; detonation; sharp, sudden sound.

**trono** *m.* throne.

**tropa** *f.* troop; crowd; *Ríopl.* herd of cattle, drove of horses (*often* **tropilla**).

**tropel** *m.* throng; bustle, rush; jumble, confusion.

**tropezar**¹,⁹ *v. irr.* to stumble; to blunder; — **con** to meet, come across, encounter.

**tropezón** *m.* stumbling; stumble; slip; **a -es** falteringly, stumbling along clumsily; **darse un —** to stumble, trip.

**tropical** *adj.* tropical.

**trópico** *m.* tropic.

**tropiezo** *m.* stumble; stumbling block; slip, fault; dispute.

**tropilla** *f.* small troop; *Am.* drove of horses guided by the **madrina;** *Mex.* pack of dogs; *Am.* group of spare saddle horses.

**tropillero** *m. Am.* horse wrangler, herdsman.

**trotar** *v.* to trot; to hurry.

**trote** *m.* trot; **al —** quickly.

**trovador** *m.* troubadour, minstrel.

**troza** *f.* log.

**trozar**[9] *v.* to cut off, break off (*a piece*); to break or cut into pieces.

**trozo** *m.* piece, bit, fragment; passage, selection.

**truco** *m.* clever trick; pocketing of a ball (*in the game of pool*); *Am.* blow with the fist; *Andes, Ríopl.* a card game; **-s** game of pool (*game similar to billiards*).

**truculencia** *f.* cruelty, ferocity, ruthlessness.

**truculento** *adj.* cruel, fierce, ruthless.

**trucha** *f.* trout; *Am.* vendor's portable stand.

**trueno** *m.* thunder; explosion, report of a gun; wild youth, troublemaker; *Am.* firecracker, rocket.

**trueque, trueco** *m.* exchange; barter; *Col., Ven., Andes* change, small money; **a** (*or* **en) — de** in exchange for.

**truhán** *m.* scoundrel; swindler; cheat; buffoon, jester.

**tu** *adj.* thy; your (*fam. sing.*).

**tú** *pers. pron.* thou; you (*fam. sing.*).

**tualet = lavabo.**

**tuberculosis** *f.* tuberculosis; **tuberculoso** *adj.* tuberculous, tubercular.

**tubería** *f.* tubing, piping; pipe line.

**tubo** *m.* tube; pipe; lamp chimney; **— de ensayo** test tube; **— de escape** tail pipe.

**tuerca** *f.* nut (*of a screw*); **llave de -s** wrench.

**tuerto** *adj.* one-eyed; blind in one eye; *m.* wrong, injustice; **a — o a derecho** (*or* **a tuertas o a derechas**) rightly or wrongly; thoughtlessly.

**tuétano** *m.* marrow; pith; innermost part; **mojado hasta los -s** soaked through and through.

**tufo** *m.* vapor, fume; disagreeable odor; airs, conceit; **tufillo** *m.* whiff, pungent odor.

**tul** *m.* tulle (*a thin, fine net for veils*); **tul, tule** *m. Mex.* a kind of reed or bulrush (*used in the manufacture of seats and backs of chairs*).

**tulipán** *m.* tulip.

**tullido** *p.p.* crippled; paralyzed; numb.

**tullirse**[20] *v. irr.* to become crippled; to become numb or paralyzed.

**tumba** *f.* tomb; grave; *Col., Cuba, Mex.* felling of timber; *Ven.* forest clearing.

**tumbar** *v.* to knock down; *Col., Mex., Cuba* to fell timber; **-se** to lie down.

**tumbo** *m.* tumble; somersault; **dar -s** to jump, bump along.

**tumor** *m.* tumor; **tumorcillo** *m.* boil; small tumor.

**tumulto** *m.* tumult, uproar; mob, throng.

**tumultuoso** *adj.* tumultuous.

**tuna** *f.* prickly pear.

**tunante** *m. & f.* rascal, rogue, scamp; loafer; *Andes, Ch., C.A.* libertine, licentious or lewd person.

**tunda** *f.* whipping, thrashing; shearing (*the nap of cloth*).

**tundir** *v.* to lash, beat, whip; to shear (*the nap of cloth*).

**túnel** *m.* tunnel.

**túnica** *f.* tunic; gown, robe.

**tupido** *adj.* dense; compact, thick; blocked, obstructed.

**tupir** *v.* to press, pack, squeeze together; to stop up, clog; **-se** to get stopped up; to stuff oneself; to become dense (*as a forest*); *Am.* to get astonished or confused.

**turba** *f.* mob, throng.

**turbación** *f.* disturbance, confusion; embarrassment.

**turbamulta** *f.* throng, mob, crowd.

**turbar** *v.* to perturb; to disturb; to trouble; **-se** to get disturbed, confused, embarrassed.

**turbio** *adj.* muddy; muddled, confused.

**turbión** *m.* thunderstorm; heavy shower.

**turborreactor** *m.* turbojet.

**turbulento** *adj.* turbulent; restless; disorderly.

**turco** *adj.* Turkish; *m.* Turk; Turkish, Turkish language; *Am.* peddler.

**turismo** *m.* tourist travel; touring, sightseeing; **oficina de —** travel bureau; **turista** *m. & f.* tourist; **turístico** *adj.* tourist; related to tourism.

**turnar** *v.* to alternate; **-se** to alternate; to take turns.

**turno** *m.* turn, alternate order.

**turrón** *m.* nougat, nut confection; almond cake; *Mex.* **romper el —** to decide to use the **tú** form of address (*as a mark of close friendship*).

**tusa** *f. Am.* corn, corncob; *Cuba, Mex.* corn husk; *Am.* corn silk, tassel of an ear of corn.

**tusar** *v. Cuba, Mex., Ríopl., Andes* to shear; *Ríopl.* to crop, cut badly (*hair*).

**tutear** *v.* to address familiarly (*using the* **tú** *form*).

**tutela** *f.* guardianship; guidance, protection.

**tutelar** *v.* to guide, coach, direct; *adj.* guiding, guardian (*used as adj.*).

**tutor** *m.* tutor; guardian.

**tuyo** *poss. adj.* your, of yours (*fam. sing.*); *poss. pron.* yours.

# U

**u** *conj.* (*before words beginning with* **o** *or* **ho**) or.

**ubicar**[6] *v. Am.* to locate; **-se** to be situated or located.

**ubre** *f.* udder.

**ufanarse** *v.* to glory (in); to be proud (of).

TR

**ufano** *adj.* proud; gay; self-satisfied.

**ujier** *m.* usher, doorman.

**úlcera** *f.* ulcer; sore.

**ulterior** *adj.* ulterior; further; later.

**ultimar** *v.* to put an end to; *Am.* to give the finishing blow, kill.

**último** *adj.* last, final; ultimate; latest; **estar en las últimas** to be on one's last legs; to be at the end of one's rope, be at the end of one's resources.

**ultrajar** *v.* to outrage, insult; to scorn.

**ultraje** *m.* outrage, insult.

**ultramar** *m.* country or place across the sea; **de —** overseas, from across the sea; **en** (*or* **a**) **—** overseas.

**ultravioleta** *adj.* ultraviolet.

**ulular** *v.* to howl, shriek, hoot.

**umbral** *m.* threshold.

**umbrío** *adj.* shady.

**un(o)** *indef. art.* a, an; **-s** some, a few; **-s cuantos** a few; **uno** *pron.* & *num.* one.

**unánime** *adj.* unanimous.

**unanimidad** *f.* unanimity, complete accord.

**unción** *f.* unction (*anointing with oil*); religious fervor; spiritual grace; **Extremaunción** Extreme Unction (*the Last Sacrament of the Church*).

**uncir**[10] *v.* to yoke.

**ungir**[11] *v.* to anoint; to consecrate.

**ungüento** *m.* ointment; salve.

**único** *adj.* only, sole; unique, singular, rare.

**unidad** *f.* unity; unit.

**unificar**[6] *v.* to unify; to unite.

**uniformar** *v.* to standardize; to make uniform; to furnish with uniforms.

**uniforme** *adj.* & *m.* uniform.

**uniformidad** *f.* uniformity.

**unilateral** *adj.* unilateral, one-sided.

**unión** *f.* union.

**unir** *v.* to unite; to join; to bring together; **-se** to unite, join together; to wed.

**universal** *adj.* universal.

**universidad** *f.* university.

**universo** *m.* universe.

**untar** *v.* to anoint; to smear; to oil, grease; to bribe; to corrupt; **-se** to smear oneself; to get smeared.

**unto** *m.* grease, fat; ointment.

**untuosidad** *f.* greasiness; **untuoso** *adj.* unctuous; oily, greasy.

**uña** *f.* fingernail; toenail; claw; hoof; hook (*on a tool*); **a — de caballo** at full gallop, at full speed; **largo de -s** prone to stealing; *Mex., C.A., Ven., Col., Andes* **largas -s** thief; **vivir de sus -s** to live by stealing; *Mex., C.A., Ven., Col., Andes* **echar la —** to steal; **ser — y carne** to be inseparable friends.

**uranio** *m.* uranium.

**urbanidad** *f.* courtesy, politeness; refinement.

**urbano** *adj.* urban; courteous, polite.

**urbe** *f.* metropolis, large city.

**urdimbre** *f.* warp (*of a fabric*); scheme.

**urdir** *v.* to warp (*in weaving*); to plot, scheme; to invent (*a lie, story, etc.*).

**uremia** *f.* uremia.

**urgencia** *f.* urgency; pressing need.

**urgente** *adj.* urgent, pressing.

**urgir**[11] *v.* to urge; to be urgent.

**urna** *f.* urn; **— electoral** ballot box.

**urraca** *f.* magpie.

**usado** *p.p.* & *adj.* used; accustomed; worn; threadbare.

**usanza** *f.* usage, custom, habit.

**usar** *v.* to use; to wear; to wear out; to be accustomed; **-se** to be in use, be in vogue.

**uso** *m.* (*empleo*) use; usage; wear; (*costumbre*) usage; practice; habit; custom; **al — de la época** according to the custom or usage of the period; **estar en buen —** to be in good condition (*said of a thing*).

**usted** *pers. pron.* (*abbreviated as* **Vd., V.,** *or* **Ud.**) you.

**usual** *adj.* usual; ordinary, customary.

**usufructo** *m.* use, enjoyment; profit.

**usufructuar**[18] *v.* to enjoy the use of; to make use of.

**usura** *f.* usury.

**usurero** *m.* usurer, loan shark.

**usurpar** *v.* to usurp.

**utensilio** *m.* utensil; implement, tool.

**útero** *m.* uterus, womb.

**útil** *adj.* useful; profitable; **-es** *m. pl.* tools, instruments.

**utilidad** *f.* utility; profit; usefulness.

**utilizar**[9] *v.* to utilize; to use.

**uva** *f.* grape; **— espina** gooseberry; **— pasa** raisin; **estar hecho una —** to be tipsy, drunk.

## V

**vaca** *f.* cow; **carne de —** beef; **cuero de —** cowhide; *Am.* **hacer —** to play hooky, play truant, cut class; to join in a quick business deal.

**vacación** *f.* vacation (*usually* **vacaciones**).

**vacada** *f.* herd of cows.

**vacancia** *f.* vacancy.

**vacante** *adj.* vacant, unfilled, unoccupied; *f.* vacancy.

**vaciar**[17] *v.* (*dejar vacío*) to empty; to drain; to flow; (*amoldar*) to cast into a mold; (*ahuecar*) to hollow out; **-se** to spill; to empty; to become empty; to flow (into).

**vaciedad** *f.* emptiness; nonsense, silliness.

**vacilación** *f.* hesitation; wavering; doubt.

**vacilante** *adj.* vacillating, hesitating, wavering; unsteady.

**vacilar** *v.* to vacillate, waver, hesitate; to sway.

**vacío** *adj.* empty; vacant; unoccupied; hollow; *m.* void; hollow; vacuum; vacancy; gap, blank.

**vacuna** *f.* vaccine; vaccination; cowpox (*eruptive disease of the cow*); **vacunación** *f.* vaccination; **— antipoliomelítica** antipolio inoculation.

**vacunar** *v.* to vaccinate.

**vadear** *v.* to ford; to wade; to avoid (*a difficulty*).

**vado** *m*. ford; **no hallar —** to find no way out.

**vagabundear** *v*. to tramp around, wander, rove; to loiter.

**vagabundo** *adj*. vagabond, wandering; *m*. vagabond, tramp; vagrant; wanderer.

**vagar**[7] *v*. to wander, roam; to loiter; to loaf; *m*. leisure; loitering.

**vago** *adj*. vague; roaming; idle; vagrant; *m*. vagrant, tramp.

**vagón** *m*. railway car or coach; **vagoneta** *f*. small railway car or tram (*used in mines*); **vagonada** *f*. carload.

**vaguear** = **vagar**.

**vahído** *m*. dizziness, dizzy spell.

**vaho** *m*. vapor, steam, fume, mist; odor.

**vaina** *f*. sheath, scabbard; case; pod, husk; *Ven., Col., C.A., Mex.* bother, nuisance; *Ven., Col.* luck.

**vainilla** *f*. vanilla.

**vaivén** *m*. sway; fluctuation, wavering; traffic, coming and going; **-es** comings and goings; ups and downs; inconstancy.

**vajilla** *f*. tableware; set of dishes; **— de plata** silverware; **— de porcelana** chinaware.

**vale** *m*. bond, promissory note; voucher; adieu, farewell; *m. & f. Col., Ven., Mex.* comrade, pal, chum.

**valedero** *adj*. valid, binding, effective.

**valedor** *m*. defender, protector; *Am*. pal, comrade.

**valenciano** *adj*. Valencian, of or from Valencia, Spain; *m*. Valencian.

**valentía** *f*. courage, valor; exploit; boast.

**valentón** *adj*. blustering, boastful; *m*. bully, braggart.

**valer**[47] *v. irr.* to favor, protect; to cost; to be worth; to be worthy; to be equivalent to; to be valid; to prevail; to be useful; **— la pena** to be worth while; **— por** to be worth; **-se de** to avail oneself of, make use of; **más vale** it is better; **¡válgame Dios!** heaven help me! good heavens!

**valeroso** *adj*. valiant, brave; valuable.

**valía** *f*. worth, value; influence.

**validez**. *f* validity; stability, soundness.

**válido** *adj*. valid.

**valiente** *adj*. valiant, brave; powerful; *m*. brave man; bully.

**valija** *f*. valise, satchel; mailbag.

**valimiento** *m*. favor, protection; **gozar de —** to enjoy protection or favor.

**valioso** *adj*. valuable; worthy; wealthy.

**valor** *m*. value; worth; price; significance; valor, courage; boldness; efficacy, power; **-es** stocks, bonds.

**valoración** *f*. valuation, appraisal.

**valorar** *v*. to evaluate, value, appraise.

**valorizar**[9] *v. Cuba, Ven., Ríopl., Andes* to value, appraise; *Am*. to realize, convert into money.

**vals** *m*. waltz.

**valsar** *v*. to waltz.

**valuación** *f*. valuation, appraisal.

**valuar**[18] *v*. to value, price, appraise; to rate.

**válvula** *f*. valve.

**valla** *f*. stockade, fence; barrier; obstacle; *Cuba, Col.* cockpit (*for cockfights*).

**vallado** *m*. stockade, fenced-in place; fence.

**valle** *m*. valley; vale.

**vanagloria** *f*. vainglory, boastful vanity.

**vanagloriarse**[17] *v*. to glory, take great pride (in), boast (of).

**vanaglorioso** *adj*. vain, boastful, conceited.

**vanguardia** *f*. vanguard.

**vanidad** *f*. vanity; conceit; emptiness.

**vanidoso** *adj*. vain, conceited.

**vano** *adj*. vain; empty; hollow; *m*. opening in a wall (*for a door or window*).

**vapor** *m*. vapor, steam, mist; steamer, steamship.

**vaporoso** *adj*. vaporous, steamy, misty; vaporlike.

**vapulear** *v*. to beat, whip, thrash.

**vapuleo** *m*. beating, whipping, thrashing.

**vaquería** *f*. herd of cows; stable for cows; dairy.

**vaquerizo** *m*. herdsman; *adj*. pertaining to cows; **vaqueriza** *f*. stable for cows.

**vaquero** *m*. cowherd, herdsman; cowboy; *Cuba* milkman; *adj*. relating to cowherds, cowboys, or cattle.

**vaqueta** *f*. sole leather; cowhide; *Mex.* **zurrar a uno la —** to tan someone's hide, beat someone up.

**vara** *f*. twig; stick; rod; wand; staff; yard, yardstick; thrust with a picador's lance.

**varadero** *m*. shipyard.

**varar** *v*. to beach (*a boat*); to run aground; to stop, come to a standstill (*said of business*).

**varear** *v*. to beat; to whip; to sell by the yard; to measure with a **vara**; *Am*. to exercise (*a horse before a race*).

**variable** *afd*. variable, unstable, changeable; *f*. variable.

**variación** *f*. variation.

**variado** *p.p. & adj* varied; variegated.

**variar**[17] *v*. to vary; to change; to shift; to differ.

**variedad** *f*. variety; variation, change.

**varilla** *f*. small rod; wand; long, flexible twig; rib (*of an umbrella or fan*); corset stay; *Mex* peddler's wares.

**varillero** *m. Mex.* peddler.

**vario** *adj*. various; different; changeable; varied; **-s** various, several.

**varón** *m*. male, man; *Am*. long beam, timber.

**varonil** *adj* manly; strong; brave.

**vasallo** *adj. & m*. vassal, subject.

**vasco, vascongado** *adj. & m*. Basque.

**vasija** *f*. vessel, container, receptacle.

**vaso** *m*. drinking glass; glassful; vase; vessel; hull of a ship; horse's hoof; **— de elección** person chosen by God.

**vástago** *m*. (*de planta*) shoot, sprout; stem; (*persona*) scion, offspring; *Mex., Col., Ven.* stem, trunk of a

UF

banana tree.

**vasto** *adj*. vast, extensive, large.

**vate** *m*. bard, poet.

**vaticinar** *v*. to prophesy, predict, foretell.

**vaticinio** *m*. prophecy, prediction.

**vecindad** *f*. vicinity; neighborhood; neighborliness; **casa de —** tenement.

**vecindario** *m*. neighborhood, neighbors; vicinity.

**vecino** *m*. neighbor; resident; citizen; *adj*. neighboring; next, near.

**vedar** *v*. to prohibit; to impede.

**vega** *f*. fertile lowland or plain; *Cuba*, *Ven*. tobacco plantation.

**vegetación** *f*. vegetation.

**vegetal** *adj*. vegetable; *m*. vegetable, plant.

**vegetar** *v*. to vegetate.

**vehemente** *adj*. vehement, passionate, impetuous; violent.

**vehículo** *m*. vehicle.

**veintena** *f*. score, twenty.

**vejestorio** *m*. wrinkled old person.

**vejete** *m*. little old man.

**vejez** *f*. old age.

**vejiga** *f*. bladder; blister; smallpox sore; **— de la bilis** (*or* **— de la hiel**) gall bladder.

**vela** *f*. vigil, watch; night watch; candle; sail; **a toda —** under full sail; at full speed; **en —** on watch, without sleep; **hacerse a la —** to set sail.

**velada** *f*. watch, vigil; evening party; evening function or meeting.

**velador** *m*. night watchman; keeper, guard; lamp table; bedside table; candlestick; *Ríopl.*, *Mex.*, *Cuba*, *Col*. lamp shade.

**velar** *v*. to keep vigil; to stay up at night; to be vigilant; to watch over; to veil; to cover, hide.

**velatorio** *m*. wake (*vigil over a corpse*). *See* **velorio**.

**veleidoso** *adj*. inconstant, fickle, changeable.

**velero** *m*. sailboat; sailmaker; candlemaker; *adj*. swift-sailing **buque —** sailboat.

**veleta** *f*. weathervane, weathercock; *m*. & *f*. fickle person.

**velís** *m*. *Mex*. valise.

**velo** *m*. veil; curtain, covering; **— del paladar** velum, soft palate.

**velocidad** *f*. velocity.

**velocímetro** *m*. speedometer.

**velorio** *m*. *Am*. wake (*vigil over a corpse*); *Mex.*, *C.A.*, *Ven.*, *Col.*, *Ch.*, *Andes* dull party.

**veloz** *adj*. swift, quick, fast.

**vello** *m*. hair (*on the body*); down, fuzz; nap (*of cloth*).

**vellón** *m*. fleece; tuft of wool; sheepskin with fleece; silver and copper alloy; an ancient copper coin.

**velloso** *adj*. hairy; downy, fuzzy.

**velludo** *adj*. hairy; downy; fuzzy; *m*. plush; velvet.

**vena** *f*. vein; lode, vein of metal ore; mood, disposition; **estar en —** to be in the mood; to be inspired.

**venado** *m*. deer; venison, deer meat; *Mex*. **pintar —** to play hooky.

**vencedor** *adj*. conquering, winning, victorious; *m*. conqueror, winner, victor.

**vencer**[10] *v*. to conquer, vanquish; to defeat; to overcome; to surpass; to win; **-se** to control oneself; to mature, fall due; **se venció el plazo** the time limit expired.

**vencido** *p.p.* & *adj*. conquered; defeated; due, fallen due.

**vencimiento** *m*. conquering, defeat; maturity (*of a debt*), falling due; expiration (*of a period of time*).

**venda** *f*. bandage.

**vendaje** *m* bandage.

**vendar** *v*. to bandage; to blindfold.

**vendaval** *m*. strong wind, gale.

**vendedor** *m*. vendor, seller, peddler.

**vender** *v*. to sell; to betray; **-se** to be sold; to sell oneself, accept a bribe.

**vendimia** *f*. vintage; profit.

**venduta** *f*. *Col*. auction; *Cuba* small fruit and vegetable store.

**veneno** *m*. venom, poison.

**venenoso** *adj*. poisonous.

**venerable** *adj*. venerable.

**veneración** *f*. veneration, reverence.

**venerando** *adj*. venerable, worthy of respect.

**venerar** *v*. to venerate, revere; to worship.

**venero** *m*. water spring; source, origin; lode, layer, seam (*of mineral*).

**venezolano** *adj*. Venezuelan; *m*. Venezuelan; *Ven*. Venezuelan silver coin.

**vengador** *adj*. avenging, revenging; *m*. avenger.

**venganza** *f*. vengeance, revenge.

**vengar**[7] to avenge, revenge; **-se de** to take revenge on.

**vengativo** *adj*. vindictive, revengeful.

**venia** *f*. pardon; permission, leave; bow, nod; *C.A.*, *Ven.*, *Ríopl*. military salute.

**venida** *f*. arrival; return; river flood, onrush of water; attack (*in fencing*).

**venidero** *adj*. coming, future; **en lo —** in the future; **-s** *m. pl*. successors.

**venir**[48] *v. irr*. to come; to arrive; to fit; **-le a uno bien** (*or* **mal**) to be becoming (*or* unbecoming); **— a menos** to decline, decay; **— a pelo** to come just at the right moment; to suit perfectly; to be pat, opportune, to the point; **— en** to agree to; **— sobre** to fall upon; **¿a qué viene eso?** what is the point of that?; **-se abajo** to fall down; to collapse; to fail.

**venoso** *adj*. veined; venous (*of or pertaining to the veins; with veins*).

**venta** *f*. sale; roadside inn; *Ur*. store, vendor's stand; **— pública** auction.

**ventaja** *f*. advantage; gain, profit; bonus; odds.

**ventajoso** *adj*. advantageous, beneficial, profitable; *Mex*. self-seeking, profiteering.

**ventana** *f*. window; window shutter; *Col*. clearing (*in a forest*); **— (or**

**ventanilla) de la nariz** nostril.
**ventarrón** *m.* gale, strong wind.
**ventear** *v.* (*oler*) to scent, sniff; (*soplar*) to blow, be windy; (*poner al aire*) to air; (*indagar*) to nose around; *Ven.* to toss in the wind; *Am.* to flee; *Am.* to outrun; **-se** to expel air, break wind; *Col.* to stay outdoors.
**ventero** *m.* innkeeper.
**ventilación** *f.* ventilation.
**ventilador** *m.* ventilator; fan (*for ventilation*).
**ventilar** *v.* to ventilate; to air.
**ventisca** *f.* blizzard, snowstorm; snowdrift.
**ventiscar**⁶ *v.* to snow hard and blow (*as in a blizzard*); to drift (*as snow in a blizzard*).
**ventisquero** *m.* blizzard, snowstorm; glacier; snowdrift; snow-capped mountain peak.
**ventolera** *f.* gust of wind; pride, vanity; whim; pin wheel; **darle a uno la — de** to take the notion to.
**ventoso** *adj.* windy.
**ventura** *f.* happiness; fortune, chance; risk, danger; **a la —** at random; **buena —** fortune; **por —** perchance.
**venturoso** *adj.* fortunate, lucky; happy.
**ver**⁴⁹ *v. irr.* to see; to look; to look at; to look into, examine; **— de** to try to, see to it that; **a más** (*or* **hasta más**) **—** good-bye; **no — la hora de** to be anxious to; **no tener nada que con** not to have anything to do with; **-se** to be seen; to be; **-se obligado a** to be obliged to, be forced, to; **a mi modo de —** in my opinion; **de buen —** good-looking; **ser de —** to be worth seeing.
**vera** *f.* edge; **a la — del camino** at the edge of the road.
**veracidad** *f.* truthfulness.
**veraneante** *m. & f.* summer resorter, vacationist, or tourist.
**veranear** *v.* to spend the summer.
**veraneo** *m.* summering, summer vacation.
**veraniego** *adj.* summer, of summer.
**verano** *m.* summer.
**veras** *f. pl.* reality, truth; **de —** in truth; truly; in earnest.
**veraz** *adj.* truthful.
**verbal** *adj.* verbal; oral.
**verbena** *f.* verbena (*a plant*); festival or carnival (*on eve of a religious holiday*).
**verbigracia** *adv.* for instance, for example.
**verbo** *m.* verb; **el Verbo** the Word (*second person of the Trinity*).
**verboso** *adj.* verbose, wordy.
**verdad** *f.* truth; **¿—?** really?; is that so?; isn't that so?; **— de Perogrullo** truism, evident truth; **de —** (*or* **a la —**) in truth, in earnest; **en —** really, truly.
**verdadero** *adj.* real; true; truthful; sincere.
**verde** *adj.* green; unripe; young; off-color, indecent; *m.* green; verdure; *Ur., Ven.* country, countryside.

**verdear** *v.* to grow green; to look green.
**verdinegro** *adj.* dark-green.
**verdor** *m.* verdure, greenness.
**verdoso** *adj.* greenish.
**verdugo** *m.* executioner; cruel person; torment; rapier (*light sword*); lash, whip; welt; shoot of a tree; **verdugón** *m.* large welt.
**verdulera** *f.* woman vendor of green vegetables; **verdulería** *f.* green vegetable store or stand.
**verdura** *f.* verdure; greenness; green vegetables.
**vereda** *f.* path; *Ch., Ríopl., Andes* sidewalk; *Col.* small village; *C.R.* bank of a stream.
**veredicto** *m.* verdict.
**vergonzoso** *adj.* shameful, disgraceful; shy, bashful; *m.* species of armadillo.
**vergüenza** *f.* shame; disgrace; shyness, bashfulness; **tener —** to have shame; to be ashamed.
**vericueto** *m.* rugged, wild place (*often rocky*).
**verídico** *adj.* truthful; true.
**verificar**⁶ *v.* to verify; to confirm; to test, check; to carry out, fulfill; **-se** to be verified; to take place.
**verijas** *f. pl. Ríopl., Mex.* groin (*hollow between lower part of abdomen and thigh*); *Am.* flanks of a horse.
**verja** *f.* grate, grating.
**verruga** *f.* wart; nuisance.
**versado** *adj.* versed, skilled, expert.
**versar** *v.* to deal (with), treat (of); **-se en** to become versed in.
**versión** *f.* version; translation.
**verso** *m.* verse; meter; **— suelto** (*or* **— libre**) free or blank verse.
**verter**¹ *v. irr.* to pour; to empty; to spill; to translate; to flow down.
**vertical** *adj.* vertical.
**vértice** *m.* top, apex, summit.
**vertiente** *f.* slope; watershed; *adj.* flowing.
**vertiginoso** *adj.* whirling, dizzy, giddy.
**vértigo** *m.* dizziness, giddiness; fit of madness.
**vestíbulo** *m.* vestibule; lobby.
**vestido** *m.* clothing, apparel; dress; garment; suit.
**vestidura** *f.* vestment; attire, apparel; raiment.
**vestigio** *m.* vestige, sign, trace.
**vestir**⁵ *v. irr.* (*cubrir*) to dress; to clothe; to put on; to adorn; to cover; (*llevar*) to wear; **-se** to dress, get dressed; to be clothed; to be covered.
**vestuario** *m.* wardrobe, apparel; theatrical costumes; cloakroom; dressing room; vestry (*room for church vestments*).
**veta** *f.* vein, seam (*of mineral*); streak, grain (*in wood*); stripe; *Am.* rope.
**veteado** *adj.* veined; striped; streaked.
**veterano** *adj. & m.* veteran.
**veterinario** *m.* veterinary.
**veto** *m.* veto.
**vetusto** *adj.* old, ancient.
**vez** *f.* time, occasion; turn; **a la —** at the same time; **cada — más** more

**VA**

and more; **cada — que** whenever; **de — en cuando** from time to time; **de una —** all at once; **en — de** instead of; **otra —** again; **una que otra —** rarely, once in a while; **tal —** perhaps; **a veces** sometimes; **raras veces** seldom; **hacer las veces de** to take the place of.

**vía** *f.* way; road; track; railroad track; conduit; **Vía Crucis** the Way of the Cross; **Vía Láctea** the Milky Way.

**viaducto** *m.* viaduct.

**viajante** *m.* traveler; **— de comercio** traveling salesman.

**viajar** *v.* to travel.

**viaje** *m.* voyage; trip; travel; **— de ida y vuelta** (*or* **— redondo**) round trip.

**viajero** *m.* traveler; *adj.* traveling.

**vianda** *f.* viands, food; meal.

**viandante** *m.* & *f.* wayfarer, walker, pedestrian; passer-by; vagabond.

**viático** *m.* provisions for a journey; viaticum (*communion given to dying persons*).

**víbora** *f.* viper.

**vibración** *f.* vibration.

**vibrante** *adj.* vibrant, vibrating.

**vibrar** *v.* to vibrate.

**vicepresidente** *m.* vice-president.

**viceversa** *adv.* vice versa, conversely.

**viciado** *adj.* contaminated, foul; corrupt; *p.p. of* **viciar.**

**viciar** *v.* to vitiate, corrupt; to adulterate; to falsify; **-se** to become corrupt.

**vicio** *m.* vice; bad habit; fault; craving; **de —** as a habit; **hablar de —** to talk too much; **-s** *Am.* articles and ingredients used for serving **mate.**

**vicioso** *adj.* vicious, evil, wicked; having bad habits; licentious; faulty, incorrect (*grammatical construction, reasoning, etc.*).

**vicisitud** *f.* vicissitude; **-es** vicissitudes, ups and downs, changes of fortune or condition.

**víctima** *f.* victim.

**victoria** *f.* victory, triumph; victoria (*carriage*).

**victorioso** *adj.* victorious.

**vicuña** *f.* vicuña (*an Andean animal allied to the alpaca and llama*); vicuña wool; vicuña cloth.

**vid** *f.* vine, grapevine.

**vida** *f.* life; living; livelihood; **— mía** dearest; **hacer —** to live together; **pasar a mejor —** to die; **tener la — en un hilo** to be in great danger.

**vidalita** *f. Am.* melancholy song of Argentina and Chile.

**vidente** *m.* seer, prophet; *adj.* seeing.

**vidriado** *m.* glaze; glazed earthenware; *p.p.* & *adj.* glazed.

**vidriar**[17] *v.* to glaze (*earthenware*).

**vidriera** *f.* glass window; glass door; *Am.* show case, show window; **— de colores** stained-glass window.

**vidriero** *m.* glazier (*one who installs windowpanes*); glass blower; glass maker; glass dealer.

**vidrio** *m.* glass; any glass article.

**vidrioso** *adj.* glassy; brittle; slippery,

icy; touchy, irritable.

**viejo** *adj.* old; ancient; worn-out; *m.* old man; **— verde** old man who boast of his youth and vigor; *Am.* **los -s** the old folks (*applied to one's parents*); **viejoto** *f.* old hag.

**viento** *m.* wind; scent; **hace —** it is windy; **a los cuatro -s** in all directions; **vientecito** *m.* gentle breeze.

**vientre** *m.* abdomen; belly; bowels; entrails; womb.

**viernes** *m.* Friday.

**viga** *f.* beam; rafter.

**vigencia** *f.* operation (*of a law*); **entrar en —** to take effect (*said of a law*); **estar en —** to be in force (*said of a law*).

**vigente** *adj.* effective, in force (*as a law*).

**vigía** *f.* lookout, watchtower; watch (*act of watching*); reef; *m.* lookout, watchman.

**vigilancia** *f.* vigilance.

**vigilante** *adj.* vigilant, watchful; *m.* watchman.

**vigilar** *v.* to keep guard; to watch over.

**vigilia** *f.* vigil, watch; wakefulness, sleeplessness; night hours (*spent in study*); eve before certain church festivals; vesper service; **día de —** day of abstinence; **comer de —** to abstain from meat.

**vigor** *m.* vigor; **en —** in force (*said of a law*); **entrar en —** to become effective (*as a law, statute, etc.*).

**vigorizar**[9] *v.* to invigorate, tone up, give vigor to, strengthen.

**vigoroso** *adj.* vigorous.

**vihuela** *f.* guitar.

**vil** *adj.* vile, base, low, mean.

**vileza** *f.* villainy; baseness; vile act.

**vilipendiar** *v.* to revile.

**vilo : en —** in the air; suspended; undecided; in suspense; **llevar en —** to waft.

**villa** *f.* village; villa, country house.

**villancico** *n.* carol; Christmas carol.

**villanía** *f.* villainy; lowliness.

**villano** *adj.* rustic, uncouth; villainous, mean, base; *m.* villain; rustic, peasant.

**villorrio** *m.* small village, hamlet.

**vinagre** *m.* vinegar; **vinagrera** *f.* vinegar cruet.

**vincular** *v.* to tie, bond, unite; to entail (*limit the inheritance of property*); to found, base (on).

**vínculo** *m.* bond, tie, chain; entailed inheritance.

**vindicar**[6] *v.* to vindicate; to avenge; to defend, assert (*one's rights*); **-se** to avenge oneself; to defend oneself.

**vino** *m.* wine; **— amontillado** good grade of pale sherry (*originally from Montilla*); **— tinto** dark-red wine; **vinería** *f. Ríopl., Andes* wineshop; **vinero** *adj. Am.* pertaining to wine; **vinoso** *adj.* winy.

**viña** *f.* vineyard.

**viñedo** *m.* vineyard.

**violación** *f.* violation.

**violado** *adj.* violet; *m.* violet, violet color; *p.p.* violated.

**violar** *v.* to violate; to rape.

**violencia** *f.* violence.

**violentar** *v.* to force; to break into (*a house*); **-se** to force oneself; to get angry.

**violento** *adj.* violent; impetuous; forced; strained; unnatural.

**violeta** *f.* violet.

**violín** *m.* violin; *m. & f.* violinist; *Ven.* **estar hecho un —** to be very thin.

**violinista** *m. & f.* violinist.

**virada** *f.* tack, change of direction, turn.

**viraje** *m.* change of direction; turn.

**virar** *v.* to turn, turn around, change direction; to tack (*said of a ship*).

**virgen** *adj. & f.* virgin.

**virginal** *adj.* virginal, virgin, pure.

**viril** *adj.* virile, manly.

**virilidad** *f.* virility, manhood, manly strength, vigor.

**virreinato** *m.* viceroyalty (*office or jurisdiction of a viceroy*).

**virrey** *m.* viceroy.

**virtud** *f.* virtue.

**virtuoso** *adj.* virtuous; *m.* virtuoso (*person skilled in an art*).

**viruela** *f.* smallpox; pock (*mark left by smallpox*); **-s locas** (*or* **-s bastardas**) chicken pox.

**viruta** *f.* wood shaving.

**visa** *f.* visa, visé; **visado** *p.p. of* **visar**; *m.* visa, visé.

**visaje** *m.* grimace; wry face; **hacer -s** to make faces.

**visar** *v.* to visé; to approve; to O.K.

**viscoso** *adj.* slimy, sticky.

**visera** *f.* visor; eye shade; *Cuba, Mex.* blinder (*on a horse's bridle*).

**visible** *adj.* visible; evident; conspicuous, notable.

**visillo** *m.* window curtain.

**visión** *f.* vision; sight; fantasy; apparition; sight (*ridiculous-looking person or thing*).

**visionario** *adj. & m.* visionary.

**visita** *f.* visit, call; visitor; callers, company; **— de cumplimiento** (*or* **— de cumplido**) formal courtesy call, **— domiciliaria** police inspection of a house; home call (*of a social worker, doctor, etc.*).

**visitación** *f.* visitation, visit.

**visitador** *m.* visitor, caller; inspector.

**visitante** *m. & f.* caller, visitor; *adj.* visiting.

**visitar** *v.* to visit; to inspect.

**vislumbrar** *v.* to catch a glimpse of; to guess, surmise; **-se** to be faintly visible.

**vislumbre** *f.* glimmer; glimpse; vague idea; faint appearance.

**viso** *m.* appearance, semblance; pretense, pretext; luster, brilliance, glitter; glass curtain; **a dos -s** with a double view; with a double purpose.

**víspera** *f.* eve, evening or day before; time just before; **-s** vespers; **en -s de** on the eve of; about to.

**vista** *f.* (*panorama*) view; landscape; sight; (*sentido*) sight; vision; (*acción*) look, glance; **a — de** in the presence of; in front of, within view of; **pagadero a la —** payable at sight or upon presentation; **¡hasta la —!** good-bye!; **bajar la —** to lower one's eyes; **conocer de —** to know by sight; **hacer la — gorda** to pretend not to see; **pasar la — por** to glance over; **perder de —** to lose sight of; **tener a la —** to have before one; to have received (*a letter*).

**vistazo** *m.* glance; **dar un — a** to glance over.

**visto** *p.p. of* **ver** seen; *adj.* evident, clear **bien —** well thought of, proper; **mal —** looked down upon, improper; **— bueno** (V°.B°.) approved (O.K.); **dar el — bueno** to approve, O.K.; **— que** whereas, considering that.

**vistoso** *adj.* showy; colorful.

**vital** *adj.* vital; important, necessary.

**vitalicio** *adj.* for life; *m.* life-insurance policy; lifetime pension.

**vitalidad** *f.* vitality.

**vitamina** *f.* vitamin.

**vítor** *m.* cheer, applause; **¡—!** hurrah!

**vitorear** *v.* to cheer, applaud.

**vitrina** *f.* glass case; show case; show window.

**vituallas** *f. pl.* victuals, food, provisions.

**vituperar** *v.* to revile, insult, call bad names.

**vituperio** *m.* affront, insult; reproach; censure.

**viuda** *f.* widow.

**viudez** *f.* widowhood.

**viudo** *m.* widower.

**vivac, vivaque** *m.* bivouac, military encampment; *Am.* police headquarters.

**vivacidad** *f.* vivacity; brightness; liveliness.

**vivaracho** *adj.* lively; vivacious, gay.

**vivaz** *adj.* vivacious, lively; bright, keen, witty.

**víveres** *m. pl.* food supplies, provisions.

**vivero** *m.* fish pond, fish hatchery, tree nursery.

**viveza** *f.* vivacity; animation, liveliness; quickness; brilliance, cleverness.

**vívido** *adj.* vivid; colorful.

**vivienda** *f.* dwelling; apartment.

**viviente** *adj.* living.

**vivir** *v.* to live; to endure, last; **¡viva!** hurrah! long live!; **¿quién vive?** who goes there?; *m.* existence, living.

**vivo** *adj.* (*no muerto*) alive; living; (*ágil*) lively; quick; (*vistoso*) vivid; bright; (*listo*) clever, wide-awake; **tío —** merry-go-round; **al —** vividly; **de viva voz** by word of mouth; **tocar en lo —** to hurt to the quick, touch the most sensitive spot.

**vizcacha** *f.* *Andes, Ríopl.* viscacha (*South American rodent about the size of a hare*).

**vizcachera** *f.* *Andes, Ríopl.* viscacha burrow or hole; *Am.* room filled with junk; **vizcacheral** *m.* *Andes, Ríopl.* ground full of viscacha burrows.

**vizcaíno** *adj.* Biscayan, of or from Biscay, Spain.

**vocablo** *m.* word, term.

**vocabulario** *m.* vocabulary.

**vocación** *f.* vocation; aptness, talent.

**vocal** *adj.* vocal; oral; vowel; *f.* vowel; *m.* voter (*in an assembly or council*).

**vocear** *v.* to shout; to cry out; to hail.

**vocecita** *f.* sweet little voice.

**vocería** *f.* clamor, shouting.

**vocerío** *m. Am.* clamor, shouting.

**vocero** *m.* spokesman.

**vociferar** *v.* to shout, clamor; to yell; to boast loudly of.

**vodevil** *m.* vaudeville.

**volante** *adj.* flying; floating: **papel** (*or* **hoja**) — handbill, circular; *m.* ruffle, frill; steering wheel; balance wheel; flywheel.

**volar**[2] *v. irr.* to fly; to fly away; to explode; to irritate, pique; to rouse (*bird game*); **-se** *Carib., Col.* to fly off the handle, lose one's temper.

**volátil** *adj.* volatile, fickle, changeable; flying.

**volcán** *m,* volcano; *Col.* precipice; *Am.* swift torrent; *C.A.* **un — de** many; lots of; a pile of.

**volcánico** *adj.* volcanic.

**volcar**[2,6] *v. irr.* to overturn; to capsize; to upset; to make dizzy; **-se** to upset, get upset.

**volear** *v.* to volley, hit (*a ball*) in the air.

**volición** *f.* volition.

**voltaje** *m.* voltage.

**voltear** *v.* to turn, turn around; to revolve; to turn inside out; to overturn; to tumble or roll over; to turn a somersault; *Am.* to go prying around; *Col., Ven., C.A., Mex., Andes* — **la espalda** to turn one's back; **-se** to turn over; to change sides.

**voltereta** *f.* somersault, tumble.

**voltio, volt** *m.* volt.

**voluble** *adj.* fickle; moody; changeable; twining (*as a climbing vine*).

**volumen** *m.* volume.

**voluminoso** *adj.* voluminous, bulky, very large.

**voluntad** *f.* will; desire; determination; benevolence, good will; consent; **última** — last will, testament; **de** (*or* **de buena**) — willingly, with pleasure.

**voluntario** *adj.* voluntary; willful; *m.* volunteer.

**voluntarioso** *adj.* willful.

**voluptuoso** *adj.* voluptuous; sensual.

**voluta** *f.* scroll, spiral-like ornament; **-s de humo** spirals of smoke.

**volver**[2,52] *v. irr.* (*regresar*) to return; (*dar vuelta*) to turn; to turn up, over, or inside out; to restore; — **loco** to drive crazy; — **a** (*+inf.*) to do again; — **en sí** to come to, recover one's senses; — **por** to return for; to defend; **-se** to become; to turn; to turn around; to change one's ideas; **-se atrás** to go back; to back out, go back to one's word; **-se loco** to go crazy.

**vomitar** *v.* to vomit.

**vómito** *m.* vomit; vomiting.

**voracidad** *f.* voraciousness, greediness.

**vorágine** *f.* vortex, whirlpool.

**voraz** *adj.* voracious, ravenous, greedy.

**vórtice** *m.* vortex, whirlpool; whirlwind, tornado; center of a cyclone.

**votación** *f.* voting; vote, total number of votes.

**votante** *m. & f.* voter.

**votar** *v.* to vote; to vow; to curse; **¡voto a tal!** by Jove!

**voto** *m.* vote; vow; prayer; votive offering; oath; wish; — **de confianza** vote of confidence.

**voz** *f.* (*capacidad*) voice; (*sonido*) shout, outcry; (*palabra*) word; rumor; — **común** common rumor or gossip; **a — en cuello** (*or* **a — en grito**) shouting; at the top of one's lungs; **en — alta** aloud; **a voces** shouting, with shouts; **secreto a voces** open secret; **dar voces** to shout, yell.

**vozarrón** *m.* loud, strong voice.

**vuelco** *m.* upset; overturning; capsizing; tumble.

**vuelo** *m.* flight; width, fullness (*of a dress or cloak*); frill, ruffle; jut, projection (*of a building*); **al** (*or* **a**) — on the fly; quickly; **levantar** (*or* **alzar**) **el** — to fly away; to soar.

**vuelta** *f.* (*giro*) turn; return; repetition; (*parte opuesta*) reverse side; cuff, facing of a sleeve; cloak lining; (*cambio*) change (*money returned*); **a la** — around the corner; on returning; **a la — de los años** within a few years; *Am.* **otra** — again; **dar -s** to turn over and over; to wander about; **dar una** — to take a walk; **estar de** — to be back; **no tiene — de hoja** there are no two ways about it.

**vuelto** *p.p. of* **volver**; *m. Am.* change (*money returned*).

**vuestro** *poss. adj.* your, of yours (*fam. pl.*); *poss. pron.* yours.

**vulgar** *adj.* common, ordinary; in common use; low, vile, base.

**vulgaridad** *f.* vulgarity, coarseness, commonness.

**vulgarismo** *m.* slang, slang expression, vulgar or ungrammatical expression.

**vulgo** *m.* populace, the common people; *adv.* commonly, popularly.

# Y

**y** *conj.* and.

**ya** *adv.* already; now; finally; soon, presently; in time; **¡—!** now I see!; I understand; enough!; **¡— lo creo!** I should say so!; yes, of course!; — **no** no longer; — **que** since; although; — **se ve** of course; it is clear; — **voy** I am coming.

**yacer**[50] *v. irr.* to lie (*in the grave*); to be lying down; to lie, be situated.

**yacimiento** *m.* bed, layer (*of ore*); — **de petróleo** oil field.

**yanqui** *m. & f.* North American, native of the United States; Yankee.

**yantar** *v.* to eat; *m.* food, meal.

**yarará** *f. Ríopl.* Argentine poisonous

snake.
**yarda** f. yard (unit of measure).
**yate** m. yacht.
**yedra** = **hiedra**.
**yegua** f. mare; Am. cigar butt; adj. Am. big, large; **yeguada** f. herd of mares.
**yelmo** m. helmet.
**yema** f. egg yolk; bud, shoot; candied egg yolk; — **del dedo** finger tip.
**yerba** = **hierba**.
**yerbabuena** f. mint; peppermint.
**yerbero** m. Mex., Cuba, Ven., Col., Andes herb vendor.
**yermo** m. desert, wilderness; adj. desert uninhabited; uncultivated; sterile.
**yerno** m. son-in-law.
**yerro** m. error, fault, mistake.
**yerto** adj. stiff, motionless, rigid.
**yesca** f. tinder; anything highly inflammable; incentive (to passion); Ríopl., Mex. **estar hecho una —** to be in great anger.
**yeso** m. gypsum, chalk; plaster; chalk (for blackboard); — **blanco** whitewash; — **mate** plaster of Paris; **yesoso** adj. chalky.
**yo** pers. pron. I.
**yodo** m. iodine.
**yugo** m. yoke; marriage tie; burden.
**yunque** f. anvil.
**yunta** f. yoke of oxen; pair of draft animals.
**yuyo** m. Cuba, Mex., Ríopl., Andes wild grass, weeds; Am. an herb sauce; Am. garden stuff; Andes **estar —** to be lifeless, insipid; Col. **volverse uno —** to faint.

## Z

**zacate** m. Mex., C.A. grass, forage; hay.
**zafado** adj. impudent, brazen, shameless; Ven. smart, wide-awake, keen; Col., Mex., Andes "touched", half-crazy; p.p. of **zafar**.
**zafar** v. to release, set free; to dislodge; Am. to exclude; **-se** to slip away; to dodge; to get rid (of); to get loose; Col., Ven., Andes to get dislocated (said of a bone); Col., Mex., Andes to go crazy; Col. to use foul language.
**zafio** adj. coarse, uncouth, rude.
**zafir, zafiro** m. sapphire.
**zafra** f. sugar-making season; sugar making; sugar crop.
**zaga** f. rear; **a la —** (a or en —) behind.
**zagal** m. young shepherd; lad; **zagala** f. young shepherdess; lass, maiden; **zagalejo** m. young shepherd; short skirt; petticoat.
**zaguán** m. vestibule.
**zaherir**[3] v. irr. to hurt (feelings); to censure, reprove; to reproach.
**zaino** adj. treacherous; vicious; chestnut-colored (horse).
**zalamero** m. fawner, flatterer, servile person; **zalamería** f. flattery, scraping and bowing.
**zalea** f. pelt, undressed sheepskin.
**zambo** adj. knock-kneed; m. Ríopl., Ven., Andes Indian and negro halfbreed; Col. a species of South

American monkey.
**zambullida** f. dive, dip, plunge.
**zambullir**[20] v. to plunge, dip, duck; **-se** to dive; to plunge.
**zambullón** m. quick, sudden dip or dive.
**zanahoria** f. carrot.
**zanca** f. long leg of any fowl; long leg; long prop; **zancada** f. stride, long step.
**zanco** m. stilt; **andar en -s** to walk on stilts.
**zancón** adj. lanky, long-legged; Col., Guat., Mex. too short (skirt or dress).
**zancudo** adj. long-legged; m. Mex., C.A., Ven., Col., Andes mosquito.
**zángano** m. drone; loafer, sponger; Am. rogue, rascal.
**zangolotear** v. to shake, jiggle; **-se** to shake; to waddle; to sway from side to side.
**zangoloteo** m. jiggle, jiggling; shaking; waddling.
**zanguanga** f. feigned illness; **hacer la —** to pretend to be ill; **zanguango** adj. lazy; silly; m. fool.
**zanja** f. ditch; trench; Am. irrigation ditch.
**zanjar** v. to excavate; to dig ditches in; to settle (disputes).
**zapallo** m. Pan., Col., Ven., Andes pumpkin; squash.
**zapapico** m. pickaxe.
**zapata** f. half-boot; — **de freno** brake shoe.
**zapateado** m. a Spanish tap dance.
**zapatear** v. to tap with the feet; to tapdance.
**zapateo** m. tapping with the feet; Am. a popular tap dance.
**zapatería** f. shoe store; shoemaker's shop.
**zapatero** m. shoemaker; shoe dealer.
**zapatilla** f. slipper, pump.
**zapato** m. shoe.
**zarandajas** f. pl. trifles, trinkets, worthless things.
**zarandear** v. to winnow (separate the chaff from grain); to sift; to sift out; to move (something) quickly, wiggle, jiggle; C.A., Ríopl. to whip, lash, mistreat, abuse; **-se** to wiggle, jiggle; to bump along; to waddle; to strut, swagger.
**zarandeo** m. jiggle, jiggling; sifting; waddling; strutting.
**zarcillo** m. earring; tendril (coil of a climbing vine); Andes, Mex. earmark (on the ear of an animal).
**zarpa** f. paw, claw; weighing anchor; **echar la —** to grasp, seize; **zarpada** f. pounce; blow with a paw; **zarpazo** m. blow with the paw; big blow, thud; hard fall.
**zarpar** v. to weigh anchor; to set sail.
**zarza** f. bramble; blackberry bush.
**zarzamora** f. blackberry.
**zarzuela** f. Spanish musical comedy.
**zigzag** m. zigzag.
**zigzaguear** v. to zigzag.
**zinc** = **cinc**.

VI

**zócalo** *m.* base (*of a pedestal*); *Mex.* public square.

**zodíaco** *m.* zodiac.

**zona** *f.* zone; band, girdle; shingles (*a disease*).

**zonzo** *adj.* dull, stupid, silly, foolish.

**zoología** *f.* zoology.

**zoológico** *adj.* zoological; **jardín —** zoo.

**zopenco** *adj.* stupid, dull, thick-headed *m.* blockhead, dunce.

**zopilote** *m. Mex. C.A.* buzzard.

**zoquete** *m.* (*cosa*) block, chunk of wood; hunk of bread; (*persona*) blockhead, dunce, fool; ugly fat person; *Am.* grease, dirt, filth; *Am.* slap.

**zorra** *f.* fox; foxy person; drunkenness; prostitute; **pillar una —** to get drunk.

**zorro** *m.* fox; foxy person; **-s** fox skins; duster made of cloth or leather strips; **estar hecho un —** to be drowsy; **hacerse uno el —** to pretend to be stupid or not to hear; *adj.* foxy; **zorrillo, zorrino** *m. Ríopl.* skunk; **zorruno** *adj.* foxy.

**zorzal** *m.* thrush; crafty fellow; *Am.* fool, scapegoat, dupe.

**zozobra** *f.* foundering; sinking; anxiety, worry.

**zozobrar** *v.* to founder; to capsize; to sink; to be in great danger; to fret, worry.

**zumbar** *v.* to buzz; to hum; to ring (*said of the ears*); to scoff at; to strike, hit; *Ven., Col.* to throw out or away; *Andes* to punish; **— una bofetada** to give a slap; **-se** *Am.* to slip away, disappear.

**zumbido** *m.* buzzing, humming; ringing (*in one's ears*); hit, blow, whack.

**zumbón** *adj.* funny, playful; sarcastic; *m.* jester.

**zumo** *f.* juice; profit; **zumoso** *adj.* juicy.

**zurcido** *m.* darn; darning; *p.p. of* **zurcir.**

**zurcir**[10] *v.* to darn; to invent, make up (*lies*).

**zurdo** *adj.* left-handed; left; **a zurdas** with the left hand; clumsily.

**zuro** *m.* cob, corncob.

**zurra** *f.* beating, flogging; tanning (*of leather*).

**zurrar** *v.* to flog, thrash; to tan (*leather*).

**zurrón** *m.* pouch; bag; leather bag; *Ven., Col.* big coward.

**Zutano** *m.* so-and-so; a certain person. (*Used often with* **Fulano** *and* **Mengano**).

# Parte Segunda Inglés-Español

## Al Estudioso

El auge que desde el principio de la Guerra Mundial II viene cobrando en la América española el aprendizaje del inglés, nos ha movido a recopilar en este breve Diccionario las voces y locuciones más indispensables de esta lengua tal como se habla y escribe en los Estados Unidos de América.

Al igual que en la Sección española-inglesa hemos antepuesto la abreviatura *Am.* y otras a aquellos vocablos o idiotismos que son de uso exclusivo en alguna región de la América española, o bien de uso frecuentísimo en ésta, aunque ya hayan caído en desuso en la Península. Todo lo cual no excluye la posibilidad de que alguna acepción así designada se oiga en labios de español o sea de uso esporádico en España.

Lo que sí hemos procurado con gran ahinco y anhelamos lograr, presentando al estudioso este caudal indispensable de palabras, es el acercamiento lingüístico de las Américas, como base para nuestra mutua comprensión y como instrumento poderosísimo para nuestra solidaridad.

LOS EDITORES

## Lista de Abreviaturas

| | | | |
|---|---|---|---|
| *adj.* | adjectivo | *irr.* | irregular |
| *adv.* | adverbio | *p.p.* | participio pasado o pasivo |
| *art.* | artículo | *pers.* | personal |
| *art. indef.* | artículo indefinido | *pl.* | plural |
| *aux.* | auxiliar | *pos.* | posesivo |
| *comp.* | comparativo | *prep.* | preposición |
| *conj.* | conjunción | *pron.* | pronombre |
| *contr.* | contracción | *pron. pers.* | pronombre personal |
| *defect.* | defectivo | *pron. pos.* | pronombre posesivo |
| *etc.* | etcétera | *s.* | sustantivo |
| *ger.* | gerundio | *sing.* | singular |
| *gram.* | gramatical, gramática | *subj.* | subjuntivo |
| *imperf.* | imperfecto | *v.* | verbo |
| *indic.* | indicativo | *v. defect.* | verbo defectivo |
| *interj.* | interjección | *v. irr.* | verbo irregular |
| *interr.* | interrogativo | | |

## Abreviaturas Especiales de Indicación Regional

| | |
|---|---|
| *Am.*[1] | Americanismo |
| *Andalucía* | |
| *Andes* | (Ecuador, Perú, Bolivia) |
| *Arg.* | Argentina |
| *Bol.* | Bolivia |
| *Carib.* | (Cuba, Puerto Rico, República Dominicana) |
| *C.A.* | Centroamérica (Guatemala, El Salvador, Honduras, Nicaragua, Costa Rica) |
| *Ch.* | Chile |
| *Col.* | Colombia |
| *C.R.* | Costa Rica |
| *Cuba* | |
| *Ec.* | El Ecuador |
| *Esp.* | España |
| *Guat.* | Guatemala |
| *Hond.* | Honduras |
| *Méx.* | México |
| *N. Esp.* | Norte de España |
| *Nic.* | Nicaragua |
| *Pan.* | Panamá |
| *Par.* | Paraguay |
| *Perú* | |
| *P.R.* | Puerto Rico |
| *Ríopl.* | Río de la Plata (La Argentina oriental, el Uruguay) |
| *S.A.* | Sudamérica |
| *Sal.* | El Salvador |
| *Ur.* | El Uruguay |
| *Ven.* | Venezuela |

## Pronunciación Inglesa[2]

### I. Vocales

| Símbolo fonético | Ortografía inglesa | Ortografía fonética | Explicación de los sonidos |
|---|---|---|---|
| i | see<br>pea | si<br>pi | Equivale a la *i* in *hilo*. |
| ɪ | bit | bɪt | El sonido más aproximado es la *i* en *virtud*, pero la [ɪ] inglesa es una *i* más abierta tirando a *e* cerrada. |
| e | late<br>they | let<br>ðe | Equivale aproximadamente a *ei*; la *i* de este diptongo es muy relajada y más abierta que en español. |

---

[1] Esta abreviatura se emplea para indicar uso general hispanoamericano; se implica a la vez carácter arcaizante en cuanto a España. Se usa también para señalar los vocablos ya poco usados que puedan encontrarse en obras literarias del siglo pasado.

[2] El estudioso puede consultar el importante diccionario de pronunciación norteamericana: Kenyon and Knott, *A Pronouncing Dictionary of American English* (Springfield, Massachusetts: G. & C. Merriam Company, Publishers, 1944).

| ɛ | bet | bɛt | El sonido más aproximado en español es la *e* abierta de *perro*. |
| æ | sat | sæt | Es una vocal intermedia entre la *a* y la *e*. |
| ɑ | car | kɑr | Equivale aproximadamente a la *a* en *cargo*. |
| ɔ | forge | fɔrdʒ | Equivale aproximadamente a la *o* en *corto, corre*. |
| o | mode | mod | Equivale aproximadamente a *ou*; la *u* de este diptongo es muy relájada y más abierta que en español. |
| ʊ | pull | pʊl | El sonido más aproximado en español es la *u* en *turrón*, pero la [ʊ] inglesa es todavía más abierta. |
| u | June<br>moon | dʒun<br>mun | Equivale aproximadamente a la *u* en *uno*. |
| ə | cudgel<br>apply | kʌdʒəl<br>əplái | Es una *e* muy relajada. No tiene equivalente en español. |
| ɚ | teacher | títʃɚ | Es una *e* muy relajada, articulada simultáneamente con la *r*. No tiene equivalente en español. |
| ɝ | earth<br>fur | ɝθ<br>fɝ | Es un sonido intermedio entre la *e* y la *o* articulado simultáneamente con la *r*. Se acerca más a la *e* que a la *o*. No tiene equivalente en español. |
| ʌ | duck | dʌk | Es una vocal intermedia entre la *e* muy abierta y la *o*. Se acerca más a la *o* que a la *e*. No tiene equivalente en español. |

## II. Diptongos

| aɪ | aisle<br>nice | aɪl<br>naɪs | Equivale aproximadamente a *ai* en *aire*. |
| aʊ | now | naʊ | Equivale aproximadamente a *au* en *causa*. |
| ɔɪ | coy | kɔɪ | Equivale aproximadamente a *oy* en *hoy*. El segundo elemento del diptongo es más abierto y débil, tirando a *e*. |
| ju | used | juzd | Equivale aproximadamente a *iu* en *ciudad*. |
| jʊ | cure | kjʊr | Equivale aproximadamente al diptongo *iu*, pero la *u* es más abierta. |

## III. Consonantes

| p | paper | pépɚ | Equivale aproximadamente a la *p* española, pero es mucho más explosiva. |
| b | bat | bæt | La *b* inglesa es semejante a la *b* inicial española, pero se pronuncia más explosivamente. |
| t | tea | ti | Es bastante diferente de la *t* española. Se articula colocando flojamente la lengua arriba de los dientes incisivos superiores. |

| | | | |
|---|---|---|---|
| d | day | de | Equivale a la *d* inicial española pronunciada con mayor énfasis. |
| k | cat<br>kill | kæt<br>kɪl | Equivale aproximadamente a la *c* española delante de *a,o,u* pronunciada con mayor énfasis. |
| g | go<br>gum<br>ago | go<br>gʌm<br>əgó | Equivale aproximadamente a la *g* inicial delante de *a,o,u*: *goma, guerra, gana*; sólo que la *g* inglesa se pronuncia con mayor explosión. |
| f | fun<br>affair | fʌn<br>əfér | Equivale aproximadamente a la *f* española. |
| v | very | vérɪ | No tiene equivalente en español. Es una labiodental que se articula con el labio inferior y los dientes incisivos superiores. |
| o | thin | θɪn | Equivale aproximadamente a la *z* en el castellano *cazar*. |
| ð | then<br>other | ðɛn<br>ʌðɚ | Equivale aproximadamente a la *d* española en *pardo*. |
| s | send<br>case<br>cent | sɛnd<br>kes<br>sɛnt | Equivale aproximadamente a la *s* inicial española: *santo*. |
| z | rose<br>these<br>zero | roz<br>ðiz<br>zíro | Equivale aproximadamente a la *s* sonora en *mismo*, pero se pronuncia con más sonoridad en inglés. |
| ʃ | sheet<br>machine<br>nation | ʃit<br>maʃín<br>néʃən | Es una *s* palatal que no tiene equivalente en español. Suena como la *ch* francesa: *chapeau*. |
| ʒ | vision | vɪʒən | No tiene equivalente en español. Es una palatal fricativa sonora, semejante a la *y* argentina y uruguaya. |
| tʃ | chase | tʃes | Equivale aproximadamente a la *ch* en *charla*. |
| dʒ | judge<br>gentle | dʒʌdʒ<br>dʒéntl̩ | No tiene equivalente exacto en español. Se parece a la *y* de *inyectar* en la pronunciación de uruguayos y argentinos. |
| m | much | mʌtʃ | Equivale aproximadamente a la *m* española. |
| n | none<br>any | nʌn<br>énɪ | Equivale aproximadamente a la *n* española en *nada*. |
| ņ | eaten<br>button<br>lesson | ítņ<br>bʌtņ<br>lésņ | No tiene equivalente en español. Representa la *n* sin la articulación de la vocal anterior. |
| ŋ | ankle<br>angle<br>ring | æŋkl̩<br>æŋgl̩<br>rɪŋ | Equivale a la *n* española en *mango, banco*. |
| l | late<br>altar<br>fall<br>folly | let<br>ɔ́ltɚ<br>fɔl<br>fálɪ | La *l* inicial equivale aproximadamente a la *l* española en *lado*. La *l* en medio de palabra es más débil que la inicial. La *l* final se pronuncia a veces de una manera tan relajada en inglés que apenas la percibe el oído español. |
| l̩ | able<br>ankle | ébl̩<br>æŋkl̩ | No tiene equivalente en español. Se pronuncia como la *l* en *hábil*, pero omitiendo la *i*. |

| w | weed<br>well<br>wall | wid<br>wɛl<br>wɔl | Equivale a la *u* de los diptongos:<br>*ui, ue, ua, uo.* |
|---|------|-----|------------------------------------------|
| h | hat<br>whole | hæt<br>hol | No tiene equivalente exacto en espa-<br>ñol. Equivale aproximadamente a<br>una *j* suave que se reduce a una<br>simple aspiración. |
| hw | where | hwɛr | Equivale a una *j* suave seguida de<br>una *w* arriba explicada. |
| j | year<br>yawn<br>yet | jɪr<br>jɔn<br>jɛt | Equivale a la *i* española en los dip-<br>tongos *ie, ia, io, iu*: *hiena.* |
| r | rose<br>bear | roz<br>bɛr | No tiene equivalente en español. La<br>punta de la lengua se arrolla hacia<br>atrás sin tocar el paladar. A veces se<br>pierde al grado de vocalizarse. |

## Pronunciación de la *S* del Plural[3]

I. La **-s** del plural es sorda cuando la palabra termina en las consonantes sordas representadas por los símbolos fonéticos [p], [t], [k], [f], [θ]. Pronúnciase como la *s* de *santo*: **caps** [kæps], **gates** [gets], **cats** [kæts], **books** [bʊks], **cliffs** [klɪfs], **lengths** [lɛŋkθs].

Las excepciones más comunes son: **oath** [oθ], **oaths** [oðz]; **leaf** [lif], **leaves** [livz], **wife** [waɪf], **wives** [waɪvz]; **knife** [naɪf], **knives** [naɪvz]; **calf** [kæf], **calves** [kævz]; **half** [hæf], **halves** [hævz].

II. La **-s** del plural es sonora cuando la palabra termina en vocal (inclu-yendo la **-y** que se cambia en **-ies**), o en las consonantes sonoras representadas por los símbolos fonéticos [b], [d], [g], [v], [ð], [m], [n], [ŋ], [l]: **cries** [kraɪz], **robes** [robz], **beds** [bɛdz], **logs** [lɔgz], **stoves** [stovz], **lathes** [leðz], **farms** [fɑrmz], **bins** [bɪnz], **kings** [kɪŋz], **falls** [fɔlz], **furs** [fɝz], **papers** [pépɝz], **plows** [plaʊz].

III. Cuando la palabra termina **-en** las consonantes representadas por los símbolos [s], [ʃ], [tʃ], [z], [ʒ], [dʒ], se añade **-es** [ɪz], o **s** [ɪz], si la palabra termina en **-ce, -se, -dge, -ge**: **face** [fes], **faces** [fésɪz]; **kiss** [kɪs], **kisses** [kísɪz]; **ash** [æʃ], **ashes** [æʃɪz]; **lunch** [lʌntʃ], **lunches** [lʌntʃɪz]; **rose** [roz], **roses** [rózɪz]; **judge** [dʒʌdʒ], **judges** [dʒʌdʒɪz].

## El Sustantivo

I. Género

Son masculinos los nombres de varón o animal macho, y son femeninos los nombres de mujer o animal hembra. Los demás son neutros. El artículo definido **the** se aplica a todos los sustantivos, singular y plural: **the man** el hombre; **the men** los hombres; **the book** el libro; **the books** los libros; **the woman** la mujer; **the women** las mujeres.

En ciertos sustantivos se distingue el género femenino por medio del sufijo **-ess: poet** poeta; **poetess** poetisa. A veces es indispensable indicar

---

[3] Las mismas reglas se aplican a la pronunciación del genitivo y de la tercera persona del presente de indicativo, singular: **keeps** [kips]; **Kate's** [kets]; **saves** [sevz]; **John's** [dʒɑnz]; **judges** [dʒʌdʒɪz]; **Alice's** [ǽlɪsɪz].

el género por medio de las palabras **male** o **female, boy** o **girl, man** o **woman, she** o **he: baby boy** niño; **baby girl** niña; **woman writer** escritora; **she-bear** osa. En otros casos hay una palabra distinta para cada género; **uncle** tío; **aunt** tía.

## II. Plural de los Sustantivos[4]

1. Generalmente se forma el plural añadiendo **-s** al singular: **paper, papers** papel, papeles; **book, books** libro, libros; **chief, chiefs** jefe, jefes.

2. Los sustantivos que terminan en **-ch** (pronunciada como la *ch* española), **-ss, -x, -sh, -z,** y **-o** añaden **-es** para formar el plural: **arch, arches** arco, arcos; **kiss, kisses** beso, besos; **box, boxes** caja, cajas; **dish, dishes** plato, platos; **buzz, buzzes** zumbido, zumbidos; **hero, heroes** héroe, héroes. Nótese que los sustantivos terminados en **-ch** (pronunciada [k]) forman el plural añadiendo **-s: monarch, monarchs** monarca, monarcas.

3. Los sustantivos que terminan en **-fe,** y ciertos sustantivos que terminan en **-f,** cambian estas letras en **v** y añaden **-es: leaf, leaves** hoja, hojas; **life, lives** vida, vidas; **wife, wives** esposa, esposas; **knife, knives** cuchillo, cuchillos.

4. Para formar el plural de los sustantivos terminados en **-y** precedida de consonante cámbiase la **-y** en **-ies: fly, flies** mosca, moscas; **cry, cries** grito, gritos; **family, families** familia, familias; **quantity, quantities** cantidad, cantidades. Nótese que los sustantivos terminados en **-y** precedida de vocal forman el plural añadiendo **-s** al singular: **day, days** día, días.

5. Ciertos sustantivos forman el plural de una manera irregular: **man, men** hombre, hombres; **woman, women** mujer, mujeres; **mouse, mice** ratón, ratones; **louse, lice** piojo, piojos; **goose, geese** ganso, gansos; **tooth, teeth** diente, dientes; **foot, feet** pie, pies; **ox, oxen** buey, bueyes.

6. Ciertos sustantivos que terminan en **-is** forman el plural cambiando la **i** de la terminación en **e: axis, axes** eje, ejes; **the crisis, the crises** la crisis, las crisis.

## El Adjetivo

El adjetivo inglés es invariable en cuanto a género y número. Normalmente se coloca delante del sustantivo: **an interesting book** un libro interesante; **a large table** una mesa grande; **beautiful women** mujeres hermosas.

*Los comparativos y superlativos.* Aunque no hay una regla general, por lo común los adjetivos monosílabos, los adjetivos acentuados en la última sílaba y algunos bisílabos fácilmente pronunciados forman *el comparativo de aumento y el superlativo* añadiendo **-er** y **-est.** Los demás adjetivos van precedidos de **more** y **most.** Nótese que (1) sólo se añaden **-r** y **-st** a los que terminan en **-e** muda; (2) los adjetivos terminados en **-y** cambian esta letra en **i;** (3) los adjetivos terminados en consonante precedida de vocal doblan la consonante:

---

[4] Véase las reglas para la pronunciación del plural.

| Positivo | Comparativo | Superlativo |
|---|---|---|
| **tall** alto | **taller** más alto | **the tallest** el más alto |
| **wise** sabio | **wiser** más sabio | **the wisest** el más sabio |
| **polite** cortés | **politer** más cortés | **the politest** el más cortés |
| **happy** feliz | **happier** más feliz | **the happiest** el más feliz |
| **fat** gordo | **fatter** más gordo | **the fattest** el más gordo |
| **careful** cuidadoso | **more careful** más cuidadoso | **the most careful** el más cuidadoso |

*El superlativo absoluto* se forma anteponiendo **very** y a veces **most**: **very intelligent** muy inteligente; **she is a most beautiful woman** es una mujer hermosísima.

*El comparativo y el superlativo de inferioridad* se forman con los adverbios **less** y **least**: **less wise** menos sabio; **the least wise** el menos sabio.

*El comparativo de igualdad* se forma con el adverbio **as**: **as poor as** tan pobre como; **as much as** tanto como; **as much money as** tanto dinero como.

Los adjetivos siguientes forman el comparativo y el superlativo de una manera irregular:

| | | |
|---|---|---|
| good, well | better | best |
| bad, ill | worse | worst |
| little | less, lesser | least |
| far | farther, further | farthest, furthest |
| much, many | more | most |
| old | older, elder | oldest, eldest |

## El Adverbio

Fórmanse muchos adverbios, añadiendo **-ly** al adjetivo: **courteous** cortés, **courteously** cortésmente; **bold** atrevido, **boldly** atrevidamente. Existen las irregularidades siguientes en la formación de los adverbios que terminan en **-ly**: (1) los adjetivos terminados en **-ble** cambian la **-e** en **-y**: **possible, possibly**; (2) los terminados en **-ic** añaden **-ally**: **poetic, poetically**; (3) los terminados en **-ll** añaden sólo la **-y**: **full, fully**; (4) los terminados en **-ue** pierden la **-e** final: **true, truly**; (5) los terminados en **-y** cambian la **-y** en **i**: **happy, happily**.

Como los adjetivos, la mayor parte de los adverbios forman el *comparativo* y el *superlativo* con los adverbios **more** (más), **most** (más), y **very** (muy). Asimismo los adverbios monosílabos añaden **-er** y **-est**:

| Positivo | Comparativo | Superlativo | Superlativo Absoluto |
|---|---|---|---|
| boldly | more boldly | most boldly | very boldly |
| generously | more generously | most generously | very generously |
| soon | sooner | soonest | very soon |
| early | earlier | earliest | very early |
| late | later | latest | very late |
| near | nearer | nearest | very near |
| fast | faster | fastest | very fast |

Los adverbios siguientes forman el comparativo y el superlativo de una manera irregular:

| | | | |
|---|---|---|---|
| well | better | best | very well |
| badly, ill | worse | worst | very badly |
| little | less | least | very little |
| much | more | most | very much |
| far | farther, further | farthest, furthest | very far |

## Sufijos Comunes en Inglés

**-dom**          denota dominio, jurisdicción, estado, condición, etc.: **kingdom** reino; **martyrdom** martirio; **boredom** aburrimiento; **freedom** libertad.

**-ed, -d**       es la terminación del pretérito y del participio pasivo o pasado de los verbos regulares: **I called** llamé; **called** llamado.

**-ee**           indica la persona que recibe la acción: **addressee** destinatario; **employee** empleado.

**-eer**          denota oficio u ocupación: **engineer** ingeniero; **auctioneer** subastador.

**-en**           a) terminación del participio de muchos verbos irregulares: **fallen, broken, shaken;**
                  b) sufijo que significa *hecho de*: **golden** dorado, de oro; **wooden** de madera; **leaden** de plomo;
                  c) terminación verbal equivalente a *hacer*: **whiten** hacer blanco, emblanquecer; **darken** hacer obscuro, obscurecer.

**-er**           a) indica la persona que hace o el agente de la acción del verbo: **player** jugador; **talker** hablador;
                  b) indica el residente de un lugar: **New Yorker** habitante o residente de Nueva York; **islander** isleño;
                  c) denota ocupación: **carpenter** carpintero; **baker** panadero.
                  d) es la terminación del comparativo de adjetivos y adverbios; **taller** más alto; **faster** más aprisa.

**-ess**          úsase para formar el género femenino de ciertos sustantivos: **patroness** patrona; **poetess** poetisa; **countess** condesa.

**-est**          terminación del superlativo: **tallest** el más alto.

**-fold**         sufijo que significa *veces*: **twofold** dos veces; **hundredfold** cien veces.

**-ful**          a) equivale a *lleno*, y tratándose de adjetivos es igual a *-oso*: **hopeful** lleno de esperanzas; **careful** cuidadoso; **wilful** voluntarioso; **merciful** misericordioso; **glassful** un vaso (*lleno*);
                  b) indica a veces hábito o inclinación: **forgetful** olvidadizo;
                  c) es a veces equivalente a los sufijos españoles *-ado*, *-ada*: **handful** puñado; *spoonful* cucharada.

**-hood**         indica estado, condición, carácter, grupo; a menudo equivale a *-dad*: **motherhood** maternidad; **brotherhood** fraternidad; **childhood** niñez; **falsehood** falsedad.

**-ician**        denota especialidad en cierto ramo: **musician** músico; **technician** técnico; **electrician** electricista.

**-ie**           sufijo diminutivo: **birdie** pajarito; **Annie** Anita.

**-ing**          a) sufijo del gerundio: **speaking** hablando;
                  b) sufijo del participio activo: **threatening** amenazante; **surprising** sorprendente;
                  c) úsase a menudo para formar adjetivos: **running water** agua corriente; **drinking water** agua potable; **waiting room** sala de espera; **washing machine** máquina lavadora;

*d)* úsase para formar sustantivos: **understanding** entendimiento; **supplying** abastecimiento; **clothing** ropa; **covering** cobertura; equivale al infinitivo castellano: **swimming is good exercise** el nadar es buen ejercicio.

**-ish**  *a)* úsase para formar ciertos adjetivos de nacionalidad: **Spanish** español; **English** inglés; **Turkish** turco;

*b)* indica semejanza: **boyish** como niño, aniñado; **womanish** como mujer, mujeril, afeminado; **whitish** blancuzco, medio blanco, que tira a blanco.

**-less**  equivale a *sin, falto de*: **childless** sin hijos; **penniless** sin dinero; en ciertos casos el sufijo inglés se traduce por medio de un prefijo: **countless** innumerable, sin número; **endless** interminable, sin fin.

**-like**  significa *semejanza*, y equivale a *como, a manera de*: **lifelike** que parece vivo; **childlike** como niño, infantil; **tigerlike** como tigre.

**-ly**  *a)* sufijo adverbial: **slowly** lentamente; **happily** felizmente; **possibly** posiblemente;

*b)* añadido a ciertos sustantivos equivale a *como, a la manera de*: **motherly** como madre, materno; **gentlemanly** como caballero, caballeroso; **friendly** amigable; **manly** varonil;

*c)* equivale a *cada* en estos ejemplos: **daily** cada día; diario; **weekly** cada semana, semanal; **monthly** cada mes, mensual; **yearly** cada año, anual.

**-ness**  úsase para formar sustantivos abstractos: **goodness** bondad; **darkness** obscuridad; **foolishness** tontería; **shamelessness** desvergüenza.

**-ship**  *a)* úsase para formar sustantivos abstractos: **friendship** amistad; **relationship** relación, parentesco;

*b)* denota arte o destreza: **horsemanship** equitación;

*c)* expresa dignidad, oficio, cargo, o título: **professorship** profesorado o cátedra; **chairmanship** presidencia (*de un comité, asamblea, etc.*); **lordship** señoría;

*d)* a veces expresa tan sólo un estado y su duración: **courtship** galanteo, cortejo, noviazgo.

**-some**  expresa en alto grado la cualidad representada por el vocablo al cual se añade: **tiresome** que cansa, cansado; **quarrelsome** dado a riñas, pendenciero; **loathsome** que repugna, asqueroso; **burdensome** gravoso.

**-th**  úsase para formar números ordinales: **fifth** quinto; **tenth** décimo.

**-ty**  *a)* terminación de los múltiples de diez: **twenty** veinte; **thirty** treinta; **forty** cuarenta;

*b)* terminación de muchos sustantivos abstractos; equivale frecuentemente al sufijo español *-tad* o *-dad*: **beauty** beldad; **paternity** paternidad; **falsity** falsedad.

**-ward, -wards**  denotan *hacia*: **homeward** hacia casa; **downward** hacia abajo.

**-ways, -wise**  expresan manera, dirección, posición, etc.: **edgewise** de lado; **sideways** de lado; **lengthwise** a lo largo.

**-y**  *a)* terminación equivalente a los sufijos españoles *-ia, -ía*:

**victory** victoria; **glory** gloria; **courtesy** cortesía; **biology** biología; **astronomy** astronomía;

*b)* sufijo diminutivo: **doggy** perrito; **Johnny** Juanito;

*c)* denota abundancia, y es a menudo equivalente a *-udo*, *-oso*, *-ado*: **rocky** lleno de rocas, rocoso, pedregoso; **rainy** lluvioso; **hairy** lleno de pelo, peludo; **bulky** abultado; **wavy** ondulado; **angry** enojado;

*d)* expresa semejanza: **rosy** rosado, como una rosa, color de rosa.

## Números

Consúltese la tabla de la página xlii de la Sección Española-Inglesa para el aprendizaje de los números cardinales y ordinales desde uno hasta un millón.

## Verbos Irregulares de la Lengua Inglesa

Se denominan verbos irregulares los que no forman el pretérito o el participio pasivo con la adición de **-d** o **-ed** al presente. Obsérvese que en ciertos verbos coexiste la forma regular al lado de la irregular. En otros coexisten dos formas irregulares juntamente con la regular.

| *Presente* | *Pretérito* | *Participio pasivo o pasado* |
|---|---|---|
| abide | abode | abode |
| am, is, are | was, were | been |
| arise | arose | arisen |
| awake | awoke, awaked | awaked, awoke |
| bear | bore | born, borne |
| beat | beat | beat, beaten |
| become | became | become |
| befall | befell | befallen |
| beget | begat | begotten |
| begin | began | begun |
| behold | beheld | beheld |
| bend | bent | bent |
| bereave | bereft, bereaved | bereft, bereaved |
| beseech | besought, beseeched | besought, beseeched |
| beset | beset | beset |
| bet | bet | bet |
| bid | bid, bade | bidden, bid |
| bind | bound | bound |
| bite | bit | bitten, bit |
| bleed | bled | bled |
| blow | blew | blown |
| break | broke | broken |
| breed | bred | bred |
| bring | brought | brought |
| build | built | built |
| burn | burnt, burned | burnt, burned |
| burst | burst | burst |
| buy | bought | bought |
| can (*verbo defectivo*) | could | — |
| cast | cast | cast |
| catch | caught | caught |
| chide | chided, chid | chided, chidden |
| choose | chose | chosen |
| cleave | cleft, clove, cleaved | cleft, cleaved, cloven |
| cling | clung | clung |

| Presente | Pretérito | Participio pasivo o pasado |
|---|---|---|
| clothe | clad, clothed | clad, clothed |
| come | came | come |
| cost | cost | cost |
| creep | crept | crept |
| crow | crew, crowed | crowed |
| cut | cut | cut |
| deal | dealt | dealt |
| dig | dug, digged | dug, digged |
| do | did | done |
| draw | drew | drawn |
| dream | dreamt, dreamed | dreamt, dreamed |
| drink | drank | drunk |
| drive | drove | driven |
| dwell | dwelt, dwelled | dwelt, dwelled |
| eat | ate | eaten |
| fall | fell | fallen |
| feed | fed | fed |
| feel | felt | felt |
| fight | fought | fought |
| find | found | found |
| flee | fled | fled |
| fling | flung | flung |
| fly | flew | flown |
| forbear | forbore | forborne |
| forbid | forbade | forbidden |
| foresee | foresaw | foreseen |
| foretell | foretold | foretold |
| forget | forgot | forgotten, forgot |
| forgive | forgave | forgiven |
| forsake | forsook | forsaken |
| freeze | froze | frozen |
| get | got | got, gotten |
| gild | gilt, gilded | gilt, gilded |
| gird | girt, girded | girt, girded |
| give | gave | given |
| go | went | gone |
| grind | ground | ground |
| grow | grew | grown |
| hang[5] | hung | hung |
| have, has | had | had |
| hear | heard | heard |
| heave | hove, heaved | hove, heaved |
| hew | hewed | hewn, hewed |
| hide | hid | hidden, hid |
| hit | hit | hit |
| hold | held | held |
| hurt | hurt | hurt |
| inlay | inlaid | inlaid |
| keep | kept | kept |
| kneel | knelt | knelt |
| knit | knit, knitted | knit, knitted |
| know | knew | known |
| lay | laid | laid |
| lead | led | led |
| lean | leaned, leant | leaned, leant |
| leap | leapt, leaped | leapt, leaped |
| learn | learned, learnt | learned, learnt |
| leave | left | left |
| lend | lent | lent |
| let | let | let |

[5] Es regular cuando significa "ahorcar."

| *Presente* | *Pretérito* | *Participio pasivo o pasado* |
|---|---|---|
| lie[6] (**yacer; echarse**) | lay | lain |
| light | lit, lighted | lit, lighted |
| load | loaded | loaded, laden |
| lose | lost | lost |
| make | made | made |
| may (*verbo defectivo*) | might | — |
| mean | meant | meant |
| meet | met | met |
| melt | melted | melted, molten |
| mistake | mistook | mistaken |
| mow | mowed | mown, mowed |
| must (*verbo defectivo*) | — | — |
| ought (*verbo defectivo*) | ought | — |
| pay | paid | paid |
| put | put | put |
| quit | quit, quitted | quit, quitted |
| read [rɛd] | read [rɛd] | read [rɛd] |
| rend | rent | rent |
| rid | rid, ridded | rid, ridded |
| ride | rode | ridden |
| ring | rang, rung | rung |
| rise | rose | risen |
| run | ran | run |
| saw | sawed | sawn, sawed |
| say | said | said |
| see | saw | seen |
| seek | sought | sought |
| sell | sold | sold |
| send | sent | sent |
| set | set | set |
| sew | sewed | sewn, sewed |
| shake | shook | shaken |
| shall | should | — |
| shave | shaved | shaved, shaven |
| shear | sheared | shorn, sheared |
| shed | shed | shed |
| shine[7] | shone | shone |
| shoe | shod | shod |
| shoot | shot | shot |
| show | showed | shown, showed |
| shred | shred, shredded | shred, shredded |
| shrink | shrank, shrunk | shrunk, shrunken |
| shut | shut | shut |
| sing | sang, sung | sung |
| sink | sank | sunk |
| sit | sat | sat |
| slay | slew | slain |
| sleep | slept | slept |
| slide | slid | slid, slidden |
| sling | slung | slung |
| slink | slunk | slunk |
| slit | slit | slit |
| smell | smelt, smelled | smelt, smelled |
| smite | smote | smitten |
| sow | sowed | sown, sowed |
| speak | spoke | spoken |
| speed | sped, speeded | sped, speeded |
| spell | spelled, spelt | spelled, spelt |
| spend | spent | spent |

[6] Es regular cuando significa "mentir."
[7] Es por lo común regular cuando significa "pulir, dar brillo."

| Presente | Pretérito | Participio pasivo o pasado |
|---|---|---|
| spill | spilled, spilt | spilled, spilt |
| spin | spun | spun |
| spit | spit, spat | spit, spat |
| split | split | split |
| spread | spread | spread |
| spring | sprang, sprung | sprung |
| stand | stood | stood |
| stave | staved, stove | staved, stove |
| steal | stole | stolen |
| stick | stuck | stuck |
| sting | stung | stung |
| stink | stank, stunk | stunk |
| strew | strewed | strewn, strewed |
| stride | strode | stridden |
| strike | struck | struck, striken |
| string | strung | strung |
| strive | strove, strived | striven, strived |
| swear | swore | sworn |
| sweep | swept | swept |
| swell | swelled | swollen, swelled |
| swim | swam | swum |
| swing | swung | swung |
| take | took | taken |
| teach | taught | taught |
| tear | tore | torn |
| tell | told | told |
| think | thought | thought |
| thrive | throve, thrived | thriven, thrived |
| throw | threw | thrown |
| thrust | thrust | thrust |
| tread | trod | trod, trodden |
| understand | understood | understood |
| undertake | undertook | undertaken |
| undo | undid | undone |
| uphold | upheld | upheld |
| upset | upset | upset |
| wake | woke, waked | waked |
| wear | wore | worn |
| weave | wove | woven |
| wed | wedded | wedded, wed |
| weep | wept | wept |
| wet | wet, wetted | wet, wetted |
| will (*verbo auxiliar*) | would | — |
| win | won | won |
| wind | wound | wound |
| withdraw | withdrew | withdrawn |
| withhold | withheld | withheld |
| withstand | withstood | withstood |
| work | worked, wrought | worked, wrought |
| wring | wrung | wrung |
| write | wrote | written |

# A

**a** [ə, e] *art. indef.* un, una; **what —** ... !
¡qué ... !; **such —** tal; tan.

**abandon** [əbǽndən] *v.* abandonar;
dejar; *s.* abandono, desahogo, desenvoltura; entrega.

**abandoned** [əbǽndənd] *adj.* abandonado; dejado; perverso; inmoral.

**abandonment** [əbǽndənmənt] *s.* abandono, abandonamiento; desamparo;
desenvoltura, desembarazo.

**abashed** [əbǽʃt] *adj.* humillado, avergonzado.

**abate** [əbét] *v.* bajar, rebajar; disminuir;
acabar con; mitigar(se); calmarse.

**abatement** [əbétmənt] *s.* diminución,
merma; rebaja, descuento; mitigación.

**abbess** [ǽbəs] *s.* abadesa.

**abbey** [ǽbɪ] *s.* abadía, monasterio.

**abbot** [ǽbət] *s.* abad.

**abbreviate** [əbríviet] *v.* abreviar, acortar, reducir.

**abbreviation** [əbriviéʃən] *s.* abreviación, abreviatura.

**abdicate** [ǽbdəket] *v.* abdicar, renunciar.

**abdomen** [ǽbdəmən] *s.* abdomen;
vientre.

**abduct** [æbdʌkt] *v.* secuestrar, raptar,
*Am.* plagiar (*a alguien*).

**abduction** [æbdʌkʃən] *s.* rapto, robo,
secuestro (*de una persona*).

**aberration** [æbəréʃən] *s.* aberración,
extravío (*de la mente*).

**abet** [əbét] *v.* incitar; fomentar.

**abeyance** [əbéəns] *s.* suspensión; **in —**
pendiente.

**abhor** [əbhɔ́r] *v.* aborrecer, odiar, abominar.

**abhorrence** [əbhɔ́rəns] *s.* aborrecimiento, aversión.

**abide** [əbáɪd] *v.* quedar, permanecer;
morar, habitar; aguardar; soportar,
tolerar; **to — by** conformarse a;
atenerse a.

**ability** [əbílətɪ] *s.* habilidad, capacidad.

**abject** [ǽbdʒékt] *adj.* abatido; vil.

**abjure** [æbdʒúr] *v.* abjurar.

**able** [ébl] *adj.* hábil, capaz; competente;
**able-bodied** de cuerpo sano; **to be
— to** poder; saber.

**ably** [éblɪ] *adv.* hábilmente.

**abnormal** [æbnɔ́rml] *adj.* anormal.

**aboard** [əbórd] *adv.* a bordo; en el tren;
**to go —** embarcarse; **all — !** ¡viajeros al tren!; *Méx., C.A.* ¡vámonos!

**abode** [əbód] *s.* morada, domicilio,
casa; *pret. & p.p. de* **to abide**.

**abolish** [əbálɪʃ] *v.* abolir; anular.

**abolition** [æbəlíʃən] *s.* abolición.

**abominable** [əbámnəbl] *adj.* abominable, aborrecible.

**abort** [əbɔ́rt] *v.* abortar.

**abortion** [əbɔ́rʃən] *s.* aborto.

**abound** [əbáund] *v.* abundar; **to —
with** abundar en.

**about** [əbáut] *prep.* (*concerning*) acerca
de, tocante a, respecto de; (*near,
surrounding*) alrededor de, por; *adv.*
(*almost*) casi, poco más o menos; **at**

**— ten o'clock** a eso de las diez; **to be
— one's business** atender a su
negocio; **to be — to** estar para, estar
a punto de; **to face —** dar media
vuelta; **to have no money — one's
person** no llevar dinero consigo.

**above** [əbʌ́v] *prep.* por encima de;
sobre; *adv.* arriba; **— all** sobre todo;
**above-mentioned** susodicho, ya
mencionado; **from —** de arriba; del
cielo, de Dios.

**abrasive** [əbrésɪv] *adj.* abrasivo; tosco.

**abreast** [əbrést] *adj., adv.* al lado; **to
keep abreast** ponerse al corriente.

**abridge** [əbrídʒ] *v.* abreviar; compendiar, condensar; privar (*a uno de sus
derechos*).

**abroad** [əbród] *adv.* en el extranjero;
fuera de casa; **to go —** ir al extranjero; **to spread —** divulgar o publicar
por todas partes.

**abrupt** [əbrʌpt] *adj.* repentino; precipitado; áspero, brusco; escarpado;
**-ly** *adv.* de repente; bruscamente.

**abscess** [ǽbsɛs] *s.* absceso.

**absence** [ǽbsn̩s] *s.* ausencia; falta; **—
of mind** abstracción; **leave of —**
licencia (*para ausentarse*).

**absent** [ǽbsn̩t] *adj.* ausente; abstraído,
distraído; **absent-minded** absorto,
abstraído; [æbsént] *v.* **to — oneself**
ausentarse.

**absolute** [ǽbsəlut] *adj.* absoluto; **the
—** lo absoluto; **-ly** *adv.* absolutamente; en absoluto.

**absolution** [æbsəlúʃən] *s.* absolución.

**absolve** [æbsálv] *v.* absolver, remitir;
perdonar, alzar la pena o el castigo.

**absorb** [əbsɔ́rb] *v.* absorber.

**absorbent** [əbsɔ́rbənt] *adj. & s.* absorbente.

**absorption** [əbsɔ́rpʃən] *s.* absorción;
abstracción, embebecimiento.

**abstain** [əbstén] *v.* abstenerse, privarse.

**abstinence** [ǽbstənəns] *s.* abstinencia.

**abstract** [ǽbstrækt] *adj.* abstracto; *s.*
sumario; extracto; **in the —** en abstracto; [æbstrǽkt] *v.* abstraer; considerar aisladamente; separar, retirar;
resumir, compendiar.

**abstraction** [æbstrǽkʃən] *s.* abstracción; idea abstracta.

**absurd** [əbsɝ́d] *adj.* absurdo; insensato;
ridículo, disparatado.

**absurdity** [əbsɝ́dətɪ] *s.* absurdo, disparate.

**abundance** [əbʌ́ndəns] *s.* abundancia,
copia.

**abundant** [əbʌ́ndənt] *adj.* abundante,
copioso.

**abuse** [əbjús] *s.* abuso; maltrato;
ultraje; [əbjúz] *v.* abusar de; maltratar; injuriar; ultrajar.

**abusive** [əbjúsɪv] *adj.* abusivo; insultante, injurioso.

**abyss** [əbís] *s.* abismo; sima.

**academic** [əkədémɪk] *adj.* académico;
escolar.

**academy** [əkǽdəmɪ] *s.* academia; colegio, instituto; escuela preparatoria.

**accede** [æksíd] *v.* acceder, consentir.

**accelerate** [ækséləret] *v.* acelerar(se).
**acceleration** [æksɛləréʃən] *s.* aceleración.
**accelerator** [ækséləretɚ] *s.* acelerador.
**accent** [æksɛnt] *s.* acento; [æksént] *v.* acentuar; recalcar.
**accentuate** [ækséntʃuet] *v.* acentuar; recalcar; realzar.
**accept** [əksépt] *v.* aceptar; admitir; acoger; aprobar.
**acceptable** [əkséptəbl] *adj.* aceptable; grato; acepto.
**acceptance** [əkséptəns] *s.* aceptación; aprobación; buena acogida, recibimiento.
**access** [æksɛs] *s.* acceso; ataque (*de una enfermedad*); arrebato (*de furia*).
**accessible** [æksésəbl] *adj.* accesible; asequible, obtenible.
**accessory** [æksésərɪ] *adj.* accesorio; adjunto; *s.* accesorio; cómplice; **accessories** cosas accesorias, adornos, adminículos.
**accident** [æksədənt] *s.* accidente; percance, contratiempo; **by —** por casualidad.
**accidental** [æksədéntl] *adj.* accidental; casual; **-ly** *adv.* accidentalmente; por casualidad.
**acclaim** [əklém] *v.* aclamar, aplaudir; *s.* aclamación, aplauso.
**acclamation** [ækləméʃən] *s.* aclamación, aplauso.
**acclimate** [əkláımət], [ækləmet] *v.* aclimatar(se); acostumbrar(se).
**acclimatize** [əkláımətaız] *v.* aclimatar(se).
**accommodate** [əkɑmədét] *v.* (*adjust*) acomodar, ajustar, ayudar, hacer un favor; (*lodge*) hospedar, alojar, tener cabida para; **to — oneself** conformarse, adaptarse.
**accommodation** [əkɑmədéʃən] *s.* favor, ayuda; conveniencia; alojamiento (*en un hotel, casa, etc.*); cabida; adaptación; ajuste.
**accompaniment** [əkʌmpənɪmənt] *s.* acompañamiento.
**accompanist** [əkʌmpənɪst] *s.* acompañador, acompañante.
**accompany** [əkʌmpənɪ] *v.* acompañar.
**accomplice** [əkʌmplɪs] *s.* cómplice.
**accomplish** [əkʌmplɪʃ] *v.* cumplir; completar; lograr, conseguir; realizar, efectuar.
**accomplished** [əkʌmplɪʃt] *adj.* cumplido; realizado; consumado; establecido; diestro; perfecto.
**accomplishment** [əkʌmplɪʃmənt] *s.* cumplimiento; logro, realización; habilidad; perfección; mérito, proeza.
**accord** [əkɔrd] *s.* acuerdo, convenio; armonía, concierto; **of one's own —** voluntariamente; espontáneamente; **in — with** de acuerdo con; **with one —** unánimemente; *v.* otorgar, conceder, dar; concordar.
**accordance** [əkɔrdns] *s.* conformidad, acuerdo; **in — with** de acuerdo con, de conformidad con.
**according** [əkɔrdɪŋ]: **— to** según; conforme a; de acuerdo con; **— as** según (que), a medida que.
**accordingly** [əkɔrdɪŋlɪ] *adv.* en conformidad; así; como tal; por lo tanto; por consiguiente.
**accordion** [əkɔrdɪən] *s.* acordeón.
**accost** [əkɔst] *v.* abordar (*a alguien*) en la calle, acosar; molestar, perseguir.
**account** [əkáunt] *s.* (*bill*) cuenta, computación; (*story*) relato; **on — of** a causa de; con motivo de; por; **on my —** por mí; **on my own —** por mi propia cuenta; **on no —** de ninguna manera; **of no —** de ningún valor o importancia; **to turn to —** aprovechar, hacer útil o provechoso; *v.* dar cuenta (a); considerar, tener por; **to — for** dar cuenta o razón de; explicar; **how do you — for that?** ¿cómo se explica eso?
**accountable** [əkáuntəbl] *adj.* responsable; explicable.
**accountant** [əkáuntənt] *s.* contador, tenedor de libros.
**accounting** [əkáuntɪŋ] *s.* contabilidad, contaduría.
**accredit** [əkrédɪt] *v.* acreditar.
**accrue** [əkrú] *v.* acumular(se).
**acculturate** [əkʌltʃõet] *v.* aculturar(se).
**accumulate** [əkjúmjəlet] *v.* acumular(se), juntar(se), amontonar(se).
**accumulation** [əkjumjəléʃən] *s.* acumulación, amontonamiento.
**accuracy** [ækjərəsɪ] *s.* precisión, exactitud, esmero.
**accurate** [ækjərɪt] *adj.* preciso, exacto, correcto; esmerado; cierto; certero; acertado; **-ly** *adv.* con exactitud; correctamente; con esmero.
**accursed** [əkɚst] *adj.* maldito; infame.
**accusation** [ækjəzéʃən] *s.* acusación.
**accuse** [əkjúz] *v.* acusar; denunciar.
**accuser** [əkjúzɚ] *s.* acusador; delator, denunciador.
**accustom** [əkʌstəm] *v.* acostumbrar; **to — oneself** acostumbrarse; **to be -ed to** tener la costumbre de, acostumbrar, soler; estar acostumbrado a, estar hecho a.
**ace** [es] *s.* as; as, el mejor de su clase (*como un aviador excelente*); **within an — of** a punto de; muy cerca de.
**acetate** [æsatet] *s.* acetato.
**acetylene** [əsétəlin] *s.* acetileno.
**ache** [ek] *s.* dolor; **tooth —** dolor de muelas; *v.* doler.
**achieve** [ətʃív] *v.* acabar, llevar a cabo; realizar; conseguir, lograr; alcanzar.
**achievement** [ətʃívmənt] *s.* logro, realización; proeza, hazaña.
**acid** [æsɪd] *adj.* ácido; agrio; *s.* ácido.
**acidity** [əsídətɪ] *s.* acidez.
**acknowledge** [əknálɪdʒ] *v.* reconocer, admitir; confesar; **to — receipt** acusar recibo.
**acknowledgment** [əknálɪdʒmənt] *s.* reconocimiento, expresión de gratitud; confesión, admisión; **— of receipt** acuse de recibo.
**acorn** [ékɔrn] *s.* bellota.
**acoustics** [əkústɪks] *s.* acústica.

**acquaint** [əkwént] v. enterar, informar; dar a conocer; familiarizar; **to — oneself with** ponerse al corriente de; enterarse de; **to be -ed with** conocer a (una persona); estar enterado de (algo); conocer (una ciudad, un país, etc.).

**acquaintance** [əkwéntəns] s. conocimiento; conocido; **-s** amistades.

**acquiesce** [ækwɪés] v. asentir; consentir, quedar conforme.

**acquiescence** [ækwɪésns] s. asentimiento, consentimiento; conformidad.

**acquire** [əkwáɪr] v. adquirir; obtener, conseguir; contraer (costumbres, vicios).

**acquisition** [ækwəzíʃən] s. adquisición.

**acquit** [əkwít] v. absolver, exonerar; pagar, redimir, librar de (una obligación); **to — oneself well** quedar bien; portarse bien.

**acquital** [əkwítl] s. absolución.

**acre** [ékɚ] s. acre (medida de superficie).

**acrobat** [ækrəbæt] s. acróbata.

**acronym** [ækrənɪm] s. acrónimo.

**across** [əkrós] prep. a través de; al otro lado de; por; por en medio de; adv. a través, de través; **to go —** atravesar; **to come —, run —** encontrarse con; tropezar con.

**acrylic** [əkrílɪk] adj. acrílico.

**act** [ækt] s. acto; acción, hecho; v. hacer, desempeñar (un papel); representar (en el teatro); obrar; actuar; portarse; funcionar; **to — as** servir de, estar de.

**acting** [æktɪŋ] s. representación, desempeño (de un papel dramático); acción, actuación; adj. interino, suplente.

**action** [ækʃən] s. acción; acto; actuación; funcionamiento.

**activate** [æktɪvet] v. activar.

**active** [æktɪv] adj. activo.

**activism** [æktəvɪzm] s. activismo.

**activist** [æktəvɪst] s. activista.

**activity** [æktívətɪ] s. actividad.

**actor** [æktɚ] s. actor.

**actress** [æktrɪs] s. actriz.

**actual** [æktʃʊəl] adj. (legitimate) verdadero, real; (current) actual, existente; **-ly** adv. realmente, en realidad; de hecho, efectivamente.

**acumen** [əkjúmɪn] s. caletre, tino, perspicacia.

**acute** [əkjút] adj. agudo; perspicaz; penetrante.

**adamant** [ædəmænt] adj. duro; firme, inflexible.

**adapt** [ədǽpt] v. adaptar; **to — oneself** adaptarse, acomodarse.

**adaptation** [ædəptéʃən] s. adaptación.

**add** [æd] v. sumar; añadir, agregar.

**addict** [ædɪkt] s. adicto (persona adicta al uso de narcóticos); **drug —** morfinómano.

**addicted** [ədíktɪd] adj. adicto, dado, entregado, habituado.

**addition** [ədíʃən] s. adición; suma; añadidura, aditamento; **in — to** además de.

**additional** [ədíʃənl] adj. adicional.

**additive** [ædətɪv] s. & adj. aditivo.

**address** [ədrés] s. (street) dirección,

domicilio, señas; sobrescrito; (speech) discurso, arenga, conferente; **form of —** tratamiento; v. dirigir, poner la dirección, señas o sobrescrito a; hablar, dirigir la palabra a; dirigirse a; **to — oneself to a task** aplicarse a una tarea.

**addressee** [ædrɛsí] s. destinatario.

**adduce** [ədús] v. aducir.

**adequate** [ædəkwɪt] adj. adecuado; proporcionado; suficiente.

**adhere** [ədhír] v. adherirse; pegarse.

**adherence** [ədhírəns] s. adherencia.

**adhesion** [ədhíʒən] s. adhesión.

**adhesive** [ədhísɪv] adj. adhesivo; pegajoso; **— tape** tela adhesiva, esparadrapo.

**adjacent** [ədʒésn̩t] adj. adyacente, contiguo.

**adjective** [ædʒɪktɪv] s. adjetivo.

**adjoin** [ədʒóɪn] v. estar contiguo o adyacente a, lindar con.

**adjourn** [ədʒɚ́n] v. aplazar, diferir; **to — the meeting** suspender o levantar la sesión; **meeting -ed** se levanta la sesión.

**adjournment** [ədʒɚ́nmənt] s. aplazamiento, levantamiento (de una sesión).

**adjunct** [ædʒʌŋkt] s. adjunto, aditamento, añadidura; asociado, acompañante; adj. adjunto, unido, subordinado.

**adjust** [ədʒʌ́st] v. ajustar; acomodar; arreglar; graduar; **to — oneself** adaptarse, conformarse.

**adjustment** [ədʒʌ́stmənt] s. ajuste; ajustamiento; arreglo; regulación.

**ad-lib** [ædlíb] v. improvisar; expresarse espontáneamente.

**administer** [ədmínəstɚ] v. administrar; dirigir, regir, gobernar; aplicar (remedio, castigo, etc.); **to — an oath** tomar juramento.

**administration** [ədmɪnəstréʃən] s. administración; dirección, gobierno; gerencia; manejo.

**administrative** [ədmínəstretɪv] adj. administrativo; ejecutivo; gubernativo.

**administrator** [ədmínəstretɚ] s. administrador.

**admirable** [ædmərəbl] adj. admirable; **admirably** adv. admirablemente.

**admiral** [ædmərəl] s. almirante.

**admiration** [ædməréʃən] s. admiración.

**admire** [ədmáɪr] v. admirar; estimar.

**admirer** [ədmáɪrɚ] s. admirador; pretendiente.

**admissible** [ədmísəbl] adj. admisible.

**admission** [ədmísʃən] s. (entrance) entrada, precio de entrada o de ingreso; (confession) confesión, admisión.

**admit** [ədmít] v. admitir; aceptar; confesar, reconocer; conceder; dar entrada.

**admittance** [ədmítn̩s] s. entrada; derecho de entrar; admisión.

**admonish** [ədmánɪʃ] v. amonestar.

**admonition** [ædməníʃən] s. amonestación, consejo.

**ado** [ədú] *s.* actividad; bulla; disturbio.
**adobe** [ədóbɪ] *s.* adobe; casa de adobe.
**adolescence** [ædlésn̩s] *s.* adolescencia.
**adolescent** [ædlésn̩t] *adj. & s.* adolescente.
**adopt** [ədápt] *v.* adoptar.
**adoption** [ədápʃən] *s.* adopción.
**adorable** [ədórəbl] *adj.* adorable; encantador.
**adoration** [ædəréʃən] *s.* adoración.
**adore** [ədór] *v.* adorar.
**adorn** [ədɔ́rn] *v.* adornar; ornar; embellecer.
**adornment** [ədɔ́rnmənt] *s.* adorno.
**adrenal** [ədrínl] *adj.* suprarrenal.
**adrenalin** [ædrénəlɪn] *s.* adrenalina.
**adrift** [ədríft] *adj. & adv.* a la deriva, flotando, flotante.
**adroit** [ədrɔ́ɪt] *adj.* hábil, diestro.
**adult** [ədʌ́lt] *adj. & s.* adulto.
**adulterate** [ədʌ́ltəret] *v.* adulterar.
**adulterer** [ədʌ́ltərɚ] *s.* adúltero.
**adultery** [ədʌ́ltərɪ] *s.* adulterio.
**advance** [ədvǽns] *v.* (*progress*) avanzar, adelantar; progresar; acelerar; (*promote*) promover; proponer; (*pay beforehand*) pagar por adelantado (*anticipado*); *s.* avance; progreso; adelanto, anticipo; alza, aumento de precio; **-s** requerimientos, pretensiones, insinuaciones; **in —** por adelantado, con anticipación.
**advanced** [ədvǽnst] *adj.* avanzado; adelantado; **— in years** entrado en años, viejo, anciano.
**advancement** [ədvǽnsmənt] *s.* adelantamiento, mejora, progreso; promoción.
**advantage** [ədvǽntɪdʒ] *s.* ventaja; beneficio, provecho; **to have the — over** llevar ventaja a; **to take — of** aprovecharse de; **to take — of a person** abusar de la confianza o paciencia de alguien.
**advantageous** [ædvəntédʒəs] *adj.* ventajoso; provechoso.
**advent** [ǽdvɛnt] *s.* advenimiento; venida.
**adventure** [ədvéntʃɚ] *s.* aventura; riesgo.
**adventurer** [ədvéntʃərɚ] *s.* aventurero.
**adventurous** [ədvéntʃərəs] *adj.* aventurero; atrevido; aventurado, arriesgado.
**adverb** [ǽdvɚb] *m.* adverbio.
**adversary** [ǽdvɚsɛrɪ] *s.* adversario, antagonista, contrario.
**adverse** [ədvɝ́s] *adj.* adverso; opuesto, contrario; hostil; desfavorable.
**adversity** [ədvɝ́sətɪ] *s.* adversidad; infortunio.
**advertise** [ǽdvɚtaɪz] *v.* anunciar; avisar, dar viso.
**advertisement** [ædvɚtáɪzmənt] *s.* anuncio, aviso.
**advertiser** [ǽdvɚtaɪzɚ] *s.* anunciador, anunciante.
**advertising** [ǽdvɚtaɪzɪŋ] *s.* anuncios; arte o negocio de anunciar.
**advice** [ədváɪs] *s.* aviso, advertencia; consejo; noticia.

**advisable** [ədváɪzəbl̩] *adj.* conveniente; prudente; recomendable.
**advise** [ədváɪz] *v.* (*counsel*) aconsejar; (*inform*) avisar, informar, advertir; **to — with** consultar con; aconsejarse con.
**adviser, advisor** [ədváɪzɚ] *s.* consejero, aconsejador.
**advocate** [ǽdvəkɪt] *s.* abogado; defensor, intercesor; partidario; [ǽdvəket] *v.* abogar por; defender.
**aerial** [ɛ́rɪəl] *adj.* aéreo; *s.* antena.
**aerodynamic** [ɛrodaɪnǽmɪk] *adj.* aerodinámico; aerodynamics *s.* aerodinámica.
**aeroplane** [ɛ́rəplen] = **airplane.**
**aerosol** [ɛ́rosol] *s.* aerosol.
**aesthetic** [ɛsθétɪk] *adj.* estético; **-s** *s.* estética.
**afar** [əfár] *adv.* lejos; **from —** desde lejos.
**affable** [ǽfəbl̩] *adj.* afable, amable.
**affair** [əfér] *s.* (*social*) función, tertulia, fiesta, convite; (*venture*) asunto; negocio; lance; cosa; **love —** amorío.
**affect** [əfékt] *v.* afectar; conmover; fingir; hacer ostentación de.
**affectation** [æfɪktéʃən] *s.* afectación.
**affected** [əféktɪd] *adj.* (*emotion*) afectado, conmovido, enternecido; (*feigned*) fingido, artificioso.
**affection** [əfékʃən] *s.* afecto, cariño; inclinación; afección, dolencia.
**affectionate** [əfékʃənɪt] *adj.* afectuoso, cariñoso.
**affidavit** [æfədévɪt] *s.* declaración jurada.
**affiliate** [əfílɪet] *v.* afiliar; afiliarse, unirse, asociarse.
**affinity** [əfínətɪ] *s.* afinidad.
**affirm** [əfɝ́m] *v.* afirmar, asegurar, aseverar.
**affirmative** [əfɝ́mətɪv] *adj.* afirmativo; *s.* afirmativa.
**affix** [əfíks] *v.* fijar, pegar; **to — one's signature** poner su firma, firmar.
**afflict** [əflíkt] *v.* afligir; **to be -ed with** padecer de, sufrir de, adolecer de.
**affliction** [əflíkʃən] *s.* aflicción; pena, dolor; achaque; angustia; infortunio.
**affluent** [ǽflʊənt] *adj.* acaudalado; abundante.
**afford** [əfórd] *v.* proveer, proporcionar; **I cannot — that expense** no puedo hacer ese gasto; **he cannot — to waste time** no le conviene perder el tiempo; no tiene tiempo que perder; **I cannot — that risk** no puedo (*o* no quiero) exponerme a ese riesgo.
**affricate** [ǽfrɪkət] *adj. & s.* africado.
**affront** [əfrʌ́nt] *s.* afrenta, agravio, ultraje; *v.* afrentar, agraviar, ultrajar.
**afire** [əfáɪr] *adj.* ardiendo, quemándose.
**afloat** [əflót] *adj. & adv.* flotante; flotando; a flote; a flor de agua; a bordo; inundado; a la deriva, sin rumbo; **the rumor is —** corre la voz.
**afoot** [əfút] *adv.* a pie; en marcha, en movimiento.
**aforesaid** [əfórsɛd] *adj.* susodicho, ya dicho.

**afraid** [əfréd] *adj.* miedoso, medroso; atemorizado, amedrentado; **to be —** temer, tener miedo.

**afresh** [əfréʃ] *adv.* de nuevo, desde el principio.

**African** [ǽfrɪkən] *adj.* & *s.* africano; negro.

**after** [ǽftɚ] *prep.* (*temporal*) después de, tras, tras de; (*position*) detrás de; (*following*) en busca de; *adv.* después; detrás; *conj.* después (de) que; *adj.* subsiguiente; siguiente; **— all** después de todo; de todos modos; **day — tomorrow** pasado mañana; **after-dinner** de sobremesa; **—effect** consecuencia, resultado; **—math** consecuencias, resultados (*usualmente desastrosos*); **—thought** idea tardía.

**afternoon** [æftɚnún] *s.* tarde.

**aftertaste** [ǽftɚtest] *s.* dejo, dejillo (*sabor que queda en la boca*).

**afterwards** [ǽftɚwɚdz] *adv.* después.

**again** [əgén] *adv.* otra vez, de nuevo; además; por otra parte; **— and —** repetidas veces; **never —** nunca jamás; **to come —** volver; **to do it —** volver a hacerlo.

**against** [əgénst] *prep.* contra; frente a; en contraste con; **— the grain** a contrapelo, a redopelo; **— a rainy day** para cuando llueva.

**age** [edʒ] *s.* edad; época; siglo; generación; **of —** mayor de edad; **old —** vejez, ancianidad; **to become of —** llegar a mayor edad; **under —** menor de edad; *v.* envejecer(se).

**aged** [édʒɪd, édʒd] *adj.* viejo, anciano; añejo; envejecido; **— forty years** de cuarenta años; **— in wood** añejado en toneles o barriles (*dícese del vino*).

**agency** [édʒənsɪ] *s.* agencia; medio, intermedio.

**agenda** [ədʒéndə] *s.* temario; asuntos que han de tratarse en una reunión.

**agent** [édʒənt] *s.* agente; intermediario, representante; apoderado.

**aggrandize** [ǽgrəndaɪz] *v.* engrandecer; agrandar.

**aggravate** [ǽgrəvet] *v.* agravar, empeorar; irritar, exasperar.

**aggregate** [ǽgrɪgɪt] *s.* agregado, conjunto, colección; *adj.* agregado, unido; **in the —** en conjunto.

**aggression** [əgréʃən] *s.* agresión.

**aggressive** [əgrésɪv] *adj.* agresivo; emprendedor.

**aggressor** [əgrésɚ] *s.* agresor.

**aghast** [əgǽst] *adj.* espantado, pasmado.

**agile** [ǽdʒəl] *adj.* ágil.

**agility** [ədʒílətɪ] *s.* agilidad.

**agitate** [ǽdʒətet] *v.* agitar; turbar, perturbar; alborotar; discutir acaloradamente; maquinar, tramar.

**agitation** [ædʒətéʃən] *s.* agitación; alboroto.

**agitator** [ǽdʒətetɚ] *s.* agitador, alborotador, revoltoso.

**ago** [əgó] *adj.* & *adv.* pasado; en el pasado; **many years —** hace muchos años; muchos años ha, mucho tiempo ha; **long —** hace mucho tiempo; ha mucho.

**agonize** [ǽgənaɪz] *v.* agonizar; sufrir angustiosamente; retorcerse de dolor; luchar.

**agony** [ǽgənɪ] *s.* agonía; angustia; tormento; dolor; lucha.

**agree** [əgrí] *v.* (*accede*) acordar, concordar, consentir, estar de acuerdo, ponerse de acuerdo; (*suit*) sentarle bien a uno (*dícese del clima, del alimento, etc.*).

**agreeable** [əgríəbl̩] *adj.* agradable, afable; complaciente; conveniente; satisfactorio.

**agreement** [əgrímənt] *s.* (*concord*) acuerdo, convenio, conformidad; (*grammatical*) concordancia; **to be in —** estar de acuerdo; **to come to an —** ponerse de acuerdo.

**agricultural** [ægrɪkʌ́ltʃərəl] *adj.* agrícola.

**agriculture** [ǽgrɪkʌltʃɚ] *s.* agricultura.

**agriculturist** [ægrɪkʌ́ltʃərɪst] *s.* agricultor.

**aground** [əgráund] *adj.* & *adv.* encallado.

**ahead** [əhéd] *adv.* delante, al frente; adelante; **— of time** adelantado; antes de tiempo; **to go —** ir adelante; **to get —** adelantar(se).

**aid** [ed] *s.* ayuda, auxilio, socorro; ayudante, auxiliar; *v.* ayudar, auxiliar, socorrer.

**ail** [el] *v.* adolecer, padecer; **what -s you?** ¿qué tienes? ¿qué te aflige?

**aileron** [élərən] *s.* alerón.

**ailment** [élmənt] *s.* achaque, dolencia.

**aim** [em] *s.* (*pointing*) puntería; tino; (*objective*) fin, objeto; proposición; *v.* apuntar (*un arma*); dirigir, asestar; dirigir la puntería; aspirar (a); **to — to please** proponerse (*o tratar de*) agradar.

**aimless** [émlɪs] *adj.* sin propósito, sin objeto.

**air** [ɛr] *s.* (*atmosphere*) aire, brisa; (*music*) tonada; **in the —** en el aire; indeciso, incierto; **in the open —** al raso, al aire libre; **to be on the —** emitir, radiodifundir; **to put on -s** darse tono; *adj.* de aire; aéreo; **— brake** freno neumático; **— line** línea aérea; ruta aérea; **by —mail** por correo aéreo, por vía aérea, por avión; **air-conditioned** de aire acondicionado; *v.* airear; orear; ventilar; publicar, pregonar; ostentar.

**airborne** [érborn] *aéreo*; aerotransportado.

**aircraft** [érkræft] *s.* avión, aeroplano; aeronave; aviones.

**airline** [érlaɪn] *s.* aerovía: línea aérea; compañía de transporte aéreo.

**airplane** [érplen] *s.* aeroplano, avión; **— carrier** portaaviones.

**airport** [érport] *s.* aeropuerto, aeródromo.

**airship** [érʃɪp] *s.* aeronave.

**airtight** [értáɪt] *adj.* hermético.

**airy** [érɪ] *adj.* airoso; aireado, ventilado; ligero; tenue.

**aisle** [aɪl] *s.* pasillo, pasadizo; nave (*de una iglesia*).

**ajar** [ədʒár] *adj.* entreabierto, entornado.

**alarm** [əlárm] *s.* alarma; rebato; inquietud; **— clock** despertador; *v.* alarmar; inquietar.

**album** [ǽlbəm] álbum.

**alcohol** [ǽlkəhɔl] *s.* alcohol.

**alcoholic** [ǽlkəhólɪk] *adj.* alcohólico.

**alcove** [ǽlkov] *s.* alcoba.

**alderman** [ɔ́ldɚmən] *s.* concejal, regidor.

**ale** [el] *s.* cerveza de tipo espeso y amargo.

**alert** [əlɚ́t] *adj.* alerto, vigilante; despierto; vivo; listo; *s.* alarma, rebato; **to be on the —** estar alerta.

**alfalfa** [ælfǽlfə] *s.* alfalfa.

**algebra** [ǽldʒəbrə] *s.* álgebra.

**alibi** [ǽləbaɪ] *s.* coartado; excusa.

**alien** [éljən] *s.* extranjero; residente extranjero; *adj.* extraño, ajeno.

**alienate** [éljənet] *v.* enajenar; apartar, alejar (*a una persona de otra*).

**alienist** [éljənɪst] *s.* alienista, psiquiatra.

**alight** [əláɪt] *v.* apearse, desmontarse, bajar(de); posarse (*dícese de pájaros, mariposas, etc.*).

**align** [əláɪn] *v.* alinear(se).

**alike** [əláɪk] *adj.* semejante; parecido; **to be —** parecerse, asemejarse; ser iguales; *adv.* del mismo modo.

**alimony** [ǽləmonɪ] *s.* asistencia de divorcio; alimento.

**alive** [əláɪv] *adj.* vivo; con vida; viviente; activo; **— with** lleno de.

**all** [ɔl] *adj.* todo (el); todos (los); *s.* todo; todo el mundo, todos; *adv.* enteramente; **— at once** de una vez; de un tirón; de repente; **— right** bueno; bien; **— the worse** tanto peor; **not at —** de ninguna manera; no hay de qué; **nothing at —** nada en absoluto; **— told** (*o* **in —**) en conjunto; **once (and) for —** por última vez; una vez por todas; **to be — in** estar agotado, estar rendido de fatiga; **it is — over** se acabó, ha terminado todo.

**allay** [əlé] *v.* aliviar; calmar.

**allegation** [æləgéʃən] *s.* alegación, alegato; aseveración.

**allege** [əlédʒ] *v.* alegar; declarar; sostener, asegurar.

**allegiance** [əlídʒəns] *s.* lealtad, fidelidad; homenaje.

**allegory** [ǽləgorɪ] *s.* alegoría.

**allergy** [ǽlədʒɪ] *s.* alergia (*sensibilidad anormal a ciertos alimentos o sustancias*).

**alleviate** [əlívɪet] *v.* aliviar.

**alley** [ǽlɪ] *s.* callejón; callejuela; **blind —** callejón sin salida; **bowling —** boliche, *Am.* bolera.

**alliance** [əláɪəns] *s.* alianza.

**allied** [əláɪd] *adj.* aliado; relacionado.

**alligator** [ǽləgetɚ] *s.* lagarto; caimán; **— pear** aguacate.

**allot** [əlát] *v.* asignar; repartir.

**allow** [əláu] *v.* permitir, dejar; conceder; admitir; asignar; abonar; **to — for**

**certain errors** tener en cuenta ciertos errores.

**allowable** [əláuəbl] *adj.* permisible, admisible, lícito.

**allowance** [əláuəns] *s.* asignación; abono, pensión; ración; rebaja, descuento; permiso; concesión; **monthly —** mesada, mensualidad; **to make — for** tener en cuenta.

**alloy** [ǽlɔɪ] *s.* aleación, liga, mezcla (*de dos o más metales*); [əlɔ́ɪ] *v.* alear, ligar, mezclar (*metales*).

**allude** [əlúd] *v.* aludir.

**allure** [əlúr] *v.* seducir, cautivar; atraer, halagar.

**allurement** [əlúrmənt] *s.* seducción, tentación; atractivo, halago.

**alluring** [əlúrɪŋ] *adj.* seductivo, halagüeño, encantador.

**allusion** [əlúʒən] *s.* alusión; indirecta, insinuación.

**ally** [əláɪ] *v.* unir; aliarse; **to — oneself (itself) with** aliarse con, unirse con; [ǽlaɪ] *s.* aliado.

**almanac** [ɔ́lmənæk] *s.* almanaque, calendario.

**almighty** [əlmáɪtɪ] *adj.* todopoderoso, omnipotente.

**almond** [ámənd] *s.* almendra; **— tree** almendro.

**almost** [ɔ́lmost] *adv.* casi; **I — fell down** por poco me caigo.

**alms** [amz] *s.* limosna; **— box** cepo o cepillo, alcancía (*para limosnas*).

**aloft** [əlɔ́ft] *adv.* en alto; arriba.

**alone** [əlón] *adj.* solo; solitario; único; *adv.* sólo, solamente; **all —** a solas; completamente solo; solito; **to let —** no tocar; no molestar; dejar en paz; no hacer caso de.

**along** [əlɔ́ŋ] *prep.* a lo largo de; por; al lado de; **— with** junto con; en compañía de; **all —** todo el tiempo; de un extremo a otro; **all — the coast** por toda la costa; **to carry — with** llevar consigo; **to go — with** acompañar; **to get —** ir bien; **to get — with** llevarse bien con; **get —!** ¡vete! ¡váyase! ¡largo de aquí!

**alongside** [əlɔ́ŋsáɪd] *prep. & adv.* al lado (de); al costado (de); lado a lado.

**aloof** [əlúf] *adj.* aislado, apartado, retirado; huraño; reservado; *adv.* aparte; lejos.

**aloofness** [əlúfnɪs] *s.* alejamiento, desapego, aislamiento.

**aloud** [əláud] *adv.* alto, recio, fuerte; en voz alta.

**alphabet** [ǽlfəbɛt] *s.* alfabeto.

**already** [ɔlrédɪ] *adv.* ya.

**also** [ɔ́lso] *adv.* también, además, igualmente.

**altar** [ɔ́ltɚ] *s.* altar; **high — altar** mayor; **—piece** retablo.

**alter** [ɔ́ltɚ] *v.* alterar; cambiar; variar.

**alteration** [ɔltɚréʃən] *s.* alteración, cambio; mudanza; modificación.

**alternate** [ɔ́ltɚnɪt] *adj.* alternativo; alterno; alternado; *s.* suplente; **-ly** *adv.* alternativamente, por turno; [ɔ́ltɚnet] *v.* alternar; variar; turnar.

**alternative** [ɔltɜ́rnətiv] *adj.* alternativo; *s.* alternativa.

**alternator** [ɔltɜ́rnétɜ] *s.* alternador.

**although** [ɔlðóǐ] *conj.* aunque, si bien, bien que.

**altimeter** [ǽltɪmətɜ] *s.* altímetro.

**altitude** [ǽltɜtjud] *s.* altitud, altura, elevación.

**alto** [ǽlto] *s.* & *adj.* contralto.

**altogether** [ɔltɜgéðɜ] *adv.* del todo, completamente; en conjunto.

**aluminum** [əlúmɪnəm] *s.* aluminio.

**alumnus** [əlʌ́mnəs] *s.* graduado, exalumno.

**always** [ɔ́lwɪz] *adv.* siempre.

**am** [æm] *1ª persona del presente de indic. del verbo* **to be**: soy, estoy.

**amalgamate** [əmǽlgəmet] *v.* amalgamar; combinar; unir.

**amass** [əmǽs] *v.* amontonar, acumular, apilar, *Am.* amasar.

**amateur** [ǽmətʃur] *s.* aficionado; novicio, principiante.

**amaze** [əméz] *v.* pasmar, maravillar, asombrar.

**amazement** [əmézmənt] *s.* pasmo, admiración, asombro.

**amazing** [əmézɪŋ] *adj.* pasmoso, asombroso, maravilloso.

**ambassador** [æmbǽsədɜ] *s.* embajador.

**amber** [ǽmbɜ] *s.* ámbar; color de ámbar; *adj.* ambarino; de ámbar.

**ambiguity** [æmbɪgjúətɪ] *s.* ambigüedad.

**ambiguous** [æmbígjuəs] *adj.* ambiguo.

**ambition** [æmbíʃən] *s.* ambición, aspiración.

**ambitious** [æmbíʃəs] *adj.* ambicioso.

**ambivalent** [æmbívələnt] *adj.* ambivalente.

**amble** [ǽmbl] *v.* andar, vagar.

**ambulance** [ǽmbjələns] *s.* ambulancia.

**ambush** [ǽmbuʃ] *s.* emboscada; celada; acecho; **to lie in —** estar emboscado, estar al acecho; *v.* emboscar; poner celada a.

**amenable** [əmínabl] *adj.* dócil; tratable.

**amend** [əménd] *v.* enmendar; rectificar; **-s** *s. pl.* satisfacción, compensación; **to make — for** resarcir, dar satisfacción por, compensar por.

**amendment** [əméndmənt] *s.* enmienda.

**American** [əmérəkən] *adj.* & *s.* (*continental*) americano; (*U.S.A.*) norteamericano.

**amethyst** [ǽməθɪst] *s.* amatista.

**amiable** [émɪəbl] *adj.* amable, afable, amistoso.

**amicable** [ǽmɪkəbl] *adj.* amigable, amistoso.

**amid** [əmíd] *prep.* en medio de; entre; **amidst** [əmídst] = **amid**.

**amiss** [əmís] *adj.* errado, equivocado; impropio; *adv.* mal; fuera de lugar, impropiamente; **to take —** llevar a mal.

**ammonia** [əmónjə] *s.* amoníaco.

**ammunition** [æmjəníʃən] *s.* munición.

**amnesia** [æmníʒjə] *s.* amnesia.

**amnesty** [ǽmnɛstɪ] *s.* amnistía.

**among** [əmʌ́ŋ] *prep.* entre, en medio de; **amongst** [əmʌ́ŋst] = **among**.

**amorous** [ǽmərəs] *adj.* amoroso.

**amorphous** [əmɔ́rfəs] *adj.* amorfo.

**amortize** [ǽmɜtaɪz] *v.* amortizar.

**amount** [əmáunt] *s.* suma; cantidad; total; importe; valor; *v.* montar, subir, importar, ascender (a); valer; **that -s to stealing** eso equivale a robar.

**ampere** [ǽmpɪr] *s.* amperio.

**amphitheater** [ǽmfəθɪətɜ] *s.* anfiteatro.

**ample** [ǽmpl] *adj.* amplio; abundante; bastante, suficiente.

**amplify** [ǽmpləfaɪ] *v.* ampliar; amplificar.

**amputate** [ǽmpjətet] *v.* amputar.

**amuse** [əmjúz] *v.* divertir, entretener, distraer; **to — oneself** divertirse.

**amusement** [əmjúzmənt] *s.* diversión, entretenimiento, pasatiempo, recreo, distracción.

**amusing** [əmjúzɪŋ] *adj.* divertido, entretenido; gracioso, chistoso.

**an** [ən, æn] *art. indef.* un, una.

**anachronism** [ənǽkrənɪzm] *s.* anacronismo.

**analogous** [ənǽləgəs] *adj.* análogo.

**analogy** [ənǽlədʒɪ] *s.* analogía, semejanza.

**analysis** [ənǽləsɪs] *s.* análisis.

**analyze** [ǽnəlaɪz] *v.* analizar.

**anarchist** [ǽnɜkɪst] *s.* anarquista.

**anarchy** [ǽnɜkɪ] *s.* anarquía.

**anatomy** [ənǽtəmɪ] *s.* anatomía.

**ancestor** [ǽnsɛstɜ] *s.* antepasado; **-s** abuelos, antepasados.

**ancestral** [ænséstrəl] *adj.* solariego, de los antepasados; hereditario.

**ancestry** [ǽnsɛstrɪ] *s.* linaje, abolengo, ascendencia.

**anchor** [ǽŋkɜ] *s.* ancla; **to drop —** anclar, echar anclas, dar fondo, fondear; **to weigh —** levar el ancla; *v.* anclar; echar anclas; fijar, asegurar.

**anchovy** [ǽntʃovɪ] *s.* anchoa, anchova.

**ancient** [énʃənt] *adj.* antiguo; vetusto; **the -s** los antiguos; la antigüedad.

**and** [ənd, ænd] *conj.* y; e (*delante de* i *o* hi); **— so forth** etcétera; y así sucesivamente; **let us try — do it** tratemos de hacerlo; **let us go — see him** vamos a verle.

**Andalusian** [ændəlúʒən] *adj.* andaluz.

**anecdote** [ǽnɪkdot] *s.* anécdota.

**anemia** [ənímɪə] *s.* anemia.

**anesthetic** [ænəsθétɪk] *adj.* & *s.* anestésico.

**anew** [ənjú] *adv.* otra vez, de nuevo; nuevamente.

**angel** [éndʒəl] *s.* ángel.

**angelic** [ændʒélɪk] *adj.* angélico.

**anger** [ǽŋgɜ] *s.* enojo, enfado, ira, cólera; *v.* enojar, enfadar, encolerizar.

**angina** [ændʒáɪnə] *s.* angina; **— pectoris** angina de pecho.

**angle** [ǽŋgl] *s.* ángulo; (*interior*) rincón; (*exterior*) esquina; punto de vista, aspecto; *v.* pescar.

**Anglo-Saxon** [ǽnglosǽksn̩] *adj.* & *s.* anglosajón.

**angry** [ǽŋgrɪ] *adj.* enojado; colérico.
**anguish** [ǽŋgwɪʃ] *s.* angustia, ansia, pena, dolor.
**angular** [ǽŋgjələ] *adj.* angular; anguloso.
**animal** [ǽnəml] *s. & adj.* animal.
**animate** [ǽnəmɪt] *adj.* animado, viviente; **animated cartoon** dibujo animado; [ǽnəmet] *v.* animar; alentar.
**animation** [ænəméʃən] *s.* animación; viveza.
**animosity** [ænəmásətɪ] *s.* animosidad, ojeriza, inquina, rencor.
**anise** [ǽnɪs] *s.* anís.
**ankle** [ǽŋkl] *s.* tobillo.
**annals** [ǽnlz] *s. pl.* anales.
**annex** [ǽnɛks] *s.* (*building*) pabellón, ala; (*dependent addition*) anexo; añadidura; [ənéks] *v.* anexar.
**annexation** [ænɛkséʃən] *s.* anexión.
**annihilate** [ənáɪəlet] *v.* aniquilar; anonadar.
**anniversary** [ænəvə́rsərɪ] *s. & adj.* aniversario.
**annotate** [ǽnotet] *v.* anotar.
**annotation** [ænotéʃən] *s.* anotación, acotación, nota.
**announce** [ənáʊns] *v.* anunciar; proclamar.
**announcement** [ənáʊnsmənt] *s.* anuncio; aviso; noticia.
**announcer** [ənáʊnsə] *s.* anunciador; **radio —** locutor.
**annoy** [ənɔ́ɪ] *v.* molestar; fastidiar; incomodar; enfadar.
**annoyance** [ənɔ́ɪəns] *s.* molestia; fastidio; enfado.
**annual** [ǽnjʊəl] *adj.* anual; *s.* anuario; planta anual; **-ly** *adv.* anualmente, cada año, todos los años.
**annuity** [ənúətɪ] *s.* anualidad, renta anual.
**annul** [ənʌ́l] *v.* anular; abolir.
**annulment** [ənʌ́lmənt] *s.* revocación; anulación.
**anoint** [ənɔ́ɪnt] *v.* ungir; untar; administrar la Extremaunción.
**anon** [ənán] *adv.* pronto, luego; otra vez.
**anonymous** [ənánəməs] *adj.* anónimo.
**another** [ənʌ́ðə] *adj. & pron.* otro; **one — uno** a otro, unos a otros.
**answer** [ǽnsə] *s.* respuesta, contestación; réplica; solución; *v.* responder; contestar; replicar; **to — for** ser responsable de (*o* por); responder de; ser (salir) fiador de; **to — the purpose** ser adecuado, servir para el objeto.
**ant** [ænt] *s.* hormiga; **—eater** oso hormiguero; **— hill** hormiguero.
**antacid** [æntǽsɪd] *s. & adj.* antiácido.
**antagonism** [æntǽgənɪzəm] *s.* antagonismo, oposición, antipatía.
**antagonist** [æntǽgənɪst] *s.* antagonista, adversario.
**antagonize** [æntǽgənaɪz] *v.* contrariar; oponerse a, hostilizar.
**antecedent** [æntəsídn̩t] *adj. & s.* antecedente.
**antelope** [ǽntlop] *s.* antílope.

**antenna** [ænténə] (*pl.* **antennae** [ænténi]) *s.* antena.
**anterior** [æntírɪə] *adj.* anterior; delantero.
**anteroom** [ǽntɪrum] *s.* antecámara; sala de espera.
**anthem** [ǽnθəm] *s.* himno.
**anthology** [ænθáləɗʒɪ] *s.* antología.
**anthracite** [ǽnθrəsaɪt] *s.* antracita.
**anthropology** [ænθrəpáləɗʒɪ] *s.* antropología.
**antiaircraft** [æntɪérkræft] *adj.* antiaéreo.
**antibiotic** [æntɪbaɪátɪk] *s. & adj.* antibiótico.
**antibody** [ǽntɪbadɪ] *s.* anticuerpo.
**anticipate** [æntísəpet] *v.* anticipar(se); prever; esperar.
**anticipation** [æntɪsəpéʃən] *s.* anticipación; expectación; previsión.
**antics** [ǽntɪks] *s. pl.* travesuras, cabriolas.
**antidote** [ǽntɪdot] *s.* antídoto.
**antifreeze** [ǽntɪfriz] *s.* anticongelante.
**antipathy** [æntípəθɪ] *s.* antipatía, repugnancia.
**antiquated** [ǽntəkwetɪd] *adj.* anticuado; desusado.
**antique** [æntík] *adj.* antiguo; anticuado; *s.* antigualla.
**antiquity** [æntíkwətɪ] *s.* antigüedad; vejez, ancianidad.
**antiseptic** [æntəséptɪk] *adj. & s.* antiséptico.
**antisocial** [æntɪsóʃəl] *adj.* antisocial; *s. Am.* criminal.
**antithesis** [æntíθəsɪs] *s.* antítesis.
**antler** [ǽntlə] *s.* asta, cuerno (*del venado, ciervo, etc.*).
**anvil** [ǽnvɪl] *s.* yunque.
**anxiety** [æŋzáɪətɪ] *s.* ansiedad, zozobra; ansia, anhelo, afán.
**anxious** [ǽŋkʃəs] *adj.* ansioso; inquieto, preocupado; anheloso, deseoso; **-ly** *adv.* con ansiedad, con ansia, ansiosamente.
**any** [énɪ] *adj. & pron.* cualquier(a), cualesquier (a); alguno, algunos; **in — case** de todos modos, en todo caso; **I have not — bread** no tengo pan; **she does not sing — more** ya no canta; **he does not want to work — more** no quiere trabajar más.
**anybody** [énɪbadɪ] *pron.* alguien, alguno; cualquiera; **not . . . —** no . . . nadie, no . . . ninguno; **he does not know —** no conoce a nadie.
**anyhow** [énɪhaʊ] *adv.* de todos modos; de cualquier modo.
**anyone** [énɪwʌn] *pron.* = **anybody.**
**anything** [énɪθɪŋ] *pron.* alguna cosa; cualquier cosa; algo; **not . . . —** no . . . nada; **not to know —** no saber nada; **— you wish** todo lo que quiera Vd.
**anyway** [énɪwe] *adv.* de todos modos; en cualquier caso.
**anywhere** [énɪhwɛr] *adv.* dondequiera; en cualquier parte o lugar; en todas partes; **not . . . —** no . . . en (*o* a) ninguna parte; **not to go —** no ir a ninguna parte.

**apart** [əpárt] *adj.* aparte; separadamente; a un lado; *adj.* aislado, separado; **to take —** desarmar, desmontar; **to tear —** despedazar, hacer pedazos.

**apartment** [əpártmənt] *s.* departamento, piso, apartamento; vivienda, habitación.

**apathy** [ǽpəθɪ] *s.* apatía, indiferencia, indolencia.

**ape** [ep] *s.* mono; *v.* remedar, imitar.

**aperture** [ǽpətʃə] *s.* abertura.

**apex** [épɛks] *s.* ápice, cumbre.

**aphasia** [əfézɪə] *s.* afasia.

**apiece** [əpís] *adv.* cada uno, a cada uno, por persona.

**apocope** [əpákəpɪ] *s.* apócope.

**apogee** [ǽpədʒɪ] *s.* apogeo.

**apologetic** [əpaledʒétɪk] *adj.* que se excusa o disculpa.

**apologize** [əpálədʒaɪz] *v.* disculparse, excusarse.

**apology** [əpálədʒɪ] *s.* apología; excusa, disculpa, justificación, satisfacción.

**apoplexy** [ǽpəplɛksɪ] *s.* apoplejía.

**apostle** [əpás]] *s.* apóstol.

**apostolic** [ǽpəstálɪk] *adj.* apostólico.

**apostrophe** [əpástrəfɪ] *s.* apóstrofe; (*punctuation*) apóstrofo.

**appall** [əpɔ́l] *v.* aterrorizar, aterrar; asombrar, espantar.

**appalling** [əpɔ́lɪŋ] *adj.* aterrador; espantoso, asombroso.

**apparatus** [ǽpərétəs] *s.* aparato; aparejo.

**apparel** [əpǽrəl] *s.* ropa; ropaje; vestidos; indumentaria.

**apparent** [əpǽrənt] *adj.* aparente; visible, claro, evidente; patente; **heir —** heredero presunto; **-ly** *adv.* aparentemente, al parecer, por lo visto.

**apparition** [æpəríʃən] *s.* aparición; aparecido, espectro, fantasma.

**appeal** [əpíl] *s.* (*legal*) apelación, recurso; (*request*) súplica; (*attraction*) atracción, atractivo, llamamiento; *v.* apelar; recurrir, acudir; atraer, despertar interés o simpatía; llamar la atención.

**appear** [əpír] *v.* aparecer(se); parecer; comparecer.

**appearance** [əpírəns] *s.* apariencia, semblante; porte, facha; aparición.

**appease** [əpíz] *v.* apaciguar, aplacar; pacificar; conciliar; sosegar.

**appeasement** [əpízmənt] *s.* apaciguamiento; conciliación.

**appendix** [əpéndɪks] *s.* apéndice.

**appertain** [əpətén] *v.* pertenecer.

**appetite** [ǽpətaɪt] *s.* apetito; gana, deseo.

**appetizer** [ǽpətaɪzə] *s.* aperitivo.

**appetizing** [ǽpətaɪzɪŋ] *adj.* apetecible; apetitoso.

**applaud** [əplɔ́d] *v.* aplaudir.

**applause** [əplɔ́z] *s.* aplauso.

**apple** [ǽp]] *s.* manzana; **— tree** manzano; **Adam's —** nuez (*de la garganta*); *Ven., C.A., Col.* manzana; **— of my eye** niña de mis ojos.

**applesauce** [ǽp]sɔs] *s.* compota de manzana.

**appliance** [əpláɪəns] *s.* utensilio, instrumento; herramienta.

**applicable** [ǽplɪkəb]] *adj.* aplicable.

**applicant** [ǽpləkənt] *s.* solicitante, aspirante, candidato.

**application** [æpləkéʃən] *s.* (*dedication*) aplicación; (*petition*) solicitud, petición; *Méx., Carib., Ven.* aplicación.

**applied** [əpláɪd] *adj. & p.p.* aplicado; **— for** pedido, solicitado.

**apply** [əpláɪ] *v.* aplicar(se); **to — to** dirigirse a, acudir a, recurrir a; **to — for** solicitar, pedir; **to — oneself** aplicarse, dedicarse; **to — on account** acreditar en cuenta.

**appoint** [əpɔ́ɪnt] *v.* (*designate*) nombrar, designar, señalar; (*furnish*) amueblar, equipar; **a well -ed house** una casa bien amueblada.

**appointee** [əpɔɪntí] *s.* electo.

**appointment** [əpɔ́ɪntmənt] *s.* (*designation*) nombramiento, disignación; (*engagement*) cita, compromiso; **-s** mobiliario, mueblaje; accesorios.

**apportion** [əpórʃən] *v.* repartir proporcionadamente, prorratear.

**apportionment** [əpórʃənmənt] *s.* prorrateo, distribución, repartimiento.

**appraisal** [əpréz]] *s.* tasa, valuación.

**appraise** [əpréz] *v.* avaluar, valuar, tasar.

**appreciable** [əpríʃɪəb]] *adj.* (*prized*) apreciable; (*perceived*) perceptible; (*quantity*) bastante.

**appreciate** [əpríʃɪet] *v.* apreciar; estimar; agradecer; **to — in value** subir de valor.

**appreciation** [əpríʃɪéʃən] *s.* apreciación; aprecio; valuación; agradecimiento; aumento, alza, subida (*de precio*).

**apprehend** [æprɪhénd] *v.* aprehender, asir, prender; comprender; percibir.

**apprehension** [æprɪhénʃən] *s.* aprehensión, aprensión, recelo, desconfianza; presentimiento; captura.

**apprehensive** [æprɪhénsɪv] *adj.* aprensivo.

**apprentice** [əpréntɪs] *s.* aprendiz; novicio, principiante; *v.* poner de aprendiz.

**apprenticeship** [əpréntɪsʃɪp] *s.* aprendizaje.

**apprise** [əpráɪz] *v.* enterar, informar; apreciar.

**approach** [əprótʃ] *s.* acercamiento; aproximación; acceso, entrada; **method of —** técnica o modo de plantear (*un problema*); *v.* acercarse, aproximarse; abordar (*a alguien*).

**approbation** [æprəbéʃən] *s.* aprobación.

**appropriate** [əpróprɪɪt] *adj.* apropiado, propio, apto, conveniente, a propósito; [əpróprɪet] *v.* apropiarse, apoderarse de; asignar (*una suma de dinero*).

**appropriation** [əproprɪéʃən] *s.* apropiación; asignación, suma asignada.

**approval** [əprúvl] *s.* aprobación, asentimiento.

**approve** [əprúv] *v.* aprobar; asentir a.

**approximate** [əpráksəmɪt] *adj.* aproximado; aproximativo; **-ly** *adv.* aproximadamente, casi, poco más o menos; [əpráksəmet] *v.* aproximar; aproximarse, acercarse.

**apricot** [éprɪkɑt] *s.* albaricoque; *Am.* chabacano.

**April** [éprəl] *s.* abril.

**apron** [éprən] *s.* delantal.

**apropos** [æprəpó] *adv.* a propósito; *adj.* oportuno; pertinente; **—of** a propósito de.

**apt** [æpt] *adj.* apto, capaz; pertinente, a propósito; **—to** propenso a.

**aptitude** [æptətjud] *s.* aptitud, capacidad; habilidad.

**aquarium** [əkwérɪəm] *s.* acuario; pecera.

**aquatic** [əkwætɪk] *adj.* acuático.

**aqueduct** [ækwɪdʌkt] *s.* acueducto.

**Arab** [ærəb] *adj.* & *s.* árabe.

**Aragonese** [ærəgəniz] *adj.* & *s.* aragonés.

**arbiter** [árbɪtɚ] *s.* árbitro, arbitrador, juez árbitro.

**arbitrary** [árbətrɛrɪ] *adj.* arbitrario; despótico.

**arbitrate** [árbətret] *v.* arbitrar; decidir; someter al arbitraje.

**arbitration** [ɑrbətréʃən] *s.* arbitraje, arbitración.

**arbitrator** [árbətretɚ] *s.* arbitrador, árbitro; medianero.

**arbor** [árbɚ] *s.* emparrado, enramada, glorieta.

**arc** [ɑrk] *s.* arco; **— lamp** lámpara de arco.

**arcade** [ɑrkéd] *s.* arcada; galería; soportal.

**arch** [ɑrtʃ] *s.* arco; bóveda; **semicircular** — arco de medio punto; **— enemy** enemigo acérrimo; *v.* arquear(se); enarcar(se).

**archaeology** [ɑrkɪáləḏʒɪ] *s.* arqueología.

**archaic** [ɑrkéɪk] *adj.* arcaico, desusado, anticuado.

**archbishop** [ártʃbíʃəp] *s.* arzobispo.

**archery** [ártʃərɪ] *s.* tiro de flechas.

**archipelago** [ɑrkəpéləgo] *s.* archipiélago.

**architect** [árkətɛkt] *s.* arquitecto.

**architectural** [ɑrkətéktʃərəl] *adj.* arquitectónico.

**architecture** [árkətɛktʃɚ] *s.* arquitectura.

**archives** [árkaɪvz] *s.* archivo.

**archway** [ártʃwe] *s.* pasadizo (*bajo un arco*); arcada, galería abovedada.

**arctic** [árktɪk] *adj.* ártico.

**ardent** [árdṇt] *adj.* ardiente; apasionado.

**ardor** [árdɚ] *s.* ardor; enardecimiento; fervor.

**arduous** [árdʒʊəs] *adj.* arduo, trabajoso.

**are** [ɑr] *2ª persona y pl. del presente de indic. del verbo* **to be:** eres, estás; somos, estamos; sois, estáis; son, están.

**area** [érɪə] *s.* área, superficie; espacio; región.

**arena** [ərínə] *s.* arena, redondel, plaza.

**Argentine** [árdʒəntin] *adj.* & *s.* argentino.

**argue** [árgjʊ] *v.* argüir; debatir; altercar; **to — into** persuadir a.

**argument** [árgjəmənt] *s.* argumento; razonamiento; sumario, resumen.

**arid** [ærɪd] *adj.* árido.

**arise** [əráɪz] *v.* levantarse; elevarse; surgir; provenir.

**arisen** [ərízṇ] *p.p. de* **to arise.**

**aristocracy** [ærəstákrəsɪ] *s.* aristocracia.

**aristocrat** [ərístəkræt] *s.* aristócrata.

**aristocratic** [ərɪstəkrǽtɪk] *adj.* aristocrático.

**arithmetic** [əríθmətik] *s.* aritmética.

**ark** [ɑrk] *s.* arca; **— of the covenant** arca del testamento; **Noah's —** arca de Noé.

**arm** [ɑrm] *s.* (*anatomy*) brazo; (*weapon*) arma; **— in —** de bracete, de bracero; *Am.* de brazo, de brazos; **at -'s length** a una brazada; **with open -s** con los brazos abiertos; *v.* armar(se).

**armada** [ɑrmádə] *s.* armada, flota.

**armament** [árməmənt] *s.* armamento.

**armature** [ármətʃɚ] *s.* armadura.

**armchair** [ármtʃɛr] *s.* silla de brazos, sillón, butaca.

**armed forces** [ármd fórsəz] *s.* fuerzas armadas.

**armful** [ármfʊl] *s.* brazada.

**armistice** [árməstɪs] *s.* armisticio.

**armor** [ármɚ] *s.* armadura; blindaje, coraza; arnés; *v.* blindar, acorazar.

**armored** [ármɚd] *p.p.* blindado, acorazado.

**armory** [ármərɪ] *s.* armería; arsenal.

**armpit** [ármpɪt] *s.* sobaco.

**army** [ármɪ] *s.* ejército; muchedumbre; **— doctor** médico militar; **regular —** tropa de línea.

**aroma** [ərómə] *s.* aroma; fragancia.

**aromatic** [ærəmǽtɪk] *adj.* aromático.

**arose** [əróz] *pret. de* **to arise.**

**around** [əráʊnd] *adv.* alrededor; en redor; a la redonda; en torno; en derredor; cerca; **all —** por todos lados; *prep.* alrededor de; cerca de; **— here** por aquí; **to go — in circles** dar vueltas; **to go — the world** dar la vuelta al mundo.

**arouse** [əráʊz] *v.* despertar, *Ríopl., C.A., Ven.* recordar (*al dormido*); excitar; promover.

**arraign** [ərén] *v.* acusar; procesar (*a un criminal*).

**arrange** [əréndʒ] *v.* arreglar; disponer, colocar; acomodar; hacer arreglos (para), hacer planes (para).

**arrangement** [əréndʒmənt] *s.* arreglo; disposición; colocación, orden; convenio.

**array** [əré] *s.* arreglo, formación, orden; orden (*de batalla*); pompa; gala, atavío; *v.* formar (*tropas*); poner en orden; ataviar, adornar.

**arrears** [ərírz] *s. pl.* atrasos, pagos o rentas vencidos y no cobrados; **in —** atrasado (*en el pago de una cuenta*).

**arrest** [ərést] *s.* arresto, captura, aprensión, detención; *v.* aprehender o prender, arrestar; detener; llamar, atraer (*la atención*).

**arrival** [ərάɪv] *s.* llegada; arribo; venida; **the new -s** los recién llegados.

**arrive** [ərάɪv] *v.* llegar; arribar; **to — at a result** lograr (*o* conseguir) un resultado.

**arrogance** [ǽrəgəns] *s.* arrogancia.

**arrogant** [ǽrəgənt] *adj.* arrogante.

**arrow** [ǽro] *s.* saeta, flecha.

**arsenal** [ársṇəl] *s.* arsenal.

**arsenic** [ársṇɪk] *s.* arsénico.

**arson** [ársən] *s.* delito de incendio.

**art** [ɑrt] *s.* arte; destreza; astucia; **fine -s** bellas artes; **master of -s** licenciado en letras, maestro en artes.

**artery** [ártərɪ] *s.* arteria.

**artful** [ártfəl] *adj.* artero, mañero, ladino.

**artichoke** [ártɪtʃok] *s.* alcachofa.

**article** [ártɪkl̩] *s.* artículo; **— of clothing** prenda de vestir; **— of merchandise** mercancía, mercadería.

**articulate** [artíkjəlɪt] *adj.* articulado; claro, inteligible; capaz de hablar; [artíkjəlet] *v.* articular; enunciar; enlazar.

**articulation** [artɪkjəléʃən] *s.* articulación; coyuntura.

**artifact** [ártəfækt] *s.* artefacto.

**artifice** [ártəfɪs] *s.* artificio; ardid.

**artificial** [artəfíʃəl] *adj.* artificial; postizo; afectado, artificioso.

**artillery** [artílərɪ] *s.* artillería; **— man** artillero.

**artisan** [ártəzṇ] *s.* artesano; artífice.

**artist** [ártɪst] *s.* artista.

**artistic** [artístɪk] *adj.* artístico; **-ally** *adv.* artísticamente.

**as** [əz] *adv., conj., prep.* como; mientras; a medida que, según; en el momento en que; **— far — hasta**, hasta donde; **— for (— to)** en cuanto a; **— if** como si; **— it were** por decirlo así; **— large —** tan grande como; **— much — tanto como**; **— well** tan bien; también; **— yet** hasta ahora, todavía; **— long — you wish** todo el tiempo que Vd. quiera; **strong — he is** aunque es tan fuerte; **the same —** lo mismo que.

**asbestos** [æsbéstəs] *s.* asbesto.

**ascend** [əsénd] *v.* ascender; subir, elevarse.

**ascension** [əsénʃən] *s.* ascensión; subida.

**ascent** [əsént] *s.* ascenso; subida; ascensión.

**ascertain** [æsɚtén] *v.* averiguar, indagar.

**ascetic** [əsétɪk] *adj.* ascético; *s.* asceta.

**ascribe** [əskráɪb] *v.* atribuir, imputar, achacar.

**ash** [æʃ] *s.* ceniza; **— tray** cenicero; **— tree** fresno; **Ash Wednesday** miércoles de ceniza; **ash-colored** *adj.* ceniciento, cenizo.

**ashamed** [əʃémd] *adj.* avergonzado, corrido; **to be —** tener vergüenza; avergonzarse.

**ashore** [əʃór] *adv.* a tierra; en tierra; **to go —** desembarcar.

**Asiatic** [əʒɪǽtɪk] *adj. & s.* asiático.

**aside** [əsáɪd] *adv.* aparte; a un lado; al lado; *s.* aparte (*en un drama*).

**ask** [æsk] *v.* (*request*) pedir, rogar, solicitar; (*inquire*) preguntar; (*invite*) invitar; **to — for** pedir; **to — for (about, after)** preguntar por; **to — a question** hacer una pregunta.

**askance** [əskǽns] *adv.* de soslayo; con recelo, recelosamente; **to look —** mirar con recelo; no aprobar.

**asleep** [əslíp] *adj.* dormido; **to fall —** dormirse; **my arm is —** se me ha dormido (entumecido *o* entumido) el brazo.

**asparagus** [əspǽrəgəs] *s.* espárrago.

**aspect** [ǽspɛkt] *s.* aspecto.

**asphalt** [ǽsfɔlt] *s.* asfalto.

**aspiration** [æspəréʃən] *s.* aspiración; anhelo.

**aspire** [əspáɪr] *v.* aspirar; anhelar, ambicionar.

**aspirin** [ǽspɜɪn] *s.* aspirina.

**ass** [æs] *s.* asno, burro; pollino.

**assail** [əsél] *v.* asaltar, acometer, agredir.

**assailant** [əsélənt] *s.* asaltador, agresor.

**assassin** [əsǽsɪn] *s.* asesino.

**assassinate** [əsǽsṇet] *v.* asesinar.

**assassination** [əsæsṇéʃən] *s.* asesinato.

**assault** [əsɔlt] *s.* asalto, acometida, ataque; *v.* asaltar, acometer, atacar; violar.

**assay** [əsé] *v.* ensayar (*metales*); analizar, examinar; contrastar (*pesas, moneda*); *s.* ensaye (*de metales*); contraste (*de pesas, moneda*).

**assemble** [əsémbl̩] *v.* reunir(se), congregar(se), juntar(se); convocar; armar, montar (*maquinaria*).

**assembly** [əsémblɪ] *s.* asamblea; reunión; montaje (*de maquinaria*); **— hall** salón de sesiones; paraninfo.

**assent** [əsént] *s.* asentimiento; consentimiento; *v.* asentir; consentir.

**assert** [əsɝt] *v.* aseverar, asegurar, afirmar; **to — oneself** hacerse valer; obrar con firmeza; vindicarse.

**assertion** [əsɝʃən] *s.* aserción, aserto, afirmación.

**assess** [əsés] *v.* avaluar; tasar; asignar, imponer (*impuestos, multas, contribuciones, etc.*).

**assessment** [əsésmənt] *s.* avaluación, tasación; imposición (*de contribuciones, multas, etc.*); contribución, impuesto.

**asset** [ǽsɛt] *s.* cualidad, ventaja; **-s** capital, fondos, caudal; haber, activo; **personal -s** bienes muebles.

**assiduous** [əsídʒʊəs] *adj.* asiduo, diligente.

**assign** [əsáɪn] *v.* asignar; señalar, designar; traspasar, ceder a favor de.

**assignment** [əsáɪnmənt] *s.* asignación; designación; cesión (*de bienes*); tarea (*asignada*); lección (*señalada*).

**assimilate** [əsímlet] *v.* asimilar(se), absorber(se).

**assist** [əsíst] *v.* asistir, ayudar.

**assistance** [əsístəns] *s.* asistencia, ayuda.

**AF**

**assistant** [əsístənt] *s.* asistente; ayudante; auxiliar; *adj.* subordinado, auxiliar.

**associate** [əsóʃɪɪt] *adj.* asociado; *s.* asociado; socio; compañero; colega; [əsóʃɪet] *v.* asociar(se); relacionar.

**association** [əsosɪéʃən] *s.* asociación; sociedad; conexión, relación.

**assort** [əsórt] *v.* ordenar, clasificar.

**assorted** [əsórtɪd] *adj.* surtido, mezclado, variado, de todas clases.

**assortment** [əsórtmənt] *s.* variedad; clasificación; surtido; colección, grupo.

**assume** [əsúm] *v.* asumir; tomar; dar por sentado, dar por supuesto; arrogarse, apropiarse.

**assumption** [əsámpʃən] *d.* suposición; toma, apropiación; presunción; asunción (*de la Virgen*).

**assurance** [əʃúrəns] *s.* seguridad, certeza; convicción; confianza; **life —** seguro de vida. *Véase* **insurance**.

**assure** [əʃúr] *v.* asegurar; afirmar; infundir confianza.

**assuredly** [əʃúrɪdlɪ] *adv.* seguramente; sin duda, con seguridad.

**asterisk** [ǽstərɪsk] *s.* asterisco.

**astigmatism** [əstígmətɪzəm] *s.* astigmatismo.

**astonish** [əstánɪʃ] *v.* asombrar, pasmar, espantar.

**astonishing** [əstánɪʃɪŋ] *adj.* asombroso, pasmoso, maravilloso.

**astonishment** [əstánɪʃmənt] *s.* asombro, pasmo, sorpresa.

**astound** [əstáund] *v.* pasmar; aterrar, aturdir.

**astray** [əstré] *adv.* fuera de camino; *adj.* desviado, extraviado, descaminado; **to go —** perderse; errar el camino; extraviarse; **to lead —** desviar, extraviar; llevar por mal camino; seducir.

**astride** [əstráɪd] *adv.* a horcajadas.

**astrodome** [ǽstrədom] *s.* astródomo.

**astrology** [əstrálədʒɪ] *s.* astrología.

**astronaut** [ǽstrənɔt] *s.* astronauta.

**astronomer** [əstránəmə] *s.* astrónomo.

**astronomy** [əstránəmɪ] *s.* astronomía.

**astrophysics** [æstrofízɪks] *s.* astrofísica.

**Asturian** [æstjúrɪən] *adj. & s.* asturiano.

**astute** [əstjút] *adj.* astuto, sagaz.

**asunder** [əsándə] *adj.* separado; **to cut —** separar, apartar; dividir en dos.

**asylum** [əsáɪləm] *s.* asilo; hospicio; **orphan —** orfanato, casa de huérfanos, *Méx., C.A., Andes* orfanatorio.

**at** [æt] *prep.* a; en; en (la) casa de; **— last** por fin, al fin; **— once** al punto; **to be — work** estar trabajando; **to enter — that door** entrar por aquella puerta.

**ate** [et] *pret. de* **to eat.**

**atheist** [éθɪɪst] *s.* ateo.

**athlete** [ǽθlit] *s.* atleta.

**athletic** [æθlétɪk] *adj.* atlético.

**athletics** [æθlétɪks] *s.* gimnasia; atletismo; deportes.

**Atlantic** [ətlǽntɪk] *adj.* atlántico; *s.* el Atlántico.

**atlas** [ǽtləs] *s.* atlas.

**atmosphere** [ǽtməsfɪr] *s.* atmósfera; ambiente.

**atmospheric** [ætməsférɪk] *adj.* atmosférico.

**atom** [ǽtəm] *s.* átomo; **— bomb** bomba atómica.

**atomic** [ətámɪk] *adj.* atómico; **— age** edad atómica; **— energy** fuerza atómica; **— pile** pila atómica; **— weight** peso atómico.

**atone** [ətón] *v.* expiar, purgar; reparar.

**atonement** [ətónmənt] *s.* expiación; reparación.

**atrocious** [ətróʃəs] *adj.* atroz.

**atrocity** [ətrásətɪ] *s.* atrocidad; maldad.

**attach** [ətǽʃ] *v.* unir, juntar; sujetar, pegar, adherir; poner (*sello o firma*); embargar (*bienes*); asignar; atribuir.

**attachment** [ətǽtʃmənt] *s.* adhesión; apego; afición, cariño; embargo (*de bienes*); accesorio.

**attack** [ətǽk] *s.* ataque, asalto; acceso; *v.* atacar; acometer, embestir.

**attain** [ətén] *v.* lograr, conseguir, alcanzar; llegar a.

**attainment** [əténmənt] *s.* logro, consecución; adquisición; dote habilidad.

**attempt** [ətémpt] *s.* tentativa; prueba, ensayo; esfuerzo; atentado; *v.* tentar, intentar; procurar, tratar (de), probar; **to — the life of** atentar contra la vida de.

**attend** [əténd] *v.* atender, cuidar, mirar por; asistir a; acompañar.

**attendance** [əténdəns] *s.* asistencia; presencia; concurrencia.

**attendant** [əténdənt] *s.* acompañante; sirviente, servidor; asistente; *adj.* acompañante.

**attention** [əténʃən] *s.* (*care*) cuidado; (*courtesy*) fineza, urbanidad, atención; **to pay —** hacer caso; prestar atención.

**attentive** [əténtɪv] *adj.* atento; cortés.

**attest** [ətést] *v.* atestiguar, atestar; certificar; dar fe.

**attic** [ǽtɪk] *s.* desván.

**attire** [ətáɪr] *s.* atavío; vestidura; vestido, traje; *v.* ataviar, adornar.

**attitude** [ǽtətjud] *s.* actitud; postura.

**attorney** [ətэ́nɪ] *s.* abogado; procurador; apoderado; **— general** fiscal (*de una nación o estado*); **district —** fiscal de distrito; **power of —** procuración, poder.

**attract** [ətrǽkt] *v.* atraer; cautivar; **to — attention** llamar la atención.

**attraction** [ətrǽkʃən] *s.* atracción; atractivo; **-s** diversiones; lugares o sitios de interés.

**attractive** [ətrǽktɪv] *adj.* atractivo; seductor; simpático.

**attractiveness** [ətrǽktɪvnɪs] *s.* atracción; atractivo.

**attribute** [ǽtrəbjut] *s.* atributo; propiedad; [ətríbjut] *v.* atribuir, achacar.

**attrition** [ətríʃən] *s.* agotamiento; atrición.

**auction** [ókʃən] *s.* subasta, almoneda, remate, *Am.* venduta; *v.* subastar; rematar.

**audacious** [ɔdéʃəs] *adj.* audaz, atrevido, osado.

**audacity** [ɔdǽsətɪ] *s.* audacia, osadía; descaro.

**audible** [ɔ́dəbl] *adj.* audible.

**audience** [ɔ́dɪəns] *s.* auditorio, concurrencia, público; audiencia.

**audio frequency** [ɔdɪofríkwensɪ] *s.* audiofrecuencia.

**audio-visual** [ɔdɪovíʒuəl] *adj.* adio-visual.

**audit** [ɔ́dɪt] *v.* intervenir [*cuentas*); asistir a (*una clase*) de oyente; *s.* intervención, comprobación de cuentas.

**audition** [ɔdíʃən] *s.* audición.

**auditor** [ɔ́dɪtɚ] *s.* interventor (*de cuentas*); oyente.

**auditorium** [ɔdətóriəm] *s.* salón de conferencias o conciertos; paraninfo.

**auditory** [ɔ́dətorɪ] *adj.* auditivo.

**auger** [ɔ́gɚ] *s.* taladro, barrena.

**aught** [ɔt] *s.* algo.

**augment** [ɔgmént] *v.* aumentar.

**augur** [ɔ́gɚ] *s.* agorero; *v.* augurar, pronosticar; **to — well** (*o* **ill**) ser de buen (*o* mal) agüero.

**August** [ɔ́gəst] *s.* agosto.

**aunt** [ænt] *s.* tía.

**auspices** [ɔ́spɪsɪz] *s. pl.* auspicios; protección.

**auspicious** [ɔspíʃəs] *adj.* propicio; favorable.

**austere** [ɔstír] *adj.* austero, adusto, severo.

**austerity** [ɔstérətɪ] *s.* austeridad, severidad.

**Austrian** [ɔ́strɪən] *adj. & s.* austríaco.

**authentic** [ɔθéntɪk] *adj.* auténtico.

**author** [ɔ́θɚ] *s.* autor; escritor.

**authoritative** [əθɔ́rətetɪv] *adj.* autorizado, que tiene autoridad; autoritario.

**authority** [əθɔ́rətɪ] *s.* autoridad; facultad; **to have on good —** saber de buena tinta.

**authorize** [ɔ́θəraɪz] *v.* autorizar.

**auto** [ɔ́to] *s.* auto, automóvil.

**autocrat** [ɔ́təkræt] *s.* autócrata.

**autograph** [ɔ́təgræf] *s.* autógrafo.

**automatic** [ɔtəmǽtɪk] *adj.* automatico; **-ally** *adv.* automáticamente.

**automobile** [ɔ́təməbil] *s.* automóvil.

**autonomy** [ɔtánəmɪ] *s.* autonomía.

**autopsy** [ɔ́tɑpsɪ] *s.* autopsia.

**autumn** [ɔ́təm] *s.* otoño.

**autumnal** [ɔtʌ́mnl] *adj.* otoñal.

**auxiliary** [ɔgzíljərɪ] *adj. & s.* auxiliar.

**avail** [əvél] *v.* aprovechar; beneficiar; **to — oneself of** aprovecharse de; *s.* provecho; ventaja; **of no —** de ninguna utilidad o ventaja.

**available** [əvéləb]) *adj.* disponible; aprovechable; obtenible.

**avalanche** [ǽv]æntʃ] *s.* alud; torrente.

**avarice** [ǽvərɪs] *s.* avaricia.

**avaricious** [ævəríʃəs] *adj.* avaro, avariento.

**avenge** [əvéndʒ] *v.* vengar; vindicar.

**avenger** [əvéndʒɚ] *s.* vengador.

**avenue** [ǽvənu] *s.* avenida.

**aver** [əvɚ́] *v.* afirmar, asegurar.

**average** [ǽvrɪdʒ] *s.* promedio, término medio; **on an —** por término medio; *adj.* medio, mediano; ordinario; *v.* promediar, calcular o sacar el promedio; **to — a loss** prorratear una pérdida; **he -s 20 miles an hour** avanza o recorre un promedio de 20 millas por hora.

**averse** [əvɚ́s] *adj.* adverso, renuente.

**aversion** [əvɚ́ʒən] *s.* aversión; malquerencia, inquina.

**avert** [əvɚ́t] *v.* apartar, desviar; evitar; impedir.

**aviation** [evɪéʃən] *s.* aviación.

**aviator** [évɪetɚ] *s.* aviador.

**avocado** [ɑvəkádo] *s.* aguacate.

**avocation** [ævəkéʃən] *s.* distracción; ocupación de distracción o diversión.

**avoid** [əvɔ́ɪd] *v.* evitar; eludir.

**avow** [əváu] *v.* confesar, reconocer, admitir.

**avowal** [əváuəl] *s.* confesión, admisión.

**await** [əwét] *v.* esperar, aguardar.

**awake** [əwék] *adj.* despierto; alerto; **wide-awake** muy despierto; avispado; *v.* despertar(se).

**awaken** [əwékən] *v.* despertar(se).

**award** [əwórd] *s.* premio; decisión, sentencia; *v.* asignar; otorgar; conferir; adjudicar (*un premio, medalla, etc.*).

**aware** [əwér] *adj.* consciente; enterado, sabedor; cauto; sobre aviso.

**away** [əwé] *adv.* lejos; fuera; *adj.* ausente; **right —** ahora mismo, ahorita; **two miles —** a diez millas de aquí; **to give —** regalar; **to go —** irse; **to take —** quitar.

**awe** [ɔ] *s.* pavor; pasmo; **to stand in —** quedarse, o estar, pasmado; pasmarse; *v.* atemorizar; infundir pavor; maravillar.

**awful** [ɔ́ful] *adj.* terrible; horroroso; tremendo; impresionante; **-ly** *adv.* terriblemente; horrorosamente; muy.

**awhile** [əhwáɪl] *adv.* (por) un rato; (por) algún tiempo.

**awkward** [ɔ́kwɚd] *adj.* torpe, desmañado; molesto, embarazoso; incómodo; inconveniente.

**awl** [ɔl] *s.* lezna, punzón.

**awning** [ɔ́nɪŋ] *s.* toldo.

**awoke** [əwók] *pret. & p.p. de* **to awake.**

**ax, axe** [æks] *s.* hacha.

**axis** [ǽksɪs] *pl.* **axes** [ǽksɪz]) *s.* eje.

**axle** [ǽksl] *s.* eje (*de una rueda*); **front —** eje delantero; **rear —** eje trasero.

**aye** [e] *adv.* sí; *s.* voto afirmativo.

**Aztec** [ǽztɛk] *adj. & s.* azteca.

**azure** [ǽʒɚ] *adj.* azul; *s.* azur, azul celeste.

# B

**babble** [bǽbl] *s.* balbuceo; parloteo, charla; *v.* balbucear; parlotear, charlar.

**babe** [beb] = **baby.**

**baboon** [bæbún] *s.* mandril (*especie de mono*).

**baby** [bébɪ] *s.* nene, bebé, criatura; *Andes, Ch.* guagua; *C.A.* tierno; *adj.* infantil; de niño; **— girl** nena; **—**

**sitter** [bébɪsítəʳ] *s.* cuidaniños, niñera por horas; *v.* mimar.
**bachelor** [bǽtʃələʳ] *s.* bachiller; soltero.
**bacillus** [bəsíləs] *s.* bacilo.
**back** [bæk] *s.* (*anatomy*) espalda; lomo (de animal); (*opposite side*) revés; respaldo (*de silla*), espaldar; **behind one's** — a espaldas de uno, a espaldas vueltas; **in — of** detrás de, tras; **to fall on one's** — caer de espaldas, caer boca arriba; **to turn one's** — volver las espaldas; *adj.* posterior; trasero; retrasado, atrasado, rezagado; — **pay** sueldo atrasado; — **yard** patio interior; corral; *adv.* atrás, detrás; — **and forth** de aquí para allá; **to come** — volver, regresar; **to give** — devolver; *v.* respaldar, endosar; sostener, apoyar, retroceder; hacer retroceder; **to — down** hacerse (para) atrás; retractarse.
**backbone** [bǽkbón] *s.* espinazo, espina dorsal; firmeza; apoyo, sostén.
**backer** [bǽkəʳ] *s.* fiador; sostenedor, defensor.
**background** [bǽkgraund] *s.* fondo; educación; experiencia; **to keep in the** — dejar en último término; quedarse en último término; mantenerse retirado.
**backhand** [bǽkhǽnd] *s.* revés; escritura inclinada a la izquierda; **-ed stroke** revés; **a -ed remark** una ironía; una indirecta.
**backing** [bǽkɪŋ] *s.* apoyo, garantía; endose, endoso; respaldo.
**backlash** [bǽklæʃ] *s.* contragolpe; culateo.
**backlog** [bǽklɔg] *s.* reserva pendiente.
**backstage** [bækstédʒ] *adv.* detrás del telón.
**backward** [bǽkwəʳd] *adj.* atrasado; retrasado; retrógrado; lerdo, tardo; huraño, tímido, esquivo; *adv.* = **backwards.**
**backwardness** [bǽkwəʳdnɪs] *s.* torpeza; atraso; timidez.
**backwards** [bǽkwəʳdz] *adv.* hacia (*o* para) atrás; de espaldas; **to go** — retroceder, andar hacia (*o* para) atrás.
**bacon** [békən] *s.* tocino.
**bacteria** [bæktíríə] *s. pl.* bacterias.
**bacteriology** [bæktɪríálədʒɪ] *s.* bacteriología.
**bad** [bæd] *adj.* malo; perverso; dañoso; podrido; **to go from — to worse** ir de mal en peor; **to look** — tener mal cariz, tener mala cara o mal aspecto; **-ly** *adv.* mal, malamente.
**bade** [bæd] *pret. de* **to bid.**
**badge** [bædʒ] *s.* insignia, divisa; distintivo.
**badger** [bǽdʒəʳ] *s.* tejón; *v.* atormentar, acosar, molestar.
**badness** [bǽdnɪs] *s.* maldad.
**baffle** [bǽfl] *v.* desconcertar, confundir; frustrar, impedir.
**bag** [bæg] *s.* (*sack*) saco, bolsa, talega; costal; (*baggage*) maleta; zurrón, morral; *v.* ensacar; cazar; agarrar; adueñarse de; inflarse; abolsarse.

**baggage** [bǽgɪdʒ] *s.* equipaje; bagaje; — **car** furgón, vagón de equipajes; — **check** talón, contraseña de equipajes; — **tag** marbete, etiqueta.
**bagpipe** [bǽgpaɪp] *s.* gaita.
**bail** [bel] *s.* fianza, caución; **to let out on** — poner en libertad bajo fianza; *v.* dar fianza; salir fiador; achicar (*agua*), vaciar; **to — out of a plane** tirarse (*con paracaídas*) de un aeroplano.
**bait** [bet] *s.* cebo; atractivo, aliciente; *v.* tentar, atraer; cebar; acosar, perseguir.
**bake** [bek] *v.* hornear, cocer al horno; calcinar.
**baker** [békəʳ] *s.* panadero, pastelero, hornero.
**bakery** [békərɪ] *s.* panadería, pastelería, tahona.
**baking** [békɪŋ] *s.* hornada; cocimiento; — **powder** levadura.
**balance** [bǽləns] *s.* (*instrument*) balanza; (*equilibrium*) contrapeso, equilibrio, balance; (*debit, credit*) saldo; — **of payments** balanza de pagos; — **wheel** volante del reloj; — **of trade** balanza comercial; — **of power** equilibrio político; **to lose one's** — perder el equilibrio; *v.* contrapesar; pesar; balancear(se); equilibrar; saldar (*una cuenta*).
**balcony** [bǽlkənɪ] *s.* balcón; galería (*de teatro*).
**bald** [bɔld] *adj.* calvo; pelado, sin vegetación; escueto, sin adornos; — **spot** calva.
**bale** [bel] *s.* bala, fardo (*de mercancías*); *v.* embalar, enfardar, empacar.
**balk** [bɔk] *v.* oponerse, rebelarse, resistirse; pararse de repente; negarse a seguir; encabritarse; **to — someone's plans** frustrar los planes de alguien.
**ball** [bɔl] *s.* (*plaything*) pelota, bola; (*string, thread*) ovillo; (*weapon*) bala; (*dance*) baile; — **bearing** cojinete de bolas; — **game** juego de pelota; beisbol; *v.* ovillar; **to — up** enredar, confundir.
**ballad** [bǽləd] *s.* romance; copla, canción; balada.
**ballast** [bǽləst] *s.* lastre; grava (*usada en terraplenes, caminos, etc.*); *v.* lastrar, poner el lastre a (*una embarcación*).
**ballet** [bǽlé] *s.* ballet.
**balloon** [bəlún] *s.* globo (*aerostático*).
**ballot** [bǽlət] *s.* balota, *Am.* boleta, cédula para votar; voto; — **box** urna electoral; *v.* balotar, votar.
**ball point** [bɔ́lpɔɪnt] *s.* bolígrafo.
**balm** [bɑm] *s.* bálsamo.
**balmy** [bámɪ] *adj.* balsámico; fragante; refrescante, suave; algo loco, chiflado.
**balsam** [bɔ́lsəm] *s.* bálsamo; especie de abeto.
**bamboo** [bæmbú] *s.* bambú.
**ban** [bæn] *s.* bando, proclama; excomunión; prohibición; **marriage -s** (*o* **banns**) amonestaciones; *v.* proscribir, prohibir; condenar.

**banana** [bənǽnə] s. banana; plátano; — **tree** banano; plátano.

**band** [bænd] s. (group) banda, partida, pandilla, cuadrilla; (musicians) banda; (strip) faja, lista, cinta, tira; partida, pandilla, cuadrilla; **rubber —** liga de goma; v. unir, juntar; atar, ligar; **to — together** confederarse, juntarse.

**bandage** [bǽndɪdʒ] s. venda, vendaje; v. vendar.

**bandit** [bǽndɪt] s. bandido bandolero.

**bang** [bæŋ] s. golpe, golpazo; estallido; fleco (de pelo); **with a —** de golpe, de golpazo; de repente; con estrépito; **—!** ¡pum!; v. golpear; hacer estrépito; cortar (el pelo) en fleco; **to — the door** dar un portazo.

**banish** [bǽnɪʃ] v. proscribir, desterrar; **to — fear** desechar el temor.

**banishment** [bǽnɪʃmənt] s. proscripción; destierro.

**banister** [bǽnɪstɚ] s. balaustre; barandilla, barandal, pasamano.

**banjo** [bǽndʒo] s. banjo.

**bank** [bæŋk] s. (institution) banco; (in card game) banca; (of a river) orilla, ribera, banda; escarpa; (pile) montón; **savings —** caja de ahorros; adj. bancario; de banco; v. depositar en un banco; amontonar (tierra o arena); cubrir con cenizas, tapar (el fuego); ladear (un aeroplano); **to — upon** (o **on**) contar con.

**bankbook** [bǽŋkbʊk] s. libreta de banco.

**banker** [bǽŋkɚ] s. banquero.

**banking** [bǽŋkɪŋ] s. transacciones bancarias, banca; adj. bancario, de banca; **— house** banca, casa de banca.

**banknote** [bǽŋknot] s. billete de banco.

**bankrupt** [bǽŋkrʌpt] adj. en quiebra, arruinado, insolvente; v. quebrar; arruinar.

**bankruptcy** [bǽŋkrʌptsɪ] s. bancarrota, quiebra; **to go into —** declararse insolvente; quebrar, hacer bancarrota.

**banner** [bǽnɚ] s. bandera, estandarte, pendón; adj. primero, principal, sobresaliente.

**banquet** [bǽŋkwɪt] s. banquete; v. banquetear.

**baptism** [bǽptɪzəm] s. bautismo; bautizo.

**Baptist** [bǽptɪst] s. bautista.

**baptize** [bæptáɪz] v. bautizar.

**bar** [bɑr] s. (of iron) barra; barrote; tranca; (obstacle) barrera, obstáculo; (of justice) tribunal; foro; (saloon) cantina, taberna; (counter) mostrador; (piece) barra (de jabón); pastilla (de chocolate); **sand —** banco de arena; **-s** reja; **to be admitted to the —** recibirse de abogado; v. atrancar (la puerta); estorbar; prohibir; excluir.

**barb** [bɑrb] s. púa.

**barbarian** [bɑrbérɪən] s. & adj. bárbaro; salvaje.

**barbarous** [bárbərəs] adj. bárbaro; salvaje; inculto.

**barbecue** [bárbɪkju] s. Méx., C.A., Col. barbacoa; Ríopl. churrasco; v. hacer

barbacoa; Ríopl. churrasquear.

**barbed** [bɑrbd] adj. con púas; **— wire** alambre de púas.

**barber** [bárbɚ] s. barbero; peluquero.

**barbershop** [bárbɚʃɑp] s. barbería; peluquería.

**bard** [bɑrd] s. bardo, vate, poeta.

**bare** [ber] adj. (naked) desnudo; descubierto; pelado; (evident) manifiesto, patente; (unfurnished) desamueblado, vacío; **— majority** mayoría escasa; **to lay —** poner de manifiesto, hacer patente, revelar; **to ride —back** montar en pelo.

**barefoot** [bérfʊt] adj. descalzo, con los pies desnudos; **-ed** [bérfʊtɪd] = **barefoot.**

**bareheaded** [bérhédɪd] adj. descubierto, sin sombrero.

**barelegged** [bérlégɪd] adj. con las piernas desnudas; sin medias.

**barely** [bérlɪ] adv. apenas; escasamente; **— three pounds** tres libras escasas.

**bareness** [bérnɪs] s. desnudez.

**bargain** [bárgɪn] s. (agreement) convenio, pacto; negocio, trato; (cheap) ganga; **— sale** ganga, Méx., C.A., Ven., Andes barata; **into the —** por añadidura; de ganancia; **to make a —** cerrar un convenio; v. regatear; negociar; **to — for** regatear; contar con, esperar.

**barge** [bɑrdʒ] s. lanchón; barca.

**baritone** [bǽrəton] s. & adj. barítono.

**barium** [bǽrɪəm] s. bario.

**bark** [bɑrk] s. ladrido; corteza (de árbol); barco velero; v. ladrar; descortezar, quitar la corteza.

**barley** [bárlɪ] s. cebada.

**barn** [bɑrn] s. establo, cuadra; granero, troje; pajar; **streetcar —** cobertizo para tranvías.

**barnacle** [bárnəkəl] s. cirrópodo.

**barnyard** [bárnjɑrd] s. corral; **— fowl** aves de corral.

**barometer** [bərámətɚ] s. barómetro.

**baron** [bǽrən] s. barón.

**baroque** [bərók] adj. & s. barroco.

**barrage** [bəráʒ] s. fuego de barrera; presa.

**barrel** [bǽrəl] s. barril, barrica, tonel, cuba; cañón (de fusil, pistola, etc.); v. embarrilar (meter en barril).

**barren** [bǽrən] adj. árido; estéril.

**barrenness** [bǽrənnɪs] s. aridez; esterilidad.

**barrette** [bərét] s. broche, prendedor (para sujetar el pelo).

**barricade** [bærəkéd] s. barricada, barrera; v. poner barricadas; obstruir el paso con barricadas.

**barrier** [bǽrɪɚ] s. barrera, valla; obstáculo.

**barter** [bártɚ] v. permutar, trocar, cambiar; s. permuta, trueque, cambio.

**base** [bes] s. base; basa; fundamento; adj. bajo, vil, ruin; inferior; v. basar, fundar; establecer.

**baseball** [bésbɔ́l] s. baseball o beisbol.

**basement** [bésmənt] s. sótano.

**baseness** [bésnɪs] s. bajeza, ruindad,

vileza.

**bashful** [bǽʃfəl] *adj.* tímido, encogido, vergonzoso.

**bashfulness** [bǽʃfəlnɪs] *s.* timidez, vergüenza, cortedad, apocamiento.

**basic** [bésɪk] *adj.* básico; fundamental.

**basin** [bésṇ] *s.* palangana, jofaina; lebrillo; tazón (*de fuente*); estanque, depósito de agua; **river** — cuenca de río.

**basis** [bésɪs] (*pl.* **bases** [bésiz]) *s.* base, fundamento.

**bask** [bæsk] *v.* calentarse (*al sol*); asolearse, tomar el sol.

**basket** [bǽskɪt] *s.* cesta, cesto, canasta.

**basketball** [bǽskɪtbɔl] *s.* basquetbol.

**basque** [bæsk] *adj.* & *s.* (*person*) vasco; (*language*) vascuence, vasco; (*territory*) vascongado, vasco.

**bass** [bes] *s.* bajo (*en música*); *adj.* bajo, grave; — **drum** tambora, bombo; — **horn** tuba.

**bastard** [bǽstəd] *s.* & *adj.* bastardo.

**baste** [best] *v.* hilvanar; pringar (*empapar la carne con grasa*); apalear.

**bat** [bæt] *s.* palo, *Méx.*, *Carib.*, *Ven.*, *C.A.* bate (*de beisbol*); garrote; golpe, garrotazo; murciélago; *v.* apalear; dar palos; *Méx.*, *Carib.*, *Ven.*, *C.A.* batear; **not to** — **an eye** no pestañear.

**batch** [bætʃ] *s.* hornada; colección, grupo, conjunto.

**bath** [bæθ] *s.* baño.

**bathe** [beð] *v.* bañar(se).

**bather** [béðɚ] *s.* bañista.

**bathhouse** [bǽθhaʊs] *s.* casa de baños; bañadero.

**bathrobe** [bǽθrob] *s.* bata de baño.

**bathroom** [bǽθrum] *s.* baño, cuarto de baño.

**bathtub** [bǽθtʌb] *s.* bañera, tina.

**bathysphere** [bǽθɪsfɪr] *s.* batisfera.

**battalion** [bətǽljən] *s.* batallón.

**batter** [bǽtɚ] *s.* batido, masa; *Am.* bateador (*de beisbol*); *v.* golpear; **to** — **down** demoler.

**battery** [bǽtərɪ] *s.* batería; acumulador; asalto.

**battle** [bǽtl̩] *s.* batalla, lucha, combate; *v.* batallar, luchar, combatir.

**battlefield** [bǽtl̩fild] *s.* campo de batalla.

**battleship** [bǽtl̩ʃɪp] *s.* buque de guerra, acorazado.

**bawl** [bɔl] *s.* aullido; grito; *v.* aullar; gritar; pregonar; **to** — **out** regañar, reprender.

**bay** [be] *s.* bahía; ladrido, balido, aullido; — **rum** ron de laurel; — **tree** laurel; — **window** ventana saliente, mirador; **to hold at** — tener a raya; *adj.* bayo; *v.* dar aullidos, ladridos o balidos.

**bayonet** [béənɪt] *s.* bayoneta; *v.* traspasar; herir con bayoneta.

**bazaar** [bəzár] *s.* bazar; feria.

**bazooka** [bəzúka] *s.* bazuca.

**be** [bi] *v.* (*innately*) ser; (*state or condition*) estar, verse, hallarse, encontrarse; — **that as it may** sea como

sea; **to** — **cold** (**warm, hungry, right,** *etc.*) tener frío (calor, hambre, razón, *etc.*); **to** — **in a hurry** tener prisa; **he is to** — ha de ser; va a ser; **it is cold** (**hot, windy,** *etc.*) hace frío (calor, viento, *etc.*).

**beach** [bitʃ] *s.* playa, ribera; *v.* varar, poner en seco (*una embarcación*), encallar.

**beachhead** [bítʃhed] *s.* cabeza de playa.

**beacon** [bíkən] *s.* faro, fanal; boya luminosa; señal; **aviation** — radiofaro.

**bead** [bid] *s.* cuenta (*de rosario, collar, etc.*); abalorio; glóbulo; gota (*de sudor*); **-s** rosario; collar de cuentas; *v.* adornar con abalorios o cuentecitas.

**beak** [bik] *s.* pico (*de ave*); espolón (*de nave*).

**beam** [bim] *s.* rayo (*de luz o de calor*); sonrisa; viga; vigueta; brazo (*de balanza*); **radio** — línea de radiación, radiofaro; *v.* emitir (*luz, rayos*); brillar; sonreír, estar radiante de alegría; radiar, transmitir por radio.

**beaming** [bímɪŋ] *adj.* radiante, resplandeciente; sonriente.

**bean** [bin] *s.* judía, habichuela; *Méx.*, *C.A.*, *Ven.*, *Col.* frijol; *Ch.*, *Ríopl.* poroto; **coffee** — grano de café; **Lima** — haba; **string** — judía o habichuela verde; *Méx.*, *C.A.* ejote; *Ch.*, *Ríopl.* poroto.

**bear** [bɛr] *s.* oso, osa; bajista (*el que hace bajar los valores en la Bolsa*); *v.* (*stand*) soportar; llevar; sobrellevar; tolerar, aguantar; (*give birth*) parir, dar a luz; producir; **to** — **down** deprimir; apretar; **to** — **a grudge** guardar rencor; **to** — **in mind** tener en cuenta; **to** — **on a subject** tener relación con un asunto; **to** — **oneself with dignity** portarse con dignidad; **to** — **out** confirmar; **to** — **testimony** dar testimonio.

**beard** [bɪrd] *s.* barba, barbas; aristas (*de trigo o maíz*); **-ed** *adj.* barbado, barbudo.

**bearer** [bérɚ] *s.* portador; mensajero.

**bearing** [bérɪŋ] *s.* (*posture*) porte, presencia; (*relation*) relación, conexión; (*direction*) rumbo, orientación; (*mechanical*) cojinete; **ball** — cojinete de bolas; **beyond** — inaguantable, insufrible; **to lose one's -s** perder el rumbo, desorientarse; **fruit-bearing** *adj.* fructífero.

**beast** [bist] *s.* bestia, animal.

**beat** [bit] *s.* golpe; toque (*de tambor*); latido, palpitación; compás; ronda (*que hace el policía*); *v.* batir; golpear; azotar; vencer, ganar; marcar (*el compás*); pulsar, latir; sonar (*tambores*); **to** — **around the bush** andarse por las ramas; valerse de rodeos; *pret.* & *p.p. de* **to beat.**

**beaten** [bítṇ] *p.p. de* **to beat** & *adj.* batido; vencido; fatigado; — **path** camino trillado.

**beater** [bítər] *s.* batidor; molinillo; golpeador; **egg —** batidor de huevos.

**beatific** [biətífɪk] *adj.* beatifico.

**beating** [bítɪŋ] *s.* paliza, tunda, zurra; latido, pulsación.

**beatitude** [bɪǽtətjud] *s.* beatitud, bienaventuranza; **the Beatitudes** las bienaventuranzas.

**beau** [bo] *s.* galán, pretendiente.

**beauteous** [bjútɪəs] *adj.* bello, hermoso.

**beautiful** [bjútəfəl] *adj.* bello, hermoso.

**beautify** [bjútəfaɪ] *v.* hermosear, embellecer.

**beauty** [bjútɪ] *s.* belleza, hermosura; beldad; **— parlor** salón de belleza.

**beaver** [bívər] *s.* castor; **— board** cartón para tabiques.

**became** [bɪkém] *pret. de* **to become.**

**because** [bɪkɔ́z] *conj.* porque; **— of** *prep.* por, a causa de.

**beckon** [békən] *s.* seña, llamada; *v.* llamar a señas.

**become** [bɪkʌ́m] *v. (suit)* sentar bien a, quedar bien a; convenir a; *(turn out to be)* hacerse; ponerse; llegar a ser; convertirse en; **to — crazy** volverse loco; enloquecer; **to — angry** enojarse; **to — frightened** asustarse; **to — old** envejecer(se); **what has — of him?** ¿qué ha sido de él?; ¿qué se ha hecho él?; *p.p. de* **to become.**

**becoming** [bɪkʌ́mɪŋ] *adj.* propio, conveniente; decente, decoroso; **that dress is — to you** le sienta bien ese traje.

**bed** [bɛd] *s.* cama, lecho; cauce *(de un río)*; fondo *(de lago o mar)*; cuadro *(de jardín)*; yacimiento *(mineral)*; **to go to —** acostarse; **to put to —** acostar.

**bedbug** [bédbʌg] *s.* chinche.

**bedclothes** [bédkloz] *s. pl.* ropa de cama.

**bedding** [bédɪŋ] = **bedclothes.**

**bedpan** [bédpæn] *s.* silleta; cómodo.

**bedridden** [bédrɪdən] *adj.* en cama; postrado.

**bedrock** [bédrák] *s.* roca sólida; lecho de roca.

**bedroom** [bédrum] *s.* cuarto de dormir, alcoba, *Méx., C.A.* recámara.

**bedside** [bédsaɪd]: **at the —** al lado de la cama; **— table** velador, mesilla de noche.

**bedspread** [bédsprɛd] *s.* colcha, sobrecama.

**bedtime** [bédtaɪm] *s.* hora de acostarse, hora de dormir.

**bee** [bi] *s.* abeja; reunión *(para trabajar o competir)*; **to have a — in one's bonnet** tener una idea metida en la cabeza.

**beech** [bitʃ] *s.* haya; **—nut** nuez de haya, hayuco.

**beef** [bif] *s.* carne de vaca o toro; vaca, toro *(engordados para matar)*; **roast — rosbif.**

**beefsteak** [bífstek] *s.* bistec, biftec o bisté.

**beehive** [bíhaɪv] *s.* colmena; abejera.

**been** [bɪn, bɛn] *p.p. de* **to be.**

**beer** [bɪr] *s.* cerveza; **— tavern** cervecería.

**beet** [bit] *s.* remolacha, *Am.* betabel.

**beetle** [bítl] *s.* escarabajo.

**befall** [bɪfɔ́l] *v.* sobrevenir, acaecer, suceder.

**befallen** [bɪfɔ́lən] *p.p. de* **to befall.**

**befell** [bɪfél] *pret. de* **to befall.**

**befit** [bɪfít] *v.* convenir.

**before** [bɪfór] *adv. (temporal)* antes; *(spatial)* delante; al frente; *prep.* antes de; delante de; enfrente de; ante; *conj.* antes (de) que.

**beforehand** [bɪfórhænd] *adv.* de antemano, por adelantado, con antelación, con anticipación.

**befriend** [bɪfrénd] *v.* ofrecer o brindar amistad a; favorecer; amparar.

**beg** [bɛg] *v.* rogar, suplicar, pedir; mendigar, pordiosear; **to — the question** dar por sentado lo mismo que se arguye.

**began** [bɪgǽn] *pret. de* **to begin.**

**beget** [bɪgét] *v.* engendrar; causar, producir.

**beggar** [bégər] *s.* mendigo, pordiosero; pobre; infeliz, miserable.

**begin** [bɪgín] *v.* comenzar, empezar, principiar.

**beginner** [bɪgínər] *s.* principiante; novicio.

**beginning** [bɪgínɪŋ] *s.* principio; comienzo, empiezo; origen; **— with** comenzando con *(o por)*; a partir de; **at the —** al principio.

**begot** [bɪgát] *pret. & p.p. de* **to beget.**

**begotten** [bɪgátn] *p.p. de* **to beget.**

**beguile** [bɪgáɪl] *v.* engañar; defraudar; seducir.

**begun** [bɪgʌ́n] *p.p. de* **to begin.**

**behalf** [bɪhǽf]: **in (on) — of** por; en nombre de; a favor de; en defensa de; **in my —** en mi nombre; a mi favor; por mí.

**behave** [bɪhév] *v.* portarse, conducirse, obrar, proceder *(bien o mal)*; **— yourself!** ¡pórtate bien!

**behavior** [bɪhévjər] *s.* comportamiento, proceder, conducta; funcionamiento; reacción.

**behead** [bɪhéd] *v.* decapitar, degollar, descabezar.

**beheld** [bɪhéld] *pret. & p.p. de* **to behold.**

**behind** [bɪháɪnd] *adv.* detrás; atrás; a la zaga, en zaga; *prep.* detrás de, tras; **— one's back** a espaldas de uno; **— time** atrasado, retrasado; **from —** por detrás; **to arrive ten minutes — time** llegar con diez minutos de retraso; **to fall —** atrasarse; retrasarse.

**behold** [bɪhóld] *v.* contemplar, mirar; **—!** ¡he aquí!

**behoove** [bɪhúv] *v.* serle necesario a uno; corresponderle a uno; atañerle a uno.

**being** [bíɪŋ] *s.* ser; ente; esencia; existencia; *ger. de* **to be** siendo; **for the time —** por ahora; por el momento.

**belated** [bɪlétɪd] *adj.* tardío; atrasado.

**belch** [bɛltʃ] *v.* eructar; **to — forth**

**BA**

echar, arrojar, vomitar; *s.* eructo.
**belfry** [bélfrɪ] *s.* campanario.
**Belgian** [béldʒɪən] *adj.* & *s.* belga.
**belief** [bəlíf] *s.* creencia; fe; convicción; opinión.
**believable** [bəlívəbl] *adj.* creíble.
**believe** [bəlív] *v.* creer; pensar; **to — in** creer en; tener fe en; confiar en.
**believer** [bəlívɚ] *s.* creyente, fiel.
**belittle** [bɪlítl] *v.* menospreciar, apocar, empequeñecer; dar poca importancia a.
**bell** [bɛl] *s.* campana; campanilla; **cow — cencerro, esquila; call — timbre; jingle — cascabel; —flower** campanilla, campánula.
**bellboy** [bélbɔɪ] *s.* mozo de hotel, botones.
**belle** [bɛl] *s.* beldad, mujer bella.
**belligerent** [bəlídʒərənt] *adj.* & *s.* beligerante.
**bellow** [bélo] *s.* bramido, rugido; *v.* rugir, bramar, berrear; gritar.
**bellows** [béloz] *s.* (*sing.* & *pl.*) fuelle.
**belly** [bélɪ] *s.* barriga; panza, vientre; estómago.
**bellyache** [béliek] *s.* dolor de barriga (*estómago*).
**belong** [bəlɔ́ŋ] *v.* pertenecer, corresponder; **it does not — here** está fuera de su sitio; está mal colocado.
**belongings** [bəlɔ́ŋɪŋz] *s. pl.* posesiones, bienes, efectos, cosas.
**beloved** [bɪlʌ́vɪd] *adj.* querido, amado.
**below** [bəló] *adv.* abajo; bajo; debajo; **here —** aquí abajo; en este mundo, de tejas abajo; *prep.* bajo, debajo de.
**belt** [bɛlt] *s.* cinturón, cinto; correa; zona; **sword —** talabarte; *v.* ceñir, fajar.
**bemoan** [bɪmón] *v.* lamentarse de, quejarse de.
**bench** [bentʃ] *s.* banco, banca; tribunal.
**bend** [bɛnd] *s.* curva; vuelta, recodo; *v.* encorvar(se), doblar(se), *Am.* enchuecar(se); inclinar(se); someter(se), ceder; **to — one's efforts** esforzarse (por), dirigir sus esfuerzos.
**beneath** [bɪníθ] *prep.* debajo de, bajo; indigno de; inferior a.
**benediction** [bɛnədíkʃən] *s.* bendición.
**benefactor** [bénəfæktɚ] *s.* benefactor, bienhechor; patrón.
**beneficent** [bənéfəsn̩t] *adj.* benéfico.
**beneficial** [bɛnəfíʃəl] *adj.* benéfico; ventajoso, provechoso.
**benefit** [bénəfɪt] *s.* beneficio; provecho, ventaja; **— performance** función de beneficio; *v.* beneficiar; hacer bien; **to — by the advice** aprovecharse del consejo; **he -ed by the medicine** le hizo bien la medicina.
**benevolence** [bənévələns] *s.* benevolencia.
**benevolent** [bənévələnt] *adj.* benévolo.
**benign** [bɪnáɪn] *adj.* benigno; afable.
**bent** [bɛnt] *s.* inclinación; tendencia; propensión; *pret.* & *p.p. de* **to bend;** *adj.* encorvado; inclinado, doblado; corvo; gacho; **to be — on** estar resuelto a.

**benzene** [bénzin] *s.* benceno.
**bequeath** [bɪkwíð] *v.* heredar, legar, dejar en testamento.
**bequest** [bɪkwést] *s.* legado, donación.
**berate** [bɪrét] *v.* regañar, reñir, reprender.
**beret** [bəré] *s.* boina.
**berry** [bérɪ] *s.* baya (*como mora, fresa, etc.*); grano (*de café*).
**berth** [bɝθ] *s.* litera (*de un camarote*); **to give a wide — to** sacarle el cuerpo a, hacerse a un lado para dejar pasar.
**beseech** [bɪsítʃ] *v.* suplicar, rogar.
**beset** [bɪsét] *v.* atacar; rodear; acosar; *pret.* & *p.p. de* **to beset.**
**beside** [bɪsáɪd] *prep.* (*spatial*) al lado de; cerca de; (*in addition*) además de; fuera de; **to be — oneself** estar fuera de sí, estar loco; **that is — the question** eso no hace al caso; no se trata de eso; *adv.* además.
**besides** [bɪsáɪdz] *adv.* además; *prep.* además de.
**besiege** [bɪsídʒ] *v.* sitiar, cercar; acosar, importunar.
**besought** [bɪsɔ́t] *pret.* & *p.p. de* **to beseech.**
**best** [bɛst] *adj.* mejor; *adv.* mejor; más; **the —** el mejor; lo mejor; **— girl** novia; querida; **— man** padrino de boda; **— seller** éxito de venta; de mayor venta; **at —** a lo más, cuando más; **to do one's —** hacer todo lo posible; **to get the — of a person** vencer o ganarle a una persona; **to make the — of** sacar el mejor partido de.
**bestow** [bɪstó] *v.* otorgar, conferir; **to — gifts upon** hacer regalos (o dádivas) a; **time well -ed** tiempo bien empleado.
**bet** [bɛt] *s.* apuesta; *v.* apostar; *pret.* & *p.p. de* **to bet.**
**betake** [bɪték] *v.* **to — oneself** encaminarse, dirigirse.
**betaken** [bɪtékən] *p.p. de* **to betake.**
**betook** [bɪtúk] *pret. de* **to betake.**
**betray** [bɪtré] *v.* traicionar, vender, hacer traición; revelar, no guardar (*un secreto*); **to — one's ignorance** hacer patente su ignorancia.
**betrayer** [bɪtréɚ] *s.* traidor, traicionera.
**betrothal** [bɪtróθəl] *s.* esponsales, compromiso, mutua promesa de matrimonio.
**betrothed** [bɪtróθt] *s.* prometido, desposado; novio, novia.
**better** [bétɚ] *adj.* mejor; *adv.* mejor; más; **— half** cara mitad; **so much the —** tanto mejor; **to be — off** estar mejor así; estar en mejores condiciones; **to change for the —** mejorar(se); **to get —** mejorar(se), restablecerse, aliviarse; *v.* mejorar; **to — oneself** mejorarse, mejorar de situación.
**betterment** [bétɚmənt] *s.* mejoramiento, mejora, mejoría.
**between** [bətwín] *prep.* entre, en medio de; *adv.* en medio.

**bevel** [bévəl] *adj.* biselado; *v.* biselar.
**beverage** [bévrɪdʒ] *s.* bebida.
**bewail** [bɪwél] *v.* lamentar; quejarse de.
**beware** [bɪwér] *v.* guardarse (de), cuidarse (de); — ! ¡cuidado! ¡guárdese!
**bewilder** [bɪwíldə·] *v.* confundir, turbar, perturbar, dejar perplejo; **to be -ed** estar turbado o perplejo; estar desorientado.
**bewilderment** [bɪwíldə·mənt] *s.* perplejidad, aturdimiento.
**bewitch** [bɪwítʃ] *v.* hechizar; aojar; encantar, cautivar.
**beyond** [bɪjánd] *adv.* más allá, más lejos; *prep.* allende; más allá de; fuera de: — **my reach** fuera de mi alcance.
**bias** [báɪəs] *s.* (*tendency*) prejuicio; inclinación, tendencia; (*diagonal*) sesgo, oblicuidad; **on the** — sesgado, al sesgo, de lado; *adj.* sesgado, oblicuo; *v.* predisponer, inclinar, influir en.
**bib** [bɪb] *s.* babero; pechera (*de delantal*).
**Bible** [báɪb] *s.* Biblia.
**biblical** [bíblɪk] *adj.* bíblico.
**bibliographer** [bɪblɪágrəfə·] *s.* bibliógrafo.
**bibliography** [bɪblɪágrəfɪ] *s.* bibliografía.
**bicker** [bíkə·] *v.* disputar, reñir.
**bicycle** [báɪsɪk] *s.* bicicleta; *v.* andar en bicicleta.
**bid** [bɪd] *s.* postura, oferta; envite (*en naipes*); turno (*para envidar*); invitación; *v.* ofrecer (*precio*); mandar; invitar, convidar; rogar; envidar (*en naipes*); **to** — **fair** parecer muy probable; **to** — **good-bye** decir adiós; despedirse; **to** — **up** alzar, pujar (*la oferta en una subasta*); *pret.* & *p.p. de* **to bid**.
**bidden** [bídn̩] *p.p. de* **to bid** & **to bide**.
**bide** [baɪd] *v.* aguardar; **to** — **one's time** esperar una buena oportunidad.
**biennium** [baɪénɪəm] *s.* bienio.
**bier** [bɪr] *s.* féretro.
**big** [bɪg] *adj.* grande; importante; imponente; — **Dipper** Osa Mayor; — **game** caza mayor; — **sister** hermana mayor; — **with child** encinta; **to talk** — darse bombo, *Am.* darse corte; **big-bellied** panzudo, panzón, barrigón; **big-hearted** magnánimo.
**bigamy** [bígəmɪ] *s.* bigamia.
**bigot** [bígət] *s.* fanático.
**bigotry** [bígətrɪ] *s.* fanatismo; intolerancia.
**bikini** [bɪkínɪ] *s.* traje bikini.
**bile** [baɪl] *s.* bilis, hiel; cólera, mal humor.
**bilingual** [baɪlíŋgwəl] *adj.* & *s.* bilingüe.
**bill** [bɪl] *s.* (*statement*) cuenta; factura; (*poster*) cartel, anuncio; (*bank note*) billete de banco; programa de teatro; (*bird*) pico; (*legislative*) proyecto de ley; — **of exchange** libranza, letra de cambio; — **of fare** lista de platos; — **of lading** conocimiento de embarque; — **of rights** declaración de derechos; — **of sale** escritura o acta

de venta; *v.* cargar en cuenta; enviar una cuenta a; **to** — **and coo** acariciarse y arrullar (*como las palomas*).
**billboard** [bílbord] *s.* cartelera.
**billfold** [bílfold] *s.* cartera.
**billiards** [bíljə·dz] *s.* billar.
**billion** [bíljən] *s.* billón, millón de millones; mil millones (*en los Estados Unidos y Francia*).
**billow** [bílo] *s.* oleada; ola grande; *v.* alzarse en olas.
**bin** [bɪn] *s.* arcón, depósito; **coal** — carbonera; **grain** — granero.
**bind** [baɪnd] *v.* (*unite*) unir, juntar; (*tie*) ligar; amarrar; vendar; ceñir; (*compel*) restringir; obligar, compeler; (*enclose*) encuadernar, empastar; rivetear.
**binding** [báɪndɪŋ] *s.* encuadernación; ribete, cinta; **cloth** — encuadernación en tela; **paper** — encuadernación en rústica; *adj.* obligatorio.
**biography** [baɪágrəfɪ] *s.* biografía.
**biology** [baɪáládʒɪ] *s.* biología.
**bipartisan** [baɪpártəzən] *adj.* de dos partidos; bipartito.
**birch** [bɜtʃ] *s.* abedul.
**bird** [bɜd] *s.* ave; pájaro; persona extraña o mal vista; — **of prey** ave de rapiña; — **seed** alpiste; — **shot** perdigones.
**birth** [bɜθ] *s.* nacimiento; parto; linaje; origen, principio; — **certificate** certificado (*o* fe) de nacimiento; — **control** control de la natalidad; limitación de partos; — **rate** natalidad; **to give** — dar a luz, parir.
**birthday** [bɜ́θde] *s.* cumpleaños, natalicio.
**birthplace** [bɜ́θples] *s.* lugar de nacimiento, suelo natal.
**birthright** [bɜ́θraɪt] *s.* derechos naturales o de nacimiento; naturalidad; primogenitura.
**biscuit** [bískɪt] *s.* bizcocho; galleta; panecillo.
**bishop** [bíʃəp] *s.* obispo; alfil (*en ajedrez*).
**bison** [báɪsn̩] *s.* bisonte, búfalo.
**bit** [bɪt] *s.* pedacito, trocito; pizca, miaja, migaja; poquito; bocado (*del freno*); taladro; **I don't care a** — no me importa un ardite; *pret.* & *p.p. de* **to bite**.
**bitch** [bɪtʃ] *s.* perra; ramera, prostituta.
**bite** [baɪt] *s.* mordedura, mordisco; bocado, bocadito; picadura (*de insecto*); *v.* morder; mordiscar; picar.
**bitten** [bítn̩] *p.p. de* **to bite**.
**bitter** [bítə·] *adj.* amargo; agrio, acre; áspero; mordaz; **to fight to the** — **end** luchar hasta morir; **-s** *s. pl.* amargo; **-ly** *adv.* amargamente; con amargura.
**bitterness** [bítə·nɪs] *s.* amargura, amargor; rencor; aspereza.
**black** [blæk] *adj.* negro; obscuro; sombrío; **black-and-blue** amoratado, lleno de moretones; — **mark** mancha, estigma, marca de deshonra; *s.* negro; luto; **—out** obscurecimiento: **to put**

**down in — and white** poner por escrito v. teñir de negro; embetunar, dar bola o betún a (los zapatos).

**blackberry** [blǽkbɛrɪ] s. zarzamora: mora.

**blackbird** [blǽkbɜ˞d] s. mirlo.

**blackboard** [blǽkbord] s. encerado; pizarrón; pizarra.

**blacken** [blǽkən] v. ennegrecer; obscurecer; teñir de negro; denigrar.

**blackhead** [blǽkhɛd] s. espinilla.

**blackish** [blǽkɪʃ] adj. negruzco.

**blackjack** [blǽkdʒæk] s. (weapon) cachiporra flexible; (card game) veintiuna.

**blackmail** [blǽkmel] s. chantaje, extorsión; v. ejercer el chantaje, extorsionar.

**blackness** [blǽknɪs] s. negrura; obscuridad.

**blacksmith** [blǽksmɪθ] s. herrero; **-'s shop** herrería.

**bladder** [blǽdɚ] s. vejiga.

**blade** [bled] s. hoja (de navaja, cuchillo, etc.); hoja (de hierba); espada; pala (de remo); aspa (de hélice); **shoulder — ** espaldilla o paletilla.

**blame** [blem] s. culpa; v. culpar, echar la culpa a; **to be to —** tener la culpa.

**blameless** [blémlɪs] adj. inculpable.

**blanch** [blæntʃ] v. blanquear; palidecer; escaldar (almendras).

**bland** [blænd] adj. blando, suave.

**blank** [blæŋk] adj. (no writing) en blanco; (void) vacío; (confused) aturdido; **— cartridge** cartucho vacío; **— face** cara sin expresión; **— form** blanco, forma en blanco, Méx., C.A., Ven. esqueleto; **— verse** verso suelto o libre; s. blanco; vacío; hueco, intermedio; papel en blanco; forma en blanco; **application —** forma (o blanco) para memorial o solicitud.

**blanket** [blǽŋkɪt] s. manta; frazada; cobertor; Ríopl., C.A., Méx., Ven., Col. cobija; Méx. sarape, poncho; adj. general, inclusivo, que abarca un grupo o clase.

**blare** [blɛr] s. fragor; son de trompetas; clarinada; v. trompetear, proclamar; sonar (las trompetas); hacer estruendo.

**blaspheme** [blæsfím] v. blasfemar.

**blasphemy** [blǽsfɪmɪ] s. blasfemia.

**blast** [blæst] s. (wind) ráfaga de viento, golpe de viento; soplo repentino; (trumpet) trompetazo; (whistle) silbido; (explosion) explosión; estallido; carga de dinamita; **— furnace** alto horno; v. volar (con dinamita, etc.); destruir.

**blaze** [blez] s. llama, llamarada, incendio; resplandor; **— of anger** arranque de ira; v. arder; resplandecer; **to — a trail** abrir (o marcar) una senda.

**bleach** [blitʃ] s. blanqueador; blanqueo; v. blanquear(se); desteñir(se).

**bleachers** [blítʃɚz] s. pl. graderías, Am. glorietas.

**bleak** [blik] adj. yermo, desierto; helado.

**blear** [blɪr] v. nublar (los ojos).

**bleary** [blírɪ] adj. nublado, inflamado,

lagrimoso, lagañoso.

**bleat** [blit] s. balido; v. balar.

**bled** [blɛd] pret. & p.p. de **to bleed**.

**bleed** [blid] v. sangrar; desangrar; extorsionar.

**blemish** [blémɪʃ] s. mancha, tacha, defecto; v. manchar; empañar.

**blend** [blɛnd] s. mezcla, entremezcla; gradación (de colores, sonidos, etc.); v. mezclar, entremezclar; graduar (colores o sonidos); entremezclarse, fundirse; armonizar.

**bless** [blɛs] v. bendecir; **God — you!** ¡que Dios te bendiga!

**blessed** [blésɪd] adj. bendito; santo, beato; bienaventurado; **the whole — day** todo el santo día; [blɛst] pret. & p.p. de **to bless**.

**blessing** [blésɪŋ] s. bendición; gracia, don, beneficio.

**blest** [blɛst] adj. = **blessed**.

**blew** [blu] pret. de **to blow**.

**blight** [blaɪt] s. pulgón (parásito); tizón (honguillo parásito); quemadura (enfermedad de las plantas); roña (de las plantas); malogro; ruina; v. destruir, arruinar; frustrar (esperanzas).

**blimp** [blɪmp] s. dirigible pequeño.

**blind** [blaɪnd] adj. ciego; tapado, oculto; hecho a ciegas; **— alley** callejón sin salida; **— choice** selección hecha a ciegas; **— flying** vuelo ciego, vuelo a ciegas; **—man** ciego; **— man's buff** juego de la gallina ciega; **— date** [blaɪnddet] s. cita a ciegas; persiana, cortinilla; biombo; venda (para los ojos); anteojera (para resguardar los ojos del caballo); **to be a — for someone** ser tapadera de alguien; v. cegar; ofuscar; encubrir, tapar.

**blinder** [blaɪndɚ] s. anteojera, Am. visera (para caballos de tiro).

**blindfold** [blaɪndfold] v. vendar (los ojos); adj. vendado (de ojos); s. venda (para los ojos).

**blindly** [blaɪndlɪ] adv. ciegamente; a ciegas.

**blindness** [blaɪndnɪs] s. ceguera, ceguedad.

**blink** [blɪŋk] s. pestañeo; parpadeo; guiño; guiñada; v. pestañear; parpadear; guiñar.

**blip** [blɪp] s. bache de radar.

**bliss** [blɪs] s. beatitud, bienaventuranza, gloria; felicidad.

**blister** [blístɚ] s. ampolla, vejiga (en la piel o en cualquier superficie); v. ampollar, levantar ampollas; ampollarse.

**blitz** [blɪts] s. ataque relámpago.

**blizzard** [blízɚd] s. ventisca; v. ventiscar.

**bloat** [blot] v. inflar(se); abotagarse.

**blob** [blɑb] s. burbuja.

**block** [blɑk] s. (piece) bloque, trozo de piedra; zoquete; (city section) manzana (de casas); Am. cuadra; (obstacle) estorbo, obstáculo; (group) grupo, sección; (hat) horma; **— pulley** polea; **chopping —** tajo; v. estorbar; tapar; bloquear; planchar (sobre horma); parar (una pelota, una *jugada*); **to — out** esbozar, bosquejar; **to — the door** impedir el paso; **to — up a door** tapiar una puerta.

**blockade** [blɑkéd] *s.* bloqueo; obstrucción; *v.* bloquear.

**blockhead** [blɑ́khɛd] *s.* zoquete, tonto, zopenco.

**blond(e)** [blɑnd] *adj.* & *s.* rubio, blondo; *Mex.* huero, güero; *Guat.* canche; *Sal., Hond.,* chele; *C.R.* macho; *Col.* mono; *Ven.* catire.

**blood** [blʌd] *s.* sangre; **— count** análisis cuantitativo de la sangre; **— pudding** (*o* **— sausage**) morcilla; **— relative** pariente consanguíneo; **— vessel** vena; arteria; **in cold —** en sangre fría; **— bank** banco de sangre; **— poisoning** septicemia.

**bloodshed** [blʌ́dʃɛd] *s.* matanza; derrame, derramiento o efusión de sangre.

**bloodshot** [blʌ́dʃɑt] *adj.* inyectado de sangre.

**bloodthirsty** [blʌ́dθɜ̃stɪ] *adj.* sanguinario.

**bloody** [blʌ́dɪ] *adj.* sangriento; ensangrentado; sanguinario, feroz.

**bloom** [blum] *s.* flor; florecimiento floración; lozanía; color rosado (*en las mejillas*) *v.* florecer, *Am.* florear.

**blooming** [blúmɪŋ] *adj.* floreciente; fresco, lozano, vigoroso.

**blossom** [blɑ́səm] *s.* flor; floración, florecimiento; *v.* florecer.

**blot** [blɑt] *s.* mancha, borrón; tacha; *v.* manchar; borrar; secar (*con papel secante*); emborronar, echar manchas o borrones; **to — out** borrar, tachar; destruir; **this pen -s** esta pluma echa borrones; **blotting paper** papel secante.

**blotch** [blɑtʃ] *v.* emborronar o borronear, manchar, cubrir con manchas; *s.* mancha, borrón.

**blotter** [blɑ́tɚ] *s.* papel secante; libro borrador.

**blouse** [blaʊs] *s.* blusa.

**blow** [blo] *s.* (*stroke*) golpe; porrazo; (*shock*) choque, sorpresa, desastre; (*wind*) soplo, soplido; **to come to -s** venir a las manos; *v.* soplar; ventear; resoplar; sonar (*una trompeta*); fanfarronear; **to — a fuse** quemar un fusible; **to — one's nose** sonarse; **to — one's brains out** levantarse la tapa de los sesos; **to — open** abrirse; **to — out** apagar(se); estallar, reventar(se) (*un neumático*); **to — over** pasar; disiparse; **to — up** inflar, hinchar; volar (*con dinamita*); estallar, reventar.

**blower** [blóɚ] *s.* soplador; fuelle; ventilador, aventador.

**blown** [blon] *p.p. de* **to blow** & *adj.* soplado; inflado; **full-blown rose** rosa abierta.

**blowout** [blóaʊt] *s.* reventón (*de neumático*); escape violento de gas, aire, etc.

**blowpipe** [blópaɪp] *s.* soplete.

**blowtorch** [blótɔrtʃ] *s.* soplete.

**blue** [blu] *adj.* azul; triste, melancólico;

*s.* azul; **the -s** melancolía, morriña, murria; *v.* azular, teñir de azul.

**bluebell** [blúbɛl] *s.* campanilla azul (*flor*).

**bluebird** [blúbɚd] *s.* pájaro azul, *Am.* azulejo.

**bluejay** [blúdʒe] *s.* gayo, especie de azulejo (*pájaro*).

**bluff** [blʌf] *s.* acantilado, escarpa, risco; fanfarronada; fanfarrón, farsante; *v.* fanfarronear; alardear, hacer alarde; echar bravatas; embaucar.

**bluffer** [blʌ́fɚ] *s.* farsante, fanfarrón.

**bluing** [blúɪŋ] *s.* añil (*para ropa blanca*).

**bluish** [blúɪʃ] *adj.* azulado, azulejo.

**blunder** [blʌ́ndɚ] *s.* disparate, desatino; despropósito; *v.* disparatar, desatinar; equivocarse.

**blunt** [blʌnt] *adj.* despuntado, embotado; brusco, grosero, *Méx.* claridoso; *v.* despuntar, embotar.

**blur** [blɚ] *s.* mancha; tacha; nube, cosa obscura o confusa; *v.* empañar, borronear, manchar; nublar, ofuscar; empañarse, nublarse.

**blush** [blʌʃ] *s.* sonrojo; rubir; *v.* sonrojarse, ruborizarse, ponerse colorado.

**bluster** [blʌ́stɚ] *v.* ventear o soplar recio (*el viento*); fanfarronear; *s.* ventolera, ventarrón, fuerte golpe de viento; jactancia, fanfarronada.

**blustering** [blʌ́stərɪŋ] *adj.* fanfarrón, jactancioso; **— wind** ventarrón.

**boar** [bor] *s.* jabalí.

**board** [bord] *s.* (*wood*) tabla, tablero; mesa; (*meals*) comidas; (*directors*) junta, consejo; (*pasteboard*) en pasta; cartón; **the -s** las tablas, el teatro; **room and —** cuarto y comida, pensión completa; asistencia; **— of directors** junta directiva; **bulletin —** tablilla para anuncios; **free on — (f.o.b.)** franco a bordo; **on — a** bordo; en el tren; **to go by the —** caer en el mar; perderse; ser descartado; *v.* ir a bordo; subir (*al tren*); entablar, cubrir con tablas; tomar a pupilaje, dar asistencia, pensión o pupilaje; residir o comer (*en casa de huéspedes*).

**boarder** [bórdɚ] *s.* huésped, pupilo, pensionista.

**boardinghouse** [bórdɪŋhaʊs] *s.* casa de huéspedes, pensión.

**boast** [bost] *s.* jactancia; alarde; bravata; gloria, orgullo; *v.* jactarse, alardear; hacer alarde de; ostentar.

**boastful** [bóstfəl] *adj.* jactancioso.

**boastfulness** [bóstfəlnɪs] *s.* jactancia; ostentación.

**boat** [bot] *s.* bote; barco, buque; lancha, chalupa.

**boathouse** [bóthaʊs] *s.* casilla o cobertizo para botes.

**boating** [bótɪŋ] *s.* paseo en lancha o bote; **to go —** pasear en bote.

**boatman** [bótmən] (*pl.* **boatmen** [bótmɛn]) *s.* barquero.

**bob** [bɑb] *s.* meneo, sacudida; pesa (*de metal*); **to wear a —** llevar el pelo corto (*o* en melena); *v.* menearse; **to — one's hair** cortarse el pelo en

melena; **to — up** aparecer de repente;
**to — up and down** saltar, brincar;
cabecear (*dícese de una embarcación*).
**bobbin** [bábɪn] *s.* carrete; bobina.
**bobwhite** [bábhwáɪt] *s.* cordorniz.
**bode** [bod] *pret. & p.p. de* **to bide.**
**bodice** [bádɪs] *s.* corpiño, jubón.
**bodily** [bádlɪ] *adj.* corpóreo; corporal;
*adv.* todos juntos, colectivamente;
**they rose —** se levantaron todos a
una, se levantaron todos juntos.
**body** [bádɪ] *s.* cuerpo; agregado, conjunto; gremio; carrocería (*de automóvil*); fuselaje (*de aeroplano*); **— of
water** extensión de agua; **— politic**
grupo político; estado.
**bodyguard** [bádɪgɑrd] *s.* guardaespal-
das.
**bog** [bɑg] *s.* pantano; tremedal; *v.*
hundir(se); atascarse.
**Bohemian** [bohímɪən] *adj. & s.* bohemio.
**boil** [bɔɪl] *s.* hervor; tumorcillo; **to
come to a —** soltar el hervor, hervir;
*v.* hervir; cocer; bullir; **to — down**
hervir hasta evaporar; abreviar.
**boiler** [bɔ́ɪlɚ] *s.* caldera, marmita; caldera de vapor; calorífero central.
**boiling point** [bɔ́ɪlɪŋpɔɪnt] *s.* punto de
ebullición.
**boisterous** [bɔ́ɪstərəs] *adj.* bullicioso;
estrepitoso, ruidoso; tumultuoso.
**bold** [bold] *adj.* atrevido, osado; arriesgado; audaz; insolente; claro, bien
delineado; **— cliff** risco escarpado;
**bold-faced** descarado; **bold-faced
type** negritas.
**boldness** [bóldnɪs] *s.* atrevimiento; osadía; audacia; descaro, insolencia.
**bologna** [bəlónɪ] *s.* especie de embutido.
**Bolshevik** [bólʃəvik] *adj. & s.* bolche-
vique.
**bolster** [bólstɚ] *s.* travesaño, almohada
larga (*para la cabecera de la cama*);
refuerzo, sostén, soporte; *v.* sostener,
apoyar; apuntalar; **to — someone's
courage** infundirle ánimo a alguien.
**bolt** [bolt] *s.* (*door lock*) pestillo,
cerrojo; (*pin*) perno, tornillo grande;
(*movement*) salida de repente; (*cloth*)
rollo; **thunder —** rayo; *v.* cerrar con
cerrojo; tragar, engullir; romper con
(*un partido político*); echarse a correr,
lanzarse de repente; caer como rayo;
**to — out** salir de golpe.
**bomb** [bɑm] *s.* bomba; *v.* bombardear;
**— shelter** [bámʃɛltɚ] *s.* refugio
antiaéreo.
**bombard** [bɑmbárd] *v.* bombardear,
cañonear.
**bombardier** [bɑmbɚdír] *s.* bombardero
**bombardment** [bɑmbárdmənt] *s.* bombardeo, cañoneo.
**bombastic** [bɑmbǽstɪk] *adj.* ampuloso,
altisonante.
**bomber** [bámɚ] *s.* bombardero, avión
de bombardeo.
**bonbon** [bánbɑn] *s.* bombón, confite.
**bond** [bɑnd] *s.* lazo, vínculo; ligadura;
fianza, vale; obligación, bono.
**bondage** [bándɪdʒ] *s.* servidumbre, es-

clavitud.
**bondsman** [bándzmən] *s.* fiador.
**bone** [bon] *s.* hueso; espina (*de pez*); **-s**
restos; osamenta; **— of contention**
materia de discordia; **to make no
-s about it** no pararse en pelillos;
obrar francamente; *v.* deshuesar, quitar los huesos o espinas.
**bonfire** [bánfaɪr] *s.* hoguera, fogata.
**bonnet** [bánɪt] *s.* gorra; sombrero (*de
mujer*).
**bonus** [bónəs] *s.* prima, premio, gratificación.
**bony** [bónɪ] *adj.* huesudo.
**boo** [bu] *v.* mofarse, burlarse (*a gritos*);
**— !** *interj.* ¡bu!; **-s** *s. pl.* rechifla,
gritos de mofa.
**booby** [búbɪ] *s.* bobo, bobalicón.
**book** [buk] *s.* libro; **The book** la Biblia;
**cash —** libro de caja; **memorandum
—** libreta; **on the -s** cargado en cuenta; **to keep -s** llevar los libros o la
contabilidad *v.* inscribir, asentar (*en
un libro*); **to — passage** reservar
pasaje.
**bookcase** [búkkes] *s.* estante, estantería,
armario para libros.
**bookend** [búkɛnd] *s.* apoyalibros,
sujetalibros.
**bookkeeper** [búkkipɚ] *s.* tenedor de
libros, contador.
**bookkeeping** [búkkipɪŋ] *s.* teneduría
de libros, contabilidad; **double entry —** partida doble.
**booklet** [búklɛt] *s.* librillo, librito,
cuaderno, folleto.
**bookseller** [búksɛlɚ] *s.* librero.
**bookshelf** [búkʃɛlf] *s.* estante, repisa
para libros.
**bookshop** [búkʃɑp] *s.* librería.
**bookstore** [búkstor] *s.* librería.
**boom** [bum] *s.* (*noise*) estampido;
(*increase*) alza, auge (*en el mercado o
bolsa*); bonanza, prosperidad mo-
mentánea; *v.* rugir, resonar, hacer
estampido; prosperar, medrar, florecer, estar en bonanza; fomentar.
**boon** [bun] *s.* don; bendición, gracia,
favor; *adj.* jovial, congenial.
**boor** [bur] *s.* patán, hombre zafio o
grosero.
**boorish** [búrɪʃ] *adj.* grosero, zafio.
**boost** [bust] *s.* empuje, empujón (*de
abajo arriba*); **— in prices** alza o auge
de precios; *v.* empujar, alzar, levantar; hacеr subir.
**booster** [bústɚ] *s.* aumentador; (*rocket*)
cohete de lanzamiento; (*electronics*)
amplificador.
**boot** [but] *s.* bota, calzado; **to — por
añadidura, de ganancia, *Méx.* de
pilón, *Ven.* de ñapa; *Ríopl., Andes* de
yapa (*llapa*); *v.* dar un puntapié; **to
— out** echar a puntapiés; echar a
patadas.
**bootblack** [bútblæk] *s.* limpiabotas.
**booth** [buθ] *s.* casilla, puesto.
**bootlegger** [bútlɛgɚ] *s.* contrabandista
(*de licores*).
**bootlicker** [bútlɪkɚ] *s.* servilón, zalamero.

**booty** [búti] *s.* botín, saqueo.

**borax** [bóræks] *s.* bórax.

**border** [bórdɚ] *s.* borde, margen, orilla; orla, franja; ribete; frontera; *v.* ribetear, guarnecer (*el borde*); orlar; **to — on** (*o* **upon**) lindar con, confinar con; rayar en; **it -s on madness** raya en locura.

**bore** [bor] *s.* taladro, barreno; agujero (*hecho con taladro*); calibre (*de un cañón, cilindro, etc.*); persona o cosa aburrida; *v.* taladrar, horadar, barrenar; aburrir, fastidiar; *pret. de* **to bear.**

**bored** [bord] *adj.* cansado, aburrido; *p.p. de* **to bore.**

**boredom** [bórdəm] *s.* aburrimiento, tedio, hastío, fastidio.

**boric acid** [bórɪk ǽsəd] *s.* ácido bórico.

**boring** [bórɪŋ] *adj.* aburrido, fastidioso, tedioso.

**born** [bɔrn] *p.p. de* **to bear** & *adj.* nacido; innato; **to be —** nacer.

**borne** [bɔrn] *p.p.* **to bear.**

**borough** [bɝo] *s.* villa; distrito de municipio.

**borrow** [bóro] *v.* pedir prestado; tomar prestado; tomar fiado.

**borrower** [bórəwɚ] *s.* el que pide prestado.

**bosom** [búzəm] *s.* seno, pecho, corazón; pechera (*de camisa*); **in the — of the family** en el seno de la familia; *adj.* querido; **— friend** amigo íntimo.

**boss** [bɔs] *s.* jefe; patrón; mayoral, capataz; **political —** cacique político; *v.* mandar, dominar, dirigir.

**bossy** [bósɪ] *adj.* mandón, autoritario.

**botany** [bátnɪ] *s.* botánica.

**botch** [batʃ] *s.* chapucería.

**both** [boθ] *adj.* & *pron.* ambos, entrambos, los dos; **— this and that** tanto esto como aquello; **— of them** ambos, ellos dos, los dos; **— (of) his friends** sus dos amigos, ambos amigos.

**bother** [báðɚ] *s.* molestia; fastidio; incomodidad; enfado; *v.* molestar(se); fastidiar, enfadar; incomodar; estorbar.

**bothersome** [báðɚsəm] *adj.* molesto.

**bottle** [bátl] *s.* botella; *v.* embotellar.

**bottleneck** [bátlnɛk] *s.* embotellamiento; gollete.

**bottom** [bátəm] *s.* fondo; base; fundamento; asiento (*de silla*); **to be at the — of the class** ser el último de la clase; **what is at the — of all this?** ¿qué hay en el fondo de todo esto?

**boudoir** [budwár] *s.* tocador.

**bough** [bau] *s.* rama.

**bought** [bɔt] *pret.* & *p.p. de* **to buy.**

**bouillon** [búljan] *s.* caldo.

**boulder** [bóldɚ] *s.* peña, roca, guijarro grande, pedrusco.

**boulevard** [búləvard] *s.* bulevar.

**bounce** [bauns] *s.* bote, rebote (*de una pelota*); salto, brinco; *v.* hacer saltar; saltar, brincar; botar; echar, arrojar (*a alguien*); echar, despedir de un empleo.

**bouncer** [baunsɚ] *s.* apagabroncas.

**bound** [baund] *s.* (*jump*) salto, brinco; (*bounce*) bote, rebote; (*limit*) límite, confín; *adj.* ligado; confinado; obligado; ceñido; encuadernado; **to be — for** ir para, ir con rumbo a; **to be — up in one's work** estar absorto en su trabajo; **it is — to happen** es seguro que sucederá; **I am — to do it** estoy resuelto a hacerlo; *v.* botar, resaltar; saltar, brincar; limitar; ceñir, cercar; *pret. & p.p. de* **to bind.**

**boundary** [báundərɪ] *s.* límite, linde; confín; frontera.

**boundless** [báundlɪs] *adj.* ilimitado, sin límite, sin término.

**bountiful** [báuntəfəl] *adj.* generoso, liberal; abundante.

**bounty** [báuntɪ] *s.* largueza, generosidad; don, favor, gracia; premio, recompensa.

**bouquet** [buké] *s.* ramillete, ramo de flores; aroma, fragancia.

**bourgeois** [burʒwá] *adj.* & *s.* burgués.

**bout** [baut] *s.* combate, lucha, contienda, asalto; **a — of pneumonia** un ataque de pulmonía.

**bow** [bau] *s.* (*inclination*) reverencia, inclinación, saludo; (*of a ship*) proa; *v.* hacer una reverencia, inclinarse (*para saludar*); someterse; **to — one's head** inclinar la cabeza **-ed down** agobiado.

**bow** [bo] *s.* arco (*para tirar flechas*); arco (*de violín*); curva; lazo, moño (*de cintas*); **bow-legged** *adj.* patizambo, patituerto; *v.* arquear; tocar (*un instrumento*) con arco.

**bowels** [báuəlz] *s. pl.* intestinos; entrañas; tripas.

**bower** [báuɚ] *s.* enramada, ramada, glorieta.

**bowl** [bol] *s.* cuenco; tazón; jícara; boliche, bola; **wash —** palangana, lavamanos; **-s** juego de bolos; *v.* bolear, jugar a los bolos, jugar al boliche.

**box** [baks] *s.* caja; estuche; palco de teatro; casilla; compartimiento; bofetada; **—car** furgón; **— office** taquilla; **— seat** asiento de palco; *v.* encajonar; meter en una caja; abofetear; boxear.

**boxer** [báksɚ] *s.* boxeador, pugilista.

**boxing** [báksɪŋ] *s.* boxeo, pugilato.

**boy** [bɔɪ] *s.* niño; muchacho; mozo.

**boycott** [bóɪkat] *v.* boycotear; *s.* boycoteo.

**boyhood** [bóɪhud] *s.* niñez; mocedad, juventud.

**boyish** [bóɪʃ] *adj.* pueril; juvenil; aniñado.

**brace** [bres] *s.* traba; tirante; apoyo, refuerzo; corchete ({ }); **carpenter's —** berbiquí; *v.* trabar; apoyar, reforzar; asegurar; estimular, fortalecer; **to — up** animarse, cobrar ánimo.

**bracelet** [bréslɪt] *s.* brazalete, pulsera.

**bracket** [brǽkɪt] *s.* ménsula, soporte, sostén; repisa; **-s** paréntesis cuadrados; *v.* colocar entre paréntesis; unir;

**agrupar.**

**brag** [bræg] *s.* jactancia; *v.* jactarse (de); hacer alarde de.

**braggart** [brǽgət] *adj.* & *s.* jactancioso, fanfarrón.

**braid** [bred] *s.* trenza; galón, trencilla; *v.* trenzar; galonear, guarnecer con galones.

**brain** [bren] *s.* cerebro; seso; **to rack one's -s** devanarse los sesos, romperse la cabeza; *v.* saltar la tapa de los sesos; **— trust** [bréntrʌst] *s.* grupo de consejeros; **— washing** [brénwɔʃɪŋ] *s.* lavado cerebral.

**brake** [brek] *s.* freno; *Ven., Col.* retranca; *Méx., Ríopl., C.A., Carib.* garrote; **— lining** forro de freno; **— shoe** zapata de freno; **— drum** tambor de freno; **— fluid** flúido de freno; **to apply the -s** frenar; *v.* frenar, enfrenar; *Ven., Col.* retrancar; *Méx., Ríopl., C.A., Carib.* dar garrote.

**brakeman** [brékmən] *s.* guardafrenos, *Ven., Col.* retranquero, *Méx., Ríopl., C.A., Carib.* garrotero.

**bramble** [brǽmbl̩] *s.* zarza, breña.

**bran** [bræn] *s.* salvado.

**branch** [bræntʃ] *s.* rama (*de árbol*); ramo (*de la ciencia*); sucursal; bifurcación; sección; tributario (*de un río*); ramificación; **— railway** ramal; *v.* ramificarse; bifurcarse.

**brand** [brænd] *s.* (*make*) marca; marca de fábrica; hechura; (*cattle mark*) hierro; *Ríopl., Méx.* fierro (*de marcar*) estigma; **brand-new** nuevecito, flamante, acabado de hacer o comprar; *v.* marcar, herrar, marcar (*con hierro candente*); difamar; **to — as** motejar de.

**brandish** [brǽndɪʃ] *v.* blandir; *s.* floreo, molinete.

**brandy** [brǽndɪ] *s.* aguardiente; coñac.

**brash** [bræʃ] *adj.* insolente; impetuoso; temerario.

**brass** [bræs] *s.* latón, bronce; desfachatez, descaro; **-es** utensilios de latón. instrumentos músicos de metal; **— band** banda, murga.

**brassière** [brəzír] *s.* corpiño, sostén (*para ceñir los pechos*).

**brat** [bræt] *s.* mocoso.

**bravado** [brəvádo] *s.* bravata; jactancia.

**brave** [brev] *adj.* bravo, valiente, valeroso; *v.* arrostrar; desafiar, hacer frente a.

**bravery** [brévərɪ] *s.* valor, valentía.

**brawl** [brɔl] *v.* reyerta, pendencia, riña; alboroto; *v.* armar una pendencia, alborotar, reñir.

**bray** [bre] *s.* rebuzno; *v.* rebuznar.

**brazen** [brézn̩] *adj.* bronceado; de bronce; de latón; descarado, desvergonzado.

**brazier** [brezjər] *s.* brasero.

**breach** [britʃ] *s.* (*opening*) brecha, abertura; (*infraction*) infracción; rompimiento; **— of faith** abuso de confianza; **— of promise** violación de un compromiso; *v.* abrir brecha.

**bread** [bred] *s.* pan; **—box** caja para pan; *v. Méx., C.A.,* empanizar; *Ríopl., Ch.* empanar.

**breadth** [bredθ] *s.* anchura, ancho; extensión; amplitud.

**break** [brek] *s.* rompimiento; rotura; interrupción, pausa; bajón (*en la bolsa o mercado*); **to have a bad (good) —** tener mala (buena) suerte; **to make a bad —** cometer un disparate; *v.* romper(se), quebrantar(se), quebrar(se); amansar, domar; arruinar; **to —away** fugarse, escaparse; **to — into** forzar la entrada en, allanar (*una morada*); **to — loose** escaparse, desprenderse, soltarse; **to — out** estallar (*una guerra*); **to — out of prison** escaparse de la cárcel; **to — a promise** faltar a la palabra; **to — up** desmenuzar, despedazar; disolver; perturbar.

**breakable** [brékəbl̩] *adj.* quebradizo.

**breakdown** [brékdaʊn] *s.* parada imprevista; (*automobile*) avería, pane.

**breaker** [brékɚ] *s.* rompiente (*ola*); **law —** infractor.

**breakfast** [brékfəst] *s.* desayuno; **to eat —** tomar el desayuno; *v.* desayunarse.

**breakthrough** [brékθru] *s.* adelanto repentino; brecha.

**breakwater** [brékwɔtɚ] *s.* rompeolas, malecón.

**breast** [brest] *s.* pecho; seno; teta; pechuga (*de ave*); **to make a clean — of it** confesarlo todo.

**breath** [breθ] *s.* aliento; resuello; respiro; soplo, hálito; **in the same —** al mismo instante, con el mismo aliento; **out of —** sin aliento, jadeante; **under one's —** en voz baja, entre dientes.

**breathe** [brið] *v.* respirar; resollar; tomar aliento; exhalar; **to — into** infundir; **he -ed his last** exhaló el último suspiro; **he did not — a word** no dijo palabra.

**breathless** [bréθlɪs] *adj.* jadeante; sin aliento.

**breathtaking** [bréθtekɪŋ] *adj.* conmovedor; emocionante.

**bred** [bred] *pret.* & *p.p. de* **to breed.**

**breeches** [brítʃɪz] *s. pl.* bragas, calzones; **riding —** pantalones de montar.

**breed** [brid] *s.* casta, raza; relea, especie; *v.* criar; procrear, engendrar; educar; producirse; multiplicarse.

**breeder** [brídɚ] *s.* criador; animal de cría.

**breeding** [brídɪŋ] *s.* cría, crianza; educación, modales.

**breeze** [briz] *s.* brisa, vientecillo.

**breezy** [brízɪ] *adj.* airoso, ventilado; refrescado (*por la brisa*); animado, vivaz; **it is —** hace brisa.

**brethren** [bréðrɪn] *s. pl.* hermanos (*los fieles de una iglesia o los miembros de una sociedad*).

**brevity** [brévətɪ] *s.* brevedad.

**brew** [bru] *s.* cerveza; mezcla; *v.* fermentar, hacer (*licores*); preparar (*té*); fomentar, tramar; fabricar cerveza; amenazar (*una tormenta, calamidad* *etc.*).

**brewery** [brúəri] *s.* cervecería, fábrica de cerveza.

**briar, brier** [bráiɚ] *s.* zarza; rosal silvestre.

**bribe** [braib] *s.* soborno, cohecho; *v.* sobornar, cohechar.

**bribery** [bráibəri] *s.* soborno, cohecho.

**brick** [brik] *s.* ladrillo; ladrillos; *v.* enladrillar.

**brickbat** [bríkbæt] *s.* pedazo de ladrillo; insulto.

**bridal** [bráidl] *adj.* nupcial; de bodas; de novia; — **dress** vestido de novia.

**bride** [braid] *s.* novia, desposada.

**bridegroom** [bráidgrum] *s.* novio, desposado.

**bridesmaid** [bráidzmed] *s.* madrina de boda.

**bridge** [bridʒ] *a.* puente; caballete de la nariz; **draw** — puente levadizo; **suspension** — puente colgante; *v.* tender un puente; **to** — **a gap** llenar un vacío.

**bridle** [bráidl] *s.* brida, freno de caballo; freno, restricción; — **path** camino de herradura; *v.* embridar, enfrenar; reprimir, subyugar; erguirse, erguir la cabeza.

**brief** [brif] *adj.* breve, corto, conciso; *s.* sumario, resumen; informe, memorial; breve apostólico; **to hold a** — **for** abogar por; **-ly** *adv.* brevemente; en resumen, en breve.

**briefcase** [brífkes] *s.* portapapeles, cartera grande.

**briefing** [brifiŋ] *s.* reunión preparatoria.

**brigade** [brigéd] *s.* brigada.

**bright** [brait] *adj.* (*light*) brillante, claro, luciente; radiante; (*smart*) inteligente; (*cheerful*) alegre; listo, vivo; — **color** color subido.

**brighten** [bráitn] *v.* abrillantar, pulir, dar lustre; avivar(se); alegrar(se); animar(se); aclararse, despejarse (*el cielo*).

**brightness** [bráitnis] *s.* brillo, lustre; esplendor; claridad; viveza, agudeza, inteligencia.

**brilliance** [bríljəns] *s.* brillantez, brillo; lustre; resplandor.

**brilliant** [bríljənt] *adj.* brillante; resplandeciente; espléndido; talentoso; *s.* brillante; diamante.

**brim** [brim] *s.* borde, margen, orilla; ala (*de sombrero*); **to fill to the** — llenar o arrasar hasta el borde; **to be filled to the** — estar hasta los topes; estar de bote en bote; *v.* **to** — **over** rebosar.

**brine** [brain] *s.* salmuera.

**bring** [briŋ] *v.* traer; llevar; ocasionar, causar; **to** — **about** producir, efectuar, ocasionar; **to** — **down** bajar; **to** — **forth** dar a luz; producir; **to** — **to** resucitar; **to** — **up** criar, educar; **to** — **up a subject** traer a discusión un asunto.

**brink** [briŋk] *s.* borde, orilla, margen; **on the** — **of** al borde de.

**brisk** [brisk] *adj.* vivo, animado; fuerte;

rápido; **-ly** *adv.* aprisa; fuerte.

**bristle** [brisl] *s.* cerda; *v.* erizar(se); **to** — **with** estar erizado (*o* lleno) de.

**bristly** [brisli] *adj.* serdoso; erizado.

**British** [brítiʃ] *adj.* británico; **the** — los ingleses.

**brittle** [brítl] *adj.* quebradizo; frágil.

**broach** [brotʃ] *v.* traer a colación, comenzar a hablar de (*un asunto*).

**broad** [brɔd] *adj.* ancho; amplio, vasto, extenso; tolerante; — **hint** insinuación clara; **in** — **daylight** en pleno día; **broad-minded** tolerante; de amplias miras.

**broadcast** [brɔ́dkæst] *s.* radiodifusión, difusión, emisión; transmisión; *v.* difundir; radiodifundir, radiar, emitir.

**broadcloth** [brɔ́dklɔθ] *s.* paño fino de algodón o de lana.

**broadside** [brɔ́dsaid] *s.* (*guns*) andanada; (*announcement*) hoja suelta de propaganda.

**brocade** [brokéd] *s.* brocado.

**broil** [brɔil] *v.* asar(se).

**broke** [brok] *pret. de* **to break**; *adj.* quebrado, arruinado; pelado, sin dinero; **to go** — quebrar, arruinarse.

**broken** [brókən] *p.p. de* **to break** & *adj.* roto; rompido; quebrado; quebrantado; arruinado; abatido; — **English** inglés champurrado o champurreado; inglés mal pronunciado.

**broker** [brókɚ] *s.* corredor, agente; bolsista; **money** — cambista, corredor de cambio.

**bronchitis** [brɑnkáitis] *s.* bronquitis.

**bronco, broncho** [brɑ́ŋko] *s.* potro o caballo bronco, *Ríopl.* redomón; — **buster** domador.

**bronze** [brɑnz] *s.* bronce; color de bronce; *v.* broncear.

**brooch** [brutʃ] *s.* broche (*alfiler de pecho*).

**brood** [brud] *s.* pollada; nidada; cría; casta; *v.* empollar; **to** — **over** cavilar.

**brook** [bruk] *s.* arroyuelo, riachuelo, *C.A.*, *Col.*, *Ven.* quebrada; *Méx.*, *Ríopl.* arroyo, cañada; *v.* tolerar, aguantar.

**broom** [brum] *s.* escoba; retama (*arbusto*); **-stick** palo o mango de escoba.

**broth** [brɔθ] *s.* caldo.

**brother** [brʌ́ðɚ] *s.* hermano; cofrade.

**brotherhood** [brʌ́ðɚhud] *s.* hermandad; fraternidad; cofradía.

**brother-in-law** [brʌ́ðɚinlɔ] *s.* cuñado.

**brotherly** [brʌ́ðɚli] *adj.* fraternal.

**brought** [brɔt] *pret. & p.p. de* **to bring**.

**brow** [brau] *s.* ceja; frente.

**brown** [braun] *adj.* moreno; café; castaño; pardo oscuro; tostado; *v.* tostar(se).

**browse** [brauz] *v.* hojear; ramonear, pacer, pastar (*el ganado*).

**bruise** [bruz] *s.* magulladura, cardenal, contusión; *v.* magullar(se); estropear(se).

**brunet, brunette** [brunét] *adj.* moreno, trigueño.

**brunt** [brʌnt] *s.* fuerza (*de un golpe o ataque*); **the** — **of the battle** lo más

reñido del combate.
**brush** [brʌʃ] *s.* (*tooth, clothes*) cepillo;
(*paint, shaving*) brocha; (*artist's*)
pincel; (*vegetation*) matorral; (*contact*) roce; encuentro; *v.* cepillar, acepillar; rozar; **to — aside** desechar,
echar a un lado; **to — up** cepillarse;
repasar (*una materia, una técnica, etc.*).
**brushwood** [brʌʃwʊd] *s.* broza; maleza,
matorral, zarzal.
**brusque** [brʌsk] *adj.* brusco.
**brutal** [brútl̩] *adj.* brutal, bruto.
**brutality** [brutǽlətɪ] *s.* brutalidad.
**brute** [brut] *s.* bruto, bestia; *adj.* bruto,
brutal; bestial.
**bubble** [bʌbl̩] *s.* burbuja; borbollón;
ampolla; *v.* borbotar; hacer espuma;
bullir; **to — over with joy** rebosar
de gozo.
**bubble gum** [bʌbl̩ gʌm] *s.* chicle
hinchable; chicle de globo.
**buck** [bʌk] *s.* macho cabrío, cabrón;
gamo; macho (*del ciervo, antílope,
etc.*); corveta, respingo (*de un caballo*);
embestida; **— private** soldado raso;
**to pass the —** *Ríopl., Andes* pasar el
fardo; *v.* cabriolear, respingar; embestir; encabritarse; bregar con (*el
viento*); **to — up** cobrar ánimo; **the
horse -ed the rider** el caballo tiró
al jinete.
**bucket** [bʌ́kɪt] *s.* cubo, cubeta, balde.
**buckle** [bʌ́kl̩] *s.* hebilla; *v.* abrochar con
hebilla; doblarse; abollarse; **to —
down to** aplicarse con empeño a; **to
— with** luchar con.
**buckshot** [bʌ́kʃɑt] *s.* posta, perdigón.
**buckskin** [bʌ́kskɪn] *s.* badana; ante.
**buckwheat** [bʌ́khwit] *s.* trigo sarraceno.
**bud** [bʌd] *s.* botón, yema; capullo, pimpollo; retoño; *v.* echar botones o retoños; florecer.
**buddy** [bʌ́dɪ] *s.* camarada, compañero.
**budge** [bʌdʒ] *v.* mover(se), menear(se),
bullir.
**budget** [bʌ́dʒɪt] *s.* presupuesto.
**buff** [bʌf] *s.* piel de ante o búfalo; color
de ante; pulidor; **blindman's —**
juego de la gallina ciega; *v.* pulir,
pulimentar.
**buffalo** [bʌ́flo] *s.* búfalo.
**buffet** [bʌfé] *s.* aparador; repostería;
mostrador para refrescos; fonda de
estación.
**buffeting** [bʌ́fətɪŋ] *s.* golpeteo, bataneo.
**buffoon** [bʌfún] *s.* bufón; payaso.
**bug** [bʌg] *s.* insecto; bicho; microbio.
**buggy** [bʌ́gɪ] *s.* cochecillo.
**bugle** [bjúgl̩] *s.* clarín; corneta; trompeta.
**build** [bɪld] *s.* estructura; talle, forma,
hechura; *v.* edificar, construir; fabricar; **to — up one's health** reconstituir su salud.
**builder** [bɪ́ldɚ] *s.* constructor.
**building** [bɪ́ldɪŋ] *s.* edificio; construcción.
**build-up** [bɪ́ldʌp] *s.* refuerzo paulatino.
**built** [bɪlt] *pret. & p.p. de* **to build.**
**bulb** [bʌlb] *s.* bulbo (*de la cebolla y
otras plantas*); planta bulbosa; **elec-**

**tric light —** bombilla, bujía eléctrica,
ampolla, *Méx., C.A., Andes* foco;
*Ríopl.* bombita.
**bulge** [bʌldʒ] *s.* bulto; protuberancia;
panza; *v.* abultar; combarse.
**bulgy** [bʌ́ldʒɪ] *adj.* abultado.
**bulk** [bʌlk] *s.* bulto, volumen; masa; **the
— of the army** el grueso del ejército.
**bulky** [bʌ́lkɪ] *adj.* abultado, voluminoso,
grueso.
**bull** [bʊl] *s.* toro; alcista (*el que hace
subir los valores en la bolsa*); disparate,
error; **Papal —** bula; **—fight** corrida
de toros; **—fighter** torero; **bull's-eye**
centro del blanco; tiro perfecto.
**bulldog** [bʊ́ldɔg] *s.* perro dogo, perro de
presa.
**bulldozer** [bʊ́ldozɚ] *s.* topadora; buldózer.
**bullet** [bʊ́lɪt] *s.* bala.
**bulletin** [bʊ́lətn̩] *s.* boletín; **— board**
tablilla para fijar anuncios o avisos.
**bullfrog** [bʊ́lfrɑg] *s.* rana grande.
**bullion** [bʊ́ljən] *s.* oro (*o plata*) en
barras; metálico; lingotes de oro o
plata.
**bully** [bʊ́lɪ] *s.* pendenciero, valentón,
fanfarrón, matón; *adj.* excelente, magnífico; *v.* intimidar; echar bravatas.
**bulwark** [bʊ́lwɚk] *s.* baluarte; defensa.
**bum** [bʌm] *s.* holgazán, vagabundo;
gorrón; borracho; **to go on a —** irse
de juerga; *adj.* malo, mal hecho, de
ínfima calidad; inútil, inservible; **to
feel —** estar indispuesto; *v.* holgazanear; vivir de gorra.
**bumblebee** [bʌ́mbl̩bi] *s.* abejorro, abejón.
**bump** [bʌmp] *s.* (*blow*) tope, choque;
golpe; (*lump*) chichón; abolladura;
hinchazón; joroba, protuberancia;
*v.* topar, topetear; chocar; abollar;
**to — along** zarandearse, ir zarandeándose; **to — off** derribar; matar.
**bumper** [bʌ́mpɚ] *s.* parachoques, defensa; tope; *adj.* grande, excelente; **—
crop** cosecha abundante.
**bun** [bʌn] *s.* bollo (*de pan*).
**bunch** [bʌntʃ] *s.* manojo, puñado;
racimo (*de uvas, plátanos, etc.*); grupo;
**— of flowers** ramillete de flores; *v.*
juntar(se), agrupar(se).
**bundle** [bʌ́ndl̩] *s.* lío, bulto, fardo, hato;
haz; paquete; *v.* liar, atar; envolver;
**to — up** abrigarse, taparse bien.
**bungalow** [bʌ́ŋgəlo] *s.* casita de un
piso.
**bungle** [bʌ́ŋgl̩] *v.* chapucear; estropear; echar a perder.
**bunion** [bʌ́njən] *s.* juanete.
**bunk** [bʌŋk] *s.* litera, camilla (*fija en la
pared*); embuste, tontería, paparrucha,
papa.
**bunny** [bʌ́nɪ] *s.* conejito.
**buoy** [bɔɪ] *s.* boya; *v.* boyar, mantener a
flote; **to — up** sostener, apoyar.
**buoyant** [bɔ́ɪənt] *adj.* boyante, flotante;
vivaz, animado, alegre.
**burden** [bɝ́dn̩] *s.* carga, peso; cuidado;
gravamen; *v.* cargar; agobiar.
**burdensome** [bɝ́dn̩səm] *adj.* gravoso;

pesado.

**bureau** [bjúro] s. oficina; despacho; división, ramo; cómoda; **travel —** oficina de turismo; **weather —** oficina de meteorología, observatorio meteorológico.

**burglar** [bə́glə] s. ladrón (que se mete en casa ajena).

**burglary** [bə́glərɪ] s. robo.

**burial** [bérɪəl] s. entierro; **— place** cementerio.

**burlap** [bə́læp] s. arpillera, tela burda de cáñamo.

**burly** [bə́lɪ] adj. corpulento, voluminoso, grandote.

**burn** [bɜn] s. quemadura; v. quemar(se); incendiar; arder; abrasar(se).

**burner** [bə́nə] s. quemador; mechero; hornilla.

**burnish** [bə́nɪʃ] v. bruñir; pulir; s. bruñido, pulimento.

**burnt** [bə́nt] pret. & p.p. de **to burn.**

**burrow** [bə́o] s. madriguera, conejera; v. hacer madrigueras en; escarbar; socavar, minar; esconderse.

**burst** [bɜst] s. reventón, explosión; estallido; **— of laughter** carcajada; v. reventar(se); abrirse; estallar; **to — into** entrar de repente; **to — into tears** prorrumpir en lágrimas; **to — with laughter** estallar o reventar de risa; pret. & p.p. de **to burst.**

**bury** [bérɪ] v. enterrar; sepultar; **to be buried in thought** estar absorto, meditabundo o pensativo.

**bus** [bʌs] s. autobús, ómnibus, Méx. camión; C.A. camioneta; Ríopl. colectivo; Ch. micro; Carib. guagua.

**busboy** [bʌ́sbɔɪ] s. ayudante de camarero.

**bush** [buʃ] s. arbusto; mata; matorral, breñal; **rose —** rosal; **to beat around the —** andarse por las ramas.

**bushel** [búʃəl] s. fanega (medida de áridos).

**bushing** [búʃɪŋ] s. buje.

**bushy** [búʃɪ] adj. matoso, espeso; lleno de arbustos.

**busily** [bízɪlɪ] adv. diligentemente.

**business** [bíznɪs] s. negocio; ocupación; comercio; asunto; **— house** casa de comercio, establecimiento mercantil; **— transaction** negocio, transacción comercial; **to do — with** negociar con, comerciar con; **he has no — doing it** no tiene derecho a hacerlo; **not to be one's —** no concernirle a uno, no importarle a uno; **to make a — deal** hacer un trato.

**businesslike** [bíznɪslaɪk] adj. eficaz, eficiente, práctico; formal.

**businessman** [bíznɪsmæn] s. hombre de negocios, comerciante.

**bust** [bʌst] s. busto; pecho (de mujer); **to go out on a —** salir o ir de parranda; v. reventar; quebrar; domar (un potro).

**bustle** [bʌ́sl] s. bulla, bullicio, trajín, alboroto; polisón (para abultar las caderas); v. bullir(se); menearse; trajinar.

**busy** [bízɪ] adj. ocupado; activo; **—body** entremetido; **— street** calle de mucho tráfico; v. **to — oneself** ocuparse.

**but** [bʌt] conj., prep. & adv. pero, mas; sino; menos, excepto; sólo, no . . . más que; **— for you** a no ser por Vd.; **not only . . . — also** no sólo . . . sino (que) también; **I cannot help —** no puedo menos de; **she is — a child** no es más que una niña.

**butcher** [bútʃə] s. carnicero; **-'s shop** carnicería; v. matar (reses); hacer una matanza o carnicería; destrozar.

**butchery** [bútʃəɪ] s. carnicería, matanza.

**butler** [bʌ́tlə] s. despensero, mayordomo; **-'s pantry** despensa.

**butt** [bʌt] s. culata (de rifle); colilla (de cigarro); tope; topetazo; cabezada; **the — of ridicule** el blanco de las burlas; v. topetear, embestir; **to — in** entremeterse; **to — into a conversation** meter baza, Am. meter su cuchara.

**butter** [bʌ́tə] s. manteca, mantequilla; v. enmantecar, untar con manteca o mantequilla.

**buttercup** [bʌ́təkʌp] s. botón de oro (flor).

**butterfly** [bʌ́təflaɪ] s. mariposa.

**buttermilk** [bʌ́təmɪlk] s. suero de mantequilla.

**butterscotch** [bʌ́təskátʃ] s. confite o jarabe de azúcar y mantequilla.

**buttocks** [bʌ́təks] s. pl. nalgas, asentaderas.

**button** [bʌ́tn̩] s. botón; **— hook** abotonador; v. abotonar(se).

**buttonhole** [bʌ́tn̩hol] s. ojal; v. hacer ojales; **to — someone** detener, demorar a uno (charlando).

**buttress** [bʌ́trɪs] s. contrafuerte; refuerzo, sostén; v. sostener, reforzar, poner contrafuerte.

**buy** [baɪ] v. comprar; **to — off** sobornar; **to — up** acaparar.

**buyer** [báɪə] s. comprador.

**buzz** [bʌz] s. zumbido; murmullo; v. zumbar; murmurar; **to — the bell** tocar el timbre.

**buzzard** [bʌ́zəd] s. buitre, Am. aura, Méx., C.A. zopilote, Ríopl. carancho; Col. Andes gallinazo.

**by** [baɪ] prep. por; cerca de; al lado de; junto a; según; **— and —** luego, pronto; **— dint of** a fuerza de; **— far** con mucho; **— night** de noche; **— the way** de paso; a propósito; entre paréntesis; **— this time** ya; a la hora de ésta; **— two o'clock** para las dos; **— days gone —** días pasados.

**bygone** [báɪgɔn] adj. pasado; **let -s be -s** lo pasado pasado, lo pasado pisado.

**bylaw** [báɪlɔ] s. estatuto; reglamento.

**bypass** [báɪpæs] s. desviación.

**bypath** [báɪpæθ] s. atajo, vereda.

**by-product** [báɪprɑdəkt] s. producto secundario o accessorio.

**bystanders** [báɪstændəz] s. circunstantes, presentes; mirones.

## C

**cab** [kæb] *s.* coche de alquiler; taxímetro, taxi; casilla (*de una locomotora*); **— driver** cochero; chófer.

**cabbage** [kǽbɪdʒ] *s.* col, repollo, berza.

**cabin** [kǽbɪn] *s.* cabaña, choza, bohío, barraca; camarote (*de buque*); **airplane —** cabina de aeroplano.

**cabinet** [kǽbənɪt] *s,* gabinete; armario; escaparate, vitrina.

**cable** [kébl] *s.* cable, amarra; cablegrama; **— address** dirección cablegráfica; *v.* cablegrafiar.

**cablegram** [kébl̩græm] *s.* cablegrama.

**cabman** [kǽbmən] *s.* cochero; chófer.

**cackle** [kǽkl̩] *s.* cacareo; charla; risotada; *v.* cacarear; parlotear, charlar.

**cactus** [kǽktəs] (*pl.* **cacti** [kǽktaɪ]) *s.* cacto.

**cad** [kæd] *s.* canalla (*m.*); malcriado.

**cadence** [kédn̩s] *s.* cadencia.

**cadet** [kədét] *s.* cadete.

**cadmium** [kǽdmɪəm] *s.* cadmio.

**café** [kəfé] *s.* café, restaurante.

**cafeteria** [kæfətírɪə] *s.* restaurante (*en donde se sirve uno mismo*).

**caffein** [kǽfiɪn] *s.* cafeína.

**cage** [kedʒ] *s.* jaula; *v.* enjaular.

**cake** [kek] *s.* pastel; bizcocho; bollo; torta; *Ven., Col.* panqué; pastilla (*de jabón*); **— of ice** témpano de hielo; *v.* apelmazarse, formar masa compacta.

**calamity** [kəlǽmətɪ] *s.* calamidad.

**calcium** [kǽlsɪəm] *s.* calcio.

**calculate** [kǽlkjəlet] *v.* calcular; **to — on** contar con.

**calculation** [kælkjəléʃən] *s.* cálculo; cómputo, cuenta.

**calculus** [kǽlkjələs] *s.* cálculo.

**calendar** [kǽləndɚ] *s.* calendario, almanaque; **— year** año corriente.

**calf** [kæf] (*pl.* **calves** [kævz] ) *s.* ternero, ternera, becerro, becerra; pantorrilla (*de la pierna*); **—skin** piel de becerro o becerrillo.

**caliber** [kǽləbɚ] *s.* calibre.

**calico** [kǽləko] *s.* calicó (*tela de algodón*).

**call** [kɔl] *s.* (*summons*) llamada; llamamiento; (*visit*) visita; (*demand*) demanda, pedido; **within —** al alcance de la voz; *v.* llamar; gritar; hacer una visita; pasar (*lista*); **to — at a port** hacer escala en un puerto; **to — for** ir por; demandar, pedir; **to — on** visitar a; acudir a (*en busca de auxilio*); **to — to order a meeting** abrir la sesión; **to — together** convocar; **to — up on the phone** llamar por teléfono.

**caller** [kɔ́lɚ] *s.* visita, visitante; llamador (*el que llama*).

**callous** [kǽləs] *adj.* calloso; duro.

**callus** [kǽləs] *s.* callo.

**calm** [kɑm] *s.* calma; sosiego; *adj.* calmo, tranquilo, quieto, sosegado; *v.* calmar, tranquilizar, sosegar; **to — down** calmarse; **-ly** *adv.* tranquilamente, con calma.

**calmness** [kɑ́mnɪs] *s.* calma, sosiego,

tranquilidad.

**calorie** [kǽlərɪ] *s.* caloría.

**calumny** [kǽləmnɪ] *s.* calumnia.

**came** [kem] *pret. de* **to come.**

**camel** [kǽml̩] *s.* camello.

**cameo** [kǽmɪo] *s.* camafeo.

**camera** [kǽmərə] *s.* cámara fotográfica.

**camouflage** [kǽməflɑʒ] *s.* camuflaje; disfraz; *v.* encubrir, disfrazar.

**camp** [kæmp] *s.* campo, campamento; **— chair** silla de tijera; **political —** partido político; *v.* acampar.

**campaign** [kæmpén] *s.* campaña; *v.* hacer campaña; hacer propaganda.

**camphor** [kǽmfɚ] *s.* alcanfor.

**campus** [kǽmpəs] *s.* campo (*de una universidad*).

**can** [kæn] *s.* lata, bote, envase; **— opener** abrelatas; *v.* envasar, enlatar; *v. defect. y aux.* (*usado sólo en las formas* **can** *y* **could**) poder, saber.

**Canadian** [kənédɪən] *adj. & s.* canadiense.

**canal** [kənǽl] *s.* canal; **irrigation —** acequia.

**canary** [kənérɪ] *s.* canario.

**cancel** [kǽns̩l] *v.* cancelar; anular; revocar; techar.

**cancellation** [kæns̩léʃən] *s.* cancelación; anulación; revocación.

**cancer** [kǽnsɚ] *s.* cáncer.

**candid** [kǽndɪd] *adj.* cándido, franco, sincero.

**candidacy** [kǽndədəsɪ] *s.* candidatura.

**candidate** [kǽndədet] *s.* candidato; aspirante.

**candle** [kǽndl̩] *s.* candela, vela; bujía; cirio; **— power** potencia lumínica (*en bujías*).

**candlestick** [kǽndl̩stɪk] *s.* candelero; palmatoria.

**candor** [kǽndɚ] *s.* candor, sinceridad.

**candy** [kǽndɪ] *s.* dulce, confite, bombón; **— shop** confitería, dulcería; *v.* confitar, azucarar; almibarar, garapiñar; cristalizarse (*el almíbar*); **candied almonds** almendras garapiñadas.

**cane** [ken] *s.* caña; **— plantation** (*o* **—field**) cañaveral; *C.A.* cañal; **— chair** silla de bejuco; **sugar —** caña de azúcar; **walking —** bastón; **to beat with a —** bastonear, apalear.

**canine** [kénaɪn] *adj.* canino, perruno.

**canned** [kænd] *adj.* enlatado, envasado, conservado (*en lata o en vidrio*); **— goods** conservas alimenticias.

**cannery** [kǽnərɪ] *s.* fábrica de conservas alimenticias.

**cannibal** [kǽnəbl̩] *s.* caníbal.

**cannon** [kǽnən] *s.* cañón.

**cannonade** [kænənéd] *s.* cañoneo; *v.* cañonear.

**cannot** [kǽnat] = **can not** no puedo, no puede, no podemos, etc.

**canny** [kǽnɪ] *adj.* sagaz; astuto.

**canoe** [kənú] *s.* canoa, *Ríopl.* piragua, *Méx.* chalupa.

**canon** [kǽnən] *s.* canon; ley, regla; criterio, norma; canónigo.

**canopy** [kǽnəpɪ] s. dosel, pabellón; (*airplane*) capota, cúpula.

**cantaloupe** [kǽntʃop] s. melón.

**canteen** [kæntín] s. cantina; cantimplora.

**canton** [kǽntən] s. cantón, región, distrito.

**canvas** [kǽnvəs] s. lona; lienzo; toldo; cañamazo.

**canvass** [kǽnvəs] s. inspección; escrutinio; indagación, encuesta, pesquisa; solicitación (*de votos*); v. examinar, escudriñar; recorrer (*un distrito solicitando algo*); hacer una encuesta; solicitar votos o pedidos comerciales.

**canyon** [kǽnjən] s. cañón, garganta.

**cap** [kæp] s. (*head covering*) gorro, gorra, boina; (*bottle, wheel*) tapa, tapón; (*mountain*) cima, cumbre; **percussion —** cápsula fulminante; v. tapar, poner tapón a; **that -s the climax** eso es el colmo.

**capability** [kepəbílətɪ] s. capacidad, aptitud.

**capable** [képəbl] adj. capaz; hábil; competente.

**capacious** [kəpéʃəs] adj. capaz, amplio, espacioso.

**capacity** [kəpǽsətɪ] s. capacidad; cabida; habilidad; aptitud; **in the — of a teacher** en calidad de maestro.

**cape** [kep] s. capa; capote; cabo, promontorio.

**caper** [képɚ] s. cabriola; voltereta, brinco; **to cut -s** cabriolar, retozar, hacer travesuras; v. cabriolar, retozar, juguetear, brincar.

**capillary** [kǽpɪlɛrɪ] s. & adj. capilar.

**capital** [kǽpətl] s. capital (*f.*), ciudad principal; capital (*m.*), caudal; capitel (*de una columna*); letra mayúscula; **to make — of** sacar partido de, aprovecharse de; adj. capital; principal; excelente; **— punishment** pena capital, pena de muerte.

**capitalism** [kǽpətlɪzəm] s. capitalismo.

**capitalist** [kǽpətlɪst] s. capitalista; -ic adj. capitalista.

**capitalization** [kæpətləzéʃən] s. capitalización.

**capitalize** [kǽpətlaɪz] v. capitalizar; sacar provecho (de); escribir con mayúscula.

**capitol** [kǽpətl] s. capitolio.

**capitulate** [kəpítʃəlet] v. capitular.

**caprice** [kəprís] s. capricho.

**capricious** [kəpríʃəs] adj. caprichoso.

**capsize** [kæpsáɪz] v. zozobrar, volcar(se).

**capsule** [kǽpsl] s. cápsula.

**captain** [kǽptɪn] s. capitán; v. capitanear, mandar; servir de capitán.

**captivate** [kǽptəvet] v. cautivar.

**captive** [kǽptɪv] s. & adj. cautivo, prisionero.

**captivity** [kæptívətɪ] s. cautiverio, prisión.

**captor** [kǽptɚ] s. aprehensor o aprensor.

**capture** [kǽptʃɚ] s. captura; aprensión; presa; toma; v. capturar; prender; tomar (*una ciudad*).

**car** [kɑr] s. coche, automóvil, auto, *Am.* carro; vagón (*de ferrocarril*); camarín (*de ascensor*), ascensor, *Am.* elevador; **dining —** coche comedor; **freight —** furgón, vagón de carga.

**caramel** [kǽrəml] s. caramelo.

**carat** [kǽrət] s. quilate.

**caravan** [kǽrəvæn] s. caravana.

**carbolic** [kɑrbálɪk] adj. carbólico.

**carbon** [kárbən] s. carbono; **— copy** copia en papel carbón; **— paper** papel carbón; **— monoxide** monóxido de carbón; **— dioxide** dióxido de carbono.

**carburetor** [kárbəretɚ] s. carburador.

**carcass** [kárkəs] s. esqueleto; cuerpo descarnado, despojo; res (*muerta*); casco (*de un buque*).

**card** [kɑrd] s. (*missive*) tarjeta; (*playing*) naipe, carta; carda (*para cardar lana*); **— index** índice de fichas; fichero; **—sharp** fullero; **file —** ficha, papeleta; **post—** tarjeta postal; **pack of -s** baraja, naipes; **to play -s** jugar a la baraja, jugar a los naipes; v. cardar (*lana*).

**cardboard** [kárdbord] s. cartón; **fine — cartulina.**

**cardiac** [kárdıæk] adj. cardiaco, cardíaco.

**cardinal** [kárdnəl] adj. cardinal; principal, fundamental; rojo, bermellón; **— number** número cardinal; s. cardenal (*dignatario eclesiástico*); **— bird** cardenal.

**care** [kɛr] s. (*worry*) cuidado; aflección; ansiedad; (*caution*) cuidado, cautela, esmero; (*responsibility*) cargo, custodia; **to take — of** cuidar de; v. tener interés (por); **to — about** tener interés en (o por); preocuparse de; importarle a uno; **to — for** cuidar de; estimar, tenerle cariño a; gustarle a uno; simpatizarle a uno (*una persona*); **to — to** querer, desear, tener ganas de; **what does he — ?** ¿a él qué le importa?

**career** [kərír] s. carrera, profesión.

**carefree** [kérfri] adj. libre de cuidado, sin cuidados, despreocupado.

**careful** [kérfəl] adj. cuidadoso; esmerado; cauteloso; **to be —** tener cuidado; **-ly** adv. cuidadosamente, con cuidado; con esmero.

**carefulness** [kérfəlnɪs] s. cuidado; esmero; cautela.

**careless** [kérlɪs] adj. descuidado; negligente; indiferente; **-ly** adv. sin cuidado; sin esmero; descuidadamente.

**carelessness** [kérlɪsnɪs] s. descuido; falta de esmero; desaliño; negligencia.

**caress** [kərés] s. caricia; v. acariciar.

**caretaker** [kértekɚ] s. cuidador, guardián, vigilante, celador.

**carfare** [kárfɛr] s. pasaje de tranvía.

**cargo** [kárgo] s. carga, cargamento; flete.

**caricature** [kǽrɪkətʃɚ] s. caricatura; v. caricaturar o caricaturizar.

**carload** [kárlod] s. furgonada, vagonada, carga de un furgón o vagón.

**CA**

**carnal** [kárnl] *adj.* carnal.

**carnation** [karnéʃən] *s.* clavel; color encarnado o rosado.

**carnival** [kárnəvl] *s.* carnaval; fiesta, holgorio; feria, verbena.

**carnivorous** [karnívərəs] *adj.* carnívoro, carnicero.

**carol** [kǽrəl] *s.* villancico; **Christmas** — villancico de Navidad; *v.* cantar villancicos; celebrar con villancicos.

**carom** [kǽrəm] *s.* carambola; rebote.

**carouse** [kəráuz] *v.* andar de parranda, *Ríopl., Ch.* andar de farra; embriagarse.

**carpenter** [kárpəntɚ] *s.* carpintero.

**carpentry** [kárpəntrɪ] *s.* carpintería.

**carpet** [kárpɪt] *s.* alfombra; **small** — tapete.

**carriage** [kǽrɪdʒ] *s.* carruaje, coche; acarreo, transporte; porte; — **paid** porte pagado; **good** — buen porte, garbo, manera airosa.

**carrier** [kǽrɪɚ] *s.* portador; mensajero; carretero, trajinante; transportador; *Am.* cargador; **airplane** — portaaviones; **disease** — transmisor de gérmenes contagiosos; **mail** — cartero.

**carrot** [kǽrət] *s.* zanahoria.

**carry** [kǽrɪ] *v.* llevar; acarrear, transportar; *Am.* cargar; sostener (*una carga*); traer consigo; ganar, lograr (*una elección, un premio, etc.*); **to** — **away** llevarse; cargar con; entusiasmar, encantar; **to** — **on** continuar; no parar; **to** — **oneself well** andar derecho, airoso, garboso; **to** — **out** llevar a cabo, realizar; sacar.

**cart** [kart] *s.* carro, carreta, vagoncillo; *v.* acarrear.

**cartage** [kártɪdʒ] *s.* carretaje, acarreo.

**carter** [kártɚ] *s.* carretero; acarreador.

**carton** [kártn̩] *s.* caja de cartón.

**cartoon** [kartún] *s.* caricatura.

**cartoonist** [kartúnɪst] *s.* caricaturista.

**cartridge** [kártrɪdʒ] *s.* cartucho; — **belt** cartuchera, canana; — **box** cartuchera; — **shell** cápsula.

**carve** [karv] *v.* tallar; labrar; cincelar; esculpir; trinchar, tajar (*carne*).

**carver** [kárvɚ] *s.* trinchador; trinchante (*cuchillo*); entallador, escultor.

**carving** [kárvɪŋ] *s.* talla, obra de escultura, entalladura; — **knife** trinchante.

**cascade** [kæskéd] *s.* cascada, salto de agua.

**case** [kes] *s.* (*instance*) caso; (*box*) caja; (*pillow*) funda, cubierta; (*scabbard*) vaina; **window** — marco de ventana; **in** — **that** caso que, en caso de que, dado que; **in any** — en todo caso; **just in** — por si acaso; — **work** trabajo con casos.

**casement** [késmənt] *s.* puerta ventana.

**cash** [kæʃ] *s.* dinero contante; — **box** cofre; — **payment** pago al contado; — **on delivery** (**c.o.d.**) contra reembolso, cóbrese al entregar; — **register** caja registradora (*de dinero*); **to pay** — pagar al contado; *v.* cambiar, cobrar (*un cheque*).

**cashew** [kǽʃju] *s.* anacardo.

**cashier** [kæʃír] *s.* cajero.

**cask** [kæsk] *s.* tonel, barril, cuba.

**casket** [kǽskɪt] *s.* ataúd; **jewel** — joyero, cofrecillo.

**casserole** [kǽsərol] *s.* cacerola.

**cassock** [kǽsək] *s.* sotana.

**cast** [kæst] *s.* tirada (*al pescar*); molde; matiz; apariencia; defecto (*del ojo*); reparto (*de papeles dramáticos*); actores; — **iron** hierro fundido o colado; *v.* echar; tirar; arrojar; lanzar; moldear; repartir (*papeles dramáticos*); escoger (*para un papel dramático*); **to** — **a ballot** votar; **to** — **a statue in bronze** vaciar una estatua en bronce; **to** — **about** buscar; hacer planes; **to** — **aside** desechar; **to** — **lots** echar suertes; **to be** — **down** estar abatido; *pret. & p.p. de* **to cast**.

**castanets** [kǽstənɛts] *s. pl.* castañuelas.

**caste** [kæst] *s.* casta; **to lose** — perder el prestigio social.

**Castilian** [kæstíljən] *s. & adj.* castellano.

**castle** [kǽsl̩] *s.* castillo; alcázar; fortaleza; torre, roque (*en ajedrez*).

**castor oil** [kǽstɚ ɔɪl] *s.* aceite de ricino.

**castrate** [kǽstret] *v.* capar, castrar.

**casual** [kǽʒuəl] *adj.* casual; accidental.

**casualty** [kǽʒuəltɪ] *s.* baja o pérdida (*en el ejército*); accidente.

**cat** [kæt] *s.* gato; gata.

**catalogue** [kǽtlɔg] *s.* catálogo; *v.* catalogar.

**cataract** [kǽtərækt] *s.* catarata.

**catarrh** [kətár] *s.* catarro.

**catastrophe** [kətǽstrəfɪ] *s.* catástrofe.

**catch** [kætʃ] *s.* presa; botín; pesca; pestillo (*de la puerta*); trampa; cogida (*de la pelota*); — **phrase** frase llamativa; — **question** pregunta tramposa; **he is a good** — es un buen partido; **to play** — jugar a la pelota; *v.* coger; prender; asir; alcanzar; enganchar; comprender; ser contagioso, pegarse; **to** — **a glimpse of** vislumbrar; **to** — **cold** coger un resfriado, resfriarse; **to** — **on** comprender, caer en la cuenta; **to** — **one's eye** llamarle a uno la atención; **to** — **sight of** avistar; **to** — **unaware** sorprender, coger desprevenido; **to** — **up with** alcanzar a, emparejarse con.

**catcher** [kǽtʃɚ] *s.* cogedor, agarrador; parador, cácher o receptor (*en beisbol*).

**catching** [kǽtʃɪŋ] *adj.* pegajoso, contagioso; atractivo.

**catechism** [kǽtəkɪzəm] *s.* catecismo.

**category** [kǽtəgorɪ] *s.* categoría.

**cater** [kétɚ] *v.* surtir, abastecer, proveer los alimentos (*para banquetes, fiestas, etc.*) **to** — **to** proveer a las necesidades o al gusto de; **to** — **to the taste of** halagar el gusto de.

**caterpillar** [kǽtəpɪlɚ] *s.* oruga; — **tractor** tractor.

**cathedral** [kəθídrəl] *s.* catedral.

**cathode** [kǽθod] *s.* cátodo; — **rays** rayos catódicos.

**Catholic** [kǽθəlɪk] *s. & adj.* católico.

**Catholicism** [kəθáləsɪzəm] *s.* catolicismo.

**catsup** [kǽtsəp] *s.* salsa de tomate.

**cattle** [kǽtl] *s.* ganado, ganado vacuno; **— raiser** ganadero, *Ríopl.* estanciero; **— raising** ganadería; **— ranch** hacienda de ganado, *Méx., C.A.* rancho, *Ríopl.* estancia; *Ven., Col.* hato.

**caught** [kɔt] *pret. & p.p. de* **to catch**.

**cauliflower** [kɔ́ləflauɚ] *s.* coliflor.

**cause** [kɔz] *s.* causa; *v.* causar; originar; **to — to** hacer; inducir a.

**caution** [kɔ́ʃən] *s.* precaución, cautela; aviso, advertencia; **—!** ¡cuidado! ¡atención!; *v.* prevenir, avisar, advertir.

**cautious** [kɔ́ʃəs] *adj.* cauto; cauteloso, cuidadoso; precavido.

**cavalier** [kævəlír] *s.* caballero; galán; *adj.* orgulloso, altivo, desdeñoso.

**cavalry** [kǽvlrɪ] *s.* caballería.

**cave** [kev] *s.* cueva; caverna; *v.* **to — in** hundirse; desplomarse.

**cavern** [kǽvən] *s.* caverna.

**cavity** [kǽvətɪ] *s.* cavidad, hueco; (*tooth*) carie.

**caw** [kɔ] *s.* graznido; *v.* graznar.

**cease** [sis] *v.* cesar; parar, desistir; dejar de.

**ceaseless** [síslɪs] *adj.* incesante.

**cedar** [sídɚ] *s.* cedro.

**cede** [sid] *v.* ceder.

**ceiling** [sílɪŋ] *s.* techo (*interior*); cielo máximo (*en aviación*); altura máxima (*en aviación*); **— price** precio máximo.

**celebrate** [séləbret] *v.* celebrar.

**celebrated** [séləbretɪd] *adj.* célebre, renombrado.

**celebration** [sɛləbréʃən] *s.* celebración; fiesta.

**celebrity** [səlébrətɪ] *s.* celebridad; renombre.

**celery** [sélərɪ] *s.* apio.

**celestial** [səléstʃəl] *adj.* celestial, celeste.

**cell** [sɛl] *s.* celda; célula; pila eléctrica.

**cellar** [sélɚ] *s.* bodega, sótano.

**celluloid** [séljəlɔɪd] *s.* celuloide.

**cement** [səmént] *s.* cemento; **reinforced —** cemento armado; *v.* unir, cementar, pegar con cemento; cubrir con cemento.

**cemetery** [sémətɛrɪ] *s.* cementerio.

**censor** [sénsɚ] *s.* censor; censurador, crítico; *v.* censurar (*cartas, periódicos, etc.*).

**censorship** [sénsɚʃɪp] *s.* censura.

**censure** [sénʃɚ] *s.* censura, crítica; reprobación; *v.* censurar, criticar, reprobar.

**census** [sénsəs] *s.* censo.

**cent** [sɛnt] *s.* centavo (*de peso o dólar*); **per —** por ciento.

**centennial** [sɛnténɪəl] *adj. & s.* centenario.

**center** [séntɚ] *s.* centro; *v.* centrar; colocar en el centro; concentrar(se).

**centigrade** [séntəgred] *adj.* centígrado.

**centipede** [séntəpid] *s.* ciempiés, cientopiés.

**central** [séntrəl] *adj.* central; céntrico; *s.* (la) central de teléfonos.

**centralize** [séntrəlaɪz] *v.* centralizar.

**centrifugal** [sɛntrífjʊgl] *adj.* centrífugo.

**centripetal** [sɛntrípətl] *adj.* centrípeto.

**century** [séntʃərɪ] *s.* siglo.

**ceramic** [sərémɪk] *adj.* cerámico; **ceramics** *s.* cerámica.

**cereal** [sírɪəl] *adj.* cereal; *s.* cereal; grano.

**ceremonial** [sɛrəmónɪəl] *adj.* ceremonial; *s.* ceremonial; rito.

**ceremonious** [sɛrəmónɪəs] *adj.* ceremonioso.

**ceremony** [sérəmonɪ] *s.* ceremonia; ceremonial.

**certain** [sɝtn̩] *adj.* cierto, seguro; **-ly** *adv.* ciertamente; por cierto; de cierto; seguramente; de seguro.

**certainty** [sɝtn̩tɪ] *s.* certeza; certidumbre; seguridad.

**certificate** [sɚtífəkɪt] *s.* certificado; documento; testimonio; **— of stock** bono, obligación; **birth —** partida de nacimiento; **death —** partida (*o* certificado) de defunción.

**certification** [sɚtɪfɪkéʃən] *s.* certificación.

**certify** [sɝtəfaɪ] *v.* certificar; dar fe, atestiguar.

**cessation** [sɛséʃən] *s.* suspensión, paro.

**cesspool** [séspul] *s.* cloaca, rezumadero.

**chafe** [tʃef] *s.* rozadura; irritación, molestia; *v.* rozar(se); frotar; irritar(se).

**chaff** [tʃæf] *s.* hollejo, cáscara; *v.* embromar, bromear.

**chagrin** [ʃəgrín] *s.* mortificación, desazón, pesar; **-ed** *p.p.* mortificado, afligido.

**chain** [tʃen] *s.* cadena; **— of mountains** cordillera; **— store** tienda sucursal (*una entre muchas de una misma empresa*); **— reaction** reacción en cadena; reacción eslabonada; *v.* encadenar.

**chair** [tʃɛr] *s.* silla; cátedra; presidencia; **arm —** sillón (de brazos); **easy —** butaca, poltrona; **folding —** silla de tijera; **rocking —** mecedora.

**chairman** [tʃérmən] *s.* presidente (*de una junta*).

**chairmanship** [tʃérmənʃɪp] *s.* presidencia (*de una junta*).

**chalice** [tʃǽlɪs] *s.* cáliz (*vaso sagrado*).

**chalk** [tʃɔk] *s.* tiza, yeso; greda; *v.* enyesar; marcar con tiza o yeso; **to — down** apuntar con tiza o yeso (*en el pizarrón*); **to — out** bosquejar, esbozar con tiza.

**chalky** [tʃɔ́kɪ] *adj.* yesoso; blanco.

**challenge** [tʃǽlɪndʒ] *s.* desafío; reto; demanda; *v.* desafiar, retar; disputar; poner a prueba; dar el quienvive.

**chamber** [tʃémbɚ] *s.* cámara; aposento; **— of commerce** cámara de comercio.

**chambermaid** [tʃémbɚmed] *s.* camarera, sirvienta.

**chamois** [ʃǽmɪ] *s.* gamuza.

**champion** [tʃǽmpɪən] *s.* campeón; defensor; *v.* defender.

**championship** [tʃǽmpɪənʃɪp] *s.* campeonato.

**chance** [tʃæns] *s.* (*opportunity*) oportunidad, ocasión; (*possibility*) posibilidad, probabilidad; (*fortune*) suerte, fortuna; casualidad, azar; (*risk*) riesgo; billete de rifa o lotería; **by** — por casualidad; **game of** — juego de azar; **to run a** — correr riesgo; *adj.* casual, accidental; *v.* arriesgar; **to** — **to** acertar a, hacer (*algo*) por casualidad.

**chancellor** [tʃǽnsələ] *s.* canciller; primer ministro; magistrado; rector de universidad.

**chandelier** [ʃændlír] *s.* araña de luces, *Am.* candil.

**change** [tʃendʒ] *s.* (*money*) cambio; vuelta, *Am.* vuelto; suelto; *Méx.* feria; (*fresh clothes*) muda de ropa; (*switch*) mudanza; **the** — **of life** la menopausia; *v.* cambiar; mudar; alterar; **to** — **clothes** mudar de ropa; **to** — **trains** transbordar(se), cambiar de tren.

**changeable** [tʃéndʒəbl] *adj.* mudable, variable; inconstante; — **silk** seda tornasolada.

**channel** [tʃǽnl] *s.* canal; cauce.

**chant** [tʃænt] *s.* canto llano o gregoriano; sonsonete; *v.* cantar (*psalmos, himnos, etc.*).

**chaos** [kéɑs] *s.* caos; desorden.

**chaotic** [keátɪk] *adj.* caótico.

**chap** [tʃæp] *s.* grieta, raja, rajadura (*en la piel*); chico; **what a fine** — **he is!** ¡qué buen tipo (*o sujeto*) es!; *v.* agrietarse, rajarse (*la piel*).

**chapel** [tʃǽpl] *s.* capilla.

**chaperon(e)** [ʃǽpəron] *s.* acompañante, persona de respeto; **to go along as a** — *Am.* ir de moscón; *v.* acompañar, servir de acompañante.

**chaplain** [tʃǽplɪn] *s.* capellán; **army** — capellán castrense.

**chapter** [tʃǽptə] *s.* capítulo; cabildo (*de una catedral*).

**char** [tʃɑr] *v.* requemar, carbonizar.

**character** [kǽrɪktə] *s.* carácter; personaje.

**characteristic** [kærɪktərístɪk] *adj.* característico; típico; *s.* característica, rasgo característico; distintivo; peculiaridad.

**characterize** [kǽrɪktəraɪz] *v.* caracterizar.

**charcoal** [tʃárkol] *s.* carbón; carboncillo (*para dibujar*); — **drawing** dibujo al carbón.

**charge** [tʃɑrdʒ] *s.* (*custody*) cargo; custodia; cuidado; (*order*) mandato, encargo; (*accusation*) cargo, acusación; (*load*) carga; peso; (*cost*) precio, coste; (*attack*) embestida, asalto, ataque; — **account** cuenta abierta; — **prepaid** porte pagado; **under my** — a mi cargo; **to be in** — **of** estar encargado de; *v.* cargar; cargar en cuenta; cobrar (*precio*); mandar; exhortar; atacar, embestir, asaltar; **to** — **with murder** acusar de homicidio.

**charger** [tʃárdʒə] *s.* cargador (*de batería*); caballo de guerra, corcel.

**chariot** [tʃǽrɪət] *s.* carroza; carruaje.

**charitable** [tʃǽrətəbl] *adj.* caritativo.

**charity** [tʃǽrətɪ] *s.* caridad; limosna; beneficencia.

**charlatan** [ʃárlətn̩] *s.* charlatán; farsante.

**charm** [tʃɑrm] *s.* encanto; atractivo; hechizo; talismán; **watch** — dije; *v.* encantar; cautivar; hechizar.

**charming** [tʃármɪŋ] *adj.* encantador, atractivo.

**chart** [tʃɑrt] *s.* carta (*hidrográfica o de navegar*); mapa; gráfica, representación gráfica; *v.* cartografiar, delinear mapas o cartas; **to** — **a course** trazar o planear una ruta o derrotero.

**charter** [tʃártə] *s.* carta constitucional, constitución, código; título; carta de privilegio; — **member** socio fundador; *v.* fletar (*un barco*); alquilar (*un ómnibus*).

**chase** [tʃes] *s.* caza; persecución; *v.* cazar; perseguir; **to** — **away** ahuyentar.

**chasm** [kǽzəm] *s.* abismo; vacío.

**chaste** [tʃest] *adj.* casto; honesto; puro.

**chastise** [tʃæstáɪz] *v.* castigar.

**chastisement** [tʃæstáɪzmənt] *s.* castigo, escarmiento.

**chastity** [tʃǽstətɪ] *s.* castidad; honestidad; pureza.

**chat** [tʃæt] *s.* charla, plática; *v.* charlar, platicar.

**chattels** [tʃǽtl̩z] *s. pl.* enseres, bienes muebles.

**chatter** [tʃǽtə] *s.* charla, parloteo; castañeteo (*de los dientes*); chirrido (*de aves*); *v.* charlar, parlotear, cotorrear; castañetear (*los dientes*).

**chauffeur** [ʃófə] *s.* chófer, cochero de automóvil.

**cheap** [tʃip] *adj.* barato; cursi, de mal gusto; **to feel** — sentir vergüenza; **-ly** *adv.* barato, a poco precio.

**cheapen** [tʃípən] *v.* abaratar.

**cheapness** [tʃípnɪs] *s.* baratura; cursilería.

**cheat** [tʃit] *s.* fraude, engaño; trampa; trampista, tramposo; estafador; embaucador; *v.* engañar; trampear; embaucar; estafar.

**check** [tʃɛk] *s.* cheque (*de banco*); talón, marbete, contraseña (*de equipajes, etc.*); marca, señal; cuenta (*de restaurante*); restricción, represión; cuadro (*de un tejido o tela*); comprobación; jaque (*en ajedrez*); — **room** vestuario; — **point** punto de inspección; depósito de equipajes, *C.A.*, *Ven.* consigna; *v.* refrenar, reprimir, restringir; facturar, depositar (*equipajes*); inspeccionar; confrontar, comprobar; marcar (*con una señal*); dar jaque (*en ajedrez*); **to** — **out of a hotel** desocupar el cuarto o alojamiento de un hotel.

**checkbook** [tʃékbʊk] *s.* libreta de cheques; libro talonario.

**checker** [tʃékə] *s.* cuadro; casilla (*de un*

**CH**

*tablero de ajedrez, etc.*); pieza (*del juego de damas*); comprobador; inspector; **-s** juego de damas; **—board** tablero; *v.* cuadricular, marcar con cuadritos; **-ed career** vida azarosa, vida llena de variedad; **-ed cloth** paño o tela a cuadros.

**cheek** [tʃik] *s.* mejilla, carrillo; cachete; descaro, desfachatez; **fat —** mejilla gorda, moflete; **— bone** pómulo.

**cheer** [tʃir] *s.* alegría; buen ánimo, jovialidad; consuelo; **-s** aplausos, vivas; *v.* alegrar, alentar, animar; aplaudir, vitorear; **to — up** alentar, dar ánimo; cobrar ánimo, animarse.

**cheerful** [tʃírfəl] *adj.* animado, alegre, jovial; **-ly** *adv.* alegremente, con alegría, con júbilo; de buena gana, de buen grado.

**cheerfulness** [tʃírfəlnɪs] *s.* jovialidad, alegría; buen humor.

**cheerily** [tʃírəlɪ] = **cheerfully.**

**cheerless** [tʃírlɪs] *adj.* abatido, desalentado, desanimado; triste, sombrío.

**cheery** [tʃírɪ] = **cheerful.**

**cheese** [tʃiz] *s.* queso; **cottage —** requesón.

**chemical** [kémɪkl̩] *adj.* químico; *s.* producto químico.

**chemist** [kémɪst] *s.* químico.

**chemistry** [kémɪstrɪ] *s.* química.

**cherish** [tʃérɪʃ] *v.* acariciar, abrigar (*una esperanza, un ideal, etc.*); apreciar.

**cherry** [tʃérɪ] *s.* cereza; **— tree** cerezo.

**chess** [tʃɛs] *s.* ajedrez; **—board** tablero de ajedrez.

**chest** [tʃɛst] *s.* cofre, arca; caja; pecho; **— of drawers** cómoda.

**chestnut** [tʃésnət] *s.* castaña; **— tree** castaño; *adj.* castaño; **— horse** caballo zaino.

**chew** [tʃu] *s.* mascada, mordisco, bocado; *v.* mascar, masticar.

**chewing gum** [tʃúɪŋ gʌm] *s.* goma de mascar; *Am.* chicle.

**chick** [tʃɪk] *s.* polluelo, pollito; pajarito; **chick-pea** garbanzo.

**chicken** [tʃíkɪn] *s.* pollo; polluelo; **— pox** viruelas locas; **chicken-hearted** cobarde, gallina.

**chicory** [tʃíkərɪ] *s.* achicoria.

**chide** [tʃaɪd] *v.* regañar, reprender, reprobar.

**chief** [tʃif] *s.* jefe, caudillo; cacique (*de una tribu*); **commander in —** comandante en jefe; *adj.* principal; **— clerk** oficial mayor; **— justice** presidente de la corte suprema; **-ly** *adv.* principalmente, mayormente; sobre todo.

**chiffon** [ʃifán] *s.* gasa.

**chilblain** [tʃílblen] *s.* sabañón.

**child** [tʃaɪld] *s.* niño, niña; hijo, hija; **-'s play** cosa de niños; **to be with —** estar encinta.

**childbirth** [tʃáɪldbɜθ] *s.* parto, alumbramiento.

**childhood** [tʃáɪldhud] *s.* niñez, infancia.

**childish** [tʃáɪldɪʃ] *adj.* pueril; infantil; **— action** niñería, niñada.

**childless** [tʃáɪldlɪs] *adj.* sin hijos.

**childlike** [tʃáɪldlaɪk] *adj.* como niño, aniñado, pueril.

**children** [tʃíldrən] *pl. de* **child.**

**Chilean** [tʃílɪən] *adj. & s.* chileno.

**chili** [tʃílɪ] *s.* *Méx., C.A.* chile, *Carib., S.A.* ají.

**chill** [tʃɪl] *s.* frío, resfrío; enfriamiento; escalofrío; calofrío; **-s and fever** escalofríos; *adj.* frío; *v.* resfriar(se); enfriar(se); **to become -ed** resfriarse, escalofriarse.

**chilly** [tʃílɪ] *adj.* frío; friolento.

**chime** [tʃaɪm] *s.* repique, campaneo; **-s** órgano de campanas, juego de campanas; *v.* repicar, campanear; tocar, sonar, tañer (*las campanas*); **to — with** estar en armonía con.

**chimney** [tʃímnɪ] *s.* chimenea; **lamp —** tubo de lámpara, *Am.* bombilla.

**chin** [tʃɪn] *s.* barba.

**china** [tʃáɪnə] *s.* loza de china, porcelana, loza fina; vajilla de porcelana; **— closet** chinero.

**chinaware** [tʃáɪnəwɛr] = **china.**

**Chinese** [tʃaɪníz] *adj.* chino; *s.* chino; idioma chino.

**chink** [tʃɪŋk] *s.* grieta, hendidura.

**chip** [tʃɪp] *s.* astilla, brizna; fragmento; desconchadura; desportilladura; ficha (*de pócar*); *v.* astillar; desconchar(se); descascarar(se); desportillar(se); picar, tajar (*con cincel o hacha*); **to — in** contribuir con su cuota.

**chipmunk** [tʃípmʌŋk] *s.* especie de ardilla.

**chirp** [tʃɜp] *s.* chirrido; pío; gorjeo; *v.* chirriar; piar; pipiar; gorjear.

**chisel** [tʃízl̩] *s.* cincel; *v.* cincelar; sisar, estafar.

**chivalrous** [ʃívlrəs] *adj.* caballeresco, caballeroso, galante, cortés.

**chivalry** [ʃívlrɪ] *s.* caballería; caballerosidad.

**chlorine** [klórin] *s.* cloro.

**chloroform** [klórəfɔrm] *s.* cloroformo.

**chocolate** [tʃóklɪt] *s.* chocolate; **— pot** chocolatera.

**choice** [tʃɔɪs] *s.* selección; preferencia; escogimiento; cosa elegida; favorito, preferido; alternativa; **to have no other —** no tener otra alternativa; *adj.* selecto; bien escogido; excelente.

**choir** [kwaɪr] *s.* coro.

**choke** [tʃok] *s.* sofoco, ahogo, tos ahogada; estrangulación; estrangulador, obturador (*de automóvil*); *v.* sofocar(se), ahogar(se); estrangular(se); obstruir, tapar; regularizar (*el motor*).

**cholera** [kálərə] *s.* cólera (*m.*).

**cholesterol** [kəléstəol] *s.* colesterol.

**choose** [tʃuz] *v.* escoger; elegir, seleccionar; **to — to** optar por; preferir; **I do not — to do it** no se me antoja (*o no es mi gusto*) hacerlo.

**chop** [tʃap] *s.* chuleta, costilla, tajada (*de carne*); **-s** quijadas (*usualmente de animal*); *v.* tajar, cortar; picar, desmenuzar (*carne*).

**choppy** [tʃápɪ] *adj.* picado, agitado.

**choral** [kórəl] *adj.* coral.

**chord** [kɔrd] *s.* cuerda; acorde.

**chore** [tʃor] *s.* tarea; quehacer.

**choreography** [korɪágrəfɪ] *s.* coreografía.

**chorus** [kórəs] *s.* coro; *v.* cantar o hablar en coro; contestar a una voz.

**chose** [tʃoz] *pret. de* **to choose.**

**chosen** [tʃózn̩] *p.p. de* **to choose.**

**christen** [krísn̩] *v.* bautizar.

**christening** [krísnɪŋ] *s.* bautizo, bautismo.

**Christian** [krístʃən] *s. & adj.* cristiano; **— name** nombre de pila o bautismo.

**Christianity** [krɪstʃɪǽnətɪ] *s.* cristiandad, cristianismo.

**Christmas** [krísməs] *s.* Navidad, Pascua de Navidad; **— Eve** Nochebuena; **— gift** regalo de Navidad; aguinaldo; **Merry —!** ¡Felices Navidades! ¡Felices Pascuas!

**chrome** [krom] *s.* cromo; *adj.* cromado.

**chromium** [krómɪəm] *s.* cromo.

**chromosome** [króməsom] *s.* cromosomo.

**chronic** [kránɪk] *adj.* crónico.

**chronicle** [kránɪkl̩] *s.* crónica; *v.* relatar; escribir la crónica de.

**chronicler** [kráni̇klə] *s.* cronista.

**chronological** [krɑnəládʒɪkl̩] *adj.* cronológico.

**chronometer** [krənámətə] *s.* cronómetro.

**chrysanthemum** [krɪsǽnθəməm] *s.* crisantema, crisantemo.

**chubby** [tʃʌ́bɪ] *adj.* rechoncho; gordiflón.

**chuck** [tʃʌk] *s.* mamola, golpecito, caricia (*debajo de la barba*); *v.* echar, tirar (*lo que no sirve*); **to — under the chin** hacer la mamola.

**chuckle** [tʃʌ́kl̩] *s.* risita; *v.* reír entre dientes.

**chum** [tʃʌm] *s.* compañero, camarada, compinche.

**chunk** [tʃʌŋk] *s.* trozo; zoquete.

**church** [tʃɚtʃ] *s.* iglesia.

**churchman** [tʃɚ́tʃmən] *s.* clérigo, eclesiástico, sacerdote.

**churchyard** [tʃɚ́tʃjard] *s.* patio de iglesia; camposanto, cementerio.

**churn** [tʃɚn] *s.* mantequera (*para hacer manteca*); *v.* batir (*en una mantequera*); agitar, revolver.

**cider** [sáɪdə] *s.* sidra.

**cigar** [sɪgár] *s.* cigarro, puro; **— store** tabaquería, estanquillo.

**cigarette** [sɪgərét] *s.* cigarrillo, pitillo, *Méx., C.A., Ven., Col.* cigarro; **— case** cigarrera, pitillera; **— holder** boquilla; **— lighter** encendedor.

**cinch** [sɪntʃ] *s.* cincha; ganga, cosa fácil; *v.* cinchar; apretar.

**cinder** [síndə] *s.* ceniza; carbón, brasa, ascua; cisco; **-s** cenizas; rescoldo.

**cinnamon** [sínəmən] *s.* canela; **— tree** canelo.

**cipher** [sáɪfə] *s.* cifra; número; cero.

**circle** [sɚ́kl̩] *s.* círculo; cerco, rueda; *v.* cercar, circundar; circular, dar vueltas.

**circuit** [sɚ́kɪt] *s.* circuito; rode o, vuelta

**circular** [sɚ́kjələ] *adj.* circular; redondo; *s.* circular; hoja volante.

**circulate** [sɚ́kjəlet] *v.* circular; poner en circulación.

**circulation** [sɚkjəléʃən] *s.* circulación.

**circumference** [sɚkʌ́mfərəns] *s.* circunferencia.

**circumflex** [sɚ́kəmflɛks] *adj.* circunflejo.

**circumlocution** [sɚkəmlokjúʃən] *s.* circunlocución, rodeo.

**circumscribe** [sɚkəmskráɪb] *v.* circunscribir, limitar.

**circumspect** [sɚ́kəmspɛkt] *adj.* circunspecto; prudente.

**circumspection** [sɚkəmspékʃən] *s.* circunspección, miramiento, prudencia.

**circumstance** [sɚ́kəmstæns] *s.* circunstancia; incidente; ceremonia, pompa.

**circus** [sɚ́kəs] *s.* circo.

**cirrhosis** [sɪrósɪs] *s.* cirrosis.

**cistern** [sístən] *s.* cisterna.

**citadel** [sítədl̩] *s.* ciudadela.

**citation** [saɪté ʃən] *s.* citación; cita; mención.

**cite** [saɪt] *v.* citar; citar a juicio; mencionar.

**citizen** [sítəzn̩] *s.* ciudadano, paisano.

**citizenship** [sítəzn̩ʃɪp] *s.* ciudadanía.

**citron** [sítrən] *s.* acitrón.

**citrus** [sítrəs] *s.* cidro.

**city** [sítɪ] *s.* ciudad, población; municipio; *adj.* municipal; urbano; **— council** ayuntamiento; **— hall** ayuntamiento, casa municipal.

**civic** [sívɪk] *adj.* cívico.

**civics** [sívɪks] *s.* derecho político.

**civil** [sívl̩] *adj.* civil; cortés; **— engineer** ingeniero civil; **— rights** derechos civiles; **— disobedience** desobediencia civil.

**civilian** [səvíljən] *s.* paisano (*persona no militar*).

**civility** [səvílətɪ] *s.* civilidad, cortesía, urbanidad.

**civilization** [sɪvləzéʃən] *s.* civilización.

**civilize** [sívl̩aɪz] *v.* civilizar.

**civilized** [sívl̩aɪzd] *adj.* civilizado.

**clad** [klæd] *pret. & p.p. de* **to clothe.**

**claim** [klem] *s.* demanda; reclamación, reclamo; derecho, título; pretensión; **miner's —** denuncia; *v.* reclamar; demandar; pedir, exigir; afirmar, sostener; **to — a mine** denunciar una mina; **to — to be** pretender ser.

**claimant** [klémənt] *s.* reclamante o reclamador; pretendiente (*a un trono*).

**clairvoyant** [klɛrvóɪənt] *adj.* clarividente.

**clam** [klæm] *s.* almeja.

**clamber** [klǽmbə] *v.* trepar, encaramarse, subir a gatas, subir gateando.

**clammy** [klǽmɪ] *adj.* frío y húmedo.

**clamor** [klǽmə] *s.* clamor; clamoreo; gritería, vocería; *v.* clamar; vociferar, gritar.

**clamorous** [klǽmərəs] *adj.* clamoroso.

**clamp** [klæmp] *s.* grapa; tornillo de banco; *v.* afianzar, sujetar; pisar recio.

**clan** [klæn] *s.* clan; tribu.

**clandestine** [klændéstɪn] *adj.* clandestino.

**clang** [klæŋ] *s.* tantán, retintín; campanada, campanillazo; —! —! ¡tan! ¡tan!; *v.* sonar, repicar (*una campana o timbre*); hacer sonar, tocar fuerte.

**clap** [klæp] *s.* palmada; golpe seco; — **of thunder** trueno; *v.* palmear, palmotear, aplaudir, dar palmadas; cerrar de golpe (*un libro*); dar una palmada, *Am.* palmear (*sobre la espalda*); **to — in jail** meter (*o* encajar) en la cárcel.

**clapper** [klǽpə] *s.* badajo.

**clarify** [klǽrəfaɪ] *v.* aclarar.

**clarinet** [klærənét] *s.* clarinete.

**clarity** [klǽrətɪ] *s.* claridad, luz.

**clash** [klæʃ] *s.* choque, encontrón, colisión; riña, conflicto; estruendo; *v.* chocar; darse un encontrón; hacer crujir; oponerse, estar en conflicto.

**clasp** [klæsp] *s.* (*fastener*) broche; hebilla; cierre; traba; (*grip*) apretón, apretón de manos; *v.* abrochar; asir; agarrar; sujetar, asegurar; abrazar; apretar (*la mano*).

**class** [klæs] *s.* clase; *v.* clasificar.

**classic** [klǽsɪk] *adj. & s.* clásico; — **scholar** humanista, erudito clásico.

**classical** [klǽsɪk!] *adj.* clásico.

**classicism** [klǽsɪsɪzm] *s.* clasicismo.

**classification** [klæsəfəkéʃən] *s.* clasificación.

**classify** [klǽsəfaɪ] *v.* clasificar.

**classmate** [klǽsmet] *s.* compañero de clase, condiscípulo.

**classroom** [klǽsrum] *s.* clase, aula.

**clatter** [klǽtə] *s.* estrépito, boruca; traqueteo; bullicio; alboroto; *v.* hacer estrépito o boruca; traquetear; meter bulla o alboroto.

**clause** [klɔz] *s.* cláusula.

**claw** [klɔ] *s.* garra; zarpa; uña; pinza (*de langosta, cangrejo, etc.*); orejas (*de un martillo*); arañazo; *v.* desgarrar; arañar; rasgar.

**clay** [kle] *s.* barro; arcilla, greda.

**clean** [klin] *adj.* limpio; puro; *adv.* limpiamente; **clean-cut** bien tallado, de buen talle, de buen parecer; *v.* limpiar; asear; **to — up** limpiar(se), asear(se).

**cleaner** [klínə] *s.* limpiador; quitamanchas.

**cleanliness** [klénlɪnɪs] *s.* limpieza, aseo.

**cleanly** [klénlɪ] *adj.* limpio; aseado; [klínlɪ] *adv.* limpiamente.

**cleanness** [klínnɪs] *s.* limpieza; aseo.

**cleanse** [klɛnz] *v.* limpiar; asear; purificar, depurar.

**cleanser** [klénzə] *s.* limpiador.

**clear** [klɪr] *adj.* (*evident*) claro; patente, manifiesto; (*clean*) límpido; despejado; libre (*de culpa, estorbos, deudas, etc.*); — **profit** ganancia neta; **clear-cut** *adj.* bien delineado; clarividente; **to pass — through** atravesar, traspasar de lado a lado; **to be in the —** estar sin deudas; estar libre de culpa; *v.* aclarar(se); despejar(se); clarificar;

quitar (*estorbos*); desmontar (*un terreno*); salvar, saltar por encima de; librar (*de culpa, deudas, etc.*); sacar (*una ganancia neta*); pasar (*un cheque*) por un banco de liquidación; liquidar (*una cuenta*); **to — the table** levantar la mesa; **to — up** aclarar(se).

**clearance** [klírəns] *s.* espacio (*libre entre dos objetos*); despacho de aduana; — **sale** saldo, venta (*de liquidación*), *Am.* barata.

**clearing** [klírɪŋ] *s.* aclaramiento; claro; terreno desmontado o desarbolado; liquidación de balances; —**house** banco de liquidación.

**clearness** [klírnɪs] *s.* claridad.

**cleavage** [klívɪdʒ] *s.* hendedura.

**cleave** [kliv] *v.* hender(se); tajar; rajar, partir.

**cleaver** [klívə] *s.* cuchilla o hacha (*de carnicero*).

**clef** [klɛf] *s.* clave (*en música*).

**cleft** [klɛft] *s.* grieta, hendedura; *adj.* hendido, partido, rajado; *pret. & p.p. de* **to cleave.**

**clemency** [klémənsɪ] *s.* clemencia.

**clement** [klémənt] *adj.* clemente.

**clench** [klɛntʃ] *s.* agarro, agarrada, agarrón; apretón; *v.* agarrar, asir; apretar (*los dientes, el puño*).

**clergy** [klə́dʒɪ] *s.* clero.

**clergyman** [klə́dʒɪmən] *s.* clérigo, eclesiástico, pastor, sacerdote.

**clerical** [klérɪk!] *adj.* clerical, eclesiástico; oficinesco, de oficina; de dependientes.

**clerk** [klɜk] *s.* dependiente; empleado (*de oficina*); escribiente; archivero (*de municipio*); **law —** escribano; *v.* estar de dependiente.

**clever** [klévə] *adj.* diestro, hábil; listo; talentoso; mañoso; **-ly** *adv.* hábilmente; con destreza; con maña.

**cleverness** [klévənɪs] *s.* destreza, habilidad, maña; talento.

**clew** [klu] *s.* indicio (*que indica el camino para resolver un misterio o problema*).

**cliché** [klɪʃé] *s.* (*plate*) clisé; *Am.* cliché; (*phrase*) cliché.

**click** [klɪk] *s.* golpecito; chasquido (*de la lengua*); gatillazo (*sonido del gatillo de una pistola*); taconeo (*sonido de tacones*); *v.* sonar (*un pestillo, un broche, un gatillo, etc.*); chasquear (*la lengua*); **to — the heels** cuadrarse (*militarmente*); taconear.

**client** [kláɪənt] *s.* cliente.

**clientele** [klaɪəntél] *s.* clientela.

**cliff** [klɪf] *s.* risco, precipicio, peñasco, escarpa.

**climate** [kláɪmɪt] *s.* clima.

**climax** [kláɪmæks] *s.* clímax, culminación; *v.* culminar; llegar al clímax.

**climb** [klaɪm] *s.* subida, ascenso; *v.* subir; trepar; encaramarse; **to — down** bajar a gatas; desprenderse (*de un árbol*).

**climber** [kláɪmə] *s.* trepador; enredadera, planta trepadora.

**clime** [klaɪm] *s.* clima.

**clinch** [klɪntʃ] *v.* remachar, redoblar (*un*

*clavo*); afianzar, sujetar, asegurar bien; cerrar (*un trato*); abrazarse fuertemente; *s.* remache; abrazo; agarrón; **to be in a** — estar agarrados o abrazados.

**cling** [klɪŋ] *v.* pegarse, adherirse.

**clinic** [klínɪk] *s.* clínica.

**clink** [klɪŋk] *s.* tintín.

**clip** [klɪp] *s.* (*fastener*) broche, presilla; (*cutting*) tijeretada (*corte con tijeras*); trasquila, trasquiladura; **paper** — sujetapapeles; **to go at a good** — ir a paso rápido; andar de prisa; *v.* recortar; cortar; trasquilar (*el pelo o lana de los animales*); **to** — **together** sujetar.

**clipper** [klípɚ] *s.* clíper (*velero o avión de gran velocidad*); trasquilador; recortador; **-s** tijeras; maquinilla (*para recortar el pelo*).

**clipping** [klípɪŋ] *s.* recorte.

**cloak** [klok] *s.* capa; manto; *v.* tapar, embozar, encubrir.

**cloakroom** [klókrum] *s.* guardarropa, vestuario.

**clock** [klɑk] *s.* reloj; **alarm** — despertador; *v.* marcar; cronometrar.

**clockwise** [klákwaɪz] *adv.* en el sentido de las manecillas de reloj.

**clockwork** [klákwɜk] *s.* maquinaria de reloj; **like** — con precisión, puntualmente; sin dificultad.

**clod** [klɑd] *s.* terrón; tonto, necio.

**clog** [klɑg] *s.* estorbo, obstáculo; zueco (*zapato de suela gruesa de madera*); — **dance** zapateado; *v.* estorbar, embarazar; obstruir, atorar, tapar; obstruirse, atascarse, azolvarse (*Am.* enzolvarse), atorarse (*un caño, acequia, etc.*).

**cloister** [klóɪstɚ] *s.* claustro; monasterio; convento; *v.* enclaustrar.

**close** [kloz] *s.* fin, terminación, conclusión; *v.* cerrar(se); concluir; **to** — **an account** saldar una cuenta; **to** — **in upon** cercar, rodear; **to** — **out** liquidar, vender en liquidación.

**close** [klos] *adj.* (*near*) cercano, próximo; aproximado; íntimo; (*tight*) estrecho, ajustado; (*stingy*) cerrado; tacaño, mezquino; (*suffocating*) opresivo; sofocante; — **attention** suma atención; — **questioning** interrogatorio detallado o minucioso; — **translation** traducción fiel; **at** — **range** de cerca; *adv.* cerca; **-ly** *adv.* aproximadamente; estrechamente; apretadamente; con sumo cuidado a atención.

**closed circuit** [klozd sɝ́kɪt] *s.* & *adj.* circuito cerrado.

**closeness** [klósnɪs] *s.* cercanía, proximidad; aproximación; estrechez; intimidad; tacañería, avaricia; mala ventilación, falta de aire; fidelidad (*de una traducción*).

**closet** [klázɪt] *s.* ropero; alacena, armario; gabinete, retrete, excusado; *v.* encerrar en un cuarto (*para una entrevista secreta*); **to** — **oneself (themselves)** encerrarse.

**clot** [klɑt] *v.* coagular(se), cuajar(se); *s.* coágulo, cuajarón.

**cloth** [klɔθ] *s.* tela, paño, género; trapo; *adj.* de paño; — **binding** encuadernación en tela.

**clothe** [kloð] *v.* vestir; cubrir; revestir; investir.

**clothes** [kloz] *s. pl.* ropa; ropaje, vestidos; **suit of** — terno, traje, *Carib.*, *Ven.* flux; — **line** tendedero; — **pin** pinzas, gancho (*para tender la ropa*).

**clothier** [klóðjɚ] *s.* comerciante en ropa o paño; ropero, pañero.

**clothing** [klóðɪŋ] *s.* ropa; ropaje, vestidos.

**cloud** [klaud] *s.* nube; **storm** — nubarrón; *v.* nublar(se), anublar(se); obscurecer; manchar.

**cloudburst** [kláudbɚst] *s.* chaparrón, aguacero.

**cloudless** [kláudlɪs] *adj.* claro, despejado; sin nubes.

**cloudy** [kláudɪ] *adj.* nublado; nubloso; sombrío.

**clove** [klov] *s.* clavo (*especia*); — **of garlic** diente de ajo.

**cloven** [klóvən] *adj.* hendido; *s.* & *adj.* — **hoof** patihendido, pie hendido.

**clover** [klóvɚ] *s.* trébol; **to be in** — estar o vivir en la abundancia; sentirse próspero.

**cloverleaf** [klóvɚlif] *s.* (*highway*) cruce en trébol.

**clown** [klaun] *s.* payaso, bufón; *v.* payasear, bufonear, hacer el payaso.

**cloy** [klɔɪ] *v.* empalagar; hastiar.

**club** [klʌb] *s.* club, círculo; casino; garrote, porra; palo; basto (*de la baraja*); *v.* golpear, aporrear, apalear; **to** — **together** formar club; escotar, pagar la cuota que le toca a cada uno, *Am.* cotizar.

**clubhouse** [klʌ́bhaus] *s.* club, casino.

**cluck** [klʌk] *s.* cloqueo; *v.* cloquear.

**clue** = **clew**.

**clump** [klʌmp] *s.* terrón; pisada fuerte; — **of bushes** matorral; — **of trees** grupo de árboles, arboleda; *v.* apiñar, amontonar; **to** — **along** andar pesadamente.

**clumsy** [klʌ́mzɪ] *adj.* torpe, desmañado; incómodo; difícil de manejar; mal hecho.

**clung** [klʌŋ] *pret.* & *p.p. de* **to cling**.

**cluster** [klʌ́stɚ] *s.* racimo; grupo; *v.* agrupar(se); arracimarse (*formar racimo*).

**clutch** [klʌtʃ] *s.* apretón fuerte; agarro, agarrón; embrague (*de automóvil*); **-es** garras; uñas; — **pedal** palanca del embrague; **to step on the** — pisar el embrague; desembragar, soltar el embrague; **to throw in the** — embragar; *v.* agarrar, asir; apretar.

**clutter** [klʌ́tɚ] *v.* obstruir; atestar (*de cosas*); poner en desorden; *s.* desorden, confusión.

**coach** [kotʃ] *s.* coche; entrenador (*e. deportes*); maestro particular; *v.* aleccionar; guiar, adiestrar, *Am.* entrenar; **to** — **with** ser instruido o entrenado por.

**coachman** [kótʃmən] *s.* cochero.

**coagulate** [koǽgjəlet] *v.* coagular(se), cuajar(se).

**coal** [kol] *s.* carbón; ascua, brasa; **hard —** carbón de piedra, antracita; **soft —** hulla; **— bin** carbonera; **— dealer** carbonero; **— oil** kerosina; **— tar** alquitrán de carbón; *v.* cargar de carbón, echar carbón; proveer(se) de carbón.

**coalition** [koəlíʃən] *s.* coalición.

**coarse** [kors] *adj.* (*crude*) burdo, basto; tosco; áspero; (*rude*) rudo; grosero; vulgar; tosco; **— sand** arena gruesa.

**coarseness** [kórsnɪs] *s.* tosquedad; vulgaridad, grosería, rudeza.

**coast** [kost] *s.* costa, litoral; **— guard** guardacostas, guarda de costas; *v.* costear, navegar por la costa; deslizar-(se), resbalar(se) cuesta abajo.

**coastal** [kóstl] *adj.* costero, costanero, de la costa.

**coastline** [kóstlaɪn] *s.* costa, litoral.

**coat** [kot] *s.* chaqueta, americana; *Am.* saco; lana, pelo (*de un animal*); **lady's —** abrigo de señora; **— hanger** colgador; **— of arms** escudo de armas; **— of paint** capa de pintura; *v.* cubrir; revestir, dar una mano (*de pintura*); **to — with sugar** azucarar, bañar en azúcar.

**coating** [kótɪŋ] *s.* capa.

**coattail** [kóttel] *s.* faldón.

**coax** [koks] *v.* rogar o persuadir con halagos, halagar, tentar.

**cob** [kab] *s.* carozo, zuro (*de la mazorca del maíz*), *Ven.*, *Col.*, *Carib.* tusa, *Méx.*, *C.A.* olote.

**cobalt** [kóbɔlt] *s.* cobalto.

**cobbler** [káblə] *s.* remendón (*zapatero*); pudín de bizcocho y fruta.

**cobblestone** [káblston] *s.* guijarro; *adj.* empedrado.

**cobweb** [kábwɛb] *s.* telaraña.

**cocaine** [kokén] *s.* cocaína.

**cock** [kak] *s.* gallo; macho de ave; espita, grifo; martillo (*de armas de fuego*); **—sure** muy seguro de sí mismo; *v.* amartillar (*un arma de fuego*); ladear (*la cabeza*), ladearse (*el sombrero*).

**cockfight** [kákfaɪt] *s.* pelea de gallos, riña de gallos.

**cockpit** [kákpɪt] *s.* gallera; (*airplane*) cabina.

**cockroach** [kákrotʃ] *s.* cucaracha.

**cocktail** [káktel] *s.* coctel; aperitivo (*de ostras, almejas, frutas, etc.*).

**cocky** [kákɪ] *adj.* arrogante, *Am.* retobado.

**cocoa** [kóko] *s.* cacao; bebida de cacao, chocolate.

**coconut** [kókənət] *s.* coco (*fruta*).

**cocoon** [kəkún] *s.* capullo (*del gusano de seda, etc.*).

**cod** [kad] *s.* *N.Esp.* abadejo; *Andalucía*, *Am.* bacalao; **cod-liver oil** aceite de hígado de bacalao.

**coddle** [kádl] *v.* mimar, consentir.

**code** [kod] *s.* código; clave; **— mes-**

**sage** comunicación en clave; **signal —** código de señales.

**codfish** [kádfɪʃ] = **cod.**

**coerce** [koɔ́s] *v.* forzar, obligar.

**coercion** [koɔ́ʃən] *s.* coacción.

**coexistence** [koɛgzístəns] *s.* coexistencia.

**coffee** [kɔ́fɪ] *s.* café; **— shop** café; **— tree** cafeto; **black —** café solo.

**coffeepot** [kɔ́fɪpat] *s.* cafetera.

**coffer** [kɔ́fə] *s.* cofre, arca.

**coffin** [kɔ́fɪn] *s.* ataúd, féretro.

**cog** [kag] *s.* diente; **— wheel** rueda dentada.

**cognate** [kágnet] *s.* cognato.

**coherent** [kohírənt] *adj.* coherente; conexo.

**cohesion** [kohíʒən] *s.* cohesión.

**coiffure** [kwafjúr] *s.* tocado, peinado.

**coil** [kɔɪl] *s.* rollo; rosca; espiral de alambre; **electric —** bobina; *v.* arrollar(se), enrollar(se); enroscar(se).

**coin** [kɔɪn] *s.* moneda; *v.* acuñar; inventar, forjar (*una frase o palabra*).

**coinage** [kɔ́ɪnɪdʒ] *s.* acuñación; sistema monetario; moneda, monedas; invención (*de una palabra o frase*).

**coincide** [koɪnsáɪd] *v.* coincidir.

**coincidence** [koínsədəns] *s.* coincidencia; casualidad.

**coke** [kok] *s.* cok, coque (*combustible*).

**cold** [kold] *adj.* frío; **— cream** crema cosmética; **— meat** fiambre; **— wave** ola de frío; **— war** guerra fría; **to be —** tener frío; **it is — today** hace frío hoy; *s.* frío; catarro, resfriado; **to catch a —** resfriarse, acatarrarse.

**coldness** [kóldnɪs] *s.* frialdad; indiferencia, despego.

**colic** [kálɪk] *s.* cólico.

**collaborate** [kəlǽbəret] *v.* colaborar.

**collaboration** [kəlæbəréʃən] *s.* colaboración.

**collapse** [kəlǽps] *s.* desplome, derrumbe, derrumbamiento; hundimiento; postración; *v.* doblar(se), plegar(se); contraer (*el volumen*); hundirse, derrumbarse, desplomarse; sufrir una postración.

**collar** [kálə] *s.* collar; cuello (*de vestido, camisa, etc.*); collera (*para mulas o caballos de tiro*); *v.* acollarar, poner collar a; coger o agarrar por el cuello; prender.

**collate** [kəlét, kólet] *v.* cotejar; colacionar.

**collateral** [kəlǽtərəl] *adj.* colateral; auxiliar, subsidiario, accesorio; *s.* garantía (*para un préstamo bancario*).

**colleague** [kálig] *s.* colega.

**collect** [kəlékt] *v.* recoger; coleccionar; cobrar; recaudar (*impuestos*); reunir(se); congregarse; **to — oneself** calmarse; sosegarse, reportarse.

**collection** [kəlékʃən] *s.* colección; agrupación (*de gente*); recolección, cobranza, cobro, recaudación, colecta.

**collective** [kəléktɪv] *adj.* colectivo.

**collectivism** [kəléktəvɪzm] *s.* colectivismo.

**collector** [kəléktɚ] *s.* colector; coleccionista (*de sellos, objetos artísticos, etc.*); cobrador (*de billetes, deudas, etc.*); recaudador (*de impuestos*).

**college** [kálɪdʒ] *s.* universidad; **— of engineering** facultad de ingeniería; **— of medicine** escuela (*facultad*) de medicina.

**collide** [kəláɪd] *v.* chocar; estar en conflicto, oponerse.

**collie** [kálɪ] *s.* perro de pastor.

**collision** [kəlíʒən] *s.* choque, colisión; oposición, pugna (*de intereses, ideas, etc.*).

**colloquial** [kəlókwɪəl] *adj.* familiar; **— expression** locución o frase familiar.

**collusion** [kəlúʒɪən] *s.* confabulación.

**colon** [kólən] *s.* colon (*del intestino*); dos puntos (*signo de puntuación*).

**colonel** [kɚ́nl] *s.* coronel.

**colonial** [kəlónɪəl] *adj.* colonial.

**colonist** [kálənɪst] *s.* colono, colonizador.

**colonization** [kalənəzéʃən] *s.* colonización.

**colonize** [kálənaɪz] *v.* colonizar; establecerse en colonia.

**colony** [kálənɪ] *s.* colonia.

**color** [kálɚ] *s.* color; colorido; **the -s** la bandera; *v.* colorar; colorear; dar colorido; pintar; teñir; iluminar (*una fotografía, grabado, etc.*); ruborizarse.

**colored** [kálɚd] *adj.* colorado, teñido, colorido, pintado; de color; coloreado; **— person** persona de color.

**colorful** [kálɚfəl] *adj.* lleno de color; colorido; vistoso; vívido; pintoresco.

**coloring** [kálɚɪŋ] *s.* colorido; coloración; colorante.

**colorless** [kálɚlɪs] *adj.* incoloro; descolorido.

**colossal** [kəlásl] *adj.* colosal.

**colt** [kolt] *s.* potro.

**Columbian** [kəlʌ́mbɪən] *adj.* colombiano, de Colombia; colombino, referente a Cristóbal Colón.

**column** [káləm] *s.* columna.

**comb** [kom] *s.* peine; peineta (*de mujer*); cresta (*de gallo*); rastrillo, carda (*para lana*); almohaza (*para caballos*); panal (*de miel*); *v.* peinar; rastrillar, cardar (*lana*); escudriñar; **to — one's hair** peinarse.

**combat** [kámbæt] *s.* combate, pelea; *v.* combatir.

**combatant** [kámbətənt] *adj. & s.* combatiente.

**combination** [kambənéʃən] *s.* combinación.

**combine** [kəmbáɪn] *v.* combinar(se), unir(se).

**combo** [kámbo] *s.* batería de jazz.

**combustible** [kəmbʌ́stəbl] *adj. & s.* combustible.

**combustion** [kəmbʌ́stʃən] *s.* combustión.

**come** [kʌm] *v.* venir; llegar; provenir; **to — about** suceder; **to — again** volver, volver a venir; **to — back** volver, regresar; **to — downstairs** bajar; **to — in** entrar; **to — out** salir;

**to — of age** llegar a mayor edad; **to — off** soltarse, zafarse; **to — to** volver en sí; **to — to terms** ponerse de acuerdo, ajustarse; **to — up** subir; surgir (*una cuestión*); *p.p. de* **to come.**

**comedian** [kəmídɪən] *s.* cómico, comediante.

**comedy** [kámədɪ] *s.* comedia.

**comely** [kʌ́mlɪ] *adj.* agradable a la vista, gentil, bien parecido.

**comet** [kámɪt] *s.* cometa.

**comfort** [kʌ́mfɚt] *s.* comodidad; bienestar; alivio, consuelo; *v.* consolar, confortar, aliviar.

**comfortable** [kʌ́mfɚtəbl] *adj.* cómodo; confortable; **— life** vida holgada; **— income** un buen pasar, renta suficiente; **comfortably** *adv.* cómodamente; con comodidad; holgadamente.

**comforter** [kʌ́mfɚtɚ] *s.* consolador; edredón, cobertor acolchado.

**comfortless** [kʌ́mfɚtlɪs] *adj.* incómodo; desconsolado.

**comic** [kámɪk] *adj.* cómico; chistoso, gracioso; **-s** *s. pl.* caricaturas, historietas cómicas.

**comical** [kámɪkl] *adj.* cómico, gracioso.

**coming** [kámɪŋ] *adj.* que viene, que llega; próximo; venidero; *s.* venida, llegada; **— of Christ** advenimiento de Cristo.

**comma** [kámə] *s.* coma.

**command** [kəmǽnd] *s.* (*order*) mando; mandato, orden; mandamiento; (*post*) comandancia; (*dominance*) dominio; **at your —** a la orden de Vd., a la disposición de Vd.; **he has a good — of English** domina bien el inglés; *v.* mandar; ordenar; dominar; comandar; **to — respect** inspirar respeto, imponerse.

**commander** [kəmǽndɚ] *s.* jefe; comandante; teniente de navío; comendador (*de ciertas órdenes*); **— in chief** comandante en jefe; general en jefe.

**commandment** [kəmǽndmənt] *s.* mandamiento; mandato, orden.

**commando** [kəmǽndo] *s.* comando.

**commemorate** [kəmémɚet] *v.* conmemorar.

**commence** [kəméns] *v.* comenzar.

**commencement** [kəménsmənt] *s.* comienzo, principio; acto de distribución de diplomas.

**commend** [kəménd] *v.* alabar, elogiar; encomendar, encargar; recomendar.

**commendation** [kaməndéʃən] *s.* encomio, alabanza.

**comment** [kámɛnt] *s.* comentario, observación, nota; *v.* comentar; hacer observaciones; hacer comentarios.

**commentary** [káməntɛrɪ] *s.* comentario.

**commentator** [káməntetɚ] *s.* comentador; comentarista; **radio —** comentarista radial.

**commerce** [kámɚs] *s.* comercio.

**commercial** [kəmɚ́ʃəl] *adj.* comercial.

**commiseration** [kəmɪzəréʃən] *s.* compasión.

**commissar** [kámɪsar] *s.* comisario.
**commissary** [kámǝserɪ] *s.* comisario.
**commission** [kǝmíʃǝn] *s.* comisión; encargo; junta; nombramiento; **to put out of** — inutilizar; descomponer, quebrar; retirar del servicio (*un navío*); *v.* comisionar; encargar; nombrar; poner en servicio (*un navío*); **-ed officer** oficial comisionado (*alférez u oficial superior a éste*).
**commissioner** [kǝmíʃǝnɚ] *s.* comisionado; comisario; **police** — comisario de policía.
**commit** [kǝmít] *v.* (*perpetrate*) cometer; (*entrust*) encargar; **to — to memory** aprender de memoria; **to — to prison** encarcelar; **to — oneself** dar o expresar su opinión, expresarse abiertamente, comprometerse.
**committee** [kǝmítɪ] *s.* comité; comisión, junta; **— of one** comisionado o delegado único.
**commodity** [kǝmádǝtɪ] *s.* mercancía; género, mercadería, artículo de comercio, producto.
**common** [kámǝn] *adj.* común; general; corriente; vulgar, ordinario; público; **— law** derecho consuetudinario; **— sense** sentido común; **— soldier** soldado raso; **— market** mercado común; **-s** *s. pl.* refectorio (*de un colegio o universidad*); ejido, campo común; **-ly** *adv.* comúnmente, por lo común.
**commonness** [kámǝnnɪs] *s.* vulgaridad, ordinariez; frecuencia.
**commonplace** [kámǝnples] *adj.* común, trivial; *s.* lugar común.
**commonwealth** [kámǝnwɛlθ] *s.* estado; república; pueblo, colectividad.
**commotion** [kǝmóʃǝn] *s.* conmoción; tumulto; bullicio; levantamiento.
**commune** [kǝmjún] *v.* comunicarse (con); comulgar.
**communicate** [kǝmjúnǝket] *v.* comunicar(se); transmitir.
**communication** [kǝmjunǝkéʃǝn] *s.* comunicación.
**communicative** [kǝmjúnǝketɪv] *adj.* comunicativo.
**communion** [kǝmjúnjǝn] *s.* comunión.
**communism** [kámjʊnɪzǝm] *s.* comunismo.
**communist** [kámjʊnɪst] *s. & adj.* comunista.
**community** [kǝmjúnǝtɪ] *s.* comunidao; sociedad; vecindario, barrio; **— chest** caja de beneficencia, fondos de beneficencia.
**commute** [kǝmjút] *v.* conmutar.
**compact** [kǝmpǽkt] *adj.* compacto; denso; apretado; conciso, sucinto; [kámpækt] *s.* pacto, trato, convenio; polvera.
**compactness** [kǝmpǽktnɪs] *s.* solidez; densidad; concisión.
**companion** [kǝmpǽnjǝn] *s.* compañero; acompañante.
**companionship** [kǝmpǽnjǝnʃɪp] *s.* compañerismo, camaradería; com-

pañía.
**company** [kʌ́mpǝnɪ] *s.* compañía; sociedad; visita; **ship's** — tripulación; **to keep — with** acompañar a; cortejar a; tener relaciones con, frecuentar la compañía de.
**comparable** [kámpǝrǝbl] *adj.* comparable.
**comparative** [kǝmpǽrǝtɪv] *adj.* comparativo.
**compare** [kǝmpér] *v.* comparar; cotejar; confrontar; contrastar; **beyond** — incomparable, sin par, sin igual, sin comparación.
**comparison** [kǝmpǽrǝsṇ] *s.* comparación; símil; **beyond** — incomparable, sin comparación; **in — with** comparado con.
**compartment** [kǝmpártmǝnt] *s.* compartimiento, sección, división; departamento.
**compass** [kʌ́mpǝs] *s.* compás (*para dibujar*); brújula; área, ámbito; alcance.
**compassion** [kǝmpǽʃǝn] *s.* compasión, lástima.
**compassionate** [kǝmpǽʃǝnɪt] *adj.* compasivo, misericordioso.
**compatible** [kǝmpǽtǝbl] *adj.* compatible.
**compatriot** [kǝmpétrɪǝt] *s.* compatriota.
**compel** [kǝmpél] *v.* compeler, obligar; exigir.
**compensate** [kámpǝnset] *v.* compensar; recompensar; remunerar.
**compensation** [kampǝnséʃǝn] *s.* compensación; recompensa; remuneración.
**compete** [kǝmpít] *v.* competir.
**competence** [kámpǝtǝns] *s.* competencia, aptitud, capacidad.
**competent** [kámpǝtǝnt] *adj.* competente; calificado; capaz.
**competition** [kampǝtíʃǝn] *s.* competencia; concurso, certamen; contienda.
**competitive** [kǝmpétǝtɪv] *adj.* en competencia; **— examination** oposición, concurso.
**competitor** [kǝmpétǝtɚ] *s.* competidor; rival; opositor.
**compile** [kǝmpáɪl] *v.* compilar, recopilar.
**complacency** [kǝmplésṇsɪ] *s.* complacencia, contentamiento.
**complacent** [kǝmplésṇt] *adj.* complaciente, satisfecho.
**complain** [kǝmplén] *v.* quejarse; querellarse.
**complaint** [kǝmplént] *s.* queja; quejido, lamento; dolencia, enfermedad; **to lodge a** — hacer una reclamación.
**complement** [kámplǝmǝnt] *s.* complemento; [kámplǝment] *v.* complementar, completar.
**complete** [kǝmplít] *adj.* completo; *v.* completar; terminar; **-ly** *adv.* completamente, por completo.
**completeness** [kǝmplítnɪs] *s.* perfección; minuciosidad; lo completo; lo

CO

cabal; lo acabado.

**completion** [kəmplíʃən] *s.* completamiento; terminación, conclusión; cumplimiento.

**complex** [kámplɛks] *s.* complejo; [kəmpléks] *adj.* complejo; compuesto; complicado.

**complexion** [kəmplékʃən] *s.* cutis, tez; aspecto.

**complexity** [kəmpléksətɪ] *s.* complejidad.

**compliance** [kəmpláɪəns] *s.* complacencia; condescendencia; conformidad; cumplimiento; **in — with** en conformidad con; de acuerdo con, conforme a.

**complicate** [kámpləket] *v.* complicar.

**complicated** [kámpləketɪd] *adj.* complicado.

**complication** [kampləkéʃən] *s.* complicación.

**complicity** [kəmplísətɪ] *s.* complicidad.

**compliment** [kámpləmənt] *s.* cumplido, cumplimiento; requiebro, lisonja, galantería; **to send one's -s** enviar saludos; [kámpləment] *v.* cumplimentar; requebrar; lisonjear; alabar.

**comply** [kəmpláɪ] *v.* consentir, conformarse (con), obrar de acuerdo (con); cumplir (con).

**component** [kəmpónənt] *adj. & s.* componente.

**compose** [kəmpóz] *v.* componer; **to — oneself** sosegarse, serenarse, calmarse.

**composed** [kəmpózd] *adj.* compuesto; tranquilo, sereno, sosegado; **to be — of** estar compuesto de, componerse de, constar de.

**composer** [kəmpózɚ] *s.* compositor; autor.

**composite** [kəmpázɪt] *adj.* compuesto; *s.* compuesto; mezcla.

**composition** [kampəzíʃən] *s.* composición; arreglo; compuesto.

**composure** [kəmpóʒɚ] *s.* compostura, calma, serenidad.

**compound** [kámpaund] *adj. & s.* compuesto; [kampáund] *v.* componer; mezclar, combinar; **to — interest** calcular el interés compuesto.

**comprehend** [kamprɪhénd] *v.* comprender; abarcar, abrazar, incluir.

**comprehensible** [kamprɪhénsəbl] *adj.* comprensible, inteligible.

**comprehension** [kamprɪhénʃən] *s.* comprensión.

**comprehensive** [kamprɪhénsɪv] *adj.* comprensivo; inclusivo.

**compress** [kámprɛs] *s.* compresa; [kəmprés] *v.* comprimir, apretar, condensar.

**compression** [kəmpréʃən] *s.* compresión.

**comprise** [kəmpráɪz] *v.* comprender, abarcar, incluir, abrazar; constar de.

**compromise** [kámprəmaɪz] *s.* compromiso; arreglo; avenencia; término medio; *v.* comprometer; avenirse, transigir, *Am.* transar.

**comptroller** [kəntrólɚ] *s.* interventor, *Am.* contralor.

**compulsion** [kəmpálʃən] *s.* compulsión, coacción.

**compulsory** [kəmpálsərɪ] *adj.* obligatorio.

**computation** [kampjətéʃən] *s.* cómputo, cálculo.

**compute** [kəmpjút] *v.* computar.

**computer** [kəmpjútɚ] *s. Esp.* calculadora electrónica; *Arg.* computadora; programadora.

**computerize** [kəmpjútɚaɪz] *v.* someter datos a la calculadora electrónica; suplir con sistema computadora.

**comrade** [kámræd] *s.* camarada, compañero.

**concave** [kankév] *adj.* cóncavo.

**conceal** [kənsíl] *v.* encubrir, ocultar, esconder.

**concealment** [kənsílmənt] *s.* encubrimiento.

**concede** [kənsíd] *v.* conceder; otorgar, admitir, reconocer.

**conceit** [kənsít] *s.* presunción, amor propio, vanagloria; concepto, agudeza.

**conceited** [kənsítɪd] *adj.* presuntuoso, presumido, vanidoso, engreído.

**conceivable** [kənsívəbl] *adj.* concebible, imaginable, comprensible.

**conceive** [kənsív] *v.* concebir; imaginar.

**concentrate** [kánsn̩tret] *v.* concentrar(se), reconcentrar(se).

**concentration** [kansn̩tréʃən] *s.* concentración; reconcentración.

**concept** [kánsɛpt] *s.* concepto, idea; opinión.

**conception** [kənsépʃən] *s.* concepción; concepto, idea.

**concern** [kənsɛ́n] *s.* (*business*) compañía, negociación; negocio; establecimiento mercantil; (*interest*) cuidado; interés; preocupación; **to be of no —** no ser de consecuencia; *v.* concernir, importar, interesar; preocupar; **in all that -s him** en cuanto le atañe, en cuanto le concierne.

**concerned** [kənsɛ́nd] *adj.* interesado; preocupado, intranquilo, inquieto, ansioso; **to be — about** interesarse por, preocuparse por; **as far as I am —** por lo que me concierne, por lo que me toca, en cuanto a mí me atañe.

**concerning** [kənsɛ́nɪŋ] *prep.* tocante a, respecto a, acerca de.

**concert** [kánsɛt] *s.* concierto; [kənsɛ́t] *v.* concertar, arreglar (*un plan*).

**concession** [kənséʃən] *s.* concesión.

**conciliate** [kənsílɪet] *v.* conciliar, poner en armonía; ganar la voluntad de.

**concise** [kənsáɪs] *adj.* conciso, sucinto.

**conciseness** [kənsáɪsnɪs] *s.* concisión, brevedad.

**conclude** [kənklúd] *v.* concluir; acabar, terminar; deducir; decidir.

**conclusion** [kənklúʒən] *s.* conclusión.

**conclusive** [kənklúsɪv] *adj.* conclusivo,

concluyente.

**concoct** [kankákt] *v.* confeccionar; preparar (*combinando diversos ingredientes*); inventar, urdir.

**concoction** [kankákʃən] *s.* cocimiento, menjurje; mezcla.

**concord** [kánkɔrd] *s.* concordia, conformidad, acuerdo; convenio, pacto.

**concrete** [kankrít] *adj.* concreto; de hormigón, de cemento; *s.* hormigón, cemento, *Am.* concreto.

**concubine** [káŋkjubaɪn] *s.* concubina.

**concur** [kənkɹ́] *v.* estar de acuerdo, ser del mismo parecer; unirse.

**concussion** [kənkʌ́ʃən] *s.* concusión.

**condemn** [kəndém] *v.* condenar; **to — a building** condenar un edificio.

**condemnation** [kandɛmnéʃən] *s.* condenación.

**condensation** [kandɛnséʃən] *s.* condensación; resumen, compendio.

**condense** [kəndéns] *v.* condensar(se).

**condescend** [kandɪsénd] *v.* condescender.

**condescension** [kandɪsénʃən] *s.* condescendencia.

**condiment** [kándəmənt] *s.* condimento.

**condition** [kəndíʃən] *s.* condición; estado; nota o calificación provisional; **on — that** a condición de que, con tal que; *v.* acondicionar; poner en buena condición; estipular; reprobar provisionalmente (*a un estudiante*).

**conditional** [kəndíʃənl] *adj.* condicional.

**condole** [kəndól] *v.* condolerse; **to — with** dar el pésame a; consolar a.

**condolence** [kəndóləns] *s.* pésame.

**condone** [kəndón] *v.* dispensar; perdonar; condonar.

**conduce** [kəndjús] *v.* conducir.

**conducive** [kəndjúsɪv] *adj.* conducente.

**conduct** [kándʌkt] *s.* (*behavior*) conducta; comportamiento, proceder; (*handling*) dirección, manejo; [kəndʌ́kt] *v.* conducir; dirigir, manejar; **to — oneself well** portarse bien.

**conductor** [kəndʌ́ktɚ] *s.* conductor; guía; **orchestra —** director de orquesta; **train —** revisor; cobrador, *Am.* conductor.

**conduit** [kándɪt] *s.* conducto; caño; cañería, tubería.

**cone** [kon] *s.* cono; **paper —** cucurucho; **pine —** piña.

**confection** [kənfékʃən] *s.* confección; confitura; confite, dulce.

**confectionery** [kənfékʃənɛrɪ] *s.* confitería; dulcería; confites, dulces.

**confederacy** [kənfédərəsɪ] *s.* confederación.

**confederate** [kənfédərɪt] *adj. & s.* confederado; [kənfédəret] *v.* confederar(se).

**confederation** [kənfɛdəréʃən] *s.* confederación.

**confer** [kənfɹ́] *v.* conferir, conceder; conferenciar, consultar.

**conference** [kánfərəns] *s.* conferencia;

consulta, junta, sesión.

**confess** [kənfés] *v.* confesar(se); reconocer, admitir.

**confession** [kənféʃən] *s.* confesión.

**confessional** [kənféʃənl] *s.* confesionario.

**confessor** [kənfésɚ] *s.* confesor.

**confidant** [kanfədǽnt] *s.* confidente.

**confide** [kənfáɪd] *v.* confiar; fiar.

**confidence** [kánfədəns] *s.* confianza; confidencia; **— game** estafa; **— man** estafador.

**confident** [kánfədənt] *adj.* confiado; seguro, cierto; **-ly** *adv.* confiadamente, con toda seguridad.

**confidential** [kanfədénʃəl] *adj.* confidencial; íntimo; secreto; **-ly** *adv.* en confianza.

**confine** [kánfaɪn] *s.* confín; [kənfáɪn] *v.* confinar; encerrar; **to — oneself to** limitarse a; **to be -ed in bed** estar encamado, guardar cama.

**confinement** [kənfáɪnmənt] *s.* encerramiento; encierro; prisión, encarcelación.

**confirm** [kənfɹ́m] *v.* confirmar.

**confirmation** [kanfɚméʃən] *s.* confirmación.

**confiscate** [kánfɪsket] *v.* confiscar.

**conflagration** [kanfləgréʃən] *s.* conflagración, incendio.

**conflict** [kánflɪkt] *s.* conflicto, oposición, choque; lucha, combate; [kənflíkt] *v.* chocar, oponerse, estar en conflicto.

**conform** [kənfɔ́rm] *v.* conformar(se).

**conformity** [kənfɔ́rmətɪ] *s.* conformidad.

**confound** [kanfáund] *v.* confundir, perturbar, desconcertar, aturdir; **— it!** ¡caramba!

**confront** [kənfrʌ́nt] *v.* confrontar; carear, poner cara a cara (*a dos reos*); encararse con, afrontar, hacer frente a, arrostrar.

**confuse** [kənfjúz] *v.* confundir; trastornar; embrollar; desconcertar.

**confused** [kənfjúzd] *adj.* confuso; revuelto; desconcertado, perplejo; **to become —** confundirse; desconcertarse.

**confusing** [kənfjúzɪŋ] *adj.* confuso, revuelto; desconcertante.

**confusion** [kənfjúʒən] *s.* confusión; desorden; tumulto; perplejidad.

**congeal** [kəndʒíl] *v.* congelar(se), helar(se), cuajar(se).

**congenial** [kəndʒínjəl] *adj.* congenial; simpático; **to be — with** congeniar con, simpatizar con.

**congestion** [kəndʒéstʃən] *s.* congestión; aglomeración.

**conglomeration** [kənglaməréʃən] *s.* aglomeración.

**congratulate** [kəngrǽtʃəlet] *v.* congratular, felicitar, dar el parabién.

**congratulation** [kəngrætʃəléʃən] *s.* congratulación, felicitación, parabién, enhorabuena.

**congregate** [káŋgrɪget] *v.* congregar(se), juntar(se), reunir(se).

**congregation** [kaŋgrɪgéʃən] *s.* congregación; asamblea, reunión; colección, agregado; fieles, feligreses (de una iglesia).

**congress** [káŋgrəs] s. congreso; asamblea.

**congressional** [kəngréʃən]] adj. perteneciente al congreso.

**congressman** [káŋgrəsmən] s. congresista, diputado, representante.

**conjecture** [kəndʒéktʃɚ] s. conjetura, suposición; v. conjeturar, suponer.

**conjugate** [kándʒəget] v. conjugar.

**conjugation** [kandʒəgéʃən] s. conjugación.

**conjunction** [kəndʒáŋkʃən] s. conjunción.

**conjure** [kándʒɚ] v. conjurar; **to — up** evocar; [kəndʒúr] rogar, implorar.

**connect** [kənékt] v. conectar; unir(se), juntar(se); enlazar(se); relacionar(se); acoplar.

**connection** [kənékʃən] s. conexión; enlace; vínculo; unión; relación; **-s** parientes; amigos, amistades.

**conniption** [kənípʃən] s. pataleta; **to have a — darle a uno una pataleta.

**connive** [kənáiv] v. conspirar; disimular; hacerse cómplice.

**connoisseur** [kanəsɚ́] s. conocedor, perito.

**conquer** [káŋkɚ] v. conquistar; vencer.

**conqueror** [káŋkərɚ] s. conquistador; vencedor.

**conquest** [kánkwɛst] s. conquista.

**conscience** [kánʃəns] s. conciencia.

**conscientious** [kanʃiénʃəs] adj. concienzudo.

**conscious** [kánʃəs] adj. consciente; sabedor; **-ly** adv. conscientemente; a sabiendas.

**consciousness** [kánʃəsnɪs] s. conciencia, estado consciente; **to lose — perder el sentido o conocimiento.

**conscript** [kənskrípt] v. reclutar; [kánskrɪpt] s. recluta.

**consecrate** [kánsɪkret] v. consagrar; dedicar.

**consecration** [kansɪkréʃən] s. consagración; dedicación.

**consecutive** [kənsékjətɪv] adj. consecutivo.

**consensus** [kənsénsəs] s. consenso.

**consent** [kənsént] s. consentimiento; permiso, asentimiento; v. consentir; permitir, asentir.

**consequence** [kánsəkwɛns] s. consecuencia.

**consequent** [kánsəkwɛnt] adj. consecuente; consiguiente; s. consecuente, consiguiente, consecuencia; **-ly** adv. por consiguiente, por consecuencia.

**consequential** [kansəkwéntʃl] adj. de consecuencia.

**conservation** [kansɚvéʃən] s. conservación; preservación.

**conservative** [kənsɚ́vətɪv] adj. conservador; conservativo; s. conservador.

**conservatory** [kənsɚ́vətorɪ] s. conservatorio; invernadero.

**conserve** [kənsɚ́v] s. conserva, dulce; v. conservar; preservar.

**consider** [kənsídɚ] v. considerar.

**considerable** [kənsídərəbl] adj. considerable; cuantioso; **considerably** adv. considerablemente; **considerably older** bastante más viejo.

**considerate** [kənsídərɪt] adj. considerado.

**consideration** [kənsɪdəréʃən] s. (respect) respeto; consideración; importancia; (pay) remuneración; **in — of** en atención a, teniendo en cuenta, en razón de, en vista de.

**considering** [kənsídərɪŋ] prep. en razón de, en vista de; en atención a, en consideración de.

**consign** [kənsáin] v. consignar; enviar; entregar.

**consignee** [kansainí] s. consignatario.

**consignment** [kənsáinmənt] s. consignación.

**consist** [kənsíst] v. consistir (en); constar (de).

**consistency** [kənsístənsı] s. consecuencia; consistencia, firmeza, solidez.

**consistent** [kənsístənt] adj. consecuente, lógico; compatible; consistente, coherente.

**consolation** [kansəléʃən] s. consolación; consuelo.

**console** [kənsól] v. consolar.

**consolidate** [kənsálədet] v. consolidar(se); unir(se), combinar(se).

**consonant** [kánsənənt] adj. consonante; conforme; s. consonante.

**consort** [kánsɔrt] s. consorte; [kənsɔ́rt] v. **to — with** asociarse con.

**conspicuous** [kənspíkjuəs] adj. conspicuo, notorio; manifiesto, sobresaliente.

**conspiracy** [kənspírəsı] s. conspiración, conjuración.

**conspirator** [kənspírətɚ] s. conspirador, conjurado.

**conspire** [kənspáir] v. conspirar; tramar, maquinar.

**constable** [kánstəbl] s. alguacil, policía; condestable (título).

**constancy** [kánstənsı] s. constancia.

**constant** [kánstənt] adj. constante; s. constante, cantidad constante; **-ly** adv. constantemente, continuamente, siempre; a menudo.

**constellation** [kanstəléʃən] s. constelación.

**consternation** [kanstɚnéʃən] s. consternación.

**constipate** [kánstəpet] v. estreñir.

**constipation** [kanstəpéʃən] s. estreñimiento.

**constituent** [kənstítʃuənt] adj. constituyente; constitutivo; componente; s. componente, elemento; elector, votante.

**constitute** [kánstətjut] v. constituir; componer; establecer.

**constitution** [kanstətjúʃən] s. constitución.

**constitutional** [kanstətjúʃən]] adj. constitucional; s. paseo a pie, caminata

CO

(*para hacer ejercicio*).

**constrain** [kənstrén] *v.* constreñir; obligar, forzar; apretar, comprimir.

**construct** [kənstrʌ́kt] *v.* construir, fabricar.

**construction** [kənstrʌ́ktʃən] *s.* construcción; estructura; interpretación.

**constructive** [kənstrʌ́ktɪv] *adj.* constructivo; de utilidad positiva; provechoso.

**construe** [kənstrú] *v.* interpretar, explicar.

**consul** [káns!] *s.* cónsul.

**consulate** [káns!ɪt] *s.* consulado.

**consult** [kənsʌ́lt] *v.* consultar.

**consultant** [kənsʌ́ltənt] *s.* consultante.

**consultation** [kansl�b téʃən] *s.* consulta.

**consume** [kənsúm] *v.* consumir; gastar; perder (*el tiempo*).

**consumer** [kənsúmɚ] *s.* consumidor.

**consummate** [kánsəmet] *v.* consumar, completar; [kənsʌ́mɪt] *adj.* consumado, perfecto, completo.

**consumption** [kənsʌ́mpʃən] *s.* consumo, gasto; consunción; tisis, tuberculosis.

**consumptive** [kənsʌ́mptɪv] *adj.* tísico.

**contact** [kántækt] *s.* contacto; *v.* tocar; poner(se) en contacto con; estar en contacto con.

**contagion** [kəntédʒən] *s.* contagio.

**contagious** [kəntédʒəs] *adj.* contagioso.

**contain** [kəntén] *v.* contener; encerrar; tener cabida para; reprimir, refrenar; **to — oneself** contenerse, refrenarse.

**container** [kənténɚ] *s.* envase, caja, recipiente.

**contaminate** [kəntǽmənet] *v.* contaminar, viciar, inficionar.

**contemplate** [kántəmplet] *v.* contemplar; meditar; tener la intención de; proyectar.

**contemplation** [kantəmpléʃən] *s.* contemplación; meditación; intención, propósito.

**contemporary** [kəntémpərɛrɪ] *adj.* contemporáneo; coetáneo.

**contempt** [kəntémpt] *s.* desdén, menosprecio; desprecio; **— of court** contumacia.

**contemptible** [kəntémptəb!] *adj.* despreciable, vil.

**contemptuous** [kəntémptʃuəs] *adj.* desdeñoso.

**contend** [kənténd] *v.* contender; competir; argüir; altercar; sostener, afirmar.

**content** [kántɛnt] *s.* contenido; sustancia; capacidad, volumen; **-s** contenido; **table of -s** tabla de materias, índice general.

**content** [kəntént] *adj.* contento; satisfecho; *s.* contento; satisfacción; **to one's heart's —** a pedir de boca; hasta saciarse; a su entera satisfacción; *v.* contentar; satisfacer.

**contented** [kənténtɪd] *adj.* contento, satisfecho.

**contention** [kənténʃən] *s.* contención, contienda, disputa, controversia; tema, argumento; aseveración.

**contentment** [kənténtmənt] *s.* contentamiento, contento.

**contest** [kántɛst] *s.* concurso, certamen; debate; contienda; torneo; [kəntést] *v.* contender; disputar; luchar por; **to — with** competir con.

**context** [kántɛkst] *s.* contexto.

**contiguous** [kəntígjuəs] *adj.* contiguo; adyacente.

**continent** [kántənənt] *s.* continente; *adj.* continente, casto, moderado.

**continental** [kantənánt!] *adj.* & *s.* continental.

**contingency** [kəntíndʒənsɪ] *s.* contingencia, eventualidad.

**contingent** [kəntíndʒənt] *adj.* & *s.* contingente.

**continual** [kəntínjuəl] *adj.* continuo; frecuente; **-ly** *adv.* de continuo, continuamente, frecuentemente.

**continuance** [kəntínjuəns] *s.* continuación; aplazamiento.

**continuation** [kəntɪnjuéʃən] *s.* continuación.

**continue** [kəntínju] *v.* continuar.

**continuity** [kantənúətɪ] *s.* continuidad.

**continuous** [kəntínjuəs] *adj.* continuo, sin parar, sin cesar.

**contortion** [kəntórʃən] *s.* contorsión.

**contour** [kántur] *s.* contorno; perímetro.

**contraband** [kántrəbænd] *s.* contrabando.

**contract** [kántrækt] *s.* contrato, pacto, convenio; contrata; **marriage —** esponsales; [kəntrǽkt] *v.* contratar; contraer(se), encoger(se); **to — an illness** contraer una enfermedad; **to — the brows** fruncir las cejas.

**contraction** [kəntrǽkʃən] *s.* contracción.

**contractor** [kəntrǽktɚ] *s.* contratista.

**contradict** [kantrədíkt] *v.* contradecir; contrariar.

**contradiction** [kantrədíkʃən] *s.* contradicción; contrariedad.

**contradictory** [kantrədíktərɪ] *adj.* contradictorio; opuesto, contrario.

**contrary** [kántrɛrɪ] *adj.* contrario; opuesto; testarudo, obstinado; *s.* contrario; **on the —** al contrario.

**contrast** [kántræst] *s.* contraste; [kəntrǽst] *v.* contrastar.

**contravene** [kantrəvín] *v.* contravenir a; oponerse a.

**contribute** [kəntríbjut] *v.* contribuir.

**contribution** [kantrəbjúʃən] *s.* contribución; aportación; cuota; dádiva.

**contributor** [kəntríbjətɚ] *s.* contribuidor; colaborador.

**contrite** [kántraɪt] *adj.* contrito.

**contrivance** [kəntráɪvəns] *s.* traza, maquinación; artificio, invención; designio; artefacto, aparato, máquina.

**contrive** [kəntráɪv] *v.* tramar, maquinar; inventar, idear; proyectar; **to —** **to** buscar el medio de, tratar de, procurar.

**control** [kəntról] *s.* (*authority*) mando, manejo; dirección; (*instrument*) freno, regulador; restricción; *Am.* control;

**-s** mandos, controles; — **stick** palanca (de un aeroplano); — **tower** torre de mando; **to lose — of one's temper** perder la paciencia; v. gobernar, manejar, Am. controlar; regular, regularizar; restringir; contener, reprimir; tener a raya; **to — oneself** contenerse, dominarse.

**controller** [kəntrólə] s. interventor, registrador, Ríopl., C.A., Andes, Ven., Col. contralor, Ch., Méx. controlador; regulador; aparato de manejo y control.

**controversy** [kántrəvʒsɪ] s. controversia, debate, disputa.

**conundrum** [kənándrəm] s. adivinanza, acertijo.

**convalesce** [kɑnvəlés] v. convalescer.

**convene** [kənvín] v. juntar, convocar; reunirse.

**convenience** [kənvínjəns] s. conveniencia, comodidad; **at one's —** cuando le convenga a uno, cuando tenga oportunidad, cuando buenamente pueda.

**convenient** [kənvínjənt] adj. conveniente; oportuno; cómodo; a propósito; **-ly** adv. convenientemente, cómodamente.

**convent** [kánvɛnt] s. convento.

**convention** [kənvénʃən] s. convención; congreso, asamblea; convenio; costumbre, regla.

**conventional** [kənvénʃənl] adj. convencional; tradicional.

**converge** [kənvʒdʒ] v. converger o convergir.

**conversant** [kánvəsnt] adj.: **— with** versado en.

**conversation** [kɑnvəséʃən] s. conversación.

**converse** [kənvʒs] v. conversar, hablar, platicar.

**conversion** [kənvʒʒən] s. conversión.

**convert** [kánvʒt] s. converso, persona convertida; catecúmeno (converso reciente); [kənvʒt] v. convertir(se).

**convex** [kɑnvéks] adj. convexo.

**convey** [kənvé] v. llevar; transportar; transferir, traspasar; transmitir; comunicar; **to — thanks** expresar agradecimiento, dar las gracias.

**conveyance** [kənvéəns] s. vehículo; transporte; transmisión; entrega; comunicación; traspaso; escritura de propiedad o traspaso.

**convict** [kánvɪkt] s. presidiario; reo; [kənvíkt] v. convencer (de un delito), declarar culpable; probar la culpabilidad de.

**conviction** [kənvíkʃən] s. convicción; convencimiento; prueba de culpabilidad.

**convince** [kənvíns] v. convencer.

**convincing** [kənvínsɪŋ] adj. convincente.

**convocation** [kɑnvəkéʃən] s. convocación; asamblea.

**convoke** [kənvók] v. convocar.

**convoy** [kánvɔɪ] s. convoy, escolta, guardia; [kənvɔ́ɪ] v. convoyar.

**convulse** [kənváls] v. crispar; agitar; convulsionar.

**convulsion** [kənválʃən] s. convulsión, agitación.

**coo** [ku] s. arrullo; v. arrullar.

**cook** [kʊk] s. cocinero, cocinera; v. cocinar, guisar; cocer; **to — up a plan** urdir un plan.

**cookery** [kúkərɪ] s. cocina, arte de cocinar.

**cookie, cooky** [kúkɪ] s. bizcochito, bollito.

**cooking** [kúkɪŋ] s. cocina, arte culinaria; **— stove** cocina de gas, cocina eléctrica, estufa; **— utensils** batería de cocina, trastos de cocina.

**cool** [kul] adj. fresco; frío, indiferente; calmo, sereno; s. fresco, frescura; v. refrescar; enfriar; templar, calmar; **to — off** enfriarse; calmarse.

**coolant** [kúlənt] s. líquido refrigerador.

**coolness** [kúlnɪs] s. fresco, frescura; frialdad, indiferencia.

**coon** [kun] s. coatí (cuadrúpedo carnívoro); negro; **a -'s age** una eternidad, mucho tiempo.

**coop** [kup] s. jaula; **chicken —** gallinero; v. enjaular; **to — up** encerrar.

**cooperate** [koápəret] v. cooperar.

**cooperation** [koapəréʃən] s. cooperación.

**cooperative** [koápəretɪv] adj. cooperativo; s. cooperativa, sociedad cooperativa.

**coördinate** [koórdnet] v. coordinar; [koórdnɪt] adj. coordinado.

**coördination** [koordnéʃən] s. coordinación.

**cop** [kɑp] s. polizonte, policía.

**cope** [kop] v. **to — with** tener suficiente fuerza para; **I cannot — with this** no puedo con esto, no puedo dar abasto a esto.

**copious** [kópɪəs] adj. copioso, abundante.

**copper** [kápə] s. cobre; polizonte, policía; **— coin** moneda de cobre, centavo; **— kettle** marmita o caldera de cobre; adj. cobrizo.

**copy** [kápɪ] s. copia; ejemplar (de un libro); manuscrito (para el impresor); v. copiar; imitar; remedar.

**copyright** [kápɪraɪt] s. derecho de propiedad literaria; v. registrar, obtener patente de propiedad literaria.

**coquette** [kokét] s. coqueta.

**coral** [kórəl] s. coral; adj. coralino, de coral.

**cord** [kɔrd] s. cuerda; cordón, cordel; cuerda (medida de leña); tendón; **-s** pantalones de pana; **spinal —** espinazo, espina dorsal.

**cordial** [kórdʒəl] adj. & s. cordial.

**corduroy** [kɔrdərɔ́ɪ] s. pana; **-s** pantalones de pana; **— road** camino de troncos o maderos.

**core** [kor] s. corazón, centro; núcleo; esencia; v. cortar el centro o corazón de; despepitar (una manzana).

**cork** [kɔrk] s. corcho; tapón; **— tree** alcornoque; v. tapar con corcho.

**45** **cor–cou**

**CO**

**corkscrew** [kɔ́rkskru] s. tirabuzón, sacacorchos; adj. espiral, de forma espiral.

**corn** [kɔrn] s. maíz; grano, cereal; callo (de los pies o manos); — **bread** pan de maíz; — **meal** harina de maíz; v. salar, curar, acecinar.

**corned beef** [kɔ́rnd bif] s. carne de vaca curada (en salmuera y salitre).

**corner** [kɔ́rnɚ] s. (interior) rincón; rinconada; ángulo; (exterior) esquina; ángulo; (monopoly) monopolio; — **stone** piedra angular; — **table** (— **shelf,** — **bracket**) rinconera; v. arrinconar; acorralar; acaparar, monopolizar.

**cornet** [kɔrnét] s. corneta.

**cornfield** [kɔ́rnfild] s. maizal, Am. milpa.

**cornice** [kɔ́rnɪs] s. cornisa.

**corollary** [kɔ́rəlɛrɪ] s. corolario; consecuencia natural.

**coronation** [kɔrənéʃən] s. coronación.

**coronet** [kɔ́rənɪt] s. coronilla, guirnalda.

**corporal** [kɔ́rpərəl] adj. corporal; corpóreo; s. cabo (militar).

**corporation** [kɔrpəréʃən] s. corporación; sociedad mercantil.

**corps** [kor] s. cuerpo (grupo organizado); **air** — cuerpo de aviación; **army** — cuerpo de ejército.

**corpse** [kɔrps] s. cadáver.

**corpulent** [kɔ́rpjələnt] adj. corpulento.

**corpuscle** [kɔ́rpəs] s. corpúsculo.

**corral** [kərǽl] s. corral; v. acorralar.

**correct** [kərékt] v. corregir; adj. correcto; **it is** — está bien; **-ly** adv. correctamente; **-ly done** bien hecho.

**correction** [kərékʃən] s. corrección.

**correctness** [kəréktnɪs] s. corrección.

**corrector** [kəréktɚ] s. corregidor, corrector.

**correlate** [kɔ́rəlet] v. correlacionar.

**correspond** [kɔrəspánd] v. corresponder; corresponderse, cartearse, escribirse.

**correspondence** [kɔrəspándəns] s. correspondencia.

**correspondent** [kɔrəspándənt] adj. correspondiente; s. correspondiente; corresponsal.

**corresponding** [kɔrəspándɪŋ] adj. correspondiente; conforme.

**corridor** [kɔ́rədɚ] s. corredor, pasillo, pasadizo.

**corroborate** [kərábəret] v. corroborar.

**corrode** [kəród] v. corroer(se).

**corrugated iron** [kɔ́rəgetəd aɪɚn] s. hierro acanalado.

**corrupt** [kərápt] adj. corrompido; perverso, depravado; **to become** — corromperse; v. corromper; pervertir; sobornar.

**corruption** [kərápʃən] s. corrupción; soborno; descomposición.

**corset** [kɔ́rsɪt] s. corsé.

**cosmetic** [kazmétɪk] adj. & s. cosmético.

**cosmic** [kázmɪk] adj. cósmico.

**cosmonaut** [kázmənɔt] s. cosmonauta.

**cosmopolitan** [kazməpálətn̩] adj. cosmopolita.

**cost** [kɔst] s. coste, costa o costo; **at all -s** a toda costa; **to sell at** — vender al costo; v. costar; pret. & p.p. de to **cost.**

**costly** [kɔ́stlɪ] adj. costoso.

**costume** [kástjum] s. vestuario, traje, vestido; atavío; indumentaria.

**cot** [kat] s. catre; **folding** — catre de tijera.

**cottage** [kátɪdʒ] s. casita, caseta; casa de campo; — **cheese** requesón.

**cotton** [kátn̩] s. algodón; —**seed** semilla de algodón; — **wool** algodón en rama; — **yarn** hilaza.

**couch** [kaʊtʃ] s. canapé, diván; v. expresar; estar escondido o en acecho; **-ed in difficult language** expresado en lenguaje difícil.

**cough** [kɔf] s. tos; — **drop** pastilla para la tos; **whooping** — tos ferina; v. toser; **to** — **up** expectorar.

**could** [kʊd] pret. del. v. defect. **can.**

**council** [káʊnsl] s. concilio; consejo; **city** — consejo muncipal.

**councilman** [káʊnslmən] s. concejal.

**councilor** [káʊnslɚ] s. concejal.

**counsel** [káʊnsl] s. (advice) consejo; parecer, dictamen; (lawyer) abogado consultor; v. aconsejar; recomendar.

**counselor** [káʊnslɚ] s. consejero; abogado consultor.

**count** [kaʊnt] s. (reckoning) cuenta, cálculo; cómputo; (charge) cargo, acusación; (noble) count; v. contar; valer, tener importancia; **to** — **on** contar con, confiar en.

**countdown** [káʊntdaʊn] s. recuento descendiente hasta cero.

**countenance** [káʊntənəns] s. semblante, aspecto; **to give** — **to** favorecer, apoyar; aprobar; v. aprobar; favorecer, apoyar; tolerar.

**counter** [káʊntɚ] s. contador; mostrador; tablero; ficha; adj. contrario, opuesto; adv. al contrario; **to run** — **to** ser contrario a, oponerse a; v. oponerse; contradecir; **to** — **a blow** devolver un golpe.

**counteract** [kaʊntɚǽkt] v. contrarrestar, neutralizar.

**counterbalance** [kaʊntɚbǽləns] v. contrapesar; equilibrar; [káʊntɚbæləns] s. contrapeso.

**counterfeit** [káʊntɚfɪt] s. falsificación; adj. falso; falsificado, falseado; contrahecho; — **money** moneda falsa; v. contrahacer, falsificar, falsear.

**countermand** [káʊntɚmænd] s. contraorden, contramando, revocación, canceleción; [kaʊntɚmǽnd] v. contramandar, revocar, cancelar.

**counterpart** [káʊntɚpart] s. contraparte.

**counterpoise** [káʊntɚpɔɪz] s. contrapeso; v. contrapesar.

**countersign** [káʊntɚsaɪn] s. contraseña.

**countess** [káʊntɪs] s. condesa.

**countless** [káʊntlɪs] adj. incontable, innumerable.

**country** [kʌ́ntrɪ] *s.* país; tierra; patria; campo; *adj.* campestre; rural; rústico; campesino.

**countryman** [kʌ́ntrɪmən] *s.* compatriota, paisano; campesino, *Méx.*, *C.A.* ranchero, *P.R.* jíbaro; *Cuba* guajiro; *Ch.* huaso; *Arg.* gaucho; *Ec.*, *Col.* paisa.

**countryside** [kʌ́ntrɪsaɪd] *s.* campiña, campo.

**county** [kʌ́untɪ] *s.* condado (*división de un estado*).

**coup d'état** [ku detá] *s.* golpe de estado; cuartelazo.

**coupé** [kupé, kup] *s.* cupé.

**couple** [kʌ́pl̩] *s.* par; pareja; *v.* parear; unir; acoplar.

**couplet** [kʌ́plɪt] *s.* copla, versos pareados.

**coupling** [kʌ́plɪŋ] *s.* unión, conexión; acoplamiento; enganche.

**coupon** [kúpan] *s.* cupón; talón.

**courage** [kɝ́ɪdʒ] *s.* coraje, ánimo, valor.

**courageous** [kərédʒəs] *adj.* valeroso, valiente, animoso.

**courier** [kúrɪɚ] *s.* mensajero.

**course** [kors] *s.* (*way*) curso; rumbo, trayecto; (*advance*) marcha, progreso; (*mode*) método; (*study*) asignatura; (*dish*) plato (*de una comida*); **— of conduct** conducta, proceder; **golf —** campo o cancha de golf; **race —** hipódromo, pista; **in the — of a year** en el transcurso de un año; **of —** claro, por supuesto; **to follow a straight —** seguir una línea recta.

**court** [kort] *s.* patio; plazuela, plazoleta; juzgado, tribunal de justicia; corte; **tennis —** cancha para tenis; **— plaster** tela adhesiva, tafetán inglés, esparadrapo; **to pay — to** hacer la corte a, cortejar, galantear; *v.* cortejar; galantear; buscar; **to — danger** exponerse al peligro.

**courteous** [kɝ́tɪəs] *adj.* cortés.

**courtesy** [kɝ́təsɪ] *s.* cortesía, fineza, atención; reverencia.

**courtier** [kórtɪɚ] *s.* cortesano, palaciego.

**court-martial** [kórtmɑrʃəl] *s.* consejo de guerra; *v.* someter a consejo de guerra.

**courtship** [kórtʃɪp] *s.* cortejo, galanteo.

**courtyard** [kórtjɑrd] *s.* patio.

**cousin** [kʌ́zn̩] *s.* primo; prima; **first —** primo hermano, primo carnal.

**cove** [kov] *s.* cala, ensenada.

**covenant** [kʌ́vənənt] *s.* convenio, pacto; contrato.

**cover** [kʌ́vɚ] *s.* (*lid*) cubierta, tapa, tapadera; (*blanket*) cobija; cobertor; (*binding*) encuadernación; envoltura; (*pillow*) funda; (*shelter*) albergue, abrido; **table —** tapete; **to send under separate —** enviar por separado; *v.* cubrir; tapar; encubrir; abrigar, proteger; abarcar; **to — a distance** recorrer una distancia.

**coverage** [kʌ́vərɪdʒ] *s.* alcance; (*journalism*) reportaje.

**covering** [kʌ́vrɪŋ] *s.* cubierta; cober-

tura; envoltura; cobija, abrigo.

**covet** [kʌ́vɪt] *v.* codiciar; ambicionar.

**covetous** [kʌ́vɪtəs] *adj.* codicioso.

**cow** [kau] *s.* vaca; hembra (*de elefante y otros cuadrúpedos*); *v.* atemorizar, acobardar.

**coward** [káuɚd] *adj.* & *s.* cobarde.

**cowardice** [káuɚdɪs] *s.* cobardía.

**cowardliness** [káuɚdlɪnɪs] *s.* cobardía.

**cowardly** [káuɚdlɪ] *adj.* cobarde; *adv.* cobardemente.

**cowboy** [káubɔɪ] *s.* vaquero, *Am.* gaucho.

**cower** [káuɚ] *v.* agacharse (*de miedo o vergüenza*), achicarse, encogerse (*de miedo*), acobardarse.

**cowhide** [káuhaɪd] *s.* cuero de vaca, vaqueta.

**cowl** [kaul] *s.* capucha.

**coxswain** [káksən] *s.* timonel.

**coy** [kɔɪ] *adj.* recatado, esquivo, modesto; tímido; gazmoño.

**coyote** [káɪot, kaɪótɪ] *s.* coyote.

**cozy** [kózɪ] *adj.* cómodo y abrigado; cómodo y agradable.

**crab** [kræb] *s.* cangrejo; cascarrabias (*persona de mal genio*); **— apple** manzana silvestre.

**crack** [kræk] *s.* (*space*) raja, grieta, rendija; (*sound*) crujido; estallido; trueno, estampido; (*blow*) golpe; (*joke*) pulla, chanza; **at the — of dawn** al romper el alba; *adj.* excelente; *v.* rajar(se), hender(se), agrietarse; crujir; estallar; **to — a joke** soltar un chiste; **to — nuts** cascar nueces.

**crackdown** [krǽkdaun] *s.* represión severa.

**cracked** [krækt] *adj.* agrietado, rajado; quebrado; chiflado, loco.

**cracker** [krǽkɚ] *s.* galleta.

**crackle** [krǽkl̩] *s.* crujido; crepitación; chasquido; *v.* crujir, crepitar.

**cradle** [krédl̩] *s.* cuna.

**craft** [kræft] *s.* maña, destreza; astucia, artificio, cautela; arte, oficio; embarcación; embarcaciones.

**craftsman** [krǽftsmən] *s.* artesano, artífice.

**crafty** [krǽftɪ] *adj.* mañoso, astuto, cauteloso, taimado.

**crag** [kræg] *s.* risco, peñasco.

**cram** [kræm] *v.* rellenar; atestar; atracar(se), hartar(se); engullir.

**cramp** [kræmp] *s.* calambre; grapa; *v.* comprimir, apretar, estrechar; afianzar, sujetar (*con grapa*).

**cranberry** [krǽnberɪ] *s.* arándano.

**crane** [kren] *s.* grulla (*ave*); grúa (*máquina para levantar pesos*); *v.* **to — one's neck** estirar el cuello.

**cranium** [krénɪəm] *s.* cráneo.

**crank** [kræŋk] *s.* cigüeña, manubrio, manija, manivela; **he is a —** es un maniático; *v.* voltear el manubrio o la cigüeña.

**crankcase** [krǽŋkes] *s.* cárter del motor.

**crankshaft** [krǽŋkʃæft] *s.* cigüeñal.

**cranky** [krǽŋkɪ] *adj.* cascarrabias; maniático; enojadizo.

**cranny** [krǽnɪ] *s.* grieta, rendija.

**crape** [krep] *s.* crespón; crespón negro.

**crash** [kræʃ] *s.* (*noise*) estallido, golpazo, estruendo; (*collision*) choque; (*failure*) fracaso; quiebra; bancarrota; — **landing** aterrizaje violento; aterrizaje de barriga; *v.* estrellar(se); estallar; chocar; **to — an airplane** aterrizar de golpe un aeroplano; **to — into** chocar con, estrellarse contra.

**crate** [kret] *s.* canasto, cesta, jaula (*para el transporte de mercancías, etc.*); *Am.* huacal; *v.* embalar en jaula.

**crater** [krétɚ] *s.* cráter.

**cravat** [krəvǽt] *s.* corbata.

**crave** [krev] *v.* ansiar, anhelar, apetecer; **to — mercy (pardon)** pedir misericordia (perdón).

**crawl** [krɔl] *s.* marcha lenta; natación a la marinera; *v.* arrastrarse; gatear, andar a gatas; marchar lentamente; **to be -ing with ants** hormiguear, estar lleno de hormigas.

**crayon** [kréɔn] *s.* lápiz de color, *Am.* creyón; pastel; tiza, yeso.

**craze** [krez] *s.* manía, locura; moda; antojo; *v.* enloquecer.

**crazy** [krézɪ] *adj.* loco; trastornado; **to go —** volverse loco, perder el juicio.

**creak** [krik] *s.* crujido, rechino, rechinamiento; *v.* crujir, rechinar.

**cream** [krim] *s.* crema; nata; — **of tomato soup** puré de tomate; **cold —** crema cosmética; **ice —** helado; *v.* desnatar; batir, mezclar (*azúcar y mantequilla*); preparar (*legumbres*) con salsa de crema.

**creamery** [krímərɪ] *s.* lechería, quesería, *Am.* mantequillería.

**creamy** [krímɪ] *adj.* natoso; lleno de crema o nata.

**crease** [kris] *s.* pliegue; arruga; *v.* plegar, hacer pliegues; arrugar.

**create** [krɪét] *v.* crear.

**creation** [krɪéʃən] *s.* creación; obra.

**creative** [krɪétɪv] *adj.* creativo, creador.

**creator** [krɪétɚ] *s.* creador.

**creature** [krítʃɚ] *s.* criatura; ser viviente; animalejo.

**credence** [krídn̩s] *s.* creencia, crédito.

**credentials** [krɪdénʃəlz] *s. pl.* credenciales.

**credible** [krédəbl̩] *adj.* creíble.

**credit** [krédɪt] *s.* crédito; buena fama; — **and debit** haber y deber; activo y pasivo; — **card** tarjeta de crédito; **on —** a crédito, al fiado, a plazo; **to give —** dar crédito, creer; acreditar; abonar; **that does him —** eso le acredita; *v.* acreditar; abonar en cuenta; creer, dar crédito; atribuir.

**creditable** [krédɪtəbl̩] *adj.* loable.

**creditor** [krédɪtɚ] *s.* acreedor.

**credulous** [krédʒələs] *adj.* crédulo.

**creed** [krid] *s.* credo; creencia.

**creek** [krik, krɪk] *s.* riachuelo, arroyo.

**creep** [krip] *v.* arrastrarse; gatear, andar a gatas; trepar (*las plantas*); andar lentamente; deslizarse; sentir hormigueo (*en le cuerpo*); *s. pl.* hormigueo;

**creeper** [krípɚ] *s.* enredadera, planta trepadora.

**cremate** [krímet] *v.* incinerar.

**creosote** [kríəsot] *s.* creosota.

**crepe** [krep] = **crape.**

**crept** [krɛpt] *pret.* & *p.p. de* **to creep.**

**crescent** [krésn̩t] *adj.* creciente; *s.* luna creciente; media luna (*emblema de turcos y mahometanos*).

**crest** [krɛst] *s.* cresta; penacho; copete; cima, cumbre; timbre (*de un escudo de armas*).

**crestfallen** [kréstfɔlən] *adj.* cabizbajo, alicaído, abatido.

**cretonne** [krɪtán] *s.* cretona.

**crevice** [krévɪs] *s.* grieta, hendedura.

**crew** [kru] *s.* tripulación; cuadrilla (*de obreros*); *pret. de* **to crow.**

**crib** [krɪb] *s.* camita de niño; pesebre; granero, arcón; armazón (*usado en la construcción de edificios*); traducción o clave fraudulenta (*en un examen*); *v.* enjaular; usar traducción o clave fraudulenta (*en un examen*).

**cricket** [kríkɪt] *s.* grillo; vilorta (*juego*).

**crime** [kraɪm] *s.* crimen.

**criminal** [krímən̩l] *adj.* & *s.* criminal.

**crimp** [krɪmp] *v.* rizar; *s.* rizo.

**crimson** [krímzn̩] *adj.* & *s.* carmesí.

**cringe** [krɪndʒ] *v.* encogerse; arrastrarse.

**cripple** [krípl̩] *s.* cojo; manco; tullido; baldado, inválido; *v.* estropear; mutilar, derrengar; baldar; incapacitar.

**crisis** [kráɪsɪs] *s.* crisis.

**crisp** [krɪsp] *adj.* (*brittle*) quebradizo; tieso; bien tostado; (*curly*) crespo, encrespado; — **answer** contestación aguda; — **wind** brisa refrescante; *v.* encrespar.

**criterion** [kraɪtírɪən] *s.* criterio.

**critic** [krítɪk] *s.* crítico; criticón.

**critical** [krítɪkl̩] *adj.* crítico; criticador, criticón.

**criticism** [krítəsɪzəm] *s.* crítica; criticismo.

**criticize** [krítəsaɪz] *v.* criticar; censurar.

**croak** [krok] *v.* croar; graznar; *s.* canto de ranas; graznido.

**crochet** [kroʃé] *s.* labor de gancho; — **hook** aguja de gancho; *v.* hacer labor de gancho.

**crock** [krak] *s.* vasija de loza, jarra.

**crockery** [krákərɪ] *s.* loza.

**crocodile** [krákədaɪl] *s.* cocodrilo, *Am.* caimán.

**crony** [krónɪ] *s.* compadre, compinche, camarada, compañero.

**crook** [krʊk] *s.* (*thief*) falsario; estafador, maleante, pícaro; (*curve*) curva, vuelta; recodo; gancho; **shepherd's —** cayado; *v.* torcer(se); **to — one's arm** doblar el brazo o codo.

**crooked** [krúkɪd] *adj.* torcido; curvo, encorvado, *Am.* chueco; *Ríopl.* chingado; falso, fraudulento.

**croon** [krun] *v.* cantar "tristes" (*con exagerado patetismo*).

**crop** [krap] *s.* cosecha; buche (*de ave*); látigo, *Am.* cuarta; — **of hair** cabe-

llera; *v.* segar; recortar; rapar; **to —
out** aparecer, asomar; **to — up** brotar, manifestarse inesperadamente.

**cross** [krɔs] *s.* cruz; cruce; cruzamiento
(*de razas*); mezcla; *v.* cruzar(se); atravesar(se); santiguar(se); encontrarse;
contrariar; *adj.* en cruz, cruzado,
transversal; malhumorado; **cross-
country** a campo traviesa; **cross-
examine** *v.* interrogar, repreguntar;
**cross-eyed** bizco; **—word puzzle**
crucigrama.

**crossbar** [krɔ́sbɑr] *s.* travesaño.

**crossing** [krɔ́siŋ] *s.* cruce; cruzamiento;
encrucijada, crucero; travesía; **railroad —** cruce; **river —** vado.

**crossroad** [krɔ́srod] *s.* vía transversal,
encrucijada, crucero.

**cross section** [krés sékʃən] *s.* corte
transversal; sección transversal.

**crouch** [krautʃ] *v.* agacharse, agazaparse.

**crow** [kro] *s.* cuervo; canto del gallo;
**crow's-foot** pata de gallo (*arrugas en
el rabo del ojo*); *v.* cantar (*el gallo*); cacarear; jactarse, hacer alarde.

**crowbar** [króbɑr] *s.* barra, palanca de
hierro.

**crowd** [kraud] *s.* muchedumbre; gentío,
gente; cuadrilla, pandilla; grupo; *v.*
agolparse, apiñar(se); estrujar, empujar.

**crowded** [kráudɪd] *adj.* atestado, lleno,
apiñado.

**crown** [kraun] *s.* corona; copa (*de sombrero*); cima; *v.* coronar.

**crucible** [krúsəbl] *s.* crisol.

**crucifix** [krúsəfɪks] *s.* crucifijo.

**crucify** [krúsəfai] *v.* crucificar.

**crude** [krud] *adj.* basto, tosco, rudo; inculto; **— oil** petróleo crudo; **— sugar**
azúcar bruto, azúcar crudo.

**cruel** [krúəl] *adj.* cruel.

**cruelty** [krúəlti] *s.* crueldad.

**cruet** [krúit] *s.* ampolla (*pequeña vasija
de cristal*); vinajera (*para servir vino en
la misa*); **oil —** aceitera; **vinegar —**
vinagrera.

**cruise** [kruz] *s.* travesía, viaje por mar;
excursión; *v.* navegar.

**cruiser** [krúzɚ] *s.* crucero (*buque*).

**crumb** [krʌm] *s.* migaja; miga; mendrugo; *v.* desmenuzar, desmigajar.

**crumble** [krʌ́mbl] *v.* desmenuzar(se);
desmoronarse.

**crumple** [krʌ́mpl] *v.* arrugar(se); ajar,
apabullar.

**crunch** [krʌntʃ] *v.* crujir; mascullar.

**crusade** [kruséd] *s.* cruzada; *v.* hacer
una campaña; hacer una cruzada.

**crusader** [kruségɚ] *s.* cruzado.

**crush** [krʌʃ] *s.* compresión, presión; estrujamiento, apiñamiento de gente; *v.*
estrujar; aplastar; majar; subyugar;
**to — stone** moler piedra.

**crust** [krʌst] *s.* corteza (*de pan, queso,
etc.*); costra; mendrugo; *v.* encostrarse, cubrir(se) de costra.

**crusty** [krʌ́sti] *adj.* costroso.

**crutch** [krʌtʃ] *s.* muleta.

**cry** [krai] *s.* grito; lloro, lamento; **a far**

**— from** muy distante de, muy lejos
de; *v.* gritar; llorar; clamar; exclamar;
vocear; **to — for help** pedir socorro.

**crystal** [krístl] *s.* cristal; **— clear** cristalino.

**crystalline** [krístlɪn] *adj.* cristalino.

**crystallize** [krístlaiz] *v.* cristalizar(se).

**cub** [kʌb] *s.* cachorro (*de oso, tigre, lobo,
león*); **— reporter** reportero novato.

**Cuban** [kjúbən] *adj. & s.* cubano.

**cube** [kjub] *s.* cubo; **— root** raíz cúbica.

**cubic** [kjúbɪk] *adj.* cúbico.

**cubism** [kjúbɪzm] *s.* cubismo.

**cuckoo** [kúku] *s.* cuco, cuclillo; *adj.* tocado, chiflado, medio loco.

**cucumber** [kjúkʌmbɚ] *s.* pepino.

**cud** [kʌd] *s.* rumia; **to chew the —**
rumiar.

**cuddle** [kʌ́dl] *v.* abrazar, tener en
brazos; estar abrazados.

**cudgel** [kʌ́dʒəl] *s.* garrote; porra; *v.* aporrear, apalear.

**cue** [kju] *s.* señal, indicación; pie (*últimas palabras de un parlamento que
sirven de señal en el teatro*); **billiard
—** taco de billar.

**cuff** [kʌf] *s.* puño (*de camisa o de vestido*);
doblez (*del pantalón*); bofetada; *v.*
abofetear, dar de bofetadas.

**cull** [kʌl] *v.* entresacar; extraer.

**culminate** [kʌ́lmənet] *v.* culminar.

**culprit** [kʌ́lprɪt] *s.* reo, delincuente, culpable.

**cult** [kʌlt] *s.* culto; secta religiosa.

**cultivate** [kʌ́ltəvet] *v.* cultivar; labrar,
barbechar.

**cultivated** [kʌ́ltəvetɪd] *adj.* cultivado;
culto.

**cultivation** [kʌltəvéʃən] *s.* cultivación,
cultivo; cultura.

**cultivator** [kʌ́ltəvetɚ] *s.* cultivador; máquina cultivadora.

**culture** [kʌ́ltʃɚ] *s.* cultura; cultivo.

**cultured** [kʌ́ltʃɚd] *adj.* culto; cultivado.

**cumbersome** [kʌ́mbɚsəm] *adj.* engorroso, embarazoso, incómodo.

**cunning** [kʌ́nɪŋ] *adj.* astuto, socarrón,
sagaz, taimado; diestro; cuco, mono,
gracioso; *s.* astucia, maña, sagacidad.

**cup** [kʌp] *s.* taza, pocillo; copa (*trofeo*).

**cupboard** [kʌ́bɚd] *s.* armario, aparador;
alacena.

**cur** [kɝ] *s.* perro mestizo, *Am.* perro
chusco; villano, vil, cobarde.

**curate** [kjúrɪt] *s.* cura.

**curator** [kjúretɚ] *s.* conservador.

**curb** [kɝb] *s.* reborde, encintado (*de la
acera*); *Ríopl.* cordón de la acera; freno,
restricción; barbada (*del freno de un
caballo*); brocal de pozo; *v.* refrenar,
reprimir.

**curd** [kɝd] *s.* cuajada; *v.* cuajar(se), coagular(se).

**curdle** [kɝ́dl] *v.* cuajar(se), coagular(se).

**cure** [kjur] *s.* cura, curación; remedio;
*v.* curar(se); sanar

**curfew** [kɝ́fju] *s.* queda.

**curio** [kjúrio] *s.* curiosidad, objeto raro
y curioso.

**curiosity** [kjuriásəti] *s.* curiosidad;
rareza.

**curious** [kjúrɪəs] *adj.* curioso; extraño, raro.

**curl** [kɜˈl] *s.* rizo, bucle; espiral (*de humo*); *v.* rizar(se); ensortijar(se); enroscar(se); retorcerse, alzarse en espirales (*el humo*).

**curly** [kɜˈlɪ] *adj.* rizo, rizoso, rizado, crespo, *Am.* chino.

**currant** [kɜˈənt] *s.* grosella; — **bush** grosellero.

**currency** [kɜˈənsɪ] *s.* moneda corriente; circulación; **paper** — papel moneda.

**current** [kɜˈənt] *adj.* corriente; común, prevaleciente, en boga; *s.* corriente.

**curriculum** [kəríkjələm] *s.* programa de estudios.

**curse** [kɜˈs] *s.* maldición; calamidad; *v.* maldecir.

**cursed** [kɜˈst] *adj.* maldito.

**cursive** [kɜˈsɪv] *adj.* cursivo.

**curt** [kɜˈt] *adj.* corto; brusco.

**curtail** [kɜˈtél] *v.* cercenar; acortar; restringir, reducir.

**curtain** [kɜˈtn̩] *s.* cortina; telón (*de teatro*); *v.* poner cortinas.

**curvature** [kɜˈvətʃɚ] *s.* curvatura.

**curve** [kɜˈv] *s.* curva; *v.* encorvar(se); torcer(se); doblar(se).

**curved** [kɜˈvd] *adj.* encorvado; torcido; curvo, corvo, *Méx.*, *C.A.* chueco.

**cushion** [kúʃən] *s.* cojín; almohadilla; almohadón; amortiguador (*para amortiguar un sonido o golpe*); *v.* acojinar; amortiguar (*un choque*).

**custard** [kʌ́stəd] *s.* flan, natillas.

**custody** [kʌ́stədɪ] *s.* custodia, cargo, cuidado; **to hold in** — custodiar.

**custom** [kʌ́stəm] *s.* costumbre, hábito, uso, usanza; **-s** derechos de aduana; — **made** hecho a la medida; — **tailor** maestro sastre; — **built** construido según pedido.

**customary** [kʌ́stəmɛrɪ] *adj.* acostumbrado, habitual, usual, de costumbre.

**customer** [kʌ́stəmɚ] *s.* parroquiano, cliente, marchante.

**customhouse** [kʌ́stəmhaʊs] *s.* aduana; — **official** aduanero; — **mark** marchamo.

**cut** [kʌt] *s.* corte (*m.*); cortadura, *Am.* cortada; rebanada, tajada; rebaja, reducción (*de precios, sueldos*); hechura (*de un traje*); ausencia (*de la clase*); grabado; **short** — atajo, camino corto; *v.* cortar; tajar; labrar, tallar; segar; rebajar, reducir (*precios, sueldos*); negar el saludo a; alzar (*los naipes*); **to** — **across** cruzar, atravesar; **to** — **capers** hacer cabriolas, cabriolar; **to** — **class** faltar a la clase; **to** — **out** recortar; excluir; **to be** — **out for** estar hecho para, tener vocación para; *pret. & p.p. de* **to cut.**

**cute** [kjut] *adj.* mono, cuco; astuto.

**cuticle** [kjútɪk|] *s.* cutícula.

**cutlery** [kʌ́tlərɪ] *s.* cuchillería, cuchillos.

**cutlet** [kʌ́tlɪt] *s.* chuleta.

**cutter** [kʌ́tɚ] *s.* cortador; máquina para cortar; trineo; **wood** — leñador; **coast guard** — barco guardacostas.

**cutting** [kʌ́tɪŋ] *adj.* cortante; penetrante; mordaz, sarcástico.

**cybernetics** [saɪbɚnétɪks] *s.* cibernética.

**cycle** [sáɪk|] *s.* ciclo.

**cyclone** [sáɪklon] *s.* ciclón; huracán.

**cylinder** [sílɪndɚ] *s.* cilindro.

**cylindrical** [sɪlíndrɪk|] *adj.* cilíndrico.

**cymbal** [símb|] *s.* címbalo, platillo; **to play the -s** tocar los platillos.

**cynic** [sínɪk] *s.* cínico.

**cynical** [sínɪk|] *adj.* cínico.

**cynicism** [sínəsɪzəm] *s.* cinismo.

**cypress** [sáɪprəs] *s.* ciprés.

**cyst** [sɪst] *s.* quiste.

# D

**dad** [dæd] *s.* papá, tata; **daddy** *s.* papaíto o papacito, tata, tatita, *Am.* taita.

**daffodil** [dǽfədɪl] *s.* narciso.

**dagger** [dǽgɚ] *s.* daga; puñal; **to look -s at** traspasar con la mirada.

**daily** [délɪ] *adj.* diario; *adv.* diariamente; *s.* diario, periódico.

**dainty** [déntɪ] *adj.* delicado, fino, primoroso, exquisito; *s.* golosina, manjar exquisito.

**dairy** [dérɪ] *s.* lechería, vaquería; quesería, quesera.

**daisy** [dézɪ] *s.* margarita, maya.

**dale** [del] *s.* cañada.

**dally** [dǽlɪ] *v.* juguetear; holgazanear; entretenerse, tardar; malgastar el tiempo.

**dam** [dæm] *s.* presa, represa; *v.* represar, estancar.

**damage** [dǽmɪdʒ] *s.* daño; perjuicio; avería; **to pay for -s** indemnizar, pagar los daños y perjuicios; *v.* dañar(se); averiar(se).

**dame** [dem] *s.* dama, señora; **old** — vieja.

**damn** [dæm] *v.* maldecir; condenar; blasfemar; — **it** ¡maldito sea!

**damnation** [dæmnéʃən] *s.* condenación, perdición.

**damp** [dæmp] *adj.* húmedo; mojado; *s.* humedad; *v.* humedecer, mojar.

**dampen** [dǽmpən] *v.* mojar, humedecer; desalentar; amortiguar.

**dampness** [dǽmpnɪs] *s.* humedad.

**damsel** [dǽmz|] *s.* damisela.

**dance** [dæns] *s.* baile; danza; — **music** música de baile; *v.* bailar; danzar.

**dancer** [dǽnsɚ] *s.* bailador; bailarín, bailarina; danzante.

**dandelion** [dǽnd|aɪən] *s.* diente de león.

**dandruff** [dǽndrəf] *s.* caspa.

**dandy** [dǽndɪ] *s.* currutaco, majo, afectado; chulo; *adj.* elegante, excelente.

**danger** [déndʒɚ] *s.* peligro, riesgo.

**dangerous** [déndʒərəs] *adj.* peligroso; arriesgado; **-ly** *adv.* peligrosamente; **-ly ill** gravemente enfermo.

**dangle** [dǽŋg|] *v.* pender, colgar, bambolear(se) (*en el aire*).

**dapple(d)** [dǽp|(d)] *adj.* rodado, con manchas (*dícese de los caballos*); **dapple-grey** rucio rodado, tordo, tordillo.

**dare** [dɛr] *s.* desafío, reto, provocación; —**devil** atrevido, osado; *v.* atreverse, osar; desafiar.

**daring** [dɛ́rɪŋ] *s.* atrevimiento, osadía; *adj.* osado, atrevido, arrojado.

**dark** [dɑrk] *adj.* obscuro; sombrío; — **horse** caballo desconocido (*que gana inesperadamente la carrera*); candidato nombrado inesperadamente; — **secret** secreto profundo; enigma; **dark-skinned** moreno, trigueño; *s.* obscuridad; sombra.

**darken** [dɑ́rkən] *v.* obscurecer(se); nublarse.

**darkness** [dɑ́rknɪs] *s.* obscuridad; tinieblas; sombra.

**darky** [dɑ́rkɪ] *s.* negro (*persona*).

**darling** [dɑ́rlɪŋ] *adj.* & *s.* amado, querido; **my** — vida mía (*o* mi vida), amor mío.

**darn** [dɑrn] *s.* zurcido; **it is not worth a** — no vale un comino, no vale un pito; *v.* zurcir;—! ¡caramba! ¡canastos!; **-ing needle** aguja de zurcir.

**dart** [dɑrt] *s.* dardo, flecha; sisa (*en un vestido*); movimiento rápido; *v.* lanzar(se); flechar; **to** — **out** salir como una flecha; **to** — **in and out** entrar y salir precipitadamente.

**dash** [dæʃ] *s.* (*line*) raya; (*run*) carrera corta; (*vigor*) ímpetu; (*grace*) garbo; pizca (*de sal, azúcar, etc.*); rociada (*de agua*); —**board** tablero de instrumentos; **with a** — **of the pen** de una plumada; *v.* lanzar(se); echar(se); estrellar(se); salpicar; frustrar (*esperanzas*); **to** — **by** pasar corriendo; **to** — **out** salir a la carrera; **to** — **off a letter** escribir de prisa una carta.

**data** [dɛ́tə] *s. pl.* datos.

**date** [det] *s.* (*time*) fecha; (*statement*) data; (*appointment*) cita, compromiso; (*fruit*) dátil; **out of** — anticuado, desusado; fuera de moda; **up to** — al día, moderno; **up to this** — hasta ahora, hasta la fecha; *v.* fechar; **to** — **from** datar de; remontarse a.

**daub** [dɔb] *v.* embarrar, untar; pintarrajear.

**daughter** [dɔ́tə] *s.* hija; **daughter-in-law** nuera.

**daunt** [dɔnt] *v.* intimidar, asustar, espantar; desanimar.

**dauntless** [dɔ́ntlɪs] *adj.* denodado, intrépido

**davenport** [dǽvənport] *s.* sofá.

**dawn** [dɔn] *s.* alba; amanecer, madrugada; *v.* amanecer; alborear, rayar (*el día*); **it just -ed upon me** acabo de darme cuenta.

**day** [de] *s.* día; — **after tomorrow** pasado mañana; — **before yesterday** anteayer o antier; — **laborer** jornalero; **by** — de día; **by the** — por día; **eight-hour** — jornada de ocho horas; **to win the** — ganar la jornada, triunfar.

**daybreak** [débrek] *s.* amanecer, alba; **at** — al amanecer, al romper el día, al rayar el día.

**daylight** [délaɪt] *s.* luz del día.

**daytime** [détaɪm] *s.* día (*tiempo de luz natural*); **in the** — durante el día; de

día.

**daze** [dez] *s.* aturdimiento; deslumbramiento; **to be in a** — estar aturdido; *v.* aturdir; ofuscar; deslumbrar.

**dazzle** [dǽzl] *s.* brillantez; *v.* deslumbrar; ofuscar.

**deacon** [díkən] *s.* diácono.

**dead** [dɛd] *adj.* muerto; — **air** aire viciado o estancado; — **letter** carta no reclamada; — **loss** pérdida absoluta; *adv.* completamente, absolutamente; sumamente, muy; — **sure** completamente seguro; — **tired** muerto de cansancio; *s.* **the** — los muertos; **in the** — **of the night** en el sigilo de la noche; **in the** — **of winter** en lo más crudo del invierno.

**deaden** [dɛ́dn̩] *v.* amortiguar.

**deadhead** [dɛ́dhɛd] *s.* persona que no paga la entrada; colado.

**deadly** [dɛ́dlɪ] *adj.* mortal; fatal; como la muerte, cadavérico; *adv.* mortalmente; — **dull** sumamente aburrido.

**deaf** [dɛf] *adj.* sordo; **deaf-mute** *s.* & *adj.* sordomudo.

**deafen** [dɛ́fən] *v.* ensordecer; amortiguar, apagar (*un sonido*).

**deafening** [dɛ́fənɪŋ] *adj.* ensordecedor, estruendoso.

**deafness** [dɛ́fnɪs] *s.* sordera.

**deal** [dil] *s.* trato, negocio; mano (*en el juego de naipes*); distribución, reparto (*de los naipes*); **a great** — **of** una gran cantidad de, mucho; **to give a square** — tratar con equidad; *v.* tallar (*en juegos de naipes*); distribuir, repartir; dar (*un golpe*); **to** — **in** comerciar en; **to** — **with** tratar de (*un asunto*); tratar con; negociar con.

**dealer** [dílə] *s.* negociante, comerciante, tratante; tallador (*en el juego de naipes*).

**dealings** [dílɪŋz] *s. pl.* relaciones (*comerciales o amistosas*); comercio, tratos; negocios.

**dealt** [dɛlt] *pret.* & *p.p. de* **to deal**.

**dean** [din] *s.* deán (*dignidad eclesiástica*); decano (*de universidad*).

**dear** [dɪr] *adj.* (*beloved*) querido, amado; (*expensive*) caro; costoso; *adv.* caro; — **me!** ¡Dios mío!; **oh** —! ¡ay!; **my** — querido mío; **Dear Sir** Muy señor mío; **-ly** *adv.* cariñosamente; a precio alto; **my -ly beloved** muy amado mío; muy amados míos.

**dearth** [dɜθ] *s.* escasez, carestía, insuficiencia.

**death** [dɛθ] *s.* muerte; mortandad; — **rate** mortalidad.

**deathbed** [dɛ́θbɛd] *s.* lecho de muerte.

**debase** [dɪbés] *v.* rebajar el valor de; degradar, humillar, envilecer.

**debatable** [dɪbétəbl] *adj.* discutible, disputable.

**debate** [dɪbét] *s.* debate, discusión; *v.* debatir, discutir; considerar; deliberar.

**debilitate** [dəbílətet] *v.* debilitar.

**debit** [débɪt] *s.* débito, adeudo, cargo; debe (*de una cuenta*); pasivo (*en contabilidad*); *v.* adeudar, cargar en cuenta.

**debriefing** [dibrífɪŋ] *s.* informe de vuelo bajo interrogación; informe.

**debris** [dəbrí] *s.* escombros; ruinas.

**debt** [dɛt] *s.* deuda; adeudo; débito; **bad — cuenta** incobrable; **to run into —** adeudarse, entramparse, cargarse de deudas.

**debtor** [détɚ] *s.* deudor.

**debunk** [dibʌ́ŋk] *v.* desbaratar; desenmascarar.

**debut** [dɪbjú] *s.* estreno; **to make a —** debutar, estrenarse.

**decade** [déked] *s.* década, decenio.

**decadence** [dɪkédn̩s] *s.* decadencia.

**decanter** [dɪkǽntɚ] *s.* garrafa; **large —** garrafón.

**decay** [dɪké] *s.* decaimiento; decadencia, ruina; podredumbre; caries (*de la dentadura*); *v.* decaer; venir a menos; pudrir(se) o podrir(se).

**decease** [dɪsís] *s.* muerte, fallecimiento; *v.* morir, fallecer.

**deceased** [dɪsíst] *adj. & s.* muerto, difunto.

**deceit** [dɪsít] *s.* engaño; fraude; trampa.

**deceitful** [dɪsítfəl] *adj.* engañador; tramposo; engañoso.

**deceive** [dɪsív] *v.* engañar.

**December** [dɪsémbɚ] *s.* diciembre.

**decency** [dísn̩sɪ] *s.* decencia.

**decent** [dísn̩t] *adj.* decente; decoroso.

**decibel** [désɪbɛl] *s.* decibelio; decibel.

**decide** [dɪsáɪd] *v.* decidir, resolver, determinar; **to — to** resolverse a, decidirse a.

**decided** [dɪsáɪdɪd] *adj.* decidido, resuelto.

**decimal** [désəml̩] *adj.* decimal; *s.* decimal, fracción decimal.

**decipher** [dɪsáɪfɚ] *v.* descifrar.

**decision** [dɪsíʒən] *s.* decisión, resolución.

**decisive** [dɪsáɪsɪv] *adj.* decisivo; terminante.

**deck** [dɛk] *s.* cubierta (*de un buque*); baraja; *v.* cubrir; ataviar; **to — one-self out** emperifollarse.

**declaration** [dɛkləréʃən] *s.* declaración.

**declare** [dɪklǽr] *v.* declarar; afirmar.

**decline** [dɪkláɪn] *s.* declinación; decadencia; mengua; baja (*de precios*); *v.* declinar; decaer; rehusar; **to — to do something** negarse a hacer algo.

**declivity** [dɪklívətɪ] *s.* declive.

**décolleté** [dekalté] *adj.* escotado.

**decompose** [dikəmpóz] *v.* descomponer(se); corromper(se), pudrir(se).

**decorate** [dékəret] *v.* decorar, adornar; condecorar.

**decoration** [dɛkəréʃən] *s.* decoración; adorno; insignia, condecoración.

**decorative** [dékəretɪv] *adj.* decorativo; ornamental.

**decorum** [dɪkórəm] *s.* decoro; circunspección.

**decoy** [dɪkɔ́ɪ] *s.* reclamo, señuelo, figura de ave (*que sirve para atraer aves*); cebo (*artificio para atraer con engaño*); trampa, lazo; *v.* atraer con señuelo o engaño.

**decrease** [díkris] *s.* disminución o dimi-

nución; merma; mengua; [dikrís] *v.* disminuir(se); mermar; menguar.

**decree** [dɪkrí] *s.* decreto; *v.* decretar; mandar.

**decrepit** [dɪkrépɪt] *adj.* decrépito.

**dedicate** [dédəket] *v.* dedicar.

**dedication** [dɛdəkéʃən] *s.* dedicación; dedicatoria.

**deduce** [dɪdjús] *v.* deducir, inferir.

**deduct** [dɪdʌ́kt] *v.* deducir, descontar, rebajar.

**deduction** [dɪdʌ́kʃən] *s.* deducción; rebaja, descuento.

**deed** [did] *s.* hecho, acción, acto; hazaña; escritura (*de venta o compra*).

**deem** [dim] *v.* juzgar, creer, considerar.

**deep** [dip] *adj.* (*down*) hondo; profundo; (*obscure*) oscuro; (*tone*) grave, bajo; **— in debt** cargado de deudas; **— in thought** absorto; **— mourning** luto riguroso; **to go off the — end** echarse a pique; caer en el abismo; **— into the night** en las tinieblas de la noche; *s.* **the —** el mar; **-ly** *adv.* profundamente, hondamente; intensamente.

**deepen** [dípən] *v.* ahondar, profundizar.

**deer** [dɪr] *s.* ciervo, venado; **—skin** piel o cuero de venado.

**deface** [dɪfés] *v.* desfigurar, estropear, mutilar.

**defame** [dɪfém] *v.* difamar, calumniar, denigrar.

**default** [dɪfɔ́lt] *s.* falla, falta, negligencia (*de un deber, pago, obligación*); deficiencia; *v.* fallar, faltar (*en el cumplimiento de un deber, pago, obligación*); no comparecer a la cita de un tribunal.

**defeat** [dɪfít] *s.* derrota, vencimiento; frustración (*de un plan*); *v.* vencer, derrotar; frustrar.

**defect** [dɪfékt] *s.* defecto.

**defective** [dɪféktɪv] *adj.* defectuoso; incompleto; subnormal, falto de inteligencia; **— verb** verbo defectivo.

**defend** [dɪfénd] *v.* defender.

**defendant** [dɪféndənt] *s.* acusado, demandado, procesado.

**defender** [dɪféndɚ] *s.* defensor; abogado defensor.

**defense** [dɪféns] *s.* defensa.

**defenseless** [dɪfénslɪs] *adj.* indefenso, inerme.

**defensive** [dɪfénsɪv] *adj.* defensivo; *s.* defensiva.

**defer** [dɪfɚ́] *v.* diferir, posponer, aplazar; **to — to another's opinion** remitirse o ceder al dictamen de otro.

**defiance** [dɪfáɪəns] *s.* reto, desafío, provocación; oposición; **in — of** en abierta oposición con, a despecho de.

**deficiency** [dɪfíʃənsɪ] *s.* deficiencia; defecto; déficit.

**deficient** [dɪfíʃənt] *adj.* deficiente; defectuoso.

**deficit** [défəsɪt] *s.* déficit.

**defile** [dɪfáɪl] *v.* viciar, corromper; profanar; manchar, ensuciar.

**define** [dɪfáɪn] *v.* definir.

**definite** [défənɪt] *adj.* definido; claro, preciso; fijo; **— article** artículo deter-

minado o definido; **-ly** *adv.* definida-
mente; claramente; **-ly not** terminan-
temente no.
**definition** [dɛfəníʃən] *s.* definición.
**definitive** [dɪfínɪtɪv] *adj.* definitivo.
**deflect** [dɪflɛ́kt] *v.* desviar(se).
**deform** [dɪfɔ́rm] *v.* deformar; desfigurar, afear.
**deformed** [dɪfɔ́rmd] *adj.* deforme, disforme; deformado; desfigurado.
**deformity** [dɪfɔ́rmətɪ] *s.* deformidad;
deformación.
**defraud** [dɪfrɔ́d] *v.* defraudar.
**defray** [dɪfré] *v.* sufragar, costear, pagar
(*gastos*).
**deft** [dɛft] *adj.* diestro, ágil.
**defunct** [dɪfʌ́ŋkt] *adj.* difunto.
**defy** [dɪfáɪ] *v.* desafiar; retar; oponerse
a, resistirse a.
**degenerate** [dɪdʒénərɪt] *adj.* & *s.* degenerado; [dɪdʒénəret] *v.* degenerar.
**degradation** [dɛgrədéʃən] *s.* degrada-
ción; envilecimiento.
**degrade** [dɪgréd] *v.* degradar; envilecer,
rebajar.
**degree** [dɪgrí] *s.* grado; rango; **by -s**
gradualmente; **to get a — graduarse.**
**dehydrate** [dɪháɪdret] *v.* deshidratar-
(se).
**deign** [den] *v.* dignarse, condescender.
**deity** [díətɪ] *s.* deidad.
**dejected** [dɪdʒɛ́ktɪd] *adj.* abatido.
**dejection** [dɪdʒɛ́kʃən] *s.* abatimiento,
melancolía, depresión.
**delay** [dɪlé] *s.* demora, tardanza, dilación, retraso; *v.* demorar: retardar,
dilatar; diferir; tardarse.
**delayed action** [dɪléd ǽkʃən] *adj.* atrasado; retardado.
**delegate** [déləget] *s.* delegado, representante; *v.* delegar, diputar.
**delegation** [deləgéʃən] *s.* delegación,
diputación.
**deletion** [dɪlíʃən] *s.* suspensión.
**deliberate** [dɪlíbərɪt] *adj.* deliberado,
premeditado; cauto, prudente; lento;
**-ly** *adv.* deliberadamente; con preme-
ditación; [dɪlíbəret] *v.* deliberar.
**deliberation** [dɪlɪbəréʃən] *s.* delibera-
ción.
**delicacy** [délǝkǝsɪ] *s.* delicadeza; sensibilidad; finura; golosina.
**delicate** [délǝkǝt] *adj.* delicado; frágil;
exquisito.
**delicatessen** [dɛlǝkǝtésn̩] *s.* tienda de
fiambres, queso, ensaladas, etc.
**delicious** [dɪlíʃǝs] *adj.* delicioso.
**delight** [dɪláɪt] *s.* deleite; delicia; *v.*
deleitar(se); encantar; agradar; **to —
in** gozarse en, deleitarse en.
**delighted** [dɪláɪtɪd] *adj.* encantado; **to
be — to** alegrarse de, tener mucho
gusto en (*o* de).
**delightful** [dɪláɪtfǝl] *adj.* deleitoso; delicioso; ameno, agradable.
**delineate** [dɪlíniet] *v.* delinear, trazar.
**delinquent** [dɪlíŋkwǝnt] *adj.* & *s.* delincuente.
**delirious** [dɪlírɪǝs] *adj.* delirante; **to be
— delirar,** desvariar.
**delirium** [dɪlírɪǝm] *s.* delirio, desvarío.

**deliver** [dɪlívǝ] *v.* entregar; librar,
libertar; pronunciar (*un discurso*); dar
(*un golpe*).
**deliverance** [dɪlívǝrǝns] *s.* liberación,
rescate.
**deliverer** [dɪlívǝrǝ] *s.* libertador; portador, mensajero.
**delivery** [dɪlívǝrɪ] *s.* (*giving*) entrega;
(*saving*) liberación; (*birth*) parto;
(*speaking*) elocuencia, manera de hacer
una conferencia; **— service** servicio
de entrega; **— truck** camión (*o*
camioneta) de reparto; **mail —**
reparto de correo.
**dell** [dɛl] *s.* cañada, hondonada.
**delta wing** [déltǝ wɪŋ] *s.* ala en delta.
**delude** [dɪlúd] *v.* engañar.
**deluge** [déljudʒ] *s.* diluvio; *v.* inundar;
abrumar.
**delusion** [dɪlúʒǝn] *s.* ilusión; engaño,
error.
**demand** [dɪmǽnd] *s.* demanda; exigencia; solicitud; **on —** a solicitud; *v.*
demandar, reclamar; exigir.
**demanding** [dɪmǽndɪŋ] *adj.* exigente.
**demeanor** [dɪmínǝ] *s.* conducta, comportamiento, proceder.
**demented** [dɪméntɪd] *adj.* demente.
**demise** [dɪmáɪz] *s.* fallecimiento.
**demobilize** [dɪmóbl̩aɪz] *v.* demovilizar.
**democracy** [dǝmákrǝsɪ] *s.* democracia.
**democrat** [démǝkræt] *s.* demócrata.
**democratic** [demǝkrǽtɪk] *adj.* democrático.
**demolish** [dɪmálɪʃ] *v.* demoler.
**demon** [dímǝn] *s.* demonio.
**demonstrate** [démǝnstret] *v.* demostrar.
**demonstration** [demǝnstréʃǝn] *s.* demostración; prueba; (*protest*) manifestación.
**demonstrative** [dɪmánstrǝtɪv] *adj.* demostrativo; efusivo.
**den** [dɛn] *s.* guarida; escondrijo; cueva,
lugar de retiro.
**denial** [dɪnáɪǝl] *s.* negación; negativa;
**self-denial** abnegación.
**denigrate** [dénɪgret] *v.* calumniar;
ennegrecer.
**denomination** [dɪnɑmǝnéʃǝn] *s.* (*name*)
denominación; nombre; título, designación; (*sect*) secta religiosa.
**denote** [dɪnót] *v.* denotar.
**denounce** [dɪnáʊns] *v.* denunciar;
delatar, acusar.
**dense** [dɛns] *adj.* denso; espeso, apretado; estúpido.
**density** [dénsǝtɪ] *s.* densidad; estupidez.
**dent** [dɛnt] *s.* abolladura; mella; *v.*
abollar; mellar.
**dental** [déntl̩] *adj.* dental; *s.* dental,
consonante dental.
**dentifrice** [déntɪfrɪs] *s.* pasta denti-
frica; dentífrico.
**dentist** [déntɪst] *s.* dentista.
**denunciation** [dɪnʌnsɪéʃǝn] *s.* denuncia, acusación.
**deny** [dɪnáɪ] *v.* negar; rehusar; **to —
oneself** sacrificarse, abnegarse; **to —
oneself to callers** negarse a recibir
visitas.

**depart** [dɪpárt] v. partir, salir, irse; desviarse, apartarse.

**departed** [dɪpártɪd] adj. ido; ausente; difunto.

**department** [dɪpártmənt] s. departamento; distrito; ramo, división; — **store** almacén.

**departure** [dɪpártʃɚ] s. salida, partida; desviación.

**depend** [dɪpénd] v. depender; **to — on** depender de; contar con, confiar en.

**dependable** [dɪpéndəbl] adj. seguro, fidedigno, digno de confianza.

**dependence** [dɪpéndəns] s. dependencia; confianza.

**dependency** [dɪpéndənsɪ] s. dependencia; sucursal.

**dependent** [dɪpéndənt] adj. dependiente; subordinado; s. dependiente, familiar.

**depict** [dɪpíkt] v. pintar, describir; representar.

**depilatory** [dɪpílətorɪ] s. depilatorio.

**deplete** [dɪplít] v. agotar; vaciar.

**deplorable** [dɪplórəbl] adj. deplorable, lamentable.

**deplore** [dɪplór] v. deplorar.

**deport** [dɪpórt] v. deportar; **to — oneself well** portarse bien.

**deportment** [dɪpórtmənt] s. comportamiento, conducta.

**depose** [dɪpóz] v. deponer; declarar, atestiguar.

**deposit** [dɪpázɪt] s. depósito; v. depositar.

**deposition** [dɛpəzíʃən] s. deposición; declaración.

**depositor** [dɪpázɪtɚ] s. depositador.

**depot** [dípo] s. depósito; almacén; estación de ferrocarril.

**deprecate** [déprɪket] v. desaprobar.

**depreciate** [dɪpríʃɪet] v. depreciar; bajar de precio, abaratar(se); menospreciar.

**depress** [dɪprés] v. deprimir; abatir; desanimar; depreciar, rebajar el valor de.

**depressed** [dɪprést] adj. abatido, decaído.

**depressing** [dɪprésɪŋ] adj. deprimente.

**depression** [dɪpréʃən] s. depresión; decaimiento, abatimiento; rebaja (de precios).

**deprive** [dɪpráɪv] v. privar.

**depth** [dɛpθ] s. profundidad; hondura; fondo; longitud (de un solar); gravedad (de los sonidos); viveza (de los colores); **in the — of the night** en las tinieblas de la noche; **in the — of winter** en lo más crudo del invierno.

**deputation** [dɛpjətéʃən] s. diputación, delegación; comisión.

**depute** [dɪpjút] v. diputar, delegar.

**deputy** [dépjətɪ] s. diputado; agente; delegado.

**derange** [dɪréndʒ] v. trastornar, desordenar.

**derby** [dɝbɪ] s. sombrero hongo, Méx., Ven., Col. sombrero de bola.

**derelict** [dérɪlɪkt] adj. abandonado; negligente.

**deride** [dɪráɪd] v. escarnecer, ridiculizar, mofarse de, burlarse de.

**derision** [dɪríʒən] s. mofa, escarnio.

**derive** [dəráɪv] v. derivar(se); provenir; sacar (provecho); recibir (placer).

**dermatology** [dɚmətálədʒɪ] s. dermatología.

**derrick** [dérɪk] s. grúa; armazón (para la explotación del petróleo).

**descend** [dɪsénd] v. descender; bajar; **to — upon** caer sobre, acometer.

**descendant** [dɪséndənt] adj. & s. descendiente.

**descent** [dɪsént] s. descenso; bajada; descendencia, linaje; descendimiento; declive.

**describe** [dɪskráɪb] v. describir; trazar.

**description** [dɪskrípʃən] s. descripción; **of all -s** de todas clases.

**descriptive** [dɪskríptɪv] adj. descriptivo; — **linguistics** lingüística descriptiva.

**desert** [dézɚt] adj. desierto, despoblado; estéril; s. desierto, yermo; páramo; [dɪzɝt] v. abandonar, desamparar; desertar.

**deserter** [dɪzɝtɚ] s. desertor.

**desertion** [dɪzɝʃən] s. deserción, abandono, desamparo.

**deserve** [dɪzɝv] v. merecer.

**deserving** [dɪzɝvɪŋ] adj. meritorio; merecedor.

**design** [dɪzáɪn] s. (sketch) dibujo, diseño; (plan) designio, propósito, intención; plan, proyecto; v. diseñar; trazar; proyectar; idear.

**designate** [dézɪgnet] v. designar; señalar, indicar, nombrar.

**designer** [dɪzáɪnɚ] s. diseñador; dibujante; proyectista; intrigante.

**desirability** [dɪzaɪrəbílətɪ] s. conveniencia, utilidad.

**desirable** [dɪzáɪrəbl] adj. deseable; agradable; conveniente.

**desire** [dɪzáɪr] s. deseo; anhelo, ansia; v. desear; anhelar, ansiar.

**desirous** [dɪzáɪrəs] adj. deseoso.

**desist** [dɪzíst] v. desistir.

**desk** [dɛsk] s. escritorio, bufete, pupitre, mesa de escribir.

**desolate** [déslɪt] adj. desolado; despoblado, desierto; solitario; [déslet] v. desolar; asolar, arrasar; despoblar.

**desolation** [dɛsléʃən] s. desolación; soledad.

**despair** [dɪspér] s. desesperación; desesperanza; v. desesperarse, perder la esperanza.

**despairing** [dɪspérɪŋ] adj. desesperado, sin esperanza.

**despatch** [dɪspætʃ] = **dispatch**.

**desperate** [désprɪt] adj. desesperado; arriesgado, temerario; — **illness** enfermedad gravísima; **-ly** adv. desesperadamente; **-ly ill** gravísimamente enfermo.

**desperation** [dɛspəréʃən] s. desesperación; temeridad.

**despicable** [déspɪkəbl] adj. despreciable; desdeñable.

**despise** [dɪspáɪz] v. despreciar; des-

DE

deñar; menospreciar.
**despite** [dıspáıt] s. despecho; prep. a despecho de, a pesar de.
**despoil** [dıspóıl] v. despojar.
**despondency** [dıspándənsı] s. abatimiento desaliento, descaecimiento o decaimiento del ánimo.
**despondent** [dıspándənt] adj. abatido, descaecido o decaído de ánimo, desalentado, desesperanzado.
**despot** [déspət] s. déspota.
**despotic** [dıspátık] adj. despótico.
**despotism** [déspətızəm] s. despotismo.
**dessert** [dızə́t] s. postre.
**destination** [dɛstənéʃən] s. destinación, destino; paradero.
**destine** [déstın] v. destinar; **-ed for** con rumbo a, con destinación a; destinado a.
**destiny** [déstənı] s. destino, sino, hado.
**destitute** [déstətjut] adj. destituido, necesitado; falto, desprovisto.
**destroy** [dıstrói] v. destruir.
**destroyer** [dıstróıə] s. destruidor; destructor, cazatorpedero, destroyer.
**destruction** [dıstrákʃən] s. destrucción; ruina.
**destructive** [dıstráktıv] adj. destructivo.
**detach** [dıtǽʃ] v. separar, despegar, desprender; destacar (una porción de tropa).
**detachment** [dıtǽtʃmənt] s. separación; desprendimiento; desapego, despego, alejamiento; destacamento (militar).
**detail** [dítel] s. detalle; pormenor; destacamento (militar); **to go into —** detallar, pormenorizar; [dıtél] v. detallar; pormenorizar; destacar, asignar.
**detain** [dıtén] v. detener; entretener, demorar, retardar.
**detect** [dıtékt] v. descubrir.
**detective** [dıtéktıv] s. detective, detectivo, policía secreto.
**detention** [dıténʃən] s. detención.
**detergent** [dıtə́dʒənt] s. detergente.
**deteriorate** [dıtírıəret] v. deteriorar(se).
**deterioration** [dıtırıəréʃən] s. deterioro.
**determination** [dıtɜmənéʃən] s. determinación; decisión; resolución, firmeza.
**determine** [dıtə́mın] v. determinar; decidir; **to — to** determinarse a, decidirse a, resolverse a.
**determined** [dıtə́mınd] adj. determinado, decidido, resuelto.
**detest** [dıtést] v. detestar, aborrecer.
**detour** [dítur] s. rodeo, desvío, desviación, vuelta; v. dar o hacer un rodeo.
**devastate** [dévəstet] v. devastar, arruinar, asolar.
**develop** [dıvéləp] v. desarrollar(se); desenvolver(se); revelar (una película o placa fotográfica); explotar (una mina).
**development** [dıvéləpmənt] s. (evolution) desarrollo; desenvolvimiento; evolución; crecimiento; (generation)

fomento; explotación; (photo) revelado.
**deviate** [dívıet] v. desviar(se).
**deviation** [divıéʃən] s. desviación; desvío, extravío.
**device** [dıváıs] s. artificio; mecanismo, aparato; ardid, recurso; divisa; **left to one's own -s** abandonado a sus propios recursos.
**devil** [dévl] s. diablo; demonio.
**devilish** [dévlıʃ] adj. diabólico; endiablado; travieso.
**deviltry** [dévltrı] s. diablura.
**devious** [dívıəs] adj. desviado; tortuoso; indirecto.
**devise** [dıváız] v. idear, trazar, urdir.
**devoid** [dıvóıd] adj. exento, libre, falto, privado, desprovisto.
**devote** [dıvót] v. dedicar; consagrar; **to — oneself to** dedicarse a, consagrarse a, aplicarse a.
**devoted** [dıvótıd] adj. dedicado, consagrado; apegado; **— friend** amigo fiel o leal.
**devotion** [dıvóʃən] s. devoción; piedad; afecto; lealtad.
**devour** [dıváur] v. devorar.
**devout** [dıváut] adj. devoto, piadoso; sincero.
**dew** [dju] s. rocío, sereno; v. rociar; caer (el rocío).
**dewdrop** [djúdrɑp] s. gota de rocío.
**dewy** [djúı] adj. rociado, húmedo de rocío.
**dexterity** [dɛkstérətı] s. destreza.
**dexterous** [dékstrəs] adj. diestro.
**dextrose** [dékstros] s. dextrosa.
**diadem** [dáıədɛm] s. diadema.
**diagnose** [daıəgnós] v. diagnosticar.
**diagonal** [daıǽgənļ] adj. diagonal, oblicuo; s. diagonal.
**diagram** [dáıəgræm] s. diagrama.
**dial** [dáıəl] s. esfera; muestra (del reloj), Méx., C.A. carátula; **— telephone** teléfono automático; v. sintonizar o captar (una estación radiotelefónica).
**dialect** [dáıəlɛkt] s. dialecto.
**dialogue** [dáıəlɔg] s. diálogo; v. dialogar.
**diameter** [daıǽmətə] s. diámetro.
**diamond** [dáımənd] s. diamante; rombo (figura geométrica).
**diaper** [dáıəpə] s. pañal.
**diarrhea** [daıəríə] s. diarrea.
**diary** [dáıərı] s. diario.
**dice** [daıs] s. pl. de **die** dados; v. cuadricular, cortar en cuarterones o cubos.
**dichotomy** [daıkátəmı] s. dicotomía.
**dictate** [díktet] s. dictado, precepto; v. dictar.
**dictation** [dıktéʃən] s. dictado; mando absoluto; **to take —** escribir al dictado.
**dictator** [díktetə] s. dictador.
**dictatorship** [dıktétəʃıp] s. dictadura.
**diction** [díkʃən] s. dicción.
**dictionary** [díkʃənɛrı] s. diccionario.
**did** [dıd] pret. de **to do**.
**die** [daı] s. (pl. **dice**) dado (para jugar); (pl. **dies**) matriz, molde; cuño (sello

*para acuñar moneda).*

**die** [daɪ] *v.* morir(se); marchitarse, secarse *(las flores, plantas, etc.)*; **to —
out** morirse, extinguirse, apagarse.

**dieresis** [daɪérəsɪs] *s.* diéresis.

**diet** [dáɪət] *s.* dieta; régimen; **to be on
a —** estar a dieta; **to put on a —**
adietar, poner a dieta; *v.* ponerse a
dieta; estar a dieta.

**differ** [dífɚ] *v.* diferir, diferenciarse,
distinguirse; disentir; **to — with** no
convenir con, no estar de acuerdo con.

**difference** [dífrəns] *s.* diferencia; distinción; discordia, controversia; **it
makes no —** no importa, es igual, da
lo mismo.

**different** [dífrənt] *adj.* diferente; distinto.

**differentiate** [dɪfərénʃɪet] *v.* diferenciar(se); distinguir(se).

**difficult** [dífəkʌlt] *adj.* difícil; dificultoso, trabajoso, penoso.

**difficulty** [dífəkʌltɪ] *s.* dificultad;
apuro, aprieto.

**diffidence** [dífədəns] *s.* timidez; desconfianza de sí propio.

**diffident** [dífədənt] *adj.* huraño;
tímido.

**diffuse** [dɪfjús] *adj.* difuso; prolijo;
[dɪfjúz] *v.* difundir.

**diffusion** [dɪfjúʒən] *s.* difusión; diseminación.

**dig** [dɪg] *v.* cavar; excavar; ahondar; escarbar; trabajar duro; **to — under**
socavar; **to — up** desenterrar; *s.* piquete; pulla, sarcasmo.

**digest** [dáɪdʒɛst] *s.* sumario, compendio; recopilación; código; [dədʒést]
*v.* digerir; recopilar.

**digestible** [dədʒéstəbl] *adj.* digestible,
digerible.

**digestion** [dədʒéstʃən] *s.* digestión.

**digestive** [dədʒéstɪv] *adj.* digestivo.

**dignified** [dígnəfaɪd] *adj.* digno, mesurado; serio, grave.

**dignitary** [dígnətɛrɪ] *s.* dignatario.

**dignity** [dígnɪtɪ] *s.* dignidad.

**digraph** [dáɪgræf] *s.* dígrafo.

**digress** [dəgrés] *v.* divagar.

**digression** [dəgréʃən] *s.* digresión, divagación.

**dike** [daɪk] *s.* dique, represa; zanja.

**dilate** [daɪlét] *v.* dilatar(se), extender(se), ensanchar(se).

**diligence** [dílədʒəns] *s.* diligencia; aplicación, esmero.

**diligent** [dílədʒənt] *adj.* diligente, activo, aplicado.

**dilute** [dɪlút] *v.* diluir, desleír; aguar;
*adj.* diluido.

**dim** [dɪm] *adj.* penumbroso, obscuro;
nublado; confuso; indistinto; deslustrado, sin brillo; *v.* obscurecer;
anublar, ofuscar; atenuar.

**dime** [daɪm] *s.* moneda de diez centavos.

**dimension** [dəménʃən] *s.* dimensión.

**diminish** [dəmínɪʃ] *v.* disminuir;
rebajar.

**diminution** [dɪmənjúʃən] *s.* diminución, mengua.

**diminutive** [dəmínjətɪv] *adj.* diminutivo; diminuto; *s.* diminutivo.

**dimness** [dímnɪs] *s.* semi-obscuridad,
penumbra; ofuscamiento.

**dimple** [dímpl] *s.* hoyuelo.

**din** [dɪn] *s.* estruendo, fragor, estrépito.

**dine** [daɪn] *v.* comer; festejar u obsequiar con una comida.

**diner** [dáɪnɚ] *s.* coche-comedor; comensal *(persona que come a la mesa).*

**dingy** [díndʒɪ] *adj.* negruzco; manchado, sucio.

**dining** [dáɪnɪŋ] *ger. de* **to dine; — car**
coche-comedor; **— room** comedor.

**dinner** [dínɚ] *s.* comida; **— coat** smoking o esmoquin.

**dint** [dɪnt]: **by — of** a fuerza de.

**diorama** [daɪəræmə] *s.* diorama.

**dip** [dɪp] *s.* zambullida; inmersión; bajada; declive; depresión; *v.* meter(se);
zambullirse; mojar *(la pluma en el
tintero)*; teñir; agachar *(la cabeza)*;
saludar *(con la bandera)*; inclinarse *(un
camino)*; dar un bajón *(un avión)*;
hundirse *(el sol en el horizonte)*; **to —
out** vaciar *(con cucharón o cazo)*.

**diphtheria** [dɪfθírɪə] *s.* difteria.

**diphthong** [dífθɔŋ] *s.* diptongo.

**diploma** [dɪplómə] *s.* diploma.

**diplomacy** [dɪplóməsɪ] *s.* diplomacia.

**diplomat** [dípləmæt] *s.* diplomático.

**diplomatic** [dɪpləmætɪk] *adj.* diplomático.

**dipper** [dípɚ] *s.* cucharón, cazo; **the
Big Dipper** la Osa Mayor.

**dire** [daɪr] *adj.* extremo; horrendo;
fatal, de mal agüero.

**direct** [dərékt] *adj. (straight)* directo;
derecho, en línea recta; *C.A.* recto;
*(immediate)* inmediato; **— current**
corriente continua; **— object** acusativo; *adv.* directamente; **-ly** *adv.*
directamente; inmediatamente; en
seguida; *v.* dirigir; guiar; encaminar;
dar direcciones ú ordenes.

**direction** [dərékʃən] *s.* dirección; administración; gerencia; rumbo.

**directional antenna** [dərékʃən‿ænténə]
*s.* antena direccional.

**directional signal** [dərékʃən‿sígnl] *s.*
señal direccional.

**directive** [dəréktɪv] *adj.* directivo; *s.*
orden, mandato.

**directness** [déréktnɪs] *s.* derechura;
franqueza; lo directo; **with — sin**
rodeos.

**director** [dəréktɚ] *s.* director; gerente.

**directory** [dəréktərɪ] *s.* directorio;
junta directiva; **telephone —** guía
telefónica.

**dirigible** [dírədʒəbl] *adj. & s.* dirigible.

**dirt** [dɚt] *s.* suciedad; mugre; tierra,
polvo, lodo.

**dirty** [dɚtɪ] *adj.* sucio; mugriento; cochino; enlodado; manchado; *v.* ensuciar; manchar; enlodar.

**disable** [dɪsébl] *v.* incapacitar.

**disadvantage** [dɪsədvǽntɪdʒ] *s.* desventaja; **to be at a —** estar en una
situación desventajosa.

**disagree** [dɪsəgrí] *v. (dissent)* diferir,

DE

disentir; no convenir, no estar de acuerdo; (*bad effect*) no sentarle bien a uno (*el clima, la comida, etc.*).

**disagreeable** [dɪsəgríəbl] *adj*. desagradable; áspero, de mal genio.

**disagreement** [dɪsəgrímənt] *s*. desavenencia, desacuerdo; disensión; discordia; discordancia.

**disallow** [dísəlaʊ] *v*. desaprobar; rechazar.

**disappear** [dɪsəpír] *v*. desaparecer.

**disappearance** [dɪsəpírəns] *s*. desaparición.

**disappoint** [dɪsəpóɪnt] *v*. chasquear; contrariar; decepcionar; faltar a lo prometido; desilusionar; **to be -ed** estar desilusionado o decepcionado; estar desengañado; quedar contrariado.

**disappointing** [dɪsəpóɪntɪŋ] *adj*. desilusionante, desengañador, decepcionante.

**disappointment** [dɪsəpóɪntmənt] *s*. desilusión, desengaño, decepción; chasco; contrariedad.

**disapproval** [dɪsəprúvl] *s*. desaprobación.

**disapprove** [dɪsəprúv] *v*. desaprobar.

**disarm** [dɪsárm] *v*. desarmar(se).

**disarmament** [dɪsármənmənt] *s*. desarme.

**disarray** [dɪsəré] *s*. desarreglo, confusión, desorden; *v*. desarreglar, desordenar.

**disaster** [dɪzǽstər] *s*. desastre.

**disastrous** [dɪzǽstrəs] *adj*. desastroso.

**disband** [dɪsbǽnd] *v*. dispersar; licenciar (*las tropas*); desbandarse.

**disbelieve** [dɪsbəlív] *v*. descreer, no creer.

**disburse** [dɪsbə́rs] *v*. desembolsar.

**disbursement** [dɪsbə́rsmənt] *s*. desembolso; gasto.

**disc** [dɪsk] = **disk**.

**discard** [dískard] *s*. descarte; desecho, cosa desechada; [dɪskárd] *v*. descartar; desechar.

**discern** [dɪsə́n] *v*. discernir, distinguir; percibir.

**discernment** [dɪsə́nmənt] *s*. discernimiento.

**discharge** [dɪstʃárdʒ] *s*. descarga (*de artillería*); descargo (*de una obligación*); desempeño (*de un deber*); exoneración; despedida; licencia (*militar*); pago (*de una deuda*); derrame, desagüe; supuración; *v*. descargar; exonerar; poner en libertad; despedir, echar, deponer; dar de baja (*a un soldado*); pagar (*una deuda*); arrojar, supurar; desaguar.

**disciple** [dɪsáɪpl] *s*. discípulo.

**discipline** [dísəplɪn] *s*. disciplina; *v*. disciplinar.

**disclose** [dɪsklóz] *v*. descubrir; revelar.

**discolor** [dɪskʌ́lər] *v*. descolorar(se), desteñir(se).

**discomfort** [dɪskʌ́mfərt] *s*. incomodidad; malestar.

**disconcert** [dɪskənsə́t] *v*. desconcertar.

**disconnect** [dɪskənékt] *v*. desconectar; desunir, separar.

**disconnected** [dɪskənéktɪd] *p.p.* & *adj*. desconectado; desunido; inconexo, incoherente.

**disconsolate** [dɪskánslɪt] *adj*. desconsolado.

**discontent** [dɪskəntént] *s*. descontento; *v*. descontentar.

**discontented** [dɪskənténtɪd] *adj*. descontento; descontentadizo.

**discontinue** [dɪskəntínju] *v*. descontinuar; parar; suspender, interrumpir; abandonar.

**discord** [dískɔrd] *s*. discordia; disonancia, discordancia; desavenencia.

**discount** [dískaʊnt] *s*. descuento; rebaja; **— rate** tipo de descuento; *v*. descontar; rebajar.

**discourage** [dɪskə́rɪdʒ] *v*. desanimar, desalentar, abatir; **to — from** disuadir de.

**discouragement** [dɪskə́rɪdʒmənt] *s*. desaliento, abatimiento.

**discourse** [dískors] *s*. discurso; conversación; [dɪskórs] *v*. disertar, discurrir, hablar.

**discourteous** [dɪskə́tɪəs] *adj*. descortés, desatento.

**discourtesy** [dɪskə́təsɪ] *s*. descortesía, desatención.

**discover** [dɪskʌ́vər] *v*. descubrir.

**discoverer** [dɪskʌ́vərər] *s*. descubridor.

**discovery** [dɪskʌ́vrɪ] *s*. descubrimiento.

**discredit** [dɪskrédɪt] *s*. descrédito; deshonra; *v*. desacreditar; deshonrar; no creer.

**discreet** [dɪskrít] *adj*. discreto, prudente.

**discrepancy** [dɪskrépənsɪ] *s*. discrepancia, diferencia; variación.

**discretion** [dɪskréʃən] *s*. discreción; prudencia; **at one's own —** a discreción.

**discriminate** [dɪskrímənet] *v*. discernir; distinguir; hacer distinciones, hacer favoritismos; dar trato de inferioridad con motivos de prejuicio; **to — against** hacer favoritismos en perjuicio de.

**discuss** [dɪskʌ́s] *v*. discutir.

**discussion** [dɪskʌ́ʃən] *s*. discusión.

**disdain** [dɪsdén] *s*. desdén, menosprecio; *v*. desdeñar, menospreciar; desdeñarse de.

**disdainful** [dɪsdénfəl] *adj*. desdeñoso.

**disease** [dɪzíz] *s*. enfermedad.

**diseased** [dɪzízd] *adj*. enfermo.

**disembark** [dɪsɪmbárk] *v*. desembarcar.

**disentangle** [dɪsɪntǽŋgl] *v*. desenredar, desenmarañar, deshacer (*una maraña o enredo*).

**disfigure** [dɪsfígjər] *v*. desfigurar; afear.

**disfranchise** [dɪsfrǽntʃaɪz] *v*. privar de derecho de voto o de ciudadanía.

**disgrace** [dɪsgrés] *s*. ignominia, deshonra; vergüenza; **to be in —** estar desacreditado, haber perdido la gracia o el favor; *v*. deshonrar; degradar; desacreditar; avergonzar.

**disgraceful** [dɪsgrésfəl] *adj*. vergonzoso.

**disguise** [dɪsgáɪz] *s.* disfraz; *v.* disfrazar.

**disgust** [dɪsgÁst] *s.* asco; repugnancia; disgusto; *v.* disgustar, dar asco; repugnar.

**disgusted** [dɪsgÁstɪd] *adj.* disgustado; descontento; asqueado.

**disgusting** [dɪsgÁstɪŋ] *adj.* asqueroso, repugnante.

**dish** [dɪʃ] *s.* plato; manjar, vianda; **-es** vajilla; *v.* servir.

**dishearten** [dɪshártn̩] *v.* desalentar, desanimar, descorazonar.

**disheveled** [dɪʃévl̩d] *adj.* desgreñado; desaliñado, desaseado.

**dishonest** [dɪsánɪst] *adj.* engañoso, falso, tramposo, falto de honradez, fraudulento.

**dishonesty** [dɪsánɪstɪ] *s.* fraude, falta de honradez.

**dishonor** [dɪsánɚ] *s.* deshonra; afrenta; *v.* deshonrar; recusar (*un giro o cheque*).

**dishonorable** [dɪsánɚəbl̩] *adj.* deshonroso; infame.

**dishwasher** [díʃwɔʃɚ] *s.* (*person*) lavaplatos; (*machine*) máquina de lavar platos.

**disillusion** [dɪsɪlúʒən] *s.* desilusión, decepción, desengaño; *v.* desilusionar, decepcionar, desengañar.

**disinfect** [dɪsɪnfékt] *v.* desinfectar.

**disinfectant** [dɪsɪnféktənt] *s.* desinfectante.

**disinterested** [dɪsíntərəstɪd] *adj.* desinteresado.

**disk** [dɪsk] *s.* disco; **— brake** freno de disco.

**dislike** [dɪsláɪk] *s.* antipatía, aversión; *v.* sentir o tener aversión por; **I — it** me repugna, no me gusta, me desagrada.

**dislocate** [dísloket] *v.* dislocar, descoyuntar.

**dislodge** [dɪslÁdʒ] *v.* desalojar.

**disloyal** [dɪslóɪəl] *adj.* desleal.

**dismal** [dízml̩] *adj.* lúgubre, sombrío, tétrico.

**dismantle** [dɪsmæntl̩] *v.* desmantelar; desmontar, desarmar.

**dismay** [dɪsmé] *s.* desmayo, desaliento, pavor; *v.* desalentar, desanimar; atemorizar.

**dismiss** [dɪsmís] *v.* (*discharge*) despedir, expulsar, destituir; (*dispel*) desechar; (*allow to leave*) licenciar, dar de baja; (*close*) dar por terminado (*un pleito o caso jurídico*); **to — the meeting** disolver la junta, levantar la sesión.

**dismissal** [dɪsmís l̩] *s.* despedida, expulsión, destitución (*de un cargo*).

**dismount** [dɪsmáunt] *v.* desmontar; apear(se); desarmar (*un cañón, una máquina*); desengastar (*joyas*).

**disobedience** [dɪsəbídɪəns] *s.* desobediencia.

**disobedient** [dɪsəbídɪənt] *adj.* desobediente.

**disobey** [dɪsəbé] *v.* desobedecer.

**disorder** [dɪsórdɚ] *s.* (*confusion*) desorden; trastorno; confusión; (*illness*) enfermedad; *v.* desordenar; trastornar; desarreglar.

**disorderly** [dɪsórdɚlɪ] *adj.* desordenado; desarreglado; revoltoso; escandaloso; *adv.* desordenadamente.

**disown** [dɪsón] *v.* repudiar; desconocer, negar.

**disparage** [dɪspǽrɪdʒ] *v.* desacreditar; desdorar.

**dispassionate** [dɪspǽʃənɪt] *adj.* desapasionado.

**dispatch** [dɪspǽtʃ] *s.* despacho; envío; parte (*m.*), comunicación, mensaje; prontitud, expedición; *v.* despachar; enviar, expedir; matar.

**dispel** [dɪspél] *v.* disipar; dispersar.

**dispensary** [dɪspénsərɪ] *s.* dispensario.

**dispensation** [dɪspənséʃən] *s.* dispensa, exención; dispensación; distribución.

**dispense** [dɪspéns] *v.* (*give*) dispensar, dar; repartir, distribuir; administrar (*la justicia*); despachar (*recetas, medicamentos*); **to — from** eximir de, dispensar de; **to — with** omitir; pasarse sin, prescindir de.

**dispersal** [dɪspɚ́sl̩] *s.* dispersión; desbandada.

**disperse** [dɪspɚ́s] *v.* dispersar(se), disipar(se), esparcir(se).

**displace** [dɪsplés] *v.* desalojar; desplazar; poner fuera de su lugar; suplantar.

**display** [dɪsplé] *s.* manifestación, exhibición; ostentación; *v.* exhibir; mostrar, manifestar; desplegar.

**displease** [dɪsplíz] *v.* desagradar; disgustar, fastidiar.

**displeasure** [dɪspléʒɚ] *s.* desagrado, disgusto, descontento.

**disposal** [dɪspóz l̩] *s.* disposición; arreglo; venta (*de bienes*).

**dispose** [dɪspóz] *v.* disponer; arreglar; influir; **to — of** deshacerse de.

**disposition** [dɪspəzíʃən] *s.* disposición; arreglo; aptitud, inclinación; venta; **good (bad) —** buen (mal) genio.

**disprove** [dɪsprúv] *v.* refutar.

**dispute** [dɪspjút] *s.* disputa; *v.* disputar.

**disqualify** [dɪskwáləfaɪ] *v.* inhabilitar, incapacitar, descalificar.

**disregard** [dɪsrɪgárd] *s.* desatención, falta de atención, negligencia, descuido; falta de respeto o consideración; *v.* desatender, no hacer caso de, desentenderse de.

**disrespect** [dɪsrɪspékt] *s.* desacato, falta de respeto.

**disrespectful** [dɪsrɪspéktfəl] *adj.* irrespetuoso.

**dissatisfied** [dɪssǽtɪsfaɪd] *adj.* descontento, malcontento, mal satisfecho.

**dissatisfy** [dɪssǽtɪsfaɪ] *v.* descontentar, no satisfacer.

**dissect** [dɪsékt] *v.* disecar, hacer una disección; analizar.

**dissemble** [dɪsémbl̩] *v.* disimular, fingir.

**dissension** [dɪsénʃən] *s.* disensión, discordia.

**dissent** [dɪsént] *v.* disentir; *s.* desacuerdo; disensión, desavenencia.

**dissimulation** [dɪsɪmjəléʃən] *s*. disimulo.

**dissipate** [dísəpet] *v*. disipar(se).

**dissipation** [dɪsəpéʃən] *s*. disipación.

**dissolute** [dísəlut] *adj*. disoluto.

**dissolution** [dɪsəlúʃən] *s*. disolución.

**dissolve** [dɪzálv] *v*. disolver(se); anular.

**dissuade** [dɪswéd] *v*. disuadir.

**distaff** [dístæf] *s*. rueca.

**distance** [dístəns] *s*. distancia; lejanía; alejamiento; **in the —** a lo lejos, en lontananza.

**distant** [dístənt] *adj*. (*far*) distante; apartado, lejano, remoto; (*aloof*) esquivo; **to be — from** distar de; **-ly** *adv*. de lejos; remotamente; a distancia; en lontananza.

**distaste** [dɪstést] *s*. disgusto, aversión, repugnancia.

**distasteful** [dɪstéstfəl] *adj*. desagradable, repugnante.

**distemper** [dɪstémpɚ] *s*. moquillo; pepita (*de las gallinas*).

**distend** [dɪsténd] *v*. dilatar, ensanchar.

**distil** [dɪstíl] *v*. destilar.

**distillation** [dɪstɪléʃən] *s*. destilación.

**distillery** [dɪstílərɪ] *s*. destilería.

**distinct** [dɪstíŋkt] *adj*. distinto, claro; diferente; **-ly** *adv*. distintamente, claramente, con claridad.

**distinction** [dɪstíŋkʃən] *s*. distinción.

**distinctive** [dɪstíŋktɪv] *adj*. distintivo.

**distinguish** [dɪstíŋgwɪʃ] *v*. distinguir; discernir.

**distinguished** [dɪstíŋgwɪʃt] *adj*. distinguido.

**distinguishing** [dɪstíŋgwɪʃɪŋ] *adj*. distintivo, característico.

**distort** [dɪstórt] *v*. desfigurar, deformar, torcer, falsear; tergiversar.

**distract** [dɪstrǽkt] *v*. distraer; perturbar.

**distraction** [dɪstrǽkʃən] *s*. distracción, diversión; perturbación; **to drive to — volver loco**.

**distress** [dɪstrés] *s*. angustia, aflicción, congoja; dolor; **to be in —** tener una aflicción; estar apurado; estar en zozobra (*un navío*); *v*. angustiar, acongojar, afligir; **to be -ed** estar afligido o apurado.

**distribute** [dɪstríbjut] *v*. distribuir, repartir.

**distribution** [dɪstrəbjúʃən] *s*. distribución; repartimiento.

**distributor** [dɪstríbjətɚ] *s*. distribuidor.

**district** [dístrɪkt] *s*. distrito; **— attorney** fiscal de distrito.

**distrust** [dɪstrʌ́st] *s*. desconfianza; recelo; *v*. desconfiar; recelar.

**distrustful** [dɪstrʌ́stfəl] *adj*. desconfiado, sospechoso, receloso.

**disturb** [dɪstɚ́b] *v*. turbar, perturbar, inquietar; desarreglar; incomodar, molestar; **don't — yourself!** ¡no se moleste Vd.!

**disturbance** [dɪstɚ́bəns] *s*. disturbio; perturbación; desorden; alboroto; molestia.

**disuse** [dɪsjús] *s*. desuso; **to fall into —** caer en desuso; caducar.

**ditch** [dɪtʃ] *s*. zanja; foso; **irrigation —** acequia; *v*. zanjar, abrir zanjas; meter en la zanja; **to — someone** deshacerse de alguien.

**ditto** [díto] *s*. ídem, lo mismo.

**diuretic** [daɪjʊrétɪk] *adj*. & *s*. diurético.

**divan** [dáɪvæn] *s*. diván.

**dive** [daɪv] *s*. zambullida (*echándose de cabeza*), buceada, chapuz; picada (*descenso rápido de un avión*); *Méx*. clavado; garito, leonera; *v*. echarse de cabeza; zambullirse (*de cabeza*); bucear; sumergirse (*un submarino*); **to — into someone** abalanzarse sobre alguien.

**diver** [dáɪvɚ] *s*. buzo; zambullidor.

**diverge** [dəvɚ́dʒ] *v*. divergir, irse apartando, separarse; diferir.

**divergence** [dəvɚ́dʒəns] *s*. divergencia; diferencia (*de opiniones*).

**divers** [dáɪvɚz] *adj*. diversos, varios.

**diverse** [dəvɚ́s] *adj*. diverso; diferente.

**diversion** [dəvɚ́ʒən] *s*. diversión, recreo; desviación.

**diversity** [dəvɚ́sətɪ] *s*. diversidad, diferencia, variedad.

**divert** [dəvɚ́t] *v*. divertir, entretener; distraer; desviar, apartar.

**divide** [dəváɪd] *v*. dividir(se); partir.

**dividend** [dívədɛnd] *s*. dividendo.

**divine** [dəváɪn] *adj*. divino; *v*. adivinar.

**divinity** [dəvínətɪ] *s*. divinidad; deidad; teología.

**division** [dəvíʒən] *s*. división.

**divorce** [dəvórs] *s*. divorcio; *v*. divorciar(se).

**divulge** [dəváldʒ] *v*. divulgar.

**dizziness** [dízɪnɪs] *s*. vahído o vaguido, desvanecimiento, mareo, vértigo.

**dizzy** [dízɪ] *adj*. desvanecido, mareado; confuso; aturdido; **— speed** velocidad vertiginosa.

**do** [du] *v*. hacer; **to — away with** deshacerse de; prescindir de; **to — a lesson** estudiar una lección; **to — one's hair** peinarse, arreglarse el pelo; **to — the dishes** lavar los platos; **to — up** envolver; limpiar, arreglar; lavar o planchar; **to — well in business** prosperar en los negocios; **to — without** pasarse sin; **to have nothing to — with** no tener nada que ver con; **that will —** basta, bastará; **that won't —** eso no sirve; eso no resultará bien; **this will have to —** habrá que conformarse con esto; **how — you — ?** ¿cómo está Vd.?; **— you hear me?** ¿me oye Vd.?; **yes, I —** sí, le oigo; **I — say it** sí lo digo.

**docile** [dásl] *adj*. dócil.

**dock** [dɑk] *s*. muelle, desembarcadero; dársena; **dry —** carenero, dique de carena; *v*. entrar en el muelle; atracar, meter (*una embarcación*) en el muelle o dique; **to — the wages** rebajar la paga.

**doctor** [dáktɚ] *s*. doctor; médico, facultativo; *v*. medicinar, curar; **to — oneself** medicinarse, tomar medicinas.

**doctrine** [dáktrɪn] *s.* doctrina.

**document** [dákjəmənt] *s.* documento; [dákjəm ent] *v.* documentar.

**dodder** [dádɚ] *v.* tambalear; temblar.

**dodge** [dɑdʒ] *s.* evasión, evasiva; *v.* evadir(se); escabullirse; hurtar el cuerpo; **to — around a corner** dar un esquinazo.

**doe** [do] *s.* cierva; hembra (*del antílope, del gamo, de la liebre*).

**dog** [dɔg] *s.* perro, perra; can; **hot —** salchicha caliente, *Ch., C.A.* perro caliente; *Ríopl.* pancho; **to put on a lot of —** emperifollarse; darse mucho tono, *Ríopl.* darse mucho corte; *v.* seguir la pista de, perseguir, acosar; *adv.* sumamente, completamente; **dog-tired** cansadísimo.

**dogma** [dɔ́gmə] *s.* dogma.

**dogmatic** [dɔgmǽtɪk] *adj.* dogmático.

**doily** [dɔ́ɪlɪ] *s.* mantelito (*para platos, vasos, lámparas, etc.*).

**doings** [dúɪŋz] *s. pl.* hechos, acciones, acontecimientos; **great —** mucha actividad, fiesta, función.

**do-it-yourself** [duɪtjʊrsɛ́lf] *adj.* proyectado para que uno pueda hacer sus propios trabajos manuales en casa.

**dole** [dol] *s.* reparto gratuito (*de dinero o alimento*); ración, limosna; *v.* repartir gratuitamente.

**doleful** [dólfəl] *adj.* lúgubre, triste, lastimoso.

**doll** [dɑl] *s.* muñeca, muñeco; *v.* **to — up** emperifollarse, ataviarse; **dolly** *s.* muñequita.

**dollar** [dálɚ] *s.* dólar.

**dolphin** [dɔ́lfɪn] *s.* delfín.

**domain** [domén] *s.* dominio; heredad.

**dome** [dom] *s.* cúpula: media naranja (*de iglesia*).

**domestic** [dəméstɪk] *adj.* doméstico; hogareño; nacional, del país, *Am.* criollo; *s.* criado, sirviente.

**domicile** [dáməsaɪl] *s.* domicilio.

**dominant** [dámənənt] *adj.* dominante.

**dominate** [dámənet] *v.* dominar.

**domination** [dəmənéʃən] *s.* dominación, dominio.

**domineer** [dəmənír] *v.* dominar, señorear.

**domineering** [dəmənírɪŋ] *adj.* dominador, mandón, imperioso, tiránico.

**dominion** [dəmínjən] *s.* dominio.

**domino** [dáməno] *s.* dominó, traje de máscara; disfraz; ficha (*de dominó*); **dominoes** dominó (*juego*).

**don** [dɑn] *s.* don (*título*); caballero; *v.* ponerse, vestirse.

**donate** [dónet] *v.* donar, regalar, hacer donación.

**donation** [donéʃən] *s.* donación; regalo, dádiva.

**done** [dʌn] *p.p. de* **to do** hecho; terminado, acabado; **to be — in** estar rendido de cansancio; **the meat is well — está** bien asada la carne.

**donkey** [dáŋkɪ] *s.* burro, asno.

**doodad** [dúdæd] *s.* chuchería, chisme.

**doom** [dum] *s.* hado, sino, destino;

mala suerte, perdición, ruina; **the day of —** el día del juicio final; *v.* condenar, sentenciar; predestinar; **to be -ed to failure** estar predestinado al fracaso.

**door** [dor] *s.* puerta; entrada.

**doorbell** [dórbɛl] *s.* campanilla o timbre (*de llamada*).

**doorknob** [dórnɑb] *s.* tirador de puerta, perilla, manija.

**doorman** [dórmæn] *s.* portero.

**doorstep** [dórstɛp] *s.* escalón de la puerta; umbral.

**doorway** [dórwe] *s.* puerta, entrada; vano (*de la puerta*).

**dope** [dop] *s.* (*narcotic*) narcótico; opio; droga; menjurje, medicamento; (*information*) información; **— fiend** morfinómano; **he is a —** es un zoquete; *v.* narcotizar; **to — out** adivinar, conjeturar; **to — oneself up** medicinarse demasiado.

**dormitory** [dórmətorɪ] *s.* dormitorio.

**dose** [dos] *s.* dosis; *v.* medicinar; **to — oneself** medicinarse.

**dot** [dɑt] *s.* punto; **on the —** en punto; *v.* marcar con puntos; poner el punto (*sobre la* i).

**dotage** [dótɪdʒ] *s.* chochez; **to be in one's —** chochear.

**dote** [dot] *v.* chochear; **to — on** estar loco por.

**double** [dʌ́bḷ] *adj.* doble; doblado; **— boiler** baño de María; **— deal** trato doble; **— entry** partida doble; **— standard** norma de conducta sexual mas restringida para la mujer; *s.* doble; **-s** juego de dobles (*en tenis*); *adv.* doblemente; **double-breasted** cruzado; **double-faced** de dos caras; *v.* doblar(se); duplicar(se); **to — up** doblarse; **doubly** *adv.* doblemente; por duplicado.

**doubt** [daʊt] *s.* duda; *v.* dudar.

**doubtful** [dáʊtfəl] *adj.* dudoso; dudable.

**doubtless** [dáʊtlɪs] *adj.* indudable, cierto, seguro; *adv.* sin duda; indudablemente; probablemente.

**douche** [duʃ] *s.* ducha; jeringa.

**dough** [do] *s.* pasta, masa; dinero.

**doughnut** [dónət] *s.* bollito o buñuelo en rosca.

**dove** [dʌv] *s.* paloma.

**dove** [dov] *pret. de* **to dive.**

**down** [daʊn] *adv.* abajo, hacia abajo; **— to** hasta; **— East** en el este; **— the street** calle abajo; **to cut — prices** reducir o rebajar precios; **to get — to work** aplicarse; **to go** (*o* **come) —** bajar; **to pay —** pagar al contado; **to put —** poner; anotar, apuntar, poner por escrito; *adj.* abatido, descorazonado; **— grade** declive, pendiente; **prices are —** han bajado los precios; **to be — on someone** tenerle ojeriza a alguien; *s.* plumón; vello; pelusa; *v.* echar por tierra, derribar; rebajar (*precios*).

**downcast** [dáʊnkæst] *adj.* cabizbajo, abatido; **with — eyes** con los ojos bajos.

**downfall** [dáunfɔl] *s.* caída; ruina.

**downpour** [dáunpor] *s.* aguacero, chaparrón.

**downright** [dáunraɪt] *adj.* claro, positivo, categórico, absoluto; **— foolishness** solemne disparate; *adv.* enteramente; absolutamente.

**downstairs** [dáunstérz] *adv.* abajo; en el piso bajo; *adj.* del piso bajo; *s.* piso bajo, piso inferior.

**downstream** [dáunstrím] *adv.* río abajo, aguas abajo; con la corriente.

**downtown** [dáuntáun] *adv.* al centro, en el centro (*de una población*); *adj.* del centro; *s.* centro.

**downward** [dáunwəd] *adj.* descendente; inclinado; *adv.* ( = **downwards**) hacia abajo.

**downy** [dáunɪ] *adj.* suave, blando; velloso; plumoso.

**dowry** [dáurɪ] *s.* dote.

**doze** [doz] *s.* siestecita, sueño ligero; *v.* dormitar.

**dozen** [dázn̩] *s.* docena.

**drab** [dræb] *adj.* pardo, pardusco; monótono.

**draft** [dræft] *s.* corriente de aire; trago; libranza, letra de cambio, giro bancario; trazado; plan; leva (*militar*); conscripción; tiro (*de estufa, hogar, etc.*); calado (*de un barco*); **— beer** cerveza de barril; **— horse** caballo de tiro; **rough —** croquis, borrador; *v.* trazar, dibujar, delinear, reclutar, echar leva; redactar (*un documento*).

**draftsman** [dræftsmən] *s.* dibujante.

**drag** [dræg] *s.* rastra; traba, obstáculo; **to have a — with someone** tener buenas aldabas con alguien; *v.* arrastrar(se); rastrear; moverse despacio; **to — on and on** prolongarse demasiado, prolongarse hasta el fastidio.

**dragon** [drǽgən] *s.* dragón.

**drain** [dren] *s.* (*channel*) desagüe; desaguadero, conducto; (*exhaust*) agotamiento; consumo; *v.* desaguar(se); apurar (*un vaso*); agotar, consumir; escurrir(se), secar(se); desecar (*un terreno*), *Am.* drenar.

**drainage** [drénɪdʒ] *s.* desagüe, *Am.* drenaje; desaguadero; sistema de desaguaderos; desecamiento, desecación (*de un terreno, laguna, etc.*).

**drake** [drek] *s.* pato.

**drama** [drámə] *s.* drama.

**dramatic** [drəmǽtɪk] *adj.* dramático.

**dramatist** [drámətɪst] *s.* dramaturgo, dramático.

**dramatize** [drǽmətaɪz] *v.* dramatizar.

**drank** [dræŋk] *pret. de* **to drink.**

**drape** [drep] *s.* colgadura, cortina, tapiz; *v.* colgar, entapizar, adornar con tapices; cubrir, revestir.

**drapery** [drépərɪ] *s.* tapicería, colgaduras, cortinas; pañería, paños, géneros.

**drastic** [drǽstɪk] *adj.* extremo, fuerte, violento; **to take — steps** tomar medidas enérgicas.

**draught** [dræft] *véase* **draft.**

**draw** [drɔ] *v.* (*pull*) tirar; estirar; jalar (*halar*); (*attract*) atraer; sacar; (*design*) debujar, trazar; (*withdraw*) girar, librar (*una libranza*); hacer (*una comparación*); correr (*la cortina*); **to — aside** apartar(se); **to — a breath** aspirar, tomar aliento; **to — lots** echar suertes, sortear; **to — near** acercarse; **to — out** sacar; sonsacar (*a una persona*); alargar, prolongar; **to — up** acercar(se); redactar (*un documento*); *s.* empate (*en deportes o juegos*); número sacado (*en una rifa*); atracción; **—bridge** puente levadizo.

**drawback** [drɔ́bæk] *s.* desventaja; obstáculo, inconveniente.

**drawer** [drɔr] *s.* cajón, gaveta; **-s** calzoncillos.

**drawer** [drɔ́ə] *s.* librador, girador; dibujante.

**drawing** [drɔ́ɪŋ] *s.* (*design*) dibujo; delineación, trazado; (*raffle*) sorteo; **— paper** papel de dibujo; **— room** sala de recibo, recibidor, recibimiento.

**drawn** [drɔn] *p.p. de* **to draw.**

**dread** [drɛd] *s.* pavor, temor, aprensión; *adj.* terrible; temido; *v.* temer; sentir aprensión de.

**dreadful** [drédfəl] *adj.* horrendo; espantoso.

**dream** [drim] *s.* sueño; ensueño; *v.* soñar; **to — of** soñar con, soñar en.

**dreamer** [drímə] *s.* soñador.

**dreamland** [drímlænd] *s.* tierra del ensueño; región de los sueños.

**dreamt** [drempt] = **dreamed.**

**dreamy** [drímɪ] *adj.* soñoliento; soñador; melancólico; como un sueño; **a — recollection** un vago recuerdo.

**dreary** [drírɪ] *adj.* sombrío; melancólico.

**dredge** [drɛdʒ] *s.* draga; *v.* dragar.

**dregs** [drɛgz] *s. pl.* heces, sedimento.

**drench** [drɛntʃ] *s.* mojada, mojadura, empapada; *v.* empapar; mojar; remojar.

**dress** [drɛs] *s.* vestido, traje; vestidura, ropaje, atavío; **— rehearsal** ensayo general y último (*antes de una función*); **— suit** traje de etiqueta; *v.* vestir(se); arreglarse, componerse; aderezar; adobar (*carne o pieles*); curar (*heridas*); alinear, formar (*las tropas*); **to — down** reprender, regañar; **to — up** emperifollarse, acicalarse, ataviarse.

**dresser** [drésə] *s.* tocador, cómoda (*con espejo*); **she is a good —** viste con elegancia o buen gusto.

**dressing** [drésɪŋ] *s.* aderezo; salsa (*para ensaladas*); relleno (*para carne, pollo, etc.*); medicamento, vendajes (*para heridas*); **a — down** regaño; **— gown** bata; **— room** tocador; **— table** tocador.

**dressmaker** [drésmekə] *s.* modista.

**drew** [dru] *pret. de* **to draw.**

**dribble** [dríbl̩] *v.* gotear; dejar caer en gotas; babear; *s.* goteo; chorrito.

**driblet** [dríblɪt] *s.* gota, gotita; **in -s** gota a gota; en pequeñas cantidades.

**dried** [draɪd] *pret.* & *p.p. de* **to dry**; *adj.*
seco; paso; — **fig** higo paso.

**drift** [drɪft] *s.* (*direction*) rumbo, dirección, tendencia, deriva; (*pile*) montón,
amontonamiento (*de arena, nieve, etc.*);
(*off course*) desvío (*de un barco o avión*);
**to get the — of a conversation**
enterarse a medias de una conversación; *v.* flotar; ir(se) a la deriva;
dejarse llevar por la corriente; amon-
tonarse (*la nieve, la arena*); esparcirse
(*la arena, la nieve, las nubes*).

**driftwood** [dríftwud] *s.* madera o leña
flotante; madera de playa.

**drill** [drɪl] *s.* (*tool*) taladro; barrena;
(*training*) ejercicio; adiestramiento;
*Am.* entrenamiento; dril (*tela*); *v.*
taladrar, barrenar, perforar; hacer
ejercicio; aleccionar; disciplinar (*un
ejército*); adiestrar(se), *Am.* entrenar-
(se).

**drily** [dráɪlɪ] *adv.* secamente.

**drink** [drɪŋk] *s.* bebida; trago; *v.* beber;
**to — a toast to** beber a la salud de,
brindar por; — **it down**! ¡bébaselo!
¡tráagueselo!

**drinkable** [dríŋkəbl̩] *adj.* potable.

**drip** [drɪp] *s.* goteo; *v.* gotear, caer gota
a gota; dejar caer gota a gota.

**drive** [draɪv] *s.* (*ride*) paseo en coche;
(*road*) calzada, carretera, paseo; (*campaign*) campaña; (*impulse*) empuje;
tiro, tirada (*de una pelota*); *v.* impulsar,
impeler, empujar; arrear (*animales*);
conducir, guiar o manejar (*un auto*);
forzar; encajar, clavar (*una estaca,
cuña, o clavo*); tirar, lanzar (*una pelota*);
dar un paseo en auto; llevar (*a alguien*) en auto; cavar (*un pozo, túnel,
etc.*); **to — away** ahuyentar; **to — a
good bargain** hacer un buen trato;
**to — mad** volver loco; **what are
you driving at?** ¿qué quieres decir
con eso?

**drivel** [drívl̩] *s.* baba; ñoñería, tontería;
*v.* babear; chochear, decir ñoñerías.

**driveling** [drívlɪŋ] *adj.* baboso.

**driven** [drívən] *p.p. de* **to drive**.

**driver** [dráɪvɚ] *s.* cochero, chófer, mecánico, conductor (*de automóvil*); arriero (*de animales*); uno de los palos de
golf; **pile** — martinete (*para clavar
pilotes*); **slave** — mandón, tirano;
**truck** — carretero, camionero.

**driveway** [dráɪvwe] *s.* calzada de entrada, carretera de entrada.

**drizzle** [drízl̩] *v.* lloviznar; *s.* llovizna.

**drone** [dron] *s.* zángano; holgazán; zumbido; *v.* zumbar; hablar con monotonía; holgazanear, perder el tiempo.

**droop** [drup] *v.* doblarse, andar o estar
alicaído, estar abatido; languidecer;
marchitarse; bajar (*los hombros, los
párpados*); **his shoulders** — tiene los
hombros caídos; **-ing eyelids** párpados caídos.

**drop** [drɑp] *s.* (*liquid*) gota; (*descent*)
baja; caída; (*incline*) declive; **cough
—** pastilla para la tos; **letter —**
buzón; — **curtain** telón (*de teatro*);
— **hammer** martinete; — **out** dimi-

tente; *v.* dejar caer, soltar; gotear;
caer; dejar (*un asunto, una amistad*); **to
— a line** ponar unos renglones; **to
— asleep** quedarse dormido, dormirse; **to — behind** dejar atrás; quedarse atrás; **to — in** hacer una visita
inesperada, *Am.* descolgarse; **to — in
a mailbox** echar al buzón; **to — out**
retirarse; desaparecer; **to — the
curtain** bajar el telón.

**drought** [draut] *s.* sequía.

**drove** [drov] *s.* manada, recua, rebaño;
tropel; *pret. de* **to drive**.

**drown** [draun] *v.* ahogar(se), anegar(se);
apagar, ahogar (*un sonido*).

**drowse** [drauz] *v.* dormitar; estar amodorrado.

**drowsiness** [dráuzɪnɪs] *s.* modorra,
somnolencia.

**drowsy** [dráuzɪ] *adj.* soñoliento; adormilado, amodorrado; **to become —**
amodorrarse.

**drudge** [drʌdʒ] *v.* afanarse, atarearse; *s.*
trabajador, esclavo del trabajo.

**drug** [drʌg] *s.* droga; narcótico; **to be a
— on the market** ser invendible (*una
mercancía*); *v.* jaropar (*administrar dro-
gas en demasía*); narcotizar.

**druggist** [drágɪst] *s.* boticario, droguista,
droguero, farmacéutico.

**drugstore** [drágstor] *s.* botica, droguería, farmacia.

**drum** [drʌm] *s.* tambor; tímpano (*del
oído*); barril, tonel; **bass —** tambora,
bombo; **—stick** bolillo de tambor; **—
major** tambor mayor; *v.* tocar el
tambor; tamborilear; **to — a lesson
into someone** meterle a uno la lección en la cabeza; **to — up trade**
solicitar o fomentar ventas.

**drummer** [drámɚ] *s.* tambor, tamborilero; viajante de comercio, agente.

**drunk** [drʌŋk] *p.p. de* **to drink**; *adj.*
borracho, ebrio, emborrachado, bebi-
do; *Ríopl.* mamado; *C.A.* bolo; *Ch.*
cufifo; **to get —** emborracharse,
embriagarse.

**drunkard** [dráŋkɚd] *s.* borracho, borrachón, beodo, bebedor.

**drunken** [dráŋkən] *adj.* borracho, ebrio.

**drunkenness** [dráŋkənnɪs] *s.* borrachera, embriaguez.

**dry** [draɪ] *adj.* seco; árido; **a — book** un
libro aburrido; **— cleaner** quitamanchas; tintorero; **— cleaning** lavado o
limpieza la seco; **— goods** lencería,
géneros, tejidos, telas; **— measure**
medida para áridos; *v.* secar(se); enjugar; **to — up** secarse, resecarse.

**dryness** [dráɪnɪs] *s.* sequedad; aridez.

**dub** [dʌb] *v.* doblar (*una película*).

**dubious** [djúbɪəs] *adj.* dudoso.

**duchess** [dátʃɪs] *s.* duquesa.

**duck** [dʌk] *s.* pato, pata; ánade; dril
(*género*); zambullida, chapuz; agacha-
da rápida (*para evitar un golpe*); *v.*
zambullir(se), chapuzar(se); agachar-
(se); agachar (*la cabeza*).

**duckling** [dáklɪŋ] *s.* patito, anadeja.

**dud** [dʌd] *s.* bomba que no estalla.

**dude** [dud] *s.* caballerete; novato.

**due** [dju] *adj.* debido; vencido, pagadero; **in — time** a su debido tiempo; **the bill is —** se ha vencido la cuenta; **the train is — at two o'clock** el tren debe llegar a las dos; *adv.* directamente; **— east** hacia el este, rumbo al oriente; *s.* derecho, privilegio; **-s** cuota.

**duel** [djúəl] *s.* duelo, desafío, combate; *v.* batirse en duelo.

**duet** [djuét] *s.* duo, dueto.

**dug** [dʌg] *pret. & p.p. de* **to dig.**

**duke** [djuk] *s.* duque.

**dukedom** [djúkdəm] *s.* ducado.

**dull** [dʌl] *adj.* (*dim*) opaco, empañado, mate; sin brillo; (*boring*) aburrido; (*blunt*) embotado, sin punta, sin filo; (*stupid*) torpe; tardo; **— pain** dolor sordo; **— sound** sonido sordo o apagado; *v.* embotar(se); empañar(se); ofuscar; amortiguar (*un dolor o sonido*).

**dullness** [dʌlnɪs] *s.* (*dimness*) falta de brillo; (*sluggishness*) estupidez, torpeza; (*bluntness*) falta de punta o filo; (*monotony*) aburrimiento; (*heaviness*) pesadez.

**duly** [djúlɪ] *adv.* debidamente.

**dumb** [dʌm] *adj.* (*silent*) mudo; silencioso, callado; (*dull*) estúpido, torpe; **— creature** animal.

**dumbness** [dʌmnɪs] *s.* mudez; mutismo; estupidez.

**dummy** [dʌmɪ] *s.* (*figure*) maniquí, figurón, muñeco; (*fool*) zoquete, tonto; *adj.* falso, fingido.

**dump** [dʌmp] *s.* montón (*de tierra, carbón, etc.*); terrero, vaciadero, escorial; **garbage —** muladar; basurero; **to be in the -s** estar abatido; *v.* echar, vaciar, descargar; echar a la basura.

**dunce** [dʌns] *s.* zopenco, zoquete, tonto.

**dune** [djun] *s.* duna o médano.

**dung** [dʌŋ] *s.* boñiga, estiércol.

**dungeon** [dʌndʒən] *s.* mazmorra, calabozo.

**dunghill** [dʌ́ŋhɪl] *s.* muladar, estercolero.

**dupe** [djup] *s.* inocentón, incauto, víctima (*de un engaño*); *v.* embaucar.

**duplicate** [djúpləkɪt] *adj. & s.* doble, duplicado; [djúpləket] *v.* duplicar, copiar.

**duplicity** [djuplísətɪ] *s.* duplicidad, doblez.

**durable** [djúrəbl] *adj.* durable, duradero.

**duration** [djuréʃən] *s.* duración.

**during** [dúrɪŋ] *prep.* durante.

**dusk** [dʌsk] *s.* crepúsculo (*vespertino*), anochecida; caída de la tarde; sombra, oscuridad; **at —** al atardecer.

**dusky** [dʌskɪ] *adj.* obscuro, negruzco; sombrío.

**dust** [dʌst] *s.* polvo; tierra; **cloud of —** polvareda; *v.* sacudir el polvo, desempolvar, quitar el polvo; empolvar, llenar de polvo; espolvorear.

**duster** [dʌstɚ] *s.* limpiador; quitapolvo; **feather —** plumero.

**dusty** [dʌstɪ] *adj.* polvoriento; empolva-

do, lleno de polvo.

**Dutch** [dʌtʃ] *adj. & s.* holandés; **— treat** convite a escote.

**Dutchman** [dʌtʃmən] *s.* holandés.

**duty** [djútɪ] *s.* deber, obligación; derechos aduanales; impuesto; **— free** libre de derechos aduanales.

**dwarf** [dwɔrf] *s. & adj.* enano; *v.* achicar, empequeñecer; impedir el desarrollo o crecimiento de.

**dwell** [dwɛl] *v.* residir, morar, habitar vivir; **to — on a subject** espaciarse o dilatarse en un asunto.

**dweller** [dwélɚ] *s.* habitante, morador.

**dwelling** [dwélɪŋ] *s.* morada, habitación, domicilio.

**dwelt** [dwɛlt] *pret. & p.p. de* **to dwell.**

**dwindle** [dwíndl] *v.* menguar, mermar; disminuir(se); gastarse.

**dye** [daɪ] *s.* tinte, tintura; *v.* teñir, tinturar.

**dyer** [dáɪɚ] *s.* tintorero; **-'s shop** tintorería.

**dying** [dáɪɪŋ] *adj.* moribundo; agonizante.

**dynamic** [daɪnǽmɪk] *adj.* dinámico; enérgico; **-s** *s.* dinámica.

**dynamite** [dáɪnəmaɪt] *s.* dinamita; *v.* dinamitar, volar con dinamita.

**dynamo** [dáɪnəmo] *s.* dínamo.

**dynasty** [dáɪnəstɪ] *s.* dinastía.

**dysentery** [dísn̩tɛrɪ] *s.* disentería.

# E

**each** [itʃ] *adj.* cada; *pron.* cada uno; **— other** el uno al otro, uno(s) a otro(s).

**eager** [ígɚ] *adj.* anhelante, ansioso, deseoso; **-ly** *adv.* con anhelo; con ahinco; ansiosamente.

**eagerness** [ígɚnɪs] *s.* anhelo, ansia, deseo vehemente; ahinco; ardor.

**eagle** [ígl] *s.* águila.

**ear** [ɪr] *s.* oreja; oído; **—drum** tímpano; **— muff** orejera; **— of corn** mazorca; **— of wheat** espiga; **by —** de oído; **within —shot** al alcance del oído.

**earl** [ɝl] *s.* conde.

**early** [ɝ́lɪ] *adv.* temprano; *adj.* temprano; primitivo, remoto; **— riser** madrugador, tempranero, mañanero; **at an — date** en fecha a próxima.

**earn** [ɝn] *v.* ganar; merecer.

**earnest** [ɝ́nɪst] *adj.* serio, formal; ardiente; **in —** en serio, con toda formalidad; de buena fe; **-ly** *adv.* seriamente; con ahinco; encarecidamente, ansiosamente.

**earnestness** [ɝ́nɪstnɪs] *s.* seriedad; celo; solicitud; sinceridad; **in all —** con todo ahinco; con toda formalidad; con toda sinceridad.

**earnings** [ɝ́nɪŋz] *s.* ganancias; sueldo, salario, paga.

**earring** [írrɪŋ] *s.* arete, zarcillo, pendiente, arracada; *C.A.* arito; *P.R.* pantalla.

**earth** [ɝθ] *s.* tierra; suelo.

**earthen** [ɝ́θən] *adj.* de tierra; de barro.

**earthenware** [ɝ́θənwɛr] *s.* loza de barro; trastos, cacharros.

**earthly** [ɝ́θlɪ] *adj.* terrenal, terrestre,

mundano; terreno; **to be of no — use** no servir para nada.

**earthquake** [ɝ́θkwek] *s.* terremoto, temblor de tierra.

**earthworm** [ɝ́θwɝm] *s.* lombriz.

**ease** [iz] *s.* (*facility*) facilidad; naturalidad; soltura; (*comfort*) comodidad; tranquilidad; **at —** tranquilo; cómodo; *v.* facilitar; aliviar; mitigar; tranquilizar; aligerar (*el peso*); aflojar.

**easel** [íz]] *s.* caballete (*de pintor*).

**easily** [ízəlɪ] *adv.* fácilmente; sin dificultad; cómodamente.

**east** [ist] *s.* este; oriente, levante; *adj.* del este, oriental; *adv.* al este, hacia el este; en el este.

**Easter** [ístɝ] *s.* Pascuas, Pascua Florida; **— Sunday** Domingo de Resurrección o de Pascuas.

**eastern** [ístɝn] *adj.* oriental; del este.

**eastward** [ístwɝd] *adv. & adj.* hacia el este u oriente.

**easy** [ízɪ] *adj.* (*simple*) fácil; (*comfortable*) cómodo; tranquilo; **— chair** silla cómoda, poltrona, butaca; **easy-going man** hombre cachazudo o calmo; **at an — pace** a paso moderado; **within — reach** al alcance; a la mano.

**eat** [it] *v.* comer; **to — away** corroer, destruir; **to — breakfast** desayunarse, tomar el desayuno; **to — dinner** tomar la comida, comer; **to — supper** tomar la cena, cenar; **to — one's heart out** sufrir en silencio; **to — one's words** retractarse.

**eaten** [ítṇ] *p.p. de* **to eat.**

**eaves** [ivz] *s. pl.* alero (*de un tejado*).

**ebb** [ɛb] *s.* reflujo; decadencia; **— tide** marea menguante; **to be at a low —** eśtar decaído; *v.* menguar, decaer.

**ebony** [ébənɪ] *s.* ébano.

**eccentric** [ɪkséntrɪk] *adj. & s.* excéntrico.

**ecclesiastic** [ɪklizɪǽstɪk] *adj. & s.* eclesiástico.

**echelon** [éʃəlɑn] *s.* escalón.

**echo** [éko] *s.* eco; *v.* hacer eco, repetir; resonar, repercutir.

**eclectic** [ɪkléktɪk] *adj.* ecléctico.

**eclipse** [ɪklíps] *s.* eclipse; *v.* eclipsar.

**economic** [ɪkənámɪk] *adj.* económico.

**economical** [ɪkənámɪkl] *adj.* económico.

**economics** [ɪkənámɪks] *s.* economía política.

**economist** [ɪkánəmɪst] *s.* economista.

**economize** [ɪkánəmaɪz] *v.* economizar.

**economy** [ɪkánəmɪ] *s.* economía; parsimonia.

**ecstasy** [ékstəsɪ] *s.* éxtasis.

**ecumenical** [ɛkjuménəkl] *adj.* ecuménico.

**eddy** [édɪ] *s.* remolino; *v.* arremolinarse.

**Eden** [ídṇ] *s.* Edén; paraíso.

**edge** [ɛdʒ] *s.* orilla, borde; filo; **to be on — estar** nervioso.

**edgewise** [édʒwaɪz] *adv.* de lado; de filo.

**edible** [édəbl] *adj. & s.* comestible.

**edifice** [édəfɪs] *s.* edificio.

**edify** [édəfaɪ] *v.* edificar (*moral espiritualmente*).

**edit** [édɪt] *v.* redactar; preparar o corregir (*un manuscrito*) para la imprenta; cuidar (*una edición*).

**edition** [ɪdíʃən] *s.* edición.

**editor** [édɪtɝ] *s.* redactor; director de un periódico; revisor (*de manuscritos*).

**editorial** [ɛdətórɪəl] *adj.* editorial; *s.* editorial (*m.*), artículo de fondo.

**editorialize** [ɛdɪtórɪəlaɪz] *v.* expresar opiniones como en artículo de fondo; editorializar.

**educate** [édʒəket] *v.* educar; instruir.

**education** [ɛdʒəkéʃən] *s.* educación; crianza; instrucción, enseñanza; pedagogía.

**educational** [ɛdʒəkéʃənl] *adj.* educativo, docente; pedagógico.

**educator** [édʒəketɝ] *s.* educador.

**eel** [il] *s.* anguila.

**effect** [əfékt] *s.* efecto; **-s** bienes, efectos; **to go into —** hacerse vigente, ponerse en operación (*una ley*); *v.* efectuar; ejecutar; realizar.

**effective** [əféktɪv] *adj.* efectivo, eficaz; vigente (*una ley*); **-ly** *adv.* eficazmente.

**effectual** [əféktʃʊəl] *adj.* eficaz.

**effeminate** [əfémənɪt] *adj.* afeminado.

**effete** [ɪfít] *adj.* gastado; estéril; decadente.

**efficacy** [éfəkəsɪ] *s.* eficacia.

**efficiency** [əfíʃənsɪ] *s.* eficiencia; eficacia.

**efficient** [əfíʃənt] *adj.* eficiente; eficaz.

**effigy** [éfɪdʒɪ] *s.* efigie; **to burn in —** quemar en efigie.

**effort** [éfɝt] *s.* esfuerzo; empeño.

**effrontery** [əfrʌ́ntərɪ] *s.* descaro, desvergüenza, desfachatez.

**effusive** [ɛfúsɪv] *adj.* efusivo, demostrativo, expansivo.

**egg** [ɛg] *s.* huevo; **fried —** huevo frito o estrellado; **hard-boiled —** huevo cocido, huevo duro; **scrambled -s** huevos revueltos; **soft-boiled —** huevo pasado por agua; *v.* **to — on** incitar.

**eggplant** [égplænt] *s.* berenjena.

**egocentric** [igoséntrɪk] *adj.* egocéntrico.

**egotism** [ígətɪzəm] *s.* egotismo; egoismo.

**Egyptian** [ɪdʒípʃən] *adj. & s.* egipcio.

**either** [íðɝ] *adj. & pron.* uno u otro; **— of the two** cualquiera de los dos; **in — case** en ambos casos; *adv.* tampoco; **nor I —** ni yo tampoco; *conj.* o.

**eject** [ɪdʒékt] *v.* echar, arrojar, expulsar.

**ejection** [ɪdʒékʃən] *s.* expulsión; **— seat** asiento lanzable.

**elaborate** [ɪlǽbərɪt] *adj.* elaborado, primoroso; esmerado; [ɪlǽbəret] *v.* elaborar.

**elapse** [ɪlǽps] *v.* transcurrir, pasar.

**elastic** [ɪlǽstɪk] *adj.* elástico; *s.* elástico; goma elástica; cordón elástico; liga elástica.

**elasticity** [ɪlæstísətɪ] *s.* elasticidad.

**elated** [ɪlétɪd] *adj.* exaltado, gozoso, alborozado.

**elbow** [élbo] s. codo; recodo, ángulo; **to be within — reach** estar a la mano; v. codear, dar codazos; **to — one's way through** abrirse paso a codazos.

**elder** [éldɚ] adj. mayor, más grande, más viejo, de más edad; s. mayor; anciano; dignatario (en ciertas iglesias); **our -s** nuestros mayores; nuestros antepasados.

**elderly** [éldɚlɪ] adj. viejo, anciano.

**eldest** [éldɪst] adj. mayor.

**elect** [ɪlɛ́kt] adj. & s. electo; elegido; v. elegir.

**election** [ɪlɛ́kʃən] s. elección.

**elector** [ɪlɛ́ktɚ] s. elector.

**electoral** [ɪlɛ́ktərəl] adj. electoral.

**electric** [ɪlɛ́ktrɪk] adj. eléctrico; **— meter** electrómetro, contador eléctrico; **— storm** tronada, tempestad; **— eye** ojo eléctrico; s. tranvía o ferrocarril eléctrico.

**electrical** [ɪlɛ́ktrɪkl] adj. eléctrico; **— engineering** electrotecnia, ingeniería eléctrica; **— engineer** ingeniero electricista; electrotécnico.

**electrician** [ɪlɛktrɪ́ʃən] s. electricista.

**electricity** [ɪlɛktrɪ́sətɪ] s. electricidad.

**electrify** [ɪlɛ́ktrəfaɪ] v. electrizar; electrificar.

**electrocardiograph** [ɪlɛktrokárdɪəgræf] s. electrocardiógrafo.

**electrocute** [ɪlɛ́ktrəkjut] v. electrocutar.

**electron** [ɪlɛ́ktrɑn] s. electrón.

**electronics** [ɪlɛktrɑ́nɪks] s. electrónica.

**elegance** [éləgəns] s. elegancia.

**elegant** [éləgənt] adj. elegante.

**element** [éləmənt] s. elemento.

**elemental** [ɛləméntl] adj. elemental.

**elementary** [ɛləméntərɪ] adj. elemental.

**elephant** [éləfənt] s. elefante.

**elevate** [éləvet] v. elevar; alzar; levantar.

**elevation** [ɛləvéʃən] s. elevación; altura; exaltación.

**elevator** [éləvetɚ] s. ascensor, Am. elevador; **grain —** almacén de granos.

**elicit** [ɪlɪ́sɪt] v. extraer, sonsacar; **to — admiration** despertar admiración; **to — applause** suscitar el aplauso o los aplausos.

**eligible** [élɪdʒəbl] adj. elegible.

**eliminate** [ɪlɪ́mənet] v. eliminar.

**elimination** [ɪlɪmənéʃən] s. eliminación.

**elite** [ɛlít] s. lo selecto; los selectos; los escogidos.

**elk** [ɛlk] s. ante.

**elliptic** [ɪlíptɪk] adj. elíptico.

**elm** [ɛlm] s. olmo.

**elope** [ɪlóp] v. fugarse (con su novio).

**eloquence** [éləkwəns] s. elocuencia.

**eloquent** [éləkwənt] adj. elocuente.

**else** [ɛls] adj. & adv. otro (úsase sólo en ciertas combinaciones); más, además; **or —** de otro modo; si no; **nobody —** ningún otro; **nothing —** nada más; **somebody —** algún otro, otra persona; **what — ?** ¿qué más?

**elsewhere** [élshwɛr] adv. en otra parte, a otra parte.

**elucidate** [ɪlúsədet] v. elucidar, esclarecer, aclarar, clarificar.

**elucidation** [ɪlusədéʃən] s. elucidación, esclarecimiento, explicación.

**elude** [ɪlúd] v. eludir, evadir.

**elusive** [ɪlúsɪv] adj. evasivo; que elude.

**emaciated** [ɪméʃɪetɪd] adj. demacrado, escuálido, macilento.

**emanate** [émənet] v. emanar, brotar.

**emanation** [ɛmənéʃən] s. emanación; efluvio.

**emancipate** [ɪmǽnsəpet] v. emancipar.

**emancipation** [ɪmænsəpéʃən] s. emancipación.

**embalm** [ɪmbám] v. embalsamar.

**embankment** [ɪmbǽŋkmənt] s. terraplén; dique.

**embargo** [ɪmbárgo] s. embargo; prohibición; **to put an — on** embargar.

**embark** [ɪmbárk] v. embarcar(se).

**embarrass** [ɪmbǽrəs] v. turbar, desconcertar; apenar; avergonzar; embarazar; **to be financially -ed** encontrarse escaso de fondos.

**embarrassing** [ɪmbǽrəsɪŋ] adj. embarazoso, penoso; desconcertante; angustioso.

**embarrassment** [ɪmbǽrəsmənt] s. turbación, vergüenza, desconcierto; aprieto, apuro, dificultad; estorbo, embarazo.

**embassy** [émbəsɪ] s. embajada.

**embellish** [ɪmbélɪʃ] v. embellecer, hermosear.

**ember** [émbɚ] s. ascua; **-s** ascuas, rescoldo.

**embezzle** [ɪmbézl] v. desfalcar.

**embezzlement** [ɪmbézlmənt] s. desfalco, peculado.

**embitter** [ɪmbítɚ] v. amargar.

**emblem** [émbləm] s. emblema.

**embody** [ɪmbádɪ] v. encarnar, dar cuerpo a; incorporar, abarcar.

**emboss** [ɪmbɔ́s] v. realzar, grabar en relieve.

**embrace** [ɪmbrés] s. abrazo; v. abrazar(se); abarcar.

**embroider** [ɪmbrɔ́ɪdɚ] v. bordar; recamar; ornar, embellecer.

**embroidery** [ɪmbrɔ́ɪdərɪ] s. bordado; bordadura; recamo.

**embryo** [émbrɪo] s. embrión.

**emerald** [émərəld] s. esmeralda.

**emerge** [ɪmɚ́dʒ] v. emerger; surtir.

**emergency** [ɪmɚ́dʒənsɪ] s. caso fortuito; aprieto; urgencia; emergencia.

**emigrant** [éməgrənt] adj. & s. emigrante.

**emigrate** [éməgret] v. emigrar.

**emigration** [ɛməgréʃən] s. emigración.

**eminence** [émənəns] s. eminencia.

**eminent** [émənənt] adj. eminente.

**emit** [ɪmít] v. emitir; exhalar, arrojar; despedir (olor, humo, etc.).

**emotion** [ɪmóʃən] s. emoción.

**emotional** [ɪmóʃənl] adj. emocional; emotivo; sentimental; sensible.

**empathy** [émpəθɪ] s. empatía.

**emperor** [émpərɚ] s. emperador.

**emphasis** [émfəsɪs] s. énfasis.

**emphasize** [émfəsaɪz] v. dar énfasis; hacer hincapié en; subrayar, recalcar; acentuar.

**emphatic** [ɪmfǽtɪk] adj. enfático; recalcado; **-ally** adv. enfáticamente.

**emphysema** [ɛmfəsímə] s. enfisema.

**empire** [émpaɪr] s. imperio.

**empirical** [ɛmpírəkl] adj. empírico.

**employ** [ɪmplɔ́ɪ] v. emplear; dar empleo a; ocupar; **to be in his —** ser su empleado; trabajar a sus órdenes.

**employee** [ɪmplɔɪí] s. empleado.

**employer** [ɪmplɔ́ɪəʔ] s. patrón, amo, principal.

**employment** [ɪmplɔ́ɪmənt] s. empleo; ocupación.

**empower** [ɪmpáuəʔ] v. autorizar; apoderar (*dar poder a un abogado*).

**empress** [émprɪs] s. emperatriz.

**emptiness** [émptɪnɪs] s. vaciedad; futilidad, vanidad.

**empty** [émptɪ] adj. vacío; vacante, desocupado; vano; v. vaciar; desaguar, desembocar.

**emulate** [émjʊlet] v. emular.

**enable** [ɪnébl] v. capacitar, hacer capaz; habilitar; dar poder; facilitar; hacer posible.

**enact** [ɪnǽkt] v. decretar, promulgar; hacer el papel de.

**enamel** [ɪnǽml] s. esmalte; v. esmaltar.

**enamor** [ɪnǽməʔ] v. enamorar, mover a amar; encantar; **to be -ed of** estar enamorado de.

**encamp** [ɪnkǽmp] v. acampar.

**enchant** [ɪntʃǽnt] v. encantar; embelesar; hechizar.

**enchanter** [ɪntʃǽntəʔ] s. encantador; hechicero, mago, brujo.

**enchantment** [ɪntʃǽntmənt] s. encanto; encantamiento; hechicería.

**enchantress** [ɪntʃǽntrɪs] s. encantadora; hechicera, bruja.

**encircle** [ɪnsǽkl] v. cercar, rodear, ceñir.

**enclose** [ɪnklóz] v. encerrar; cercar, rodear, circundar; incluir.

**enclosure** [ɪnklóʒəʔ] s. recinto, cercado, vallado; remesa, lo remitido (*dentro de una carta*), lo adjunto; encerramiento.

**encompass** [ɪnkámpəs] v. abarcar; encuadrar; rodear, ceñir, circundar.

**encounter** [ɪnkáuntəʔ] s. encuentro; combate; v. encontrar(se); encontrarse con; tropezar con.

**encourage** [ɪnkɹ́ɪdʒ] v. alentar, animar; fomentar.

**encouragement** [ɪnkɹ́ɪdʒmənt] s. aliento, ánimo; estímulo; fomento.

**encroach** [ɪnkrótʃ] v. **to — upon** usurpar, invadir, meterse en; quitar (*el tiempo*).

**encumber** [ɛnkámbəʔ] v. impedir; estorbar.

**encyclopedia** [ɪnsaɪkləpídɪə] s. enciclopedia.

**end** [ɛnd] s. (*temporal*) fin; cabo; término; (*spatial*) término; extremo; **no — of things** un sin fin de cosas; **odds and -s** retazos; **on —** de punta;

**to put an — to** acabar con, poner fin a; v. acabar; terminar; concluir, dar fin.

**endanger** [ɪndéndʒəʔ] v. poner en peligro, arriesgar.

**endear** [ɪndír] v. hacer amar, hacer querer; **to — oneself** hacerse querer.

**endeavor** [ɪndévəʔ] s. esfuerzo, empeño; tentativa; tarea; v. procurar, tratar de, intentar; esforzarse por o en.

**endemic** [ɛndémɪk] adj. endémico.

**ending** [éndɪŋ] s. final; terminación; conclusión.

**endless** [éndlɪs] adj. sin fin, interminable, inacabable; eterno.

**endorse** [ɛndórs] v. endosar; repaldar; apoyar, garantizar.

**endorsement** [ɛndórsmənt] s. (*signature*) endose, endoso; (*backing*) respaldo; garantía, apoyo.

**endorser** [ɛndórsəʔ] s. endosante.

**endow** [ɪndáu] v. dotar.

**endowment** [ɪndáumənt] s. dotación; dote, don.

**endurance** [ɪndjúrəns] s. resistencia; aguante; paciencia; duración.

**endure** [ɪndjúr] v. aguantar, soportar, sufrir; durar, perdurar.

**enema** [énəmə] s. lavativa.

**enemy** [énəmɪ] s. enemigo.

**energetic** [enəʔdʒétɪk] adj. enérgico.

**energy** [énəʔdʒɪ] s. energía.

**enervate** [énəʔvet] v. enervar, debilitar.

**enfold** = **infold**.

**enforce** [ɪnfórs] v. dar fuerza a; hacer cumplir (*una ley*); **to — obedience** hacer obedecer, imponer obediencia.

**enforcement** [ɪnfórsmənt] s. coacción; cumplimiento forzoso (*de una ley*).

**engage** [ɪngédʒ] v. (*employ*) ocupar; emplear, contratar; (*reserve*) alquilar; (*attract*) atraer; (*mesh*) engranar, acoplar; **to — in battle** trabar batalla; **to — (oneself) to do it** comprometerse a hacerlo; **to be -ed in something** estar ocupado en algo; **to be -ed to be married** estar comprometido para casarse.

**engagement** [ɪngédʒmənt] s. compromiso; cita; noviazgo; convenio, contrato; pelea; traba, engrane, acoplamiento (*de maquinaria*).

**engender** [ɪndʒéndəʔ] v. engendrar, producir.

**engine** [éndʒən] s. máquina; motor; locomotora.

**engineer** [ɛndʒənír] s. ingeniero; maquinista (*de locomotora*); v. dirigir, planear.

**engineering** [ɛndʒənírɪŋ] s. ingeniería; manejo, planeo.

**English** [íŋglɪʃ] adj. inglés; s. inglés, idioma inglés; **the —** los ingleses.

**Englishman** [íŋglɪʃmən] s. inglés.

**engrave** [ɪngrév] v. grabar, esculpir.

**engraving** [ɪngrévɪŋ] s. grabado; estampa, lámina; **wood —** grabado en madera.

**engross** [ɛngrós] v. absorber; redactar en limpio.

**engrossed** [ɪngróst] adj. absorto, ensi-

EL

mismado.

**engulf** [ɪngʎlf] v. engolfar, absorber, tragar.

**enhance** [ɪnhǽns] v. realzar; engrandecer.

**enigma** [ɪnígmə] s. enigma.

**enjoin** [ɪndʒɔ́ɪn] v. mandar, ordenar; **to — from** prohibir, vedar.

**enjoy** [ɪndʒɔ́ɪ] v. gozar de; disfrutar de; **to — oneself** divertirse, gozar, deleitarse; **to — the use of** usufructuar.

**enjoyable** [ɪndʒɔ́ɪəbl̩] adj. agradable, deleitable.

**enjoyment** [ɪndʒɔ́ɪmənt] s. placer, goce; disfrute; usufructo.

**enlarge** [ɪnlárdʒ] v. agrandar(se); ensanchar; ampliar; **to — upon** explayarse en, extenderse en; comentar.

**enlargement** [ɪnlárdʒmənt] s. (photo) ampliación; ensachamiento.

**enlighten** [ɪnláɪtn̩] v. alumbrar; iluminar; ilustrar, instruir.

**enlist** [ɪnlíst] v. alistar(se); sentar plaza (de soldado); reclutar.

**enlistment** [ɪnlístmənt] s. reclutamiento; alistamiento.

**enliven** [ɪnláɪvən] v. avivar, animar, alegrar.

**enmity** [ɛ́nmətɪ] s. enemistad.

**ennoble** [ɪnóbl̩] v. ennoblecer.

**enormous** [ɪnɔ́rməs] adj. enorme.

**enough** [ənʎf] adj. & adv. bastante; s. lo bastante, lo suficiente; **that is —** eso basta, con eso basta; **—!** ¡basta!

**enquire = inquire.**

**enrage** [ɪnrédʒ] v. enrabiar, hacer rabiar; enfurecer.

**enrapture** [ɪnrǽptʃɚ] v. extasiar, embelesar, enajenar.

**enrich** [ɪnrítʃ] v. enriquecer.

**enroll** [ɪnról] v. alistar(se); matricular(se); inscribir(se); hacerse miembro.

**enrollment** [ɪnrólmənt] s. alistamiento; registro, matrícula.

**ensemble** [ɑnsámbl̩] s. (music) conjunto musical; (dress) traje armonioso.

**ensign** [ɛ́nsn̩] s. alférez (de la marina); [ɛ́nsaɪn] bandera; insignia.

**enslave** [ɪnslév] v. esclavizar.

**ensnare** [ɛnsnér] v. enredar, entrampar, embaucar.

**ensue** [ɛnsú] v. sobrevenir, seguir(se), resultar.

**entail** [ɪntél] v. envolver, ocasionar; vincular (una herencia).

**entangle** [ɪntǽŋgl̩] v. enredar, enmarañar, embrollar.

**enter** [ɛ́ntɚ] v. entrar en; ingresar en; asentar (una partida, cantidad, etc.); registrar; salir (al escenario).

**enterprise** [ɛ́ntɚpraɪz] s. empresa.

**enterprising** [ɛ́ntɚpraɪzɪŋ] adj. emprendedor.

**entertain** [ɛntɚtén] v. divertir; agasajar; obsequiar; banquetear; acariciar (una idea); abrigar (una esperanza, un rencor); **she -s a great deal** es muy fiestera u obsequiosa.

**entertaining** [ɛntɚténɪŋ] adj. entrete-

nido, divertido, chistoso.

**entertainment** [ɛntɚténmənt] s. entretenimiento; pasatiempo; diversión; fiesta; convite.

**enthusiasm** [ɪnθjúzɪæzəm] s. entusiasmo.

**enthusiast** [ɪnθjúzɪæst] s. entusiasta.

**enthusiastic** [ɪnθjuzɪǽstɪk] adj. entusiasta, entusiástico; **to be —** estar entusiasmado.

**entice** [ɪntáɪs] v. atraer, tentar, seducir, halagar.

**entire** [ɪntáɪr] adj. entero, cabal; **the — world** todo el mundo; **-ly** adv. enteramente, por entero.

**entirety** [ɪntáɪrtɪ] s. totalidad, entereza; conjunto; todo.

**entitle** [ɪntáɪtl̩] v. titular, intitular; autorizar, dar derecho.

**entity** [ɛ́ntətɪ] s. entidad; ente, ser.

**entrails** [ɛ́ntrəlz] s. pl. entrañas; tripas.

**entrance** [ɛ́ntrəns] s. entrada; ingreso.

**entreat** [ɪntrít] v. suplicar, rogar; instar.

**entreaty** [ɪntrítɪ] s. súplica, ruego; instancia.

**entrench = intrench.**

**entrust** [ɪntrʎst] v. confiar; depositar, entregar.

**entry** [ɛ́ntrɪ] s. entrada; ingreso; partida, registro, anotación; **double —** partida doble (en teneduría).

**enumerate** [ɪnjúməret] v. enumerar.

**enunciate** [ɪnʎnsɪet] v. articular; enunciar, declarar.

**envelop** [ɪnvɛ́ləp] v. envolver.

**envelope** [ɛ́nvəlop] s. sobre, cubierta (de una carta).

**enviable** [ɛ́nvɪəbl̩] adj. envidiable.

**envious** [ɛ́nvɪəs] adj. envidioso.

**environment** [ɪnváɪrənmənt] s. ambiente, medio ambiente.

**environs** [ɪnváɪrənz] s. pl. cercanías, contornos, alrededores.

**envisage** [ɛnvízɪdʒ] v. prever; encararse con.

**envoy** [ɛ́nvɔɪ] s. enviado.

**envy** [ɛ́nvɪ] s. envidia; v. envidiar.

**ephemeral** [ɪfɛ́mɚl] adj. efímero.

**epic** [ɛ́pɪk] s. epopeya, poema, épico; adj. épico.

**epidemic** [ɛpədémɪk] s. epidemia; peste; adj. epidémico.

**Epiphany** [ɪpífənɪ] s. Epifanía.

**episode** [ɛ́pəsod] s. episodio.

**epistle** [ɪpísl̩] s. epístola, carta.

**epitaph** [ɛ́pətæf] s. epitafio.

**epoch** [ɛ́pək] s. época.

**equal** [íkwəl] adj. igual; **to be — to a task** ser competente (o tener suficientes fuerzas) para una tarea; s. igual; cantidad igual; v. igualar; ser igual a; **-ly** adv. igualmente; por igual.

**equality** [íkwálətɪ] s. igualdad.

**equalize** [íkwəlaɪz] v. igualar; emparejar; equilibrar; nivelar.

**equation** [ɪkwéʒən] s. ecuación.

**equator** [ɪkwétɚ] s. ecuador.

**equilibrium** [ikwəlíbrɪəm] s. equilibrio.

**equip** [ɪkwíp] v. equipar; proveer; habilitar.

**equipment** [ɪkwípmənt] s. equipo;

aparatos; avíos; habilitación.

**equitable** [ékwɪtəbḷ] *adj.* equitativo.

**equity** [ékwətɪ] *s.* equidad; justicia.

**equivalent** [ɪkwívələnt] *adj.* & *s.* equivalente.

**equivocal** [ɪkwívəkḷ] *adj.* equívoco, ambiguo.

**era** [írə] *s.* era, época.

**eradicate** [ɪrǽdɪket] *v.* desarraigar, extirpar.

**erase** [ɪrés] *v.* borrar; tachar.

**eraser** [ɪrésɚ] *s.* goma, *Am.* borrador; **blackboard —** cepillo.

**erasure** [ɪréʃɚ] *s.* borradura, raspadura.

**ere** [ɛr] *prep.* antes de; *conj.* antes (de) que.

**erect** [ɪrékt] *adj.* erguido; derecho; levantado; *Am.* parado; *v.* erigir; levantar, alzar.

**ermine** [ɚ́mɪn] *s.* armiño.

**erode** [ɪród] *v.* erosionar.

**erosion** [ɪróʒən] *s.* erosión; desgaste.

**erotic** [ɪrátɪk] *adj.* erótico.

**err** [ɚ] *v.* errar; equivocarse; descarriarse.

**errand** [érənd] *s.* mandado, recado, encargo; **— boy** mandadero.

**errant** [érənt] *adj.* errante; **knight-errant** caballero andante.

**erratic** [ɛrǽtɪk] *adj.* inconstante errático; vagabundo.

**erroneous** [ərónɪəs] *adj.* erróneo, errado.

**error** [érɚ] *s.* error.

**erudition** [ɛrʊdíʃən] *s.* erudición.

**eruption** [ɪrʌ́pʃən] *s.* erupción.

**escalate** [éskəlet] *v.* aumentar; intensificar.

**escapade** [éskəped] *s.* trapisonda, travesura.

**escape** [əskép] *s.* escape; fuga, huída; escapada; escapatoria; *v.* escapar(se); fugarse; huir(se); eludir, evadir; **it -s me** se me escapa.

**escort** [éskɔrt] *s.* escolta; acompañante; convoy; [ɪskɔ́rt] *v.* escoltar; convoyar; acompañar.

**escutcheon** [ɪskʌ́tʃən] *s.* escudo de armas, blasón.

**especial** [əspéʃəl] *adj.* especial; **-ly** *adv.* especialmente.

**espionage** [éspɪənɪdʒ] *s.* espionaje.

**essay** [ése] *s.* ensayo; [əsé] *v.* ensayar.

**essence** [ésn̩s] *s.* esencia.

**essential** [əsénʃəl] *adj.* esencial.

**establish** [əstǽblɪʃ] *v.* establecer.

**establishment** [əstǽblɪʃmənt] *s.* establecimiento.

**estate** [əstét] *s.* hacienda, heredad; bienes, propiedades; estado, condición; **country —** finca rural.

**esteem** [əstím] *s.* estima, estimación, aprecio; *v.* estimar, apreciar; considerar, juzgar.

**estimable** [éstəməbḷ] *adj.* estimable.

**estimate** [éstəmɪt] *s.* (*calculation*) tasa, cálculo aproximado; presupuesto; (*judgment*) opinión; [éstəmet] *v.* estimar, tasar, calcular aproximadamente; hacer un presupuesto; juzgar, opinar.

**estimation** [ɛstəméʃən] *s.* juicio, opinión; estima; estimación.

**estrange** [əstréndʒ] *v.* enajenar; apartar.

**estuary** [éstʃʊɛrɪ] *s.* estuario o estero, desembocadura de un rio.

**etch** [ɛtʃ] *v.* grabar al agua fuerte.

**etching** [étʃɪŋ] *s.* agua fuerte, grabado al agua fuerte.

**eternal** [ɪtɚ́nḷ] *adj.* eterno.

**eternity** [ɪtɚ́nətɪ] *s.* eternidad.

**ether** [íθɚ] *s.* éter.

**ethereal** [ɪθírɪəl] *adj.* etéreo.

**ethical** [éθɪkḷ] *adj.* ético, moral.

**ethics** [éθɪks] *s.* ética, moral.

**ethnic** [éθnɪk] *adj.* étnico.

**etiquette** [étɪkɛt] *s.* etiqueta (*regla de conducta social*).

**etymology** [ɛtəmálədʒɪ] *s.* etimología.

**eucalyptus** [jukəlíptəs] *s.* eucalipto.

**euphemism** [júfəmɪzm] *s.* eufemismo.

**European** [jʊrəpíən] *adj.* & *s.* europeo.

**evacuate** [ɪvǽkjuet] *v.* evacuar; desocupar.

**evade** [ɪvéd] *v.* evadir.

**evaluate** [ɪvǽljuet] *v.* valorar, avaluar.

**evaporate** [ɪvǽpəret] *v.* evaporar(se).

**evaporation** [ɪvæpəréʃən] *s.* evaporación.

**evasion** [ɪvéʒən] *s.* evasión, evasiva.

**evasive** [ɪvésɪv] *adj.* evasivo.

**eve** [iv] *s.* víspera, vigilia; **Christmas Eve** Nochebuena; **New Year's Eve** víspera del Año Nuevo; **on the — of** en vísperas de.

**even** [ívən] *adj.* (*level*) liso, plano, llano, a nivel; (*same*) parejo; uniforme; igual; **— dozen** docena cabal; **— number** número par; **— temper** genio apacible; **to be — with someone** estar mano a mano (*o* estar a mano) con alguien; **to get — with someone** desquitarse de alguien; *adv.* aun, hasta; **— if** (*o* **— though**) aun cuando; **— so** aun así; **not —** ni siquiera, ni aun; *v.* allanar; nivelar(se); igualar(se); emparejar; **-ly** *adv.* igualmente; de un modo igual; con uniformidad; con suavidad.

**evening** [ívnɪŋ] *s.* tarde; noche (*las primeras horas*); **— gown** vestido de etiqueta; **— star** estrella vespertina, lucero de la tarde.

**evenness** [ívənnɪs] *s.* lisura; igualdad; **— of temper** apacibilidad o suavidad de genio.

**event** [ɪvént] *s.* suceso, acontecimiento; incidente, evento; resultado, coneecuencia; **in any —** en todo caso; **in the — of** en caso de.

**eventful** [ɪvéntfəl] *adj.* lleno de sucesos; importante, memorable.

**eventual** [ɪvéntʃuəl] *adj.* eventual; último, final, terminal; **-ly** *adv.* finalmente, por fin, con el tiempo; eventualmente.

**ever** [évɚ] *adv.* siempre; jamás; alguna vez; **— so much** muchísimo; **for — and —** por (*o* para) siempre jamás; **hardly —** casi nunca, apenas; **if —** si alguna vez; **more than —** más que nunca; **the best friend I — had** el mejor amigo que en mi vida he tenido.

**evergreen** [évəʌgrin] *s.* siempreviva, sempiterna; *adj.* siempre verde.

**everlasting** [ɛvəʌlǽstıŋ] *adj.* sempiterno, eterno, perpetuo; duradero; *s.* eternidad; sempiterna (*planta*); siempreviva; perpetua, flor perpetua.

**evermore** [ɛvəʌmór] *adv.* para siempre; **for —** para siempre jamás.

**every** [évrı] *adj.* cada; todo; todos los, todas las; **— bit of it** todo, todito; **— day** todos los días; **— once in a while** de vez en cuando; **— one of them** todos ellos; **— other day** cada dos días, un día sí y otro no.

**everybody** [évrıbɑdı] *pron.* todos, todo el mundo.

**everyday** [évrıdé] *adj.* diario, cuotidiano, de todos los días; ordinario.

**everyone** [évrıwʌn] *pron.* todos; todo el mundo; cada uno.

**everything** [évrıθıŋ] *pron.* todo.

**everywhere** [évrıhwɛr] *adv.* por (*o* en) todas partes; a todas partes.

**evict** [ıvíkt] *v.* desalojar; expulsar.

**evidence** [évədəns] *s.* evidencia; prueba; demostración, señal; testimonio; **to be in —** mostrarse; *v.* hacer evidente, evidenciar; patentizar, revelar, mostrar.

**evident** [évədənt] *adj.* evidente, patente.

**evil** [ívl] *adj.* malo, malvado, maligno; aciago, de mal agüero; **to cast the — eye** aojar; **the Evil One** el Diablo; *s.* mal; maldad; *adv.* mal.

**evildoer** [ívldúəʌ] *s.* malhechor.

**evoke** [ıvók] *v.* evocar; **to — laughter** provocar a risa.

**evolution** [ɛvəlúʃən] *s.* evolución.

**evolve** [ıválv] *v.* desarrollar(se), desenvolver(se); urdir; evolucionar.

**ewe** [ju] *s.* oveja.

**exact** [ıgzǽkt] *adj.* exacto; *v.* exigir; **-ly** *adv.* exactamente; en punto.

**exacting** [ıgzǽktıŋ] *adj.* exigente.

**exaggerate** [ıgzǽdʒəret] *v.* exagerar.

**exalt** [ıgzólt] *v.* exaltar, ensalzar.

**exaltation** [ɛgzɔltéʃən] *s.* exaltación.

**examination** [ıgzæmənéʃən] *s.* examen; reconocimiento (*médico*).

**examine** [ıgzǽmın] *v.* examinar; reconocer (*dícese del médico*).

**example** [ıgzǽmpl] *s.* ejemplo.

**exasperate** [ıgzǽspəret] *v.* exasperar, irritar.

**excavate** [ékskəvet] *v.* excavar.

**exceed** [ıksíd] *v.* exceder; sobrepasar; propasarse.

**exceedingly** [ıksídıŋlı] *adv.* sumamente, extremamente; **— well** extremamente bien.

**excel** [ıksél] *v.* sobresalir (en *o* entre); sobrepugar (a).

**excellence** [éksləns] *s.* excelencia.

**excellency** [ékslənsı] *s.* excelencia.

**excellent** [ékslənt] *adj.* excelente.

**except** [ıksépt] *prep.* excepto, menos; *v.* exceptuar.

**excepting** [ıkséptıŋ] *prep.* excepto, salvo, menos, exceptuando.

**exception** [ıksépʃən] *s.* (*exclusion*) excepción; (*opposition*) objeción; **with the — of** a excepción de, con excepción de; **to take —** objetar; ofenderse.

**exceptional** [ıksépʃənl] *adj.* excepcional.

**excess** [ıksés] *s.* exceso; sobrante; **— baggage (weight)** exceso de equipaje (de peso); **to drink to —** beber en exceso.

**excessive** [ıksésıv] *adj.* excesivo; **-ly** *adv.* excesivamente, en exceso, demasiado.

**exchange** [ıkstʃéndʒ] *s.* (*money*) cambio; (*interchange*) trueque; intercambio, canje (*de publicaciones, prisioneros*); (*stock*) lonja, bolsa; **rate of —** cambio, *Am.* tipo de cambio; **telephone —** central de teléfonos; *v.* cambiar; trocar; canjear (*publicaciones, prisioneros*); **to — greetings** saludarse; mandarse felicitaciones.

**excite** [ıksáıt] *v.* excitar; acalorar; agitar.

**excited** [ıksáıtıd] *adj.* excitado, acalorado; animado; **to get —** entusiasmarse; sobreexcitarse; acalorarse; **-ly** *adv.* acaloradamente, agitadamente.

**excitement** [ıksáıtmənt] *s.* excitación; acaloramiento; agitación, alboroto; animación.

**exciting** [ıksáıtıŋ] *adj.* excitante, excitador; estimulante.

**exclaim** [ıksklém] *v.* exclamar.

**exclamation** [ɛksklméʃən] *s.* exclamación; **— point** punto de admiración.

**exclude** [ıksklúd] *v.* excluir.

**exclusion** [ıksklúʒən] *s.* exclusión.

**exclusive** [ıksklúsıv] *adj.* exclusivo; privativo; **— of** sin contar.

**excommunicate** [ɛkskəmjúnəket] *v.* excomunicar.

**excommunication** [ɛkskəmjunəkéʃən] *s.* excomunión.

**excrement** [ékskrımənt] *s.* excremento.

**excursion** [ıkskɜ́ʒən] *s.* excursión; correría; expedición.

**excusable** [ıkskjúzəbl] *adj.* excusable, disculpable.

**excuse** [ıkskjús] *s.* excusa; disculpa; [ıkskjúz] *v.* excusar; disculpar; perdonar, dispensar; eximir; **— me!** ¡dispense Vd.!; ¡perdone Vd.!

**execute** [éksıkjut] *v.* ejecutar; ajusticiar; llevar a cabo.

**execution** [ɛksıkjúʃən] *s.* ejecución; desempeño.

**executioner** [ɛksıkjúʃənəʌ] *s.* verdugo.

**executive** [ıgzékjutıv] *adj.* ejecutivo; *s.* ejecutivo, poder ejecutivo; gerente, administrador.

**executor** [ıgzékjətəʌ] *s.* albacea, ejecutor testamentario; [éksıkjutəʌ] ejecutor.

**exemplary** [ıgzémplərı] *adj.* ejemplar.

**exempt** [ıgzémpt] *adj.* exento, libre; *v.* eximir, exentar.

**exemption** [ıgzémpʃən] *s.* exención.

**exercise** [éksəʌsaız] *s.* ejercicio; *v.* ejercitar(se); ejercer (*poder o autoridad*); hacer ejercicio, hacer gimnasia; **to be -d about something** estar preocupado o sobreexcitado por algo.

**exert** [ɪgzɜ́t] *v.* ejercer; **to — oneself** esforzarse, hacer esfuerzos, empeñarse.

**exertion** [ɪgzɜ́ʃən] *s.* ejercicio; esfuerzo, empeño.

**exhale** [ɛkshél] *v.* exhalar, emitir; espirar, soplar.

**exhaust** [ɪgzɔ́st] *s.* escape (*de gas o vapor*); *v.* agotar; consumir; debilitar, fatigar; **I am -ed** no puedo más; estoy agotado.

**exhaustion** [ɪgzɔ́stʃən] *s.* agotamiento; fatiga, postración.

**exhaustive** [ɛgzɔ́stɪv] *adj.* comprensivo; detallado.

**exhibit** [ɪgzíbɪt] *v.* exhibir; mostrar, exponer.

**exhibition** [ɛksəbíʃən] *s.* exhibición; exposición, manifestación.

**exhilarate** [ɪgzíləret] *v.* alborozar, excitar, animar, entusiasmar.

**exhort** [ɪgzɔ́rt] *v.* exhortar.

**exile** [égzaɪl] *s.* destierro, exilio; desterrado; *v.* desterrar; expatriar.

**exist** [ɪgzíst] *v.* existir.

**existence** [ɪgzístəns] *s.* existencia.

**existent** [ɪgzístənt] *adj.* existente.

**exit** [égzɪt] *s.* salida; salida (*del foro*); *v.* vase o vanse (*un personaje o personajes al fin de una escena*).

**exodus** [éksədəs] *s.* éxodo.

**exonerate** [ɪgzánəret] *v.* exonerar.

**exorbitant** [ɪgzɔ́rbətənt] *adj.* exorbitante.

**exotic** [ɪgzátɪk] *adj.* exótico; raro, extraño.

**expand** [ɪkspǽnd] *v.* ensanchar(se); dilatar(se); extender(se); agrandar(se); desarrollar (*una ecuación*).

**expanse** [ɪkspǽns] *s.* espacio, extensión.

**expansion** [ɪkspǽnʃən] *s.* expansión; ensanche; desarrollo (*de una ecuación*).

**expansive** [ɪkspǽnsɪv] *adj.* expansivo; efusivo.

**expect** [ɪkspékt] *v.* esperar; contar con; **I — so** supongo que sí.

**expectation** [ɛkspɛktéʃən] *s.* expectación; expectativa; esperanza.

**expectorate** [ɪkspéktəret] *v.* expectorar, desgarrar.

**expedient** [ɪkspídiənt] *adj.* conveniente, oportuno; ventajoso; prudente; *s.* expediente, medio.

**expedite** [ékspədaɪt] *v.* facilitar; despachar.

**expedition** [ɛkspɪdíʃən] *s.* expedición.

**expeditionary** [ɛkspɪdíʃənɛrɪ] *adj.* expedicionario.

**expel** [ɪkspél] *v.* expeler; expulsar.

**expend** [ɪkspénd] *v.* gastar; consumir.

**expenditure** [ɪkspéndɪtʃɚ] *s.* gasto; desembolso.

**expense** [ɪkspéns] *s.* gasto; coste, costa o costo.

**expensive** [ɪkspénsɪv] *adj.* costoso.

**expensiveness** [ɪkspénsɪvnɪs] *s.* precio subido, coste elevado.

**experience** [ɪkspíriəns] *s.* experiencia; aventura, lance; *v.* experimentar; pasar (*penas, sufrimientos*); sentir.

**experienced** [ɪkspíriənst] *adj.* experimentado; ducho, perito, experto.

**experiment** [ɪkspérəmənt] *s.* experimento, prueba; *v.* experimentar, hacer un experimento.

**experimental** [ɪksperəmént̬l] *adj.* experimental.

**expert** [ékspɜt] *s.* experto, perito; [ɪkspɜ́t] *adj.* experto, perito, experimentado.

**expiration** [ɛkspəréʃən] *s.* terminación; vencimiento (*de un plazo*); espiración (*del aire*).

**expire** [ɪkspáɪr] *v.* expirar, morir; acabar; vencerse (*un plazo*); expeler (*el aire aspirado*).

**explain** [ɪksplén] *v.* explicar.

**explainable** [ɪksplénəbl̩] *adj.* explicable.

**explanation** [ɛksplənéʃən] *s.* explicación.

**explanatory** [ɪksplǽnətorɪ] *adj.* explicativo.

**explicit** [ɛksplísɪt] *adj.* explícito.

**explode** [ɪksplód] *v.* estallar, hacer explosión, *Am.* explotar; reventar; volar (*con dinamita*); desacreditar (*una teoría*).

**exploit** [éksplɔɪt] *s.* hazaña, proeza; [ɪksplɔ́ɪt] *v.* explotar; sacar partido de, abusar de.

**exploitation** [ɛksplɔɪtéʃən] *s.* explotación.

**exploration** [ɛkspləréʃən] *s.* exploración.

**explore** [ɪksplór] *v.* explorar.

**explorer** [ɪksplórɚ] *s.* explorador.

**explosion** [ɪksplóʒən] *s.* explosión, estallido.

**explosive** [ɪksplósɪv] *adj. & s.* explosivo.

**export** [éksport] *s.* exportación; artículo exportado, mercancía exportada; [ɪkspórt] *v.* exportar.

**exportation** [ɛksportéʃən] *s.* exportación.

**expose** [ɪkspóz] *v.* exponer; exhibir, mostrar, poner a la vista; revelar; desenmascarar.

**exposition** [ɛkspəzíʃən] *s.* exposición; exhibición.

**exposure** [ɪkspóʒɚ] *s.* exposición; revelación; **to die of —** morir a efecto de la intemperie.

**expound** [ɪkspáund] *v.* exponer, explicar.

**express** [ɪksprés] *adj.* (*rapid*) expreso; (*explicit*) explícito, claro; **— company** compañía de expreso; expreso, *Am.* exprés; **— train** tren expreso; *adv.* por expreso, por exprés; *s.* expreso; tren expreso, *Am.* exprés; *v.* expresar; enviar por expreso (*o por exprés*).

**expression** [ɪkspréʃən] *s.* expresión.

**expressive** [ɪksprésɪv] *adj.* expresivo.

**expulsion** [ɪkspʌ́lʃən] *s.* expulsión.

**exquisite** [ɛkskwízɪt] *adj.* exquisito.

**exquisiteness** [ɪkskwízɪtnɪs] *s.* exquisitez; primor.

**extant** [ɪkstǽnt] *adj.* existente.

**extemporaneous** [εkstεmpərénɪəs] *adj.* improvisado.

**extend** [ɪksténd] *v.* extender(se); tender; prolongar(se); alargar(se); agrandar; dilatar, prorrogar (*un plazo*); dar (*el pésame, el parabién, ayuda, etc.*).

**extended** [ɪkséndɪd] *adj.* extenso; prolongado; extendido.

**extension** [ɪksténʃən] *s.* extensión; prolongación; prórroga (*de un plazo*); añadidura, anexo.

**extensive** [ɪksténsɪv] *adj.* extenso, ancho, dilatado; extensivo; **-ly** *adv.* extensamente, por extenso; extensivamente; **-ly used** de uso general o común.

**extent** [ɪkstént] *s.* extensión; grado; **to a great —** en gran parte, generalmente; **to such an — that** a tal grado que; **to the — of one's ability** en proporción a su habilidad; **up to a certain —** hasta cierto punto.

**extenuate** [ɪksténjʊet] *v.* atenuar, mitigar.

**exterior** [ɪkstírɪə] *adj.* exterior; externo; *s.* exterioridad; exterior, porte, aspecto.

**exterminate** [ɪkstə́rmənet] *v.* exterminar, destruir por completo, extirpar.

**extermination** [ɪkstə́rmənéʃən] *s.* exterminio.

**external** [ɪkstə́rnl] *adj.* externo; exterior; *s.* exterioridad; lo externo.

**extinct** [ɪkstíŋkt] *adj.* extinto; extinguido, apagado.

**extinguish** [ɪkstíŋgwɪʃ] *v.* extinguir; apagar.

**extol** [ɪkstól] *v.* enaltecer; ensalzar.

**extort** [ɪkstórt] *v.* obtener por fuerza o amenaza, exigir (*dinero, promesa, etc.*), *Am.* extorsionar.

**extortion** [ɪkstórʃən] *s.* extorsión.

**extra** [ékstrə] *adj.* extraordinario; de sobra, de más, adicional; suplementario; **— tire** neumático de repuesto o de recambio; **— workman** obrero supernumerario; *adv.* extraordinariamente; *s.* extra; extraordinario (*de un periódico*); suplemento; gasto extraordinario; recargo (*cargo adicional*); actor suplente o supernumerario.

**extract** [ékstrækt] *s.* extracto; cita, trozo (*entresacado de un libro*); resumen; [ɪkstrǽkt] *v.* extraer; seleccionar; citar.

**extraordinary** [ɪkstrórdnɛrɪ] *adj.* extraordinario; **extraordinarily** *adv.* extraordinariamente; de manera extraordinaria.

**extravagance** [ɪkstrǽvəgəns] *s.* despilfarro, derroche, gasto excesivo; lujo excesivo; extravagancia, capricho.

**extravagant** [ɪkstrǽvəgənt] *adj.* gastador, despilfarrado; extravagante, disparatado; **— praise** elogios excesivos; **— prices** precios exorbitantes.

**extreme** [ɪkstrím] *adj.* (*last*) último; extremo; más remoto; (*excessive*) excesivo; riguroso; radical; **— opinions** opiniones extremadas; *s.* extremo;

cabo; **to go to -s** extremar, exagerar; hacer extremos; tomar las medidas más extremas; **-ly** *adv.* extremamente, en extremo.

**extremity** [ɪkstrémətɪ] *s.* extremidad, extremo; medida extrema; **in —** en gran peligro; en un apuro.

**exuberant** [ɪgzjúbərənt] *adj.* exuberante.

**exult** [ɪgzʌ́lt] *v.* alborozarse, regocijarse.

**eye** [aɪ] *s.* ojo; **— shade** visera; **in a twinkling of an —** en un abrir y cerrar de ojos; **hook and —** macho y hembra; **to catch one's —** llamar la atención; **to have good -s** tener buena vista; **to have before one's -s** tener a (*o* tener ante) la vista; **to keep an — on** cuidar, vigilar; **to see — to —** estar completamente de acuerdo; *v.* mirar, observar.

**eyeball** [áɪbɔl] *s.* globo del ojo.

**eyebrow** [áɪbraʊ] *s.* ceja.

**eyeglass** [áɪglæs] *s.* lente, cristal (*de anteojo*); ocular (*de microscopio o telescopio*); **-es** lentes, anteojos.

**eyelash** [áɪlæʃ] *s.* pestaña.

**eyelid** [áɪlɪd] *s.* párpado.

**eyesight** [áɪsaɪt] *s.* vista; **poor —** male vista.

## F

**fable** [fébl] *s.* fábula.

**fabric** [fǽbrɪk] *s.* género, tela; tejido; textura; estructura.

**fabulous** [fǽbjələs] *adj.* fabuloso.

**façade** [fəsád] *s.* fachada.

**face** [fes] *s.* (*human*) cara, rostro; (*building*) fachada, frente; (*surface*) haz, superficie; (*watch*) muestra; *Ríopl.* esfera; *Méx., C.A., Ven., Col.* carátula; **— value** valor nominal; **in the — of** en presencia de, ante, frente a; **to lose —** perder prestigio; **to make -s** hacer muecas o gestos; **to save one's —** salvar el amor propio; *v.* encararse con; enfrentarse con; hacer frente a; mirar hacia; forrar; **to — about** volverse, *Méx., C.A., Ven., Col., Andes* voltearse; **to — danger** afrontar o arrostrar el peligro; **to — with marble** revestir de mármol; **it -s the street** da a la calle.

**facilitate** [fəsílətet] *v.* facilitar.

**facility** [fəsílətɪ] *s.* facilidad.

**fact** [fækt] *s.* hecho; dato; verdad, realidad; **in —** de hecho; en realidad.

**faction** [fǽkʃən] *s.* facción, bando, partido, pandilla.

**factor** [fǽktə] *s.* factor; elemento; agente; *v.* descomponer en factores.

**factory** [fǽktrɪ] *s.* fábrica.

**faculty** [fǽkltɪ] *s.* facultad; (*college*) profesorado; cuerpo docente.

**fad** [fæd] *s.* novedad; manía; moda.

**fade** [fed] *v.* descolorar(se), desteñir(se); marchitar(se); apagarse (*un sonido*); desvanecerse.

**fagged** [fægd] *adj.* agotado, rendido de cansancio.

**fail** [fel] *v.* (*not effect*) faltar; fallar;

fracasar; no tener éxito; (*wane*) decaer; debilitarse; (*go broke*) quebrar, hacer bancarrota; **to — in an examination** fallar en un examen, salir mal en un examen; **to — a student** reprobar o suspender a un estudiante; **to — to do it** dejar de hacerlo, no hacerlo; **don't — to come** no deje Vd. de venir; **without —** sin falta.

**failure** [féljə˞] *s.* fracaso; malogro; falta; descuido, negligencia; quiebra, bancarrota; debilitamiento.

**faint** [fent] *adj.* (*weak*) débil, languido; (*indistinct*) imperceptible, tenue, vago, indistinto; **to feel —** sentirse desvanecido; **—hearted** tímido, cobarde; *s.* desmayo; *v.* desmayarse; languidecer; **-ly** *adv.* débilmente; lánguidamente; indistintamente, vagamente, tenuemente; apenas.

**faintness** [féntnɪs] *s.* languidez, debilidad, desfallecimiento; falta de claridad; vaguedad.

**fair** [fer] *adj.* (*just*) justo, recto, honrado; imparcial; equitativo; (*mediocre*) regular, mediano; (*complexion*) rubio, blondo; *Méx.* huero; *Guat.* canche; *C.R.* macho; *Pan.* fulo; *Col.* mono; *Ven.* catire; (*weather*) claro, despejado; **— chance of success** buena probabilidad de éxito; **— complexion** tez blanca; **— hair** pelo rubio; **— name** reputación sin mancilla; **— play** juego limpio; **— sex** sexo bello; **— weather** buen tiempo, tiempo bonancible; **to act —** obrar con imparcialidad (*o* con equidad); **to play —** jugar limpio; *s.* feria; mercado; exposición; **-ly** *adv.* justamente; imparcialmente; medianamente; **-ly difficult** medianamente difícil; **-ly well** regular, bastante bien.

**fairness** [férnɪs] *s.* justicia, equidad, imparcialidad; blancura (*de la tez*); belleza.

**fairy** [férɪ] *s.* hada; **— godmother** hada madrina; **— tale** cuento de hadas.

**fairyland** [férɪlænd] *s.* tierra de las hadas.

**faith** [feθ] *s.* fe; fidelidad; **in good —** de buena fe; **to have — in** tener fe o confianza en; **to keep —** cumplir con la palabra.

**faithful** [féθfəl] *adj.* fiel; leal; **-ly** *adv.* fielmente; con fidelidad; puntualmente; **-ly yours** suyo afectísimo; siempre suyo.

**faithfulness** [féθfəlnɪs] *s.* fidelidad; lealtad; exactitud.

**faithless** [féθlɪs] *adj.* infiel; sin fe; desleal; falso.

**fake** [fek] *s.* fraude, trampa; falsedad; embustero; *adj.* falso, fingido; *v.* falsear; fingir; simular.

**falcon** [fólkən] *s.* halcón.

**fall** [fɔl] *s.* (*drop*) caída; bajada; (*collapse*) ruina; baja (*de precios*); (*season*) otoño; **-s** cascada, catarata, salto de agua; *v.* caer(se); decaer; ba-

jar; **to — asleep** dormirse, quedarse dormido; **to — back** retroceder; **to — behind** atrasarse, rezagarse, quedarse atrás; **to — in love** enamorarse; **to — out with** reñir con, enemistarse con; **to — to one** tocarle a uno, corresponderle a uno; **his plans fell through** fracasaron (*o* se malograron) sus planes.

**fallacy** [fǽləsɪ] *s.* falsedad; error.

**fallen** [fólən] *p.p.* *de* **to fall.**

**fallout** [fólaʊt] *s.* precipitación radiactiva.

**fallow** [fǽlo] *adj.* baldío; *s.* barbecho; *v.* barbechar.

**false** [fɔls] *adj.* falso; postizo (*dientes, barba, etc.*); fingido, simulado.

**falsehood** [fólshʊd] *s.* falsedad, mentira.

**falseness** [fólsnɪs] *s.* falsedad.

**falsify** [fólsəfaɪ] *v.* falsificar, falsear; mentir.

**falsity** [fólsətɪ] *s.* falsedad; mentira.

**falter** [fóltə˞] *v.* vacilar; titubear; tambalearse; bambolearse; **to — an excuse** balbucear una excusa; *s.* temblor, vacilación.

**fame** [fem] *s.* fama.

**famed** [femd] *adj.* afamado, famoso, renombrado.

**familiar** [fəmíljə˞] *adj.* familiar, íntimo; confianzudo; **to be — with a subject** conocer bien, estar versado en o ser conocedor de una materia; *s.* familiar.

**familiarity** [fəmɪlɪǽrətɪ] *s.* familiaridad; confianza, franqueza.

**family** [fǽmlɪ] *s.* familia; **— name** apellido; **— tree** árbol genealógico; **to be in the — way** estar encinta.

**famine** [fǽmɪn] *s.* hambre; escasez, carestía.

**famished** [fǽmɪʃt] *adj.* hambriento, muerto de hambre; **to be —** morirse de hambre.

**famous** [féməs] *adj.* famoso.

**fan** [fæn] *s.* abanico; aventador; ventilador; aficionado (*a deportes*); admirador; *v.* abanicar; ventilar.

**fanatic** [fənǽtɪk] *adj.* & *s.* fanático.

**fanaticism** [fənǽtəsɪzəm] *s.* fanatismo.

**fanciful** [fǽnsɪfəl] *adj.* fantástico; caprichoso; imaginario.

**fancy** [fǽnsɪ] *s.* fantasía, antojo, capricho; imaginación; afición, gusto; **to have a — for** tener afición a; **to strike one's —** antojársele a uno; **to take a — to a person** caerle a uno bien (*o* simpatizarle a uno) una persona; *adj.* fantástico, de fantasía; de adorno; elegante; **— ball** baile de fantasía o disfraces; **— free** libre de cuidados; **—work** labor ;bordado fino; *v.* imaginar(se); fantasear; forjar, concebir (*una idea*); **to — oneself** imaginarse; **just — the idea!** ¡figúrate qué idea! **I don't — the idea of** no me gusta la idea de.

**fang** [fæŋ] *s.* colmillo (*de ciertos animales*).

**fantastic** [fæntǽstɪk] *adj.* fantástico; extravagante.

EX

**fantasy** [fǽntəsɪ] *s.* fantasía.

**far** [fɑr] *adv.* lejos; **— away** muy lejos; **— and wide** por todas partes; **— better** mucho mejor; **— off** muy lejos; a lo lejos; **by —** con mucho; **as — as** hasta; en cuanto a; **as — as I know** según parece; a lo que parece; que yo sepa; **so —** hasta ahora; hasta aquí; hasta entonces; **how —?** ¿hasta dónde?; *adj.* lejano, distante, remoto; **— journey** largo viaje; **it is a — cry from** dista mucho de.

**faraway** [fárəwé] *adj.* muy lejano, distante, remoto; abstraído.

**farce** [fɑrs] *s.* farsa.

**fare** [fɛr] *s.* pasaje, tarifa de pasajes; pasajero; comida, alimento; *v.* pasarla (*bien o mal*); irle a uno (*bien o mal*); **to — forth** salir.

**farewell** [fɛrwél] *s.* despedida, adiós; **to bid —** to despedirse de; **—!** ¡adiós!

**farfetched** [fárfétʃt] *adj.* traído de muy lejos; forzado; traído por los cabellos; que no hace al caso; improbable, poco creíble.

**far-flung** [fárflʌ́ŋ] *adj.* extenso, de gran alcance.

**farm** [fɑrm] *s.* hacienda, granja, *Ríopl.* estancia, *Méx.* rancho; **— hand** péon; **— produce** productos agrícolas; *v.* cultivar, labrar (*la tierra*); **to — out** dar en arriendo; repartir.

**farmer** [fɑ́rmɚ] *s.* labrador; granjero; agricultor; *Méx.* ranchero, *Ríopl.* estanciero, *Am.* hacendado.

**farmhouse** [fármhaʊs] *s.* alquería, finca.

**farming** [fármɪŋ] *s.* labranza, agricultura, cultivo de los campos; *adj.* agrícola.

**farmyard** [fármjard] *s.* corral (*de una alquería*).

**far-off** [fárɔ́f] *adj.* distante, remoto.

**far-sighted** [farsáɪtəd] *adj.* (*sight*) présbite; (*foresighted*) precavido.

**farther** [fárðɚ] *adv.* más lejos; más; **— on** más adelante; *adj.* más remoto, más lejano.

**farthest** [fárðɪst] *adj.* más lejano; más remoto; *adv.* más lejos.

**fascinate** [fǽsnet] *v.* fascinar.

**fascination** [fæsnéʃən] *s.* fascinación.

**fashion** [fǽʃən] *s.* (*style*) moda, boga; estilo; (*way*) manera, modo; **— plate** figurín; **the latest —** la última moda (*o novedad*); **after a —** medianamente, no muy bien; **to be in —** estar de moda; estilarse; *v.* forjar, hacer, formar; idear.

**fashionable** [fǽʃnəbl] *adj.* de moda; de buen tono; elegante.

**fast** [fæst] *adj.* rápido, veloz; adelantado (*dícese del reloj*); firme; fiel (*amigo*); fijo; disipado, disoluto; *adv.* aprisa, de prisa; firmemente, fijamente; **— asleep** profundamente dormido; *s.* ayuno; *v.* ayunar.

**fasten** [fǽsn̩] *v.* fijar(se); sujetar(se), asegurar(se); atar, unir; abrochar(se).

**fastener** [fǽsnɚ] *s.* broche; abrochador.

**fastidious** [fæstídɪəs] *adj.* melindroso.

**fat** [fæt] *adj.* gordo; grasiento; mantecoso; **— profits** ganancias pingües; *s.* grasa, manteca; gordura; **the — of the land** lo mejor y más rico de la tierra.

**fatal** [fét] *adj.* fatal.

**fatality** [fətǽlətɪ] *s.* fatalidad; muerte.

**fate** [fet] *s.* hado, sino, destino; fortuna, suerte.

**father** [fáðɚ] *s.* padre.

**fatherhood** [fáðɚhʊd] *s.* paternidad.

**father-in-law** [fáðɚɪnlɔ] *s.* suegro.

**fatherland** [fáðɚlænd] *s.* patria.

**fatherly** [fáðɚlɪ] *adv.* paternal.

**fathom** [fǽðəm] *v.* sondar, sondear; penetrar; *s.* braza (*medida de profundidad*).

**fathomless** [fǽðəmlɪs] *adj.* insondable.

**fatigue** [fətíg] *s.* fatiga, cansancio; *v.* fatigar(se), cansar(se).

**fatness** [fǽtnɪs] *s.* gordura.

**fatten** [fǽtn̩] *v.* engordar.

**faucet** [fɔ́sɪt] *s.* grifo, llave, espita, canilla, *Am.* bitoque.

**fault** [fɔlt] *s.* (*defect*) falta; defecto, tacha; (*blame*) culpa; (*geological*) falla; **to a —** excesivamente; **to be at —** ser, culpable; **to find — with** criticar a.

**faultfinder** [fɔ́ltfaɪndɚ] *s.* criticón, criticador.

**faultless** [fɔ́ltlɪs] *adj.* intachable, sin tacha, perfecto.

**faulty** [fɔ́ltɪ] *adj.* defectuoso, imperfecto.

**favor** [févɚ] *s.* favor; **your — of the ...** su grata (*carta*) del ...; *v.* favorecer.

**favorable** [févrəbl] *adj.* favorable; **favorably** *adv.* favorablemente.

**favorite** [févrɪt] *adj.* & *s.* favorito.

**favoritism** [févrɪtɪzəm] *s.* favoritismo.

**fawn** [fɔn] *s.* cervato; color de cervato; *v.* adular; halagar.

**fear** [fɪr] *s.* temor, miedo; pavor; *v.* temer.

**fearful** [fírfəl] *adj.* terrible, espantoso; temible, temeroso; miedoso.

**fearless** [fírlɪs] *adj.* sin temor, intrépido, atrevido, arrojado.

**fearlessness** [fírlɪsnɪs] *s.* intrepidez, arrojo, osadía, atrevimiento.

**feasible** [fízəbl] *adj.* factible, hacedero, dable.

**feast** [fist] *s.* fiesta; festín, banquete; *v.* festejar, obsequiar; banquetear; **to — one's eyes on** deleitar la vista en.

**feat** [fit] *s.* proeza, hazaña; acto de destreza; suerte (*en el circo*).

**feather** [féðɚ] *s.* pluma; **-s** plumaje; **a — in one's cap** un triunfo para uno; **— weight** de peso mínimo; *v.* emplumar.

**feathery** [féðərɪ] *adj.* plumoso; ligero, como una pluma.

**feature** [fítʃɚ] *s.* facción, rasgo distintivo; película principal (*en el cine*); **-s** facciones (*de la cara*); **— article** artículo sobresaliente o principal; *v.* destacar, hacer sobresalir; dar realce a; mostrar, exhibir (*como cosa principal*); hacer resaltar.

**February** [fébrʊɛrɪ] *s.* febrero.

**fed** [fɛd] *pret.* & *p.p. de* **to feed; to be**
— **up** estar harto; estar hasta la coronilla, estar hasta el copete.
**federal** [fédərəl] *adj.* federal.
**federation** [fɛdəréʃən] *s.* federación,
confederación, liga.
**fee** [fi] *s.* honorario (honorarios); derechos; cuota; **admission** — derechos
de entrada; precio de entrada.
**feeble** [fíbl] *adj.* débil, endeble; **feebly**
*adv.* débilmente.
**feed** [fid] *s.* forraje, pasto, pienso (*para
los caballos*); comida; *v.* alimentar(se);
dar de comer; pacer, pastar; **to** —
**coal** echar carbón.
**feedback** [fídbæk] *s.* regeneración.
**feel** [fil] *v.* sentir; tocar, tentar; palpar;
**to** — **better** (**sad, happy,** *etc.*) sentirse mejor (triste, feliz, *etc.*); **to** —
**one's way** tantear el camino; **to** —
**for someone** compadecer a alguien;
**it -s soft** está suave; **it -s hot in here**
se siente calor aquí; *s.* tacto, sentido
del tacto; **this cloth has a nice** —
esta tela es suave al tacto.
**feeler** [fílər] *s.* tentáculo, antena (*de los
insectos*); tiento; propuesta (*para averiguar la inclinación o pensamiento de
alguien*).
**feeling** [fílɪŋ] *s.* (*touch*) tacto; sensación; (*emotion*) sentimiento; emoción;
pasión; (*pity*) compasión; ternura; **to
hurt someone's -s** ofender la
sensibilidad de alguien; *adj.* sensible, compasivo.
**feet** [fit] *pl. de* **foot.**
**feign** [fen] *v.* fingir.
**fell** [fɛl] *v.* derribar, echar abajo; cortar
(*un árbol*); *pret. de* **to fall.**
**fellow** [félo] *s.* socio, miembro (*de una
sociedad, colegio, etc.*); becario (*estudiante que disfruta una beca*); camarada; compañero; individuo, tipo, sujeto, hombre; — **citizen** conciudadano; — **man** prójimo; — **member**
consocio; colega; — **student** condiscípulo.
**fellowship** [féloʃɪp] *s.* compañerismo;
unión; confraternidad; sociedad;
beca; **to get a** — obtener una beca.
**felony** [félənɪ] *s.* crimen.
**felt** [fɛlt] *s.* fieltro; *adj.* de fieltro; *pret.*
& *p.p. de* **to feel.**
**female** [fímel] *s.* hembra; *adj.* hembra;
femenino, mujeril, de la mujer; — **cat**
(**dog,** *etc.*) gata (perra, *etc.*); — **screw**
tuerca, hembra de tornillo.
**feminine** [fémənɪn] *adj.* femenino,
femenil.
**femininity** [femɪnínɪtɪ] *s.* feminidad.
**fence** [fɛns] *s.* cerca, valla, vallado; receptor de cosas robadas; **to be on
the** — estar indeciso; *v.* esgrimir; **to**
— **in** cercar, rodear con cerca.
**fencing** [fénsɪŋ] *s.* esgrima; cercado.
**fender** [féndər] *s.* guardabarros, guardafango; *Am.* trompa (*de locomotora*);
*Ríopl.* parrilla.
**ferment** [fɜ́ment] *s.* fermento; fermen-
tación; [fəmént] *v.* fermentar; hacer
fermentar.

**fermentation** [fɜmentéʃən] *s.* fermen-
tación.
**fern** [fɜn] *s.* helecho.
**ferocious** [fəróʃəs] *adj.* feroz, fiero.
**ferocity** [fərásətɪ] *s.* ferocidad, fiereza.
**ferret** [fɛ́rɪt] *v.* **to** — **out** buscar, cazar;
escudriñar, indagar.
**ferry** [fɛ́rɪ] *s.* barca de pasaje (*a través
de un rio o bahía*); embarcadero; *v.*
transportar de una orilla a otra; atravesar (*un rio*) en barca de pasaje.
**fertile** [fɜ́tl] *adj.* fértil; fecundo.
**fertility** [fɜtílətɪ] *s.* fertilidad.
**fertilize** [fɜ́tlaɪz] *v.* fertilizar; abonar;
fecundar.
**fertilizer** [fɜ́tlaɪzər] *s.* abono (*para la
tierra*).
**fervent** [fɜ́vənt] *adj.* ferviente; fervoroso.
**fervor** [fɜ́vər] *s.* fervor; ardor.
**fester** [féstər] *v.* supurar; enconarse (*una
llaga*); *s.* llaga, úlcera.
**festival** [féstəvl] *s.* fiesta.
**festive** [féstɪv] *adj.* festivo; alegre.
**festivity** [festívətɪ] *s.* júbilo, regocijo;
festividad.
**fetch** [fɛtʃ] *v.* ir a buscar; coger; traer.
**fete** [fet] *s.* fiesta; *v.* festejar; agasajar.
**fetid** [fétɪd] *adj.* fétido.
**fetish** [fétɪʃ] *s.* fetiche.
**fetter** [fétər] *v.* engrillar, meter en grillos
encadenar; **-s'** *s. pl.* grillos, cadenas,
trabas.
**fetus** [fítəs] *s.* feto.
**feud** [fjud] *s.* riña, pelea, contienda;
**old** — enemistad antigua (*entre dos
personas o familias*).
**feudal** [fjúdl] *adj.* feudal.
**fever** [fívər] *s.* fiebre, calentura.
**feverish** [fívərɪʃ] *adj.* calenturiento, febril.
**feverishness** [fívərɪʃnɪs] *s.* calentura;
agitación febril.
**few** [fju] *adj.* & *pron.* pocos; **a** — unos
pocos, unos cuantos.
**fiancé** [fiɑnsé] *s.* novio; **fiancée** *f.*
novia.
**fiasco** [fɪǽsko] *s.* fiasco.
**fib** [fɪb] *s.* bola, mentirilla, paparrucha,
papa; *v.* echar papas, decir o contar
paparruchas.
**fibber** [fíbər] *s.* paparruchero, cuentero,
mentirosillo.
**fiber** [fáɪbər] *s.* fibra.
**fibrous** [fáɪbrəs] *adj.* fibroso.
**fickle** [fíkl] *adj.* inconstante, voluble,
veleidoso, mudable.
**fiction** [fíkʃən] *s.* ficción.
**fictional** [fíkʃənl] *adj.* novelesco; ficticio.
**fictitious** [fɪktíʃəs] *adj.* ficticio.
**fiddle** [fídl] *s.* violin; *v.* tocar el violín;
**to** — **around** malgastar el tiempo;
juguetear.
**fidelity** [faɪdélətɪ] *s.* fidelidad.
**fidget** [fídʒɪt] *v.* estar inquieto; agitarse,
menearse nerviosamente.
**field** [fild] *s.* campo o cancha (*de
deportes*); — **artillery** artillería de
campaña; — **glasses** anteojos de
larga vista; — **work** trabajo de

**FA**

investigación en el campo.

**fiend** [find] *s.* demonio, diablo; **dope —** morfinómano.

**fiendish** [fíndɪʃ] *adj.* diabólico.

**fierce** [fɪrs] *adj.* feroz, fiero; furioso, espantoso.

**fierceness** [fɪrsnɪs] *s.* ferocidad; fiereza; vehemencia.

**fiery** [fáɪrɪ] *adj.* fogoso; ardiente; vehemente.

**fife** [faɪf] *s.* pífano.

**fig** [fɪg] *s.* higo; **— tree** higuera.

**fight** [faɪt] *s.* lucha; pelea; riña, pleito; **he has a lot of — left** le sobra fuerza para luchar; *v.* luchar (con); pelear; combatir; reñir; batirse; **to — it out** decidirlo a golpes o con argumentos; **to — one's way through** abrirse camino a la fuerza.

**fighter** [fáɪtɚ] *s.* luchador; combatiente; guerrero; **— airplane** avión de caza.

**fighting** [fáɪtɪŋ] *s.* lucha, combate, pelea; *adj.* combatiente; luchador.

**figure** [fígjɚ] *s.* (*form*) figura; forma; talle (*de una persona*); (*numerical*) cifra, número; valor; precio; **-s** cuentas, cálculos; **— of speech** figura de dicción; **to be good at -s** sabe hacer bien las cuentas; ser listo en aritmética; **to cut a poor —** tener mala facha, hacer el ridículo; *v.* figurar; imaginarse, figurarse; adornar con dibujos; calcular; **to — on** contar con, confiar en; tener la intención de, proponerse; tomar en cuenta; **to — out** descifrar, resolver.

**filament** [fíləmənt] *s.* filamento.

**file** [faɪl] *s.* (*records*) fichero; archivo; registro, lista; (*cabinet*) guardapapeles; (*line*) fila; (*tool*) lima; **— card** ficha, papeleta; *v.* archivar; guardar en el fichero; registrar, asentar en el registro; limar; desfilar, marchar en fila.

**filial** [fíliəl] *adj.* filial.

**filigree** [fíligri] *s.* filigrana.

**fill** [fɪl] *v.* llenar(se); ocupar (*un puesto*); empastar (*un diente*); servir, atender, despachar (*un pedido*); inflar (*un neumático*); tapar (*un agujero*); **to — out a blank** llenar un formulario (forma o esqueleto).

**fillet** [fɪlé] *s.* filete; [fíllɪt] cinta, lista de adorno.

**filling** [fíllɪŋ] *s.* relleno; empaste (*dental*); **gold —** orificación.

**filly** [fíllɪ] *s.* potranca.

**film** [fɪlm] *s.* película; membrana; tela (*formada sobre la superficie de un líquido*); nube (*en el ojo*); *v.* filmar (*cinematografiar*); **her eyes -ed with tears** se le arrasaron los ojos de lágrimas.

**filter** [fíltɚ] *s.* filtro; *v.* filtrar(se).

**filth** [fɪlθ] *s.* suciedad; porquería; mugre.

**filthiness** [fíllθɪnɪs] *s.* suciedad, porquería.

**filthy** [fíllθɪ] *adj.* sucio; puerco, cochino; mugriento.

**fin** [fɪn] *s.* aleta (*de pez*).

**final** [fáɪnl] *adj.* final; terminante; definitivo; **-ly** *adv.* finalmente; en fin, por fin.

**finance** [fənǽns] *s.* teoría bancaria, *Am.* finanza; **-s** fondos, recursos monetarios; negocios bancarios, *Am.* finanzas; *v.* hacer operaciones bancarias; fomentar (*un negocio o empresa*), *Am.* financiar.

**financial** [fənǽnʃəl] *adj.* financiero; monetario.

**financier** [fɪnənsír] *s.* financiero, *Am.* financista.

**financing** [fənǽnsɪŋ] *s. Am.* financiamiento.

**find** [faɪnd] *v.* hallar; encontrar; declarar; **to — fault with** criticar a, censurar a; **to — guilty** declarar o encontrar culpable; **to — out** descubrir; averiguar; *s.* hallazgo.

**finding** [fáɪndɪŋ] *s.* descubrimiento; hallazgo; fallo, decisión; **-s** resultados, datos (*de una investigación*).

**fine** [faɪn] *adj.* fino; perfecto, excelente; superior; primoroso; **— arts** bellas artes; **— sand** arena fina o menuda; **— weather** tiempo claro o despejado; **to feel —** sentirse muy bien de salud; **to have a — time** pasar un rato muy divertido; **fine-looking** bien parecido, guapo; *s.* multa; **in —** finalmente, en fin, en resumen; *v.* multar; **-ly** *adv.* finamente; con primor; excelentemente; muy bien, perfectamente.

**fineness** [fáɪnnɪs] *s.* finura; fineza; primor; excelencia, perfección.

**finery** [fáɪnərɪ] *s.* galas; atavíos, adornos.

**finesse** [fɪnés] *s.* sutileza; artificio; soltura.

**finger** [fíŋgɚ] *s.* dedo (*de la mano*); **—print** impresión digital; **the little —** el dedo meñique; **middle —** dedo del corazón, dedo de enmedio; **ring —** dedo anular; *v.* tocar; manosear.

**fingernail** [fíŋgɚnel] *s.* uña.

**finicky** [fíniki] *adj.* melindroso.

**finish** [fíniʃ] *s.* fin término, conclusión; (*varnish*) acabado; pulimiento; **to have a rough —** estar sin pulir, sin pulimento o al natural; *v.* acabar, acabar con, terminar, finalizar; pulir, pulimentar.

**finished** [fíniʃt] *adj.* acabado; pulido, pulimentado; excelente.

**fir** [fɝ] *s.* abeto.

**fire** [faɪr] *s.* (*flame*) fuego; lumbre; (*destructive*) quemazón; incendio; **— alarm** alarma de incendios; **— department** cuerpo o servicio de bomberos; servicio de incendios; **— engine** bomba (*para incendios*); **— escape** escalera de salvamento; **— insurance** seguro contra incendios; **to be on —** estar ardiendo, estar quemándose; **to catch —** incendiarse, quemarse; **to set on —** pegar fuego, incendiar; **to be under enemy —** estar expuesto al fuego del enemigo; *v.* incendiar; pegar fuego; inflamar; disparar; **to — an em-**

**ployee** despedir (*o* expulsar) a un empleado.

**firearm** [fáɪrɑrm] *s.* arma de fuego.

**firebrand** [fáɪrbrænd] *s.* tizón; pavesa.

**firecracker** [fáɪrkrækə] *s.* triquitraque

**firefly** [fáɪrflaɪ] *s.* luciérnaga.

**fireman** [fáɪrmən] *s.* bombero; fogonero.

**fireplace** [fáɪrples] *s.* chimenea, hogar.

**fireproof** [fáɪrpruf] *adj.* incombustible; a prueba de incendio; *v.* hacer incombustible.

**fireside** [fáɪrsaɪd] *s.* hogar.

**firewood** [fáɪrwʊd] *s.* leña.

**fireworks** [fáɪrwɜks] *s.* fuegos artificiales.

**firm** [fɜm] *adj.* firme; fijo; estable; *s.* firma, razón social (*nombre de una casa comercial*); compañía (*comercial o industrial*); **-ly** *adv.* firmemente, con firmeza.

**firmament** [fɜməmənt] *s.* firmamento.

**firmness** [fɜmnɪs] *s.* firmeza; estabilidad.

**first** [fɜst] *adj.* primero; *adv.* primero, en primer lugar, al principio; **from the —** desde el principio; **first-born** primogénito; **first-class** de primera clase; **first-cousin** primo hermano; **first-rate** de primera clase; muy bien; **—hand** de primera mano.

**first aid** [fɜst éd] *s.* primeros auxilios.

**fish** [fɪʃ] *s.* pez; pescado; **— market** pescadería; **— story** patraña, cuento extravagante o increíble; **neither — nor fowl** ni chicha ni limonada; *v.* pescar.

**fisher** [fíʃə] *s.* pescador.

**fisherman** [fíʃəmən] *s.* pescador.

**fishery** [fíʃərɪ] *s.* pesquera; pesquería, pesca.

**fishhook** [fíʃhʊk] *s.* anzuelo.

**fishing** [fíʃɪŋ] *s.* pesca, pesquería; **— rod** caña de pescar; **— tackle** avíos o enseres de pescar; **to go —** ir de pesca.

**fissure** [fíʃə] *s.* grieta, hendedura, *Am.* rajadura.

**fist** [fɪst] *s.* puño; **to shake one's — at** amenazar con el puño.

**fit** [fɪt] *adj.* (*proper*) apto; a propósito, propio, conveniente; (*healthy*) sano, de buena salud, en buen estado; capaz; **— to be tied** frenético; **not to see — to do it** no tener a bien hacerlo; *s.* talle (*de un traje*); ajuste; encaje (*de una pieza en otra*); ataque, convulsión; **— of anger** acceso, arrebato o arranque de cólera; **by -s and starts** espasmódicamente; **that suit is a good —** ese traje le entalla (*o le viene*) bien; *v.* ajustar(se); adaptar; encajar(se), caber (en); acomodar; entallar (*un vestido*); venir bien (*un vestido, zapatos, sombrero, etc.*); ser a propósito para, ser propio para; capacitar, preparar; **to — in with** armonizar con; llevarse bien con; **to — out** equipar, proveer; **it does not — the facts** no está de acuerdo con los hechos; no hace al caso.

**fitness** [fítnɪs] *s.* aptitud; capacidad; conveniencia; propiedad (*de una idea, de una palabra, etc.*); **physical —** buena salud.

**fitting** [fítɪŋ] *adj.* propio, apropiado; a propósito, conveniente; *s.* ajuste; **dress —** prueba de un traje o vestido; **-s** avíos, guarniciones, accesorios.

**fix** [fɪks] *v.* (*repair*) remendar; componer; reparar; ajustar; arreglar; (*prearrange*) fijar; asegurar; **to — up** arreglar(se); componer(se); *s.* apuro, aprieto.

**fixed** [fɪkst] *adj.* fijo, firme.

**fixture** [fíkstʃə] *s.* (*thing*) accesorio fijo; (*person*) persona firmemente establecida (*en un sitio o empleo*); **electric light -s** instalaciones eléctricas (*como brazos de lámparas, arañas*).

**flabby** [flæbɪ] *adj.* blanducho.

**flag** [flæg] *s.* bandera; banderola; **— lily** flor de lis; *v.* hacer señas con banderola; adornar con banderas; decaer, debilitarse, menguar, flaquear.

**flagrant** [flégrənt] *adv.* flagrante, notorio, escandaloso.

**flagstaff** [flægstæf] *s.* asta de bandera.

**flagstone** [flægston] *s.* losa.

**flair** [flɛr] *s.* instinto, penetración, cacumen; disposición o aptitud natural.

**flak** [flæk] *s.* fuego antiaéreo.

**flake** [flek] *s.* copo (*de nieve*); escama; hojuela; **corn -s** hojuelas de maíz; *v.* descostrarse, descascararse.

**flamboyant** [flæmbójənt] *adj.* rimbombante; flameante.

**flame** [flem] *s.* llama; flama; **— thrower** lanzallamas; *v.* llamear, flamear, echar llamas; inflamar(se); enardecer(se).

**flaming** [flémɪŋ] *adj.* llameante; flameante; encendido; ardiente, apasionado; **— red** rojo encendido.

**flank** [flæŋk] *s.* flanco; costado; lado; ijar (*de un animal*); *v.* flanquear; rodear.

**flannel** [flænl] *s.* franela.

**flap** [flæp] *s.* (*thing*) aleta; cubierta (*del bolsillo*); (*action*) golpeteo; aleteo; *v.* golpetear; aletear, batir (*las alas*); hojear con violencia (*las páginas*).

**flare** [flɛr] *s.* llamarada; llama; arranque (*de ira*); vuelo (*de una falda*); *v.* llamear, echar llamaradas; tener vuelo (*una falda*); **to — up** enfurecerse; encenderse; **the illness -ed up** recrudeció la enfermedad.

**flash** [flæʃ] *s.* rayo; destello, llamarada; fogonazo; **— of hope** rayo de esperanza; **— of lightning** relámpago; **— of wit** agudeza; **— bulb** bombilla de destello; bombilla flash; **in a —** en un instante; **news —** última noticia (*enviada por radio o telégrafo*); *v.* relampaguear; destellar; brillar; centellear; radiar o telegrafiar (*noticias*); **to — by** pasar como un relámpago.

**flashing** [flæʃɪŋ] *s.* relampagueo, centello; *adj.* relumbrante; flameante.

**flashlight** [flæʃlaɪt] *s.* linterna eléctrica.

**flashy** [flǽʃɪ] *adj*. relumbrante; llamativo, de relumbrón, ostentoso; chillante, chillón (*dícese de los colores*).

**flask** [flæsk] *s*. frasco.

**flat** [flæt] *adj*. (*no curves*) plano, llano, chato; aplastado; (*tasteless*) insípido; monótono; (*without air*) desinflado; — **denial** negativa terminante; — **note** nota desentonada; — **rate** precio o número redondo; **D** — re bemol (*nota musical*); —**car** vagón de plataforma; **to be** — **broke** estar completamente pelado, estar sin dinero; **to fall** — caer de plano; caer mal (*un discurso, chiste, etc.*); **to sing** — desafinarse, cantar desentonadamente; **to refuse -ly** negarse absolutamente; *s*. plano; palma (*de la mano*); apartamento, departamento, piso; bemol (*en música*).

**flatiron** [flǽtaɪən] *s*. plancha.

**flatness** [flǽtnɪs] *s*. llanura; lisura; insipidez; desafinamiento (*en música*).

**flatten** [flǽtn̩] *v*. aplastar(se); aplanar(se); allanar(se).

**flatter** [flǽtə] *v*. lisonjear; adular.

**flatterer** [flǽtərə] *s*. lisonjero, adulador.

**flattering** [flǽtərɪŋ] *adj*. lisonjero, halagüeño, adulador.

**flattery** [flǽtərɪ] *s*. lisonja, halago; adulación.

**flatulence** [flǽtjʊləns] *s*. hinchazón, flatulencia.

**flaunt** [flɔnt] *v*. ostentar; hacer gala de.

**flavor** [flévə] *s*. sabor; gusto; condimento; *v*. sazonar; dar sabor a; condimentar.

**flavorless** [flévəlɪs] *adj*. insípido, sin sabor.

**flaw** [flɔ] *s*. defecto; falta; tacha; imperfección.

**flawless** [flɔ́lɪs] *adj*. sin tacha; intachable, irreprochable; perfecto.

**flax** [flæks] *s*. lino.

**flay** [fle] *s*. desollar.

**flea** [fli] *s*. pulga.

**fled** [flɛd] *pret*. & *p.p. de* **to flee**.

**flee** [fli] *v*. huir; huir de.

**fleece** [flis] *s*. vellón, lana; *v*. trasquilar, esquilar; despojar, estafar, defraudar.

**fleet** [flit] *s*. flota; armada; *adj*. veloz.

**fleeting** [flítɪŋ] *adj*. fugaz, transitorio, pasajero, efímero.

**Flemish** [flɛ́mɪʃ] *adj*. flamenco; *s*. flamenco, idioma flamenco; **the** — los flamencos.

**flesh** [flɛʃ] *s*. carne; — **and blood** carne y hueso; — **color** color encarnado; **in the** — en persona.

**fleshy** [flɛ́ʃɪ] *adj*. carnoso; gordo, gordiflón.

**flew** [flu] *pret. de* **to fly**.

**flexibility** [flɛksəbílətɪ] *s*. flexibilidad.

**flexible** [flɛ́ksəbl] *adj*. flexible.

**flicker** [flíkə] *s*. titilación, parpadeo, luz trémula; temblor momentáneo (*de emoción*); aleteo; especie de pájaro carpintero; *v*. titilar; temblar; parpadear; vacilar; aletear; **to** — **one's eyelash** pestañear.

**flier** [flái̯ə] *s*. volador; aviador; tren rápido.

**flight** [flaɪt] *s*. vuelo; bandada (*de pájaros*); escuadrilla (*de aviones*); fuga, huída; — **of stairs** tramo de escalera; **to put to** — poner en fuga.

**flimsy** [flímzɪ] *adj*. endeble, débil; tenue; quebradizo; frágil; baladí; **a** — **excuse** una excusa baladí.

**fling** [flɪŋ] *v*. arrojar(se), lanzar(se); tirar; echar; **to** — **open (shut)** abrir (cerrar) de golpe; *s*. tiro; tirada; lanzamiento; tentativa; **to go out on a** — irse a echar una cana al aire.

**flint** [flɪnt] *s*. pedernal.

**flip** [flɪp] *v*. arrojar, lanzar al aire; sacudir; dar un dedazo.

**flippancy** [flípənsɪ] *s*. ligereza; frivolidad; impertinencia; petulancia.

**flippant** [flípənt] *adj*. ligero (*en sus acciones y modales*), ligero de cascos; frívolo; inpertinente; petulante.

**flirt** [flɜt] *s*. coqueta; coquetón, coquetona; *v*. coquetear.

**flirtation** [flɜtéʃən] *s*. coquetería; **to carry on a** — coquetear.

**flit** [flɪt] *v*. pasar velozmente; volar; revolotear.

**float** [flot] *s*. boya; cosa flotante, flotador; corcho (*de una caña de pescar*); balsa; carro o carroza (*de procesiones, fiestas, etc.*); *v*. flotar; sobrenadar; boyar; poner a flote; lanzar al mercado (*una nueva emisión de valores, bonos, etc.*).

**flock** [flak] *s*. bandada (*de pájaros, niños, etc.*); rebaño, grey; manada (*de animales*); grupo; — **of people** gentío, muchedumbre; *v*. agruparse, congregarse; **to** — **to** acudir juntos (*o en bandadas*) a; **to** — **together** andar juntos, volar en bandadas, ir en grupo.

**flog** [flag] *v*. azotar.

**flood** [flʌd] *s*. inundación; diluvio; avenida (*de agua*), crecida; creciente; torrente; —**gate** compuerta (*de una presa*); esclusa (*de un canal*); — **light** reflector; proyector de luz; — **tide** flujo (*o marea ascendiente*); *v*. inundar.

**floor** [flor] *s*. (*surface*) suelo; piso; (*story*) piso; (*bottom*) fondo; **to have the** — tener la palabra; *v*. solar; entarimar, enladrillar, enlosar; echar al suelo, derribar; asombrar.

**flop** [flap] *v*. (*flap*) caer o colgar flojamente; aletear; menearse; (*throw*) lanzar; dejar caer; (*fail*) fracasar; fallar; **to** — **down** dejarse caer; desplomarse, tumbarse; **to** — **over** voltear(se); dar vueltas; *s*. fracaso.

**florist** [flórɪst] *s*. florero, florera; **-'s shop** florería.

**floss** [flɔs] *s*. seda floja; pelusa; fibra sedosa; **dental** — seda dental.

**flounder** [flǎʊndə] *v*. patalear (*en el lodo, nieve, etc.*); forcejear (*por salir del lodo, nieve, o cualquier aprieto*); revolcarse; tropezar, cometer errores; *s*. lenguado (*pez*).

**flour** [flaʊr] *s*. harina.

**flourish** [flə́rɪʃ] v. (*prosper*) florecer, prosperar, medrar; (*blandish*) blandir; agitar en el aire; (*with the signature*) rúbrica; s. floreo; adorno o rasgo caprichoso; ostentación.

**floury** [fláʊrɪ] adj. harinoso.

**flow** [flo] s. flujo; corriente; **— of words** torrente de palabras; v. fluir; correr; flotar, ondear; **to — into** desembocar en; **to be -ing with riches** nadar en la abundancia.

**flower** [fláʊə] s. flor; **— bed** cuadro de jardín; **— vase** florero; v. florecer, *Am.* florear.

**flowerpot** [fláʊrpɑt] s. tiesto, maceta.

**flowery** [fláʊrɪ] adj. florido.

**flowing** [flóɪŋ] adj. fluído, corriente, fluente; suelto, ondeante.

**flown** [flon] p.p. de **to fly.**

**flu** [flu] s. influenza, gripe.

**fluctuate** [flʌ́ktʃuet] s. fluctuar.

**fluctuation** [flʌktʃuéʃən] s. fluctuación.

**flue** [flu] s. cañon (*de chimenea*); tubo de escape.

**fluency** [flúənsɪ] s. fluidez; labia.

**fluent** [flúənt] adj. fluente, flúido; **to speak -ly** hablar con facilidad.

**fluff** [flʌf] v. mullir; esponjar.

**fluffy** [flʌ́fɪ] adj. mullido, suave, blando; cubierto de vello o plumón; **— hair** pelo esponjado o esponjoso.

**fluid** [flúɪd] adj. & s. flúido.

**flung** [flʌŋ] pret. & p.p. de **to fling.**

**flunk** [flʌŋk] s. reprobación (*en un examen o asignatura*); v. reprobar, suspender (*en un examen*); salir mal, fracasar o fallar (*en un examen*).

**flunky** [flʌ́ŋkɪ] s. lacayo; ayudante servil; zalamero, persona servil.

**flurry** [flə́rɪ] s. (*weather*) ráfaga; nevisca; (*action*) agitación.

**flush** [flʌʃ] s. sonrojo, rubor; bochorno; flujo rápido; flux (*de naipes*); adj. lleno; rico; parejo, al mismo nivel; **— with** a flor de, a ras de; v. sonrojar(se), ruborizar(se), poner(se) colorado; hacer rebosar (*de agua*); **to — out** vaciar (*un depósito*), enjuagar.

**flute** [flut] s. flauta; estría (*de una columna*); v. acanalar, estriar (*una columna*).

**flutter** [flʌ́tə] s. aleteo; agitación; alboroto; vuelco (*del corazón*); v. aletear; revolotear; agitar(se); palpitar; menear(se); tremolar (*una bandera*).

**flux** [flʌks] s. flujo.

**fly** [flaɪ] s. mosca; pliegue (*para cubrir botones*); braguета (*abertura de los pantalones*); **on the —** al vuelo; **to hit a —** pegar una planchita o elevar una palomita (*en beisbol*); v. volar; pasar velozmente; huir; ondear; enarbolar (*una bandera*); **to — at** lanzarse sobre; **to — away** volar, irse, escaparse; **to — off the handle** perder los estribos (*o la paciencia*); **to — open (shut)** abrirse (cerrarse) de repente; **to — up in anger** montar en cólera.

**flyer** = **flier.**

**flyleaf** [fláɪlif] s. guarda (*hoja en blanco al principio y al fin de un libro*).

**foam** [fom] s. espuma; v. espumar, hacer espuma.

**focus** [fókəs] s. foco; distancia focal; v. enfocar(se).

**fodder** [fádə] s. forraje.

**foe** [fo] s. enemigo.

**fog** [fɑg] s. niebla, neblina, bruma; velo; nube (*en una película o fotografía*); **—horn** sirena; v. anublar, ofuscar, obscurecer; ponerse brumoso; velar(se) (*una película*).

**foggy** [fágɪ] adj. brumoso, nublado; obscuro, confuso.

**foil** [fɔɪl] s. oropel, hojuela, laminita de metal; florete (*de esgrima*); realce, contraste; **tin —** hojuela de estaño; v. frustrar.

**fold** [fold] s. (*double over*) pliegue, doblez; (*enclosure*) redil; grey; **three —** tres veces; **hundred —** cien veces; v. doblar(se); plegar(se); envolver; **to — one's arms** cruzarse de brazos.

**folder** [fóldə] s. (*pamphlet*) folleto, circular; (*holder*) papelera; plegadera (*máquina para plegar*).

**folding** [fóldɪŋ] adj. plegadizo; **—chair** silla plegadiza, silla de tijera; **— machine** plegadora, máquina plegadora; **— screen** biombo.

**foliage** [fólɪɪdʒ] s. follaje, fronda.

**folio** [fólɪo] s. folio; infolio, libro en folio; pliego; **— edition** edición en folio.

**folk** [fok] s. gente; pueblo; **-s** parientes, allegados; familia; personas; amigos (*vocativo familiar*); adj. popular, del pueblo; **— dance** danza o baile tradicional; **—lore** folklore; cuentos, leyendas y tradiciones populares; **— song** canción popular, canción típica o tradicional; **— music** música del pueblo; música tradicional.

**follow** [fálo] v. seguir; ejercer (*un oficio o profesión*); seguir el hilo de (*un argumento*); seguirse (*como consecuencia*); **to — suit** jugar el mismo palo (*en naipes*); seguir el ejemplo, imitar.

**follower** [fáləwə] s. seguidor; imitador; partidario.

**following** [fáləwɪŋ] s. séquito, comitiva, partidarios; adj. siguiente; subsiguiente.

**folly** [fálɪ] s. locura; necedad, tontería; desatino.

**foment** [fomént] v. fomentar.

**fond** [fɑnd] adj. aficionado (a); amigo (de), amante (de), encariñado (con); cariñoso, afectuoso; tierno; **to be — of** querer a (*una persona*); estar encariñado con, ser aficionado a; gustar de (*algo*); **-ly** adv. cariñosamente, afectuosamente.

**fondle** [fándḷ] v. acariciar.

**fondness** [fándnɪs] s. cariño, afecto; afición.

**font** [fɑnt] s. pila bautismal; fuente.

**food** [fud] s. alimento, sustento; comida.

**foodstuff** [fúdstʌf] s. alimento; producto alimenticio; comestibles.

**fool** [ful] s. tonto, necio, zonzo; payaso; **to play the —** payasear, hacer el payaso; v. chasquear, chancear(se);

bromear, embromar; engañar; **to —
away the time** malgastar el tiempo.

**foolish** [fúlıʃ] *adj.* tonto; necio, bobo,
zonzo.

**foolishness** [fúlıʃnıs] *s.* tontería, necedad, bobería.

**foot** [fut] *s.* pie; pata (*de animal*); **on —**
a pie; **— soldier** soldado de infantería;
**to put one's — in it** meter la pata;
*v.* andar a pie; **to — it** andar a pie;
**to — the bill** pagar la cuenta; sufragar los gastos.

**football** [fútbɔl] *s.* futbol, football.

**foothold** [fúthold] *s.* arraigo; puesto
establecido.

**footing** [fútıŋ] *s.* base; posición firme;
**to be on a friendly — with** tener
relaciones amistosas con; **to lose
one's —** perder pie.

**footlights** [fútlaıts] *s. pl.* candilejas (*del
teatro*); tablas, teatro.

**footman** [fútmən] *s.* lacayo.

**footnote** [fútnot] *s.* nota al pie de una
página.

**footpath** [fútpæθ] *s.* vereda, senda, trocha (*para gente de a pie*).

**footprint** [fútprınt] *s.* huella, pisada.

**footstep** [fútstɛp] *s.* (*action*) pisada,
paso; (*trace*) huella; **to follow in the
-s of** seguie las pisadas o huellas de.

**footstool** [fútstul] *s.* banquillo, taburete,
escabel.

**fop** [fɑp] *s.* currutaco.

**for** [fɔr] *prep.* por; para; **— all of her
intelligence** a pesar de su inteligencia; **— fear that** por miedo (de) que;
**— the present** por el presente, por
ahora; **as — him** en cuanto a él; **to
know — a fact** saber de cierto, saber
de hecho; **to pay him — it** pagár-
selo; **to thank him — it** agradecér-
selo; *conj.* porque, pues.

**forage** [fɔ́rıdʒ] *s.* forraje; *v.* forrajear;
dar forraje a.

**foray** [fɔ́re] *s.* correría, incursión; saqueo; *v.* pillar, saquear.

**forbade** [fəbǽd] *pret. de* **to forbid.**

**forbear** [fɔ́rber] *s.* antepasado; [fɔrbér]
*v.* abstenerse de; tener paciencia.

**forbid** [fəbíd] *v.* prohibir; vedar.

**forbidden** [fəbídṇ] *adj.* prohibido;
vedado; *p.p. de* **to forbid.**

**forbidding** [fəbídıŋ] *adj.* austero, reservado; pavoroso; impenetrable.

**forbore** [fɔrbór] *pret. de* **to forbear.**

**forborne** [fɔrbórn] *p.p. de* **to forbear.**

**force** [fors] *s.* fuerza; cuerpo (*de policía,
de empleados, etc.*); **in —** en vigor,
vigente; **armed -s** fuerzas armadas;
*v.* forzar, obligar; **to — one's way**
abrirse paso por fuerza; **to — out**
echar por fuerza, echar a la fuerza.

**forced** [forst] *adj.* forzado.

**forceful** [fórsfəl] *adj.* vigoroso; enérgico.

**forceps** [fórsəps] *s.* gatillo (*tenazas para
sacar muelas*); pinzas.

**forcible** [fórsəbl] *adj.* (*strong*) fuerte,
enérgico; potente; eficaz; (*by force*)
violento; hecho a la fuerza; **forcibly**
*adv.* fuertemente; con energía; forzo-

samente; por fuerza.

**ford** [ford] *s.* vado; *v.* vadear.

**fore** [for] *adj.* anterior, delantero; de
proa; *s.* frente; puesto delantero; *adv.*
delante, hacia adelante; *interj.* ¡cuidado! (*dícese en el campo de golf*).

**forearm** [fórɑrm] *s.* antebrazo.

**forebode** [forbód] *v.* presagiar; presentir.

**foreboding** [forbódıŋ] *s.* presentimiento; presagio.

**forecast** [fórkæst] *s.* pronóstico; [for-
kǽst] *v.* pronosticar; predecir; *pret. &
p.p. de* **to forecast.**

**forefather** [fórfaðɚ] *s.* antepasado.

**forefinger** [fórfıŋgɚ] *s.* (dedo) índice.

**forefoot** [fórfut] *s.* pata delantera, mano
(*de cuadrúpedo*).

**forego** [forgó] *v.* abstenerse de.

**foregone** [forgón] *p.p. de* **to forego; a
— conclusion** una conclusión inevitable.

**foreground** [fórgraund] *s.* frente, primer plano, primer término.

**forehead** [fórıd] *s.* frente (*f.*).

**foreign** [fɔ́rın] *adj.* extranjero; foráneo;
extraño; **— to his nature** ajeno a su
índole; **— office** ministerio de relaciones exteriores; departamento de
negocios extranjeros; **— trade** comercio exterior; **foreign-born** extranjero
de nacimiento.

**foreigner** [fɔ́rınɚ] *s.* extranjero; forastero.

**forelock** [fórlak] *s.* guedeja.

**foreman** [fórmən] *s.* capataz; presidente
(*de una jurado*); *Méx., C.A., Ven.,
Col.* caporal (*de un rancho o hacienda*);
*Ríopl.* capataz.

**foremost** [fórmost] *adj.* (*first*) primero;
delantero; (*most important*) principal,
más notable, más distinguido.

**forenoon** [fornún] *s.* (la) mañana.

**forerunner** [forrʌ́nɚ] *s.* precursor; presagio.

**foresaw** [forsɔ́] *pret. de* **to foresee.**

**foresee** [forsí] *s.* prever.

**foreseen** [forsín] *p.p. de* **to foresee**
previsto.

**foresight** [fórsaıt] *s.* previsión.

**forest** [fórıst] *s.* bosque, selva; **— ranger** guardabosques; *v.* arbolar, plantar de árboles.

**forestall** [forstɔ́l] *v.* prevenir; madrugar.

**forester** [fórıstɚ] *s.* guardabosques; silvicultor; habitante de un bosque.

**forestry** [fórıstrı] *s.* silvicultura.

**foretell** [fortél] *v.* predecir, pronosticar,
presagiar.

**foretold** [fortóld] *pret. & p.p. de* **to foretell.**

**forever** [fɚévɚ] *adv.* por (*o* para) siempre.

**forfeit** [fórfıt] *s.* multa; pena; prenda
perdida; **game of -s** juego de prendas; *v.* perder, perder el derecho a.

**forgave** [fɚgév] *pret. de* **to forgive.**

**forge** [fordʒ] *s.* fragua; forja; *v.* fraguar;
forjar; falsear, falsificar; **to — ahead**
abrirse paso; avanzar.

**forgery** [fórdʒɚrı] *s.* falsificación.

**forget** [fɚgét] v. olvidar; olvidarse de; to — **oneself** cometer un desmán impensadamente; perder el tino o la paciencia.

**forgetful** [fɚgétfəl] adj. olvidadizo; negligente.

**forgetfulness** [fɚgétfəlnɪs] s. olvido; negligencia.

**forget-me-not** [fɚgétmɪnɑt] s. nomeolvides.

**forgive** [fɚgív] v. perdonar.

**forgiven** [fɚgívən] p.p. de **to forgive**.

**forgiveness** [fɚgívnɪs] s. perdón.

**forgiving** [fɚgívɪŋ] adj. perdonador, misericordioso, de buen corazón.

**forgot** [fɚgát] pret. & p.p. de **to forget**.

**forgotten** [fɚgátn] p.p. de **to forget**.

**fork** [fɔrk] s. tenedor, Méx., Col., Ven., Andes trinche; horquilla (para heno); horcón; bifurcación; v. bifurcarse; levantar o arrojar (heno) con horquilla.

**forlorn** [fɚlórn] adj. desamparado, desdichado.

**form** [fɔrm] s. forma; condición, estado; **blank** — blanco, forma en blanco, Méx., Ven. esqueleto; v. formar(se).

**formal** [fɔrml] adj. formal, perteneciente a la forma; convencional, ceremonioso; — **party** reunión de etiqueta; **-ly** adv. formalmente, con ceremonia, solemnemente.

**formality** [fɔrmǽlətɪ] s. formalidad, ceremonia; formalismo.

**formation** [fɔrméʃən] s. formación.

**formative** [fɔrmətɪv] adj. formativo.

**former** [fɔrmɚ] adj. primero, precedente, anterior; antiguo; **in** — **times** en otro tiempo, en días de antaño, antiguamente, anteriormente; **the** — aquél (aquélla, aquéllos, aquéllas); **-ly** adv. anterioremente; antes, en tiempos pasados.

**formidable** [fɔrmɪdəbl] adj. formidable.

**formula** [fɔrmjələ] s. fórmula.

**formulate** [fɔrmjəlet] v. formular.

**forsake** [fɚsék] v. desamparar; abandonar.

**forsaken** [fɚsékən] p.p. de **to forsake** & adj. desamparado, abandonado.

**forsook** [fɚsúk] pret. de **to forsake**.

**forswear** [fɔrswér] v. abjurar.

**fort** [fort] s. fuerte, fortín, fortaleza.

**forth** [forθ] adv. adelante; hacia adelante; **to go** — salir; **and so** — etcétera, y así succesivamente.

**forthcoming** [fórθkʌmɪŋ] adj. venidero, próximo; **funds will not be** — **until** no habrá fondos disponibles hasta.

**forthwith** [forθwíθ] adv. en seguida, pronto, al punto.

**fortification** [fɔrtəfəkéʃən] s. fortificación.

**fortify** [fɔrtəfaɪ] v. fortificar; fortalecer.

**fortitude** [fɔrtətjud] s. fortaleza.

**fortnight** [fɔrtnaɪt] s. quincena, quince días, dos semanas.

**fortress** [fɔrtrɪs] s. fortaleza, fuerte.

**fortuitous** [fɔrtjúətəs] adj. fortuito; inopinado, inesperado.

**fortunate** [fɔrtʃənɪt] adj. afortunado; **-ly** adv. afortunadamente, por fortuna.

**fortune** [fɔrtʃən] s. fortuna; —**teller** agorero, adivino.

**forum** [fórəm] s. foro; tribunal.

**forward** [fɔrwɚd] adj. (leading) delantero; (progressive) precoz; progresista; (daring) atrevido; descarado; adv. adelante, hacia adelante; v. transmitir; despachar; reenviar; **to** — **a plan** fomentar un plan.

**fossil** [fásl] adj. fósil; anticuado; s. fósil.

**foster** [fɔstɚ] v. criar, nutrir; fomentar, promover; adj. putativo; adoptivo.

**fought** [fɔt] pret. & p.p. de **to fight**.

**foul** [faul] adj. sucio; asqueroso; puerco, cochino; fétido; vil; injusto; — **air** aire viciado; — **ball** pelota foul (en beisbol); —**mouthed** mal hablado, obsceno; — **play** juego sucio; fraude; violencia; — **weather** mal tiempo; s. mala jugada (contraria a las reglas del juego), trampa, Am. chapuza, foul; v. ensuciar; violar (las reglas de un juego); Am. pegar un foul (en beisbol).

**found** [faund] v. fundar, establecer; pret. & p.p. de **to find**.

**foundation** [faundéʃən] s. fundación; base, fundamento; dotación.

**founder** [fáundɚ] s. fundador; fundidor (de metales); v. zozobrar, irse a pique; fracasar; tropezar; hacer zozobrar.

**foundry** [fáundrɪ] s. fundición.

**fountain** [fáuntn] s. fuente; manantial; — **pen** pluma (de) fuente, pluma estilográfica.

**fourscore** [fórskór] adj. cuatro veintenas, ochenta.

**fourth** [forθ] adj. cuarto; s. cuarto, cuarta parte; **the** — **of July** el cuatro de julio.

**fowl** [faul] s. ave; gallo, gallina; pollo.

**fox** [faks] s. zorra; zorro; persona astuta.

**foxy** [fáksɪ] adj. zorro, zorruno, astuto.

**fraction** [frǽkʃən] s. fracción; quebrado.

**fracture** [frǽktʃɚ] s. fractura; quiebra, rotura; v. fracturar; quebrar, romper.

**fragile** [frǽdʒəl] adj. frágil.

**fragment** [frǽgmənt] s. fragmento.

**fragrance** [frégrəns] s. fragancia.

**fragrant** [frégrənt] adj. fragante, oloroso.

**frail** [frel] adj. frágil; endeble, débil.

**frailty** [fréltɪ] s. debilidad, flaqueza.

**frame** [frem] s. armazón, armadura, esqueleto; estructura; marco (de un cuadro, ventana, puerta, etc.); disposición (de ánimo); **embroidery** — bastidor para bordar; — **house** casa con armazón de madera; v. formar, forjar; fabricar; enmarcar (poner en marco); inventar; **to** — **someone** conspirar contra una persona; **to** — **up a charge** forjar un cargo o acusación.

**framework** [frémwɚk] s. armazón, esqueleto; estructura.

**franc** [fræŋk] s. franco (moneda francesa).

**franchise** [frǽntʃaɪz] s. (privilege) fran-

**FO**

quicia; derecho o privilegio político; (*vote*) sufragio, voto.

**frank** [fræŋk] *adj.* franco, sincero; **very — francote;** *s.* sello de franqueo; franquicia de correos; *v.* franquear, despachar, enviar (*carta*) exenta de franqueo.

**frankfurter** [fræŋkfətə] *s.* salchicha.

**frankness** [fræŋknɪs] *s.* franqueza, sinceridad.

**frantic** [fræntɪk] *adj.* frenético; **-ally** *adv.* frenéticamente.

**fraternal** [frətɜ́nl] *adj.* fraternal.

**fraternity** [frətɜ́nətɪ] *s.* fraternidad; confraternidad.

**fraternize** [frǽtənaɪz] *v.* fraternizar.

**fraud** [frɔd] *s.* fraude, engaño; trampa, *Am.* chapuza; trampista, tramposo.

**fraudulent** [frɔ́dʒələnt] *adj.* fraudulento.

**fray** [fre] *s.* reyerta, riña, pelea, alboroto; raedura; *v.* raer(se); deshilacharse.

**frayed** [fred] *adj.* raído, deshilachado.

**freak** [frik] *s.* capricho; rareza, hombre o cosa rara; monstruosidad, fenómeno.

**freckle** [frékl] *s.* peca; *v.* ponerse pecoso.

**freckled** [frékld] *adj.* pecoso.

**freckly** [fréklɪ] *adj.* pecoso.

**free** [fri] *adj.* (*not bound*) libre; suelto; (*gratis*) gratuito; exento; (*generous*) liberal, generoso; **— of charge** gratis; **— on board (f.o.b.)** libre a bordo; **— port** puerto franco; **postage —** franco de porte; **to give someone a — hand** dar rienda suelta o libertad de acción a una persona; **— hand drawing** dibujo a pulso, dibujo a mano; **— thinker** libre pensador; *adv.* libremente; gratis, de balde; *v.* librar; libertar; soltar; eximir; **-ly** *adv.* libremente; con soltura.

**freedom** [frídəm] *s.* libertad; libre uso; exención.

**freeze** [friz] *v.* helar(se); congelar(se).

**freezing** [frizɪŋ] *adj.* helado, glacial; **— point** punto de congelación.

**freight** [fret] *s.* flete; carga; **— train** tren de carga, tren de mercancías; **by —** por carga; *v.* fletar, cargar; enviar por carga.

**French** [frɛntʃ] *adj.* francés; **to take — leave** marcharse a la francesa, irse sin despedirse; *s.* francés, idioma francés; **the —** los franceses.

**Frenchman** [frɛntʃmən] *s.* francés.

**frenzy** [frɛnzɪ] *s.* frenesí.

**frequency** [fríkwənsɪ] *s.* frecuencia.

**frequent** [fríkwənt] *adj.* frecuente; *v.* frecuentar; **-ly** *adv.* frecuentemente, a menudo.

**fresh** [frɛʃ] *adj.* (*not stale*) fresco; (*new*) reciente; nuevo; (*bold*) impertinente, entremetido; **— water** agua dulce; **-ly** *adv.* frescamente; con frescura; nuevamente, recientemente; **-ly painted** recién pintado, acabado de pintar.

**freshen** [frɛ́ʃən] *v.* refrescar(se).

**freshman** [frɛ́ʃmən] *s.* novato, novicio, estudiante del primer año.

**freshness** [frɛ́ʃnɪs] *s.* frescura; frescor, fresco; descaro.

**fret** [fret] *v.* irritar(se); apurarse; estar nervioso; agitarse; *s.* agitación, apuro, preocupación; traste (*de guitarra, mandolina, etc.*); **—work** calado.

**fretful** [frɛ́tfəl] *adj.* descontentadizo, malhumorado, enojadizo; nervioso.

**friar** [fráɪə] *s.* fraile.

**friction** [fríkʃən] *s.* fricción; rozamiento; frotación; desavenencia.

**Friday** [fráɪdɪ] *s.* viernes.

**fried** [fraɪd] *adj.* frito; freído; *p.p. de* **to fry.**

**friend** [frɛnd] *s.* amigo, amiga.

**friendless** [frɛ́ndlɪs] *adj.* sin amigos, solo.

**friendliness** [frɛ́ndlɪnɪs] *s.* afabilidad; amistad.

**friendly** [frɛ́ndlɪ] *adj.* amistoso, afable, amigable; propicio, favorable; *adv.* amistosamente.

**friendship** [frɛ́nʃɪp] *s.* amistad.

**frigate** [frígət] *s.* fragata.

**fright** [fraɪt] *s.* espanto, susto; terror; espantajo, **she is a —** es un adefesio.

**frighten** [fráɪtn] *v.* espantar, asustar, atemorizar; **to — away** espantar, ahuyentar; **to get -ed** espantarse, asustarse.

**frightened** [fráɪtnd] *adj.* espantado, asustado.

**frightful** [fráɪtfəl] *adj.* espantoso, terrible, horroroso.

**frigid** [frídʒɪd] *adj.* frígido, frío.

**fringe** [frɪndʒ] *s.* fleco; flequillo; orla; *v.* adornar con fleco; orlar.

**frippery** [frípərɪ] *s.* perifollos, moños, perejiles; cursilería.

**frisk** [frɪsk] *v.* retozar, cabriolar, saltar, brincar; registrar (*los bolsillos*), *Ven.*, *Méx.* escular.

**frisky** [frískɪ] *adj.* retozón, juguetón.

**fritter** [frítə] *s.* fritura, fruta de sartén; *v.* **to — away** malgastar, desperdiciar poco a poco.

**frivolity** [frɪvɑ́lətɪ] *s.* frivolidad.

**frivolous** [frívələs] *adj.* frívolo.

**fro** [fro]: **to and —** de una parte a otra; de aquí para allá.

**frock** [frɑk] *s.* vestido (*de mujer*); **— coat** levita.

**frog** [frɑg] *s.* rana; broche (*de cordoncillos o galones*); **— in the throat** gallo en la garganta.

**frolic** [frɑ́lɪk] *s.* retozo, juego; holgorio, diversión; *v.* retozar, travesear, juguetear.

**from** [frɑm, frʌm] *prep.* de; desde; **to take something away — a person** quitarle algo a una persona.

**front** [frʌnt] *s.* frente (*m.*); fachada; frontispicio; **in — of** enfrente de; delante de; **shirt —** pechera; *adj.* delantero; frontal; frontero; *v.* hacer frente a; **to — towards** mirar hacia; dar a, caer a.

**frontier** [frʌntír] *s.* frontera; *adj.* fronterizo.

**frost** [frɔst] *s.* escarcha; helada; *v.* escarchar; helar; cubrir de escarcha.

**frosting** [fróstɪŋ] s. escarcha, confitura (*para cubrir un pastel*).

**frosty** [fróstɪ] adj. escarchado, cubierto de escarcha; helado.

**froth** [frɔθ] s. espuma; v. espumar, hacer espuma; echar espuma o espumarajos; **to — at the mouth** echar espumarajos por la boca; enfurecerse.

**frown** [fraun] s. ceño; entrecejo; v. fruncir el ceño o las cejas; **to — at** mirar con ceño; desaprobar (*algo*).

**froze** [froz] *pret. de* **to freeze**.

**frozen** [frózn̩] *p.p. de* **to freeze**.

**frugal** [frúgl̩] adj. frugal.

**fruit** [frut] s. fruto (*en general*); fruta (*comestible*); **to eat —** comer fruta; **— tree** árbol frutal; v. fructificar, producir frutas.

**fruitful** [frútfəl] adj. fructuoso; productivo; provechoso.

**fruitless** [frútlɪs] adj. infructuoso, improductivo, estéril.

**frustrate** [frʌ́stret] v. frustrar.

**frustration** [frʌstréʃən] s. frustración.

**fry** [fraɪ] v. freír(se); s. fritada; **small —** pececillos; gente menuda; **French fries** patatas fritas a la francesa; **-ing pan** sartén.

**fudge** [fʌdʒ] s. dulce (*usualmente de chocolate y nueces*).

**fuel** [fjúəl] s. combustible; incentivo.

**fugitive** [fjúdʒətɪv] adj. fugitivo; transitorio; s. fugitivo, prófugo.

**fulfill** [fulfíl] v. cumplir; cumplir con; realizar; llevar a cabo; llenar (*un requisito*).

**fulfillment** [fulfílmənt] s. cumplimiento.

**full** [ful] adj. lleno; completo; harto; pleno; **— dress** traje de etiqueta; **— moon** plenilunio, luna llena; **— skirt** falda de vuelo entero; **— of fun** muy divertido, muy chistoso; **at — speed** a toda velocidad; **in — completa-** mente; por completo; **to the —** por completo, por entero, totalmente; adv. completamente, enteramente; **to know — well** saber perfectamente, saber a ciencia cierta; **full-blooded** de raza pura; **full-fledged** hecho y derecho; maduro; completo; **-y** adv. completamente, enteramente, por completo.

**fullness** [fúlnɪs] s. plenitud; llenura.

**fumble** [fʌ́mbl̩] v. tentalear, buscar a tientas; chapucear, no coger la pelota o soltarla al correr.

**fume** [fjum] v. exhalar vapor o gas; rabiar; **-s** s. pl. vapores, emanaciones, gases.

**fumigate** [fjúməget] v. fumigar, sahumar, *Ríopl.* humear.

**fun** [fʌn] s. diversión; burla, broma, chanza, *Carib.*, *Méx.*, *C.A.* choteo; **for —** en (*o* de) broma; de chanza; de chiste; **full of —** muy divertido; **to have —** divertirse; **to make — of** burlarse de, chancearse con, *Carib.*, *Méx.*, *C.A.* chotear, chotearse con; *Ríopl.* jorobar.

**function** [fʌ́ŋkʃən] s. función; v. funcio-

nar.

**fund** [fʌnd] s. fondo, caudal; **-s** fondos, recursos; v. consolidar (*una deuda*); prorrogar el plazo de (*una deuda*).

**fundamental** [fʌndəmént l̩] adj. fundamental; s. fundamento, principio.

**funeral** [fjúnərəl] adj. funeral, fúnebre; s. funeral, exequias, funerales.

**fungus** [fʌ́ŋgəs] s. hongo; fungosidad.

**funnel** [fʌ́nl̩] s. embudo; humero (*cañón de chimenea*).

**funny** [fʌ́nɪ] adj. (*comical*) chistoso, cómico, gracioso, divertido; (*odd*) extraño, raro; **the funnies** la sección cómica (*de un periódico*).

**fur** [fɝ] s. piel (*de animales peludos o lanudos*); sarro (*en la lengua*); **— coat** abrigo de pieles; v. forrar, cubrir o adornar con pieles.

**furbish** [fɝ́bɪʃ] v. acicalar, pulir.

**furious** [fjúrɪəs] adj. furioso.

**furl** [fɝl] v. arrollar, enrollar; plegar.

**furlough** [fɝ́lo] s. licencia militar; v. dar licencia militar.

**furnace** [fɝ́nɪs] s. horno.

**furnish** [fɝ́nɪʃ] v. (*equip*) equipar; amueblar; (*provide*) proveer, suministrar, surtir; **to — a room** amueblar un cuarto.

**furniture** [fɝ́nɪtʃɚ] s. muebles, mobiliario, moblaje, mueblaje.

**furrow** [fɝ́o] s. surco; arruga; v. surcar; arar.

**further** [fɝ́ðɚ] adj. adicional; más lejano; más remoto; adv. además; más; más lejos; v. promover, fomentar, adelantar.

**furthermore** [fɝ́ðɚmor] adv. además.

**furthest** [fɝ́ðɪst] adj. (el) más lejano, (el) más remoto; adv. más lejos.

**furtive** [fɝ́tɪv] adj. furtivo.

**fury** [fjúrɪ] s. furia; frenesí.

**fuse** [fjuz] s. fusible; mecha; v. fundir(se).

**fuselage** [fjúzl̩ɪdʒ] s. fuselaje.

**fusion** [fjúʒən] s. fusión; **nuclear —** fusión nuclear.

**fuss** [fʌs] s. melindre, preocupación inútil; bulla innecesaria; **to make a — over someone** darle a alguien demasiada importancia, desvivirse por alguien; v. hacer melindres, inquietarse (*por bagatelas*).

**fussy** [fʌ́sɪ] adj. melindroso; minucioso (*en demasía*); inquieto, nervioso; **— dress** vestido con demasiados adornos.

**futile** [fjútl̩] adj. fútil; vano.

**future** [fjútʃɚ] adj. futuro; s. futuro; porvenir.

**fuzz** [fʌz] s. vello; pelusa.

**fuzzy** [fʌ́zɪ] adj. velloso; cubierto de plumón fino; cubierto de pelusa.

## G

**gab** [gæb] v. charlar, parlotear; s. charla; **gift of —** labia, facundia.

**gabardine** [gǽbɚdin] s. gabardina (*paño*).

**gabble** [gǽbl̩] s. charla, cotorreo; v. charlar, cotorrear.

**gable** [gébl] *s.* gablete (*de un tejado*); —
**roof** tejado de caballete o de dos
aguas; — **window** ventana con gablete.

**gad** [gæd] *v.* vagar, callejear; andar de
aquí para allá.

**gadget** [gǽdʒɪt] *s.* adminículo, artefacto,
chisme.

**gag** [gæg] *s.* (*obstacle*) mordaza; (*joke*)
broma, burla; morcilla, chiste (*improvisado por un actor*); *v.* amordazar; dar náuseas, hacer vomitar,
basquear; interpolar chistes (*en la
escena*).

**gage** *véase* **gauge.**

**gaiety** [géətɪ] *s.* alegría, viveza, alborozo.

**gaily** [gélɪ] *adv.* alegremente; vistosa-
mente.

**gain** [gen] *s.* ganancia, provecho; *v.*
ganar.

**gainful** [génfl] *adj.* ganancioso.

**gait** [get] *s.* paso, andadura, marcha.

**gale** [gel] *s.* ventarrón; — **of laughter**
risotada, carcajada, risada.

**gall** [gɔl] *s.* (*bile*) bilis, hiel; (*bitterness*)
amargura; odio; descaro; — **bladder**
vejiga de la bilis; *v.* irritar.

**gallant** [gǽlənt] *adj.* valiente; noble;
vistoso; [gəlǽnt] *adj.* galante, atento,
cortés; galanteador; *s.* galán.

**gallantry** [gǽləntrɪ] *s.* galantería; gallardía, valor.

**gallery** [gǽlərɪ] *s.* galería; paraíso, gallinero *del* (*teatro*).

**galley** [gǽlɪ] *s.* galera; cocina (*de un
buque*); — **proof** galerada; — **slave**
galeote.

**gallon** [gǽlən] *s.* galón (*aproximadamente cuatro litros*).

**gallop** [gǽləp] *s.* galope; *v.* galopar,
galopear; ir a galope.

**gallows** [gǽloz] *s.* horca.

**galoshes** [gəlɑ́ʃɪz] *s. pl.* chanclos,
zapatos fuertes, zapatones.

**gamble** [gǽmbl] *v.* jugar, apostar,
aventurar (*algo*) en el juego; **to —
away** perder en el juego; **to — everything** jugar el todo por el todo;
arriesgarlo todo; *s.* jugada (*en juegos de
azar*), apuesta, riesgo.

**gambol** [gǽmbəl] *v.* retozar; cabriolar;
juguetear; *s.* retozo, cabriola.

**game** [gem] *s.* juego; deporte; caza
(*animales de caza y su carne*); **to make
— of** mofarse de, burlarse de; *adj.*
valiente, atrevido; resuelto; — **bird**
ave de caza.

**gamut** [gǽmət] *s.* gama.

**gander** [gǽndɚ] *s.* ánsar, ganso.

**gang** [gæŋ] *s.* cuadrilla; pandilla; juego
(*de herramientas o máquinas*); *v.* agru-
par(se); **to — up against** conspirar
contra.

**gangplank** [gǽŋplæŋk] *s.* plancha, pasamano (*de un buque*), pasarela.

**gangrene** [gǽŋgrin] *s.* gangrena; *v.*
gangrenar(se).

**gangster** [gǽŋstɚ] *s.* bandolero, bandido, maleante, atracador.

**gangway** [gǽŋwe] *s.* paso, pasadizo;
plancha, pasamano; portalón (*de un

barco*); —! ¡a un lado! ¡ábranse!

**gantlet** = **gauntlet.**

**gap** [gæp] *s.* brecha, abertura; boquete;
hueco; intervalo.

**gape** [gep] *s.* (*breach*) brecha, abertura;
(*open jaws*) bostezo; boqueada; *v.*
boquear, abrir la boca; estar boquiabierto (*mirando*); estar embobado;
bostezar.

**garage** [gɔráʒ] *s.* garaje.

**garb** [gɑrb] *s.* vestido; vestidura; aspecto, apariencia; *v.* vestir, ataviar.

**garbage** [gɑ́rbɪdʒ] *s.* desperdicios,
basura.

**garden** [gɑ́rdn̩] *s.* jardín; huerta;
huerto; *v.* cultivar un jardín.

**gardener** [gɑ́rdnɚ] *s.* jardinero, hortelano; horticultor.

**gargle** [gɑ́rgl] *s.* gargarismo, *Am.* gárgaras; *v.* gargarizar, hacer gárgaras,
*Am.* gargarear.

**garland** [gɑ́rlənd] *s.* guirnalda.

**garlic** [gɑ́rlɪk] *s.* ajo.

**garment** [gɑ́rmənt] *s.* prenda (*de vestir*).

**garnet** [gɑ́rnɪt] *s.* granate.

**garnish** [gɑ́rnɪʃ] *s.* aderezo; adorno; *v.*
aderezar; adornar; guarnecer.

**garret** [gǽrɪt] *s.* desván, buhardilla.

**garrison** [gǽrəsn̩] *s.* guarnición; *v.*
guarnecer o guarnicionar (*una fortaleza*).

**garter** [gɑ́rtɚ] *s.* liga (*para sujetar las
medias*); *v.* sujetar con liga.

**gas** [gæs] *s.* (*gaseous*) gas; (*petroleum*)
gasolina; — **burner** mechero; —
**stove** estufa o cocina de gas; **tear —**
gas lacrimante o lacrimógeno; *v.*
asfixiar con gas; envenenar con gas.

**gaseous** [gǽsɪəs] *adj.* gaseoso.

**gash** [gæʃ] *s.* cuchillada, herida, incisión;
*v.* dar una cuchillada, acuchillar.

**gasoline** [gǽslin] *s.* gasolina.

**gasp** [gæsp] *s.* boqueada; grito sofo-
cado; *v.* boquear; jadear; sofocarse;
abrir la boca (*de asombro*).

**gastric** [gǽstrɪk] *adj.* gástrico.

**gastrointestinal** [gǽstroɪntéstɪnl̩] *adj.*
gastrointestinal.

**gate** [get] *s.* portón, entrada; puerta;
*Ven., Col.* tranquera (*puerta de
trancas*).

**gateway** [gétwe] *s.* paso, entrada.

**gather** [gǽðɚ] *v.* recoger; coger; reu-
nir(se), juntar(se); deducir, colegir;
fruncir (*en pliegues*); cobrar (fuerzas);
**to — dust** llenarse de polvo, empolvarse; *s.* pliegue.

**gathering** [gǽðrɪŋ] *s.* asamblea, reunión; muchedumbre; pliegue.

**gaudy** [gɔ́dɪ] *adj.* vistoso, llamativo,
chillón, chillante.

**gauge** [gedʒ] *s.* calibrador; indicador;
instrumento para medir; medida;
calibre (*de un cañón, pistola, etc.*);
ancho (*del ferrocarril*), *Ven.* trocha;
*v.* medir; calibrar; estimar, calcular.

**gaunt** [gɔnt] *adj.* macilento, demacrado,
flaco.

**gauntlet** [gɔ́ntlɪt] *s.* guantelete; manopla; **to throw down the —** retar,
desafiar.

**gauze** [gɔz] *s.* gasa; cendal.

**gave** [gev] *pret. de* **to give.**

**gavel** [gǽvl] *s.* mazo del que preside.

**gawk** [gɔk] *v.* bobear, mirar embobado; *s.* simplón, bobo.

**gawky** [gɔ́kɪ] *adj.* torpe, desmañado; bobo.

**gay** [ge] *adj.* alegre; vivo; vistoso; festivo.

**gayety** *véase* **gaiety.**

**gaze** [gez] *s.* mirada (fija); *v.* contemplar, mirar con fijeza, clavar la mirada.

**gazette** [gəzét] *s.* gaceta.

**gear** [gɪr] *s.* (*equipment*) aperos; herramientas; aparejo; equipo; (*wheel*) rueda dentada; (*assembly*) engranaje (*de ruedas dentadas*); **foot—** calzado; **low —** primera velocidad; **steering —** mecanismo de dirección; **to be in —** estar engranado; **to shift —** cambiar de engrane o velocidad; **to throw in —** engranar; **to throw out of —** desengranar; **—shift lever** palanca de engrane, palanca de cambios; *v.* engranar.

**geese** [gis] *pl. de* **goose.**

**Geiger counter** [gáɪgɚkáʊntɚ] *s.* contador (de) Geiger.

**gelatin** [dʒélətn̩] *s.* gelatina, jaletina.

**gem** [dʒem] *s.* gema, piedra preciosa; joya, alhaja, panecillo, bollo.

**geminate** [dʒémənet] *v.* geminar(se).

**gender** [dʒéndɚ] *s.* género.

**gene** [dʒin] *s.* gen.

**general** [dʒénərəl] *adj. & s.* general; **in — en** general, por lo común, por lo general.

**generality** [dʒenərǽlətɪ] *s.* generalidad.

**generalize** [dʒénərəlaɪz] *v.* generalizar.

**generate** [dʒénəret] *v.* engendrar; producir; originar.

**generation** [dʒenəréʃən] *s.* generación; producción.

**generator** [dʒénɚetɚ] *s.* generador.

**generic** [dʒənérɪk] *adj.* genérico.

**generosity** [dʒenərásətɪ] *s.* generosidad.

**generous** [dʒénərəs] *adj.* generoso; magnánimo, liberal; amplio; abundante.

**genetics** [dʒənétɪks] *s.* genética.

**genial** [dʒínjəl] *adj.* genial, afable.

**genitive** [dʒénətɪv] *adj. & s.* genitivo.

**genius** [dʒínjəs] *s.* genio; ingenio, talento.

**genteel** [dʒentíl] *adj.* gentil, cortés; elegante; gallardo.

**gentile** [dʒéntaɪl] *adj. & s.* gentil.

**gentle** [dʒéntl̩] *adj.* suave; afable; apacible; manso; gentil.

**gentleman** [dʒéntlmən] *s.* caballero; **gentlemen** *pl.* caballeros; señores.

**gentlemanly** [dʒéntlmənlɪ] *adj.* caballeroso, caballero, cortés.

**gentleness** [dʒéntl̩nɪs] *s.* suavidad, dulzura, apacibilidad; mansedumbre.

**gently** [dʒéntlɪ] *adv.* suavemente; despacio; dulcemente; con ternura; mansamente.

**genuine** [dʒénjʊɪn] *adj.* genuino; sincero.

**geographical** [dʒiəgrǽfɪkl̩] *adj.* geográfico.

**geography** [dʒiágrəfɪ] *s.* geografía.

**geological** [dʒiəládʒɪkl̩] *adj.* geológico.

**geology** [dʒiálədʒɪ] *s.* geología.

**geometric** [dʒiəmétrɪk] *adj.* geométrico.

**geometry** [dʒiámətrɪ] *s.* geometría.

**geophysics** [dʒiofízɪks] *s.* geofísica.

**geranium** [dʒəréniəm] *s.* geranio.

**germ** [dʒɜm] *s.* germen; microbio.

**German** [dʒɝmən] *adj. & s.* alemán.

**germane** [dʒɚmen] *adj.* pertinente, relacionado.

**germinate** [dʒɝmənet] *v.* germinar.

**gerund** [dʒɛrənd] *s.* gerundio.

**gestation** [dʒestéʃən] *s.* gestación.

**gesticulate** [dʒestíkjəlet] *v.* gesticular, hacer gestos o ademanes, accionar, manotear.

**gesture** [dʒéstʃɚ] *s.* gesto; ademán; **a mere —** una pura formalidad; *v.* gesticular, hacer gestos.

**get** [gɛt] *v.* (*obtain*) obtener, adquirir, lograr, conseguir; (*earn*) recibir, ganar; (*reach*) llegar (a); traer; (*catch*) coger, atrapar; preparar (*la lección, la comida, etc.*); **to — along** llevarse bien (*con alguien*); ir pasándolo (*o* ir pasándola); **to — angry** ponerse enojado, enojarse; **to — away** escaparse; irse; **to — down** bajar; **to — ill** ponerse enfermo, enfermar(se); **to — in** entrar; meter(se); llegar; **to — married** casarse; **to — off the train** bajar del tren; apearse del tren; **to — old** envejecer(se); **to — on** subir a; montar; **to — out** salir; irse; sacar; divulgarse (*un secreto*); **to — over** pasar por encima de; recuperarse de (*una enfermedad*); olvidar (*una ofensa*); pasársele a uno (*el susto*); **to — ready** preparar(se); alistar(se); **to — rich** enriquecerse, hacerse rico; **to — rid of** deshacerse de, desprenderse de; **to — through** pasar; terminar; **to — together** juntar(se), reunir(se); ponerse de acuerdo; **to — up** levantarse; **I got him to do it** le persuadí a que lo hiciese; **I (have) got to do it** tengo que hacerlo; **I don't — it** no lo comprendo; **that's what -s me** (*or* **-s my goat**) eso es lo que me irrita.

**ghastly** [gǽstlɪ] *adj.* horrible; pálido, lívido, cadavérico.

**ghost** [gost] *s.* espectro, fantasma; **the Holy Ghost** el Espíritu Santo; **not to have the — of a notion of** no tener la más remota idea de; **— writer** colaborador anónimo.

**ghostly** [góstlɪ] *adj.* como un espectro; de espectros, de aparecidos.

**giant** [dʒáɪənt] *s.* gigante; *adj.* gigantesco; enorme.

**giddy** [gídɪ] *adj.* ligero de cascos, frívolo; voluble, inconstante; desvanecido; **— speed** velocidad vertiginosa.

**gift** [gɪft] *s.* regalo; dádiva; don; dote, talento, prenda; donación.

**gifted** [gíftɪd] *adj.* talentoso, de talento.

**GA**

**gigantic** [dʒaɪgǽntɪk] *adj.* gigantesco.
**giggle** [gígl] *s.* risita, risilla; risa falsa;
*v.* reírse falsamente; reírse sofocando
la voz; reír con una risilla afectada.
**gild** [gɪld] *v.* dorar.
**gill** [gɪl] *s.* agalla (*de pez*).
**gilt** [gɪlt] *adj.* & *s.* dorado; *pret.* & *p.p.*
*de* **to gild**.
**gimmick** [gímɪk] *s.* adminículo.
**gin** [dʒɪn] *s.* ginebra (*licor*).
**ginger** [dʒíndʒɚ] *s.* jengibre; **— ale**
cerveza de jengibre.
**gingerbread** [dʒíndʒɚbrɛd] *s.* pan de
jengibre; ornato de mal gusto.
**gingham** [gíŋəm] *s.* guinga (*tela de algodón*).
**gipsy** *véase* **gypsy**.
**giraffe** [dʒɔræf] *s.* jirafa.
**gird** [gɚd] *v.* ceñir; rodear; **to — oneself for** prepararse para.
**girdle** [gɚ́dl] *s.* ceñidor; cinto; faja; *v.*
ceñir; fajar; cercar.
**girl** [gɚl] *s.* niña; muchacha; joven;
chica, moza; criada.
**girlhood** [gɚ́lhʊd] *s.* niñez; mocedad,
juventud.
**girlish** [gɚ́lɪʃ] *adj.* pueril; de niña, de
muchacha; juvenil.
**girt** [gɚt] *pret.* & *p.p. de* **to gird**; *v.
véase* **gird**.
**girth** [gɚθ] *s.* circunferencia; cincha
(*para caballos*); faja; *v.* cinchar; ceñir.
**gist** [dʒɪst] *s.* substancia, esencia.
**give** [gɪv] *v.* dar; regalar; ceder, dar de
sí; **to — away** regalar; entregar; revelar (*un secreto*); **to — back** devolver;
**to — birth** dar a luz, parir; **to — in**
ceder; darse por vencido; **to — off**
emitir; **to — out** divulgar; repartir;
agotarse; **to — up** abandonar; desistir; renunciar a; perder la esperanza;
rendir(se); ceder, darse por vencido;
*s.* elasticidad.
**given** [gívən] *p.p. de* **to give**; *adj.*
(*presented*) dado; regalado; (*inclined*)
adicto, entregado; dispuesto, inclinado; **— name** nombre de pila,
nombre de bautismo; **— time** hora
determinada; **— that** dada que, supuesto que.
**giver** [gívɚ] *s.* dador, donador.
**glacial** [gléʃəl] *adj.* glacial.
**glacier** [gléʃɚ] *s.* glaciar, helero.
**glad** [glæd] *adj.* contento; alegre; **to be
— to** alegrarse de, tener mucho gusto
en (*o* de); **-ly** *adv.* alegremente; con
mucho gusto; de buena gana.
**gladden** [glǽdn̩] *v.* regocijar, alegrar.
**glade** [gled] *s.* claro herboso (*en un
bosque*).
**gladness** [glǽdnɪs] *s.* alegría, gozo.
**glamour** [glǽmɚ] *s.* encanto, hechizo;
fascinación, embrujo; **— girl** niña
hechicera.
**glamorous** [glǽmərəs] *adj.* fascinador,
hechicero.
**glance** [glæns] *s.* mirada, vistazo,
ojeada; vislumbre; *v.* echar (*o* dar) un
vistazo; vislumbrar; pegar de soslayo;
**to — off** rebotar de soslayo (*o* de
lado).

**gland** [glænd] *s.* glándula.
**glare** [glɛr] *s.* (*light*) resplandor,
relumbre; (*stare*) mirada furiosa;
*v.* resplandecer, relumbrar; **to — at**
mirar enfurecido a.
**glass** [glæs] *s.* (*substance*) vidrio; cristal;
(*receptacle*) vaso; copa (*de cristal*);
(*eye*) lente; **looking —** espejo; **-es**
anteojos, lentes, gafas; *adj.* de vidrio;
**— blower** vidriero, soplador de
vidrio; **— case** escaparate.
**glassware** [glǽswɛr] *s.* vajilla de cristal,
cristalería; **— shop** cristalería.
**glassy** [glǽsɪ] *adj.* vidrioso.
**glaze** [glez] *s.* vidriado; lustre; superficie lustrosa o glaseada; *v.* vidriar;
glasear; lustrar; poner vidrios a.
**glazier** [gléʒɚ] *s.* vidriero.
**gleam** [glim] *s.* destello, rayo, fulgor,
viso; *v.* destellar, fulgurar, centellear.
**glean** [glin] *v.* recoger; espigar.
**glee** [gli] *s.* regocijo; júbilo; **— club** orfeón, masa coral.
**glib** [glɪb] *adj.* locuaz; de mucha labia;
**— excuse** excusa fácil.
**glide** [glaɪd] *s.* deslizamiento; ligadura
(*en música*); planeo (*de un aeroplano*);
*v.* deslizarse; resbalarse; planear (*un
aeroplano*).
**glider** [gláɪdɚ] *s.* deslizador, planeador
(*aeroplano*).
**glimmer** [glímɚ] *s.* vislumbre; viso;
titileo; **— of hope** rayo de esperanza;
*v.* titilar, centellear.
**glimpse** [glɪmps] *s.* vislumbre; vistazo,
ojeada; **to catch a — of** vislumbrar;
*v.* vislumbrar.
**glint** [glɪnt] *s.* fulgor, rayo, destello.
**glisten** [glísn̩] *v.* relucir, brillar.
**glitter** [glítɚ] *s.* lustre, brillo, resplandor; *v.* relumbrar, relucir, brillar.
**gloat** [glot] *v.* gozarse (en), deleitarse
(en); relamerse (*de gusto*).
**globe** [glob] *d.* globo; esfera.
**gloom** [glum] *s.* lobreguez, sombra;
abatimiento, tristeza, melancolía.
**gloomy** [glúmɪ] *adj.* lóbrego, sombrío;
triste, melancólico; abatido.
**glorify** [glórəfaɪ] *v.* glorificar.
**glorious** [glórɪəs] *adj.* glorioso; espléndido.
**glory** [glórɪ] *s.* gloria; *v.* gloriarse; vanagloriarse.
**gloss** [glɔs] *s.* (*shine*) lustre, brillo; pulimento; (*note*) glosa, comentario;
*v.* lustrar, dar brillo a; pulir; glosar,
comentar; **to — over** encubrir, dar
colorido de bueno (*a algo que no lo es*).
**glossary** [glásərɪ] *s.* glosario.
**glossy** [glósɪ] *adj.* lustroso; pulido.
**glove** [glʌv] *s.* guante; *v.* enguantar,
poner guantes.
**glow** [glo] *s.* incandescencia; brillo (*de
un ascua*); calor vivo; fosforescencia;
*v.* lucir, brillar (*como un ascua*); fosforecer; estar encendido o enarde-
cido.
**glowing** [glóɪŋ] *adj.* encendido, ardiente.
**glowworm** [glówɚm] *s.* luciérnaga.
**glue** [glu] *s.* cola (*para pegar*); *v.* en-

colar, pegar (*con cola*).
**glum** [glʌm] *adj.* hosco.
**glutton** [glʌ́tn̩] *s.* glotón.
**gluttonous** [glʌ́tn̩əs] *adj.* glotón; goloso.
**gluttony** [glʌ́tn̩ɪ] *s.* gula, glotonería.
**glycerin** [glísəɪn] *s.* glicerina.
**gnarled** [nɑrld] *adj.* nudoso, torcido.
**gnash** [næʃ] *v.* crujir, rechinar (*los
dientes*).
**gnat** [næt] *s.* jején (*insecto*).
**gnaw** [nɔ] *v.* roer.
**go** [go] *v.* (*move*) ir(se); andar; (*function*)
marchar, funcionar, servir; **to —
around** andar alrededor de; dar
vueltas; **to — away** irse; **to — back
on one's word** faltar a la palabra; **to
— by** pasar por; guiarse por (*una
regla*); **to — down** bajar; **to —
insane** volverse loco; **to — into**
entrar en; investigar; caber en; **to —
off** hacer explosión; dispararse; irse,
salir disparado; **to — on** proseguir,
continuar; **to — out** salir; apagarse;
**to — over** pasar por encima de;
examinar con cuidado; releer; repasar; recorrer; **to — to sleep**
dormirse; **to — under** ir o pasar por
debajo de; hundirse; **to — up** subir;
**to let —** soltar; **there is not enough
to — around** no hay (bastante) para
todos; *s.* empuje, energía; **it is a —**
trato hecho; **to be on the —** estar en
continuo movimiento.
**goad** [god] *s.* aguijón; *v.* aguijonear;
aguijar, incitar.
**goal** [gol] *s.* meta; fin, objetivo.
**goat** [got] *s.* cabra; **male —** macho cabrío; **to be the —** ser la víctima,
pagar el pato.
**goatee** [gotí] *s.* perilla.
**gobble** [gábl̩] *v.* tragar, engullir; **to —
up** engullirse.
**gobbler** [gáblə] *s.* pavo.
**go-between** [góbətwin] *s.* medianero.
**goblet** [gáblɪt] *s.* copa grande.
**goblin** [gáblɪn] *s.* duende.
**god** [gɑd] *s.* dios; **God** Dios.
**godchild** [gádtʃaɪld] *s.* ahijado, ahijada.
**goddess** [gádɪs] *s.* diosa.
**godfather** [gádfaðə] *s.* padrino.
**godless** [gádlɪs] *adj.* impío, ateo.
**godlike** [gádlaɪk] *adj.* como Dios;
divino.
**godly** [gádlɪ] *adj.* pío, devoto; divino.
**godmother** [gádmʌðə] *s.* madrina.
**goggles** [gáglz̩] *s. pl.* antiparras, gafas.
**going** [góɪŋ] *ger.* & *adj.* que anda,
marcha o funciona bien; **to be —** ir,
irse; *s.* ida, partida; **comings and -s**
idas y venidas.
**goiter** [gɔ́ɪtə] *s.* papera; bocio; *Ríopl.*,
*Méx.*, *C.A.* buche; *C.A.* güecho.
**gold** [gold] *s.* oro; **— standard** patrón
de oro.
**golden** [góldn̩] *adj.* de oro; áureo; dorado.
**goldfinch** [góldfɪntʃ] *s.* jilguero amarillo.
**goldfish** [góldfɪʃ] *s.* carpa dorada.
**goldsmith** [góldsmɪθ] *s.* orfebre.

**golf** [gɑlf] *s.* golf.
**gondola** [gándələ] *s.* góndola; cabina
(*de una aeronave*); **— car** vagón de
mercancías (*sin techo*), *Am.* jaula.
**gone** [gɔn] *p.p. de* **to go** & *adj.* ido; perdido; **he is —** se fué; **it is all —** se
acabó; ya no hay más.
**gong** [gɔŋ] *s.* gong, batintín.
**good** [gʊd] *adj.* bueno; válido; valedero; **— afternoon** buenas tardes;
**— day** buenos días; adiós; **— evening** buenas noches; **— morning**
buenos días; **— night** buenas noches;
**Good Friday** Viernes Santo; **for —**
para siempre, permanentemente; **to
have a — time** pasar un buen rato;
divertirse; **to make —** pagar, compensar; cumplir (*una promesa*); salir
bien, tener buen éxito; *s.* bien; beneficio, provecho, ventaja; **-s** bienes,
efectos; mercancías.
**good-bye** [gʊdbáɪ] *s.* & *interj.* adiós.
**good-looking** [gúdlúkɪŋ] ·*adj.* bien
parecido, guapo.
**goodly** [gúdlɪ] *adj.* grande, considerable; de buena apariencia.
**good-natured** [gúdnétʃəd] *adj.* de buen
genio, bonachón, afable.
**goodness** [gúdnɪs] *s.* bondad; **—!**
¡Dios mío! ¡cielos!
**goody** [gúdɪ] *s.* golosina, bonbón,
dulce; *interj.* ¡qué gusto!; **goody-
goody** beatuco (*el que afecta virtud*),
papanatas.
**goof** [guf] *v.* chapucear.
**goose** [gus] *s.* ganso; bobo, tonto; **—
flesh** carne de gallina.
**gooseberry** [gúsberɪ] *s.* grosella; grosellero (*arbusto*).
**gopher** [gófə] *s.* roedor semejante a la
ardilla.
**gore** [gor] *s.* (*blood*) cuajarón de sangre;
sangre; (*cloth*) cuchillo (*Am.* chuchilla),
sesga (*tira de lienzo en figura de
cuchilla*); *v.* acornear, herir con los
cuernos; hacer una sesga en (*un
traje*).
**gorge** [gɔrdʒ] *s.* cañada, barranco, barranca; *v.* engullir(se), atracarse.
**gorgeous** [gɔ́rdʒəs] *adj.* primoroso, vistoso, hermosísimo.
**gorilla** [gərílə] *s.* gorila.
**gory** [górɪ] *adj.* sangriento, ensangrentado.
**gospel** [gáspl̩] *s.* evangelio; **it is the —
truth** es la pura verdad.
**gossip** [gásɪp] *s.* (*rumors*) chisme,
chismería; murmuración, hablilla;
(*person*) murmurador, chismero, chismoso; *v.* chismear, murmurar.
**gossipy** [gásəpɪ] *adj.* chismero, chismoso.
**got** [gɑt] *pret.* & *p.p. de* **to get.**
**Gothic** [gáθɪk] *adj.* gótico; *s.* gótico
(*idioma de los godos*); estilo gótico.
**gotten** [gátn̩] *p.p. de* **to get.**
**gouge** [gaʊdʒ] *s.* gubia (*especie de formón o escoplo curvo*); *v.* excavar con
gubia, formón o escoplo; **to — someone's eyes out** sacarle los ojos a alguien.

GI

**gourd** [gord] s. calabaza.

**gourmet** [gurmé] s. gastrónomo.

**gout** [gaut] s. gota (*enfermedad*).

**govern** [gávən] v. gobernar; regir.

**governess** [gávənis] s. institutriz.

**government** [gávəmənt] s. gobierno.

**governmental** [gavəméntl] adj. gubernativo.

**governor** [gávənə] s. gobernador; regulador (*de una máquina*).

**gown** [gaun] s. vestido (*de mujer*); toga (*de un juez, profesor, etc.*); **dressing — bata.**

**grab** [græb] v. agarrar asir; arrebatar; s. arrebatiña; agarro, agarrón; presa.

**grace** [gres] s. gracia; favor; donaire, garbo; **to say —** bendecir la mesa, dar gracias; **to be in the good -s of someone** gozar del favor de uno; v. agraciar, adornar.

**graceful** [grésfəl] adj. gracioso, agraciado, garboso; **-ly** adv. graciosamente, con gracia, con garbo.

**gracefulness** [grésfəlnis] s. gracia, donaire, gallardía, garbo.

**gracious** [gréʃəs] adj. afable; cortés; —! ¡válgame Dios!

**gradation** [gredéʃən] s. graduación; gradación; grado.

**grade** [gred] s. (*degree*) grado; (*mark*) nota, calificación; (*slope*) cuesta, declive, pendiente; *Am.* gradiente; **— crossing** cruce a nivel (*de un ferrocarril con una carretera*); **the -s** la escuela primaria; v. graduar, clasificar; calificar, dar una calificación; nivelar (*un camino*).

**gradual** [grédʒuəl] adj. gradual; **-ly** adv. gradualmente, poco a poco.

**graduate** [grédʒuit] adj. graduado, que ha recibido un grado académico; **to do — work** cursar asignaturas superiores (*al bachillerato*); s. estudiante graduado (*que estudia para licenciado o doctor*); [grédʒuet] v. graduar(se).

**graduation** [grædʒuéʃən] s. graduación.

**graft** [græft] s. (*insertion*) injerto; tejido injertado; (*extortion*) sisa, malversación (*de caudales públicos*); ganancia ilegal, *Am.* mordida; v. injertar; malversar fondos ajenos; sisar, exigir pago ilegal, *Am.* morder.

**grafter** [gréftə] s. malversador (*de fondos públicos*), estafador. *C.A.* coyote, *Méx.* mordelón.

**grain** [gren] s. (*cereal*) grano; (*markings*) fibra (*de la madera*), veta (*del mármol o madera*); **against the —** a (o al) redopelo, a contrapelo.

**gram** [græm] s. gramo.

**grammar** [græmə] s. gramática; **— school** escuela primaria.

**grammatical** [grəmǽtik̩l] adj. gramatical, gramático.

**granary** [grǽnəri] s. granero.

**grand** [grænd] adj. grande; grandioso, admirable; magnífico.

**grandchild** [grǽntʃaild] s. nieto.

**grandchildren** [grǽntʃildrən] s. pl.
nietos.

**granddaughter** [grǽndɔtə] s. nieta.

**grandeur** [grǽndʒə] s. grandeza, grandiosidad; majestad.

**grandfather** [grǽnfaðə] s. abuelo.

**grandiose** [grǽndios] adj. grandioso, magnífico.

**grandma** [grǽnma] s. abuela, abuelita, *Am.* mamá grande.

**grandmother** [grǽnmʌðə] s. abuela.

**grandness** [grǽndnis] s. grandeza; grandiosidad; magnificencia.

**grandpa** [grǽnpa] s. abuelo, abuelito, *Am.* papá grande.

**grandparent** [grǽnpɛrənt] s. abuelo, abuela; **-s** abuelos.

**grandson** [grǽnsʌn] s. nieto.

**grandstand** [grǽnstænd] s. andanada, gradería cubierta.

**grange** [grendʒ] s. granja; asociación de agricultores.

**granite** [grǽnit] s. granito (*roca*).

**granny** [grǽni] s. abuelita; viejecita, viejita.

**grant** [grænt] s. concesión; subvención; donación; transferencia de propiedad (*mediante escritura*); v. conceder; otorgar; ceder, transferir (*derechos, propiedad, etc.*); **to take for -ed** dar por supuesto, dar por sentado.

**granulate** [grǽnjələt] v. granular(se).

**grape** [grep] s. uva.

**grapefruit** [grépfrut] s. toronja.

**grapevine** [grépvain] s. vid; parra.

**graph** [græf] s. diagrama, gráfica; v. hacer una gráfica o diagrama.

**graphic** [grǽfik] adj. gráfico.

**graphite** [grǽfait] s. grafito.

**grapple** [grǽpl̩] v. luchar, pelear cuerpo a cuerpo; aferrar, agarrar.

**grasp** [græsp] v. (*seize*) agarrar; asir; apretar; (*understand*) comprender; abarcar; s. agarro, asimiento; apretón de manos; **to be within one's —** estar al alcance de uno; **to have a good — of a subject** estar fuerte en una materia, saber a fondo una materia.

**grass** [græs] s. hierba; césped; pasto; *Méx.* zacate; *Méx., Ven., Col.* grama.

**grasshopper** [grǽshapə] s. saltamontes, saltón, *Méx., C.A.* chapulín.

**grassroots** [grǽsruts] adj. del pueblo; de la gente.

**grassy** [grǽsi] adj. herboso, *Am.* pastoso.

**grate** [gret] s. (*window*) reja, verja, enrejado; (*grill*) parrilla, brasero; v. enrejar, poner enrejado; crujir, rechinar (*los dientes*); rallar (*queso*); **to — on** molestar, irritar.

**grateful** [grétfəl] adj. agradecido; grato, agradable.

**grater** [grétə] s. rallador.

**gratify** [grǽtəfai] v. complacer, dar gusto, agradar; satisfacer.

**grating** [grétiŋ] s. reja, enrejado, verja; adj. rechinante; molesto, áspero.

**gratis** [grétis] adv. gratis, de balde.

**gratitude** [grǽtətjud] s. gratitud.

**gratuitous** [grətjúətəs] adj. gratuito;

sin fundamento; — **statement** afirmación arbitraria.

**grave** [grev] *adj.* grave; serio; *s.* tumba sepulcro, sepultura; acento grave; —**stone** losa o lápida sepulcral.

**gravel** [grǽvl] *s.* grava, guijo, cascajo; cálculos (*en los riñones, la vejiga, etc.*); mal de piedra; *v.* cubrir con grava.

**graveyard** [grévjɑrd] *s.* cementerio.

**gravitation** [grævɪtéʃən] *s.* atracción; gravitación.

**gravity** [grǽvətɪ] *s.* gravedad; seriedad.

**gravy** [grévɪ] *s.* salsa; jugo (*de carne*).

**gray** [gre] *adj.* gris; cano; entrecano (*que empieza a encanecer*); — **horse** rucio, tordo, tordillo; — **matter** seso; **gray-headed** canoso; *s.* gris, color gris; *v.* encanecer; poner(se) gris.

**grayish** [gréɪʃ] *adj.* grisáceo, pardusco; — **hair** pelo entrecano.

**grayness** [grénɪs] *s.* grisura, gris, calidad de gris; encanecimiento.

**graze** [grez] *v.* (*feed*) pacer; apacentar, *Am.* pastear, pastar; (*brush*) rozar; raspar; *s.* roce, rozón, raspadura.

**grease** [gris] *s.* grasa; *v.* engrasar; untar; lubricar; **to — the palm** untar la mano, sobornar.

**greasy** [grísɪ] *adj.* grasiento, grasoso.

**great** [gret] *adj.* gran(de); eminente; magnífico, excelente; **a — deal** una gran cantidad; muchos; mucho; **a — many** muchos; **a — while** un largo rato o tiempo; **-ly** *adv.* grandemente; mucho; muy; en gran parte; sobremanera.

**great-grandchild** [grétgrǽntʃɑɪld] *s.* biznieto.

**great-grandfather** [grétgrǽnfɑðɚ] *s.* bisabuelo.

**great-grandmother** [grétgrǽnmʌðɚ] *s.* bisabuela.

**greatness** [grétnɪs] *s.* grandeza.

**Grecian** [gríʃən] *adj. & s.* griego.

**greed** [grid] *s.* codicia; avaricia; gula.

**greedily** [grídḷɪ] *adv.* vorazmente; con avaricia; con gula.

**greediness** [grídɪnɪs] *s.* codicia; avaricia; gula; voracidad.

**greedy** [grídɪ] *adj.* codicioso; avaro; goloso; voraz.

**Greek** [grik] *adj. & s.* griego.

**green** [grin] *adj.* (*color*) verde; (*novice*) novato, inexperto; **to grow —** verdear; **the fields look —** verdean los campos; *s.* verde, verdor; césped, prado; campo de golf; **-s** verduras, hortalizas.

**greenhorn** [grínhɔrn] *s.* novato, pipiolo.

**greenhouse** [grínhaʊs] *s.* invernáculo, invernadero.

**greenish** [grínɪʃ] *adj.* verdoso.

**greenness** [grínnɪs] *s.* (*color*) verdor, verdura; (*experience*) inmadurez; impericia.

**greet** [grit] *v.* saludar; **to — each other** saludarse.

**greeting** [grítɪŋ] *s.* saludo; salutación; **-s!** ¡salud! ¡saludos!

**grenade** [grɪnéd] *s.* granada, bomba epqueña.

**grew** [gru] *pret. de* **to grow.**

**grey** = **gray.**

**greyish** = **gray.**

**greyness** = **grayness.**

**greyhound** [gréhaʊnd] *s.* lebrel, galgo.

**griddle** [grídl] *s.* tartera; plancha (*para tapar el hornillo*).

**grief** [grif] *s.* dolor, pesar; **to come to —** sobrevenirle a uno una desgracia; fracasar.

**grievance** [grívəns] *s.* queja; resentimiento; motivo de queja, injusticia, ofensa.

**grieve** [griv] *v.* afligir(se); lamentar(se), acongojar(se).

**grievous** [grívəs] *adj.* doloroso, penoso; grave, altroz.

**grill** [grɪl] *s.* parrilla; **men's —** restaurante para hombres; *v.* asar en parrillas; interrogar (*a un sospechoso*).

**grim** [grɪm] *adj.* austero, áspero; fiero; torvo, siniestro.

**grimace** [grɪmés] *s.* mueca, gesto; *v.* hacer muecas o gestos.

**grime** [graɪm] *s.* mugre; *v.* ensuciar.

**grimy** [gráɪmɪ] *adj.* mugriento.

**grin** [grɪn] *s.* sonrisa abierta; sonrisa maliciosa; sonrisa canina; *v.* sonreír (*mostrando mucho los dientes*).

**grind** [graɪnd] *v.* (*crush*) moler; machacar; (*sharpen*) afilar, amolar; (*study hard*) afanarse demasiado; estudiar con empeño; **to — a hand organ** tocar el organillo; **to — one's teeth** rechinar los dientes; *s.* molienda; faena, trabajo penoso; estudiante tesonero; **the daily —** la rutina diaria.

**grinder** [gráɪndɚ] *s.* moledor; molinillo (*para moler café*); amolador, afilador; muela (*piedra para afilar*); muela (*diente molar*).

**grindstone** [gráɪndston] *s.* piedra de amolar.

**grip** [grɪp] *v.* (*seize*) agarrar; asir; apretar; empuñar; (*impress*) impresionar; conmover; *s.* agarro; asimiento; apretón; asidero, asa; (*suitcase*) valija, maletín; *Méx.*, velís; **to have a — on someone** tener agarrado a alguien.

**grippe** [grɪp] *s.* gripe, influenza.

**grit** [grɪt] *s.* (*gravel*) arenilla, arena; piedra arenisca; (*pluck*) firmeza, tesón; **-s** maíz, avena, o trigo a medio moler; *v.* rechinar, crujir.

**gritty** [grítɪ] *adj.* arenoso; valeroso, firme.

**grizzly** [grízlɪ] *adj.* grisáceo, pardusco; — **bear** oso pardo.

**groan** [gron] *s.* gemido, quejido; *v.* gemir; quejarse; crujir (*por exceso de peso*).

**grocer** [grósɚ] *s.* abacero, *Méx.* abarrotero, *Carib., C.A.* bodeguero; *Ríopl.* almacenero.

**grocery** [grósərɪ] *s.* abacería, tienda de comestibles, *Méx.* abarrotería, *Méx.* tienda de abarrotes; *Carib., C.A.* bodega; **groceries** comestibles, *Méx.* abarrotes.

**groom** [grum] *s.* (*bridegroom*) novio; (*stable groom*) caballerizo, mozo de caballeriza; establero; *v.* almohazar, limpiar con la almohaza (*a los caballos*), cuidar (*a los caballos*); **to — oneself** asearse, peinarse, componerse; **well-groomed** bien vestido, aseado, limpio.

**groove** [gruv] *s.* estría, ranura, acanaladura; surco (*en un camino*); muesca, encaje; *v.* acanalar, estriar.

**grope** [grop] *v.* tentalear, tentar, andar a tientas; **to — for** buscar tentando, buscar a tientas.

**gross** [gros] *adj.* grueso; burdo; tosco; grosero; **— earnings** ganancias totales; **— ignorance** ignorancia crasa; **— weight** peso bruto; *s.* grueso, totalidad; gruesa (*doce docenas*).

**grotesque** [grotésk] *adj.* & *s.* grotesco.

**grotto** [gráto] *s.* gruta.

**grouch** [grautʃ] *s.* mal humor; gruñón, refunfuñón, cascarrabias; **to have a — against someone** tenerle ojeriza (*o* mala voluntad) a una persona; guardarle rencor a alguien; *v.* gruñir, refunfuñar; estar de mal humor.

**grouchy** [gráutʃɪ] *adj.* gruñón, refunfuñón, malhumorado, cascarrabias.

**ground** [graund] *s.* (*earth*) suelo, tierra; terreno; (*motive*) motivo, rezón; base, fundamento; **— crew** personal de tierra; **-s** heces, desperdicios, sedimento; **— floor** piso bajo, planta baja, **to break —** roturar, arar, cavar; **to give —** retroceder, ceder; **to hold one's —** mantenerse firme; *v.* conectar (*un alambre*) con la tierra; encallar (*una embarcación*); aterrizar (*un aeroplano*); **to be well -ed** poseer las bases o principios fundamentales; *pret.* & *p.p. de* **to grind.**

**groundless** [gráundlɪs] *adj.* infundado.

**group** [grup] *s.* grupo; **— insurance** seguros sociales; *v.* agrupar.

**grove** [grov] *s.* arboleda, bosquecillo.

**grow** [gro] *v.* crecer; brotar; cultivar; criar; producir; **to — angry** ponerse enojado o enfadado, enfadarse, enojarse; **to — better** ponerse mejor, mejorar; **to — difficult** dificultarse, hacerse difícil; **to — late** hacerse tarde; **to — old** ponerse viejo, envejecer; **to — out of a habit** perder la costumbre; **to — pale** ponerse pálido, palidecer; **to — tired** cansarse.

**growl** [graul] *s.* gruñido; *v.* gruñir.

**growler** [gráulɚ] *s.* gruñón; regañón.

**grown** [gron] *p.p. de* **to grow** & *adj.* crecido; desarrollado; **— man** hombre maduro, hombre hecho; **— with trees** poblado de árboles.

**grown-up** [grónʌp] *adj.* crecido, adulto; *s.* adulto.

**growth** [groθ] *s.* (*increase*) crecimiento, acrecentamiento; aumento; (*development*) desarrollo; (*vegetation*) vegetación; (*tissue*) tumor, lobanillo, excrecencia.

**grubby** [grábɪ] *adj.* roñoso; sucio.

**grudge** [grʌdʒ] *s.* inquina, rencor, resentimiento, mala voluntad; *v.* tener inquina, envidia o mala voluntad; dar de mala gana.

**gruff** [grʌf] *adj.* áspero, rudo; grosero.

**grumble** [grámbl] *s.* refunfuño, gruñido, queja; *v.* refunfuñar, gruñir, quejarse.

**grumbler** [grámblɚ] *s.* gruñón; regañón.

**grumpy** [grámpɪ] *adj.* malhumorado; gruñón.

**grunt** [grʌnt] *s.* gruñido, *Méx.*, *C.A.*, *Col.*, *Ven.* pujido; *v.* gruñir, *Ríopl.*, *Méx.*, *C.A.*, *Ven.*, *Andes* pujar.

**guarantee** [gærəntí] *s.* garantía; fianza; fiador; *v.* garantizar; dar fianza; salir fiador de.

**guarantor** [gærəntɚ] *s.* fiador.

**guaranty** [gærəntɪ] *s.* garantía; fianza; fiador; *v. véase* **guarantee.**

**guard** [gard] *s.* guarda; guardia; resguardo; **to be on —** estar alerta; estar en guardia; **to keep —** vigilar; *v.* guardar; resguardar; vigilar; **to — (oneself) against** guardarse de.

**guardian** [gárdɪən] *s.* guardián, custodio; tutor; **— angel** ángel custodio, ángel de la guarda.

**guardianship** [gárdɪənʃɪp] *s.* tutela; guarda, custodia.

**guardrail** [gárdrel] *s.* baranda.

**Guatemalan** [gwɑtəmálən] *adj.* & *s.* guatemalteco.

**guess** [gɛs] *s.* conjetura, suposición; adivinación; *v.* adivinar; suponer, creer.

**guest** [gɛst] *s.* convidado; visita; huésped, pensionista, inquilino.

**guffaw** [gʌfɔ́] *s.* risotada, carcajada.

**guidance** [gáidns] *s.* guía, dirección.

**guide** [gaid] *s.* guía.

**guidebook** [gáidbuk] *s.* guía del viajero; **railway —** guía de ferrocarriles.

**guideline** [gáidlain] *s.* norma; precepto.

**guild** [gild] *s.* gremio; cofradía; asociación.

**guile** [gail] *s.* engaño, astucia.

**guilt** [gilt] *s.* culpa, delito; culpabilidad.

**guiltless** [gíltlɪs] *adj.* libre de culpa; inocente.

**guilty** [gíltɪ] *adj.* culpable; reo, delincuente.

**guise** [gaiz] *s.* aspecto, apariencia; modo; **under the — of** so capa de; disfrazado de.

**guitar** [gitár] *s.* guitarra.

**gulf** [gʌlf] *s.* golfo; abismo.

**gull** [gʌl] *s.* gaviota.

**gullet** [gálɪt] *s.* gaznate.

**gully** [gálɪ] *s.* barranco, barranca; hondonada.

**gulp** [gʌlp] *s.* trago; *v.* tragar; engullir; **to — it down** tragárselo.

**gum** [gʌm] *s.* (*product*) goma; (*of mouth*) encía; **chewing —** goma de mascar, *Am.* chicle; **— tree** arbol gomífero, *Col.* gomero; *v.* engomar, pegar con goma.

**gun** [gʌn] *s.* (*cannon*) cañón; (*rifle*) fusil, rifle; (*shotgun*) escopeta; pistola, revólver; **a 21 — salute** una salva de 21 cañonazos.

**gunboat** [gʌ́nbot] *s.* cañonero, lancha cañonera.

**gunner** [gʌ́nɚ] *s.* artillero, cañonero; ametrallador.

**gunpowder** [gʌ́npaʊdɚ] *s.* pólvora.

**gurgle** [gɚ́gl] *v.* borbotar, hacer borbollones; *s.* borbollón, borbotón.

**gush** [gʌʃ] *s.* chorro; borbollón, borbotón; efusión (*de cariño o entusiasmo*); *v.* chorrear, borbotar, borbollar, borbollonear; brotar; ser demasiado efusivo.

**gust** [gʌst] *s.* ráfaga, ventolera.

**gut** [gʌt] *s.* tripa, intestino; cuerda de tripa; **to have -s** tener agallas (*ánimo*).

**gutter** [gʌ́tɚ] *s.* arroyo (*de la calle o de un camino*); gotera (*del techo*); zanja.

**guy** [gaɪ] *s.* (*person*) sujeto, tipo, individuo; (*wire*) tirante, alambre, cadena (*para sostener algo*); *v.* sostener (*algo*) con tirantes; burlarse de, mofarse de.

**gymnasium** [dʒɪmnéziəm] *s.* gimnasio.

**gymnastics** [dʒɪmnǽstɪks] *s. pl.* gimnasia.

**gyrate** [dʒaɪret] *v.* girar.

**gyroscope** [dʒaɪrəskop] *s.* giroscopio.

**gypsy** [dʒípsɪ] *s. & adj.* gitano.

# H

**habit** [hǽbɪt] *s.* hábito; costumbre; **drinking —** vicio de la bebida; **riding —** traje de montar.

**habitual** [həbítʃʊəl] *adj.* habitual; acostumbrado.

**hack** [hæk] *s.* (*cut*) tajo; (*cough*) tos seca; (*horse*) caballo de alquiler; rocín; (*writer*) escritor mercenario; *v.* tajar, picar; toser con tos seca.

**hackneyed** [hǽknɪd] *adj.* trillado, muy común.

**had** [hæd] *pret. & p.p.* de **to have; you — better do it** es bueno que Vd. lo haga; sería bueno que Vd. lo hiciese; **I — rather go than stay** preferiría irme a quedarme.

**hag** [hæg] *s.* hechicera, bruja; viejota.

**haggard** [hǽgəd] *adj.* macilento, flaco.

**haggle** [hǽgl] *v.* regatear.

**hail** [hel] *s.* (*storm*) granizo; (*greeting*) saludo; llamada, grito; **Hail Mary** Ave María; *interj.* ¡salud!; ¡salve!; *v.* granizar; saludar; llamar; aclamar; **to — from** proceder de, ser oriundo de.

**hailstorm** [hélstɔrm] *s.* granizada.

**hair** [hɛr] *s.* pelo; cabello; vello; filamento (*de las plantas*); **— net** red para el cabello.

**hairbrush** [hérbrʌʃ] *s.* cepillo para el cabello.

**haircut** [hérkʌt] *s.* corte de pelo; **to have a —** hacerse cortar el pelo.

**hairdo** [hérdu] *s.* peinado.

**hairdresser** [hérdrɛsɚ] *s.* peluquero; peinadora.

**hairless** [hérlɪs] *adj.* sin pelo, pelado; lampiño.

**hairpin** [hérpɪn] *s.* horquilla, *Am.* gancho (*para el pelo*).

**hairy** [hérɪ] *adj.* peludo, cabelludo; hirsuto, velloso, velludo.

**hale** [hel] *adj.* sano, fuerte, robusto; *v.* llevar (*a una persona*) por fuerza.

**half** [hæf] *s.* mitad; **— an apple** media manzana; *adj.* medio; **— brother** hermanastro; **— cooked** a medio cocer, medio cocido; **half-past one** la una y media; **half-baked** a medio cocer; a medio planear.

**half-breed** [hǽfbrid] *adj. & s.* mestizo.

**half-hour** [hǽfáʊr] *s.* media hora; *adj.* de media hora.

**half-mast** [hǽfmǽst] *s.* media asta; *v.* poner a media asta (*la bandera*).

**half-open** [hǽfópən] *adj.* entreabierto; medio abierto, entornado.

**halfway** [hǽfwe] *adj. & adv.* a medio camino; parcial, incompleto; **— between** equidistante de; **— finished** a medio acabar; **to do something —** hacer algo a medias.

**half-witted** [hǽfwítɪd] *adj.* imbécil, zonzo.

**halibut** [hǽləbət] *s.* mero, hipogloso (*pez*).

**hall** [hɔl] *s.* salón (*para asambleas, funciones, etc.*); edificio (*de un colegio o universidad*); vestíbulo; corredor, pasillo; **town —** ayuntamiento.

**hallmark** [hólmark] *s.* distintivo.

**hallo** = **hello**.

**hallow** [hǽlo] *v.* santificar; consagrar.

**Halloween** [hæloín] *s.* víspera de Todos los Santos.

**hallway** [hólwe] *s.* corredor, pasillo; zaguán.

**halo** [hélo] *s.* halo; aureola.

**halt** [hɔlt] *s.* alto, parada; *v.* parar(se), detener(se); hacer alto; vacilar.

**halter** [hóltɚ] *s.* ronzal, cabestro.

**halting** [hóltɪŋ] *adj.* vacilante; **-ly** *adv.* con vacilación.

**halve** [hæv] *v.* partir por la mitad; partir en dos.

**halves** [hævz] *pl.* de **half; to go —** ir a medias.

**ham** [hæm] *s.* jamón.

**hamburger** [hǽmbɚgɚ] *s.* carne picada de vaca; bocadillo o emparedado de carne picada, *Am.* hamburguesa.

**hamlet** [hǽmlɪt] *s.* caserío, aldehuela.

**hammer** [hǽmɚ] *s.* martillo; martinete (*de piano*); **sledge —** macho; *v.* martillar; machacar; clavar.

**hammock** [hǽmək] *s.* hamaca, *Ven.*, *Col.* chinchorro; *Ríopl.* mangangá; coy.

**hamper** [hǽmpɚ] *s.* canasto, cesto grande, cuévano; *v.* estorbar, impedir, embarazar.

**hand** [hænd] *s.* mano; manecilla; aguja (*de reloj*); obrero; letra (*modo de escribir*); **— and glove** uña y carne; **— in —** (cogidos) de la mano; **at —** a la mano, cerca; **made by —** hecho a mano; **on —** disponible; en existencia; listo; a la mano, presente; **on the other —** en cambio, por otra

parte; **to have one's -s full** estar
ocupadísimo; *v.* entregar, dar; **to —
down** bajar (*una cosa para dársela a
alguien*); transmitir (*de una a otra
generación*); pronunciar (*un fallo*); **to
— in** entregar; **to — over** entregar.

**handbag** [hǽndbæg] *s.* bolsa o bolso;
saco de noche, maletín.

**handball** [hǽndbɔl] *s.* pelota; juego de
pelota.

**handbill** [hǽndbɪl] *s.* hoja volante
(*anuncio*).

**handcuff** [hǽndkʌf] *v.* maniatar; **-s** *s.
pl.* esposas, manillas de hierro.

**handful** [hǽndfəl] *s.* manojo, puñado.

**handicap** [hǽndɪkæp] *s.* desventaja, estorbo, impedimento, obstáculo; ventaja o desventaja (*impuesta en ciertas
contiendas*); **— race** carrera de handicap; *v.* estorbar, poner trabas a.

**handiwork** [hǽndɪwɜ̃k] *s.* labor, trabajo hecho a mano; artefacto.

**handkerchief** [hǽŋkɚtʃɪf] *s.* pañuelo.

**handle** [hǽndḷ] *s.* mango, asa; tirador
(*de puerta o cajón*); puño (*de espada*);
manubrio (*de bicicleta, organillo, etc.*);
*v.* manejar; manipular; manosear, tocar; comerciar en; **-s easily** se
maneja con facilidad, es muy manuable.

**handmade** [hǽndméd] *adj.* hecho a
mano.

**handsaw** [hǽndsɔ] *s.* serrucho.

**handshake** [hǽndʃek] *s.* apretón de
manos.

**handsome** [hǽnsəm] *adj.* (*good-looking*) hermoso, guapo, bien parecido;
(*generous*) generoso; **a — sum** una
suma considerable.

**handwriting** [hǽndraɪtɪŋ] *s.* letra (*modo de escribir*), escritura.

**handy** [hǽndɪ] *adj.* a la mano, próximo;
hábil, diestro; manuable, fácil de manejar.

**hang** [hæŋ] *v.* colgar; suspender; ahorcar; inclinar (*la cabeza*); **sentenced
to —** condenado a la horca; **to —
around** andar holgazaneando por un
sitio; rondar; esperar sin hacer nada;
**to — on** colgarse de; depender de;
estar pendiente de; persistir; **to —
paper on a wall** empapelar una
pared; **to — with tapestries** entapizar; *s.* modo de caerle la ropa a una
persona; modo de manejar (*un mecanismo*); modo de resolver (*un problema*);
significado (*de un argumento*); **I don't
care a —** no me importa un ardite.

**hangar** [hǽŋɚ] *s.* hangar, cobertizo.

**hanger** [hǽŋɚ] *s.* colgadero; percha, clavijero; **paper —** empapelador.

**hanging** [hǽŋɪŋ] *s.* muerte en la horca;
**-s** colgaduras; *adj.* colgante; colgado.

**hangman** [hǽŋmən] *s.* verdugo.

**hangnail** [hǽŋnel] *s.* padrastro (*pedacito de pellejo que se levanta junto a las
uñas*).

**hang-over** [hǽŋovɚ] *s.* sobrante, remanente, resto; **to have a —** *Ven., Col.,
Andes* tener un ratón o estar enratona-
do (*tras una borrachera*), *Méx.*, estar

crudo o tener una cruda; *Ch.* la mona;
*C.A.* de goma; *Ríopl.* resaca.

**haphazard** [hæphǽzɚd] *adv.* al azar, al
acaso, a la ventura, a la buena de
Dios; *adj.* casual; impensado.

**haphazardly** [hæphǽzɚdlɪ] *adv.* =
**haphazard.**

**hapless** [hǽplɪs] *adj.* desventurado, desgraciado.

**happen** [hǽpən] *v.* suceder, pasar,
acontecer, sobrevenir, acaecer; **to —
to hear** (**do, be,** *etc.*) oír (hacer,
estar, *etc.*) por casualidad; **to — to
pass by** acertar a pasar; **to — on**
(**upon**) encontrarse con, tropezar con.

**happening** [hǽpənɪŋ] *s.* acontecimiento, suceso.

**happily** [hǽplɪ] *adv.* felizmente; afortunadamente.

**happiness** [hǽpɪnɪs] *s.* felicidad, dicha,
contento.

**happy** [hǽpɪ] *adj.* feliz; dichoso, alegre;
afortunado; **to be — to** alegrarse de.

**harangue** [hərǽŋ] *s.* arenga, perorata;
*v.* arengar, perorar.

**harass** [hǽrəs] *v.* acosar, hostigar,
molestar.

**harbor** [hárbɚ] *s.* puerto; asilo, refugio,
abrigo; *v.* abrigar; hospedar; albergar.

**hard** [hard] *adj.* (*firm*) duro; (*stiff*)
tieso; (*difficult*) arduo, difícil; **—
cash** dinero contante y sonante,
metálico; **— coal** antracita; **— liquor** licor espiritoso (*aguardiente,
ron, etc.*); **— luck** mala suerte; **— of
hearing** medio sordo; **— water** agua
cruda; *adv.* fuerte, recio, con fuerza;
con empeño, con ahinco; **— by** muy
cerca; **— core** núcleo resistente (*de
un grupo*); **—hearted** de corazón
duro; **hard-working** muy trabajador,
industrioso, aplicado.

**harden** [hárdṇ] *v.* endurecer(se).

**hardening** [hárdṇɪŋ] *s.* endurecimien-
to.

**hardly** [hárdlɪ] *adv.* apenas; a duras
penas; difícilmente; duramente, con
aspereza; probablemente no.

**hardness** [hárdnɪs] *s.* dureza; aspereza;
dificultad.

**hardship** [hárdʃɪp] *s.* apuro, aflicción;
trabajo, penalidad.

**hardware** [hárdwer] *s.* quincalla, quincallería; **— shop** quincallería, ferretería.

**hardy** [hárdɪ] *adj.* robusto, fuerte,
recio, atrevido.

**hare** [her] *s.* liebre.

**harebrained** [hérbrénd] *adj.* atolondrado, ligero de cascos.

**harelip** [hérlɪp] *s.* labio leporino.

**harem** [hérəm] *s.* harén.

**harlot** [hárlət] *s.* ramera, prostituta.

**harm** [harm] *s.* daño, mal; perjuicio;
*v.* dañar; hacer mal, hacer daño;
perjudicar.

**harmful** [hármfəl] *adj.* dañoso; dañino,
nocivo, perjudicial.

**harmless** [hármlɪs] *adj.* innocuo; inofensivo; no dañoso, inocente.

**harmlessness** [hármlɪsnɪs] *s.* innocuidad; inocencia, falta de malicia.
**harmonic** [hɑrmánɪk] *adj.* armónico.
**harmonious** [hɑrmóniəs] *adj.* armonioso.
**harmonize** [hármənaɪz] *v.* armonizar; concordar; congeniar.
**harmony** [hármənɪ] *s.* armonía.
**harness** [hárnɪs] *s.* guarniciones (*de caballerías*); jaez, aparejo; **to get back in** — volver al servicio activo, volver a trabajar; volver a la rutina; *v.* enjaezar, poner guarniciones a (*un caballo, mula, etc.*).
**harp** [hɑrp] *s.* arpa; *v.* tocar el arpa; **to** — **on** repetir constantemente (*una nota, palabra, tema, etc.*); porfiar en.
**harpoon** [hɑrpún] *s.* arpón; *v.* arponear, pescar con arpón.
**harrow** [hǽro] *s.* rastro, rastrillo, grada; *v.* rastrear, rastrillar; atormentar; horrorizar.
**harrowing** [hǽrəwɪŋ] *adj.* horrendo, horripilante, que pone los cabellos de punta; espeluznante.
**harry** [hǽrɪ] *v.* acosar, molestar; asolar.
**harsh** [hɑrʃ] *adj.* tosco, áspero; severo, austero.
**harshness** [hárʃnɪs] *s.* aspereza; tosquedad; severidad.
**harvest** [hárvɪst] *s.* cosecha; siega, agosto; recolección; *v.* cosechar; segar.
**hash** [hæʃ] *s.* picadillo.
**haste** [hest] *s.* prisa; apresuramiento; **in** — de prisa; **to make** — darse prisa, apresurarse; *Am.* apurarse.
**hasten** [hésn̩] *v.* apresurar(se), precipitar(se); darse prisa.
**hastily** [héstlɪ] *adv.* aprisa, de prisa, apresuradamente, precipitadamente.
**hasty** [héstɪ] *adj.* apresurado; precipitado.
**hat** [hæt] *s.* sombrero.
**hatch** [hætʃ] *v.* empollar; criar pollos; idear, maquinar; *s.* cría, nidada, pollada; escotillón, trampa (*puerta en el suelo*); —**way** escotilla.
**hatchet** [hǽtʃɪt] *s.* hacha; **to bury the** — echar pelillos a la mar, olvidar rencores o enemistades.
**hate** [het] *s.* odio; aborrecimiento; *v.* odiar; aborrecer; detestar.
**hateful** [hétfəl] *adj.* odioso, aborrecible.
**hatred** [hétrɪd] *s.* odio, aversión.
**haughtily** [hɔ́tlɪ] *adv.* con altivez, altaneramente, arrogantemente.
**haughtiness** [hɔ́tɪnɪs] *s.* altanería, altivez.
**haughty** [hɔ́tɪ] *adj.* altivo, altanero, arrogante.
**haul** [hɔl] *v.* (*transport*) acarrear, transportar; (*pull*) jalar (*halar*); tirar de; (*drag*) arrastrar; **to** — **down the flag** arriar (*o* bajar) la bandera; *s.* acarreo; transporte; tirón, estirón; buena pesca; ganancia, botín.
**haunch** [hɔntʃ] *s.* anca.
**haunt** [hɔnt] *v.* frecuentar a menudo; andar por, vagar por (*como fantasma o espectro*); **that idea -s me** me persigue esa idea; **-ed house** casa de espantos, fantasmas o aparecidos; *s.* guarida.
**have** [hæv] *v.* tener; poseer; haber (*v. aux.*); **to** — **a suit made** mandar hacer un traje; **to** — **a look at** dar un vistazo a, echar una mirada a; **to** — **to** tener que; deber; **I'll not** — **it so** no lo toleraré, no lo permitiré; **what did she** — **on?** ¿qué vestido llevaba (puesto)?
**haven** [hévən] *s.* asilo, abrigo, refugio; puerto.
**havoc** [hǽvək] *s.* estrago, estropicio, ruina; **to cause** — hacer estragos.
**hawk** [hɔk] *s.* halcón; *v.* pregonar (*mercancías*).
**hawthorn** [hɔ́θrn] *s.* espino.
**hay** [he] *s.* heno, paja, hierba seca; — **fever** catarro asmático.
**hayloft** [hélɔft] *s.* henil, pajar.
**haystack** [héstæk] *s.* montón de heno o paja.
**hazard** [hǽzəd] *s.* azar; riesgo, peligro; estorbo, obstáculo (*en el campo de golf*); *v.* arriesgar, aventurar.
**hazardous** [hǽzədəs] *adj.* peligroso.
**haze** [hez] *s.* bruma, neblina, niebla; *v.* atormentar, hostigar (*con bromas estudiantiles*).
**hazel** [hézl̩] *s.* avellano; —**nut** avellana; *adj.* de avellano; avellanado, color de avellana.
**hazy** [hézɪ] *adj.* (*weather*) nublado, brumoso; (*mind*) confuso.
**he** [hi] *pron. pers.* él; — **who** el que, quien; **he-goat** macho cabrío.
**head** [hɛd] *s.* cabeza; cabecera (*de cama*); jefe; — **of hair** cabellera; **game of -s or tails** juego de cara y cruz, juego de las chapas, *Ven., Col., Andes, Ch.* juego de cara y sello; *Méx.* juego de aguila y sol; **to be out of one's** — delirar, estar delirante; **to come to a** — madurar; supurar (*un absceso*); **to keep one's** — conservar la calma, no perder la cabeza; **it goes to his** — le desvanece; se le sube a la cabeza; *adj.* principal, primero; de proa, de frente; **head-on** de frente; *v.* encabezar; ir a la cabeza de; acaudillar; mandar, dirigir; **to** — **off** atajar; detener, refrenar; **to** — **towards** dirigirse a, encaminarse a.
**headache** [hédek] *s.* dolor de cabeza.
**headdress** [héddrɛs] *s.* tocado, adorno para la cabeza.
**headgear** [hédgɪr] *s.* sombrero, gorro, gorra; tocado, toca (*de mujer*); cabezada (*de guarnición para caballo*).
**heading** [hédɪŋ] *s.* encabezamiento, título.
**headland** [hédlənd] *s.* cabo, promontorio.
**headlight** [hédlaɪt] *s.* linterna delantera, faro delantero.
**headline** [hédlaɪn] *s.* título, encabezado.
**headlong** [hédlɔ́ŋ] *adv.* de cabeza; precipitadamente.
**headquarters** [hédkwɔ́rtəz] *s.* cuartel general; jefatura; oficina principal.

**HA**

**headset** [hédsɛt] s. receptor de cabeza.
**headstrong** [hédstrɔŋ] adj. testarudo, porfiado, obstinado.
**headway** [hédwe] s. progreso, avance; **to make —** avanzar, adelantar, progresar.
**heal** [hil] v. curar; sanar; cicatrizar.
**health** [hɛlθ] s. salud; sanidad; salubridad.
**healthful** [hélθfəl] adj. sano; salubre; saludable.
**healthfulness** [hélθfəlnɪs] s. salubridad; sanidad.
**healthy** [hélθɪ] adj. sano; saludable.
**heap** [hip] s. montón; pila; v. amontonar; apilar.
**hear** [hɪr] v. (listen) oír; escuchar; (get news) tener noticias; **to — about someone** oír hablar de alguien; **to — from someone** tener noticias de alguien; **to — of** saber de, tener noticias de, oír hablar de; **I -d that . . .** oí decir que . . .
**heard** [hɝd] pret. & p.p. de **to hear.**
**hearer** [hírɚ] s. oyente.
**hearing** [hírɪŋ] s. (sense) oído; (trial) audiencia; examen de testigos; **hard of —** medio sordo, algo sordo; **within —** al alcance del oído; **— aid** aparato auditivo.
**hearsay** [hírse] s. habilla, rumor; **by —** de oídas.
**hearse** [hɝs] s. carroza fúnebre.
**heart** [hart] s. (organ) corazón; (spirit) ánimo; **at —** en realidad, en el fondo; **from the bottom of one's —** de corazón, con toda el alma; con toda sinceridad; **to learn by —** aprender de memoria; **to take —** cobrar ánimo; **to take to —** tomar en serio; tomar a pechos; **— attack** ataque cardíaco.
**heartache** [hártek] s. dolor del corazón; angustia, pesar, congoja.
**heartbroken** [hártbrokən] adj. traspasado de dolor, acongojado, angustiado; desengañado.
**hearten** [hártn̩] v. animar.
**heartfelt** [hártfɛlt] adj. sentido, cordial, sincero; **my — sympathy** mi más sentido pésame.
**hearth** [harθ] s. hogar; fogón.
**heartily** [hártɪlɪ] adv. de corazón; cordialmente; de buena gana; **to eat —** comer con apetito; comer bien (o mucho).
**heartless** [hártlɪs] adj. de mal corazón; cruel; insensible.
**heart-rending** [hártrɛndɪŋ] adj. angustioso; agudo.
**hearty** [hártɪ] adj. sincero, cordial; sano, fuerte; **— food** alimento nutritivo; **a — laugh** una buena carcajada; **— meal** comida abundante.
**heat** [hit] s. (hot) calor; ardor; (emotion) vehemencia; celo (ardor sexual de la hembra); calefacción (para las habitaciones); corrida, carrera (de prueba); v. calentar(se); acalorar(se).
**heater** [hítɚ] s. calentador; calorífero.
**heathen** [híðən] s. pagano, gentil, idóla-

tra; paganos; adj. pagano; irreligioso.
**heating** [hítɪŋ] s. calefacción.
**heave** [hiv] v. levantar, alzar (con esfuerzo); arrojar, lanzar; exhalar (un suspiro); jalar (un cable); jadear; basquear, hacer esfuerzos por vomitar.
**heaven** [hévən] s. cielo.
**heavenly** [hévənlɪ] adj. celeste; celestial; divino.
**heavily** [hévlɪ] adv. pesadamente, lentamente; copiosamente, excesivamente.
**heaviness** [hévɪnɪs] s. pesadez, pesantez; opresión, abatimiento.
**heavy** [hévɪ] adj. (weight) pesado; (thick) grueso; (coarse) burdo; (oppressive) opresivo; **— rain** aguacero recio o fuerte; **with a — heart** abatido, acongojado.
**heavyweight** [héviwet] s. & adj. peso pesado (fuerte).
**hectic** [héktɪk] adj. febril; inquieto.
**hedge** [hɛdʒ] s. seto; vallado, barrera; v. cercar; poner valla o seto a; evitar o evadir contestaciones.
**hedgehog** [hédʒhag] s. erizo.
**hedonism** [hídənɪzm] s. hedonismo.
**heed** [hid] v. atender; hacer caso; prestar atención; s. atención, cuidado; **to pay — to** prestar atención a; hacer caso de.
**heedless** [hídlɪs] adj. descuidado; desatento.
**heel** [hil] s. talón (del pie o de una media); tacón (del zapato); **head over -s** patas arriba; v. poner tacón a; poner talón a.
**hegemony** [hɪdʒémənɪ] s. hegemonía.
**heifer** [héfɚ] s. novilla, vaquilla.
**height** [haɪt] s. altura; elevación; **— of folly** colmo de la locura.
**heighten** [háɪtn̩] v. avivar; aumentar(se); realzar.
**heinous** [hénəs] adj. aborrecible, odioso; malvado.
**heir** [ɛr] s. heredero.
**heiress** [érɪs] s. heredera.
**held** [hɛld] pret. & p.p. de **to hold.**
**helicopter** [héləkaptɚ] s. helicóptero.
**helium** [hílɪəm] s. helio.
**hell** [hɛl] s. infierno.
**hello** [hɛló] interj. ¡hola!; ¡halo!
**helm** [hɛlm] s. timón.
**helmet** [hélmɪt] s. yelmo.
**help** [hɛlp] s. (aid) ayuda; auxilio; remedio; alivio; (employee) criado o criados, empleado o empleados; v. ayudar, asistir; auxiliar; remediar; servir (algo de comer); **to — down** ayudar a bajar **— yourself** sírvase Vd. (de comer o beber); tómelo Vd., está a la disposición de Vd.; **he cannot — it** no puede evitarlo; **he cannot — doing it** no puede menos de hacerlo; **he cannot — but come** no puede menos de venir.
**helper** [hélpɚ] s. ayudante, asistente.
**helpful** [hélpfəl] adj. útil, servicial; provechoso.
**helping** [hélpɪŋ] s. ayuda; porción (que se sirve en la mesa).

**helpless** [hélplɪs] *adj.* (*defenseless*) desamparado; (*handicapped*) desvalido; imposibilitado; incapaz; (*confused*) perplejo, indeciso (*sin saber qué hacer*); **a — situation** una situación irremediable.

**helplessness** [hélplɪsnɪs] *s.* incapacidad; incompetencia; impotencia, debilidad; abandono, desamparo.

**hem** [hɛm] *s.* dobladillo, bastilla; *v.* dobladillar, bastillar, hacer dobladillos en (*la ropa*); **to — in** rodear, cercar; **to — and haw** toser y retoser (*fingidamente*); tartamudear, vacilar.

**hemisphere** [hémɪsfɪr] *s.* hemisferio.

**hemlock** [hémlɑk] *s.* cicuta (*hierba venenosa*); abeto americano.

**hemoglobin** [hímoglobɪn] *s.* hemoglobina.

**hemp** [hɛmp] *s.* cáñamo, *Am.* sisal.

**hemstitch** [hémstɪtʃ] *s.* dobladillo de ojo; *v.* hacer (*o* echar) dobladillo de ojo.

**hen** [hɛn] *s.* gallina; ave hembra.

**hence** [hɛns] *adv.* de (*o* desde) aquí; desde ahora; por lo tanto, por consiguiente; **a week —** de hoy en ocho días; de aquí a una semana.

**henceforth** [hɛnsfórθ] *adv.* de aquí en adelante; de hoy en adelante; desde ahora.

**hepatitis** [hɛpətáɪtɪs] *s.* hepatitis.

**her** [hɜ] *pron.* la; le, a ella; ella (*con preposición*); *adj.* su (sus), de ella.

**herald** [hérəld] *s.* heraldo; anunciador, proclamador; precursor; *v.* anunciar, proclamar, publicar.

**herb** [ɜb] *s.* hierba (yerba).

**herd** [hɜd] *s.* (*animals*) hato; rebaño; manada; tropel; tropilla; (*cattle*) ganado; (*people*) muchedumbre; **the common —** el populacho, la chusma; *v.* reunir, juntar (*el ganado*); ir en manadas, ir juntos.

**herdsman** [hɜdʒmən] *s.* vaquero, vaquerizo; pastor.

**here** [hɪr] *adv.* aquí; acá; **— it is** aquí está, helo aquí, aquí lo tiene Vd., **— is to you!** ¡a la salud de Vd.!; **that is neither — nor there** eso no viene al caso.

**hereafter** [hɪræftɚ] *adv.* de aquí (*o* de hoy) en adelante; desde ahora en adelante; en lo futuro; *s.* **the —** la otra vida.

**hereby** [hɪrbáɪ] *adv.* por este medio; mediante la presente, por la presente; con estas palabras.

**hereditary** [hərédətɛrɪ] *adj.* hereditario.

**heredity** [hérédətɪ] *s.* herencia.

**herein** [hɪrín] *adv.* aquí dentro; en esto.

**heresy** [hérəsɪ] *s.* herejía.

**heretic** [hérətɪk] *s.* hereje.

**heretofore** [hɪrtəfór] *adv.* hasta ahora, hasta el presente.

**herewith** [hɪrwíθ] *adv.* aquí dentro, con esto, adjunto, incluso.

**heritage** [hérətɪdʒ] *s.* herencia.

**hermetic** [hɜmétɪk] *adj.* hermético.

**hermit** [hɜmɪt] *s.* ermitaño.

**hernia** [hɜnɪə] *s.* hernia, ruptura, relajamiento.

**hero** [híro] *s.* héroe; protagonista.

**heroic** [hɪróɪk] *adj.* heroico.

**heroin** [héroɪn] *s.* heroína.

**heroine** [héroɪn] *s.* heroína.

**heroism** [héroɪzəm] *s.* heroísma.

**heron** [hérən] *s.* garza.

**herring** [hérɪŋ] *s.* arenque.

**hers** [hɜz] *pron. pos.* suyo (suya, suyos, suyas), de ella; el suyo (la suya, los suyos, las suyas); el (la, los, las) de ella; **a friend of —** un amigo suyo.

**herself** [hɜsélf] *pron.* ella misma; se (*como reflexivo*); **by —** sola; por sí (sola); **she — did it** ella misma lo hizo; **she talks to —** ella habla para sí, habla consigo misma, habla para sus adentros, habla sola.

**hesitant** [hézətənt] = **hesitating.**

**hesitate** [hézətet] *v.* vacilar; titubear; dudar.

**hesitating** [hésətetɪŋ] *adj.* vacilante; indeciso; irresoluto; **-ly** *adv.* con vacilación.

**hesitation** [hɛzətéʃən] *s.* vacilación; titubeo, duda.

**hew** [hju] *v.* tajar, cortar; picar (*piedra*); labrar (*madera, piedra*).

**hewn** [hjun] *p.p. de* **to hew.**

**hey** [he] *interj.* ¡he!; ¡oiga!; ¡oye!

**hibernate** [háɪbɚnet] *v.* invernar.

**hiccup, hiccough** [híkʌp] *s.* hipo; *v.* hipar, tener hipo.

**hickory** [híkəri] *s.* nogal americano; **— nut** nuez (*del nogal americano*).

**hid** [hɪd] *pret. & p.p. de* **to hide.**

**hidden** [hídn̩] *p.p. de* **to hide;** *adj.* oculto, escondido.

**hide** [haɪd] *v.* ocultar(se); esconder(se); **to — from** esconderse de, recatarse de; *s.* cuero, piel; **to play — and seek** jugar al escondite.

**hideous** [hídɪəs] *adj.* horrendo, horripilante, feote.

**hierarchy** [háɪərɑrki] *s.* jerarquía.

**hieroglyphic** [haɪəroglífɪk] *adj. & s.* jeroglífico.

**high** [haɪ] *adj.* alto; **— altar** altar mayor; **— and dry** enjuto; en seco; solo, abandonado; **— antiquity** antigüedad remota; **— explosive** explosivo de gran potencia; **— tide** pleamar; **— wind** ventarrón, viento fuerte; **in — gear** en directa, en tercera velocidad; **two feet —** dos pies de alto; **it is — time that** ya es hora de que; **to be in — spirits** estar muy animado; *adv.* alto; a precio subido; en alto; **to look — and low** buscar por todas partes; **high-grade** de calidad superior; **high-handed** arbitrario, despótico; **high-minded** magnánimo; orgulloso; **high-sounding** altisonante, rimbombante; **high-strung** muy tenso.

**highland** [háɪlənd] *s.* tierra montañosa; **the Highlands** las montañas de Escocia.

**highlight** [háɪlaɪt] *s.* lo más notable.

**highly** [háɪlɪ] *adv.* altamente; sumamente, muy; **— paid** muy bien pagado.

**highness** [háɪnɪs] *s.* altura; elevación; Alteza (*título*).

**highway** [háɪwe] *s.* camino real; carretera, calzada.

**highwayman** [háɪwemən] *s.* forajido, salteador de caminos, bandido.

**hike** [haɪk] *s.* caminata, paseo largo, *Am.* andada; *v.* dar (*o* echar) una caminata.

**hill** [hɪl] *s.* colina, collado, cerro; montoncillo de tierra; *Andes, Am.* loma; **ant —** hormiguero; **down—** cuesta abajo; **up—** cuesta arriba.

**hillock** [hílək] *s.* collado, otero, montecillo.

**hillside** [hílsaɪd] *s.* ladera.

**hilltop** [híltɑp] *s.* cumbre, cima (*de una colina*).

**hilly** [hílɪ] *adj.* montuoso; accidentado.

**hilt** [hɪlt] *s.* empuñadura, puño (*de una espada o daga*).

**him** [hɪm] *pron.* le; lo; él (*con preposición*).

**himself** [hɪmsélf] *pron.* él mismo; se (*como reflexivo*); a sí mismo; *véase* **herself**.

**hind** [haɪnd] *adj.* trasero; posterior; *s.* cierva; **—most** *adj.* último, postrero.

**hinder** [híndɚ] *v.* estorbar, impedir, obstruir.

**hindrance** [híndrəns] *s.* estorbo, obstáculo, impedimento.

**hinge** [hɪndʒ] *s.* gozne; bisagra; *v.* engoznar, poner goznes; **to — on** girar sobre; depender de.

**hint** [hɪnt] *s.* indirecta, insinuación; sugestión; **not to take the —** no darse por entendido; *v.* insinuar, intimar, sugerir indirectamente.

**hip** [hɪp] *s.* cadera.

**hippopotamus** [hɪpəpátəməs] *s.* hipopótamo.

**hire** [haɪr] *s.* (*rent*) alquiler; (*pay*) paga, sueldo; *v.* alquilar; emplear, dar empleo, *C.A., Ven., Col.* enganchar, *Am.* conchabar; **to — out** alquilarse, ponerse a servir a otro.

**his** [hɪz] *pron. pos.* suyo (suya, suyos, suyas), de él; el suyo (la suya, los suyos, las suyas); el (la, los, las) de él; **a friend of —** un amigo suyo; *adj.* su (sus), de él.

**hiss** [hɪs] *s.* silbido, chiflido; siseo; *v.* sisear, silbar, chiflar.

**historian** [hɪstórɪən] *s.* historiador.

**historic** [hɪstórɪk] *adj.* histórico.

**historical** [hɪstórɪk]] *adj.* histórico.

**history** [hístrɪ] *s.* historia.

**histrionics** [hɪstrɪánɪks] *s.* histrionismo.

**hit** [hɪt] *v.* pegar, golpear; dar (*un golpe*); dar en (*o* con); chocar; **they — it off well** se llevan bien, congenian; **to — the mark** acertar, atinar, dar en el blanco; **to — upon** dar con; encontrarse con, encontrar por casualidad; *pret. & p.p. de* **to hit**; *s.* golpe; choque; golpe de fortuna; pulla, dicharacho;

**to be a great —** ser un gran éxito; **to make a — with someone** caerle en gracia a una persona; **hit-and-run** *adj.* que abandona a su víctima atropellada.

**hitch** [hɪtʃ] *v.* atar, amarrar; enganchar; uncir (*bueyes*); dar un tirón; **to — one's chair nearer to** acercar su silla a; *s.* tirón; obstáculo, impedimento, tropiezo; enganche, enganchamiento.

**hitchhike** [hítʃhaɪk] *v.* viajar de gorra (*en automóvil*), *Méx.* irse o viajar de mosca; *Ch., Ríopl.* hacer dedo, ir a dedo.

**hither** [híðɚ] *adv.* acá; **— and thither** acá y allá.

**hitherto** [híðɚtú] *adv.* hasta aquí, hasta ahora, hasta hoy.

**hive** [haɪv] *s.* colmena; enjambre; **-s** ronchas (*de la piel*).

**hoard** [hord] *s.* tesoro escondido; acumulamiento secreto de provisiones; *v.* atesorar, guardar (*con avaricia*); acumular secretamente.

**hoarse** [hors] *adj.* bronco, áspero, ronco.

**hoarseness** [hórsnɪs] *s.* ronquera; carraspera.

**hoary** [hórɪ] *adj.* cano, encanecido, canoso.

**hobble** [hábl] *v.* (*limp*) cojear, renquear; (*tie*) maniatar o manear (*un animal*); (*impede*) impedir, estorbar; *s.* cojera; traba, maniota o manea (*cuerda con que se atan las manos de una bestia*).

**hobby** [hábɪ] *s.* afición; trabajo hecho por afición (*no por obligación*).

**hobo** [hóbo] *s.* vagabundo.

**hodgepodge** [hádʒpadʒ] *s.* mezcolanza, baturrillo.

**hoe** [ho] *s.* azada, azadón; *v.* cavar, escardar, limpiar con azadón.

**hog** [hɑg] *s.* puerco, cerdo, cochino; *v.* apropiárselo todo.

**hoist** [hɔɪst] *v.* alzar, levantar; izar (*la bandera, las velas*); *s.* elevador, *Am.* malacate.

**hold** [hold] *v.* tener(se); retener; detener; tener cabida para; sostener; mantener(se); opinar; celebrar (*una reunión, etc.*); ocupar (*un puesto*); ser válido (*un argumento o regla*); **to — back someone** detener (*o* refrenar) a alguien; **to — forth** perorar, hablar largamente; **to — in place** sujetar, **to — off** mantener(se) a distancia; mantenerse alejado; **to — on** agarrar(se); asir(se); persistir; **— on!** ¡agárrese bien!; ¡deténgase! ¡pare!; **to — someone responsible** hacerle a uno responsable; **to — someone to his word** obligar a uno a cumplir su palabra; **to — oneself erect** tenerse o andar derecho; **to — one's own** mantenerse firme; **to — one's tongue** callarse; **to — out** continuar, durar; mantenerse firme; **to — over** aplazar; durar; continuar en un cargo; **to — still** estarse quieto o callado; **to — tight** apretar; **to — to one's promise**

cumplir con la promesa; **to — up** levantar, alzar; detener; asaltar, atracar (*para robar*); **how much does it —?** ¿cuánto le cabe? *s.* agarro; dominio; influencia; autoridad; bodega (*de un barco*); cabina de carga (*de un aeroplano*); **to get — of** asir, agarrar; atrapar; **to take — of** coger, agarrar, asir.

**holder** [hóldɚ] *s.* (*person*) tenedor, posesor; (*device*) receptáculo; cojinillo (*para coger un trasto caliente*); **cigarette —** boquilla; **pen—** portaplumas.

**holdup** [hóldʌp] *s.* asalto, atraco.

**hole** [hol] *s.* agujero; abertura; hoyo, hueco, cavidad; bache (*de un camino*); **swimming —** charco, remanso; **to be in a —** hallarse en un apuro o aprieto.

**holiday** [hálǝde] *s.* día de fiesta, día festivo, festividad; **-s** días de fiesta; vacaciones.

**holiness** [hólɪnɪs] *s.* santidad.

**hollow** [hálo] *adj.* (*empty*) hueco; vacío; (*concave*) cóncavo; hundido; (*insincere*) falso; *s.* hueco, hoyo; cavidad; concavidad; depresión; cañada, hondonada; *v.* ahuecar; excavar; ahondar.

**holly** [hálɪ] *s.* agrifolio, acebo.

**holster** [hólstɚ] *s.* pistolera, funda (*de pistola*).

**holy** [hólɪ] *adj.* santo; sagrado, sacro; **— water** agua bendita.

**homage** [hámɪdʒ] *s.* homenaje; reverencia, acatamiento; **to do —** acatar, rendir homenaje, honrar.

**home** [hom] *s.* casa, hogar; habitación, domicilio; **at —** en casa; *adj.* doméstico; casero; **— office** oficina matriz o central; **— rule** autonomía; **— run** *Méx., C.A., Ven., Col.* jonrón (*en beisbol*); **— stretch** último trecho (*de una carrera*); *adv.* a casa; en casa; **to strike —** herir en lo vivo; dar en el clavo o en el blanco.

**homeland** [hómlænd] *s.* tierra natal, suelo patrio.

**homeless** [hómlɪs] *adj.* sin casa; destituido.

**homelike** [hómlaɪk] *adj.* hogareño, cómodo.

**homely** [hómlɪ] *adj.* feo; llano; sencillo; casero, doméstico.

**homemade** [hómmédɩ] *adj.* hecho en casa; doméstico, nacional, del país.

**homesick** [hómsɪk] *adj.* nostálgico.

**homesickness** [hómsɪknɪs] *s.* nostalgia.

**homestead** [hómstɛd] *s.* heredad; casa y terrenos adyacentes.

**homeward** [hómwɚd] *adv.* a casa; hacia la patria; **— voyage** retorno, viaje de vuelta.

**homework** [hómwɝk] *s.* trabajo de casa; trabajo hecho en casa.

**homicide** [hámǝsaɪd] *s.* homicidio; homicida, asesino.

**homogeneous** [homǝdʒínɪǝs] *adj.* homogéneo.

**homogenize** [homádʒǝnaɪz] *v.* homogenizar.

**homosexual** [homǝsékʃjʊl] *adj. & s.* homosexual.

**hone** [hon] *v.* amolar, asentar, afilar; *s.* piedra de afilar.

**honest** [ánɪst] *adj.* honrado, recto; genuino; **— goods** mercancías genuinas; **-ly** *adv.* honradamente; de veras.

**honesty** [ánɪstɪ] *s.* honradez, rectitud.

**honey** [hánɪ] *s.* miel; dulzura; querido, querida.

**honeycomb** [hánɪkom] *s.* panal.

**honeyed** [hánɪd] *adj.* meloso; dulce; melífluo.

**honeymoon** [hánɪmun] *s.* luna de miel; viaje de novios, viaje de bodas; *v.* pasar la luna de miel.

**honeysuckle** [hánɪsʌkl] *s.* madreselva.

**honk** [hɔŋk] *s.* pitazo (*de automóvil*); graznido (*voz del ganso*); *v.* donar la bocina; graznar.

**honor** [ánɚ] *s.* honor; honra; señoría (*título*); **upon my —** sobre mi palabra; *v.* honrar; dar honra.

**honorable** [ánɚǝbl] *adj.* honorable; honroso; honrado.

**honorary** [ánɚɛrɪ] *adj.* honorario, honorífico.

**hood** [hʊd] *s.* capucha, caperuza; capirote, cubierta (*del motor*); *v.* encapuchar, encapirotar.

**hoodlum** [húdlǝm] *s.* maleante; antisocial.

**hoof** [hʊf] *s.* casco, pezuña; pata (*de caballo, toro, etc.*).

**hook** [hʊk] *s.* gancho, garfio; anzuelo (*para pescar*); **— and eye** corchete; macho y hembra, **by — or crook** por la buena o por la mala, por angas o por mangas; **on his own —** por su propia cuenta; *v.* enganchar(se); abrochar(se); pescar, coger con anzuelo; robar, hurtar.

**hooky** [húkɪ]: **to play —** hacer novillos, *Carib.* capear la escuela, *Méx.* pintar venado, *C.A., Ven., Col.* jubilarse; *Ríopl.* hacerse la rata (*la rabona*).

**hoop** [hup] *s.* aro; argolla; *v.* poner aro a; ceñir, cercar.

**hoot** [hut] *v.* ulular (*dícese del buho, lechuza, etc.*); rechiflar, ridiculizar; *s.* alarido, chillido.

**hooting** [hútɪŋ] *s.* grita, rechifla.

**hop** [hɑp] *s.* salto, brinco; baile; *v.* saltar; brincar.

**hope** [hop] *s.* esperanza; *v.* esperar; **to — for** esperar; **to — against —** esperar desesperando; esperar lo que no puede ser, esperar lo imposible.

**hopeful** [hópfǝl] *adj.* esperanzado, lleno de esperanza; **a young —** un joven prometedor; **-ly** *adv.* con esperanza; con ansia; lleno de esperanza.

**hopeless** [hóplɪs] *adj.* sin esperanza; falto de esperanza, desesperanzado; desesperado; irremediable; **— cause** causa perdida; **— illness** enfermedad incurable; **it is —** no tiene remedio; **-ly** *adv.* sin esperanza, sin remedio.

**hopelessness** [hóplɪsnɪs] *s.* falta de es-

HI

peranza; falta de remedio; desesperanza, desaliento.

**horde** [hord] *s.* horda; muchedumbre, gentío; enjambre.

**horizon** [hɔráɪzn̩] *s.* horizonte.

**horizontal** [hɔrəzántl̩] *adj.* horizontal.

**horn** [hɔrn] *s.* (*animal*) cuerno; asta; (*automobile*) bocina, klaxon, trompa; (*musical*) corneta; trompeta; **— of plenty** cuerno de la abundancia; *v.* acornear, dar cornadas; **to — in** entremeterse.

**hornet** [hɔ́rnɪt] *s.* avispón; **-'s nest** avispero.

**horoscope** [hɔ́rəskop] *s.* horóscopo.

**horrible** [hɔ́rəbl̩] *adj.* horrible; **horribly** *adv.* horriblemente.

**horrid** [hɔ́rɪd] *adj.* horrendo, horrible.

**horrify** [hɔ́rəfaɪ] *v.* horrorizar, aterrorizar, espantar.

**horror** [hɔ́rɚ] *s.* horror.

**hors d'oeuvre** [ɔrdɑ́vrə] *s.* entremés; bocadillos.

**horse** [hɔrs] *s.* caballo; caballete (*de madera*), borriquete (*de carpinteros*); **saddle —** caballo de silla; **— dealer** chalán; **— race** carrera de caballos; **— sense** sentido común.

**horseback** [hɔ́rsbæk] *s.* lomo de caballo; **to ride —** montar a caballo, cabalgar, jinetear.

**horsefly** [hɔ́rsflaɪ] *s.* tábano, mosca de caballo.

**horselaugh** [hɔ́rslæf] *s.* carcajada, risotada.

**horseman** [hɔ́rsmən] *s.* jinete.

**horsemanship** [hɔ́rsmənʃɪp] *s.* equitación.

**horsepower** [hɔ́rspauɚ] *s.* caballo de fuerza.

**horseradish** [hɔ́rsrædɪʃ] *s.* rábano picante.

**horseshoe** [hɔ́rsʃu] *s.* herradura.

**hose** [hoz] *s.* medias; manga o manguera (*para regar*); **men's —** calcetines.

**hosiery** [hóʒrɪ] *s.* medias; calcetines; calcetería (*negocio*); **— shop** calcetería.

**hospitable** [háspɪtəbl̩] *adj.* hospitalario.

**hospital** [háspɪtl̩] *s.* hospital.

**hospitality** [háspɪtǽlətɪ] *s.* hospitalidad.

**host** [host] *s.* huésped (*el que hospeda*), anfitrión (*el que convida*); hospedero, mesonero; hueste; ejército, multitud; hostia; **sacred —** hostia consagrada.

**hostage** [hástɪdʒ] *s.* rehén (*persona que queda como prenda en poder del enemigo*).

**hostess** [hóstɪs] *s.* huéspeda (*la que hospeda o convida*).

**hostile** [hást] *adj.* hostil.

**hostility** [hastílətɪ] *s.* hostilidad.

**hot** [hat] *adj.* caliente; caluroso; cálido; picante (*como el pimentón, chile, ají, etc.*); furioso; fresco, reciente; **—bed** semillero; **hot-headed** enojadizo, impetuoso; exaltado; **— house** invernáculo, invernadero; **it is — today** hace calor hoy.

**hotel** [hotél] *s.* hotel.

**hotel-keeper** [hotélkipɚ] *s.* hotelero.

**hotly** [hátlɪ] *adv.* calurosamente, con vehemencia.

**hound** [haʊnd] *s.* perro de busca, lebrel, galgo, sabueso, podenco; *v.* acosar, perseguir; azuzar, incitar.

**hour** [aʊr] *s.* hora; **— hand** horario.

**hourly** [áʊrlɪ] *adv.* por horas; a cada hora; a menudo; *adj.* frecuente; por horas.

**house** [haʊs] *s.* (*residence*) casa; domicilio; (*legislature*) cámara, asamblea legislativa; **country —** casa de campo; **a full —** un lleno completo (*en el teatro*); [haʊz] *v.* alojar; hospedar.

**household** [háʊshold] *s.* casa, familia; *adj.* casero; doméstico.

**housekeeper** [háʊskipɚ] *s.* casera; ama de llaves; **to be a good —** ser una mujer hacendosa.

**housekeeping** [háʊskipɪŋ] *s.* gobierno de casa; quehaceres domésticos.

**housetop** [háʊstap] *s.* techumbre, tejado.

**housewife** [háʊswaɪf] *s.* mujer de su casa; madre de familia.

**housework** [háʊswɜk] *s.* trabajo de casa; quehaceres domésticos.

**housing** [háʊzɪŋ] *s.* viviendas; programa de construcción de viviendas.

**hove** [hov] *pret. & p.p. de* **to heave**.

**hovel** [hávl̩] *s.* choza, cabaña, *Carib.*, *Ven.* bohío, *Méx.* jacal; cobertizo; *Ríopl.* tapera.

**hover** [hávɚ] *v.* cernerse (*como un pájaro*); vacilar; **to — around** revolotear; rondar.

**how** [haʊ] *adv.* cómo; **— beautiful!** ¡qué hermoso!; **— early (late, soon)** ¿cuándo? ¿a qué hora?; **— far is it?** ¿a qué distancia está? ¿cuánto dista de aquí?; **— long?** ¿cuánto tiempo?; **— many?** ¿cuántos? **— much is it?** ¿cuánto es? ¿a cómo se vende? ¿cuál es el precio?; **— old are you?** ¿cuántos años tiene Vd.? **no matter — much** por mucho que; **he knows — difficult it is** él sabe lo difícil que es; él sabe cuán difícil es.

**however** [haʊévɚ] *adv. & conj.* sin embargo, no obstante, con todo, empero; **— difficult it may be** por muy difícil que sea; **— much** por mucho que.

**howl** [haʊl] *s.* aullido, alarido, chillido, grito; *v.* aullar; chillar, dar alaridos; gritar.

**hub** [hʌb] *s.* cubo (*de una rueda*); eje, centro de actividad.

**hubbub** [hʌ́bʌb] *s.* ajetreo; barullo.

**huckster** [hʌ́kstɚ] *s.* vendedor ambulante.

**huddle** [hʌ́dl̩] *s.* montón, confusión, tropel; **to be in a —** estar agrupados (*en futbol para planear una jugada*); **to get in a —** agruparse (*para aconsejarse o planear algo*); *v.* amontonar(se); acurrucarse.

**hue** [hju] *s.* tinte, matiz.

**huff** [hʌf] *s.* enojo, rabieta; **to get into a —** enojarse.

**hug** [hʌg] *v.* abrazar, estrechar; **to —**

**the coast** costear; *s.* abrazo fuerte.
**huge** [hjudʒ] *adj.* enorme; descomunal.
**hull** [hʌl] *s.* casco (*de una nave*); armazón (*de una aeronave*); vaina, hollejo (*de ciertas legumbres*); *v.* mondar, pelar desvainar, deshollejar.
**hum** [hʌm] *v.* canturrear (*o* canturriar), tararear; zumbar (*dícese de insectos, máquinaria, etc.*); **to — to sleep** arrullar; *s.* canturreo, tarareo; zumbido; *interj.* ¡hum!; ¡ejém!
**human** [hjúmən] *adj.* humano; *s.* ser humano.
**humane** [hjumén] *adj.* humano; humanitario.
**humanism** [hjúmənɪzm] *s.* humanismo.
**humanitarian** [hjumænətériən] *adj.* humanitario; *s.* filántropo.
**humanity** [hjumǽnətɪ] *s.* humanidad; **-ies** humanidades.
**humble** [hámbl] *adj.* humilde; *v.* humillar; **humbly** *adv.* humildemente, con humildad.
**humbleness** [hámblnɪs] *s.* humildad.
**humid** [hjúmɪd] *adj.* húmedo.
**humidify** [hjumídəfaɪ] *v.* humedecer.
**humidity** [hjumídətɪ] *d.* humedad.
**humiliate** [hjumílɪet] *v.* humillar.
**humiliation** [hjumɪlɪéʃən] *s.* humillación.
**humility** [hjumílətɪ] *s.* humildad.
**hummingbird** [hámɪŋbɝd] *s.* colibrí, pájaro mosca, *Méx.* chuparrosa, *Am.'* chupaflor, *Am.* guainumbí; *Ríopl., Ch.* picaflor.
**humor** [hjúmɚ] *s.* humor, humorismo, gracia; capricho; **out of —** de mal humor, malhumorado, disgustado; *v.* seguir el humor (*a una persona*), complacer; mimar.
**humorous** [hjúmərəs] *adj.* humorístico, gracioso, cómico, chistoso.
**hump** [hʌmp] *s.* joroba, corcova, giba; *v.* encorvarse.
**humpback** [hámpbæk] = **hunchback**.
**hunch** [hʌntʃ] *s.* joroba, corcova, giba; presentimiento, corazonada; *v.* encorvar (*la espalda*).
**hunchback** [hántʃbæk] *s.* joroba; jorobado.
**hundred** [hándrəd] *adj.* cien(to); *s.* ciento; **-s** centenares, cientos.
**hundredth** [hándrədθ] *adj.* centésimo.
**hung** [hʌŋ] *pret.* & *p.p. de* **to hang.**
**hunger** [háŋgɚ] *s.* hambre; *v.* tener hambre, estar hambriento; **to — for** ansiar, anhelar.
**hungrily** [háŋgrɪlɪ] *adv.* con hambre, hambrientamente.
**hungry** [háŋgrɪ] *adj.* hambriento; **to be — tener hambre.**
**hunk** [hʌŋk] *s.* pedazo grande; mendrugo (*de pan*).
**hunt** [hʌnt] *v.* cazar; perseguir; buscar; escudriñar; **to — down** dar caza a; seguir la pista de; **to — for** buscar; *s.* caza, cacería; busca, búsqueda; perseguimiento.
**hunter** [hántɚ] *s.* cazador; buscador; perro de caza, perro de busca.

**huntsman** [hántsmən] *s.* cazador.
**hurl** [hɝl] *v.* arrojar, lanzar.
**hurrah** [hərɔ́] *interj.* ¡hurra! ¡viva!; *v.* vitorear.
**hurricane** [hɝɪken] *s.* huracán.
**hurried** [hɝɪd] *adj.* apresurado; **-ly** *adv.* de prisa, apresuradamente, a escape.
**hurry** [hɝɪ] *v.* apresurar(se); precipitar(se); dar(se) prisa; apurarse; correr; **to — in (out)** entrar (salir) de prisa; **to — up** apresurar(se); dar(se) prisa; *s.* prisa; precipitación; **to be in a —** tener prisa, ir de prisa, estar de prisa.
**hurt** [hɝt] *v.* hacer daño; dañar; perjudicar; herir; lastimar; doler; **to — one's feelings** darle a uno que sentir; lastimar a uno; **my tooth -s** me duele la muela; *pret.* & *p.p. de* **to hurt;** *s.* daño; herida; lesión; dolor.
**husband** [házbənd] *s.* marido, esposo.
**hush** [hʌʃ] *v.* acallar, aquietar; callar(se); **—!** ¡chitón! ¡silencio! ¡cállese! ¡quieto!; **to — up a scandal** encubrir un escándalo; *s.* silencio, quietud.
**husk** [hʌsk] *s.* cáscara, hollejo, vaina; *v.* mondar, pelar, deshollejar.
**husky** [háskɪ] *adj.* ronco; forzudo, fuerte; cascarudo.
**hustle** [hásl] *v.* apresurar(se); apurarse; menear(se); atropellar; *s.* prisa, apresuramiento, meneo; actividad; **— and bustle** vaivén.
**hut** [hʌt] *s.* choza, cabaña, *Am.* bohío.
**hyacinth** [háɪəsɪnθ] *s.* jacinto.
**hybrid** [háɪbrɪd] *adj.* híbrido.
**hydraulic** [haɪdrɔ́lɪk] *adj.* hidráulico.
**hydroelectric** [haɪdroiléktrɪk] *adj.* hidroeléctrico.
**hydrogen** [háɪdrədʒen] *s.* hidrógeno.
**hydrophobia** [haɪdrofóbɪə] *s.* hidrofobia.
**hydroplane** [háɪdrəplen] *s.* hidroplano, hidroavión.
**hygiene** [háɪdʒin] *s.* higiene.
**hymn** [hɪm] *s.* himno.
**hyphen** [háɪfən] *s.* guión.
**hypnosis** [hɪpnósɪs] *s.* hipnosis.
**hypocrisy** [hɪpákrəsɪ] *s.* hipocresía.
**hypocrite** [hípəkrɪt] *s.* hipócrita.
**hypocritical** [hɪpəkrítɪkl] *adj.* hipócrita.
**hypothesis** [haɪpáθəsɪs] *s.* hipótesis.
**hysterical** [hɪstérɪkl] *adj.* histérico.

**I**

**I** [aɪ] *pron. pers.* yo.
**Iberian** [aɪbíriən] *adj.* ibérico, ibero.
**ice** [aɪs] *s.* (*solid*) hielo; (*food*) helado; sorbete; **— cream** helado; **icecream parlor** *Am.* heladería; **— skates** patines de cuchilla; **— water** agua helada; *v.* helar; escarchar, alfeñicar, cubrir con escarcha (*un pastel*).
**iceberg** [áɪsbɝg] *s.* montaña de hielo, témpano.
**icebox** [áɪsbaks] *s.* nevera, *Am.* refrigerador.
**iceman** [áɪsmæn] *s.* vendedor de hielo.
**icicle** [áɪsɪkl] *s.* carámbano.

**HO**

**iconoclasm** [aɪkánəklæzəm] *s.* iconoclasmo.

**icy** [áɪsɪ] *adj.* helado, frío; congelado; cubierto de hielo.

**idea** [aɪdíə] *s.* idea.

**ideal** [aɪdíəl] *adj.* & *s.* ideal.

**idealism** [aɪdíəlɪzəm] *s.* idealismo.

**idealist** [aɪdíəlɪst] *s.* idealista.

**idealistic** [aɪdɪəlístɪk] *adj.* idealista.

**identical** [aɪdéntɪkl̩] *adj.* idéntico.

**identify** [aɪdéntəfaɪ] *v.* identificar.

**identity** [aɪdéntətɪ] *s.* identidad.

**ideology** [aɪdɪólədʒɪ] *s.* ideología.

**idiom** [ídɪəm] *s.* modismo, idiotismo.

**idiosyncrasy** [ɪdɪosínkrəsi] *s.* idiosincrasia.

**idiot** [ídɪət] *s.* idiota.

**idiotic** [ɪdɪátɪk] *adj.* idiota.

**idle** [áɪdl̩] *adj.* ocioso; perezoso, holgazán; vano; desocupado; *v.* holgazanear; perder el tiempo; funcionar (*el motor solo, sin engranar*); **idly** *adv.* ociosamente; inútilmente; perezosamente.

**idleness** [áɪdlnɪs] *s.* ociosidad; ocio, desocupación; pereza, holgazanería.

**idler** [áɪdlɚ] *s.* holgazán, haragán.

**idol** [áɪdl̩] *s.* ídolo.

**idolatry** [aɪdálətrɪ] *s.* idolatría.

**idolize** [áɪdlaɪz] *v.* idolatrar,

**idyl** [áɪdl̩] *s.* idilio.

**if** [ɪf] *conj.* si.

**ignite** [ɪgnáɪt] *v.* encender(se), inflamar(se); prender, pegar fuego a.

**ignition** [ɪgníʃən] *s.* ignición, encendido (*de un motor*); **— switch** interruptor de encendido, *Méx.*, *C.A.*, *Ven.*, *Carib.* switch de ignición.

**ignoble** [ɪgnóbl̩] *adj.* innoble; bajo, vil.

**ignorance** [ígnərəns] *s.* ignorancia.

**ignorant** [ígnərənt] *adj.* ignorante.

**ignore** [ɪgnór] *v.* no hacer caso de, desatender; desairar.

**ill** [ɪl] *adj.* enfermo; malo; **— nature** mal genio, mala índole; **— will** mala voluntad, ojeriza, inquina; *s.* mal; enfermedad; calamidad, infortunio; *adv.* mal, malamente; **— at ease** inquieto, intranquilo; **ill-bred** mal criado; **ill-clad** mal vestido; **ill-humored** malhumorado; **ill-mannered** descortés, grosero; **ill-natured** de mala índole, *Ven.*, *Col.*, *Méx.* mal genioso; **ill-advised** mal aconsejado.

**illegal** [ɪlígl̩] *adj.* ilegal; ilícito.

**illegitimate** [ɪlɪdʒítəmɪt] *adj.* ilegítimo; bastardo.

**illicit** [ɪlísɪt] *adj.* ilícito.

**illiteracy** [ɪlítərəsɪ] *s.* analfabetismo.

**illiterate** [ɪlítərɪt] *adj.* & *s.* analfabeto.

**illness** [ílnɪs] *s.* mal, enfermedad.

**illuminate** [ɪlúmənet] *v.* iluminar; alumbrar; esclarecer.

**illumination** [ɪlumənéʃən] *s.* iluminación; alumbrado.

**illusion** [ɪlúʒən] *s.* ilusión.

**illusive** [ɪlúsɪv] *adj.* ilusorio, ilusivo, falaz.

**illusory** [ɪlúsərɪ] *adj.* ilusorio, ilusivo, engañoso.

**illustrate** [ɪləstrét] *v.* ilustrar; esclare-

cer.

**illustration** [ɪləstréʃən] *s.* ilustración; grabado, estampa; aclaración, esclarecimiento.

**illustrator** [íləstretɚ] *s.* ilustrador.

**illustrious** [ɪlʌstrɪəs] *adj.* ilustre.

**image** [ímɪdʒ] *s.* imagen.

**imagery** [ímɪdʒrɪ] *s.* conjunto de imágenes, figuras; fantasía.

**imaginary** [ɪmædʒənɛrɪ] *adj.* imaginario.

**imagination** [ɪmædʒənéʃən] *s.* imaginación; imaginativa.

**imaginative** [ɪmædʒənetɪv] *adj.* imaginativo.

**imagine** [ɪmædʒɪn] *v.* imaginar(se); figurarse.

**imbecile** [ímbəsɪl] *adj.* & *s.* imbécil.

**imbibe** [ɪmbáɪb] *v.* embeber, absorber; beber.

**imbue** [ɪmbjú] *v.* imbuir, infundir; impregnar, empapar.

**imitate** [ímətet] *v.* imitar; remedar.

**imitation** [ɪmətéʃən] *s.* imitación; remedo; *adj.* imitado, de imitación.

**imitator** [ímətetɚ] *s.* imitador; remedador.

**immaculate** [ɪmækjəlɪt] *adj.* inmaculado, sin mancha.

**immaterial** [ɪmətírɪəl] *adj.* inmaterial, espiritual; **it is — to me** me es indiferente.

**immediate** [ɪmídɪɪt] *adj.* inmediato; próximo; **-ly** *adv.* inmediatamente; en seguida; al punto, en el acto, al instante.

**immense** [ɪméns] *adj.* inmenso.

**immensity** [ɪménsətɪ] *s.* inmensidad.

**immerse** [ɪmɚ́s] *v.* sumergir, sumir.

**immigrant** [íməgrənt] *adj.* & *s.* inmigrante.

**immigrate** [íməgret] *v.* inmigrar.

**immigration** [ɪməgréʃən] *s.* inmigración.

**imminent** [ímənənt] *adj.* inminente.

**immobile** [ɪmóbɪl] *adj.* inmóbil.

**immodest** [ɪmádɪst] *adj.* deshonesto, impúdico, indecente.

**immoral** [ɪmórəl] *adj.* inmoral; licencioso.

**immorality** [ɪmərǽlətɪ] *s.* inmoralidad.

**immortal** [ɪmórtl̩] *adj.* & *s.* inmortal.

**immortality** [ɪmortǽlətɪ] *s.* inmortalidad.

**immovable** [ɪmúvəbl̩] *adj.* inmovible (o inamovible); inmóvil; inmutable.

**immune** [ɪmjún] *adj.* inmune.

**immunity** [ɪmjúnətɪ] *s.* inmunidad.

**immutable** [ɪmjútəbl̩] *adj.* inmutable.

**imp** [ɪmp] *s.* diablillo.

**impair** [ɪmpér] *v.* dañar, perjudicar, menoscabar, desvirtuar, debilitar.

**impairment** [ɪmpérmənt] *s.* menoscabo; perjuicio; deterioro.

**impart** [ɪmpárt] *v.* impartir, dar, comunicar.

**impartial** [ɪmpárʃəl] *adj.* imparcial.

**impartiality** [ɪmpɑrʃǽlətɪ] *s.* imparcialidad.

**impassible** [ɪmpǽsəbl̩] *adj.* impasible.

**impassioned** [ɪmpǽʃənd] *adj.* apasionado, vehemente, ardiente.

**impassive** [ɪmpǽsɪv] *adj.* impasible.

**impatience** [ɪmpéʃəns] *s.* impaciencia.

**impatient** [ɪmpéʃənt] *adj.* impaciente.

**impeach** [ɪmpítʃ] *v.* demandar o acusar formalmente (*a un alto funcionario de gobierno*); **to — a person's honor** poner en tela de juicio el honor de uno.

**impede** [ɪmpíd] *v.* impedir, estorbar, obstruir.

**impediment** [ɪmpédəmənt] *s.* impedimento, obstáculo, estorbo; traba.

**impel** [ɪmpél] *v.* impeler, impulsar.

**impending** [ɪmpéndɪŋ] *adj.* inminente, amenazador.

**imperative** [ɪmpérətɪv] *adj.* imperativo; imperioso, urgente; *s.* imperativo.

**imperceptible** [ɪmpɚséptəbl] *adj.* imperceptible.

**imperfect** [ɪmpɚ́fɪkt] *adj.* imperfecto; defectuoso; *s.* imperfecto (*tiempo del verbo*).

**imperial** [ɪmpírɪəl] *adj.* imperial.

**imperialism** [ɪmpírɪəlɪzm] *s.* imperialismo.

**imperil** [ɪmpérəl] *v.* poner en peligro, arriesgar.

**imperious** [ɪmpírɪəs] *adj.* imperioso; urgente.

**impersonal** [ɪmpɚ́sn̩l] *adj.* impersonal.

**impersonate** [ɪmpɚ́snet] *v.* representar (*un personaje*); remedar, imitar; fingirse otro, pretender ser otro.

**impertinence** [ɪmpɚ́tn̩əns] *s.* impertinencia; insolencia, descaro.

**impertinent** [ɪmpɚ́tn̩ənt] *adj.* impertinente; insolente, descarado.

**impervious** [ɪmpɚ́vɪəs] *adj.* impermeable; impenetrable; **— to reason** refractario, testarudo.

**impetuous** [ɪmpétʃʊəs] *adj.* impetuoso.

**impetus** [ímpətəs] *s.* ímpetu.

**impious** [ímpɪəs] *adj.* impío.

**implacable** [ɪmplékəbl] *adj.* implacable.

**implant** [ɪmplǽnt] *v.* implantar, plantar; inculcar, infundir.

**implement** [ímpləmənt] *s.* herramienta, instrumento; **-s** utensilios, aperos, enseres.

**implicate** [ímplɪket] *v.* implicar, envolver, enredar.

**implicit** [ɪmplísɪt] *adj.* implícito.

**implore** [ɪmplór] *v.* implorar, rogar; suplicar.

**imply** [ɪmplái] *v.* implicar; querer decir; insinuar.

**impolite** [ɪmpəláɪt] *adj.* descortés.

**import** [ímport] *s.* significado, significación, sentido; importancia; importación; **-s** artículos importados; [ɪmpórt] *v.* importar; significar, querer decir.

**importance** [ɪmpórtn̩s] *s.* importancia.

**important** [ɪmpórtn̩t] *adj.* importante.

**impose** [ɪmpóz] *v.* imponer; **to — upon** abusar de (*la amistad, hospitalidad, confianza de alguien*); engañar.

**imposing** [ɪmpózɪŋ] *adj.* imponente; impresionante.

**imposition** [ɪmpəzíʃən] *s.* imposición; carga, impuesto; abuso (*de confianza*).

**impossibility** [ɪmpɑsəbílətɪ] *s.* imposibilidad.

**impossible** [ɪmpásəbl] *adj.* imposible.

**impostor** [ɪmpástɚ] *s.* impostor, embaucador.

**imposture** [ɪmpástʃɚ] *s.* impostura, fraude, engaño.

**impotence** [ímpətəns] *s.* impotencia.

**impotent** [ímpətənt] *adj.* impotente.

**impoverish** [ɪmpávərɪʃ] *v.* empobrecer.

**impregnate** [ɪmprégnet] *v.* impregnar; empapar; empreñar.

**impress** [ímprɛs] *s.* impresión, marca, señal, huella; [ɪmprés] *v.* imprimir, estampar, marcar, grabar; impresionar.

**impression** [ɪmpréʃən] *s.* impresión, marca.

**impressive** [ɪmprésɪv] *adj.* impresionante; imponente.

**imprint** [ímprɪnt] *s.* impresión; pie de imprenta; [ɪmprínt] *v.* imprimir; estampar.

**imprison** [ɪmprísn̩] *v.* aprisionar, encarcelar.

**imprisonment** [ɪmprízn̩mənt] *s.* prisión, encarcelación o encarcelamiento.

**improbable** [ɪmprábəbl] *adj.* improbable.

**impromptu** [ɪmprámptu] *adv.* de improviso.

**improper** [ɪmprápɚ] *adj.* impropio.

**improve** [ɪmprúv] *v.* mejorar(se); **to — upon** mejorar; **to — one's time** aprovechar el tiempo.

**improvement** [ɪmprúvmənt] *s.* mejoramiento; mejora; progreso, adelanto; mejoría (*de una enfermedad*).

**improvise** [ímprəvaɪz] *v.* improvisar.

**imprudent** [ɪmprúdn̩t] *adj.* imprudente.

**impudence** [ímpjədəns] *s.* impudencia, descaro, insolencia.

**impudent** [ímpjədənt] *adj.* impudente, descarado, insolente.

**impulse** [ímpʌls] *s.* impulso; ímpetu; inclinación; **to act on —** obrar impulsivamente.

**impulsive** [ɪmpʌ́lsɪv] *adj.* impulsivo.

**impunity** [ɪmpjúnətɪ] *s.* impunidad, falta o exención de castigo.

**impure** [ɪmpjúr] *adj.* impuro; sucio; adulterado.

**impurity** [ɪmpjúrətɪ] *s.* impureza.

**impute** [ɪmpjút] *v.* imputar, achacar, atribuir.

**in** [ɪn] *prep.* en; dentro de; de (*después de un superlativo*); **— haste** de prisa; **— the morning** por (*o* en) la mañana; **— writing** por escrito; **at two — the morning** a las dos de la mañana; **dressed — white** vestido de blanco; **the tallest — his class** el más alto de su clase; **to come — a week** venir de hoy en ocho días, venir dentro de ocho días; *adv.* dentro; adentro; en casa; **to be — and out** estar entrando y saliendo; **to be all —** no poder más, estar rendido de can-

IC

sancio; **to be — with someone** estar asociado con alguien; disfrutar el aprecio de una persona; **to come —** entrar; **to have it — for someone** tenerle ojeriza a una persona; **to put — meter; is the train —?** ¿ha llegado el tren?

**inability** [ɪnəbílətɪ] *s.* inhabilidad, incapacidad.

**inaccessible** [ɪnəksésəbļ] *adj.* inaccesible; inasequible.

**inaccurate** [ɪnǽkjərɪt] *adj.* inexacto, impreciso, incorrecto.

**inactive** [ɪnǽktɪv] *adj.* inactivo; inerte.

**inactivity** [ɪnæktívətɪ] *s.* inactividad, inacción, inercia.

**inadequate** [ɪnǽdəkwɪt] *adj.* inadecuado; insuficiente.

**inadvertent** [ɪnədvə́tn̩t] *adj.* inadvertido; descuidado; **-ly** *adv.* inadvertidamente; descuidadamente.

**inadvisable** [ɪnədváɪzəbļ] *adj.* imprudente.

**inanimate** [ɪnǽnəmɪt] *adj.* inanimado.

**inasmuch** [ɪnəzmʌ́tʃ]: **— as** visto que, puesto que; en cuanto.

**inattentive** [ɪnətɛ́ntɪv] *adj.* desatento.

**inaugurate** [ɪnɔ́gjəret] *v.* inaugurar, iniciar; investir de una dignidad o cargo.

**inauguration** [ɪnɔgjəréʃən] *s.* inauguración.

**inboard** [ínbord] *adj.* interior.

**inborn** [ɪnbɔ́rn] *adj.* innato, connatural.

**incandescent** [ɪnkəndɛ́sn̩t] *adj.* incandescente, candente.

**incapable** [ɪnképəbļ] *adj.* incapaz.

**incapacitate** [ɪnkəpǽsɪtet] *v.* incapacitar.

**incendiary** [ɪnsɛ́ndɪɛrɪ] *adj.* incendiario; **— bomb** bomba incendiaria.

**incense** [ínsɛns] *s.* incienso; [ɪnsɛ́ns] *v.* inflamar, exasperar.

**incentive** [ɪnsɛ́ntɪv] *s.* incentivo, estímulo.

**incessant** [ɪnsɛ́sn̩t] *adj.* incesante, continuo.

**inch** [ɪntʃ] *s.* pulgada (*2.54 centímetros*); **by -es** poco a poco, gradualmente; **every — a man** nada menos que todo un hombre; **to be within an — of** estar a dos pulgadas de, estar muy cerca de; *v.* avanzar muy despacio (*por pulgadas*).

**incidence** [ínsɪdəns] *s.* incidencia.

**incident** [ínsədənt] *s.* incidente, suceso, acontecimiento.

**incidental** [ɪnsədɛ́ntļ] *adj.* incidental; accidental; contingente; **-s** *s. pl.* gastos imprevistos; **-ly** *adv.* incidentalmente; de paso.

**incipient** [ɪnsípɪənt] *adj.* incipiente.

**incision** [ɪnsíʒən] *s.* incisión.

**incite** [ɪnsáɪt] *v.* incitar.

**inclement** [ínklɛmənt] *adj.* inclemente.

**inclination** [ɪnklənéʃən] *s.* inclinación.

**incline** [ínklaɪn] *s.* declive, pendiente, cuesta; [ɪnkláɪn] *v.* inclinar(se).

**inclose** = **enclose.**

**inclosure** = **enclosure.**

**include** [ɪnklúd] *v.* incluir, encerrar;

abarcar.

**inclusive** [ɪnklúsɪv] *adj.* inclusivo; **from Monday to Friday —** del lunes al viernes inclusive.

**incoherent** [ɪnkohírənt] *adj.* incoherente, inconexo.

**income** [ínkʌm] *s.* renta, rédito, ingreso, entrada; **— tax** impuesto sobre rentas.

**incomparable** [ɪnkʌ́mpərəbļ] *adj.* incomparable, sin par, sin igual.

**incompatible** [ɪnkəmpǽtəbļ] *adj.* incompatible.

**incompetent** [ɪnkʌ́mpətənt] *adj.* incompetente.

**incomplete** [ɪnkəmplít] *adj.* incompleto.

**incomprehensible** [ɪnkʌmprɪhénsəbļ] *adj.* incomprensible.

**inconceivable** [ɪnkənsívəbļ] *adj.* inconcebible.

**inconsiderate** [ɪnkənsídərɪt] *adj.* inconsiderado, falto de miramiento.

**inconsistency** [ɪnkənsístənsɪ] *s.* inconsecuencia; falta de uniformidad (*en la aplicación de una regla o principio*).

**inconsistent** [ɪnkənsístənt] *adj.* inconsecuente; falto de uniformidad.

**inconspicuous** [ɪnkənspíkjuəs] *adj.* poco llamativo.

**inconstancy** [ɪnkʌ́nstənsɪ] *s.* inconstancia, mudanza.

**inconstant** [ɪnkʌ́nstənt] *adj.* inconstante, mudable, voluble.

**incontestable** [ɪnkəntéstəbļ] *adj.* incontestable.

**inconvenience** [ɪnkənvínjəns] *s.* inconveniencia; molestia; *v.* incomodar; molestar.

**inconvenient** [ɪnkənvínjənt] *adj.* inconveniente; inoportuno.

**incorporate** [ɪnkɔ́rpərɪt] *adj.* incorporado; asociado; [ɪnkɔ́rpəret] *v.* incorporar; incorporarse, asociarse (*para formar un cuerpo*).

**incorrect** [ɪnkərékt] *adj.* incorrecto.

**incorrigible** [ɪnkɔ́rɪdʒəbļ] *adj.* incorregible.

**increase** [ínkris] *s.* aumento; acrecentamiento; crecimiento; incremento; [ɪnkrís] *v.* aumentar(se); acrecentar(se), crecer.

**increasingly** [ɪnkrísɪŋlɪ] *adv.* más y más; cada vez más.

**incredible** [ɪnkrédəbļ] *adj.* increíble.

**incredulity** [ɪnkrədúlətɪ] *s.* incredulidad.

**incredulous** [ɪnkrédʒələs] *adj.* incrédulo, descreído.

**increment** [ínkrəmənt] *s.* incremento.

**incriminate** [ɪnkrímənet] *v.* acriminar.

**incubator** [ínkjubetɚ] *s.* incubadora.

**inculcate** [ɪnkʌ́lket] *v.* inculcar, infundir.

**incur** [ɪnkə́] *v.* incurrir en.

**incurable** [ɪnkjúrəbļ] *adj.* incurable, irremediable; *s.* incurable.

**indebted** [ɪndétɪd] *adj.* adeudado, endeudado; obligado, agradecido.

**indebtedness** [ɪndétɪdnɪs] *s.* deuda; obligación.

**indecency** [ɪndísn̩sɪ] *s.* indecencia.
**indecent** [ɪndisn̩t] *adj.* indecente.
**indecision** [ɪndəsíʒən] *s.* indecisión.
**indeed** [ɪndíd] *adv.* en verdad, a la verdad; de veras; realmente.
**indefensible** [ɪndɪfénsəbl̩] *adj.* indefendible.
**indefinite** [ɪndéfənɪt] *adj.* indefinido.
**indelible** [ɪndéləbl̩] *adj.* indeleble.
**indelicate** [ɪndéləkət] *adj.* indelicado, indecoroso.
**indemnify** [ɪndémnəfaɪ] *v.* indemnizar.
**indemnity** [ɪndémnətɪ] *s.* indemnización.
**indent** [ɪndént] *v.* dentar, endentar; sangrar (*comenzar un renglón más adentro que los otros*).
**independence** [ɪndɪpéndəns] *s.* independencia.
**independent** [ɪndɪpéndənt] *adj.* independiente.
**indescribable** [ɪndɪskráɪbəbl̩] *adj.* indescriptible.
**index** [índɛks] *s.* índice; *v.* alfabetizar, ordenar alfabéticamente; poner en un índice; — **finger** índice.
**Indian** [índɪən] *adj. & s.* indio; — **Ocean** Océano Indico.
**indicate** [índəket] *v.* indicar.
**indication** [ɪndəkéʃən] *s.* indicación.
**indicative** [ɪndíkətɪv] *adj. & s.* indicativo.
**indict** [ɪndáɪt] *v.* procesar, demandar (*ante un juez*); enjuiciar, formar causa a.
**indictment** [ɪndáɪtmənt] *s.* acusación (*hecha por el Gran Jurado*), denuncia, proceso judicial.
**indifference** [ɪndífrəns] *s.* indiferencia; apatía.
**indifferent** [ɪndífrənt] *adj.* indiferente; apático.
**indigenous** [ɪndídʒənəs] *adj.* indígena, autóctono, nativo.
**indigent** [índədʒənt] *adj. & s.* indigente.
**indigestion** [ɪndədʒéstʃən] *s.* indigestión.
**indignant** [ɪndígnənt] *adj.* indignado; **-ly** *adv.* con indignación.
**indignation** [ɪndɪgnéʃən] *s.* indignación.
**indignity** [ɪndígnətɪ] *s.* indignidad, afrenta.
**indigo** [índɪgo] *s.* índigo, añil; — **blue** azul de añil.
**indirect** [ɪndərékt] *adj.* indirecto.
**indiscreet** [ɪndɪskrít] *adj.* indiscreto.
**indiscretion** [ɪndɪskréʃən] *s.* indiscreción.
**indispensable** [ɪndɪspénsəbl̩] *adj.* indispensable.
**indispose** [ɪndɪspóz] *v.* indisponer.
**indisposed** [ɪndɪspózd] *adj.* indispuesto.
**indisposition** [ɪndɪspəzíʃən] *s.* indisposición; malestar.
**indistinct** [ɪndɪstíŋkt] *adj.* indistinto.
**individual** [ɪndəvídʒuəl] *adj.* individual; *s.* individuo, sujeto, persona.
**individuality** [ɪndəvɪdʒuǽlətɪ] *s.* individualidad; individuo, persona.

**indivisible** [ɪndəvízəbl̩] *adj.* indivisible.
**indoctrinate** [ɪndáktrɪnet] *v.* adoctrinar.
**indolence** [índələns] *s.* indolencia, desidia, apatía.
**indolent** [índələnt] *adj.* indolente, desidioso, apático.
**indomitable** [ɪndámətəbl̩] *adj.* indomable.
**indoor** [índor] *adj.* interior, de casa.
**indoors** [índórz] *adv.* dentro, en casa; adentro; **to go** — entrar; ir adentro.
**indorse** = **endorse**.
**indorsement** = **endorsement**.
**indorser** = **endorser**.
**induce** [ɪndjús] *v.* inducir.
**inducement** [ɪndjúsmənt] *s.* aliciente, incentivo.
**induct** [ɪndʌkt] *v.* introducir; iniciar; instalar (*en un cargo*).
**induction** [ɪndʌkʃən] *s.* inducción; instalación (*en un cargo*).
**indulge** [ɪndʌldʒ] *v.* gratificar, complacer; seguir el humor a (*una persona*); mimar, consentir (*a un niño*); **to** — **in** darse a, entregarse a (*un placer*); darse el lujo de, permitirse el placer de.
**indulgence** [ɪndʌldʒəns] *s.* indulgencia; complacencia (*en el vicio o placer*).
**indulgent** [ɪndʌldʒənt] *adj.* indulgente.
**industrial** [ɪndʌstrɪəl] *adj.* industrial.
**industrialist** [ɪndʌstrɪəlɪst] *s.* industrial; fabricante.
**industrious** [ɪndʌstrɪəs] *adj.* industrioso, aplicado, diligente.
**industry** [índəstrɪ] *s.* industria; aplicación, diligencia.
**ineffable** [ɪnéfəbl̩] *adj.* inefable.
**ineffective** [ɪnəféktɪv] *adj.* inefectivo, ineficaz.
**inefficient** [ɪnɪfíʃənt] *adj.* ineficaz.
**ineligible** [ɪnélədʒəbl̩] *adj.* inelegible.
**inequality** [ɪnɪkwálətɪ] *s.* desigualdad; disparidad.
**inert** [ɪnɜ́t] *adj.* inerte.
**inertia** [ɪnɜ́ʃə] *s.* inercia.
**inestimable** [ɪnéstəməbl̩] *adj.* inestimable.
**inevitable** [ɪnévətəbl̩] *adj.* inevitable.
**inexhaustible** [ɪnɪgzóstəbl̩] *adj.* inagotable.
**inexpedient** [ɪnɛkspídjənt] *adj.* inoportuno; imprudente.
**inexpensive** [ɪnɪkspénsɪv] *adj.* económico, barato.
**inexperience** [ɪnɪkspírɪəns] *s.* inexperiencia, falta de experiencia.
**inexperienced** [ɪnɪkspírɪənst] *adj.* inexperto, falto de experiencia.
**inexplicable** [ɪnéksplɪkəbl̩] *adj.* inexplicable.
**inexpressible** [ɪnɪksprésəbl̩] *adj.* inexpresable, indecible, inefable.
**infallible** [ɪnfǽləbl̩] *adj.* infalible.
**infamous** [ínfəməs] *adj.* infame, ignominioso.
**infamy** [ínfəmɪ] *s.* infamia.
**infancy** [ínfənsɪ] *s.* infancia.
**infant** [ínfənt] *s.* infante, bebé, criatura, nene.

**infantile** [ínfəntaɪl] *adj.* infantil.
**infantry** [ínfəntrɪ] *s.* infantería.
**infect** [ɪnfékt] *v.* infectar, inficionar; contagiar; contaminar.
**infection** [ɪnfékʃən] *s.* infección; contagio.
**infectious** [ɪnfékʃəs] *adj.* infeccioso; contagioso.
**infer** [ɪnfɝ] *v.* inferir, deducir, colegir.
**inference** [ínfərəns] *s.* inferencia, deducción.
**inferior** [ɪnfírɪɚ] *adj. & s.* inferior.
**inferiority** [ɪnfɪrɪórətɪ] *s.* inferioridad; — **complex** complejo de inferioridad.
**infernal** [ɪnfɝnl] *adj.* infernal.
**inferno** [ɪnfɝno] *s.* infierno.
**infest** [ɪnfést] *v.* infestar, plagar.
**infidel** [ínfədl] *adj. & s.* infiel.
**infiltrate** [ɪnfíltret] *v.* infiltrar(se).
**infinite** [ínfənɪt] *adj. & s.* infinito.
**infinitive** [ɪnfínətɪv] *adj. & s.* infinitivo.
**infinity** [ɪnfínətɪ] *s.* infinidad; infinito.
**infirm** [ɪnfɝm] *adj.* enfermizo, achacoso, débil.
**infirmary** [ɪnfɝmərɪ] *s.* enfermería.
**infirmity** [ɪnfɝmətɪ] *s.* enfermedad, achaque; flaqueza.
**inflame** [ɪnflém] *v.* inflamar(se); enardecer(se).
**inflammation** [ɪnfləméʃən] *s.* inflamación.
**inflate** [ɪnflét] *v.* inflar; hinchar.
**inflation** [ɪnfléʃən] *s.* inflación; hinchazón.
**inflection** [ɪnflékʃən] *s.* inflexión.
**inflict** [ɪnflíkt] *v.* infligir, imponer.
**influence** [ínfluəns] *s.* influencia, influjo; *v.* influir en; ejercer influencia o influjo sobre.
**influential** [ɪnfluénʃəl] *adj.* influyente.
**influenza** [ɪnfluénzə] *s.* influenza, gripe.
**influx** [ínflʌks] *s.* entrada, afluencia (*de gente*).
**infold** [ɪnfóld] *v.* envolver; abrazar; abarcar.
**inform** [ɪnfórm] *v.* informar; enterar; avisar; **to — against** delatar a, denunciar a.
**informal** [ɪnfórml] *adj.* informal, sin ceremonia; **— visit** visita de confianza; **-ly** *adv.* informalmente, sin ceremonia, de confianza.
**informant** [ɪnfórmənt] *s.* informante.
**information** [ɪnfəméʃən] *s.* (*service*) información; (*details*) informes; (*news*) noticias; (*knowledge*) conocimientos, saber.
**infraction** [ɪnfrǽkʃən] *s.* infracción.
**infringe** [ɪnfrínʤ] *v.* infringir, violar; **to — upon** violar.
**infuriate** [ɪnfjúrɪet] *v.* enfurecer.
**infuse** [ɪnfjúz] *v.* infundir; inculcar.
**ingenious** [ɪnʤínjəs] *adj.* ingenioso.
**ingenuity** [ɪnʤənúətɪ] *s.* ingeniosidad.
**ingratitude** [ɪnɡrǽtətjud] *s.* ingratitud.
**ingredient** [ɪnɡrídɪənt] *s.* ingrediente.
**inhabit** [ɪnhǽbɪt] *v.* habitar, vivir en, residir en.
**inhabitant** [ɪnhǽbətənt] *s.* habitante.
**inhale** [ɪnhél] *v.* inhalar, aspirar, inspirar.

**inherent** [ɪnhírənt] *adj.* inherente.
**inherit** [ɪnhérɪt] *v.* heredar.
**inheritance** [ɪnhérətəns] *s.* herencia.
**inhibit** [ɪnhíbɪt] *v.* inhibir, cohibir, refrenar, reprimir; impedir.
**inhibition** [ɪnɪbíʃən] *s.* inhibición, cohibición; prohibición, restricción.
**inhospitable** [ɪnháspɪtəbl] *adj.* inhospitalario.
**inhuman** [ɪnhjúmən] *adj.* inhumano.
**inimitable** [ɪnímətəbl] *adj.* inimitable.
**iniquity** [ɪníkwɪtɪ] *s.* iniquidad, maldad.
**initial** [ɪníʃəl] *adj. & s.* inicial; *v.* marcar o firmar con iniciales.
**initiate** [ɪníʃɪet] *v.* iniciar.
**initiative** [ɪníʃɪetɪv] *s.* iniciativa.
**inject** [ɪnʤékt] *v.* inyectar; injerir, introducir.
**injection** [ɪnʤékʃən] *s.* inyección.
**injunction** [ɪnʤʌ́ŋkʃən] *s.* mandato, orden; entredicho.
**injure** [ínʤɚ] *v.* dañar; herir, lesionar; lastimar.
**injurious** [ɪnʤúrɪəs] *adj.* dañoso, dañino, perjudicial.
**injury** [ínʤərɪ] *s.* daño; herida, lesión; perjuicio.
**injustice** [ɪnʤʌ́stɪs] *s.* injusticia.
**ink** [ɪŋk] *s.* tinta; *v.* entintar; teñir o manchar con tinta.
**inkling** [íŋklɪŋ] *s.* indicación, indicio, idea, sospecha, noción vaga.
**inkstand** [íŋkstænd] *s.* tintero.
**inkwell** [íŋkwel] *s.* tintero.
**inlaid** [ɪnléd] *adj.* incrustado, embutido; **— work** embutido, incrustación; *pret. & p.p. de* **to inlay.**
**inland** [ínlənd] *s.* interior (*de un país*); *adj.* interior, del interior de un país; *adv.* tierra adentro.
**inlay** [ɪnlé] *v.* incrustar, embutir; [ínle] *s.* embutido.
**inmate** [ínmet] *s.* residente, asilado (*de un hospicio, asilo, casa de corrección, etc.*); presidiario; hospiciano.
**inmost** [ínmost] *adj.* más interior, más íntimo, más secreto o recóndito; más profundo.
**inn** [ɪn] *s.* posada, mesón, fonda.
**innate** [ɪnét] *adj.* innato, connatural.
**inner** [ínɚ] *adj.* interior; íntimo, recóndito; **—most** = **inmost.**
**inning** [ínɪŋ] *s.* entrada, cuadro (*en beisbol*); turno (*del bateador en beisbol y otros juegos*).
**innkeeper** [ínkipɚ] *s.* ventero, mesonero, posadero.
**innocence** [ínəsns] *s.* inocencia.
**innocent** [ínəsn̩t] *adj. & s.* inocente.
**innocuous** [ɪnákjuəs] *adj.* innocuo, inofensivo.
**innovation** [ɪnəvéʃən] *s.* innovación.
**innuendo** [ɪnjuéndo] *s.* insinuación, indirecta.
**innumerable** [ɪnjúmərəbl] *adj.* innumerable.
**inoculate** [ɪnákjəlet] *v.* inocular; contaminar.
**inoffensive** [ɪnəfénsɪv] *adj.* inofensivo.

**inopportune** [ɪnɑpɚtjún] *adj.* inoportuno.

**input** [ínput] *s.* potencia consumida; (*electric*) entrada.

**inquire** [ɪnkwáɪr] *v.* inquirir, indagar; preguntar; **to — about** preguntar por; **to — into** indagar, investigar.

**inquiry** [ɪnkwáɪrɪ] *s.* indagación, investigación; pregunta; interrogatorio.

**inquisition** [ɪnkwəzíʃən] *s.* inquisición; indagación.

**inquisitive** [ɪnkwízətɪv] *adj.* inquisitivo, investigador; preguntón; curioso.

**inroad** [ínrod] *s.* incursión, invasión, ataque; **to make -s upon** atacar; mermar.

**insane** [ɪnsén] *adj.* insano, loco; **— asylum** manicomio, casa de locos.

**insanity** [ɪnsǽnətɪ] *s.* locura.

**insatiable** [ɪnséʃɪəbl] *adj.* insaciable.

**inscribe** [ɪnskráɪb] *v.* inscribir.

**inscription** [ɪnskrípʃən] *s.* inscripción; letrero.

**insect** [ínsɛkt] *s.* insecto.

**insecure** [ɪnsɪkjúr] *adj.* inseguro.

**insensible** [ɪnsénsəbl] *adj.* insensible.

**insensitive** [ɪnsénsətɪv] *adj.* insensible.

**inseparable** [ɪnsépərəbl] *adj.* inseparable.

**insert** [íns ɚt] *s.* inserción; intercalación; hoja (*insertada en un libro*); circular, folleto (*insertado en un periódico*); [ɪnsɚt] *v.* insertar; intercalar; encajar; meter.

**insertion** [ɪnsɚ́ʃən] *s.* inserción; introducción.

**inside** [ínsáɪd] *s.* interior; **-s** entrañas; *adj.* interior, interno; secreto; *adv.* dentro; adentro; **to turn — out** volver(se) al revés; *prep.* dentro de.

**insight** [ínsaɪt] *s.* penetración, discernimiento; intuición; perspicacia; comprensión.

**insignia** [ɪnsígnɪə] *s. pl.* insignias.

**insignificant** [ɪnsɪgnífəkənt] *adj.* insignificante.

**insinuate** [ɪnsínjuet] *v.* insinuar.

**insinuation** [ɪnsɪnjuéʃən] *s.* insinuación; indirecta.

**insipid** [ɪnsípɪd] *adj.* insípido.

**insist** [ɪnsíst] *v.* insistir en; empeñarse (en); porfiar, persistir.

**insistence** [ɪnsístəns] *s.* insistencia, empeño, porfía.

**insistent** [ɪnsístənt] *adj.* insistente; porfiado, persistente.

**insolence** [ínsələns] *s.* insolencia.

**insolent** [ínsələnt] *adj.* insolente.

**insoluble** [ɪnsáljəbl] *adj.* insoluble.

**inspect** [ɪnspékt] *v.* inspeccionar; examinar, registrar.

**inspection** [ɪnspékʃən] *s.* inspección; registro.

**inspector** [ɪnspéktɚ] *s.* inspector.

**inspiration** [ɪnspəréʃən] *s.* inspiración.

**inspire** [ɪnspáɪr] *v.* inspirar.

**install** [ɪnstól] *v.* instalar.

**installation** [ɪnstəléʃən] *s.* instalación.

**installment, instalment** [ɪnstólmənt] *s.* instalación; abono (*pago*); entrega o continuación (*semanal o mensual de una novela*); **to pay in -s** pagar por plazos; pagar en abonos.

**instance** [ínstəns] *s.* ejemplo, caso; vez, ocasión; instancia; **for —** por ejemplo.

**instant** [ínstənt] *s.* instante; *adj.* inmediato; urgente; **the 10th —** el 10 del (mes) corriente; **-ly** *adv.* al instante, inmediatamente.

**instantaneous** [ɪnstənténɪəs] *adj.* instantáneo.

**instead** [ɪnstéd] *adv.* en lugar de ello (eso, él, ella, *etc.*); **— of** en lugar de, en vez de.

**instep** [ínstɛp] *s.* empeine (*del pie, del zapato*).

**instigate** [ínstəget] *v.* instigar.

**instill** [ɪnstíl] *v.* inculcar, infundir.

**instinct** [ínstɪŋkt] *s.* instinto.

**instinctive** [ɪnstíŋktɪv] *adj.* instintivo.

**institute** [ínstətjut] *s.* instituto; *v.* instituir.

**institution** [ɪnstətjúʃən] *s.* institución.

**instruct** [ɪnstrÁkt] *v.* instruir; dar instrucciones.

**instruction** [ɪnstrÁkʃən] *s.* instrucción; enseñanza; **lack of —** falta de saber o conocimientos; **-s** órdenes, instrucciones.

**instructive** [ɪnstrÁktɪv] *adj.* instructivo.

**instructor** [ɪnstrÁktɚ] *s.* instructor.

**instrument** [ínstrəmənt] *s.* instrumento.

**instrumental** [ɪnstrəméntl] *adj.* instrumental; **to be — in** ayudar a, servir de instrumento para.

**insubordinate** [ɪnsəbórdɪnət] *adj.* insubordinado.

**insufferable** [ɪnsÁfrəbl] *adj.* insufrible, inaguantable.

**insufficiency** [ɪnsəfíʃənsɪ] *s.* insuficiencia; incompetencia; falta, escasez.

**insufficient** [ɪnsəfíʃənt] *adj.* insuficiente; inadecuado.

**insulate** [ínsəlet] *v.* aislar.

**insulation** [ɪnsəléʃən] *s.* aislamiento; aislación.

**insulator** [ínsəletɚ] *s.* aislador.

**insult** [ínsÁlt] *s.* insulto; (ɪnsÁlt) *v.* insultar.

**insurance** [ɪnʃúrəns] *s.* aseguramiento; seguro; prima, premio (*de una póliza de seguro*); **— agent** agente de seguros; **— company** cómpañía de seguros; **— policy** póliza de seguro; **accident —** seguro contra accidentes; **fire —** seguro contra incendios; **life —** seguro sobre la vida.

**insure** [ɪnʃúr] *v.* asegurar; asegurarse de.

**insurgent** [ɪnsɚ́dʒənt] *adj. & s.* insurgente, insurrecto.

**insurmountable** [ɪnsɚmáuntəbl] *adj.* insuperable.

**insurrection** [ɪnsərékʃən] *s.* insurrección, rebelión, alzamiento.

**intact** [ɪntǽkt] *adj.* intacto.

**integral** [íntəgrəl] *adj.* integral; integrante; *s.* integral.

**integrate** [íntəgret] *v.* integrar.

**integrity** [ɪntégrətɪ] *s.* integridad, en-

IN

tereza.

**intellect** [íntlɛkt] *s.* intelecto; entendimiento.

**intellectual** [ıntléktʃuəl] *adj.* & *s.* intelectual.

**intelligence** [ıntélədʒəns] *s.* inteligencia; información, noticias; policía secreta.

**intelligent** [ıntélədʒənt] *adj.* inteligente.

**intelligible** [ıntélədʒəbl] *adj.* inteligible.

**intemperance** [ıntémpərəns] *s.* intemperancia.

**intend** [ınténd] *v.* intentar, pensar, tener la intención de; proponerse; destinar; **to — to do it** pensar hacerlo.

**intense** [ınténs] *adj.* intenso.

**intensify** [ınténsıfaı] *v.* intensificar.

**intensity** [ınténsətı] *s.* intensidad.

**intensive** [ınténsıv] *adj.* intenso; intensivo.

**intent** [ıntént] *s.* intento, intención, propósito; significado; **to all -s and purposes** en todo caso, en todos sentidos; en realidad; *adj.* atento; **— on** absorto en, reconcentrado en; resuelto a, decidido a.

**intention** [ınténʃən] *s.* intención.

**intentional** [ınténʃənl] *adj.* intencional; **-ly** *adv.* intencionalmente, adrede, a propósito.

**inter** [ıntɜ́] *v.* enterrar, sepultar.

**intercede** [ıntɜ·síd] *v.* interceder.

**intercept** [ıntɜ·sépt] *v.* interceptar; atajar.

**interception** [ıntɜ·sépʃən] *s.* interceptación.

**intercession** [ıntɜ·séʃən] *s.* intercesión.

**interchange** [íntɜ·tʃendʒ] *s.* intercambio; cambio, trueque; [ıntɜ·tʃéndʒ] *v.* cambiar, trocar; permutar; alternar.

**intercourse** [íntɜ·kors] *s.* comunicación; comercio, trato; intercambio (*de ideas, sentimientos, etc.*).

**interdental** [ıntɜ·déntl] *adj.* interdental.

**interest** [íntɜrıst] *s.* interés; rédito; participación (*en un negocio*); *v.* interesar.

**interested** [íntɜrıstıd] *adj.* interesado; **to be** (*o* **become**) **— in** interesarse en (*o* por).

**interesting** [íntɜrıstıŋ] *adj.* interesante.

**interfere** [ıntɜ·fír] *v.* intervenir; interponerse, entremeterse; estorbar; **to — with** estorbar, frustrar; dificultar.

**interference** [ıntɜ·fírəns] *s.* intervención; obstáculo; interferencia (*en la radio*).

**interior** [ıntírıɜ·] *adj.* interior; interno; *s.* interior.

**interjection** [ıntɜ·dʒékʃən] *s.* interjección, exclamación; intercalación.

**interlace** [ıntɜ·lés] *v.* entrelazar, enlazar, entretejer.

**interlock** [ıntɜ·lák] *v.* entrelazar(se); trabar(se).

**interlude** [íntɜ·lud] *s.* intervalo.

**intermediate** [ıntɜ·mídııt] *adj.* intermedio.

**interminable** [ıntɜ́mınəbl] *adj.* interminable, inacabable.

**intermingle** [ıntɜ·míŋgl] *v.* entremezclar(se), entreverar(se); mezclar(se).

**intermission** [ıntɜ·míʃən] *s.* intermisión; intermedio, entreacto.

**intermittent** [ıntɜ·mítņt] *adj.* intermitente.

**intern** [ıntɜ́n] *v.* internar, confinar, encerrar; [íntɜn] *s.* practicante (*de medicina en un hospital*).

**internal** [ıntɜ́nl] *adj.* interno; interior.

**international** [ıntɜ·nǽʃənl] *adj.* internacional.

**interoceanic** [ıntɜ·oʃıǽnık] *adj.* interoceánico.

**interpose** [ıntɜ·póz] *v.* interponer(se).

**interpret** [ıntɜ́prıt] *v.* interpretar.

**interpretation** [ıntɜprıtéʃən] *s.* interpretación.

**interpreter** [ıntɜ́prıtɜ·] *s.* intérprete.

**interrogate** [ıntérəget] *v.* interrogar.

**interrogation** [ıntɜrəgéʃən] *s.* interrogación.

**interrogative** [ıntɜrágətıv] *adj.* interrogativo; *s.* pronombre o palabra interrogativa.

**interrupt** [ıntɜrápt] *v.* interrumpir.

**interruption** [ıntɜrápʃən] *s.* interrupción.

**intersect** [ıntɜ·sékt] *v.* cortar(se); cruzar(se).

**intersection** [ıntɜ·sékʃən] *s.* intersección; **street —** bocacalle.

**intersperse** [ıntɜ·spɜ́s] *v.* entremezclar, esparcir.

**intertwine** [ıntɜ·twáın] *v.* entrelazar, entretejer, trenzar.

**interval** [íntɜ·vl] *s.* intervalo.

**intervene** [ıntɜ·vín] *s.* intervenir; interponerse; mediar.

**intervention** [ıntɜ·vénʃən] *s.* intervención.

**interview** [íntɜ·vju] *s.* entrevista; *v.* entrevistar, entrevistarse con.

**intestine** [ıntéstın] *s.* intestino; *adj.* intestino, interno.

**intimacy** [íntəməsı] *s.* intimidad.

**intimate** [íntəmıt] *adj.* íntimo; *s.* amigo íntimo; [íntəmet] *v.* intimar, insinuar; indicar, dar a entender.

**intimation** [ıntəméʃən] *s.* intimación, insinuación.

**intimidate** [ıntímədet] *v.* intimidar, acobardar, infundir miedo.

**into** [íntu, íntə] *prep.* en; dentro de; hacia el interior.

**intolerable** [ıntálərəbl] *adj.* intolerable, inaguantable.

**intolerance** [ıntálərəns] *s.* intolerancia.

**intolerant** [ıntálərənt] *adj.* intolerante.

**intonation** [ıntonéʃən] *s.* entonación.

**intoxicate** [ıntáksəket] *v.* embriagar; emborrachar.

**intoxication** [ıntaksəkéʃən] *s.* embriaguez; envenenamiento, intoxicación (*estado tóxico o envenenamiento parcial*).

**intransigent** [ıntrǽnsədʒənt] *adj.* intransigente.

**intravenous** [ıntrəvínəs] *adj.* intravenoso.

**intrench** [ıntréntʃ] *v.* atrincherar; **to —**

**oneself** atrincherarse; **to — upon another's rights** infringir los derechos ajenos; **to be -ed** estar atrincherado; estar firmemente establecido.
**intrepid** [ɪntrépɪd] *adj.* intrépido.
**intricate** [íntrəkɪt] *adj.* intrincado, enredado.
**intrigue** [ɪntríg] *s.* intriga; enredo; trama; lío, embrollo; *v.* intrigar; tramar, maquinar.
**intriguer** [ɪntrígɚ] *s.* intrigante.
**introduce** [ɪntrədjús] *v.* introducir; presentar.
**introduction** [ɪntrədʌ́kʃən] *s.* introducción; presentación.
**introspection** [ɪntrospékʃən] *s.* introspección.
**introvert** [íntrovɚt] *s.* introvertido.
**intrude** [ɪntrúd] *v.* entremeterse (*o* entrometerse); introducir, meter.
**intruder** [ɪntrúdɚ] *s.* intruso, entremetido.
**intrusion** [ɪntrúʒən] *s.* intrusión, entremetimiento.
**intrusive** [ɪntrúsɪv] *adj.* intruso.
**intrust** = **entrust.**
**intuition** [ɪntuíʃən] *s.* intuición.
**inundate** [ínəndet] *v.* inundar.
**inure** [ɪnjúr] *v.* habituar, acostumbrar.
**invade** [ɪnvéd] *v.* invadir.
**invader** [ɪnvédɚ] *s.* invasor.
**invalid** [ɪnvǽlɪd] *adj.* inválido (*que no vale*), nulo, de ningún valor.
**invalid** [ínvəlɪd] *adj.* inválido, enfermizo, achacoso; **— diet** dieta para inválidos; *s.* inválido.
**invaluable** [ɪnvǽljebl] *adj.* de gran precio o valor, inapreciable, inestimable.
**invariable** [ɪnvérɪəbl] *adj.* invariable; **invariably** *adv.* invariablemente; sin falta, sin excepción.
**invasion** [ɪnvéʒən] *s.* invasión.
**invent** [ɪnvént] *v.* inventar.
**invention** [ɪnvénʃən] *s.* invención; invento; inventiva, facultad para inventar.
**inventive** [ɪnvéntɪv] *adj.* inventivo.
**inventiveness** [ɪnvéntɪvnɪs] *s.* inventiva.
**inventor** [ɪnvéntɚ] *s.* inventor.
**inventory** [ínvəntori] *s.* inventario; *v.* inventariar.
**inverse** [ɪnvɚ́s] *adj.* inverso.
**invert** [ɪnvɚ́t] *v.* invertir; trastrocar; volver al revés.
**invest** [ɪnvést] *v.* invertir, colocar (*fondos*); investir (*de una dignidad o cargo*); revestir (*de autoridad*); sitiar.
**investigate** [ɪnvéstəget] *v.* investigar, indagar.
**investigation** [ɪnvɛstəgéʃən] *s.* investigación; indagación.
**investigator** [ɪnvéstəgetɚ] *s.* investigador; indagador.
**investment** [ɪnvéstmənt] *s.* inversión (*de fondos*).
**investor** [ɪnvéstɚ] *s.* el que invierte fondos.
**invigorate** [ɪnvígəret] *v.* vigorizar, fortalecer.
**invincible** [ɪnvínsəbl] *adj.* invencible.

**invisible** [ɪnvízəbl] *adj.* invisible.
**invitation** [ɪnvətéʃən] *s.* invitación.
**invite** [ɪnváɪt] *v.* invitar; convidar.
**inviting** [ɪnváɪtɪŋ) *adj.* atractivo; seductivo, tentador.
**invocation** [ɪnvəkéʃən] *s.* invocación.
**invoice** [ínvɔɪs] *s.* factura; envío, mercancías enviadas; *v.* facturar.
**invoke** [ɪnvók] *v.* invocar.
**involuntary** [ɪnválənterɪ] *adj.* involuntario.
**involve** [ɪnválv] *v.* complicar, enredar; envolver; implicar; comprometer; **to get -d in difficulties** embrollarse, meterse en embrollos.
**inward** [ínwɚd] *adj.* interior; interno; secreto; *adv.* hacia el interior; hacia dentro, adentro, para dentro; **-s** *adv.* = **inward.**
**iodine** [áɪədaɪn] *s.* yodo.
**ire** [aɪr] *s.* ira.
**iridescent** [ɪrədésn̩t] *adj.* iridiscente, tornasolado, irisado.
**iris** [áɪrɪs] *s.* iris; arco iris; flor de lis.
**Irish** [áɪrɪʃ] *adj.* irlandés; *s.* irlandés, idioma irlandés; **the —** los irlandeses.
**irksome** [ɚ́ksəm] *adj.* fastidioso, engorroso, molesto, tedioso.
**iron** [áɪɚn] *s.* hierro; plancha (*de planchar ropa*); *adj.* férreo, de hierro; **—work** herraje, trabajo en hierro; **—works** herrería; fábrica de hierro; *v.* planchar; **to — out a difficulty** allanar una dificultad.
**ironical** [aɪránɪkl] *adj.* irónico.
**ironing** [áɪɚnɪŋ] *s.* planchado.
**irony** [áɪrənɪ] *s.* ironía.
**irradiate** [ɪrédɪet] *v.* irradiar.
**irrational** [ɪrǽʃənl] *adj.* irracional.
**irregular** [ɪrégjəlɚ] *adj.* irregular.
**irrelevant** [ɪréləvənt] *adj.* fuera de propósito, inaplicable al caso, inoportuno, que no viene (*o* no hace) al caso.
**irreligious** [ɪrɪlídʒəs] *adj.* irreligioso, impío.
**irremediable** [ɪrɪmídɪəbl] *adj.* irremediable; incurable.
**irreproachable** [ɪrɪprótʃəbl] *adj.* irreprochable, intachable.
**irresistible** [ɪrɪzístəbl] *adj.* irresistible.
**irresolute** [ɪrézəlut] *adj.* irresoluto, indeciso.
**irreverence** [ɪrévərəns] *s.* irreverencia, desacato.
**irreverent** [ɪrévərənt] *adj.* irreverente.
**irrigate** [írəget] *v.* regar; irrigar, bañar.
**irrigation** [ɪrəgéʃən] *s.* riego; irrigación; **— canal** acequia, canal de irrigación.
**irritable** [írətəbl] *adj.* irritable; colérico.
**irritate** [írətet] *v.* irritar.
**irritating** [írətetɪŋ] *adj.* irritante.
**irritation** [ɪrətéʃən] *s.* irritación.
**irrupt** [ɪrʌ́pt] *v.* irrumpir.
**island** [áɪlənd] *s.* isla.
**islander** [áɪləndɚ] *s.* isleño.
**isle** [aɪl] *s.* isla, ínsula.
**isolate** [áɪslet] *v.* aislar.
**isolation** [aɪsléʃən] *s.* aislamiento.
**isolationism** [aɪséʃənɪzəm] *s.* aislamiento.
**isometric** [aɪsométrɪk] *adj.* isométrico.

**IN**

**Israel** [ízriəl] *s.* Israel.

**issue** [íʃu] *s.* (*printing*) tirada, impresión; (*stock, bonds*) emisión (*de valores*); (*problem*) problema, tema; (*result*) resultado, consecuencia; **without —** sin prole, sin sucesión; **to take — with** disentir o diferir de; *v.* publicar, dar a luz; dar, promulgar (*un decreto*); emitir (*valores, acciones, etc.*); emanar; fluir; salir; brotar; provenir.

**isthmus** [ísməs] *s.* istmo.

**it** [ɪt] *pron. neutro* lo, la (*acusativo*); ello, él, ella (*después de una preposición*); *por lo general no se traduce cuando es sujeto del verbo:* **— is there** está allí; **— is I** soy yo; **— is raining** llueve, está lloviendo; **what time is —?** ¿qué hora es?; **— is two o'clock** son las dos; **how goes —?** ¿qué tal?

**Italian** [ɪtǽljən] *adj. & s.* italiano.

**italic** [ɪtǽlɪk] *adj.* itálico; **-s** *s.* letra bastardilla.

**italicize** [ɪtǽləsaɪz] *v.* poner en letra bastardilla.

**itch** [ɪtʃ] *s.* comezón; picazón; sarna (*enfermedad de la piel*); *v.* picar, darle a uno comezón; sentir comezón; **to be -ing to** tener ansias de.

**itchy** [ítʃɪ] *adj.* sarnoso, *Méx., Ven.* sarniento; **to feel —** sentir comezón.

**item** [áɪtəm] *s.* artículo; detalle; noticia, suelto (*de un periódico*); partida (*de una lista*).

**itemize** [áɪtəmaɪz] *v.* pormenorizar detallar; hacer una lista de.

**itinerant** [aɪtínəənt] *adj.* ambulante.

**itinerary** [aɪtínərɛrɪ] *s.* itinerario; ruta; guía de viajeros.

**its** [ɪts] *pos. neutro* su (sus), de él, de ella, de ello.

**itself** [ɪtsélf] *pron. neutro* mismo, misma; **by —** por sí, de por sí, por sí solo; solo, aislado; **in —** en sí.

**ivory** [áɪvrɪ] *s.* marfil; **— tower** torre de marfil.

**ivy** [áɪvɪ] *s.* hiedra (yedra).

## J

**jab** [dʒæb] *v.* picar; pinchar; *s.* piquete, pinchazo.

**jack** [dʒæk] *s.* gato (*para alzar cosas pesadas*); sota (*en naipes*); macho (*del burro y otros animales*); bandera de proa; **— of all trades** aprendiz de todo y oficial de nada; **— pot** premio gordo, premio mayor; **— rabbit** liebre americana; *v.* **to — up** solevantar, alzar con gato (*un objeto pesado*).

**jackass** [dʒǽkæs] *s.* asno, burro.

**jacket** [dʒǽkɪt] *s.* chaqueta; envoltura; forro (*de un libro*); hollejo (*de la patata*).

**jackknife** [dʒǽknaɪf] *s.* navaja.

**jagged** [dʒǽgɪd] *adj.* serrado, dentado.

**jail** [dʒel] *s.* cárcel; *v.* encarcelar.

**jailer** [dʒélə] *s.* carcelero.

**jam** [dʒæm] *v.* estrujar, apachurrar; atorar(se); obstruir(se), atascar(se); apiñar(se), agolpar(se); **to — on the brakes** frenar de golpe; **to — one's fingers** machucarse los dedos; **to —**

**through** forzar por, meter a la fuerza; *s.* conserva, compota; apretura; atascamiento; **traffic —** aglomeración de transeúntes o automóviles, *Am.* bola; **to be in a —** estar en un aprieto.

**janitor** [dʒǽnətə] *s.* conserje; portero; casero (*encargado de un edificio*).

**January** [dʒǽnjuɛrɪ] *s.* enero.

**Japanese** [dʒæpəníz] *adj. & s.* japonés.

**jar** [dʒɑr] *s.* jarra, jarro; tarro; choque; sacudida; trepidación, vibración; **large earthen —** tinaja; *v.* trepidar; hacer vibrar; hacer temblar; menear; **to — one's nerves** ponerle a uno los nervios de punta.

**jargon** [dʒárgən] *s.* jerga, jerigonza.

**jasmine** [dʒǽzmɪn] *s.* jazmín.

**jasper** [dʒǽspə] *s.* jaspe.

**jaunt** [dʒɔnt] *s.* caminata, excursión; *v.* dar un paseíto, hacer una corta caminata.

**jaw** [dʒɔ] *s.* quijada, mandíbula, *Am.* carretilla; **-s** grapa (*de herramienta*).

**jawbone** [dʒɔbón] *s.* mandíbula, quijada.

**jay** [dʒe] *s.* grajo; rústico, bobo; **blue —** azulejo; **—walker** el que cruza las bocacalles descuidadamente.

**jazz** [dʒæz] *s.* jazz (*cierta clase de música sincopada*); *v.* tocar el jazz; bailar el jazz; **to — up** sincopar; animar, alegrar.

**jealous** [dʒéləs] *adj.* celoso; envidioso; **to be — of someone** tener celos de una persona, tenerle celos a una persona.

**jealousy** [dʒéləsɪ] *s.* celos; envidia.

**jeer** [dʒɪr] *s.* mofa, befa, escarnio, *Carib.* choteo; *v.* mofar, befar, *Carib.* chotear; **to — at** mofarse de.

**jelly** [dʒélɪ] *s.* jalea; *v.* convertir(se) en jalea, hacer(se) gelatinoso.

**jeopardy** [dʒépədɪ] *s.* riesgo.

**jerk** [dʒɜk] *s.* tirón; sacudida, *Méx., C.A., Ven., Col.* jalón; espasmo muscular; *v.* sacudir(se); dar un tirón; atasajar (*la carne*); **to — out** sacar de un tirón; **-ed beef** tasajo, *Am.* charqui.

**jerkwater** [dʒɜkwɔtə] *adj.* de mala muerte.

**jersey** [dʒɜzɪ] *s.* tejido de punto, tejido elástico, *Am.* jersey; chaqueta, blusa, camisa (*de punto*), *Am.* jersey.

**jest** [dʒɛst] *s.* broma; chanza; chiste; *v.* bromear; chancearse.

**jester** [dʒéstə] *s.* chancero, burlón; bufón.

**Jesuit** [dʒéʒuɪt] *s.* jesuita.

**jet** [dʒɛt] *s.* chorro; surtidor (*de fuente*); **— airplane** avión de reacción; **— engine** motor de reacción; **gas —** mechero de gas; *adj.* de azabache; **jet-black** negro como el azabache; *v.* chorrear, salir en chorro.

**Jew** [dʒu] *s.* judío.

**jewel** [dʒúəl] *s.* joya, alhaja; gema; **— box** estuche, joyero.

**jeweler** [dʒúələ] *s.* joyero; **-'s shop** joyería.

**jewelry** [dʒúəlrɪ] *s.* joyas, alhajas, pe-

drería; — **store** joyería.
**Jewish** [dʒúɪʃ] *adj.* judío.
**jiffy** [dʒífɪ] *s.* instante; **in a —** en un instante, en dos paletas; en un decir Jesús, en un santiamén.
**jig** [dʒɪg] *s.* jiga (*música y baile*); — **saw** sierra mecánica (*para recortar figuras*); —**saw puzzle** rompecabezas (*de recortes*); *v.* tocar una jiga; bailar una jiga; bailotear; menear(se).
**jiggle** [dʒígl] *v.* zangolotear(se), zarandear(se), menear(se); *s.* zarandeo, meneo, zangoloteo.
**jilt** [dʒɪlt] *v.* desairar, dar calabazas, dejar plantado.
**jingle** [dʒíŋgl] *s.* retintín; verso o rima infantil; — **bell** cascabel; *v.* hacer retintín.
**job** [dʒab] *s.* tarea, faena; trabajo; empleo, ocupación; **to be out of a —** estar sin trabajo; estar desocupado.
**jockey** [dʒákɪ] *s.* jockey; *v.* maniobrar (*para sacar ventaja o ganar un puesto*).
**join** [dʒɔɪn] *v.* juntar(se); enlazar(se); acoplar; unirse a, asociarse a.
**joint** [dʒɔɪnt] *s.* (*point*) juntura, coyuntura; (*function*) articulación; conexión; bisagra; (*public place*) garito (*casa de juego*); fonducho, restaurante de mala muerte; **out of —** descoyuntado; desunido; *adj.* unido, asociado; copartícipe; colectivo; — **account** cuenta en común; — **action** acción colectiva; — **committee** comisión mixta; — **creditor** acreedor copartícipe; — **heir** coheredero; — **session** sesión plena; **-ly** *adv.* juntamente, juntos, unidamente, colectivamente.
**joke** [dʒok] *s.* broma; chiste, chanza; *v.* bromear; chancear(se), *Carib.* chotear; *Ríopl.* farrear; jorobar.
**joker** [dʒókɚ] *s.* bromista, chancero, guasón, *Carib.* choteador; naipe especial (*que no pertenece a ningún palo*).
**jokingly** [dʒókɪŋlɪ] *adv.* en (o de) chanza, en (o de) broma; de chiste.
**jolly** [dʒálɪ] *adj.* jovial; alegre; festivo; *v.* bromear, chancearse.
**jolt** [dʒolt] *s.* sacudida; sacudimiento; choque; *v.* sacudir.
**jostle** [dʒásl] *v.* rempujar o empujar, dar empellones; codear; *s.* rempujón, empujón, empellón.
**jot** [dʒat] *v.* **to — down** apuntar, tomar apuntes; *s.* jota, pizca.
**journal** [dʒɚnl] *s.* diario; periódico; revista; acta (*de una junta o concilio*).
**journalism** [dʒɚnlɪzəm] *s.* periodismo.
**journalist** [dʒɚnlɪst] *s.* periodista.
**journalistic** [dʒɚnlístɪk] *adj.* periodístico.
**journey** [dʒɚnɪ] *s.* viaje, jornada; *v.* viajar.
**joy** [dʒɔɪ] *s.* júbilo, regocijo; alegría, gusto, deleite; felicidad.
**joyful** [dʒɔɪfəl] *adj.* regocijado, jubiloso; alegre; **-ly** *adv.* con regocijo, regocijadamente, con júbilo, alegremente.
**joyous** [dʒɔɪəs] *adj.* jubiloso, alegre,

gozoso.
**jubilant** [dʒúbələnt] *adj.* jubiloso, alegre.
**jubilee** [dʒúblɪ] *s.* jubileo; júbilo.
**judge** [dʒʌdʒ] *s.* juez; — **advocate** auditor de un consejo militar; *v.* juzgar.
**judgment** [dʒʌdʒmənt] *s.* juicio; sentencia, fallo; opinión; discernimiento; — **day** día del juicio final.
**judicial** [dʒudíʃəl] *adj.* judicial.
**judicious** [dʒudíʃəs] *adj.* juicioso, cuerdo.
**jug** [dʒʌg] *s.* cántaro; jarro, jarra; botija; chirona (*cárcel*) *Am.* chirola.
**juggle** [dʒʌgl] *v.* hacer juegos de manos; hacer suertes; **to — the accounts** barajar (o manipular) las cuentes; *s.* juego de manos, suerte; trampa.
**juggler** [dʒʌglɚ] *s.* prestidigitador, malabarista.
**juice** [dʒus] *s.* jugo; zumo.
**juiciness** [dʒúsɪnɪs] *s.* jugosidad.
**juicy** [dʒúsɪ] *adj.* jugoso, zumoso; suculento; **a — story** un cuento picante.
**juke box** [dʒúkbaks] *s.* tragamonedas; tragaquintos.
**July** [dʒulái] *s.* julio.
**jumble** [dʒʌmbl] *s.* revolver(se), barajar; mezclar(se); *s.* mezcolanza, revoltijo; confusión.
**jump** [dʒʌmp] *v.* saltar; brincar; salvar (*de un salto*); hacer saltar; comerse una pieza (*en el juego de damas*); **to — at the chance** asir o aprovechar la oportunidad; **to — bail** perder la fianza por evasión; **to — over** saltar por encima de, salvar de un salto; **to — the track** descarrilarse; **to — to conclusions** hacer deducciones precipitadas; *s.* salto; brinco; subida repentina (*del precio*); **to be always on the —** andar siempre de aquí para allá; trajinar, trafagar, ser muy activo.
**jumper** [dʒʌmpɚ] *s.* saltador; chaquetón holgado (*de obrero*); vestido sin mangas (*puesto sobre la blusa de mujer*); **-s** traje de juego (*para niños*).
**jumpy** [dʒʌmpɪ] *adj.* saltón; asustadizo, nervioso.
**junction** [dʒʌŋkʃən] *s.* unión, juntura; confluencia (*de dos ríos*); empalme (*de ferrocarriles*).
**juncture** [dʒʌŋktʃɚ] *s.* juntura; coyuntura; **at this —** a esta sazón, en esta coyuntura.
**June** [dʒun] *s.* junio.
**jungle** [dʒʌŋgl] *s.* selva; matorral; *Am.* jungla; *Carib.* manigua.
**junior** [dʒúnjɚ] *adj.* menor, más joven; — **college** colegio para los dos primeros años del bachillerato; **John Smith, Junior (Jr.)** John Smith, hijo; *s.* estudiante del tercer año (*en escuela superior, colegio o universidad*).
**juniper** [dʒúnɪpɚ] *s.* junípero; enebro.
**junk** [dʒʌŋk] *s.* basura, desperdicios; trastos viejos; cosa inservible; **Chinese —** junco chino (*embarcación pequeña*); *v.* desechar, echar a la basura.

IS

**jurisdiction** [dʒurɪsdíkʃən] s. jurisdicción.

**jurisprudence** [dʒurɪsprúdn̩s] s. jurisprudencia, derecho.

**juror** [dʒúrɚ] s. jurado, miembro de un jurado.

**jury** [dʒúrɪ] s. jurado; **grand —** jurado de acusación.

**just** [dʒʌst] adj. justo; recto; exacto; adv. ni más ni menos, exactamente, justamente; precisamente; sólo, no más, nada más; apenas; **— now** ahora mismo; **he — left** acaba de salir, Am. salió recién; **she is — a little girl** no es más que una niña, es una niña no más; **to have —** acabar de.

**justice** [dʒʌ́stɪs] s. justicia; juez; magistrado.

**justification** [dʒʌstəfəkéʃən] s. justificación.

**justify** [dʒʌ́stəfaɪ] v. justificar.

**justly** [dʒʌ́stlɪ] adv. justamente; con razón.

**jut** [dʒʌt] v. sobresalir, proyectarse, extenderse; s. salidizo, proyección.

**juvenile** [dʒʒúvən̩l] adj. juvenil.

# K

**kangaroo** [kæŋgərú] s. canguro.

**keel** [kil] s. quilla; v. dar de quilla (voltear un barco); **to — over** volcar(se); zozobrar; caerse patas arriba, desplomarse.

**keen** [kin] adj. agudo; afilado; perspicaz; ansioso.

**keenness** [kínnɪs] s. agudeza; perspicacia; anhelo, ansia.

**keep** [kip] v. guardar; tener guardado; tener; retener; conservar(se); preservar(se); mantener(se); **to — accounts** llevar las cuentas; **to — at it** persistir, seguir dale que dale; **to — away** mantener(se) alejado; **to — back** tener a raya; detener; reprimir, restringir; **to — from** impedir; guardar(se) de; abstenerse de; **to — going** seguir andando, seguir adelante; seguir viviendo; **to — off** no arrimarse, no acercarse; no entrar; mantener(se) a distancia; **to — one's hands off** no tocar; **to — one's temper** contenerse, refrenarse, reprimirse; **to — quiet** estarse quieto o callado; **to — something up** seguir o continuar haciendo algo; **to — to the right** seguir a la derecha; mantenerse a la derecha; **to — track of** llevar la cuenta de; no perder de vista; s. manutención, subsistencia; **for -s** para siempre; para guardar; dado, no prestado.

**keeper** [kípɚ] s. guardián, custodio; **jail —** carcelero.

**keeping** [kípɪŋ] s. custodia; mantenimiento; preservación, conservación; **in — with** en armonía con.

**keepsake** [kípsek] s. prenda, recuerdo, regalo.

**keg** [kɛg] s. tonel, barril.

**kennel** [kén̩l] s. perrera.

**kept** [kɛpt] pret. & p.p. de **to keep.**

**kerchief** [kɝ́tʃɪf] s. pañuelo, pañolón.

**kernel** [kɝ́nl̩] s. simiente; grano (de trigo o maíz); meollo (de ciertas frutas como la nuez); núcleo.

**kerosene** [kérəsin] s. kerosina, petróleo para lámparas.

**kettle** [kétl̩] s. caldera; **—drum** tímpano; **tea—** marmita, tetera, Am. pava (para el mate).

**key** [ki] s. (lock) llave; (music) clave; (instrument) tecla; (land) cayo; isleta; **— ring** llavero; **to be in —** estar a tono, estar templado; estar en armonía; v. poner a tono, afinar, templar (con llave); armonizar; **to — up** elevar el tono de; **to be -ed up** estar sobre-excitado, estar en tensión nerviosa.

**keyboard** [kíbord] s. teclado.

**keyhole** [kíhol] s. ojo de la cerradura.

**keynote** [kínot] s. nota tónica; idea o principio fundamental.

**keystone** [kíston] s. clave (de un arco); base, fundamento principal.

**khaki** [káki] s. kaki, ·caqui; adj. de kaki.

**kick** [kɪk] s. (foot) Esp. coz; puntapié; Am. patada; (complaint) queja; protesta; fuerza (de una bebida); estímulo; **to have a —** Am. patear (dícese del licor); v. cocear; dar coces o patadas; dar puntapiés; patear; quejarse, protestar; **to — out** echar a patadas; echar, expulsar; **to — the bucket** estirar la pata, morir, Am. patear el balde; **to — up a lot of dust** levantar una polvareda.

**kid** [kɪd] s. cabrito; cabritilla (piel curtida de cabrito); niño, niña; **— gloves** guantes de cabritilla; v. bromear, embromar; chancearse con, Carib., Méx. chotear.

**kidnap** [kídnæp] v. secuestrar, raptar.

**kidnapper** [kídnæpɚ] s. secuestrador; robachicos, ladrón de niños.

**kidnapping** [kídnæpɪŋ] s. rapto, secuestro.

**kidney** [kídnɪ] s. riñon; **— bean** judía, frijol; **— stones** cálculos.

**kill** [kɪl] v. matar; destruir; amortiguar; parar (el motor); s. animal o animales matados (en la caza).

**killer** [kílɚ] s. matador; asesino.

**kiln** [kɪln] s. horno.

**kilo** [kílo], **kilogram** [kíləgræm] s. kilo, kilogramo.

**kilometer** [kíləmitɚ] s. kilómetro.

**kimono** [kəmónə] s. quimono; bata.

**kin** [kɪn] s. parentela, parientes, familia; **to notify the nearest of —** avisar al pariente o deudo más cercano.

**kind** [kaɪnd] adj. bondadoso; benévolo; amable; **to send one's — regards to** enviar afectuosos saludos a; **kind-hearted** de buen corazón; **— of tired** algo cansado; s.·clase, especie, género; **to pay in —** pagar en especie; pagar en la misma moneda.

**kindergarten** [kíndɚgɑrtn̩] s. escuela de párvulos.

**kindle** [kíndl̩] v. encender(se); inflamar(se); incitar; prender (el fuego).

**kindling** [kíndlɪŋ] s. encendimiento;

leña ligera, astillas, *Andes* charamuscas.

**kindly** [káɪndlɪ] *adj.* bondadoso; benigno; benévolo; amable, apacible; *adv.* bondadosamente, ambablemente; con benevolencia; por favor; **not to take — to criticism** no aceptar de buen grado las correcciones.

**kindness** [káɪndnɪs] *s.* bondad, amabilidad; gentileza; benevolencia; favor.

**kindred** [kíndrɪd] *adj.* emparentado; allegado; semejante; **— facts** hechos relacionados; **— spirits** espíritus afines.

**kinesics** [kaɪnízɪks] *s.* kinésica; quinésica.

**king** [kɪŋ] *s.* rey; rey (*en ajedrez*); dama (*en el juego de damas*).

**kingdom** [kíŋdəm] *s.* reino.

**kingly** [kíŋlɪ] *adj.* regio; real; majestuoso; *adv.* regiamente; majestuosamente.

**kink** [kɪŋk] *s.* (*bend*) enroscadura; (*pain*) tortícolis.

**kinky** [kíŋkɪ] *adj.* crespo, ensortijado, *Am.* grifo.

**kinship** [kínʃɪp] *s.* parentesco; afinidad; semejanza.

**kinsman** [kínzmən] *s.* pariente, deudo.

**kiss** [kɪs] *s.* beso; *v.* besar.

**kit** [kɪt] *s.* estuche, caja de herramientas; saco, envoltura (*para guardar instrumentos, herramientas, etc.*); gatito; **medicine —** botiquín; **soldier's —** mochila.

**kitchen** [kítʃɪn] *s.* cocina; **—ware** trastos de cocina.

**kite** [kaɪt] *s.* cometa (*f.*), *Méx.* papalote; *Ch.* volantín; *Arg.* barrilete; milano (*pájaro*).

**kitten** [kítṇ] *s.* gatito.

**kitty** [kítɪ] *s.* gatito, minino.

**knack** [næk] *s.* destreza, maña, habilidad.

**knapsack** [nǽpsæk] *s.* mochila, morral, alforja.

**knave** [nev] *s.* bribón, bellaco, pícaro; sota (*de naipes*).

**knead** [nid] *v.* amasar, sobar.

**knee** [ni] *s.* rodilla; **knee-deep** hasta la rodilla; metido hasta las rodillas.

**kneel** [nil] *v.* arrodillarse; hincarse.

**knell** [nɛl] *s.* doble (*toque de campanas por los difuntos*); *v.* doblar, tocar a muerto.

**knelt** [nɛlt] *pret. & p.p. de* **to kneel.**

**knew** [nju] *pret. de* **to know.**

**knickknack** [níknæk] *s.* chuchería, baratija, chisme.

**knife** [naɪf] *s.* cuchillo; cuchilla; **carving —** trinchante; **pocket —** cortaplumas; navaja; *v.* acuchillar.

**knight** [naɪt] *s.* caballero; campeón; caballo (*en ajedrez*); **— errant** caballero andante; *v.* armar caballero.

**knighthood** [náɪthud] *s.* caballería, orden de la caballería.

**knit** [nɪt] *v.* tejer (*a punto de aguja*); hacer calceta o malla; enlazar; soldarse (*un hueso*) **to — one's brow** fruncir las cejas, arrugar la frente; *pret. & p.p.*

*de* **to knit.**

**knitting** [nítɪŋ] *s.* labor de punto; **— needle** aguja de media.

**knives** [naɪvz] *pl. de* **knife.**

**knob** [nɑb] *s.* perilla, botón, tirador (*de puerta, cajón, etc.*); protuberancia.

**knock** [nɑk] *v.* (*pound*) golpear, golpetear; llamar o tocar a la puerta; (*criticize*) criticar, censurar o hablar mal de; **to — down** derribar; desmontar (*una máquina o aparato*); **to — off** suspender (*el trabajo*); rebajar (*del precio*); derribar, echar abajo; **to — out** aplastar de un golpe, poner fuera de combate; dejar sin sentido; *s.* golpe; golpeteo; toque, llamada, aldabonazo; crítica, censura; **knock-kneed** zambo, patizambo.

**knocker** [nɑ́kɚ] *s.* llamador, aldaba, aldabón; criticón, murmurador.

**knoll** [nol] *s.* colina, loma; eminencia.

**knot** [nɑt] *s.* nudo; lazo; *v.* anudar(se).

**knotty** [nɑ́tɪ] *adj.* nudoso; dificultoso, enredado.

**know** [no] *v.* (*to be acquainted with*) conocer; (*to have knowledge of;* **to know how to**) saber; (*to recognize*) reconocer; distinguir; **to — how to swim** saber nadar; **to — of** saber de; tener conocimiento de; tener noticias de; estar enterado de.

**knowingly** [nóɪŋlɪ] *adv.* a sabiendas; adrede.

**knowledge** [nálɪdʒ] *s.* conocimiento; saber, sabiduría; pericia; **not to my — no que yo sepa.**

**known** [non] *p.p. de* **to know.**

**knuckle** [nʌ́kḷ] *s.* nudillo; coyuntura, articulación; artejo; *v.* someterse; **to — down** someterse; aplicarse con empeño al trabajo.

## L

**label** [lébḷ] *s.* marbete, etiqueta, rótulo; *v.* marcar, rotular; apodar, llamar.

**labor** [lébɚ] *s.* trabajo; labor; obra; mano de obra; la clase obrera; **— union** unión de obreros; **to be in —** estar de parto; *v.* trabajar; afanarse; estar de parto; elaborar (*un punto*).

**laboratory** [lǽbrətorɪ] *s.* laboratorio.

**laborer** [lébərɚ] *s.* trabajador, obrero; jornalero, peón.

**laborious** [ləbórɪəs] *adj.* laborioso, trabajoso, penoso; industrioso.

**labyrinth** [lǽbərɪnθ] *s.* laberinto.

**lace** [les] *s.* (*cloth*) encaje; (*cord*) cordón, cordoncillo, cinta (*de corsé, etc.*); **gold —** galón de oro (*para guarnecer uniformes*); *v.* atar con cinta o cordón; guarnecer con encajes; enlazar, entrelazar.

**lack** [læk] *s.* falta; escasez, carencia; deficiencia; *v.* carecer de, faltarle a uno; necesitar; **he -s courage** le falta ánimo.

**lackey** [lǽkɪ] *s.* lacayo.

**lacking** [lǽkɪŋ] *adj.* falto, carente.

**lacquer** [lǽkɚ] *s.* laca; *v.* barnizar con laca.

**lad** [læd] *s.* rapaz, chico.

**ladder** [lǽdɚ] *s.* escalera de mano.
**laden** [lédn̩] *adj.* cargado; agobiado, abrumado; *v.* cargar; agobiar.
**ladies** [lédɪz] *pl. de* lady.
**ladle** [lédl] *s.* cucharón; *v.* servir (*sopa*) con cucharón.
**lady** [lédɪ] *s.* señora; dama; —**like** como señora, muy fina, elegante; —**love** amada, querida.
**lag** [læg] *v.* rezagarse, quedarse atrás, atrasarse; andar lentamente; *s.* retardo o retardación, retraso.
**lagoon** [lagún] *s.* laguna.
**laid** [led] *pret. & p.p. de* to lay; **to be — up** estar incapacitado o estropeado.
**lain** [len] *p.p. de* to lie.
**lair** [lɛr] *s.* guarida; cueva de fieras.
**lake** [lek] *s.* lago.
**lamb** [læm] cordero; —**kin** corderito.
**lame** [lem] *adj.* cojo; lisiado; estropeado; —**excuse** disculpa falsa; *v.* hacer cojo; estropear, incapacitar.
**lament** [ləmént] *s.* lamento; *v.* lamentar(se).
**lamentable** [lǽməntəbl̩] *adj.* lamentable; doloroso.
**lamentation** [læməntéʃən] *s.* lamentación, lamento.
**laminate** [lǽmənet] *v.* laminar.
**lamp** [læmp] *s.* lámpara; linterna; farol; —**post** poste (de farol); —**shade** pantalla de lámpara.
**lance** [læns] *s.* lanza; *v.* alancear, lancear, herir con lanza; picar con bisturí.
**land** [lænd] *s.* tierra; terreno; suelo; *v.* desembarcar; aterrizar (*un avión*); llegar; coger (*un pez*); **to — a job** conseguir una colocacion, lograr un empleo.
**land-grant** [lǽndgrænt] *adj.* mediante donación federal de tierras.
**landholder** [lǽndholdɚ] *s.* terrateniente, propietario, hacendado.
**landing** [lǽndɪŋ] *s.* (*act*) desembarco, desembarque; aterrizaje (*de un avión*); (*place*) desembarcadero; descanso (*de escalera*); —**field** campo de aterrizaje; aeropuerto; —**strip** pista de aterrizaje.
**landlady** [lǽndledɪ] *s.* patrona, casera, dueña (*de la casa*).
**landlord** [lǽndlɔrd] *s.* amo, patrón, propietario, dueño; casero.
**landmark** [lǽndmark] *s.* mojón, señal (*para fijar los confines*); marca; suceso culminante.
**landowner** [lǽndonɚ] *s.* terrateniente, propietario, hacendado.
**landscape** [lǽndskep] *s.* paisaje.
**landslide** [lǽndslaɪd] *s.* derrumbe, derrumbamiento, desplome; gran mayoría de votos.
**lane** [len] *s.* senda, vereda; callejuela; ruta, derrotero (*de vapores o aviones*).
**language** [lǽŋgwɪdʒ] *s.* lengua; idioma; lenguaje.
**languid** [lǽŋgwɪd] *adj.* lánguido.
**languish** [lǽŋgwɪʃ] *v.* languidecer.
**languor** [lǽŋgɚ] *d.* languidez.
**lank** [læŋk] *adj.* alto y delgado, largucho.
**lanky** [lǽŋkɪ] *adj.* largucho, zancón,

zancudo.
**lantern** [lǽntɚn] *s.* linterna; farol.
**lap** [læp] *s.* falda, regazo; aleta; etapa, trecho (*de una carrera*); *v.* lamer; **to — over** cruzar(se) sobre, entrecruzar(se).
**lapel** [ləpél] *s.* solapa.
**lapidary** [lǽpɪdɛrɪ] *s. & adj.* lapidario.
**lapse** [læps] *s.* lapso; transcurso; desliz; error; *v.* deslizarse; pasar, transcurrir; caer en un desliz; decaer (*el entusiasmo, el interés, etc.*); caducar (*un plazo, un contrato, etc.*).
**larboard** [lárbɚd] *s.* babor; *adj.* de babor; —**side** banda de babor.
**larceny** [lársn̩ɪ] *s.* latrocinio, hurto; ratería.
**lard** [lɑrd] *s.* lardo, manteca de puerco; *v.* mechar.
**large** [lɑrdʒ] *adj.* grande; **at —** suelto, libre; sin trabas; en general; **-ly** *adv.* grandemente, en gran parte.
**large-scale** [lárdʒskél] *adj.* en grande escala.
**lariat** [lǽrɪət] *s.* reata.
**lark** [lɑrk] *s.* (*bird*) alondra; (*fun*) diversión, holgorio, jarana; **to go on a —** ir o andar de jarana.
**larva** [lárvə] *s.* larva.
**larynx** [lǽrɪŋks] *s.* laringe.
**lascivious** [ləsívɪəs] *adj.* lascivo.
**lash** [læʃ] *s.* látigo; azote, latigazo; pestaña; *v.* fustigar; azotar; censurar, reprender; amarrar.
**lass** [læs] *s.* moza, muchacha, doncella.
**lassitude** [lǽsətjud] *s.* dejadez, flojedad, decaimiento de fuerzas.
**lasso** [lǽso] *s.* lazo, reata, mangana; *v.* lazar, *Am.* enlazar.
**last** [læst] *adj.* (*in a series*) último; final; (*just passed*); pasado; —**night** anoche; —**year** el año pasado; **at —** por fin, finalmente, al fin; **next to the —** penúltimo; **to arrive —** llegar el último; *s.* fin, término; horma (*de zapato*); *v.* durar; perdurar; **-ly** *adv.* finalmente, en conclusión.
**lasting** [lǽstɪŋ] *adj.* duradero; perdurable.
**latch** [lætʃ] *s.* pestillo, picaporte, aldaba, cerrojo; *v.* cerrar con aldaba.
**late** [let] *adj.* (*tardy*) tardío; tardo; (*recent*) reciente; último; —**comer** recién llegado; rezagado; **a — hour** una hora avanzada; **the — Mr. X** el finado (*o difunto*) Sr. X; **to have a — supper** cenar tarde; *adv.* tarde; **— in the night** a una hora avanzada de la noche; **— into the night** a deshoras de la noche; **— in the week** a fines de la semana; **of —** últimamente, recientemente; hace poco; **to be —** ser tarde; llegar tarde; estar atrasado; venir o llegar con retraso (*el tren*); **the train was ten minutes —** el tren llegó con diez minutos de retraso; **-ly** últimamente, recientemente; hace poco, poco ha.
**latent** [létn̩t] *adj.* latente.
**later** [létɚ] *adv. & adj.* (*comp. de* late) más tarde; después, luego; más re-

ciente; posterior.

**lateral** [lǽtərəl] *adj.* lateral.

**latest** [létɪst] *adv.* & *adj.* (*superl. de* **late**) más tarde; más reciente, más nuevo; último; **the — fashion** la última moda, las últimas novedades; **the — news** las últimas novedades, las noticias más recientes; **at the —** a más tardar.

**lathe** [leð] *s.* torno (*de carpintero o mecánico*).

**lather** [lǽðə] *s.* jabonadura, espuma de jabón; *v.* jabonar, enjabonar; espumar, hacer espuma.

**Latin** [lǽtn̩] *adj.* latino; *s.* latín.

**latitude** [lǽtətjud] *s.* latitud; libertad; amplitud.

**latter** [lǽtə] *adj.* último; **towards the — part of the week** a (*o* hacia) fines de la semana; **the —** éste (ésta, esto, etc.).

**lattice** [lǽtɪs] *s.* celosía; enrejado, rejilla.

**laud** [lɔd] *v.* loar, encomiar, alabar.

**laudable** [lɔ́dəbl] *adj.* laudable, loable.

**laugh** [læf] *v.* reír(se); **to — at** reírse de; **to — loudly** reírse a carcajadas; **to — in one's sleeve** reírse para sus adentros; **she -ed in his face** se rió en sus barbas; *s.* risa; **loud —** risotada, carcajada, risada.

**laughable** [lǽfəbl] *adj.* risible; ridículo.

**laughter** [lǽftə] *s.* risa.

**launch** [lɔntʃ] *v.* (*put into water*) botar o echar (*un barco*) al agua; (*a rocket*) lanzar; (*begin*) empezar, poner en operación; **to — forth** lanzarse; **to — forth on a journey** emprender un viaje; *s.* lancha.

**launder** [lɔ́ndə] *v.* lavar y planchar (*la ropa*).

**laundress** [lɔ́ndrɪs] *s.* lavandera.

**laundry** [lɔ́ndrɪ] *s.* lavandería; lavado; ropa (lavada).

**laurel** [lɔ́rəl] *s.* laurel; gloria, honor.

**lava** [lávə] *s.* lava.

**lavatory** [lǽvətorɪ] *s.* lavabo; lavamanos; lavatorio.

**lavender** [lǽvəndə] *s.* espliego, lavándula; *adj.* lila, morado claro.

**lavish** [lǽvɪʃ] *adj.* gastador, pródigo, dadivoso; abundante, copioso; profuso; lujoso; *v.* prodigar; malgastar, despilfarrar; **to — praise upon** colmar de alabanzas a; **-ly** pródigamente; copiosamente; lujosamente.

**law** [lɔ] *s.* ley; derecho, jurisprudencia; regla; **— student** estudiante de leyes, estudiante de derecho; **law-abiding** observante de la ley.

**lawbreaker** [lɔ́brekə] *s.* infactor, transgresor.

**lawful** [lɔ́fəl] *adj.* legal; lícito; válido; permitido.

**lawless** [lɔ́lɪs] *adj.* sin ley; ilegal; desenfrenado; revoltoso; licencioso.

**lawmaker** [lɔ́mekə] *s.* legislador.

**lawn** [lɔn] *s.* césped, prado; linón (*tela de hilo o algodón*); **— mower** cortadora de césped.

**lawsuit** [lɔ́sut] *s.* pleito, litigio.

**lawyer** [lɔ́jə] *s.* abogado, jurisconsulto.

**lax** [læks] flojo; suelto; relajado.

**laxative** [lǽksətɪv] *adj.* & *s.* laxante, purgante.

**laxity** [lǽksətɪ] *s.* flojedad, flojera; relajamiento (*de une regla, ley, etc.*).

**lay** [le] *pret. de* **to lie.**

**lay** [le] *v.* colocar; poner; tender, extender; poner (*huevos*); echar (*la culpa*); atribuir (*la responsabilidad*); presentar, exponer; asentar (*el polvo*); **to — a wager** apostar; **to — aside** poner a un lado; ahorrar; **to — away** (*o* by) guardar; **to — bare** revelar; exponer; **to — down** poner, colocar; rendir (*las armas*); **to — down the law** mandar, dictar; **to — hold of** asir, agarrar; **to — off a workman** suspender a un obrero; **to — open** exponer a la vista; **to — out a plan** trazar un plan; **to — up** almacenar; guardar, ahorrar; **to be laid up** estar incapacitado o estropeado; **to — waste** asolar; *s.* lay, balada, canción; situación, orientación (*del terreno*); *adj.* lego, laico; profano (*no iniciado en una ciencia*).

**layer** [léə] *s.* capa; estrato; gallina ponedora.

**layman** [lémən] *s.* lego, seglar, laico.

**lazily** [lézɪlɪ] *adv.* perezosamente.

**laziness** [lézɪnɪs] *s.* pereza.

**lazy** [lézɪ] *adj.* perezoso, holgazán.

**lead** [lɛd] *s.* plomo; plomada, pesa de plomo.

**lead** [lid] *v.* (*guide*) guiar, dirigir; llevar; conducir; mandar (*un ejército*); (*precede*) ir a la cabeza de; sobresalir entre; ser mano (*en el juego de naipes*); **to — an orchestra** dirigir una orquesta, llevar la batuta; **to — astray** llevar por mal camino, extraviar, descarriar; **to — the way** ir por delante, mostrar el camino; *s.* delantera, primer lugar; mando, dirección; indicio; papel principal; primer actor.

**leaden** [lédn̩] *adj.* plomizo; aplomado, color de plomo; pesado.

**leader** [lídə] *s.* jefe, caudillo, *Am.* líder; director; guía; caballo delantero; **-s** puntos suspensivos.

**leadership** [lídəʃɪp] *s.* dirección, mando; iniciativa.

**leading** [lídɪŋ] *adj.* principal; delantero; **— man** primer actor.

**leadoff** [lídɔf] *adj.* delantero; puntero.

**leaf** [lif] *s.* hoja; *v.* echar hojas (*un árbol*), cubrirse de hojas; **to — through a book** hojear un libro.

**leafless** [líflɪs] *adj.* sin hojas, deshojado.

**leaflet** [líflɪt] *s.* hojilla; folleto, hoja volante, papel volante, circular.

**leafy** [lífɪ] *adj.* frondoso.

**league** [lig] *s.* (*alliance*) liga, confederación; sociedad; (*distance*) legua; *v.* asociar(se); ligarse, coligarse.

**leak** [lik] *s.* gotera (*en un techo*); agujero, grieta (*por donde se escapa el agua o el gas*); escape (*de gas, vapor, electricidad, etc.*); *v.* gotear(se); rezumar(se);

LA

hacer agua (*dícese de un barco*); salirse, escaparse (*el gas, el vapor, etc.*).

**lean** [lin] *v.* (*incline*) inclinar(se); recostar(se), reclinar(se); (*support*) apoyar(se); *adj.* magro; flaco; — **year** año estéril, año improductivo.

**leant** [lɛnt] = **leaned.**

**leap** [lip] *v.* saltar; brincar; *s.* salto, brinco; — **year** año bisiesto.

**leapt** [lɛpt] *pret. & p.p. de* **to leap.**

**learn** [lɜn] *v.* aprender; saber, averiguar, enterarse de.

**learned** [lɜnɪd] *adj.* erudito; docto.

**learner** [lɜnə] *s.* aprendedor; estudiante, estudioso.

**learning** [lɜnɪŋ] *s.* erudición, saber; aprendizaje.

**learnt** [lɜnt] *pret. & p.p. de* **to learn.**

**lease** [lis] *v.* arrendar, dar o tomar en arriendo; *s.* arriendo, contrato de arrendamiento.

**leash** [liʃ] *s.* traílla; cuerda.

**least** [list] *adj.* (el) mínimo, (el) más pequeño; *adv.* menos; **at** — al menos, a lo menos, por lo menos; **the** — lo (el, la) menos.

**leather** [léðə] *s.* cuero, piel; *adj.* de cuero, de piel; — **strap** correa.

**leave** [liv] *v.* dejar; abandonar; salir (de); partir; irse; **to** — **out** dejar fuera; omitir; *s.* permiso, licencia; — **of absence** licencia; **to take** — **of** despedirse de.

**leaven** [lévən] *s.* levadura, fermento; *v.* fermentar (*la masa*).

**leaves** [livz] *pl. de* **leaf.**

**leavings** [lívɪŋz] *s.* sobras, desperdicios.

**lecture** [léktʃə] *s.* conferencia, discurso; reprensión; *v.* dar una conferencia; explicar; reprender.

**lecturer** [léktʃərə] *s.* conferenciante; lector (*de universidad*).

**led** [lɛd] *pret. & p.p. de* **to lead.**

**ledge** [lɛdʒ] *s.* borde; salidizo.

**ledger** [lédʒə] *s.* libro mayor (*en contabilidad*).

**leech** [litʃ] *s.* sanguijuela.

**leer** [lɪr] *s.* mirada de soslayo, mirada lujuriosa; *v.* mirar de soslayo; mirar con lujuria.

**leeward** [líwəd] *s. & adv.* sotavento.

**left** [lɛft] *pret. & p.p. de* **to leave; I have two books** — me quedan dos libros; *adj.* izquierdo; *s.* izquierda; **mano izquierda; at (on, to) the** — a la izquierda.

**left-handed** [léfthǽndɪd] *adj.* zurdo; a la izquierda; torpe; malicioso, insincero; — **compliment** alabanza irónica.

**leftist** [léftɪst] *s.* izquierdista.

**leftover** [léftovə] *adj.* sobrante; **-s** *s. pl.* sobras.

**left-wing** [léftwɪŋ] *adj.* izquierdista.

**leg** [lɛg] *s.* pierna; pata (*de animal, mesa, etc.*); pie o pata (*de banquillo, silla, etc.*); etapa, trecho (*de una carrera o viaje*); **to be on one's last -s** estar en las últimas.

**legacy** [légəsɪ] *s.* legado, herencia.

**legal** [lígl] *adj.* legal; lícito.

**legalize** [líglaɪz] *v.* legalizar; sancionar, autorizar.

**legate** [légɪt] *s.* legado; delegado.

**legation** [lɪgéʃən] *s.* legación; embajada.

**legend** [lédʒənd] *s.* leyenda; letrero, inscripción.

**legendary** [lédʒəndɛrɪ] *adj.* legendario.

**leggings** [légɪŋz] *s. pl.* polainas.

**legible** [lédʒəbl] *adj.* legible.

**legion** [lídʒən] *s.* legión.

**legislate** [lédʒɪslet] *v.* legislar.

**legislation** [lɛdʒɪsléʃən] *s.* legislación.

**legislative** [lédʒɪsletɪv] *adj.* legislativo.

**legislator** [lédʒɪsletə] *s.* legislador.

**legislature** [lédʒɪsletʃə] *s.* legislatura, asamblea legislativa.

**legitimate** [lɪdʒítəmɪt] *adj.* legítimo.

**leisure** [líʒə] *s.* ocio; — **hours** horas de ocio; **to be at** — estar ocioso; estar libre o desocupado; **do it at your** — hágalo Vd. cuando pueda o le convenga; hágalo Vd. en sus ratos de ocio.

**leisurely** [líʒəlɪ] *adj.* lento, deliberado, pausado; *adv.* sin prisa, despacio, a sus (mis, tus, *etc.*) anchas.

**lemon** [lémən] *s.* limón; — **tree** limonero; *adj.* de limón; — **color** cetrino.

**lemonade** [lɛmənéd] *s.* limonada.

**lend** [lɛnd] *v.* prestar.

**lender** [léndə] *s.* prestador; **money** — prestamista.

**length** [lɛŋkθ] *s.* largo, largor, largura, longitud; duración; cantidad (*de una sílaba*); **at** — largamente, detenidamente; al fin; **to go to any** — hacer cuanto esté de su parte.

**lengthen** [léŋkθən] *v.* alargar(se); prolongar(se).

**lengthwise** [léŋkθwaɪz] *adv.* a lo largo; longitudinalmente; *adj.* longitudinal.

**lengthy** [léŋkθɪ] *adj.* largo, prolongado.

**lenient** [líniənt] *adj.* indulgente, clemente, poco severo.

**lens** [lɛnz] *s.* lente; cristalino (*del ojo*).

**lent** [lɛnt] *pret. & p.p. de* **to lend.**

**Lent** [lɛnt] *s.* cuaresma.

**leopard** [lépəd] *s.* leopardo.

**less** [lɛs] *adj.* menor; *adv. & prep.* menos; — **and** — cada vez menos.

**lessen** [lésṇ] *v.* aminorar(se), disminuir(se), reducir(se); mermar.

**lesser** [lésə] *adj.* menor, más pequeño.

**lesson** [lésṇ] *s.* lección.

**lest** [lɛst] *conj.* no sea que, por miedo de que.

**let** [lɛt] *v.* (*permit*) dejar, permitir; (*rent*) alquilar, arrendar; — **us** (*o* **let's**) **do it** vamos a hacerlo, hagámoslo; — **him come** que venga; **to** — **be** no molestar, dejar en paz; no tocar; **to** — **down** bajar; desilusionar; **to** — **go** soltar; **to** — **in** dejar entrar, admitir; **to** — **know** avisar, enterar, hacer saber; **to** — **off** soltar; dejar libre; **to** — **through** dejar pasar; **to** — **up** disminuir; *pret. & p.p. de* **to let.**

**letdown** [létdɑʊn] *s.* aflojamiento; desilusión.

**lethal** [líθəl] *adj.* letal.

**lethargy** [léθədʒɪ] *s.* letargo; **to fall into a** — aletargarse.

**letter** [létæ] *s. (alphabet)* letra; *(missive)* carta; **— box** buzón; **— carrier** cartero; **—head** membrete; *v.* rotular, hacer a mano letras de molde.

**lettuce** [létɪs] *s.* lechuga.

**level** [lévl] *adj.* llano, plano; a nivel; igual; parejo; **level-headed** bien equilibrado, sensato; *adv.* a nivel; a ras; *s.* nivel; **to be on the —** obrar rectamente, obrar sin engaño; ser o decir la pura verdad; *v.* nivelar; igualar; allanar; apuntar, asestar *(un arma)*; **to — to the ground** arrasar, echar por tierra.

**lever** [lévæ] *s.* palanca; **control —** palanca de mando.

**levity** [lévɪtɪ] *s.* frivolidad; levedad.

**levy** [lévɪ] *s.* imposición, recaudación *(de tributos, impuestos, etc.)*; leva, enganche, reclutamiento; embargo *(de propiedad)*; *v.* imponer, exigir, recaudar *(tributos o multas)*; reclutar; **to — on someone's property** embargar la propiedad de alguien.

**lewd** [lud] *adj.* lujurioso, lascivo, deshonesto.

**lewdness** [lúdnɪs] *s.* lascivia, lujuria.

**lexicon** [léksɪkɑn] *s.* léxico.

**liability** [laɪəbílətɪ] *s.* responsabilidad; obligación; desventaga; **liabilities** obligaciones, deudas; pasivo.

**liable** [láɪəbl] *adj.* responsable, obligado; sujeto, expuesto; propenso; probable.

**liaison** [liezán] *s.* enlace; unión.

**liar** [láɪæ] *s.* mentiroso, embustero.

**libel** [láɪbl] *s.* libelo; difamación; *v.* difamar.

**liberal** [líbərəl] *adj. & s.* liberal.

**liberalism** [líbərəlɪzm] *s.* liberalismo.

**liberality** [lɪbərǽlətɪ] *s.* liberalidad; largueza, generosidad.

**liberalize** [líbəəlaɪz] *v.* liberalizar(se).

**liberate** [líbəret] *v.* libertar, librar; soltar.

**liberation** [lɪbəréʃən] *s.* liberación.

**liberator** [líbəretæ] *s.* libertador.

**libertine** [líbətin] *adj. & s.* libertino.

**liberty** [líbətɪ] *s.* libertad; **at —** libre.

**librarian** [laɪbrérɪən] *s.* bibliotecario.

**library** [láɪbrɛrɪ] *s.* biblioteca.

**lice** [laɪs] *pl. de* **louse.**

**license, licence** [láɪsn̩s] *s.* licencia; permiso; título; **driver's —** licencia *(pase, certificado o patente)* de chófer; título de conductor; licencia para manejar; **— plate** placa *(o* chapa*)* de numeración, chapa de circulación, chapa de matrícula; *v.* licenciar, dar licencia a; permitir, autorizar.

**licentious** [laɪsénʃəs] *adj.* licencioso, disoluto.

**lick** [lɪk] *v. (tongue)* lamer; *(thrash)* dar una tunda o zurra; vencer; **to — someone's boots** adular a uno con servilismo; **to — the dust** morder el polvo; adular; *s.* lamedura, *Am.* lamida; lengüetada; *C.A.* lambida; **salt —** lamedero *(lugar salino donde lame el ganado)*; **not to do a — of work** no hacer absolutamente nada.

**licking** [líkɪŋ] *s.* zurra, tunda.

**lid** [lɪd] *s.* tapadera, tapa; **eye—** párpado.

**lie** [laɪ] *s.* mentira; embuste; **to give the — to** desmentir, dar un mentís; *v.* mentir *(pret. & p.p.* **lied***)*; tenderse, acostarse; yacer; estar; estar situado; consistir (en); **to — back** recostarse, echarse hacia atrás; **to — down** acostarse, echarse, tenderse; **to — in wait** acechar, espiar.

**lieutenant** [luténənt] *s.* teniente; **second —** subteniente.

**life** [laɪf] *s.* vida; **from —** del natural; **still —** naturaleza muerta; **—boat** bote de salvamento, lancha salvavidas; **— imprisonment** prisión perpetua; **— insurance** seguro sobre la vida; **— pension** pensión vitalicia; **— preserver** salvavidas, cinto o chaqueta de salvamento.

**lifeless** [láɪflɪs] *adj.* sin vida; muerto; exánime; inanimado; desanimado.

**lifelessness** [láɪflɪsnɪs] *s.* falta de vida; inercia; falta de animación.

**lifelike** [láɪflaɪk] *adj.* como la vida; natural, que parece vivo.

**lifelong** [láɪflɔ́ŋ] *adj.* perpetuo, de toda la vida.

**lifetime** [láɪftaɪm] *s.* vida, transcurso de la vida.

**lift** [lɪft] *v.* levantar; alzar; elevar; disiparse *(las nubes, la niebla, las tinieblas)*; **to — one's hat** quitarse el sombrero *(para saludar)*; *s.* elevación; exaltación de ánimo; alzamiento, levantamiento; carga; ayuda *(para levantar una carga)*; alza *(de un zapato)*; ascensor, *Am.* elevador; **to give someone a — in a car** llevar a alguien en el auto.

**ligature** [lígətʃur] *s.* ligadura.

**light** [laɪt] *s.* luz; lumbre; **tail —** *Am.* farito trasero, *Am.* farol de cola, *Méx.* calavera; *adj.* claro; con luz; de tez blanca; ligero; leve; frívolo; **— drink** bebida suave; **—headed** frívolo, ligero de cascos; **—hearted** alegre; **— opera** opereta; **to make — of** dar poca importancia a; *v.* encender(se); iluminar, alumbrar; **to — upon** caer sobre; posarse en *(dícese de los pájaros, mariposas, etc.)*.

**lighten** [láɪtn̩] *v.* aligerar; iluminar; aclarar; relampaguear; alegrar.

**lighter** [láɪtæ] *s.* encendedor.

**lighthouse** [láɪthaus] *s.* faro.

**lighting** [láɪtɪŋ] *s.* iluminación; alumbrado.

**lightly** [láɪtlɪ] *adv.* ligeramente; levemente; frívolamente; sin seriedad.

**lightness** [láɪtnɪs] *s.* ligereza; frivolidad; claridad.

**lightning** [láɪtnɪŋ] *s.* relampagueo; relámpago; **— rod** pararrayos.

**lightweight** [láɪtwet] *s.* peso liviano; peso ligero.

**likable** [láɪkəbl] *adj.* agradable, simpático, placentero.

**like** [laɪk] *adv. & prep.* como; del mismo modo que; semejante a; *adj.* seme-

LE

jante, parecido; **in — manner** de manera semejante, del mismo modo; **to feel — going** tener ganas de ir; **to look — someone** parecerse a alguien; **it looks — rain** parece que va a llover, quiere llover; *s.* semejante, igual; **-s** gustos; preferencias; *v.* gustarle a uno; **he -s books** le gustan los libros; **do whatever you —** haz lo que gustes.

**likely** [láɪklɪ] *adj.* probable, creíble; prometedor; **— place** lugar a propósito; **it is — to happen** es probable que suceda; *adv.* probablemente.

**liken** [láɪkən] *v.* asemejar, comparar.

**likeness** [láɪknɪs] *s.* semejanza; parecido; retrato.

**likewise** [láɪkwaɪz] *adv.* igualmente, asimismo; del mismo modo; también.

**liking** [láɪkɪŋ] *s.* simpatía; afición; preferencia, gusto.

**lilac** [láɪlək] *s.* lila; *adj.* lila, morado claro.

**lily** [lílɪ] *s.* lirio; azucena.

**lily-white** [lɪlihwáɪt] *adj.* blanquísimo; puro; racialmente segregado.

**limb** [lɪm] *s.* rama (*de árbol*); miembro (*del cuerpo*), pierna, brazo.

**limber** [límbər] *adj.* flexible; ágil; *v.* hacer flexible; **to — up** agilitar(se), hacer(se) flexible.

**lime** [laɪm] *s.* cal; lima (*fruta*); liga (*para cazar pájaros*).

**limelight** [láɪmlaɪt] *s.* luz de calcio; proscenio; **to be in the —** estar a la vista del público.

**limestone** [láɪmston] *s.* piedra caliza.

**limit** [límɪt] *s.* límite; confín; *v.* limitar.

**limitation** [lɪmɪtéʃən] *s.* limitación; restricción.

**limited** [límɪtɪd] *adj.* limitado; restringido.

**limitless** [límɪtlɪs] *adj.* ilimitado, sin límites.

**limp** [lɪmp] *s.* cojera; *v.* cojear; renquear; *adj.* flojo; flexible.

**limpid** [límpɪd] *adj.* límpido; claro, transparente.

**line** [laɪn] *s.* (*mark*) línea; renglón; raya; (*cord*) cuerda; (*business*) ramo; giro (*de negocios*); especialidad; **— of goods** surtido, línea (*Am.* renglón) de mercancías; **branch railway —** ramal; **pipe —** cañería, tubería; **to bring into —** alinear; obligar a proceder de acuerdo con un plan; poner de acuerdo; **to get in —** meterse en fila, hacer (*o* formar) cola; *v.* linear, rayar; alinear; forrar; **to — up** alinear(se); formarse, formar fila.

**lineage** [líniɪdʒ] *s.* linaje.

**linear** [líniər] *adj.* lineal.

**lined** [laɪnd] *adj.* rayado; forrado.

**linen** [línɪn] *s.* lino; ropa blanca.

**liner** [láɪnər] *s.* vapor, buque; **air —** avión, transporte aéreo.

**lineup** [láɪnəp] *s.* formación.

**linger** [líŋgər] *v.* tardar(se), demorarse, dilatarse; andar ocioso, vagar; perdurar; prolongarse.

**lingerie** [lǽnʒəri] *s.* ropa interior de mujer.

**linguistics** [lɪŋgwístɪks] *s.* lengüística.

**lining** [láɪnɪŋ] *s.* forro.

**link** [lɪŋk] *s.* eslabón; enlace; **cuff -s** gemelos; *v.* eslabonar(se); enlazar(se).

**linnet** [línɪt] *s.* jilguero.

**linoleum** [lɪnólɪəm] *s.* linóleo (*tela impermeable para cubrir el suelo*).

**linseed** [línsid] *s.* linaza; **— oil** aceite de linaza.

**lint** [lɪnt] *s.* hilas; hilachas.

**lion** [láɪən] *s.* león.

**lioness** [láɪənɪs] *s.* leona.

**lip** [lɪp] *s.* labio.

**lipstick** [lípstɪk] *s.* lápiz para los labios.

**liquid** [líkwɪd] *adj.* líquido; **— assets** valores líquidos (*o* realizables); **— measure** medida para líquidos; *s.* líquido.

**liquidate** [líkwɪdet] *v.* liquidar, saldar (*cuentas*); poner término a.

**liquidation** [lɪkwɪdéʃən] *s.* liquidación; saldo de cuentas.

**liquor** [líkər] *s.* licor; bebida espiritosa (*como aguardiente, ron, etc.*).

**lisp** [lɪsp] *v.* ceceo; *v.* cecear; balbucir.

**list** [lɪst] *s.* lista; registro; escora (*inclinación de un barco*); *v.* alistar, registrar poner o apuntar en una lista; hacer una lista de; escorar, inclinarse a la banda.

**listen** [lísn̩] *v.* escuchar; atender, dar oídos, prestar atención; **—!** ¡oye! ¡escucha!; ¡oiga! ¡escuche!; **to — in** escuchar por radio; escuchar a hurtadillas (*una conversación*).

**listener** [lísnər] *s.* escuchador, oyente; **radio —** radioescucha, radioyente.

**listless** [lístlɪs] *adj.* abstraído; indiferente; indolente; desatento.

**listlessness** [lístlɪsnɪs] *s.* indiferencia, inatención, abstracción.

**lit** [lɪt] *pret. & p.p. de* **to light**; *adj.* alumbrado; algo borracho.

**literal** [lítərəl] *adj.* literal; **-ly** *adv.* al pie de la letra, literalmente.

**literary** [lítərɛrɪ] *adj.* literario.

**literature** [lítərətʃur] *s.* literatura; impresos, folletos, circulares.

**litigation** [lɪtəgéʃən] *s.* litigio, pleito.

**litter** [lítər] *s.* (*young animals*) camada, cría; (*stretcher*) litera; camilla; cama de paja para animales; (*disorder*) cosas esparcidas; desorden; revoltillo; *v.* desarreglar, revolver, esparcir cosas por.

**little** [lítl] *adj.* pequeño; poco; **— Bear** Osa Menor; **a — coffee** un poco de café; **a — while** un ratito (*o* ratico), un poco; *adv. & s.* poco; **— by —** poco a poco.

**live** [lɪv] *v.* vivir; **to — down** hacer olvidar, borrar (*el pasado*); **to — up to** vivir en conformidad con, vivir de acuerdo con.

**live** [laɪv] *adj.* (*not dead*) vivo; (*lively*) enérgico; vivo, activo; **— coal** ascua encendida; **— oak** encina; **— question** cuestión palpitante, cuestión de actualidad; **— wire** alambre cargado;

persona muy activa.

**livelihood** [láɪvlɪhʊd] *s.* vida, alimento, subsistencia, manutención.

**liveliness** [láɪvlɪnɪs] *s.* viveza, animación; agilidad.

**livelong** [lívlɔŋ] *adj.* todo; absolutamente todo.

**lively** [láɪvlɪ] *adj.* vivo; vivaz; animado, alegre; airoso; — **horse** caballo brioso; *adv.* vivamente; de prisa.

**liver** [lívɚ] *s.* hígado; vividor.

**livery** [lívɚɪ] *s.* librea; caballeriza (*para caballos de alquiler*); **auto** — garage para autos de alquiler.

**lives** [laɪvz] *pl. de* **life**.

**livestock** [láɪvstak] *s.* ganado.

**live wire** [láɪvwáɪr] *s.* persona alerta y vivaz.

**livid** [lívɪd] *adj.* lívido; amoratado.

**living** [lívɪŋ] *s.* (*state*) vida; (*means*) manutención, subsistencia; *adj.* vivo; viviente; — **room** sala; — **wage** sueldo suficiente para vivir; **the** — los vivos.

**lizard** [lízɚd] *s.* lagarto; **small** — lagartija.

**load** [lod] *s.* carga; **ship** — cargamento; **-s of** gran cantidad de; montones de; *v.* cargar; agobiar; colmar.

**loaf** [lof] *s.* hogaza de pan; **sugar** — azúcar de pilón; *v.* holgazanear, haraganear.

**loafer** [lófɚ] *s.* holgazán, haragán, zángano.

**loan** [lon] *s.* préstamo; empréstito; — **shark** usurero; — **word** préstamo semántico; *v.* prestar (*dinero*).

**loath** [loθ] *adj.* maldispuesto, renuente; **to be** — **to** repugnarle a uno.

**loathe** [loð] *v.* repugnarle a uno; abominar.

**loathsome** [lóðsəm] *adj.* repugnante, asqueroso; aborrecible.

**loaves** [lovz] *pl. de* **loaf**.

**lob** [lab] *v.* volear.

**lobby** [lábɪ] *s.* (*place*) vestíbulo; antecámara; salón de entrada; hall; (*influence*) camarilla (*que busca ventajas ante un cuerpo legislativo*); **hotel** — vestíbulo o patio del hotel; *v.* cabildear (*procurar ventajas o partidarios en una asamblea*).

**lobe** [lob] *s.* lóbulo.

**lobster** [lábstɚ] *s.* langosta de mar.

**local** [lókḷ] *adj.* local; — **train** tren ordinario.

**locality** [lokǽlətɪ] *s.* localidad; comarca.

**localize** [lókḷaɪz] *v.* localizar.

**locate** [lóket] *v.* situar, establecer; localizar, averiguar la posición de; avecindarse, radicarse, establecerse.

**location** [lokéʃən] *s.* situación; sitio, localidad.

**lock** [lak] *s.* (*door*) cerradura; (*canal*) esclusa (*de un canal*); llave (*de un arma de fuego*); guedeja (*de pelo*); bucle, rizo; *v.* cerrar con llave; trabar(se), juntar(se); entrelazar(se); **to** — **in** encerrar; **to** — **out** cerrar la puerta (*a alguien*), dejar afuera; **to** —

**up** encerrar; encarcelar.

**locker** [lákɚ] *s.* alacena; armario.

**locket** [lákɪt] *s.* guardapelo.

**lockout** [lákaʊt] *s.* paro (*suspensión del trabajo por parte de los empresarios*); cierre de fábrica.

**locksmith** [láksmɪθ] *s.* cerrajero.

**locomotive** [lokəmótɪv] *s.* locomotora; — **engineer** maquinista

**locust** [lókəst] *s.* langosta, saltamontes; cigarra; — **tree** algarrobo; acacia falsa.

**lodge** [ladʒ] *s.* logia; casita accesoria; casa de campo; *v.* alojar(se); hospedar(se); colocar; **to** — **a complaint** presentar una queja.

**lodger** [ládʒɚ] *s.* huésped, inquilino.

**lodging** [ládʒɪŋ] *s.* alojamiento, hospedaje; vivienda.

**loft** [lɔft] *s.* desván; galería, balcón interior (*de un templo*); **choir** — coro; **hay** — pajar.

**lofty** [lɔ́ftɪ] *adj.* elevado; sublime; altivo.

**log** [lɔg] *s.* leño, troza, tronco aserrado; corredera (*aparato para medir las millas que anda la nave*); diario de navegación; — **cabin** cabaña de troncos; *v.* cortar (*árboles*); cortar leños y transportarlos; registrar (*en el diario de navegación*).

**logic** [ládʒɪk] *s.* lógica.

**logical** [ládʒɪkḷ] *adj.* lógico.

**logroll** [lógrol] *v.* lograr aprobación de leyes mediante favores.

**loin** [lɔɪn] *s.* ijada, ijar, lomo.

**loiter** [lɔ́ɪtɚ] *v.* holgazanear, vagar, malgastar el tiempo; **to** — **behind** rezagarse.

**loll** [lal] *v.* arrellanarse o repantigarse, recostarse con toda comodidad.

**lone** [lon] *adj.* solo, solitario.

**loneliness** [lónlɪnɪs] *s.* soledad.

**lonely** [lónlɪ] *adj.* solo, solitario; triste, desamparado.

**lonesome** [lónsəm] *adj.* solo, solitario; triste, nostálgico.

**long** [lɔŋ] *adj.* largo; **the whole day** — todo el santo día; **three feet** — tres pies de largo; **to be** — **in coming** tardar en venir; *adv.* mucho, mucho tiempo; — **ago** hace mucho tiempo; **as** (*o* **so**) — **as** en tanto que, mientras que; **how** — **is it since . . . ?** ¿cuánto tiempo hace que . . . ?; **so** —! ¡hasta luego! ¡adiós!; **long-suffering** sufrido, paciente; **long-winded** prolijo, largo (*en hablar*); **long-distance** de larga distancia; *v.* anhelar; ansiar; **to** — **for** anhelar; suspirar por.

**longer** [lɔ́ŋgɚ] *adj.* más largo; *adv.* más, más tiempo; **no** — ya no; **not . . . any** — ya no; no . . . más.

**longevity** [landʒévətɪ] *s.* longevidad.

**longing** [lɔ́ŋɪŋ] *s.* anhelo, añoranza, nostalgia; *adj.* anhelante, anheloso, nostálgico; **-ly** *adv.* con anhelo, anhelosamente, con ansia.

**longitude** [lándʒətjud] *s.* longitud.

**longshoreman** [lɔ́ŋʃormən] *s.* estibador (*de barco o muelle*), cargador.

**long-term** [lɔ́ŋtɚm] *adj.* a largo plazo.
**look** [luk] *v.* (*see*) mirar; (*seem*) parecer; **it -s well on you** le cae (*o* le sienta) bien; **to — after** atender, cuidar; **to — alike** parecerse; asemejarse; **to — down on a person** mirar con desprecio (*o* menospreciar) a alguien; **to — for** buscar; esperar; **to — forward to** anticipar con placer; **to — into** examinar, investigar; **— out!** ¡cuidado!; ¡tenga cuidado!; **to — out of** asomarse a; **to — over** examinar; dar un vistazo a; **to — up** levantar la vista; buscar; **to — up to** admirar, mirar con respeto; *s.* mirada, vistazo; **-s** apariencia, aspecto; **to have good -s** ser bien parecido.
**looking glass** [lúkiŋglæs] *s.* espejo.
**lookout** [lúkaut] *s.* vigía; atalaya; mirador; vista, perspectiva; **that is your —** ¡eso a usted!; **to be on the —** estar alerta.
**loom** [lum] *s.* telar; *v.* destacarse, descollar; asomar(se), aparecer.
**loop** [lup] *s.* (*closed*) lazo, gaza, presilla; (*road*) vuelta, curva; (*electric*) circuito; *v.* hacer una gaza (con *o* en); atar con gaza o presilla; hacer un circuito.
**loophole** [lúphol] *s.* agujero, abertura; salida; escapatoria.
**loose** [lus] *adj.* (*slack*) suelto; flojo; (*unfettered*) desatado; (*licentious*) desoluto; **— change** suelto, moneda suelta; **— jointed** de articulaciones flojas; **to let —** soltar; *v.* soltar, desatar; aflojar; **-ly** *adv.* sueltamente; flojamente; con poca exactitud, sin fundamento.
**loosen** [lúsn̩] *v.* soltar(se); aflojar(se); desatar(se); **to — one's hold** desasirse, soltarse.
**looseness** [lúsnɪs] *s.* (*limberness*) soltura; flojedad; (*laxness*) flojera; holgura; relajación; (*of bowel*) flujo.
**loot** [lut] *s.* botín, pillaje, saqueo; *v.* saquear, pillar, robar.
**lop** [lap] *v.* tronchar, desmochar (*Am.* mochar).
**loquacious** [lokwéʃəs] *adj.* locuaz, hablador, lenguaraz.
**lord** [lɔrd] *s.* señor; dueño, amo; lord; **Lord's Prayer** Padre Nuestro; **Our Lord** Nuestro Señor; *v.* señorear, mandar; **to — it over** señorear, dominar.
**lordly** [lɔ́rdlɪ] *adj.* señoril; noble; altivo; despótico; *adv.* altivamente, imperiosamente.
**lordship** [lɔ́rdʃɪp] *s.* señoría (*título*); señorío, dominio.
**lose** [luz] *v.* perder; **to — sight of** perder de vista.
**loss** [lɔs] *s.* pérdida; **to be at a —** estar perplejo; no saber qué hacer; **to sell at a —** vender con pérdida.
**lost** [lɔst] *pret. & p.p.* de **to lose**; *adj.* perdido; extraviado; **— in thought** absorto, abstraído; **to get —** perderse, extraviarse.
**lot** [lat] *s.* (*land*) lote; (*section*) parte,

porción; (*luck*) suerte; solar, porción de terreno; **a — of** (*o* **-s of**) una gran cantidad de; mucho; muchos; **to draw -s** echar suertes; **to fall to one's —** tocarle a uno, caerle en suerte; *adv.* mucho; **a — better** mucho mejor.
**lotion** [lófən] *s.* loción.
**lottery** [látərɪ] *s.* lotería.
**loud** [laud] *adj.* ruidoso; recio, fuerte; chillón (*dícese también de los colores*); *adv.* ruidosamente, fuerte, recio; alto, en voz alta.
**loud-speaker** [láudspíkɚ] *s.* altavoz, altoparlante.
**lounge** [laundʒ] *s.* sala de descanso; sofá, diván, canapé; *v.* arrellanarse, repantigarse, recostarse cómodamente; sestear; holgazanear.
**louse** [laus] *s.* piojo.
**lousy** [láuzɪ] *adj.* piojoso; asqueroso.
**lovable** [lʌ́vəbl] *adj.* amable.
**love** [lʌv] *s.* (*affection*) amor; cariño; (*fondness*) afición; **— affair** amorío; **to be in —** estar enamorado; **to fall in — with** enamorarse de; **to make — to** enamorar; *v.* amar, querer; gustar mucho de, gustarle a uno mucho; encantarle a uno algo.
**loveliness** [lʌ́vlɪnɪs] *s.* belleza, hermosura; amabilidad.
**lovely** [lʌ́vlɪ] *adj.* amable; lindo, bello; exquisito; encantador; ameno.
**lover** [lʌ́vɚ] *s.* amante; **music —** aficionado a (*o* amante de) la música.
**loving** [lʌ́vɪŋ] *adj.* amante, amoroso, cariñoso, afectuoso; **-ly** *adv.* cariñosamente, afectuosamente.
**low** [lo] *adj.* (*not high*) bajo; (*base*) vil; (*humble*) humilde; (*downcast*) abatido, débil; (*lacking*) deficiente; (*sick*) gravemente enfermo; **— comedy** farsa, sainete; **— gear** primera velocidad; **— Mass** misa rezada; **— key** de intensidad mínima; **dress with a — neck** vestido escotado (*o* con escote); **to be — on something** estar escaso de algo; **to be in — spirits** estar abatido o desanimado; *adv.* bajo; en voz baja, quedo, quedito; con bajeza, a precio bajo vilmente; *s.* mugido; *v.* mugir.
**lower** [lóɚ] *adj.* más bajo; inferior; **— case letter** letra minúscula; **— classman** estudiante de los dos primeros años; **— house** cámara de diputados; *v.* bajar; disminuir; rebajar; abatir; humillar.
**lowland** [lólænd] *s.* tierra baja.
**lowliness** [lólɪnɪs] *s.* bajeza; humildad.
**lowly** [lólɪ] *adj.* bajo, humilde; inferior; *adv.* humildemente.
**lowness** [lónɪs] *s.* bajeza; humildad; abatimiento; gravedad (*de tono*); debilidad (*de un sonido*); baratura.
**loyal** [lɔ́ɪəl] *adj.* leal, fiel.
**loyalty** [lɔ́ɪəltɪ] *s.* lealtad, fidelidad.
**lubricant** [lúbrɪkənt] *adj. & s.* lubricante.
**lubricate** [lúbrɪket] *v.* lubricar.
**lucid** [lúsɪd] *adj.* lúcido; claro;

luciente.

**luck** [lʌk] s. suerte; fortuna; **in —** de buena suerte; **in bad —** de mala suerte.

**luckily** [lʌkılı] adv. afortunadamente, por fortuna.

**lucky** [lʌkı] adj. afortunado, feliz; **to be —** tener suerte, tocarle a uno la suerte.

**lucrative** [lúkrətıv] adj. lucrativo.

**ludicrous** [lúdıkrəs] adj. ridículo.

**lug** [lʌg] v. llevar, traer, Am. cargar; **to — away** cargar con, llevarse (una cosa pesada).

**luggage** [lʌgıdʒ] s. equipaje.

**lukewarm** [lúkwɔ́rm] adj. tibio, templado; indiferente.

**lull** [lʌl] v. arrullar; sosegar; calmar(se); s. calma, momento de calma.

**lullaby** [lʌləbaı] s. arrullo, canción de cuna.

**lumber** [lʌ́mbɚ] s. madera, maderaje; **—man** maderero, negociante en madera; **—yard** depósito de maderas; **— jack** leñador; v. cortar y aserrar madera; explotar los bosques; moverse pesadamente.

**luminous** [lúmənəs] adj. luminoso.

**lump** [lʌmp] s. (mass) terrón; bulto; (swelling) hinchazón, chichón; protuberancia; **— of sugar** terrón de azúcar; v. amontonar; consolidar (gastos); apelotonarse, aterronarse, formar terrones.

**lumpy** [lʌ́mpı] adj. aterronado.

**lunatic** [lúnətık] adj. & s. lunático, loco.

**lunch** [lʌntʃ] s. almuerzo; merienda; **—room** merendero, Méx., Ven., Carib. lonchería; Ríopl. confitería; Spain cafetería; v. almorzar; merendar; Am. tomar el lonche.

**luncheon** [lʌ́ntʃən] s. almuerzo; merienda.

**lung** [lʌŋ] s. pulmón.

**lurch** [lɝtʃ] s. sacudida; tambaleo repentino; **to give a —** tambalearse; **to leave someone in the —** dejar a uno plantado, dejar a uno a buenas noches; v. tambalearse; dar un tambaleo repentino.

**lure** [lur] s. aliciente, atractivo; tentación; cebo o reclamo (para atraer); v. atraer; seducir; atraer (con cebo o reclamo).

**lurk** [lɝk] v. estar oculto; estar en acecho; moverse furtivamente.

**luscious** [lʌ́ʃəs] adj. exquisito, delicioso, sabroso.

**lust** [lʌst] s. lujuria; deseo vehemente; codicia; v. **to — after** codiciar.

**luster** [lʌ́stɚ] s. lustre, brillo.

**lustrous** [lʌ́strəs] adj. lustroso.

**lusty** [lʌ́stı] adj. vigoroso, fornido, robusto.

**lute** [lut] s. laúd.

**luxuriant** [lʌgʒúrıənt] adj. lozano, frondoso, exuberante.

**luxurious** [lʌgʒúrıəs] adj. lujoso; dado al lujo; frondoso.

**luxury** [lʌ́kʃərı] s. lujo.

**lye** [laı] s. lejía.

**lying** [láııŋ] ger. de **to lie**; adj. mentiroso; **lying-in hospital** casa de maternidad.

**lymph** [lımpf] s. linfa.

**lynch** [lıntʃ] v. linchar.

**lynx** [lıŋks] s. lince.

**lyre** [laır] s. lira.

**lyric** [lírık] s. poema lírico; adj. lírico.

**lyrical** [lírıkl] adj. lírico.

**lyricism** [lírəsızəm] s. lirismo.

## M

**macaroni** [mækərónı] s. macarrón o macarrones.

**macaroon** [mækərún] s. macarrón, almendrado, bollito de almendra.

**machine** [məʃín] s. máquina; automóvil; **— gun** ametralladora; **— made** hecho a máquina; **political —** camarilla política; **sewing —** máquina para coser.

**machinery** [məʃínərı] s. maquinaria.

**machinist** [məʃínıst] s. mecánico, maquinista.

**mackerel** [mǽkərəl] s. escombro, caballa (pez).

**mad** [mæd] adj. loco; rabioso; furioso, enojado; **to drive —** enloquecer, volver loco; **to get —** encolerizarse; **to go —** volverse loco, enloquecerse; **-ly** adv. locamente.

**madam, madame** [mǽdəm] s. madama, señora.

**madcap** [mǽdkæp] s. calavera (m.), adj. temerario; temerario; atolondrado.

**madden** [mǽdn̩] v. enloquecer(se).

**made** [med] pret. & p.p. de **to make; to be — of** estar hecho de; ser de; **to have something —** mandar hacer algo; **made-up** fingido, falso; artificial, pintado (con afeites).

**made-to-order** [medtuɔ́rdɚ] adj. hecho a la medida.

**madman** [mǽdmæn] s. loco.

**madness** [mǽdnıs] s. locura; rabia.

**magazine** [mægəzín] s. revista; almacén (especialmente para provisiones militares); **powder —** polvorín.

**magic** [mǽdʒık] s. magia; adj. mágico.

**magician** [mədʒíʃən] s. mágico; brujo.

**magistrate** [mǽdʒıstret] s. magistrado.

**magnanimous** [mægnǽnəməs] adj. magnánimo.

**magnesium** [mægnízıəm] s. magnesio.

**magnet** [mǽgnıt] s. imán.

**magnetic** [mægnétık] adj. magnético; **— pole** polo magnético; **— tape** cinta magnética.

**magnetize** [mǽgnətaız] v. magnetizar; cautivar.

**magnificence** [mægnífəsn̩s] s. magnificencia.

**magnificent** [mægnífəsn̩t] adj. magnífico.

**magnify** [mǽgnəfaı] v. agrandar, engrandecer; amplificar; exagerar.

**magnitude** [mǽgnətjud] s. magnitud.

**magpie** [mǽgpaı] s. urraca; cotorra, hablador, habladora.

**mahogany** [məhágənɪ] *s.* caoba.

**maid** [med] *s.* criada, sirvienta, camarera, *Méx.* recamarera, *Ríopl.*, *Andes* mucama; doncella; — **of honor** doncella de honor; **old** — solterona.

**maiden** [médṇ] *s.* doncella; virgen; mozuela; soltera; — **lady** mujer soltera; — **voyage** primer viaje (*de un vapor*).

**mail** [mel] *s.* correo; correspondencia; **air** — correo aéreo; **coat of** — malla; —**bag** valija; — **train** tren correo; *v.* echar al correo.

**mailbox** [mélbɑks] *s.* buzón.

**mailman** [mélmæn] *s.* cartero.

**maim** [mem] *v.* mutilar, estropear.

**main** [men] *adj.* principal, mayor, de mayor importancia; *s.* tubería, cañería principal (*de agua o gas*); alta mar, océano; **in the** — en su mayor parte; en general, en conjunto; **-ly** *adv.* principalmente.

**mainland** [ménlænd] *s.* continente, tierra firme.

**mainspring** [ménsprɪŋ] *s.* muelle real; origen.

**maintain** [mentén] *v.* mantener; sostener, afirmar; guardar.

**maintenance** [méntənəns] *s.* mantenimiento; sustento; manutención; sostén, sostenimiento.

**maize** [mez] *s.* maíz.

**majestic** [mədʒéstɪk] *adj.* majestuoso.

**majesty** [mædʒɪstɪ] *s.* majestad.

**major** [médʒɚ] *adj.* (*greater*) mayor, más grande; (*principal*) principal; — **key** tono mayor; *s.* comandante, mayor, mayor de edad; curso o asignatura de especialización (*en la universidad*); — **league** liga mayor; *v.* especializarse (*en un curso de estudios*).

**majority** [mədʒɔ́rətɪ] *s.* mayoría; mayor edad.

**make** [mek] *v.* (*do*) hacer; (*create*) fabricar; formar; (*deliver*) pronunciar (*un discurso*); **to** — **a clean breast of** confesar; **to** — **a train** alcanzar un tren; **to** — **a turn** dar vuelta; **to** — **away with** llevarse, robar; matar; **to** — **fast** asegurar, afianzar; **to** — **headway** progresar, adelantar, avanzar; **to** — **much of** dar mucha importancia a; **to** — **neither head nor tail of** no comprender nada de; **to** — **nothing out of** no comprender nada de, no sacar nada en limpio; **to** — **out in the distance** distinguir a lo lejos; **to** — **over** rehacer, alterar (*un traje*); **to** — **sure** asegurarse; **to** — **toward** dirigirse a, encaminarse a; **to** — **up a story** inventar un cuento; **to** — **up after a quarrel** hacer las paces; **to** — **up for a loss** compensar por una pérdida; **to** — **up one's face** pintarse la cara; **to** — **up one's mind** resolverse, decidirse; *s.* hechura, forma; marca (*de fábrica*); manufactura.

**maker** [mékɚ] *s.* hacedor; fabricante; artífice.

**makeshift** [mékʃɪft] *adj.* provisional.

**make-up** [mékʌp] *s.* (*composition*) compostura, composición, hechura; (*character*) naturaleza, carácter; **facial** — afeite, cosmético.

**malady** [mælədɪ] *s.* mal, enfermedad.

**malaria** [məlérɪə] *s.* malaria, fiebre palúdica, paludismo.

**malcontent** [mælkəntɛnt] *adj.* & *s.* malcontento.

**male** [mel] *adj.* macho; varón; masculino; varonil; de hombres, de varones; *s.* macho; varón; hombre.

**malice** [mælɪs] *s.* malicia.

**malicious** [məlíʃəs] *adj.* malicioso, perverso, malévolo.

**malign** [məláɪn] *v.* calumniar, difamar; *adj.* maligno; pernicioso.

**malignant** [məlígnənt] *adj.* maligno; malévolo.

**mallet** [mælɪt] *s.* mazo, maceta.

**malnutrition** [mælnutríʃən] *s.* desnutrición.

**malt** [mɔlt] *s.* malta; **-ed milk** leche malteada.

**mama, mamma** [mámə] *s.* mamá.

**mammal** [mæmḷ] *s.* mamífero.

**mammoth** [mæməθ] *adj.* gigantesco, enorme.

**mammy** [mæmɪ] *s.* mamita; niñera negra; criada negra.

**man** [mæn] *s.* hombre; varón; pieza (*de ajedrez*); — **and wife** marido y mujer; **to a** — unánimente, todos a una; **officers and men** oficiales y soldados; **man-of-war** buque de guerra; — **cook** cocinero; *v.* armar, proveer de gente armada; guarnecer (*una fortaleza*); tripular (*una embarcación*).

**manage** [mænɪdʒ] *v.* manejar; gobernar, dirigir; gestionar; **to** — **to do something** arreglárselas para hacer algo.

**manageable** [mænɪdʒəbḷ] *adj.* manejable; domable, dócil.

**management** [mænɪdʒmənt] *s.* manejo; dirección; gobierno, administración; gerencia.

**manager** [mænɪdʒɚ] *s.* gerente; director, administrador; empresario.

**mandate** [mændet] *s.* mandato; *v.* asignar por mandato.

**mane** [men] *s.* melena (*del león*), crin (*del caballo*).

**maneuver** [mənúvɚ] *s.* maniobra; gestión; *v.* maniobrar; manipular, manejar.

**manful** [mænfəl] *adj.* varonil; viril.

**manganese** [mǽŋɡənis] *s.* manganeso.

**mange** [mendʒ] *s.* sarna, roña.

**manger** [méndʒɚ] *s.* pesebre.

**mangle** [mǽŋɡl] *v.* magullar, mutilar; destrozar, estropear; planchar en máquina de planchar; *s.* planchadora (*máquina de planchar*).

**mangy** [méndʒɪ] *adj.* sarnoso, *Am.* sarniento.

**manhood** [mǽnhud] *s.* virilidad; edad viril; hombres.

**mania** [ménɪə] *s.* manía.

**manicure** [mǽnɪkjur] *s.* manicura; *v.*

manicurar.

**manifest** [mǽnəfɛst] *adj.* manifiesto; *s.* manifiesto (*lista de la carga de un buque*); *v.* manifestar; poner de manifiesto; declarar.

**manifestation** [mænəfɛstéʃən] *s.* manifestación.

**manifesto** [mænɪféstɔ] *s.* manifiesto, bando, proclama.

**manifold** [mǽnəfold] *adj.* múltiple; numeroso, diverso.

**manikin** [mǽnəkɪn] *s.* maniquí; muñeco; hombrecillo.

**manila** [mənílə] *s.* abacá (*cáñamo de Manila*); — **paper** papel de Manila.

**manipulate** [mənípjəlet] *v.* manipular; manejar.

**manipulation** [mənɪpjəléʃən] *s.* manipulación.

**mankind** [mænkáɪnd] *s.* humanidad, género humano; los hombres.

**manly** [mǽnlɪ] *adj.* varonil; viril; *adv.* varonilmente.

**manner** [mǽnɚ] *s.* (*way*) manera; modo; género; (*air*) aire, ademán; **-s** maneras, modales; costumbres; **after the — of** a la manera de; **by no — of means** de ningún modo.

**mannerism** [mǽnɚɪzm] *s.* costumbre; amaneramiento.

**mannish** [mǽnɪʃ] *adj.* hombruno.

**manoeuvre** = **maneuver.**

**manor** [mǽnɚ] *s.* solar, casa solariega.

**mansion** [mǽnʃən] *s.* mansión; palacio.

**manslaughter** [mǽnslɔtɚ] *s.* homicidio impremeditado o casual.

**mantel** [mǽnt1] *s.* manto (*de una chimenea*); repisa de chimenea.

**mantle** [mǽnt1] *s.* manto; capa.

**manual** [mǽnjʊəl] *adj.* manual; — **training school** escuela de artes y oficios; *s.* manual; teclado de órgano.

**manufacture** [mænjəfǽktʃɚ] *s.* fabricación; manufactura; *v.* fabricar, manufacturar.

**manufacturer** [mænjəfǽktʃərɚ] *s.* fabricante.

**manufacturing** [mænjəfǽktʃərɪŋ] *s.* fabricación; *adj.* fabril, manufacturero.

**manure** [mənúr] *s.* estiércol, abono; *v.* estercolar, abonar (*la tierra*).

**manuscript** [mǽnjəskrɪpt] *adj.* & *s.* manuscrito.

**many** [ménɪ] *adj.* muchos; — **a time** muchas veces; **a great —** muchísimos; **as — as** tantos como; cuantos; **as — as five** hasta cinco; **how —?** ¿cuántos?; **three books too —** tres libros de más; **too —** demasiados.

**map** [mæp] *s.* mapa; *v.* trazar un mapa de; **to — out** proyectar, planear.

**maple** [mép1] *s.* arce, *Méx.* meple; *Ríopl.* maple.

**mar** [mɑr] *v.* desfigurar, estropear.

**marble** [mɑ́rb1] *s.* mármol; canica (*para jugar*); **to play -s** jugar a las canicas; *adj.* de mármol; marmóreo.

**march** [mɑrtʃ] *s.* marcha; *v.* marchar, caminar; hacer marchar; **to — in** entrar marchando; **to — out** mar-

charse; salirse marchando.

**March** [mɑrtʃ] *s.* marzo.

**mare** [mɛr] *s.* yegua.

**margarine** [mɑ́rdʒərɪn] *s.* margarina.

**margin** [mɑ́rdʒɪn] *s.* margen; orilla; sobrante; reserva (*fondos*).

**marginal** [mɑ́rdʒɪn1] *adj.* marginal; — **note** nota marginal, acotación.

**marigold** [mǽrəgold] *s.* caléndula, maravilla.

**marine** [mərín] *adj.* marino; marítimo; — **corps** cuerpo de marinos; *s.* marino; soldado de marina; **merchant —** marina mercante.

**mariner** [mǽrənɚ] *s.* marinero.

**maritime** [mǽrətaɪm] *adj.* marítimo.

**mark** [mɑrk] *s.* marca; señal, seña; nota, calificación; **question —** punto de interrogación; **to come up to the —** alcanzar la norma requerida; **to hit the —** dar en el blanco; **to make one's —** distinguirse; **to miss one's —** fallar; errar el tiro; fracasar; *v.* marcar; señalar; notar; observar; calificar; — **my words!** ¡advierte lo que te digo!; **to — down** anotar, apuntar; rebajar el precio de.

**marker** [mɑ́rkɚ] *s.* marcador; marca, señal; jalón.

**market** [mɑ́rkɪt] *s.* mercado, plaza; — **place** mercado, plaza; — **price** precio corriente; **meat —** carnicería; **stock —** mercado de valores, bolsa; *v.* vender; vender o comprar en el mercado; **to go -ing** ir de compras.

**marmalade** [mɑ́rm1ed] *s.* mermelada.

**maroon** [mərún] *s.* & *adj.* rojo obscuro.

**marooned** [mərúnd] *adj.* abandonado (*en lugar desierto*) aislado; **to get —** encontrarse aislado, perdido o incomunicado.

**marquis** [mɑ́rkwɪs] *s.* marqués.

**marquise** [mɑrkíz] *s.* marquesa.

**marriage** [mǽrɪdʒ] *s.* matrimonio; casamiento, boda; unión, enlace; — **license** licencia para casarse.

**marriageable** [mǽrɪdʒəb1] *adj.* casadero.

**married** [mǽrɪd] *adj.* casado; conyugal; — **couple** matrimonio, cónyuges; pareja de casados; **to get —** casarse.

**marrow** [mǽro] *s.* meollo, tuétano, medula (*de los huesos*).

**marry** [mǽrɪ] *v.* casar; casarse; casarse con.

**marsh** [mɑrʃ] *s.* pantano; ciénaga.

**marshal** [mɑ́rʃəl] *s.* mariscal; alguacil; jefe de policía (*en ciertas regiones*); maestro de ceremonia; **fire —** jefe de bomberos; *v.* ordenar, arreglar; guiar, conducir con ceremonia.

**marshmallow** [mɑ́rʃmælo] *s.* pastilla o bombón de altea.

**marshy** [mɑ́rʃɪ] *adj.* pantanoso, cenagoso.

**mart** [mɑrt] *s.* mercado.

**martial** [mɑ́rʃəl] *adj.* marcial; — **law** estado de guerra.

**martin** [mɑ́rtɪn] *s.* avión (*pájaro*).

**martyr** [mɑ́rtɚ] *s.* mártir; *v.* martirizar, torturar, atormentar.

**MA**

**martyrdom** [mártərdəm] *s.* martirio.
**marvel** [márvl] *s.* maravilla; *v.* maravillarse.
**marvelous** [márvləs] *adj.* maravilloso.
**mascot** [mæskɑt] *s.* mascota.
**masculine** [mæskjəlɪn] *adj.* masculino; varonil; hombruno.
**mash** [mæʃ] *v.* majar, amasar; machacar, magullar; **-ed potatoes** puré de papas (*o* patatas); patatas majadas.
**mask** [mæsk] *s.* máscara; disfraz; careta; *v.* disfrazar, enmascarar; encubrir; **-ed ball** baile de máscaras.
**mason** [mésn̩] *s.* albañil; **Mason** masón, francmasón.
**masonry** [mésn̩rɪ] *s.* albañilería; mampostería; **Masonry** masonería, francmasonería.
**masquerade** [mæskəréd] *s.*·mascarada; disfraz, máscara; *v.* enmascararse, disfrazarse; andar disfrazado.
**mass** [mæs] *s.* masa; montón; mole; mayoría, mayor parte; misa; **— meeting** mitin popular; **— communication** comunicación extensa; **— media** los medios de comunicarse con el publico (*radio, televisión, periódicos, etc.*); **the -es** las masas, el pueblo; *v.* juntar(se) en masa.
**massacre** [mæsəkə] *s.* hecatombe, matanza, carnicería, destrozo; *v.* hacer matanza o hecatombe, destrozar.
**massage** [məsáʒ] *v.* friccionar, dar masaje; *s.* masaje.
**massive** [mæsɪv] *adj.* sólido, macizo; voluminoso, imponente.
**mast** [mæst] *s.* mástil, palo.
**master** [mæstə] *s.* (*head*) amo, dueño, señor; maestro; patrón; (*skilled*) experto, perito; **band —** director de la banda; **— of arts** maestro en artes, licenciado; **-'s degree** licenciatura, grado de licenciado; *adj.* maestro; **builder** maestro de obras; **— key** llave maestra; *v.* dominar; domar; gobernar; **to — a language** dominar un idioma.
**masterful** [mæstəfəl] *adj.* magistral; dominante.
**masterly** [mæstəlɪ] *adj.* magistral; *adv.* magistralmente.
**masterpiece** [mæstəpis] *s.* obra maestra.
**mastery** [mæstərɪ] *s.* maestría, arte, destreza; dominio.
**mastiff** [mæstɪf] *s.* mastín, alano.
**mat** [mæt] *s.* (*covering*) estera; esterilla, felpudo, tapete; (*gymnasium*) colchoncillo (*de gimnasia*); borde de cartón (*para hacer resaltar una pintura*).
**match** [ɪnætʃ] *s.* (*pair*) pareja; (*game*) partida, contienda, juego; (*light*) fósforo, cerilla; *Méx.* cerillo; **he has no — no tiene igual; he is a good —** es un buen partido; **the hat and coat are a good —** el abrigo y el sombrero hacen juego; *v.* igualar; aparear; hacer juego, armonizar; **to — one's strength** medir uno sus fuerzas; **these colors do not — well** estos colores no casan bien.

**matchless** [mætʃlɪs] *adj.* sin par, sin igual, incomparable.
**mate** [met] *s.* compañero, compañera; consorte; macho o hembra (*entre animales o aves*); piloto (*el segundo de un buque mercante*); oficial subalterno (*en la marina*); *v.* aparear(se).
**material** [mətírɪəl] *adj.* material; esencial; *s.* material; tejido, género; materia; **raw —** materia prima.
**maternal** [mətə́n̩l] *adj.* maternal, materno.
**maternity** [mətə́n̩ɑtɪ] *s.* maternidad.
**mathematical** [mæθəmǽtɪkl] *adj.* matemático.
**mathematician** [mæθəmətíʃən] *s.* matemático.
**mathematics** [mæθəmǽtɪks] *s.* matemáticas.
**matinée** [mætn̩é] *s.* función de la tarde, *Am.* matiné.
**matriarch** [métrɪɑrk] *s.* matriarca.
**matriculate** [mətríkjəlet] *v.* matricular(se).
**matriculation** [mətrɪkjəléʃən] *s.* matriculación, matrícula.
**matrimony** [mætrəmonɪ] *s.* matrimonio, casamiento.
**matrix** [métrɪks] *s.* matriz; molde.
**matron** [métrən] *s.* matrona, madre de familia; ama de llaves; vigilante, cuidadora (*de un asilo, cárcel par mujeres, etc.*).
**matter** [mætə] *s.* (*substance*) material, materia; sustancia; (*affair*) asunto, cuestión; cosa; (*discharge*) pus; **— for complaint** motivo de queja; **— of two minutes** cosa de dos minutos; **as a — of fact** de hecho; en verdad, en realidad; **business -s** negocios; **printed —** impresos; **serious —** cosa seria; **it is of no —** no tiene importancia; **to do something as a — of course** hacer algo por rutina; **what is the —?** ¿qué pasa?; ¿qué tiene Vd.?; **matter-of-fact person** persona de poca imaginación; *v.* importar; supurar; **it does not —** no importa, no le hace.
**mattress** [mætrɪs] *s.* colchón; **spring —** colchón de muelles.
**mature** [mətjúr] *adj.* maduro; **a — note** un pagaré vencido; *v.* madurar(se); vencerse, hacerse cobrable o pagadero (*un pagaré, una deuda*).
**maturity** [mətjúrətɪ] *s.* madurez; vencimiento (*de una deuda u obligación*).
**maul** [mɔl] *v.* magullar; maltratar; manejar rudamente; golpear.
**maverick** [mǽvəɪk] *s.* animal sin marca; becerro suelto.
**maxim** [mæksɪm] *s.* máxima.
**maximum** [mæksəməm] *adj. & s.* máximo.
**may** [me] *v. irr. y defect.* (*able*) poder; (*permitted*) tener permiso para, serle permitido a uno; (*possible*) ser posible; **— I sit down?** ¿puedo sentarme?; **— you have a good time** que se divierta Vd.; **it — be that** puede ser que, tal vez sea que; **it — rain** puede

(ser) que llueva, es posible que llueva; **she — be late** puede (ser) que llegue ella tarde.

**May** [me] *s.* mayo, mes de mayo; **— Day** primero de mayo; **—pole** mayo; **— Queen** maya (*reina de la fiesta del primero de mayo*).

**maybe** [mébɪ] *adv.* quizás, tal vez, acaso.

**mayonnaise** [meənéz] *s.* mayonesa.

**mayor** [méɚ] *s.* alcalde, alcalde mayor.

**maze** [mez] *s.* laberinto; confusión; **to be in a —** estar confuso o perplejo.

**me** [mi] *pron. pers.* me; mí (*después de preposición*); **give it to —** démelo (a mí); **for —** para mí; **with —** conmigo.

**meadow** [médo] *s.* pradera, prado; **— lark** alondra de los prados.

**meager** [mígɚ] *adj.* escaso, insuficiente; magro, flaco.

**meal** [mil] *s.* comida; harina (*a medio moler*); **corn —** harina de maíz; **—time** hora de comer.

**mean** [min] *adj.* (*malicious*) ruin, bajo; vil; (*humble*) humilde; (*stingy*) mezquino, tacaño; (*difficult*) de mal genio; (*sick*) malo, indispuesto; (*middle*) mediano; medio; intermedio; **— distance** distancia media; *s.* medio; término medio; **-s** medios; recursos; **a man of -s** un hombre pudiente o rico; **by -s of** por medio de; **by all -s** de todos modos; a toda costa; por supuesto; **by no -s** de ningún modo; *v.* querer decir, significar; pensar, proponerse, tener la intención de; intentar; destinar; **he -s well** tiene buenas intenciones.

**meander** [miǽndɚ] *v.* serpentear.

**meaning** [mínɪŋ] *s.* (*sense*) significado, sentido; significación; (*intent*) propósito, intención; *adj.* significativo; **well-meaning** bien intencionado.

**meaningless** [mínɪŋlɪs] *adj.* sin sentido, vacío de sentido.

**meanness** [mínnɪs] *s.* ruindad, vileza, bajeza; mezquindad.

**meant** [mɛnt] *pret. & p.p. de* **to mean**.

**meantime** [míntaɪm] *adv.* mientras tanto, entretanto; *s.* ínterin, entretanto; **in the —** en el ínterin, mientras tanto.

**meanwhile** [mínhwaɪl] = **meantime**.

**measles** [mízlz] *s.* sarampión.

**measurable** [méʒrəbl] *adj.* medible, mensurable; **measurably** *adv.* marcadamente.

**measure** [méʒɚ] *s.* (*dimension*) medida; compás (*de música*); cadencia, ritmo; (*law*) proyecto de ley; ley; **beyond —** sobremanera; con exceso; **dry —** medida para áridos; **in large —** en gran parte, en gran manera; *v.* medir.

**measured** [méʒɚd] *adj.* medido; moderado; acompasado.

**measurement** [méʒɚmənt] *s.* medida; dimensión; tamaño; medición.

**meat** [mit] *s.* carne; meollo, sustancia; **— ball** albóndiga; **— market** carnicería; **cold —** fiambre.

**meaty** [mítɪ] *adj.* carnoso; sustancioso.

**mechanic** [məkǽnɪk] *adj. & s.* mecánico; **-s** *s.* mecánica.

**mechanical** [məkǽnɪkl] *adj.* mecánico; maquinal.

**mechanism** [mékənɪzəm] *s.* mecanismo.

**medal** [médl] *s.* medalla.

**meddle** [médl] *v.* entrometerse o entremeterse; meterse.

**meddler** [médlɚ] *s.* entremetido.

**meddlesome** [médlsəm] *adj.* entremetido.

**median** [mídɪən] *adj.* mediano, del medio; *s.* punto, línea o número del medio; mediana.

**mediate** [mídɪet] *v.* mediar; intervenir; arbitrar.

**mediation** [midɪéʃən] *s.* mediación, intervención, intercesión.

**mediator** [mídɪetɚ] *s.* mediador, medianero, árbitro.

**medical** [médɪkl] *adj.* médico; **— school** escuela de medicina.

**medication** [mɛdɪkéʃən] *s.* medicación.

**medicine** [médəsn] *s.* medicina; medicamento; **— ball** pelota grande de cuero; **— cabinet** botiquín; **— man** curandero indio.

**medieval** [midíívl] *adj.* medioeval o medieval.

**mediocre** [midióukɚ] *adj.* mediocre, mediano; ordinario.

**mediocrity** [midɪákrətɪ] *s.* mediocridad, medianía.

**meditate** [médətet] *v.* meditar.

**meditation** [mɛdətéʃən] *s.* meditación.

**medium** [mídɪəm] *s.* medio; medio ambiente; *adj.* mediano; intermedio; a medio cocer, a medio asar; **— of exchange** mediador de cambio.

**medley** [médlɪ] *s.* baturrillo, mezcla, mezcolanza.

**meek** [mik] *adj.* manso, dócil, paciente, sufrido.

**meekness** [míknɪs] *s.* mansedumbre, docilidad.

**meet** [mit] *v.* encontrar(se); reunirse; conocer (*personalmente*), ser presentado a; ir a esperar (*un tren, vapor, o a alguien*); satisfacer (*deseos, requisitos, etc.*); pagar (*una deuda*); sufragar (*gastos*); responder a (*una acusación*); **to —** in battle trabar batalla; **to — with** encontrarse con; tropezar con; topar con; reunirse con; *s.* concurso; contienda (*tratándose de deportes*); **track —** competencia de atletas.

**meeting** [mítɪŋ] *s.* reunión; mitin; sesión; asamblea; encuentro.

**megaphone** [mégəfon] *s.* megáfono, portavoz, bocina.

**melancholy** [mélənkɑlɪ] *s.* melancolía; *adj.* melancólico.

**melee** [méle] *s.* reyerta; zafarrancho.

**mellow** [mélo] *adj.* maduro, sazonado; dulce, blando, suave; *v.* madurar(se), sazonar(se); ablandar(se), suavizar(se).

**melodious** [məlódɪəs] *adj.* melodioso.

**melodrama** [mélodramə] *s.* melodrama.

**melody** [mélədɪ] *s.* melodía.

MA

**melon** [mélən] s. melón.
**melt** [mɛlt] v. derretir(se); disolver(se); fundir(se).
**member** [mémbɚ] s. miembro; socio.
**membership** [mémbɚʃɪp] s. número de miembros o socios; asociación; (los) miembros (de un club o sociedad).
**membrane** [mémbren] s. membrana.
**memento** [mɪménto] s. memento, memoria, recuerdo.
**memoir** [mémwɑr] s. memoria, apuntaciones; **-s** memorias; autobiografía.
**memorable** [mémərəbl] adj. memorable.
**memorandum** [mɛmərǽndəm] s. memorándum; memoria, apunte; — **book** memorándum, librito de apuntes, memorial.
**memorial** [məmóriəl] s. (monument) monumento conmemorativo; (occasion) obra o fiesta conmemorativa; memorial, petición; adj. conmemorativo.
**memorize** [méməraɪz] v. aprender de memoria.
**memory** [méməri] s. memoria; recuerdo.
**men** [mɛn] pl. de **man**.
**menace** [ménɪs] s. amenaza; v. amenazar.
**mend** [mɛnd] v. remendar; reparar; componer; enmendar; **to — one's ways** enmendarse, reformarse; s. remiendo; reparación; **to be on the —** ir mejorando.
**menial** [míniəl] adj. servil, bajo.
**menstruation** [mɛnstruéʃən] s. menstruo o menstruación.
**mental** [méntl] adj. mental.
**mentality** [mɛntǽlətɪ] s. mentalidad, ingenio.
**mention** [ménʃən] s. mención; alusión; v. mencionar, mentar; **don't — it** no hay de qué (contestación a "thank you").
**menu** [ménju] s. menú, lista de platos.
**meow** [mjaʊ] = **mew**.
**mercantile** [mɚ́kəntɪl] adj. mercantil.
**mercenary** [mɚ́sn̩ɛrɪ] adj. mercenario.
**merchandise** [mɚ́tʃəndaɪz] s. mercancías, mercaderías; **piece of —** mercancía.
**merchant** [mɚ́tʃənt] s. comerciante; negociante; mercader; adj. mercante, mercantil; — **marine** marina mercante.
**merciful** [mɚ́sɪfəl] adj. misericordioso, piadoso.
**merciless** [mɚ́sɪlɪs] adj. sin piedad, despiadado, incompasivo.
**mercury** [mɚ́kjərɪ] s. mercurio; azogue.
**mercy** [mɚ́sɪ] s. (favor) merced; favor, gracia; (compassion) misericordia, piedad, compasión; **to be at the — of** estar a merced de.
**mere** [mɪr] adj. mero; simple, puro; **a — formality** una pura formalidad, no más que una formalidad, una formalidad no más; **a — trifle** una nonada; **-ly** adv. meramente; sólo, solamente; simplemente.

**merge** [mɚdʒ] v. combinar(se), unir(se); absorber(se); fundirse.
**merger** [mɚ́dʒɚ] s. amalgamación comercial.
**meridian** [mərídɪən] adj. & s. meridiano.
**merit** [mérɪt] s. mérito; v. merecer.
**meritorious** [mɛrətórɪəs] adj. meritorio.
**mermaid** [mɚ́med] s. ninfa marina.
**merrily** [mérəlɪ] adv. alegremente, con regocijo.
**merriment** [mérɪmənt] s. alegría, regocijo, júbilo.
**merry** [mérɪ] adj. alegre; jovial; divertido; festivo; — **Christmas** Felices Navidades, Felices Pascuas; **to make —** divertirse.
**merry-go-round** [mérɪgəraʊnd] s. tío vivo, Méx., C.A. los caballitos; Ríopl. calesita.
**merrymaker** [mérɪmekɚ] s. fiestero; juerguista.
**merrymaking** [mérɪmekɪŋ] s. regocijo; jaleo, juerga, jolgorio; adj. regocijado, alegre, festivo, fiestero.
**mesh** [mɛʃ] s. malla; red; **-es** red, redes; v. enredar, coger con red; **to — gears** engranar.
**mess** [mɛs] s. (food) rancho, comida (en el ejército o la marina); (confusion) lío, confusión; (dirt) suciedad; — **of fish** plato o ración de pescado; **to make a — of** revolver, confundir; ensuciar; echar a perder; v. revolver, confundir; ensuciar, echar a perder (generalmente: **to — up**); **to — around** revolver o mezclar las cosas; entrometerse; **messy** [mésɪ] adj. desordenado, desarreglado; sucio.
**message** [mésɪdʒ] s. mensaje; parte (m.), comunicación; recado.
**messenger** [mésn̩dʒɚ] s. mensajero; mandadero.
**met** [mɛt] pret. & p.p. de **to meet**.
**metabolism** [mətǽbəlɪzm] s. metabolismo.
**metal** [métl] s. metal; adj. de metal, metálico.
**metallic** [mətǽlɪk] adj. metálico.
**metallurgy** [métl̩ɚdʒɪ] s. metalurgia.
**metaphor** [métəfɚ] s. metáfora.
**metathesis** [mətǽθəsɪs] s. metátesis.
**meteor** [mítɪɚ] s. meteoro; estrella fugaz.
**meteorite** [mítɪoraɪt] s. meteorito.
**meteorological** [mitɪərəládʒɪkl̩] adj. meteorológico.
**meteorology** [mitɪərálədʒɪ] s. meteorología.
**meter** [mítɚ] s. metro; contador (de gas, agua, electricidad, etc.).
**method** [méθəd] s. método; técnica.
**methodical** [məθádɪkl̩] adj. metódico.
**metre** = **meter**.
**metric** [métrɪk] adj. métrico; — **system** sistema métrico.
**metropolis** [mətrápl̩ɪs] s. metrópoli.
**metropolitan** [mɛtrəpálətn̩] adj. metropolitano.
**mettle** [métl̩] s. temple, brío, ánimo, valor.

**mew** [mju] s. maullido, maúllo, miau; v. maullar.

**Mexican** [méksɪkən] adj. & s. mejicano o mexicano.

**mezzanine** [mézənin] s. entresuelo.

**mice** [maɪs] pl. de **mouse**.

**microbe** [máɪkrob] s. microbio.

**microfilm** [máɪkrəfɪlm] s. microfilm.

**microphone** [máɪkrəfon] s. micrófono.

**microscope** [máɪkrəskop] s. microscopio.

**microscopic** [maɪkrəskápɪk] adj. microscópico.

**mid** [mɪd] adj. medio (úsase por lo general en composición); **in — air** en el aire; prep. en medio de, entre.

**midday** [mídde] s. mediodía; adj. del mediodía.

**middle** [mídl] adj. medio; intermedio; **Middle Ages** Edad Media; **— finger** dedo de en medio, dedo del corazón; **— size** tamaño mediano; s. medio, centro, mitad; **in the — of** en medio de, a la mitad de; **towards the — of the month** a mediados del mes; **— class** clase media.

**middle-aged** [mídléʤd] adj. de edad mediana, de edad madura.

**middleman** [mídlmæn] s. revendedor; medianero, corredor, agente.

**middle-sized** [mídlsáɪzd] adj. de mediano tamaño, de mediana estatura.

**middy** [mídɪ] s. guardiamarina (m.); **— blouse** blusa a la marinera.

**midget** [míʤɪt] s. enanillo.

**midnight** [mídnaɪt] s. medianoche; adj. de (la) medianoche; **— blue** azul oscuro; **— Mass** misa de gallo.

**midriff** [mídrɪf] s. diafragma.

**midshipman** [mídʃɪpmən] s. guardiamarina (m.).

**midst** [mɪdst] s. medio, centro; **in the — of** en medio de, entre; **in our —** entre nosotros.

**midstream** [mídstrim] s. el medio (o el centro) de la corriente.

**midsummer** [mídsámər] s. pleno verano, solsticio estival, la mitad del verano.

**midterm** [mídtɜm]; **— examination** examen a mitad del curso.

**midway** [mídwé] adj. situado a medio camino; equidistante; adv. a medio camino; en medio del camino.

**midwife** [mídwaɪf] s. partera, comadrona.

**mien** [min] s. facha, aspecto.

**might** [maɪt] imperf. de **may** podía; podría; pudiera, pudiese; s. poder, poderío, fuerza.

**mighty** [máɪtɪ] adj. poderoso, potente, fuerte; adv. muy, sumamente.

**migrant** [máɪgrənt] adj. migratorio.

**migrate** [máɪgret] v. emigrar.

**migration** [maɪgréʃən] s. migración.

**mike** [maɪk] = **microphone**.

**mild** [maɪld] adj. (gentle) suave; blando; apacible; (moderate) templado, moderado.

**mildew** [míldu] s. moho; enmohecimiento.

**mildness** [máɪldnɪs] s. suavidad; mansedumbre; apacibilidad; templanza, dulzura.

**mile** [maɪl] s. milla; **—stone** mojón.

**mileage** [máɪlɪʤ] s. millaje, número de millas; recorrido (en millas). Compárese kilometraje, número de kilómetros.

**militant** [mílɪtənt] s. militante; belicoso.

**military** [mílətɛrɪ] adj. militar; de guerra; s. **the —** el ejército; los militares.

**militia** [məlíʃə] s. milicia.

**milk** [mɪlk] s. leche; **— diet** régimen lácteo; v. ordeñar.

**milkmaid** [mílkmed] s. lechera.

**milkman** [mílkmən] s. lechero, Am. vaquero.

**milky** [mílkɪ] adj. lácteo; lechoso; **Milky Way** Vía Láctea.

**mill** [mɪl] s. (grinder) molino; (factory) fábrica; (money) la milésima parte de un dólar; **saw —** aserradero; **spinning —** hilandería; **sugar —** ingenio de azúcar; **textile —** fábrica de tejidos; v. moler; aserrar (madera); fabricar; acordonar (el canto de la moneda); **to — around** arremolinarse (una muchedumbre).

**miller** [mílər] s. molinero; mariposa nocturna.

**milliner** [mílənər] s. modista (de sombreros para señoras).

**millinery** [mílənɛrɪ] s. sombreros de señora; artículos para sombreros de señora; oficio de modista; **— shop** sombrerería.

**million** [míljən] s. millón; **a — dollars** un millón de dólares.

**millionaire** [mɪljənér] adj. & s. millonario.

**millionth** [míljənθ] adj. & s. millonésimo.

**millstone** [mílston] s. muela o piedra de molino; carga pesada.

**mimic** [mímɪk] adj. mímico, imitativo; **— battle** simulacro; s. imitador, remedador; v. imitar, remedar.

**mince** [mɪns] v. picar, desmenuzar; **not to — words** hablar con toda franqueza.

**mincemeat** [mínsmit] s. picadillo (especialmente el de carne, pasas, manzanas y especias).

**mind** [maɪnd] s. (brain) mente; (thought) pensamiento; inteligencia; (spirit) ánimo, espíritu; (purpose) propósito, intención; (opinion) parecer, opinión; **to be out of one's —** estar loco, haber perdido el juicio; **to change one's —** cambiar de parecer; **to give someone a piece of one's —** cantarle a alguien la verdad; echarle a alguien un buen regaño; **to have a — to** estar por; sentir ganas de; **to make up one's —** decidirse, resolverse; **to my —** a mi modo de ver; **to speak one's — freely** hablar con toda franqueza; v. cuidar; atender a, hacer caso de; obedecer; **I don't —** no tengo inconveniente en ello; **never —** no importa; no se preocupe; no se

moleste; no haga Vd. caso; **to —
one's own business** atendar a lo
suyo, no meterse en lo ajeno.
**mindful** [máɪndfəl] *adj.* atento (a);
cuidadoso (de).
**mine** [maɪn] *pron. pos.* mío (mía, míos,
mías); el mío (la mía, los míos, las
mías); **a book of —** un libro mío.
**mine** [maɪn] *s.* mina; **— sweeper**
dragaminas; *v.* minar; explotar (*una
mina*); extraer (*mineral*).
**miner** [máɪnɚ] *s.* minero.
**mineral** [mínərəl] *adj.* & *s.* mineral.
**mingle** [míngl] *v.* mezclar(se); entre-
mezclar(se); confundir(se); juntarse.
**miniature** [mínɪtʃɚ] *s.* miniatura; *adj.*
en miniatura; diminuto.
**minimal** [mínəml] *adj.* mínimo.
**minimize** [mínəmaɪz] *v.* empequeñecer.
**minimum** [mínəməm] *adj.* & *s.* mínimo.
**mining** [máɪnɪŋ] *s.* minería, explotación de minas; *adj.* minero; **— engineer** ingeniero de minas.
**miniskirt** [mínɪskɚt] *s.* minifalda.
**minister** [mínɪstɚ] *s.* ministro; pastor,
clérigo; *v.* ministrar; atender; proveer,
socorrer.
**ministry** [mínɪstrɪ] *s.* ministerio; socorro, ayuda.
**mink** [mɪŋk] *s.* visón.
**minnow** [míno] *s.* pececillo de río.
**minor** [máɪnɚ] *adj.* (*young*) menor; de
menor edad; (*secondary*) secundario;
**— key** tono menor; *s.* menor de edad;
premisa menor (*de un silogismo*); tono
menor; curso o asignatura menor.
**minority** [mənórətɪ] *s.* minoría; minoridad, menor edad; menor parte.
**minstrel** [mínstrəl] *s.* trovador; bardo,
vate; actor cómico que remeda al
negro norteamericano.
**mint** [mɪnt] *s.* (*flavor*) menta, hierbabuena (*yerbabuena*); (*candy*) pastilla o
bombón de menta; (*money*) casa de
moneda; **a — of money** un montón
de dinero, la mar de dinero; *v.*
acuñar.
**mintage** [míntədʒ] *s.* acuñación; moneda acuñada.
**minuet** [mɪnjuét] *s.* minué.
**minus** [máɪnəs] *adj.* negativo; sin, falto
de; **seven — four** siete menos cuatro;
*s.* menos, signo menos.
**minute** [mínɪt] *s.* minuto; **-s** acta (*de
una junta*); **— hand** minutero.
**minute** [mənjút] *adj.* menudo, diminuto; minucioso, detallado.
**miracle** [mírək]] *s.* milagro.
**miraculous** [mərǽkjələs] *adj.* milagroso.
**mirage** [mərɑ́ʒ] *s.* espejismo.
**mire** [maɪr] *s.* cieno, fango, lodo; *v.*
atascar(se) en el fango; enlodar(se).
**mirror** [mírɚ] *s.* espejo; *v.* reflejar.
**mirth** [mɚθ] *s.* júbilo, regocijo, alegría.
**mirthful** [mɚ́θfəl] *adj.* jubiloso, regocijado, gozoso, alegre.
**miry** [máɪrɪ] *adj.* cenagoso, fangoso,
lodoso.

**misadventure** [mɪsədvéntʃɚ] *s.* desgracia; contratiempo.
**misbehave** [mɪsbihév] *v.* portarse mal,
obrar mal.
**miscarriage** [mɪskǽrɪdʒ] *s.* aborto, malparto; mal éxito; extravío (*de una
carta, papel, etc.*).
**miscarry** [mɪskǽrɪ] *v.* (*fail*) malograrse,
frustrarse; extraviarse (*una carta*);
(*abort*) abortar.
**miscellaneous** [mɪslénɪəs] *adj.* misceláneo, diverso.
**mischief** [místʃɪf] *s.* travesura; diablura;
mal, daño; diablillo, persona travie-
sa.
**mischievous** [místʃɪvəs] *adj.* travieso;
malicioso; dañino.
**misconception** [mɪskənsépʃən] *s.* concepto erróneo.
**misconduct** [mɪskándʌkt] *s.* mala conducta; mala administración; [mɪskən-
dʌ́kt] *v.* maladministrar, manejar mal;
**to — oneself** portarse mal, conducirse mal.
**misdeed** [mɪsdíd] *s.* fechoría, mala
acción.
**misdemeanor** [mɪsdimínɚ] *s.* mal
comportamiento; fechoría.
**miser** [máɪzɚ] *s.* avaro, avariento.
**miserable** [mízrəbl] *adj.* miserable; infeliz, desdichado.
**miserly** [máɪzɚlɪ] *adj.* avariento, avaro;
tacaño, mezquino.
**misery** [mízrɪ] *s.* miseria, desgracia;
estrechez, pobreza; dolor.
**misfortune** [mɪsfórtʃən] *s.* infortunio,
desgracia, desastre.
**misgiving** [mɪsgívɪŋ] *s.* mal presentimiento, aprensión, recelo, temor.
**misguided** [mɪsgáɪdəd] *adj.* mal aconsejado.
**mishap** [míshæp] *s.* desgracia, contratiempo, accidente.
**misjudge** [mɪsdʒʌ́dʒ] *v.* juzgar mal.
**mislaid** [mɪsléd] *pret.* & *p.p. de* **to mislay.**
**mislay** [mɪslé] *v.* extraviar, perder;
poner fuera de su sitio, colocar mal;
traspapelar (*una carta, documento,
etc.*).
**mislead** [mɪslíd] *v.* guiar por mal
camino; extraviar, descarriar; engañar.
**misled** [mɪsléd] *pret.* & *p.p. de* **to mislead.**
**mismanage** [mɪsmǽnɪdʒ] *v.* administrar.
**misplace** [mɪsplés] *v.* extraviar, poner
fuera de su sitio, colocar mal; traspapelar (*una carta, documento, etc.*).
**misprint** [mɪsprínt] *s.* errata, error ti-
pográfico, error de imprenta.
**mispronounce** [míspronauns] *v.* pronunciar mal.
**misrepresent** [mɪsreprɪzént] *v.* falsear,
falsificar; tergiversar.
**miss** [mɪs] *v.* (*not hit*) errar, no acertar;
fallar; (*omit*) equivocar; perder; faltar a; (*feel absence of*) echar de menos;
*Am.* extrañar; **he just -ed being
killed** por poco lo matan; *s.* error;

falla, falta.

**miss** [mɪs] s. señorita; **Miss Smith** la señorita Smith.

**missile** [mísl̩] s. proyectil; arma arrojadiza; adj. arrojadizo, que se puede arrojar o tirar.

**missing** [mísɪŋ] adj. ausente; perdido; **one book is —** falta un libro.

**mission** [míʃən] s. misión.

**missionary** [míʃənɛrɪ] adj. & s. misionero.

**misspell** [mɪsspél] v. escribir con mala ortografía, deletrear mal.

**mist** [mɪst] s. neblina, niebla; llovizna, Ven., Col., Andes garúa; v. lloviznar; anublar.

**mistake** [məsték] s. error, yerro, equivocación; errata (de imprenta); **to make a —** equivocarse; v. equivocar.

**mistaken** [məstékən] p.p. de **to mistake** & adj. equivocado; errado; erróneo, incorrecto; **to be —** estar equivocado, equivocarse, errar.

**mister** [místɚ] s. señor.

**mistook** [mɪstúk] pret. de **to mistake**.

**mistreat** [mɪstrít] v. maltratar.

**mistress** [místrɪs] s. señora; ama, dueña; querida, amante; **school—** maestra.

**mistrial** [mɪstráɪl] s. pleito viciado de nulidad.

**mistrust** [mɪstrʌ́st] s. desconfianza; v. desconfiar de.

**mistrustful** [mɪstrʌ́stfəl] adj. desconfiado, sospechoso, receloso.

**misty** [místɪ] adj. brumoso; nublado; empañado; vago, indistinto.

**misunderstand** [mɪsʌndɚstǽnd] v. comprender mal; entender mal; interpretar mal; no comprender.

**misunderstanding** [mɪsʌndɚstǽndɪŋ] s. equivocación; mala interpretación, mala inteligencia; desavenencia.

**misunderstood** [mɪsʌndɚstúd] pret. & p.p. de **to misunderstand**.

**misuse** [mɪsjús] s. abuso; mal uso; malversación (de fondos); [mɪsjúz] v. abusar de; maltratar; usar o emplear mal; malversar (fondos).

**mite** [maɪt] s. óbolo, friolera, pequeñez; criatura.

**miter** [máɪtɚ] s. mitra; dignidad de obispo.

**mitigate** [mítəget] v. mitigar.

**mitten** [mítn̩] s. mitón (guante de una pieza y sin dedos).

**mix** [mɪks] v. mezclar(se); unir(se), juntar(se), asociar(se); **to — someone up** confundir a uno; s. mezcla; confusión, lío.

**mixture** [míkstʃɚ] s. mezcla; mezcolanza.

**mix-up** [míksʌp] s. equívoco; enredo.

**moan** [mon] s. quejido, gemido; v. gemir; quejarse; lamentar(se).

**moat** [mot] s. foso.

**mob** [mɑb] s. populacho; muchedumbre, gentío, Am. bola (de gente); v. atropellar; apiñarse o agolparse alrededor de.

**mobile** [móbl̩] adj. móvil; movible; movedizo.

**mobilization** [mobl̩əzéʃən] s. movilización.

**mobilize** [móblaɪz] v. movilizar.

**moccasin** [mákəsn̩] s. Am. mocasín (zapato burdo de cuero); Am. mocasín (víbora venenosa).

**mock** [mɔk] v. (ridicule) mofar, mofarse de; (imitate) remedar, imitar; **to — at** mofarse de; burlarse de; s. mofa, burla, escarnio; mímica; remedo; adj. falso, ficticio, imitado; **— battle** simulacro, batalla fingida.

**mockery** [mɔ́kərɪ] s. burla, mofa, escarnio; remedo.

**mockup** [mɑ́kʌp] s. maqueta; modelo.

**mode** [mod] s. modo, manera; moda.

**model** [mádl̩] s. (guide) modelo; (pattern) patrón; (figure) figurín, maniquí; adj. ejemplar; modelo; **— school** escuela modelo; v. modelar; moldear, formar; posar, servir de modelo.

**moderate** [mádərɪt] adj. moderado; templado; módico; [mádəret] v. moderar(se); templar(se).

**moderation** [madəréʃən] s. moderación; templanza.

**modern** [mádɚn] adj. moderno.

**modernize** [mádɚnaɪz] v. modernizar.

**modest** [mádɪst] adj. modesto.

**modesty** [mádəstɪ] s. modestia.

**modification** [madəfəkéʃən] s. modificación.

**modify** [mádəfaɪ] v. modificar.

**modulate** [mádʒəlet] v. modular.

**mohair** [móhɛr] s. moer.

**Mohammedan** [mohǽmədən] adj. & s. mahometano.

**moist** [mɔɪst] adj. húmedo; mojado.

**moisten** [mɔ́ɪsn̩] v. humedecer, mojar.

**moisture** [mɔ́ɪstʃɚ] s. humedad.

**molar** [mólɚ] adj. molar; s. muela.

**molasses** [məlǽsɪz] s. melaza, miel de caña.

**mold** [mold] s. (form) molde, matriz; (substance) moho; tierra vegetal; v. moldear, amoldar; modelar; enmohecer(se), cubrir(se) de moho.

**molder** [móldɚ] v. desmoronarse.

**molding** [móldɪŋ] s. moldura; moldeamiento.

**moldy** [móldɪ] adj. mohoso.

**mole** [mol] s. lunar; topo (animal); dique, malecón, rompeolas.

**molecule** [máləkjul] s. molécula.

**molest** [məlést] v. molestar.

**mollify** [máləfaɪ] v. apaciguar.

**molten** [móltn̩] adj. derretido, fundido, en fusión.

**moment** [mómənt] s. momento; importancia, consecuencia.

**momentary** [mómənterɪ] adj. momentáneo.

**momentous** [moméntəs] adj. importante.

**momentum** [moméntəm] s. momento (de una fuerza); ímpetu.

**monarch** [mánɚk] s. monarca.

**monarchy** [mánɚkɪ] s. monarquía.

**MI**

**monastery** [mánəstɛrɪ] *s.* monasterio.
**Monday** [mʌ́ndɪ] *s.* lunes.
**monetary** [mánətɛrɪ] *adj.* monetario.
**money** [mʌ́nɪ] *s.* dinero; — **changer** cambista; — **order** giro postal; **paper** — papel moneda; **silver** — moneda de plata; **money-making** lucrativo, provechoso, ganancioso.
**monger** [mʌ́ŋgəˈ] *s.* traficante; defensor.
**mongrel** [mʌ́ŋgrəl] *adj.* & *s.* mestizo, mixto, cruzado, *Am.* chusco (*perro*).
**monk** [mʌŋk] *s.* monje.
**monkey** [mʌ́ŋkɪ] *s.* mono; —**shine** monada, monería; — **wrench** llave inglesa; *v.* juguetear; hacer monerías; payasear; entremeterse; **to** — **with** juguetear con; meterse con.
**monogram** [mánəgræm] *s.* monograma.
**monograph** [mánəgræf] *s.* monógrafía.
**monologue** [mánɔg] *s.* monólogo, soliloquio.
**monopolize** [mənápl̩aɪz] *v.* monopolizar, acaparar.
**monopoly** [mənápl̩ɪ] *s.* monopolio.
**monosyllable** [mánəsɪləbl̩] *s.* monosílabo.
**monotone** [mánəton] *adj.* monótono.
**monotonous** [mənátn̩əs] *adj.* monótono.
**monotony** [mənátn̩ɪ] *s.* monotonía.
**monster** [mánstəˈ] *s.* monstruo; *adj.* enorme.
**monstrosity** [mʌnstrásətɪ] *s.* monstruosidad; monstruo.
**monstrous** [mánstrəs] *adj.* monstruoso.
**month** [mʌnθ] *s.* mes.
**monthly** [mʌ́nθlɪ] *adj.* mensual; *s.* publicación mensual; *adv.* mensualmente.
**monument** [mánjəmənt] *s.* monumento.
**monumental** [mʌnjəmɛ́ntl̩] *adj.* monumental; colosal, grandioso.
**moo** [mu] *s.* mugido; *v.* mugir.
**mood** [mud] *s.* humor, disposición de ánimo; modo (*del verbo*); **to be in a good** — estar de buen humor; **to be in the** — **to** estar dispuesto a, tener gana de.
**moody** [múdɪ] *adj.* (*changing*) caprichoso, voluble, mudable; (*sad*) melancólico, mohino.
**moon** [mun] *s.* luna; mes lunar; **once in a blue** — de Pascuas a San Juan, muy rara vez, *Am.* por campanada de vacante, *Am.* a cada muerte de (*o* por la muerte de un) obispo.
**moonlight** [múnlaɪt] *s.* luz de la luna; — **dance** baile a la luz de la luna; — **night** noche de luna.
**moor** [mur] *v.* amarrar, atracar (*un buque*); anclar; estar anclado; *s.* terreno inculto o baldío.
**Moor** [mur] *s.* moro.
**Moorish** [múrɪʃ] *adj.* morisco, moro.
**mop** [map] *s.* *Am.* trapeador; **dust** — limpiapolvo; — **of hair** greñas, cabellera abundante; *v.* limpiar (*el suelo*), *Am.* trapear; **to** — **one's brow**

limpiarse (*o* secarse) la frente; **to** — **up** limpiar; vencer; acabar con.
**mope** [mop] *v.* andar quejumbroso o abatido.
**moral** [mɔ́rəl] *adj.* moral; — **philosophy** ética, moral; *s.* moraleja; **-s** moral, ética.
**morale** [mərǽl] *s.* moral, entereza de ánimo.
**moralist** [mɔ́rəlɪst] *s.* moralista.
**morality** [mərǽlətɪ] *s.* moralidad.
**moralize** [mɔ́rəlaɪz] *v.* moralizar.
**morbid** [mɔ́rbɪd] *adj.* mórbido, morboso: malsano.
**mordant** [mɔ́rdənt] *adj.* mordaz.
**more** [mor] *adj.* & *adv.* más; — **and** — cada vez más, más y más; — **or less** poco más o menos; **there is no** — no hay más, ya no hay; se acabó.
**moreover** [moróvəˈ] *adv.* además.
**morning** [mɔ́rnɪŋ] *s.* mañana; **good** —! ¡buenos días!; **tomorrow** — mañana por la mañana; *adj.* de la mañana; matutino, matinal; **morning-glory** dondiego de día; — **star** lucero del alba.
**morphine** [mɔ́rfin] *s.* morfina.
**morrow** [mɔ́ro]: **on the** — el día de mañana; mañana.
**morsel** [mɔ́rsl̩] *s.* bocado; manjar sabroso.
**mortal** [mɔ́rtl̩] *adj.* & *s.* mortal.
**mortality** [mɔrtǽlətɪ] *s.* mortalidad; mortandad.
**mortar** [mɔ́rtəˈ] *s.* mortero; argamasa, mezcla; **metal** — almirez.
**mortgage** [mɔ́rgɪdʒ] *s.* hipoteca, gravamen; *v.* hipotecar.
**mortify** [mɔ́rtəfaɪ] *v.* mortificar; avergonzar.
**mosaic** [mozéɪk] *adj.* & *s.* mosaico.
**Moslem** [mázləm] *adj.* & *s.* musulmán.
**mosquito** [məskíto] *s.* mosquito; — **net** mosquitero.
**moss** [mɔs] *s.* musgo; **moss-grown** musgoso, cubierto de musgo; anticuado.
**mossy** [mɔ́sɪ] *adj.* musgoso.
**most** [most] *adv.* más; sumamente, muy; *s.* la mayoría, la mayor parte, el mayor número o cantidad; los más; — **people** la mayoría (*o* la mayor parte) de la gente; **at the** — a lo más, a lo sumo; **for the** — **part** por la mayor parte; generalmente, mayormente; **the** — **that I can do** lo más que puedo hacer; **the** — **votes** el mayor número de votos, los más votos.
**mostly** [móstlɪ] *adv.* por la mayor parte; mayormente, principalmente.
**moth** [mɔθ] *s.* polilla; mariposa nocturna; —**ball** bolita de naftalina; **moth-eaten** apolillado.
**mother** [mʌ́ðəˈ] *s.* madre; **mother-of-pearl** madreperla, nácar; *adj.* de madre; materno, maternal; nativo, natal; — **country** madre patria; país natal; — **Superior** superiora; — **tongue** lengua materna; *v.* servir de madre a, cuidar de.

**motherhood** [mʌ́ðɚhʊd] s. maternidad.
**mother-in-law** [mʌ́ðɚɪnlɔ] s. suegra.
**motherly** [mʌ́ðɚlɪ] adj. maternal, materno.
**motif** [motíf] s. motivo, tema.
**motion** [móʃən] s. (movement) moción; movimiento; (signal) ademán; señal, seña; — **sickness** mareo; v. hacer una seña o señas; indicar.
**motionless** [móʃənlɪs] adj. inmóvil, inmoble.
**motion picture** [móʃənpíktʃɚ] s. cine o cinematógrafo; película; fotografía cinematográfica; **motion-picture** adj. cinematográfico.
**motive** [mótɪv] s. motivo; tema; adj. motriz.
**motley** [mátlɪ] adj. abigarrado, multicolor, de diversos colores; variado, mezclado; s. mezcla, mezcolanza.
**motor** [mótɚ] s. motor; automóvil; v. pasear o ir en automóvil.
**motorbike** [mótɚbaɪk] s. motocicleta pequeña; moto.
**motorboat** [mótɚbot] s. autobote, lancha de gasolina, bote de motor.
**motorcar** [mótɚkar] s. automóvil.
**motorcoach** [mótɚkotʃ] s. autobús, ómnibus, Méx. camión, Carib. guagua; Ríopl., Ch. micro; C.A. bus.
**motorcycle** [mótɚsaɪkḷ] s. motocicleta.
**motorist** [mótɚrɪst] s. motorista, automovilista.
**motorman** [mótɚmən] s. motorista.
**motor scooter** [mótɚskutɚ] s. motoneta.
**mottled** [mátḷd] adj. moteado; jaspeado, manchado.
**motto** [máto] s. mote, divisa, lema.
**mould** = **mold.**
**moulder** = **molder.**
**moulding** = **molding.**
**mouldy** = **moldy.**
**mound** [maʊnd] s. montecillo, montículo, montón de tierra.
**mount** [maʊnt] s. (elevation) monte; (horse) montura, cabalgadura, caballo; v. montar; montar a caballo; subir, ascender; armar (una máquina); engastar (joyas).
**mountain** [máʊntṇ] s. montaña; adj. montañés; de montaña; — **goat** cabra montés; — **lion** puma; — **range** cordillera, cadena de montañas.
**mountaineer** [maʊntṇír] s. montañés.
**mountainous** [máʊntṇəs] adj. montañoso.
**mourn** [morn] v. lamentar; deplorar; **to** — **for** llorar a; estar de duelo por.
**mournful** [mórnfəl] adj. fúnebre; lúgubre; lastimero; triste.
**mourning** [mórnɪŋ] s. luto; duelo; lamentación; **to be in** — estar de luto, estar de duelo; adj. de luto.
**mouse** [maʊs] s. ratón; — **trap** ratonera.
**moustache** = **mustache.**
**mouth** [maʊθ] s. boca; abertura; desembocadura, embocadura (de un río).
**mouthful** [máʊθfəl] s. bocado.
**mouthpiece** [máʊθpis] s. boquilla (de

un instrumento de viento); portavoz.
**movable** [múvəbḷ] adj. movible, móvil; **-s** s. pl. muebles, bienes muebles.
**move** [muv] v. (motion) mover(se); (change) mudar(se), mudar de casa; (propose) proponer, hacer la moción de; (game) hacer una jugada (en ajedrez o damas); (emotion) conmover; inducir; — **away** irse; alejarse; apartarse; **to** — **forward** avanzar; **to** — **on** seguir adelante, caminar; **to** — **out** irse, mudarse, mudar de casa; s. movimiento; mudanza (de una casa a otra); paso, trámite (para conseguir algo); jugada, turno (en juegos); **get a** — **on there!** ¡ande! ¡dése prisa!; Am. ¡ándele!
**movement** [múvmənt] s. (motion) movimiento; maniobra; meneo; acción; (mechanism) mecanismo, movimiento (de un reloj); (bowel) evacuación.
**movie** [múvɪ] s. cine, película; **-s** cine.
**mow** [mo] v. segar; cortar (césped).
**mower** [móɚ] s. segador; segadora, cortadora mecánica; máquina segadora.
**mown** [mon] adj. & p.p. segado.
**Mr.** [místɚ] Sr., señor; **Mrs.** [mísɪz] Sra., señora.
**much** [mʌtʃ] adj., adv. & s. mucho; — **the same** casi lo mismo; **as** — **as** tanto como; **how** — ? ¿cuánto?; **not** — **of a book** un libro de poco valor; **not** — **of a poet** un poetastro; **so** — **that** tanto que; **too** — demasiado; **very** — muchísimo; **to make** — **of** dar mucha importancia a.
**muck** [mʌk] s. (manure) estiércol húmedo; (mire) cieno; (filth) porquería, suciedad.
**mucous** [mjúkəs] adj. mucoso; — **membrane** membrana mucosa.
**mud** [mʌd] s. lodo, fango, cieno; — **wall** tapia.
**muddle** [mʌ́dḷ] v. enturbiar; confundir; embrollar; s. confusión, embrollo, lío, desorden.
**muddy** [mʌ́dɪ] adj. fangoso, lodoso; turbio; confuso; v. enlodar, ensuciar; enturbiar.
**muff** [mʌf] s. manguito (para las manos); falla, error (en ciertos juegos); v. no coger, dejar escapar (la pelota).
**muffin** [mʌ́fɪn] s. bollo, panecillo.
**muffle** [mʌ́fḷ] v. embozar; tapar; apagar, amortiguar (un sonido).
**muffler** [mʌ́flɚ] s. bufanda; silenciador (para maquinaria); mofle.
**mug** [mʌg] s. pichel, vaso con asa.
**mulatto** [məlǽto] s. mulato.
**mulberry** [mʌ́lbɛrɪ] s. mora; — **tree** moral.
**mule** [mjul] s. mulo, mula; **muleteer** [mjulətír] s. arriero.
**mull** [mʌl] v. meditar, ponderar, revolver en la mente; calentar (vino, sidra, etc.) con azúcar y especias.
**multiple** [mʌ́ltəpḷ] s. múltiplo; adj. múltiple.
**multiplication** [mʌltəpləkéʃən] s. mul-

tiplicación; — **table** tabla de multiplicar.

**multiplicity** [mʌltəplísətɪ] s. multiplicidad.

**multiply** [mʌ́ltəplaɪ] v. multiplicar(se).

**multitude** [mʌ́ltətjud] s. multitud.

**mum** [mʌm] adj. callado, silencioso; **to keep** — estarse (o quedarse) callado.

**mumble** [mʌ́mbl] v. murmurar, hablar entre dientes; mascullar; s. murmullo; **to talk in a** — mascullar las palabras, hablar entre dientes.

**mummy** [mʌ́mɪ] s. momia.

**mumps** [mʌmps] s. parótidas, paperas.

**munch** [mʌntʃ] v. mascar ruidosamente, mascullar.

**mundane** [məndén] adj. mundano.

**municipal** [mjunísəpl] adj. municipal.

**municipality** [mjunɪsəpǽlətɪ] s. municipio; municipalidad.

**munition** [mjunɪ́ʃən] s. munición; — **plant** fábrica de municiones, arsenal; v. guarnecer, abastecer de municiones.

**mural** [mjúrəl] adj. & s. mural.

**murder** [mɝ́dɚ] s. asesinato, homicidio; v. asesinar.

**murderer** [mɝ́dərɚ] s. asesino, homicida.

**murderess** [mɝ́dərɪs] s. asesina, homicida.

**murderous** [mɝ́dərəs] adj. asesino, homicida.

**murmur** [mɝ́mɚ] s. (noise) murmullo; susurro; (complaint) queja; v. murmurar; susurrar; quejarse.

**muscle** [mʌ́sl] s. músculo.

**muscular** [mʌ́skjələ] adj. muscular; musculoso.

**muse** [mjuz] v. meditar; s. meditación; **Muse** musa.

**museum** [mjuzíəm] s. museo.

**mush** [mʌʃ] s. potaje espeso de maíz; masa de maíz; cualquier masa blanda; sentimentalismo.

**mushroom** [mʌ́ʃrum] s. seta, hongo.

**music** [mjúzɪk] s. música; — **stand** atril.

**musical** [mjúzɪkl] adj. musical, músico; melodioso; armonioso; aficionado a la música; — **comedy** zarzuela, comedia musical.

**musician** [mjuzíʃən] s. músico.

**muskmelon** [mʌ́skmɛlən] s. melón.

**muskrat** [mʌ́skræt] s. almizclera (roedor semejante a la rata).

**muslin** [mʌ́zlɪn] s. muselina.

**muss** [mʌs] v. desarreglar, desordenar; arrugar.

**must** [mʌst] v. defect. (por lo general se usa sólo en el presente) deber; deber de, haber de; tener que.

**mustache** [mʌ́stæʃ] s. bigote, mostacho.

**mustard** [mʌ́stɚd] s. mostaza; — **plaster** sinapismo.

**muster** [mʌ́stɚ] v. pasar lista o revista; juntarse para una formación militar; reunir(se); **to** — **out** dar de baja; **to** — **up one's courage** cobrar valor o ánimo; s. revista (de soldados o marinos); **to pass** — pasar lista o revista; ser aceptable (en una inspección).

**musty** [mʌ́stɪ] adj. mohoso; rancio; añejo.

**mute** [mjut] adj. mudo; s. mudo; letra muda; sordina (de violín).

**mutilate** [mjútlet] v. mutilar.

**mutiny** [mjútn̩ɪ] s. motín; v. amotinarse.

**mutter** [mʌ́tɚ] v. murmurar, refunfuñar; hablar entre dientes; s. murmullo, refunfuño.

**mutton** [mʌ́tn̩] s. carne de carnero; — **chop** chuleta de carnero.

**mutual** [mjútʃʊəl] adj. mutuo.

**muzzle** [mʌ́zl] s. hocico; bozal (para el hocico); boca (de arma de fuego); v. abozalar, poner bozal a; amordazar; hacer callar.

**my** [maɪ] adj. mi (mis).

**myriad** [mírɪəd] s. miríada, diez mil; millares, gran cantidad.

**myrtle** [mɝ́tl] s. mirto, arrayán.

**myself** [maɪsélf] pron. yo mismo; me (como reflexivo); a mí mismo; **by** — solo; **I** — **did it** yo mismo lo hice; **I talk to** — hablo conmigo mismo, hablo para mis adentros.

**mysterious** [mɪstírɪəs] adj. misterioso.

**mystery** [místrɪ] s. misterio.

**mystic** [místɪk] adj. & s. místico.

**mystical** [místɪkl] adj. místico.

**myth** [mɪθ] s. mito, fábula.

**mythology** [mɪθálədʒɪ] s. mitología.

## N

**nab** [næb] v. agarrar, coger; arrestar.

**nag** [næg] s. rocín, caballejo, jaco; v. importunar, irritar (con repetidos regaños).

**nail** [nel] s. clavo; uña (del dedo); — **file** lima (para las uñas); v. clavar; clavetear; agarrar, atrapar.

**naive** [naív] adj. simple, ingenuo, cándido.

**naked** [nékɪd] adj. desnudo.

**nakedness** [nékɪdnɪs] s. desnudez.

**name** [nem] s. (designation) nombre; (fame) renombre, fama; —**sake** tocayo; **by the** — **of** nombrado, llamado; apellidado; **family** — apellido; **to call someone** -**s** motejar o decirle groserías a uno; ponerle apodos a uno; **to make a** — **for oneself** ganar fama; **what is your** —? ¿cómo se llama Vd.?; v. nombrar; mentar, mencionar; llamar.

**nameless** [némlɪs] adj. sin nombre; anónimo.

**namely** [némlɪ] adv. a saber, esto es, es decir.

**nap** [næp] s. siesta; pelo (de un tejido); **to take a** — echar un sueño, echar una siesta; v. dormitar; echar un sueño; sestear.

**nape** [nep] s. nuca, cogote.

**naphtha** [nǽfθə] s. nafta.

**napkin** [nǽpkɪn] s. servilleta.

**narcissus** [nɑrsísəs] s. narciso.

**narcotic** [nɑrkátɪk] adj. & s. narcótico.

**narrate** [nærét] v. narrar.

**narration** [næréʃən] s. narración.

**narrative** [nǽrətɪv] adj. narrativo; s.

narración; narrativa; relato.

**narrow** [nǽro] *adj.* (*cramped*) estrecho; angosto; limitado; (*intolerant*) intolerante; **— escape** trance difícil, escapada difícil; **— search** búsqueda esmerada; **narrow-minded** fanático, intolerante; **-s** *s. pl.* desfiladero, paso; estrecho o estrechos; *v.* angostar(se), estrechar(se); limitar, restringir, reducir; **-ly** *adv.* estrechamente; **he -ly escaped** por poco no se escapa.

**narrowness** [nǽrənɪs] *s.* (*cramped*) estrechez, estrechura, angostura; limitación; (*intolerance*) intolerancia.

**nasal** [nézl] *adj.* nasal.

**nastiness** [nǽstɪnɪs] *s.* suciedad, porquería; grosería.

**nasturtium** [næstɝ́ʃəm] *s.* mastuerzo.

**nasty** [nǽstɪ] *adj.* (*foul*) sucio, asqueroso; feo; (*indecent*) grosero; indecente; **a — fall** una caída terrible; **a — disposition** un genio horrible.

**natal** [nétl] *adj.* natal.

**nation** [néʃən] *s.* nación.

**national** [nǽʃən] *adj.* nacional; *s.* nacional, ciudadano.

**nationalism** [nǽʃənəlɪzm] *s.* nacionalismo.

**nationality** [næʃənǽlətɪ] *s.* nacionalidad.

**native** [nétɪv] *adj.* nativo; natal; natural; indígena; del país, *Am.* criollo; **— of** oriundo de, natural de; *s.* nativo, natural, indígena; habitante.

**nativity** [nətívətɪ] *s.* nacimiento; natividad (*de la Virgen María*); **the Nativity** la Navidad.

**natural** [nǽtʃərəl] *adj.* natural; sencillo, sin afectación; *s.* becuadro (*signo musical*); **he is a — for that job** tiene aptitud natural para ese puesto; **-ly** *adv.* naturalmente; con naturalidad.

**naturalism** [nǽtʃərəlɪzəm] *s.* naturalismo.

**naturalist** [nǽtʃərəlɪst] *s.* naturalista.

**naturalization** [nætʃərələzéʃən] *s.* naturalización.

**naturalize** [nǽtʃərəlaɪz] *v.* naturalizar.

**naturalness** [nǽtʃərəlnɪs] *s.* naturalidad.

**nature** [nétʃɚ] *s.* naturaleza; natural, genio, índole; instinto; especie; **to copy from** — copiar del natural.

**naught** [nɔt] *s.* cero; nada.

**naughty** [nɔ́tɪ] *adj.* malo, desobediente; travieso, pícaro; malicioso.

**nausea** [nɔ́zɪə] *s.* náusea.

**nauseate** [nɔ́zɪet] *v.* dar náuseas, dar bascas, asquear, dar asco; sentir náusea; **to be — ed** tener náuseas.

**nauseating** [nɔ́zɪetɪŋ] *adj.* nauseabundo, asqueroso.

**nautical** [nɔ́tɪkl] *adj.* náutico, naval.

**naval** [névl] *adj.* naval; **— officer** oficial de marina.

**nave** [nev] *s.* nave (*de una iglesia*).

**navel** [névl] *s.* ombligo; **— orange** naranja california (*sin semillas*).

**navigable** [nǽvəgəbl] *adj.* navegable.

**navigate** [nǽvəget] *v.* navegar.

**navigation** [nævəgéʃən] *s.* navegación; náutica.

**navigator** [nǽvəgetɚ] *s.* navegador, navegante.

**navy** [névɪ] *s.* marina de guerra; armada; **— blue** azul marino; **— yard** astillero, arsenal.

**nay** [ne] *adv.* no; no sólo . . . sino (que) también; *s.* no, voto negativo.

**near** [nɪr] *adv.* (*space, time*) cerca; (*almost*) casi; **— at hand** cerca, a la mano; **I came — forgetting to do it** por poco se me olvida hacerlo; **to come (go, draw) —** acercarse; **— sighted** miope; *prep.* cerca de; **— the end of the month** hacia fines del mes; *adj.* cercano, próximo; estrecho, íntimo; **— silk** seda imitada; **I had a — accident** por poco me sucede un accidente; *v.* acercarse (a).

**near-by** [nɪrbáɪ] *adv.* cerca, a la mano; *adj.* cercano, próximo.

**nearly** [nírlɪ] *adv.* casi, cerca de; aproximadamente, próximamente; **I — did it** estuve al punto de hacerlo, estuve para hacerlo.

**nearness** [nírnɪs] *s.* cercanía, proximidad.

**neat** [nit] *adj.* pulcro, aseado, limpio; ordenado; esmerado; hábil, diestro; **-ly** *adv.* aseadamente; esmeradamente; ordenadamente; hábilmente.

**neatness** [nítnɪs] *s.* pulcritud, aseo; limpieza; esmero; claridad.

**nebulous** [nébjuləs] *adj.* nebuloso.

**necessarily** [nɛsəsérəlɪ] *adv.* necesariamente.

**necessary** [nésəsɛrɪ] *adj.* necesario; **necessaries** *s. pl.* necesidades, requisitos.

**necessitate** [nəsésətet] *v.* necesitar, precisar.

**necessity** [nəsésətɪ] *s.* necesidad.

**neck** [nɛk] *s.* cuello; pescuezo; garganta; **— of land** istmo; **low —** escote; **— and —** parejos (*en una carrera*).

**necklace** [néklɪs] *s.* collar; gargantilla.

**necktie** [néktaɪ] *s.* corbata.

**necrology** [nɛkrálədʒɪ] *s.* necrología.

**need** [nid] *s.* (*lack*) necesidad; (*poverty*) pobreza; **for — of** por falta de; **if — be** si fuere menester, en caso de necesidad; *v.* necesitar; tener necesidad de; hacerle falta a uno; tener que.

**needful** [nídfəl] *adj.* necesario; necesitado.

**needle** [nídl] *s.* aguja.

**needlepoint** [nídlpɔɪnt] *s.* encaje de mano.

**needless** [nídlɪs] *adj.* innecesario, inútil.

**needlework** [nídlwɝk] *s.* labor, bordado; costura.

**needy** [nídɪ] *adj.* necesitado, menesteroso.

**ne'er** [nɛr] *adv. contr.* de **never**; **ne'er-do-well** *s.* persona incompetente; haragán.

**negation** [nɪgéʃən] *s.* negación; negativa.

MU

**negative** [négətɪv] *adj.* negativo; *s.* negativa; negación, partícula o voz negativa; negativa (*de una fotografía*).

**neglect** [nɪglékt] *s.* negligencia; descuido; abandono; *v.* descuidar; desatender; abandonar; **to — to** dejar de, olvidar, olvidarse de.

**neglectful** [nɪgléktfəl] *adj.* negligente, descuidado.

**negligence** [néglədʒəns] *s.* negligencia.

**negligent** [néglədʒənt] *adj.* negligente, descuidado.

**negotiate** [nɪgóʃɪet] *v.* negociar; agenciar; vencer (*un obstáculo o dificultad*), dar cima a.

**negotiation** [nɪgoʃɪéʃən] *s.* negociación.

**negro** [nígro] *s.* & *adj.* negro.

**Negroid** [nígrɔɪd] *adj.* negroide.

**neigh** [ne] *s.* relincho; *v.* relinchar.

**neighbor** [nébɚ] *s.* vecino; prójimo; *adj.* vecino; cercano.

**neighborhood** [nébɚhud] *s.* vecindad; vecindario; inmediación; **in the — of a hundred dollars** cerca de cien dólares.

**neighboring** [nébərɪŋ] *adj.* vecino; cercano; colindante.

**neither** [níðɚ] *pron.* ninguno, ni (el) uno ni (el) otro; **— of the two** ninguno de los dos; *adj.* ninguno; **— one of us** ninguno de nosotros; *conj.* ni; **— . . . nor** ni . . . ni; **— will I** tampoco yo, ni yo tampoco.

**neologism** [nɪálədʒɪzm] *s.* neologismo.

**neophyte** [níofaɪt] *s.* neófito.

**nephew** [néfju] *s.* sobrino.

**nepotism** [népətɪzm] *s.* nepotismo.

**nerve** [nɚv] *s.* (*anatomy*) nervio; (*courage*) valor, ánimo; audacia; (*effrontery*) descaro; **-s** nervios; nerviosidad; **to strain every —** esforzarse hasta más no poder, poner el mayor empeño posible.

**nervous** [nɚvəs] *adj.* nervioso.

**nervousness** [nɚvəsnɪs] *s.* nerviosidad; agitación.

**nest** [nɛst] *s.* nido; nidada; **— egg** nidal; ahorros; **— of baskets (boxes, tables)** juego graduado de cestas (cajas, mesitas); **wasp's —** avispero; *v.* anidar.

**nestle** [nésl] *v.* acurrucarse; abrigar(se); anidar.

**net** [nɛt] *s.* red; malla; tejido de mallas; *adj.* de mallas, de punto de malla; *v.* redar, enredar, coger con red; cubrir con una red.

**net** [nɛt] *adj.* neto; **— price** precio neto; **— profit** ganancia neta o líquida; *v.* producir una ganancia neta o líquida; obtener una ganancia líquida.

**nettle** [nétl] *s.* ortiga; *v.* picar, irritar, enfadar.

**network** [nétwɚk] *s.* red; malla; **radio —** red de estaciones radiofónicas.

**neurotic** [njʊrátɪk] *adj.* & *s.* neurótico.

**neuter** [njútɚ] *adj.* neutro.

**neutral** [njútrəl] *adj.* neutral; neutro.

**neutrality** [njútrǽlətɪ] *s.* neutralidad.

**neutralize** [njútrəlaɪz] *v.* neutralizar.

**never** [névɚ] *adv.* nunca, jamás; **—**

**mind** no importa; no haga Vd. caso; no se moleste Vd.; **never-ending** perpetuo, eterno; de nunca acabar.

**nevertheless** [nɛvɚðəlés] *adv.* & *conj.* sin embargo, no obstante, con todo, empero.

**new** [nju] *adj.* (*not old*) nuevo; moderno; (*fresh*) fresco; reciente; *adv.* recién; **—born baby** criatura recién nacida.

**newcomer** [njúkʌmɚ] *s.* recién llegado.

**newly** [njúlɪ] *adv.* nuevamente, recientemente; **— arrived** recién llegado; **— wed** recién casado.

**newness** [njúnɪs] *s.* novedad, calidad de nuevo.

**news** [njuz] *s.* noticias, nuevas; novedades; **piece of —** noticia, nueva; **—boy** vendedor de periódicos; **— reel** película noticiera; película de noticias mundiales; **—stand** puesto de periódicos.

**newsmonger** [njúzmʌŋgɚ] *s.* chismoso, chismero, gacetilla.

**newspaper** [njúzpepɚ] *s.* periódico.

**next** [nɛkst] *adj.* (*future*) próximo; entrante, que viene; (*following*) siguiente; contiguo; **in the — life** en la otra vida; **to be — in turn** tocarle a uno, ser su turno; *adv.* después, luego; **— best** segundo en cualidad o importancia; *prep.*; **— to** junto a; al lado de; después de.

**nibble** [níbl] *s.* mordisco; *v.* mordiscar, mordisquear; picar, morder.

**nice** [naɪs] *adj.* (*attractive*) fino; bueno; amable, simpático; lindo; primoroso; (*refined*) refinado; esmerado; preciso, exacto; **-ly** *adv.* con esmero; con finura o primor; sutilmente, con delicadeza; amablemente; bien; **to get along -ly with** llevarse bien con.

**nicety** [náɪsətɪ] *s.* fineza, finura; delicadeza; exactitud.

**niche** [nɪtʃ] *s.* nicho.

**nick** [nɪk] *s.* mella, desportilladura; **in the — of time** en el momento crítico; *v.* mellar, desportillar.

**nickel** [níkl] *s.* níquel; moneda de cinco centavos; **nickel-plated** niquelado.

**nickname** [níknem] *s.* mote, apodo; *v.* apodar, poner apodo a.

**niece** [nis] *s.* sobrina.

**niggardly** [nígɚdlɪ] *adj.* mezquino, ruin, tacaño; *adv.* mezquinamente, ruinmente.

**night** [naɪt] *s.* noche; **good —!** ¡buenas noches!; **tomorrow —** mañana por la noche; *adj.* nocturno; de noche; **— owl** buho; trasnochador; **— watchman** sereno, vigilante nocturno.

**nightfall** [náɪtfɔl] *s.* anochecer, caída de la tarde, anochecida.

**nightgown** [náɪtgaʊn] *s.* camisa de dormir, camisa de noche, *Am.* camisón.

**nightingale** [náɪtŋgel] *s.* ruiseñor.

**nightly** [náɪtlɪ] *adv.* cada noche, todas las noches; *adj.* nocturno, de noche.

**nightmare** [náɪtmɛr] *s.* pesadilla.

**nihilism** [náɪɪlɪzm] *s.* nihilismo.

**nimble** [nímbl̩] *adj.* ágil, ligero; listo.

**nip** [nɪp] *v.* (*pinch*) pellizcar; (*bite*) mordiscar; (*frostbite*) marchitar, helar (*por la acción del frío*); **to — in the bud** cortar en germen, destruir al nacer; **to — off** despuntar; podar; *s.* pellizco; mordisco; trago.

**nipple** [nípl̩] *s.* teta, tetilla, pezón; pezón de goma.

**nitrate** [náɪtret] *s.* nitrato.

**nitric acid** [náɪtrɪkǽsɪd] *s.* ácido nítrico.

**nitrogen** [naítrədʒən] *s.* nitrógeno.

**no** [no] *adv.* no; **— longer** ya no; **there is — more** no hay más; *adj.* ningun(o); **— matter how much** por mucho que; **— one** ninguno, nadie; **— smoking** se prohibe fumar; **I have — friend** no tengo ningún amigo; **of — use** inútil, sin provecho; *s.* no, voto negativo.

**nobility** [nobílətɪ] *s.* nobleza.

**noble** [nóbl̩] *s.* & *adj.* noble.

**nobleman** [nóbl̩mən] *s.* noble.

**nobleness** [nóbl̩nɪs] *s.* nobleza.

**nobly** [nóblɪ] *adv.* noblemente.

**nobody** [nóbadɪ] *pron.* nadie, ninguno.

**nocturnal** [naktə́nl̩] *adj.* nocturno.

**nod** [nad] *v.* inclinar la cabeza (*para hacer una seña, saludar, o asentir*); cabecear, dar cabezadas (*dormitando*); *s.* inclinación de cabeza, saludo; señal de asentimiento (*con la cabeza*).

**noise** [nɔɪz] *s.* ruido; barullo; sonido; *v.* divulgar; **it is being -d about that** corre el rumor que.

**noiseless** [nɔ́ɪzlɪs] *adj.* sin ruido, silencioso, quieto; **-ly** *adv.* sin ruido, silenciosamente.

**noisily** [nɔ́ɪzɪlɪ] *adv.* ruidosamente.

**noisy** [nɔ́ɪzɪ] *adj.* ruidoso.

**nominal** [námən l̩] *adj.* nominal.

**nominate** [námənet] *v.* nombrar, designar.

**nomination** [namənéʃən] *s.* nombramiento, nominación.

**nonconformist** [nankənfɔ́rmɪst] *adj.* & *s.* disidente.

**none** [nʌn] *pron.* ninguno; ningunos; nada; **I want — of that** no quiero nada de eso; **that is — of his business** no le importa a él eso; *adv.* no, de ningún modo; **— the less** no menos; **to be — the happier for that** no estar por eso más contento.

**nonentity** [nanéntətɪ] *s.* nulidad, persona o cosa inútil.

**nonintervention** [nanɪntəvénʃən] *s.* no intervención.

**nonpartisan** [nanpártəzən] *adj.* imparcial; independiente.

**nonsense** [nánsɛns] *s.* tontería, necedad; disparate, desatino.

**noodle** [núdl̩] *s.* tallarín, fideo, pasta (*para sopa*).

**nook** [nʊk] *s.* rincón; **breakfast —** desayunador.

**noon** [nun] *s.* mediodía.

**noonday** [núnde] *s.* mediodía; *adj.* meridiano, de mediodía; **— meal** comida de mediodía.

**noontide** [núntaɪd] *s.* mediodía.

**noontime** [núntaɪm] *s.* mediodía.

**noose** [nus] *s.* dogal; lazo, nudo corredizo, *Am.* gaza; *v.* lazar, coger con lazo; hacer un lazo corredizo en.

**nor** [nɔr] *conj.* ni; **neither . . . —** ni . . . ni.

**norm** [nɔrm] *s.* norma.

**normal** [nɔ́rml̩] *adj.* normal; *s.* norma; normal, línea perpendicular.

**north** [nɔrθ] *s.* norte; *adj.* septentrional; norteño; del norte; **— pole** polo norte, polo ártico; **— wind** cierzo, norte; **North American** norteamericano; *adv.* al norte, hacia el norte.

**northeast** [nɔrθíst] *adj.* & *s.* nordeste; *adv.* hacia el nordeste, rumbo al nordeste.

**northeastern** [nɔrθístən] *adj.* del nordeste, nordeste.

**northern** [nɔ́rðən] *adj.* septentrional; norteño; del norte; hacia el norte; **— lights** aurora boreal.

**northerner** [nɔ́rðənə] *s.* norteño, habitante del norte.

**northward** [nɔ́rθwəd] *adv.* hacia el norte, rumbo al norte.

**northwest** [nɔrθwést] *adj.* & *s.* noroeste; *adv.* hacia el noroeste.

**northwestern** [nɔrθwéstən] *adj.* noroeste, del noroeste.

**Norwegian** [nɔrwídʒən] *adj.* & *s.* noruego.

**nose** [noz] *s.* nariz; proa (*de un barco*); **— dive** picada (*de un avíon*); *v.* olfatear; **to — around** husmear, curiosear.

**nostalgia** [nastǽldʒɪə] *s.* nostalgia, añoranza.

**nostrils** [nástrəlz] *s. pl.* narices, ventanas de la nariz.

**not** [nat] *adv.* no; **— at all** de ningún modo; de nada (*contestación a* "thank you"); **— at all sure** nada seguro; **— even a word** ni siquiera una palabra.

**notable** [nótəbl̩] *adj.* notable.

**notary** [nótərɪ] *s.* notario.

**notation** [notéʃən] *s.* notación; apunte; anotación.

**notch** [natʃ] *s.* muesca, ranura; hendidura; *v.* ranurar, hacer una ranura en.

**note** [not] *s.* nota; apunte, apuntación; **bank —** billete de banco; **promissory —** pagaré, abonaré; *v.* notar, observar, reparar; **to — down** apuntar.

**notebook** [nótbʊk] *s.* libreta, cuaderno, libro de apuntes.

**noted** [nótɪd] *adj.* notable, célebre, famoso.

**noteworthy** [nótwɜðɪ] *adj.* notable, célebre.

**nothing** [nʌ́θɪŋ] *s.* nada; cero; **for —** por nada; inútilmente; de balde, gratis.

**notice** [nótɪs] *s.* noticia; aviso, advertencia, anuncio; mención; **to give a short —** avisar a última hora; **to take — of** hacer caso de, prestar

NE

atención a; *v.* notar, observar; prestar atención a; hacer caso a (*o* de); notificar.

**noticeable** [nótɪsəbl̩] *adj.* notable; conspicuo; perceptible.

**notify** [nótəfaɪ] *v.* notificar, avisar.

**notion** [nóʃən] *s.* noción; idea; capricho; **-s** mercería, artículos menudos (*como alfileres, botones, etc.*), chucherías.

**notorious** [notórɪəs] *adj.* notorio.

**notwithstanding** [nɑtwɪθstǽndɪŋ] *prep.* a pesar de; *adv.* & *conj.* no obstante, sin embargo; — **that** a pesar (de) que.

**nought** = **naught.**

**noun** [naun] *s.* nombre, sustantivo.

**nourish** [nɝ́ɪʃ] *v.* nutrir, alimentar.

**nourishing** [nɝ́ɪʃɪŋ] *adj.* nutritivo, alimenticio.

**nourishment** [nɝ́ɪʃmənt] *s.* nutrimento, sustento, alimento; nutrición.

**novel** [návl̩] *s.* novela; *adj.* novel, nuevo; raro, original.

**novelist** [návl̩ɪst] *s.* novelista.

**novelty** [návl̩tɪ] *s.* novedad; innovación; **novelties** novedades.

**November** [novémbɚ] *s.* noviembre.

**novice** [návɪs] *s.* novicio; novato, principiante.

**now** [nau] *adv.* ahora; ya; — ... — ya ... ya, ora ... ora; — **and then** de vez en cuando, de cuando en cuando; — **that** ahora que; — **then** ahora bien; **he left just** — salió hace poco, *Ríopl., Ch., Andes* recién salió.

**nowadays** [náuədez] *adv.* hoy día.

**nowhere** [nóhwɛr] *adv.* en ninguna parte, a ninguna parte.

**noxious** [nákʃəs] *adj.* nocivo.

**nucleus** [njúklɪəs] *s.* núcleo.

**nude** [njud] *adj.* desnudo.

**nudge** [nʌdʒ] *v.* codear, tocar con el codo; *s.* codazo ligero.

**nugget** [nʌ́gɪt] *s.* pepita; pedazo.

**nuisance** [njúsn̩s] *s.* molestia; lata, fastidio; persona o cosa fastidiosa.

**null** [nʌl] *adj.* nulo; — **and void** nulo e inválido.

**nullify** [nʌ́lɪfaɪ] *v.* invalidar; anular.

**numb** [nʌm] *adj.* entumecido o entumido, aterido; **to become** — entumecerse, entumirse, aterirse; *v.* entumecer.

**number** [nʌ́mbɚ] *s.* número; *v.* numerar; ascender a (*cierto número*); **to** — **him among one's friends** contarle entre sus amigos.

**numberless** [nʌ́mbɚlɪs] *adj.* innumerable, sin número.

**numeral** [njúmrəl] *s.* número, cifra; guarismo; *adj.* numeral.

**numerical** [njumérɪkl̩] *adj.* numérico.

**numerous** [njúmrəs] *adj.* numeroso; numerosos, muchos.

**nun** [nʌn] *s.* monja.

**nuptial** [nʌ́pʃəl] *adj.* nupcial; **-s** *s. pl.* nupcias, bodas.

**nurse** [nɝs] *s.* (*for the sick*) enfermera, enfermero; (*for children*) niñera, aya; *Méx., Ven., Col., Andes* nana, *Am.* manejadora, *Andes* pilmama; *C.A.*

china; **wet** — nodriza, ama de cría; *v.* criar, amamantar, dar de mamar, lactar; mamar; cuidar (*a un enfermo*); abrigar (*rencor*).

**nursery** [nɝ́srɪ] *s.* cuarto para niños; criadero, semillero (*de plantas*); **day** — sala donde se cuida y divierte a los niños.

**nurture** [nɝ́tʃɚ] *s.* crianza; nutrimento; *v.* criar; nutrir; cuidar; fomentar.

**nut** [nʌt] *s.* nuez (*nombre genérico de varias frutas como la almendra, la castaña, la avellana, etc.*); tuerca; loco, tipo raro o extravagante.

**nutcracker** [nʌ́tkrækɚ] *s.* cascanueces.

**nutmeg** [nʌ́tmeg] *s.* nuez moscada.

**nutrient** [nútrɪənt] *s.* nutritivo.

**nutrition** [njutríʃən] *s.* nutrición; nutrimento, alimento.

**nutritious** [njutríʃəs] *adj.* nutritivo, alimenticio.

**nutritive** [njútrɪtɪv] *adj.* nutritivo.

**nutshell** [nʌ́tʃɛl] *s.* cáscara de nuez (*o de otro fruto semejante*); **in a** — en suma, en breve, en pocas palabras.

**nymph** [nɪmf] *s.* ninfa.

## O

**oak** [ok] *s.* roble; encina; — **grove** robledo o robledal; **live** — encina siempreverde.

**oar** [or] *s.* remo; *v.* remar, bogar.

**oasis** [oésɪs] *s.* oasis.

**oat** [ot] *s.* avena (*planta*); **-s** avena, granos de avena.

**oath** [oθ] *s.* juramento; blasfemia, reniego.

**oatmeal** [ótmɪl] *s.* harina de avena; gachas de avena.

**obedience** [əbídɪəns] *s.* obediencia.

**obedient** [əbídɪənt] *adj.* obediente.

**obesity** [obísətɪ] *s.* obesidad, gordura.

**obey** [əbé] *v.* obedecer.

**object** [ábdʒɪkt] *s.* objeto; cosa; complemento (*del verbo*); [əbdʒékt] *v.* objetar; oponerse; tener inconveniente.

**objection** [əbdʒékʃən] *s.* objeción, reparo; inconveniente.

**objective** [əbdʒéktɪv] *adj.* objetivo; — **case** caso complementario; *s.* objetivo; fin, propósito.

**obligate** [ábləget] *v.* obligar, constreñir; comprometer.

**obligation** [abləgéʃən] *s.* (*duty*) obligación; deber (*debt*) deuda; **to be under** — estar obligado a; estar agradecido a, deber favores a.

**obligatory** [əblígətorɪ] *adj.* obligatorio.

**oblige** [əbláɪdʒ] *v.* obligar; complacer; **much -ed!** ¡muchas gracias! ¡muy agradecido!; **to be very much -ed to someone** quedar muy agradecido con alguien.

**obliging** [əbláɪdʒɪŋ] *adj.* complaciente, obsequioso, comedido, cortés.

**oblique** [əblík] *adj.* oblicuo.

**obliterate** [əblítəret] *v.* borrar; arrasar, destruir.

**oblivion** [əblívɪən] *s.* olvido.

**oblivious** [əblívɪəs] *adj.* olvidado, abstraído.

**oblong** [ábləŋ] *adj.* cuadrilongo; oblongo.

**obnoxious** [əbnákʃəs] *adj.* ofensivo; molesto; odioso.

**oboe** [óbo] *s.* oboe.

**obscene** [əbsín] *adj.* obsceno.

**obscenity** [əbsénətɪ] *s.* obscenidad, indecencia.

**obscure** [əbskjúr] *adj.* obscuro; *v.* obscurecer; ofuscar.

**obscurity** [əbskjúrətɪ] *s.* obscuridad.

**obsequies** [ábsɪkwɪz] *s.* exequias, honras, funerales.

**obsequious** [əbsíkwɪəs] *adj.* obsequioso; servil, zalamero.

**observable** [əbzɜvəbl̩] *adj.* observable.

**observance** [əbzɜ́vəns] *s.* observancia; ceremonia, rito.

**observant** [əbzɜ́vənt] *adj.* observador; observante.

**observation** [abzɜvéʃən] *s.* observación.

**observatory** [əbzɜ́vətorɪ] *s.* observatorio; mirador.

**observe** [əbzɜ́v] *v.* observar; guardar (*las fiestas religiosas*); celebrar (*una fiesta*).

**observer** [əbzɜ́vɚ] *s.* observador.

**obsess** [əbsés] *v.* obsesionar, causar obsesión.

**obsession** [əbséʃən] *s.* obsesión; idea fija.

**obsolete** [ábsəlit] *adj.* anticuado; desusado.

**obstacle** [ábstəkl̩] *s.* obstáculo.

**obstinacy** [ábstənəsɪ] *s.* obstinación, terquedad, porfía.

**obstinate** [ábstənɪt] *adj.* obstinado, terco, porfiado.

**obstreperous** [abstrépɚəs] *adj.* estrepitoso, turbulento.

**obstruct** [əbstrákt] *v.* obstruir.

**obstruction** [əbstrákʃən] *s.* obstrucción; impedimento, estorbo.

**obtain** [əbtén] *v.* obtener, conseguir, alcanzar, adquirir.

**obtainable** [əbténəbl̩] *adj.* obtenible, asequible.

**obtrusive** [əbtrúsɪv] *adj.* intruso, entremetido.

**obviate** [ábvɪet] *v.* obviar; allanar (*una dificultad*)

**obvious** [ábvɪəs] *adj.* obvio, evidente.

**occasion** [əkéʒən] *s.* (*timely*) ocasión; (*chance*) oportunidad; (*cause*) motivo, causa; (*event*) acontecimiento; *v.* ocasionar, causar.

**occasional** [əkéʒənl̩] *adj.* ocasional; infrecuente, poco frecuente; **-ly** *adv.* de vez en cuando, a veces.

**occidental** [aksədéntl̩] *adj.* & *s.* occidental.

**occlusive** [oklúsɪv] *adj.* & *s.* oclusivo.

**occult** [əkʌ́lt] *adj.* oculto, misterioso.

**occupant** [ákjəpənt] *s.* ocupante; inquilino.

**occupation** [akjəpéʃən] *s.* ocupación; trabajo, empleo, oficio.

**occupy** [ákjəpaɪ] *v.* ocupar.

**occur** [əkɜ́] *v.* ocurrir, suceder; **to — to one** ocurrírsele a uno, venirle a la mente.

**occurrence** [əkɜ́əns] *s.* ocurrencia, suceso, caso, acontecimiento.

**ocean** [óʃən] *s.* océano.

**o'clock** [əklák] *contr. de* of the clock; **it is two —** son las dos.

**octave** [áktɪv] *s.* octava.

**October** [aktóbɚ] *s.* octubre.

**oculist** [ákjəlɪst] *s.* oculista.

**odd** [ɑd] *adj.* (*rare*) extraño, singular, raro; (*not even*) non, impar; **— change** suelto, cambio sobrante; **— moments** momentos libres, momentos de ocio; **— shoe** zapato suelto (*sin compañero*); **— volume** tomo suelto; **thirty —** treinta y tantos, treinta y pico; **-ly** *adv.* extrañamente, de un modo raro.

**oddity** [ádətɪ] *s.* rareza.

**odds** [ɑdz] *s. pl. o sing.* diferencia, disparidad (*en apuestas*); ventaja, puntos de ventaja (*en apuestas*); **— and ends** retazos, trozos sobrantes, pedacitos varios; **the — are against me** la suerte me es contraria, estoy de mala suerte; **to be at -s with** estar reñido o enemistado con.

**ode** [od] *s.* oda.

**odious** [ódɪəs] *adj.* odioso.

**odor** [ódɚ] *s.* olor; **bad —** mal olor, hedor.

**odorous** [ódərəs] *adj.* oloroso.

**o'er** [or] *contr. de* over.

**of** [av, ʌv] *prep.* de; **— course** por supuesto, claro, ya se ve; **— late** últimamente; **a quarter — five** las cinco menos cuarto; **to smell —** oler a; **to taste —** saber a.

**off** [ɔf] *adv.* (*distant*) lejos, fuera, a distancia; (*not attached*) suelto; apagado (*la luz*); (*equivale al reflexivo se en ciertos verbos*: marcharse, irse, *etc.*); **— and on** de vez en cuando; a intervalos; **ten cents —** rebaja de diez centavos; **ten miles —** a una distancia de diez millas; **to take a day —** ausentarse por un día; descansar por un día; *adj.* ausente; distante, más remoto; quitado; **the — side** el lado más remoto; **with his hat —** con el sombrero quitado; **the electricity is —** está cortada la electricidad; **to be — in one's accounts** estar errado en sus cuentas; **to be — to war** haberse ido a la guerra; **to be well —** ser persona acomodada, estar en buenas circunstancias; *prep.* lejos de; **off-color** de mal color; verde (*indecente*); **— shore** a vista de la costa; **— standard** de calidad inferior; **— the road** desviado, descarriado; a un lado del camino; **to be — duty** no estar de turno; estar libre.

**offend** [əfénd] *v.* ofender.

**offender** [əféndɚ] *s.* ofensor; transgresor, delincuente.

**offense** [əféns] *s.* ofensa; agravio; delito, culpa; **no — was meant** lo hice (*o* lo dije) sin malicia; **weapon of —** arma ofensiva.

**offensive** [əfénsɪv] *adj.* ofensivo; *s.* ofensiva.

**offer** [ɔ́fɚ] v. ofrecer; **to — to do it** ofrecerse a hacerlo; s. oferta; ofrecimiento; promesa; propuesta.

**offering** [ɔ́fɚɪŋ] s. ofrenda; oferta, ofrecimiento.

**offhand** [ɔ́fhǽnd] adv. de improviso, por el momento, sin pensarlo, impensadamente; adj. impensado, hecho de improviso; **in an — manner** con indiferencia; descuidadamente; sin plan.

**office** [ɔ́fɪs] s. (function) oficio; cargo; función; (place) oficina, despacho; — **building** edificio para oficinas; **post — correo; box —** taquilla, Ch., Ríopl. boletería; **through the good -s of** por el intermedio de.

**officer** [ɔ́fɪsɚ] s. (office holder) oficial; funcionario; (police) policía, gendarme; agente de policía; v. comandar, dirigir (como oficial); proveer de oficiales.

**official** [əfíʃəl] adj. oficial; s. oficial, funcionario; empleado público.

**officiate** [əfíʃɪet] v. oficiar.

**officious** [əfíʃəs] adj. oficioso, intruso, entremetido.

**offset** [ɔfsét] v. compensar por; contrapesar.

**offshore** [ɔfʃór] adj. & adv. (land) terral; (at sea) lejos de la playa.

**offspring** [ɔ́fsprɪŋ] s. prole, hijos, descendientes; hijo, vástago; resultado, consecuencia.

**offstage** [ɔfstédʒ] adv. & adj. entre bastidores.

**oft** [ɔft] = **often.**

**often** [ɔ́fən] adv. muchas veces, con frecuencia, frecuentemente, a menudo; **how —?** ¿cuántas veces?; ¿cada cuándo?

**ogre** [ógɚ] s. ogro, gigante, monstruo.

**oil** [ɔɪl] s. aceite; óleo; petróleo; — **can** alcuza; — **painting** pintura al óleo; — **well** pozo de petróleo; **motor —** aceite para motores; v. aceitar, engrasar, lubricar; untar.

**oilcloth** [ɔ́ɪlklɔθ] s. hule, tela de hule.

**oily** [ɔ́ɪlɪ] adj. aceitoso, oleoso; grasiento.

**ointment** [ɔ́ɪntmənt] s. ungüento.

**O.K.** [óké] adj. bueno; corriente, convenido; adv. bien; **it's —** está bien; **to give one's —** dar el V°. B°. (visto bueno); v. dar el V°. B°., aprobar.

**old** [old] adj. viejo; antiguo; añejo; — **maid** solterona; — **man** anciano, viejo; — **wine** vino añejo; **days of —** días de antaño; **how — are you?** ¿cuántos años tiene Vd.? ¿qué edad tiene Vd.?; **to be — enough to . . .** tener bastante edad para . . . ; **to be an — hand at** ser ducho en, ser muy perito o experto en.

**olden** [óldn̩] adj. viejo, antiguo, de antaño.

**old-fashioned** [óldfǽʃənd] adj. pasado de moda; anticuado; chapado a la antigua.

**old-time** [óldtáɪm] adj. vetusto, de tiempos antiguos; de antaño.

**old-timer** [óldtáɪmɚ] s. antiguo residente.

**olive** [álɪv] s. oliva, aceituna; — **grove** olivar; — **oil** aceite de oliva; — **tree** olivo; — **branch** ramo de olivo; adj. aceitunado, verde aceituna.

**omelet** [ámlɪt] s. tortilla de huevos.

**omen** [ómən] s. agüero, presagio.

**ominous** [ámənəs] adj. siniestro, de mal agüero, amenazador.

**omission** [omíʃən] s. omisión.

**omit** [omít] v. omitir; dejar de.

**omnipotent** [amnípətənt] adj. omnipotente, todopoderoso.

**on** [an] prep. en; a; sobre, encima de; — **all sides** por todos lados; — **arriving** al llegar; — **board** a bordo; en el tren; — **condition that** con la condición de que; — **credit** al fiado; — **foot** a pie; — **horseback** a caballo; — **Monday** el lunes; — **purpose** a propósito, adrede; — **sale** de venta; — **time** a tiempo; a plazo; adv. adelante; **farther** — más adelante; **later** — después; — **and** — sin parar, sin cesar, continuamente; adj. puesto; **his hat is —** lleva puesto el sombrero; **the light is —** está encendida la luz.

**once** [wʌns] adv. una vez; en otro tiempo; — **and for all** una vez por todas, definitivamente; — **in a while** de vez en cuando; — **upon a time** érase que se era; en otro tiempo; **at —** al punto; a un mismo tiempo; **just this —** siquiera esta vez, sólo esta vez; conj. una vez que, cuando; luego que.

**one** [wʌn] adj. un, uno; — **hundred** cien, ciento; — **thousand** mil; **his — chance** su única oportunidad; **the — and only** el único; **one-armed** manco; **one-eyed** tuerto; **one-sided** de un solo lado; unilateral; parcial; desigual; **one-way** de un sentido; s. & pron. uno; — **another** uno a otro; — **by** — uno a uno; uno por uno; **the — who** el que, la que; **the green —** el verde; **this —** éste, ésta.

**oneself** [wʌnsélf] pron. se (reflexivo); **to speak to —** hablar consigo mismo; **by —** solo; por sí, por sí solo.

**ongoing** [ángoɪŋ] adj. que está haciéndose; corriente; que cursa.

**onion** [ʌ́njən] s. cebolla.

**onlooker** [ánlukɚ] s. espectador, mirón.

**only** [ónlɪ] adj. solo, único; adv. sólo, solamente; conj. sólo que.

**onset** [ánset] s. embestida, ataque; impulso inicial, primer ímpetu; arranque.

**onto** [ántu] prep. a; sobre.

**onward** [ánwɚd] adv. adelante; hacia adelante.

**onyx** [ániks] s. onix, ónice.

**ooze** [uz] v. rezumar(se), escurrir(se).

**opal** [ópl] s. ópalo.

**opaque** [opék] adj. opaco; mate.

**open** [ópən] v. abrir(se); **to — into** comunicarse con, tener paso a; **to — onto** dar a, caer a, mirar a; adj. abierto; franco, sincero; expuesto (a); — **country** campo raso, campo abierto;

— **question** cuestión discutible; — **to temptation** expuesto a caer en la tentación; — **winter** invierno sin nieve; **in the — air** al (o en el) aire libre; **open-minded** receptivo; de amplias miras; **—mouthed** boquiabierto, con la boca abierta; **open-end** [ópənénd] sin límites; sin trabas; s. campo raso, aire libre.

**opening** [ópənɪŋ] s. (hole) abertura; (beginning) apertura, comienzo; (clearing) claro (en un bosque); (vacancy) puesto vacante; oportunidad; adj. primero; — **night of a play** estreno de una comedia; **the — number** el primer número (de un programa).

**opera** [ápərə] s. ópera; — **glasses** gemelos; — **house** ópera, teatro de la ópera; **comic** — ópera cómica, zarzuela.

**operate** [ápəret] v. (function) operar; funcionar; obrar; (manage) maniobrar; manejar; **to — on a person** operar a una persona.

**operation** [apəréʃən] s. (function) operación; funcionamiento; (management) manipulación; manejo; maniobra; **to be in** — funcionar, estar funcionando.

**operator** [ápəretə] s. operador, cirujano; maquinista, mecánico, operario; especulador (en la Bolsa); **mine** — explotador de minas; **telegraph** — telegrafista; **telephone** — telefonista.

**operetta** [apərétə] s. opereta, zarzuela.

**opinion** [əpínjən] s. opinión, parecer.

**opium** [ópiəm] s. opio.

**opponent** [əpónənt] s. contrario, adversario, antagonista.

**opportune** [apətjún] adj. oportuno; a propósito.

**opportunist** [apətúnɪst] s. oportunista.

**opportunity** [apətjúnəti] s. oportunidad; ocasión.

**oppose** [əpóz] v. oponer(se); oponerse a.

**opposing** [əpózɪŋ] adj. opuesto, contrario.

**opposite** [ápəzɪt] adj. (contrary) opuesto; contrario; (facing) frontero, de enfrente; — **to** frente a; prep. frente a, en frente de; s. contrario; **the** — lo opuesto, lo contrario.

**opposition** [apəzíʃən] s. oposición; resistencia.

**oppress** [əprés] v. oprimir; agobiar.

**oppression** [əpréʃən] s. opresión.

**oppressive** [əprésɪv] adj. (harsh) opresivo; (distressing) abrumador; gravoso; bochornoso, sofocante.

**oppressor** [əprésə] s. opresor.

**optic** [áptɪk] adj. óptico; **-s** s. óptica.

**optical** [áptɪkl] adj. óptico.

**optician** [aptíʃən] s. óptico.

**optimism** [áptəmɪzəm] s. optimismo.

**optimist** [áptəmɪst] s. optimista.

**optimistic** [aptəmístɪk] adj. optimista.

**option** [ápʃən] s. opción, derecho de escoger; alternativa.

**optional** [ápʃənl] adj. discrecional.

**opulence** [ápjələns] s. opulencia, riqueza, abundancia.

**opulent** [ápjələnt] adj. opulento, rico; abundante.

**or** [ɔr] conj. o; u (delante de o, ho).

**oracle** [ɔ́rəkl] s. oráculo.

**oral** [órəl] adj. oral; bucal.

**orange** [ɔ́rɪndʒ] s. naranja; — **blossom** azahar; — **grove** naranjal; — **tree** naranjo; adj. de naranja; anaranjado.

**orangeade** [ɔrɪndʒéd] s. naranjada.

**oration** [oréʃən] s. discurso, peroración, arenga.

**orator** [ɔ́rətə] s. orador.

**oratory** [ɔ́rətori] s. oratoria, elocuencia; oratorio, capilla.

**orb** [ɔrb] s. orbe.

**orbit** [ɔ́rbɪt] s. órbita; v. moverse en órbita.

**orbital** [ɔ́rbɪt] adj. orbital.

**orchard** [ɔ́rtʃəd] s. huerto.

**orchestra** [ɔ́rkɪstrə] s. orquesta; — **seat** butaca, luneta, Am. platea (de orquesta).

**orchid** [ɔ́rkɪd] s. orquídea.

**ordain** [ɔrdén] v. ordenar; decretar.

**ordeal** [ɔrdíl] s. prueba penosa.

**order** [ɔ́rdə] s. (request) orden (s.); pedido; (group) clase; orden; (arrangement) orden (m.); **holy -s** órdenes sagradas; **in** — en orden; en buen estado; en regla; **in — to** para, a fin de; **in — that** para que, a fin de que; **made to** — mandado hacer, hecho a la medida; **to be out of** — estar descompuesto; estar desordenado; no estar en regla; v. ordenar; mandar; arreglar; pedir (hacer un pedido); **to — away** echar, despedir, expulsar.

**orderly** [ɔ́rdəli] adj. ordenado; en orden, bien arreglado; bien disciplinado; s. ordenanza (soldado); asistente de hospital.

**ordinal** [ɔ́rdɪnl] adj. ordinal; — **number** número ordinal.

**ordinance** [ɔ́rdnəns] s. ordenanza, ley, reglamento.

**ordinarily** [ɔrdņérəli] adv. ordinariamente, por lo común.

**ordinary** [ɔ́rdņeri] adj. ordinario.

**ore** [or] s. mineral.

**organ** [ɔ́rgən] s. órgano; **hand** — organillo.

**organic** [ɔrgǽnɪk] adj. orgánico; constitutivo, fundamental.

**organism** [ɔ́rgənɪzəm] s. organismo.

**organist** [ɔ́rgənɪst] s. organista.

**organization** [ɔrgənəzéʃən] s. organización; organismo; entidad; sociedad.

**organize** [ɔ́rgənaɪz] v. organizar(se).

**organizer** [ɔ́rgənaɪzə] s. organizador.

**orgy** [ɔ́rdʒɪ] s. orgía.

**orient** [ɔ́rɪent] s. oriente; v. orientar.

**oriental** [orɪéntl] adj. & s. oriental.

**orientate** [ɔ́rɪentet] v. orientar.

**orientation** [orɪentéʃən] s. orientación.

**orifice** [ɔ́rəfɪs] s. orificio.

**origin** [ɔ́rədʒɪn] s. origen.

**original** [ərídʒənl] adj. & s. original; **-ly** adv. originalmente, originariamente; en el principio, al principio.

**originality** [ərɪdʒənǽləti] s. originali-

**OF**

dad.

**originate** [ərídʒənet] *v.* originar(se).

**oriole** [óriol] *s.* oriol (*pájaro*).

**ornament** [ɔ́rnəmənt] *s.* ornamento, adorno; [ɔ́rnəmɛnt] *v.* ornamentar, adornar, ornar.

**ornamental** [ɔrnəmɛ́ntl] *adj.* ornamental, de adorno, decorativo.

**ornate** [ɔrnét] *adj.* ornado, adornado en exceso; — **style** estilo florido.

**orphan** [ɔ́rfən] *adj.* & *s.* huérfano; — **asylum** hospicio, orfanato, asilo de huérfanos; *v.* dejar huérfano a.

**orthodox** [ɔ́rθədaks] *adj.* ortodoxo.

**orthography** [ɔrθágrəfɪ] *s.* ortografía.

**oscillate** [ásəlet] *v.* oscilar.

**ostentation** [astəntéʃən] *s.* ostentación, boato.

**ostentatious** [astəntéʃəs] *adj.* ostentoso.

**ostrich** [ɔ́strɪtʃ] *s.* avestruz.

**other** [ʌ́ðɚ] *adj.* & *s.* otro; — **than** otra cosa que; más que; **every** — **day** cada dos días, un día sí y otro no; **some** — **day** otro día.

**otherwise** [ʌ́ðɚwaɪz] *adv.* de otro modo; en otros respetos; *adj.* otro, diferente.

**otter** [átɚ] *s.* nutria; piel de nutria.

**ought** [ɔt] *v. defect.* (*por lo general se traduce por el presente y el condicional de* deber) debo, debes, etc.; debería, deberías, etc.; debiera, debieras, etc.

**ounce** [auns] *s.* onza.

**our** [aur] *adj.* nuestro (nuestra, nuestros, nuestras).

**ours** [aurz] *pron. pos.* nuestro (nuestra, nuestros, nuestras); el nuestro (la nuestra, los nuestros, las nuestras); **a friend of** — un amigo nuestro.

**ourselves** [aursélvz] *pron.* nosotros mismos; nos (*reflexivo*); a nosotros mismos; **we** — nosotros mismos; **by** — solos; por nosotros; *véase* **herself.**

**oust** [aust] *v.* echar, expulsar.

**out** [aut] *adv.* fuera; afuera; hacia fuera; — **of fear** por miedo, de miedo; — **of humor** malhumorado; — **of money** sin dinero; — **of print** agotado; — **of touch with** aislado de, sin contacto con; — **of tune** desentonado; **made** — **of** hecho de; **to fight it** — decidirlo luchando; **to have it** — **with** habérselas con; **to speak** — hablar francamente; *adj.* ausente; apagado; — **and** — **criminal** criminal empedernido; — **and** — **refusal** una negativa redonda; — **size** tamaño poco común o extraordinario; **before the week is** — antes de que termine la semana; **the book is just** — acaba de publicarse el libro; **the secret is** — se ha divulgado el secreto.

**outbreak** [áutbrek] *s.* (*eruption*) erupción; (*revolt*) motín, insurrección, tumulto; (*attack*) ataque, arranque (*de ira*); **at the** — **of the war** al estallar la guerra.

**outburst** [áutbɚst] *s.* explosión; estallido; arranque (*de pasión*); erupción.

**outcast** [áutkæst] *adj.* excluido, desechado; desterrado; *s.* paria (*persona excluida de la sociedad*).

**outcome** [áutkʌm] *s.* resultado, consecuencia.

**outcry** [áutkraɪ] *s.* grito; clamor.

**outdoor** [áutdor] *adj.* externo; fuera de la casa; — **games** juegos al aire libre.

**outdoors** [autdórz] *adv.* puertas afuera, fuera de casa, al aire libre, al raso; *s.* aire libre, campo raso, campiña.

**outer** [áutɚ] *adj.* exterior, externo.

**outfit** [áutfɪt] *s.* equipo; pertrechos; *v.* equipar, habilitar, aviar.

**outgoing** [áutgoɪŋ] *adj.* (*leaving*) saliente; (*extrovert*) extrovertido.

**outguess** [autgés] *v.* anticipar; madrugar.

**outing** [áutɪŋ] *s.* excursión, gira (jira), caminata.

**outlaw** [áutlɔ] *s.* forajido, bandido; prófugo, fugitivo; *v.* proscribir, declarar ilegal.

**outlay** [áutle] *s.* gasto, desembolso; [áutlé] *v.* gastar, desembolsar.

**outlet** [áutlet] *s.* salida; desaguadero, desagüe.

**outline** [áutlaɪn] *s.* (*abstract*) bosquejo, esbozo; (*boundary*) contorno; *v.* bosquejar, esbozar; delinear.

**outlive** [autlív] *v.* sobrevivir.

**outlook** [áutluk] *s.* vista; perspectiva.

**outlying** [áutlaɪɪŋ] *adj.* circundante, exterior, remoto (*del centro*).

**out-of-date** [áutəvdét] *adj.* fuera de moda, anticuado.

**outpost** [áutpost] *s.* avanzada.

**output** [áutput] *s.* rendimiento; producción total.

**outrage** [áutredʒ] *s.* ultraje; *v.* ultrajar.

**outrageous** [autrédʒəs] *adj.* afrentoso; atroz.

**outran** [autræn] *pret. de* **to outrun.**

**outright** [autráɪt] *adv.* & *adj.* sin rodeos; cabal; completo.

**outrun** [autrʌ́n] *v.* aventajar (*en una carrera*); dejar atrás; *p.p. de* **to outrun.**

**outset** [áutsɛt] *s.* comienzo, principio.

**outshine** [autʃáɪn] *v.* eclipsar, sobrepasar (*en brillo o lucidez*).

**outshone** [autʃón] *pret. & p.p. de* **to outshine.**

**outside** [áutsáɪd] *adj.* (*external*) exterior; externo; (*foreign*) foráneo, extranjero; *adv.* fuera, afuera; fuera de casa; *prep.* fuera de; *s.* exterior, parte exterior; superficie; lado de afuera; **in a week, at the** — en una semana, a lo sumo; **to close on the** — cerrar por fuera.

**outsider** [autsáɪdɚ] *s.* foráneo, persona de fuera; extraño.

**outskirts** [áutskɚts] *s. pl.* alrededores, arrabales, cercanías.

**outspoken** [áutspókən] *adj.* franco, francote, *Ven., Méx., C.A., Carib.* claridoso.

**outstanding** [áutstǽndɪŋ] *adj.* sobresaliente; destacado, notable; — **bills** cuentas por cobrar; — **debts** deudas por pagar.

**outstretched** [autstrétʃt] *adj.* extendido; **with — arms** con los brazos abiertos.

**outward** [áutwɘᵈd] *adj.* (*external*) exterior, externo; (*apparent*) aparente; superficial; *adv.* fuera, hacia fuera; **— bound** que sale, de salida; para fuera, para el extranjero; **-ly** *adv.* exteriormente; por fuera; aparentemente.

**outweigh** [autwé] *v.* exceder en peso o valor; sobrepujar.

**oval** [óvl̩] *adj.* oval, ovalado; *s.* óvalo.

**ovary** [óvɘrɪ] *s.* ovario.

**ovation** [ovéʃɘn] *s.* ovación.

**oven** [ʌ́vɘn] *s.* horno.

**over** [óvɘ·] *prep.* sobre; por; por encima de; encima de; a través de; al otro lado de; más de; **— night** por la noche, durante la noche; (*véase* **overnight**); **— to** a; **all — the city** por toda la ciudad; *adv.* encima; al otro lado; otra vez, de nuevo; **— again** otra vez, de nuevo; **— against** en contraste con; **— and —** una y otra vez, repetidas veces; **—curious** demasiado curioso; **—generous** demasiado generoso; **— here** acá, aquí; **— there** allá, allí; **two years and —** más de dos años; **to do it —** hacerlo otra vez, volver a hacerlo; *adj.* excesivo; **it is all —** ya se acabó, se ha acabado; ha pasado.

**overalls** [óvɘ·ɔlz] *s. pl. Am.* overol, overoles (*pantalones de trabajo*).

**overate** [ovɘ·ét] *pret. de* **to overeat.**

**overboard** [óvɘ·bord] *adv.* al mar, al agua.

**overcame** [ovɘ·kém] *pret. de* **to overcome.**

**overcast** [óvɘ·kæst] *adj.* encapotado, nublado; **to become —** encapotarse, nublarse; [ovɘ·kǽst] *v.* nublar o anublar; sobrehilar (*dar puntadas sobre el borde de una tela*); *pret. & p.p. de* **to overcast.**

**overcharge** [ovɘ·tʃárdʒ] *v.* cargar demasiado; cobrar demasiado.

**overcoat** [óvɘ·kot] *s.* sobretodo, abrigo.

**overcome** [ovɘ·kʌ́m] *v.* vencer; rendir; *p.p. & adj.* vencido; rendido; agobiado; **to be — by weariness** estar rendido de fatiga.

**overdue** [ovɘ·dú] *adj.* atrasado; vencido sin pago.

**overeat** [ovɘ·ít] *v.* hartarse.

**overeaten** [ovɘ·ítn̩] *p.p. de* **to overeat.**

**overexcite** [óvɘrɪksáit] *v.* sobreexcitar.

**overflow** [óvɘ·flo] *s.* derrame, desbordamiento; inundación; superabundancia; [ovɘ·fló] *v.* derramarse, desbordarse; rebosar; inundar.

**overgrown** [óvɘ·grón] *adj.* denso, frondoso, poblado (*de follaje, herbaje, etc.*); **— boy** muchachón, muchacho demasiado crecido para su edad.

**overhang** [ovɘ·hǽŋ] *v.* colgar por encima de; proyectarse o sobresalir por encima de; adornar con colgaduras; amenazar (*dícese de un desastre o calamidad*).

**overhaul** [ovɘ·hól] *v.* reparar (*de cabo a rabo*); remendar; alcanzar (*en una*

carrera).

**overhead** [óvɘ·hɛd] *s.* gastos generales (*renta, seguro, alumbrado, calefacción, etc.*); *adj.* de arriba; elevado; **— expenses** gastos generales; [óvɘ·hɛ́d] *adv.* encima de la cabeza, arriba; en lo alto.

**overhear** [ovɘ·hír] *v.* oír por casualidad, alcanzar a oír, acertar a oír.

**overheard** [ovɘ·hɘ́d] *pret. & p.p. de* **to overhear.**

**overheat** [óvɘ·hít] *v.* recalentar(se); calentar(se) demasiado.

**overhung** [ovɘ·hʌ́ŋ] *pret. & p.p. de* **to overhang.**

**overland** [óvɘ·lænd] *adv. & adj.* por tierra.

**overlap** [ovɘ·lǽp] *v.* solapar.

**overlay** [ovɘ·lé] *v.* cubrir; incrustar.

**overload** [ovɘ·lód] *v.* sobrecargar; [óvɘ·lod] *s.* sobrecarga.

**overlook** [ovɘ·lúk] *v.* mirar a (*desde lo alto*); dar a, tener vista a; pasar por alto, omitir; perdonar (*faltas*); descuidar, no notar; inspeccionar, examinar.

**overly** [óvɘ·lɪ] *adv.* excesivamente.

**overnight** [óvɘ·náit] *adv.* durante la noche; toda la noche; *adj.* de noche; nocturno; **— bag** saco de noche; **— trip** viaje de una noche.

**overpass** [óvɘ·pǽs] *v.* viaducto.

**overpower** [ovɘ·páuɘ·] *v.* subyugar, abrumar, vencer.

**overran** [ovɘ·rǽn] *pret. de* **to overrun.**

**override** [ovɘ·ráid] *v.* anular; invalidar.

**overrule** [ovɘrúl] *v.* anular.

**overrun** [ovɘ·rʌ́n] *v.* desbordarse, mundar; sobrepasar; infestar, invadir; *p.p. de* **to overrun.**

**overseas** [óvɘ·síz] *adv.* en ultramar, allende los mares; *adj.* de ultramar.

**oversee** [ovɘ·sí] *v.* dirigir; vigilar.

**overseer** [óvɘ·sir] *s.* sobrestante, capataz; inspector, superintendente.

**overshoe** [óvɘ·ʃu] *s.* chanclo; zapato de goma, caucho o hule.

**oversight** [óvɘ·sait] *s.* inadvertencia, negligencia, descuido.

**overstep** [ovɘ·stép] *v.* sobrepasarse, propasarse; traspasar; **to — the bounds** traspasar los límites; propasarse.

**overtake** [ovɘ·ték] *v.* alcanzar.

**overtaken** [ovɘ·tékɘn] *p.p. de* **to overtake.**

**overthrew** [ovɘ·θrú] *pret. de* **to overthrow.**

**overthrow** [óvɘ·θro] *s.* (*overturn*) derrocamiento; (*defeat*) derrota, destrucción; caída; [ovɘ·θró] *v.* derrocar; derribar, echar abajo, volcar; destronar.

**overthrown** [ovɘ·θrón] *p.p. de* **to overthrow.**

**overtime** [óvɘ·taim] *adv. & adj.* en exceso de las horas estipuladas; **— pay** sobresueldo.

**overtook** [ovɘ·túk] *pret. de* **to overtake.**

**overture** [óvɘ·tʃɘ·] *s.* obertura, preludio; propuesta, proposición.

**overturn** [ovɘ·tɘ́n] *v.* volcar(se); trastornar; derribar; echar abajo.

**overwhelm** [ovəhwélm] *v.* abrumar, agobiar; oprimir; arrollar.

**overwhelming** [ovəhwélmɪŋ] *adj.* abrumador; opresivo; arrollador, irresistible, poderoso.

**overwork** [óvəwə́k] *v.* atarearse, afanarse más de lo debido, trabajar demasiado; *s.* exceso de trabajo.

**owe** [o] *v.* deber, adeudar.

**owing** [óɪŋ] *adj.* debido; — **to** debido a.

**owl** [aul] *s.* lechuza, buho, *Méx., C.A.* tecolote.

**own** [on] *adj.* propio; **a house of his —** una casa suya; **his — people** los suyos; **to be on one's —** no estar a merced ajena; trabajar por su propia cuenta; **to come into one's —** entrar en posesión de lo suyo; **to hold one's —** mantenerse firme; *v.* poseer, tener; admitir, reconocer; **to — to** confesar; **to — up** confesar.

**owner** [ónə] *s.* dueño, amo; propietario; poseedor.

**ownership** [ónəʃɪp] *s.* posesión, propiedad.

**ox** [aks] (pl. **oxen** [áksn̩]) *s.* buey.

**oxygen** [áksədʒən] *s.* oxígeno.

**oyster** [óɪstə] *s.* ostra, ostión.

**ozone** [ózon] *s.* ozono.

## P

**pace** [pes] *s.* paso; *v.* pasear, andar; andar al paso; marchar; medir a pasos.

**pacemaker** [pésmekə] *s.* marcapaso.

**pacific** [pəsífɪk] *adj.* pacífico.

**pacify** [pǽsəfaɪ] *v.* pacificar, apaciguar; calmar.

**pack** [pæk] *s.* fardo, lío, carga; manada (*de lobos*); cuadrilla, pandilla (*de ladrones*); jauría (*de perros*); muchedumbre; baraja (*de naipes*); — **animal** acémila, bestia de carga; *v.* empacar, empaquetar; embalar; enlatar; envasar; apiñar(se); cargar (*una bestia*); hacer (*el baúl, la maleta*); **to — off** despedir de repente; echar a la calle; largarse, irse.

**package** [pǽkɪdʒ] *s.* paquete; fardo, bulto; cajetilla (*de cigarrillos*).

**packer** [pǽkə] *s.* empacador; embalador, envasador.

**packet** [pǽkɪt] *s.* paquetillo; cajetilla.

**packing** [pǽkɪŋ] *s.* (*covering*) embalaje; envase; (*filling*) relleno; — **box** caja para embalar o empacar; — **house** establecimiento frigorífico, fábrica para envasar o enlatar comestibles.

**pact** [pækt] *s.* pacto, convenio.

**pad** [pæd] *s.* almohadilla, cojincillo; tableta, bloc de papel; *v.* rellenar; forrar; acolchar.

**padding** [pǽdɪŋ] *s.* relleno (*de pelo, algodón, paja, etc.*), *Andes* guata; ripio, palabras o frases inútiles.

**paddle** [pǽdl̩] *s.* pala; remo de canoa; — **wheel** rueda de paleta; *v.* remar con pala; apalear; chapotear (*en el agua*).

**paddock** [pǽdək] *s.* dehesa.

**padlock** [pǽdlɑk] *s.* candado; *v.* cerrar con candado.

**pagan** [pégən] *s.* & *adj.* pagano.

**paganism** [pégənɪzəm] *s.* paganismo.

**page** [pedʒ] *s.* página; paje; "botones" (*de hotel*), mensajero; *v.* paginar; vocear, llamar a voces.

**pageant** [pǽdʒənt] *s.* (*parade*) manifestación, desfile, procesión, pompa; (*drama*) representación al aire libre.

**paid** [ped] *pret.* & *p.p. de* **to pay.**

**pail** [pel] *s.* balde, cubo, cubeta.

**pain** [pen] *s.* dolor; sufrimiento; **-s** esmero; **on** (**under**) — **of** so pena de; **to be in —** estar sufriendo, tener dolores; **to take -s** esmerarse, extremarse; *v.* doler; causar dolor; afligir.

**painful** [pénfəl] *adj.* doloroso; penoso; arduo.

**painless** [pénlɪs] *adj.* sin dolor; libre de dolor.

**painstaking** [pénztekɪŋ] *adj.* esmerado, cuidadoso; aplicado.

**paint** [pent] *s.* (*mixture*) pintura, color; (*rouge*) colorete; *v.* pintar; pintarse (*la cara*); **to — the town red** irse de juerga o de parranda, *Am.* irse de farra.

**paintbrush** [péntbrʌʃ] *s.* (*art*) pincel; (*house*) brocha.

**painter** [péntə] *s.* pintor.

**painting** [péntɪŋ] *s.* pintura.

**pair** [pɛr] *s.* par; pareja; **a — of scissors** unas tijeras; *v.* aparear(se); hacer pareja, hacer pares; **to — off** aparear(se).

**pajamas** [pədʒǽməz] *s. pl.* pijama.

**pal** [pæl] *s.* compañero, camarada.

**palace** [pǽlɪs] *s.* palacio.

**palate** [pǽlɪt] *s.* paladar.

**palatial** [pəléʃl̩] *adj.* suntuoso.

**pale** [pel] *adj.* pálido; descolorido; *v.* palidecer, ponerse pálido o descolorido.

**paleness** [pélnɪs] *s.* palidez.

**palisade** [pǽləsed] *s.* palizada, estacada; **-s** riscos, acantilados.

**pall** [pɔl] *v.* empalagar; aburrir; **it -s on me** me empalaga; me aburre; *s.* paño de ataúd; palia (*lienzo que se pone encima del cáliz*).

**palliative** [pǽljətɪv] *adj.* & *s.* paliativo.

**pallid** [pǽlɪd] *adj.* pálido.

**pallor** [pǽlə] *s.* palidez.

**palm** [pɑm] *s.* palma; palmera; — **Sunday** Domingo de Ramos; — **tree** palma, palmera; *v.* **to — something off on someone** pasar o dar algo indeseable a una persona (*sin que se dé cuenta de ello*).

**palpable** [pǽlpəbl̩] *adj.* palpable, tangible; evidente.

**palpitate** [pǽlpətet] *v.* palpitar, latir.

**palpitation** [pælpətéʃən] *s.* palpitación; latido.

**paltry** [pɔ́ltrɪ] *adj.* mezquino, miserable, despreciable, insignificante.

**pamper** [pǽmpə] *v.* mimar, consentir (*a un niño*).

**pamphlet** [pǽmflɪt] *s.* folleto, *Am.* panfleto.

**pan** [pæn] *s.* cazuela, cacerola; cazo; platillo (*de balanza*); **dish** — cazo para lavar platos; **frying** — sartén; *v.* **to** — **out** (**well**) salir bien, dar buen resultado.

**Pan American** [pǽnəmérəkən] *adj.* panamericano.

**pancake** [pǽnkek] *s.* tortita de harina, *Ven.*, *Col.* panqué; *Ríopl.* panqueque.

**pander** [pǽndɚ] *s.* alcahuete, encubridor *v.* alcahuetear, servir de alcahuete.

**pane** [pen] vidrio, cristal (*de ventana o puerta*); cuadro (*de vidrio*).

**panel** [pǽnl̩] *s.* panel, tablero; cuarterón (*de puerta, ventana, etc.*); tabla (*doble pliegue de una falda o vestido*); **jury** — jurado; *v.* proveer de (*o adornar con*) paneles.

**pang** [pæŋ] *s.* dolor agudo; angustia, tormento.

**panhandle** [pǽnhændl̩] *s.* mango de sartén; territorio en forma de mango; *v.* mendigar.

**panic** [pǽnɪk] *adj. & s.* pánico; **panic-stricken** sobrecogido de pánico.

**panorama** [pænərǽmə] *s.* panorama.

**pansy** [pǽnzɪ] *s.* pensamiento (*flor*).

**pant** [pænt] *v.* jadear; palpitar; **to** — **for** anhelar, ansiar.

**panther** [pǽnθɚ] *s.* pantera.

**panting** [pǽntɪŋ] *s.* jadeo, palpitación; *adj.* jadeante.

**pantomime** [pǽntəmaɪm] *s.* pantomima.

**pantry** [pǽntrɪ] *s.* despensa.

**pants** [pænts] *s. pl.* pantalones.

**papa** [púpə] *s.* papá.

**papacy** [pépəsɪ] *s.* papado.

**papal** [pépl̩] *adj.* papal.

**paper** [pépɚ] *s.* (*material*) papel; (*daily*) periódico; (*essay*) tema, ensayos; **-s** papeles, documentos, credenciales; **naturalization -s** carta de naturaleza, certificado de ciudadanía; — **of pins** cartón de alfileres; **on** — escrito; por escrito; *adj.* de papel; para papel; — **doll** muñeca de papel; — **money** papel moneda; —**weight** pisapapeles; *v.* empapelar.

**paperback** [pépɚbæk] *s. & adj.* libro en rústica.

**paperwork** [pépɚwɚk] *s.* preparación de escritos; papeleo.

**paprika** [pæpríkə] *s.* pimentón.

**par** [pɑr] *s.* (*equality*) paridad, igualdad; (*standard*) valor nominal; — **value** valor a la par; **above** — sobre par, a premio, con prima; **at** — a la par; **below** — bajo par, a descuento; **on a** — **with** al par de, al nivel de, igual a; **to feel above** — sentirse mejor que de ordinario; **to feel below** — sentirse menos bien que de ordinario.

**parable** [pǽrəbl̩] *s.* parábola (*alegoría bíblica*).

**parachute** [pǽrəʃut] *s.* paracaídas.

**parachutist** [pǽrəʃutɪst] *s.* paracaidista.

**parade** [pəréd] *s.* (*procession*) desfile, procesión, manifestación; paseo; (*re-view*) parada; — **ground** campo de maniobras; **to make a** — **of** ostentar, hacer ostentación de; *v.* desfilar, pasar en desfile; marchar en parada; hacer ostentación de.

**paradigm** [pǽrədɪm], [pǽrədaɪm] *s.* paradigma.

**paradise** [pǽrədaɪs] *s.* paraíso.

**paradox** [pǽrədɑks] *s.* paradoja.

**paraffin** [pǽrəfɪn] *s.* parafina.

**paragraph** [pǽrəgræf] *s.* párrafo; *v.* dividir en párrafos.

**Paraguayan** [pærəgwáɪən] *adj. & s.* paraguayo.

**parallel** [pǽrəlɛl] *adj. & s.* paralelo; *v.* ser (*o correr*) paralelo a; comparar, cotejar.

**paralysis** [pərǽləsɪs] *s.* parálisis.

**paralyze** [pǽrəlaɪz] *v.* paralizar.

**paramount** [pǽrəmaʊnt] *adj.* importantísimo, superior, supremo, máximo.

**paranoia** [pærənója] *s.* paranoia.

**parapet** [pǽrəpɪt] *s.* parapeto.

**paraphrase** [pǽrəfrez] *v.* parafrasear.

**parasite** [pǽrəsaɪt] *s.* parásito.

**parasol** [pǽrəsɔl] *s.* parasol, sombrilla.

**paratroops** [pǽrətrups] *s.* tropas paracaidistas.

**parcel** [pársl̩] *s.* paquete; parcela, porción, lote (*de terreno*); — **post** paquete postal; *v.* parcelar, dividir en porciones o parcelas; hacer paquetes; **to** — **out** repartir.

**parch** [pɑrtʃ] *v.* resecar(se); tostar(se).

**parchment** [pártʃmənt] *s.* pergamino.

**pardon** [párdn̩] *s.* perdón; indulto; **I beg your** — perdone Vd.; dispense Vd.; *v.* perdonar; dispensar; indultar.

**pare** [pɛr] *v.* mondar, pelar (*manzanas, patatas, etc.*); cortar, recortar; **to** — **down expenditures** reducir gastos.

**parent** [pérənt] *s.* padre, madre; origen; **-s** padres.

**parentage** [pérəntɪdʒ] *s.* linaje; padres.

**parental** [pərént l̩] *adj.* parental.

**parenthesis** [pərénθəsɪs] (*pl.* **parentheses** [pərénθəsiz]) *s.* paréntesis.

**parish** [pǽrɪʃ] *s.* parroquia.

**parishioner** [pəríʃənɚ] *s.* parroquiano, feligrés; **-s** fieles, feligreses.

**park** [pɑrk] *s.* parque; *v.* estacionar, dejar (*un automóvil*); estacionarse; **-ing lot** *Ch.*, *Ríopl.* playa de estacionamiento; *Mex.*, *Ven.* estacionamiento; *Col.* parqueadero; **-ing space** sitio o lugar para estacionarse; **free -ing** estacionamiento gratis; **no -ing** se prohibe estacionarse; no estacionarse.

**parlance** [párləns] *s.* lenguaje.

**parley** [párlɪ] *s.* parlamento, discusión, conferencia; *v.* parlamentar, discutir.

**parliament** [párləmənt] *s.* parlamento.

**parliamentary** [pɑrləméntərɪ] *adj.* parlamentario.

**parlor** [párlɚ] *s.* sala, salón; sala de recibo; — **car** coche salón; **beauty** — salón de belleza.

**parochial** [pərókɪəl] *adj.* parroquial.

OV

**parody** [pǽrədɪ] s. parodia; v. parodiar.
**parole** [pəról] s. palabra de honor; **to put on** — dejar libre (a un prisionero) bajo palabra de honor; v. dejar libre bajo palabra de honor.
**parrot** [pǽrət] s. cotorra, loro, perico, papagayo; v. remedar, repetir como loro.
**parry** [pǽrɪ] v. parar, quitar o reparar (un golpe); s. quite, reparo.
**parsley** [párslɪ] s. perejil.
**parsnip** [pársnəp] s. chirivía (legumbre).
**parson** [pársn̩] s. pastor, clérigo.
**part** [part] s. parte (f.); papel (dramático); raya (del cabello); — **and parcel** parte esencial o inherente; — **owner** condueño, dueño en parte; — **time** parte del tiempo; **in foreign -s** en el extranjero, en países extranjeros; **spare -s** piezas accesorias, piezas de repuesto (o de refacción); **do your** — haga Vd. cuanto esté de su parte; v. partir(se); separar(se); **to** — **company** separarse; **to** — **from** separarse de, despedirse de; **to** — **one's hair** hacerse la raya; **to** — **with** separarse de, despedirse de, deshacerse de.
**partake** [parték] v. tomar parte, tener parte, participar.
**partaken** [partékən] p.p. de **to partake**.
**partial** [párʃəl] adj. parcial; **-ly** adv. parcialmente, en parte; con parcialidad.
**partiality** [parʃǽlətɪ] s. parcialidad.
**participant** [partísəpənt] adj. & s. participante, partícipe, copartícipe.
**participate** [partísəpet] v. participar.
**participation** [partɪsəpéʃən] s. participación.
**participle** [pártəsɪpl̩] s. participio; **present** — gerundio.
**particle** [pártɪkl̩] s. partícula.
**particular** [partíkjələ] adj. (single) particular, peculiar; (special) esmerado, exacto; escrupuloso; (demanding) quisquilloso; exigente; s. particular, detalle, circunstancia; **in** — en particular, especialmente; **-ly** adv. particularmente; en particular.
**parting** [pártɪŋ] s. (departure) despedida; (division) separación; bifurcación; **the** — **of the ways** encrucijada, bifurcación, cruce de caminos; adj. de despedida, último.
**partisan** [pártəzn̩] adj. partidario; parcial; s. partidario; secuaz, seguidor.
**partition** [partíʃən] s. (division) partición; división, separación; (wall) tabique; Am. medianía; v. partir, dividir; repartir.
**partitive** [pártətɪv] adj. partitivo.
**partly** [pártlɪ] adv. en parte.
**partner** [pártnə] s. socio, consocio; compañero; **dancing** — pareja de baile.
**partnership** [pártnəʃɪp] s. sociedad, compañía.
**partook** [partúk] pret. de **to partake**.
**partridge** [pártrɪdʒ] s. perdiz.
**party** [pártɪ] s. (get-together) tertulia, reunión, fiesta; (group) grupo, par-

tida (de gente); (legal) parte; **hunting** — partida de caza; **political** — partido político.
**pass** [pæs] s. paso; pase, permiso de entrar; aprobación (en un examen); trance, situación; — **key** llave maestra; **to come to** — suceder; v. pasar; pasar por; pronunciar (sentencia), dar (un juicio o parecer); aprobar (a un estudiante); adoptar (una ley); ser aprobado en (un examen); **to** — **away** pasar a mejor vida, morir; desaparecer; pasar (el tiempo).
**passable** [pǽsəbl̩] adj. (penetrable) transitable; (acceptable) pasadero, regular, mediano.
**passage** [pǽsɪdʒ] s. pasaje; paso, tránsito; transcurso (del tiempo); pasillo, pasadizo; travesía, viaje por mar; aprobación (de un proyecto de ley); adopción (de una ley).
**passageway** [pǽsədʒwe] s. corredor; pasaje.
**passbook** [pǽsbuk] s. libreta de banco.
**passenger** [pǽsn̩dʒə] s. pasajero; **the -s** los pasajeros; el pasaje.
**passer-by** [pǽsəbáɪ] s. transeúnte, viandante.
**passion** [pǽʃən] s. pasión; **Passion play** drama de la Pasión; **to fly into a** — montar en cólera, encolerizarse.
**passionate** [pǽʃənɪt] adj. apasionado.
**passive** [pǽsɪv] adj. pasivo; s. voz pasiva.
**passport** [pǽsport] s. pasaporte.
**password** [pǽswɜd] s. consigna, contraseña, santo y seña.
**past** [pæst] adj. pasado; último; — **master** perito; **the** — **president** el expresidente, el último presidente; — **tense** tiempo pasado; pretérito; **for some time** — desde hace algún tiempo, de poco tiempo a esta parte; prep. — **bearing** insoportable; — **understanding** incomprensible; **half** — **two** las dos y media; **woman** — **forty** cuarentona, mujer de más de cuarenta años; **to go** — **the house** pasar por (o por enfrente de) la casa; s. pasado; pretérito; pretérito imperfecto; **man with a** — hombre de dudosos antecedentes.
**paste** [pest] s. pasta; engrudo; v. pegar (con engrudo).
**pasteboard** [péstbord] s. cartón; — **box** caja de cartón.
**pasteurize** [pǽstəraɪz] v. pasterizar (o pasteurizar).
**pastime** [pǽstaɪm] s. pasatiempo.
**pastor** [pǽstə] s. pastor, clérigo, cura.
**pastoral** [pǽstərəl] adj. pastoril; pastoral; s. pastoral, carta pastoral; égloga; pastorela, idilio.
**pastry** [péstrɪ] s. pastelería, pasteles; — **cook** pastelero; — **shop** pastelería.
**pasture** [pǽstʃə] s. pastura, pasto; dehesa; v. pastar, pacer; apacentar(se).
**pat** [pæt] adj. apto, oportuno; **to have a lesson** — saber al dedillo la lección; **to stand** — mantenerse firme;

*adv.* a propósito; oportunamente; de molde; *s.* palmadita, caricia, golpecito; — **of butter** cuadrito de mantequilla; *v.* dar palmaditas a; acariciar; pasar la mano (*para alisar o acariciar*).

**patch** [pætʃ] *s.* (*repair*) remiendo; parche; mancha; (*plot*) pedazo (*de terreno*); sembrado; *v.* remendar; **to — up a quarrel** hacer las paces.

**pate** [pet] *s.* coronilla (*de la cabeza*); **bald —** calva.

**patent** [pǽtnt] *adj.* patente, evidente, manifiesto; de patente; — **leather** charol; — **medicine** medicina de patente; — **right** patente; *s.* patente; *v.* patentar.

**paternal** [pətɜ́rnl] *adj.* paternal, paterno.

**paternity** [pətɜ́rnətɪ] *s.* paternidad.

**path** [pæθ] *s.* senda, sendero; vereda; ruta; trayectoria (*de una bala*).

**pathetic** [pəθétɪk] *adj.* patético.

**pathology** [pæθálədʒɪ] *s.* patología.

**pathos** [péθɑs] *s.* patetismo, cualidad patética.

**pathway** [pǽθwe] *s.* senda, vereda, vía.

**patience** [péʃəns] *s.* paciencia.

**patient** [péʃənt] *adj.* paciente; pacienzudo; *s.* paciente, enfermo.

**patriarch** [pétrɪɑrk] *s.* patriarca.

**patriarchal** [petrɪárkl] *adj.* patriarcal.

**patrimony** [pǽtrəmonɪ] *s.* patrimonio.

**patriot** [pétrɪət] *s.* patriota.

**patriotic** [petrɪátɪk] *adj.* patriótico.

**patriotism** [pétrɪətɪzəm] *s.* patriotismo.

**patrol** [pətról] *s.* patrulla; ronda; *v.* patrullar, rondar.

**patron** [pétrən] *s.* patrón, patrono; benefactor; cliente, parroquiano; — **saint** santo patrón.

**patronage** [pétrənɪdʒ] *s.* (*support*) patrocinio, amparo; (*clientele*) clientela; (*manner*) condescendencia; **political —** control de nombramientos políticos.

**patroness** [pétrənɪs] *s.* patrona, protectora.

**patronize** [pétrənaɪz] *v.* patrocinar, amparar; tratar con condescendencia; favorecer, ser parroquiano de.

**patter** [pǽtɚ] *v.* golpetear ligeramente; talonear; charlar, parlotear; *s.* golpeteo; golpecitos; taloneo; charla, parloteo.

**pattern** [pǽtɚn] *s.* (*model*) modelo; dechado; muestra; ejemplo; patrón, molde; (*design*) diseño, dibujo (*en tejidos, telas, etc.*); *v.* **to — oneself after** seguir el ejemplo de; **to — something after (on, upon)** forjar o modelar algo a imitación de.

**paucity** [pósɪtɪ] *s.* escasez; falta.

**paunch** [pɔntʃ] *s.* panza, barriga.

**pause** [pɔz] *s.* pausa; *s.* pausar, hacer pausa; detenerse, parar.

**pave** [pev] *v.* pavimentar; **to — the way for** preparar o abrir el camino para; **to — with bricks** enladrillar; **to — with flagstones** enlosar.

**pavement** [pévmənt] *s.* pavimento; **brick —** enladrillado.

**pavilion** [pəvíljən] *s.* pabellón.

**paw** [pɔ] *s.* garra, zarpa; *v.* echar la zarpa; arañar; manosear; **to — the ground** patear la tierra (*dícese del caballo*).

**pawn** [pɔn] *s.* prenda, empeño; peón (*de ajedrez*); **—broker** prestamista, prendero; **—shop** empeño, casa de empeños, montepío; **in —** en prenda; *v.* empeñar, dejar en prenda.

**pay** [pe] *v.* (*remit*) pagar; (*pay for*) costear; (*profit*) ser provechoso; (*worthwhile*) valer la pena; **to — attention** prestar atención; **to — back** restituir, devolver; **to — court** hacer la corte; **to — down** pagar al contado; **to — homage** hacer o rendir homenaje; **to — one's respects** presentar sus respetos; **to — a visit** hacer una visita; *s.* pago; recompensa; paga; sueldo; **— day** día de pagos, *Am.* día de raya; **—master** pagador, *Am.* rayador; — **roll** nómina.

**payable** [péəbl] *adj.* pagadero.

**payment** [pémənt] *s.* pago; paga; **— in full** pago total.

**payoff** [péɔf] *s.* arreglo; pago.

**pea** [pi] *s.* guisante, chícharo; **sweet —** guisante de olor.

**peace** [pis] *s.* paz.

**peaceable** [písəbl] *adj.* pacífico, tranquilo.

**peaceful** [písfəl] *adj.* pacífico; tranquilo, quieto, sosegado.

**peach** [pitʃ] *s.* melocotón, durazno; persona bella o admirable; — **tree** durazno, duraznero, melocotonero.

**peacock** [píkɑk] *s.* pavón, pavo real; **to act like a —** pavonearse, hacer ostentación.

**peak** [pik] *s.* pico, cumbre, cima; cúspide; punto máximo.

**peal** [pil] *s.* repique (*de campanas*); **— of laughter** carcajada, risotada; **— of thunder** trueno; *v.* repicar (*las campanas*).

**peanut** [pínət] *s.* cacahuate, *Carib.*, *Ven.*, *Col.*, *Ch.*, *Ríopl.*, *Andes* maní.

**pear** [pɛr] *s.* pera; — **tree** peral; **alligator —** aguacate, *Ch.*, *Andes*, *Ríopl.* palta (*variedad sudamericana*).

**pearl** [pɜrl] *s.* perla; — **necklace** collar de perlas; **mother-of-pearl** nácar, madreperla.

**pearly** [pɜ́rlɪ] *adj.* perlino; nacarado; aperlado.

**peasant** [péznt] *adj.* & *s.* campesino, rústico, *P.R.* jíbaro, *Cuba* guajiro; *Col.* paisa; *Ch.* guaso; *Ríopl.* gaucho.

**pebble** [pébl] *s.* guija, china, guijarro, piedrecilla.

**pecan** [pikán] *s.* pacana.

**peck** [pɛk] *v.* picar, picotear; *s.* picotazo, picotada; medida de áridos (*aproximadamente 9 litros*); **a — of trouble** la mar de disgustos o molestias.

**peculiar** [pɪkjúljɚ] *adj.* peculiar; raro, singular, extraño.

**peculiarity** [pɪkjulɪǽrətɪ] *s.* peculiaridad; particularidad; rareza.

**pedagogue** [pédəgɑg] *s.* pedagogo, dó-

**PA**

mine.

**pedagogy** [pédəgodʒɪ] *s.* pedagogía.

**pedal** [pédl] *s.* pedal; *v.* pedalear, mover los pedales.

**pedant** [pédṇt] *s.* pedante.

**pedantic** [pɪdǽntɪk] *adj.* pedante, pedantesco.

**peddle** [pédl] *v.* ir vendiendo de puerta en puerta; **to — gossip** chismear.

**peddler** [pédlɚ] *s.* buhonero; vendedor ambulante.

**pedestal** [pédɪstl] *s.* pedestal.

**pedestrian** [pədéstrɪən] *s.* peatón, transeúnte, viandante; *adj.* pedestre.

**pediatrics** [pidɪǽtrɪks] *s.* pediatría.

**pedigree** [pédəgri] *s.* linaje, genealogía.

**peek** [pik] *v.* atisbar, espiar; *s.* atisbo.

**peel** [pil] *s.* corteza, cáscara (*de algunas frutas*); pellejo (*de patatas*); *v.* pelar(se), descortezar(se), deshollejar(se); **to keep one's eye -ed** tener los ojos muy abiertos, estar alerta.

**peep** [pip] *v.* atisbar, espiar; asomar(se); pipiar, piar; *s.* atisbo; ojeada; pío (*de pollo o ave*).

**peer** [pir] *s.* (*equal*) par, igual; (*noble*) noble; *v.* mirar con atención, atisbar; asomar; **to — into other people's business** fisgar, curiosear.

**peer group** [pírgrup] *s.* conjunto de personas de la misma edad y condiciones.

**peerless** [pírlɛs] *adj.* incomparable; sin par.

**peeve** [piv] *v.* irritar, poner de mal humor; **to get -d** amoscarse, ponerse de mal humor.

**peevish** [pívɪʃ] *adj.* enojadizo; malhumorado.

**peg** [pɛg] *s.* espiga, clavo de madera, estaquilla; clavija (*de violin*); **to take a person down a —** rebajar o humillar a alguien; *v.* clavar, clavetear; poner estaquillas; **to — along** atarearse, trabajar con tesón.

**pejorative** [pədʒórətɪv] *adj.* peyorativo; despectivo.

**pellet** [pélɪt] *s.* (*ball*) pelotilla; bola; (*pill*) píldora.

**pell-mell** [pélmél] *adj.* confuso, tumultuoso; *adv.* a trochemoche, atropelladamente, en tumulto.

**pelt** [pɛlt] *s.* zalea, cuero (*especialmente de oveja*); piel; *v.* golpear; **to — with stones** apedrear, arrojar piedras a.

**pelvis** [pélvɪs] *s.* pelvis.

**pen** [pɛn] *s.* pluma (*para escribir*); corral; redil; **—holder** mango de pluma, portapluma; **— name** nombre de pluma; **fountain —** pluma fuente, pluma estilográfica; **pig —** pocilga; *v.* escribir (*con pluma*); acorralar, encerrar.

**penal** [pínl] *adj.* penal.

**penalize** [pínəlaɪz] *v.* penar; aplicar sanción.

**penalty** [péntɪ] *s.* pena, castigo; multa.

**penance** [pénəns] *s.* penitencia.

**pencil** [pénsl] *s.* lápiz; lapicero; **— sharpener** tajalápiz.

**pendant** [péndənt] *s.* pendiente (*adorno que cuelga*); *adj.* pendiente.

**pending** [péndɪŋ] *adj.* pendiente; colgado; *prep.* durante.

**pendulum** [péndʒələm] *s.* péndulo.

**penetrate** [pénətret] *v.* penetrar.

**penetrating** [pénətretɪŋ] *adj.* penetrante.

**penetration** [pɛnətréʃən] *s.* penetración.

**penguin** [péngwɪn] *s.* pingüino.

**penicillin** [pɛnəsílɪn] *s.* penicilina.

**peninsula** [pənínsələ] *s.* península.

**penitent** [pénətənt] *adj.* arrepentido, penitente; *s.* penitente.

**penitentiary** [pɛnəténʃərɪ] *s.* penitenciaría, presidio.

**penknife** [pénnaɪf] *s.* cortaplumas; navaja.

**penmanship** [pénmənʃɪp] *s.* escritura, caligrafía.

**pennant** [pénənt] *s.* banderola, gallardete.

**penniless** [pénɪlɪs] *adj.* pobre, sin dinero.

**penny** [pénɪ] *s.* centavo (*de dólar*); **to cost a pretty —** costar un ojo de la cara, costar un dineral.

**pension** [pénʃən] *s.* pensión; retiro (*de un militar*); *v.* pensionar.

**pensive** [pénsɪv] *adj.* pensativo.

**pent** [pɛnt] *adj.* encerrado; acorralado; **pent-up emotions** sentimientos reprimidos.

**penthouse** [pénthaʊs] *s.* casa de azotea; colgadizo.

**people** [pípl] *s.* gente; pueblo *v.* poblar.

**pepper** [pépɚ] *s.* pimienta; **— plant** pimentero; **— shaker** pimentero; **green -s** pimientos verdes; **red —** pimentón, chile, *Carib., Col., Ven., Andes, Ch., Ríopl.* ají; *v.* sazonar con pimienta; **to — with bullets** acribillar a balazos.

**peppermint** [pépɚmɪnt] *s.* menta; pastilla o bombón de menta.

**per** [pɚ] *prep.* por; **— capita** por cabeza; **— cent** por ciento; **— year** al año; **ten cents — dozen** diez centavos por docena (*o diez centavos la docena*).

**percale** [pɚkél] *s.* percal.

**perceive** [pɚsív] *v.* percibir.

**percentage** [pɚséntɪdʒ] *s.* porcentaje, tanto por ciento.

**perceptible** [pɚséptəbl] *adj.* perceptible.

**perception** [pɚsépʃən] *s.* percepción.

**perceptive** [pɚséptɪv] *adj.* perceptivo; sensible.

**perch** [pɚtʃ] *s.* percha (*para pájaros*); perca (*pez*); *v.* encaramar(se); posarse (*en una percha o rama*).

**perchance** [pɚtʃǽns] *adv.* por ventura, acaso, quizás, tal vez.

**percolate** [pɚkəlet] *v.* filtrar(se), colar(se); rezumarse; penetrar.

**perdition** [pɚdíʃən] *s.* perdición.

**perennial** [pərénɪəl] *adj.* perenne; continuo; perpetuo.

**perfect** [pɚfɪkt] *adj.* perfecto; completo;

*s.* tiempo perfecto (*del verbo*); [pɚfékt] *v.* perfeccionar.

**perfection** [pɚfékʃən] *s.* perfección.
**perfidious** [pɚfídɪəs] *adj.* pérfido.
**perfidy** [pɚ́fədɪ] *s.* perfidia.
**perforate** [pɚ́fəret] *v.* perforar.
**perforce** [pɚfɔ́rs] *adj.* necesariamente; por fuerza.
**perform** [pɚfɔ́rm] *v.* ejecutar; llevar a cabo, cumplir, hacer; funcionar (*una máquina*); desempeñar o representar un papel.
**performance** [pɚfɔ́rməns] *s.* ejecución; desempeño, cumplimiento; funcionamiento (*de una máquina o motor*); función, representación; acto, acción.
**perfume** [pɚ́fjum] *s.* perfume; [pɚfjúm] *v.* perfumar.
**perfumery** [pɚfjúmərɪ] *s.* perfumería; perfumes.
**perhaps** [pɚhǽps] *adv.* acaso, tal vez, quizá (*o* quizás), puede ser.
**perigee** [pérədʒɪ] *s.* perigeo.
**peril** [pérəl] *s.* peligro; riesgo; *v.* poner en peligro.
**perilous** [pérələs] *adj.* peligroso.
**perimeter** [pərímətɚ] *s.* perímetro.
**period** [pírɪəd] *s.* período; punto final; fin, término.
**periodic** [pɪrɪádɪk] *adj.* periódico.
**periodical** [pɪrɪádɪkl̩] *adj.* periódico; *s.* revista, publicación periódica.
**periphery** [pərífərɪ] *s.* periferia.
**perish** [pérɪʃ] *v.* perecer.
**perishable** [pérɪʃəbl̩] *adj.* perecedero; deleznable.
**perjure** [pɚ́dʒɚ] *v.* **to — oneself** perjurar.
**perjury** [pɚ́dʒrɪ] *s.* perjurio, juramento falso.
**permanence** [pɚ́mənəns] *s.* permanencia.
**permanent** [pɚ́mənənt] *adj.* permanente; duradero.
**permeate** [pɚ́mɪet] *v.* penetrar, saturar; difundirse por, filtrarse por.
**permissible** [pɚmísəbl̩] *adj.* lícito.
**permission** [pɚmíʃən] *s.* permiso, licencia.
**permissive** [pɚmísɪv] *adj.* permisivo.
**permit** [pɚ́mɪt] *s.* permiso, pase; licencia; [pɚmít] *v.* permitir.
**permutation** [pɚmjutéʃən] *s.* permutación.
**pernicious** [pɚníʃəs] *adj.* pernicioso.
**perpendicular** [pɚpəndíkjələ] *adj.* & *s.* perpendicular.
**perpetrate** [pɚ́pətret] *v.* perpetrar, cometer.
**perpetual** [pɚpétʃuəl] *adj.* perpetuo.
**perpetuate** [pɚpétʃuet] *v.* perpetuar.
**perplex** [pɚpléks] *v.* confundir, turbar, aturdir.
**perplexed** [pɚplékst] *adj.* perplejo, confuso.
**perplexity** [pɚpléksətɪ] *s.* perplejidad, confusión.
**persecute** [pɚ́sɪkjut] *v.* perseguir, acosar.
**persecution** [pɚsɪkjúʃən] *s.* persecución.

**persecutor** [pɚ́sɪkjutɚ] *s.* perseguidor.
**perseverance** [pɚsəvírəns] *s.* perseverancia.
**persevere** [pɚsəvír] *v.* perseverar; persistir.
**persist** [pɚzíst] *v.* persistir; porfiar.
**persistence** [pɚzístəns] *s.* persistencia; porfía.
**persistent** [pɚzístənt] *adj.* persistente; porfiado.
**person** [pɚ́sn̩] *s.* persona.
**personable** [pɚ́sənəbl̩] *adj.* presentable; bien parecido.
**personage** [pɚ́sn̩ɪdʒ] *s.* personaje.
**personal** [pɚ́sn̩l̩] *adj.* personal; en persona.
**personality** [pɚsnǽlətɪ] *s.* personalidad; persona, personaje; alusión personal.
**personnel** [pɚsnél] *s.* personal.
**perspective** [pɚspéktɪv] *s.* perspectiva; **— drawing** dibujo en perspectiva.
**perspicacious** [pɚspɪkéʃəs] *adj.* perspicaz.
**perspiration** [pɚspəréʃən] *s.* sudor.
**perspire** [pɚspáɪr] *v.* sudar.
**persuade** [pɚswéd] *v.* persuadir.
**persuasion** [pɚswéʒən] *s.* persuasión; creencia.
**persuasive** [pɚswésɪv] *adj.* persuasivo.
**pert** [pɚt] *adj.* insolente, descarado, atrevido, *Am.* retobado.
**pertain** [pɚtén] *v.* pertenecer; atañer.
**pertinent** [pɚ́tn̩ənt] *adj.* pertinente, a propósito, al caso.
**perturb** [pɚtɚ́b] *v.* perturbar.
**perusal** [pərúzl̩] *s.* lectura.
**peruse** [pərúz] *v.* leer con cuidado.
**Peruvian** [pərúvɪən] *adj.* & *s.* peruano.
**pervade** [pɚvéd] *v.* llenar, penetrar, difundirse por.
**perverse** [pɚvɚ́s] *adj.* perverso; terco, obstinado.
**pervert** [pɚvɚ́t] *v.* pervertir; falsear; [pɚ́vɚt] *s.* perverso.
**pessimism** [pésəmɪzəm] *s.* pesimismo.
**pessimist** [pésəmɪst] *s.* pesimista; **-ic** *adj.* pesimista.
**pest** [pest] *s.* peste, plaga; pestilencia.
**pester** [péstɚ] *v.* importunar, molestar.
**pesticide** [péstəsaɪd] *s.* & *adj.* insecticida.
**pestilence** [péstl̩əns] *s.* pestilencia.
**pet** [pet] *s.* animal mimado, animal casero o doméstico; niño mimado; favorito; *adj.* favorito; mimado; **— name** nombre de cariño (*por lo general diminutivo*); *v.* mimar, acariciar.
**petal** [pétl̩] *s.* pétalo.
**petcock** [pétkɑk] *s.* llave de desagüe (*purga*).
**petition** [pətíʃən] *s.* petición, súplica; instancia, memorial, solicitud, *Am.* ocurso; *v.* solicitar, pedir, dirigir una instancia o memorial a; suplicar, rogar.
**petrify** [pétrɪfaɪ] *v.* petrificar.
**petroleum** [pətrólɪəm] *s.* petróleo.
**petticoat** [pétɪkot] *s.* enaguas.
**petty** [pétɪ] *adj.* insignificante, pequeño; mezquino; inferior, subordinado; **— cash** fondos para gastos menores; **—**

PE

**larceny** ratería; **— officer** oficial subordinado (*en la marina*); **— treason** traición menor.

**pew** [pju] *s.* banco de iglesia.

**phalanx** [félǽŋks] *s.* falanje.

**phantom** [fǽntəm] *s.* fantasma.

**pharmacist** [fármᵊsɪst] *s.* farmacéutico, boticario.

**pharmacy** [fármᵊsɪ] *s.* farmacia, botica.

**pharynx** [fǽrɪŋks] *s.* faringe.

**phase** [fez] *s.* fase.

**pheasant** [fézᵊnt] *s.* faisán.

**phenomena** [fənámᵊnə] *pl. de* **phenomenon.**

**phenomenon** [fənámᵊnɑn] *s.* fenómeno.

**philanthropy** [fɪlǽnθrᵊpɪ] *s.* filantropía.

**philharmonic** [fɪlharmánɪk] *adj.* filarmónico.

**philology** [fɪláldʒɪ] *s.* filología.

**philosopher** [fᵊlásᵊfᵊ] *s.* filósofo.

**philosophical** [fɪlᵊsáfɪkl] *adj.* filosófico.

**philosophy** [fᵊlásᵊfɪ] *s.* filosofía.

**phlegm** [flɛm] *s.* flema.

**phone** [fon] *s.* teléfono; *v.* telefonear.

**phoneme** [fónim] *s.* fonema.

**phonetics** [fonétɪks] *s.* fonética.

**phonograph** [fónᵊgrǽf] *s.* fonógrafo.

**phonology** [fonáldʒɪ] *s.* fonología.

**phosphate** [fásfet] *s.* fosfato.

**phosphorus** [fásfᵊrᵊs] *s.* fósforo (*elemento quimico*).

**photo** [fóto] *s.* fotografía, retrato.

**photograph** [fótᵊgrǽf] *s.* fotografía, retrato; *v.* fotografiar, retratar.

**photographer** [fᵊtágrᵊfᵊ] *s.* fotógrafo.

**photography** [fᵊtágrᵊfɪ] *s.* fotografía.

**phrase** [frez] *s.* frase; expresión, locución; *v.* frasear; expresar, formular.

**physic** [fízɪk] *s.* purga, purgante; *v.* purgar.

**physical** [fízɪkl] *adj.* físico.

**physician** [fᵊzíʃən] *s.* médico.

**physicist** [fízᵊsɪst] *s.* físico.

**physics** [fízɪks] *s.* física.

**physiological** [fɪzɪᵊládʒɪkl] *adj.* fisiológico.

**physiology** [fɪzɪálᵊdʒɪ] *s.* fisiología.

**physique** [fɪzík] *s.* físico, constitución física, talle, cuerpo.

**piano** [pɪǽno] *s.* piano; **— bench** banqueta de piano; **— stool** taburete de piano; **grand —** piano de cola; **upright —** piano vertical.

**picaresque** [pɪkᵊrésk] *adj.* picaresco.

**pick** [pɪk] *v.* (*choose*) escoger; coger; (*break*) picar; (*clean*) mondarse, limpiarse (*los dientes*); desplumar (*un ave*); roer (*un hueso*); falsear (*una cerradura*); armar (*una pendencia*); **to — flaws** criticar, censurar; **to — out** escoger; **to — pockets** ratear; **to — up** recoger; **to — up speed** acelerar la marcha; *s.* pico (*herramienta*); selección; lo selecto, lo mejor; recolección, cosecha; **ice —** punzón para romper hielo; **tooth—** mondadientes, palillo de dientes.

**pickaxe** [píkæks] *s.* pico, zapapico.

**picket** [píkɪt] *s.* piquete (*estaca o palo clavado en la tierra*); piquete (*vigilante huelguista*); piquete de soldados; *v.* estacionar piquetes cerca de (*una fábrica, campamento, etc.*); vigilar (*por medio de piquetes*); estar de guardia.

**pickle** [píkl] *s.* encurtido; **to be in a —** hallarse en un aprieto; *v.* encurtir, escabechar; **-d cucumbers** pepinillos encurtidos; **-d fish** escabeche, pescado en escabeche.

**pickpocket** [píkpɑkɪt] *s.* rata (*m.*); ratero; *Méx., Ven., Col.* carterista.

**picnic** [píknɪk] *s.* partida de campo, día de campo, comida campestre, *Am.* picnic; *v.* hacer una comida campestre; ir a un picnic.

**picture** [píktʃᵊ] *s.* (*painting*) cuadro, pintura; (*portrait*) retrato; (*photo*) fotografía; (*engraving*) grabado; (*movie*) película; **— frame** marco; **— gallery** museo o galería de pinturas; *v.* pintar, dibujar; describir; imaginar(se).

**picturesque** [pɪktʃᵊrésk] *adj.* pintoresco.

**pie** [paɪ] *s.* pastel; empanada.

**piece** [pis] *s.* (*section*) pieza; pedazo; parte; sección; (*passage*) trozo; **— of advice** consejo; **— of land** parcela; **— of money** moneda; **— of news** noticia; **— of nonsense** tontería; **—meal** en pedazos, a pedazos, por partes; *v.* remendar; **to — between meals** comer a deshoras; **to — on to** juntar a, pegar a; **to — together** unir, pegar, juntar.

**pier** [pɪr] *s.* muelle, embarcadero; rompeolas; pilar (*de puente o arco*).

**pierce** [pɪrs] *v.* atravesar, traspasar; taladrar, agujerear, perforar.

**piety** [páɪᵊtɪ] *s.* piedad, religiosidad.

**pig** [pɪg] *s.* puerco, cerdo, cochino; *S.A.* chancho; *C.A.* tunco; cuchi; **— iron** hierro en lingotes; **—headed** cabezón, testarudo; **guinea —** conejillo de Indias.

**pigeon** [pídʒᵊn] *s.* pichón; paloma.

**pigeonhole** [pídʒᵊnhol] *s.* casilla; *v.* encasillar.

**pigment** [pígmᵊnt] *s.* pigmento, color.

**pigmy** [pígmɪ] *s.* pigmeo.

**pike** [paɪk] *s.* pica, lanza; lucio (*pez*).

**pile** [paɪl] *s.* pila, montón; pelo (*de ciertos tejidos*); pilote; **-s** almorranas (*enfermedad*); **— driver** martinete (*para clavar pilotes*); *v.* apilar(se), amontonar(se); acumular(se).

**pilfer** [pílfᵊ] *v.* pillar, ratear, hurtar, sisar.

**pilgrim** [pílgrɪm] *s.* peregrino, romero.

**pilgrimage** [pílgrᵊmɪdʒ] *s.* peregrinación, romería.

**pill** [pɪl] *s.* píldora; persona fastidiosa.

**pillage** [pílɪdʒ] *v.* pillar, saquear; *s.* pillaje, saqueo.

**pillar** [pílᵊ] *s.* pilar, columna; **to go from — to post** ir de Ceca en Meca.

**pillow** [pílo] *s.* almohada; cojín.

**pillowcase** [pílokes] *s.* funda de almohada.

**pilot** [páɪlət] *s.* piloto; guía; — **light** (*o* — **burner**) mechero, encendedor (*de una cocina o estufa de gas*); **harbor** — práctico de puerto; *v.* pilotar o pilotear; dirigir, guiar.

**pimple** [pímpl] *s.* grano, barro.

**pin** [pɪn] *s.* alfiler; prendedor; espiga; bolo (*del juego de bolos*); — **money** dinero para alfileres; — **wheel** molinete, *Am.* remolino; **breast** — broche; **safety** — imperdible; *v.* prender (*con alfiler*); asegurar, fijar, clavar; **to** — **down** fijar, inmovilizar; hacer dar una contestación definitiva; **to** — **one's hope to** poner toda su esperanza en; **to** — **up** prender con alfileres; colgar (*un dibujo o retrato*), fijar con tachuelas.

**pincers** [pínsɚz] *s. pl.* pinzas; tenazas; **small** — tenacillas.

**pinch** [pɪntʃ] *v.* (*squeeze*) pellizcar; apretar; (*economize*) economizar; (*arrest*) prender, arrestar; **to** — **one's finger in the door** machucarse el dedo en la puerta; *s.* pellizco; pizca, porción pequeña; punzada, dolor agudo; aprieto, apuro; — **hitter** suplente, sustituto.

**pinchers** [píntʃɚz] = **pincers.**

**pine** [paɪn] *s.* pino; — **cone** piña; — **grove** pinar; — **nut** piñón; *v.* languidecer; **to** — **away** consumirse; **to** — **for** anhelar, suspirar por.

**pineapple** [páɪnæpl] *s.* piña, ananá o ananás.

**pinion** [pínjən] *s.* piñón.

**pink** [pɪŋk] *s.* clavel; color de rosa; **in the** — **of condition** en la mejor condición; *adj.* rosado, color de rosa.

**pinnacle** [pínəkl] *s.* pináculo, cumbre.

**pint** [paɪnt] *s.* pinta (*aproximadamente medio litro*).

**pioneer** [paɪənír] *s.* explorador, colonizador; fundador, iniciador, precursor; pionero; *v.* explorar, colonizar; fundar, preparar.

**pious** [páɪəs] *adj.* pío, piadoso.

**pipe** [paɪp] *s.* pipa (*de fumar*); tubo, caño; cañón (*de órgano*); caramillo, flauta; — **line** cañería, tubería; *v.* conducir por cañerías; desaguar por cañería; proveer de tuberías o cañerías; chillar; **to** — **down** bajar la voz.

**piper** [páɪpɚ] *s.* gaitero, flautista.

**piping** [páɪpɪŋ] *s.* cañería, tubería; cordoncillo (*de adorno para costuras*); chillido, silbido; *adj.* agudo, chillón; — **hot** muy caliente; hirviendo.

**pippin** [pípɪn] *s.* camuesa.

**pique** [pik] *s.* enojo, resentimiento; *v.* picar, excitar; enojar, irritar; **to** — **oneself on** picarse de, preciarse de.

**pirate** [páɪrət] *s.* pirata; *v.* piratear; plagiar.

**pistol** [pístl] *s.* pistola; revólver.

**piston** [pístn] *s.* pistón, émbolo; — **ring** aro de pistón; — **rod** vástago del émbolo.

**pit** [pɪt] *s.* hoyo; foso; hueso (*de ciertas frutas*); — **of the stomach** boca del estómago.

**pitch** [pɪtʃ] *s.* (*throw*) tiro, lanzamiento (*de una pelota*); cabezada (*de un barco*); (*music*) diapasón, tono; (*inclination*) grado, declive, grado de inclinación; pez (*f.*), brea; resina; — **dark** oscurísimo; *v.* tirar, lanzar, arrojar; cabecear (*un barco*); graduar el tono de (*un instrumento o voz*); echarse de cabeza; inclinarse; **to** — **a tent** armar una tienda de campaña; acampar; **to** — **into** arremeter contra; reprender, regañar; — **in!** ¡manos a la obra!

**pitcher** [pítʃɚ] *s.* cántaro, jarro o jarra; tirador, lanzador (*en beisbol*).

**pitchfork** [pítʃfɔrk] *s.* horca, horquilla (*para hacinar las mieses, levantar la paja, etc.*).

**piteous** [pítɪəs] *adj.* lastimero, lastimoso.

**pith** [pɪθ] *s.* meollo, médula; esencia, sustancia.

**pitiful** [pítɪfəl] *adj.* lastimoso; lamentable; miserable.

**pitiless** [pítɪlɪs] *adj.* despiadado, incompasivo, cruel.

**pity** [pítɪ] *s.* piedad; lástima; compasión; **for** -**'s sake** por piedad, por Dios; **what a** —**!** ¡qué lástima!; *v.* compadecer; tener lástima por; apiadarse de, tener piedad de.

**placard** [plækard] *s.* letrero, cartel; *v.* fijar carteles.

**place** [ples] *s.* (*site*) lugar, sitio; localidad; (*position*) puesto; empleo; posición; — **of business** oficina, despacho; — **of worship** templo, iglesia; **market** — plaza, mercado; **in** — **of** en lugar de, en vez de; **it is not my** — **to do it** no es mi deber hacerlo, no me toca a mí hacerlo; *v.* colocar; situar; poner; acomodar, dar empleo a.

**placid** [plǽsɪd] *adj.* plácido, apacible, sosegado.

**plagiarism** [pléʒɚɪzəm] *s.* plagio.

**plague** [pleg] *s.* plaga; peste, pestilencia; calamidad; *v.* plagar, infestar; importunar.

**plaid** [plæd] *s.* tartán, tela a cuadros; manta escocesa a cuadros; diseño a cuadros; *adj.* a cuadros.

**plain** [plen] *adj.* (*flat*) llano; (*simple*) sencillo; claro; franco; ordinario; — **fool** tonto de capirote; — **woman** mujer sin atractivo; **in** — **sight** en plena vista; **plain-clothes man** detective; *adv.* claramente; — **stupid** completamente estúpido; **plain-spoken** franco, francote, sincero; *s.* llano, llanura.

**plaintiff** [pléntɪf] *s.* demandante.

**plaintive** [pléntɪv] *adj.* lastimero, triste.

**plan** [plæn] *s.* plan; proyecto; plano (*dibujo o mapa*); *v.* planear; proyectar, idear; pensar, proponerse.

**plane** [plen] *s.* (*airplane*) avión; aeroplano; (*surface*) plano, superficie plana; cepillo (*de carpintero*); *adj.* plano, llano; — **tree** plátano falso;

**PE**

*v.* acepillar, alisar con cepillo (*la madera o los metales*).

**planet** [plǽnɪt] *s.* planeta.

**plank** [plæŋk] *s.* tabla, tablón; principio, base (*del programa de un partido político*); *v.* entablar, entarimar, cubrir con tablas; asar (*carne*) en una tabla.

**plant** [plænt] *s.* (*vegetation*) planta; (*industry*) fábrica; taller; *v.* plantar; sembrar; implantar; establecer.

**plantation** [plæntéʃən] *s.* plantación; plantío; sembrado; **coffee** — cafetal; **cotton** — algodonal; **rubber** — cauchal; **sugar** — ingenio de azúcar.

**planter** [plǽntɚ] *s.* plantador, cultivador.

**plaque** [plæk] *s.* placa.

**plasma** [plǽzmə] *s.* plasma.

**plaster** [plǽstɚ] *s.* yeso; emplasto; **of Paris** yeso, yeso mate; **court** — esparadrapo, tafetán inglés; **mustard** — sinapismo; *v.* enyesar; emplastar, poner emplastos a; pegar (*carteles, anuncios*); embarrar.

**plastic** [plǽstɪk] *adj.* plástico.

**plat** [plæt] *s.* plano; parcela; *v.* levantar o trazar un plano.

**plate** [plet] *s.* (*eating*) plato; (*metal*) placa; plancha; lámina; **dental** — dentadura postiza; *v.* platear; dorar; niquelar; blindar, proteger con planchas de metal.

**plateau** [plætó] *s.* antiplanicie, mesa, meseta.

**plated** [plétəd] *adj.* chapeado; blindado.

**plateful** [plétful] *s.* plato, plato lleno.

**platform** [plǽtfɔrm] *s.* plataforma; tablado; programa de un partido político; **railway** — andén.

**platinum** [plǽtnəm] *s.* platino.

**platitude** [plǽtətjud] *s.* lugar común, perogrullada.

**platter** [plǽtɚ] *s.* platel, platón.

**play** [ple] *v.* (*game*) jugar; juguetear; (*instrument*) tocar; (*drama*) representar; hacer, desempeñar (*un papel*); manipular (*un instrumento, radio, fonógrafo, etc.*); **to — a joke** hacer una broma, dar un chasco; **to — cards** jugar a los naipes, jugar a la baraja; **to — havoc** hacer estragos, causar daño; **to — tennis** jugar al tenis; **to — the fool** hacerse el tonto, fingirse tonto; **to be all -ed out** no poder más, estar agotado; *s.* juego; jugada (*acción, movimiento en un juego*); pieza, drama, comedia, representación; recreación, diversión; **— on words** juego de palabras, equívoco; **to give full — to** dar rienda suelta a.

**player** [pléɚ] *s.* (*games*) jugador; (*music*) músico; (*plays*) cómico, actor; artista; **— piano** piano mecánico, pianola; **piano —** pianista; **violin —** violinista.

**playful** [pléfəl] *adj.* juguetón, retozón; bromista.

**playground** [plégraʊnd] *s.* campo o patio de recreo.

**playmate** [plémet] *s.* compañero de juego.

**plaything** [pléθɪŋ] *s.* juguete.

**playwright** [pléraɪt] *s.* dramático, dramaturgo.

**plea** [pli] *s.* súplica; ruego; alegato, defensa; pretexto; **on the — that** con el pretexto de que.

**plead** [plid] *v.* abogar; suplicar; argüir; alegar; defender (*una causa*); **to — guilty** declararse o confesarse culpable.

**pleasant** [plézn̩t] *adj.* grato; agradable; simpático.

**pleasantry** [plézn̩trɪ] *s.* chanza, broma, chiste, humorada.

**please** [pliz] *v.* agradar, gustar, dar gusto a; complacer; **— do it** haga Vd. el favor de hacerlo, tenga Vd. la bondad de hacerlo, sírvase hacerlo; **as you —** como Vd. quiera, como Vd. guste; **if you —** si me hace Vd. (el) favor; **to be -ed to** complacerse en, tener gusto en; alegrarse de; **to be -ed with** gustarle a uno, estar satisfecho de (*o con*).

**pleasing** [plízɪŋ] *adj.* agradable.

**pleasure** [plézɚ] *s.* placer, gusto; deleite, alegría, gozo; **— trip** viaje de recreo; **what is your —?** ¿qué deseaba Vd.? ¿en qué puedo servirle?

**pleat** [plit] *s.* pliegue, doblez; *v.* plegar, hacer pliegues (*en*).

**plebeian** [plɪbíən] *adj.* & *s.* plebeyo.

**pledge** [plɛdʒ] *s.* promesa; prenda (*garantía*); fianza; **as a — of** en prenda de; *v.* prometer; empeñar, dar en prenda; hacer firmar una promesa; **to — one's word** empeñar (*o dar*) su palabra; **to — to secrecy** exigir promesa de sigilo.

**plenary** [plénərɪ] *adj.* plenario.

**plenipotentiary** [plɛnəpəténʃərɪ] *adj.* & *s.* plenipotenciario.

**plentiful** [pléntɪfəl] *adj.* abundante, copioso.

**plenty** [pléntɪ] *s.* abundancia, copia; **— of time** bastante tiempo; **that is —** con eso basta; basta.

**pliable** [pláɪəbl̩] *adj.* flexible; manejable, dócil; transigente.

**pliant** [pláɪənt] *adj.* flexible; dócil, sumiso.

**pliers** [pláɪɚz] *s. pl.* alicates, tenazas.

**plight** [plaɪt] *s.* apuro, aprieto, situación difícil.

**plod** [plɑd] *v.* bregar, trafagar, afanarse, trabajar asiduamente.

**plosive** [plósɪv] *adj.* & *s.* oclusivo.

**plot** [plɑt] *s.* (*outline*) trama, enredo; argumento; (*conspiracy*) complot, conspiración; (*land*) parcela (*de tierra*), solar; (*plan*) plano, diagrama; *v.* tramar, urdir; maquinar, conspirar; hacer el plano o diagrama de; **to — a curve** hacer una gráfica.

**plotter** [plátɚ] *s.* conspirador; tramador; conjurado.

**plough = plow.**

**plow** [plaʊ] *s.* arado; **—share** reja de arado; *v.* arar; surcar.

**pluck** [plʌk] *v.* coger; arrancar; desplumar (*un ave*); puntear (*las cuerdas de una guitarra*); **to — at** tirar de; **to — up** arrancar; cobrar ánimo; *s.* ánimo, valor; tirón.

**plucky** [plʌ́kɪ] *adj.* valeroso, animoso.

**plug** [plʌg] *s.* (*stopper*) taco, tapón; (*horse*) caballejo, penco; (*boost*) elogio incidental (*de un producto comercial o de una persona*); **— of tobacco** tableta de tabaco; **electric —** clavija de conexión; **fire —** boca de agua para incendios; **spark —** bujía; *v.* tapar; **to — along** afanarse, atarearse; **to — in** enchufar, conectar; **to — up** tapar, obstruir.

**plum** [plʌm] *s.* (*fruit*) ciruela; (*prize*) la cosa mejor; la mejor colocación; **— pudding** pudín inglés con pasas; **— tree** ciruelo.

**plumage** [plúmɪdʒ] *s.* plumaje.

**plumb** [plʌm] *s.* plomo, pesa de plomo; sonda; **out of —** no vertical; *adj.* vertical, a plomo, recto; **— bob** plomo, plomada; *adv.* a plomo, verticalmente; **— crazy** completamente loco; *v.* sondear; aplomar (*una pared*).

**plumber** [plʌ́mɚ] *s.* plomero.

**plumbing** [plʌ́mɪŋ] *s.* plomería; cañerías (*de un edificio*); oficio de plomero.

**plume** [plum] *s.* pluma; plumaje; penacho; *v.* adornar con plumas; **to — its wing** alisarse o componerse el plumaje del ala.

**plump** [plʌmp] *adj.* rechoncho, regordete, rollizo; *adv.* de golpe; *v.* **to — down** dejar(se) caer; desplomarse, sentarse de golpe.

**plunder** [plʌ́ndɚ] *s.* pillaje, saqueo; botín; *v.* pillar; saquear.

**plunge** [plʌndʒ] *v.* zambullir(se), sumergir(se); hundir(se); lanzar(se), arrojar(se), precipitar(se); **to — headlong** echarse de cabeza; *s.* zambullida; salto (*de arriba abajo*).

**plunk** [plʌŋk] *v.* (*instrument*) puntear; (*place*) arrojar.

**plural** [plúrəl] *adj.* & *s.* plural.

**plurality** [plurǽlɪtɪ] *s.* pluralidad.

**plus** [plʌs] *s.* más, signo más; **— quantity** cantidad positiva; **two — three** dos más tres.

**plush** [plʌʃ] *s.* felpa; velludo.

**Pluto** [plúto] *s.* Plutón.

**plutonic** [plutánɪk] *adj.* plutónico.

**ply** [plaɪ] *v.* manejar con tesón (*un instrumento o herramienta*); importunar (*con preguntas*); hacer con regularidad un recorrido (*entre dos puntos*); **to — a trade** seguir o ejercer un oficio; **to — oneself with** saturarse de, rellenarse de; *s.* doblez, pliegue; capa (*de tejido, goma, etc.*).

**pneumatic** [njumǽt k] *adj.* neumático.

**pneumonia** [njumónjə] *s.* pulmonía.

**poach** [potʃ] *v.* escalfar (*huevos*); invadir (*un vedado*); cazar o pescar en vedado; robar caza o pesca (*de un vedado*).

**pocket** [pákɪt] *s.* bolsillo, faltriquera,

*C.A.* bolsa; tronera (*de billar*); cavidad; hoyo; *v.* embolsarse; apropiarse; ocultar (*el orgullo o rencor*); aguantar (*un insulto*).

**pocketbook** [pákɪtbʊk] *s.* cartera; portamonedas; **woman's —** bolsa.

**pocketknife** [pákɪtnaɪf] *s.* navaja; cortaplumas.

**pod** [pɑd] *s.* vaina (*de guisante, frijol, etc.*).

**podium** [pódɪəm] *s.* podio.

**poem** [póɪm] *s.* poema, poesía.

**poet** [póɪt] *s.* poeta; vate.

**poetess** [póɪtɪs] *s.* poetisa.

**poetic** [poétɪk] *adj.* poético; **-s** *s.* arte poética, poética.

**poetical** [poétɪkl̩] *adj.* poético.

**poetry** [póɪtrɪ] *s.* poesía.

**poignant** [póɪnjənt] *adj.* intenso; picante.

**point** [pɔɪnt] *s.* punto; punta (*de lápiz, espada, tierra, etc.*); **it is not to the —** no viene al caso; **not to see the —** no caer en la cuenta; no ver el chiste; propósito o intención; **on the — of** a punto de; *v.* apuntar; señalar; indicar; **to — out** señalar, mostrar, indicar.

**pointblank** [pɔɪntblǽŋk] *adj.* a quema ropa.

**pointed** [pɔ́ɪntɪd] *adj.* puntiagudo, agudo; satírico; apto; a propósito, al caso; **— arch** arco apuntado, arco ojival.

**pointer** [pɔ́ɪntɚ] *s.* (*indicator*) puntero; indicador, señalador; (*dog*) perro de punta y vuelta; (*advice*) indicación, consejo.

**poise** [pɔɪz] *s.* equilibrio; porte, compostura; *v.* equilibrar(se); balancear(se).

**poison** [pɔ́ɪzn̩] *s.* veneno; ponzoña; *v.* envenenar, emponzoñar.

**poisonous** [pɔ́ɪznəs] *adj.* venenoso, ponzoñoso.

**poke** [pok] *v.* atizar, remover (*el fuego*); picar (*con el dedo o cualquier objeto puntiagudo*); **to — along** andar perezosamente; **to — around** husmear, curiosear; **to — fun at** burlarse de; **to — into** meter en; **to — out** sacar; proyectarse; *s.* pinchazo; piquete; codazo; aguijonada; **slow —** tardón.

**polar** [pólɚ] *adj.* polar; **— bear** oso blanco.

**polarity** [polǽrɪtɪ] *s.* polaridad.

**polarization** [polərɪzéʃən] *s.* polarización.

**pole** [pol] *s.* poste; pértiga, palo largo; asta (*de bandera*); garrocha; polo; **Pole** polaco; **north —** polo norte, polo ártico; **south —** polo sur, polo antártico; **— vault** salto con garrocha.

**polemics** [polémɪks] *s.* polémica.

**police** [pəlís] *s.* policía; *v.* vigilar; guardar el orden.

**policeman** [pəlísmən] *s.* policía (*m.*), guardia de policía, polizonte, *Ven. Col.* vigilante, *Méx.* gendarme; *Ch.* carabinero.

**policy** [páləsɪ] *s.* política; **insurance —** póliza de seguro.

**Polish** [pólɪʃ] *adj.* polaco; *s.* polaco, idioma polaco.

**polish** [pálɪʃ] *s.* pulimento; lustre, brillo; urbanidad, cultura; **shoe —** betún, bola; *v.* pulir, pulimentar; dar brillo o lustre a; embolar, dar bola o brillo a (*zapatos*).

**polite** [pəláɪt] *adj.* cortés, fino, urbano, político.

**politeness** [pəláɪtnɪs] *s.* cortesía; fineza, urbanidad.

**politic** [pálətɪk] *adj.* político, prudente; conveniente.

**political** [pəlítɪk] *adj.* político.

**politician** [palətíʃən] *s.* político; politicastro.

**politics** [pálətɪks] *s.* política.

**poll** [pol] *s.* votación; lista electoral; **-s** comicios; urnas electorales; casilla (*donde se vota*); **— tax** impuesto (*de tanto por cabeza*); *v.* registrar los votos de; votar; recibir (*votos*).

**pollen** [pálən] *s.* polen.

**pollinate** [pálənet] *v.* polinizar.

**polo** [pólo] *s.* polo.

**polyglot** [pálɪɡlɑt] *s.* políglota.

**pomegranate** [pámɡrænɪt] *s.* granada; **— tree** granado.

**pomp** [pɑmp] *s.* pompa, boato.

**pompous** [pámpəs] *adj.* pomposa, ostentoso.

**pond** [pɑnd] *s.* charca; estanque; **fish —** vivero.

**ponder** [pándɚ] *v.* ponderar, pesar, examinar; **to — over** reflexionar.

**ponderous** [pándərəs] *adj.* ponderoso; pesado.

**pontoon** [pɑntún] *s.* pontón, chata, barco chato; flotador (*de hidroavión*); **— bridge** pontón, puente flotante.

**pony** [póni] *s.* caballito, potrillo; clave o traducción (*usada ilícitamente en un examen*).

**poodle** [púdl] *s.* perro de lanas.

**pool** [pul] *s.* charco; charca; trucos (*juego parecido al billar*); polla o puesta (*en ciertos juegos*); fondos en común, combinación de fondos (*para una empresa o para especular*); "trust"; **swimming —** piscina; *v.* formar una polla; combinar fondos.

**poor** [pur] *adj.* pobre; malo; de mala calidad; **— student** estudiante pobre; mal estudiante; **— little thing** pobrecito; **the —** los pobres; **-ly** *adv.* pobremente; mal.

**poorhouse** [púrhaus] *s.* hospicio, casa de pobres.

**pop** [pɑp] *s.* tronido, trueno, estallido; detonación; **— of a cork** taponazo; **soda —** gaseosa; *v.* reventar, estallar; detonar; saltar (*un tapón*); **to — a question** espetar una pregunta; **to — corn** hacer palomitas de maíz, hacer rosetas de maíz; **to — in and out** entrar y salir de sopetón; **to — one's head out** sacar o asomar de repente la cabeza.

**popcorn** [pápkɔrn] *s.* rosetas, palomitas de maíz, *Andes* alborotos; *Ch.* cabritas; *Méx.* esquite.

**Pope** [pop] *s.* Papa.

**popeyed** [pápaɪd] *adj.* de ojos saltones, *Am.* desorbitado.

**poplar** [páplɚ] *s.* álamo; **black —** chopo; **— grove** alameda.

**poppy** [pápɪ] *s.* amapola.

**populace** [pápjəlɪs] *s.* pueblo, populacho.

**popular** [pápjəlɚ] *adj.* popular.

**popularity** [pɑpjelǽrətɪ] *s.* popularidad.

**populate** [pápjələt] *v.* poblar.

**population** [pɑpjəléʃən] *s.* población.

**populous** [pápjələs] *adj.* populoso.

**porcelain** [pórslɪn] *s.* porcelana.

**porch** [pórtʃ] *s.* pórtico, porche; galería.

**porcupine** [pórkjəpaɪn] *s.* puerco espín.

**pore** [por] *s.* poro; *v.* **to — over a book** engolfarse en la lectura.

**pork** [pork] *s.* puerco, carne de puerco **— chop** chuleta de puerco; **salt —** tocino salado.

**pornography** [pɔrnáɡrəfɪ] *s.* pornografía.

**porous** [pórəs] *adj.* poroso.

**porridge** [pórɪdʒ] *s.* potaje, gachas.

**port** [pɔrt] *s.* (*harbor*) puerto; (*wine*) oporto; (*left side*) babor (*de un barco*); **—hole** porta, portilla.

**portable** [pórtəbl] *adj.* portátil.

**portal** [pórtl] *s.* portal.

**portent** [pórtent] *s.* portento, presagio, agüero.

**portentous** [pɔrténtəs] *adj.* portentoso; prodigioso; de mal agüero.

**porter** [pórtɚ] *s.* mozo de cordel, *Méx.*, *C.A.* cargador; *Ríopl.* changador; camarero (*en un coche-cama*); portero.

**portfolio** [pɔrtfólɪo] *s.* portafolio, cartera; carpeta; ministerio.

**portion** [pórʃən] *s.* porción; *v.* repartir.

**portly** [pórtlɪ] *adj.* corpulento.

**portrait** [pórtret] *s.* retrato.

**portray** [pɔrtré] *v.* retratar, pintar, dibujar, representar.

**portrayal** [pɔrtréəl] *s.* retrato, delineación, delineamiento, representación.

**Portuguese** [pórtʃəɡiz] *adj.* & *s.* portugués.

**pose** [poz] *s.* (*posture*) postura, actitud; (*affected attitude*) afectación; *v.* posar (*como modelo*); colocar(se) en cierta postura; afectar una actitud o postura; proponer, plantear (*una cuestión o problema*); **to — as** fingirse, hacerse pasar por.

**position** [pəzíʃən] *s.* posición; postura; situación, empleo, puesto.

**positive** [pázətɪv] *adj.* positivo; cierto; seguro; categórico; dogmático.

**possess** [pəzés] *v.* poseer.

**possession** [pəzéʃən] *s.* posesión.

**possessive** [pəzésɪv] *adj.* & *s.* posesivo.

**possessor** [pəzésɚ] *s.* poseedor, posesor, dueño.

**possibility** [pasəbílətɪ] *s.* posibilidad.

**possible** [pásəbl] *adj.* posible; **possibly** *adv.* posiblemente; acaso, tal vez.

**post** [post] *s.* (*pole*) poste, pilar; (*position*) puesto; empleo; **army —** guarnición militar; **— haste** por la posta, rápidamente; **— office** correo, casa de correos; **post-office box** apartado, casilla postal; **—paid** porte pagado, franco de porte; *v.* fijar (*anuncios, carteles*); anunciar; poner en lista; apostar, situar; echar al correo; **to — an entry** asentar o hacer un asiento (*en teneduría*); **to be well -ed** estar al corriente, estar bien enterado.

**postage** [póstɪdʒ] *s.* porte, franqueo; **— stamp** sello de correo, *Am.* estampilla, *Méx., Ríopl.* timbre.

**postal** [póstl̩] *adj.* postal; **— card** tarjeta postal; **— money order** giro postal.

**postcard** [póstkard] *s.* tarjeta postal.

**poster** [póstɚ] *s.* cartel, cartelón; fijador de carteles.

**posterior** [pastíriɚ] *adj.* posterior; trasero.

**posterity** [pastérətɪ] *s.* posteridad.

**posthumous** [pástʃuməs] *adj.* póstumo.

**postman** [póstmən] *s.* cartero.

**postmaster** [póstmæstɚ] *s.* administrador de correos.

**postpone** [postpón] *v.* posponer; aplazar, diferir; postergar.

**postponement** [postpónmənt] *s.* aplazamiento.

**postscript** [pósskript] *s.* posdata.

**posture** [pástʃɚ] *s.* postura, actitud; posición; *v.* adoptar una postura.

**posy** [pózɪ] *s.* flor.

**pot** [pat] *s.* pote; olla, puchero, cacharro (*de cocina*); bacín, bacinica (*de cámara o recámara*); **flower —** tiesto, maceta; **—bellied** panzudo, barrigón; **— hole** bache.

**potassium** [pətǽsiəm] *s.* potasio.

**potato** [pətéto] *s.* patata, papa; **sweet — batata,** *Méx., C.A., Ch., Andes* camote, *Carib., Ríopl.* boniato.

**potency** [pótn̩sɪ] *s.* potencia, poder, fuerza.

**potent** [pótn̩t] *adj.* potente, poderoso, fuerte.

**potential** [pəténʃəl] *adj. & s.* potencial.

**pottage** [pátɪdʒ] *s.* potaje.

**potter** [pátɚ] *s.* alfarero, fabricante de vasijas o cacharros de barro; **-'s field** cementerio de pobres y desconocidos.

**pottery** [pátərɪ] *s.* cerámica, alfarería; vasijas de barro.

**pouch** [pautʃ] *s.* bolsa, saquillo; **mail —** valija; **tobacco —** tabaquera, petaca.

**poultice** [póltɪs] *s.* emplasto.

**poultry** [póltrɪ] *s.* aves de corral.

**pounce** [pauns] *s.* salto (*para agarrar*); zarpada; *v.* **to — into** entrar de sopetón; **to — upon** abalanzarse sobre, saltar sobre, agarrar.

**pound** [paund] *s.* libra; golpazo; **— sterling** libra esterlina; *v.* golpear; machacar, martillar.

**pour** [por] *v.* vaciar, verter; servir (*una taza*); fluir; llover a cántaros, llover recio.

**pout** [paut] *v.* hacer pucheros, lloriquear; poner cara de enfado; *s.* puchero, pucherito.

**poverty** [pávɚtɪ] *s.* pobreza.

**powder** [páudɚ] *s.* polvo; pólvora (*explosivo*); polvos (*de tocador*); **— compact** polvera; **— magazine** polvorín; **— puff** polvera, borla, *Ríopl., Ch.* cisne, *Méx., Andes* mota; *v.* empolvar(se); polvorear, espolvorear; pulverizar(se); **to — one's face** empolvarse la cara, ponerse polvos.

**power** [páuɚ] *s.* poder; poderío; potencia; fuerza; **motive —** fuerza motriz; **— of attorney** poder; **— plant** planta de fuerza motriz.

**powerful** [páuɚfəl] *adj.* poderoso.

**powerless** [páuɚlɪs] *adj.* impotente.

**practicable** [prǽktɪkəbl̩] *adj.* practicable; factible, hacedero; práctico; **— road** camino transitable.

**practical** [prǽktɪkl̩] *adj.* práctico; **— joke** chasco, burla pesada; **-ly** *adv.* casi, virtualmente; realmente, en realidad; prácticamente.

**practice** [prǽktɪs] *s.* práctica; ejercicio (*de una profesión*); método; regla, costumbre; clientela; *v.* practicar; ejercer (*una profesión*); ejercitarse.

**practiced** [prǽktɪst] *adj.* práctico, experimentado; experto, perito.

**practitioner** [prǽktíʃənɚ] *s.* profesional; práctico.

**prairie** [prérɪ] *s.* pradera, llanura.

**praise** [prez] *s.* alabanza; elogio; encomio; *v.* alabar; elogiar; encomiar.

**praiseworthy** [prézwɚðɪ] *adj.* laudable.

**prance** [præns] *v.* cabriolar, hacer cabriolas.

**prank** [præŋk] *s.* travesura, burla; **to play -s** hacer travesuras.

**prate** [pret] *v.* parlotear, charlar; *s.* parloteo, charla.

**prattle** [prǽtl̩] *v.* parlotear, charlar; *s.* parloteo, charla.

**pray** [pre] *v.* orar, rezar; rogar, suplicar; **— tell me** dígame por favor, le ruego que me diga.

**prayer** [prer] *s.* oración, rezo; ruego, súplica; **— book** devocionario; **Lord's — Padre Nuestro.**

**preach** [pritʃ] *v.* predicar; sermonear.

**preacher** [prítʃɚ] *s.* predicador.

**preaching** [prítʃɪŋ] *s.* predicación; sermón; sermoneo.

**preamble** [príæmbl̩] *s.* preámbulo.

**prearranged** [priərǽndʒd] *adj.* arreglado de antemano.

**precarious** [prɪkériəs] *adj.* precario; inseguro.

**precaution** [prɪkóʃən] *s.* precaución.

**precede** [prɪsíd] *v.* preceder.

**precedence** [prɪsídn̩s] *s.* precedencia; prioridad.

**precedent** [présədənt] *s.* precedente.

**preceding** [prɪsídɪŋ] *adj.* precedente, anterior.

**precept** [prísɛpt] *s.* precepto.

**precinct** [prísɪŋkt] *s.* distrito; recinto; **-s** límites, inmediaciones.

**precious** [préʃəs] *adj.* precioso; querido, amado, caro; **— little** poquísimo, muy poco.

**precipice** [présəpɪs] *s.* precipicio.

PO

**precipitate** [prɪsípətet] v. precipitar-(se); adj. precipitado, apresurado, atropellado; s. precipitado.

**precipitation** [prɪsɪpətéʃən] s. precipitación; lluvia (o nieve, rocío, granizo, etc.); cantidad de agua pluvial.

**precipitous** [prɪsípətəs] adj. precipitoso, escarpado; precipitado.

**precise** [prɪsáɪs] adj. preciso, exacto.

**precision** [prɪsíʒən] s. precisión, exactitud.

**preclude** [prɪklúd] v. excluir; impedir.

**precocious** [prɪkóʃəs] adj. precoz.

**precursor** [prɪkəsə] s. precursor.

**predecessor** [prɛdɪsésə] s. predecesor.

**predestine** [prɪdéstɪn] v. predestinar.

**predicament** [prɪdíkəmənt] s. aprieto, apuro, dificultad.

**predicate** [prédɪkɪt] adj. & s. predicado.

**predict** [prɪdíkt] v. predicir, vaticinar.

**prediction** [prɪdíkʃən] s. predicción, pronóstico, vaticinio.

**predilection** [prɪdlékʃən] s. predilección, preferencia.

**predispose** [prɪdɪspóz] v. predisponer.

**predominance** [prɪdámənəns] s. predominio; ascendiente.

**predominant** [prɪdámənənt] adj. predominante.

**predominate** [prɪdámənet] v. predominar.

**preface** [préfɪs] s. prefacio; prólogo; v. prologar.

**prefect** [prífɛkt] s. prefecto.

**prefer** [prɪfə́] v. preferir; **to — a claim** presentar una demanda.

**preferable** [préfrəbl] adj. preferible; preferente; **preferably** adv. preferiblemente; preferentemente, de preferencia.

**preference** [préfrəns] s. preferencia.

**preferred** [prɪfə́d] p.p. & adj. preferido; **— shares** acciones preferentes.

**prefix** [prífɪks] s. prefijo; [prifíks] v. prefijar, anteponer.

**pregnancy** [prégnənsɪ] s. preñez, embarazo.

**pregnant** [prégnənt] adj. preñado; lleno, repleto, encinta.

**prejudice** [prédʒədɪs] s. (preconception) prejuicio, prevención; (harm) daño; v. predisponer, prevenir; perjudicar.

**prelate** [prélɪt] s. prelado.

**preliminary** [prɪlímənɛrɪ] adj. & s. preliminar.

**prelude** [préljud] s. preludio; v. preludiar.

**premature** [primətjúr] adj. prematuro.

**premeditated** [prɪmédətetɪd] adj. premeditado.

**premier** [prímɪə] s. primer ministro; adj. primero; principal.

**premise** [prémɪs] s. premisa; -s terrenos; local.

**premium** [prímɪəm] s. premio; **at a —** muy escaso, muy caro; **insurance —** prima de seguro.

**prenatal** [prinétl] adj. prenatal.

**preoccupy** [priákjəpaɪ] v. preocupar; ocupar de antemano.

**preorbital** [priórbɪtl] adj. preorbital.

**prepaid** [pripéd] adj. pagado de antemano; **to send —** enviar porte pagado, enviar franco de porte.

**preparation** [prɛpəréʃən] s. preparación; preparativo.

**preparatory** [prɪpǽrətorɪ] adj. preparatorio.

**prepare** [prɪpér] v. preparar(se).

**preparedness** [prɪpérɪdnɪs] s. preparación, prevención.

**preponderant** [pripándrənt] adj. preponderante.

**preposition** [prɛpəzíʃən] s. preposición.

**prepossess** [pripozés] v. preocupar; predisponer.

**preposterous** [prɪpástrəs] adj. absurdo, insensato.

**prerequisite** [prirékwəzɪt] s. requisito previo.

**prerogative** [prɪrágətɪv] s. prerrogativa.

**presage** [présɪdʒ] s. presagio; [prɪsédʒ] v. presagiar.

**prescribe** [prɪskráɪb] v. prescribir; recetar.

**prescription** [prɪskrípʃən] s. receta; prescripción, precepto, mandato.

**presence** [prézns] s. presencia; **— of mind** aplomo, serenidad.

**present** [prézṇt] s. (time) presente; (gift) regalo; **at —** al presente, ahora; **for the —** por ahora; adj. presente; corriente, actual; **— company excepted** mejorando lo presente; **— participle** gerundio; **to be —** asistir, estar presente; [prɪzént] v. presentar; regalar, obsequiar.

**presentation** [prezṇtéʃən] s. presentación; regalo, obsequio.

**presentiment** [prɪzéntəmənt] s. presentimiento; corazonada.

**presently** [prézṇtlɪ] adv. luego, pronto, dentro de poco.

**preservation** [prezəvéʃən] s. preservación; conservación.

**preserve** [prɪzə́v] v. preservar, guardar; conservar; mantener; s. conserva, compota; **forest —** vedado.

**preside** [prizáɪd] v. presidir; **to — at (— over) a meeting** presidir una junta.

**presidency** [prézədənsɪ] s. presidencia.

**president** [prézədənt] s. presidente.

**presidential** [prezədénʃəl] adj. presidencial.

**press** [prɛs] v. (bear down) prensar; apretar; comprimir; planchar (ropa); (force) forzar; apremiar, urgir; empujar; **to — forward** empujar hacia adelante; avanzar, ganar terreno; **to — one's point** porfiar; insistir en su argumento; **to — through the crowd** abrirse paso por entre la multitud; **to be hard -ed by work** estar abrumado de trabajo; **to be hard -ed for money** estar escaso de fondos; s. prensa; imprenta.

**pressing** [présɪŋ] adj. apremiante, urgente.

**pressure** [préʃə] s. presión; apremio,

urgencia; — **cooker** cocinilla de presión; — **gauge** manómetro.
**pressurize** [préʃəaɪz] *v.* sobrecargar.
**prestige** [prɛstíʒ] *s.* prestigio.
**presumable** [prɪsúməbl̩] *adj.* presumible, probable.
**presume** [prɪzúm] *v.* presumir; suponer; **to — on (upon)** abusar de; **to — to** atreverse a.
**presumption** [prɪzʌ́mpʃən] *s.* presunción; pretensión; suposición.
**presumptuous** [prɪzʌ́mptʃʊəs] *adj.* presuntuoso, pretencioso, presumido.
**presuppose** [prisəpóz] *v.* presuponer.
**pretend** [prɪténd] *v.* pretender; fingir.
**pretense** [prɪténs] *s.* pretensión; presunción; ostentación; apariencia; pretexto; **under — of** so pretexto de.
**pretension** [prɪténʃən] *s.* pretensión; pretexto.
**pretentious** [prɪténʃəs] *adj.* pretencioso.
**pretext** [prítɛkst] *s.* pretexto.
**prettily** [prítɪlɪ] *adv.* lindamente; agradablemente.
**prettiness** [prítɪnɪs] *s.* lindeza, gracia.
**pretty** [prítɪ] *adj.* lindo, bonito, bello, *Am.* chulo; *adv.* medianamente; bastante; un poco, algo; — **well** regular, así así; bastante bien, medianamente.
**prevail** [prɪvél] *v.* prevalecer; **to — on (upon)** persuadir.
**prevailing** [prɪvélɪŋ] *adj.* predominante; en boga.
**prevalent** [prévələnt] *adj.* prevaleciente; común, corriente.
**prevent** [prɪvént] *v.* prevenir, evitar; impedir; estorbar.
**prevention** [prɪvénʃən] *s.* prevención; precaución.
**preventive** [prɪvéntɪv] *adj.* impeditivo.
**preview** [prívju] *s.* vista previa (*anticipada*).
**previous** [prívɪəs] *adj.* previo; **-ly** *adv.* previamente; antes; de antemano.
**prey** [pre] *s.* presa; víctima; **birds of —** aves de rapiña; *v.* **to — on** cazar; rapiñar, pillar; robar; **it -s upon my mind** me tiene preocupado, me tiene en zozobra.
**price** [praɪs] *s.* precio; valor; costo (coste *o* costa); **at any —** a toda costa, a todo trance; *v.* apreciar, valuar, fijar el precio de; averiguar el precio de.
**priceless** [práɪslɪs] *adj.* sin precio, inapreciable.
**prick** [prɪk] *v.* picar; pinchar; punzar; sentir comezón; sentir picazón; **to — up one's ears** aguzar las orejas; *s.* picadura; punzada; pinchazo; piquete; aguijón; púa.
**prickly** [príklɪ] *adj.* espinoso, lleno de espinas; lleno de púas; — **heat** picazón causada por el calor; — **pear** tuna (*de nopal*).
**pride** [praɪd] *s.* orgullo; soberbia; *v.* **to — oneself on (upon)** enorgullecerse de, preciarse de.
**priest** [prist] *s.* sacerdote.
**priesthood** [prísthʊd] *s.* sacerdocio.

**prim** [prɪm] *adj.* remilgado; repulido; peripuesto; estirado.
**primarily** [praɪmérəlɪ] *adv.* primariamente, principalmente; en primer lugar.
**primary** [práɪmɛrɪ] *adj.* (*first*) primario; primero; (*basic*) fundamental; principal; — **colors** colores elementales; — **election** elección primaria; — **school** escuela primaria.
**prime** [praɪm] *adj.* (*main*) principal; primario, primero; (*select*) selecto, de primera calidad; — **minister** primer ministro; — **number** número primo; *s.* flor (*de la vida o de la edad*); la flor y nata (*lo mejor*); plenitud; número primo; **to be in one's —** estar en la flor de la edad; *v.* preparar, informar, instruir de atemano; cebar (*un carburador, bomba o arma de fuego*).
**primer** [prímɚ] *s.* abecedario, cartilla de lectura; compendio.
**primeval** [praɪmívl̩] *adj.* primitivo.
**primitive** [prímətɪv] *adj.* primitivo.
**primness** [prímnɪs] *s.* remilgo, tiesura, demasiada formalidad, dengue, afectación.
**primp** [prɪmp] *v.* acicalar(se), adornar(se), arreglar(se).
**primrose** [prímroz] *s.* prímula o primavera (*flor*); color amarillo pálido.
**prince** [prɪns] *s.* príncipe.
**princely** [prínslɪ] *adj.* noble, regio, magnífico, propio de un príncipe.
**princess** [prínsɪs] *s.* princesa.
**principal** [prínsəpl̩] *adj.* principal; *s.* principal, capital; principal, jefe, director.
**principle** [prínsəpl̩] *s.* principio; regla, ley; fundamento, base.
**print** [prɪnt] *s.* (*type*) tipo, letra de molde; (*art*) lámina, grabado; estampado (*tejido estampado*); diseño (*estampado*); impresión; **in —** impreso, publicado; **out of —** agotado; *v.* imprimir; estampar; escribir en letra de molde; **-ed fabric** estampado.
**printer** [príntɚ] *s.* impresor.
**printing** [príntɪŋ] *s.* imprenta; impresión; tipografía; — **office** imprenta; — **press** prensa.
**prior** [práɪɚ] *adj.* previo, anterior, precedente; — **to** anterior a, con antelación a; *s.* prior (*de un monasterio*).
**priority** [praɪɔ́rətɪ] *s.* prioridad, precedencia, antelación.
**prism** [prízəm] *s.* prisma.
**prison** [prízn̩] *s.* prisión, cárcel; *v.* encarcelar.
**prisoner** [prízn̩ɚ] *s.* prisionero, preso.
**privacy** [práɪvəsɪ] *s.* secreto, reserva; retiro; **to have no —** carecer de sitio privado; estar a la vista del público.
**private** [práɪvɪt] *adj.* privado; personal; particular; secreto; confidencial; **a — citizen** un particular; — **school** escuela particular; *s.* soldado raso; **in —** en secreto; a solas, privadamente.
**privation** [praɪvéʃən] *s.* privación.
**privilege** [prívlɪdʒ] *s.* privilegio.

**PR**

**privileged** [prívlɪdʒd] *adj.* privilegiado;
**to be — to** tener el privilegio de.
**privy** [prívɪ] *adj.* privado; enterado de;
*s.* excusado exterior.
**prize** [praɪz] *s.* (*reward*) premio,
galardón; (*booty*) presa, botín de
guerra; **— fight** boxeo público,
pugilato; **— fighter** boxeador, pugilista; **— medal** medalla de premio;
*v.* apreciar, estimar, tener en gran
estima.
**probability** [prabəbílətɪ] *s.* probabilidad.
**probable** [prábəbl] *adj.* probable; **probably** *adv.* probablemente.
**probation** [probéʃən] *s.* probación;
noviciado; prueba; **to put a prisoner
on —** poner a un prisionero en libertad bajo la vigilancia de un juez.
**probe** [prob] *v.* tentar, reconocer, sondear (*una herida*); escudriñar, examinar a fondo; indagar; *s.* tienta (*instrumento de cirujano*); indagación.
**problem** [prábləm] *s.* problema.
**procedure** [prəsídʒəˑ] *s.* procedimiento;
proceder.
**proceed** [prəsíd] *v.* proceder; proseguir; seguir adelante; **to — to** proceder a, comenzar a, ponerse a.
**proceeding** [prəsídɪŋ] *s.* procedimiento; transacción; **-s** transacciones;
actas; proceso.
**proceeds** [prósidz] *s. pl.* producto, ganancia.
**process** [práses] *s.* (*series*) proceso;
(*method*) procedimiento, método; **in
— of time** con el transcurso del
tiempo, con el tiempo, andando el
tiempo; **in the — of being made**
en vía de preparación; *v.* preparar
mediante un procedimiento especial,
someter a un procedimiento; procesar (*ante un juez*).
**procession** [prəséʃən] *s.* procesión;
desfile; **funeral —** cortejo fúnebre.
**proclaim** [proklém] *v.* proclamar; promulgar.
**proclamation** [prakləméʃən] *s.* proclamación; proclama.
**proclivity** [proklívɪtɪ] *s.* inclinación.
**procure** [prokjúr] *v.* procurar, conseguir, obtener.
**prod** [prad] *v.* aguijonear; picar.
**prodigal** [prádɪgl] *adj. & s.* pródigo,
gastador.
**prodigious** [prədídʒəs] *adj.* prodigioso.
**prodigy** [prádədʒɪ] *s.* prodigio.
**produce** [prádjus] *s.* producto; productos agrícolas; [prədjús] *v.* producir.
**producer** [prədjúsəˑ] *s.* productor; **theatrical —** empresario.
**product** [prádəkt] *s.* producto.
**production** [prədʌ́kʃən] *s.* producción;
producto; obra, composición; representación teatral.
**productive** [prədʌ́ktɪv] *adj.* productivo.
**profanation** [prafənéʃen] *s.* profanación, desacato.
**profane** [prəfén] *adj.* profano; *v.* profanar.

**profess** [prəfés] *v.* profesar; pretender.
**profession** [prəféʃən] *s.* profesión.
**professional** [prəféʃənl] *adj.* profesional; *s.* profesional, *Méx.* profesionista.
**professor** [prəfésəˑ] *s.* profesor, catedrático.
**proffer** [práfəˑ] *s.* oferta, propuesta; *v.*
ofrecer, proponer.
**proficiency** [prəfíʃənsɪ] *s.* pericia, destreza.
**proficient** [prəfíʃənt] *adj.* proficiente,
perito, experto.
**profile** [prófaɪl] *s.* perfil; contorno.
**profit** [práfɪt] *s.* (*gain*) ganancia; lucro;
(*usefulness*) provecho, utilidad, beneficio; **— and loss** pérdidas y ganancias; **net —** ganancia neta o líquida;
*v.* aprovechar; ganar, sacar provecho;
**to — by** aprovecharse de, sacar
provecho de.
**profitable** [práfɪtəbl] *adj.* provechoso;
lucrativo.
**profiteer** [prafətír] *s.* extorsionista, carero, explotador, logrero; *v.* extorsionar, explotar, cobrar más de lo justo.
**profound** [prəfáund] *adj.* profundo.
**profuse** [prəfjús] *adj.* profuso, abundante; pródigo.
**progeny** [prádʒenɪ] *s.* prole.
**prognosis** [pragnósɪs] *s.* pronóstico.
**program** [prógræm] *s.* programa; plan.
**progress** [prágres] *s.* progreso; [prəgrés]
*v.* progresar.
**progressive** [prəgrésɪv] *adj.* progresivo;
progresista; *s.* progresista.
**prohibit** [prohíbɪt] *v.* prohibir; vedar.
**prohibition** [proəbíʃən] *s.* prohibición.
**project** [prádʒɛkt] *s.* proyecto, plan;
[prədʒékt] *v.* proyectar(se); exten-
der(se), sobresalir.
**projectile** [prədʒéktl] *s.* proyectil; *adj.*
arrojadizo; **— weapon** arma arrojadiza.
**projection** [prədʒékʃən] *s.* proyección;
saliente, salidizo.
**projector** [prədʒéktəˑ] *s.* proyector.
**proletarian** [prolətériən] *adj. & s.*
proletario.
**proletariat** [prolətériət] *s.* proletariado.
**prolific** [prolífɪk] *adj.* prolífico.
**prologue** [prólɔg] *s.* prólogo.
**prolong** [prəlɔ́ŋ] *v.* prolongar.
**prolongation** [prolɔŋgéʃən] *s.* prolongación.
**promenade** [praménéd] *s.* paseo; baile
(*usualmente* **prom**); *v.* pasearse.
**prominent** [prámənənt] *adj.* prominente; notable; saliente; conspicuo.
**promiscuous** [prəmískjuəs] *adj.* pro-
miscuo.
**promise** [prámɪs] *s.* promesa; *v.* prometer; **Promised Land** Tierra de
Promisión.
**promising** [prámɪsɪŋ] *adj.* prometedor.
**promissory** [práməsorɪ] *adj.* promisorio; **— note** pagaré.
**promontory** [práməntorɪ] *s.* promontorio.
**promote** [prəmót] *v.* (*favor*) promover;
fomentar; explotar; adelantar; (*raise*)
ascender; elevar.

**promoter** [prəmótəˈ] *s.* promotor, promovedor.

**promotion** [prəmóʃən] *s.* promoción; ascenso; adelantamiento.

**prompt** [prɑmpt] *adj.* pronto, puntual; listo, presto; *v.* mover, incitar, inducir; apuntar *(servir de apuntador en el teatro)*; soplar *(sugerir a otro lo que debe decir en una clase o junta).*

**promptly** [prámptlɪ] *adv.* pronto, prontamente, presto; puntualmente; con prontitud, con presteza.

**promptness** [prámptnɪs] *s.* prontitud, presteza; puntualidad.

**promulgate** [prəmʌ́lget] *v.* promulgar.

**prone** [pron] *adj.* inclinado; propenso, dispuesto; boca abajo; postrado.

**prong** [prɔŋ] *s.* púa, punta.

**pronoun** [prónaʊn] *s.* pronombre.

**pronounce** [prənáʊns] *v.* pronunciar; declarar.

**pronounced** [prənáʊnst] *adj.* pronunciado, marcado; **— opinions** opiniones decididas.

**pronunciation** [prənʌnsɪéʃən] *s.* pronunciación.

**proof** [pruf] *s.* prueba; comprobación; *adj.* impenetrable, resistente; **— against** a prueba de; **—reader** corrector de pruebas de imprenta; **— sheet** prueba, pliego de prueba; **galley —** galerada; **bomb—** a prueba de bomba; **fire —** a prueba de incendios; **water—** impermeable.

**prop** [prɑp] *s.* puntal; sostén, apoyo; *v.* apuntalar, sostener.

**propaganda** [prɑpəgǽndə] *s.* propaganda.

**propagate** [prápəget] *v.* propagar(se).

**propagation** [prɑpəgéʃen] *s.* propagación; diseminación.

**propel** [prəpél] *v.* propulsar, impeler.

**propeller** [prəpéləˈ] *s.* hélice *(de un buque o avión)*; propulsor, impulsor.

**proper** [prápəˈ] *adj.* propio; conveniente a propósito; justo; correcto; **— noun** nombre propio; **-ly** *adv.* propiamente; con propiedad, correctamente.

**property** [prápəˈtɪ] *s.* propiedad; posesión; posesiones, bienes.

**prophecy** [práfəsɪ] *s.* profecía.

**prophesy** [práfəsaɪ] *v.* profetizar, predecir, pronosticar, augurar.

**prophet** [práfɪt] *s.* profeta.

**prophetic** [prəfétɪk] *adj.* profético.

**propitious** [prəpíʃəs] *adj.* propicio, favorable.

**proportion** [prəpórʃən] *s.* proporción; **out of —** desproporcionado; *v.* proporcionar; **well -ed** bien proporcionado.

**proposal** [prəpóz]] *s.* propuesta; proposición; declaración *(de amor).*

**propose** [prəpóz] *v.* proponer; declararse, hacer propuesta de matrimonio; **to — to do something** proponerse hacer algo.

**proposition** [prɑpəzíʃən] *s.* proposición; propuesta; asunto.

**proprietor** [prəpráɪətəˈ] *s.* propietario, dueño.

**propriety** [prəpráɪətɪ] *s.* propiedad, corrección; decoro.

**propulsion** [propʌ́lʃən] *s.* propulsión.

**prorate** [prorét] *v.* prorratear, repartir proporcionalmente.

**prosaic** [prozéɪk] *adj.* prosaico.

**prose** [proz] *s.* prosa; *adj.* prosaico.

**prosecute** [prásɪkjut] *v.* procesar, enjuiciar, demandar ante un juez; llevar adelante *(un negocio, empresa, demanda, etc.).*

**prosecution** [prɑsɪkjúʃən] *s.* prosecución, seguimiento; parte acusadora *(en un pleito).*

**prosecutor** [prásɪkjutəˈ] *s.* fiscal; acusador.

**prospect** [práspɛkt] *s.* *(hope)* perspectiva, vista; esperanza; espectativa; *(candidate)* cliente; *(chances)* probabilidad de éxito; *v.* explorar, andar en busca de.

**prospective** [prəspéktɪv] *adj.* probable, posible, esperado; presunto.

**prospector** [prəspéktəˈ] *s.* explorador, buscador *(de minas, petróleo, etc.).*

**prosper** [práspəˈ] *v.* prosperar, medrar.

**prosperity** [prɑspérətɪ] *s.* prosperidad.

**prosperous** [prásprəs] *adj.* próspero.

**prostitute** [prástətjut] *s.* ramera, prostituta; *v.* prostituir.

**prostrate** [prástret] *adj.* postrado; abatido; *v.* postrar; abatir.

**protagonist** [protǽgənɪst] *s.* protagonista.

**protect** [prətékt] *v.* proteger.

**protection** [prətékʃen] *s.* protección; amparo.

**protective** [prətéktɪv] *adj.* protector; **— tariff** tarifa proteccionista.

**protector** [prətéktəˈ] *s.* protector.

**protectorate** [prətéktrɪt] *s.* protectorado.

**protégé** [prótəge] *s.* protegido.

**protein** [prótiɪn] *s.* proteína.

**protest** [prótest] *s.* protesta protestación; [prətést] *v.* protestar.

**protestant** [prátɪstənt] *adj. & s.* protestante.

**protestation** [prɑtəstéʃən] *s.* protestación, protesta.

**protoplasm** [prótəplæzəm] *s.* protoplasma.

**prototype** [prótotaɪp] *s.* prototipo.

**protract** [protrǽkt] *v.* alargar, extender, prolongar.

**protrude** [protrúd] *v.* sobresalir; resaltar; proyectar(se).

**protuberance** [protjúbərəns] *s.* protuberancia.

**proud** [praʊd] *adj.* orgulloso; soberbio.

**prove** [pruv] *v.* probar; demostrar; comprobar; resultar.

**proverb** [právɝb] *s.* proverbio; refrán.

**provide** [prəváɪd] *v.* proveer; abastecer; suplir; estipular; **to — for** hacer provisión para; **to — with** proveer de.

**provided** [prəváɪdɪd] *conj.* con tal (de) que, a condición (de) que; **— that** con tal (de) que.

**providence** [právədəns] *s.* providencia.

**providential** [prɑvədénʃəl] *adj.* providencial.

**provider** [prəváidə] s. proveedor.

**province** [právɪns] s. provincia; juris-dicción; **it isn't within my —** no está dentro de mi jurisdicción; no es de mi incumbencia.

**provincial** [prəvínʃəl] adj. provincial; s. provinciano.

**provision** [prəvíʒən] s. (goods) provi-sión; abastecimiento; (plan) estipula-ción; **-s** provisiones; víveres; **to make the necessary -s** tomar las medidas (o precauciones) necesarias.

**proviso** [prəváizo] s. condición, estipu-lación.

**provocation** [pravəkéʃən] s. provoca-ción.

**provoke** [prəvók] v. provocar; irritar; enfadar.

**prow** [prau] s. proa.

**prowess** [práuɪs] s. proeza.

**prowl** [praul] v. rondar en acecho; fisgonear.

**proximity** [praksímətɪ] s. proximidad.

**proxy** [práksɪ] s. apoderado, substituto, delegado; **by —** mediante apoderado.

**prude** [prud] s. mojigato, persona gaz-moña.

**prudence** [prúdn̩s] s. prudencia.

**prudent** [prúdn̩t] adj. prudente.

**prudery** [prúdərɪ] s. mojigatería, gaz-moñería, remilgo.

**prudish** [prúdɪʃ] adj. gazmoño, remil-gado.

**prune** [prun] s. ciruela; ciruela pasa; v. podar, recortar.

**pry** [praɪ] v. atisbar, espiar; fisgar, fis-gonear; curiosear; **to — a secret out** extraer (o arrancar) un secreto; **to — apart** separar por fuerza; **to — into other people's affairs** entre-meterse en lo ajeno; **to — open** abrir a la fuerza; **to — up** levantar con una palanca.

**psalm** [sɑm] s. salmo.

**pseudonym** [sjúdn̩ɪm] s. seudónimo.

**psychiatrist** [saɪkáɪətrɪst] s. psiquiatra, alienista.

**psychiatry** [saɪkáɪətrɪ] s. psiquiatría.

**psychological** [saɪkəládʒɪk!] adj. psico-lógico.

**psychologist** [saɪkálədʒɪst] s. psicólogo.

**psychology** [saɪkálədʒɪ] s. psicología.

**psychosis** [saɪkósɪs] s. sicosis.

**public** [páblɪk] adj. público; **— prose-cutor** fiscal; s. público.

**publication** [pablɪkéʃən] s. publicación.

**publicity** [pablísətɪ] s. publicidad, pro-paganda.

**publish** [páblɪʃ] v. publicar; editar; **-ing house** editorial o editora.

**publisher** [páblɪʃə] s. publicador; edi-tor.

**pucker** [pákə] v. fruncir.

**pudding** [púdɪŋ] s. budín, pudín.

**puddle** [pád!] s. charco.

**puff** [pʌf] s. resoplido; bocanada (de humo, vapor, etc.); bullón (de vestido); **— of wind** ráfaga, soplo; **— paste** hojaldre; **cream —** bollo de crema; **powder —** polvera, borla, Méx.

mota; Ríopl. cisne; v. resoplar, jadear; echar bocanadas; **to — up** inflar(se); ahuecar(se); hinchar(se).

**pug** [pʌg] s. perro dogo; **— nose** nariz chata, ñata o respingada.

**pull** [pul] v. (tug) tirar de; jalar (halar); (extract) sacar; arrancar; (stretch) estirar; **to — apart** desgarrar; despedazar; descomponer; desmon-tar; **to — down the curtain** bajar la cortinilla; **to — oneself together** componerse, serenarse; **to — over to the right** hacerse a la derecha, desviarse hacia la derecha; **to — up** arrancar; parar (un caballo, un auto); parar, hacer alto; **to — through** salir de un apuro; sacar (a alguien) de un apuro; **the train -ed into the station** el tren llegó a la estación; s. tirón; estirón; ascenso difícil; esfuerzo (para subir); **to have —** tener buenas aldabas, tener influencia.

**pullet** [púlɪt] s. polla.

**pulley** [púlɪ] s. polea; garrucha.

**pulp** [pʌlp] s. pulpa.

**pulpit** [púlpɪt] s. púlpito.

**pulsate** [pálset] v. pulsar, latir.

**pulse** [pʌls] s. pulso; pulsación.

**pulverize** [pálvəraɪz] v. pulverizar.

**pumice** [pámɪs] s. piedra pómez.

**pump** [pʌmp] s. bomba (para sacar agua); zapatilla; **gasoline —** bomba de gasolina; **hand —** bomba de mano; **tire —** bomba para neumáti-cos; v. manejar la bomba, Am. bom-bear; inflar (un neumático); **to — someone** sacarle (o sonsacarle) a una persona la verdad o un secreto.

**pumpkin** [pámpkɪn] s. calabaza.

**pun** [pʌn] s. equívoco, retruécano, juego de palabras; v. decir retruécanos o equívocos, jugar del vocablo.

**punch** [pʌntʃ] s. (blow) puñetazo, puñada; (drink) ponche; (vitality) pun-zón, sacabocados; (vitality) fuerza, empuje; vitalidad; **— bowl** pon-chera; v. dar un puñetazo, dar una puñada; punzar, horadar, perforar; **to — a hole** hacer un agujero o per-foración.

**punctual** [páŋktʃuəl] adj. puntual.

**punctuality** [pʌŋktʃuǽlətɪ] s. puntuali-dad.

**punctuate** [páŋktʃuet] v. puntuar.

**punctuation** [pʌŋktʃuéʃən] s. puntua-ción.

**puncture** [páŋktʃə] v. picar, punzar, pinchar; agujerear, perforar; **-d tire** neumático picado; s. picadura; pin-chazo; perforación; **to have a tire —** tener un neumático picado, tener una llanta o goma picada.

**punish** [pánɪʃ] v. castigar.

**punishment** [pánɪʃmənt] s. castigo.

**punt** [pʌnt] s. puntapié, patada.

**puny** [pjúnɪ] adj. endeble, débil, flaco, enfermizo; insignificante.

**pup** [pʌp] s. cachorro.

**pupil** [pjúp!] s. discípulo; **— of the eye** pupila, niña del ojo.

**puppet** [pápɪt] s. títere, muñeco, mo-

nigote; — **show** títeres.
**puppy** [pʌ́pɪ] *s.* cachorrito.
**purchase** [pɜ́tʃəs] *v.* comprar; mercar; *s.* compra; merca; **to get a — upon** agarrarse fuerte a.
**purchaser** [pɜ́tʃəsə˞] *s.* comprador, marchante.
**pure** [pjʊr] *adj.* puro; **-ly** *adv.* puramente; meramente.
**purée** [pjuré] *s.* puré.
**purgative** [pɜ́gətɪv] *adj.* purgante; *s.* purga, purgante.
**purgatory** [pɜ́gətorɪ] *s.* purgatorio.
**purge** [pɜdʒ] *v.* purgar(se); limpiar; purificar(se); *s.* purga, purgante.
**purify** [pjʊ́rəfaɪ] *v.* purificar(se); depurar.
**purist** [pjʊ́rɪst] *s.* purista.
**purity** [pjʊ́rətɪ] *s.* pureza.
**purple** [pɜ́pl] *s.* púrpura; *adj.* purpúreo, morado.
**purport** [pɜ́port] *s.* significado; tenor, sustancia; [pə˞pórt] *v.* pretender, aparentar.
**purpose** [pɜ́pəs] *s.* (*intention*) propósito, intención; (*goal*) fin, objeto; **for no —** sin objeto, inútilmente, en vano, para nada; **on —** adrede, de propósito; *v.* proponerse.
**purr** [pɜ] *s.* ronroneo (*del gato*); zumbido (*del motor*); *v.* ronronear (*el gato*).
**purse** [pɜs] *s.* bolsillo, portamonedas, bolsa; *v.* **to — one's lips** fruncir los labios.
**pursuant** [pə˞súənt] *adv.* conforme; de acuerdo con.
**pursue** [pə˞sú] *v.* perseguir; seguir; dedicarse a (*una carrera, un estudio*).
**pursuer** [pə˞sú˞ə] *s.* perseguidor.
**pursuit** [pə˞sút] *s.* perseguimiento; busca; ocupación; ejercicio (*de una profesión, cargo, etc.*); **in — of** a caza de, en seguimiento de, en busca de.
**pus** [pʌs] *s.* pus, podre.
**push** [pʊʃ] *v.* (*shove*) empujar; (*promote*) fomentar, promover; (*hurry*) apresurar; **to — aside** hacer a un lado, rechazar, apartar; **to — forward** empujar, abrirse paso; avanzar; **to — through** encajar (*por un agujero o rendija*); abrirse paso a empujones; *s.* empuje; empujón, empellón; **— button** botón eléctrico.
**pushcart** [pʊ́ʃkart] *s.* carretilla de mano.
**pussy** [pʊ́sɪ] *s.* minino, gatito; **— willow** especie de sauce americano.
**put** [pʊt] *v.* poner; colocar; **to — a question** hacer una pregunta; **to — across an idea** darse a entender bien; hacer aceptar una idea; **to — away** apartar; guardar; **to — before** poner delante, anteponer; proponer ante; **to — by money** ahorrar o guardar dinero; **to — down** apuntar, anotar; sofocar (*una revolución*); rebajar (*los precios*); **to — in words** expresar; **to — in writing** poner por escrito; **to — off** aplazar, posponer; diferir; **to — on** ponerse (*ropa*); **to — on airs** darse tono o ínfulas; **to**

**— on weight** engordar; **to — out** apagar, extinguir; **to — someone out** echar o expulsar a alguien; molestar o incomodar a alguien; **to — to shame** avergonzar; **to — up** enlatar, envasar (*frutas, legumbres*); apostar (*dinero*); alojar(se); erigir; **to — up for sale** poner de venta; **to — up with** aguantar, tolerar; *pret. & p.p. de* **to put.**
**putrefy** [pjútrəfaɪ] *v.* podrir (*o* pudrir), corromper.
**putrid** [pjútrɪd] *adj.* putrefacto, podrido.
**putter** [pʌ́tə˞] *v.* trabajar sin orden ni sistema; ocuparse en cosas de poca monta; malgastar el tiempo.
**putty** [pʌ́tɪ] *s.* masilla; *v.* tapar o rellenar con masilla.
**puzzle** [pʌ́zl] *s.* rompecabezas, acertijo; enigma; **crossword —** crucigrama; *v.* embrollar, poner perplejo, confundir; **to — out** desenredar, descifrar; **to — over** ponderar; tratar de resolver o descifrar; **to be -d** estar perplejo.
**pyramid** [pírəmɪd] *s.* pirámide.

## Q

**quack** [kwæk] *s.* graznido (*del pato*); curandero, matasanos, medicastro; charlatán; *adj.* falso; *v.* graznar.
**quagmire** [kwǽgmaɪr] *s.* tremedal, cenagal.
**quail** [kwel] *s.* codorniz.
**quaint** [kwent] *adj.* raro, extraño; pintoresco.
**quake** [kwek] *s.* temblor; terremoto; *v.* temblar.
**qualification** [kwaləfəkéʃən] *s.* (*condition*) calificación; cualidad, calidad; (*requirement*) requisito; aptitud.
**qualify** [kwáləfaɪ] *v.* calificar; capacitar; **to — for a position** estar capacitado para una posición; **his studies — him for the job** sus estudios le capacitan para el puesto.
**quality** [kwálətɪ] *s.* cualidad; calidad.
**qualm** [kwam] *s.* escrúpulo.
**quantify** [kwántɪfaɪ] *v.* cuantificar.
**quantity** [kwántɪtɪ] *s.* cantidad.
**quarantine** [kwórəntin] *s.* cuarentena; *v.* poner en cuarentena, aislar.
**quarrel** [kwórəl] *s.* riña, reyerta, pendencia; querella; *v.* reñir; pelear, disputar.
**quarrelsome** [kwórəlsəm] *adj.* reñidor, pendenciero.
**quarry** [kwórɪ] *s.* cantera; presa, caza (*animal perseguido*); *v.* explotar (*una cantera*); trabajar en una cantera.
**quart** [kwɔrt] *s.* cuarto de galón (*0.9463 de un litro*).
**quarter** [kwórtə˞] *s.* (*one-fourth*) cuarto, cuarta parte; (*coin*) moneda de 25 centavos; (*district*) barrio, distrito; **-s** morada, vivienda; alojamiento; **from all -s** de todas partes; **to give no — to the enemy** no dar cuartel al enemigo; *adj.* cuarto; *v.* cuartear, dividir en cuartos; descuartizar;

acuartelar, acantonar, alojar (*tropas*).
**quarterly** [kwɔ́rtəlɪ] *adv.* trimestral-
mente, por trimestres; *adj.* trimestral;
*s.* publicación trimestral.
**quartet** [kwɔrtét] *s.* cuarteto.
**quartz** [kwɔrts] *s.* cuarzo.
**quaver** [kwévə] *v.* temblar; *s.* temblor;
trémolo (*de la voz*).
**quay** [ki] *s.* muelle, embarcadero.
**queen** [kwin] *s.* reina.
**queer** [kwɪr] *adj.* raro, extraño, singular; excéntrico; **to feel —** sentirse
raro, no sentirse bien; *v.* poner en
ridículo, comprometer; **to — oneself
with** quedar mal con, ponerse mal
con.
**quell** [kwɛl] *v.* reprimir; sofocar (*una
revuelta*); calmar.
**quench** [kwɛntʃ] *v.* apagar (*el fuego, la
sed*); reprimir, sofocar, ahogar, templar el ardor de.
**query** [kwírɪ] *s.* (*interrogation*) pregunta; interrogación, signo de interrogación; (*doubt*) duda; *v.* preguntar, expresar duda; marcar con
signo de interrogación.
**quest** [kwɛst] *s.* busca; pesquisa.
**question** [kwɛ́stʃən] *s.* (*interrogation*)
pregunta; (*issue*) cuestión; problema;
duda; proposición; **— mark** signo
de interrogación; **beyond —** fuera de
duda; **that is out of the —** ¡imposible!; ¡ni pensar en ello!; *v.*
preguntar; interrogar; dudar.
**questionable** [kwɛ́stʃənəbl] *adj.* dudoso; discutible.
**questioner** [kwɛ́stʃənə] *s.* interrogador,
preguntador.
**questioning** [kwɛ́stʃənɪŋ] *s.* interrogatorio; *adj.* interrogador.
**questionnaire** [kwɛstʃənér] *s.* cuestionario, lista de preguntas, interrogatorio.
**quibble** [kwíbl] *v.* sutilizar, valerse de
argucias o sutilezas; andar en dimes y
diretes; *s.* sutileza, argucia.
**quick** [kwɪk] *adj.* (*soon*) pronto, presto;
(*smart*) listo; (*speedy*) rápido, veloz;
agudo; **— temper** genio violento; **—
wit** mente aguda; *adv.* rápidamente,
de prisa, con prisa, pronto; *s.* carne
viva; **to cut to the —** herir en lo vivo,
herir en el alma.
**quicken** [kwíkən] *v.* acelerar(se); avi-
var(se); aguzar (*la mente, el entendimiento*).
**quickly** [kwíklɪ] *adv.* pronto, presto, de
prisa, aprisa, rápidamente.
**quickness** [kwíknɪs] *s.* (*speed*) rapidez;
presteza, prontitud; (*alertness*) vive-
zal; agudeza (*de ingenio*).
**quicksand** [kwíksænd] *s.* arena movediza.
**quicksilver** [kwíksɪlvə] *s.* mercurio,
azogue.
**quiet** [kwáɪət] *adj.* quieto; callado;
tranquilo; en calma; reposado; *s.*
quietud; sosiego, reposo; calma;
silencio; *v.* aquietar; sosegar; calmar,
tranquilizar; **to — down** aquietarse;
calmarse; **-ly** *adv.* quietamente, con

quietud; calladamente; tranquilamente.
**quietness** [kwáɪətnɪs] *s.* quietud; sosiego, calma.
**quill** [kwɪl] *s.* pluma; cañón (*de pluma
de ave*); púa (*de puerco espín*).
**quilt** [kwɪlt] *s.* colcha; *v.* acolchar.
**quince** [kwɪns] *s.* membrillo.
**quinine** [kwáɪnaɪn] *s.* quinina.
**quip** [kwɪp] *s.* pulla, dicharacho; agudeza.
**quirk** [kwɜk] *s.* chifladura, extravagancia, capricho; peculiaridad mental.
**quit** [kwɪt] *v.* (*abandon*) dejar, abandonar; irse; (*cease*) parar, cesar; **to
— doing something** dejar de hacer
algo; **-s** *adj.* desquitado; **we are -s**
no nos debemos nada, estamos des-
quitados, *Am.* estamos a mano; *pret.*
& *p.p. de* **to quit**.
**quite** [kwaɪt] *adv.* bastante; del todo,
enteramente; **— a person** una persona admirable; **— so** así es, en
efecto; **it's — the fashion** está muy
en boga.
**quitter** [kwítə] *s.* el que deja fácilmente lo empezado, el que se da fácilmente por vencido; evasor; desertor.
**quiver** [kwívə] *v.* temblar; estremece-
cerse; *s.* temblor; estremecimiento.
**quiz** [kwɪz] *s.* examen; interrogatorio;
cuestionario; *v.* examinar, interrogar,
hacer preguntas.
**quizzical** [kwízəkl] *adj.* curioso; burlón.
**quota** [kwótə] *s.* cuota.
**quotation** [kwotéʃen] *s.* citación, cita;
cotización (*de precios*); **— marks**
comillas.
**quote** [kwot] *v.* citar; cotizar (*precios*);
**to — from** citar a, entresacar una
cita de; *s.* cita, citación; **-s** comillas;
**in -s** entre comillas.
**quotient** [kwóʃent] *s.* cociente.

## R

**rabbi** [ræbaɪ] *s.* rabí, rabino.
**rabbit** [ræbɪt] *s.* conejo.
**rabble** [ræbl] *s.* populacho, plebe; canalla.
**rabid** [ræbəd] *adj.* rabioso.
**rabies** [rébiz] *s.* rabia, hidrofobia.
**raccoon** [rækún] *s.* *Méx.*, *C.A.*, *Andes*
mapache.
**race** [res] *s.* (*lineage*) raza; (*competition*)
corrida, carrera; contienda; **—track**
(*o* **—course**) pista; **boat —** regata;
*v.* correr; competir en una carrera;
ir corriendo; regatear (*competir en
una regata*); acelerar (*un motor*).
**racer** [résə] *s.* corredor; caballo de
carrera; auto de carrera.
**racial** [réʃəl] *adj.* racial.
**racism** [résɪzm] *s.* racismo.
**rack** [ræk] *s.* (*framework*) percha, colgadero, clavijero; (*torture*) potro de
tormento; **baggage —** red; **towel —**
toallero; **to fall into — and ruin**
caer en un estado de ruina total; *v.*
atormentar; **to — one's brain**
devanarse los sesos, quebrarse uno la

cabeza.

**racket** [rǽkɪt] *s.* (*instrument*) raqueta (*de tenis*); (*noise*) boruca, estrépito, baraúnda; bullicio; trapacería.

**racketeer** [rækɪtír] *s.* trapacista, trapacero, extorsionista; *v.* trapacear, extorsionar.

**radar** [rédɑr] *s.* radar.

**radial** [rédɪəl] *adj.* radial.

**radiance** [rédɪəns] *s.* resplandor, brillo.

**radiant** [rédɪənt] *adj.* radiante; resplandeciente, brillante.

**radiate** [rédɪet] *v.* irradiar; radiar.

**radiator** [rédɪetɚ] *s.* radiador; calorífero.

**radical** [rǽdɪkl] *adj. & s.* radical.

**radio** [rédɪo] *s.* radio (*m. o f.*); radiotelefonía; radiotelegrafía; — **commentator** comentarista radial; — **listener** radioescucha, radioyente; — **program** programa radiofónico; **by** — por radio; *v.* radiar, emitir, transmitir, radiodifundir o difundir.

**radioactive** [redɪoǽktɪv] *adj.* radiactivo.

**radiology** [redɪálədʒɪ] *s.* radiología.

**radish** [rǽdɪʃ] *s.* rábano.

**radium** [rédɪəm] *s.* radio (*elemento químico*).

**radius** [rédɪəs] *s.* radio (*de un círculo*).

**raffle** [rǽfl] *s.* rifa, sorteo; *v.* rifar, sortear.

**raft** [ræft] *s.* balsa; **a — of things** un montón (*o la mar*) de cosas.

**rafter** [rǽftɚ] *s.* viga (*del techo*).

**rag** [ræg] *s.* trapo; harapo, andrajo, *Am.* hilacho; — **doll** muñeca de trapo; **to be in -s** estar hecho andrajos, *Am.* estar hecho tiras.

**ragamuffin** [rǽgəmʌfɪn] *s.* pelagatos, golfo; granuja, pilluelo.

**rage** [redʒ] *s.* rabia, furor; ira; **to be all the** — estar en boga, estar de moda; *v.* rabiar; enfurecerse; estar enfurecido; bramar; **to — with anger** bramar de ira.

**ragged** [rǽgɪd] *adj.* andrajoso, haraposo, harapiento, desharrapado, roto; — **edge** borde raído o deshilachado; **to be on the — edge** estar al borde del precipicio; estar muy nervioso.

**raid** [red] *s.* incursión, invasión repentina; allanamiento (*de un local*); **air** — ataque aéreo, bombardeo aéreo; *v.* hacer una incursión; invadir de repente; caer sobre; allanar (*un local*), entrar a la fuerza.

**rail** [rel] *s.* (*steel bar*) riel, carril; (*railroad*) ferrocarril; (*railing*) barandal, barandilla; — **fence** empalizada, estacada; **by** — por ferrocarril.

**railing** [rélɪŋ] *s.* baranda, barandilla; pasamano (*de escalera*), balaustrada, barrera; rieles.

**railroad** [rélrod] *s.* ferrocarril; *adj.* ferroviario; de ferrocarril.

**railway** [rélwe] *s.* ferrocarril; *adj.* ferroviario; de ferrocarril; — **crossing** cruce, crucero.

**raiment** [rémənt] *s.* vestidura, ropaje.

**rain** [ren] *s.* lluvia; — **water** agua llovediza; *v.* llover; — **or shine** que llueva o no; llueva o truene; a todo trance.

**rainbow** [rénbo] *s.* arco iris.

**raincoat** [rénkot] *s.* impermeable; *Ch.* capa de agua, *Méx.* manga o capa de hule; *Ríopl.* piloto.

**raindrop** [réndrɑp] *s.* gota de agua.

**rainfall** [rénfɔl] *s.* lluvia, lluvias; cantidad de agua pluvial; aguacero.

**rainy** [rénɪ] *adj.* lluvioso.

**raise** [rez] *v.* (*lift*) levantar, alzar; subir; eregir; (*cultivate*) criar; cultivar; (*collect*) reunir; reclutar; **to — a question** hacer una observación o suscitar una duda; **to — a racket** armar un alboroto; *s.* aumento de sueldo.

**raisin** [rézn] *s.* pasa, uva seca.

**rake** [rek] *s.* rastro, rastrillo; libertino, perdulario; *v.* rastrear, rastrillar (*la tierra*); raspar; barrer (*con rastrillo*); atizar (*el fuego*).

**rally** [rǽlɪ] *v.* (*unite*) reunir(se); juntar(se); (*improve*) recobrar(se); mejorar (*de salud*); fortalecerse; revivir; tomar nueva vida; **to — to the side of** acudir al lado de; *s.* junta popular, junta libre; recuperación.

**ram** [ræm] *s.* (*animal*) carnero; (*tool*) ariete o martillo hidráulico; espolón de buque; **battering** — ariete; *v.* apisonar, aplanar a golpes; aplastar de un choque; rellenar, atestar; **to — a boat** chocar con un barco; arremeter contra un barco.

**ramble** [rǽmbl] *v.* vagar; divagar; callejear; *s.* paseo, andanza.

**rampage** [rǽmpedʒ] *s.* alboroto.

**rampant** [rǽmpənt] *adj.* extravagante; desenfrenado.

**rampart** [rǽmpɑrt] *s.* baluarte, muralla.

**ran** [ræn] *pret. de* **to run.**

**ranch** [ræntʃ] *s.* hacienda, *Méx., C.A.* rancho; **cattle** — hacienda de ganado, *Méx., C.A.* rancho, *Ríopl.* estancia; *Ch.* fundo; *Ven., Col.* hato.

**rancid** [rǽnsɪd] *adj.* rancio, acedo.

**rancor** [rǽnkɚ] *s.* rencor, encono.

**random** [rǽndəm] *adj.* impensado; fortuito, al azar; **at** — al azar, a la ventura.

**rang** [ræŋ] *pret. de* **to ring.**

**range** [rendʒ] *v.* (*align*) alinear; poner en fila; arreglar; (*wander*) vagar por; rondar; fluctuar; **to — ten miles** tener un alcance de diez millas (*un arma de fuego*); *s.* fila, hilera; alcance; extensión; fluctuación, variación (*dentro de ciertos* límites); distancia; pastizal, *C.A.* pastal; estufa; **gas** — cocina de gas; — **of mountains** cordillera, cadena de montañas; — **of vision** campo de visión; **in** — **with** en línea con; **shooting** — campo de práctica para tirar.

**rank** [ræŋk] *s.* (*position*) rango, categoría; orden; calidad; grado; (*line*) fila; línea, hilera; **the — and file** el pueblo, la gente ordinaria; la tropa; *v.* poner en fila; ordenar, arreglar; clasificar; **to — above** sobrepasar a;

QU

ser de grado superior a; **to — high** tener un alto rango, categoría o renombre; ser tenido en alta estima; **to — second** tener el segundo lugar; **to — with** estar al nivel de, tener el mismo grado que; **he -s high in athletics** sobresale en los deportes.

**ransack** [rǽnsæk] *v.* escudriñar; saquear.

**ransom** [rǽnsəm] *s.* rescate; *v.* rescatar; redimir.

**rant** [rænt] *v.* desvariar; disparatar, gritar necedades.

**rap** [ræp] *v.* (*strike*) golpear, dar un golpe; (*censure*) criticar, censurar; **to — on the door** llamar o tocar a la puerta; *s.* golpe; **not to care a —** no importarle a uno un ardite.

**rapacious** [rəpéʃəs] *adj.* rapaz.

**rape** [rep] *s.* estupro, violación (*de una mujer*); *v.* forzar, violar (*a una mujer*).

**rapid** [rǽpɪd] *adj.* rápido; **-s** *s. pl.* raudal, rápidos (*de un río*).

**rapidity** [rəpídətɪ] *s.* rapidez, velocidad.

**rapport** [rəpór] *s.* relación de confianza mutua.

**rapt** [ræpt] *adj.* extasiado; absorto.

**rapture** [rǽptʃɚ] *s.* éxtasis, rapto.

**rare** [rɛr] *adj.* (*strange*) extraordinario, extraño; raro; (*precious*) raro; precioso; (*not well-done*) a medio asar, a medio freír, medio crudo; **-ly** *adv.* rara vez, raras veces; raramente; extraordinariamente.

**rarity** [rɛ́rətɪ] *s.* rareza; enrarecimiento (*de la atmósfera*).

**rascal** [rǽskl] *s.* bribón, bellaco, pícaro.

**rash** [ræʃ] *adj.* temerario, atrevido; precipitado; imprudente; *s.* salpullido, erupción (*de la piel*).

**rashness** [rǽʃnɪs] *s.* temeridad.

**rasp** [ræsp] *v.* chirriar; irritar; *s.* chirrido, sonido áspero; ronquera, carraspera.

**raspberry** [rǽzberɪ] *s.* frambuesa; **— bush** frambueso.

**raspy** [rǽspɪ] *adj.* ronco; áspero.

**rat** [ræt] *s.* rata; postizo (*para el pelo*).

**rate** [ret] *s.* proporción; porcentaje, tanto por ciento, *Am.* tipo (*de interés*); tarifa; precio; **— of exchange** cambio, *Am.* tipo de cambio; **— of increase** incremento proporcional; **at any —** en todo caso, de todos modos; **at that —** a ese paso; en esa proporción; **at the — of** a razón de; **first —** de primera clase o calidad; muy bien; *v.* calificar, clasificar, considerar; tasar, valuar; **he -s as the best** se le considera como el mejor; **he -s high** se le tiene en alta estima.

**rather** [rǽðɚ] *adv.* algo, un poco, un tanto; más bien; mejor; mejor dicho; **— than** más bien que; **I would — die than** prefiero antes la muerte que; **I would — not go** preferiría no ir.

**ratify** [rǽtəfaɪ] *s.* ratificar.

**rating** [rétɪŋ] *s.* clasificación; rango, grado; clase.

**ratio** [réʃo] *s.* razón, proporción; relación.

**ration** [réʃən] *s.* ración; *v.* racionar.

**rational** [rǽʃənl] *adj.* racional.

**rationalize** [rǽʃənlaɪz] *v.* buscar excusas.

**rationing** [réʃənɪŋ] *s.* racionamiento.

**rattle** [rǽtl] *v.* traquetear; golpetear; sacudir ruidosamente; confundir, desconcertar; **to — off** decir de corrido (*o* decir muy aprisa); *s.* traqueteo; golpeteo; **child's —** sonaja, sonajero; **death —** estertor de la muerte.

**rattlesnake** [rǽtlsnek] *s.* culebra de cascabel, *Ríopl.*, *Ch.* cascabel o cascabela.

**raucous** [rókəs] *adj.* ronco; estentóreo.

**ravage** [rǽvɪdʒ] *s.* estrago, ruina, destrucción, asolamiento; saqueo, pillaje; *v.* asolar, arruinar; pillar, saquear.

**rave** [rev] *v.* desvariar, delirar, disparatar; bramar; **to — about someone** deshacerse en elogios de alguien.

**raven** [révən] *s.* cuervo; *adj.* negro lustroso.

**ravenous** [rǽvənəs] *adj.* voraz; devorador; **to be —** tener un hambre canina.

**ravine** [rəvín] *s.* quebrada, hondonada, barranco (*o* barranca).

**ravish** [rǽvɪʃ] *v.* encantar; arrebatar; violar (*a una mujer*).

**raw** [rɔ] *adj.* (*crude*) crudo; áspero; pelado, descarnado; (*untrained*) inexperto, nuevo; **— material** materia prima; **— recruit** recluta nuevo; **— silk** seda en rama, seda cruda; **— sugar** azúcar bruto, azúcar crudo.

**rawhide** [róhaɪd] *s.* cuero crudo; **— whip** rebenque.

**ray** [re] *s.* rayo; raya (*especie de pez*).

**rayon** [réɑn] *s.* seda artificial.

**raze** [rez] *v.* arrasar, asolar.

**razor** [rézɚ] *s.* navaja de afeitar; **— blade** hoja de afeitar; **safety —** navaja de seguridad.

**reach** [ritʃ] *v.* (*go as far as*) llegar a; alcanzar; (*touch*) tocar; (*extend*) extenderse; **to — for** tratar de coger; echar mano a; **to — into** meter la mano en; penetrar en; **to — out one's hand** alargar o tender la mano; *s.* alcance; extensión; **beyond his —** fuera de su alcance; **within his —** a su alcance.

**react** [rɪǽkt] *v.* reaccionar.

**reaction** [rɪǽkʃən] *s.* reacción.

**reactionary** [rɪǽkʃənɛrɪ] *adj. & s.* reaccionario.

**read** [rid] *v.* leer; indicar (*dícese de un contador, termómetro, etc.*); **to — law** estudiar derecho; **it -s thus** dice así, reza así; **it -s easily** se lee fácilmente o sin esfuerzo.

**read** [rɛd] *pret. & p.p. de* **to read.**

**reader** [rídɚ] *s.* lector; libro de lectura.

**readily** [rédlɪ] *adv.* pronto, con presteza; fácilmente, sin esfuerzo.

**readiness** [rédnɪs] *s.* prontitud, presteza, facilidad; buena disposición; **to be in —** estar preparado, estar listo.

**reading** [rídɪŋ] *s.* lectura; indicación (*de un barómetro, termómetro, etc.*); — **room** sala o salón de lectura.

**readjust** [riədʒʌ́st] *v.* reajustar, ajustar de nuevo; arreglar de nuevo; readaptar.

**readjustment** [riədʒʌ́stmənt] *s.* reajuste; readaptación; nuevo arreglo.

**ready** [rédɪ] *adj.* pronto, listo; preparado; propenso; dispuesto; — **cash** fondos disponibles; dinero a la mano.

**ready-made** [rédɪméd] *adj.* hecho, ya hecho.

**real** [ríəl] *adj.* real, verdadero; — **estate** bienes raíces, bienes inmuebles; **-ly** *adv.* realmente, verdaderamente.

**realism** [ríəlɪzəm] *s.* realismo.

**realist** [ríəlɪst] *s.* realista; **-ic** *adj.* realista, vivo, natural.

**reality** [riǽlətɪ] *s.* realidad.

**realization** [riələzéʃən] *s.* realización; comprensión.

**realize** [ríəlaɪz] *v.* (*comprehend*) darse cuenta de, hacerse cargo de; (*achieve*) realizar, efectuar; convertir en dinero.

**realm** [rɛlm] *s.* reino; dominio, región.

**realtor** [ríəltɚ] *s.* corredor de bienes raíces.

**reap** [rip] *v.* segar; cosechar; recoger; obtener, sacar (*provecho, fruto, etc.*).

**reaper** [rípɚ] *s.* segador; segadora, máquina segadora.

**reappear** [riəpír] *v.* reaparecer.

**rear** [rir] *adj.* trasero, posterior; de atrás; — **admiral** contraalmirante; — **guard** retaguardia; *s.* espalda, parte de atrás; trasero; fondo (*de una sala, salón, etc.*); cola (*de una fila*); **in the** — detrás, atrás, a la espalda; *v.* criar, educar; encabritarse, empinarse (*el caballo*).

**reason** [rízn̩] *s.* razón; causa, motivo; **by** — **of a** causa de; **it stands to** — es razonable; *v.* razonar; **to** — **out** discurrir, razonar.

**reasonable** [ríznəbl̩] *adj.* razonable, justo; racional; módico, moderado; **reasonably** *adv.* razonablemente; con razón; bastante.

**reasoning** [ríznɪŋ] *s.* razonamiento, raciocinio.

**reassure** [riəʃúr] *v.* tranquilizar, restaurar la confianza a; asegurar de nuevo.

**rebate** [ríbet] *s.* rebaja (*de precio*); *v.* rebajar (*precio*).

**rebel** [rébl̩] *s. & adj.* rebelde; [rɪbél] *v.* rebelarse.

**rebellion** [rɪbéljən] *s.* rebelión.

**rebellious** [rɪbéljəs] *adj.* rebelde.

**rebirth** [ribɚ́θ] *s.* renacimiento.

**rebound** [rɪbáʊnd] *v.* rebotar; repercutir; [ríbaʊnd] *s.* rebote; **on the** — de rebote.

**rebuff** [rɪbʌ́f] *s.* desaire; repulsa; *v.* desairar; rechazar.

**rebuild** [ribíld] *v.* reconstruir, reedificar.

**rebuilt** [ribílt] *pret. & p.p. de* **to rebuild.**

**rebuke** [rɪbjúk] *s.* reprensión, reproche, reprimenda, repulsa; *v.* reprender, reprochar.

**recall** [ríkɔl] *s.* llamada, aviso (*para hacer volver*); retirada (*de un diplomático*); revocación; [rɪkɔ́l] *v.* recordar; retirar; revocar.

**recapitulate** [rikəpítʃəlet] *v.* recapitular.

**recede** [rɪsíd] *v.* retroceder; retirarse.

**receipt** [rɪsít] *s.* recibo; fórmula, receta; **-s** entradas, ingresos; **on** — **of** al recibo de; **we are in** — **of your kind letter** ... obra en nuestro poder su grata ... ; *v.* sellar (*con el recibí*), dar recibo.

**receive** [rɪsív] *v.* recibir.

**receiver** [rɪsívɚ] *s.* receptor; recibidor, depositario, síndico; recipiente, receptáculo.

**recent** [rísn̩t] *adj.* reciente; **-ly** *adv.* recientemente, *Ch., Ríopl.* recién (*como en* salió recién); **-ly married** recién casados.

**receptacle** [rɪséptəkl̩] *s.* receptáculo.

**reception** [rɪsépʃən] *s.* recepción; recibimiento; acogida, acogimiento.

**recess** [rɪsés] *s.* (*niche*) nicho, hueco; (*cessation*) tregua, intermisión; (*period*) hora de recreo o asueto; **in the -es of** en lo más recóndito de; *v.* suspender el trabajo; levantar (*por corto tiempo*) una sesión; hacer un hueco o nicho en (*la pared*).

**recession** [rɪséʃən] *s.* retroceso; contracción económica.

**recipe** [résəpɪ] *s.* receta, fórmula.

**recipient** [rɪsípɪənt] *s.* recipiente, recibidor; *adj.* receptivo.

**reciprocal** [rɪsíprəkl̩] *adj.* recíproco, mutuo.

**reciprocate** [rɪsíprəket] *v.* corresponder.

**recital** [rɪsáɪtl̩] *s.* recitación; relación; narración; recital (*músico*).

**recitation** [rɛsətéʃən] *s.* recitación.

**recite** [rɪsáɪt] *v.* recitar; relatar; decir o dar la lección.

**reckless** [réklɪs] *adj.* temerario, atrevido, precipitado; descuidado; — **with one's money** derrochador.

**recklessness** [réklɪsnɪs] *s.* temeridad, osadía, descuido.

**reckon** [rékən] *v.* contar, computar, calcular; juzgar; suponer; **to** — **on** contar con.

**reckoning** [rékənɪŋ] *s.* cuenta; ajuste de cuentas; cálculo; **the day of** — el día del juicio.

**reclaim** [rɪklém] *v.* recobrar, aprovechar (*tierras baldías*); aprovechar o utilizar (*el hule usado*); pedir la devolución de, tratar de recobrar.

**recline** [rɪkláɪn] *v.* reclinar(se), recostar(se).

**recluse** [rɪklús] *adj.* recluso, solitario; *s.* recluso, solitario, ermitaño.

**recognition** [rɛkəgníʃən] *s.* reconocimiento.

**recognize** [rékəgnaɪz] *v.* reconocer.

**recoil** [rɪkóɪl] *v.* recular, *Am.* patear (*un*

**RA**

*arma de fuego*); retroceder, retirarse; *s.* reculada; rebote.

**recollect** [rɛkəlɛ́kt] *v.* recordar; [rikəlɛ́kt] recobrar, volver a cobrar; recoger, reunir.

**recollection** [rɛkəlɛ́kʃən] *s.* recuerdo.

**recommend** [rɛkəmɛ́nd] *v.* recomendar.

**recommendation** [rɛkəmɛndéʃən] *s.* recomendación.

**recompense** [rɛ́kəmpɛns] *v.* recompensar; *s.* recompensa.

**reconcile** [rɛ́kənsaɪl] *v.* reconciliar; ajustar, conciliar; **to — oneself to** resignarse a, conformarse con.

**reconciliation** [rɛkənsɪlɪéʃən] *f.* reconciliación; ajuste, conciliación; conformidad, resignación.

**reconnoiter** [rikənɔ́ɪtəʳ] *v.* reconocer, explorar; hacer un reconocimiento o exploración.

**reconsider** [rikənsídəʳ] *v.* reconsiderar.

**reconstruct** [rikənstrʌ́kt] *v.* reconstruir, reedificar.

**reconstruction** [rikənstrʌ́kʃən] *s.* reconstrucción.

**record** [rɛ́kəʳd] *s.* registro; copia oficial de un documento; memoria; historial (*de una persona*), hoja de servicios; disco (*fonográfico*); record (*en deportes*); **to break the speed —** batir el record de velocidad; **an off-the-record remark** una observación que no ha de constar en el acta; observación hecha en confianza; *adj.* notable, extraordinario; sobresaliente; [rɪkɔ́rd] *v.* registrar; asentar, apuntar; inscribir; grabar en disco fonográfico.

**recording** [rɪkɔ́rdɪŋ] *s.* grabación.

**recount** [rɪ́kaʊnt] *s.* recuento, segunda cuenta; [rɪkáʊnt] *v.* contar, narrar, relatar, referir; [rikáʊnt] recontar, volver a contar.

**recourse** [ríkors] *s.* recurso, refugio, auxilio; **to have — to** recurrir a.

**recover** [rɪkʌ́vəʳ] *v.* recobrar(se), recuperar(se); recobrar la salud; reponerse; [rikʌ́vəʳ] volver a cubrir.

**recovery** [rɪkʌ́vrɪ] *s.* recobro; recuperación; cobranza.

**recreation** [rɛkrɪéʃən] *s.* recreación, recreo.

**recriminate** [rikrímənet] *v.* recriminar.

**recruit** [rɪkrút] *v.* reclutar; alistar; *s.* recluta; novato, nuevo miembro (*de una organización*).

**rectangle** [rɛ́ktæŋgl] *s.* rectángulo.

**rectify** [rɛ́ktəfaɪ] *v.* rectificar.

**rector** [rɛ́ktəʳ] *s.* rector.

**rectum** [rɛ́ktəm] *s.* recto.

**recuperate** [rɪkjúpəret] *v.* recuperar, recobrar; recobrar la salud.

**recur** [rɪkɝ́] *v.* volver a ocurrir; repetirse; **to — to a matter** volver a un asunto.

**red** [rɛd] *adj.* rojo; colorado, encarnado; **red-hot** candente; enfurecido, furioso; muy caliente; **— tape** formalismo, trámites enojosos; **— wine** vino tinto; **to see —** enfurecerse; *s.*

color rojo; rojo.

**redden** [rɛ́dn̩] *v.* enrojecer(se); ruborizarse, ponerse rojo; teñir de rojo.

**reddish** [rɛ́dɪʃ] *adj.* rojizo.

**redeem** [rɪdím] *v.* redimir; rescatar; desempeñar (*una prenda*); cumplir (*una promesa*).

**redeemer** [rɪdíməʳ] *s.* salvador, redentor; **the Redeemer** el Redentor.

**redemption** [rɪdɛ́mpʃən] *s.* redención; rescate; **— of a note** pago de una obligación.

**redness** [rɛ́dnɪs] *s.* rojez o rojura; inflamación.

**redouble** [rɪdʌ́bl̩] *v.* redoblar; repetir; repercutir.

**redound** [rɪdáʊnd] *v.* redundar.

**redress** [rídrɛs] *s.* reparación, enmienda; compensación; desagravio; [rɪdrés] *v.* enmendar, rectificar, remediar, reparar; desagraviar.

**reduce** [rɪdjús] *v.* reducir; mermar; rebajar; adelgazar(se); subyugar.

**reduction** [rɪdʌ́kʃən] *s.* reducción; merma; rebaja.

**redundant** [rɪdʌ́ndənt] *adj.* redundante.

**redwood** [rɛ́dwʊd] *s. Am.* secoya o secuoya (*árbol gigantesco de California*); madera roja de la secoya.

**reed** [rid] *s.* caña; junco, junquillo; lengüeta, boquilla (*de ciertos instrumentos de viento*); caramillo.

**reef** [rif] *s.* arrecife, escollo; banco de arena (*en el mar*).

**reek** [rik] *v.* (*fume*) exhalar, echar (*vaho o vapor*); (*stink*) heder, oler mal; *s.* hedor, mal olor.

**reel** [ril] *s.* (*spool*) carrete; carretel; (*film*) cinta cinematográfica; *v.* aspar, enredar (*en carretel*); bambolearse, tambalearse; **to — off stories** ensartar cuento tras cuento.

**re-elect** [riəlɛ́kt] *v.* reelegir.

**re-election** [riəlɛ́kʃən] *s.* reelección.

**re-enter** [riɛ́ntəʳ] *v.* volver a entrar.

**re-establish** [riəstǽblɪʃ] *v.* restablecer.

**refer** [rɪfɝ́] *v.* referir; transmitir, remitir; dejar al juicio o decisión de; referirse, aludir; acudir, recurrir (*a un tratado, diccionario, etc.*).

**referee** [rɛfərí] *s.* árbitro; *v.* arbitrar.

**reference** [rɛ́frəns] *s.* (*mention*) referencia; mención, alusión; (*sponsor*) fiador, el que recomienda a otro; **— book** libro de referencia, libro de consulta; **commercial -s** fiadores, referencias comerciales; **letter of —** carta de recomendación; **with — to** con respecto a, respecto de, en cuanto a.

**refill** [rifíl] *v.* rellenar.

**refine** [rɪfáɪn] *v.* refinar, purificar; pulir; perfeccionar.

**refined** [rɪfáɪnd] *adj.* refinado; pulido, fino, culto.

**refinement** [rɪfáɪnmənt] *s.* refinamiento, finura; buena crianza; refinación, purificación; perfeccionamiento.

**refinery** [rɪfáɪnərɪ] *s.* refinería.

**reflect** [rɪflɛ́kt] *v.* reflejar (*luz, calor*);

reflexionar; meditar; **to — on one's character** desdecir del carácter de uno.

**reflection** [rɪflékʃən] *s.* reflexión; reflejo, imagen; tacha, discrédito; **on —** después de reflexionarlo.

**reflective** [rɪfléktɪv] *adj.* reflexivo.

**reflex** [ríflɛks] *adj.* reflejo; *s.* reflejo; acción refleja.

**reflexive** [rɪfléksɪv] *adj.* reflexivo.

**reform** [rɪfɔ́rm] *v.* reformar(se); *s.* reforma.

**reformation** [rɛfəméʃən] *s.* reforma.

**reformatory** [rɪfɔ́rmətorɪ] *s.* reformatorio.

**reformer** [rɪfɔ́rmə] *s.* reformador; reformista.

**refraction** [rɪfrǽkʃən] *s.* refracción.

**refractory** [rɪfrǽktorɪ] *adj.* refractario; terco, obstinado, rebelde.

**refrain** [rɪfrén] *v.* refrenarse, abstenerse; *s.* estribillo.

**refresh** [rɪfréʃ] *v.* refrescar(se); renovar.

**refreshing** [rɪfréʃɪŋ] *adj.* refrescante; renovador, que renueva; placentero.

**refreshment** [rɪfréʃmənt] *s.* refresco.

**refrigeration** [rɪfrɪdʒəréʃən] *s.* refrigeración, enfriamiento.

**refrigerator** [rɪfrídʒəretə] *s.* nevera, *Am.* refrigerador.

**refuge** [réfjudʒ] *s.* refugio, asilo, amparo.

**refugee** [rɛfjʊdʒí] *s.* refugiado.

**refund** [rɪfʌnd] *s.* reembolso, reintegro; [rɪfʌnd] *v.* reembolsar, restituir, reintegrar; [rɪfʌnd] consolidar (*una deuda*).

**refurbish** [rɪfɚ́bɪʃ] *v.* retocar.

**refusal** [rɪfjúz] *s.* negativa; desaire; opción (*derecho de recusar un convenio provisional*).

**refuse** [rɪfjúz] *v.* rehusar; negar; desechar; rechazar; **to — to** rehusarse a, negarse a.

**refuse** [réfjus] *s.* desechos, basura, sobras, desperdicios.

**refute** [rɪfjút] *v.* refutar.

**regain** [rɪgén] *v.* recobrar; ganar de nuevo.

**regal** [rígl] *adj.* regio, real.

**regale** [rɪgél] *v.* regalar, agasajar; recrear.

**regalia** [rɪgéliə] *s. pl.* galas, decoraciones, insignias.

**regard** [rɪgárd] *v.* (*look*) mirar; (*consider*) considerar; juzgar; estimar; **as -s this** tocante a esto, en cuanto a esto; por lo que toca a esto; *s.* miramiento, consideración; respeto; estima; mirada; **-s** recuerdos, memorias; **in** (*o* **with**) **— to** con respecto a, tocante a, respecto de.

**regarding** [rɪgárdɪŋ] *prep.* tocante a, con respecto a, respecto de, relativo a.

**regardless** [rɪgárdlɪs]: **— of** sin hacer caso de, prescindiendo de.

**regency** [rídʒənsɪ] *s.* regencia.

**regent** [rídʒənt] *s.* regente.

**regime** [rɪʒím] *s.* régimen.

**regiment** [rédʒəmənt] *s.* regimiento.

**region** [rídʒən] *s.* región.

**register** [rédʒɪstə] *s.* (*recording*) regis-

tro; matrícula; (*entry*) archivo; lista; (*machine*) contador; indicador; (*voice*) registro; **cash —** caja registradora; *v.* registrar; matricular(se); inscribir(se); marcar, indicar; mostrar, manifestar; certificar (*una carta*).

**registrar** [rédʒɪstrar] *s.* registrador, archivero.

**registration** [redʒɪstréʃən] *s.* registro; asiento (*en un libro*); matrícula; inscripción.

**regret** [rɪgrét] *s.* pesadumbre, dolor; sentimiento, remordimiento; **to send -s** enviar sus excusas (*al rehusar una invitación*); *v.* sentir, lamentar; arrepentirse de.

**regretful** [rigrétful] *adj.* deplorable.

**regrettable** [rɪgrétəbl] *adj.* lamentable.

**regular** [régjələ] *adj.* regular; metódico, ordenado; **a — fool** un verdadero necio, un tonto de capirote; **— price** precio corriente; **— soldier** soldado de línea.

**regularity** [regjəlǽrətɪ] *s.* regularidad.

**regulate** [régjəlet] *v.* regular, regularizar.

**regulation** [regjəléʃən] *s.* regulación; regla, orden; **-s** reglamento; **— uniform** uniforme de regla, uniforme de ordenanza.

**regulator** [régjəletə] *s.* regulador; registro (*de reloj*).

**rehabilitate** [rihæbílətet] *v.* rehabilitar.

**rehearsal** [rɪhɚ́sl] *s.* ensayo (*de un drama, concierto, etc.*); enumeración, repetición.

**rehearse** [rɪhɚ́s] *v.* ensayar; repetir, repasar.

**reign** [ren] *s.* reino, reinado; *v.* reinar.

**reimburse** [riɪmbɚ́s] *v.* reembolsar.

**reimbursement** [riɪmbɚ́smənt] *s.* reembolso, reintegro.

**rein** [ren] *s.* rienda; *v.* guiar, gobernar; refrenar (*un caballo*).

**reincarnate** [riɪnkárnet] *v.* reencarnar.

**reindeer** [réndɪr] *s.* reno (*especie de ciervo*).

**reinforce** [riɪnfɔ́rs] *v.* reforzar.

**reinforcement** [riɪnfɔ́rsmənt] *s.* refuerzo.

**reiterate** [riítəret] *v.* reiterar, repetir.

**reject** [ridʒékt] *v.* rechazar; desechar; descartar; rehusar.

**rejoice** [ridʒɔ́ɪs] *v.* regocijar(se).

**rejoicing** [ridʒɔ́ɪsɪŋ] *s.* regocijo, júbilo.

**rejoin** [ridʒɔ́ɪn] *v.* reunirse con; volver(se) a unir; [ridʒɔ́ɪn] replicar.

**rejuvenate** [rɪdʒúvənet] *v.* rejuvenecer.

**relapse** [rɪlǽps] *s.* recaída; *v.* recaer, reincidir.

**relate** [rɪlét] *v.* relatar, narrar; relacionar; **it -s to** se relaciona con, se refiere a.

**related** [rɪlétɪd] *adj.* relatado, narrado; relacionado; **to become — by marriage** emparentar; **we are —** somos parientes; estamos emparentados.

**relation** [rɪléʃən] *s.* (*association*) relación; (*story*) narración; (*kinship*) parentesco; pariente; **-s** parientes, parentela; **with — to** con relación a,

RE

con respecto a, tocante a.

**relationship** [rɪléʃənʃɪp] *s.* relación; parentesco.

**relative** [rélətɪv] *adj.* relativo; *s.* relativo, pronombre relativo; pariente, deudo; — **to** relativo a; tocante a; referente a.

**relax** [rɪlǽks] *v.* relajar; aflojar; mitigar(se); esparcirse, recrearse.

**relaxation** [rilækséʃən] *s.* (*loosening*) expansión, esparcimiento; aflojamento o relajamiento; (*recreation*) solaz, recreo; — **of discipline** relajación de la disciplina; — **of one's mind** esparcimiento del ánimo.

**relay** [ríle] *s.* relevo, remuda; — **race** carrera de relevo; **electric** — relevador; [rɪlé] *v.* transmitir, despachar; hacer cundir (*una noticia*); **to** — **a broadcast** reemitir (*o* redifundir) un programa de radio.

**release** [rɪlís] *v.* soltar; librar; poner en libertad; relevar, aliviar; **to** — **a piece of news** hacer pública una nueva; **to** — **from blame** exonerar; *s.* liberación; alivio; exoneración; escape.

**relegate** [réləget] *v.* relegar; **to** — **to a corner** arrinconar, arrumbar.

**relent** [rɪlént] *v.* mitigar(se); ceder; aplacarse.

**relentless** [rɪléntlɪs] *adj.* implacable.

**relevant** [réləvənt] *adj.* pertinente; a propósito.

**reliability** [rɪlaɪəbíləti] *s.* formalidad; puntualidad; integridad.

**reliable** [rɪláɪəb̩l] *adj.* formal; puntual; digno de confianza.

**reliance** [rɪláɪəns] *s.* confianza; **self-reliance** confianza en sí, confianza en sus propias fuerzas.

**relic** [rélɪk] *s.* reliquia.

**relief** [rɪlíf] *s.* (*ease*) alivio; descanso, consuelo; (*help*) ayuda, socorro; (*projection*) relieve, realce; **low** — bajo relieve; **to be on** — recibir manutención gratuita; **to put in** — realzar, poner en relieve.

**relieve** [rɪlív] *v.* relevar; librar; ayudar; aliviar; mitigar.

**religion** [rɪlídʒən] *s.* religión.

**religious** [rɪlídʒəs] *adj. & s.* religioso.

**relinquish** [rɪlíŋkwɪʃ] *v.* abandonar, dejar.

**relish** [rélɪʃ] *s.* (*zest*) buen sabor; gusto; apetito; goce; (*condiment*) condimento; entremés; *v.* saborear, paladear; gustarle a uno, agradarle a uno.

**relocate** [rilóket] *v.* restablecer.

**reluctance** [rɪlʌ́ktəns] *s.* repugnancia, renuencia, aversión, desgana.

**reluctant** [rɪlʌ́ktənt] *adj.* renuente, refractario, opuesto; **-ly** *adv.* renuentemente, con renuencia, de mala gana; a redopelo.

**rely** [rɪláɪ] *v.* **to** — **on** contar con, confiar en, fiarse de.

**remain** [rɪmén] *v.* quedar(se), permanecer, estarse; restar, faltar.

**remainder** [rɪméndər] *s.* resto; restante; residuo.

**remains** [rɪménz] *s. pl.* restos; reliquias; sobras.

**remake** [rimék] *v.* rehacer, hacer de nuevo.

**remark** [rɪmárk] *s.* observación, nota, reparo; *v.* notar, observar; **to** — **on** comentar; aludir a.

**remarkable** [rɪmárkəb̩l] *adj.* notable; extraordinario; **remarkably** *adv.* notablemente; extraordinariamente.

**remedy** [rémədɪ] *s.* remedio; cura; *v.* remediar; curar.

**remember** [rɪmémbər] *v.* recordar; acordarse; — **me to him** déle Vd. recuerdos (*o* memorias) de mi parte.

**remembrance** [rɪmémbrəns] *s.* recuerdo; recordación; memoria; **-s** recuerdos, saludos.

**remind** [rɪmáɪnd] *v.* recordar.

**reminder** [rɪmáɪndər] *s.* recordatorio, recordativo, memorándum, memoria; advertencia.

**reminiscence** [remənísn̩s] *s.* reminiscencia, memoria, recuerdo.

**remiss** [rɪmís] *adj.* descuidado, negligente.

**remission** [rɪmíʃən] *s.* remisión, perdón.

**remit** [rɪmít] *v.* remitir; remesar, enviar una remesa; perdonar, absolver.

**remittance** [rɪmítn̩s] *s.* remisión, envío, remesa (*de fondos*).

**remnant** [rémnənt] *s.* resto; residuo; retazo (*de tela, paño, etc.*); vestigio.

**remodel** [rimád̩l] *v.* rehacer, reconstruir; modelar de nuevo.

**remorse** [rɪmɔ́rs] *s.* remordimiento.

**remote** [rɪmót] *adj.* remoto; lejano; *s.* — **control** telecontrol; comando a distancia.

**removal** [rɪmúvḷ] *s.* mudanza, traslado; deposición (*de un empleo*); eliminación; extracción; alejamiento.

**remove** [rɪmúv] *v.* remover; mudar(se), trasladar(se); quitar; eliminar; extirpar; sacar, extraer; deponer (*de un empleo*); apartar; alejar.

**removed** [rɪmúvd] *adj.* remoto, distante.

**renaissance** [renəsáns] *s.* renacimiento.

**renascence** [rɪnǽsn̩s] *s.* renacimiento.

**rend** [rend] *v.* desgarrar, rasgar; rajar.

**render** [réndər] *v.* dar; entregar; hacer; ejecutar, interpretar (*música o un papel dramático*); traducir; **to** — **an account of** rendir o dar cuenta de; **to** — **homage** rendir homenaje; **to** — **thanks** rendir gracias, dar las gracias; **to** — **useless** inutilizar, incapacitar.

**rendition** [rɛndíʃən] *s.* (*surrender*) rendición; (*version*) traducción, ejecución.

**renew** [rɪnjú] *v.* renovar; restaurar; reanudar; prorrogar (*un préstamo*).

**renewal** [rɪnjúəl] *s.* renovación; reanudación; prórroga.

**renounce** [rɪnáúns] *v.* renunciar.

**renovate** [rénəvet] *v.* renovar.

**renown** [rɪnáún] *s.* renombre.

**renowned** [rɪnáʊnd] *adj.* renombrado.

**rent** [rɛnt] *s.* alquiler; renta, arrendamiento; **it is for —** se alquila, se arrienda; *v.* alquilar, arrendar.

**rent** [rɛnt] *pret.* & *p.p. de* **to rend;** *s.* grieta, hendidura; rasgadura, rotura.

**rental** [rént]] *s.* renta, alquiler.

**reopen** [riópən] *v.* reabrir(se), volver a abrir(se).

**repair** [rɪpér] *v.* reparar; remendar; componer; restaurar; **to — to** dirigirse a; *s.* reparo, reparación; remiendo; compostura; **in —** en buen estado; compuesto.

**reparation** [rɛpəréʃən] *s.* reparación; desagravio.

**repartee** [rɛpartí] *s.* respuesta viva; agudeza en el diálogo.

**repay** [rɪpé] *v.* resarcir; compensar; reembolsar; pagar.

**repayment** [rɪpémənt] *s.* reintegro, pago, devolución, restitución.

**repeal** [rɪpíl] *v.* derogar, abrogar, revocar, abolir (*una ley*); *s.* abrogación, derogación, revocación, abolición (*de una ley*).

**repeat** [rɪpít] *v.* repetir; *s.* repetición.

**repeated** [rɪpítɪd] *adj.* repetido; **-ly** *adv.* repetidamente; repetidas veces, una y otra vez.

**repel** [rɪpél] *v.* repeler; rechazar; repugnar; **that idea -s me** me repugna (*o* me es repugnante) esa idea.

**repellent** [rɪpélənt] *s.* repelente; (*water*) impermeable.

**repent** [rɪpént] *v.* arrepentirse (de).

**repentance** [rɪpéntəns] *s.* arrepentimiento.

**repentant** [rɪpéntənt] *adj.* arrepentido; penitente.

**repertoire** [répɚtwɑr] *s.* repertorio.

**repetition** [rɛpɪtíʃən] *s.* repetición.

**replace** [rɪplés] *v.* reponer, volver a colocar; reemplazar; restituir; remudar.

**replaceable** [rɪplésəb]] *adj.* reemplazable; substituible.

**replacement** [rɪplésmənt] *s.* reposición; reemplazo; devolución, restitución; substitución.

**replenish** [rɪplénɪʃ] *v.* reabastecer; rellenar, llenar.

**replete** [rɪplít] *adj.* repleto, atestado.

**replica** [réplɪkə] *s.* reproducción, copia exacta.

**reply** [rɪplái] *v.* replicar, contestar, responder; *s.* réplica, contestación, respuesta.

**report** [rɪpórt] *v.* dar cuenta de; avisar; informar; presentar un informe; rendir informe; hacer un reportaje, *Am.* reportar; denunciar, delatar; presentarse; **to — for duty** presentarse; **it is -ed that** dizque, se dice que, corre la voz que; *s.* noticia, reporte; informe; memorial; relación; rumor; estallido, disparo; **news —** reportaje.

**reporter** [rɪpórtɚ] *s.* reportero, repórter.

**repose** [rɪpóz] *v.* reposar, decansar; **to**

**— one's confidence in** confiar en; depositar su confianza en; *s.* reposo.

**repository** [rɪpázətorɪ] *s.* depósito; almacén.

**represent** [rɛprɪzént] *v.* representar.

**representation** [rɛprɪzɛntéʃən] *s.* representación.

**representative** [rɛprɪzéntətɪv] *adj.* representativo; representante; típico; *s.* representante; delegado, diputado.

**repress** [rɪprés] *v.* reprimir; refrenar, restringir; cohibir.

**repression** [rɪpréʃən] *s.* represión.

**reprieve** [rɪprív] *v.* suspensión temporal de pena; alivio.

**reprimand** [réprəmænd] *v.* reprender, regañar; *s.* reprimenda, reprensión, regaño.

**reprisal** [rɪpráɪz]] *s.* represalia.

**reproach** [rɪprótʃ] *v.* reprochar; censurar, criticar; echar en cara; *s.* reproche, reprimenda; censura.

**reproduce** [riprədjús] *v.* reproducir.

**reproduction** [riprədʌkʃən] *s.* reproducción.

**reproof** [rɪprúf] *s.* represión, reproche, regaño.

**reprove** [rɪprúv] *v.* reprobar, reprender, censurar.

**reptile** [répt]] *s.* reptil.

**republic** [rɪpʌ́blɪk] *s.* república.

**republican** [rɪpʌ́blɪkən] *adj.* & *s.* republicano.

**repudiate** [rɪpjúdiet] *v.* repudiar.

**repugnance** [rɪpʌ́gnəns] *s.* repugnancia; aversión.

**repugnant** [rɪpʌ́gnənt] *adj.* repugnante; antipático.

**repulse** [rɪpʌ́ls] *v.* repulsar, repeler; rechazar; *s.* repulsa; desaire.

**repulsive** [rɪpʌ́lsɪv] *adj.* repulsivo, repugnante.

**reputable** [répjətəb]] *adj.* de buena reputación.

**reputation** [repjətéʃən] *s.* reputación, renombre.

**repute** [rɪpjút] *v.* reputar; estimar, considerar; *s.* reputación; renombre, fama; **of ill —** de mala fama.

**request** [rɪkwést] *v.* solicitud, petición, demanda; súplica, ruego; **at the — of** a solicitud de, a instancias de; *v.* solicitar, pedir, rogar, suplicar.

**require** [rɪkwáɪr] *v.* requerir; exigir, demandar.

**requirement** [rɪkwáɪrmənt] *s.* requerimiento, requisito; exigencia; necesidad.

**requisite** [rékwəzɪt] *s.* requisito; *adj.* requerido, necesario.

**requisition** [rɛkwəzíʃən] *s.* requisición, demanda, orden; *v.* demandar, pedir, ordenar.

**rescind** [rɪsínd] *v.* rescindir.

**rescue** [réskju] *v.* rescatar; librar; salvar; *s.* rescate, salvamento, salvación, socorro; **to go to the — of** acudir al socorro de, ir a salvar a.

**research** [rísɚtʃ] *s.* rebusca, búsqueda, investigación; [rɪsɚ́tʃ] *v.* rebuscar, investigar.

RE

**resemblance** [rɪzémbləns] *s.* semejanza, parecido.

**resemble** [rɪzémbl] *v.* asemejarse a, semejar, parecerse a.

**resent** [rɪzént] *v.* resentirse de, sentirse de, darse por agraviado de.

**resentful** [rɪzéntfəl] *adj.* resentido; rencoroso.

**resentment** [rɪzéntmənt] *s.* resentimiento.

**reservation** [rɛzɚvéʃən] *s.* reservación; reserva.

**reserve** [rɪzɚ́v] *v.* reservar; *s.* reserva.

**reservoir** [rézɚvwɔr] *s.* depósito (*de agua, aceite, gas, provisiones, etc.*); receptáculo; **water —** alberca, aljibe, tanque, estanque.

**reside** [rɪzáɪd] *v.* residir, vivir.

**residence** [rézədəns] *s.* residencia; domicilio.

**resident** [rézədənt] *adj. & s.* residente.

**residential** [rɛzɪdénʃəl] *adj.* residencial.

**residue** [rézədju] *s.* residuo; resto.

**resign** [rɪzáɪn] *v.* renunciar; dimitir; **to — oneself to** resignarse a.

**resignation** [rɛzɪgnéʃən] *s.* renuncia, dimisión; resignación.

**resilience** [rizíljəns] *s.* elasticidad.

**resin** [rézn̩] *s.* resina.

**resist** [rɪzíst] *v.* resistir; oponerse, resistirse a.

**resistance** [rɪzístəns] *s.* resistencia.

**resistant** [rɪzístənt] *adj.* resistente.

**resolute** [rézəlut] *adj.* resuelto.

**resolution** [rɛzəlúʃən] *s.* resolución; acuerdo.

**resolve** [rɪzálv] *v.* resolver(se); **to — into** resolverse en, reducirse a, transformarse en; **to — to** acordar; proponerse, resolverse a.

**resonance** [rézənəns] *s.* resonancia.

**resonant** [rézənənt] *adj.* resonante.

**resort** [rɪzɔ́rt] *v.* recurrir, acudir; **to — to force** recurrir a la fuerza; *s.* refugio; morada; **as a last —** como último recurso; **summer —** lugar de veraneo; **vice —** garito; casa de mala fama; **to have — to** recurrir a.

**resorter** [rɪzɔ́rtɚ] *s.* **summer —** veraneante.

**resound** [rɪzáund] *v.* resonar; repercutir; retumbar.

**resource** [rɪsórs] *s.* recurso; **natural -s** recursos o riquezas naturales.

**respect** [rɪspékt] *v.* respetar; **as -s** por lo que respecta a, por lo que toca a, tocante a; *s.* respeto; consideración; **with — to** (con) respecto a, respecto de; por lo que atañe a.

**respectable** [rɪspéktəbl] *adj.* respetable.

**respectful** [rɪspéktfəl] *adj.* respetuoso.

**respecting** [rɪspéktɪŋ] *prep.* con respecto a, tocante a.

**respective** [rɪspéktɪv] *adj.* respectivo.

**respiration** [rɛspəréʃən] *s.* respiración, respiro.

**respite** [réspɪt] *s.* tregua, pausa, descanso; intervalo; prórroga.

**resplendent** [rɪspléndənt] *adj.* resplandeciente.

**respond** [rɪspúnd] *v.* responder; corres-

ponder; reaccionar.

**response** [rɪspáns] *s.* respuesta, contestación; reacción.

**responsibility** [rɪspɑnsəbíləti] *s.* responsabilidad.

**responsible** [rɪspánsəbl] *adj.* responsable; formal, digno de confianza.

**rest** [rɛst] *s.* (*repose*) descanso; reposo; quietud; tregua; pausa; (*support*) apoyo; **at —** en paz; en reposo; tranquilo; **the —** el resto; los demás; *v.* descansar; reposar; apoyar; **to — on** descansar sobre; apoyar(se) en; basar(se) en; contar con, confiar en, depender de.

**restaurant** [réstərənt] *s.* restaurante. *Am.* restorán.

**restful** [réstfəl] *adj.* reposado, sosegado, tranquilo.

**restitution** [rɛstətjúʃən] *s.* restitución; devolución.

**restive** [réstɪv] *adj.* intranquilo.

**restless** [réstlɪs] *adj.* inquieto, intranquilo.

**restlessness** [réstlɪsnɪs] *s.* inquietud, desasosiego, intranquilidad.

**restoration** [rɛstəréʃən] *s.* restauración; restitución; renovación.

**restore** [rɪstór] *v.* restaurar; renovar; restituir; restablecer.

**restrain** [rɪstrén] *v.* refrenar, contener, cohibir, reprimir, coartar; restringir.

**restraint** [rɪstrént] *s.* restricción; reserva, circunspección; moderación; cohibición.

**restrict** [rɪstríkt] *v.* restringir, limitar.

**restriction** [rɪstríkʃən] *s.* restricción.

**result** [rɪzált] *v.* resultar; **to — from** resultar de; **to — in** parar en; causar; dar por resultado; *s.* resulta, resultado; **as a —** de resultas, como resultado.

**resume** [rɪzúm] *v.* reasumir, volver a tomar; recomenzar; reanudar, continuar.

**résumé** [rɛzumé] *s.* resumen, sumario.

**resurgent** [rɪsɚ́dʒənt] *adj.* resurgente.

**resurrection** [rɛzərékʃən] *s.* resurrección.

**resuscitate** [rɪsásətet] *v.* resucitar; revivir.

**retail** [rítel] *s.* venta al por menor; **at — al** al por menor; **— merchant** detallista, comerciante al por menor; **— price** precio al por menor; *v.* detallar; vender al menudeo (*o* vender al por menor), *Méx.*, *C.A.*, *Ven.*, *Col.* menudear.

**retailer** [rítelɚ] *s.* detallista, revendedor, comerciante al por menor.

**retain** [rɪtén] *v.* retener; emplear.

**retaliate** [rɪtǽliet] *v.* desquitarse, vengarse.

**retaliation** [rɪtæliéʃən] *s.* desquite; desagravio; represalia, venganza.

**retard** [rɪtárd] *v.* retardar, retrasar, atrasar.

**retention** [rɪténʃən] *s.* retención.

**reticence** [rétəsəns] *s.* reserva.

**retinue** [rétn̩ju] *s.* comitiva, séquito, acompañamiento.

**retire** [rɪtáɪr] *v.* retirar(se); jubilar(se);

acostarse; apartarse.

**retirement** [rɪtáɪrmənt] *s.* retiro; jubilación.

**retort** [rɪtɔ́rt] *v.* replicar; redargüir; *s.* réplica.

**retouch** [rɪtʌ́tʃ] *v.* retocar; *s.* retoque.

**retrace** [rɪtrés] *v.* repasar; volver a trazar; **to — one's steps** volver sobre sus pasos, retroceder.

**retract** [rɪtrǽkt] *v.* retractar, retractarse de; desdecirse (de); retraer.

**retreat** [rɪtrít] *s.* retiro, refugio, asilo; retirada; retreta (*toque de retirada*); *v.* retirarse; retroceder.

**retrench** [rɪtréntʃ] *v.* cercenar, reducir, disminuir; economizar.

**retrieve** [rɪtrív] *v.* cobrar (*la caza*); recobrar, recuperar; reparar (*una pérdida*).

**retroactive** [rɛtroǽktɪv] *adj.* retroactivo.

**retroflex** [rétroflɛks] *adj.* retroflejo.

**retrospect** [rétrospɛkt] *s.* retrospección; **in —** retrospectivamente.

**return** [rɪtɜ́n] *v.* volver, regresar; retornar; devolver; replicar; redituar; producir; restar (*la pelota en tenis*); **to — a favor** corresponder a un favor; **to — a report** rendir un informe; *s.* vuelta, regreso; retorno; recompensa; restitución, devolución; réplica; resto (*en un juego de pelota*); rédito, ganancia; informe; **— game** desquite, juego de desquite; **— ticket** boleto de vuelta; **by — mail** a vuelta de correo; **election -s** reportaje de elecciones; **in —** en cambio; **in — for** a cambio de, a trueque de; **income tax —** declaración de rentas; **many happy -s** muchas felicidades (en su día).

**reunion** [rijúnjən] *s.* reunión; junta.

**reunite** [rijʊnáɪt] *v.* reunir(se), volver a unirse; reconciliar(se).

**reveal** [rɪvíl] *v.* revelar.

**revel** [révl] *v.* deleitarse, gozarse; parrandear, *Am.* farrear; andar de parranda, *Ríopl.* andar de farra; *s.* parranda, juerga, jarana.

**revelation** [rɛvléʃən] *s.* revelación; **Revelation(s)** Apocalipsis.

**revelry** [révlrɪ] *s.* jaleo, juerga, jarana.

**revenge** [rɪvéndʒ] *v.* vengar, vindicar; *s.* venganza; desquite.

**revengeful** [rɪvéndʒfəl] *adj.* vengativo.

**revenue** [révənju] *s.* renta; rédito; rentas públicas, ingresos.

**revere** [rɪvír] *v.* venerar.

**reverence** [révrəns] *s.* reverencia; veneración; *v.* reverenciar, venerar.

**reverend** [révrənd] *adj.* reverendo; venerable.

**reverent** [révrənt] *adj.* reverente.

**reverie, revery** [révərɪ] *s.* ensueño; arrobamiento.

**reverse** [rɪvɜ́s] *adj.* inverso, invertido; contrario, opuesto; *s.* revés; reverso, dorso; lo contrario; contratiempo; *v.* invertir; voltear; revocar (*una sentencia*).

**revert** [rɪvɜ́t] *v.* revertir, volver atrás, retroceder.

**review** [rɪvjú] *v.* (*study*) repasar, revisar; revistar; (*inspect*) pasar revista a (*las tropas*); (*criticize*) reseñar, hacer una reseña de (*un libro*); *s.* revista; repaso; reseña, crítica (*de un libro, drama, etc.*); revisión (*de un caso jurídico, sentencia, etc.*).

**revile** [rɪváɪl] *v.* vilipendiar, vituperar, denigrar.

**revise** [rɪváɪz] *v.* revisar, repasar, releer (*para corregir*); corregir, enmendar.

**revision** [rɪvíʒən] *s.* revisión; enmienda; edición enmendada o mejorada.

**revival** [rɪváɪvl] *s.* (*renewal*) renovación; revivificación; (*repeating*) renacimiento; nueva presentación (*teatral*); **— meeting** junta para revivir el fervor religioso; **religious —** despertamiento (*o nuevo fervor*) religioso.

**revive** [rɪváɪv] *v.* revivir, resucitar; volver en sí; renacer; reavivar, reanimar(se); avivar.

**revoke** [rɪvók] *v.* revocar, abrogar, anular; renunciar (*en los juegos de naipes*).

**revolt** [rɪvólt] *s.* revuelta, rebelión; sublevación; *v.* rebelarse, sublevarse; **it -s me** me da asco, me repugna.

**revolting** [rɪvóltɪŋ] *adj.* repugnante; asqueroso.

**revolution** [rɛvəlúʃən] *s.* revolución; vuelta (*que da una rueda*).

**revolutionary** [rɛvəlúʃənɛrɪ] *adj. & s.* revolucionario.

**revolutionist** [rɛvəlúʃənɪst] *s.* revolucionario.

**revolve** [rɪválv] *v.* girar, dar vueltas; rodar; voltear, dar vueltas a; **to — in one's mind** revolver en la mente, ponderar, reflexionar.

**revolver** [rɪválvə] *s.* revólver.

**reward** [rɪwɔ́rd] *v.* premiar; recompensar; *s.* premio, gratificación, recompensa, galardón; albricias (*por haber hallado algún objeto perdido*).

**rewrite** [riráɪt] *v.* volver a escribir; refundir (*un escrito*).

**rhapsody** [rǽpsədɪ] *s.* rapsodia.

**rhetoric** [rétərɪk] *s.* retórica.

**rheumatism** [rúmətɪzəm] *s.* reumatismo, reuma.

**rhinoceros** [raɪnásərəs] *s.* rinoceronte.

**rhubarb** [rúbɑrb] *s.* ruibarbo.

**rhyme** [raɪm] *s.* rima; **without — or reason** sin ton ni son; *v.* rimar.

**rhythm** [ríðəm] *s.* ritmo.

**rhythmical** [ríðmɪkl] *adj.* rítmico, acompasado, cadencioso.

**rib** [rɪb] *s.* costilla; varilla (*de paraguas*); cordoncillo (*de ciertos tejidos*).

**ribbon** [ríbən] *s.* cinta; listón, banda; tira.

**rice** [raɪs] *s.* arroz; **— field** arrozal.

**rich** [rɪtʃ] *adj.* rico; costoso, suntuoso; sabroso; **— color** color vivo; **— food** alimento muy mantecoso o dulce.

**riches** [rítʃɪz] *s. pl.* riqueza, riquezas.

**rickety** [ríkɪtɪ] *adj.* desvencijado; raquítico.

**rid** [rɪd] *v.* librar, desembarazar; **to get — of** librarse de, deshacerse de, des-

**RE**

embarazarse de; *pret. & p.p. de* **to rid.**

**ridden** [rídn̩] *p.p. de* **to ride.**

**riddle** [rídl̩] acertijo, adivinanza, enigma; *v.* acribillar, perforar; **to — with bullets** acribillar a balazos.

**ride** [raɪd] *v. (horse)* cabalgar, montar; *(vehicle)* pasear; ir en *(tranvía, tren)*; **to — a bicycle** andar o montar en bicicleta; **to — a horse** montar un caballo; **to — horseback** montar a caballo; **to — over a country** pasar o viajar por un país *(en auto, a caballo o por tren)*; **to — someone** dominar a alguien; burlarse de alguien; *s.* paseo *(a caballo o en automóvil)*; viaje *(a caballo, en automóvil, por ferrocarril, etc.).*

**rider** [ráɪdɚ] *s.* jinete; pasajero *(de automóvil)*; biciclista; motociclista; aditamento, cláusula añadida *(a un proyecto de ley).*

**ridge** [rɪdʒ] *s.* espinazo; lomo *(entre dos surcos)*; arista, intersección *(de dos planos)*; cordillera; cerro; caballete *(de tejado)*; cordoncillo *(de ciertos tejidos).*

**ridicule** [rídɪkjul] *s.* ridículo; burla, mofa; *v.* ridiculizar, poner en ridículo.

**ridiculous** [rɪdíkjələs] *adj.* ridículo.

**rifle** [ráɪfl̩] *s.* rifle; *v.* pillar, robar; despojar.

**rift** [rɪft] *s. (opening)* raja; abertura; *(disagreement)* desacuerdo.

**rig** [rɪg] *v.* aparejar, equipar; enjarciar *(un barco de vela)*; **to — oneself up** emperifollarse, ataviarse; *s.* aparejo, equipo; aparato; atavío, traje.

**rigging** [rígɪŋ] *s.* jarcia, aparejo.

**right** [raɪt] *adj. (not left)* derecho; diestro; *(proper)* recto; justo; propio; adecuado; correcto; **— angle** ángulo recto; **— side** lado derecho; derecho *(de un tejido, traje, etc.)*; **it is — that** está bien que, es justo que; **to be — tener razón; **to be all —** estar bien; estar bien de salud; **to be in one's — mind** estar en sus cabales; *adv.* derecho, directamente; rectamente; justamente; bien; correctamente; a la derecha; **— about-face** media vuelta; **— hungry** muy hambriento; **— now** ahora mismo, inmediatamente; **— there** allí mismo, *Am.* allí mero; **go — home!** ¡vete derechito a casa!; **it is — where you left it** está exactamente *(o en el mero lugar)* donde lo dejaste; **to hit — in the eye** dar de lleno en el ojo, *Am.* dar en el mero ojo; *s.* derecho; autoridad; privilegio; **— of way** derecho de vía; **by — (by -s)** justamente, con justicia; según la ley; **from — to left** de derecha a izquierda; **to the —** a la derecha; **to be in the —** tener razón; *v.* enderezar; corregir.

**righteous** [ráɪtʃəs] *adj.* recto, justo, virtuoso.

**righteousness** [ráɪtʃəsnɪs] *s.* rectitud, virtud.

**rightful** [ráɪtfəl] *adj.* justo; legítimo.

**right-hand** [ráɪthænd] *adj.* derecho, de la mano derecha; **— man** brazo derecho.

**rightist** [ráɪtɪst] *s.* derechista.

**rightly** [ráɪtlɪ] *adv.* con razón; justamente, rectamente; propiamente, aptamente, debidamente.

**right-wing** [ráɪtwɪŋ] *adj.* derechista.

**rigid** [rídʒɪd] *adj.* rígido.

**rigidity** [rɪdʒídətɪ] *s.* rigidez; tiesura.

**rigor** [rígɚ] *s.* rigor; rigidez; severidad.

**rigorous** [rígɚəs] *adj.* riguroso *(o riguroso)*, severo.

**rim** [rɪm] *s.* borde, orilla; aro.

**rime** = **rhyme.**

**rind** [raɪnd] *s.* corteza, cáscara.

**ring** [rɪŋ] *s. (finger)* anillo, sortija; argolla; aro; *(circle)* arena; pista; *(sound)* toque; tañido; repique; *(telephone)* timbrazo; telefonazo; **—leader** cabecilla; **— of defiance** tono de reto; **— of shouts** gritería; **— of a telephone** llamada de teléfono; **ring-shaped** en forma de anillo, anular; **key— llavero; **sarcastic —** retintín; *v.* tocar *(un timbre, una campanilla o campana)*; sonar; tañer, repicar; resonar; zumbar *(los oídos)*; **to — for something** llamar para pedir algo; **to — the nose of an animal** ponerle una argolla en la nariz a un animal; **to — up on the phone** llamar por teléfono.

**ringlet** [ríŋlɪt] *s.* rizo, bucle; pequeña sortija.

**rink** [rɪŋk] *s.* patinadero *(cancha para patinar).*

**rinse** [rɪns] *v.* enjuagar; lavar; aclarar *(la ropa)*; *s.* enjuague.

**riot** [ráɪət] *s.* motín, desorden, alboroto, tumulto; **— of color** riqueza o exceso de colores chillantes; *v.* amotinarse, alborotar, armar un tumulto.

**rip** [rɪp] *v.* rasgar(se), romper(se); descoser(se); **to — off** rasgar, arrancar, cortar; **to — out a seam** descoser una costura; *s.* rasgón, rasgadura, rotura; descosido.

**ripe** [raɪp] *adj.* maduro, sazonado; en sazón; **— for** maduro para, sazonado para; bien preparado para, listo para.

**ripen** [ráɪpən] *v.* madurar(se), sazonar(se).

**ripeness** [ráɪpnɪs] *s.* madurez, sazón.

**ripple** [rípl̩] *v.* rizar(se), agitar(se), ondear, temblar *(la superficie del agua)*; murmurar *(un arroyo)*; *s.* onda, temblor, ondulación *(en la superficie del agua)*; murmullo *(de un arroyo).*

**rise** [raɪz] *v.* subir; ascender; alzarse, levantarse; elevarse; surgir; salir *(el sol, la luna, un astro)*; hincharse *(la masa del pan)*; **to — up in rebellion** sublevarse, levantarse, alzarse *(en rebelión)*; *s.* subida; ascenso; pendiente; elevación; salida *(del sol, de la luna, etc.)*; subida, alza *(de precios).*

**risen** [rízn̩] *p.p. de* **to rise.**

**risk** [rɪsk] *s.* riesgo; *v.* arriesgar, aventurar, poner en peligro; exponerse a; **to—defeat** correr el riesgo de perder, exponerse a perder.

**risky** [rískı] *adj.* arriesgado, peligroso, aventurado.

**risqué** [rıské] *adj.* escabroso.

**rite** [raıt] *s.* rito, ceremonia.

**ritual** [rítʃuǝl] *adj.* & *s.* ritual, ceremonial.

**rival** [ráıvl]] *s.* rival, competidor, émulo; *adj.* competidor; **the — party** el partido opuesto; *v.* rivalizar con, competir con.

**rivalry** [ráıvlrı] *s.* rivalidad.

**river** [rívɚ] *s.* río.

**rivet** [rívıt] *s.* remache; *v.* remachar; fijar.

**rivulet** [rívjǝlıt] *s.* riachuelo, arroyuelo.

**road** [rod] *s.* camino; carretera; vía.

**roadside** [ródsaıd] *s.* borde del camino.

**roadway** [ródwe] *s.* camino, carretera.

**roam** [rom] *v.* vagar, errar, andar errante.

**roar** [ror] *v.* rugir, bramar; **to — with laughter** reír a carcajadas; *s.* rugido, bramido; **— of laughter** risotada, carcajada.

**roast** [rost] *v.* asar(se); tostar (*café, maíz, etc.*); ridiculizar, criticar; *s.* asado, carne asada; *adj.* asado; **— beef** rosbif, rosbí.

**rob** [rab] *v.* robar, hurtar; **to — someone of something** robarle algo a alguien.

**robber** [rábɚ] *s.* ladrón; **highway —** salteador.

**robbery** [rábrı] *s.* robo, hurto.

**robe** [rob] *s.* manto, traje talar, túnica, toga (*de un juez, letrado, etc.*); bata; **automobile —** manta de automóvil.

**robin** [rábın] *s.* petirrojo.

**robust** [róbʌst] *adj.* robusto, fuerte.

**rock** [rak] *s.* roca, peña; peñasco; **— crystal** cristal de roca; **— salt** sal de piedra, sal gema o sal mineral; **to go on the -s** tropezar en un escollo, *Am.* escollar; *v.* mecer(se), balancear(se); bambolear(se); estremecer; **to — to sleep** adormecer (*meciendo*), arrullar.

**rocker** [rákɚ] *s.* mecedora; arco de una mecedora o cuna.

**rocket** [rákıt] *s.* cohete.

**rocketry** [rákǝtrı] *s.* cohetería.

**rocking** [rákıŋ] *s.* balanceo; *adj.* oscilante; **— chair** silla mecedora.

**rocky** [rákı] *adj.* roqueño, rocoso, rocalloso, peñascoso; pedregoso; movedizo; tembloroso; débil, desvanecido.

**rod** [rad] *s.* vara, varilla; medida de longitud (*aproximadamente 5 metros*); **fishing —** caña de pescar.

**rode** [rod] *pret. de* **to ride**.

**rodent** [ródǝnt] *s.* roedor.

**rogue** [rog] *s.* pícaro, bribón, tunante, pillo; **-s' gallery** colección policíaca de retratos de criminales.

**roguish** [rógıʃ] *adj.* pícaro, pillo, picaresco; travieso.

**role** [rol] *s.* papel, parte.

**roll** [rol] *v.* (*move*) rodar; girar; balancearse (*un barco*); bambolearse; ondular, retumbar (*el trueno, un cañón*); aplanar, alisar con rodillo; arrollar, enrollar, hacer un rollo o bola; envolver; redoblar (*un tambor*); pronunciar (*la rr doble*); **to — over in the snow** revolverse o revolcarse en la nieve; **to — up** arrollar, enrollar, envolver; *s.* rollo (*de papel, paño, tela, etc.*); balanceo (*de un barco*); retumbo (*del trueno, de un cañón*); redoble (*de un tambor*); lista ondulación; oleaje; bollo, rosca, panecillo; **to call the —** pasar lista.

**roller** [rólɚ] *s.* rodillo, cilindro (*para aplanar o alisar*); rollo (*rodillo de pastelero*); oleada; **— coaster** montaña rusa; **— skate** patín de ruedas.

**Roman** [rómǝn] *adj.* & *s.* romano; **— nose** nariz aguileña.

**romance** [románs] *s.* (*literature*) romance; novela; cuento; fábula; (*affair*) aventura romántica; amorío, lance amoroso; *v.* contar o fingir fábulas; andar en amoríos o aventuras; **Romance** *adj.* romance, románico, neolatino.

**romantic** [romántık] *adj.* romántico; novelesco.

**romanticism** [romántǝsızǝm] *s.* romanticismo.

**romanticist** [romántǝsıst] *s.* romántico, escritor romántico.

**romp** [ramp] *v.* triscar, juguetear, retozar, travesear.

**roof** [ruf] *s.* techo, techumbre, techado; tejado; **— garden** azotea-jardín; **— of the mouth** paladar; **flat —** azotea; *v.* techar.

**room** [rum] *s.* (*in building*) cuarto, pieza, sala, habitación; (*space*) espacio; lugar, sitio; **there is no — for more** no cabe(n) más, no hay lugar o cabida para más; **to make —** hacer lugar; **—mate** compañero de cuarto; *v.* vivir, hospedarse, alojarse.

**roomer** [rúmɚ] *s.* inquilino.

**roominess** [rúmınıs] *s.* holgura.

**roomy** [rúmı] *adj.* espacioso, amplio, holgado.

**roost** [rust] *s.* gallinero; percha de gallinero; *v.* acurrucarse (*las aves en la percha*); pasar la noche.

**rooster** [rústɚ] *s.* gallo.

**root** [rut] *s.* raíz; *v.* arraigar(se); echar raíces; hocicar, hozar (*dícese de los cerdos*); **to — for** vitorear, aclamar; **to — out** (*o* **— up**) desarraigar, arrancar de raíz; **to become -ed** arraigarse.

**rope** [rop] *s.* (*cord*) soga, cuerda; (*lasso*) reata, lazo; **to be at the end of one's —** haber agotado el último recurso; estar (*o* andar) en las últimas; no saber qué hacer; **to know the -s** saber todas las tretas de un asunto o negocio; *v.* amarrar; lazar, enlazar; **to — off** acordelar, poner cuerdas tirantes alrededor de (*un sitio*); **to — someone in** embaucar a alguien.

**rosary** [rózǝrı] *s.* rosario.

**rose** [roz] *pret. de* **to rise**.

**rose** [roz] *s.* rosa; color de rosa; **—bush** rosal; **— window** rosetón.

RI

**rosebud** [rózbʌd] *s.* capullo o botón de rosa, yema, pimpollo.

**rosette** [rozét] *s.* roseta; rosetón.

**roster** [rɑ́stɚ] *s.* registro; lista.

**rostrum** [rɑ́strəm] *s.* tribuna.

**rosy** [rózɪ] *adj.* (color) rosado; color de rosa; (condition) alegre, risueño; — future porvenir risueño.

**rot** [rɑt] *v.* pudrir(se); corromperse; *s.* podre, podredumbre, putrefacción.

**rotary** [rótərɪ] *adj.* rotatorio, giratorio, rotativo.

**rotate** [rótet] *v.* girar, dar vueltas; hacer girar; turnarse; cultivar en rotación.

**rotation** [rotéʃən] *s.* rotación, vuelta; — of crops rotación de cultivos.

**rote** [rot] *s.* rutina, repetición maquinal; by — maquinalmente.

**rotten** [rɑ́tn̩] *adj.* podrido, putrefacto; hediondo; corrompido, corrupto.

**rouge** [ruʒ] *s.* colorete; *v.* pintar(se), poner(se) colorete.

**rough** [rʌf] *adj.* (course) áspero; tosco; fragoso; escabroso; (rude) brusco; grosero; (stormy) borrascoso, tempestuoso; — diamond diamante en bruto; — draft borrador; bosquejo; — estimate cálculo aproximativo, tanteo; — ground terreno escabroso; — idea idea aproximada; — sea mar picado; — weather tiempo borrascoso; *adv.* véase roughly; *v.* to — it vivir sin lujos ni comodidades, hacer vida campestre.

**roughen** [rʌ́fən] *v.* hacer o poner áspero; picar, rascar (una superficie); rajarse, agrietarse (la piel).

**roughly** [rʌ́flɪ] *adv.* ásperamente; groseramente, rudamente; aproximadamente; to estimate — tantear.

**roughness** [rʌ́fnɪs] *s.* aspereza; escabrosidad; rudeza; tosquedad; the — of the sea lo picado del mar; the — of the weather lo borrascoso del tiempo.

**round** [raund] *adj.* redondo; rotundo; circular; — trip viaje redondo, viaje de ida y vuelta; round-trip ticket boleto (o billete) de ida y vuelta; *s.* vuelta, rotación, revolución; ronda; vuelta (en el juego de naipes); tanda, turno (en ciertos deportes); escalón, travesaño (de escalera de mano); danza en rueda; — of ammunition carga de municiones; descarga; — of applause explosión de aplausos; — of pleasures sucesión de placeres; to make the -s rondar; *prep.* & *adv.* véase around; — about a la redonda; por todos lados; round-shouldered cargado de espaldas; to come — again volver otra vez; to go — a corner doblar una esquina; *v.* redondear; dar vuelta a; to — a corner doblar una esquina; to — out redondear; completar; to — up cattle juntar el ganado, *Am.* rodear el ganado.

**roundabout** [ráundəbaut] *adj.* indirecto.

**roundup** [ráundʌp] *s.* rodeo (de ganado).

**rouse** [rauz] *v.* despertar(se), *Ríopl.* recordar; excitar; incitar, provocar; levantar (la caza).

**rout** [raut] *s.* derrota, fuga desordenada; *v.* derrotar; poner en fuga; to — out echar, hacer salir a toda prisa.

**route** [rut] *s.* ruta, camino, vía; itinerario; *v.* dirigir o enviar por cierta ruta.

**routine** [rutin] *s.* rutina.

**rove** [rov] *v.* vagar, errar, andar errante.

**rover** [róvɚ] *s.* vagabundo.

**row** [rau] *s.* riña, pelea, pelotera; *v.* pelearse, reñir, armar una riña o pelotera.

**row** [ro] *s.* fila, hilera; paseo en lancha; *v.* remar, bogar; llevar en lancha o bote.

**rowboat** [róbot] *s.* bote de remos, lancha.

**rower** [róɚ] *s.* remero.

**royal** [rɔ́ɪəl] *adj.* real, regio.

**royalist** [rɔ́ɪəlɪst] *s.* realista.

**royalty** [rɔ́ɪəltɪ] *s.* realeza, soberanía real; persona o personas reales; derechos (pagados a un autor o inventor).

**rub** [rʌb] *v.* (apply friction) frotar; restregar; fregar; (scrape) raspar; irritar; to — out borrar; to — someone the wrong way irritar, contrariar, llevarle a uno la contraria; *s.* fricción, friega, frotación; roce; sarcasmo; there is the — allí está la dificultad.

**rubber** [rʌ́bɚ] *s.* caucho, goma, *Méx.*, *C.A.* hule; goma elástica; goma de borrar; partida (en ciertos juegos de naipes); jugada decisiva (en ciertos juegos de naipes); -s chanclos, zapatos de goma o hule; *adj.* de caucho, de goma, *Méx.*, *C.A.* de hule; — band faja o banda de goma; — plantation cauchal; — tree *Am.* caucho, *Am.* gomero.

**rubbish** [rʌ́bɪʃ] *s.* basura, desechos, desperdicios; tonterías.

**rubble** [rʌ́bl̩] *s.* escombros; ripio, cascajo, fragmentos de ladrillos o piedras; piedra en bruto, piedra sin labrar.

**rubric** [rúbrɪk] *s.* rúbrica.

**ruby** [rúbɪ] *s.* rubí.

**rudder** [rʌ́dɚ] *s.* timón.

**ruddy** [rʌ́dɪ] *adj.* rojo; rojizo; rubicundo.

**rude** [rud] *adj.* rudo; grosero; áspero; brusco; tosco.

**rudeness** [rúdnɪs] *s.* rudeza; grosería, descortesía; tosquedad.

**rueful** [rúfəl] *adj.* triste; lastimoso, lamentable.

**ruffian** [rʌ́fɪən] *s.* rufián, hombre brutal.

**ruffle** [rʌ́fl̩] *v.* rizar, fruncir (tela); arrugar; desarreglar; rizar (la superficie del agua); perturbar; molestar; *s.* volante (de un traje); frunce, pliegue; ondulación (en el agua).

**rug** [rʌg] *s.* alfombra, tapete.

**rugged** [rʌ́gɪd] *adj.* escabroso, fragoso; áspero; recio, robusto; tosco; borrascoso, tempestuoso.

**ruin** [rúɪn] *s.* ruina; **to go to —** arruinarse, caer en ruinas, venir a menos; *v.* arruinar; echar a perder; estropear.

**ruinous** [rúɪnəs] *adj.* ruinoso; desastroso.

**rule** [rul] *s.* (*regulation*) regla; reglamento; precepto; (*control*) mando, gobierno; **as a —** por regla general; *v.* regir, gobernar; mandar; dirigir, guiar; dominar; fallar, decidir; rayar (*con regla*); **to — out** excluir; **to — over** regir, gobernar.

**ruler** [rúlə] *s.* gobernante; soberano; regla (*para medir o trazar líneas*).

**ruling** [rúlɪŋ] *s.* fallo, decisión; gobierno; *adj.* predominante, prevaleciente; principal.

**rum** [rʌm] *s.* ron.

**rumble** [rʌmbl] *v.* retumbar, hacer estruendo, rugir; *s.* retumbo, estruendo, rumor, ruido sordo; **— seat** asiento trasero (*de cupé*).

**ruminate** [rúmənet] *v.* rumiar; reflexionar, meditar.

**rummage** [rʌmɪdʒ] *v.* escudriñar revolviéndolo todo; *s.* búsqueda desordenada; **— sale** venta de prendas usadas (*para beneficencia*).

**rumor** [rúmə] *s.* rumor; runrún; *v.* murmurar; **it is -ed that** corre la voz que.

**rump** [rʌmp] *s.* anca; trasero.

**rumple** [rʌmpl] *v.* estrujar, ajar; arrugar; *s.* arruga (*en un traje*).

**rumpus** [rʌmpəs] *s.* barullo, alharaca, boruca, batahola.

**run** [rʌn] *v.* (*on foot*) correr; (*function*) andar; marchar; funcionar; (*flow*) fluir; chorrear; (*go over*) recorrer; (*direct*) dirigir, manejar; (*un negocio, empresa, máquina, casa, etc.*); extenderse (*de un punto a otro*); correrse (*los colores*); ser candidato (*a un puesto político*); **to — a fever** tener calentura; **to — away** huir; fugarse, escaparse; **to — across a person** encontrarse o tropezar con una persona; **to — down** dejar de funcionar (*una máquina, reloj, etc.*); aprehender a (*un criminal*); hablar mal de; atropellar; **to get — down in health** quebrantársele a uno la salud; **to — dry** secarse; **to — into** tropezar con, encontrarse con; chocar con; **— around with** asociarse con; tener amores con; **to — into debt** adeudarse; **to — something into** meter algo en, clavar algo en; **to — out** salirse; **to — out of money** acabársele a uno el dinero; **to — over** derramarse (*un líquido*); atropellar; pasar por encima de; repasar, echar un vistazo a (*la lección, un libro, etc.*); **to — through a book** hojear un libro; **the play ran for three months** se dió la comedia durante tres meses; *s.* carrera, corrida; curso, marcha; recorrido; manejo; **— of good luck** serie de repetidos éxitos; **— of performances** serie de representaciones; **— on a bank** corrida, demanda extraordinaria de fondos bancarios; **in the long —** a la larga; **stocking —** carrera; **the common — of mankind** el común de las gentes; **to have the — of** tener el libre uso de; *p.p. de* **to run.**

**runaway** [rʌnəwe] *adj.* fugitivo; **— horse** caballo desbocado; **— marriage** casamiento de escapatoria; *s.* fugitivo; caballo desbocado; fuga.

**rung** [rʌŋ] *s.* barrote, travesaño (*de silla, escalera de mano, etc.*); *pret. & p.p. de* **to ring.**

**runner** [rʌnə] *s.* corredor; tapete (*para un pasillo o mesa*), *Ríopl.* pasillo; carrera (*en una media*); cuchilla (*de patín o de trineo*); contrabandista.

**running** [rʌnɪŋ] *s.* (*race*) corrida, carrera; (*direction*) manejo, dirección; (*flow*) flujo; **to be out of the —** estar fuera de combate; *adj.* corriente; **— board** estribo; **— expenses** gastos corrientes; **— knot** nudo corredizo; **— water** agua corriente; **in — condition** en buen estado; **for ten days — por diez días seguidos.**

**runt** [rʌnt] *s.* enano; hombrecillo.

**runway** [rʌnwe] *s.* senda; vía; pista (*de aterrizaje*).

**rupture** [rʌptʃə] *s.* ruptura; rompimiento, rotura; hernia; *v.* romper(se); reventar.

**rural** [rúrəl] *adj.* rural, campestre.

**rush** [rʌʃ] *v.* (*hurry*) apresurar(se); *Am.* apurarse; despachar con prisa; (*attack*) lanzar(se), precipitar(se); abalanzarse; acometer; **to — out** salir a todo correr; **to — past** pasar a toda prisa; *s.* precipitación, prisa; acometida; junco; **— chair** silla de junco; **— of business** gran movimiento comercial; **— of people** tropel de gente; **— order** pedido urgente.

**Russian** [rʌʃən] *adj. & s.* ruso.

**rust** [rʌst] *s.* moho, orín; tizón (*enfermedad de las plantas*); **— color** color rojizo; *v.* enmohecer(se), oxidar(se).

**rustic** [rʌstɪk] *adj. & s.* rústico, campesino.

**rustle** [rʌsl] *v.* susurrar, crujir; menear; **to — cattle** robar ganado; *s.* susurro, crujido.

**rusty** [rʌstɪ] *adj.* mohoso, cubierto de orín, oxidado; rojizo; entorpecido, falto de uso; falto de práctica.

**rut** [rʌt] *s.* rodada; rutina, método rutinario; **to be in a —** hacer una cosa por rutina, ser esclavo de la rutina.

**ruthless** [rúθlɪs] *adj.* despiadado, cruel, brutal.

**ruthlessness** [rúθlɪsnɪs] *s.* fiereza, falta de miramiento, truculencia, crueldad.

**rye** [raɪ] *s.* centeno.

## S

**saber** [sébə] *s.* sable.

**sabotage** [sǽbəta3] *s.* sabotaje; *v.* sabotear.

**sack** [sæk] *s.* (*bag*) saco; costal; (*looting*) saqueo, pillaje; *v.* ensacar, meter en un saco; saquear, pillar.

RO

**sacrament** [sǽkrəmənt] *s.* sacramento.

**sacred** [sékrɪd] *adj.* sagrado, sacro.

**sacredness** [sékrɪdnɪs] *s.* santidad; lo sagrado.

**sacrifice** [sǽkrəfaɪs] *s.* sacrificio; **to sell at a** — vender con pérdida; *v.* sacrificar.

**sacrilege** [sǽkrəlɪdʒ] *s.* sacrilegio.

**sacrilegious** [sækrɪlídʒəs] *adj.* sacrílego.

**sacrosanct** [sǽkrosænkt] *adj.* sacrosanto.

**sad** [sæd] *adj.* triste.

**sadden** [sǽdn̩] *v.* entristecer(se).

**saddle** [sǽdl̩] *s.* silla de montar; silla de bicicleta o motocicleta; —**bag** alforja; — **horse** caballo de silla —**tree** arzón; *v.* ensillar; **to — someone with responsibilities** cargar a alguien de responsabilidades.

**sadistic** [sədístɪk] *adj.* sádico, cruel.

**sadness** [sǽdnɪs] *s.* tristeza.

**safe** [sef] *adj.* (*secure*) seguro; salvo; sin riesgo, sin peligro; (*trustworthy*) digno de confianza; — **and sound** sano y salvo; **safe-conduct** salvoconducto; **to be** — no correr peligro, estar a salvo; *s.* caja fuerte; **-ly** *adv.* seguramente; con seguridad; sin peligro; **to arrive -ly** llegar bien, llegar sin contratiempo alguno.

**safeguard** [séfgɑrd] *s.* salvaguardia; resguardo, defensa; *v.* resguardar, proteger, salvaguardar.

**safety** [séftɪ] *s.* seguridad; protección; **in** — con seguridad; sin peligro; *adj.* de seguridad; — **device** mecanismo de seguridad; — **pin** imperdible, alfiler de seguridad.

**saffron** [sǽfrən] *s.* azafrán; *adj.* azafranado, color de azafrán.

**sag** [sæg] *v.* combarse, pandearse; doblegarse; deprimirse, hundirse (*en el centro*); encorvarse; **his shoulders** — tiene las espaldas caídas; *s.* pandeo, flexión, depresión; concavidad.

**sagacious** [səgéʃəs] *adj.* sagaz, ladino, astuto.

**sagacity** [səgǽsətɪ] *s.* sagacidad; astucia.

**sage** [sedʒ] *adj.* sabio; cuerdo, prudente; *s.* sabio; salvia (*planta*).

**said** [sɛd] *pret.* & *p.p. de* **to say**.

**sail** [sel] *s.* (*canvas*) vela (*de barco*); (*trip*) viaje o paseo en barco de vela; **under full** — a toda vela; **to set** — hacerse a la vela; *v.* navegar; hacerse a la vela; zarpar, salir (*un buque*); viajar, ir (*en barco, bote, etc.*); pasear en bote de vela; **to — a kite** volar una cometa o papalote; **to — along** deslizarse; navegar; ir bien; **to — along the coast** costear.

**sailboat** [sélbot] *s.* bote o barco de vela.

**sailor** [sélɚ] *s.* marinero; marino.

**saint** [sent] *s.* santo; *adj.* santo; san (*delante de nombres masculinos excepto: Santo Tomás, Santo Domingo, Santo Toribio*); *v.* canonizar.

**saintly** [séntlɪ] *adj.* santo; pío, devoto.

**sake** [sek]: **for the — of** por; por amor a; por consideración a; **for my — por**

mí; **for pity's** — por piedad; ¡caramba!; **for the — of argument** por vía de argumento.

**salacious** [səléʃəs] *adj.* salaz.

**salad** [sǽləd] *s.* ensalada; — **dressing** aderezo (*para ensalada*).

**salary** [sǽlərɪ] *s.* salario, sueldo.

**sale** [sel] *s.* venta; saldo, *Méx., C.A., Andes* barata; *Ríopl., Andes* realización; — **by auction** almoneda, subasta; **-s tax** impuesto sobre ventas; **for (on)** — de venta.

**salesman** [sélzmən] *s.* vendedor; dependiente (*de tienda*); **traveling** — agente viajero, viajante de comercio.

**saleswoman** [sélzwumən] *s.* vendedora; dependiente (*de tienda*).

**salient** [sélɪənt] *adj.* saliente, sobresaliente; prominente.

**saline** [sélɪn] *adj.* salino.

**saliva** [səláɪvə] *s.* saliva.

**sallow** [sǽlo] *adj.* amarillento, pálido.

**sally** [sǽlɪ] *s.* salida; agudeza, chiste agudo; *v.* salir, hacer una salida; **to — forth** salir.

**salmon** [sǽmən] *s.* salmón.

**saloon** [səlún] *s.* salón (*de un vapor*); taberna, *Am.* cantina; *Ríopl.* bar; **dining — of a ship** salón-comedor de un vapor.

**salt** [sɔlt] *s.* (*sodium chloride*) sal; (*wit*) chiste, agudeza; **smelling -s** sales aromáticas; **the — of the earth** la flor y nata de la humanidad; *adj.* salado; salobre; —**cellar** salero; — **mine** salina; — **pork** tocino salado; — **shaker** salero; — **water** agua salada, agua de mar; *v.* salar; **to — one's money away** guardar o ahorrar su dinero.

**saltpeter** [sɔltpítɚ] *s.* salitre, nitro; — **mine** salitral, salitrera.

**salty** [sɔltɪ] *adj.* salado; salobre.

**salutary** [sǽljuterɪ] *adj.* saludable.

**salutation** [sæljətéʃən] *s.* salutación, saludo.

**salute** [səlút] *s.* saludo; **gun —** salva; *v.* saludar; cuadrarse (*militarmente*).

**salvage** [sǽlvɪdʒ] *s.* salvamento.

**salvation** [sælvéʃən] *s.* salvación.

**salve** [sæv] *s.* untura, ungüento; alivio; *v.* aliviar, aquietar, calmar; untar.

**salvo** [sǽlvo] *s.* salva.

**same** [sem] *adj.* mismo; igual; idéntico; **it is all the — to me** me es igual, me da lo mismo; **the —** lo mismo; el mismo (la misma, los mismos, las mismas).

**sample** [sǽmpl̩] *s.* muestra, prueba; **book of -s** muestrario; *v.* probar, calar.

**sanatorium** [sænətorɪəm] *s.* sanatorio.

**sanctify** [sǽŋktəfaɪ] *v.* santificar.

**sanction** [sǽŋkʃən] *s.* sanción; aprobación; autorización; *v.* sancionar; ratificar; aprobar, autorizar.

**sanctity** [sǽŋktətɪ] *s.* santidad.

**sanctuary** [sǽŋktʃuerɪ] *s.* santuario; asilo.

**sand** [sænd] *s.* arena; — **pit** arenal; *v.* enarenar, cubrir de arena; mezclar con

arena; refregar con arena.
**sandal** [sǽndl̩] s. sandalia; alpargata; *Méx.* guarache (huarache); *Andes* ojota.
**sandpaper** [sǽndpepɚ] s. papel de lija; *v.* lijar, pulir o alisar con papel de lija.
**sandstone** [sǽndston] s. piedra arenisca.
**sandwich** [sǽndwɪtʃ] s. bocadillo, emparedado, sandwich; *v.* intercalar, meter (entre).
**sandy** [sǽndɪ] *adj.* arenoso; arenisco; — **hair** pelo rojizo.
**sane** [sen] *adj.* sano, sensato; cuerdo.
**sang** [sæŋ] *pret. de* **to sing.**
**sanitarium** [sænətɛrɪəm] s. sanatorio.
**sanitary** [sǽnətɛrɪ] *adj.* sanitario.
**sanitation** [sænətéʃən] s. saneamiento; salubridad; sanidad.
**sanity** [sǽnətɪ] s. cordura.
**sank** [sæŋk] *pret. de* **to sink.**
**sap** [sæp] s. savia; tonto, bobo; *v.* agotar, debilitar, minar.
**sapling** [sǽplɪŋ] s. vástago, renuevo; arbolillo.
**sapphire** [sǽfaɪr] s. zafiro; color de zafiro.
**sarcasm** [sárkæzəm] s. sarcasmo.
**sarcastic** [sɑrkǽstɪk] *adj.* sarcástico.
**sardine** [sɑrdín] s. sardina.
**sardonic** [sɑrdánɪk] *adj.* burlón; sarcástico.
**sash** [sæʃ] s. faja (*cinturón de lana, seda o algodón*); banda, cinta ancha; **window** — bastidor (*o* marco) de ventana.
**sat** [sæt] *pret. & p.p. de* **to sit.**
**satchel** [sǽtʃəl] s. valija, maletín, maleta, saco.
**sate** [set] *v.* saciar.
**sateen** [sætín] s. satén o rasete (*raso de inferior calidad*).
**satellite** [sǽtl̩aɪt] s. satélite.
**satiate** [séʃɪet] *v.* saciar, hartar.
**satin** [sǽtn̩] s. raso.
**satire** [sǽtaɪr] s. sátira.
**satirical** [sətírɪkl̩] *adj.* satírico.
**satirize** [sǽtəraɪz] *v.* satirizar.
**satisfaction** [sætɪsfǽkʃən] s. satisfacción.
**satisfactorily** [sætɪsfǽktrəlɪ] *adv.* satisfactoriamente.
**satisfactory** [sætɪsfǽktrɪ] *adj.* satisfactorio.
**satisfied** [sǽtɪsfaɪd] *adj.* satisfecho, contento.
**satisfy** [sǽtɪsfaɪ] *v.* satisfacer.
**saturate** [sǽtʃəret] *v.* saturar, empapar.
**Saturday** [sǽtɚdɪ] s. sábado.
**sauce** [sɔs] s. salsa; — **dish** salsera; *v.* aderezar con salsa; sazonar, condimentar; insolentarse con.
**saucepan** [sɔ́spæn] s. cacerola.
**saucer** [sɔ́sɚ] s. platillo.
**sauciness** [sɔ́sɪnɪs] s. descaro, insolencia.
**saucy** [sɔ́sɪ] *adj.* descarado, respondón, insolente, *Am.* retobado.
**saunter** [sɔ́ntɚ] *v.* pasearse, vagar.
**sausage** [sɔ́sɪdʒ] s. salchicha, salchichón; longaniza; chorizo.

**savage** [sǽvɪdʒ] *adj.* salvaje; fiero; bárbaro, brutal, feroz; *s.* salvaje.
**savagery** [sǽvɪdʒrɪ] s. salvajismo; crueldad, fiereza.
**savant** [səvánt] s. sabio.
**save** [sev] *v.* (*rescue*) salvar; (*hoard*) ahorrar; economizar; (*keep*) guardar; resguardar; **to — from** librar de; **to — one's eyes** cuidarse la vista; *prep.* salvo, menos, excepto.
**saver** [sévɚ] s. salvador; libertador; ahorrador; **life—** salvavidas.
**saving** [sévɪŋ] *adj.* (*rescuer*) salvador; (*economizing*) ahorrativo, económico; frugal; *s.* ahorro, economía; **-s** ahorros; **-s bank** caja o banco de ahorros; *prep.* salvo, excepto, con excepción de.
**savior** [sévjɚ] s. salvador.
**savor** [sévɚ] s. sabor; dejo; *v.* saborear; sazonar; **to — of** saber a, tener el sabor de; **it -s of treason** huele a traición.
**savory** [sévərɪ] *adj.* sabroso.
**saw** [sɔ] s. sierra; **—horse** caballete; *v.* aserrar, serrar; **it -s easily** es fácil de aserrar; *pret. de* **to see.**
**sawdust** [sɔ́dʌst] s. aserrín, serrín.
**sawmill** [sɔ́mɪl] s. aserradero.
**sawn** [sɔn] *p.p. de* **to saw.**
**Saxon** [sǽksn̩] *adj. & s.* sajón.
**saxophone** [sǽksəfon] s. saxófono; saxofón.
**say** [se] *v.* decir; declarar; —! ¡diga! ¡oiga usted!; **that is to —** es decir; **to — one's prayers** rezar, decir o recitar sus oraciones; **to — the least** por lo menos; **it is said that** dizque, se dice que, dicen que; *s.* afirmación, aserto; **the final —** la autoridad decisiva; **to have a — in a matter** tener voz y voto en un asunto; **to have one's —** expresarse, dar su opinión.
**saying** [séɪŋ] s. dicho, refrán; aserto; **as the — goes** como dice el refrán.
**scab** [skæb] s. costra (*de una herida*); roña; esquirol (*obrero que sustituye a un huelguista*); obrero que acepta un jornal inferior; *v.* encostrarse (*una herida*), cubrirse de una costra.
**scabbard** [skǽbɚd] s. vaina, funda (*de espada, puñal, etc.*).
**scabby** [skǽbɪ] *adj.* costroso; roñoso, sarnoso, tiñoso.
**scabrous** [skébrəs] *adj.* escabroso.
**scaffold** [skǽfl̩d] s. andamio, tablado; patíbulo, cadalso.
**scaffolding** [skǽfl̩dɪŋ] s. andamiada (*Am.* andamiaje), andamios.
**scald** [skɔld] *v.* escaldar; **to — milk** calentar la leche hasta que suelte el hervor; *s.* escaldadura, quemadura.
**scale** [skel] s. escala; platillo de balanza; balanza; escama (*de pez o de la piel*); costra; **pair of -s** balanza; **platform —** báscula; *v.* escalar; subir, trepar por; graduar (*a escala*); medir según escala; pesar; escamar, quitar las escamas a; pelarse, despellejarse; descostrar(se); **to — down prices**

**SA**

rebajar proporcionalmente los precios.

**scallop** [skáləp] *s.* onda, pico (*adorno*); molusco bivalvo; **-s** festón (*recortes en forma de ondas o picos*); *v.* festonear, recortar en forma de ondas o picos; asar con salsa o migas de pan.

**scalp** [skælp] *s.* cuero cabelludo; *v.* desollar el cráneo; revender (*boletós, billetes*) a precio subido.

**scaly** [skélɪ] *adj.* escamoso, lleno de escamas; — **with rust** mohoso.

**scamp** [skæmp] *s.* pícaro, bribón, bellaco.

**scamper** [skǽmpɚ] *v.* correr, escabullirse, escaparse; *s.* escabullida, carrera, corrida.

**scan** [skæn] *v.* escudriñar; examinar, mirar detenidamente; echar un vistazo a (*en el habla popular*); medir (*el verso*).

**scandal** [skǽndḷ] *s.* escándalo; maledicencia, murmuración.

**scandalize** [skǽndḷaɪz] *v.* escandalizar, dar escándalo.

**scandalous** [skǽndḷəs] *adj.* escandaloso; difamatorio; vergonzoso.

**scant** [skænt] *adj.* escaso; corto; insuficiente; *v.* escatimar, limitar.

**scanty** [skǽntɪ] *adj.* escaso; insuficiente.

**scar** [skɑr] *s.* (*skin blemish*) cicatriz; costurón; (*mark*) raya, marca (*en una superficie pulida*); *v.* marcar, rayar; hacer o dejar una cicatriz en.

**scarce** [skɛrs] *adj.* escaso; raro; **-ly** *adv.* escasamente; apenas.

**scarcity** [skɛ́rsətɪ] *s.* escasez; carestía; insuficiencia.

**scare** [skɛr] *v.* espantar, asustar; alarmar; sobresaltar; **he -s easily** se asusta fácilmente; **to — away** ahuyentar, espantar; *s.* susto, sobresalto.

**scarecrow** [skɛ́rkro] *s.* espantajo; espantapájaros.

**scarf** [skɑrf] *s.* bufanda; mantilla; pañuelo (*para el cuello o la cabeza*); tapete (*para una mesa, tocador, etc.*).

**scarlet** [skɑ́rlɪt] *s.* escarlata; *adj.* de color escarlata; **— fever** escarlata, escarlatina.

**scary** [skɛ́rɪ] *adj.* espantadizo, asustadizo, miedoso.

**scat** [skæt] *interj.* ¡zape!

**scatter** [skǽtɚ] *v.* esparcir(se); desparramar(se); dispersar(se); **—brained** ligero de cascos, aturdido.

**scene** [sin] *s.* escena; escenario; decoración; vista; **to make a —** causar un escándalo.

**scenery** [sínɚɪ] *s.* paisaje, vista; **stage —** decoraciones.

**scent** [sɛnt] *s.* (*odor*) olor; (*substance*) perfume; (*trace*) pista, rastro; **to be on the — of** seguir el rastro de; **to have a keen —** tener buen olfato; *v.* oler, olfatear, ventear, husmear; perfumar.

**scepter** [séptɚ] *s.* cetro.

**sceptic** [sképtɪk] *adj.* & *s.* escéptico.

**scepticism** [sképtəsɪzəm] *s.* escepti-

cismo.

**schedule** [skédʒʊl] *s.* horario; itinerario (*de trenes*); lista, inventario (*adjunto a un documento*); *v.* fijar el día y la hora (*para una clase, conferencia, etc.*); establecer el itinerario para (*un tren o trenes*).

**scheme** [skim] *s.* (*plan*) esquema, plan, proyecto; empresa; (*plot*) ardid, trama, maquinación; **color —** combinación de colores; **metrical —** sistema de versificación; *v.* proyectar, urdir; maquinar, intrigar, tramar.

**schemer** [skímɚ] *s.* maquinador, intrigante; proyectista.

**scheming** [skímɪŋ] *adj.* maquinador, intrigante; *s.* maquinación.

**schism** [sɪzəm] *s.* cisma.

**schizophrenia** [skɪzofrínɪə] *s.* esquizofrenia.

**scholar** [skálɚ] *s.* escolar, estudiante; becario (*el que disfruta una beca*); erudito, docto.

**scholarly** [skálɚlɪ] *adj.* erudito, sabio, docto; *adv.* eruditamente, doctamente.

**scholarship** [skálɚʃɪp] *s.* saber; erudición; beca; **to have a —** disfrutar una beca.

**scholastic** [skolǽstɪk] *adj.* escolástico; escolar.

**school** [skul] *s.* escuela; **— of fish** banco de peces; *adj.* de escuela; **— day** día de escuela; **— board** consejo de enseñanza; *v.* enseñar, educar, instruir, aleccionar.

**schoolboy** [skúlbɔɪ] *s.* muchacho de escuela.

**schoolgirl** [skúlgɝl] *s.* muchacha de escuela.

**schoolhouse** [skúlhaʊs] *s.* escuela.

**schooling** [skúlɪŋ] *s.* instrucción; enseñanza, educación.

**schoolmaster** [skúlmæstɚ] *s.* maestro de escuela.

**schoolmate** [skúlmet] *s.* condiscípulo, compañero de escuela.

**schoolroom** [skúlrum] *s.* clase, aula.

**schoolteacher** [skúltitʃɚ] *s.* maestro de escuela.

**schooner** [skúnɚ] *s.* goleta; vaso grande para cerveza; **prairie —** galera con toldo.

**science** [sáɪəns] *s.* ciencia.

**scientific** [saɪəntífɪk] *adj.* científico; **-ally** *adv.* científicamente.

**scientist** [sáɪəntɪst] *s.* científico, hombre de ciencia.

**scintillate** [síntəlet] *v.* centellear; chispear.

**scion** [sáɪən] *s.* vástago.

**scissors** [sízɚz] *s. pl.* tijeras.

**sclerosis** [sklɚósɪs] *s.* esclerosis.

**scoff** [skɔf] *s.* mofa, burla, befa, escarnio; *v.* escarnecer; mofarse; **to — at** mofarse de, burlarse de, escarnecer a.

**scold** [skold] *v.* reñir, reprender, regañar; *s.* regañón, persona regañona.

**scolding** [skóldɪŋ] *s.* regaño, reprensión; *adj.* regañón.

**scoop** [skup] *s.* (*tool*) cuchara, cucharón;

pala; (*quantity*) palada, cucharada; (*winnings*) buen ganancia; **newspaper** — primera publicación de una noticia; *v.* cavar, excavar; ahuecar; cucharear, sacar con cucharón o pala; achicar (*agua*); **to — in a good profit** sacar buena ganancia.

**scoot** [skut] *v.* escabullirse, correr, irse a toda prisa; —! ¡largo de aquí!

**scooter** [skútəˠ] *s.* motoneta (*de motor*); monopatín.

**scope** [skop] *s.* alcance, extensión; esfera, campo.

**scorch** [skɔrtʃ] *v.* chamuscar; resecar, agostar; *s.* chamusquina, *Am.* chamuscada o chamuscadura.

**score** [skor] *s.* cuenta; escor (*en el juego*); raya, línea; calificación (*expresada numéricamente*); veintena; **musical —** partitura; **on that** — a ese respecto; **on the — of** a causa de, con motivo de; **to keep the —** llevar el escor, llevar la cuenta; **to settle old -s** desquitarse; *v.* marcar el escor, señalar los tantos en un juego; calificar (*numéricamente*); instrumentar (*música*); rayar, marcar con rayas; **to — a point** ganar un punto o tanto; **to — a success** lograr éxito, obtener un triunfo.

**scorn** [skɔrn] *s.* desdén, menosprecio; *v.* desdeñar, menospreciar.

**scornful** [skɔ́rnfəl] *adj.* desdeñoso.

**scorpion** [skɔ́rpɪən] *s.* escorpión, alacrán.

**Scotch** [skɑtʃ] *adj.* escocés; **the —** los escoceses, el pueblo escocés.

**scoundrel** [skáʊndrəl] *s.* bellaco, bribón, pícaro.

**scour** [skaʊr] *v.* fregar, restregar, limpiar; pulir; **to — the country** recorrer la comarca (*en busca de algo*).

**scourge** [skɝdʒ] *s.* azote; *v.* azotar; castigar.

**scout** [skaʊt] *s.* explorador (*usualmente militar*); **a good —** un buen explorador; una buena persona, un buen compañero; *v.* explorar; reconocer.

**scowl** [skaʊl] *s.* ceño; *v.* fruncir el ceño, mirar con ceño; poner mala cara.

**scramble** [skræmbl] *v.* (*move*) gatear; (*eggs*) hacer un revoltillo; (*mix up*) revolver, mezclar; **to — for something** forcejear por coger algo; pelearse por coger algo; **to — up** trepar o subir a gatas (*una cuesta*); **-d eggs** revoltillo, huevos, revueltos; *s.* revoltillo, confusión; pelea.

**scrap** [skræp] *s.* (*fragment*) fragmento, pedacito; migaja; (*fight*) riña, reyerta; **-s** sobras; desperdicios; desechos; retales; **—book** álbum de recortes; **— iron** recortes o desechos de hierro; *v.* desechar; tirar a la basura; descartar; pelear, reñir.

**scrape** [skrep] *v.* (*abrasively*) raspar; rasguñar; rascar; (*rub*) raer; rozar; **to — along** ir tirando, ir pasándola; **to — together** recoger o acumular poco a poco; **to bow and — ser**

muy servil; *s.* raspadura; rasguño; aprieto, dificultad, lío.

**scraper** [skrépəˠ] *s.* (*tool*) raspador; (*scrimping person*) tacaño.

**scratch** [skrætʃ] *v.* (*mark*) arañar, rasguñar; (*rub*) rascar; raspar; (*line*) rayar; escarbar; (*write badly*) hacer garabatos; **to — out** borrar, tachar; sacar (*los ojos*) con las uñas; *s.* arañazo, araño, rasguño; raya, marca; **to start from —** empezar sin nada; empezar desde el principio; empezar sin ventaja.

**scrawl** [skrɔl] *s.* garabato; *v.* hacer garabatos, escribir mal.

**scrawny** [skrɔ́nɪ] *adj.* huesudo, flaco.

**scream** [skrim] *s.* chillido, alarido, grito; **he's a —** es muy cómico o chistoso; *v.* chillar, gritar.

**screech** [skritʃ] *s.* chillido; **— owl** lechuza; *v.* chillar.

**screen** [skrin] *s.* (*projection*) pantalla; (*divider*) biombo; mampara; resguardo; (*sifter*) tamiz, cedazo; **—door** antepuerta de tela metálica; **motion-picture —** pantalla de cinematógrafo; **wire —** pantalla de tela metálica; *v.* tapar; resguardar, proteger con una pantalla o biombo; cerner; proyectar sobre la pantalla; filmar; **to — windows** proteger las ventanas con tela metálica.

**screw** [skru] *s.* tornillo; **— eye** armella; **— nut** tuerca; **— propeller** hélice; **— thread** rosca; *v.* atornillar; torcer, retorcer; **to — a lid on** atornillar una tapa; **to — up one's courage** cobrar ánimo.

**screwdriver** [skrúdraɪvəˠ] *s.* destornillador.

**scribble** [skríbl] *v.* garrapatear, hacer garabatos, borronear, escribir mal o de prisa; *s.* garabato.

**script** [skrɪpt] *s.* letra cursiva, escritura; manuscrito (*de un drama, de una película*).

**scripture** [skríptʃəˠ] *s.* escritura sagrada; **the Scriptures** la Sagrada Escritura, la Biblia.

**scroll** [skrol] *s.* rollo de pergamino o papel; voluta, adorno en espiral; rúbrica (*de una firma*).

**scrub** [skrʌb] *v.* fregar; restregar; *s.* friega, fregado; *adj.* achaparrado; bajo, inferior; **— oak** chaparro; **— pine** pino achaparrado; **— team** equipo de jugadores suplentes o menos bien entrenados; **— woman** fregona.

**scruple** [skrúpl] *s.* escrúpulo; *v.* escrupulizar, tener escrúpulos.

**scrupulous** [skrúpjələs] *adj.* escrupuloso.

**scrutinize** [skrútn̩aɪz] *v.* escudriñar, escrutar.

**scrutiny** [skrútn̩ɪ] *s.* escrutinio.

**scuff** [skʌf] *v.* raspar; arrastrar los pies.

**scuffle** [skʌ́fl] *s.* refriega, riña, pelea; *v.* forcejear; luchar, pelear; arrastrar los pies.

**sculptor** [skʌ́lptəˠ] *s.* escultor.

**SC**

**sculpture** [skʌ́lptʃɚ] *s.* escultura; *v.* esculpir, cincelar, tallar.

**scum** [skʌm] *s.* nata, capa, espuma; escoria; residuo, desechos; canalla, gente baja; *v.* espumar.

**scurry** [skɚ́ɪ] *v.* escabullirse; echar a correr; apresurarse; *s.* apresuramiento; corrida, carrera.

**scuttle** [skʌ́tl] *v.* echar a correr; barrenar (*un buque*); echar a pique; *s.* escotilla, escotillón; balde (*para carbón*).

**scythe** [saɪð] *s.* guadaña.

**sea** [si] *s.* mar; **to be at —** estar en el mar; estar perplejo o confuso; **to put to —** hacerse a la mar; *adj.* marino, marítimo, de mar; **— biscuit** galleta; **— green** verdemar; **— gull** gaviota; **— level** nivel del mar; **— lion** león marino, foca; **— power** potencia naval.

**seaboard** [síbord] *s.* costa, litoral; *adj.* costanero, litoral.

**seacoast** [síkost] *s.* costa, litoral.

**seal** [sil] *s.* (*stamp*) sello; timbre; (*animal*) foca, león marino; **to set one's —** to sellar; aprobar; *v.* sellar; estampar; cerrar; tapar; **to — in** encerrar, cerrar herméticamente; **to — with sealing wax** lacrar.

**sealing wax** [sílɪŋ wæks] *s.* lacre.

**seam** [sim] *s.* costura; juntura; cicatriz; filón, veta; *v.* echar una costura, coser.

**seaman** [símən] *s.* marino, marinero.

**seamstress** [símstrɪs] *s.* costurera.

**seaplane** [síplen] *s.* hidroavión.

**seaport** [síport] *s.* puerto de mar.

**sear** [sɪr] *v.* chamuscar(se), tostar(se); resecar(se); herrar, marcar con hierro candente; *adj.* reseco, marchito.

**search** [sɚtʃ] *v.* buscar; escudriñar; registrar; examinar; **to — a prisoner** registrar a un prisionero; **to — for something** buscar algo; **to — into** investigar, indagar; *s.* busca, búsqueda; registro, inspección; investigación, pesquisa, indagación; **— warrant** mandato judicial de practicar un registro; **in — of** en busca de.

**searchlight** [sɚ́tʃlaɪt] *s.* reflector.

**seashore** [síʃor] *s.* costa, playa, orilla o ribera del mar.

**seasick** [sísɪk] *adj.* mareado; **to get —** marearse.

**seasickness** [sísɪknɪs] *s.* mareo.

**seaside** [sísaɪd] *s.* costa, litoral; playa.

**season** [sízn̩] *s.* estación (*del año*); temporada; sazón, ocasión, tiempo; **— ticket** billete de abono; **Christmas —** navidades; **harvest —** siega, tiempo de la cosecha; **opera —** temporada de la ópera; **to arrive in good —** llegar en sazón, llegar a tiempo; *v.* sazonar; condimentar; aclimatar.

**seasoning** [sízn̩ɪŋ] *s.* condimento; salsa; desecación (*de la madera*).

**seat** [sit] *s.* (*furniture*) asiento; silla; (*site*) sitio; (*headquarters*) residencia; sede (*episcopal, del gobierno, etc.*); (*body*) nalgas; fondillos, parte trasera (*de los pantalones o calzones*); **— of learning** centro de estudios, centro de erudición; *v.* sentar; asentar; dar asiento a; **to — oneself** sentarse; **it -s a thousand people** tiene cabida para mil personas.

**seaweed** [síwid] *s.* alga marina.

**secede** [sisíd] *v.* separarse (*de una federación o unión*).

**seclude** [sɪklúd] *v.* recluir, apartar, aislar; **to — oneself from** recluirse de, apartarse de.

**secluded** [sɪklúdɪd] *adj.* apartado, aislado; solitario.

**seclusion** [sɪklúʒən] *s.* apartamiento, soledad, aislamiento; retiro.

**second** [sékənd] *adj.* segundo; inferior; **— hand** segundero (*de reloj*); **— lieutenant** subteniente; **second-rate** de segunda clase; mediocre, inferior; **on — thought** después de pensarlo bien; *s.* segundo; padrino (*en un desafío*); ayudante; mercancía de segunda calidad; mercancía defectuosa; *v.* secundar (*o segundar*), apoyar; apadrinar.

**secondary** [sékəndɪ] *adj.* secundario; **— education** segunda enseñanza; **— school** escuela secundaria, escuela de segunda enseñanza.

**second-hand** [sékəndhænd] *adj.* de segunda mano; usado; de ocasión; indirecto, por intermedio de otro.

**secondly** [sékəndlɪ] *adv.* en segundo lugar.

**secrecy** [síkrəsɪ] secreto, sigilo, reserva.

**secret** [síkrɪt] *s.* secreto; *adj.* secreto; escondido, oculto; **— service** policía secreta; **-ly** *adv.* secretamente, en secreto.

**secretariat** [sɛkrətǽrɪət] *s.* secretaría.

**secretary** [sékrətɛrɪ] *s.* secretario; escritorio (*con estantes para libros*).

**secrete** [sɪkrít] *v.* secretar (*una secreción*); esconder, ocultar.

**secretion** [sɪkríʃən] *s.* secreción.

**secretive** [sɪkrítɪv] *adj.* reservado, callado; **— gland** glándula secretoria.

**sect** [sɛkt] *s.* secta.

**section** [sékʃən] *s.* sección; trozo; tajada; región; barrio; *v.* seccionar, dividir en secciones.

**secular** [sékjələ] *adj. & s.* secular.

**secure** [sɪkjúr] *adj.* seguro; firme; *v.* asegurar; afianzar; obtener; resguardar; **-ly** *adv.* seguramente, con seguridad; firmemente.

**security** [sɪkjúrətɪ] *s.* seguridad; fianza, garantía, prenda; resguardo, protección; **securities** bonos, obligaciones, acciones, valores.

**sedan** [sɪdǽn] *s.* sedán.

**sedate** [sɪdét] *adj.* sosegado; tranquilo, sereno; serio.

**sedation** [sədéʃən] *d.* sedación.

**sedative** [sédətɪv] *adj. & s.* calmante, sedativo.

**sedentary** [sédn̩tɛrɪ] *adj.* sedentario; inactivo.

**sediment** [sédəmənt] *s.* sedimento, heces, residuo.

**sedition** [sɪdíʃən] s. sedición.
**seditious** [sɪdíʃəs] adj. sedicioso.
**seduce** [sɪdjús] v. seducir.
**seduction** [sɪdʌ́kʃən] s. seducción.
**see** [si] v. ver; — **that you do it** no deje Vd. de hacerlo; tenga Vd. cuidado de hacerlo; **I'll — to it** me encargaré de ello; **let me —** a ver; **to — a person home** acompañar a una persona a casa; **to — a person off** ir a la estación para despedir a una persona; **to — a person through a difficulty** ayudar a una persona a salir de un apuro; **to — through a person** adivinar lo que piensa una persona, darse cuenta de sus intenciones; **to — to one's affairs** atender a sus asuntos; **to have seen military service** haber servido en el ejército; s. sede, silla; **Holy See** Santa Sede.
**seed** [sid] s. (grains) semilla; (semen) simiente; (fruit) pepita; **to go to —** producir semillas; decaer, declinar; descuidar de su persona, andar desaseado; v. sembrar; despepitar, quitar las pepitas o semillas de; producir semillas.
**seedling** [sídlɪŋ] s. planta de semillero; arbolillo (de menos de tres pies de altura).
**seedy** [sídɪ] adj. semilloso, lleno de semillas; raído; desaseado.
**seek** [sik] v. buscar; pedir, solicitar; **to — after** buscar; **to — to** tratar de, esforzarse por.
**seem** [sim] v. parecer; **it -s to me** me parece.
**seemingly** [símɪŋlɪ] adv. aparentemente, en apariencia, al parecer.
**seemly** [símlɪ] adj. propio, decente, decoroso.
**seen** [sin] p.p. de **to see.**
**seep** [sip] v. escurrirse, rezumarse, colarse, filtrarse.
**seer** [sɪr] s. vidente, adivino, profeta.
**seethe** [sið] v. bullir, hervir; burbujear.
**segment** [ségmənt] s. segmento.
**segregate** [ségrəget] v. segregar.
**seize** [siz] v. (grasp) asir, coger, agarrar; apoderarse de; (arrest) prender o aprehender; (take advantage of) aprovecharse de; (capture) embargar, secuestrar; **to — upon** asir; **to become -d with fear** sobrecogerse de miedo.
**seizure** [síʒɚ] s. cogida; captura; aprehensión (de un criminal); secuestro, embargo (de bienes); ataque (de una enfermedad).
**seldom** [séldəm] adv. rara vez, raras veces, raramente.
**select** [səlékt] adj. selecto, escogido; v. elegir, escoger; entresacar.
**selection** [səlékʃən] s. selección, elección.
**self** [sɛlf]: **by one—** por sí, por sí mismo; **for one—** para sí; **one's other —** su otro yo; **his wife and —** su esposa y él (véase **herself, himself, ourselves, themselves,** etc.);
**self-centered** egoísta, egocéntrico;

**self-conscious** consciente de sí, cohibido, tímido; **self-control** dominio de sí mismo (o de sí propio); **self-defense** defensa propia; **self-denial** abnegación; **self-evident** patente, manifiesto; **self-esteem** respeto de sí mismo; amor propio; **self-government** gobierno autónomo, autonomía; gobierno democrático; **self-interest** propio interés; egoísmo; **self-love** amor propio; **self-possessed** sereno, dueño de sí, tranquilo; **self-sacrifice** abnegación; **self-satisfied** pagado de sí, satisfecho de sí.
**selfish** [sélfɪʃ] adj. egoísta; **-ly** adv. con egoísmo, por egoísmo.
**selfishness** [sélfɪʃnɪs] s. egoísmo.
**selfsame** [sélfsém] adj. mismo, idéntico, mismísimo.
**sell** [sɛl] v. vender; venderse, estar de venta; **to — at auction** vender en almoneda o subasta, subastar; **to — out** venderlo todo.
**seller** [sélɚ] s. vendedor.
**selves** [sɛlvz] pl. de **self.**
**semblance** [sémbləns] s. semejanza; apariencia.
**semicircle** [sémɚsəkl] s. semicírculo.
**semicolon** [sémɚkolən] s. punto y coma.
**seminary** [sémɚnɛrɪ] s. seminario.
**senate** [sénɪt] s. senado.
**senator** [sénɪtɚ] s. senador.
**send** [sɛnd] v. enviar; mandar; despachar; remitir, expedir; lanzar (una flecha, pelota, etc.); **to — away** despedir, despachar; **to — forth** despachar, enviar; emitir; exhalar; echar; **to — someone up for 15 years** condenar a un reo a 15 años de prisión; **to — word** avisar, mandar decir, mandar recado.
**sender** [séndɚ] s. remitente; transmisor.
**senile** [sínaɪl] adj. senil, caduco; chocho.
**senility** [sənílətɪ] s. senectud; chochera o chochez.
**senior** [sínjɚ] adj. (older) mayor, de más edad; más antiguo; (superior) superior; **— class** clase del cuarto año; s. persona o socio más antiguo; estudiante del último año; **to be somebody's — by two years** ser dos años mayor que alguien.
**sensation** [sɛnséʃən] s. sensación.
**sensational** [sɛnséʃənl] adj. sensacional; emocionante.
**sense** [sɛns] s. (function) sentido; (sentiment) sentimiento; sensación; (judgment) juicio, sensatez; (meaning) significado; **common — sentido** común; **to make —** tener sentido; **to be out of one's -s** estar fuera de sí, estar loco; v. percibir, sentir; darse cuenta de.
**senseless** [sénslɪs] adj. sin sentido; insensato, absurdo; insensible, privado de sentido.
**sensibility** [sɛnsəbílətɪ] s. sensibilidad.
**sensible** [sénsəbl] adj. (aware) sensato,

**SC**

razonable, cuerdo; (*appreciable*) sensible, perceptible; **sensibly** *adv.* sensatamente, con sensatez, con sentido común; sensiblemente, perceptiblemente.

**sensitive** [sɛ́nsətɪv] *adj.* sensitivo; sensible; quisquilloso, susceptible.

**sensitiveness** [sɛ́nsətɪvnɪs] *s.* sensibilidad.

**sensitize** [sɛ́nsətaɪz] *v.* sensibilizar.

**sensual** [sɛ́nʃuəl] *adj.* sensual, carnal, lujurioso.

**sensuality** [sɛnʃuǽlətɪ] *s.* sensualidad; lujuria.

**sent** [sɛnt] *pret.* & *p.p. de* to send.

**sentence** [sɛ́ntəns] *s.* sentencia, fallo, decisión; oración (*gramatical*); **death —** pena capital; *v.* sentenciar.

**sentiment** [sɛ́ntəmənt] *s.* sentimiento; sentido.

**sentimental** [sɛntəmɛ́ntl̩] *adj.* sentimental.

**sentimentality** [sɛntəmɛntǽlətɪ] *s.* sentimentalismo, sentimentalidad.

**sentinel** [sɛ́ntənl̩] *s.* centinela.

**sentry** [sɛ́ntrɪ] *s.* centinela.

**separate** [sɛ́prɪt] *adj.* (*apart*) separado; apartado; solitario; (*different*) distinto, diferente; **-ly** *adv.* separadamente, por separado; aparte; [sɛ́pəret] *v.* separar(se); apartar(se).

**separation** [sɛpəréʃən] *s.* separación.

**September** [sɛptɛ́mbɚ] *s.* septiembre.

**sepulcher** [sɛ́plkɚ] *s.* sepulcro, sepultura.

**sequel** [síkwəl] *s.* secuela; continuación, consecuencia; resultado.

**sequence** [síkwəns] *s.* (*continuity*) secuencia, sucesión; serie, continuación; (*result*) consecuencia, resultado; runfla (*serie de tres o más naipes de un mismo palo*).

**serenade** [sɛrənéd] *s.* serenata; *v.* dar serenata a.

**serene** [sərín] *adj.* sereno; tranquilo; claro, despejado.

**serenity** [sərénətɪ] *s.* serenidad; calma.

**sergeant** [sárdʒənt] *s.* sargento; **— at arms** oficial que guarda el orden (*en un cuerpo legislativo*).

**serial** [síriəl] *s.* cuento o novela por entregas; *adj.* consecutivo, en serie; **— novel** novela por entregas.

**series** [síriz] *s.* serie; series.

**serious** [síriəs] *adj.* serio; grave; **-ly** *adv.* seriamente, con seriedad, en serio; gravemente.

**seriousness** [síriəsnɪs] *s.* seriedad; gravedad.

**sermon** [sɚ́mən] *s.* sermón.

**serpent** [sɚ́pənt] *s.* serpiente; sierpe.

**serum** [sírəm] *s.* suero.

**servant** [sɚ́vənt] *s.* sirviente; criado; servidor; **— girl** criada, *Ríopl.* mucama; *Andes, Col., Ven.* muchacha de servicio.

**serve** [sɚv] *v.* (*wait on*) servir; (*supply*) surtir, abastecer; **to — a term in prison** cumplir una condena; **to — a warrant** entregar una citación; **to — as** servir de; **to — for** servir de,

servir para; **to — notice on** notificar, avisar, advertir; **to — one's purpose** servir para el caso o propósito; **it -s me right** bien me lo merezco; *s.* saque (*de la pelota en tenis*).

**server** [sɚ́vɚ] *s.* servidor; saque (*el que saca la pelota en el juego de tenis*); bandeja; mesa de servicio.

**service** [sɚ́vɪs] *s.* servicio; saque (*de la pelota en tenis*); entrega (*de una citación judicial*); **at your —** a la disposición de Vd., servidor de Vd.; **funeral —** honras fúnebres, funerales, exequias; **mail —** servicio de correos; **table —** servicio de mesa, vajilla; **tea —** juego o servicio de té; **— entrance** entrada para el servicio; **— man** militar; **— station** estación de servicio; *v.* servir; reparar; surtir (*una tienda*).

**serviceable** [sɚ́vɪsəbl̩] *adj.* servible; útil; duradero.

**servile** [sɚ́vl̩] *adj.* servil.

**servitude** [sɚ́vətjud] *s.* servidumbre; esclavitud.

**session** [sɛ́ʃən] *s.* sesión.

**set** [sɛt] *v.* (*place*) poner; colocar, asentar; (*fix*) fijar; establecer; ajustar; engastar (*piedras preciosas*); solidificar(se), endurecer(se) (*el cemento, yeso, etc.*); ponerse (*el sol, la luna*); empollar; **to — a bone** componer un hueso dislocado; **to — a trap** armar una trampa; **to — about** ponerse a; **to — an example** dar ejemplo; **to — aside** poner a un lado, poner aparte; apartar; ahorrar; **to — back** retrasar, atrasar; **to — forth** exponer, expresar; manifestar; **to — forth on a journey** ponerse en camino; **to — off** disparar, hacer estallar (*unexplosivo*); hacer resaltar; salir; **to — on fire** pegar o poner fuego a, incendiar; **to — one's jaw** apretar las quijadas; **to — one's heart on** tener la esperanza puesta en; **to — one's mind on** resolverse a, aplicarse a; **to — out for** partir para, salir para; **to — out to** empezar a; **to — right** colocar bien; enderezar; rectificar; **to — sail** hacerse a la vela; **to — the brake** frenar, apretar el freno; **to — up** erigir, levantar; armar, montar (*una máquina*); parar (*tipo de imprenta*); establecer, poner (*una tienda, un negocio*); **to — upon someone** acometer, asaltar a alguien; *pret.* & *p.p. de* to set; *adj.* fijo; firme; sólido; resuelto; rígido; puesto; establecido; engastado; **— to go** listo para partir; *s.* juego, colección; serie; grupo, clase; partida (*de tenis*); **— of dishes** servicio de mesa, vajilla; **— of teeth** dentadura; **radio —** radio, radiorreceptor; **tea —** servicio para té.

**setback** [sɛ́tbæk] *s.* atraso, revés, retroceso inesperado.

**settee** [sɛtí] *s.* canapé.

**setting** [sɛ́tɪŋ] *s.* engaste (*de una joya*); escena, escenario; puesta (*del sol, de un astro*); **— sun** sol poniente.

**settle** [sétl] *v.* (*colonize*) colonizar, poblar; establecer(se); fijar(se); asentar(se); (*solve*) arreglar, poner en orden, ajustar (*cuentas*); zanjar (*una disputa*); pagar, liquidar, saldar; **to — down** formalizarse; asentarse; calmarse; poner casa; **to — on a date** fijar o señalar una fecha; **to — property on** (**upon**) asignar bienes o propiedad a; **to — the matter** decidir el asunto, concluir con el asunto.

**settlement** [sétlmənt] *s.* (*community*) establecimiento; colonia; poblado; población; colonización; (*arrangement*) asignación o traspaso (*de propiedad*); ajuste, arreglo; pago; saldo, finiquito, liquidación; **— house** casa de beneficencia; **marriage —** dote.

**settler** [sétlɚ] *s.* colono, poblador; **— of disputes** zanjador de disputas.

**setup** [sétəp] *s.* arreglo; organización.

**sever** [sévɚ] *v.* desunir(se), partir(se), dividir(se), separar(se); cortar, romper.

**several** [sévrəl] *adj.* varios, diversos; distintos, diferentes.

**severe** [səvír] *adj.* severo; áspero; austero; rígido; riguroso; grave; recio, fuerte.

**severity** [səvérətɪ] *s.* severidad; austeridad; rigidez; gravedad; rigor.

**sew** [so] *v.* coser.

**sewer** [sjúɚ] *s.* albañal, cloaca.

**sewing** [sóɪŋ] *s.* costura; modo de coser; **— machine** máquina de coser; **— room** cuarto de costura.

**sewn** [son] *p.p. de* **to sew.**

**sex** [sɛks] *s.* sexo; **— appeal** atracción sexual.

**sextant** [sékstənt] *s.* sextante.

**sexton** [sékstən] *s.* sacristán.

**sexual** [sékʃʊəl] *adj.* sexual.

**shabby** [ʃǽbɪ] *adj.* raído, gastado; andrajoso; mal vestido; vil, injusto; **to treat someone shabbily** tratar a alguien injustamente o con menosprecio.

**shack** [ʃæk] *s.* cabaña, choza, *Am.* bohío, *Am.* jacal.

**shackle** [ʃǽkl] *v.* encadenar; trabar, echar trabas a, poner grillos a; estorbar; **-s** *s. pl.* cadenas, trabas, grillos; esposas; estorbo.

**shade** [ʃed] *s.* (*shadow*) sombra; (*nuance*) tinte, matiz; (*cover*) visillo, cortinilla; pantalla (*de lámpara*); visera (*para los ojos*); **a — longer** un poco más largo; **— of meaning** matiz; **in the — of** a la sombra de; *v.* sombrear; dar sombra; resguardar de la luz; matizar.

**shadow** [ʃǽdo] *s.* (*darkness*) sombra; oscuridad; (*phantom*) espectro; **under the — of** al abrigo de, a la sombra de; **without a — of doubt** sin sombra de duda; *v.* sombrear; obscurecer; **to — someone** espiarle a alguien los pasos, seguirle por todas partes.

**shadowy** [ʃǽdəwɪ] *adj.* lleno de sombras; tenebroso; vago, indistinto.

**shady** [ʃédɪ] *adj.* sombrío, sombreado, umbrío; **— business** negocio sospechoso; **— character** persona de carácter dudoso, persona de mala fama.

**shaft** [ʃæft] *s.* pozo o tiro (*de mina, de elevador*); cañón de chimenea; columna; eje, árbol (*de maquinaria*); flecha.

**shaggy** [ʃǽgɪ] *adj.* peludo, velludo; lanudo; desaseado; áspero.

**shake** [ʃek] *v.* menear(se); estremecer(se); temblar; sacudir(se); agitar(se); titubear, vacilar; hacer vacilar; dar, estrechar (*la mano*); **to — hands** dar un apretón de manos, darse la mano; **to — one's head** mover o menear la cabeza; cabecear; **to — with cold** tiritar de frío, estremecerse de frío; **to — with fear** temblar de miedo, estremecerse de miedo; *s.* sacudida; sacudimiento; estremecimiento, temblor; apretón (*de manos*); **hand— shake** apretón de manos.

**shaken** [ʃékən] *p.p. de* **to shake.**

**shake-up** [ʃékəp] *s.* reorganización.

**shaky** [ʃékɪ] *adj.* tembloroso; vacilante.

**shall** [ʃæl] *v. aux. del futuro del indicativo en las primeras personas* (**I, we**); *en las demás expresa mayor énfasis, mandato u obligación*; **he — not do it** no lo hará, no ha de hacerlo; **thou shalt not steal** no hurtarás.

**shallow** [ʃǽlo] *adj.* bajo, poco profundo; superficial; ligero de cascos.

**shallowness** [ʃǽlonɪs] *s.* poca hondura, poca profundidad; superficialidad; ligereza de juicio.

**sham** [ʃæm] *s.* fingimiento, falsedad, farsa; *adj.* fingido, simulado; falso; **— battle** simulacro, batalla fingida; *v.* fingir, simular.

**shambles** [ʃǽmblz] *s.* desorden.

**shame** [ʃem] *s.* vergüenza; deshonra; **— on you!** ¡qué vergüenza!; **it is a —** es una vergüenza; es una lástima; **to bring — upon** deshonrar; *v.* avergonzar; deshonrar.

**shameful** [ʃémfəl] *adj.* vergonzoso.

**shameless** [ʃémlɪs] *adj.* desvergonzado, descarado.

**shamelessness** [ʃémlɪsnɪs] *s.* desvergüenza; descaro, desfachatez.

**shampoo** [ʃæmpú] *s.* champú, lavado de la cabeza; *v.* dar un champú, lavar (*la cabeza*).

**shamrock** [ʃǽmrɑk] *s.* trébol.

**shank** [ʃæŋk] *s.* canilla (*parte inferior de la pierna*); zanca.

**shanty** [ʃǽntɪ] *s.* choza, cabaña, casucha.

**shape** [ʃep] *s.* (*form*) forma; (*figure*) figura; (*condition*) estado, condición; **to be in a bad —** estar mal; **to put into —** arreglar, poner en orden, ordenar; *v.* formar, dar forma a; tomar forma; **to — one's life** dar forma a, ajustar o disponer su vida; **his plan is shaping well** va desarrollándose bien su plan.

**shapeless** [ʃéplɪs] *adj.* informe, sin forma.

**share** [ʃɛr] *s.* (*portion*) porción, parte;

SE

(*participation*) participación; acción (*participación en el capital de una compañía*); v. compartir; repartir; participar; **to — in** participar en, tener parte en; **to — a thing with** compartir una cosa con.

**shareholder** [ʃérholdɚ] s. accionista.

**shark** [ʃɑrk] s. (*fish*) tiburón; (*usurer*) estafador; (*expert*) perito, experto; **loan —** usurero; **to be a — at** ser un águila (o ser muy listo) para.

**sharp** [ʃɑrp] adj. (*acute*) agudo, puntiagudo; cortante; punzante; (*biting*) mordaz; picante; (*bright*) astuto; (*clear*) claro, distinto, bien marcado; (*sudden*) repentino; **— curve** curva abrupta, curva pronunciada o muy cerrada; **— ear** oídofino; **— features** facciones bien marcadas; **— struggle** lucha violenta; **— taste** sabor acre; **— temper** genio áspero; **— turn** vuelta repentina; s. sostenido (*en música*); **card—** tahur, fullero; adv. véase **sharply**; **at ten o'clock —** a las diez en punto.

**sharpen** [ʃárpən] v. afilar(se); sacar punta a; aguzar(se); amolar.

**sharply** [ʃárpli] adv. agudamente; mordazmente, ásperamente; repentinamente; claramente; **to arrive —** llegar en punto.

**sharpness** [ʃárpnɪs] s. agudeza; sutileza; mordacidad; rigor; aspereza; acidez.

**shatter** [ʃǽtɚ] v. estrellar(se), astillar(se), hacer(se) añicos; quebrar(se), romper(se); **to — one's hopes** frustrar sus esperanzas; **his health was -ed** se le quebrantó la salud; **-s** s. pl. pedazos, trozos, añicos, fragmentos; **to break into —** hacer(se) añicos.

**shave** [ʃev] v. afeitar(se), rasurar(se); rapar(se); acepillar (*madera*); s. rasura, *Am.* afeitada; **he had a close —** por poco no se escapa; se salvó por milagro.

**shaven** [ʃévən] p.p. de **to shave; cleanshaven** bien afeitado.

**shaving** [ʃévɪŋ] s. rasura, *Am.* afeitada; **wood -s** virutas; **— brush** brocha de afeitar; **— soap** jabón de afeitar.

**shawl** [ʃɔl] s. mantón, chal.

**she** [ʃi] pron. pers. ella; **— who** la que; s. hembra; **she-bear** osa; **she-goat** cabra.

**sheaf** [ʃif] s. haz, gavilla, manojo; lío; v. hacer gavillas.

**shear** [ʃɪr] v. trasquilar, esquilar (*las ovejas*); cortar (*con tijeras grandes*).

**shears** [ʃɪrz] s. pl. tijeras grandes.

**sheath** [ʃiθ] s. vaina; funda, envoltura.

**sheathe** [ʃið] v. envainar.

**sheaves** [ʃivz] pl. de **sheaf.**

**shed** [ʃed] s. cobertizo; tejadillo; *Ríopl., Andes* galpón (*de una estancia*); v. derramar; difundir; esparcir; mudar (*de piel plumas, etc.*); ser impermeable (*un paño, abrigo, sombrero, etc.*); **to — leaves** deshojarse; pret. & p.p. de **to shed.**

**sheen** [ʃin] s. lustre, viso.

**sheep** [ʃip] s. oveja; carnero; ovejas; **— dog** perro de pastor; **—fold** redil; **—skin** zalea; badana; pergamino; diploma (*de pergamino*).

**sheepish** [ʃipɪʃ] adj. vergonzoso, encogido, tímido.

**sheer** [ʃɪr] adj. (*pure*) pure; completo; (*thin*) fino, delgado, transparente, diáfano; (*steep*) escarpado; **by — force** a pura fuerza.

**sheet** [ʃit] s. (*bed*) sábana; (*paper*) hoja, pliego (*de papel*); lámina (*de metal*); extensión (*de agua, hielo*); **— lightning** relampagueo.

**shelf** [ʃelf] s. estante, anaquel; repisa; saliente de roca.

**shell** [ʃel] s. concha; cáscara (*de huevo, nuez, etc.*); vaina (*de guisantes, frijoles, garbanzos, etc.*); casco (*de una embarcación*); armazón (*de un edificio*); granada, bomba; cápsula (*para cartuchos*); v. cascar (*nueces*); desvainar, quitar la vaina a, pelar; desgranar (*maíz, trigo, etc.*); bombardear.

**shellac** [ʃəlǽk] s. laca; v. barnizar con laca.

**shellfish** [ʃélfɪʃ] s. marisco; mariscos.

**shelter** [ʃéltɚ] s. abrigo, refugio, asilo; resguardo, protección; **to take —** refugiarse, abrigarse; v. abrigar, refugiar, guarecer; proteger, amparar.

**shelve** [ʃelv] v. poner o guardar en un estante; poner a un lado, arrinconar, arrumbar.

**shelves** [ʃelvz] s. pl. estantes, anaqueles; estantería.

**shepherd** [ʃépɚd] s. pastor; zagal; **— dog** perro de pastor.

**sherbet** [ʃɚ́bɪt] s. sorbete.

**sheriff** [ʃérɪf] s. alguacil mayor (*de un condado en los Estados Unidos*).

**sherry** [ʃérɪ] s. jerez, vino de Jerez.

**shield** [ʃild] s. escudo, rodela, broquel; resguardo, defensa; v. escudar, resguardar, proteger.

**shift** [ʃɪft] v. (*change*) cambiar; mudar(se); alternar(se); variar; desviar(se); (*transfer*) trasladar, transferir; **to — for oneself** valerse o mirar por sí mismo; **to — gears** cambiar de marcha; **to — the blame** echar a otro su propio culpa; s. cambio; desvío, desviación; tanda, grupo de obreros; turno; **gear—** cambio de marcha.

**shiftless** [ʃíftlɪs] adj. negligente; holgazán.

**shilling** [ʃílɪŋ] s. chelín.

**shimmy** [ʃími] s. (*dance*) shimmy; (*vibration*) abaniqueo.

**shin** [ʃɪn] s. espinilla (*de la pierna*); v. **to — up** trepar.

**shine** [ʃaɪn] v. (*beam*) brillar, resplandecer, lucir; (*polish*) pulir; dar brillo, lustre o bola, embolar (zapatos); s. brillo, lustre, resplandor; **rain or —** llueva o truene; **to give a shoe —** dar bola (brillo o lustre) a los zapatos; embolar o embetunar los zapatos; limpiar el calzado.

**shingle** [ʃíŋgl] s. ripia, tabla delgada, *Méx.* tejamanil o tejamaní; pelo corto escalonado; letrero de oficina; **-s** zona (*erupcion de la piel*); *v.* cubrir con tejamaniles; techar con tejamaniles.

**shining** [ʃáɪnɪŋ] *adj.* brillante; resplandeciente.

**shiny** [ʃáɪnɪ] *adj.* brillante; lustroso.

**ship** [ʃɪp] *s.* (*naval*) buque, barco, navío, nave; (*air*) aeronave, avión; **—builder** ingeniero naval, constructor de buques; **—mate** camarada de a bordo **—yard** astillero; **on —board** a bordo; *v.* embarcar(se); despachar, enviar; remesar; transportar; alistarse como marino.

**shipment** [ʃípmənt] *s.* embarque; cargamento; despacho, envío; remesa.

**shipper** [ʃípɚ] *s.* embarcador; remitente.

**shipping** [ʃípɪŋ] *s.* embarque; despacho, envío; **— charges** gastos de embarque; **— clerk** dependiente de muelle; dependiente encargado de embarques.

**shipwreck** [ʃíprɛk] *s.* naufragio; *v.* echar a pique, hacer naufragar; naufragar, irse a pique.

**shipyard** [ʃípyard] *s.* astillero.

**shirk** [ʃɝk] *v.* evadir, evitar.

**shirt** [ʃɝt] *s.* camisa; **—waist** blusa; **in — sleeves** en camisa, en mangas de camisa.

**shiver** [ʃívɚ] *v.* tiritar; temblar; estremecerse; *s.* escalofrío, temblor, estremecimiento.

**shoal** [ʃol] *s.* bajío, banco de arena; banco (*de peces*).

**shock** [ʃak] *s.* (*blow*) choque; sacudida; sacudimiento; golpe; (*surprise*) sobresalto; **— absorber** amortiguador; **— of grain** hacina o gavilla de mieses; **— of hair** guedeja, greña; **— troops** tropas de asalto; *v.* chocar, ofender; escandalizar; causar fuerte impresión; horrorizar; sacudir; conmover; hacinar, hacer gavillas de (*mieses*).

**shocking** [ʃákɪŋ] *adj.* chocante, ofensivo, repugnante; espantoso, escandaloso.

**shod** [ʃad] *pret. & p.p. de* **to shoe.**

**shoe** [ʃu] *s.* zapato; botín; **brake —** zapata de freno; **horse—** herradura; **— blacking** betún, bola; **— polish** brillo, lustre, bola; **— store** zapatería; *v.* calzar; herrar (*un caballo*).

**shoeblack** [ʃúblæk] *s.* limpiabotas.

**shoehorn** [ʃúhɔrn] *s.* calzador.

**shoelace** [ʃúles] *s.* lazo, cinta, cordón de zapato.

**shoemaker** [ʃúmekɚ] *s.* zapatero.

**shoestring** [ʃústrɪŋ] *s.* lazo, cinta, cordón de zapato.

**shone** [ʃon] *pret. & p.p. de* **to shine.**

**shook** [ʃuk] *pret. de* **to shake.**

**shoot** [ʃut] *v.* (*firearm*) tirar, disparar; descargar; hacer fuego; fusilar; dar un balazo; (*throw*) lanzar, disparar (*una instantánea*); fotografiar, filmar (*una escena*); echar (*los dados*); brotar (*las plantas*); **to — by** pasar rápidamente; **to — forth** brotar, salir; germinar; lanzarse; **to — it out with someone** pelearse a balazos; **to — up**

**a place** entrarse a balazos por un lugar; *s.* vástago, retoño, renuevo; **to go out for a —** salir a tirar; ir de caza.

**shooter** [ʃútɚ] *s.* tirador.

**shooting** [ʃútɪŋ] *s.* tiroteo; **— match** certamen de tiradores (*o de tiro al blanco*); **— pain** punzada, dolor agudo; **— star** estrella fugaz.

**shop** [ʃap] *s.* tienda; taller; **— window** escaparate, vitrina, aparador, *Ríopl.*, *Andes* vidriera; **barber—** barbería; **beauty —** salón de belleza; **to talk —** hablar uno de su oficio o profesión; *v.* ir de tiendas; ir de compras, comprar.

**shopkeeper** [ʃápkipɚ] *s.* tendero.

**shopper** [ʃápɚ] *s.* comprador.

**shopping** [ʃápɪŋ] *s.* compra, compras; **to go —** ir de compras, ir de tiendas.

**shore** [ʃor] *s.* costa, playa, orilla, ribera; puntal; **ten miles off —** a diez millas de la costa; *v.* **to — up** apuntalar, poner puntales.

**shorn** [ʃorn] *p.p. de* **to shear.**

**short** [ʃɔrt] *adj.* (*duration*) corto; breve; (*height*) bajo; *Méx.* chaparro; escaso; brusco; **— cut** atajo; **— circuit** cortocircuito; **— wave** onda corta; método corto; **short-legged** de piernas cortas; **— loan** préstamo a corto plazo; **for —** para abreviar; **in —** en resumen, en suma, en conclusión; **in — order** rápidamente, prontamente; **in a — time** en poco tiempo; al poco tiempo; **to be — of** estar falto o escaso de; **to cut —** acortar, abreviar; terminar de repente; **to run — of something** acabársele (írsele acabando) a uno algo; **to stop —** parar de repente, parar en seco.

**shortage** [ʃórtɪdʒ] *s.* escasez, carestía; déficit; falta.

**shortcoming** [ʃórtkʌmɪŋ] *s.* falta, defecto.

**shorten** [ʃórtn̩] *v.* acortar(se), abreviar(se), disminuir(se).

**shortening** [ʃórtnɪŋ] *s.* manteca, grasa (*para hacer pasteles*); acortamiento; abreviación.

**shorthand** [ʃórthænd] *s.* taquigrafía.

**shortly** [ʃórtlɪ] *adj.* brevemente; en breve; al instante, pronto, luego; bruscamente, secamente.

**shortness** [ʃórtnɪs] *s.* cortedad; brevedad; pequeñez; escasez, deficiencia.

**shorts** [ʃɔrts] *s. pl.* calzoncillos, calzones cortos.

**shortsighted** [ʃórtsáɪtɪd] *adj.* miope; corto de vista.

**shot** [ʃat] *pret. & p.p. de* **to shoot;** *s.* (*discharge*) tiro; disparo; balazo; cañonazo; (*pellet*) bala; balas; (*injection*) inyección; (*throw*) tirada; **— of liquor** trago de aguardiente; **buck—** municiones, postas; **not by a long —** ni con mucho, ni por pienso, nada de eso; **he is a good —** es buen tirador, tiene buen tino; **to take a — at** disparar un tiro a; hacer una tentativa de; **within rifle —** a tiro de rifle.

**shotgun** [ʃátgʌn] *s.* escopeta.

**SH**

**should** [ʃud] *v. aux. del condicional en las primeras personas* (**I, we**): **I said that I — go** dije que iría; *equivale al imperfecto de subjuntivo*; **if it — rain** si lloviera; *se usa con la significación de deber*: **you — not do it** no debiera (*o* no debería) hacerlo.

**shoulder** [ʃóldər] *s.* (*person*) hombro; (*animal*) lomo, pernil (*de puerco, cordero*); borde, saliente (*de un camino*); **-s** espalda, espaldas; **— blade** espaldilla, paletilla; **straight from the —** con toda franqueza; **to turn a cold — to** volver las espaldas a, tratar fríamente; *v.* cargar al hombro, echarse sobre las espaldas; cargar con, asumir; empujar con el hombro.

**shout** [ʃaut] *v.* gritar; vocear; *s.* grito.

**shove** [ʃʌv] *v.* empujar, dar empellones; **to — aside** echar a un lado, rechazar; **to — off** partir, zarpar (*un buque*); salir, irse; *s.* empujón, empellón; empuje.

**shovel** [ʃʌvl] *s.* pala; *v.* traspalar.

**show** [ʃo] *v.* (*exhibit*) mostrar, enseñar; exhibir; (*prove*) probar, demostrar; indicar; (*appear*) verse; asomarse; **— him in** que pase, hágale entrar; **to — off** alardear, hacer ostentación de; lucirse; **to — up** aparecer, presentarse; **to — someone up** hacer subir a alguien; mostrarle el camino (*para subir*); desenmascarar a alguien, poner a alguien en la evidencia; *s.* exhibición; demostración; ostentación; espectáculo; representación; función; apariencia; **— window** escaparate, vitrina, aparador, *Am.* vidriera; **to go to the —** ir al teatro, ir al cine; **to make a — of oneself** exhibirse, hacer ostentación.

**showcase** [ʃókes] *s.* vitrina, aparador.

**showdown** [ʃódaun] *s.* arreglo terminante.

**shower** [ʃáuər] *s.* aguacero, chubasco, chaparrón, lluvia; ducha, baño de ducha; *Méx.* regadera; **bridal —** tertulia para obsequiar a una novia; *v.* llover; caer un aguacero.

**shown** [ʃon] *p.p. de* **to show**.

**showy** [ʃói] *adj.* ostentoso; vistoso, chillón.

**shrank** [ʃræŋk] *pret. de* **to shrink**.

**shred** [ʃrɛd] *s.* tira, triza; andrajo; fragmento; pizca; **to be in -s** estar raído; estar andrajoso; estar hecho trizas; **to tear to -s** hacer trizas; *v.* desmenuzar; hacer trizas, hacer tiras; *pret. & p.p. de* **shred**.

**shrew** [ʃru] *s.* arpía, mujer brava, mujer de mal genio.

**shrewd** [ʃrud] *adj.* astuto, sagaz, agudo.

**shriek** [ʃrik] *v.* chillar, gritar; *s.* chillido, grito.

**shrill** [ʃrɪl] *adj.* agudo, penetrante, chillón; *v.* chillar.

**shrimp** [ʃrɪmp] *s.* camarón; hombrecillo insignificante.

**shrine** [ʃraɪn] *s.* santuario; altar; lugar venerado.

**shrink** [ʃrɪŋk] *v.* encoger(se); contraer-(se); disminuir; **to — back** retroceder; **to — from** retroceder ante, apartarse de; huir de, rehuir.

**shrinkage** [ʃrínkɪdʒ] *s.* encogimiento; contracción; merma.

**shrivel** [ʃrívl] *v.* encoger(se); fruncir(se), marchitar(se); disminuir(se).

**shroud** [ʃraud] *s.* mortaja; *v.* amortajar; cubrir, ocultar.

**shrub** [ʃrʌb] *s.* arbusto.

**shrubbery** [ʃrʌbərɪ] *s.* arbustos.

**shrug** [ʃrʌg] *v.* encogerse de hombros; *s.* encogimiento de hombros.

**shrunk** [ʃrʌŋk] *pret. & p.p. de* **to shrink**.

**shrunken** [ʃrʌŋkən] *p.p. de* **to shrink**.

**shuck** [ʃʌk] *s.* hollejo; cáscara.

**shudder** [ʃʌdər] *v.* temblar, estremecerse; *s.* temblor, estremecimiento.

**shuffle** [ʃʌfl] *v.* barajar; revolver, mezclar; arrastrar (*los pies*); **to — along** ir arrastrando los pies; *s.* mezcla, confusión; evasiva; **— of feet** arrastramiento de pies; **it is your —** a Vd. le toca barajar.

**shun** [ʃʌn] *v.* esquivar, evadir, rehuir, evitar.

**shut** [ʃʌt] *v.* cerrar(se); **to — down** parar el trabajo; cerrar (*una fábrica*); **to — in** encerrar; **to — off** cortar (*el gas, la electricidad, el agua, etc.*); **to — off from** incomunicar, aislar de, cortar la comunicación con; excluir; **to — out** impedir la entrada de; cerrar la puerta a; **to — up** cerrar bien; tapar; encerrar; tapar la boca, hacer callar; callarse; *pret. & p.p. de* **to shut**; *adj.* cerrado.

**shutter** [ʃʌtər] *s.* contraventana; postigo (*de ventana*); cerrador; obturador (*de una cámara fotográfica*).

**shuttle** [ʃʌtl] *s.* lanzadera; *v.* ir y venir acompasadamente (*como una lanzadera*).

**shy** [ʃaɪ] *adj.* tímido, apocado, vergonzoso; asustadizo; esquivo; **to be — on** estar escaso de; **to be — two cents** faltarle a uno dos centavos; *v.* esquivarse, hacerse a un lado; asustarse; **to — at something** retroceder ante algo; respingar (*un caballo*) al ver algo; espantarse con algo; **to — away** esquivarse de repente; respingar (*un caballo*); desviarse, apartarse.

**shyness** [ʃáɪnɪs] *s.* apocamiento, timidez, vergüenza.

**shyster** [ʃáɪstər] *s.* leguleyo, abogadillo tramposo, picapleitos.

**sibilant** [síbələnt] *s.* sibilante.

**sick** [sɪk] *adj.* enfermo, malo; nauseado; angustiado; **— leave** licencia por enfermedad; **to be — for** languidecer por, suspirar por; **to be — of** estar cansado de; estar harto de; **to be — to** (*o* **at**) **one's stomach** tener náuseas; **to make —** enfermar; dar pena, dar lástima; *s.* **the —** los enfermos; *v.* incitar, azuzar (*a un perro*) **— him** ¡síguele!

**sicken** [síkən] *v.* enfermar(se), poner-(se) enfermo; dar asco; tener asco; sentir náuseas.

**sickening** [síknɪŋ] *adj.* nauseabundo, repugnante; lastimoso.

**sickle** [síkl] *s.* hoz.

**sickly** [síklɪ] *adj.* enfermizo; achacoso, enclenque; malsano.

**sickness** [síknɪs] *s.* enfermedad; malestar; náusea.

**side** [saɪd] *s.* (*surface*) lado; cara; costado; ladera; falda (*de una colina*); (*faction*) partido, facción; — **by** lado a lado; **by his** — a su lado; **by the** — **of** al lado de; **on all -s** por todos lados; **to take -s with** ser partidario de, ponerse al lado de; *adj.* lateral; de lado; oblicuo; incidental; secundario, de menos importancia; — **glance** mirada de soslayo, de través o de reojo; — **issue** cuestión secundaria; — **light** luz lateral; noticia, detalle o ilustración incidental; *v.* **to** — **with** estar por, ser partidario de, apoyar a, opinar con.

**sideboard** [sáɪdbord] *s.* aparador.

**sideslip** [sáɪdslɪp] *s.* deslizamiento.

**sidetrack** [sáɪdtræk] *v.* desviar; echar a un lado.

**sidewalk** [sáɪdwɔk] *s.* acera, *Méx.* banqueta, *Ríopl.*, *Ch.*, *Andes* vereda; *C.A..*, *Col.*, andén.

**sideways** [sáɪdwez] *adv.* de lado, de costado; oblicuamente; hacia un lado; *adj.* lateral, de lado, oblicuo.

**siege** [sidʒ] *s.* cerco, sitio, asedio; **to lay** — **to** sitiar, cercar.

**sieve** [sɪv] *s.* tamiz, cedazo; criba; *v.* *véase* **sift**.

**sift** [sɪft] *v.* cerner, tamizar; cribar.

**sigh** [saɪ] *v.* suspirar; *s.* suspiro.

**sight** [saɪt] *s.* (*sense*) vista; (*view*) visión; espectáculo, escena; (*gun*) mira (*de un arma de fuego*); **in** — **of** a vista de; **payable at** — pagadero a la vista; **he is a** — es un adefesio o mamarracho; **this room is a** — este cuarto es un horror; **to catch** — **of** vislumbrar, avistar; **to know by** — conocer de vista; **to lose** — **of** perder de vista; **to see the -s** ver de visitar los puntos de interés; *v.* avistar; ver.

**sightseeing** [sáɪtsiɪŋ] *s.* turismo; — **tour** paseo en auto para ver puntos de interés.

**sign** [saɪn] *s.* (*signal*) signo; seña, señal; (*indication*) muestra; (*placard*) letrero; —**board** cartel; tablero (*para fijar anuncios*); *v.* firmar; contratar, hacer firmar; **to** — **over property** ceder una propiedad mediante escritura, hacer cesión legal de propiedad; **to** — **up for a job** firmar el contrato para un empleo; contratar para un empleo.

**signal** [sígnl] *s.* señal, seña; *v.* señalar, indicar, hacer seña, dar la señal; *adj.* señalado, notable; extraordinario; — **beacon** faro; — **code** código de señales.

**signature** [sígnətʃɚ] *s.* firma.

**signer** [sáɪnɚ] *s.* firmante.

**significance** [sɪgnífəkəns] *s.* significa-

ción; significado.

**significant** [sɪgnífəkənt] *adj.* significativo.

**signify** [sígnəfaɪ] *v.* significar.

**silence** [sáɪləns] *s.* silencio; *v.* acallar; apagar (*un sonido*); aquietar, sosegar.

**silent** [sáɪlənt] *adj.* silencioso; callado; tácito; — **partner** socio comanditario (*que no tiene voz ni voto*).

**silhouette** [sɪluét] *s.* silueta; *v.* perfilar; **to be -d against** perfilarse contra.

**silk** [sɪlk] *s.* seda; *adj.* de seda; — **industry** industria sedera; — **ribbon** cinta de seda.

**silken** [sílkən] *adj.* sedoso; de seda.

**silkworm** [sílkwɜrm] *s.* gusano de seda.

**silky** [sílkɪ] *adj.* sedoso, sedeño; de seda.

**sill** [sɪl] *s.* umbral; **window** — antepecho de ventana.

**silly** [sílɪ] *adj.* necio, tonto, bobo, simple; absurdo, insensato.

**silt** [sɪlt] *s.* cieno.

**silver** [sílvɚ] *s.* (*metal*) plata; (*tableware*) cubierto; (*dishes*) vajilla de plata; (*color*) color de plata; *adj.* de plata; plateado; argentino; — **wedding** bodas de plata; *v.* platear; argentar; **to** — **a mirror** azogar un espejo.

**silversmith** [sílvɚsmɪθ] *s.* platero.

**silverware** [sílvɚwɛr] *s.* vajilla de plata, vajilla plateada; cuchillos, cucharas y tenedores (*por lo general de plata o plateados*).

**silvery** [sílvɚrɪ] *adj.* plateado; argentino.

**similar** [símələ-] *adj.* semejante; **-ly** *adv.* semejantemente; de la misma manera.

**similarity** [sɪmələ̌rətɪ] *s.* semejanza, parecido.

**simile** [síməli] *s.* símil.

**simmer** [símɚ] *v.* hervir a fuego lento.

**simple** [símpl] *adj.* simple; sencillo; llano; tonto, mentecato; **simple-minded** ingenuo, simple, simplón; *s.* simple.

**simpleton** [símpltən] *s.* simplón, papanatas, papamoscas.

**simplicity** [sɪmplísətɪ] *s.* sencillez; simplicidad; simpleza; ingenuidad.

**simplify** [símpləfaɪ] *v.* simplificar.

**simply** [símplɪ] *adv.* simplemente; sencillamente; solamente.

**simulate** [símjəlet] *v.* simular.

**simultaneous** [saɪml̩téniəs] *adj.* simultáneo.

**sin** [sɪn] *s.* pecado, culpa; *v.* pecar.

**since** [sɪns] *conj.* desde que; después (de) que; puesto que, como, visto que; dado que; *prep.* desde, despues de; *adv.* desde entonces; **ever** — desde entonces; **he died long** — murió hace mucho tiempo; **we have been here** — **five** estamos aquí desde las cinco.

**sincere** [sɪnsír] *adj.* sincero.

**sincerity** [sɪnsérətɪ] *s.* sinceridad.

**sinecure** [sínɪkjur] *s.* sinecura (*trabajo fácil y bien pagado*).

**sinew** [sínju] s. tendón; fibra, vigor.

**sinewy** [sínjəwı] adj. nervudo, nervioso o nervoso; fuerte, vigoroso.

**sinful** [sínfəl] adj. pecaminoso; pecador.

**sing** [sıŋ] v. cantar; **to — out of tune** desentonar(se), desafinar; **to — to sleep** arrullar.

**singe** [sındʒ] v. chamuscar; s. chamusquina, Am. chamuscada, Am. chamuscadura.

**singer** [síŋɚ] s. cantor; cantora, cantatriz.

**single** [síŋgl] adj. (unique) solo; (distinct) individual; particular; (unmarried) soltero; **— entry bookkeeping** teneduría por partida simple; **— room** cuarto para uno; **— woman** mujer soltera; **not a — word** ni una sola palabra; s. billete de un dólar; v. **to — out** singularizar, distinguir, escoger; entresacar.

**singlehanded** [síŋglhændıd] adj. solo, sin ayuda.

**singsong** [síŋsɔŋ] s. sonsonete, cadencia monótona.

**singular** [síŋgjəlɚ] adj. singular; raro, extraordinario; s. singular, número singular.

**sinister** [sínıstɚ] adj. siniestro, aciago, funesto.

**sink** [sıŋk] v. hundir(se); sumir(se), sumergir(se); echar a pique; irse a pique, naufragar; cavar (un pozo); enterrar, clavar (un puntal o poste); **to — into one's mind** grabarse en la memoria; **to — one's teeth into** clavar el diente en; **to — to sleep** caer en el sueño; s. sumidero; fregadero.

**sinner** [sínɚ] s. pecador.

**sinuous** [sínjuəs] adj. sinuoso, tortuoso; con vueltas y rodeos.

**sinus** [sáınəs] s. seno, cavidad (en un hueso); **frontal —** seno frontal.

**sip** [sıp] v. sorber; chupar; s. sorbo.

**siphon** [sáıfən] s. sifón; v. sacar (agua) con sifón.

**sir** [sɝ] s. señor.

**siren** [sáırən] s. sirena.

**sirloin** [sɝlɔın] s. solomillo, solomo.

**sirup** [sírəp] s. jarabe.

**sissy** [sísı] adj. & s. afeminado, maricón.

**sister** [sístɚ] s. hermana; **Sister Mary** Sor María.

**sister-in-law** [sístɚınlɔ] s. cuñada, hermana política.

**sit** [sıt] v. sentar(se); colocar, asentar; posarse (un pájaro); estar sentado; estar situado; empollar (las gallinas); apoyarse; reunirse, celebrar sesión (un cuerpo legislativo, un tribunal); sentar, venir o caer (bien o mal un traje); **to — down** sentarse; **to — out a dance** quedarse sentado durante una pieza de baile; **to — still** estarse quieto; **to — tight** mantenerse firme en su puesto; **to — up** incorporarse; **to — up all night** velar toda la noche; **to — up and take**

**notice** despabilarse.

**site** [saıt] s. sitio, local, situación.

**sitting** [sítıŋ] s. sesión (de un cuerpo legislativo, tribunal, etc.); sentada; **at one —** de una sentada; adj. sentado; **— hen** gallina ponedora; **— room** sala (de descanso); sala de espera; antesala.

**situated** [sítʃuetıd] adj. situado, sito, ubicado, colocado.

**situation** [sıtʃuéfən] s. (location) situación, colocación; (employment) empleo; posición; (status) situación.

**size** [saız] s. tamaño; medida; v. clasificar según el tamaño; **to — up** tantear, formarse una idea de, juzgar.

**sizzle** [sízl] v. chirriar (aplícase al sonido que hace la carne al freírse); s. chirrido (de la carne al freírse).

**skate** [sket] s. patín; **ice —** patín de hielo, patín de cuchilla; **roller —** patín de ruedas; v. patinar.

**skein** [sken] s. madeja.

**skeleton** [skélətn] s. esqueleto; armazón; **— key** llave maestra.

**skeptic** = **sceptic**.

**sketch** [skɛtʃ] s. (drawing) boceto; diseño; croquis; (outline) esbozo; boquejo; v. bosquejar; delinear; esbozar, dibujar.

**ski** [ski] s. esquí; v. esquiar, patinar con esquís.

**skid** [skıd] v. patinar, resbalar(se); patinar (una rueda); deslizarse.

**skill** [skıl] s. destreza, maña, habilidad, pericia.

**skilled** [skıld] adj. experto, práctico, experimentado, hábil.

**skillet** [skílıt] s. sartén; cacerola.

**skillful, skilful** [skílfəl] adj. experto, diestro, ducho, hábil, perito.

**skim** [skım] v. (remove layer) desnatar, quitar la nata a; espumar, quitar la espuma a; (read) leer superficialmente; **to — over the surface** rozar la superficie.

**skimp** [skımp] v. escatimar; economizar; ser tacaño; hacer (las cosas) con descuido.

**skimpy** [skímpı] adj. escaso; tacaño.

**skin** [skın] s. piel; cutis; pellejo; cuero; cáscara, hollejo; **to save one's —** salvar el pellejo; **skin-deep** superficial; v. desollar; pelar; **to — someone (out of his money)** desplumar a una persona, quitarle a uno el dinero.

**skinny** [skínı] adj. flaco; descarnado.

**skip** [skıp] v. saltar; brincar; saltarse (unos renglones, un párrafo, etc.), omitir; saltar por encima de, salvar de un brinco; **to — out** salir de escape, escabullirse, escaparse, s. salto, brinco; omisión.

**skipper** [skípɚ] s. patrón (de barco); capitán; saltador, brincador.

**skirmish** [skɝmıʃ] s. escaramuza; v. escaramuzar, sostener una escaramuza.

**skirt** [skɝt] s. falda, Ríopl. pollera; orilla, borde; **under—** enaguas; v. bordear, orillar, ir por la orilla de; circundar;

**to — along a coast** costear.

**skit** [skɪt] *s.* parodia, juguete o paso cómico; boceto satírico o burlesco.

**skull** [skʌl] *s.* cráneo; calavera.

**skunk** [skʌŋk] *s. C.A., Méx., Ríopl.* zorrillo o zorrino, *Ven., Col.* mapurite.

**sky** [skaɪ] *s.* cielo; — **blue** azul celeste.

**skylark** [skáɪlɑrk] *s.* alondra, calandria.

**skylight** [skáɪlaɪt] *s.* claraboya, tragaluz.

**skyrocket** [skáɪrɑkɪt] *s.* cohete.

**skyscraper** [skáɪskrepɚ] *s.* rascacielos.

**slab** [slæb] *s.* tabla, plancha, losa; tajada gruesa; **marble —** losa de mármol.

**slack** [slæk] *adj.* (*not taut*) flojo; (*sluggish*) tardo, lento; inactivo; **— season** temporada inactiva; *s.* flojedad, flojera; inactividad; **to take up the —** apretar, estirar; **-s** pantalones anchos con pliegues, *v. véase* **slacken.**

**slacken** [slǽkən] *v.* aflojar(se); flojear; retardar(se); disminuir.

**slag** [slæg] *s.* escoria.

**slain** [slen] *p.p. de* **to slay.**

**slam** [slæm] *v.* cerrar(se) de golpe; dejar caer de golpe; **to — someone** decirle a alguien una claridad o grosería; **to — the door** dar un portazo; *s.* golpazo; claridad, grosería; **— of a door** portazo; **to make a grand —** ganar todas las bazas (*en el juego de bridge*).

**slander** [slǽndɚ] *s.* calumnia, maledicencia; *v.* calumniar.

**slanderous** [slǽndərəs] *adj.* calumnioso.

**slang** [slæŋ] *s.* jerga, jerigonza; vulgarismo.

**slant** [slænt] *s.* sesgo; inclinación; punto de vista; *adj.* sesgado; inclinado; oblicuo; *v.* sesgar; inclinar(se); ladear.

**slap** [slæp] *s.* palmada, manazo, manotada; insulto, desaire; *v.* dar una palmada a, dar un manazo a.

**slapstick** [slǽpstɪk] *adj.* de golpe y porrazo.

**slash** [slæʃ] *v.* acuchillar; dar cuchilladas o tajos; cortar; hacer fuerte rebaja de (*precios, sueldos*); *s.* cuchillada; tajo, tajada, cortadura.

**slat** [slæt] *s.* tabla, tablilla.

**slate** [slet] *s.* pizarra; color de pizarra; lista de candidatos; **— pencil** pizarrín.

**slaughter** [slɔ́tɚ] *s.* carnicería, matanza, *Ríopl.* carneada; **—house** matadero, *Méx., C.A.* rastro; *v.* matar; *Ríopl.* carnear; hacer una matanza; destrozar.

**slave** [slev] *s.* esclavo; **— driver** capataz de esclavos; persona que agobia de trabajo a otra; **— labor** trabajo de esclavos; trabajadores forzados; *v.* trabajar como esclavo.

**slaver** [slǽvɚ] *s.* baba; *v.* babosear, babear.

**slavery** [slévrɪ] *s.* esclavitud.

**slavish** [slévɪʃ] *adj.* servil.

**slay** [sle] *v.* matar.

**sled** [slɛd] *s.* trineo, rastra.

**sleek** [slik] *adj.* liso; pulido, resbaloso; suave; artero, mañoso; *v.* alisar; pulir.

**sleep** [slip] *v.* dormir; **to — it off** dormir la mona; **to — off a headache** curarse con sueño un dolor de cabeza; **to — on it** consultarlo con la almohada; *s.* sueño; **to go to —** dormirse, quedarse dormido; **to put to —** adormecer; arrullar (*al nene*).

**sleeper** [slípɚ] *s.* durmiente; coche-cama, coche-dormitorio.

**sleepily** [slípɪlɪ] *adv.* con somnolencia.

**sleepiness** [slípɪnɪs] *s.* sueño, modorra, somnolencia.

**sleeping** [slípɪŋ] *adj.* durmiente; dormido; **— car** coche-cama, coche-dormitorio; **— pills** píldoras para dormir; **— sickness** encefalitis letárgica.

**sleepless** [slíplɪs] *adj.* desvelado, insomne, sin sueño.

**sleepy** [slípɪ] *adj.* soñoliento; amodorrado; **to be —** tener sueño.

**sleet** [slit] *s.* cellisca; *v.* cellisquear.

**sleeve** [sliv] *s.* manga.

**sleigh** [sle] *s.* trineo; **— bell** cascabel; *v.* pasearse en trineo.

**sleight** [slaɪt]: **— of hand** juego de manos; prestidigitación, escamoteo.

**slender** [sléndɚ] *adj.* delgado; tenue; escaso, insuficiente.

**slept** [slept] *pret. & p.p. de* **to sleep.**

**sleuth** [sluθ] *s.* detective (*o* detectivo).

**slew** [slu] *pret. de* **to slay.**

**slice** [slaɪs] *s.* rebanada, tajada; lonja; *v.* rebanar, tajar; cortar.

**slick** [slɪk] *v.* alisar; pulir; **to — up** alisar bien, pulir bien; pulirse, acicalarse, componerse; *adj.* liso; meloso, suave; aceitoso; astuto, mañoso.

**slicker** [slíkɚ] *s.* impermeable de hule (*o* de caucho); embaucador.

**slid** [slɪd] *pret. & p.p. de* **to slide.**

**slidden** [slídṇ] *p.p. de* **to slide.**

**slide** [slaɪd] *v.* resbalar(se); deslizar(se); hacer resbalar; patinar; **to — into** meter(se) en; **to — out** (*o* **— away**) deslizarse, colarse, escabullirse, escaparse; **to let something —** dejar pasar algo; no hacer caso de algo; *s.* resbalón; resbaladero, lugar resbaladizo; ligado (*en música*); *véase* **landslide; — cover** tapa corrediza; **— rule** regla de cálculo; **microscope —** platina.

**slight** [slaɪt] *s.* desaire, menosprecio, desdén, desatención; *v.* desairar, menospreciar; descuidar, desatender; *adj.* delgado; delicado; leve, ligero; pequeño; insignificante; escaso; **-ly** *adv.* escasamente; ligeramente; un poco, apenas.

**slim** [slɪm] *adj.* delgado; esbelto; escaso.

**slime** [slaɪm] *s.* limo, cieno, fango; baba, secreción viscosa.

**slimy** [sláɪmɪ] *adj.* viscoso, mucoso, fangoso; baboso.

**sling** [slɪŋ] *s.* honda (*para tirar piedras*); cabestrillo (*para sostener el brazo*); eslinga (*maroma provista de ganchos para levantar pesos*); **—shot** tirador de goma o hule; *v.* tirar, arrojar; **to — a rifle over one's shoulder** echarse el rifle al hombro.

**slink** [slɪŋk] *v.* andar furtivamente; **to — away** escurrirse, escabullirse, deslizarse.

**slip** [slɪp] *v.* (*slide*) deslizar(se); resbalar(se); (*err*) cometer un desliz; equivocarse; **to — away** escaparse, escabullirse, escurrirse; **to — in** meter(se); **to — one's dress on** ponerse de prisa el vestido; **to — out** salirse; sacar a hurtadillas; **to — out of joint** dislocarse, *Am.* zafarse (*un hueso*); **to — something off** quitar(se) algo; **to let an opportunity —** dejar pasar una oportunidad; **it slipped my mind** se me olvidó, se me pasó; **it slipped off** se zafó; *s.* desliz; resbalón; error, equivocación; funda (*de muebles, de almohada*); combinación-enagua; pedazo (*de papel*), papeleta; embarcadero; guía, sarmiento (*para transplantar*); **— knot** nudo corredizo.

**slipper** [slípɚ] *s.* zapatilla; babucha; pantufla.

**slippery** [slíprɪ] *adj.* resbaloso, resbaladizo; evasivo.

**slit** [slɪt] *v.* cortar, hacer una rendija, abertura o incisión; **to — into strips** cortar en tiras; *pret.* & *p.p. de* **to slit**; *s.* abertura, hendedura, rendija; cortada, incisión.

**slobber** [slábɚ] *s.* baba; *v.* babosear, babear.

**slobbering** [slábərɪŋ] *adj.* baboso.

**slogan** [slógən] *s.* lema, mote.

**sloop** [slup] *s.* chalupa.

**slop** [slɑp] *v.* (*soil*) ensuciar; (*splash*) salpicar; (*spill*) derramar(se); *s.* fango suciedad; **-s** lavazas, agua sucia; desperdicios.

**slope** [slop] *v.* inclinar(se); *s.* inclinación; declive; falda, ladera; cuesta, bajada; vertiente.

**sloppy** [slápɪ] *adj.* puerco, sucio, cochino; desaseado; mal hecho.

**slot** [slɑt] *s.* (*opening*) abertura, hendedura; (*groove for coins*) ranura (*en que se introduce una moneda*); **— machine** máquina automática que funciona por medio de una moneda, "traganíqueles," "tragamonedas"; *v.* hacer una abertura o hendedura.

**sloth** [sloθ] *s.* pereza; perezoso (*cuadrúpedo*).

**slouch** [slautʃ] *s.* (*posture*) postura muy relajada o floja; (*person*) persona perezosa o desaseada; **— hat** sombrero gacho; **to walk with a —** andar con los hombros caídos y la cabeza inclinada; *v.* andar agachado; andar caído de hombros; andar alicaído; arrellanarse, repantigarse (*en una silla*).

**sloveliness** [slávənlɪnɪs] *s.* desaseo, desaliño; suciedad.

**slovenly** [slávənlɪ] *adj.* desaseado,

desaliñado; desarreglado.

**slow** [slo] *adj.* (*low speed*) lento, despacio; (*late*) tardo; atrasado; (*sluggish*) lerdo; torpe; *adv.* lentamente, despacio; *v.* **to — down** (*o* **— up**) retardar disminuir (*el paso, la marcha, la velocidad*); aflojar el paso; **-ly** *adv.* despacio, lentamente.

**slowness** [slónɪs] *s.* lentitud; torpeza; cachaza.

**slug** [slʌg] *s.* bala; porrazo, puñetazo; babosa (*molusco sin concha*); haragán; trago (*de aguardiente*); lingote (*de imprenta*); *c.* aporrear, abofetear, dar puñetazos.

**sluggard** [slʌgɚd] *s.* holgazán, haragán.

**sluggish** [slʌgɪʃ] *adj.* tardo; inactivo.

**sluice** [slus] *s.* compuerta; caño, canal; **—gate** compuerta.

**slum** [slʌm] *s.* barrio bajo; *v.* visitar los barrios bajos.

**slumber** [slʌmbɚ] *v.* dormitar; dormir; *s.* sueño, sueño ligero.

**slump** [slʌmp] *v.* hundirse; desplomarse; bajar repentinamente (*los precios o valores*); *s.* desplome, hundimiento, bajón, baja repentina (*de precios, valores, etc.*).

**slung** [slʌŋ] *pret.* & *p.p. de* **to sling.**

**slunk** [slʌŋk] *pret.* & *p.p. de* **to slink.**

**slush** [slʌʃ] *s.* (*snow*) nieve a medio derretir; (*mud*) lodazal, fango; (*refuse*) desperdicios; (*drivel*) sentimentalismo.

**sly** [slaɪ] *adj.* astuto, socarrón, zorro, taimado; **on the —** a hurtadillas, a escondidas.

**slyness** [sláɪnɪs] *s.* disimulo, astucia.

**smack** [smæk] *s.* (*taste*) sabor, dejo; (*kiss*) beso ruidoso; (*crack*) chasquido (*de látigo*); (*slap*) palmada, manotada; **a — of something** una pizca de algo; *v.* dar un beso ruidoso; chasquear (*un látigo*); dar un manazo; **to — of** saber a, tener el sabor de; oler a; **to — one's lips** chuparse los labios, saborearse, rechuparse, relamerse.

**small** [smɔl] *adj.* (*size*) pequeño, chico; bajo; (*insignificant*) insignificante; mezquino; **— change** dinero menudo, suelto; **— hours** primeras horas de la mañana; **— letters** letras minúsculas; **— talk** conversación insubstancial, charladuría; **— voice** vocecita; **to feel —** sentirse pequeño o insignificante.

**smallness** [smólnɪs] *s.* pequeñez; bajeza.

**smallpox** [smólpɑks] *s.* viruelas.

**smart** [smɑrt] *adj.* (*intelligent*) listo, inteligente; (*astute*) ladino; astuto; agudo; (*stylish*) elegante; **— remark** observación aguda o penetrante; **— set** gente de buen tono; *s.* escozor, *Ríopl.*, *C.A.*, *Méx.* ardor; *v.* picar, escocer, *Ríopl.*, *C.A.*, *Méx.* arder.

**smash** [smæʃ] *v.* quebrantar, quebrar, romper; destrozar; aplastar; **to — into** chocar con; topar con, darse un tope contra; *s.* quebrazón, quiebra; fracaso; choque o tope violento; derrota completa.

**smattering** [smǽtəɾɪŋ] *s.* conocimiento superficial y rudimental.

**smear** [smɪr] *v.* embarrar, untar, manchar; **to — with paint** pintorrear, pintarrajear; *s.* mancha.

**smell** [smɛl] *v.* oler; **to — of** oler a; *s.* olor; olfato; **— of** olor a; **to take a —** oler.

**smelly** [smɛ́lɪ] *adj.* oloroso; hediondo.

**smelt** [smɛlt] *v.* fundir (*metales*); *pret.* & *p.p. de* **to smell.**

**smile** [smaɪl] *v.* sonreír(se); *s.* sonrisa.

**smiling** [smáɪlɪŋ] *adj.* risueño, sonriente; **-ly** *adv.* sonriendo, con cara risueña.

**smite** [smaɪt] *v.* golpear; herir; castigar; afligir; *véase* **smitten.**

**smith** [smɪθ] *s.* forjador; *véase* **blacksmith, goldsmith, silversmith.**

**smithy** [smíθɪ] *s.* herrería, fragua, forja.

**smitten** [smítn̩] *p.p. de* **to smite** & *adj.* afligido; castigado; enamorado; **to be — with a disease** darle a uno una enfermedad.

**smock** [smɑk] *s.* bata corta, batín.

**smoke** [smok] *s.* humo; **— screen** cortina de humo; **cloud of —** humareda; **to have a —** dar una fumada, fumar; *v.* fumar, *Am.* chupar (*un cigarro*); humear; ahumar; **to — out** ahuyentar o echar fuera con humo.

**smoker** [smókɚ] *s.* fumador; vagón de fumar; reunión o tertulia de fumadores.

**smokestack** [smókstæk] *s.* chimenea.

**smoking** [smókɪŋ] *adj.* humeante; de fumar; para fumadores; **— car** vagón de fumar; **— room** fumadero, cuarto de fumar.

**smoky** [smókɪ] *adj.* humeante; humoso, lleno de humo; ahumado.

**smooth** [smuð] *adj.* (*even*) liso; terso; igual, parejo; plano, llano; (*serene*) tranquilo; (*pleasant*) suave; (*wise*) sagaz; **— disposition** genio afable; **— manners** maneras o modales afables; **— style** estilo flúido y fácil; **— talker** hablador melifluo y sagaz; *v.* alisar; allanar; pulir; emparejar; **to — over** allanar, alisar, arreglar; **-ly** *adv.* suavemente; blandamente; fácilmente; con facilidad.

**smoothness** [smúðnɪs] *s.* (*evenness*) lisura; igualdad, uniformidad; (*pleasantness*) suavidad; afabilidad; tranquilidad; facilidad, fluidez.

**smote** [smot] *pret. de* **to smite.**

**smother** [smʌ́ðɚ] *v.* ahogar(se); sofocar(se); asfixiar(se).

**smudge** [smʌdʒ] *v.* tiznar, manchar o ensuciar con tizne; ahumar; *s.* tiznón, mancha (*hecha con tizne*); humareda, nube espesa de humo.

**smuggle** [smʌ́gl̩] *v.* contrabandear, hacer contrabando; **to — in** meter de contrabando; **to — out** sacar de contrabando.

**smuggler** [smʌ́glɚ] *s.* contrabandista.

**smut** [smʌt] *s.* (*smudge*) tizne; suciedad, mancha; (*obscenity*) obscenidad, dicho obseno o indecente; tizón (*enfermedad de ciertas plantas*); *v.* tiznar; ensuciar, manchar.

**smutty** [smʌ́tɪ] *adj.* tiznado, manchado de tizne; sucio.

**snack** [snæk] *s.* bocado, bocadillo, tentempié, bocadito; merienda, comida ligera.

**snag** [snæg] *s.* (*protuberance*) tocón; raigón; (*obstacle*) tropiezo, obstáculo; **to hit a —** tropezar con un obstáculo; *v.* rasgar; enredar.

**snail** [snel] *s.* caracol.

**snake** [snek] *s.* culebra, víbora; *v.* culebrear.

**snap** [snæp] *v.* (*make sound*) chasquear, dar un chasquido; estallar; (*break*) quebrar(se); (*photograph*) fotografiar instantaneamente; **his eyes —** le chispean los ojos; **to — at** echar una mordida o mordisco a; dar una tarascada a, morder; asir (*una oportunidad*); **to — back at** tirar una mordida a; dar una respuesta grosera a; **to — off** soltarse, saltar; quebrar(se); **to — one's fingers** tronar los dedos, castañetear con los dedos; **to — shut** cerrar(se) de golpe; **to — together** apretar, abrochar; **to — up** agarrar, asir; morder; *s.* chasquido; estallido; mordida, mordisco, dentellada; broche de presión; energía, vigor; galleta; cosa fácil, ganga; **cold —** nortazo; repentino descenso de temperatura; **not to care a —** no importarle a uno un ardite o un comino; *adj.* hecho de prisa, impensado; instantáneo; **— fastener** broche de presión; **— judgment** decisión atolondrada; **— lock** cerradura de golpe.

**snappy** [snǽpɪ] *adj.* mordedor, *Ven.*, *C.A.*, *Andes* mordelón; enojadizo, *Méx.* enojón; violento, vivo; elegante; **— cheese** queso acre o picante; **— eyes** ojos chispeantes.

**snapshot** [snǽpʃat] *s.* instantánea, fotografía instantánea; *v.* sacar una instantánea.

**snare** [snɛr] *s.* (*trap*) trampa, lazo; (*ambush*) acechanza; red; *v.* enredar; atrapar, coger con trampa; tender lazos a.

**snarl** [snɑrl] *v.* gruñir; enmarañar(se), enredar(se); *s.* gruñido; maraña, enredo; pelo enmarañado.

**snatch** [snætʃ] *v.* arrebatar; agarrar; **to — at** tratar de asir o agarrar; *s.* arrebatiña, arrebatamiento; trozo, pedacito; **to make a — at** tratar de arrebatar, tratar de agarrarse a.

**sneak** [snik] *v.* andar furtivamente; obrar solapadamente; **to — in** meter(se) a escondidas; colarse; **to — out** escurrirse, salirse a hurtadillas; sacar, llevarse (*algo*) a escondidas; *s.* persona solapada.

**sneer** [snɪr] *v.* (*smile*) sonreír con sorna; (*gesture*) hacer un gesto de desdén;

SL

(*ridicule*) mofarse; **to — at** mofarse de; *s.* sorna, mofa, rechifla; gesto desdeñoso.

**sneeze** [sniz] *v.* estornudar; *s.* estornudo.

**sniff** [snɪf] *v.* husmear, olfatear; sorber (*por las narices*); resollar para adentro; **to — at** husmear; menospreciar; *s.* husmeo, olfateo; sorbo (*por las narices*).

**sniffle** [snɪfl̩] *v.* sorber por las narices.

**snip** [snɪp] *v.* tijeretear; **to — off** cortar de un tijeretazo, recortar; *s.* tijeretada, tijeretazo; pedacito, recorte.

**snipe** [snaɪp] *v.* tirar, disparar desde un escondite.

**sniper** [snáɪpɚ] *s.* francotirador; tirador emboscado.

**snitch** [snɪtʃ] *v.* arrebatar; ratear, hurtar.

**snivel** [snɪvl̩] *v.* moquear; gimotear.

**snob** [snɑb] *s.* esnob.

**snoop** [snup] *v.* fisgar, fisgonear, curiosear; *s.* curioso, fisgón.

**snooze** [snuz] *v.* dormitar, sestear; *s.* siestecita, siestita; **to take a —** echar un sueñecito o siestita; descabezar el sueño.

**snore** [snor] *v.* roncar; *s.* ronquido.

**snorkel** [snórkl̩] *s.* tubo esnorkel.

**snort** [snɔrt] *v.* resoplar; bufar; *s.* resoplido, bufido.

**snout** [snaʊt] *s.* hocico, jeta.

**snow** [sno] *s.* nieve; *v.* nevar; **to be -ed under** estar totalmente cubierto por la nevada.

**snowball** [snóbɔl] *s.* bola de nieve; *v.* tirar bolas de nieve.

**snowdrift** [snódrɪft] *s.* ventisca, ventisquero, montón de nieve.

**snowfall** [snófɔl] *s.* nevada.

**snowflake** [snóflek] *s.* copo de nieve.

**snowstorm** [snóstɔrm] *s.* fuerte nevada, nevasca.

**snowy** [snóɪ] *adj.* nevado; níveo, blanco como la nieve.

**snub** [snʌb] *v.* desairar, menospreciar; *s.* desaire; **snub-nosed** chato, *Am.* ñato.

**snuff** [snʌf] *v.* olfatear, husmear, ventear; aspirar (*por la nariz*); despabilar (*una candela*); **to — at** olfatear, ventear; **to — out** apagar, extinguir; **to — up** sorber (*por las narices*); *s.* sorbo (*por la nariz*); rapé, tabaco en polvo; pabilo, mecha quemada (*de una vela*).

**snug** [snʌg] *adj.* (*squeezed*) apretado; ajustado; compacto; (*comfortable*) abrigado; cómodo.

**so** [so] *adv.* así; tan, muy; tanto; **so-so** regular; **so-and-so** Fulano (de tal); **— as to** para; **— far** tan lejos; hasta ahora, hasta aquí; **— many** tantos; **— much** tanto; **— much for that** basta por ese lado; **— much the better** tanto mejor; **— that** de modo que; para que; a fin de que; de suerte que; **— then** conque, pues bien, así pues; **and — forth** etcétera; y así sucesivamente; **I believe —** así

lo creo; **is that — ?** ¿de veras? ¿de verdad?; ¡no diga!; **ten minutes or —** poco más o menos diez minutos, como diez minutos.

**soak** [sok] *v.* remojar(se); empapar(se); **to — up** absorber, embeber; chupar; **to be -ed through** estar empapado; estar calado hasta los huesos; *s.* remojo, mojada; borrachín; golpe, puñetazo.

**soap** [sop] *s.* jabón; **— bubble** pompa de jabón, *Ven.*, *Col.* bombita; *Andes*, *Méx.* burbuja de jabón; **— dish** jabonera; **soft —** jabón blando; lisonja, adulación; *v.* enjabonar.

**soapy** [sópɪ] *adj.* lleno de jabón.

**soar** [sor] *v.* remontarse; encumbrarse; subir muy alto; remontar el vuelo.

**sob** [sab] *v.* sollozar; *s.* sollozo.

**sober** [sóbɚ] *adj.* (*temperate*) sobrio; moderado, templado; (*serious*) serio, grave; (*sane*) cuerdo, sensato; (*calm*) tranquilo, sereno; **to be —** estar en su juicio; no estar borracho; *v.* **to — down** sosegar(se), calmar(se); formalizarse; **to — up** desembriagarse, desemborracharse; bajársele a uno la borrachera.

**soberly** [sóbɚlɪ] *adv.* sobriamente; cuerdamente, con sensatez; seriamente.

**soberness** [sóbɚnɪs] *s.* sobriedad; seriedad.

**sobriety** [səbráɪətɪ] *s.* sobriedad; cordura.

**so-called** [sókɔld] *adj.* así llamado, llamado.

**sociable** [sóʃəbl̩] *adj.* sociable, social, tratable.

**social** [sóʃəl] *adj.* social; sociable; tratable, de buen trato; *s.* reunión social; tertulia.

**socialism** [sóʃəlɪzəm] *s.* socialismo.

**socialist** [sóʃəlɪst] *adj.* & *s.* socialista.

**socialize** [sóʃəlaɪz] *v.* socializar.

**society** [səsáɪətɪ] *s.* sociedad; compañía.

**sociology** [soʃiálədʒɪ] *s.* sociología.

**sock** [sak] *s.* (*garment*) calcetín; (*blow*) porrazo, golpe, puñetazo; *v.* pegar, apalear, golpear; *Am.* batear (*una pelota*).

**socket** [sákɪt] *s.* cuenca (*del ojo*); portalámparas, enchufe, *Carib.* sóquet.

**sod** [sad] *s.* césped; terrón (*de tierra sembrada de césped*); *v.* cubrir de césped.

**soda** [sódə] *s.* soda, sosa; **— fountain** *Am.* fuente de soda; **— water** agua gaseosa; **baking —** bicarbonato de sodio.

**sodium** [sódɪəm] *s.* sodio.

**sofa** [sófə] *s.* sofá.

**soft** [sɔft] *adj.* (*bland*) blando; muelle; suave; (*gentle*) tierno; dulce; **soft-boiled eggs** huevos pasados por agua; **— coal** carbón bituminoso; **— drink** bebida no alcohólica; **— metal** metal dulce, metal maleable; **— soap** jabón blando; adulación; **— water** agua dulce; *adv. véase* **softly.**

**soften** [sɔfən] *v.* ablandar(se); suavizar-

(se); enternecer(se); templar(se); **to
— one's voice** bajar la voz, hablar
quedo (*o* quedito).

**soft-hearted** [sɔfthártəd] *adj.* de buen
corazón.

**softly** [sɔ́ftlɪ] *adv.* blandamente; suavemente; quedo, quedito.

**softness** [sɔ́ftnɪs] *s.* blandura; molicie;
suavidad; ternura; dulzura.

**soggy** [ságɪ] *adj.* remojado; empapado.

**soil** [sɔɪl] *s.* suelo, terreno, tierra; mancha; *v.* ensuciar(se); manchar(se).

**sojourn** [sódʒɚn] *s.* estada, estancia,
permanencia, *Andes, Méx., Ríopl.*
estadía; [sodʒɚ́n] *v.* permanecer;
estarse, residir por una temporada.

**solace** [sálɪs] *s.* solaz; *v.* solazar.

**solar** [sólɚ] *adj.* solar, del sol; — **plexis**
plexo solar.

**sold** [sold] *pret. & p.p. de* **to sell; to be
— on an idea** estar bien convencido
de una idea.

**solder** [sádɚ] *v.* soldar; *s.* soldadura.

**soldier** [sóldʒɚ] *s.* soldado.

**sole** [sol] *adj.* solo, único; exclusivo; *s.*
suela (*del zapato*); planta (*del pie*);
lenguado (*pez*); *v.* solar, echar suelas
a; **to half-sole** echar o poner medias
suelas a.

**solely** [sóllɪ] *adv.* sólamente, única-
mente.

**solemn** [sáləm] *adj.* solemne.

**solemnity** [səlémnətɪ] *s.* solemnidad.

**solicit** [səlísɪt] *v.* solicitar.

**solicitor** [səlísətɚ] *s.* solicitador, agente.

**solicitous** [səlísɪtəs] *adj.* solícito.

**solicitude** [səlísətjud] *s.* solicitud, cuidado.

**solid** [sálɪd] *s.* sólido; *adj.* sólido; firme;
macizo; sensato; unánime; — **blue**
todo azul; — **gold** oro puro; **for one
— hour** por una hora entera, por una
hora sin parar; **the country is —
for** el país está firmemente unido en
favor de.

**solidarity** [salədǽrətɪ] *s.* solidaridad.

**solidify** [səlídəfaɪ] *v.* solidificar(se).

**solidity** [səlídətɪ] *s.* solidez.

**solid-state** [salədstét] *adj.* física del
estado sólido.

**soliloquy** [səlíləkwɪ] *s.* soliloquio.

**solitary** [sáləterɪ] *adj.* solitario; solo; *s.*
solitario, ermitaño.

**solitude** [sálətjud] *s.* soledad.

**solo** [solo] *s.* solo.

**soloist** [sóloɪst] *s.* solista.

**soluble** [sáljəbl] *adj.* soluble, que se
disuelve fácilmente.

**solution** [səlúʃən] *s.* solución.

**solve** [salv] *v.* resolver; explicar, aclarar,
desenredar.

**somber** [sámbɚ] *adj.* sombrío.

**some** [sʌm] *adj.* algún, alguno; algunos,
unos; algo de, un poco de; —**one**
alguien, alguno; — **twenty people**
unas veinte personas; *pron.* algunos,
unos; algo, un poco; una parte.

**somebody** [sámbadɪ] *pron.* alguien; **a
—** un personaje de importancia.

**somehow** [sámhaʊ] *adv.* de algún
modo, de alguna manera; — **or**

**other** de una manera u otra; por
alguna razón.

**someone** [sámwʌn] *pron.* alguno, alguien.

**somersault** [sámɚsɔlt] *s.* voltereta; *v.*
dar una voltereta.

**something** [sámθɪŋ] *s.* algo, alguna
cosa; un poco; — **else** alguna otra
cosa, otra cosa.

**sometime** [sámtaɪm] *adv.* algún día;
alguna vez; en algún tiempo; **-s** *adv.*
a veces, algunas veces, de vez en
cuando.

**somewhat** [sámhwat] *s.* algo, alguna
cosa, un poco; *adv.* algo, un tanto.

**somewhere** [sámhwɛr] *adv.* en alguna
parte; — **else** en alguna otra parte.

**son** [sʌn] *s.* hijo.

**song** [sɔŋ] *s.* canción; canto; **the Song
of Songs** el Cantar de los Cantares;
— **bird** ave canora, pájaro cantor; **to
buy something for a —** comprar
algo muy barato.

**sonic barrier** [sɑnɪkbǽrɪɚ] *s.* barrera
sónica.

**son-in-law** [sánɪnlɔ] *s.* yerno, hijo político.

**sonnet** [sánɪt] *s.* soneto.

**sonorous** [sənórəs] *adj.* sonoro.

**soon** [sun] *adv.* pronto, presto; luego;
— **after** poco después (de); al poco
tiempo; **as — as** tan pronto como;
luego que, así que; **how — ?**
¿cuándo?

**soot** [sʊt] *s.* hollín; tizne.

**soothe** [suð] *v.* calmar, sosegar; aliviar.

**soothsayer** [súθseɚ] *s.* adivino.

**sooty** [sútɪ] *adj.* tiznado, cubierto de
hollín.

**sop** [sap] *v.* empapar; **to — up** absorber; **to be sopping wet** estar hecho
una sopa, estar mojado hasta los
huesos; *s.* sopa (*pan u otra cosa
empapada en leche, caldo, etc.*);
soborno, regalo (*para acallar, conciliar, o sobornar*).

**sophisticated** [səfístəketəd] *adj.* mundano; exento de simplicidad.

**sophomore** [sáfəmor] *s.* estudiante de
segundo año.

**soprano** [səprǽno] *s.* soprano; **high —**
tiple; — **voice** voz de soprano.

**sorcerer** [sɔ́rsərɚ] *s.* brujo, hechicero.

**sordid** [sɔ́rdɪd] *adj.* sórdido; vil, indecente; mezquino.

**sore** [sor] *adj.* (*painful*) dolorido; inflamado, enconado; (*grievous*) afligido, apenado; (*injured*) lastimado;
picado; (*offended*) ofendido; — **eyes**
mal de ojos; **to be — at** estar enojado con; **to have a — throat** tener
mal de garganta, dolerle a uno la
garganta; *s.* úlcera, llaga; inflamación,
lastimadura; pena, aflicción; **-ly**
*adv.* dolorosamente, penosamente;
**to be -ly in need of** necesitar con
urgencia.

**soreness** [sórnɪs] *s.* dolor, dolencia; inflamación.

**sorrel** [sɔ́rəl] *adj.* alazán (*rojo canela*); *s.*
color alazán; caballo alazán.

SN

**sorrow** [sáro] s. (sadness) dolor, pena, pesar; (grieving) pesadumbre; (repentance) arrepentimiento; v. apenarse, afligirse, sentir pena.

**sorrowful** [sárəfəl] adj. pesaroso, doloroso, lastimoso, afligido; **-ly** adv. tristemente, dolorosamente, con pena, desconsoladamente.

**sorry** [sóri] adj. triste, pesaroso, afligido; arrepentido; lastimoso; **I am** — lo siento; me pesa; **I am — for her** la compadezco.

**sort** [sɔrt] s. suerte, clase, especie; — **of tired** algo cansado, un tanto cansado; **all -s of** toda suerte de, toda clase de; **out of -s** de mal humor, malhumorado; indispuesto; v. clasificar, ordenar, arreglar; **to — out** separar, clasificar; entresacar; escoger.

**sought** [sɔt] pret. & p.p. de **to seek.**

**soul** [sol] s. alma; **not a** — nadie, ni un alma.

**sound** [saund] adj. (healthy) sano; cuerdo; sensato; (firm) firme, sólido; ileso; **a — beating** una buena zurra o tunda; **— business** buen negocio, negocio bien oganizado; **— reasoning** raciocinio sólido; **— sleep** sueño profundo; **— title** título válido o legal; **of — mind** en su juicio cabal; **safe and —** sano y salvo; **to sleep —** dormir profundamente; s. son, sonido; tono; brazo de mar; **— wave** onda sonora; v. sonar, tocar; sondear; tantear; auscultar (el pecho, los pulmones); cantar, entonar (alabanzas); **to — out** tantear, sondear.

**soundness** [sáundnɪs] s. (firmness) solidez; (healthiness) cordura, buen juicio; (validity) rectitud; validez; **— of body** buena salud corporal.

**soup** [sup] s. sopa.

**sour** [saur] adj. (acid-like) agrio; acre; ácido; desabrido; rancio; (peevish) malhumorado; **— milk** leche cortada; v. agriar(se); cortarse (la leche); fermentar; poner(se) de mal humor.

**source** [sors] s. origen; manantial, fuente.

**sourness** [sáurnɪs] s. acidez, agrura, desabrimiento.

**souse** [saus] v. zambullir; chapuzar.

**south** [sauθ] s. sur, sud; adj. meridional; del sur; austral; **South American** sudamericano, suramericano; **— pole** polo sur, polo antártico; adv. hacia el sur.

**southeast** [sauθíst] s. & adj. sudeste; adv. hacia el sudeste.

**southeastern** [sauθístɚn] adj. del sudeste, sudeste.

**southern** [sʌðɚn] adj. meridional, del sur, austral, sureño; **— Cross** Cruz del Sur.

**southerner** [sʌðɚnɚ] s. sureño, meridional, habitante del sur.

**southward** [sáuθwɚd] adv. hacia el sur, rumbo al sur.

**southwest** [sauθwést] s. & adj. sudoeste (o suroeste); adv. hacia el sudoeste.

**southwestern** [sauθwéstɚn] adj. sudoeste (o suroeste), del sudoeste.

**souvenir** [suvənír] s. recuerdo, memoria.

**sovereign** [sávrɪn] s. & adj. soberano.

**sovereignty** [sávrɪntɪ] s. soberanía.

**soviet** [sóvɪɪt] s. sóviet; adj. soviético.

**sow** [sau] s. puerca.

**sow** [so] v. sembrar.

**sown** [son] p.p. de **to sow.**

**space** [spes] s. espacio; **— science** ciencia del espacio; ciencia espacial; **— station** estación espacial; **— suit** traje espacial; v. espaciar.

**spacecraft** [spéskræft] s. nave espacial; astronave.

**spaceman** [spésmæn] s. astronauta.

**spacious** [spéʃəs] adj. espacioso; dilatado, vasto.

**spade** [sped] s. azada, azadón; espada (del juego de naipes); v. cavar con la azada.

**span** [spæn] s. palmo; espacio; tramo; arco u ojo (de puente); envergadura (de un aeroplano); **— of life** longevidad; v. medir a palmos; atravesar.

**spangle** [spǽŋgl] s. lentejuela; v. adornar con lentejuelas; brillar, centellear; **-d with stars** estrellado, sembrado (o tachonado) de estrellas.

**Spaniard** [spǽnjɚd] s. español.

**spaniel** [spǽnjəl] s. perro de aguas.

**Spanish** [spǽnɪʃ] adj. español; s. español, idioma español.

**spank** [spæŋk] v. zurrar, dar una tunda, dar nalgadas; s. palmada, nalgada.

**spanking** [spǽŋkɪŋ] s. zurra, tunda, nalgadas.

**spar** [spɑr] v. boxear, pelear.

**spare** [spɛr] v. ahorrar; evitar (molestias, trabajo, etc.); perdonar; **I cannot — another dollar** no dispongo de otro dólar, no tengo más dinero disponible; **I cannot — the car today** no puedo pasarme hoy sin el automóvil; **to — no expense** no escatimar gastos; **to — the enemy** usar de clemencia con el enemigo; **to have time to —** tener tiempo de sobra; adj. flaco, descarnado; escaso, frugal; mezquino; sobrante; de sobra; de repuesto; **— cash** dinero disponible o de sobra; **— time** tiempo libre, tiempo disponible; **— tire** neumático de repuesto.

**spark** [spɑrk] s. chispa; **— plug** bujía; v. chispear, echar chispas, chisporrotear.

**sparkle** [spárkl̩] s. (flash) chispa, centella; brillo, centelleo; (spirit) viveza, animación; v. centellear; chispear; relucir, brillar.

**sparkling** [spárklɪŋ] adj. centelleante; reluciente; chispeante; **— wine** vino espumoso.

**sparrow** [spǽro] s. gorrión, pardal.

**sparse** [spɑrs] adj. escaso; esparcido; poco denso, poco poblado; **— hair** pelo ralo.

**spasm** [spǽzəm] s. espasmo.

**spastic** [spǽstɪk] adj. espástico.

**spat** [spæt] *pret. & p.p. de* **to spit;** *v.*
reñir, disputar; dar un manazo o so-
papo; *s.* sopapo, manotada; riña, desavenencia; **-s** polainas cortas.

**spatter** [spǽtɚ] *v.* salpicar; rociar;
manchar; *s.* salpicadura; rociada.

**speak** [spik] *v.* hablar; decir; recitar;
— **to the point!** ¡vamos al grano!;
**so to** — por decirlo así; **to** — **for**
hablar por, hablar en nombre o en
favor de; pedir, solicitar; apalabrar,
reservar; **to** — **one's mind** hablar
sin rodeos, decir claramente lo que se
piensa; **to** — **out** (*o* — **up**) hablar
claro; hablar con toda franqueza;
hablar en voz alta.

**speaker** [spíkɚ] *s.* orador; conferenciante, conferencista; el que habla; —
**of the House** presidente de la cámara de representantes; **loud-speak-**
**er** altavoz, altoparlante.

**spear** [spɪr] *s.* lanza; arpón (*para
pescar*); brote, retoño, hoja (*de
hierba*); *v.* alancear, lancear, herir con
lanza.

**spearmint** [spírmɪnt] *s.* yerbabuena
(hierbabuena), menta.

**special** [spéʃəl] *adj.* especial; particular;
— **delivery** entrega especial de correo; *s.* tren o autobús especial; carta
urgente, entrega especial; **-ly** *adv.*
especialmente; en especial; sobre
todo.

**specialist** [spéʃəlɪst] *s.* especialista.

**specialization** [spɛʃəlɪzéʃən] *s.* especialización.

**specialize** [spéʃəlaɪz] *v.* especializarse.

**specialty** [spéʃəltɪ] *s.* especialidad.

**species** [spíʃɪz] *s.* especie; especies.

**specific** [spɪsífɪk] *adj.* específico; peculiar, característico; — **gravity** peso
específico; *s.* específico; **-ally** *adv.*
específicamente; especificadamente;
particularmente, en particular.

**specify** [spésəfaɪ] *v.* especificar; estipular.

**specimen** [spésəmən] *s.* espécimen,
muestra, ejemplar.

**speck** [spɛk] *s.* mota; manchita; partícula; **not a** — ni pizca; *v. véase*
**speckle.**

**speckle** [spékl] *s.* manchita; mota; *v.*
motear, salpicar de motas o manchas;
manchar.

**speckled** [spékld] *adj.* moteado; —
**with freckles** pecoso.

**spectacle** [spéktək̮l] *s.* espectáculo; **-s**
gafas, anteojos; **to make a** — **of**
**oneself** ponerse en la evidencia, ponerse en ridículo.

**spectacular** [spɛktǽkjələ̩] *adj.* espectacular, ostentoso, aparatoso.

**spectator** [spéktetɚ] *s.* espectador.

**specter** [spéktɚ] *s.* espectro, fantasma,
aparecido.

**spectrograph** [spéktrogræf] *s.* espectró-
grafo.

**spectrum** [spéktrəm] *s.* espectro.

**speculate** [spékjəlet] *v.* especular; reflexionar.

**speculation** [spɛkjəléʃən] *s.* especula-

ción; reflexión.

**speculative** [spékjəletɪv] *adj.* especulativo; teórico.

**speculator** [spékjəletɚ] *s.* especulador.

**sped** [spɛd] *pret. & p.p. de* **to speed.**

**speech** [spitʃ] *s.* habla; lenguaje, idioma;
discurso, arenga; conferencia; parlamento (*de un actor*); **to make a** —
pronunciar un discurso, hacer una
perorata.

**speechless** [spítʃlɪs] *adj.* sin habla; mudo; estupefacto.

**speed** [spid] *s.* velocidad; rapidez; presteza, prontitud; — **limit** velocidad
máxima; **at full** — a toda velocidad;
*v.* apresurar(se), acelerar(se), dar(se)
prisa; correr; ir con exceso de velocidad; despachar.

**speedily** [spídɪlɪ] *adv.* velozmente,
rápidamente; a todo correr; de prisa,
con prontitud.

**speedometer** [spidúmətɚ] *s.* velocímetro.

**speedy** [spídɪ] *adj.* veloz, rápido.

**spell** [spɛl] *s.* (*charm*) hechizo, encanto;
(*period*) temporada, corto período;
(*sickness*) ataque (*de una enfermedad*);
**to put under a** — aojar; hechizar,
encantar; *v.* deletrear; significar,
indicar; **how is it -ed?** ¿cómo se
escribe?

**speller** [spélɚ] *s.* silabario; deletreador.

**spelling** [spélɪŋ] *s.* ortografía; deletreo;
— **book** silabario.

**spelt** [spɛlt] *pret. & p.p. de* **to spell.**

**spend** [spɛnd] *v.* gastar; usar, agotar,
consumir; **to** — **a day** pasar un día.

**spendthrift** [spéndθrɪft] *s.* derrochador,
gastador, pródigo.

**spent** [spɛnt] *pret. & p.p. de* **to spend.**

**sphere** [sfɪr] *s.* esfera; globo, orbe.

**spherical** [sférɪk̮l] *adj.* esférico.

**sphynx** [sfɪŋks] *s.* esfinge.

**spice** [spaɪs] *s.* especia; picante; aroma;
*v.* condimentar, sazonar con especias.

**spicy** [spáɪsɪ] *adj.* sazonado con especias; picante; aromático.

**spider** [spáɪdɚ] *s.* araña; sartén; —
**web** telaraña.

**spigot** [spígət] *s.* espita, grifo, canilla.

**spike** [spaɪk] *s.* espiga; perno; clavo
largo; alcayata; pico; *v.* clavar; clavetear.

**spill** [spɪl] *v.* verter; derramar(se); des-
parramar(se); hacer caer (*de un caballo*); revelar (*una noticia, un secreto*);
*s.* derrame, derramamiento; vuelco;
caída (*de un caballo*).

**spilt** [spɪlt] *pret. & p.p. de* **to spill.**

**spin** [spɪn] *v.* hilar; girar, dar vueltas,
rodar; bailar (*un trompo*); **to** — **out**
prolongar, alargar; **to** — **yarns** contar cuentos; *s.* giro, vuelta; paseo
(*en automóvil, bicicleta, etc.*); barrena
(*hablando de aeroplanos*).

**spinach** [spínɪtʃ] *s.* espinaca.

**spinal** [spáɪnl] *adj.* espinal; — **column**
columna vertebral, espina dorsal.

**spindle** [spíndl] *s.* huso; eje.

**spine** [spaɪn] *s.* espina; espinazo, espina
dorsal, columna vertebral.

**spinner** [spínəˠ] *s*. hilandero, hilandera; máquina de hilar.

**spinning** [spínɪŋ] *s*. hilandería, arte de hilar; — **machine** aparato para hilar, máquina de hilar; — **mill** hilandería; — **top** trompo; — **wheel** torno de hilar.

**spinster** [spínstəˠ] *s*. soltera; solterona.

**spiral** [spáɪrəl] *adj*. espiral; —**staircase** caracol, escalera espiral; *s*. espiral.

**spire** [spaɪr] *s*. aguja, chapitel de torre; cúspide, ápice; punto más alto; — **of grass** brizna de hierba.

**spirit** [spírɪt] *s*. (*essence*) espíritu; temple; (*animation*) viveza, animación; ánimo; **low -s** abatimiento; **to be in good -s** estar de buen humor; **to be out of -s** estar triste o abatido; *v*. **to — away** llevarse misteriosamente.

**spirited** [spírɪtɪd] *adj*. vivo, brioso, fogoso.

**spiritual** [spírɪtʃuɛl] *adj*. espiritual; *s*. espiritual (*tonada religiosa de los negros del sur de los Estados Unidos*).

**spit** [spɪt] *v*. escupir; expectorar; *pret*. & *p.p. de* **to spit;** *s*. esputo, saliva; · asador.

**spite** [spaɪt] *s*. despecho, rencor, inquina, ojeriza; **in — of** a despecho de; a pesar de; **out of —** por despecho; *v*. picar, irritar, hacer rabiar.

**spiteful** [spáɪtfəl] *adj*. rencoroso.

**splash** [splæʃ] *v*. salpicar; rociar; enlodar, manchar; chapotear (*en el agua*); *s*. salpicadura; rociada; chapoteo.

**spleen** [splin] *s*. bazo; mal humor, rencor.

**splendid** [spléndɪd] *adj*. espléndido.

**splendor** [spléndəˠ] *s*. esplendor; esplendidez.

**splice** [splaɪs] *v*. empalmar, unir, juntar; *s*. empalme; junta.

**splint** [splɪnt] *s*. tablilla; astilla; *v*. entablillar.

**splinter** [splíntəˠ] *s*. astilla; raja; *v*. astillar(se), hacer(se) astillas; romper(se) en astillas.

**split** [splɪt] *v*. hender(se), rajar(se); resquebrajar(se); partir(se), dividir(se); **to — hairs** pararse en pelillos; **to — one's sides with laughter** desternillarse de risa, reventar de risa; **to — the difference** partir la diferencia; *pret*. & *p.p. de* **to split;** *adj*. partido, hendido, rajado; dividido; resquebrajado; *s*. raja, hendedura, grieta; cisma, rompimiento.

**splurge** [spləˠdʒ] *s*. ostentación; fachenda.

**spoil** [spɔɪl] *v*. (*decay*) dañar(se); echar(se) a perder, podrir(se), corromper(se); (*harm*) estropear(se); arruinar; (*overindulge*) consentir, mimar; *s*. botín, presa; **-s of war** botín o despojos de guerra.

**spoke** [spok] *s*. rayo (*de rueda*); *pret*. *de* **to speak.**

**spoken** [spókən] *p.p. de* **to speak.**

**spokesman** [spóksmən] *s*. portavoz, vocero.

**sponge** [spʌndʒ] *s*. (*absorbent*) esponja; (*dependent person*) gorrón, parásito; *v*. lavar o limpiar con esponja; vivir de gorra, vivir a costa ajena; **to — up** chupar, absorber.

**spongecake** [spʌndʒkek] *s*. bizcocho esponjoso.

**sponger** [spʌndʒəˠ] *s*. esponja, gorrón, pegote, parásito, *Am*. pavo.

**spongy** [spʌndʒɪ] *adj*. esponjoso, esponjado.

**sponsor** [spʌnsəˠ] *s*. padrino, madrina; patrón (*el que patrocina una empresa*); defensor; fiador; fomentador, promovedor; *v*. apadrinar; promover, fomentar; patrocinar; ser fiador de.

**spontaneity** [spɑntəníətɪ] *s*. espontaneidad.

**spontaneous** [spɑnténɪəs] *adj*. espontáneo.

**spook** [spuk] *s*. espectro, fantasma, aparecido.

**spool** [spul] *s*. carrete, carretel; *v*. devanar, enredar (*hilo*) en carrete.

**spoon** [spun] *s*. cuchara; *v*. cucharear, sacar con cuchara.

**spoonful** [spúnfəl] *s*. cucharada.

**sport** [sport] *s*. deporte; **in —** en broma, de burla; **to make — of** reírse de, burlarse de; **to be a good —** ser buen perdedor (*en el juego*); ser un buen compañero; *v*. jugar; divertirse; bromear, chancearse; **to — a new dress** lucir un traje nuevo; **-s** *adj*. deportivo; — **clothes** trajes deportivos.

**sports car** [spórtskar] *s*. coche (*carro*) deportivo.

**sportsman** [spórtsmən] *s*. deportista; jugador generoso, buen perdedor (*en deportes*).

**spot** [spɑt] *s*. (*blemish*) mancha, mota; (*place*) sitio, lugar; **in -s** aquí y allí; aquí y allá; **on the —** allí mismo; al punto; **to pay — cash** pagar al contado; *v*. manchar, ensuciar; motear; echar de ver, distinguir; avistar; localizar.

**spotless** [spátlɪs] *adj*. sin mancha, limpio.

**spotlight** [spátlaɪt] *s*. faro giratorio.

**spotted** [spátɪd] *adj*. manchado; moteado.

**spouse** [spauz] *s*. esposo, esposa.

**spout** [spaut] *v*. chorrear; brotar; salir en chorro; emitir; declamar, perorar; hablar mucho; *s*. chorro; surtidor; pico (*de tetera, cafetera, jarra, etc.*); espita.

**sprain** [spren] *v*. torcer (*una coyuntura o músculo*); **to — one's ankle** torcerse el tobillo; *s*. torsión, torcedura.

**sprang** [spræŋ] *pret*. *de* **to spring.**

**sprawl** [sprɔl] *v*. despatarrarse; estar despatarrado; tenderse; **to — one's legs** abrir las piernas; *s*. postura floja (*abiertos los brazos y piernas*).

**spray** [spre] *s*. (*liquid*) rocío, rociada; líquido para rociar; (*branch*) ramita; **sea —** espuma del mar; *v*. rociar.

**spread** [sprɛd] *v*. extender(se); desparramar(se); esparcir(se); difundir(se), diseminar(se), dispersar(se);

propalar(se) (*noticias, rumores, etc.*), propagar(se); **to — apart** abrir(se), separar(se); **to — butter on** poner mantequilla en; **to — out the tablecloth** tender el mantel; **to — paint on** dar una mano de pintura a; **to — with** cubrir de; untar con; *s.* extensión; amplitud, anchura; envergadura (*de un aeroplano*); difusión; diseminación; propagación; cubierta, sobrecama; comilitona, festín; mantequilla, queso, etc., que se le unta al pan; *pret.* & *p.p. de* **to spread.**

**spree** [spri] *s.* juerga, parranda, holgorio; **to go on a —** andar (*o* ir) de parranda o juerga, *Am.* ir de farra.

**sprig** [sprɪg] *s.* ramita.

**sprightly** [spráɪtlɪ] *adj.* vivo, animado, brioso; alegre.

**spring** [sprɪŋ] *v.* saltar; brincar; hacer saltar; **to — a leak** hacer agua (*un barco*); comenzar a gotearse (*la cañería, el techo, etc.*); formarse una gotera; **to — a trap** hacer saltar una trampa; **to — at** abalanzarse sobre; **to — from** salir de, nacer de, brotar de; **to — news of a surprise** dar de sopetón una noticia o sorpresa; **to — something open** abrir algo a la fuerza; **to — to one's feet** levantarse de un salto; **to — up** brotar; surgir; crecer; levantarse de un salto; *s.* primavera; muelle (*de metal*); resorte; elasticidad; salto, brinco; manantial, fuente; origen; *adj.* primaveral; **— board** trampolín; **— mattress** colchón de muelles; **— water** agua de manantial.

**springtime** [sprɪ́ŋtaɪm] *s.* primavera.

**sprinkle** [sprɪ́ŋkl̩] *v.* (*scatter*) rociar; regar; espolvorear; salpicar; (*rain*) lloviznar; *s.* rociada, rocío; llovizna; **— of salt** pizca de sal.

**sprint** [sprɪnt] *v.* echar una carrera; *s.* carrera, carrerilla, corrida corta.

**sprout** [spraʊt] *v.* brotar; retoñar, germinar; hacer germinar o brotar; *s.* retoño, renuevo; **Brussels -s** bretones, coles de Bruselas.

**spruce** [sprus] *s.* abeto; *adj.* pulcro, aseado, pulido; elegante; *v.* **to — up** asearse, componerse, emperifollarse.

**sprung** [sprʌŋ] *pret.* & *p.p. de* **to spring.**

**spun** [spʌn] *pret.* & *p.p. de* **to spin.**

**spur** [spɜ] *s.* espuela; acicate; aguijón, estímulo; espolón (*del gallo*); estirbación (*de una montaña*); **— track** ramal corto (*de ferrocarril*); **on the — of the moment** impensadamente, sin la reflexión debida; por el momento; *v.* espolear, aguijar, picar, incitar; **to — on** animar, incitar a obrar o a seguir adelante.

**spurious** [spúrɪəs] *adj.* espurio.

**spurn** [spɜn] *v.* rechazar, desdeñar, menospreciar.

**spurt** [spɜt] *v.* salir a borbotones; chorrear; echar chorros; hacer un repentino esfuerzo (*para ganar una carrera*); *s.* borbotón, chorrazo, chorro repentino; esfuerzo repentino; **— of anger**

arranque de ira; **-s of flame** llamaradas.

**sputter** [spʌ́tɚ] *v.* chisporrotear; refunfuñar; *s.* chisporroteo; refunfuño.

**sputum** [spjútəm] *s.* esputo.

**spy** [spaɪ] *s.* espía; *v.* espiar; acechar; atisbar; **to — on** espiar, atisbar.

**spyglass** [spáɪglæs] *s.* anteojo de larga vista.

**squab** [skwɑb] *s.* pichón.

**squabble** [skwábl̩] *s.* reyerta; *v.* reñir, disputar.

**squad** [skwɑd] *s.* escuadra, patrulla, partida.

**squadron** [skwádrən] *s.* escuadra; escuadrón.

**squalid** [skwálɪd] *adj.* escuálido.

**squall** [skwɔl] *s.* chubasco; chillido; *v.* chillar.

**squander** [skwándɚ] *v.* despilfarrar, derrochar, malgastar, disipar.

**square** [skwɛr] *s.* (*rectangle*) cuadro; cuadrado; (*central park*) plaza; (*block*) manzana de casas; *Am.* cuadra; escuadra (*de carpintero*); casilla (*de tablero de ajedrez, damas, etc.*); **he is on the —** obra de buena fe; *v.* cuadrar; ajustar, arreglar, saldar (*cuentas*); justificar; cuadricular; **to — one's shoulders** enderezar los hombros; cuadrarse; **to — oneself with** sincerarse con, justificarse ante; **to — a person with another** poner bien a una persona con otra; *adj.* cuadrado, en cuadro, a escuadra, en ángulo recto; saldado; justo, recto, equitativo; franco; **— corner** esquina en ángulo recto; **— meal** comida completa, comida en regla; **— mile** milla cuadrada; **— root** raíz cuadrada; **— dance** danza de figuras; cuadrilla; **to be — with someone** estar en paz con alguien, no deberle nada, *Am.* estar a mano; *adv.* véase **squarely.**

**squarely** [skwɛ́rlɪ] *adv.* equitativamente, honradamente; firmemente; de buena fe; derecho, derechamente; **to hit the target — in the middle** pegar de lleno en el blanco.

**squash** [skwɑʃ] *s.* calabaza; *v.* aplastar, despachurrar o apachurrar.

**squat** [skwɑt] *v.* agazaparse, sentarse en cuclillas; ocupar tierras baldías para ganar título de propietario; *adj.* agazapado, sentado en cuclillas; rechoncho, achaparrado, *Méx., C.A., Andes* chaparro.

**squawk** [skwɔk] *v.* (*noise*) graznar; chillar; (*complain*) quejarse; *s.* graznido; chillido; queja.

**squeak** [skwik] *v.* rechinar, chirriar; chillar; *s.* rechinamiento; chirrido, chillido.

**squeal** [skwil] *v.* chillar; quejarse, protestar; soplar, delatar; *s.* chillido.

**squeamish** [skwímɪʃ] escrupuloso; delicado; remilgado.

**squeeze** [skwiz] *v.* estrujar; despachurrar o apachurrar; exprimir; prensar; apretar; **to — into** meter(se) a estrujones, encajar(se) en; **to — out the**

**juice** exprimir el jugo; **to — through a crowd** abrirse paso a estrujones por entre la muchedumbre; *s.* estrujón; apretón; abrazo fuerte; apretura.

**squelch** [skwɛltʃ] *v.* aplastar; acallar, imponer silencio; reprender; **to — a revolt** sofocar o apagar una revuelta.

**squid** [skwɪd] *s.* calamar.

**squint** [skwɪnt] *v.* mirar de través; mirar de soslayo; mirar achicando los ojos; mirar furtivamente; bizquear (*mirar bizco*); *s.* mirada de soslayo; mirada bizca; mirada furtiva; **squint-eyed** *adj.* bisojo o bizco.

**squire** [skwaɪr] *s.* escudero; *v.* acompañar, escoltar.

**squirm** [skwɝm] *v.* retorcerse; **to — out of a difficulty** forcejear para salir de un aprieto.

**squirrel** [skwɝ́əl] *s.* ardilla.

**squirt** [skwɝt] *v.* jeringar; echar un chisguete; salir a chorritos (*o a chisguetes*); *s.* jeringazo; chisguete.

**stab** [stæb] *v.* apuñalar, dar una puñalada, dar de puñaladas, acuchillar; pinchar; *s.* puñalada, cuchillada, estocada; pinchazo.

**stability** [stəbíləti] *s.* estabilidad.

**stable** [stébl] *adj.* estable; *s.* establo, cuadra; caballeriza; *v.* poner (*los animales*) en la caballeriza.

**stack** [stæk] *s.* pila, montón, rimero; hacina (*de paja o heno*); chimenea, cañón de chimenea; **library -s** estanterías o anaqueles de biblioteca; *v.* amontonar, apilar.

**stadium** [stédɪəm] *s.* estadio.

**staff** [stæf] *s.* (*stick*) báculo, cayado, bastón, vara; (*pole*) asta (*de bandera, de lanza*); (*group*) cuerpo, consejo administrativo; **— of life** sostén de la vida; **— officer** oficial de estado mayor; **army —** estado mayor; **editorial —** redacción; **musical —** pentagrama; **teaching —** cuerpo docente; *v.* proveer de funcionarios y empleados (*una organización*).

**stag** [stæg] *s.* venado, ciervo; macho, hombre; **— dinner** banquete exclusivo para hombres.

**stage** [stedʒ] *s.* (*platform*) tablado; tablas, escenario; escena; (*theater*) teatro; (*period*) etapa, tramo; período; (*stop*) parada; **—coach** ómnibus, autobús; **—hand** tramoyista; **by easy -s** por grados, gradualmente; *v.* representar, poner en escena; **to — a hold-up** hacer un asalto, atracar; **to — a surprise** dar una sorpresa.

**stagger** [stǽgɚ] *v.* (*totter*) tambalearse, tratabillar, bambolearse; hacer tambalear; (*overwhelm*) azorar, asombrar; **to — working hours** escalonar las horas de trabajo; *s.* tambaleo, bamboleo.

**stagnant** [stǽgnənt] *adj.* estancado; **to become —** estancarse.

**staid** [sted] *adj.* grave, serio.

**stain** [sten] *v.* manchar; teñir; colorar; **stained-glass window** vidriera de colores; *s.* mancha, mancilla; tinte, tintura; materia colorante.

**stainless** [sténlɪs] *adj.* sin mancha, inmaculado, limpio; **— steel** acero inempañable o inoxidable.

**stair** [ster] *s.* peldaño, escalón; **-s** escalera.

**staircase** [stérkes] *s.* escalera.

**stairway** [stérwe] *s.* escalera.

**stake** [stek] *s.* estaca; puesta, apuesta; **his future is at —** su porvenir está en peligro o riesgo; **to die at the —** morir en la hoguera; **to have a — in the future of** tener interés en el porvenir de; **to have much at —** irle a uno mucho en una cosa; haber aventurado mucho; *v.* estacar; atar a una estaca; apostar; arriesgar, aventurar; **to — off** señalar con estacas (*un perímetro*).

**stale** [stel] *adj.* viejo; rancio; gastado, improductivo.

**stalemate** [stélmet] *s.* punto muerto; estancación.

**stalk** [stɔk] *s.* tallo; caña.

**stall** [stɔl] *s.* casilla, puesto (*de un mercado o feria*); casilla o sección de un establo; *v.* encasillar, meter en casilla; atascarse (*un auto*); pararse (*el motor*); **he is -ing** está haciendo la pala; **to be -ed in the mud** estar atascado en el lodo.

**stallion** [stǽljən] *s.* caballo de cría, caballo padre, *Ven., Col., Ríopl.* padrillo; *Méx., C.A.* garañón.

**stammer** [stǽmɚ] *v.* tartamudear, balbucear; *s.* tartamudeo, balbuceo.

**stammerer** [stǽmərɚ] *s.* tartamudo.

**stammering** [stǽmərɪŋ] *s.* tartamudeo; *adj.* tartamudo.

**stamp** [stæmp] *v.* (*affix*) sellar; timbrar; poner un sello a; estampar; (*mark*) marcar, imprimir, señalar; (*with foot*) patear, patalear; **to — one's foot** dar patadas en el suelo; **to — out** extirpar, borrar; *s.* sello; timbre, estampilla; estampa; marca, impresión; patada (*en el suelo*); **postage —** sello, *Am.* estampilla, *Am.* timbre; **revenue —** timbre.

**stampede** [stæmpíd] *s.* estampida; huída en desorden; tropel; éxodo repentino; *v.* arrancar, huir en tropel; ir en tropel; ahuyentar, hacer huir en desorden.

**stanch** [stɑntʃ] *v.* restañar, estancar; *adj.* fuerte, firme; leal, constante, fiel.

**stand** [stænd] *v.* poner derecho, colocar verticalmente; (*rise*) ponerse de pie, levantarse; *Am.* parar(se); (*be erect*) estar de pie; *Am.* estar parado; (*withstand*) aguantar, sufrir, tolerar; **to — a chance of** tener probabilidad de; **to — an expense** sufragar un gasto; **to — aside** apartarse; mantenerse apartado; **to — back of** colocarse detrás de; salir fiador de, garantizar a, respaldar a; **to — by** mantenerse a corta distancia; apoyar, defender; estar alerta; **to — for** significar; estar por, apoyar; tolerar; **to — in the way** estorbar; **to — on end** poner(se) de punta; erizarse (*el pelo*); **to — one's ground** mantenerse firme; **to — out** resaltar, destacarse; sobre-salir; **to — six feet** tener seis pies de altura; **to — up for** apoyar, defender; **it -s to reason** es razonable, es lógico; *s.* puesto; mesilla; pedestal; posición; actitud; alto, parada (*para resistir*); quiosco; **grand—** andanada, gradería cubierta (*para espectadores*); **music —** atril; **umbrella —** paragüero.

**standard** [stǽndəd] *s.* (*norm*) norma; nivel normal; criterio; (*model*) modelo, patrón; *Am.* estándar; (*base*) base, pedestal; (*banner*) estandarte; **gold —** patrón de oro; **to be up to —** satisfacer las normas requeridas; *adj.* normal, que sirve de norma; de uso general; corriente; **standard-bearer** portaestandarte.

**standardization** [stændədəzéʃən] *s.* normalización, uniformación, igualación.

**standardize** [stǽndədaɪz] *v.* normalizar, uniformar, *Méx.*, *C.A.*, *Carib.* estandardizar.

**standby** [stǽndbaɪ] *s.* sustituto.

**standing** [stǽndɪŋ] *s.* (*position*) posición; (*fame*) fama, reputación; **of long —** que ha prevalecido largo tiempo; muy antiguo; *adj.* derecho, en pie; de pie; establecido, permanente; **— water** agua estancada; **there is — room only** no quedan asientos.

**standpoint** [stǽndpɔɪnt] *s.* punto de vista.

**standstill** [stǽndstɪl] *s.* alto; pausa; **to come to a —** pararse; hacer alto.

**stank** [stæŋk] *pret. de* **to stink.**

**stanza** [stǽnzə] *s.* estrofa.

**staple** [stépl] *s.* broche de alambre (*para sujetar papeles*); grapa, argolla, armella; artículo principal; **-s** artículos de necesidad prima; *adj.* principal; de uso corriente; indispensable; *v.* asegurar (*papeles*) con broche de alambre; sujetar con armellas.

**star** [stɑr] *s.* estrella; asterisco; **star-spangled** estrellado; *adj.* sobresaliente, excelente; *v.* estrellar, adornar o señalar con estrellas; marcar con asterisco; presentar como estrella (*a un actor*); lucir(se) en las tablas o el cine, hacer el papel principal.

**starboard** [stárbord] *s.* estribor; *adj.* de estribor; **— side** banda de estribor; *adv.* a estribor.

**starch** [stɑrtʃ] *s.* almidón; fecula; *v.* almidonar.

**stare** [ster] *v.* mirar, mirar con fijeza o curiosidad; mirar azorado; clavar la mirada, fijar la vista; *s.* mirada fija, mirada persistente.

**starfish** [stárfɪʃ] *s.* estrella de mar.

**stark** [stɑrk] *adj.* (*utter*) tieso; (*grim*) escueto; **— folly** pura tontería; **— in death** tieso, muerto; **— narrative** narración escueta, sin adornos; *adv.* completamente, totalmente; **— mad** loco de remate; **— naked** enteramente desnudo, en cueros, *Am.* encue-

rado.

**starlight** [stárlaɪt] *s.* luz estelar, luz de las estrellas.

**starry** [stárɪ] *adj.* estrellado, sembrado de estrellas; como estrellas, brillante.

**start** [stɑrt] *v.* comenzar, empezar, principiar; poner(se) en marcha; partir, salir; dar un salto, sobresaltarse; **the motor -s** el motor arranca; **to — after someone** salir en busca de alguien; **to — off** salir, partir; dar principio a; **to — out on a trip** empezar una jornada, emprender un viaje; **to — the motor** hacer arrancar el motor; *s.* comienzo, empiezo, principio; sobresalto; respingo (*de un caballo*); arranque; ventaja (*en una carrera*).

**starter** [stártə] *s.* (*automobile*) arranque; (*person*) arrancador; iniciador; (*first*) primero de la serie; **self-starter** arranque automático.

**startle** [stártl] *v.* asustar(se), sobresaltar(se), espantar(se).

**startling** [stártlɪŋ] *adj.* sobresaltante, pasmoso, asombroso, sorprendente.

**starvation** [starvéʃən] *s.* inanición, hambre.

**starve** [starv] *v.* morir(se) de hambre; hambrear; matar de hambre.

**state** [stet] *s.* estado; condición, situación; **in great —** con gran pompa; *adj.* de estado; del estado; de ceremonia; *v.* declarar, decir; expresar, exponer.

**stately** [stétlɪ] *adj.* majestuoso, imponente.

**statement** [stétmənt] *s.* (*declaration*) declaración; exposición; (*information*) informe, relato; (*bill*) cuenta, estado de cuentas.

**stateroom** [stétrum] *s.* camarote (*de un buque*).

**statesman** [stétsmən] *s.* estadista, hombre de estado.

**static** [stǽtɪk] *adj.* estático; *s.* estática.

**station** [stéʃən] *s.* (*operations point*) estación; (*post*) paradero; puesto; (*condition*) estado, posición social; **broadcasting —** transmisora o emisora; *v.* estacionar, colocar, apostar; **— wagon** *Esp.* rubia; *Méx.* camioneta, huayin; *C.A.* camionetilla.

**stationary** [stéʃənɛrɪ] *adj.* estacionario; fijo.

**stationery** [stéʃənɛrɪ] *s.* papelería.

**statistics** [stətístɪks] *s.* estadística; datos estadísticos.

**statuary** [stǽtʃuɛrɪ] *s.* estatuaria, arte de hacer estatuas; colección de estatuas.

**statue** [stǽtʃu] *s.* estatua.

**stature** [stǽtʃə] *s.* estatura.

**status** [stétəs] *s.* estado, condición; posición social o profesional.

**statute** [stǽtʃut] *s.* estatuto, ordenanza.

**staunch** = **stanch.**

**stave** [stev] *s.* duela de barril; *v.* poner duelas (*a un barril*); **to — off** mantener a distancia; evitar; rechazar.

**stay** [ste] *v.* (*remain*) quedarse, per-

SQ

manecer; parar(se); detener(se); (*sojourn*) hospedarse, alojarse; (*check*) resistir; **to — an execution** diferir o aplazar una ejecución; **to — one's hunger** engañar el hambre; **to — up all night** velar toda la noche; *s.* estada, estancia, permanencia; suspensión; sostén, apoyo; varilla o ballena de corsé; **to grant a —** conceder una prórroga.

**stead** [stɛd]: **in her (his) —** en su lugar; **to stand one in good —** servirle a uno, ser de provecho para uno.

**steadfast** [stédfæst] *adj.* fijo, firme; constante.

**steadily** [stédɪlɪ] *adv.* constantemente; firmemente; sin parar, de continuo; sin vacilar.

**steadiness** [stédɪnɪs] *s.* firmeza; constancia; estabilidad.

**steady** [stédɪ] *adj.* firme; estable; invariable, constante; continuo; *v.* afianzar, mantener firme, asegurar; calmar (*los nervios*).

**steak** [stek] *s.* biftec o bisté; tajada (*para asar o freir*).

**steal** [stil] *v.* (*rob*) robar, hurtar; (*move*) andar furtivamente; **to — away** colarse, escabullirse, escaparse; **to — into a room** meterse a hurtadillas en un cuarto; **to — out of a room** salirse a escondidas de un cuarto, colarse, escabullirse; *s.* robo, hurto.

**stealth** [stɛlθ]: **by — a** hurtadillas, a escondidas, con cautela.

**stealthy** [stélθɪ] *adj.* cauteloso, furtivo, secreto.

**steam** [stim] *s.* vapor; vaho; *adj.* de vapor; por vapor; **— engine** máquina de vapor; **— heat** calefacción por vapor; *v.* cocer al vapor; dar un baño de vapor; saturar de vapor; echar vapor; **to — into port** llegar a puerto (*un vapor*).

**steamboat** [stímbot] *s.* buque de vapor.

**steamer** [stímɚ] *s.* vapor, buque de vapor.

**steamship** [stímʃɪp] *s.* vapor, buque de vapor.

**steed** [stid] *s.* corcel, caballo de combate; caballo brioso.

**steel** [stil] *s.* acero; *adj.* acerado, de acero; *v.* acerar, revestir de acero; **to — oneself against** fortalecerse contra.

**steep** [stip] *adj.* empinado, escarpado, pendiente; muy alto; **— price** precio alto o excesivo; *v.* remojar, empapar; saturar; poner o estar en infusión.

**steeple** [stípl] *s.* aguja, chapitel; cúspide.

**steepness** [stípnɪs] *s.* inclinación abrupta; lo empinado, lo escarpado; altura (*de precios*).

**steer** [stɪr] *s.* novillo; buey; *v.* guiar, conducir, manejar, gobernar; timonear; **to — a course** seguir un rumbo; **the car -s easily** se maneja fácilmente el auto, es de fácil manejo.

**stellar** [stélɚ] *adj.* estelar.

**stem** [stɛm] *s.* tallo; tronco; pedúnculo (*de hoja, flor o fruto*); raíz (*de una palabra*); pie (*de copa*); cañón (*de pipa de fumar*); proa; *v.* estancar, represar; resistir, refrenar; contraponerse a; **to — from** provenir de.

**stench** [stɛntʃ] *s.* hedor, hediondez.

**stencil** [sténsl] *s.* patrón picado; esténcil.

**stenographer** [stənágrəfɚ] *s.* estenógrafo, taquígrafo, mecanógrafo.

**step** [stɛp] *s.* (*walking*) paso; pisada; (*staircase*) peldaño, escalón, grada; (*degree*) grado; (*effort*) gestión; **— by — paso** a paso; **to be in — with** marchar a compás con; estar de acuerdo con; **to take -s** dar pasos; tomar medidas; gestionar; *v.* andar, caminar; dar un paso; **to — aside** hacerse a un lado, apartarse; **to — back** dar un paso o pasos atrás; retroceder; **to — down** bajar; **to — off a distance** medir a pasos una distancia; **to — on** pisar, pisotear; **to — on the gas** pisar el acelerador; darse prisa; **to — out** salir; **to — up** subir; acelerar.

**stepfather** [stépfaðɚ] *s.* padrastro.

**stepmother** [stépmʌðɚ] *s.* madrastra.

**steppe** [stɛp] *s.* estepa.

**stereotype** [stírɪotaɪp] *s.* estéreotipo.

**sterile** [stérəl] *adj.* estéril.

**sterility** [stərílətɪ] *s.* esterilidad.

**sterilize** [stérəlaɪz] *v.* esterilizar.

**sterling** [stɚ́lɪŋ] *s.* vajilla de plata esterlina; *adj.* genuino; de ley; **— silver** plata de ley, plata esterlina; **pound —** libra esterlina.

**stern** [stɚn] *adj.* austero, severo; firme; *s.* popa.

**sternness** [stɚ́nnɪs] *s.* austeridad, severidad; firmeza.

**stethoscope** [stéθəskop] *s.* estetoscopio.

**stevedore** [stívədor] *s.* estibador, cargador.

**stew** [stju] *v.* estofar; preocuparse, apurarse; *s.* estofado, guisado; **to be in a —** estar preocupado o apurado.

**steward** [stjúwəd] *s.* mayordomo; camarero (*de buque o avión*).

**stewardess** [stjúwədɪs] *s.* camarera (*de buque o avión*).

**stick** [stɪk] *s.* palo; vara; garrote; raja de leña; **— of dynamite** barra de dinamita; **control —** palanca (*de aeroplano*); **walking —** bastón; **stick-up** atraco (*para robar*), asalto; *v.* pegar(se), adherir(se); permanecer; estar pegado; picar, pinchar; herir (*con cuchillo, puñal, etc.*); fijar (*con clavos, alfileres, tachuelas, etc.*); atascarse (*en el fango un carro, auto, etc.*); **to — something in** (*o* into) clavar o meter algo en; encajar en; **to — out** salir, sobresalir; proyectarse; **to — out one's head** asomar la cabeza; **to — out one's tongue** sacar la lengua; **to — to a job** perseverar (*o* persistir) en una tarea; **to — up** sobresalir, destacarse; estar de punta (*el pelo*); **to — one's hands up** alzar las manos; **to — someone**

**up** asaltar o atracar a alguien (*para robar*); *véase* **stuck.**

**sticker** [stíkə] *s.* marbete engomado; etiqueta.

**sticky** [stíkɪ] *adj.* pegajoso.

**stiff** [stɪf] *adj.* tieso; rígido; entumido; duro; terco; fuerte; **— climb** subida ardua o difícil; **— price** precio alto o subido; **stiff-necked** terco, obstinado; **scared —** yerto, muerto de miedo; *s.* cadáver.

**stiffen** [stífən] *v.* atiesar(se), poner(se) tieso; entumir(se); endurecer(se); espesar(se); subir de punto, aumentar (*la resistencia*).

**stiffness** [stífnɪs] *s.* tiesura; rigidez; dureza; rigor; terquedad.

**stifle** [stáɪfl] *v.* ahogar(se), asfixiar(se), sofocar(se); apagar, extinguir.

**stigma** [stígmə] *s.* estigma; baldón.

**stigmatize** [stígmətaɪz] *v.* estigmatizar.

**still** [stɪl] *adj.* (*quiet*) quieto; callado, silencioso; (*at ease*) tranquilo; inmóvil; **—born** nacido muerto; **— life** naturaleza muerta; *v.* aquietar; calmar; acallar; *adv.* todavía, aún; *conj.* empero, no obstante, sin embargo; *s.* destiladera, alambique; silencio.

**stillness** [stílnɪs] *s.* quietud, calma, silencio.

**stilt** [stɪlt] *s.* zanco; pilote, puntal, soporte.

**stilted** [stíltɪd] *adj.* tieso, afectado, pomposo.

**stimulant** [stímjələnt] *adj.* & *s.* estimulante.

**stimulate** [stímjəlet] *v.* estimular.

**stimulation** [stɪmjəléʃən] *s.* estimulación, estímulo.

**stimulus** [stímjələs] *s.* estímulo.

**sting** [stɪŋ] *v.* (*pierce*) picar; pinchar, aguijonear; (*irritate*) escocer; *Am.* arder; (*cheat*) embaucar; estafar; *s.* picadura, piquete, mordedura, picazón; aguijón; escozor; **— of remorse** remordimiento.

**stinginess** [stíndʒɪnɪs] *s.* tacañería, mezquindad.

**stingy** [stíndʒɪ] *adj.* mezquino, ruin, tacaño; escaso; *Ríopl., Mex.* codo.

**stink** [stɪŋk] *v.* heder, oler mal; apestar; *s.* hedor, mal olor, hediondez.

**stint** [stɪnt] *v.* escatimar; ser frugal o económico; **to — oneself** privarse de lo necesario, economizar demasiado; *s.* tarea, faena; **without —** sin límite; sin escatimar; generosamente.

**stipulate** [stípjəlet] *v.* estipular.

**stipulation** [stɪpjəléʃən] *s.* estipulación, condición.

**stir** [stɜ] *v.* menear(se); mover(se), bullir(se); atizar (*el fuego*); incitar; conmover; perturbar; revolver; **to — up** incitar; conmover; revolver; suscitar (*un argumento, pelea*, etc.); *s.* meneo, agitación, movimiento; alboroto.

**stirring** [stɜ́ɪŋ] *adj.* conmovedor.

**stirrup** [stíɾəp] *s.* estribo.

**stitch** [stɪtʃ] *v.* coser; dar puntadas; *s.* puntada; punzada; **to be in -es** des-

ternillarse de risa.

**stock** [stak] *s.* (*supply*) surtido; existencias, provisión; (*cattle*) ganado; (*lineage*) cepa, linaje, estirpe; (*shares*) acciones, valores; **in —** en existencia; **live—** ganado; **meat —** caldo de carne; *adj.* en existencia, existente, disponible; común, trivial; **—answer** contestación corriente, común o trivial; **— company** sociedad anónima; compañía teatral; **— exchange** bolsa; **— farm** hacienda de ganado, *Am.* rancho, *Am.* estancia; **— market** mercado de valores, bolsa; **— room** almacén; **— size** tamaño ordinario (*regularmente en existencia*); **—yard** matadero; *v.* surtir, abastecer; tener en existencia (*para vender*); **to — a farm** surtir o proveer de ganado un rancho; **to — up with** surtirse de, acumular.

**stockade** [stakéd] *s.* estacada, empalizada; vallado; *v.* empalizar, rodear de empalizadas.

**stockbroker** [stákbrokə] *s.* bolsista, corredor de bolsa.

**stockholder** [stákholdə] *s.* accionista.

**stocking** [stákɪŋ] *s.* media.

**stoic** [stóɪk] *adj.* & *s.* estoico.

**stoke** [stok] *v.* atizar (*el fuego*); cebar, alimentar (*un horno*).

**stole** [stol] *pret. de* **to steal.**

**stolen** [stólən] *p.p. de* **to steal.**

**stolid** [stálɪd] *adj.* estólido, insensible.

**stomach** [stʌmək] *s.* estómago; *v.* aguantar, tolerar.

**stomp** [stamp] *v.* pisar violentamente.

**stone** [ston] *s.* piedra; hueso (*de las frutas*); **within a -'s throw** a tiro de piedra; *adj.* pétreo, de piedra; **Stone Age** Edad de Piedra; **stone-deaf** totalmente sordo, sordo como una tapia; *v.* apedrear; deshuesar (*las frutas*).

**stony** [stónɪ] *adj.* pedregoso; pétreo, de piedra; duro.

**stood** [stud] *pret. & p.p. de* **to stand.**

**stool** [stul] *s.* (*furniture*) taburete; *C.A.* banquillo; (*toilet*) bacín, bacinica; (*excrement*) excremento; **— pigeon** soplón (*el que delata a otro*).

**stoop** [stup] *v.* agacharse; doblarse, inclinarse; encorvarse; andar encorvado o caído de hombros; rebajarse, humillarse, abajarse; *s.* encorvamiento, inclinación (*de espaldas*); **to walk with a —** andar encorvado o caído de hombros; **stoop-shouldered** cargado de espaldas, encorvado.

**stop** [stap] *v.* (*pause*) parar(se), hacer alto, detener(se); (*cease*) acabar(se); cesar; parar de, dejar de; (*block*) atajar; reprimir; suspender; obstruir, tapar; **to — at a hotel** hospedarse o alojarse en un hotel; **to — at nothing** no pararse en escrúpulos; **to — from** impedir; **to — over at** hacer escala en; **to — short** parar(se) de sopetón, parar(se) en seco; **to — up** tapar, obstruir; atascar; *s.* parada; alto, pausa; estada, estancia; detención;

suspensión; llave (*de instrumento de viento*); traste (*de guitarra*); registro (*de órgano*); — **consonant** consonante explosiva.

**stopover** [stápovɚ] *s.* parada, escala; **to make a — in** hacer escala en.

**stoppage** [stápidʒ] *s.* detención; obstrucción; **work —** paro.

**stopper** [stápɚ] *s.* tapón.

**storage** [stóridʒ] *s.* almacenaje; — **battery** acumulador; **to keep in —** almacenar.

**store** [stor] *s.* (*shop*) tienda; almacén; (*supply*) depósito; acopio; **-s** provisiones; bastimentos; víveres; **department —** almacén; **dry-goods —** lencería, *Méx., Riopl., Andes* mercería, *Am.* cajón de ropa; **fruit —** frutería; **hat —** sombrerería; **grocery —** abacería, tienda de comestibles, *Méx., C.A.* tienda de abarrotes, *Carib.* bodega; **shoe —** zapatería; **to have in —** tener guardado; *v.* almacenar; guardar; abastecer; **to — up** acumular.

**storehouse** [stórhaʊs] *s.* almacén, depósito.

**storekeeper** [stórkipɚ] *s.* tendero; almacenista; guardalmacén.

**storeroom** [stórrum] *s.* almacén; bodega; despensa.

**stork** [stɔrk] *s.* cigüeña.

**storm** [stɔrm] *s.* (*weather*) tormenta, tempestad, borrasca, temporal; (*disturbance*) tumulto; asalto; — **troops** tropas de asalto; **hail —** granizada; **snow—** nevasca; **wind—** vendaval; *v.* asaltar, atacar; rabiar; **it is -ing** hay tormenta, hay tempestad.

**stormy** [stórmɪ] *adj.* tempestuoso, borrascoso; turbulento.

**story** [stórɪ] *s.* (*tale*) cuento, historia, historieta; relato; (*gossip*) chisme; rumor; bola; (*plot*) argumento, trama; (*floor*) piso (*de un edificio*); **newspaper —** artículo de periódico, gacetilla.

**stout** [staʊt] *adj.* corpulento, robusto, fornido; fuerte; firme; leal; valiente.

**stove** [stov] *s.* estufa; cocina de gas, cocina eléctrica; *pret. & p.p. de* **to stave**.

**stow** [sto] *v.* meter, guardar; esconder; estibar, acomodar la carga de un barco; rellenar; **to — away on a ship** embarcarse clandestinamente, esconderse en un barco.

**straddle** [strǽdl] *v.* ponerse o estar a horcajadas; ponerse a caballo, cabalgar; favorecer ambos lados (*de un pleito, controversia, etc.*).

**strafe** [stref] *v.* ametrallar; *Am.* abalear.

**straggle** [strǽgl] *v.* vagar, desviarse; extraviarse; andar perdido; dispersarse; **to — behind** rezagarse.

**straight** [stret] *adj.* (*direction*) recto; derecho; directo; (*proper*) honrado; franco; erguido; correcto; en orden; — **face** cara seria; — **hair** pelo lacio; — **hand of five cards** runfla de cinco

naipes del mismo palo; — **rum** ron puro, sin mezcla; **for two hours —** por dos horas seguidas, por dos horas sin parar; **to set a person —** dar consejo a una persona; mostrarle el camino, modo o manera de hacer algo; *adv.* directamente, derecho, en línea recta; francamente; honradamente; **—away** (*o* **— off**) en seguida, al punto; **to talk — from the shoulder** hablar con toda franqueza o sinceridad.

**straighten** [strétn̩] *v.* enderezar(se); arreglar, poner en orden.

**straightforward** [stretfórwɚd] *adj.* derecho, recto; honrado; franco, sincero; *adv.* directamente, en línea recta.

**straightness** [strétnɪs] *s.* derechura; rectitud; honradez.

**straightway** [strétwe] *adv.* luego, inmediatamente, en seguida.

**strain** [stren] *v.* (*force*) estirar demasiado, hacer fuerza; poner tirante; violentar, forzar (*los músculos, los nervios, la vista, etc.*); (*sift*) colar, tamizar; **to — one's wrist** torcerse la muñeca; *s.* tensión excesiva; tirantez; torcedura; esfuerzo excesivo; linaje, rasgo racial; aire, tonada.

**strainer** [strénɚ] *s.* coladera; cedazo.

**strait** [stret] *s.* estrecho; **-s** estrecho; aprieto, apuro; **—jacket** camisa de fuerza.

**straitlaced** [strétlest] *adj.* estricto.

**strand** [strænd] *v.* encallar; dejar perdido (*sin medios de salir*), dejar aislado, extraviar; **to be -ed** estar encallado; estar extraviado (*sin medios de salir*), estar aislado, andar perdido; *s.* ribera, playa; ramal (*de cuerda, cable, etc.*); hebra, hilo; — **of hair** guedeja; trenza; — **of pearls** hilera de perlas.

**strange** [strendʒ] *adj.* extraño; raro, singular; desconocido.

**strangeness** [stréndʒnɪs] *s.* extrañeza, rareza.

**stranger** [stréndʒɚ] *s.* extraño, desconocido; forastero.

**strangle** [strǽŋgl] *v.* estrangular(se).

**strap** [stræp] *s.* correa; tira de cuero o de tela; correón; tirante; **metal —** banda de metal; *v.* amarrar o atar con correas; azotar (*con correa*); *véase* **strop**.

**stratagem** [strǽtədʒəm] *s.* estratagema.

**strategic** [strətídʒɪk] *adj.* estratégico.

**strategy** [strǽtədʒɪ] *s.* estrategia.

**stratosphere** [strǽtəsfɪr] *s.* estratosfera.

**straw** [strɔ] *s.* paja; **I don't care a —** no me importa un comino; *adj.* de paja; pajizo; **straw-colored** pajizo, color de paja; — **hat** sombrero de paja; — **vote** voto no oficial (*para averiguar la opinion pública*).

**strawberry** [stróberɪ] *s.* fresa.

**stray** [stre] *v.* extraviarse, descarriarse, desviarse; perderse, errar el camino; vagar; *adj.* extraviado, perdido; —

**remark** observación aislada; *s.* animal perdido o extraviado.

**streak** [strik] *s.* (*line*) raya, línea, lista; (*vein*) vena; (*trace*) rasgo; (*beam*) rayo (*de luz*); **— of lightning** relámpago, rayo; *v.* rayar, *Am.* listar, hacer rayas o listas en.

**stream** [strim] *s.* corriente; chorro; río, arroyo, arroyuelo; **— of cars** desfile de autos; **down—** río abajo, agua abajo, con la corriente; **up—** río arriba, agua arriba, contra la corriente; *v.* correr (*el agua*), fluir; brotar, manar; derramarse; flotar (*en el viento*), ondear; **to — out of** salir a torrentes de.

**streamer** [strímæ] *s.* banderola; gallardete; listón, cinta (*que flota en el aire*).

**streamlined** [strímlaɪnd] *adj.* aerodinámico.

**street** [strit] *s.* calle.

**streetcar** [strítkɑr] *s.* tranvía.

**strength** [strɛŋkθ] *s.* fuerza; poder; potencia; fortaleza; **on the — of his promise** fundado en su promesa.

**strengthen** [strɛ́ŋkθən] *v.* fortalecer(se); reforzar(se).

**strenuous** [strɛ́njuəs] *adj.* arduo; enérgico, vigoroso.

**streptomycin** [strɛptomáɪsɪn] *s.* estreptomicina.

**stress** [strɛs] *s.* (*force*) fuerza, esfuerzo; tensión, torsión, compresión; (*importance*) urgencia; énfasis; (*intensity*) acento; *v.* acentuar; recalcar, dar énfasis a, hacer hincapié en.

**stretch** [strɛtʃ] *v.* estirar(se); alargar(se); tender(se); ensanchar; **to — oneself** estirarse, desperezarse; **to — out one's hand** tender o alargar la mano; *s.* trecho, distancia; extension; período de tiempo; elasticidad; tensión; esfuerzo (*de la imaginación*); estirón; **home —** último trecho (*de una carrera*).

**stretcher** [strɛ́tʃæ] *s.* estirador, ensanchador, dilatador; camilla (*para los heridos*).

**strew** [stru] *v.* regar, esparcir.

**strewn** [strun] *p.p. de* **to strew**; **— with** regado de, cubierto de.

**stricken** [stríkən] *p.p. de* **to strike**; *adj.* herido; afligido; agobiado; atacado.

**strict** [strɪkt] *adj.* estricto; **in — confidence** en absoluta confianza, con toda reserva.

**stridden** [strídn̩] *p.p. de* **to stride**.

**stride** [straɪd] *v.* tranquear, caminar a paso largo, dar zancadas, andar a trancos; *s.* zancada, tranco, paso largo.

**strife** [straɪf] *s.* refriega, contienda, pleito.

**strike** [straɪk] *v.* (*hit*) dar, golpear, pegar; azotar; herir; atacar; (*collide with*) chocar con; dar con, encontrar (*oro, petróleo, etc.*); ocurrírsele a uno (*una idea*); asumir, afectar (*una postura, una actitud*); dar (*la hora un reloj*); encender (*un fósforo*); acuñar (*moneda*); declararse o estar

en huelga; **to — at** amagar; acometer; **to — off** borrar, tachar; cortar; **to — one's attention** atraer o llamar la atención; **to — one's fancy** antojársele a uno; **to — one's head against** darse un cabezazo contra; **to — out in a certain direction** tomar cierto rumbo, encaminarse o irse en cierta dirección; **to — someone for a loan** darle un sablazo a alguien; **to — up a friendship** trabar amistad; **to — with terror** sobrecoger de terror; **how does she — you?** ¿qué tal le parece?; ¿qué piensa Vd. de ella;? *s.* golpe; huelga; descubrimiento repentino (*de petróleo, de una mina, etc.*); **—breaker** esquirol (*obrero que sustituye a un huelguista*).

**striker** [stráɪkæ] *s.* (*person on strike*) huelguista; (*device*) golpeador.

**striking** [stráɪkɪŋ] *adj.* notable; llamativo; conspicuo, manifiesto; sorprendente; extraordinario; (*on strike*) que está de huelga; que está en huelga.

**string** [strɪŋ] *s.* cuerda; cordel, cinta, cordón; sarta (*de perlas, cuentas, etc.*); fibra (*de habichuelas, porotos, etc.*); fila, hilera; **— bean** habichuela, judía verde, *Méx.* ejote, *Ch.*, *Ríopl.* poroto; **— of lies** sarta de mentiras; *v.* ensartar; tender (*un cable, un alambre*); desfibrar, quitar las fibras a; encordar (*una raqueta, un violín*); encordelar, atar con cordeles, lazos o cuerdas; tomar el pelo, engañar; **to — out** extender(se), prolongar(se); **to — up** colgar.

**strip** [strɪp] *v.* despojar; robar; desnudar(se); desvestir(se), desmantelar; **to — the gears** estropear el engranaje; **to — the skin from** desollar, pelar; *s.* tira, lista, listón; **— of land** faja de tierra.

**stripe** [straɪp] *s.* (*band*) franja, raya, lista, tira; banda, galón; (*kind*) tipo, índole; *v.* rayar, *Am.* listar, adornar con listas.

**striped** [stráɪpɪd, straɪpt] *adj.* listado.

**strive** [straɪv] *v.* esforzarse; luchar, forcejear; hacer lo posible; **to — to** esforzarse por.

**striven** [strívən] *p.p. de* **to strive**.

**strode** [strod] *pret. de* **to stride**.

**stroke** [strok] *s.* golpe; ataque, apoplejía; **— of a bell** campanada; **— of a painter's brush** pincelada; **— of lightning** rayo; **— of the hand** caricia; **— of the pen** plumada; **at the — of ten** al dar las diez; *v.* frotar suavemente, pasar suavemente la mano, acariciar; alisar.

**stroll** [strol] *v.* dar un paseo, pasearse; vagar; **to — the streets** callejear; *s.* paseo, paseíto.

**strong** [strɔŋ] *adj.* fuerte; forzudo, fornido; vigoroso; recio; enérgico; firme; bien marcado; acérrimo; **— chance** buena probabilidad; **— coffee** café cargado; **— market** mercado firme; **strong-willed** de voluntad fuerte, de-

**ST**

cidido; **strong-arm** violento; *adv.* fuertemente; firmemente.

**stronghold** [stróŋhold] *s.* fuerte, plaza fuerte.

**strop** [strɑp] *v.* asentar *(navajas de afeitar)*; *s.* asentador de navajas.

**strove** [strov] *pret. de* **to strive.**

**struck** [strʌk] *pret. & p.p. de* **to strike; to be — with a disease** darle a uno una enfermedad; **to be — with terror** estar o quedar sobrecogido de terror.

**structural** [strʌ́ktʃərəl] *adj.* estructural, relativo a la estructura.

**structure** [strʌ́ktʃɚ] *s.* estructura; construcción; edificio.

**struggle** [strʌ́gl] *v.* bregar, luchar, pugnar; forcejear; esforzarse; *s.* esfuerzo; contienda; lucha, pugna.

**strung** [strʌŋ] *pret. & p.p. de* **to string.**

**strut** [strʌt] *v.* pavonearse, contonearse; *s.* contoneo; tirante, puntal.

**stub** [stʌb] *s.* trozo, fragmento, pedazo mochado; tocón *(de árbol)*; talón *(de libro talonario, boleto, etc.)*; **— book** libro talonario; **— pen** pluma de punta mocha; *v.* **to — one's foot** dar(se) un tropezón.

**stubble** [stʌ́bl] *s.* rastrojo; cañones *(de la barba).*

**stubborn** [stʌ́bɚn] *adj.* terco, testarudo, obstinado, porfiado, cabezón.

**stubbornness** [stʌ́bɚnnɪs] *s.* terquedad, testarudez, porfía, obstinación.

**stucco** [stʌ́ko] *s.* estuco; *v.* estucar, cubrir de estuco.

**stuck** [stʌk] *pret. & p.p. de* **to stick** pegado; atorado; atascado; **— full of holes** agujereado; **stuck-up** tieso, estirado, orgulloso.

**stud** [stʌd] *s.* *(knob)* tachón, tachuela de adorno; *(button)* botón postizo para camisa; *(bolt)* perno; **—horse** caballo padre; *v.* tachonar; clavetear.

**student** [stjúdn̩t] *s.* estudiante.

**studied** [stʌ́dɪd] *adj.* estudiado.

**studio** [stjúdɪo] *s.* estudio, taller.

**studious** [stjúdɪəs] *adj.* estudioso; aplicado; estudiado.

**study** [stʌ́dɪ] *s.* estudio; cuidado, solicitud; gabinete de estudio; *v.* estudiar.

**stuff** [stʌf] *s.* *(material)* materia; material; *(cloth)* género, tela; *(thing)* cosa; *(medicine)* menjurje, medicina; *(junk)* cachivaches, baratijas; **of good — de** buena estofa; *v.* rellenar; henchir; hartar(se), atracar(se), atiborrar(se).

**stuffing** [stʌ́fɪŋ] *s.* relleno; material para rellenar.

**stumble** [stʌ́mbl] *v.* tropezar, dar(se) un tropezón; dar un traspié; hablar o recitar equivocándose a cada paso; **to — upon** tropezar con; *s.* tropiezo, tropezón, traspié.

**stump** [stʌmp] *s.* tocón *(tronco que queda de un árbol)*; raigón *(de muela)*; muñón *(de brazo o pierna cortada)*; **— of a tail** rabo; **to be up a —** hallarse en un apuro, estar perplejo; *v.* trozar el tronco de *(un árbol)*; renquear, cojear; dejar confuso, confundir; **to —**

**the country** recorrer el país pronunciando discursos políticos.

**stumpy** [stʌ́mpɪ] *adj.* rechoncho, *Am.* chaparro; lleno de tocones.

**stun** [stʌn] *v.* aturdir, pasmar; atolondrar.

**stung** [stʌŋ] *pret. & p.p. de* **to sting.**

**stunk** [stʌŋk] *pret. & p.p. de* **to stink.**

**stunning** [stʌ́nɪŋ] *adj.* aplastante; elegante, bellísimo.

**stunt** [stʌnt] *v.* achaparrar, impedir el desarrollo de, no dejar crecer; hacer suertes; hacer piruetas; *s.* suerte; pirueta, suerte acrobática, maniobra gimnástica; hazaña sensacional.

**stupefy** [stjúpəfaɪ] *v.* atontar; entorpecer; aturdir, atolondrar, pasmar, dejar estupefacto.

**stupendous** [stjupéndəs] *adj.* estupendo.

**stupid** [stjúpɪd] *adj.* estúpido; atontado.

**stupidity** [stjupídətɪ] *s.* estupidez.

**stupor** [stjúpɚ] *s.* letargo, modorra; aturdimiento; **in a —** aletargado.

**sturdy** [stɚ́dɪ] *adj.* fornido, fuerte, robusto; firme.

**stutter** [stʌ́tɚ] *v.* tartamudear; *s.* tartamudeo; tartamudez.

**stutterer** [stʌ́tərɚ] *s.* tartamudo.

**stuttering** [stʌ́tərɪŋ] *adj.* tartamudo; *s.* tartamudeo.

**sty** [staɪ] *s.* pocilga; orzuelo *(en el párpado)*, *Méx.* perilla; *Ríopl.* chiquero.

**style** [staɪl] *s.* estilo; moda; **to be in —** estar de moda, estilarse; *v.* intitular, nombrar; **to — a dress** cortar un vestido a la moda.

**stylish** [stáɪlɪʃ] *adj.* elegante; a la moda.

**stylize** [stáɪlaɪz] *v.* estilizar.

**subdivision** [sʌbdəvíʒən] *s.* subdivisión; parcelación de terrenos.

**subdue** [səbdjú] *v.* subyugar, someter; sujetar, dominar; amansar, domar.

**subdued** [səbdjúd] *p.p. de* **to subdue;** *adj.* sumiso; sujeto; manso; suave; tenue; **— light** luz tenue.

**subject** [sʌ́bdʒɪkt] *s.* súbdito; sujeto; asunto, tema, materia; *adj.* sujeto; sometido; inclinado, propenso; expuesto; [səbdʒékt] *v.* sujetar; someter; subyugar, sojuzgar.

**subjection** [səbdʒékʃən] *s.* sujeción; dominación; sumisión.

**subjective** [səbdʒéktɪv] *adj.* subjetivo.

**subjugate** [sʌ́bdʒəget] *v.* subyugar, sojuzgar.

**sublimate** [sʌ́bləmet] *v.* sublimar.

**sublime** [səbláɪm] *adj.* sublime.

**submarine** [sʌbmərín] *adj.* submarino; [sʌ́bmərɪn] *s.* submarino.

**submerge** [səbmɚ́dʒ] *v.* sumergir(se), hundir(se), sumir(se).

**submission** [səbmíʃən] *s.* sumisión, sometimiento.

**submissive** [səbmísɪv] *adj.* sumiso.

**submit** [səbmít] *v.* someter; **to — a report** someter (presentar o rendir) un informe; **to — to punishment** someterse a un castigo.

**subordinate** [səbɔ́rdn̩ɪt] *adj. & s.* subordinado; subalterno; dependiente; [səbɔ́rdn̩et] *v.* subordinar.

**subscribe** [səbskráɪb] v. subscribir(se); firmar; **to — five dollars** prometer una cuota o subscripción de cinco dólares; **to — for** subscribirse a, abonarse a; **to — to a plan** subscribirse a (o aprobar) un plan.

**subscriber** [səbskráɪbɚ] s. suscritor, abonado; infrascrito (que firma un documento), firmante.

**subscription** [səbskrípʃən] s. subscripción, abono.

**subsequent** [sʌ́bsɪkwɛnt] adj. subsiguiente, subsecuente, posterior; **-ly** adv. después, posteriormente, subsiguientemente.

**subservient** [səbsɚ́vɪənt] adj. servil, servilón.

**subside** [səbsáɪd] v. menguar, disminuir; bajar (de nivel); calmarse, aquietarse.

**subsidize** [sʌ́bsədaɪz] v. subvencionar.

**subsidy** [sʌ́bsədɪ] s. subvención.

**subsist** [səbsíst] v. subsistir.

**substance** [sʌ́bstəns] s. substancia (sustancia).

**substantial** [səbstǽnʃəl] adj. substancial, substancioso; sólido; considerable; importante; **to be in — agreement** estar en substancia de acuerdo.

**substantiate** [səbstǽnʃɪet] v. comprobar; verificar.

**substantive** [sʌ́bstəntɪv] adj. & s. sustantivo.

**substitute** [sʌ́bstətjut] v. sustituir (substituir); reemplazar; s. sustituto, suplente; reemplazo.

**substitution** [sʌbstətjúʃən] s. sustitución (substitución); reemplazo.

**substratum** [sʌ́bstrætəm] s. sustrato.

**subterfuge** [sʌ́btɚfjudʒ] s. escapatoria; subterfugio.

**subterranean** [sʌbtərénɪən] adj. subterráneo.

**subtle** [sʌ́tl̩] adj. sutil.

**subtlety** [sʌ́tl̩tɪ] s. sutileza; agudeza.

**subtract** [səbtrǽkt] v. sustraer (substraer); restar.

**subtraction** [səbtrǽkʃən] s. sustracción (substracción), resta.

**suburb** [sʌ́bɚb] s. suberbio, arrabal.

**suburban** [səbɚ́bən] adj. & s. suburbano.

**subversive** [səbvɚ́sɪv] adj. subversivo (en contra de la autoridad constituida); trastornador, destructivo.

**subway** [sʌ́bwe] s. subterráneo, túnel; metro, ferrocarril subterráneo.

**succeed** [səksíd] v. suceder a; medrar, tener buen éxito, salir bien.

**success** [səksés] s. éxito, buen éxito; triunfo.

**successful** [səksésfəl] adj. afortunado; próspero; **to be —** tener buen éxito; **-ly** adv. con buen éxito, prósperamente.

**succession** [səkséʃən] s. sucesión.

**successive** [səksésɪv] adj. sucesivo.

**successor** [səksésɚ] s. sucesor; heredero.

**succor** [sʌ́kɚ] s. socorro; v. socorrer.

**succumb** [səkʌ́m] v. sucumbir.

**such** [sʌtʃ] adj. tal; semejante; **— a** tal, semejante; **— a good man** un

hombre tan bueno; **— as** tal como, tales como; **at — an hour** a tal hora; **at — and — a place** en tal o cual lugar.

**suck** [sʌk] v. chupar; mamar; **to — up** chupar; sorber; s. chupada; mamada.

**sucker** [sʌ́kɚ] s. chupador; mamón, mamantón; dulce (que se chupa); primo (persona demasiado crédula).

**suckle** [sʌ́kl̩] v. mamar; amamantar, dar de mamar.

**suction** [sʌ́kʃən] s. succión; chupada, aspiración.

**sudden** [sʌ́dn̩] adj. súbito, repentino; precipitado; inesperado; **all of a —** de súbito, de repente, de sopetón; **-ly** adv. de súbito, de repente, de sopetón.

**suddenness** [sʌ́dn̩nɪs] s. precipitación; rapidez.

**suds** [sʌdz] s. espuma, jabonadura.

**sue** [su] v. demandar; **to — for damages** demandar por daños y perjuicios; **to — for peace** pedir la paz.

**suet** [súɪt] s. sebo, gordo, grasa.

**suffer** [sʌ́fɚ] v. sufrir; padecer.

**sufferer** [sʌ́fərɚ] s. sufridor.

**suffering** [sʌ́fərɪŋ] s. sufrimiento, padecimiento; adj. doliente; sufrido, paciente.

**suffice** [səfáɪs] v. bastar, ser bastante o suficiente.

**sufficient** [səfíʃənt] adj. suficiente, bastante; **-ly** adv. suficientemente, bastante.

**suffix** [sʌ́fɪks] s. sufijo.

**suffocate** [sʌ́fəket] v. sofocar(se), ahogar(se), asfixiar(se).

**suffocation** [sʌfəkéʃən] s. asfixia, sofoco.

**suffrage** [sʌ́frɪdʒ] s. sufragio; voto.

**sugar** [ʃúgɚ] s. azúcar; **— bowl** azucarera; **— cane** caña de azúcar; **lump of —** terrón de azúcar; v. azucarar; cristalizarse (el almíbar), Am. azucararse.

**suggest** [səgdʒést] v. sugerir, indicar.

**suggestion** [səgdʒéstʃən] s. sugestión, Am. sugerencia; indicación.

**suggestive** [səgdʒéstɪv] adj. sugestivo.

**suicide** [súəsaɪd] s. suicidio; suicida; **to commit —** suicidarse.

**suit** [sut] s. traje, terno, Carib., Ven. flux (o flus); palo (de la baraja); demanda, pleito; petición; galanteo; v. adaptar, acomodar; agradar; satisfacer; sentar bien, venir bien; caer bien; convenir; ser a propósito; **— yourself** haz lo que quieras, haga Vd. lo que guste.

**suitable** [sútəbl̩] adj. propio, conveniente, debido, a propósito, apropiado, adecuado.

**suitably** [sútəblɪ] adv. propiamente, adecuadamente, convenientemente.

**suitcase** [sútkes] s. maleta, valija.

**suite** [swit] s. serie; comitiva, acompañamiento; **— of rooms** vivienda, apartamento, habitación; **bedroom —** juego de muebles para alcoba.

**suitor** [sútɚ] s. pretendiente, galán; demandante (en un pleito).

**sulk** [sʌlk] v. tener murria; estar hosco

**ST**

o malhumorado; *s.* murria.

**sulky** [sʌ́lkɪ] *adj.* malcontento, hosco, malhumorado; **to be —** tener murria.

**sullen** [sʌ́lɪn] *adj.* hosco, sombrío, tétrico; malhumorado, taciturno.

**sully** [sʌ́lɪ] *v.* manchar, ensuciar; empañar.

**sulphate** [sʌ́lfet] *s.* sulfato.

**sulphide** [sʌ́lfaɪd] *s.* sulfuro.

**sulphur** [sʌ́lfɚ] *s.* azufre.

**sulphuric** [sʌlfjúrɪk] *adj.* sulfúrico.

**sultan** [sʌ́ltn̩] *s.* sultán.

**sultry** [sʌ́ltrɪ] *adj.* bochornoso, sofocante; **— heat** bochorno, calor sofocante.

**sum** [sʌm] *s.* suma; cantidad; esencia, substancia; **— total** total; *v.* sumar; **to — up** resumir, recapitular.

**summarize** [sʌ́mǝraɪz] *v.* resumir, compendiar.

**summary** [sʌ́mǝrɪ] *s.* sumario, resumen; compendio; *adj.* sumario; breve.

**summer** [sʌ́mɚ] *s.* verano; estío; *adj.* veraniego, estival de verano; **— resort** balneario, lugar de veraneo; *v.* veranear.

**summit** [sʌ́mɪt] *s.* cima, cúspide, cumbre.

**summon** [sʌ́mǝn] *v.* citar; convocar, llamar; **-s** *s.* notificación; cita judicial, citación, emplazamiento.

**sumptuous** [sʌ́mptʃʊǝs] *adj.* suntuoso.

**sun** [sʌn] *s.* sol; **— bath** baño de sol; **— lamp** lámpara de rayos ultravioletas; **— porch** solana; *v.* asolear; **to — oneself** asolearse, tomar el sol.

**sunbeam** [sʌ́nbim] *s.* rayo de sol.

**sunburn** [sʌ́nbɚn] *s.* quemadura de sol; *v.* asolear(se); quemar(se) al sol, tostar(se) al sol.

**Sunday** [sʌ́ndɪ] *s.* domingo.

**sundial** [sʌ́ndaɪǝl] *s.* cuadrante solar, reloj de sol.

**sundown** [sʌ́ndaʊn] *s.* puesta del sol.

**sundry** [sʌ́ndrɪ] *adj.* varios, diversos.

**sunflower** [sʌ́nflaʊɚ] *s.* girasol.

**sung** [sʌŋ] *pret. & p.p. de* **to sing.**

**sunglasses** [sʌ́nglæsǝz] *s.* gafas (*anteojos*) de sol.

**sunk** [sʌŋk] *pret. & p.p. de* **to sink.**

**sunken** [sʌ́ŋkǝn] *adj.* hundido, sumido.

**sunlight** [sʌ́nlaɪt] *s.* luz del sol, luz solar.

**sunny** [sʌ́nɪ] *adj.* asoleado o soleado; alegre, risueño, resplandeciente; **— day** día de sol.

**sunrise** [sʌ́nraɪz] *s.* salida del sol, amanecer, amanecida.

**sunset** [sʌ́nset] *s.* puesta del sol.

**sunshine** [sʌ́nʃaɪn] *s.* luz del sol, solana.

**sunstroke** [sʌ́nstrok] *s.* insolación.

**sup** [sʌp] *v.* cenar.

**superb** [supɚ́b] *adj.* soberbio.

**superficial** [supɚfíʃǝl] *adj.* superficial.

**superfluous** [supɚ́fluǝs] *adj.* superfluo.

**superhuman** [supɚhjúmǝn] *adj.* sobrehumano.

**superintend** [suprɪnténd] *v.* dirigir, inspeccionar, vigilar.

**superintendent** [suprɪnténdǝnt] *s.* superintendente; inspector; capataz.

**superior** [sǝpíriɚ] *adj. & s.* superior.

**superiority** [sǝpɪriɔ́rǝtɪ] *s.* superioridad.

**superlative** [sǝpɚ́lǝtɪv] *adj. & s.* superlativo.

**supermarket** [súpɚmɑrkǝt] *s.* supermercado.

**supernatural** [supɚnǽtʃrǝl] *adj.* sobrenatural; **the —** lo sobrenatural.

**supersede** [supɚsíd] *v.* reemplazar.

**superstition** [supɚstíʃǝn] *s.* superstición.

**superstitious** [supɚstíʃǝs] *adj.* supersticioso.

**supervise** [supɚváɪz] *v.* dirigir, inspeccionar, vigilar.

**supervision** [supɚvíʒǝn] *s.* inspección, vigilancia.

**supervisor** [supɚváɪzɚ] *s.* superintendente, inspector; interventor.

**supper** [sʌ́pɚ] *s.* cena.

**supplant** [sǝplǽnt] *v.* suplantar; reemplazar.

**supple** [sʌ́pl̩] *adj.* flexible; dócil.

**supplement** [sʌ́plǝmǝnt] *s.* suplemento; apéndice; [sʌ́plǝmǝnt] *v.* suplementar, completar.

**suppliant** [sʌ́plɪǝnt] *adj. & s.* suplicante.

**supplication** [sʌplɪkéʃǝn] *s.* súplica, plegaria; ruego.

**supply** [sǝpláɪ] *v.* proveer; abastecer, surtir; suplir; dar, suministrar; *s.* provisión, abastecimiento; bastimento; abasto; surtido; **supplies** provisiones; materiales; víveres; pertrechos; **— pipe** cañería o caño de abastecimiento, tubería o tubo de suministro.

**support** [sǝpórt] *v.* (*keep from falling*) sostener; apoyar; (*provide for*) mantener; sustentar; (*bear*) soportar, aguantar; *s.* apoyo; sostén, soporte, puntal; sustento, manutención; amparo.

**supporter** [sǝpórtɚ] *s.* defensor; partidario; mantenedor; sostén, apoyo; tirante (*para medias*).

**suppose** [sǝpóz] *v.* suponer.

**supposed** [sǝpózd] *adj.* supuesto; presunto; **-ly** *adv.* supuestamente.

**supposition** [sʌpǝzíʃǝn] *s.* suposición.

**suppress** [sǝprés] *v.* suprimir; reprimir; parar, suspender; **to — a revolt** sofocar una revuelta o motín.

**suppression** [sǝpréʃǝn] *s.* supresión; represión.

**supremacy** [sǝprémǝsɪ] *s.* supremacía.

**supreme** [sǝprím] *adj.* supremo.

**sure** [ʃur] *adj.* seguro; cierto; estable; *adv. véase* **surely; be — to do it** hágalo sin falta, no deje Vd. de hacerlo; **-ly** *adv.* seguramente; ciertamente; con toda seguridad; sin falta.

**surety** [ʃúrtɪ] *s.* seguridad; garantía, fianza; fiador.

**surf** [sɚf] *s.* oleaje, rompientes; resaca.

**surface** [sɚ́fɪs] *s.* superficie; cara; *v.*

alisar, allanar; poner superficie a.

**surfboard** [sə́fbord] *s.* patín de mar.

**surfeit** [sə́fɪt] *s.* hastío, exceso; *v.* hastiar; empalagar.

**surge** [sɜ́dʒ] *s.* oleada, oleaje; *v.* agitarse, hinchar(se) (*el mar*); surgir.

**surgeon** [sɜ́dʒən] *s.* cirujano.

**surgery** [sɜ́dʒərɪ] *s.* cirujía.

**surgical** [sɜ́dʒɪkl̩] *adj.* quirúrgico.

**surly** [sɜ́lɪ] *adj.* rudo, hosco, malhumorado.

**surmise** [sɚmáɪz] *v.* conjeturar, suponer, presumir; *s.* conjetura, suposición.

**surmount** [sɚmáunt] *v.* superar, vencer; coronar.

**surname** [sɜ́nem] *s.* sobrenombre, apellido; *v.* apellidar, llamar.

**surpass** [sɚpǽs] *v.* sobrepasar, superar, sobrepujar, exceder, aventajar.

**surpassing** [sɚpǽsɪŋ] *adj.* sobresaliente, excelente.

**surplus** [sɜ́plʌs] *s.* sobra, sobrante, exceso, excedente; superávit; *adj.* sobrante, excedente, de sobra.

**surprise** [səpráɪz] *s.* sorpresa; *v.* sorprender.

**surprising** [səpráɪzɪŋ] *adj.* sorprendente.

**surrender** [sərɛ́ndɚ] *v.* rendir(se), entregar(se), darse; ceder; *s.* rendición; entrega; cesión; sumisión.

**surround** [səráund] *v.* rodear, cercar, circundar.

**surrounding** [səráundɪŋ] *adj.* circundante, circunvecino, circunstante.

**surroundings** [səráundɪŋz] *s. pl.* alrededores, inmediaciones, cercanías; ambiente.

**survey** [sɜ́ve] *s.* (*inspection*) examen, reconocimiento, enspección, estudio; (*measure*) medición agrimensura (*de un terreno*); plano (*de un terreno*); bosquejo o esbozo general (*de historia, literatura, etc.*); — **course** curso general o comprensivo; [sɚvé] *v.* examinar, inspeccionar, reconocer medir (*un terreno*), levantar un plano (*el agrimensor*).

**surveyor** [sɚvéɚ] *s.* agrimensor.

**survival** [sɚváɪvl̩] *s.* supervivencia; sobreviviente; resto.

**survive** [sɚváɪv] *c.* sobrevivir; quedar vivo, salvarse.

**survivor** [sɚváɪvɚ] *s.* sobreviviente.

**susceptible** [səsɛ́ptəbl̩] *adj.* susceptible; — **of proof** capaz de probarse; — **to** propenso a.

**suspect** [sʌ́spɛkt] *s.* sospechoso; [səspékt] *v.* sospechar.

**suspend** [səspɛ́nd] *v.* suspender.

**suspenders** [səspɛ́ndɚz] *s.* tirantes (*de pantalón*).

**suspense** [səspɛ́ns] *s.* (*uncertainty*) suspensión, incertidumbre; (*anxiety*) ansiedad; **to keep in** — tener en suspenso, tener en duda.

**suspension** [səspɛ́nʃən] *s.* suspensión; — **bridge** puente colgante.

**suspicion** [səspíʃən] *s.* sospecha.

**suspicious** [səspíʃəs] *adj.* sospechoso; suspicaz.

**sustain** [səstén] *v.* (*prolong*) sostener; mantener; (*support*) sustentar; (*bear, endure*) aguantar; (*defend*) apoyar, defender; (*undergo*) sufrir (*un daño o pérdida*).

**sustenance** [sʌ́stənəns] *s.* sustento; subsistencia; alimentos; mantenimiento.

**swagger** [swǽgɚ] *v.* pavonearse, contonearse; fanfarronear; *s.* pavoneo, contoneo; fanfarronada.

**swain** [swen] *s.* galán.

**swallow** [swálo] *s.* golondrina; trago; *v.* tragar; deglutir.

**swam** [swæm] *pret. de* **to swim**.

**swamp** [swamp] *s.* pantano; ciénaga; — **land** cenagal, terreno pantanoso; *v.* inundar(se); sumergir(se); **to be -ed with work** estar abrumado de trabajo.

**swampy** [swámpɪ] *adj.* pantanoso, cenagoso, fangoso.

**swan** [swan] *s.* cisne.

**swap** [swap] *v.* cambalachear, cambiar, trocar; *s.* cambalache, cambio, trueque.

**swarm** [swɔrm] *s.* enjambre; *v.* pulular; bullir, hervir, hormiguear.

**swarthy** [swɔ́rðɪ] *adj.* trigueño, moreno, *Am.* prieto.

**swat** [swat] *v.* pegar, aporrear; aplastar de un golpe (*una mosca*); *s.* golpe.

**sway** [swe] *v.* mecer(se); cimbrar(se); balancearse; ladear(se); oscilar; tambalear; influir; *s.* oscilación; vaivén; balanceo; influjo, influencia; mando; predominio.

**swear** [swer] *v.* jurar; renegar, blasfemar, echar maldiciones; juramentar, tomar juramento; **to — by** jurar por; poner toda su confianza en; **to — in** juramentar; **to — off smoking** jurar no fumar más, renunciar al tabaco.

**sweat** [swɛt] *v.* sudar; trasudar; hacer sudar; *s.* sudor; trasudor.

**sweater** [swɛ́tɚ] *s. Am.* suéter; sudador, el que suda.

**sweaty** [swɛ́tɪ] *adj.* sudoroso.

**Swede** [swid] *s.* sueco.

**Swedish** [swídɪʃ] *adj.* sueco; *s.* sueco, idioma sueco.

**sweep** [swip] *v.* barrer; dragar (*puertos, rios, etc.*); extenderse; **to — down upon** caer sobre; asolar; **to — everything away** barrer con todo; **she swept into the room** entró garbosamente en la sala; *s.* barrida; extensión; soplo (*del viento*).

**sweeper** [swípɚ] *s.* barrendero; **carpet** — escoba mecánica.

**sweeping** [swípɪŋ] *s.* barrido; **-s** basura; *adj.* abarcador, que lo abarca todo, vasto; asolador; — **victory** victoria completa.

**sweet** [swit] *adj.* dulce; oloroso; fresco; — **butter** mantequilla sin sal; — **corn** maíz tierno; — **milk** leche fresca; — **pea** guisante de olor; — **potato** batata, *Am.* camote, *Am.* boniato; **to have a — tooth** ser goloso, gustarle a uno los dulces; *s.*

dulce, golosina; **my —** mi vida, mi alma.

**sweeten** [swítn̩] *v.* endulzar(se), dulcificar(se); suavizar.

**sweetheart** [swíthɑrt] *s.* querida, novia, prometida; amante, querido, galán, novio.

**sweetmeat** [swítmit] *s.* confite, confitura dulce, golosina.

**sweetness** [swítnɪs] *s.* dulzura; melosidad; suavidad.

**swell** [swɛl] *v.* hinchar(se), henchir(se), inflar(se); dilatar(se), abultar(se); acrecentar; *s.* hinchazón; protuberancia; oleaje; *adj.* elegante; muy bueno, excelente, magnífico; **to have a — head** creerse gran cosa; ser vanidoso.

**swelling** [swɛ́lɪŋ] *s.* hinchazón; chichón, bulto; protuberancia.

**swelter** [swɛ́ltɚ] *v.* sofocarse de calor.

**swept** [swɛpt] *pret.* & *p.p. de* **to sweep**.

**swerve** [swɝv] *v.* desviar(se); torcer; cambiar repentinamente de rumbo; *s.* desvío brusco, cambio repentino de dirección; **to make a — to the right** torcer a la derecha.

**swift** [swɪft] *adj.* veloz, rápido.

**swiftness** [swíftnɪs] *s.* velocidad, rapidez, presteza, prontitud.

**swim** [swɪm] *v.* nadar; flotar; **to — across** pasar a nado, atravesar nadando; **my head is swimming** tengo vértigo, se me va la cabeza, estoy desvanecido; *s.* nadada; **— suit** traje de baño o natación.

**swimmer** [swímɚ] *s.* nadador.

**swindle** [swíndl̩] *v.* estafar; *s.* estafa.

**swine** [swaɪn] *s.* marrano, puerco, cerdo, cochino; marranos, puercos, cerdos.

**swing** [swɪŋ] *v.* columpiar(se), mecer(se), balancear(se); oscilar; hacer oscilar; blandir (*un bastón, espada, etc.*); colgar; girar; hacer girar; **to — a deal** llevar a cabo un negocio; **to — around** dar vuelta, girar; **to — one's arms** girar o menear los brazos; **to — open** abrirse de pronto (*una puerta*); *s.* columpio; hamaca; balanceo; vaivén; compás, ritmo; golpe, guantada, puñetazo; **— door** puerta giratoria; **— shift** turno de trabajo desde las dieciséis hasta medianoche; **in full —** en su apogeo, en pleno movimiento; **to give someone a full —** darle a alguien completa libertad de acción.

**swipe** [swaɪp] *v.* hurtar, sisar.

**swirl** [swɝl] *v.* arremolinarse; girar, dar vueltas; *s.* remolino; torbellino; vuelta, movimiento giratorio.

**Swiss** [swɪs] *adj.* & *s.* suizo.

**switch** [swɪtʃ] *s.* (*change*) mudanza; (*whip*) látigo, (*blow*) azote; *Méx.*, *Andes* chicote, *Ríopl.* rebenque; *Méx.*, *Andes* fuete; latigazo; pelo postizo; cambio; **electric —** interruptor, conmutador; **railway —** aguja, cambio; **—man** guardagujas, *Andes*, *Ríopl.* cambiavía; *Méx.* guardavía; *v.* azotar; desviar(se); cambiar(se); **to — off** cortar (*la comunicación o la*

*corriente eléctrica*); apagar (*la luz eléctrica*); **to — on the light** encender la luz.

**switchboard** [swítʃbɔrd] *s.* cuadro o tablero de distribución; cuadro conmutador.

**swivel** [swívl̩] *adj.* giratorio.

**swollen** [swólən] *p.p. de* **to swell**.

**swoon** [swun] *v.* desvanecerse, desmayarse; *s.* desmayo.

**swoop** [swup] *v.* **to — down upon** caer de súbito sobre; abalanzarse sobre; acometer; **to — off** cortar de un golpe; **to — up** agarrar, arrebatar; *s.* descenso súbito; arremetida; **at one — de un golpe.

**sword** [sord] *s.* espada; **— belt** talabarte.

**swore** [swor] *pret. de* **to swear**.

**sworn** [sworn] *p.p. de* **to swear**.

**swum** [swʌm] *p.p. de* **to swim**.

**swung** [swʌŋ] *pret.* & *p.p. de* **to swing**.

**syllable** [síləbl̩] *s.* sílaba.

**syllabus** [síləbəs] *s.* sílabo.

**symbol** [símbl̩] *s.* símbolo.

**symbolic** [sɪmbálɪk] *adj.* simbólico.

**symbolism** [símbl̩ɪzəm] *s.* simbolismo.

**symmetrical** [sɪmétrɪkl̩] *adj.* simétrico.

**symmetry** [símɪtrɪ] *s.* simetría.

**sympathetic** [sɪmpəθétɪk] *adj.* compasivo; favorablemente dispuesto; que compadece; **— towards** favorablemente dispuesto a (*o* hacia).

**sympathize** [símpəθaɪz] *v.* compadecer(se); condolerse.

**sympathy** [símpəθɪ] *s.* compasión, lástima; armonía; **to extend one's —** dar el pésame.

**symphony** [símfənɪ] *s.* sinfonía; **— orchestra** orquesta sinfónica.

**symposium** [sɪmpósɪəm] *s.* coloquio.

**symptom** [símptəm] *s.* síntoma.

**syndicate** [síndɪkɪt] *s.* sindicato; **newspaper —** sindicato periodístico; [síndɪket] *v.* sindicar, formar un sindicato; sindicarse, combinarse para formar un sindicato; vender (*un cuento, caricatura, serie de artículos, etc.*) a un sindicato.

**syndrome** [síndrom] *s.* síndrome.

**synonym** [sínənɪm] *s.* sinónimo.

**synonymous** [sɪnánəməs] *adj.* sinónimo.

**synopsis** [sɪnápsɪs] *s.* sinopsis.

**syntax** [síntæks] *s.* sintaxis.

**synthesis** [sínθəsɪs] *s.* síntesis.

**synthesize** [sínθəsaɪz] *v.* sintetizar.

**synthetic** [sɪnθétɪk] *adj.* sintético.

**syringe** [sírɪndʒ] *s.* jeringa.

**syrup** = **sirup**.

**system** [sístəm] *s.* sistema.

**systematic** [sɪstəmǽtɪk] *adj.* sistemático.

**systemic** [sɪstémɪk] *adj.* sistemático.

# T

**tab** [tæb] *s.* (*flap*) lengüeta; (*bill*) cuenta.

**tabernacle** [tǽbɚnækl̩] *s.* tabernáculo.

**table** [tébl̩] *s.* mesa; tabla (*de materias, de multiplicar, etc.*); **— cover** tapete, cubremesa; **—land** mesa, meseta; v. poner sobre la mesa; formar tabla o índice; **to — a motion** dar carpetazo a una moción, aplazar la discusión de una moción.

**tablecloth** [tébļklɔθ] s. mantel.

**tablespoon**[tébļspun]s. cuchara grande.

**tablespoonful** [tébļspunfʊl] s. cucharada.

**tablet** [tǽblɪt] s. tableta; tablilla, pastilla; bloc de papel; lápida, placa.

**tableware** [tébļwɛr] s. vajilla, servicio de mesa.

**taboo** [tæbú] s. tabú.

**tabulate** [tǽbjəlet] v. formar tablas o listas.

**tacit** [tǽsɪt] adj. tácito.

**taciturn** [tǽsətɚn] adj. taciturno, silencioso.

**tack** [tæk] s. tachuela; hilván; virada o cambio de rumbo (de una embarcación); amura, jarcia (para sostener el ángulo de una vela); **to change —** cambiar de amura, cambiar de rumbo; v. clavetear con tachuelas; coser, hilvanar; pegar, clavar; juntar, unir; virar, cambiar de rumbo; zigzaguear (un barco de vela).

**tackle** [tǽkļ] s. aparejo, equipo, enseres, avíos; agarrada (en futbol); atajador (en futbol); **fishing —** avíos de pescar; v. agarrar, asir, atajar (en futbol); atacar (un problema); acometer (una empresa).

**tact** [tækt] s. tacto, tino, tiento.

**tactful** [tǽktfəl] adj. cauto, prudente, diplomático.

**tactics** [tǽktɪks] s. táctica.

**tactless** [tǽktlɪs] adj. falto de tacto o de tino; imprudente, incauto.

**taffeta** [tǽfɪtə] s. tafetán.

**tag** [tæg] s. (label) marbete, etiqueta; cartela; (loose end) pingajo, rabito, cabo; **to play —** jugar al tócame tú, jugar a la pega; v. pegar un marbete a, marcar; **to — after** seguir de cerca a, pisar los talones a; **to — something on to** juntar, añadir o agregar algo a.

**tail** [tel] s. (animal) cola, rabo; (object) cabo, extremo, extremidad; **— light** farol trasero, farol de cola; **— spin** barrena.

**tailor** [télɚ] s. sastre.

**taint** [tent] s. tacha, mancha; corrupción; v. manchar; corromper(se), inficionar(se).

**take** [tek] v. tomar; coger; llevar; conducir; dar (un paseo, vuelta, paso, salto); asumir (un viaje); asumir; sacar o tomar (una fotografía); **to—a chance** aventurarse, correr un riesgo; **to — a fancy to** caerle en gracia a uno; aficionarse a; antojársele a uno; **to — a look at** mirar a, echar una mirada a; **to — a notion to** antojársele a uno; **to — after** salir a, parecerse a; seguir el ejemplo de; **to — amiss** interpretar mal, echar a mala parte; **to — an oath** prestar juramento; **to — apart** desarmar, desmontar; **to — away** llevarse; **to — back one's**

**words** desdecirse, retractarse; **to — back to** devolver (algo) a; **to — by surprise** coger desprevenido, coger de sorpresa; **to — care of** cuidar de, atender a; **to — charge of** encargarse de; **to — cold** resfriarse, acatarrarse; **to — down in writing** poner por escrito, apuntar; **to — effect** surtir efecto, dar resultado; entrar en vigencia (una ley); **to — exercise** hacer ejercicio; hacer gimnasia; **to — from** quitar a; sustraer de, restar de; **to — in** meter en; recibir; abarcar; embaucar; reducir, achicar (un vestido); **to — leave** decir adiós, despedirse; **to — off** quitar; descontar, rebajar; despegar (un aeroplano); remedar, parodiar (a alguien); **to — offense** ofenderse, darse por ofendido; **to — on a responsibility** asumir una responsabilidad; **to — out** sacar; **to — place** tener lugar, suceder, ocurrir; **to — stock** hacer inventario; **to — stock in** creer, tener confianza en; **to — the floor** tomar la palabra; **to — to heart** tomar a pechos, tomar en serio; **to — to one's heels** poner pies en polvorosa; **to — to task** reprender, regañar; **to — up a matter** tratar un asunto; **to — up space** ocupar espacio; **I — it that** supongo que; s. toma; **take-off** despegue (de un aeroplano); remedo, parodia.

**taken** [tékən] p.p. de **to take**; **to be — ill** caer enfermo.

**talcum** [tǽlkəm] s. talco; **— powder** talco en polvo.

**tale** [tel] s. (story) cuento, relato, fábula; (gossip) chisme; **to tell -s** contar cuentos o chismes; chismear, murmurar.

**talebearer** [télbɛrɚ] s. soplón, chismoso.

**talent** [tǽlənt] s. talento.

**talented** [tǽləntɪd] adj. talentoso.

**talk** [tɔk] v. hablar; charlar, platicar, conversar; **to — into** inducir o persuadir a; **to — nonsense** decir tonterías, hablar disparates; **to — out of** disuadir de; **to — over** discutir; **to — up** alabar; hablar claro o recio, hablar en voz alta; s. charla, conversación, plática; habla; discurso; conferencia; rumor; **— of the town** comidilla, tema de murmuración.

**talkative** [tɔ́kətɪv] adj. hablador, locuaz, platicador.

**talker** [tɔ́kɚ] s. hablador; conversador; platicador; orador.

**tall** [tɔl] adj. alto; **— tale** cuento exagerado o increíble; **six feet —** seis pies de altura o de alto.

**tallow** [tǽlo] s. sebo.

**tally** [tǽlɪ] s. cuenta; **— sheet** plana para llevar la cuenta; v. llevar la cuenta; **to — up** contar, sumar; **to — with** corresponder con, concordar con.

**tame** [tem] adj. manso; dócil; **— amusement** diversión poco animada o desabrida; v. amansar, domar, domeñar; domesticar.

**tamper** [tǽmpə] v. to — with meterse con, juguetear con; falsificar (un documento); to — with a lock tratar de forzar una cerradura.

**tan** [tæn] v. (cure) curtir, adobar (pieles); (punish) zurrar, azotar; (sunburn) tostar(se), requemar(se); adj. tostado, requemado; color de canela; bayo, amarillento; s. color moreno, de canela o café con leche.

**tang** [tæŋ] s. sabor u olor picante.

**tangent** [tǽndʒənt] adj. & s. tangente; to go off at a — salirse por la tangente.

**tangerine** [tǽndʒərin] s. naranja tangerina o mandarina.

**tangible** [tǽndʒəbl] adj. tangible, palpable; corpóreo.

**tangle** [tǽŋgl] v. enredar(se), enmarañar(se); confundir(se), embrollar(se); s. enredo, maraña, embrollo; confusión.

**tank** [tæŋk] s. tanque; depósito; swimming — piscina.

**tanner** [tǽnə] s. curtidor.

**tannery** [tǽnəri] s. curtiduría, tenería.

**tannic acid** [tǽnɪkǽsəd] s. ácido tánico.

**tantalize** [tǽntlaɪz] v. molestar; hacer desesperar; exasperar.

**tantamount** [tǽntəmaʊnt] adj. equivalente.

**tantrum** [tǽntrəm] s. berrinche.

**tap** [tæp] s. (blow) palmadita; golpecito; (faucet) espita, grifo, llave; — dance zapateado, Andes, Ríopl. zapateo; —room bar; beer on — cerveza del barril, cerveza de sifón; v. tocar, golpear ligeramente; dar una palmadita o golpecito; taladrar; extraer; to — a tree sangrar un árbol.

**tape** [tep] s. cinta, cintilla; — measure cinta para medir; —worm solitaria; — recorder magnetófono; grabadora; adhesive — tela adhesiva, esparadrapo; v. atar o vendar con cinta; medir con cinta.

**taper** [tépə] s. (candle) velita, candela; (diminished size) adelgazamiento paulatino; v. adelgazar, disminuir gradualmente; to — off ahusar(se), ir disminuyendo (hasta rematar en punta).

**tapestry** [tǽpɪstri] s. tapiz, colgadura; tapicería; tela (para forrar muebles).

**tapeworm** [tépwəm] s. tenia, solitaria.

**tapioca** [tæpɪókə] s. tapioca.

**tar** [tar] s. alquitrán, brea, pez (f.); v. alquitranar, embrear, poner brea o alquitrán.

**tardy** [tárdɪ] adj. tardo, tardió; to be — llegar tarde o retrasado.

**target** [tárgɪt] s. blanco; — practice tiro al blanco.

**tariff** [tǽrɪf] s. tarifa; arancel, impuesto.

**tarnish** [tárnɪʃ] v. empañar(se); manchar; perder el lustre; s. deslustre, falta de lustre, empañamiento; mancha.

**tarry** [tǽrɪ] v. demorarse, tardar(se).

**tart** [tart] s. acre, agridulce; agrio; picante; — reply respuesta mordaz o

agria; s. tarta, torta rellena con dulce de frutas.

**task** [tæsk] s. faena, tarea, quehacer; to take to — reprender, regañar.

**task force** [tǽskfɔrs] s. agrupación de fuerzas militares para cierta misión.

**tassel** [tǽsl] s. borla.

**taste** [test] v. gustar; probar; saborear, paladear; to — of onion saber a cebolla; it -s sour sabe agrio, tiene un sabor o gusto agrio; s. gusto; sabor; prueba; afición; after— dejo; in good— de buen gusto; to take a—of probar.

**tasteless** [téstlɪs] adj. insípido; desabrido; de mal gusto.

**tasty** [téstɪ] adj. sabroso, gustoso; de buen gusto.

**tatter** [tǽtə] s. harapo, Carib. hilacho.

**tattered** [tǽtəd] adj. roto, harapiento, andrajoso.

**tattle** [tǽtl] v. chismear, murmurar; s. habladuría, murmuración, hablilla; —tale chismoso, soplón.

**tattoo** [tætú] s. tatuaje.

**taught** [tɔt] pret. & p.p. de to teach.

**taunt** [tɔnt] v. mofarse de, echar pullas; reprochar; s. mofa, pulla.

**tavern** [tǽvən] s. taberna; posada.

**tax** [tæks] s. impuesto, contribución; esfuerzo; v. imponer contribuciones a; tasar; abrumar; reprender, reprobar; cobrar (un precio); to — one's patience abusar de la paciencia.

**taxation** [tækséʃən] s. impuestos, contribuciones; imposición de contribuciones.

**taxi** [tǽksɪ] s. taxímetro, taxi, automóvil de alquiler; v. ir en taxímetro; taxear (un aeroplano).

**taxicab** [tǽksɪkæb] = taxi.

**taxidermy** [tǽksɪdəmɪ] s. taxidermia.

**taxpayer** [tǽkspeə] s. contribuyente.

**tea** [ti] s. té.

**teach** [titʃ] v. enseñar; instruir.

**teacher** [títʃə] s. maestro, maestra.

**teaching** [títʃɪŋ] s. enseñanza; instrucción; doctrina.

**teacup** [tíkʌp] s. taza para té.

**teakettle** [tíkɛtl] s. marmita, tetera, Ríopl. pava (para el mate).

**team** [tim] s. equipo (de jugadores); partido, grupo; tronco (de caballos, mulas, etc.); yunta (de bueyes): — work cooperación; v. uncir, enganchar; formar pareja; acarrear, transportar; to — up unirse, formar un equipo.

**teamster** [tímstə] s. carretero.

**teapot** [típat] s. tetera.

**tear** [tɪr] s. lágrima; — gas gas lacrimógeno o lacrimante; to burst into -s romper a llorar; deshacerse en lágrimas.

**tear** [ter] v. rasgar(se); desgarrar, romper; to — along ir a toda velocidad; andar aprisa, correr; to — apart desarmar, desmontar; separar, apartar; to — away arrancar; irse; to — down demoler, derribar (un edificio); desarmar, desmontar (una máquina);

**to — off in a hurry** salir corriendo, salir a la carrera; **to — one's hair** mesarse los cabellos; *s.* desgarradura, rasgadura; rasgón, rotura; prisa; **wear and —** desgaste.

**tearful** [tírfəl] *adj.* lloroso.

**tease** [tiz] *v.* embromar; molestar; importunar.

**teaspoon** [tíspun] *s.* cucharilla, cucharita.

**teaspoonful** [tíspunfʋl] *s.* cucharadita.

**teat** [tit] *s.* teta.

**technical** [tɛ́knɪkl] *adj.* técnico.

**technician** [tɛkníʃən] *s.* técnico.

**technique** [tɛkník] *s.* técnica.

**technology** [tɛknálədʒɪ] *s.* tecnología.

**tedious** [tídɪəs] *adj.* tedioso, pesado, aburrido, fastidioso.

**tediousness** [tídɪəsnɪs] *s.* tedio.

**teem** [tim] *v.* **to — with** abundar en, estar lleno de.

**teen-ager** [tínedʒəˠ] *s.* joven de la edad de 13 a 19 años; *Col.* cocacolo.

**teens** [tinz] *s. pl.* edad de trece a diecinueve años; números de trece a diecinueve; **to be in one's —** tener de trece a diecinueve años.

**teeth** [tiθ] *s. pl. de* **tooth; he escaped by the skin of his —** por poco no se escapa, se escapó por milagro.

**telecast** [télǝkæst] *s.* teledifusión.

**telegram** [télǝgræm] *s.* telegrama.

**telegraph** [télǝgræf] *s.* telégrafo; *v.* telegrafiar.

**telegraphic** [tɛlǝgrǽfɪk] *adj.* telegráfico.

**telegraphy** [tǝlégrǝfɪ] *s.* telegrafía.

**telepathy** [tǝlépǝθɪ] *s.* telepatía.

**telephone** [télǝfon] *s.* teléfono; **— booth** casilla de teléfono; **— operator** telefonista; **— receiver** receptor telefónico; *v.* telefonear, llamar por teléfono.

**telescope** [télǝskop] *s.* telescopio; *v.* enchufar(se), encajar(se) un objeto en otro.

**television** [télǝvɪʒǝn] *s.* televisión.

**tell** [tɛl] *v.* (*recount*) decir; contar; expresar; explicar; (*identify*) adivinar; **to — on someone** delatar a alguien, contar chismes de alguien; **to — someone off** decirle a alguien cuatro verdades; **his age is beginning to —** ya comienza a notársele la edad.

**teller** [télǝˠ] *s.* narrador, relator; pagador o recibidor (*de un banco*); escrutador de votos.

**tellurium** [tǝlúrɪǝm] *s.* telurio.

**temerity** [tǝmérǝtɪ] *s.* temeridad.

**temper** [tempǝˠ] *v.* templar; *s.* temple (*de un metal*); genio, temple, humor; mal genio; **to keep one's —** contenerse, dominarse; **to lose one's —** perder la calma, encolerizarse.

**temperament** [témprǝmǝnt] *s.* temperamento; disposición; temple.

**temperance** [témprǝns] *s.* templanza, sobriedad.

**temperate** [témprɪt] *adj.* templado, moderado; sobrio.

**temperature** [témprǝtʃǝˠ] *s.* temperatura; **to have a —** tener calentura o fiebre.

**tempest** [témpɪst] *s.* tempestad.

**tempestuous** [tɛmpéstʃʋǝs] *adj.* tempestuoso, borrascoso.

**temple** [témpl] *s.* templo; sien.

**temporal** [témpǝrǝl] *adj.* temporal.

**temporarily** [témpǝrɛrǝlɪ] *adv.* temporalmente.

**temporary** [témpǝrɛrɪ] *adj.* temporal, transitorio, provisorio; interino.

**tempt** [tɛmpt] *v.* tentar; incitar; provocar; atraer.

**temptation** [tɛmptéʃǝn] *s.* tentación.

**tempter** [témptǝˠ] *s.* tentador.

**tempting** [témptɪŋ] *adj.* tentador, atractivo.

**tenable** [ténǝbl] *adj.* defendible.

**tenacious** [tɪnéʃǝs] *adj.* tenaz, aferrado.

**tenacity** [tɪnǽsǝtɪ] *s.* tenacidad; aferramiento; tesón.

**tenant** [ténǝnt] *s.* inquilino, arrendatario.

**tend** [tɛnd] *v.* cuidar, vigilar, guardar; atender; tender, inclinarse.

**tendency** [téndǝnsɪ] *s.* tendencia; propensión.

**tender** [téndǝˠ] *adj.* tierno; delicado; sensible; **tender-hearted** de corazón tierno; *s.* oferta, ofrecimiento; ténder (*de un tren*); lancha (*de auxilio*); cuidador, vigilante; **legal —** moneda corriente; *v.* ofrecer.

**tenderloin** [téndǝˠlɔɪn] *s.* filete.

**tenderness** [téndǝˠnɪs] *s.* ternura, terneza; delicadeza.

**tendon** [téndǝn] *s.* tendón.

**tendril** [téndrɪl] *s.* zarcillo (*tallito de una planta trepadora*).

**tenement** [ténǝmǝnt] *s.* casa de vecindad.

**tennis** [ténɪs] *s.* tenis; **— court** cancha de tenis.

**tenor** [ténǝˠ] *s.* tenor; significado; **— voice** voz de tenor.

**tense** [tɛns] *adj.* tenso; tirante; *s.* tiempo (*del verbo*).

**tension** [ténʃǝn] *s.* tensión; tirantez.

**tent** [tɛnt] *s.* tienda de campaña; pabellón; *v.* acampar.

**tentacle** [téntǝkl] *s.* tentáculo.

**tentative** [téntǝtɪv] *adj.* tentativo.

**tenuous** [ténjʋǝs] *adj.* tenue.

**tenure** [ténjʋr] *s.* tenencia.

**tepid** [tépɪd] *adj.* tibio.

**term** [tɜˠm] *s.* término; período; plazo; sesión; **-s** términos, expresiones, palabras; condiciones; **to be on good -s** estar en buenas relaciones; **not to be on speaking -s** no hablarse, no dirigirse la palabra; **to come to -s** ajustarse, ponerse de acuerdo; *v.* nombrar, llamar, denominar.

**terminable** [tǝmɪnǝbl] *adj.* terminable.

**terminal** [tɜˠmǝnl] *adj.* terminal, final, último; *s.* término, fin; estación terminal; **electric —** toma de corriente; borne (*de aparato eléctrico*).

**terminate** [tɜˠmǝnet] *v.* terminar, acabar.

**termination** [tɜ̃mənéʃən] *s.* terminación, fin; desinencia (*gramatical*).

**termite** [tɜ̃maɪt] *s.* termita.

**terrace** [térɪs] *s.* terraplén; terraza, terrado; *v.* terraplenar.

**terrestrial** [təréstrɪəl] *adj.* terrestre, terreno, terrenal.

**terrible** [térəbl] *adj.* terrible; **terribly** *adv.* terriblemente.

**terrier** [térɪɚ] *s.* perro de busca.

**terrific** [tərífɪk] *adj.* terrífico.

**terrify** [térəfaɪ] *v.* aterrar, aterrorizar.

**territory** [térətorɪ] *s.* territorio.

**terror** [térɚ] *s.* terror, espanto.

**test** [tɛst] *s.* prueba, ensayo, experimento; comprobación; examen; **— tube** probeta, tubo de ensayo; **to undergo a —** sufrir una prueba; *v.* probar, ensayar, comprobar, experimentar; poner a prueba; examinar.

**testament** [tɛ́stəmənt] *s.* testamento.

**testify** [tɛ́stəfaɪ] *v.* atestiguar, atestar.

**testimony** [tɛ́stəmonɪ] *s.* testimonio.

**tetanus** [tɛ́tənəs] *s.* tétanos.

**text** [tɛkst] *s.* texto.

**textbook** [tɛ́kstbʊk] *s.* texto, libro de texto.

**textile** [tɛ́kstl] *adj.* textil; de tejidos; **— mill** fábrica de tejidos; *s.* tejido, materia textil.

**texture** [tɛ́kstʃɚ] *s.* textura, contextura; tejido.

**than** [ðæn] *conj.* que; **more — once** más de una vez; **more — he knows** más de lo que él sabe.

**thank** [θæŋk] *v.* dar gracias, agradecer; **— heaven!** ¡gracias a Dios!; **— you** gracias; **to have oneself to — for** tener la culpa de; ser responsable de; **-s** *s. pl.* gracias.

**thankful** [θǽŋkfəl] *adj.* agradecido; **-ly** *adv.* agradecidamente, con agradecimiento, con gratitud.

**thankfulness** [θǽŋkfəlnɪs] *s.* gratitud, agradecimiento.

**thankless** [θǽŋklɪs] *adj.* ingrato; **— task** tarea ingrata o infructuosa.

**thanksgiving** [θæŋksgívɪŋ] *s.* acción de gracias; **— Day** día de acción de gracias.

**that** [ðæt] *adj.* ese, esa, aquel, aquella; **— one** ése, ésa, aquél, aquélla; *pron.* ése, ésa, eso, aquél, aquélla, aquello; *pron. rel.* que; **— is** es decir; **— of** el de, la de, lo de; **— which** el que, la que, lo que; *conj.* que; para que, a fin de que; **so —** para que; de modo que, a fin de que, de suerte que, de tal manera que; *adv.* tan; **— far** tan lejos; hasta allá, hasta allí; **— long** así de largo; de este tamaño; tanto tiempo.

**thatch** [θætʃ] *s.* paja (*para techar*); *v.* techar con paja; **-ed roof** techumbre o techo de paja.

**thaw** [θɔ] *v.* deshelar(se), derretir(se); volverse más tratable o amistoso; *s.* deshielo, derretimiento.

**the** [*delante de consonante* ðə; *delante de vocal* ðɪ] *art.* el, la; lo; los, las; *adv.* **— more ... — less** cuanto más ... tanto menos; mientras más ... tanto menos.

**theater** [θíətɚ] *s.* teatro.

**theatrical** [θɪǽtrɪkl] *adj.* teatral.

**thee** [ðɪ] *pron.* te.

**theft** [θɛft] *s.* hurto, robo.

**their** [ðɛr] *adj.* su (sus), de ellos, de ellas.

**theirs** [ðɛrz] *pron. pos.* suyo (suya, suyos, suyas), de ellos, de ellas; el suyo (la suya, los suyos, las suyas); el (la, los, las) de ellos; **a friend of —** un amigo suyo, un amigo de ellos.

**them** [ðɛm] *pron.* los, las; les; ellos, ellas (*con preposición*).

**thematic** [θimǽtɪk] *adj.* temático.

**theme** [θim] *s.* tema; ensayo; **— song** tema central.

**themselves** [ðəmsélvz] *pron.* ellos mismos, ellas mismas; se (*como reflexivo*); **to —** a sí mismos; *véase* **herself.**

**then** [ðɛn] *adv.* entonces; en aquel tiempo; en aquella ocasión; después, luego, en seguida; *conj.* pues, en tal caso; **now —** ahora bien; **now and —** de vez en cuando, de cuando en cuando; **now ... —** ora ... ora; ya ... ya; **well —** conque, pues entonces; ahora bien.

**thence** [ðɛns] *adv.* desde allí, de allí; desde entonces, desde aquel tiempo; por eso, por esa razón; **—forth** de allí en adelante, desde entonces.

**theological** [θiəládʒɪkl] *adj.* teológico; teologal.

**theology** [θiálədʒɪ] *s.* teología.

**theoretical** [θiərétɪkl] *adj.* teórico.

**theory** [θíərɪ] *s.* teoría.

**therapeutic** [θɛrəpjútɪk] *adj.* terapéutico.

**therapy** [θɛ́rəpɪ] *s.* terapia.

**there** [ðɛr] *adv.* allí, allá, ahí; **— is, — are** hay; **— followed an argument** siguió una disputa.

**thereabouts** [ðɛrəbáʊts] *adv.* por allí, por ahí; aproximadamente.

**thereafter** [ðɛrǽftɚ] *adv.* después de eso, de allí en adelante.

**thereby** [ðɛrbáɪ] *adv.* en relación con eso; así, de ese modo; por allí cerca.

**therefore** [ðɛ́rfor] *adv.* por eso, por consiguiente, por lo tanto.

**therein** [ðɛrín] *adv.* en eso, en ello; allí dentro.

**thereof** [ðɛráv] *adv.* de eso, de ello.

**thereon** [ðɛrán] *adv.* encima; encima de (*o sobre*) él, ella, ello, etc.

**thereupon** [ðɛrəpán] *adv.* luego, después, en eso, en esto; por consiguiente, por eso, por lo tanto; encima de (*o sobre*) él, ella, ello, etc.

**therewith** [ðɛrwíθ] *adv.* con eso, con ello, con esto; luego, en seguida.

**thermal** [θɝml] *adj.* termal.

**thermometer** [θɚmámətɚ] *s.* termómetro.

**thermonuclear** [θɚmonúkljɚ] *adj.* termonuclear.

**Thermos** [θɝ́məs] (*marca de fábrica*): **— bottle** termos.

**thermostat** [θɝ́məstæt] *s.* termóstato.

**these** [ðiz] *adj.* estos, estas; *pron.* éstos, éstas.

**thesis** [θísɪs] s. tesis.

**they** [ðe] *pron.* ellos, ellas.

**thick** [θɪk] *adj.* (*not thin*) espeso; grueso; (*dense*) denso; tupido; (*slow*) torpe, estúpido; — **voice** voz ronca; **one inch** — una pulgada de espesor; *adv. véase* **thickly; thickheaded** cabezudo, testarudo; estúpido; **thick-set** grueso, rechoncho; **thick-skinned** insensible; que no se avergüenza fácilmente; *s.* espesor; densidad, lo más denso; **the — of the crowd** lo más denso de la muchedumbre; **the — of the fight** lo más reñido del combate; **through — and thin** por toda suerte de penalidades.

**thicken** [θíkən] *v.* espesar(se); engrosar; **the plot -s** se complica el enredo.

**thicket** [θíkɪt] *s.* espesura, maleza, matorral, *Am.* manigua.

**thickly** [θíklɪ] *adv.* espesamente; densamente.

**thickness** [θíknɪs] *s.* espesor; espesura, grueso, grosor; densidad.

**thief** [θif] *s.* ladrón.

**thieve** [θiv] *v.* hurtar, robar.

**thieves** [θivz] *pl. de* **thief.**

**thigh** [θaɪ] *s.* muslo.

**thimble** [θímbl] *s.* dedal.

**thin** [θɪn] *adj.* (*slim*) delgado; flaco; (*sparse*) ralo; escaso; (*fine*) tenue, fino; transparente; (*weak*) débil; aguado; — **broth** caldo aguado; — **hair** pelo ralo; *v.* adelgazar(se); enflaquecer; aguar (*el caldo*); **to — out** ralear (*el pelo*); ralear o aclarar (*un bosque*).

**thine** [ðaɪn] *pron. pos.* tuyo (tuya, tuyos, tuyas); el tuyo (la tuya, los tuyos, las tuyas); *adj.* tu, tus.

**thing** [θɪŋ] *s.* cosa; **no such** — nada de eso; **that is the — to do** eso es lo que debe hacerse; eso es lo debido.

**think** [θɪŋk] *v.* (*cerebrate*) pensar; (*believe*) creer, juzgar; opinar; **to — it over** pensarlo; **to — of** pensar en; pensar de; **to — up an excuse** urdir una excusa; **to — well of** tener buena opinión de; — **nothing of it** no haga Vd. caso de ello, no le dé Vd. importancia; **what do you — of her?** ¿qué piensa Vd. de ella?; **to my way of -ing** a mi modo de ver.

**thinker** [θíŋkə] *s.* pensador.

**thinly** [θínlɪ] *adv.* delgadamente; escasamente.

**thinness** [θínnɪs] *s.* delgadez; flacura; raleza (*del cabello*); enrarecimiento (*del aire*).

**third** [θɜd] *adj.* tercero; *s.* tercio, tercera parte.

**thirst** [θɜst] *s.* sed; anhelo, ansia; *v.* tener sed; **to — for** tener sed de; anhelar, ansiar.

**thirsty** [θɜ́stɪ] *adj.* sediento; **to be —** tener sed.

**this** [ðɪs] *adj.* este, esta; *pron.* éste, ésta, esto.

**thistle** [θísl] *s.* abrojo; cardo.

**thither** [θíðə] *adv.* allá, hacia allá, para allá.

**tho** [ðo] = **though.**

**thong** [θɔŋ] *s.* correa, tira de cuero, *Am.* guasca.

**thorn** [θɔrn] *s.* espina, púa; espino; abrojo.

**thorny** [θɔ́rnɪ] *adj.* espinoso; arduo, difícil.

**thorough** [θɜ́o] *adj.* (*finished*) completo, entero, cabal, cumplido, acabado; (*careful*) esmerado.

**thoroughbred** [θɜ́obrɛd] *adj.* de casta pura, de raza pura; bien nacido; *s.* animal o persona de casta; caballo de casta.

**thoroughfare** [θɜ́ofɛr] *s.* vía pública, carretera, camino real; pasaje.

**thoroughly** [θɜ́olɪ] *adj.* completamente, enteramente, cabalmente; a fondo.

**those** [ðoz] *adj.* esos, esas, aquellos, aquellas; *pron.* ésos, ésas, aquéllos, aquéllas; — **of** los de, las de; — **which** los que, las que; aquellos que; — **who** los que, las que, quienes.

**thou** [ðau] *pron.* tú.

**though** [ðo] *conj.* aunque, si bien, bien que; aun cuando; sin embargo; **as —** como si.

**thought** [θɔt] *s.* (*cogitation*) pensamiento; (*idea*) idea, intención; reflexión, meditación; (*concern*) consideración; cuidado; **to be lost in —** estar abstraído; **to give it no —** no pensar en ello, no darle importancia, no hacerle caso; *pret. & p.p. de* **think.**

**thoughtful** [θɔ́tfəl] *adj.* pensativo; considerado; atento, solícito, cuidadoso; **to be — of others** pensar en los demás, tener consideración o solicitud por los demás; **-ly** *adv.* con reflexión; consideradamente, con consideración; con solicitud.

**thoughtfulness** [θɔ́tfəlnɪs] *s.* consideración, atención, cuidado, solicitud.

**thoughtless** [θɔ́tlɪs] *adj.* inconsiderado; descuidado; irreflexivo, atolondrado; **-ly** *adv.* inconsideradamente, sin consideración; sin reflexión, sin pensar; descuidadamente, irreflexivamente, atolondradamente.

**thoughtlessness** [θɔ́tlɪsnɪs] *s.* irreflexión, inadvertencia, descuido; atolondramiento.

**thrash** [θræʃ] *v.* trillar, desgranar (*las mieses*); zurrar, azotar; **to — around** revolcarse, agitarse, menearse; **to — out a matter** ventilar un asunto.

**thread** [θrɛd] *s.* hilo; hebra, fibra; **screw —** rosca de tornillo; *v.* ensartar, enhebrar; **to — a screw** roscar un tornillo; **to — one's way through a crowd** colarse por entre la muchedumbre.

**threadbare** [θrɛ́dbɛr] *adj.* raído, gastado.

**threat** [θrɛt] *s.* amenaza; amago.

**threaten** [θrɛ́tn] *v.* amenazar; amagar.

**threatening** [θrɛ́tnɪŋ] *adj.* amenazante, amenazador.

**thresh** [θrɛʃ] *véase* **thrash.**

**threshold** [θrɛ́ʃold] *s.* umbral, entrada.

**threw** [θru] *pret. de* **to throw.**

TE

**thrice** [θraɪs] *adv.* tres veces.

**thrift** [θrɪft] *s.* economía, frugalidad.

**thrifty** [θrɪ́ftɪ] *adj.* económico, frugal; próspero.

**thrill** [θrɪl] *v.* emocionar(se), conmover-(se); estremecerse de emoción, sobreexcitarse; *s.* emoción viva, estremecimiento emotivo, sobreexcitación.

**thrive** [θraɪv] *v.* medrar, prosperar; florecer.

**thriven** [θrɪ́vən] *p.p. de* **to thrive**.

**throat** [θrot] *s.* garganta.

**throb** [θrɑb] *v.* latir, pulsar, palpitar; *s.* latido, palpitación.

**throe** [θro] *s.* agonía; congoja.

**throne** [θron] *s.* trono.

**throng** [θrɔŋ] *s.* muchedumbre, multitud, tropel, gentío; *v.* agolparse, apiñarse; atestar.

**throttle** [θrɑ́tl] *s.* válvula reguladora, obturador, regulador; **— lever** palanca del obturador o regulador; *v.* ahogar; estrangular; **to — down** disminuir o reducir la velocidad.

**through** [θru] *prep.* por; a través de; por medio de; por conducto de; por entre; *adv.* de un lado a otro; de parte a parte, a través; de cabo a cabo; desde el principio hasta el fin; completamente, enteramente; **loyal — and —** leal a toda prueba; **to be wet —** estar empapado; estar mojado hasta los tuétanos; **to carry a plan —** llevar a cabo un plan; *adj.* directo, continuo; **— ticket** billete (*Am.* boleto) directo; **— train** tren rápido, tren de servicio directo; **to be — with** haber acabado con; no querer ocuparse más de.

**throughout** [θruáut] *prep.* (*all through*) por todo; por todas partes de; (*during*) desde el principio; hasta el fin de; **— the year** durante todo el año; *adv.* por todas partes; en todas partes; en todo, en todos respetos; desde el principio hasta el fin.

**throve** [θrov] *pret. de* **to thrive**.

**throw** [θro] *v.* tirar, arrojar, lanzar; echar; **to — away** tirar, arrojar; malgastar; **to — down** arrojar, echar por tierra, derribar; **to — in gear** engranar; **to — in the clutch** embragar; **to — off a burden** librarse o deshacerse de una carga; **to — out** echar fuera; expeler; **to — out of gear** desengranar; **to — out of work** privar de trabajo, quitar el empleo a; **to — out the clutch** desembragar; **to — overboard** echar al agua; **to — up** vomitar; *s.* tiro, tirada.

**thrown** [θron] *p.p. de* **to throw**.

**thrush** [θrʌʃ] *s.* tordo, zorzal.

**thrust** [θrʌst] *v.* (*push into*) meter; hincar, clavar; encajar; (*shove*) empujar; **to — a task upon someone** imponer una tarea a una persona, obligar a alguien a desempeñar un quehacer; **to — aside** echar o empujar a un lado; rechazar; **to — in** (*o* **into**) meter en, encajar en, intercalar en; **to — out** sacar; echar fuera;

**to — someone through with a sword** atravesar a alguien de parte a parte con la espada; *pret. & p.p. de* **to thrust**; *s.* estocada, cuchillada, puñalada, lanzada; empuje, empujón o empellón; arremetida, acometida.

**thud** [θʌd] *s.* porrazo, golpazo, golpe sordo.

**thug** [θʌg] *s.* ladrón, salteador.

**thumb** [θʌm] *s.* pulgar; **under the — of** bajo el poder o influencia de; *v.* hojear (*con el pulgar*).

**thumbtack** [θʌ́mtæk] *s.* chinche.

**thump** [θʌmp] *s.* golpazo, porrazo, trastazo; golpe sordo; *v.* golpear, golpetear, aporrear, dar un porrazo.

**thunder** [θʌ́ndɚ] *s.* trueno; tronido; estruendo; *v.* tronar.

**thunderbolt** [θʌ́ndɚbolt] *s.* rayo.

**thundering** [θʌ́ndərɪŋ] *adj.* atronador.

**thunderous** [θʌ́ndərəs] *adj.* atronador, estruendoso.

**thunderstorm** [θʌ́ndɚstɔrm] *s.* tronada, tormenta o tempestad de truenos.

**Thursday** [θɝ́zdɪ] *s.* jueves.

**thus** [θʌs] *adv.* así; **— far** hasta aquí, hasta ahora, hasta hoy.

**thwart** [θwɔrt] *v.* frustrar; estorbar; impedir.

**thy** [ðaɪ] *adj.* tu, tus.

**thyme** [taɪm] *s.* tomillo.

**thyroid** [θáɪrɔɪd] *s.* tiroides.

**thyself** [ðaɪsélf] *pron.* tú mismo; a tí mismo; te (*como reflexivo*); *véase* **herself**.

**tick** [tɪk] *s.* tic tac; funda (*de colchón o almohada*); garrapata (*insecto parásito*); *v.* hacer tic tac (*como un reloj*); latir (*el corazón*); **to — off** marcar.

**ticket** [tíkɪt] *s.* billete, *Am.* boleto; lista de candidatos (*de un partido*); balota (*para votar*); **— office** taquilla; despacho de boletos, *Am.* boletería.

**tickle** [tíkl] *v.* (*touch*) cosquillear, hacer cosquillas; (*feel*) sentir o tener cosquillas; (*please*) halagar, gustarle a uno; **to be -d to death** morirse de gusto, estar muy contento; *s.* cosquilleo, cosquillas.

**ticklish** [tíklɪʃ] *adj.* cosquilloso; delicado, arriesgado, difícil.

**tidbit** [tídbɪt] *s.* bocado, bocadito, golosina.

**tide** [taɪd] *s.* marea; corriente; **Christmas —** navidades, temporada de navidad; *v.* **to — someone over a difficulty** ayudar a alguien durante una crisis o dificultad.

**tidewater** [táɪdwɔtɚ] *adj.* costanero.

**tidings** [táɪdɪŋz] *s. pl.* noticias, nuevas.

**tidy** [táɪdɪ] *adj.* aseado, limpio, ordenado; **a — sum** una suma considerable; *v.* asear, arreglar, poner en orden; **to — oneself up** asearse.

**tie** [taɪ] *v.* (*fasten*) atar, liar, ligar; *Am.* amarrar; (*unite*) enlazar, vincular; (*equal*) empatar (*en juegos, etc.*); **to — tight** amarrar bien, apretar fuerte; **to — up the traffic** obstruir el tráfico; *s.* lazo, ligadura, atadura; enlace, vínculo; corbata; empate (*en ca-*

*rreras, juegos, etc.*); **railway** — traviesa, *Andes*, *C.A.*, *Méx.* durmiente; *Ríopl.*, *Ch.* travesaño.

**tier** [tɪr] *s.* fila, hilera, ringlera.

**tiger** [táɪgɚ] *s.* tigre; — **cat** gato montés.

**tight** [taɪt] *adj.* (*squeezed*) apretado, ajustado, estrecho; (*sealed*) hermético; (*firm*) firme, tieso; (*stingy*) tacaño, mezquino; (*drunk*) borracho; **to be in a — spot** estar en un aprieto; **to close —** apretar, cerrar herméticamente; **to hold on —** agarrarse bien; **it fits —** está muy estrecho o ajustado.

**tighten** [táɪtn̩] *v.* apretar; estrechar; estirar, poner tirante.

**tightness** [táɪtnɪs] *s.* estrechez; tirantez, tensión; mezquindad, tacañería.

**tightwad** [táɪtwɑd] *s.* tacaño; cicatero.

**tigress** [táɪgrɪs] *s.* tigre hembra.

**tile** [taɪl] *s.* teja; baldosa, azulejo; — **roof** tejado; *v.* tejar, cubrir con tejas; cubrir con azulejos, embaldosar.

**till** [tɪl] *prep.* hasta; *conj.* hasta que; *v.* cultivar, labrar, arar; *s.* gaveta o cajón para el dinero.

**tillage** [tílədʒ] *s.* labranza, cultivo, labor.

**tilt** [tɪlt] *s.* ladeo, inclinación; declive; altercación disputa; **at full —** a toda velocidad; *v.* ladear(se), inclinar(se).

**timber** [tímbɚ] *s.* madera de construcción; maderaje; madero; viga.

**time** [taɪm] *s.* tiempo; hora; vez; plazo; **at -s** a veces; **at one and the same — a** la vez; **at this —** ahora, al presente; **behind —** atrasado, retrasado; **from — to —** de vez en cuando; **in —** a tiempo; andando el tiempo; **on —** puntual; con puntualidad; a tiempo; a la hora debida; **several -s** varias veces; **to beat —** marcar el compás; **to buy on —** comprar a plazo; **to have a good —** divertirse, pasar un buen rato; **what — is it?** ¿qué hora es?; *v.* cronometrar, medir el tiempo de; regular, poner en punto (*el reloj, el motor*); escoger el momento oportuno para; — **zone** zona horaria; huso horario.

**timeless** [táɪmləs] *adj.* eterno, infinito.

**timely** [táɪmlɪ] *adj.* oportuno.

**timepiece** [táɪmpis] *s.* reloj; cronómetro.

**timetable** [táɪmtebl̩] *s.* itinerario, horario.

**timid** [tímɪd] *adj.* tímido.

**timidity** [tɪmídətɪ] *s.* timidez.

**timing** [táɪmɪŋ] *s.* medida del tiempo; cronometraje; (*pace*) selección del momento oportuno; sincronización.

**timorous** [tímərəs] *adj.* timorato, tímido, miedoso.

**tin** [tɪn] *s.* estaño; hojalata, lata; cosa de hojalata; — **can** lata; — **foil** hoja de estaño; *v.* estañar, cubrir con estaño; enlatar.

**tincture** [tíŋktʃɚ] *s.* tintura; tinte; — **of iodine** tintura de yodo; *v.* tinturar, teñir.

**tinder** [tíndɚ] *s.* yesca.

**tinge** [tɪndʒ] *v.* teñir; matizar; *s.* tinte, matiz; dejo, saborcillo.

**tingle** [tíŋgl̩] *v.* hormiguear, sentir hormigueo; **to — with excitement** estremecerse de entusiasmo; *s.* hormigueo, picazón, comezón.

**tinker** [tíŋkɚ] *v.* ocuparse vanamente.

**tinkle** [tíŋkl̩] *v.* tintinear; hacer retintín; *s.* tintineo; retintín.

**tinsel** [tínsl̩] *s.* oropel; *adj.* de oropel.

**tint** [tɪnt] *s.* tinte, matiz; *v.* teñir, matizar.

**tiny** [táɪnɪ] *adj.* diminuto, menudo, chiquito, chiquitín.

**tip** [tɪp] *s.* (*point*) punta, extremo, extremidad; (*money*) propina; (*hint*) noticia o aviso secreto; *v.* ladear(se), inclinar(se); dar propina (a); **to — a person off** dar aviso secreto a; **to — one's hat** tocarse el sombrero; **to — over** volcar(se), voltear(se).

**tipsy** [típsɪ] *adj.* alumbrado, algo borracho; ladeado.

**tiptoe** [típto] *s.* punta del pie; **on —** de puntillas; *v.* andar de puntillas.

**tirade** [táɪred] *s.* invectiva.

**tire** [taɪr] *s.* llanta, neumático, goma; **flat —** llanta o goma reventada; *v.* cansar(se), fatigar(se).

**tired** [taɪrd] *adj.* cansado, fatigado; — **out** extenuado de fatiga, rendido.

**tireless** [táɪrlɪs] *adj.* incansable, infatigable.

**tiresome** [táɪrsəm] *adj.* cansado, aburrido, pesado.

**tissue** [tíʃu] *s.* tejido; — **paper** papel de seda.

**titanic** [taɪtǽnɪk] *adj.* titánico.

**titanium** [taɪténɪəm] *s.* titanio.

**tithe** [taɪð] *s.* diezmo.

**title** [táɪtl̩] *s.* título; — **page** portada.

**to** [tu] *prep.* a; hasta; hacia; para; — **try —** tratar de; esforzarse por; **a quarter — five** las cinco menos cuarto; **bills — be paid** cuentas por pagar; **frightened — death** muerto de susto; **from house — house** de casa en casa; **he has — go** tiene que ir; **near —** cerca de; **not — my knowledge** no que yo sepa; *adv.* — **and fro** de acá para allá; **to come —** volver en sí.

**toad** [tod] *s.* sapo o escuerzo.

**toast** [tost] *v.* tostar(se); brindar por, beber a la salud de; *s.* tostada; brindis.

**toaster** [tóstɚ] *s.* tostador.

**tobacco** [təbǽko] *s.* tabaco.

**today** [tədé] *adv.* hoy; hoy día.

**toe** [to] *s.* dedo del pie; punta (*de la media, del zapato, etc.*); *v.* **to — in** andar con la punta de los pies para dentro.

**toenail** [tónel] *s.* uña del dedo del pie.

**together** [təgéðɚ] *adv.* juntamente; a un mismo tiempo, a la vez; juntos; — **with** junto con; **all —** juntos; en junto; **to call —** convocar, juntar; **to come —** juntarse, unirse; ponerse de acuerdo; **to walk —** andar juntos.

**toil** [tɔɪl] *v.* afanarse, trafagar, atarearse; *s.* esfuerzo, trabajo, faena, fatiga.

TH

**toilet** [tɔ́ɪlɪt] s. retrete, excusado, común, *Am.* inodoro; — **articles** artículos de tocador; — **case** neceser; — **paper** papel de excusado, papel higiénico.

**token** [tókən] s. señal, símbolo; prenda; recuerdo; prueba, muestra; ficha (*de metal*); — **payment** pago nominal.

**told** [told] *pret. & p.p. de* **to tell.**

**tolerance** [tálərəns] s. tolerancia.

**tolerant** [tálərənt] *adj.* tolerante.

**tolerate** [táləret] *v.* tolerar.

**toleration** [taləréʃən] s. tolerancia.

**toll** [tol] s. doble, tañido (*de las campanas*); peaje; portazgo; — **bridge** puente de peaje; —**gate** barrera de peaje; — **call** llamada por cobrar; **to pay** — pagar peaje o portazgo; *v.* tañer, doblar (*las campanas*).

**tomato** [təméto] s. tomate, *Méx.* jitomate.

**tomb** [tum] s. tumba.

**tombstone** [túmston] s. lápida sepulcral.

**tomcat** [támkæt] s. gato.

**tome** [tom] s. tomo.

**tomorrow** [təmóro] *adv.* mañana; — **morning** mañana por la mañana; — **noon** mañana al mediodía; **day after** — pasado mañana.

**ton** [tʌn] s. tonelada.

**tone** [ton] s. (*pitch*) tono; timbre; (*sound*) sonido; *v.* dar tono a, modificar el tono de; **to** — **down** bajar de tono; suavizar; **to** — **down one's voice** moderar la voz; **to** — **in well with** armonizar con, entonar bien con; **to** — **up** subir de tono; tonificar, vigorizar.

**tongs** [tɔŋz] s. *pl.* tenazas.

**tongue** [tʌŋ] s. lengua; idioma; **to be tongue-tied** tener trabada la lengua.

**tonic** [tánɪk] s. & *adj.* tónico.

**tonight** [tənáɪt] *adv.* esta noche, a la noche.

**tonnage** [tʌ́nɪdʒ] s. tonelaje.

**tonsil** [tánsl] s. amígdala.

**tonsilitis** [tansláɪtɪs] s. amigdalitis.

**too** [tu] *adv.* también; demasiado; — **many** demasiados; — **much** demasiado; **it is** — **bad!** ¡es una lástima!

**took** [tʊk] *pret. de* **to take.**

**tool** [tul] s. instrumento; herramienta; — **box** caja de herramientas.

**toot** [tut] *v.* tocar o sonar la bocina; pitar; tocar (*un cuerno, trompa o trompeta*); **to** — **one's own horn** alabarse, cantar sus propias alabanzas; s. toque o sonido (*de bocina, trompeta, etc.*); silbido, pitido; pitazo (*de locomotora*).

**tooth** [tuθ] s. diente; muela; — **mark** dentellada; **to fight** — **and nail** luchar a brazo partido; **to have a sweet** — ser amigo de golosinas.

**toothache** [túθek] s. dolor de muelas.

**toothbrush** [túθbrʌʃ] s. cepillo de dientes.

**toothed** [tuθt] *adj.* dentado.

**toothless** [túθlɪs] *adj.* desdentado.

**toothpaste** [túθpest] s. pasta para los dientes, pasta dentífrica.

**toothpick** [túθpɪk] s. mondadientes, palillo de dientes.

**top** [tɑp] s. (*peak*) cumbre, cima; cúspide; tope; pináculo; remate; cabeza; (*surface*) superficie; copa (*de árbol*); (*cover*) tapa, cubierta; (*toy*) trompo; **at the** — **of his class** a la cabeza de su clase; **at the** — **of one's voice** a voz en cuello; **filled up to the** — lleno hasta el tope; **from** — **to bottom** de arriba abajo; **from** — **to toe** de pies a cabeza; **on** — **of** encima de, sobre; *adj.* superior; más alto; —**coat** abrigo, sobretodo; **at** — **speed** a velocidad máxima; *v.* coronar; exceder; sobresalir, sobrepujar; rematar; **to** — **off** rematar; terminar.

**topaz** [tópæz] s. topacio.

**toper** [tópɚ] s. bebedor, borrachín.

**top-heavy** [tɑphévɪ] *adj.* más pesado arriba que abajo.

**topic** [tápɪk] s. tema, asunto, materia, tópico.

**topmost** [tápmost] *adj.* más alto; superior.

**topography** [təpágrəfɪ] s. topografía.

**topple** [tápl] *v.* echar abajo, derribar; volcar; **to** — **over** venirse abajo; volcarse.

**topsy-turvy** [tápsɪtɝvɪ] *adj. & adv.* patas arriba; en confusión; trastornado; enrevesado, al revés.

**torch** [tɔrtʃ] s. antorcha; **blow** — soplete.

**tore** [tor] *pret. de* **to tear.**

**torment** [tɔ́rmɛnt] s. tormento; [tɔrmɛ́nt] *v.* atormentar; afligir.

**torn** [torn] *p.p. de* **to tear** roto, rompido, rasgado.

**tornado** [tɔrnédo] s. tornado.

**torpedo** [tɔrpído] s. torpedo; — **boat** torpedero; *v.* torpedear.

**torque** [tɔrk] s. fuerza rotatoria.

**torrent** [tɔ́rənt] s. torrente.

**torrid** [tɔ́rɪd] *adj.* tórrido.

**torsion** [tɔ́rʃən] s. torsión.

**tortoise** [tɔ́rtəs] s. tortuga.

**tortuous** [tɔ́rtʃʊəs] *adj.* tortuoso.

**torture** [tɔ́rtʃɚ] s. tortura, tormento; *v.* torturar, atormentar.

**toss** [tɔs] *v.* tirar, echar, arrojar, lanzar; menear(se); cabecear (*un buque*); **to** — **aside** echar a un lado; desechar; **to** — **up** echar para arriba; aventar; s. tiro, tirada; meneo, sacudida.

**tot** [tɑt] s. chiquitín, chiquitina, chiquitico, chiquitica, niñito, niñita, nene, nena.

**total** [tótl] *adj. & s.* total.

**totalitarian** [totælətérɪən] *adj.* totalitario.

**totter** [tátɚ] *v.* tambalear(se), bambolear(se); estar para desplomarse.

**touch** [tʌtʃ] *v.* tocar; palpar, tentar; conmover, enternecer; compararse con, igualar; **to** — **at a port** hacer escala en un puerto; **to** — **off an explosive** prender la mecha de un explosivo; **to** — **up** retocar; s. toque;

tacto, sentido del tacto; tiento; —**stone** piedra de toque; **a — of fever** algo de calentura; **to keep in — with** mantener(se) en comunicación con.

**touch-and-go** [tʌtʃəndgó] *adj.* arriesgado.

**touching** [tʌtʃɪŋ] *adj.* conmovedor, enternecedor.

**touchy** [tʌtʃɪ] *adj.* quisquilloso, susceptible, sensible, sensitivo.

**tough** [tʌf] *adj.* correoso; fuerte; firme; duro; arduo, difícil; terco; empedernido, malvado.

**toughen** [tʌfn̩] *v.* curtir(se); endurecer(se), empedernir(se); hacer(se) correoso.

**toughness** [tʌfnɪs] *s.* dureza; correosidad; flexibilidad; tenacidad; resistencia; dificultad.

**toupee** [tupé] *s.* peluca.

**tour** [tur] *s.* viaje, excursión; vuelta; jira; *v.* viajar por; recorrer; hacer una jira; hacer un viaje de turismo.

**tourism** [túrɪzəm] *s.* turismo.

**tourist** [túrɪst] *s.* turista.

**tournament** [tɝnəmənt] *s.* torneo; certamen, concurso.

**tow** [to] *v.* remolcar; *s.* remolque; —**boat** remolcador; —**rope** cuerda de remolque; **to take in —** remolcar, llevar a remolque.

**toward** [tord] *prep.* hacia; rumbo a; alrededor de; para, para con; — **four o'clock** a eso de las cuatro.

**towards** [tordz] = **toward.**

**towel** [taul] *s.* toalla.

**tower** [táuɚ] *s.* torre; torreón; **bell —** campanario; *v.* sobresalir, sobrepujar; destacarse, descollar; elevarse.

**towering** [táurɪŋ] *adj.* encumbrado; elevado, muy alto; sobresaliente.

**town** [taun] *s.* (*center*) población, ciudad, pueblo, aldea; (*administration*) municipio; — **hall** ayuntamiento.

**township** [táunʃɪp] *s.* unidad primaria de gobierno local; sección de seis millas cuadradas (*en terrenos públicos*).

**toxin** [táksɪn] *s.* toxina.

**toy** [tɔɪ] *s.* juguete; *adj.* de juego, de juguete; pequeñito; *v.* jugar, juguetear.

**trace** [tres] *s.* señal, indicio, vestigio; huella, rastro; tirante (*de una guarnición*); *v.* trazar; calcar; rastrear, seguir la huella de; rebuscar, investigar; **to — the source of** remontarse al origen de, buscar el origen de.

**trachea** [trékɪə] *s.* tráquea.

**trachoma** [trəkomə] *s.* tracoma.

**track** [træk] *s.* pista, huella, rastro; pisada; vereda, senda; vía; — **sports** deportes de pista; **race —** pista; **railroad —** rieles, vía del tren, vía férrea o ferrovía; **to be off the —** estar extraviado, estar descarrilado; **to be on the — of** rastrear, ir siguiendo la pista de; **to keep — of** llevar la cuenta de; no perder de

vista; *v.* rastrear, seguir la huella de; **to — down** coger, atrapar; descubrir; **to — in mud** traer lodo en los pies, entrar con los pies enlodados.

**tract** [trækt] *s.* área; terreno; folleto; **digestive —** canal digestivo.

**traction** [trǽkʃən] *s.* tracción.

**tractor** [trǽktɚ] *s.* tractor.

**trade** [tred] *s.* (*business*) comercio; trato, negocio; (*swap*) trueque, cambio; (*occupation*) oficio; (*customers*) clientela, parroquianos; — **school** escuela de artes y oficios; — **union** gremio obrero o de obreros; *v.* comerciar, negociar, traficar, tratar; trocar, cambiar.

**trademark** [trédmɑrk] *s.* marca de fábrica.

**trader** [trédɚ] *s.* mercader, comerciante, negociante, traficante.

**tradesman** [trédzmən] *s.* mercader, comerciante, traficante; tendero.

**tradition** [trədíʃən] *s.* tradición.

**traditional** [trədíʃənl] *adj.* tradicional.

**traffic** [trǽfɪk] *s.* tráfico; tráfago; tránsito; circulación; *v.* traficar, comerciar, negociar.

**tragedy** [trǽdʒədɪ] *s.* tragedia.

**tragic** [trǽdʒɪk] *adj.* trágico.

**trail** [trel] *s.* (*trace*) pista, rastro, huella; (*path*) senda, sendero, trocha, vereda; cola (*de vestido*); *v.* arrastrar(se); rastrear, seguir la pista de; andar detrás de; **to — behind** ir rezagado, rezagarse.

**train** [tren] *s.* (*railroad*) tren; (*dress*) cola (*de vestido*); (*retinue*) séquito, comitiva; *v.* amaestrar(se), ejercitar(se); adiestrar(se) o adestrar(se), *Am.* entrenar(se); educar; disciplinar (*tropas*); apuntar (*un cañón*).

**trainer** [trénɚ] *s.* amaestrador; *Méx., C.A., Andes, Ven., Col., Carib.* entrenador.

**training** [trénɪŋ] *s.* adiestramiento, disciplina, *Méx., C.A., Andes, Ven., Col., Carib.,* entrenamiento; educación; — **camp** campo de entrenamiento o práctica.

**trait** [tret] *s.* rasgo, característica; cualidad.

**traitor** [trétɚ] *s.* traidor.

**tram** [træm] *s.* vagoneta (*de una mina de carbón*).

**tramp** [træmp] *v.* pisotear; andar a pie; vagabundear; *s.* vago, vagabundo; caminata, marcha; pisadas.

**trample** [trǽmpl] *v.* pisar, hollar, pisotear; **to — on** pisotear, hollar; *s.* pisadas.

**trance** [træns] *s.* rapto, arrobamiento, enajenamiento, éxtasis; **to be in a —** estar arrobado, estar enajenado; estar distraído o ensimismado.

**tranquil** [trǽnkwɪl] *adj.* tranquilo.

**tranquilizer** [trǽnkwəlaɪzɚ] *s.* tranquilizador.

**tranquillity** [trænkwílətɪ] *s.* tranquilidad.

**transact** [trænsǽkt] *v.* tramitar, despa-

**TO**

char, llevar a cabo.

**transaction** [trænsǽkʃən] s. transacción, trato, negocio; trámite; negociación; **-s** actas; memorias.

**transatlantic** [trænsətlǽntɪk] adj. transatlántico.

**transcend** [trænsénd] v. trascender, ir más allá de.

**transcontinental** [trænskʌntənéntl] adj. transcontinental.

**transcribe** [trænskráɪb] v. transcribir.

**transcript** [trǽnskrɪpt] s. transcripción, copia.

**transfer** [trǽnsfɚ] s. transferencia; traslado; traspaso; trasbordo; **— of ownership** cesión o traspaso de propiedad; **streetcar —** transferencia, contraseña, cupón de trasbordo; [trænsfɚ] v. transferir; trasbordar (de un tren a otro), cambiar (de tren, de tranvía); traspasar (propiedad), trasladar.

**transfigure** [trænsfígjɚ] v. transfigurar.

**transform** [trænsfórm] v. transformar(se).

**transformation** [trænsfɚméʃən] s. transformación.

**transgress** [trænsgrés] v. transgredir, violar, quebrantar (una ley); pecar; **to — the bounds of** traspasar los límites de.

**transgression** [trænsgréʃən] s. transgresión; violación de una ley; pecado.

**transgressor** [trænsgrésɚ] s. transgresor.

**transient** [trǽnʃənt] s. transeúnte; adj. transeúnte; transitorio, pasajero.

**transistor** [trænzístɚ] s. transistor.

**transit** [trǽnsɪt] s. tránsito; **in —** en tránsito, de paso.

**transition** [trænzíʃən] s. transición; tránsito, paso.

**transitive** [trǽnsətɪv] adj. transitivo.

**transitory** [trǽnsətorɪ] adj. transitorio, pasajero.

**translate** [trænslét] v. traducir, verter; trasladar.

**translation** [trænsléʃən] s. traducción, versión; translación (de un lugar a otro).

**translator** [trænslétɚ] s. traductor.

**translucent** [trænslúsn̩t] adj. translúcido; **to be —** traslucirse.

**transmission** [trænsmíʃən] s. transmisión; caja de velocidades.

**transmit** [trænsmít] v. transmitir; emitir.

**transmitter** [trænsmítɚ] s. transmisor; emisor.

**transom** [trǽnsəm] s. montante.

**transparent** [trænspérənt] adj. transparente.

**transplant** [trænsplǽnt] v. trasplantar.

**transport** [trǽnsport] s. (moving) transporte; acarreo; (rapture) éxtasis; **— plane** aeroplano de transporte; [trænspórt] v. transportar; acarrear; **to be -ed with joy** estar enajenado de placer.

**transportation** [trænspɚtéʃən] s. transportación, transporte; boleto, pasaje.

**transpose** [trænspóz] v. transponer.

**transverse** [trænsvɝ́s] adj. transverso, transversal, puesto de través.

**trap** [træp] s. trampa, lazo, red; **— door** trampa; **mouse —** ratonera; v. entrampar, coger con trampa; atrapar.

**trapeze** [træpíz] s. trapecio.

**trapezoid** [trǽpəzɔɪd] s. trapezoide; trapecio.

**trappings** [trǽpɪŋz] s. pl. arreos, jaeces, guarniciones.

**trash** [træʃ] s. basura; hojarasca; cachivaches; gentuza, plebe.

**travel** [trǽvl̩] v. viajar; viajar por; recorrer; s. viaje; tráfico.

**traveler** [trǽvlɚ] s. viajero; **—'s check** cheque de viajero.

**traveling** [trǽvlɪŋ] adj. de viaje, para viaje; **— expenses** gastos de viaje; **— salesman** agente viajero, viajante de comercio.

**travelogue** [trǽvəlɔg] s. conferencia sobre viajes.

**traverse** [trǽvɚs] v. atravesar, cruzar; recorrer; s. travesaño.

**travesty** [trǽvɪstɪ] s. parodia; v. parodiar, falsear.

**tray** [tre] s. bandeja; batea.

**treacherous** [trétʃərəs] adj. traicionero, traidor, alevoso.

**treachery** [trétʃərɪ] s. traición, perfidia, alevosía.

**tread** [trɛd] v. (trample) pisar, hollar; pisotear; (walk) andar a pie, caminar; s. paso; pisada, huella; Am. pise (de una rueda); **tire —** rodadura del neumático, Am. banda rodante.

**treadmill** [trédmɪl] s. noria; rueda de andar.

**treason** [trízn̩] s. traición.

**treasonable** [tríznəbl̩] adj. traidor, traicionero.

**treasure** [trézɚ] s. tesoro; v. atesorar.

**treasurer** [trézərɚ] s. tesorero.

**treasury** [trézərɪ] s. tesorería; tesoro, erario; **Secretary of the Treasury** ministro de hacienda.

**treat** [trit] v. tratar; curar; convidar, invitar; s. obsequio, agasajo, convite; placer, gusto.

**treatise** [trítɪs] s. tratado.

**treatment** [trítmənt] s. trato; **medical —** tratamiento médico.

**treaty** [trítɪ] s. tratado, pacto, convenio.

**treble** [trébl̩] adj. triple; **— voice** voz atiplada; s. tiple; v. triplicar.

**tree** [tri] s. árbol; **apple —** manzano; **family —** árbol genealógico; **shoe —** horma de zapato; **to be up a —** estar subido a un árbol; estar en un gran aprieto; estar perplejo.

**treeless** [trílɪs] adj. pelado, sin árboles, despoblado de árboles.

**treetop** [trítɑp] s. copa de árbol.

**trellis** [trélɪs] s. emparrado, enrejado.

**tremble** [trémbl̩] v. temblar; estremecerse; s. temblor; estremecimiento.

**tremendous** [trɪméndəs] adj. tremendo.

**tremor** [trémɚ] s. temblor.

**tremulous** [trémjələs] *adj.* trémulo; tembloroso.

**trench** [trɛntʃ] *s.* trinchera; zanja, foso.

**trend** [trɛnd] *s.* tendencia; rumbo, dirección.

**trespass** [tréspəs] *v.* invadir, traspasar; violar, infringir; pecar; **to — on property** meterse sin derecho en la propiedad ajena; **no -ing** prohibida la entrada; *s.* transgresión; pecado.

**tress** [trɛs] *s.* trenza; bucle.

**trestle** [trɛsl] *s.* caballete; puente de caballetes.

**trial** [tráɪəl] *s.* ensayo, prueba; tentativa; aflicción; juicio, proceso; **— flight** vuelo de prueba.

**triangle** [tráɪæŋgl] *s.* triángulo.

**triangular** [traɪæŋgjələ] *adj.* triangular.

**tribe** [traɪb] *s.* tribu.

**tribulation** [trɪbjəléʃən] *s.* tribulación.

**tribunal** [trɪbjúnl] *s.* tribunal, juzgado.

**tributary** [tríbjətɛrɪ] *adj.* & *s.* tributario.

**tribute** [tríbjut] *s.* tributo; homenaje.

**trick** [trɪk] *s.* treta; suerte; maña, ardid, trampa; travesura; baza (*en el juego de naipes*); **to be up to one's old -s** hacer de las suyas; *v.* embaucar, trampear, hacer trampa; burlar; **to — oneself up** componerse, emperifollarse.

**trickery** [tríkərɪ] *s.* engaños, malas mañas, astucia.

**trickle** [tríkl] *v.* gotear; escurrir; *s.* goteo.

**tricky** [tríkɪ] *adj.* tramposo, *Am.* mañero; intrincado, complicado.

**tried** [traɪd] *p.p. de* **to try** & *adj.* probado.

**trifle** [tráɪfl] *s.* fruslería, friolera, nadería, nonada; bagatela; *v.* chancear(se), bromear; jugar, juguetear.

**trigger** [trígɚ] *s.* gatillo (*de pistola, rifle, etc.*).

**trill** [trɪl] *v.* trinar; **to — the r** pronunciar la erre doble; *s.* trino.

**trilogy** [trílədʒɪ] *s.* trilogía.

**trim** [trɪm] *v.* guarnecer, adornar; recortar; podar, mondar; despabilar (*una vela*); ganarle a uno (*en el juego*); **to — up** adornar, componer; *adj.* aseado, limpio, pulcro, acicalado; *s.* adorno, franja, ribete, guarnición; **to be in — for** estar en buena salud para; estar bien entrenado para.

**trimming** [trímɪŋ] *s.* adorno, aderezo, guarnición; orla, ribete, franja; paliza, zurra; **-s** adornos; accesorios; recortes.

**trinity** [trínətɪ] *s.* trinidad.

**trinket** [tríŋkɪt] *s.* chuchería, baratija.

**trip** [trɪp] *s.* viaje, travesía; recorrido, jira, tropezón; *v.* tropezar; dar un traspié; equivocarse; hacer tropezar, hacer caer; saltar, brincar, corretear.

**triphthong** [trífθɔŋ] *s.* triptongo.

**triple** [trípl] *adj.* & *s.* triple; *v.* triplicar.

**triplicate** [trípləkət] *adj.* triplicado.

**tripod** [tráɪpad] *s.* trípode.

**trite** [traɪt] *adj.* trillado, trivial, vulgar.

**triumph** [tráɪəmf] *s.* triunfo; *v.* triunfar.

**triumphal** [traɪʌmfl] *adj.* triunfal.

**triumphant** [traɪʌmfənt] *adj.* triunfante; **-ly** *adv.* triunfantemente, en triunfo.

**trivial** [trívjəl] *adj.* trivial, insignificante.

**trod** [trad] *pret.* & *p.p. de* **to tread.**

**trodden** [trádn] *p.p. de* **to tread.**

**trolley** [trálɪ] *s.* trole; tranvía de trole.

**trombone** [trámbon] *s.* trombón.

**troop** [trup] *s.* tropa; cuadrilla.

**trophy** [trófɪ] *s.* trofeo.

**tropic** [trápɪk] *s.* trópico; **— of Cancer** trópico de Cáncer; **— of Capricorn** trópico de Capricornio; *adj.* tropical.

**tropical** [trápɪkl] *adj.* tropical.

**trot** [trat] *v.* trotar; hacer trotar; *s.* trote.

**troubadour** [trúbədor] *s.* trovador.

**trouble** [trʌbl] *v.* perturbar, turbar; molestar, incomodar; afligir; preocupar(se); **don't — to come** no se moleste Vd. en venir; *s.* pena, aflicción; inquietud, perturbación; dificultad; molestia; panne, avería, accidente (*a un mecanismo*); **heart —** enfermedad del corazón; **to be in —** estar en un aprieto o apuro; **it is not worth the —** no vale la pena; **— shooter** investigador de fallas o averías.

**troublemaker** [trʌblmekɚ] *s.* agitador, alborotador, malcontento.

**troublesome** [trʌblsəm] *adj.* molesto, fastidioso, enfadoso, dificultoso; penoso.

**trough** [trɔf] *s.* comedero; artesa; batea; **eaves —** canal, gotera del tejado; **drinking —** abrevadero.

**trousers** [tráuzɚz] *s. pl.* pantalones.

**trousseau** [trúso] *s.* ajuar de novia.

**trout** [traut] *s.* trucha.

**trowel** [tráuəl] *s.* llana, *Am.* cuchara (*de albañil*).

**truant** [trúənt] *s.* novillero, holgazán (*que se ausenta de la escuela*); **to play —** hacer novillos, *Am.* capear la escuela, *Am.* pintar venado, *Am.* jubilarse; *adj.* vago, perezoso.

**truce** [trus] *s.* tregua.

**truck** [trʌk] *s.* camión; carretón; carreta; basura; baratijas; **garden —** hortalizas, legumbres y verduras; **— garden** hortaliza, huerta de legumbres; *v.* acarrear, transportar en camión o carretón.

**trudge** [trʌdʒ] *v.* caminar, caminar con esfuerzo; *s.* caminata.

**true** [tru] *adj.* (*not false*) verdadero; cierto; verídico; fiel; (*exact*) exacto, preciso; legítimo.

**truly** [trúlɪ] *adv.* (*not falsely*) verdaderamente, en verdad; en realidad; (*exactly*) exactamente, correctamente; fielmente; **very — yours** su seguro servidor.

**trump** [trʌmp] *s.* triunfo (*en el juego de naipes*); *v.* matar con un triunfo (*en el juego de naipes*); **to — up an**

**TR**

**excuse** forjar o inventar una excusa.
**trumpet** [trámpɪt] s. trompeta; clarín; **ear —** trompetilla acústica; v. trompetear; tocar la trompeta; pregonar, divulgar.
**trunk** [trʌŋk] s. tronco; baúl; trompa (de elefante); **-s** calzones cortos (para deportes); **— line** línea principal.
**trust** [trʌst] s. (reliance) confianza, fe; (credit) crédito; (charge) cargo; custodia; depósito; (firms) trust, sindicato monopolista; v. confiar; fiar en, tener confianza en, fiarse de; esperar; dar crédito a.
**trustee** [trʌstí] s. fideicomisario, depositario; **university -s** regentes universitarios; **board of -s** patronato; consejo.
**trustful** [trʌstfəl] adj. confiado.
**trusting** [trʌstɪŋ] adj. confiado.
**trustworthy** [trʌstwɜðɪ] adj. fidedigno, digno de confianza.
**trusty** [trʌstɪ] adj. fidedigno; honrado, leal; s. presidiario fidedigno (a quien se le conceden ciertos privilegios).
**truth** [truθ] s. verdad.
**truthful** [trúθfəl] adj. verdadero; verídico; veraz.
**truthfulness** [trúθfəlnɪs] s. veracidad.
**try** [traɪ] v. probar, ensayar; hacer la prueba; poner a prueba; intentar, procurar; procesar, enjuiciar, formar causa (a un acusado); ver (una causa); **to — on a suit** probarse un traje; **to — one's luck** probar fortuna; **to — someone's patience** poner a prueba la paciencia de alguien; **to —** to tratar de, procurar, intentar; s. prueba, tentativa, ensayo.
**trying** [tráɪŋ] adj. molesto; penoso, irritante.
**tub** [tʌb] s. tina; bañera; baño; batea, cuba; v. lavar en tina o cuba.
**tuba** [túbə] s. tuba.
**tube** [tjub] s. tubo; **inner —** cámara (de un neumático); **radio —** lámpara o tubo de radio.
**tubercular** [tjubɜ́kjələ] adj. tuberculoso, tísico.
**tuberculosis** [tjubɜkjəlósɪs] s. tuberculosis.
**tuck** [tʌk] v. alforzar, hacer o echar alforzas; **to — in** meter en; **to — in bed** arropar; **to — under one's arm** meter bajo el brazo; **to — up** arremangar, recoger; **to — up one's sleeves** arremangarse; s. alforza.
**Tuesday** [tjúzdɪ] s. martes.
**tuft** [tʌft] s. (cluster) penacho, copete; borla; (clump) macizo (de plantas).
**tug** [tʌg] v. remolcar; jalar (halar); arrastrar; trabajar con esfuerzo; **to — at** tirar de, jalar; s. tirón, estirón, Am. jalón; remolcador; **—boat** remolcador; **— of war** lucha a tirones de cuerda.
**tuition** [tjuíʃən] s. derechos de enseñanza, Am. colegiatura.
**tulip** [tjúləp] s. tulipán.
**tumble** [tʌmbl] v. caer(se); voltear; dar volteretas; **to — down** caerse;

desplomarse; **to — down** caerse; desplomarse; **to — into someone** tropezar con alguien; **to — over** volcar, tumbar, derribar; venirse abajo; s. caída, tumbo, vuelco, voltereta, Am. rodada; desorden.
**tumbler** [tʌmblə] s. vaso (de mesa); acróbata.
**tumor** [tjúmə] s. tumor.
**tumult** [tjúmʌlt] s. tumulto.
**tumultuous** [tjumʌltʃuəs] adj. tumultuoso.
**tuna** [túnə] s. atún (pez).
**tune** [tjun] s. (melody) tonada; (pitch) tono; armonía; **to be in —** estar a tono, estar afinado o templado; estar entonado; **to be out of —** estar desentonado o desafinado; desentonar; v. afinar, templar; armonizar; **to — in** sintonizar; **to — up the motor** poner al punto el motor.
**tunic** [tjúnɪk] s. túnica.
**tunnel** [tʌnl] s. túnel; socavón; v. socavar; abrir un túnel.
**turban** [tɜ́bən] s. turbante.
**turbine** [tɜ́baɪn], [tɜ́bɪn] s. turbina.
**turbulent** [tɜ́bjələnt] adj. turbulento; revoltoso.
**turf** [tɜf] s. césped; terrón de tierra (con césped); hipódromo, pista (para carreras).
**Turk** [tɜk] s. turco.
**turkey** [tɜ́kɪ] s. pavo, Méx. guajolote (o guajalote); C.A. jolote, chumpe, chompipe; Col. pisco.
**Turkish** [tɜ́kɪʃ] adj. turco; s. turco, idioma turco.
**turmoil** [tɜ́mɔɪl] s. alboroto; confusión.
**turn** [tɜn] v. (rotate) volver(se); voltear(se); girar, dar vueltas, rodar; virar; (shape) tornear, labrar al torno; (become) ponerse (pálido, rojo, etc.); **to — back** volver atrás; volverse, retroceder; devolver; **to — down an offer** rechazar una oferta; **to — in** entregar; recogerse, acostarse; **to — inside out** voltear o volver al revés; **to — into** convertir(se) en; **to — off** apagar (la luz); cortar (el agua, el gas, etc.); **to — off the main road** salirse o desviarse de la carretera; **to — on** encender (la luz); abrir la llave (del gas, del agua); **to — on someone** volverse contra, acometer o caer sobre alguien; **to — out** apagar (la luz); echar, expulsar, arrojar; producir; **to — out well** salir o resultar bien; **to — over** volcar(se), voltear(se); doblar; revolver (en la mente); entregar; **to — over and over** dar repetidas vueltas; **to — sour** agriarse, fermentarse; **to — the corner** doblar la esquina; **to —to** acudir a; volverse a; dirigirse a; convertir(se) en; **to — to the left** doblar o torcer a la izquierda; **to — up** aparecer; **to — up one's nose at** desdeñar; hacer ascos a; **to — up one's sleeves** arremangarse; **to —upside down** trastornar; volcar; **it -s my stomach** me da asco o

náusea; s. vuelta; revolución; giro;
recodo (*del camino*); turno; virada,
cambio de rumbo; — **of mind**
actitud mental; **at every** — a cada
paso; **to be one's** — tocarle a uno;
**to do one a good** — hacerle a uno un
favor; **to take -s** turnarse.

**turnip** [tə́nəp] s. nabo.

**turnover** [tə́novə] s. vuelco (*de un coche*); cambio (*de empleados*); **business**
— movimiento de mercancías, nú-
mero de transacciones; **labor** —
movimiento de obreros, cambio
frecuente de trabajadores; **apple** —
pastel de manzana; — **collar** cuello
doblado.

**turntable** [tə́ntebl̩] s. plato giratorio.

**turpentine** [tə́pəntaın] s. trementina;
aguarrás.

**turpitude** [tə́pətjud] s. torpeza, vileza.

**turquoise** [tə́kwɔız] s. turquesa.

**turret** [tə́ıt] s. torrecilla; torre blindada;
alminar.

**turtle** [tə́tl̩] s. tortuga; —**dove** tórtola.

**tusk** [tʌsk] s. colmillo.

**tutor** [tútə] s. tutor, maestro particular;
v. enseñar, instruir.

**tuxedo** [tʌksído] s. esmoquin.

**twang** [twæŋ] s. tañido (*de una cuerda
de guitarra*); nasalidad, tonillo gangoso; v. puntear, tañer (*una cuerda*);
hablar con voz nasal, hablar con tonillo gangoso.

**twangy** [twǽŋı] adj. gangoso, nasal.

**tweed** [twid] s. mezclilla de lana; —
**suit** traje de mezclilla.

**tweezers** [twízəz] s. pl. pinzas, tenacillas.

**twice** [twaıs] adv. dos veces.

**twig** [twıg] s. ramita; varita.

**twilight** [twáılaıt] s. crepúsculo; **at** —
entre dos luces; adj. crepuscular.

**twin** [twın] adj. & s. gemelo, mellizo,
*Méx.* cuate.

**twine** [twaın] s. cuerda, cordel; v. en-
roscar(se), torcer(se), retorcer(se);
entrelazar.

**twinge** [twındʒ] s. punzada (*dolor agudo*); v. punzar.

**twinkle** [twíŋkl̩] v. titilar, parpadear,
pestañear; chispear; s. titilación, parpadeo; pestañeo; guiño, guiñada; **in
the** — **of an eye** en un abrir y cerrar
de ojos.

**twirl** [twɜl] v. girar; dar vueltas; s. giro,
vuelta; molinete, floreo.

**twist** [twıst] v. (*turn*) torcer(se); re-
torcer(se); (*coil*) enroscar(se); s. torsión, torcedura; torzal, cordoncillo
(*hecho de varias hebras torcidas*);
curva, recodo, vuelta; rosca (*de pan*);
**mental** — sesgo de la mente, sesgo
mental.

**twitch** [twıtʃ] v. crisparse, contraerse,
torcerse convulsivamente (*un músculo*); temblar (*los párpados*); dar un
tirón; s. temblor, ligera, convulsión,
contracción nerviosa; tirón.

**twitter** [twítə] v. gorjear (*los pájaros*);
temblar; agitarse; s. gorjeo; agitación,
estremecimiento nervioso.

**two-faced** [túfest] adj. de dos caras.

**two-fisted** [túfıstəd] adj. vigoroso; de
dos puños.

**twofold** [túfold] adj. doble.

**two-way** [túwe] adj. de dos sentidos.

**type** [taıp] s. tipo; v. escribir a máquina.

**typewrite** [táıpraıt] v. escribir a máquina.

**typewriter** [táıpraıtə] s. máquina de
escribir.

**typewriting** [táıpraıtıŋ] s. mecanografía; trabajo de mecanógrafo.

**typewritten** [táıprıtn̩] adj. escrito a
máquina.

**typhoid** [táıfɔıd] s. tifoidea, fiebre tifoidea.

**typhus** [táıfəs] s. tifo.

**typical** [típık l̩] adj. típico.

**typist** [táıpıst] s. mecanógrafo; mecanó-
grafa.

**typographical** [taıpográfık l̩] adj. tipo-
gráfico; — **error** error de máquina.

**tyrannical** [tırǽnık l̩] adj. tiránico,
tirano.

**tyranny** [tírənı] s. tiranía.

**tyrant** [táırənt] s. tirano.

# U

**ubiquitous** [jubíkwıtəs] adj. ubicuo.

**udder** [ʌ́də] s. ubre.

**ugliness** [ʌ́glınıs] s. fealdad; fiereza.

**ugly** [ʌ́glı] adj. feo; fiero; repugnante;
de mal genio; desagradable.

**ulcer** [ʌ́lsə] s. úlcera.

**ulterior** [ʌltírıə] adj. ulterior.

**ultimate** [ʌ́ltəmıt] adj. último; final;
fundamental; **-ly** adv. finalmente, a la
larga.

**ultramodern** [ʌltrəmádən] adj. ultra-
moderno.

**ultraviolet** [ʌltrəvaíələt] adj. ultravioleta.

**umbilical cord** [ʌmbíləkl̩kɔrd] s. cordón umbilical.

**umbrella** [ʌmbrélə] s. paraguas; sombrilla.

**umpire** [ʌ́mpaır] s. árbitro, arbitrador;
v. arbitrar.

**un-** [ʌn-] *prefijo negativo equivalente a* :
sin, no, in-, des-.

**unable** [ʌnébl̩] adj. incapaz, inhábil;
**to be** — **to come** no poder venir.

**unaccented** [ʌnǽksentəd] adj. in-
acentuado.

**unaccustomed** [ʌnəkʌ́stəmd] adj. desacostumbrado; insólito, inusitado.

**unaffected** [ʌnəfǽktıd] adj. inafectado,
sin afectación, natural, sincero.

**unalterable** [ʌnɔ́ltərəbl̩] adj. inalterable.

**unanimity** [junənímətı] s. unanimidad.

**unanimous** [junǽnəməs] adj. unánime.

**unarmed** [ʌnármd] adj. desarmado.

**unattached** [ʌnətǽtʃt] adj. suelto;
libre; (*law*) no embargado.

**unavoidable** [ʌnəvɔ́ıdəbl̩] adj. inevitable, ineludible.

**unaware** [ʌnəwér] adj. desprevenido;
inadvertido; ignorante; incauto; **-s**
adv. inesperadamente, inopinada-

TR

mente; impensadamente.

**unbalanced** [ʌnbǽlənst] *adj.* desequilibrado; **— account** cuenta no saldada.

**unbearable** [ʌnbérəbl] *adj.* inaguantable, insoportable.

**unbecoming** [ʌnbɪkʌ́mɪŋ] *adj.* impropio; **an — dress** un vestido que no sienta bien o que cae mal.

**unbelief** [ʌnbəlíf] *s.* incredulidad.

**unbelievable** [ʌnbəlívəbl] *adj.* increíble.

**unbeliever** [ʌnbəlívɚ] *s.* descreído, incrédulo.

**unbelieving** [ʌnbəlívɪŋ] *adj.* descreído, incrédulo.

**unbending** [ʌnbéndɪŋ] *adj.* inflexible.

**unbiased** [ʌnbáɪəst] *adj.* imparcial, libre de prejuicio.

**unbosom** [ʌnbúzəm] *v.* revelar, confesar, descubrir (*secretos*); **to — oneself** desahogarse con alguien, revelarle sus más íntimos secretos.

**unbound** [ʌnbáund] *adj.* desencuadernado, no encuadernado; suelto, desatado.

**unbroken** [ʌnbrókən] *adj.* intacto, entero; indómito; ininterrumpido, continuo.

**unbutton** [ʌnbʌ́tn̩] *v.* desabotonar, desabrochar.

**uncanny** [ʌnkǽnɪ] *adj.* extraño, raro, misterioso.

**unceasing** [ʌnsísɪŋ] *adj.* incesante.

**uncertain** [ʌnsɚ́tn̩] *adj.* incierto; dudoso; indeciso.

**uncertainty** [ʌnsɚ́tn̩tɪ] *s.* incertidumbre; falta de certeza.

**unchangeable** [ʌntʃénʒəbl] *adj.* inmutable, inalterable, invariable.

**unchanged** [ʌntʃénʒd] *adj.* inalterado, igual.

**uncharitable** [ʌntʃǽrətəbl] *adj.* duro falto de caridad.

**uncle** [ʌŋkl̩] *s.* tío.

**unclean** [ʌnklín] *adj.* inmundo, sucio; impuro.

**uncomfortable** [ʌnkʌ́mfɚtəbl] *adj.* incómodo; molesto.

**uncommon** [ʌnkʌ́mən] *adj.* poco común, insólito, raro.

**uncompromising** [ʌnkʌ́mprəmaɪzɪŋ] *adj.* intransigente; inflexible.

**unconcern** [ʌnkənsɚ́n] *s.* indiferencia.

**unconditional** [ʌnkəndíʃən] *adj.* incondicional, absoluto.

**uncongenial** [ʌnkəndʒínjəl] *adj.* que no congenia, incompatible.

**unconquerable** [ʌnkʌ́ŋkərəbl] *adj.* invencible, inconquistable.

**unconquered** [ʌnkʌ́ŋkɚd] *adj.* no conquistado, no vencido.

**unconscious** [ʌnkʌ́nʃəs] *adj.* inconsciente; privado.

**unconsciousness** [ʌnkʌ́nʃəsnɪs] *s.* inconsciencia; insensibilidad.

**unconstitutional** [ʌnkʌ́nstɪtuʃən] *adj.* inconstitucional.

**uncontrollable** [ʌnkəntróləbl] *adj.* irrefrenable, ingobernable.

**unconventional** [ʌnkənvénʃən] *adj.* despreocupado, libre de trabas o

reglas.

**uncouth** [ʌnkúθ] *adj.* rudo, tosco, inculto, grosero; desmañado.

**uncover** [ʌnkʌ́vɚ] *v.* descubrir(se); revelar; destapar(se); desabrigar(se).

**unction** [ʌ́ŋkʃən] *s.* unción; fervor; **Extreme Unction** Extremaunción.

**unctuous** [ʌ́ŋkʃəs] *adj.* untuoso.

**uncultivated** [ʌnkʌ́ltəvetɪd] *adj.* inculto; baldío.

**uncultured** [ʌnkʌ́ltʃɚd] *adj.* inculto; grosero.

**undaunted** [ʌndɔ́ntəd] *adj.* impávido.

**undecided** [ʌndɪsáɪdɪd] *adj.* indeciso.

**undeniable** [ʌndɪnáɪəbl] *adj.* innegable.

**under** [ʌ́ndɚ] *prep.* (*beneath*) bajo; debajo de; (*less*) menos de; **— age** menor de edad; **— cover** a cubierto; **— the cover of** al abrigo de, al amparo de; **— pretense of** so pretexto de; **— twelve** menos de doce; **to be — obligation to** deber favores a; *adv.* debajo; abajo; menos; *adj.* inferior, de abajo (*en ciertas combinaciones*); **— dose** dosis escasa o corta; **— secretary** subsecretario; **— side** lado de abajo, lado inferior; **the — dogs** los de abajo.

**underbrush** [ʌ́ndɚbrʌʃ] *s.* maleza.

**underclothes** [ʌ́ndɚkloz] *s. pl.* ropa interior.

**underdog** [ʌ́ndɚdɔg] *s.* perdidoso, víctima.

**underestimate** [ʌ́ndɚéstəmet] *v.* menospreciar, apreciar en menos de lo justo; salir corto en un cálculo.

**underfed** [ʌ́ndɚféd] *adj.* malnutrido.

**undergo** [ʌndɚgó] *v.* sufrir, aguantar, padecer.

**undergone** [ʌndɚgón] *p.p. de* **to undergo**

**undergraduate** [ʌndɚgrǽdʒuɪt] *s.* estudiante del bachillerato; **— course** cursos o asignaturas para el bachillerato.

**underground** [ʌ́ndɚgraund] *adj.* subterráneo; *s.* subterráneo; *adv.* bajo tierra; en secreto; ocultamente.

**underhanded** [ʌ́ndɚhǽndɪd] *adj.* socarrón, secreto, disimulado, clandestino.

**underline** [ʌ́ndɚlaɪn] *v.* subrayar.

**underlying** [ʌndɚláɪɪŋ] *adj.* fundamental.

**undermine** [ʌndɚmáɪn] *v.* minar, socavar.

**underneath** [ʌndɚníθ] *prep.* bajo, debajo de; *adv.* debajo.

**underpay** [ʌ́ndɚpé] *v.* malpagar; escatimar la paga.

**underpinning** [ʌ́ndɚpɪnɪŋ] *s.* apuntalamiento.

**underscore** [ʌ́ndɚskor] *v.* subrayar.

**undersell** [ʌndɚsél] *v.* malbaratar; vender a menos precio que.

**undershirt** [ʌ́ndɚʃɚt] *s.* camiseta.

**undersigned** [ʌndɚsáɪnd] *s.* firmante, infrascrito; **the —** el infrascrito, los infrascritos; el que suscribe.

**undersized** [ʌ́ndɚsáɪzd] *adj.* achaparrado, de tamaño inferior al normal.

**underskirt** [ʌ́ndɚskɜt] s. enaguas, refajo.

**understaffed** [ʌndɚstǽft] adj. de personal insuficiente.

**understand** [ʌndɚstǽnd] v. entender; comprender; sobrentender.

**understandable** [ʌndɚstǽndəbl] adj. comprensible.

**understanding** [ʌndɚstǽndɪŋ] s. comprensión; entendimiento, inteligencia; acuerdo; adj. comprensivo.

**understood** [ʌndɚstúd] pret. & p.p. de to understand; adj. entendido; convenido; sobrentendido.

**understudy** [ʌ́ndɚstʌdɪ] s. sobresaliente, actor suplente; v. servir de sobresaliente o actor suplente.

**undertake** [ʌndɚték] v. emprender; tratar de, intentar; comprometerse a.

**undertaken** [ʌndɚtékən] p.p. de to undertake.

**undertaker** [ʌ́ndɚtekɚ] s. director de funeraria; embalsamador.

**undertaking** [ʌndɚtékɪŋ] s. empresa.

**undertook** [ʌndɚtúk] pret. de to undertake.

**undertow** [ʌ́ndɚto] s. resaca.

**underwater** [ʌ́ndɚwɔtɚ] adj. submarino; subacuático.

**underwear** [ʌ́ndɚwɛr] s. ropa interior.

**underwent** [ʌndɚwént] pret. de to undergo.

**underworld** [ʌ́ndɚwɜld] s. hampa, bajos fondos de la sociedad; clase criminal.

**underwrite** [ʌ́ndɚraɪt] v. asegurar; subscribir.

**undesirable** [ʌndɪzáɪrəbl] adj. indeseable; inconveniente.

**undid** [ʌndíd] pret. de to undo.

**undisturbed** [ʌndɪstɝbd] adj. impasible; sereno, tranquilo; intacto.

**undo** [ʌndú] v. deshacer; desatar; desabrochar; desenredar; anular; to — one's hair soltarse el cabello.

**undoing** [ʌndúɪŋ] s. destrucción; pérdida.

**undone** [ʌndʌ́n] p.p. de to undo; inacabado, sin hacer; sin terminar; it is still — está todavía por hacer, está inacabado; to come — desatarse.

**undoubtedly** [ʌndáʊtɪdlɪ] adv. indudablemente, sin duda.

**undress** [ʌndrés] v. desnudar(se), desvestir(se).

**undue** [ʌndjú] adj. indebido; impropio; excesivo.

**undulate** [ʌ́ndjəlet] v. ondular, ondear.

**unduly** [ʌndjúlɪ] adv. indebidamente.

**undying** [ʌndáɪɪŋ] adj. imperecedero, eterno.

**unearth** [ʌnɝ́θ] v. desenterrar.

**uneasily** [ʌníz̩lɪ] adv. intranquilamente, inquietamente, con inquietud; incómodamente.

**uneasiness** [ʌnízɪnɪs] s. malestar, inquietud, intranquilidad, desasosiego.

**uneasy** [ʌnízɪ] adj. ansioso, inquieto, intranquilo; cohibido; incómodo.

**uneducated** [ʌnédʒəketɪd] adj. inculto, indocto, falto de instrucción, igno-

rante.

**unemployed** [ʌnɪmplɔ́ɪd] adj. desocupado, desempleado, cesante; ocioso; — funds fondos no invertidos o inactivos.

**unemployment** [ʌnɪmplɔ́ɪmənt] s. desempleo, cesantía, falta de empleo, desocupación.

**unending** [ʌnéndɪŋ] adj. inacabable, interminable.

**unequal** [ʌníkwəl] adj. desigual; insuficiente, ineficaz.

**unequivocal** [ʌnɪkwívəkl] adj. inequívoco.

**unerring** [ʌnérɪŋ] adj. infalible.

**unessential** [ʌnɪsénʃl] adj. no esencial.

**uneven** [ʌnívən] adj. desigual, disparejo; irregular, accidentado; — numbers números impares o nones.

**unevenness** [ʌnívənnɪs] s. desigualdad; desnivel; irregularidad, escabrosidad (del terreno).

**uneventful** [ʌnɪvéntfl] adj. sin novedad.

**unexpected** [ʌnɪkspéktɪd] adj. inesperado; -ly adv. de improviso, inesperadamente.

**unexpressive** [ʌnɪksprésɪv] adj. sin emoción.

**unfailing** [ʌnfélɪŋ] adj. que nunca falta, constante, indefectible; infalible.

**unfair** [ʌnfér] adj. injusto; tramposo; to act -ly obrar de mala fe.

**unfaithful** [ʌnféθfəl] adj. infiel; desleal.

**unfamiliar** [ʌnfəmíljɚ] adj. poco familiar; desconocido; to be — with no tener conocimiento de; no estar al tanto de, ignorar; no conocer bien.

**unfasten** [ʌnfǽsn̩] v. desabrochar; desatar; aflojar.

**unfavorable** [ʌnfévrəbl] adj. desfavorable, contrario, adverso.

**unfeeling** [ʌnfílɪŋ] adj. insensible; incompasivo.

**unfinished** [ʌnfínɪʃt] adj. inacabado, sin terminar, sin acabar; sin barnizar, sin pulir.

**unfit** [ʌnfít] adj. incompetente, inepto, incapaz; inservible; impropio; v. incapacitar.

**unfold** [ʌnfóld] v. desenvolver(se), desarrollar(se); desdoblar; revelar.

**unforeseen** [ʌnforsín] adj. imprevisto.

**unforgettable** [ʌnfɚgétəbl] adj. inolvidable.

**unfortunate** [ʌnfɔ́rtʃənɪt] adj. desventurado, infeliz, desgraciado, desdichado; -ly adv. desgraciadamente, por desgracia.

**unfounded** [ʌnfáʊndəd] adj. infundado.

**unfrequented** [ʌnfríkwəntəd] adj. poco frecuentado.

**unfriendly** [ʌnfréndlɪ] adj. hostil, enemigo; poco amistoso; adv. hostilmente.

**unfruitful** [ʌnfrútfl] adj. infructuoso.

**unfurl** [ʌnfɝ́l] v. desplegar.

**unfurnished** [ʌnfɝ́nɪʃt] adj. desamueblado.

UN

**ungainly** [ʌngénlɪ] *adj.* desgarbado, torpe.

**ungrateful** [ʌngrétfəl] *adj.* ingrato, desagradecido.

**unguarded** [ʌngárdəd] *adj.* desprevenido; descuidado.

**unhappy** [ʌnhǽpɪ] *adj.* infeliz; desgraciado, desventurado, desdichado.

**unharmed** [ʌnhármd] *adj.* sin daño, ileso.

**unhealthy** [ʌnhélθɪ] *adj.* malsano; insalubre; enfermizo.

**unheard-of** [ʌnhɝ́dɑv] *adj.* inaudito; desconocido.

**unhitch** [ʌnhítʃ] *v.* desenganchar; desatar.

**unholy** [ʌnhólɪ] *adj.* impío, malo.

**unhook** [ʌnhúk] *v.* desenganchar; desabrochar.

**unhurt** [ʌnhɝ́t] *adj.* ileso.

**uniform** [júnəfɔrm] *adj. & s.* uniforme.

**uniformity** [junəfɔ́rmətɪ] *s.* uniformidad.

**unify** [júnəfaɪ] *v.* unificar, unir.

**unilateral** [junɪlǽtɚl] *adj.* unilateral.

**unimportant** [ʌnɪmpɔ́rtn̩t] *adj.* insignificante, poco importante.

**uninhibited** [ʌnɪnhíbətəd] *adj.* sin inhibición.

**union** [júnjən] *s.* unión; — **leader** jefe de un gremio obrero; **trade-union** gremio obrero; — **shop** obreros sindicados o agremiados.

**unique** [juník] *adj.* único, singular.

**unison** [júnəzn̩]: **in** — al unísono (*en el mismo tono*); al compás.

**unit** [júnɪt] *s.* unidad.

**unite** [junáɪt] *v.* unir(se).

**unity** [júnətɪ] *s.* unidad; unión.

**universal** [junəvɝ́sl̩] *adj.* universal; — **joint** cruceta.

**universe** [júnəvɝs] *s.* universo.

**university** [junəvɝ́sətɪ] *s.* universidad.

**unjust** [ʌndʒʌ́st] *adj.* injusto.

**unjustifiable** [ʌndʒʌ́stəfaɪəbl̩] *adj.* injustificable, injustificado.

**unkempt** [ʌnkémpt] *adj.* desaseado, desaliñado; desgreñado.

**unkind** [ʌnkáɪnd] *adj.* falto de bondad; descortés; cruel.

**unknown** [ʌnnón] *adj.* desconocido; no sabido; ignoto; — **quality** incógnita; **it is** — se ignora, no se sabe, se desconoce.

**unlawful** [ʌnlɔ́fəl] *adj.* ilegal, ilícito.

**unleash** [ʌnlíʃ] *v.* soltar.

**unless** [ʌnlés] *conj.* a menos que, a no ser que.

**unlicensed** [ʌnláɪsənzd] *adj.* sin autorización.

**unlike** [ʌnláɪk] *adj.* desemejante, distinto, diferente; *prep.* a diferencia de.

**unlikely** [ʌnláɪklɪ] *adj.* improbable, inverosímil.

**unlimited** [ʌnlímɪtɪd] *adj.* ilimitado.

**unload** [ʌnlód] *v.* descargar; vaciar; deshacerse de (*acciones, mercancías*).

**unlock** [ʌnlák] *v.* abrir (*con llave*); soltar, destrabar; revelar, penetrar (*secretos*).

**unloose** [ʌnlús] *v.* soltar.

**unlucky** [ʌnlʌ́kɪ] *adj.* (*unfortunate*) desdichado, desventurado, desgraciado, desafortunado; (*of bad omen*) aciago, de mal agüero, funesto; **an — number** un número de mala suerte.

**unmanageable** [ʌnmǽnɪdʒəbl̩] *adj.* inmanejable, ingobernable, intratable, indomable.

**unmanned** [ʌnmǽnd] *adj.* desguarnecido; sin tripulación.

**unmarked** [ʌnmárkt] *adj.* sin identificación.

**unmarried** [ʌnmǽrɪd] *adj.* soltero.

**unmask** [ʌnmǽsk] *v.* desenvascar(se).

**unmerciful** [ʌnmɝ́sɪfəl] *adj.* despiadado, inclemente.

**unmistakable** [ʌnməstékəbl̩] *adj.* inequívoco, claro, inconfundible.

**unmoved** [ʌnmúvd] *adj.* fijo; inmutable, impasible; indiferente.

**unnatural** [ʌnnǽtʃərəl] *adj.* afectado, artificial; anormal; **an — mother** una madre desnaturalizada.

**unnecessary** [ʌnnésəsɛrɪ] *adj.* innecesario.

**unnoticed** [ʌnnótɪst] *adj.* inadvertido.

**unobliging** [ʌnəbláɪdʒɪŋ] *adj.* poco complaciente, descortés, descomedido.

**unobserved** [ʌnəbzɝ́vd] *adj.* inadvertido; sin ser visto.

**unobtainable** [ʌnəbténəbl̩] *adj.* inobtenible, inasequible, inaccesible.

**unobtrusive** [ʌnəbtrusɪv] *adj.* discreto; sin ser visto.

**unoccupied** [ʌnákjəpaɪd] *adj.* desocupado; vacío; desalquilado.

**unofficial** [ʌnəfíʃl̩] *adj.* extraoficial.

**unorganized** [ʌnɔ́rgənaɪzd] *adj.* sin organización; inorganizado.

**unoriginal** [ʌnəɾídʒənl̩] *adj.* trivial; ordinario.

**unorthodox** [ʌnɔ́rθədɑks] *adj.* heterodoxo.

**unpack** [ʌnpǽk] *v.* desempacar; desembalar.

**unpaid** [ʌnpéd] *adj.* no pagado; sin pagar; — **bills** cuentas por pagar.

**unpleasant** [ʌnpléznt] *adj.* desagradable.

**unpleasantness** [ʌnplézntnɪs] *s.* manera desagradable; desazón; desavenencia; **the — of a situation** lo desagradable de una situación; **to have an — with** tener una desavenencia con.

**unprecedented** [ʌnprésədɛntɪd] *adj.* sin precedente; inaudito.

**unpremeditated** [ʌnprimédətetəd] *adj.* impremeditado.

**unprepared** [ʌnprɪpérd] *adj.* desprevenido; no preparado; no listo.

**unpretentious** [ʌnpriténʃəs] *adj.* modesto; sin pretenciones.

**unprintable** [ʌnpríntəbl̩] *adj.* que no puede imprimirse.

**unproductive** [ʌnprədʌ́ktɪv] *adj.* improductivo.

**unprofessional** [ʌnprəféʃənl̩] *adj.* no profesional.

**unprofitable** [ʌnpráfɪtəbl̩] *adj.* infructuoso.

**unpublished** [ʌnpʌ́blɪʃt] *adj.* inédito, no publicado.

**unqualified** [ʌnkwáləfaɪd] *adj.* incompetente; inepto.

**unquenchable** [ʌnkwéntʃəbl̩] *adj.* inapagable, inextinguible.

**unquestionable** [ʌnkwéstʃənəbl̩] *adj.* indisputable, indudable; irreprochable.

**unravel** [ʌnrǽvl̩] *v.* desenredar; desenmarañar; deshilachar(se); deshilar.

**unreal** [ʌnríəl] *adj.* irreal; ilusorio, imaginario.

**unreasonable** [ʌnrízənəbl̩] *adj.* desrazonable, fuera de razón; irracional.

**unrecognizable** [ʌnrékəgnaɪzəbl̩] *adj.* irreconocible, no conocible, incapaz de reconocerse; desconocido.

**unrefined** [ʌnrɪfáɪnd] *adj.* no refinado; inculto, grosero.

**unreliable** [ʌnrɪlaíəbl̩] *adj.* informal; indigno de confianza.

**unrest** [ʌnrést] *s.* inquietud, desasosiego.

**unroll** [ʌnról] *v.* desenrollar(se), desenvolver(se).

**unruly** [ʌnrúlɪ] *adj.* indómito; indócil; desobediente.

**unsafe** [ʌnséf] *adj.* inseguro, peligroso.

**unsalable** [ʌnséləbl̩] *adj.* invendible.

**unsatisfactory** [ʌnsætɪsfǽktrɪ] *adj.* no satisfactorio, inaceptable.

**unscrupulous** [ʌnskrúpjʊləs] *adj.* poco escrupuloso.

**unseasonable** [ʌnsízənəbl̩] *adj.* intempestivo.

**unseat** [ʌnsít] *v.* destituir.

**unseen** [ʌnsín] *adj.* no visto, oculto; invisible.

**unselfish** [ʌnsélfɪʃ] *adj.* desinteresado.

**unselfishness** [ʌnsélfɪʃnɪs] *s.* desinterés, abnegación.

**unsettled** [ʌnsétl̩d] *adj.* (*disturbed*) desordenado, en desorden; turbio; inestable; (*uncertain*) incierto; indeciso; (*unpopulated*) deshabitado; no establecido; **— bills** cuentas no liquidadas, cuentas pendientes; **— weather** tiempo variable; **an — liquid** un líquido revuelto o turbio.

**unshaken** [ʌnʃékən] *adj.* inmóvil, inmovible, firme.

**unsightly** [ʌnsáɪtlɪ] *adj.* feo, desagradable a la vista.

**unskilled** [ʌnskíld] *adj.* inexperto.

**unskillful** [ʌnskílfəl] *adj.* inhábil, desmañado, inexperto.

**unsociable** [ʌnsóʃəbl̩] *adj.* insociable, huraño, intratable, arisco.

**unsophisticated** [ʌnsəfístəketəd] *adj.* cándido, sencillo.

**unsound** [ʌnsáund] *adj.* erróneo, falso.

**unspeakable** [ʌnspíkəbl̩] *adj.* indecible; inefable; atroz.

**unstable** [ʌnstébl̩] *adj.* inestable.

**unsteady** [ʌnstédɪ] *adj.* inseguro, inestable; movedizo; variable, inconstante.

**unsuccessful** [ʌnsəksésfəl] *adj.* sin éxito; desafortunado; **to be —** no tener

éxito.

**unsuitable** [ʌnsútəbl̩] *adj.* impropio, inapropiado; inepto; inconveniente; incongruente; incompatible.

**unsuspected** [ʌnsəspéktɪd] *adj.* insospechado.

**untenable** [ʌnténəbl̩] *adj.* insostenible.

**unthinkable** [ʌnθíŋkəbl̩] *adj.* impensable.

**untidy** [ʌntáɪdɪ] *adj.* desaliñado, desaseado; desarreglado, en desorden.

**untie** [ʌntáɪ] *v.* desatar(se); desamarrar; deshacer (*un nudo o lazo*).

**until** [ʌntíl] *prep.* hasta; *conj.* hasta que.

**untimely** [ʌntáɪmlɪ] *adj.* inoportuno; prematuro; *adv.* inoportunamente; fuera de sazón; demasiado pronto.

**untiring** [ʌntáɪrɪŋ] *adj.* incansable.

**untold** [ʌntóld] *adj.* indecible, innumerable, incalculable, inestimable.

**untouched** [ʌntʌ́ʃt] *adj.* (*unscathed*) intacto, no tocado, íntegro; (*impassive*) impasible, no conmovido; **to leave —** no tocar, dejar intacto; dejar impasible, no conmover.

**untrained** [ʌntrénd] *adj.* indisciplinado, falto de disciplina; sin educación; inexperto.

**untried** [ʌntráɪd] *adj.* no probado, no ensayado, no experimentado; **— law case** causa todavía no vista.

**untroubled** [ʌntrʌ́bl̩d] *adj.* sosegado, tranquilo, quieto.

**untrue** [ʌntrú] *adj.* falso; infiel; desleal; mentiroso.

**untruth** [ʌntrúθ] *s.* falsedad; mentira.

**untutored** [ʌntútəd] *adj.* sin instrucción; ingenuo.

**unused** [ʌnjúzd] *adj.* no usado; desacostumbrado; **— to** no hecho a, desacostumbrado a.

**unusual** [ʌnjúʒʊəl] *adj.* inusitado, insólito; desusado; raro, extraño; extraordinario.

**unvarnished** [ʌnvárnɪʃt] *adj.* sin barnizar; sin adornos.

**unveil** [ʌnvél] *v.* quitar el velo a; revelar, descubrir.

**unwarranted** [ʌnwɔ́rəntəd] *adj.* no justificado.

**unwary** [ʌnwέrɪ] *adj.* incauto.

**unwashed** [ʌnwɔ́ʃt] *adj.* no lavado, sin lavar; sucio.

**unwelcome** [ʌnwélkəm] *adj.* indeseable, no deseado; mal acogido, mal recibido, mal quisto.

**unwholesome** [ʌnhólsəm] *adj.* malsano; insalubre, dañino.

**unwieldy** [ʌnwíldɪ] *adj.* inmanejable, difícil de manejar, embarazoso, engorroso.

**unwilling** [ʌnwílɪŋ] *adj.* renuente, maldispuesto, reacio; **to be —** **to** no querer, no estar dispuesto a; **-ly** *adv.* de mala gana, sin querer.

**unwillingness** [ʌnwílɪŋnɪs] *s.* renuencia, falta de voluntad; mala gana.

**unwise** [ʌnwáɪz] *adj.* imprudente, indiscreto; necio.

**unwonted** [ʌnwʌ́ntəd] *adj.* inusitado, inacostumbrado; inédito.

**UN**

**unworthy** [ʌnwɜ́ði] *adj.* indigno.
**unwrap** [ʌnrǽp] *v.* desenvolver.
**unwritten** [ʌnrítən] *adj.* no escrito.
**up** [ʌp] *adv.* (*above*) arriba, hacia arriba; en lo alto; (*standing*) de pie; *adj.* levantado, derecho, erecto; (*finished*) terminado, concluido; **— and down** de arriba abajo; de acá para allá; **-s and downs** altibajos; fluctuaciones, vaivenes; **— the river** río arriba; **— to now** hasta ahora; **his time is —** ha expirado su tiempo; se ha cumplido su plazo; **prices are —** los precios han subido; **that is — to you** queda a la discreción de Vd.; eso es cosa suya; **to be — against it** estar perplejo, no saber qué hacer; estar en un aprieto; **to be — on the news** estar al corriente (*o* al tanto) de las noticias); **to be — to one's old tricks** hacer de las suyas; **to eat it —** comérselo; **what's —?** ¿qué pasa?; *v.* levantar, alzar.
**upbraid** [ʌpbréd] *v.* reprender, regañar.
**update** [ʌpdét] *v.* poner al día.
**upgrade** [ʌpgréd] *v.* adelantar; mejorar.
**upheaval** [ʌphívl] *s.* trastorno.
**upheld** [ʌphéld] *pret.* & *p.p. de* **to uphold.**
**uphill** [ʌphíl] *adv.* cuesta arriba; *adj.* ascendente; trabajoso, arduo.
**uphold** [ʌphóld] *v.* sostener; apoyar.
**upholster** [ʌphólstɚ] *v.* entapizar y rellenar (*muebles*).
**upholstery** [ʌphólstrɪ] *s.* tapicería.
**upkeep** [ʌ́pkip] *s.* manutención.
**upland** [ʌ́plənd] *s.* altiplanicie, tierra alta.
**uplift** [ʌ́plɪft] *s.* elevación; edificación (*espiritual*); [ʌplíft] *v.* elevar; edificar (*espiritualmente*).
**upon** [əpán] *prep.* en, sobre, encima de; **— arriving** al llegar.
**upper** [ʌ́pɚ] *adj.* superior; alto; **— berth** litera alta, cama alta (*de un coche dormitorio*); **to have the — hand** ejercer dominio o mando; llevar la ventaja; *s.* litera alta, cama alta; pala (*parte superior del calzado*).
**upright** [ʌ́pratt] *adj.* recto; derecho; vertical; justo, honrado; **— piano** piano vertical; *s.* poste; puntal; piano vertical.
**uprightness** [ʌ́praɪtnɪs] *s.* rectitud.
**uprising** [ʌpráɪzɪŋ] *s.* alzamiento, levantamiento; revuelta.
**uproar** [ʌ́pror] *s.* tumulto, alboroto, bulla, gritería.
**uproarious** [ʌprórɪəs] *adj.* estruendoso, bullicioso, tumultuoso.
**uproot** [ʌprút] *v.* desarraigar, arrancar de raíz.
**upset** [ʌpsét] *v.* (*capsize*) volcar, tumbar; (*distress*) trastornar; perturbar, turbar; **to become —** volcarse; turbarse; trastornársele a uno el estómago; *pret.* & *p.p. de* **to upset**; *adj.* indispuesto, descompuesto; desarreglado, trastornado; [ʌpset] *s.* vuelco; trastorno; desorden; indisposición.

**upshot** [ʌ́pʃɑt] *s.* resultado, fin.
**upside** [ʌ́psáɪd] *s.* lado o parte superior; **— down** al revés; patas arriba; en desorden.
**upstage** [ʌpstédʒ] *v.* quitarle la escena a uno.
**upstairs** [ʌpstérz] *adv.* arriba, en el piso de arriba; *adj.* de arriba; *s.* piso (*o* pisos) de arriba.
**upstart** [ʌ́pstɑrt] *s.* advenedizo, principiante presuntuoso.
**up-to-date** [ʌ́ptədét] *adj.* moderno; al corriente, al tanto.
**upturn** [ʌ́ptɜrn] *s.* alza, subida (*de precios*); mejora.
**upward** [ʌ́pwɚd] *adv.* arriba, para arriba, hacia arriba; más; **— of** más de; *adj.* ascendente, hacia arriba, para arriba.
**upwards** [ʌ́pwɚdz] *adv.* = **upward.**
**uranium** [juréniəm] *s.* uranio.
**urban** [ɜ́bən] *adj.* urbano.
**urchin** [ɜ́tʃɪn] *s.* granuja, pilluelo; **sea —** erizo de mar.
**urge** [ɜdʒ] *v.* urgir, instar; exhortar; recomendar o solicitar con instancia; apremiar, incitar, estimular; *s.* impulso; gana, ganas; estímulo.
**urgency** [ɜ́dʒənsɪ] *s.* urgencia; apremio.
**urgent** [ɜ́dʒənt] *adj.* urgente, apremiante.
**urinal** [júrɪnl] *s.* urinario.
**urinate** [júrənet] *v.* orinar.
**urine** [júrɪn] *s.* orina, (los) orines.
**urn** [ɜrn] *s.* urna; **coffee —** cafetera.
**us** [ʌs] *pron.* nos; nosotros (*con preposición*).
**usage** [júsɪdʒ] *s.* usanza; uso; **hard —** uso constante.
**use** [jus] *s.* (*application*) uso; empleo; (*goal*) utilidad; **it is of no —** es inútil; no sirve; **out of —** desusado, ya no usado; pasado de moda; **to have no further — for** ya no necesitar, ya no tener necesidad de; **what is the —of it?** ¿para qué sirve?; ¿qué ventaja tiene?; ¿qué objeto tiene?; [juz] *v.* usar; emplear; servirse de, hacer uso de; acostumbrar, soler, *Am.* saber; **— your judgment** haz lo que te parezca; **to — up** gastar, agotar; consumir; **to be -d to** estar hecho, acostumbrado o habituado a; **he -d to do it** solía hacerlo, lo hacía.
**useful** [júsfəl] *adj.* útil.
**usefulness** [júsfəlnɪs] *s.* utilidad.
**useless** [júslɪs] *adj.* inútil; inservible.
**uselessness** [júslɪsnɪs] *s.* inutilidad.
**usher** [ʌ́ʃɚ] *s.* acomodador (*en un teatro o iglesia*); ujier; *v.* conducir, llevar, acompañar; introducir.
**usual** [júʒuəl] *adj.* usual; corriente, común, general; **-ly** *adv.* usualmente, generalmente, por lo general.
**usurer** [júʒərɚ] *s.* usurero.
**usurp** [juzɜ́p] *v.* usurpar.
**usury** [júʒərɪ] *s.* usura.
**utensil** [juténsl] *s.* utensilio.
**uterus** [jútərəs] *s.* útero.

**utilitarian** [jʊtɪlətériən] *adj.* utilitario.

**utility** [jutíləti] *s.* utilidad; servicio.

**utilize** [jútḷaɪz] *v.* utilizar; aprovechar.

**utmost** [ʌ́tmost] *adj.* (*extreme*) sumo, extremo; más distante; más grande, mayor; más alto; (*last*) último; **he did his —** hizo cuanto pudo; **to the —** hasta más no poder.

**utter** [ʌ́tɚ] *v.* proferir; decir, expresar; **to — a cry** dar un grito; *adj.* completo, total; absoluto.

**utterance** [ʌ́tərəns] *s.* declaración; expresión; modo de hablar.

**uttermost** [ʌ́tɚmost] = **utmost.**

**uvula** [júvjələ] *s.* campanilla, galillo de la garganta.

**uvular** [júvjʊlɚ] *adj.* uvular.

# V

**vacancy** [vékənsɪ] *s.* vacante, empleo vacante; vacío; habitación o apartamento desocupado.

**vacant** [vékənt] *adj.* vacante; vacío; desocupado; libre.

**vacate** [véket] *v.* desocupar, dejar vacío; dejar vacante.

**vacation** [vekéʃən] *s.* vacación; vacaciones.

**vaccinate** [vǽksṇet] *v.* vacunar.

**vaccination** [væksṇéʃən] *s.* vacunación.

**vaccine** [vǽksin] *s.* vacuna,

**vacillate** [vǽsḷet] *v.* vacilar.

**vacuum** [vǽkjʊəm] *s.* vacío; **— cleaner** escoba eléctrica.

**vagabond** [vǽgəbɑnd] *adj.* & *s.* vagabundo.

**vagrancy** [végrənsɪ] *s.* vagancia.

**vagrant** [végrənt] *adj.* vago, vagabundo, errante; *s.* vago, vagabundo.

**vague** [veg] *adj.* vago.

**vain** [ven] *adj.* vano; vanidoso; **in —** en vano.

**vainglory** [venglórɪ] *s.* vanagloria.

**vale** [vel] *s.* valle; cañada.

**valentine** [vǽləntaɪn] *s.* tarjeta o regalo del día de San Valentín (*el día de los enamorados*); **to my —** a mi querido, a mi querida.

**valet** [vǽlɪt] *s.* criado, camarero; planchador de trajes.

**valiant** [vǽljənt] *adj.* valiente, valeroso.

**valid** [vǽlɪd] *adj.* válido; valedero.

**validity** [vəlídətɪ] *s.* validez.

**valise** [vəlís] *s.* valija, maleta, *Méx.* velís, *Méx.* petaca.

**valley** [vǽlɪ] *s.* valle.

**valor** [vǽlɚ] *s.* valor, ánimo, valentía.

**valorous** [vǽlərəs] *adj.* valeroso, valiente.

**valuable** [vǽljəbḷ] *adj.* valioso; precioso; preciado; **-s** *s. pl.* objetos de valor, joyas, alhajas.

**valuation** [væljuéʃən] *s.* valuación, valoración; avalúo; tasa.

**value** [vǽlju] *s.* (*price*) valor; precio; (*merit*) mérito; (*consideration*) estimación, aprecio; *v.* valorar, avaluar, valuar; apreciar, estimar.

**valueless** [vǽljʊlɪs] *adj.* sin valor.

**valve** [vǽlv] *s.* válvula; valva (*de los*

*moluscos*); **safety —** válvula de seguridad.

**vampire** [vǽmpaɪr] *s.* vampiro.

**van** [væn] *s.* camión (*para transportar muebles*); **—guard** vanguardia.

**vandal** [vǽndḷ] *s.* vándalo.

**vane** [ven] *s.* veleta; aspa (*de molino de viento*); paleta (*de hélice*).

**vanguard** [vǽngɑrd] *s.* vanguardia.

**vanilla** [vənílə] *s.* vainilla.

**vanish** [vǽnɪʃ] *v.* desvanecerse, desaparecer(se).

**vanity** [vǽnətɪ] *s.* vanidad; **— case** neceser; **— table** tocador.

**vanquish** [vǽnkwɪʃ] *v.* vencer.

**vantage** [vǽntɪdʒ] *s.* ventaja; **point of —** lugar estratégico.

**vapor** [vépɚ] *s.* vapor; vaho.

**vaporize** [vépɚaɪz] *v.* vaporizar.

**variable** [vérɪəbḷ] *adj.* & *s.* variable.

**variance** [vérɪəns] *s.* variación, cambio; desavenencia; **to be at —** estar desavenidos; no estar de acuerdo.

**variant** [vǽrɪənt] *s.* variante.

**variation** [vɛrɪéʃən] *s.* variación; variedad.

**varied** [vérɪd] *adj.* variado, vario.

**variegated** [vérɪgetɪd] *adj.* abigarrado.

**variety** [vəráɪətɪ] *s.* variedad.

**various** [vérɪəs] *adj.* varios; diferentes, distintos.

**varnish** [vɑ́rnɪʃ] *s.* barniz; *v.* barnizar.

**vary** [vérɪ] *v.* variar; cambiar.

**vase** [ves] *s.* vaso, jarrón.

**Vaseline** [vǽsəlin] *s.* vaselina.

**vassal** [vǽsḷ] *adj.* & *s.* vasallo.

**vast** [væst] *adj.* vasto; inmenso; anchuroso; **-ly** *adv.* vastamente, sumamente, muy.

**vastness** [vǽstnɪs] *s.* inmensidad.

**vat** [væt] *s.* tina, tanque.

**vaudeville** [vódəvɪl] *s.* vodevil, función de variedades.

**vault** [vɔlt] *s.* bóveda; tumba; **bank —** caja fuerte; depósito; **pole —** salto con garrocha; *v.* abovedar, edificar una bóveda; dar figura de bóveda; saltar con garrocha; saltar por encima de.

**vaunt** [vɔnt] *v.* jactarse; ostentar, alardear; *s.* jactancia.

**veal** [vil] *s.* carne de ternera; **— cutlet** chuleta de ternera.

**veer** [vɪr] *v.* virar; *s.* virada.

**vegetable** [védʒtəbḷ] *s.* (*plant*) vegetal, planta; (*food*) legumbre; **-s** hortaliza, legumbres; **green -s** verduras; *adj.* vegetal; de legumbres, de hortaliza; **— garden** hortaliza.

**vegetate** [védʒətet] *v.* vegetar.

**vegetation** [vedʒətéʃən] *s.* vegetación.

**vehemence** [víəməns] *s.* vehemencia.

**vehement** [víəmənt] *adj.* vehemente.

**vehicle** [víɪkḷ] *s.* vehículo.

**veil** [vel] *s.* velo; *v.* velar, tapar, encubrir.

**vein** [ven] *s.* vena; veta, filón.

**veined** [vend] *adj.* veteado, jaspeado; venoso.

**velocity** [vəlásətɪ] *s.* velocidad.

**velvet** [vélvɪt] *s.* terciopelo; velludo;

UN

*adj.* de terciopelo; aterciopelado.
**velvety** [vélvɪtɪ] *adj.* aterciopelado.
**vendor** [véndɚ] *s.* vendedor; buhonero, vendedor ambulante.
**veneer** [vənír] *s.* chapa; *v.* chapar o chapear, *Am.* enchapar.
**venerable** [vénərəb]] *adj.* venerable; venerando.
**venerate** [vénəret] *v.* venerar.
**veneration** [vɛnəréʃən] *s.* veneración.
**venereal** [vəníriəl] *adj.* venéreo.
**Venezuelan** [vɛnəzwílən] *adj.* & *s.* venezolano.
**vengeance** [véndʒəns] *s.* venganza; **with a —** con furia; con violencia.
**venison** [vénəzn̩] *s.* venado, carne de venado.
**venom** [vénəm] *s.* veneno, ponzoña.
**venomous** [vénəməs] *adj.* venenoso, ponzoñoso.
**vent** [vɛnt] *s.* (*opening*) abertura; (*escape*) escape; (*utterance*) desahogo; fogón (*de arma de fuego*); **to give — to anger** desahogar la ira, dar desahogo a la cólera; *v.* dar salida o desahogo; desahogar, descargar.
**ventilate** [vént]et] *v.* ventilar.
**ventilation** [vɛnt]éʃən] *s.* ventilación.
**ventilator** [vént]etɚ] *s.* ventilador.
**venture** [véntʃɚ] *s.* ventura, riesgo; **business —** especulación; empresa o negocio arriesgado; *v.* aventurar, arriesgar; **to — outside** aventurarse a salir; **to — to** aventurarse a, atreverse a, osar.
**venturous** [véntʃərəs] *adj.* aventurado.
**veranda** [vərǽndə] *s.* galería; terraza; balcón corrido.
**verb** [vɝb] *s.* verbo.
**verbal** [vɝb]] *adj.* verbal; oral.
**verbalize** [vɝbəlaɪz] *v.* expresar por medio de palabras.
**verbose** [vɚbós] *adj.* verboso; palabrero.
**verdict** [vɝdɪkt] *s.* veredicto; fallo, decisión, sentencia; **— of "not guilty"** veredicto de inculpabilidad.
**verdure** [vɝdʒɚ] *s.* verdura, verdor, verde.
**verge** [vɝdʒ] *s.* borde, margen, orilla; **on the —** al borde de; a punto de; *v.* **to — on** rayar en, estar al margen de; **to — toward** tender a, inclinarse a.
**verify** [vérəfaɪ] *v.* verificar; comprobar.
**verily** [vérəlɪ] *adv.* en verdad.
**veritable** [vérətəb]] *adj.* verdadero.
**vermillion** [vɚmíljən] *adj.* bermejo.
**vernacular** [vɚnǽkjulɚ] *adj.* vernáculo; *s.* idioma corriente.
**versatile** [vɝsət]] *adj.* hábil para muchas cosas; flexible.
**verse** [vɝs] *s.* verso.
**versed** [vɝst] *adj.* versado, experto, perito.
**version** [vɝʒən] *s.* versión.
**vertebrate** [vɝtəbrɪt] *adj.* vertebrado.
**vertical** [vɝtɪk]] *adj.* vertical.
**very** [vérɪ] *adv.* muy; **— much** muchísimo; **— many** muchísimos; **it is — cold today** hace mucho frío hoy;

*adj.* mismo; mismísimo; mero; **the — man** el mismísimo hombre; **the — thought of** la mera idea de.
**vespers** [véspɚz] *s. pl.* vísperas.
**vessel** [vés]] *s.* vasija; vaso; barco, embarcación; **blood —** vaso, vena, arteria.
**vest** [vɛst] *s.* chaleco; *v.* conferir; **to — with power** revestir de autoridad, conferir poder a.
**vestibule** [véstəbjul] *s.* vestíbulo; zaguán.
**vestige** [véstɪdʒ] *s.* vestigio.
**vestment** [véstmənt] *s.* vestidura.
**veteran** [vétərən] *adj.* & *s.* veterano.
**veterinary** [vétrənɛrɪ] *s.* veterinario o albéitar.
**veto** [víto] *s.* veto; prohibición; *v.* vedar, prohibir; poner el veto a; negarse a aprobar.
**vex** [vɛks] *v.* molestar, hostigar; incomodar, enfadar; perturbar.
**vexation** [vɛkséʃən] *s.* molestia, incomodidad; enojo.
**via** [váɪə] *prep.* por, por la vía de.
**viable** [váɪəb]] *adj.* viable.
**viaduct** [váɪədʌkt] *s.* viaducto.
**vial** [váɪəl] *s.* frasco, redoma; **small — ampolleta.**
**viands** [váɪəndz] *s. pl.* vianda, alimentos, comida.
**vibrate** [váɪbret] *v.* vibrar.
**vibration** [vaɪbréʃən] *s.* vibración.
**vicarious** [vaɪkérɪəs] *adj.* vicario.
**vice** [vaɪs] *s.* vicio; falta, defecto.
**vice-president** [váɪsprézədənt] *s.* vicepresidente.
**viceroy** [váɪsrɔɪ] *s.* virrey.
**vice versa** [váɪsivɝ́sə] viceversa.
**vicinity** [vəsínətɪ] *s.* vecindad; cercanía; inmediaciones.
**vicious** [víʃəs] *adj.* vicioso; malo; maligno; malicioso; **— dog** pero mordedor, perro bravo.
**vicissitude** [vəsísətjud] *s.* vicisitud, peripecia.
**victim** [víktɪm] *s.* víctima.
**victimize** [víktɪmaɪz] *v.* inmolar; engañar.
**victor** [víktɚ] *s.* vencedor.
**victorious** [vɪktórɪəs] *adj.* victorioso.
**victory** [víktrɪ] *s.* victoria.
**victuals** [vít]z] *s. pl.* vituallas, víveres.
**vie** [vaɪ] *v.* competir.
**view** [vju] *s.* (*field of vision*) vista; paisaje; (*opinion*) parecer, opinion; (*inspection*) inspección; (*aim*) mira, propósito; **in — of** en vista de; **to be within —** estar al alcance de la vista; **with a —** to con el propósito de; con la esperanza o expectación de; con la mira puesta en; *v.* mirar; examinar.
**viewpoint** [vjúpɔɪnt] *s.* punto de vista.
**vigil** [vídʒəl] *s.* vigilia, velada; **to keep — velar.**
**vigilance** [vídʒələns] *s.* vigilancia, desvelo.
**vigilant** [vídʒələnt] *adj.* vigilante.
**vigor** [vígɚ] *s.* vigor.
**vigorous** [vígərəs] *adj.* vigoroso.

**vile** [vaɪl] *adj*. vil, bajo, ruin; pésimo.
**villa** [vílə] *s*. quinta, casa de campo.
**village** [vílɪdʒ] *s*. villa, aldea.
**villager** [vílɪdʒɚ] *s*. aldeano.
**villain** [vílən] *s*. villano, malvado, bellaco.
**villainous** [vílənəs] *adj*. villano, ruin, vil, bellaco.
**villainy** [víləni] *s*. villanía, vileza.
**vim** [vɪm] *s*. vigor, fuerza, energía.
**vindicate** [víndəket] *v*. vindicar, vengar.
**vindictive** [vɪndíktɪv] *adj*. vengativo.
**vine** [vaɪn] *s*. vid, parra; enredadera.
**vinegar** [vínɪgɚ] *s*. vinagre.
**vineyard** [vínjɚd] *s*. viña, viñedo.
**vintage** [víntɪdʒ] *s*. vendimia; edad, época.
**violate** [váɪəlet] *v*. violar; infringir.
**violation** [vaɪəléʃən] *s*. violación; infracción.
**violence** [váɪələns] *s*. violencia.
**violent** [váɪələnt] *adj*. violento.
**violet** [váɪəlɪt] *s*. violeta; violado, color de violeta; *adj*. violado.
**violin** [vaɪəlín] *s*. violín.
**violinist** [vaɪəlínɪst] *s*. violinista.
**viper** [váɪpɚ] *s*. víbora.
**virgin** [vɝdʒɪn] *adj*. & *s*. virgen.
**virginal** [vɝdʒɪnl] *adj*. virginal.
**virile** [vírl] *adj*. viril.
**virtual** [vɝtʃʊəl] *adj*. virtual; **-ly** *adv*. virtualmente.
**virtue** [vɝtʃʊ] *s*. virtud.
**virtuous** [vɝtʃʊəs] *adj*. virtuoso.
**visa** [vízə] *s*. visa, visado; *v*. visar, refrendar.
**visceral** [vísɚl] *adj*. visceral.
**visé** = **visa**.
**vise** [vaɪs] *s*. tornillo de banco.
**visible** [vízəbl] *adj*. visible.
**vision** [víʒən] *s*. visión; vista.
**visionary** [víʒəneri] *adj*. visionario; imaginario; *s*. visionario, iluso, soñador.
**visit** [vízɪt] *v*. visitar; **to — punishment upon** mandar un castigo a, castigar a; *s*. visita.
**visitation** [vɪzətéʃən] *s*. visitación, visita; castigo, calamidad.
**visitor** [vízɪtɚ] *s*. visita; visitador.
**visor** [váɪzɚ] *s*. visera.
**vista** [vístə] *s*. vista, paisaje.
**visual** [vízjʊl] *adj*. visual; visible.
**visualize** [vízjʊalaɪz] *v*. representarse en la mente.
**vital** [váɪtl] *adj*. vital.
**vitality** [vaɪtǽlətɪ] *s*. vitalidad.
**vitalize** [váɪtəlaɪz] *v*. vitalizar.
**vitamin** [váɪtəmɪn] *s*. vitamina.
**vivacious** [vaɪvéʃəs] *adj*. vivaz, vivaracho, vivo, alegre, animado.
**vivacity** [vaɪvǽsətɪ] *s*. viveza, vivacidad.
**vivid** [vívɪd] *adj*. vívido, vivo; animado.
**vivify** [vívəfaɪ] *v*. vivificar.
**vocabulary** [vəkǽbjəleri] *s*. vocabulario.
**vocal** [vókl] *adj*. vocal; oral; **— cords** cuerdas vocales; **to be —** hablar, expresarse.
**vocation** [vokéʃən] *s*. vocación.

**vogue** [vog] *s*. boga, moda; **in —** en boga, de moda.
**voice** [vɔɪs] *s*. (*vocalization*) voz; (*speech*) habla; (*opinion*) voto; *v*. expresar, decir; **-d consonant** consonante sonora.
**voiceless** [vɔ́ɪslɪs] *adj*. mudo; sin voz; **— consonant** consonante sorda.
**void** [vɔɪd] *adj*. vacío; nulo, inválido; **— of** falto de, desprovisto de; *s*. vacío; *v*. vaciar, evacuar; anular, invalidar.
**volatile** [válətl] *adj*. volátil; inconstante.
**volcanic** [valkǽnɪk] *adj*. volcánico.
**volcano** [valkéno] *s*. volcán.
**volition** [volíʃən] *s*. volición; voluntad.
**volley** [válɪ] *s*. descarga, lluvia (*de piedras, flechas, balas, etc.*); voleo (*de la pelota*); *v*. descargar una lluvia de proyectiles; volear una pelota.
**volt** [volt] *s*. voltio.
**voltage** [vóltɪdʒ] *s*. voltaje.
**voluble** [váljəbl] *adj*. facundo.
**volume** [váljəm] *s*. volumen; tomo; bulto; suma, cantidad.
**voluminous** [vəlúmənəs] *adj*. voluminoso.
**voluntary** [válənteri] *adj*. voluntario.
**volunteer** [valəntír] *s*. voluntario; *adj*. voluntario; de voluntarios; *v*. ofrecer, dar voluntariamente; ofrecerse.
**voluptuous** [vəláptʃʊəs] *adj*. voluptuoso.
**vomit** [vámɪt] *s*. vómito; *v*. vomitar, *Méx.* deponer.
**voracious** [voréʃəs] *adj*. voraz.
**vortex** [vɔ́rtɛks] *s*. vórtice; vorágine.
**vote** [vot] *s*. voto; votación; *v*. votar; votar por.
**voter** [vótɚ] *s*. votante, elector.
**vouch** [vautʃ] *v*. **to — for** dar fe de; garantizar, responder de; salir fiador de.
**voucher** [váutʃɚ] *s*. comprobante, justificante; recibo; fiador.
**vouchsafe** [vautʃséf] *v*. otorgar, conceder.
**vow** [vau] *s*. voto; juramento; *v*. votar, jurar, hacer voto de.
**vowel** [váuəl] *s*. & *adj*. vocal.
**voyage** [vɔɪɪdʒ] *s*. viaje; travesía; *v*. viajar.
**vulgar** [válgɚ] *adj*. soez, ordinario, grosero; vulgar.
**vulnerable** [válnɚəbl] *adj*. vulnerable.
**vulture** [váltʃɚ] *s*. buitre, *Andes, Ríopl.* cóndor.

# W

**wabble** [wábl] *v*. tambalear(se), bambolear(se); vacilar; temblar; *s*. tambaleo, bamboleo; balanceo.
**wad** [wad] *s*. taco; bodoque; pelotilla, bolita, rollo; **— of money** rollo de billetes (*de banco*); dinero; *v*. atacar (*un arma de fuego*); rellenar; hacer una pelotilla de.
**waddle** [wádl] *v*. anadear; contonearse, zarandearse (*al andar*); *s*. anadeo; zarandeo, contoneo.
**wade** [wed] *v*. vadear; chapotear;

andar descalzo por la orilla del agua; **to — through a book** leer con dificultad un libro.

**wafer** [wéfə] *s.* oblea; hostia (*consagrada*).

**waft** [wæft] *v.* llevar en vilo, llevar por el aire; llevar a flote; *s.* ráfaga de aire; movìmiento (*de la mano*).

**wag** [wæg] *v.* menear; sacudir; **to — the tail** colear, menear la cola; *s.* meneo; bromista, farsante.

**wage** [wedʒ] *v.* hacer (*guerra*); dar (*batalla*); *s.* (*usualmente* **wages**) paga, jornal; **— earner** jornalero, obrero; trabajador; **— scale** escala de salarios (*sueldos*).

**wager** [wédʒə] *s.* apuesta; *v.* apostar.

**waggle** [wǽgl] *s.* meneo rápido.

**wagon** [wǽgən] *s.* carro, carreta; carretón.

**wail** [wel] *v.* gemir, lamentar; *s.* gemido, lamento.

**waist** [west] *s.* cintura; talle; blusa; **—band** pretina.

**waistcoat** [wéstkot] *s.* chaleco.

**waistline** [wéstlaɪn] *s.* talle.

**wait** [wet] *v.* (*stay*) esperar, aguardar; (*serve*) servir; **to — for** esperar, aguardar; **to — on** (**upon**) servir a; atender a; **to — table** servir la mesa, servir de mozo o camarero (*en un restaurante*); *s.* espera; **to lie in — for** estar en acecho de.

**waiter** [wétə] *s.* mozo, camarero, sirviente, *Méx., C.A.* mesero.

**waiting** [wétɪŋ] *s.* espera; **— room** sala de espera.

**waitress** [wétrɪs] *s.* camarera, moza, *Am.* mesera.

**waive** [wev] *v.* renunciar a; **to — one's right** renunciar voluntariamente a sus derechos.

**waiver** [wévə] *s.* renuncia.

**wake** [wek] *v.* despertar(se); **to — up** despertar(se); despabilarse; *s.* velatorio (*acto de velar a un muerto*), *Am.* velorio; estela (*huella que deja un barco en el agua*); **in the — of** después de, detrás de.

**wakeful** [wékfəl] *adj.* desvelado, despierto; insomne.

**waken** [wékən] *v.* despertar(se); *Ríopl.* recordar (*a una persona que está dormida*).

**walk** [wɔk] *v.* andar, caminar, ir a pie; recorrer a pie; pasear; **to — away** irse, marcharse; **to — back home** volverse a casa (a pie); **to — down** bajar; **to — in** entrar; **to — out** salirse, irse; parar el trabajo, declararse en huelga; **to — the streets** callejear; **to — up** subir; *s.* paseo; senda, vereda; acera; paso (*del caballo*); manera de andar; **— of life** vocación; **a ten minutes' —** una caminata de diez minutos.

**wall** [wɔl] *s.* (*interior*) pared; (*garden*) muro; (*fort*) muralla; **low mud —** tapia; **to drive to the —** poner entre la espada y la pared, poner en un aprieto.

**wallet** [wálɪt] *s.* cartera.

**wallflower** [wɔ́lflauə] *s.* alelí; **to be a — at a dance** comer pavo, *Andes, Méx.* planchar el asiento.

**wallop** [wáləp] *v.* pegar, zurrar, golpear; *s.* guantada, bofetón, golpazo.

**wallow** [wálo] *v.* revolcarse; chapalear o chapotear (*en el lodo*).

**wallpaper** [wɔ́lpepə] *s.* papel (de empapelar).

**walnut** [wɔ́lnət] *s.* nuez de nogal; nogal; **— tree** nogal.

**waltz** [wɔlts] *s.* vals; *s.* valsar, bailar el vals.

**wan** [wɑn] *adj.* pálido, enfermizo, enclenque; lánguido.

**wand** [wɑnd] *s.* vara, varita; **magic —** varita de virtud.

**wander** [wándə] *v.* vagar, errar; **to — away** extraviarse; **to — away from** apartarse de, desviarse de; **my mind -s easily** me distraigo fácilmente.

**wanderer** [wándərə] *s.* vago, vagabundo.

**wane** [wen] *v.* menguar; decaer; *s.* mengua; diminución; **to be on the —** ir menguando; ir desapareciendo.

**want** [wɑnt] *v.* (*desire*) querer, desear; (*lack*) necesitar; *s.* falta; necesidad; escasez, carencia; **to be in —** estar necesitado.

**wanting** [wántɪŋ] *adj.* falto; deficiente; necesitado.

**wanton** [wántən] *adj.* desenfrenado, libre; licencioso; inconsiderado; temerario.

**war** [wɔr] *s.* guerra; *v.* guerrear, hacer guerra; **to — on** guerrear con.

**warble** [wɔ́rbl] *v.* gorjear; trinar; *s.* gorjeo; trino.

**warbler** [wɔ́rblə] *s.* cantor; pájaro gorjeador.

**ward** [wɔrd] *s.* pupilo, menor o huérfano (*bajo tutela*); cuadra (*de hospital, prision, etc.*); distrito (*de una ciudad*); *v.* **to — off** resguardarse de; evitar; parar (*un golpe*).

**warden** [wɔ́rdṇ] *s.* guardián; alcaide; **prison —** alcaide de una prisión.

**wardrobe** [wɔ́rdrob] *s.* (*closet*) guardarropa, ropero, armario; (*garments*) vestuario; ropa.

**warehouse** [wérhaus] *s.* almacén, depósito.

**wares** [werz] *s. pl.* artículos, mercancías, mercaderías, efectos.

**warfare** [wɔ́rfer] *s.* guerra.

**warhead** [wɔ́rhɛd] *s.* punta de combate.

**warlike** [wɔ́rlaɪk] *adj.* guerrero, bélico.

**warm** [wɔrm] *adj.* (*temperature*) caliente, cálido, caluroso; (*enthusiastic*) acalorado; (*fresh*) reciente; **— hearted** de buen corazón; **— blooded** apasionado; ardiente; **he is —** tiene calor; **it is — today** hace calor hoy; *v.* calentar(se); **to — over** recalentar; **to — up** calentar(se); acalorarse; entusiasmarse.

**warmth** [wɔrmpθ] *s.* (*heat*) calor; (*friendship*) cordialidad.

**warn** [wɔrn] *v.* avisar, advertir, amonestar; prevenir, precaver.

**warning** [wɔ́rnɪŋ] *s.* aviso, advertencia, amonestación; escarmiento; **let that be a — to you** que te sirva de escarmiento.

**warp** [wɔrp] *s.* urdimbre (*de un tejido*); torcedura, deformación; comba; *v.* combar(se), deformar(se), torcer(se); urdir (*los hilos de un telar*).

**warrant** [wɔ́rənt] *s.* (*sanction*) autorización; (*right*) garantia, justificación; (*writ*) comprobante; orden, mandato, citación (*ante un juez*); *v.* autorizar; garantizar; justificar.

**warrior** [wɔ́rɪɚ] *s.* guerrero.

**warship** [wɔ́rʃɪp] *s.* buque de guerra, acorazado.

**wart** [wɔrt] *s.* verruga.

**wary** [wɛ́rɪ] *adj.* cauteloso, cauto, precavido, prevenido; **to be — of** desconfiar de.

**was** [wɑz] *pret. de* **to be** (*primera y tercera persona del singular*).

**wash** [wɑʃ] *v.* lavar(se); **to — away** deslavar(se); **to be -ed away by the waves** ser arrastrado por las olas; *s.* lavado; lavadura; lavatorio; lavazas, agua sucia; **mouth —** enjuague o enjuagatorio; **—bowl** lavabo, palangana, lavamanos; **—cloth** paño para lavarse; **— dress** vestido lavable; **— room** lavabo, lavatorio.

**washable** [wɑ́ʃəbl] *adj.* lavable.

**wash and wear** [wɔ́ʃændwɛ́r] *adj.* de lava y pon.

**washed-out** [wɑ́ʃtáut] *adj.* desteñido; agotado, sin fuerzas.

**washed up** [wɔ́ʃtʌ́p] *adj.* fracasado.

**washer** [wɑ́ʃɚ] *s.* lavador; máquina de lavar; arandela (*para una tuerca*); **—woman** lavandera.

**washing** [wɑ́ʃɪŋ] *s.* lavado; ropa sucia o para lavar; ropa lavada; **— machine** lavadora, máquina de lavar.

**washout** [wɔ́ʃaut] *s.* derrubio; fracaso.

**wasp** [wɑsp] *s.* avispa.

**waste** [west] *v.* gastar; desgastar; malgastar, desperdiciar, derrochar; disipar; **to — away** gastarse, consumirse; desgastarse; *s.* desperdicio; gasto inútil; desgaste; desechos, desperdicios; terreno baldío, desierto; *adj.* inútil, desechado; desierto; baldío; **— of time** pérdida de tiempo; **— basket** cesto para papeles; **— land** terreno baldío; **— paper** papeles inútiles, papel de desecho; **to go to —** gastarse, perderse; malgastarse, desperdiciarse; **to lay —** asolar, arruinar.

**wasteful** [wéstfəl] *adj.* despilfarrado, gastador; desperdiciado; ineconómico.

**watch** [wɑtʃ] *v.* (*look*) mirar; observar; (*be alert*) vigilar; velar; cuidar; **— out!** ¡cuidado!; **to — out for** tener cuidado con; cuidar; vigilar; *s.* reloj (de bolsillo); vela, vigilia; guardia; centinela, vigilante; **— chain** cadena de reloj, *Ven.*, *Méx.* leontina; **— charm** dije; **wrist —** reloj de pulsera; **to be on the —** tener cuidado;

**estar alerta; to keep — over** vigilar a.

**watchful** [wɑ́tʃfəl] *adj.* alerto, vigilante, despertio, atento.

**watchman** [wɑ́tʃmən] *s.* vigilante, guardia, sereno.

**watchtower** [wɑ́tʃtauɚ] *s.* atalaya, mirador.

**watchword** [wɑ́tʃwɝd] *s.* contraseña, santo y seña, consigna; lema.

**water** [wɔ́tɚ] *s.* agua; **— color** acuarela; color para acuarela; **— power** fuerza hidráulica; **—shed** vertiente; **— sports** deportes acuáticos; **— supply** abastecimiento de agua; *v.* regar; aguar, diluir con agua; abrevar, dar de beber (*al ganado*); beber agua (*el ganado*); tomar agua (*un barco, locomotora, etc.*); **my eyes —** me lloran los ojos; **my mouth -s** se me hace agua la boca.

**waterfall** [wɔ́tɚfɔl] *s.* cascada, catarata, caída de agua.

**waterfront** [wɔ́tɚfrʌnt] *s.* terreno ribereño.

**watermelon** [wɔ́tɚmɛlən] *s.* sandía.

**waterpower** [wɔ́tɚpauɚ] *s.* fuerza hidráulica.

**waterproof** [wɔ́tɚpruf] *adj. & s.* impermeable; *v.* hacer impermeable.

**water ski** [wɔ́tɚski] *s.* esquí acuático.

**waterspout** [wɔ́tɚspaut] *s.* surtidor; tromba, manga de agua.

**waterway** [wɔ́tɚwe] *s.* vía de agua, río navegable, canal.

**watery** [wɔ́tɚɪ] *adj.* aguado; acuoso; mojado, húmedo.

**wave** [wev] *v.* ondear; ondular; agitar; blandir (*una espada, bastón, etc.*); **to — aside** apartar, rechazar; **to — good-bye** hacer una seña o ademán de despedida; **to — hair** ondular el pelo; **to — one's hand** hacer una seña o señas con la mano; mover la mano; *s.* onda; ola; ondulación; **— of the hand** ademán, movimiento de la mano; **permanent —** ondulación permanente.

**wavelength** [wévlɛŋθ] *s.* longitud de onda.

**waver** [wévɚ] *v.* oscilar; vacilar, titubear; tambalear(se); *s.* vacilación, titubeo.

**wavy** [wévɪ] *adj.* rizado, ondulado; ondulante.

**wax** [wæks] *s.* cera; **— candle** vela de cera; **— paper** papel encerado; *v.* encerar; pulir con cera; hacerse, ponerse; crecer (*la luna*).

**way** [we] *s.* (*road*) camino; ruta; senda; (*manner*) modo, manera; **— in** entrada; **— out** salida; **— through** paso, pasaje; **a long — off** muy lejos, a una larga distancia; **by — of** por, por vía de; **by — of comparison** a modo de comparación; **by the —** de paso; **in no —** de ningún modo; **on the — to** camino de, rumbo a; **out of the —** fuera del camino; apartado; a un lado; impropio; extraordinario; **to be in a bad —**

**WA**

hallarse en mal estado; **to be well under** — estar (*un trabajo*) ya bastante avanzado; **to give** — ceder; quebrarse; **to have one's** — hacer su capricho, salirse con la suya; **to make** — **for** abrir paso para.

**wayfarer** [wéfɛrɚ] *s.* caminante.

**waylay** [welé] *v.* estar en acecho de (*alguien*); asaltar; detener (*a una persona*).

**wayside** [wésaɪd] *s.* borde del camino; — **inn** posada al borde del camino.

**wayward** [wéwɚd] *adj.* voluntarioso, desobediente.

**we** [wi] *pron.* nosotros, nosotras.

**weak** [wik] *adj.* débil; flaco; endeble; — **market** mercado flojo; **weak-minded** de voluntad débil; simple; — **tea** té claro o suave.

**weaken** [wíkən] *v.* debilitar(se); desmayar, flaquear, perder ánimo.

**weakly** [wíklɪ] *adv.* débilmente; *adj.* enfermizo, débil, enclenque.

**weakness** [wíknɪs] *s.* debilidad; flaqueza.

**wealth** [wɛlθ] *s.* riqueza; copia, abundancia.

**wealthy** [wélθɪ] *adj.* rico.

**wean** [win] *v.* destetar; apartar gradualmente (*de un hábito, de una amistad*).

**weapon** [wépən] *s.* arma.

**wear** [wɛr] *v.* (*have on*) llevar, tener o traer puesto; usar; (*waste away*) gastar, desgastar; **to** — **away** gastar(se), desgastar(se); consumir(se); **to** — **off** desgastar(se), gastar(se); borrarse; **to** — **out** gastar(se); desgastar(se), consumir(se); agotar; cansar; **it -s well** es duradero; dura mucho; **as the day wore on** a medida que pasaba el día; *s.* uso, gasto; durabilidad; — **and tear** desgaste; uso; **men's** — ropa para hombres; **clothes for summer** — ropa de verano.

**wearily** [wírɪlɪ] *adv.* penosamente, con cansancio, con fatiga, fatigadamente.

**weariness** [wírɪnɪs] *s.* cansancio, fatiga.

**wearing** [wérɪŋ] *adj.* cansado, aburrido, fastidioso.

**wearisome** [wírɪsəm] *adj.* fatigoso, molesto, fastidioso.

**weary** [wírɪ] *adj.* cansado, fatigado; aburrido; *v.* cansar(se), fatigar(se).

**weasel** [wíz] *s.* comadreja.

**weather** [wéðɚ] *s.* tiempo; **weather-beaten** desgastado o curtido por la intemperie; — **bureau** oficina meteorológica; — **conditions** condiciones atmosféricas; —**vane** veleta; **it is fine** —hace buen tiempo; **to be under the** — estar enfermo; estar indispuesto; *v.* exponer a la intemperie; orear, secar al aire; **to** — **a storm** aguantar un chubasco; salir ileso de una tormenta.

**weave** [wiv] *v.* (*cloth*) tejer, entretejer; (*to plan*) urdir; **to** — **together** entretejer, entrelazar; combinar; *s.* tejido.

**weaver** [wívɚ] *s.* tejedor.

**web** [wɛb] *s.* tela; membrana (*entre los dedos de los pájaros acuáticos*); **spider's** — telaraña.

**wed** [wɛd] *v.* casarse; casarse con; casar; *p.p. de* **to wed.**

**wedded** [wédɪd] *p.p.* & *adj.* casado; unido; — **to an idea** aferrado a una idea.

**wedding** [wédɪŋ] *s.* boda, casamiento, nupcias, enlace; — **day** día de bodas; — **trip** viaje de novios; **silver** — bodas de plata.

**wedge** [wɛdʒ] *s.* cuña; **entering** — cuña, entrada, medio de entrar, modo de penetrar; *v.* acuñar, meter cuñas; **to be -d between** estar encajado entre.

**Wednesday** [wénzdɪ] *s.* miércoles.

**wee** [wi] *adj.* diminuto, chiquitico, pequeñito.

**weed** [wid] *s.* cizaña, mala hierba; *v.* desherbar (*o* desyerbar), quitar o arrancar la mala hierba; **to** — **a garden** desherbar un huerto; **to** — **out** escardar; eliminar, arrancar, entresacar.

**weedy** [wídɪ] *adj.* herboso, lleno de malas hierbas.

**week** [wik] *s.* semana; —**day** día de trabajo, día laborable, día hábil; — **end** fin de semana; **a** — **from today** de hoy en ocho días.

**weekly** [wíklɪ] *adj.* semanal, semanario; *adv.* semanalmente, por semana; *s.* semanario, periódico o revista semanal.

**weep** [wip] *v.* llorar.

**weeping** [wípɪŋ] *adj.* llorón; lloroso; — **willow** sauce llorón; *s.* llanto, lloro, lágrimas.

**weevil** [wívl] *s.* gorgojo.

**weigh** [we] *v.* pesar; ponderar, considerar; **to** — **anchor** zarpar, levar el ancla; **to** — **down** agobiar; abrumar; **to** — **on one's conscience** serle a uno gravoso, pesarle a uno.

**weight** [wet] *s.* peso; pesa (*de reloj o medida para pesar*); carga; **paper—** pisapapeles; *v.* cargar, sobrecargar; añadir peso a; asignar un peso o valor relativor a.

**weighty** [wétɪ] *adj.* grave, ponderoso; de mucho peso; importante.

**weird** [wɪrd] *adj.* extraño, raro, misterioso, fantástico.

**welcome** [wélkəm] *s.* bienvenida; buena acogida; *adj.* grato, agradable; bien acogido, bien quisto; bienvenido; bien recibido; — **home!** ¡bienvenido!; — **rest** grato reposo o descanso; **you are** — no hay de qué, de nada (*para contestar a* "thank you"); **you are** — **here** está Vd. en su casa; **you are** — **to use it** se lo presto con todo gusto; está a su disposición; *v.* dar la bienvenida a; acoger o recibir con gusto.

**weld** [wɛld] *v.* soldar(se); *s.* soldadura.

**welfare** [wélfɛr] *s.* bienestar; bien; felicidad; — **work** labor social o de beneficencia.

**well** [wɛl] *adv.* bien; **he is — over fifty** tiene mucho más de cincuenta años; **—  then** pues bien, ahora bien, conque; **well-being** bienestar; **well-bred** bien criado; bien educado; **well-done** bien cocido; **well-fixed** acomodado; **well-groomed** acicalado; **well-meaning** bien intencionado; **well-nigh** casi, muy cerca de; *adj.* bueno; bien de salud, sano; conveniente; **— and good** santo y muy bueno; **well-off** acomodado, adinerado; en buenas condiciones; **well-to-do** próspero, adinerado; **all is —** no hay novedad, todo va bien; **it is — to do it** conviene hacerlo, es conveniente hacerlo.

**well** [wɛl] *s.* (*shaft*) pozo; (*cistern*) cisterna; (*spring*) manantial; **artesian — pozo** artesiano; *v.* manar; **tears -ed up in her eyes** se le arrasaron los ojos de lágrimas.

**welt** [wɛlt] *s.* verdugo, verdugón, roncha.

**went** [wɛnt] *pret. de* **to go.**

**wept** [wɛpt] *pret. & p.p. de* **to weep.**

**were** [wɝ] *pret. de* **to be** (*en el plural y en la segunda persona del singular del indicativo; es además el imperfecto del subjuntivo*); **if I — you** si yo fuera Vd.; **there —** había, hubo.

**west** [wɛst] *s.* oeste, occidente, ocaso; *adj.* occidental, del oeste; **West Indies** Antillas; *adv.* hacia el oeste, al oeste; en el oeste.

**western** [wéstɚn] *adj.* occidental, del oeste.

**westerner** [wéstɚnɚ] *s.* natural del oeste, habitante del oeste, occidental.

**westward** [wéstwɚd] *adv.* hacia el oeste; *adj.* occidental, oeste.

**wet** [wɛt] *adj.* húmedo; mojado; **— nurse** nodriza, ama de leche; *s.* humedad; antiprohibicionista (*el que favorece la venta de bebidas alcohólicas*); *v.* mojar; humedecer; *pret. & p.p. de* **to wet.**

**wetback** [wétbæk] *s.* panza mojada.

**wetness** [wétnɪs] *s.* humedad.

**whack** [hwæk] *v.* golpear, pegar; *s.* golpe; golpazo; tentativa, prueba.

**whale** [hwel] *s.* ballena; *v.* pescar ballenas.

**wharf** [hwɔrf] *s.* muelle, embarcadero.

**what** [hwɑt] *pron. interr.* qué; qué cosa; cuál; *pron. rel.* lo que; **— for?** ¿para qué? *adj.* qué; **— book?** ¿qué libro? **— a man!** ¡qué hombre!; **— happy children!** ¡qué niños más (*o* tan) felices!; **take — books you need** tome Vd. los libros que necesite.

**whatever** [hwɑtévɚ] *pron.* cualquiera cosa que, lo que, cuanto, todo lo que; **— do you mean?** ¿qué quiere Vd. decir?; **do it, — happens** hágalo suceda lo que suceda; *adj.* cualquiera; **any person —** una persona cualquiera; **no money —** nada de dinero.

**whatsoever** [hwɑtsoévɚ] = **whatever.**

**wheat** [hwit] *s.* trigo; **cream of —** crema de trigo.

**wheedle** [hwidl] *v.* engatusar.

**wheel** [hwil] *s.* (*disc*) rueda; rodaja; disco; (*bike*) bicicleta; **— chair** silla rodante, silla de ruedas; **steering —** volante (*de automóvil*); rueda del timón; *v.* rodar; hacer rodar; girar; acarrear; andar en bicicleta; **to — around** dar una vuelta; girar sobre los talones; **to — the baby** pasear al bebé en su cochecito.

**wheelbarrow** [hwílbæro] *s.* carretilla.

**wheeze** [hwiz] *s.* resuello ruidoso.

**when** [hwɛn] *adv. & conj.* cuando; *adv. interr.* ¿cuándo?

**whence** [hwɛns] *adv.* de donde; de que.

**whenever** [hwɛnévɚ] *adj. & conj.* cuando, siempre que, cada vez que.

**where** [hwɛr] *adv.* donde; adonde; en donde; por donde; **—?** ¿dónde?; ¿adónde?

**whereabouts** [hwérəbauts] *s.* paradero; *adv. interr.* ¿dónde?

**whereas** [hwɛrǽz] *conj.* mientras que; puesto que, visto que, considerando que.

**whereby** [hwɛrbái] *adv.* por donde, por lo cual; con lo cual.

**wherefore** [hwérfor] *adv.* por qué; por lo cual; por eso, por lo tanto.

**wherein** [hwɛrín] *adv.* en qué; en donde; en lo cual.

**whereof** [hwɛráv] *adv.* de que; de donde; de quien, de quienes.

**whereupon** [hwɛrəpán] *adv.* después de lo cual; entonces.

**wherever** [hwɛrévɚ] *adv.* dondequiera que, adondequiera que, por dondequiera que.

**wherewithal** [hwérwɪðɔl] *s.* medios, fondos; dinero.

**whet** [hwɛt] *v.* amolar, afilar; aguzar, estimular.

**whether** [hwéðɚ] *conj.* si; ya sea que, sea que; **— we escape or not** ya sea que escapemos o no; **I doubt —** dudo (de) que.

**which** [hwɪtʃ] *pron. interr.* ¿cuál?; ¿cuáles?; *pron. rel.* que; el cual, la cual, los cuales, las cuales; el que, la que, los que, las que; *adj. interr.* ¿qué?; **— boy has it?** ¿cuál de los muchachos lo tiene? ¿qué muchacho lo tiene?; **— way did he go?** ¿por qué camino se fue?; ¿por dónde se fue?; **during — time** tiempo durante el cual.

**whichever** [hwɪtʃévɚ] *pron. & adj.* cualquiera (que), cualesquiera (que); el que, la que; **— road you take** cualquier camino que Vd. siga.

**whiff** [hwɪf] *s.* (*waft*) soplo; fumada, bocanada; (*odor*) repentino olor o hedor; *v.* soplar; echar bocanadas.

**while** [hwaɪl] *s.* rato; tiempo, temporada; **a short —** un ratito; **a short — ago** hace poco, hace poco rato; **to be worth —** valer la pena; *conj.* mientras, mientras que; *v.* **to — away the time** pasar el tiempo.

**whilst** [hwaɪlst] *conj.* mientras, mientras que.

**whim** [hwɪm] *s.* capricho, antojo.

**whimper** [hwímpɚ] *v.* lloriquear, gimotear; quejarse; *s.* lloriqueo, gimoteo; quejido.

**whimsical** [hwímzɪk]] *adj.* caprichoso.

**whine** [hwaɪn] *v.* lloriquear; quejarse; *s.* gemido, quejido.

**whiner** [hwáɪnɚ] *s.* llorón, persona quejosa, *Méx.* quejumbres; *Andes* quejumbroso; *Ríopl.* rezongón.

**whip** [hwɪp] *v.* azotar, fustigar; zurrar, dar una paliza a, dar latigazos a; batir (*crema, huevos*); vencer; **to — up** *batir*; coger o asir de repente; hacer de prisa; *s.* azote, látigo, fuete; batido.

**whipping** [hwípɪŋ] *s.* tunda, zurra, paliza; **— cream** crema para batir.

**whir** [hwɝ] *v.* zumbar; *s.* zumbido.

**whirl** [hwɝl] *v.* girar, dar vueltas; arremolinarse; **my head -s** siento vértigo, estoy desvanecido; *s.* giro, vuelta; remolino; espiral (*de humo*); confusión.

**whirlpool** [hwɝ́lpul] *s.* remolino, vorágine, vórtice.

**whirlwind** [hwɝ́lwɪnd] *s.* remolino, torbellino.

**whisk** [hwɪsk] *v.* barrer; desempolvar (*con escobilla*); batir (*huevos*); **to — away** barrer de prisa; llevarse de prisa, arrebatar; irse de prisa, escaparse; **to — something out of sight** escamotear algo, esconder algo de prisa; *s.* — **broom** escobilla; **with a — of the broom** de un escobillazo.

**whisker** [hwískɚ] *s.* pelo de la barba; **-s** barbas; patillas; bigotes (*del gato*).

**whiskey** [hwískɪ] *s.* whisky (*aguardiente de maíz, centeno, etc.*).

**whisper** [hwíspɚ] *v.* cuchichear, hablar en secreto; soplar, decir al oído; susurrar; secretearse; **it is -ed that** corre la voz que; dizque, dicen que; *s.* cuchicheo, secreteo; susurro; murmullo; **to talk in a —** hablar en secreto; susurrar.

**whistle** [hwísl] *v.* silbar; chiflar; pitar; **to — for someone** llamar a uno con un silbido; *s.* silbido, chiflido; silbato, pito.

**whit** [hwɪt] *s.* jota, pizca.

**white** [hwaɪt] *adj.* (*color*) blanco; (*pure*) puro; inocente; (*honorable*) honrado, recto; **—caps** cabrillas o palomas (*olas con crestas blancas*); **— lead** albayalde; **— lie** mentirilla, mentira venial; **white-livered** cobarde; **white-collar** de oficina; **to show the — feather** mostrar cobardía, portarse como cobarde; *s.* blanco; clara (*del huevo*).

**whiten** [hwáɪtn] *v.* blanquear; emblanquecer(se), poner(se) blanco.

**whiteness** [hwáɪtnɪs] *s.* blancura; palidez; pureza.

**whitewash** [hwáɪtwaʃ] *v.* (*paint*) blanquear, enjalbegar; (*gloss over*) encubrir, disimular (*faltas, errores*); ab-

solver (*sin justicia*); *s.* lechada.

**whither** [hwíðɚ] *adv.* adonde; **—?** ¿adónde?

**whitish** [hwáɪtɪʃ] *adj.* blancuzco, blanquecino, blanquizco.

**whittle** [hwítl] *v.* cortar, mondar, tallar; tajar, sacar punta a (*un lápiz*); **to — down expenses** cercenar o reducir los gastos.

**whiz** [hwɪz] *v.* zumbar; *s.* zumbido, silbido; **to be a —** ser un águila, ser muy listo.

**who** [hu] *pron. rel.* quien, quienes, que, el que, la que, los que, las que; **he —** el que, quien; *pron. interr.* ¿quién?; ¿quiénes?; **— is it?** ¿quién es?

**whoever** [huévɚ] *pron.* quienquiera que, cualquiera que; el que.

**whole** [hol] *adj.* todo; entero; íntegro; **the — day** todo el día; **—hearted** sincero, cordial; **—heartedly** de todo corazón; con todo ánimo; *s.* todo, total, totalidad; **as a —** en conjunto; **on the —** en general, en conjunto.

**wholesale** [hólsel] *s.* venta al por mayor, *Am.* mayoreo; **by —** al por mayor; *adj.* al por mayor; en grandes cantidades; **— dealer** comerciante al por mayor, *Am.* mayorista; **— slaughter** matanza; gran hecatombe; **— trade** comercio al por mayor, *Am.* comercio mayorista; *adv.* al por mayor, por mayor; *v.* vender al por mayor, *Am.* mayorear.

**wholesome** [hólsəm] *adj.* saludable, sano; salubre; **— man** hombre normalmente bueno o de buena índole.

**wholly** [hólɪ] *adv.* enteramente, completamente, totalmente.

**whom** [hum] *pron. pers.* a quien, a quienes; que; al que (a la que, a los que, *etc.*); al cual (a la cual, a los cuales, *etc.*); **for —** para quien; **— did you see?** ¿a quién vió Vd.?

**whoop** [hup] *s.* grito, chillido, alarido; respiro convulsivo (*que acompaña a la tos ferina*); *v.* gritar, vocear, echar gritos; respirar convulsivamente (*al toser*); **to — it up** armar una gritería, gritar; **whooping cough** tos ferina.

**whore** [hor] *s.* ramera, puta, prostituta.

**whose** [huz] *pron.* cuyo, cuya, cuyos, cuyas; *pron. interr.* ¿de quién?; ¿de quiénes?; **— book is this?** ¿de quién es este libro?

**why** [hwaɪ] *adv.* ¿por qué?; **the reason — la** razón por la que (o la cual) **—, of course!** ¡sí, por supuesto!; ¡claro que sí!; **—, that is not true!** ¡si eso no es verdad! *s.* porqué, causa, razón, motivo.

**wick** [wɪk] *s.* mecha, pabilo.

**wicked** [wíkɪd] *adj.* malvado, malo, inicuo.

**wickedness** [wíkɪdnɪs] *s.* maldad, iniquidad, perversidad.

**wicker** [wíkɚ] *s.* mimbre; **— chair** silla de mimbre.

**wicket** [wíkɪt] *s.* postigo; ventanilla.

**wide** [waɪd] *adj.* ancho; amplio; vasto;

extenso; — **apart** muy apartados; **wide-awake** muy despierto; alerta, vigilante; — **of the mark** muy lejos del blanco; — **open** muy abierto; abierto de par en par; **far and —** por todas partes, extensamente; **to open** — abrir mucho; abrir (*la puerta*) de par en par; **two feet —** dos pies de ancho (*o de anchura*).

**widely** [wáɪdlɪ] *adv.* ampliamente; extensamente; muy; mucho.

**widen** [wáɪdn̞] *v.* ensanchar(se), ampliar(se), dilatar(se).

**widespread** [wáɪdspréd] *adj.* muy esparcido, muy extensivo; bien difundido; extendido; general, extendido por todas partes.

**widow** [wído] *s.* viuda.

**widower** [wídəwɚ] *s.* viudo.

**width** [wɪdθ] *s.* ancho, anchura.

**wield** [wild] *v.* manejar; esgrimir (*la espada o la pluma*); ejercer (*el poder*).

**wife** [waɪf] *s.* esposa.

**wig** [wɪg] *s.* peluca.

**wiggle** [wígl̞] *v.* menear(se); *s.* meneo.

**wigwam** [wígwɑm] *s.* choza de los indios norteños.

**wild** [waɪld] *adj.* salvaje; (*animal*) feroz, fiero; indómito; montaraz; (*plant*) silvestre; *Ven., Méx.* cimarrón; impetuoso, desenfrenado; bullicioso; violento; loco; enojado; desatinado; ansioso; **to talk —** disparatar, desatinar; *s.* yermo, desierto, monte.

**wildcat** [wáɪldkæt] *s.* gato montés; — **scheme** empresa arriesgada.

**wilderness** [wíldɚnɪs] *s.* yermo, desierto, monte; inmensidad.

**wild-eyed** [wáɪldaɪd] *adj.* de ojos huraños.

**wildness** [wáɪldnɪs] *s.* salvajez; ferocidad, fiereza; locura.

**wile** [waɪl] *s.* ardid, engaño; astucia.

**wilful, willful** [wílfəl] *adj.* voluntarioso, testarudo, caprichudo; intencional.

**will** [wɪl] *v.* (*desire*) querer, decidir; (*order*) ordenar, mandar; (*dispose of legally*) legar; *v. defect. y aux.* querer; *rigurosamente debe usarse para formar el futuro en las segundas y terceras personas*: **she — go** ella irá; *en las primeras personas indica voluntad o determinación*: **I — not do it** no lo haré, no quiero hacerlo.

**will** [wɪl] *s.* (*wish*) voluntad; albedrío; (*legal disposition*) testamento; **free —** libre albedrío; **ill — mala** voluntad, malquerencia.

**willful** [wílfʊl] *adj.* voluntario.

**willing** [wílɪŋ] *adj.* bien dispuesto, deseoso, complaciente; voluntario; **-ly** *adv.* con gusto, de buena gana, de buena voluntad; voluntariamente.

**willingness** [wílɪŋnɪs] *s.* buena voluntad, buena gana.

**willow** [wílo] *s.* sauce; mimbrera; **weeping —** sauce llorón.

**wilt** [wɪlt] *v.* marchitar(se); ajar(se); desmayar; languidecer.

**wily** [wáɪlɪ] *adj.* astuto, artero.

**win** [wɪn] (*achieve*) ganar; lograr, obtener; alcanzar; (*persuade*) persuadir; **to — out** ganar, triunfar; salirse con la suya; **to — over** persuadir; atraer; alcanzar o ganar el favor de.

**wince** [wɪns] *v.* cejar (*ante una dificultad o peligro*); encogerse (*de dolor, susto, etc.*).

**winch** [wɪntʃ] *s.* malacate.

**wind** [wɪnd] *s.* viento, aire; resuello; — **instrument** instrumento de viento; **to get — of** barruntar; tener noticia de.

**wind** [waɪnd] *v.* enredar; devanar, ovillar; dar cuerda a (*un reloj*); serpentear (*un camino*); dar vueltas; **to — someone around one's finger** manejar fácilmente a alguien, gobernarle; **to — up one's affairs** terminar o concluir uno sus negocios; *s.* vuelta; recodo.

**windbag** [wíndbæg] *s.* (*instrument*) fuelle; (*person*) parlanchín, hablador.

**windfall** [wíndfɔl] *s.* golpe de fortuna, ganancia repentina, herencia inesperada.

**winding** [wáɪndɪŋ] *adj.* sinuoso, tortuoso, que da vueltas; — **staircase** escalera de caracol.

**windmill** [wíndmɪl] *s.* molino de viento.

**window** [wíndo] *s.* ventana; **show —** escaparate, vitrina, aparador, *Am.* vidriera; — **shade** visillo, cortinilla; — **sill** antepecho, repisa de ventana.

**windowpane** [wíndopen] *s.* cristal de ventana, vidriera.

**windpipe** [wíndpaɪp] *s.* tráquea, gaznate.

**windshield** [wíndʃild] *s.* parabrisa, guardabrisa.

**wind tunnel** [wíndtʌnl] *s.* túnel aerodinámico.

**windy** [wíndɪ] *adj.* airoso; ventoso; **it is —** hace aire, ventea, sopla el viento.

**wine** [waɪn] *s.* vino; — **cellar** bodega.

**wing** [wɪŋ] *s.* ala; bastidor (*de escenario*); **under the — of** bajo la tutela de; **to take —** levantar el vuelo.

**winged** [wɪŋd, wíŋɪd] *adj.* alado.

**wingspread** [wíŋspred] *s.* envergadura.

**wink** [wɪŋk] *v.* guiñar; pestanear, parpadear; *s.* guiño, guiñada; **I didn't sleep a —** no pegué los ojos en toda la noche.

**winner** [wínɚ] *s.* ganador; vencedor; — **of a prize** agraciado, premiado.

**winning** [wínɪŋ] *adj.* (*successful*) ganancioso; triunfante, victorioso; (*charming*) atractivo, encantador; **-s** *s. pl.* ganancias.

**winsome** [wínsəm] *adj.* simpático, atractivo, gracioso.

**winter** [wíntɚ] *s.* invierno; — **clothes** ropa de invierno; *v.* invernar, pasar el invierno.

**wintry** [wíntrɪ] *adj.* invernal, de invierno; frío, helado.

**wipe** [waɪp] *v.* secar; enjugar; limpiar; **to — away one's tears** limpiarse las

WH

lágrimas; **to — off** borrar; limpiar; **to — out a regiment** destruir o aniquilar un regimiento.

**wire** [waɪr] *s. (strand)* alambre; *(telegram)* telegrama; **by — por** telégrafo; **— entanglement** alambrada; **— fence** alambrado; **— netting** tela metálica, alambrado; **to pull -s** mover los hilos; *v.* poner alambrado, instalar alambrado eléctrico; atar con alambre; telegrafiar.

**wireless** [wáɪrlɪs] *adj.* inalámbrico, sin hilos; **— telegraphy** radiotelegrafía; *s.* radio, radiotelegrafía; telegrafía sin hilos; radiotelefonía; radiograma.

**wire tapping** [wáɪrtæpɪŋ] *s.* secreta conexión interceptora de teléfono.

**wiry** [wáɪrɪ] *adj.* de alambre; como alambre; nervudo.

**wisdom** [wízdəm] *s.* sabiduría, saber; cordura; prudencia; **— tooth** muela del juicio.

**wise** [waɪz] *adj. (judicious)* sabio, cuerdo, sensato; *(prudent)* discreto, prudente; **the Three Wise Men** los Tres Reyes Magos; **to get — to** darse cuenta de; *s.* modo, manera; **in no —** de ningún modo.

**wisecrack** [wáɪzkræk] *s.* bufonada, dicho agudo o chocarrero, dicharacho.

**wish** [wɪʃ] *v.* desear, querer; **to — for** desear; anhelar; **I — it were true!** ¡ojalá (que) fuera verdad!; *s.* deseo.

**wishful thinking** [wíʃful θíŋkɪŋ] *s.* optimismo ilusorio.

**wistful** [wístfəl] *adj.* anhelante, anheloso, ansioso; tristón, melancólico.

**wit** [wɪt] *s.* agudeza, sal, chiste; ingenio; hombre agudo o de ingenio; **to be at one's wit's end** haber agotado todo su ingenio; **to be out of one's -s** estar fuera de sí, estar loco; **to lose one's -s** perder el juicio; **to use one's -s** valerse de su industria o ingenio.

**witch** [wɪtʃ] *s.* hechicera; bruja.

**witchcraft** [wítʃkræft] *s.* hechicería.

**with** [wɪð, wɪθ] *prep.* con; para con; en compañía de; **filled —** lleno de; **ill —** enfermo de; **the one — the black hat** el del (*o* la del) sombrero negro.

**withdraw** [wɪðdrɔ́] *v.* retirar(se); apartar(se); separar(se); **to — a statement** retractarse.

**withdrawal** [wɪðdrɔ́əl] *s.* retirada, retiro.

**withdrawn** [wɪðdrɔ́n] *p.p. de* **to withdraw.**

**withdrew** [wɪðdrú] *pret. de* **to withdraw.**

**wither** [wíðɚ] *v.* marchitar(se); ajar(se); secar(se).

**withheld** [wɪθhéld] *pret. & p.p. de* **to withhold.**

**withhold** [wɪθhóld] *v.* retener; detener; **to — one's consent** negarse a dar su consentimiento.

**within** [wɪðín] *prep.* dentro de; **— call** al alcance de la voz; **— five miles** a poco menos de cinco millas; **it is —**

**my power** está en mi mano; *adv.* dentro, adentro.

**without** [wɪðáut] *prep.* sin; **— my seeing him** sin que yo le viera; *adv.* fuera, afuera.

**withstand** [wɪθstǽnd] *v.* resistir; aguantar, padecer.

**withstood** [wɪθstúd] *pret. & p.p. de* **to withstand.**

**witness** [wítnɪs] *s.* testigo; testimonio; *v.* ver, presenciar; ser testigo de; atestiguar, dar fe de.

**witticism** [wítəsɪzəm] *s.* ocurrencia, agudeza, dicho agudo.

**witty** [wítɪ] *adj.* agudo, ocurrente, gracioso, divertido, chistoso; **— remark** dicho agudo, agudeza, ocurrencia.

**wives** [waɪvz] *s. pl. de* **wife.**

**wizard** [wízɚd] *s.* genio, hombre de ingenio; mago, mágico.

**wobble** [wábl] *s.* bamboleo.

**woe** [wo] *s.* miseria, aflicción, infortunio; **— is me!** ¡miserable de mí!

**woeful** [wóful] *adj.* miserable; abatido.

**woke** [wok] *pret. de* **to wake.**

**wolf** [wulf] *(pl.* **wolves** [wulvz]) *s.* lobo.

**woman** [wúmən] *(pl.* **women** [wímɪn]) *s.* mujer; **— writer** escritora.

**womanhood** [wúmənhud] *s.* estado de mujer; la mujer (las mujeres); integridad femenil; feminidad.

**womankind** [wúmənkaɪnd] *s.* la mujer, las mujeres, el sexo femenino.

**womanly** [wúmənlɪ] *adj.* femenil, mujeril, femenino; *adv.* femenilmente, como mujer.

**womb** [wum] *s.* vientre, entrañas; útero, matriz.

**won** [wʌn] *pret. & p.p. de* **to win.**

**wonder** [wʌ́ndɚ] *s. (marvel)* maravilla; prodigio; *(emotion)* admiración; **in —** maravillado; **no — that** no es mucho que; no es extraño que; *v.* asombrarse, maravillarse, pasmarse, admirarse; **to — at** admirarse de, maravillarse de; **I — what time it is** ¿qué hora será? **I — when he came** ¿cuándo vendría? **I should not —** if no me extrañaría que.

**wonderful** [wʌ́ndɚfəl] *adj.* maravilloso, admirable; **-ly** *adv.* maravillosamente, admirablemente, a las mil maravillas; **-ly well** sumamente bien.

**wondrous** [wʌ́ndrəs] *adj.* maravilloso, pasmoso, extraño.

**wont** [wʌnt] *adj.* acostumbrado; **to be — to** soler, acostumbrar, *C.A.* saber; *s.* costumbre, hábito, uso.

**woo** [wu] *v.* cortejar, enamorar, galantear.

**wood** [wud] *s. (material)* madera; *(stick)* palo; *(firewood)* leña; **-s** bosque; selva; **— engraving** grabado en madera; **—shed** leñera, cobertizo par leña; **fire—** leña; **piece of fire—** leño.

**woodcut** [wúdkʌt] *s.* grabado en madera.

**woodcutter** [wúdkʌtɚ] *s.* leñador.

**wooded** [wúdɪd] *adj.* arbolado, poblado de árboles.

**wooden** [wúdn̩] *adj.* de madera, de palo; tieso.

**woodland** [wúdlænd] *s.* monte, bosque, selva.

**woodman** [wúdmən] *s.* (*vendor*) leñador; (*dweller*) habitante del bosque.

**woodpecker** [wúdpɛkɚ] *s.* pájaro carpintero.

**woodwork** [wúdwɜk] *s.* maderamen; labrado en madera; obra de carpintería.

**woof** [wuf] *s.* trama (*de un tejido*); tejido.

**wool** [wʊl] *s.* lana; *adj.* de lana; lanar; **wool-bearing** lanar; **— dress** vestido de lana.

**woolen** [wúlɪn] *adj.* de lana; lanudo; **— mill** fábrica de tejidos de lana; *s.* tejido de lana; género o paño de lana.

**woolly** [wúlɪ] *adj.* lanudo; de lana.

**word** [wɜd] *s.* (*vocable*) palabra; vocablo, voz; (*news*) noticia, aviso; (*order*) mandato, orden; **pass— **contraseña; **by — of mouth** de palabra, verbalmente; *v.* expresar; redactar, formular.

**wordy** [wárdɪ] *adj.* palabrero, verboso, ampuloso.

**wore** [wor] *pret. de* to wear.

**work** [wɜk] *s.* (*effort*) trabajo; (*masterpiece*); obra maestra (*task*) tarea, faena; (*employment*) empleo, ocupación; oficio; (*accomplishment*) labor; **-s** taller, fábrica; maquinaria, mecanismo; **at —** trabajando; ocupado; *v.* trabajar; funcionar; obrar; surtir efecto; manejar, manipular; resolver (*un problema*); explotar (*una mina*); hacer trabajar; **to — havoc** hacer estropicios, causar daño; **to — loose** soltarse, aflojarse; **to — one's way through college** sufragar los gastos universitarios con su trabajo; **to — one's way up** subir por sus propios esfuerzos; **to — out a plan** urdir un plan; **to be all -ed up** estar sobreexcitado; **it didn't — out** no dió resultado; **the plan -ed well** tuvo buen éxito el plan.

**workable** [wɚkəbl̩] *adj.* practicable; explotable.

**worker** [wɚkɚ] *s.* trabajador; obrero; operario.

**working** [wɚkɪŋ] *s.* funcionamiento, operación; cálculo (*de un problema*); explotación (*de una mina*); *adj.* obrero, trabajador; **— class** clase obrera o trabajadora; **— hours** horas de trabajo; **a hard-working man** un hombre muy trabajador.

**workingman** [wɚkɪŋmæn] *s.* trabajador; obrero.

**workman** [wɚkmən] *s.* trabajador, obrero, operario.

**workmanship** [wɚkmənʃɪp] *s.* hechura; trabajo; mano de obra.

**workshop** [wɚkʃɑp] *s.* taller.

**world** [wɜld] *s.* mundo; **the World**

**War** la Guerra Mundial; **world-shaking** de gran importancia.

**worldly** [wɚldlɪ] *adj.* mundano, mundanal, terreno, terrenal.

**worm** [wɜm] *s.* gusano; lombriz; **worm-eaten** comido de gusanos; carcomido, apolillado; *v.* **to — a secret out of someone** extraerle o sonsacarle un secreto a una persona; **to — oneself into** insinuarse en, meterse en.

**worn** [worn] *p.p. de* to wear; **worn-out** gastado, roto; rendido de fatiga.

**worry** [wɚɪ] *s.* inquietud, ansiedad, cuidado, preocupación, apuro, apuración; *v.* inquietar(se), preocupar(se), afligir(se), apurar(se).

**worse** [wɜs] *adj.* peor; más malo; *adv.* peor; **— and —** cada vez peor; **— than ever** peor que nunca; **from bad to —** de mal en peor; **so much the —** tanto peor; **to be — off** estar peor que antes; **to change for the —** empeorar(se); **to get —** empeorar(se).

**worship** [wɚʃəp] *s.* adoración, culto; veneración; *v.* adorar; reverenciar.

**worshiper** [wɚʃəpɚ] *s.* adorador; **the -s** los fieles.

**worst** [wɜst] *adj.* peor; *adv.* peor; **the — el** peor; la peor; lo peor; *v.* derrotar.

**worth** [wɜθ] *s.* valor, valía, mérito; precio; **ten cent's — of** diez centavos de; **to get one's money's — out of** sacar todo el provecho posible del dinero gastado en; *adj.* digno de; **— hearing** digno de oírse; **to be — doing** valer la pena de hacerse; **to be — while** valer la pena.

**worthless** [wɚθlɪs] *adj.* sin valor; inútil; despreciable.

**worthy** [wɚðɪ] *adj.* digno; valioso, apreciable; meritorio, merecedor; *s.* benemérito, hombre ilustre.

**would** [wʊd] *imperf. de indic. y de subj. del verbo defect.* will: she **— come every day** solía venir (*o venía*) todos los días; **if you — do it** si lo hiciera Vd.; *expresa a veces deseo:* **— that I knew it!** ¡quién lo supiera!; ¡ojalá que yo lo supiera!; *v. aux. del condicional:* **she said she — go** dijo que iría.

**wound** [wund] *s.* herida; llaga, lesión; *v.* herir; lastimar; agraviar.

**wound** [waʊnd] *pret. & p.p. de* to wind.

**wove** [wov] *pret. de* to weave.

**woven** [wóvən] *p.p. de* to weave.

**wow** [waʊ] *v.* entusiasmar.

**wrangle** [ræŋgl̩] *v.* (*quarrel*) altercar, disputar; reñir; (*herd*) juntar; *Am.* rodear (*el ganado*); *s.* riña, pendencia.

**wrap** [ræp] *v.* envolver; enrollar, arrollar; **to — up** envolver(se); abrigar(se), tapar(se); **to be wrapped up in** estar envuelto en; estar absorto en; *s.* abrigo, manto.

**wrapper** [ræpɚ] *s.* envoltura, cubierta; **woman's —** bata.

**wrapping** [ræpɪŋ] *s.* envoltura; **—**

**WI**

**paper** papel de envolver.
**wrath** [ræθ] *s.* ira, cólera, rabia.
**wrathful** [ræθfəl] *adj.* colérico, rabioso, iracundo.
**wreath** [riθ] *s.* guirnalda, corona; **— of smoke** espiral de humo.
**wreathe** [rið] *v.* hacer guirnaldas; adornar con guirnaldas; **-d in smiles** sonriente.
**wreck** [rɛk] *s.* (*destruction*) ruina; destrucción; (*shipwreck*) naufragio; (*accident*) accidente; (*wreckage*) destrozos, despojos (*de un naufragio*); *v.* arruinar; naufragar; echar a pique; destrozar, demoler; **to — a train** descarrilar un tren.
**wrench** [rɛntʃ] *v.* torcer, retorcer; arrancar, arrebatar; *s.* torcedura, torsión; tirón, arranque, *Andes, Méx., C.A.* jalón; llave de tuercas; **monkey — llave inglesa.**
**wrest** [rɛst] *v.* arrebatar, arrancar; usurpar.
**wrestle** [rɛsl] *v.* luchar a brazo partido; luchar; *s.* lucha a brazo partido.
**wrestler** [rɛslɚ] *s.* luchador (*a brazo partido*).
**wretch** [rɛtʃ] *s.* miserable, infeliz; villano.
**wretched** [rɛtʃɪd] *adj.* (*miserable*) miserable; afligido; (*unfortunate*) desdichado, infeliz; (*bad*) bajo, vil; malísimo; **a — piece of work** un trabajo pésimo o malísimo.
**wriggle** [rɪgl] *v.* menear(se); retorcer(se); **to — out of** salirse de, escaparse de; escabullirse de.
**wring** [rɪŋ] torcer, retorcer; exprimir, estrujar; **to — money from someone** arrancar dinero a alguien; **to — out** exprimir (*la ropa*).
**wrinkle** [rɪŋkl] *s.* arruga; surco; **the latest — in style** la última novedad; *v.* arrugar(se).
**wrist** [rɪst] *s.* muñeca; **— watch** reloj de pulsera.
**writ** [rɪt] *s.* auto, orden judicial, mandato jurídico; **the Holy Writ** la Sagrada Escritura.
**write** [raɪt] *v.* escribir; **to — back** contestar por carta; **to — down** apuntar, poner por escrito; **to — off** cancelar (*una deuda*); **to — out** poner por escrito; escribir por entero; **to — up** relatar, describir; redactar.
**writer** [ráɪtɚ] *s.* escritor; autor.
**writhe** [raɪð] *v.* retorcerse.
**writing** [ráɪtɪŋ] *s.* escritura; escrito; composición literaria; forma o estilo literario; **hand—** letra; **— desk** escritorio; **— paper** papel de escribir; **to put in —** poner por escrito.
**written** [rítn] *p.p. de* **to write.**
**wrong** [rɔŋ] *adj.* (*incorrect*) falso, incorrecto; equivocado; (*wicked*) malo; injusto; mal hecho; (*improper*) inoportuno, inconveniente; **the — side of a fabric** el envés o el revés de un tejido; **the — side of the road** el lado izquierdo o contrario del camino; **that is the — book** ése no es el

libro; **it is in the — place** no está en su sitio, está mal colocado; *adv.* mal; al revés; **to go —** extraviarse, descaminarse; resultar mal; *s.* mal, daño perjuicio; injusticia; agravio; **to be in the —** no tener razón, estar equivocado; **to do —** hacer mal; *v.* perjudicar; agraviar; hacer mal a.
**wrote** [rot] *pret. de* **to write.**
**wrought** [rɔt] *pret. & p.p. irr. de* **to work;** *adj.* labrado; forjado; **— iron** hierro forjado; **— silver** plata labrada; **to be wrought-up** estar sobreexcitado.
**wrung** [rʌŋ] *pret. & p.p. de* **to wring.**
**wry** [raɪ] *adj.* torcido; **to make a — face** hacer una mueca.

## Y

**yacht** [jɑt] *s.* yate; *v.* navegar en yate.
**Yankee** [jǽŋkɪ] *adj. & s.* yanqui.
**yard** [jɑrd] *s.* (*measure*) yarda (*medida*); (*enclosure*) patio; cercado; terreno (*adyacente a una casa*); **back —** corral; **barn—** corral; **navy —** arsenal; **ship—** astillero.
**yardstick** [jɑ́rdstɪk] *s.* yarda (*de medir*); medida (*metro, vara, etc.*); patrón, norma.
**yarn** [jɑrn] *s.* estambre; hilado, hilaza; cuento enredado y poco probable.
**yawn** [jɔn] *v.* bostezar; *s.* bostezo.
**yea** [je] *adv.* sí; *s.* sí, voto afirmativo.
**year** [jɪr] *s.* año; **—book** anuario; **-'s income** renta anual; **by the —** por año; **leap —** año bisiesto.
**yearling** [jɪ́rlɪŋ] *s.* primal; becerro.
**yearly** [jɪ́rlɪ] *adj.* anual; *adv.* anualmente; una vez al año, cada año.
**yearn** [jɜn] *v.* anhelar; **to — for** anhelar; suspirar por.
**yearning** [jɜ́rnɪŋ] *s.* anhelo.
**yeast** [jist] *s.* levadura, fermento.
**yell** [jɛl] *v.* gritar, dar gritos, vociferar; *s.* grito, alarido.
**yellow** [jélo] *adj.* amarillo; cobarde; **— fever** fiebre amarilla; *s.* amarillo; *v.* poner(se) amarillo.
**yellowish** [jéloɪʃ] *adj.* amarillento.
**yelp** [jɛlp] *v.* aullar, ladrar; *s.* aullido, ladrido.
**yes** [jɛs] *adv.* sí.
**yesterday** [jéstɚdɪ] *adv. & s.* ayer; **day before —** anteayer o antier.
**yet** [jɛt] *adv. & conj.* todavía, aún; con todo, sin embargo; no obstante; **as — todavía, aún; **not —** todavía no.
**yield** [jild] *v.* (*surrender*) ceder; rendir; someterse; (*produce*) producir; **to — five percent** redituar el cinco por ciento; *s.* rendimiento, rendición; rédito.
**yodel** [jódl] *s.* canto en que la voz fluctúa entre natural y falsete.
**yoke** [jok] *s.* yugo; yunta (*de bueyes, mulas, etc.*); *v.* uncir; unir.
**yolk** [jok] *s.* yema (*de huevo*).
**yonder** [jándɚ] *adj.* aquel, aquella, aquellos, aquellas; *adv.* allá, allí, más allá, acullá.
**yore** [jor]: **in days of —** antaño, en

días de antaño.

**you** [ju] *pron. pers.* tú, usted, vosotros, ustedes; te, le, lo, la, os, las, los; **to —** a tí, a usted, a vosotros, a ustedes; te, le, les; *pron. impers.* se, uno.

**young** [jʌŋ] *adj.* joven; nuevo; **— leaves** hojas tiernas; **— man** joven; **her — ones** sus niños, sus hijitos; **the — people** la gente joven, los jóvenes, la juventud; *s.* jóvenes; cría, hijuelos (*de los animales*).

**youngster** [jʌ́ŋstɚ] *s.* muchacho, niño, jovencito, chiquillo.

**your** [jʊr] *adj.* tu (tus), vuestro (vuestra, vuestros, vuestras), su (sus), de usted, de ustedes.

**yours** [jʊrz] *pron. pos.* tuyo (tuya, tuyos, tuyas); vuestro (vuestra, vuestros, vuestras); suyo (suya, suyos, suyas), de usted, de ustedes; el tuyo (la tuya, los tuyos, las tuyas); el suyo (la suya, los suyos, las suyas); el (la, los, las) de usted; el (la, los, las) de ustedes; **a friend of —** un amigo tuyo, un amigo vuestro; un amigo suyo, un amigo de usted o ustedes.

**yourself** [jʊrsélf] *pron.* te, se (*como reflexivo*); **to —** a tí mismo; a usted mismo; **you —** tú mismo; usted mismo; *véase* **herself.**

**yourselves** [jʊrsélvz] *pron.* os, se (*como reflexivo*); **to —** a vosotros mismos; a

ustedes mismos; **you —** vosotros mismos; ustedes mismos.

**youth** [juθ] *s.* joven; juventud; jóvenes.

**youthful** [júθfəl] *adj.* joven; juvenil.

**Yuletide** [júltaɪd] *s.* Pascua de Navidad; Navidades.

## Z

**zeal** [zil] *s.* celo, fervor, ardor, entusiasmo.

**zealot** [zélət] *s.* fanático.

**zealous** [zéləs] *adj.* celoso, ardiente, fervoroso.

**zenith** [zínɪθ] *s.* cenit, cumbre.

**zephyr** [zéfɚ] *s.* céfiro.

**zero** [zíro] *s.* cero.

**zest** [zɛst] *s.* entusiasmo; buen sabor.

**zigzag** [zígzæg] *s.* zigzag; *adj. & adv.* en zigzag; *v.* zigzaguear, culebrear, andar en zigzag, serpentear.

**zinc** [zɪŋk] *s.* cinc (zinc).

**zip code** [zíp kod] *s.* sistema de cifras norteamericano, establecido para facilitar la entrega de cartas.

**zipper** [zípɚ] *s.* cierre relámpago, abrochador corredizo o de corredera, *Am.* riqui.

**zodiac** [zódɪæk] *s.* zodíaco.

**zone** [zon] *s.* zona; *v.* dividir en zonas.

**zoo** [zu] *s.* jardín zoológico.

**zoological** [zoəládʒɪkl̩] *adj.* zoológico.

**zoology** [zoúlədʒɪ] *s.* zoología.

WR